AF901452

Antisemitism and the Law

Antisemitism and the Law

Robert Katz

PROFESSOR OF LAW AND JOHN S. GRIMES FELLOW
INDIANA UNIVERSITY ROBERT H. MCKINNEY SCHOOL OF LAW
FOUNDER AND DIRECTOR
THE CENTER FOR THE STUDY OF LAW AND ANTISEMITISM

CAROLINA ACADEMIC PRESS
Durham, North Carolina

Copyright © 2025
Robert Katz
All Rights Reserved

ISBN 978-1-5310-2842-8
eISBN 978-1-5310-2843-5
LCCN 2025019172

CAROLINA ACADEMIC PRESS
700 Kent Street
Durham, North Carolina 27701
(919) 489-7486
www.cap-press.com

Printed in the United States of America

For Daniela, my compass and anchor
For my father, Joe Katz of blessed memory, my captain
For Jonah and Natanya, my fearless crew

Contents

PART THREE · ANTISEMITIC SPEECH

Foreword

*Jonathan Greenblatt**

In your hands is a groundbreaking casebook—one that spans three thousand years of legal history yet arrives at a critical moment. In the aftermath of Hamas's October 7th terror attack on Israel, the pronounced global resurgence of antisemitism makes clear that hatred against Jews is not a relic of the past but a living, breathing threat. Worse yet, it is a symptom of a deeper virus: hatred and bigotry directed at "the other." By collecting and synthesizing the cases and commentary within, Professor Robert Katz compels us to confront prejudice with every tool at our disposal, including—and especially—the law.

Central to Professor Katz's thesis is the legal system's paradoxical role as both a historic enforcer of Jews' subordination and an instrument for achieving full citizenship. From the Spanish Inquisition to the Dreyfus Affair to the Nazi racial state, the casebook dissects the codification of Jewish oppression. More hopefully, it analyzes landmark victories in Jews' struggle for safety and equality under law, including the Nuremberg trials, civil rights statutes, and hate crimes legislation. Throughout, it chronicles how Jewish defense organizations have leveraged the law to advance Jews' legal interests.

A consistent thread emerges across these diverse cases: a fuller understanding of the relationship between law and antisemitism enhances our capacity to combat it effectively and create a safer, more just world. This insight has guided the Anti-Defamation League (ADL) since its founding in 1913 with the mission "to stop the defamation of the Jewish people and to secure justice and fair treatment to all." ADL takes great pride in supporting Professor Katz's pioneering work. *Antisemitism and the Law* can empower the next generation of lawyers to combat antisemitism and all forms of hate through the law. Thankfully, this casebook fills a long-overlooked gap in legal education—and not a moment too soon.

* National Director and CEO, Anti-Defamation League

Foreword

*Stephen Macedo**

I am delighted to introduce a pioneering work, *Antisemitism and the Law*, which stands as the first comprehensive examination of this critical and timely subject within legal scholarship.

My association with Professor Katz dates back to my early years at Harvard, when his professor and my illustrious colleague, Judith N. Shklar, recommended that I advise Rob's senior thesis. Rob proved himself as dedicated a student and insightful a scholar as I have ever encountered. His senior thesis—an incisive critique of communitarianism using Israel as a case study—was so original and penetrating that Michael Sandel, a founder of communitarian theory, remarked it was better than most of the published work on the subject. The Harvard Government Department agreed, awarding it the prize for the best undergraduate thesis in political philosophy. Even then, Rob demonstrated a profound capacity to dissect the interplay between identity, justice, and political philosophy, a set of concerns that have shaped his career ever since.

This casebook is a natural outgrowth of that early work. In his thesis, Rob explored the tensions between group identity and universal justice, particularly how dominant communities define themselves in relation to outsiders. That inquiry has matured into a rigorous examination of how the law classifies and marginalizes Jews—whether as a race, a religion, an ethnicity, or a nationality. He meticulously analyzes seminal cases and legal texts, unraveling the complexities in legal approaches to anti-Jewish discrimination and defamation.

Yet, *Antisemitism and the Law* is more than a thoughtful and comprehensive casebook. With it, Professor Katz is building the foundation for a new field of study, identifying canonical texts and organizing questions. It is a call for sustained scholarly engagement with the legal dimensions of antisemitism.

At a time when antisemitism is re-emerging as a force in public and legal discourse, this casebook is essential reading. I am honored to introduce it, just as I was honored to advise the initial iteration of this inquiry decades ago.

* Laurance S. Rockefeller Professor of Politics and Human Values, Princeton University

Preface

Law has the power both to oppress and to liberate. This book examines how legal systems have wielded that power over Jews, drawing lessons that extend beyond them. We learn these lessons by reading legal and related texts that document Jewish oppression and liberation. In this way, we see how law has codified antisemitism, often with severity and exactitude, but also how Jews and their allies can mobilize law to oppose antisemitism, sometimes with lasting impact. Moreover, by examining how antisemitism is refracted through multiple legal systems across millennia, we gain unique insight into how law operates. This inquiry promises to make us better readers, thinkers, and advocates—and potentially, more just and empathetic citizens.

This comprehensive volume can help the reader navigate some of law and antisemitism's complexities through discussions of anti-discrimination law, Jewish identity, hate speech, hate crimes, education, the rule of law, and the Catholic Church, among other areas of law. Its remedial purpose is to equip Jewish rights advocates with a shared vocabulary, key precedents, and a toolkit of strategies, surveying the legal landscape they must navigate and examining how it has been shaped by broader societal, political, and ideological forces.

The narrative unfolds in a logical order. First, it examines Judaism, Jews, and Zionism; then, antisemitism, anti-Semites, and anti-Zionism. First, it acknowledges that Jews are not a race and that Judaism is open to all comers; then, it exposes the lies that Jews are a race and that Judaism is racist. First, it relates the Catholic Church's troubled history with Jews; then, the Church's embrace of a positive attitude.

The Holocaust is the book's connecting theme. The perceptive reader will sense its presence on every page. In law and antisemitism, the Holocaust is the brooding omnipresence in the sky.

My aim is to make the subject of antisemitism and the law widely known, accessible within the legal community and beyond it. Selected chapters can augment courses on race and the law, the First Amendment, cyberlaw, trusts and estates, torts, criminal law, international human rights law, comparative law, education law, law and religion, and Catholic law. The book can also be useful as a cross-disciplinary reference and can support graduate and undergraduate courses in other fields. General readers may think of it as a historical narrative developed through primary sources, annotations, and commentary. Non-Jews can use it to improve their "antisemitism radar."

The book has five parts: **Part One**, "Anti-Discrimination Law," examines laws that prohibit racial discrimination but do not explicitly prohibit religious discrimination.

Jews were initially excluded from these laws' coverage, which were enacted primarily to protect African Americans and members of other marginalized groups generally regarded as biologically non-white. This part traces how U.S. and U.K. courts came to interpret these laws as applying to Jews and other groups not defined by race, and these doctrinal developments reveal how Jews' racial identity in U.S. and U.K. law and society has changed over time. It raises the question, pursued throughout the book, of how advocates can best negotiate for Jewish rights in the shadow of antisemitism.

Part Two, "Jewish Identity," considers "Who is a Jew?"—that is, the legal meaning of "Jew"—in various laws and legal systems. It first examines this term as defined by Jews—Jewish law (Halakha), the State of Israel's Law of Return, and the U.S. Reform Movement—and by Jews' adversaries: the Spanish Inquisition and Nazi race laws. Examining the latter through legal lenses reveals the madness of antisemitism with chilling precision. Contemporary anti-Semites connect Jews and Judaism to racism. A single definition of "Jew" does not emerge from this analysis.

Part Three, "Antisemitic Speech," examines the regulation of hate speech law in general and antisemitic speech in particular. It traces the evolution of such regulation through group defamation laws; the First Amendment; cyberlaw; the International Military Tribunal's trial of Julius Streicher, Hitler's preeminent anti-Jewish propagandist; and hate speech laws in Canada and contemporary Germany.

Part Four, "Anti-Jewish Activities," examines hate crimes legislation in the U.S. and Germany, and Title VI of the Civil Rights Act of 1964, which addresses antisemitism on campus. It revisits definitional issues from Part One by examining how federal authorities have extended these race-based civil rights statutes to cover Jews. Additionally, this part considers the legal treatment of hateful conduct and speech that combine classical antisemitism with anti-Zionist expression.

Part Five, "Allies Against Antisemitism," considers two essential claims that must be true for Jews to obtain equal justice under law. The first claim is that antisemitism is antithetical to Christianity. The Catholic Church proclaimed the truth of this statement on October 28, 1965, when Pope Paul VI promulgated *Nostra aetate* ("In Our Times"), which repudiated the charge that Jews are collectively guilty for the death of Jesus.

The second essential claim is that antisemitism is antithetical to the rule of law. Émile Zola, a French novelist born into a Catholic family, asserted the truth of this claim on January 13, 1898, in *J'Accuse . . . !* ("I Accuse . . . !"), an open letter accusing the French military of wrongfully convicting Alfred Dreyfus, a Jewish army officer, of treason. In the short term, *J'Accuse . . . !* triggered anti-Jewish riots throughout France, including attacks on Jews, synagogues, and Jewish shops, amidst cries of "Death to the Jews!" In the long term, Zola's intervention forced French society to confront antisemitism and was instrumental in Dreyfus's eventual exoneration. Zola's courageous act, performed at great cost to himself, demonstrates the power of citizens to oppose antisemitism by appealing to liberal democratic principles.

Zola's headline appears on the cover of this book, which also features a caricature of Dreyfus as a six-headed serpent, pierced by a dagger labeled *Le Traître* ("the traitor"). The caricaturist dehumanized Dreyfus by portraying him as the embodiment of Jews' supposed perfidy and disloyalty. He used the words "Jew" and "traitor" interchangeably. Stereotypes in general are dehumanizing, but the world dehumanizes Jews in specific and predictable ways. This grotesque image provides a window into the minds of anti-Semites, for whom every Jew is, on some level, a monster. By symbolically stabbing a Jew, it condones violence against all Jews.

To provide a comprehensive picture of antisemitism as a legal phenomenon, this book includes collaborations and contributions by over a dozen recognized scholars and experts from diverse countries, disciplines, and religious traditions. Each embraced this project as their own and pursued it with passion and rigor. Their work enabled me to realize my vision for this book. (I say more about each in the "Contributors" section below.)

I am especially grateful to contributor Steven M. Freeman, Senior Counsel and Director of Legacy for the Anti-Defamation League (ADL). Steve was sold on my elevator pitch halfway through the ride up. His insights, experience, and erudition—combined with level-headedness and sound judgment—have made him an indispensable partner in this project.

Until recently, few perceived the need for courses on law and antisemitism and the pivotal role that a casebook could play in their adoption. Four visionary organizations saw this need and took action: ADL, which provided the major funding for this project; the Leon Levy Foundation; the Rieders Foundation; and the Academic Engagement Network (AEN). Beyond financial assistance, they provided invaluable encouragement, guidance, and social capital. (I say more about each in the "Acknowledgements" section below.) With their help, I was able to summon extraordinary talent and resources for this project, and to accomplish in an hourglass what might have taken many years.

Robert Katz
PROFESSOR OF LAW AND JOHN S. GRIMES FELLOW
INDIANA UNIVERSITY ROBERT H. MCKINNEY SCHOOL OF LAW
FOUNDER AND DIRECTOR
THE CENTER FOR THE STUDY OF LAW AND ANTISEMITISM

Acknowledgments

The Anti-Defamation League (ADL), founded in 1913 with the mission "to stop the defamation of the Jewish people and to secure justice and fair treatment to all," is the world's leading organization dedicated to combating antisemitism. ADL was pleased to provide the major funding for this casebook and encourages its use in law schools and other educational institutions nationwide.

The Leon Levy Foundation supports initiatives to promote human rights and Jewish culture. Its generous support enabled me to secure essential research leave and focus my full attention on this work.

The Rieders Foundation, led by its president, Clifford Rieders, serves the Jewish community of North America by fighting discrimination in all aspects of Jewish life. Its generous support enabled me to complete this work in record time by hiring top-notch research assistants. Mr. Rieders provided me with critical advice and assistance in gaining recognition and allies for the project.

The Academic Engagement Network (AEN) mobilizes faculty and university leaders to action to oppose antisemitism and to support an inclusive, welcoming campus learning community where Jewish and all students can feel like they belong, which it accomplishes through education about antisemitism, Israel, Jewish identity, and the diversity of the Jewish experience. Led by Director Miriam Elman, AEN was the first organization to recognize the casebook's potential and has supported it generously and enthusiastically to its completion.

I was immeasurably aided by the most industrious and inspirational librarians in the world, fortuitously housed at Indiana University McKinney School of Law's Ruth Lilly Law Library: Miriam Murphy, Director and Senior Lecturer in Law, who encouraged me to include Dreyfus and Zola; Lee Little, Research and Instruction Librarian, Lecturer in Law, and a whaler of books; Jackie Cooper, Cory Hinojosa, Sydney Schrock, Kim Schwant, Allison Siegel-Hirsch, and Mariah White. Indiana University McKinney School of Law advanced this project by providing summer research grants and funds for professional development and research assistants.

I have benefited enormously from the comments of Yael Eisenstat, Miriam Galston, Mark Goldfeder, Günther Jikeli, Kenneth Marcus, Antony Page, Steven Resnicoff, Marc Stern, Kenneth Stern, and IU McKinney colleagues Frank Emmert, Nicholas Georgakopoulos, the Honorable Frank Sullivan, and R. George Wright. Also critical were the work of research assistants Jordan Aberle, Kara Boyles, Rivkah Bunes,

Joshua Blustein, Ilise Feitshans, Annie Flowers, Chelsie Vonne Henderson, Gavin Hunter, Farrah Goodall, Gabriela Kaganovich, Natanya Katz, Ronnie Kawak, Courtney Knapp, Adam Lenkowsky, Jacob O'Donnell, Gina Ortiz, Kayden Poindexter, Julian Max Katz Rapaport, Mia Sacks, Andrew Scheer, Grace Van Metter, and Clare Van Prooyen. I gleaned priceless pearls of wisdom from Stanley Katz, Doris Katz, Gloria Brettner, Bruce Katz, Marie Christovao, Mark Katz, Jenny Zaslow, Elias Katz, Ruth Katz, Michael Rapaport, Manu Rapaport, and Jill Troderman. Artificial intelligence was a useful proofreader.

I would also like to express my appreciation to Steven Sheinberg, ADL's Chief Legal Officer, who championed this project, and to Peri Ayzidor, Elinor Citron, Alexander Nazareth, Christopher Wolf, and the Herbert Simon Family Foundation for their assistance under ADL's auspices.

This casebook was edited by Rachel Miranda: her meticulous attention to nuance, tone, and focus, and her ability to highlight themes, made her an exceptional editor. She guided me through completing this work with precision and care. She is a master of her craft, and I am honored to have worked with her.

This book owes its existence to Carolina Academic Press, whose steady hand guided it from idea to reality, and to Scott Sipe, Associate Publisher, a steadfast ally for Jews in legal publishing. I am grateful to Meg Mitchell, Acquisitions Editor, who set the book afloat; Ryland Bowman, Managing Editor, who guided it into port; and Jennifer Hill, Head of Design, who fitted it with a cover that encapsulates its thesis.

Contributors

Steven Freeman (Online Hate Speech) has had a distinguished career at the Anti-Defamation League (ADL) spanning more than four decades. Joining ADL in 1985 as an assistant director in the Legal Affairs Department, Freeman has since held several key positions, including Director of Legal Affairs, leader of a national team of area counsels, and Vice President of Civil Rights. He currently serves as ADL's Senior Counsel and Director of Legacy, overseeing the staff responsible for the organization's Library and Archives, which contain over a century of historical materials. Freeman's legal expertise has been instrumental in shaping ADL's advocacy efforts and coordinating the organization's amicus activity, including ADL's Supreme Court brief in the important *Moody v. NetChoice* case. His work on hate crime laws led to a keynote address at the 2nd Annual Law vs. Antisemitism Conference, which was later published in the *Lewis & Clark Law Review*. He is a graduate of Yale University and Stanford Law School.

Joan S. Friedman (Jewish Status in Reform Judaism) is Lincoln Professor of Religion and Professor of History Emerita at the College of Wooster. She was ordained a rabbi at Hebrew Union College–Jewish Institute of Religion in 1980 and chairs the CCAR Responsa Committee. She is the author of *Guidance, Not Governance: Rabbi Solomon B. Freehof and Reform Responsa* (Hebrew Union College Press, 2013), a 2013 National Jewish Book Award Finalist.

Kenneth Grad (Willful Promotion of Hatred) is Assistant Professor at the Faculty of Law, University of Manitoba, where his teaching and research focuses on criminal law, evidence, and legal history. He earned his JD from Osgoode Hall Law School and his LLM from Harvard Law School. He is currently pursuing his PhD at Osgoode Hall Law School, with an emphasis on the efficacy of criminal sanctions and other regulatory measures as tools for combating hate and racist speech. He is the author of several scholarly papers on criminal law, human rights, antisemitism, freedom of expression, and other topics.

Hans-Christian Jasch (Jews as Sub-Human) is a lawyer and legal historian by training. He holds a doctoral degree in legal history from Humboldt University in Berlin. From 2014 to 2020 he served as the executive director of the Memorial and Educational Site House of the Wannsee Conference, following the publication of his critically acclaimed 2012 book on the Nazi state secretary Wilhelm Stuckart, who represented the Ministry of the Interior at the Wannsee Conference. Parallel to his academic research on law and public administration in Nazi Germany, Dr. Jasch worked as a lawyer in the public administration for the German Federal Ministry of the Interior in the field of countering right-wing extremist hate crime and terrorism (2012–2014) and as a seconded national expert on preventing violent radicalization for the counter-terrorism unit of the European Commission in DG Home Affairs from 2007 to 2011. Between 2016 and 2019, he co-authored books on the participants of the Wannsee Conference, the Nuremberg Laws, public administration and the Holocaust, post-1945 German justice system and Holocaust crimes, a book on amateur war photography during the German attack on Poland, and an exhibition and a catalogue titled "Crimes Uncovered: The First Generation of Holocaust Researchers." He directed the curation of the new permanent exhibition in Wannsee, opened in 2020. Since 2023, he has served as the General Secretary of the German Section of the International Institute for Administrative Sciences in the Federal Ministry of the Interior.

Fr. John Paul Kimes (Antisemitism Is Antithetical to Christianity) was ordained a Maronite Catholic priest in 2000 and completed his doctorate in canon law in 2006 at the Pontifical Oriental Institute in Rome. From 2009–2019, he served as an official of the Supreme Apostolic Tribunal of the Congregation for the Doctrine of the Faith, which adjudicates the most serious crimes in the Catholic Church. He has lectured internationally and written extensively on various topics of law in the Catholic Church, primarily in criminal law. Since 2020, he has been an Associate Professor of the Practice at Notre Dame Law School, where he teaches courses on specific areas of law in the Catholic Church and the interaction between canon law and civil law in Western history. He is an advisor to more than 50 dioceses and religious orders worldwide. He serves as the Raymond of Peñafort Fellow of the de Nicola Center for Ethics and Culture, a Fellow of the Lindsay and Matt Maroun Religious Liberty Initiative, Consultant of the Canon Law Centre of the Thomas More Law School of Australian Catholic University, and a Board Member of the Institute for Families and Technology.

Lesley Klaff (Jews as Ethnic; Are Halakhically-Based Admissions Policies a Form of Racism and Racial Discrimination?) is a Senior Lecturer in Law at Sheffield Hallam University, an Affiliate Professor of Law at the University of Haifa in Israel, and editor-in-chief of the *Journal of Contemporary Antisemitism*. She is also a research fellow at the London Centre for the Study of Contemporary Antisemitism (LCSCA) and is an Academic Advisory Board Member of the Institute for Holocaust Research and Education (IHRE) in Minnesota and of the Louis D Brandeis Center for Human Rights under Law in Washington, D.C. She has published on a variety of topics relating to contemporary antisemitism, including Holocaust inversion, campus antisemitism, antisemitism in British politics, the IHRA definition, the intersection of antisemitism and misogyny, antisemitism and the law, and the legal construction of Jewish identity.

Albert Lindemann (Antisemitism Is Inimical to Democracy) is Professor of History at the University of California Santa Barbara, Emeritus. He is the author or co-editor of seven books: *The 'Red Years': European Socialism versus Bolshevism, 1919–1921*

(University of California Press, 1974); *History of European Socialism* (Yale University Press, 1983); *The Jew Accused, Three Anti-Semitic Affairs* (Cambridge University Press, 1991); *Esau's Tears: Modern Anti-Semitism and the Rise of the Jews* (Cambridge University Press, 1997); *Anti-Semitism before the Holocaust* (Pearson Education Press, 2000); *Antisemitism: A History* (co-editor, Oxford University Press, 2010); and *A History of Modern Europe from 1815 to the Present* (Wiley-Blackwell Press, 2013).

Paula Rhein-Fischer (Glorification of the Nazi Regime) is a Postdoctoral Researcher at the Academy for European Human Rights Protection at the University of Cologne (Germany). She is Principal Investigator of the German, Lithuanian and Portuguese research consortium 'Mnemonic Reality' and a Postdoctoral Fellow of the Danish, Dutch, German and Polish research consortium 'Memocracy,' both funded by the Volkswagen Foundation. She holds both German state exams in law as well as a Maîtrise en Droit from Université Paris I Panthéon Sorbonne. Dr. Rhein-Fischer completed her PhD at the Institute for International Peace and Security Law at the University of Cologne with a dissertation on the prohibition to use force and factual mistakes (Nomos 2020). She is a member of the Young College of the North-Rhine Westphalian Academy of Science and the Arts. Her current research focuses on law and time, memory laws, human rights, and constitutional law.

Jack Olsburgh (Defamation) is a graduate of City, University of London Law School, where he achieved a Distinction in the Graduate Diploma in Law and was a Lincoln's Inn Lord Bowen GDL Scholar. He is a First-Class graduate in Philosophy, Politics & Economics (PPE) from Oriel College, the University of Oxford, where he ranked fourth in his cohort and topped three Finals papers and was awarded the John Hicks Foundation Prize for best performance in the Macroeconomics Finals Honour School. Mr. Olsburgh worked as an academic research assistant to Professor Anthony Julius, who represented Ambassador Deborah Lipstadt in *Irving v. Lipstadt*. He is training to become a barrister at the Inns of Court College of Advocacy in London, and is a recipient of Lincoln's Inn's 'Lord Denning Scholarship' for the bar course.

M.M. Silver (Louis Brandeis and Louis Marshall v. Anti-Zionists; The Legal Battles of Louis Marshall: Marshall v. Ford (1920–1927)) is Professor of Jewish History and Modern History at the Max Stern Yezreel Valley College. His book and articles in Hebrew and English include *Louis Marshall and the Rise of Jewish Ethnicity in America: A Biography* (Syracuse University Press, 2013), which was a National Jewish Book Award Finalist, and *Zionism and the Melting Pot: Preachers, Pioneers, and Modern Jewish Politics* (University of Alabama Press, 2020). He lives in Galilee, Israel.

Daniel Sinclair (The Definition of "Jew" Under the Law of Return) is a Senior Fellow at the Institute on Law, Religion and Lawyer's Work, Fordham University Law School, New York, and annual Visiting Professor of Law at the Law School. He is also Adjunct Professor of Comparative Public Health Law at Tel-Aviv University, Israel, and Adjunct Professor of Law and Religion at the Sir Zelman Cowen Centre, Victoria University Law

School, Melbourne, Australia. Prof. Sinclair is Emeritus Professor of Jewish Law and Comparative Biomedical Law at the Haim Striks Faculty of Law, College of Management Academic Studies in Israel. He has published widely in the fields of comparative and Jewish biomedical law, Jewish law, the influence of Jewish law on the legal system of the State of Israel, the relationship between Halakhah and ethics, the jurisprudence of Jewish law, and Jewish identity. In addition to over seventy scholarly articles, Prof. Sinclair has published three books, including *Tradition and the Biological Revolution* (Edinburgh University Press 1989); *Law, Judicial Policy and Jewish Identity in the State of Israel* (SUNY Binghamton 2000); and *Jewish Biomedical Law: Legal and Extra-Legal Dimensions* (Oxford University Press in 2003). An ordained rabbi, he served as the rabbi of Edinburgh, Scotland, and Dean of Jews' College, London.

Gretchen Starr-LeBeau (Jews as Heretical) is Jeanne and George Todd Professor of Religious Studies at Principia College. Her first book, *In the Shadow of the Virgin: Inquisitors, Friars, and Conversos in Guadalupe, Spain* (Princeton University Press, 2003), was a finalist for the National Jewish Book Award in History. Her most recent book is *Seven Myths about the Spanish Inquisition* (Hackett, 2023). She also co-edited *Judging Faith, Punishing Sin: Inquisitions and Consistories in the Early Modern World* (Cambridge University Press, 2017), with a Spanish translation from Catedra Press in 2020. Her research focuses on the Spanish Inquisition, particularly investigations of Jewish converts to Christianity. She has received funding for her work from the Mellon Foundation, the Fulbright Foundation, the American Philosophical Society, the National Endowment for the Humanities, and the Spanish Ministry for Education, Culture, and Sport.

Victoria Saker Woeste (Non-Litigation Responses to Antisemitic Speech) is a legal historian whose interests span several major fields, from political economy to constitutional law, religion, and civil rights. Her degrees are from the University of Virginia and the University of California at Berkeley. She is the author of *The Farmer's Benevolent Trust: Law and Cooperation in Industrial America* (North Carolina, 1998), and *Henry Ford's War on Jews and the Legal Battle Against Hate Speech* (Stanford, 2012); she is also the co-editor of *Jews and the Law* (Quid Pro Books, 2014). *Henry Ford's War* is currently in development for film and television under option to Leviathan Productions. Professor Woeste has taught at Amherst College, Northwestern University, Indiana University McKinney School of Law, and Cairo University Egypt. For twenty-five years, she was a member of the research faculty at the American Bar Foundation before retiring in 2019.

Part One

Jews and Anti-Discrimination Law

Chapter 1

Jews as Non-White

This chapter examines the extension of federal civil rights protection to groups whose members, while not distinct biological races, nonetheless function like disadvantaged races in the U.S. context. The chapter begins with *Manzanares v. Safeway Stores, Inc.* (10th Cir. 1979), which tested the application of the Civil Rights Act of 1866 to Latinos. The Act's §§ 1981 and 1982 were designed to ensure that "all persons" and "all citizens" have the same contract and property rights, respectively, as "white citizens." These traditionally barred only discrimination against African Americans and other groups widely regarded as distinct biological races. In *Manzanares*, the court extended § 1981's scope to include Latinos, therefore laying the groundwork for extending laws barring race discrimination to Jews.

The remainder of this chapter is devoted to *Shaare Tefila Congregation v. Cobb* (1987), a landmark decision that involved a hate crime against Shaare Tefila Congregation, whose building neo-Nazis defaced with swastikas. The congregation brought suit under § 1982. The *Shaare Tefila* case presented the question of whether Jews could, like Latinos, be deemed a protected racial group under the Civil Rights Act of 1866. The chapter follows the case's course as it travelled through the judicial process, including the divergent opinions of a divided court of appeals; the unanimous decision of the Supreme Court, per Justice White, in favor of the congregation, and in the companion case of *St. Francis Coll. of Al-Khazraji* (1987); and a historical account of the role Jewish advocacy groups played in the litigation. Also included is a transcript of oral arguments before the Supreme Court, where the case elicited perhaps the most thoughtful discussion of Jewish identity in U.S. court history.

In the final section, we consider the limits of §§ 1981 and 1982 coverage for anti-Jewish discrimination. Is such coverage limited to discrimination based on Jews' ancestry, ethnicity, or perceived racial identity? Does it also bar discrimination against Jews that appears to reflect animus towards Jewish religious beliefs and practices? If limited to racial antisemitism, how are courts to distinguish between racial and religious antisemitism?

A. Latinos as Non-White for Remedial Purposes

Manzanares v. Safeway Stores, Inc.

593 F.2d 968 (10th Cir. 1979)

[This case involved a plaintiff of Mexican American descent—a category the court equated with Hispanics or Latinos—who alleged employment discrimination in violation of 42 USC. § 1981 (§ 1981), which provides that "all persons" shall enjoy the same right to contract as "White citizens." The district court dismissed the lawsuit. The Court of Appeals, per Chief Judge Oliver Seth, reversed the lower court's ruling and allowed the plaintiff's § 1981 claim to proceed.]

Chief Judge Oliver Seth delivered the opinion of the Court.

The plaintiff was discharged by Safeway, and charges of theft of Safeway property were brought against him.

The plaintiff describes himself in the complaint as of "Mexican American descent," and alleges that "Anglo employees of the Company, who have admitted to thefts of Company property have been subjected to suspension rather than discharge."...

The sole issue on this appeal is whether the allegations in the complaint that plaintiff was discriminated against because he was of "Mexican American descent," and the employees who were alleged to have received different treatment were "Anglos," were sufficient to permit plaintiff to seek relief under 42 USC. § 1981.

Of course, section 1981 makes no mention of race, national origin, or alienage. The only reference is that "all persons" shall have described rights and benefits of "white citizens." Thus, the standard against whom the measure was to be made were the rights and benefits of white citizens. The measure is group to group, and plaintiff has alleged that the "group" to which he belongs—those he describes as of Mexican American descent—is to be measured against the Anglos as the standard. This is perfectly clear and well understood in the context, and in the geographical area concerned. The allegation is direct that discrimination was directed to members of his group, and to him individually because of his affiliation. We hold that this was sufficient to have withstood the motions to dismiss. In this holding we consider that Mexican American, Spanish American, Spanish-surname individuals, and Hispanos [*sic*] are equivalents, and it makes no difference whether these are terms of national origin, alienage, or whatever. It is apparent that a group so described is of such an identifiable nature that the treatment afforded its members may be measured against that afforded the Anglos.

Thus, plaintiff has alleged that there has been or is discrimination against him by defendants by reason of the fact he is of Mexican American origin, and this is a sufficient identification of a group within the protection of section 1981. The group-to-group comparison or contrast is made, and with the other allegations a cause of action is alleged. This is a failure of "any person" to have the rights of "white citizens."...

In *Valdez v. Van Landingham* (10th Cir. 1973), we considered an allegation of discrimination arising from plaintiff's name. We stated in that opinion, citing *McDonald v. Santa Fe Trail Transportation Co.* (1976):

> The issue is whether a Spanish surname constitutes a 'racial' class which is protected by section 1981. The term 'race' in our language has evolved to encompass some non-racial but ethnic groups. This Circuit has recognized Spanish speaking or Spanish-surnamed Americans as a minority for purposes of sections 1981, 1983, and 1985(3)....

We also stated that the trial court was "in error to exclude Spanish-surnamed persons as a protected group."

Section 1981 is directed to racial discrimination primarily but is not necessarily limited to the technical or restrictive meaning of "race." We have considered carefully *McDonald v. Santa Fe Trail Transportation Co.* with its references to discrimination against "whites." This is significant in equating "whites" with "other persons." As to section 1981, the Court there said: "We have previously held, where discrimination against Negroes was in question, that § 1981 affords a federal remedy against discrimination in private employment on the basis of race...."

The Court in *Santa Fe Trail* clearly and directly holds that section 1981 applies to "whites" as being with[in] the "all persons" phrase. The legislative history is fully described to support the view that section 1981 does protect white persons. Thus, here the plaintiff by the allegations in the complaint has placed himself within this "all persons" protection. The Court in *Santa Fe Trail* held the trial court was in error in dismissing petitioner's claims on the ground that white persons were not protected. We must also so hold in the case before us....

If "white citizens" means a race, which technically does not seem particularly clear, it would seem that a group which is discriminated against because they are somehow different as compared to "white citizens" is within the scope of section 1981. We cannot consider this as a "national origin" case and that alone. Prejudice is as irrational as is the selection of groups against whom it is directed. It is thus a matter of practice or attitude in the community, it is usage or image based on all the mistaken concepts of "race." Webster's Third New International Dictionary includes in a lengthy definition of race a class of individuals with common characteristics, appearance, or habits. Also, "In technical discriminations, all more or less controversial and often lending themselves to great popular misunderstanding or misuse, RACE is anthropological... implying a distinct physical type...." The allegations in this case thus equate the prejudices to those based on race. The allegations demonstrate that the defendants may be poor anthropologists, but the prejudice is asserted to be directed against plaintiff in contrast to the Anglos. This in our view is sufficient. It is equivalent to the "all persons" compared to "white citizens" discrimination contemplated by section 1981.

It would not seem to serve a useful purpose to analyze the Reasons for the acts of prejudice, as that can be left to the sociologists. We are not considering prejudice based on sex or religion, as those are wholly outside the basic framework of section 1981.... It is sufficient for our purposes that as a matter of common knowledge, and as described in the opinions, a prejudice as alleged in this complaint does exist. It is directed against persons with Spanish surnames. It is a group whose rights can be measured against the standard group or control group referred to in section 1981.

Latinos Are Not a Race

1. In *The Complexities of Latino/Hispanic Identity*,[1] Scholar Kaitlin Smith explains the distinction between Latino and Hispanic as follows:

> ["Hispanic"] describes all individuals born in (or who have descended from individuals born in) Spanish-speaking countries, "Latino/a/x" is used to describe individuals who hail from (or whose ancestors hail from) countries in Latin America which includes Central America, South America, and the Caribbean. This term encompasses Portuguese-speaking Brazilians and others who are not considered Hispanic because their societies do not speak Spanish.[2]

According to the 2020 Census data, there were over 62 million Hispanics or Latinos in the U.S., comprising 18.7 percent of the U.S. population.[3] The nation's 456,000 Latino Jews comprise 1.4 percent of the U.S. Latino population.[4] Approximately 6 percent of Jewish adults in the U.S. identify as Hispanic, as do 11 percent of Gen Z Jews and 8 percent of Gen X Jews.[5]

2. *Latinidad.*[6] Professor Ángel R. Oquendo argues that "what really unites Latino/as is their unique history of oppression," most notably their entry into the U.S. through

---

1. Oxford English Dictionary (OED) defines "Hispanic" as "[a] Spanish-speaking person, esp. one of Latin American descent, living in the U.S." *Hispanic*, OXFORD ENG. DICTIONARY, https://www.oed.com/dictionary/hispanic_adj?tab=meaning_and_use#1656419 (last visited Sept. 11, 2024).

2. Kaitlin Smith, *Latinx vs. Hispanic: A History of Terms*, FACING HIST. & OURSELVES (Oct. 15, 2021), https://www.facinghistory.org/ideas-week/latinx-vs-hispanic-history-terms. OED defines "Latino" as "[a] Latin American inhabitant of the United States," *Latino*, OXFORD ENG. DICTIONARY, https://www.oed.com/dictionary/latino_n?tab=meaning_and_use#39786575 (last visited Sept. 11, 2024). On Smith's definition, Americans of Spanish descent are Hispanic but not Latino, while Americans of Portuguese descent are neither. As between the various pan-ethnic terms, 52 percent of Hispanics or Latinos prefer "Hispanic," 29 percent prefer "Latino," 2 percent prefer "Latinx," 1 percent prefer "Latine," and 15 percent have no preference. This casebook uses the term "Latino."

3. *Racial and Ethnic Diversity in the United States: 2010 Census and 2020 Census*, U.S. CENSUS BUREAU (Aug. 12, 2021), https://www.census.gov/library/visualizations/interactive/racial-and-ethnic-diversity-in-the-united-states-2010-and-2020-census.html.-xix.

4. LEONARD SAXE ET AL., BRANDEIS STEINHARDT SOC. RSCH. INST., AMERICAN JEWISH POPULATION ESTIMATES 2020 SUMMARY & HIGHLIGHTS 19 (Mar. 2021), https://ajpp.brandeis.edu/us_jewish_population_2020.

5. *Id.* Latino was not presented as an option.

6. *Latinidad*, WIKIPEDIA, https://en.wikipedia.org/wiki/Latinidad (last visited Oct. 16, 2024). The National Museum of the American Latino showcases "the contributions and experiences of Latinos in the United States" and presents them as "an essential part of our nation's history and culture." NAT'L MUSEUM OF THE AM. LATINO, https://latino.si.edu (last visited Oct. 17, 2024). The foundational

U.S. imperial expansion. "This common experience," he writes, "has caused them to form a unified community, which now includes other people of Latin American ancestry."[7]

Compare Oquendo's account of Latino identity with author David Baddiel's account of Jewish identity:

> My sense of Jewishness as an ethnicity is to some extent about what Nazis did to us. Of course it is. It's not just about that—it's about many positive things as well—but the way that positive and negative associations combine to create minority identity is complex. Identity, particularly ethnic identity, is created in the story of survival against the odds, which is why the blues are songs of sadness, and fightback, and celebration, all mixed up. That's what identity is.... Think of the old joke that Jews tell each other about how you can boil down all Jewish festivals to a simple mantra: they tried to kill us, they failed, let's eat. That is the Jewish blues, and we should all sing it.[8]

3. *Whiteness and § 1981 coverage.* Fifty-eight percent of Latinos identify their race as White, 27 percent as "some other race" category, 8 percent as two or more races, and 2 percent as Black or African American.[9] Assuming a higher percentage of Latinos self-identified as White, how would this affect Judge Seth's analysis? Is there a tipping point at which Latinos, if collectively too White, would forfeit § 1981's coverage? Consider *Martinez v. Hazelton Research Animals, Inc.*, 430 F. Supp. 186 (D. Md. 1977), in which the court restricted coverage to non-White Latinos.

> The court is of the opinion that the mere assertion that the plaintiff is an Hispanic male is an insufficient allegation of racial background to support an allegation of racial discrimination. While it might be true that Hispanic individuals may suffer discrimination closely akin to that experienced by members of the black race, it is not necessarily true of all Hispanic people.... Many people of Hispanic origin cannot be classified as "non-whites."[10]

The court granted the plaintiff leave to amend his complaint to allege that he was non-White. In *Gonzalez v. Stanford Applied Engineering, Inc.*, 597 F.2d 1298 (9th Cir. 1979), the court recognized a § 1981 claim by a brown-skinned Mexican American of indig-

---

casebook in this field (and a source of inspiration for the instant casebook) is Richard Delgado et al., LATINOS AND THE LAW: CASES AND MATERIALS 2d ed. (West Academic Publishing, 2021).

7. Ángel R. Oquendo, *Re-Imagining the Latino/a Race*, 12 HARV. BLACKLETTER L.J. 93, 93–94 (1995).

8. DAVID BADDIEL, JEWS DON'T COUNT: HOW IDENTITY POLITICS FAILED ONE PARTICULAR IDENTITY xviii–xix (2021).

9. Luis Noe-Bustamante et al., *4. Measuring the Racial Identity of Latinos*, PEW RSCH. CTR. (Nov. 4, 2021), https://www.pewresearch.org/race-and-ethnicity/2021/11/04/measuring-the-racial-identity-of-latinos/.

10. Martinez v. Hazelton Rsch. Animals, Inc., 430 F. Supp. 186, 187–88.

enous ancestry. The plaintiff stated that he believed that if "Mexican Americans were not brown ... they would [not] suffer discrimination."[11]

Should § 1981 apply to all Latinos or only non-White Latinos?

4. *Prejudice based on religion.* Judge Seth states that "we are not considering prejudice based on sex or religion, as those are wholly outside the basic framework of section 1981." 50 percent of Latinos are Catholic, 24 percent Protestant, and 19 percent are unaffiliated.[12] Is the religious demography of Latinos relevant to the question of whether 1981 applies to them? Would the analysis differ if the vast majority of Latinos were Catholic, and vice versa?

Latinos Are a Race for Remedial Purposes

1. *Anti-Latino discrimination.* In the southwestern U.S., the term "Anglo" refers to the subset of Caucasians who are not Latino.[13] Latinos suffer from stereotypes that they are foreigners, outsiders, immigrants—especially undocumented immigrants—criminals, and gang members, and prone to violence.[14] Latinos have suffered segregated schools[15] and hate crimes,[16] including the horrific rampage on August 3, 2019, in an El Paso Walmart that left 23 dead.[17] In a 2021 survey, Latinos reported experiencing various forms of discrimination, including being treated as if they were not smart (35 percent), criticized for speaking Spanish (23 percent), told to go back to their country (21 percent), fearing for their safety (21 percent), being called offensive names (20 percent), and being unfairly stopped by the police (9 percent).[18] Darker-skinned Latinos

---

11. *See also* Lopez v. Sears, Roebuck & Co., 493 F. Supp. 801, 807 (D. Md. 1980) (recognizing § 1981 claim by a "non-white Spanish surnamed Maylay (brown)" plaintiff).

12. PRRI Staff, *2020 PRRI Census of American Religion: County-Level Data on Religious Identity and Diversity,* PRRI (July 8, 2021), https://www.prri.org/research/2020-census-of-american-religion/#:~:text=Three%20in%20four%20Hispanic%20Americans,identity%20with%20other%20religious%20groups.

13. *Anglo,* Oxford Eng. Dictionary, https://www.oed.com/dictionary/anglo (last visited July 5, 2023).

14. Cynthia Kwei Yung Lee, *Race and Self-Defense: Toward a Normative Conception of Reasonableness,* 81 Minn. L. Rev. 367, 441–452 (1996).

15. Westminster Sch. Dist. v. Mendez, 161 F.2d 774 (9th Cir. 1947).

16. In 2022, the FBI recorded: 991 hate crimes against Latinos; 4,210 against African Americans; and 1,305 against Jews. *See U.S. Crime Data Explorer,* Fed. Bureau of Investigation Crime Data Explorer, https://cde.ucr.cjis.gov/LATEST/webapp/#/pages/explorer/crime/hate-crime (last visited Oct. 15, 2024) (select "Year"; then search 2022).

17. Albinson Linares, *Rise in Hate Crimes Includes a 'Significant Increase' Against Latinos,* NBC News (Nov. 3, 2023, 10:30 AM), https://www.nbcnews.com/news/latino/hate-crimes-latinos-see-significant-increase-rcna123211.

18. Luis Noe-Bustamante et al., *1. Half of U.S. Latinos Experienced Some Form of Discrimination During the First Year of the Pandemic,* Pew Rsch. Ctr. (Nov. 4, 2021), https://www.pewresearch.org/race-and-ethnicity/2021/11/04/half-of-u-s-latinos-experienced-some-form-of-discrimination-during-the-first-year-of-the-pandemic/.

experience more discrimination than lighter-skinned Latinos; the former sometimes experience discrimination by the latter.[19]

2. *Latinos and national origin discrimination.* According to a 2024 Pew Research Center survey, 52 percent of Hispanics or Latinos describe their identity by their family's country of origin, 30 percent describe themselves as Hispanic, Latino, Latinx, or Latine, and 17 percent as American.[20] A majority of Latinos thus connect their identity to national origin, defined as "the country where a person was born, or, more broadly, the country from which his or her ancestors came." *Espinoza v. Farah Mfg. Co., Inc.* (1973) (Marshall, J.). This can pose a challenge to Latinos seeking to raise § 1981 claims, which a court may reject if the plaintiff alleges only national origin discrimination.[21] However, if a Latino qualifies for § 1981 coverage on some other basis, the claim will not be denied on grounds that the plaintiff is *also* discriminated against based on national origin. In *Manzanares,* Judge Seth states, "we cannot consider this as a 'national origin' case and that alone."

3. *Added value.* If § 1981 did not cover Latinos as such, it would still permit non-Caucasian Latinos to bring claims for anti-non-Caucasian discrimination and Caucasian Latinos to bring claims for anti-Caucasian discrimination. Given this, what is the added value of recognizing Latinos as a distinct group for § 1981 purposes?

Dyads of Discrimination: White/Non-White, Anglo/Latino, Non-Jew/Jew

1. *Common perception.* Judge Seth does not specify who are "white citizens" under § 1981, a term whose racial meaning he wrote "technically does not seem particularly clear." Moving beyond a "technical or restrictive meaning of 'race,'" he looks at whether a non-Anglo group "is discriminated against because they are somehow different as compared to 'white citizens.'" He takes judicial notice of the perception that Latinos are an "identifiable" group, and that anti-Latino prejudice is "a matter of common knowledge." See also *Budinsky v. Corning Glass Works*, 425 F. Supp. 786 (W. D. Pa. 1977) ("courts which have extended the coverage of § 1981 [to groups other than African Americans] have done so on a realistic basis, within the framework of this common meaning and understanding"); *Ramos v. Flagship International, Inc.*, 612 F. Supp. 148, 151 (E.D.N.Y. 1985) (whether Latinos may sue under § 1981 is a question of fact that turns on whether they "'are popularly understood' to constitute a group or groups 'readily distinguishable ... from the various groups of persons in this country commonly recognized as white'").

---

19. Luis Noe-Bustamante, *Latinos Experience Discrimination from Other Latinos About as Much as from Non-Latinos,* Pew Rsch. Ctr. (May 2, 2022), https://www.pewresearch.org/short-reads/2022/05/02/latinos-experience-discrimination-from-other-latinos-about-as-much-as-from-non-latinos/.

20. Lopez et al., *Who is Hispanic?*, Pew Rsch. Ctr. (Sept. 12, 2024), https://www.pewresearch.org/short-reads/2024/09/12/who-is-hispanic/.

21. *See, e.g.*, Davis v. Boyle-Midway, Inc., 615 F. Supp. 560 (N.D. Ga. 1985).

2. *The Anglo/Latino dyad.* In Judge Seth's analysis, § 1981's "white citizens" is the placeholder category for the privileged group in an advantaged/disadvantaged dyad or binary. The terms "white citizens" and "all persons" are defined situationally. The term "all persons" consists of persons belonging to discrete groups that experience discrimination relative to the relevant group of "white citizens." In *Manzanares*, Anglos function as "white citizens" and Latinos as the discrete disadvantaged subset of "all persons." Anglos are "the standard group" or "control group" against which we measure the relative denial of rights to Latinos.

3. *Disadvantaged concerning what?* What variable or variables does Judge Seth use to compare Latinos to Anglos? Is it relevant for his analysis whether and to what extent Latinos experience one or more of the following vis-à-vis Anglos?:

a. Unlawful discrimination in employment, housing, education, etc.[22]

b. Lower socio-economic status—separate and apart from whether this is the result of unlawful discrimination

c. Pervasive and hateful stereotypes[23]

d. Hate crimes[24] and fear of them[25]

e. Hate speech and group defamation[26]

f. Contemptuous treatment[27]

4. *Non-Jew/Jew dyad.* On what basis if any can § 1981 register anti-Jewish discrimination? Is there some non-Jew/Jew dyad whereby non-Jews correspond to "white citizens" and Jews constitute a subset of "all persons" against whom non-Jews/"white persons" discriminate? If the sole variable or comparator is socio-economic status, then anti-Jewish discrimination does not register. In 2019, the proportion of Jewish households with incomes below the federal poverty level ranged between 1 and 4 percent.[28] If not economic inequality, what would be the relevant metric or axis of anti-Jewish oppression?

---

22. Westminster Sch. Dist. v. Mendez, 161 F.2d 774 (9th Cir. 1947).

23. Yung Lee, *supra* note 14.

24. In 2022, the FBI recorded: 991 hate crimes against Latinos; 4,210 against African Americans; and 1,305 against Jews. *See U.S. Crime Data Explorer*, Fed. Bureau of Investigation Crime Data Explorer, https://cde.ucr.cjis.gov/LATEST/webapp/#/pages/explorer/crime/hate-crime (last visited Oct. 15, 2024) (select "Year"; then search 2022).

25. Noe-Bustamante, *supra* note 18.

26. *Id.*

27. *Id.*

28. Jonathan Hornstein, The Harry & Jeanette Weinberg Found., Jewish Poverty in the United States: A Summary of Recent Research, (2019), https://cdn.fedweb.org/fed-42/2892/jewish-poverty-in-the-united-states%2520Weinberg%2520Report.pdf.

Are Sephardic Jews Hispanic?

1. *Sephardic Jews.* Sephardic Jews trace their ancestry back to the Jews of the Iberian Peninsula prior to the expulsion from Spain in 1492 and Portugal in 1497. The word "Sephardic" comes from the Hebrew word for Spain, Sephara,[29] and historically Sephardic Jews spoke Ladino, a language based on Old Spanish.[30] Roughly 3 percent of American Jews identify as Sephardic.[31] Most American Jews are Ashkenazi, that is, they are descended from the cultural group of Jews whose medieval "hub" was in Italy and Germany and whose hub later became Eastern Europe."[32]

2. *Are Sephardic Jews Hispanic?*[33] A Spaniard or person of Spanish descent living in the U.S. is considered Hispanic. Should Sephardic Jews living in the U.S. be considered Hispanic? Sephardic Jews' racial classification has varied historically, including being considered "Oriental," "Black," "White," and "Hispanic" at different times. Sephardic Jews' racial status was contested in the context of affirmative action and desegregation efforts in the 1970s. In *DeFunis v. Odegaard* (1974), Marco DeFunis, Jr., a Sephardic Jew, sued the University of Washington Law School for denying him admission despite test scores that were higher than some of the minorities admitted, due to affirmative action policies. DeFunis was considered simply as a White male in the case, with his Sephardic identity not playing a significant role. (Since DeFunis was months from graduating, the case was dismissed as moot.)

3. *Redesignation as Hispanic.* In 1978, Sephardic Jewish teachers in the Los Angeles Unified School District (LAUSD) petitioned to be reclassified as "Hispanic" rather than "White" in order to avoid being reassigned, along with other non-Hispanic White teachers, to minority-majority schools as part of racial integration efforts. In response, the school board declared that Sephardic Jews "are white." To increase their odds of being classified as Hispanic, some Sephardic Jewish teachers downplayed or concealed their Jewishness, emphasizing instead conventional markers of Hispanic identity. In one case, a Jewish teacher's Hispanic classification was questioned when she missed school to observe Yom Kippur.[34]

4. *Are Sephardic Jews Spanish?* In 2015, Spain enacted Law 12/2015, which grants Spanish citizenship to Sephardic Jews with a special connection to Spain, such as

---

29. Sarah Aroeste, *Latino, Hispanic or Sephardic?*, MY JEWISH LEARNING (Dec. 13, 2018), https://www.myjewishlearning.com/2018/12/13/latino-hispanic-or-sephardic/.

30. *Ladino*, OXFORD ENG. DICTIONARY, https://doi.org/10.1093/OED/3786941859 (last visited, Dec. 2023).

31. PEW RSCH. CTR., JEWISH AMERICANS IN 2020 38 (2021), https://www.pewresearch.org/religion/2021/05/11/the-size-of-the-u-s-jewish-population/.

32. STEVEN H. RESNICOFF, UNDERSTANDING JEWISH LAW 253, 262 (2d ed. 2019).

33. For discussion of this and related questions, *see* AVIVA BEN-UR, SEPHARDIC JEWS IN AMERICA: A DIASPORIC HISTORY (2009); Max Daniel, *Sephardic Jewish persons are classified as white: Education, Race, and Sephardic Jews in the 1970s*, *in* JEWISH IDENTITIES IN THE AMERICAN WEST: RELATIONAL PERSPECTIVES 290–325 (Ellen Eisenberg ed., 2022).

34. JEWISH IDENTITIES IN THE AMERICAN WEST: RELATIONAL PERSPECTIVES 290–325 (Ellen Eisenberg ed., 2022).

knowledge of Ladino and Spanish history and culture.[35] Kiku Adatto describes Law 12/2015 "as a powerful gesture of atonement" for Spain's expulsion of Jews.[36] How does this affect Sephardic Jews' claims to be Hispanic?[37]

B. Jews as Non-White for Remedial Purposes

On November 1, 1982, several individuals spray-painted anti-Jewish propaganda on the outside walls of the Shaare Tefila Congregation, a synagogue in Silver Spring, Maryland, causing $3,000 in damages.[38] Rather than removing the graffiti, the Congregation left it up for a week, sparking widespread expressions of support from the larger community and inspiring some community members to join congregants in cleaning the synagogue's walls.[39]

After two defendants were convicted in state court for destruction of property, the Congregation filed a civil suit for damages in federal district court under 42 USC. § 1982 (§ 1982), which, like § 1981, originated in the Civil Rights Act of 1866: it provides that "all citizens" shall enjoy the same property rights as "white citizens."[40] In *Shaare Tefila Congregation v. Cobb*, 606 F. Supp. 1504 (D. Md. 1985), the district court, per Judge Ramsey, dismissed the Congregation's § 1982 claim. Citing no evidence, Judge Ramsey concluded that "Jews do not constitute a "distinct or recognizable 'race' and are not commonly identified as such." The Congregation appealed this dismissal to the court of appeals, which affirmed the district court's judgment in a split decision: Judge K.K. Hall, wrote the opinion of the court; Judge Murnaghan filed a concurring opinion; and Judge Wilkinson filed a dissenting opinion.

Shaare Tefila Congregation v. Cobb

785 F.2d 523 (4th Cir. 1986), *rev'd*, 481 U.S. 615 (1987)

CIRCUIT JUDGE K.K. HALL delivered the opinion of the Court.

Shaare Tefila Congregation is a Jewish community of approximately 500 member families, who assemble at their synagogue in Silver Spring, Maryland, in order to wor-

---

35. *Bill Granting Spanish Citizenship to Sephardic Jews with Spanish Origins*, MINISTRY OF FOREIGN AFFS., EUR. UNION & COOP. OF SPAIN (June 11, 2015), https://www.exteriores.gob.es/Consulados/jerusalen/es/Consulado/Paginas/BILL%20GRANTING%20SPANISH%20CITIZENSHIP%20TO%20SEPHARDIC%20JEWS%20%20Jerusalem.pdf.

36. Kiku Adatto, *Spain's Attempt to Atone for a 500-Year-Old Sin*, THE ATLANTIC (Sept. 21, 2019), https://www.theatlantic.com/international/archive/2019/09/spain-offers-citizenship-sephardic-jews/598258/.

37. REPARATIVE CITIZENSHIP FOR SEPHARDI DESCENDANTS (Rina Benmayor & Dalia Kandiyoti eds., 2023).

38. *Daily News Bulletin*, JEWISH TELEGRAPHIC AGENCY, Mar. 8, 1984.

39. *Id.*; *see also* Kenneth L. Marcus, *The Landmark Case of Shaare Tefila v. Cobb*, 25 FEDERALIST SOC'Y REV. 17, 19 (2024).

40. Plaintiffs brought this action pursuant to 42 USC. §§ 1981, 1982 and 1985(3) and the Maryland common law of trespass, nuisance, and intentional infliction of emotional distress.

Figure 1.1. The community helps to clean Shaare Tefila. Photo by Dave Slade.

ship and engage in community activities. On the evening of November 2, 1982, members and employees of Shaare Tefila Congregation met at the synagogue for activities, including a board of directors' meeting. Marshall S. Levin, the Executive Director of Shaare Tefila Congregation, remained at the synagogue after the meeting. There, he received a telephone call from Dr. Jacob Teller, one of the board members, informing him that Teller's car had been spray-painted with a swastika while parked at the synagogue for the meeting. When Levin went outside to search for possible further damage, he discovered that the white outside walls of the synagogue had been spray-painted in red and black with large anti-Semitic slogans and symbols, which included the words, "Death to the Jude," "In, Take a Shower Jew," "Toten Kamf Raband," and "Dead Jew," swastikas, a skull and crossbones, and Ku Klux Klan symbols....

The Congregation alleges that the district court erred in dismissing its section 1982 claim. Section 1982 states that "all citizens of the United States shall have the same right, in every State and Territory, as is enjoyed by white citizens thereof to inherit, purchase, lease, sell, hold, and convey real and personal property." Appellant's section 1982 claim, as stated in its complaint, was that "defendants' desecration of the synagogue ... deprived plaintiffs of the right to hold real and personal property. Defendants' desecration of the synagogue was motivated by racial prejudice in that defendants perceive plaintiffs as racially distinct because they are Jews."

Appellant argues that the district court's dismissal of its section 1982 claim is erroneous as a matter of law because defendants' desecration of the synagogue had a racial character, was motivated by racial animus and, thus, is actionable under section 1982. The Congregation maintains that Jews are not members of a racially distinct group and do not wish to be so considered. It nevertheless argues that because defendants viewed Jews as a racially distinct group, defendants' acts constituted racial discrimination in violation of section 1982. In support of its argument, the Congregation relies upon the Tenth Circuit's decision in *Manzanares v. Safeway Stores, Inc.* We reject appellant's contentions and find nothing in the statute, its legislative history, or subsequent case law which would lead us to conclude that section 1982 was intended to apply to situations in which a plaintiff is not a member of a racially distinct group but is merely *perceived* to be so by defendants. We conclude that *Manzanares* is, if correct at all, inapposite.

Manzanares involved a section 1981 action brought by a plaintiff of Mexican American descent against his employer and labor union, alleging that he was discriminated against due to his race and/or national origin in that he was treated differently from Anglo-Americans. The Tenth Circuit concluded that "section 1981 is directed to racial discrimination primarily but is not necessarily limited to the technical or restrictive meaning of 'race,'" and held that the plaintiff's contentions were sufficient to state a claim under section 1981. Appellants urge us to extend the Tenth Circuit's reasoning here. We decline to do so. *Manzanares* did not hold that a defendant's mere perception of a plaintiff as racially distinct is sufficient to constitute racial discrimination in violation of section 1981. Instead, the Tenth Circuit emphasized that Mexican Americans, as a group, are commonly treated differently from Anglo-Americans, as a group. We do not find the position of Jews in this society to be analogous to that of Mexican Americans or others commonly considered to be non-whites.

Although we sympathize with appellant's position, we conclude that it cannot support a claim of racial discrimination solely on the basis of defendants' perception of Jews as being members of a racially distinct group. To allow otherwise would permit charges of racial discrimination to arise out of nothing more than the subjective, irrational perceptions of defendants. Such perceptions are not what section 1982 was intended to protect against. Because discrimination against Jews is not racial discrimination, and the Supreme Court has stated that section 1982 does not address discrimination on account of religion or national origin, *Jones v. Alfred H. Mayer Co.*, we find that the district court properly dismissed the Congregation's section 1982 claim....

Circuit Judge Murnaghan, concurring.

Bearing in mind that hard cases pose the risk of making bad law, the present controversy constitutes a hard case. The behavior of which the defendants stand accused was execrable. In also reaching the conclusion Judge Hall has expressed, I nevertheless steadfastly hope that, if the allegations are supported by proof, stern retribution under the laws of Maryland will be meted out to the defendants.

Yet the law is grounded on facts, not on misperceptions of fact. For persons of the ilk which the defendants, at the present posture of the case, are revealed to be to have the power to confer jurisdiction on the federal courts would, in all probability, lead to very regrettable consequences.

I think not only of Jews and the regrettable indignities they may well have suffered here at the hands of the defendants. I cannot say that my sympathies for the first time go out to them only because those sympathies have already gone out to the Jews long ago and on many occasions as bad as or far worse than the instant one.

My ethnic origins are principally Hibernian. On March 17, for one group of Irish hotheads and on July 12 for another (as well as other dates during the year), violence deriving from misperceptions, of Catholics on the one hand, or of Protestants on the other, as an inferior human sort or race has broken out, to my everlasting regret from time to time. Yet it will but contribute to disruption of our nation to accord such ill-mannered and unreasoned fracases the dignity of status as civil rights controversies. They belong in the state courts, where justice, more immediate and more personalized, is likely to be at hand.

Accordingly, I concur in the conclusion that 42 USC. §§ 1981, 1982 and 1985(3) do not afford a basis for bringing suit in the circumstances here involved.

Circuit Judge Wilkinson, concurring in part, dissenting in part.

I cannot accept the majority's view that the civil rights statutes invoked here fail to protect against racial discrimination based on "nothing more than the subjective, irrational perceptions of defendants." All racial prejudice is the result of subjective, irrational perceptions, which drain individuals of their dignity because of their perceived equivalence as members of a racial group. The Civil Rights Acts of 1866 and 1871 were enacted precisely to halt the spread of violence and hatred by those motivated by such perceptions, and plaintiffs in this case, no less than those in the usual racial discrimination case, have suffered the consequences of abhorrent notions concerning racial identity and its relevance. Rather than allowing ignorance and misperception to provide their own defense, I would find the erroneous but all too sincere view of defendants that Jews constitute a separate race worthy of humiliation and degradation sufficient to bring the claim within 42 USC. §§ 1982 and 1985(3).

I.

Because the majority opinion leaves the impression that the incident at issue here was an isolated event with only speculative racial overtones, it is necessary to examine the broader context in which the desecration of Shaare Tefila Synagogue occurred.... Here, we find that defendants' activities on the evening of November 1, 1982, started when they gathered behind a Drug Fair store at a shopping center in Silver Spring, Maryland. While the eight defendants drank and talked, they spray-painted the outside walls of the store with anti-Semitic slogans and symbols, including "Arian [*sic*] Brotherhood," "white Power," "KKK," an eagle with a swastika, and a Star of David with an arrow through it. Defendants also painted their initials on the Drug Fair wall.

During this time, one of the group suggested that "somebody should do that to a synagogue." Apparently heeding this suggestion, defendants proceeded toward the nearby grounds of Shaare Tefila Congregation. On their way, they painted a swastika on the car of synagogue member Jacob Teller, parked outside the synagogue. Defendants then entered the grounds of the synagogue and painted offensive symbols and slogans on the building similar to those painted at the Drug Fair. These included swastikas, a skull and crossbones, a burning cross, and the slogans "Dead Jew," "Death to the Jude," "Ku Klux Klan," and on a doorway the words "In, Take a Shower Jew." Also found on the building was the phrase "Toten Kamf Raban," apparently a reference to the *Totenkopfverbände*—"death head units" of Nazi concentration camp guards from 1936 through World War II. The skull and crossbones was the insignia of the *Totenkopfverbände.* As one would expect, these actions caused members of the congregation great emotional distress and fear.

The complaint alleges that the racial character of defendants' actions is established by their perception "of plaintiffs as racially distinct because they are Jews," and the procedural posture of this case requires us to assume that defendants do indeed view Jews as racially distinct. This assumption is further supported by the nature of the slogans and symbols painted on the synagogue and by the statements of defendants themselves. The paintings found on the synagogue align the defendants with both the Ku Klux Klan and the Nazis, two groups infamous for their persistence in the view that Jews constitute a separate and inferior race. Depositions of defendants reveal that they understood the message of these groups and ascribed to the validity of their racial theories. Defendant Heine, for example, understood that the Nazis wanted to develop a superior race, one distinct from the Jewish race. Defendant Hunt believed that the phrase "Dead Jew" would make a Jew uncomfortable because "it's an insult to your race." Thus, there is no question on appeal that defendants considered Jews to be a racially distinct group.

II.

Without so much as a hint as to the affirmative reach of § 1982, the majority asserts *ipse dixit*[41] that defendants' actions "are not what section 1982 was intended to protect against." This conclusion cannot withstand analysis. Federal civil rights laws protect citizens from acts of discriminatory intent. The discrimination found here is no different in character or consequence from that found in every racial discrimination case. Misperception lies at the heart of prejudice, and the animus formed of such ignorance sows malice and hatred wherever it operates without restriction. By removing the restriction of federal laws, the majority allows racial motivations greater latitude to effect their intolerable aims. There is simply no good reason why we should interpret this statute to protect against some forms of racial animus but not others.

There is, of course, no question that the Civil Rights Act of 1866, the genesis of §§ 1981 and 1982, was aimed at the evil fostered by racially discriminatory animus. Though not intended to provide recovery for discrimination based on religion, or national origin, these sections clearly prohibit "*all* racially motivated deprivations of the rights enumerated in the statute." The focus on discriminatory intent is not unique to §§ 1981 and 1982, for the presence of such intent is sufficient to establish violations of other laws aimed at the eradication of racial prejudice. The effort to eliminate racially

41. Editor's note: *Ipse dixit* [Latin "he himself said it"]; something asserted but not proved; "His testimony that she was a liar was nothing more than an *ipse dixit.*" *Ipse Dixit*, BLACK'S LAW DICTIONARY (12th ed. 2024).

motivated actions, moreover, is not to be obstructed by narrow interpretations. The laws at issue here offer protection to "all persons" (§ 1981) and "all citizens" (§ 1982), and "establish[ed] in the federal law a broader principle than would have been necessary simply to meet the particular and immediate plight of the newly freed Negro slaves." Put simply, the laws established the right of every person to be free of enumerated deprivations motivated by racial animus.

The focus on the subjective intent of the actor reflects the reality that discrimination and prejudice is grounded in erroneous perceptions. In the more familiar case, racial discrimination is based on the misperception of the relevance of racial identity. Bigots are motivated by the belief that those of another race are inferior and hence worthy of physical, mental and social repression. Broad, stereotypical assumptions about race have always formed the basis for both private and official acts of prejudice. One would think it preposterous to require that these beliefs be objectively true before federal law provides protection. To the contrary, it is precisely because such beliefs are false and reprehensible that federal civil rights laws were enacted. These laws provide redress for the harms suffered by misperceptions about the relevance of race as a basis for action in our society.

Plaintiffs here were confronted not only with these misperceptions about the relevance of racial identity but also with the misperception that Jews are a distinct and inferior race. The evil visited upon them was thus a dual one. It is, of course, clear to this court, the district court, and counsel that Jews are not, under any legitimate view, a distinct race, but are in fact members of a religious community with a rich cultural heritage. Yet the majority finds that the misperceptions at work here deprive the claim of the "racial character" necessary to bring it within § 1982. This conclusion must rest upon the view that the racial fallacies here are so different from those routinely prohibited by federal law as to fall outside the scope of it. I fail to see any relevant distinction between the racial attitudes that prompted defendants' actions and those at work in actions clearly within the scope of § 1982.

It is undeniable that the misguided view of the racial distinctiveness of Jews has led to atrocities of no less consequence than those generated by other fallacious beliefs about race. Though history is unfortunately replete with examples of repression of Jews as a people, one need not trace these problems through the ages to discern the consequences of distorted racial views about Jews, for it is during this century that their most terrible effects have been witnessed. Hitler was driven by the belief that Jews constituted a separate race that threatened his goal of racial purity. *See*, G. Gilbert, Nuremberg Diary 43 (1947) (testimony of Julius Streicher). "The fact that the Nazi 'race' theories represented the most ludicrous and vicious mythology that had ever been perpetuated upon a people did not... prevent those myths from functioning as if they were perfectly true." History teaches, then, that misperceptions about racial identity are no different in the misery and hatred they spread than misperceptions about the relevance of race.[42]

42. There can be no question that the Nazi theory and practice was racial. "The Nazi attitude and discrimination against the Jews was not founded upon their religious practices; it did not cease upon

Nor is the danger of warped racial classification of Jews simply a matter of history. Neo-Nazi groups in the United States make no effort to hide their racist heritage or their ultimate goals. The National Socialist Party of America, for example, has proclaimed among its fundamental principles "acceptance of Adolf Hitler" and "the Jew as the Ultimate Enemy." These principles are expressed in explicitly racist terms: "The single serious enemy facing the white man is the Jew. The Jews are not a religion, they are an Asiatic *race*, locked in mortal conflict with Aryan man which has lasted for millennia, and which will continue until one of the two combat peoples are extinct." A group called Aryan Nations, in a publication of the same name, has implored its readers: "Aryans Awake! Jews are the Race of Satan!" The racist view of Jews is also a major tenet of the Ku Klux Klan. An expert on the Klan, in an affidavit prepared for this litigation, noted that "a prevalent belief among the various Ku Klux Klan groups is that Jewish people are racially distinct from whites."

These views, like those of the Nazis, have resulted in numerous instances of violence against Jewish citizens. The facts of this case, unfortunately, are not isolated but instead representative of such incidents. In 1985 alone there were, in the estimate of one organization, 638 incidents of anti-Semitic vandalism against Jewish institutions, private Jewish homes, and Jewish businesses in the United States. Anti-Semitic physical assaults against Jews, and anti-Semitic threats and harassment of Jewish institutions reportedly totaled 306. Even were such events less prevalent, it would not lessen the sufferings of those subjected to them.

Of course, not every wrong against a Jewish citizen would be actionable under the civil rights laws. Here, however, we deal with the adherents of organizations whose aims are avowedly racial. It is clear that this case, like every case of racial discrimination, is the result of racial misperceptions. These misperceptions, moreover, result from the same catalyst for fear and violence that caused Congress to enact the Civil Rights Acts of 1866 and 1871. Defendants appropriate the very symbols of the Ku Klux Klan, the organization that visited the most virulent brand of racial violence in the Reconstruction era. In acting against it, Congress proclaimed the right of "all persons" to be free of "all racially motivated deprivations of the rights enumerated in the statute." The majority now denies that right to plaintiffs by allowing defendants' misperceptions and ignorance to serve as a defense to their actions.

III.

The failure to allow this claim under § 1982 is not only inconsistent with the purpose of the statutory scheme but also saddles the courts with the difficult and inappropriate burden of delineating racial distinctions in a context where they are irrelevant and unnecessary. The majority, apparently fearful that § 1982 actions might rest "entirely on the

religious conversion. Indeed, it even manifested itself in hunting down and 're-judaizing' assimilated Christians of Jewish extraction. Nor was this discrimination based upon national origin, since Jews of impeccable German ancestry were equally subject to the atrocities visited upon French, Polish, Danish, and Russian Jews. The Nazi discrimination against Jews was racial in that the Nazis defined the Jews as separate from their 'Aryan' race and maintained that Jews were a physically distinct people."

idiosyncrasies of individual defendants," rejects the racial nature of the actions here because the victims did not actually belong to the distinct racial class in which defendants placed them. This approach, I presume, requires courts to determine by some more objective criteria whether an individual is a member of a distinct race before the Civil Rights Act of 1866 may apply. Yet the majority offers little guidance about how courts should undertake the troubling task it requires. Careful consideration of the burden imposed by the majority reveals significant deficiencies in the approach it establishes.

It is unrealistic to expect that a biological or anthropological perspective on the question of race will help courts to determine those protected under the majority's approach. The scientific concept of "race" is anything but definite. As one court has noted, scientists generally agree that "the notion of race is a taxonomic device [that] exists in the human mind and not as a division in the objective universe." Scientists engaged in racial classification recognize that the choice of characteristics used to determine racial groups is arbitrary and depends upon the reason for classification rather than objective reality. Moreover, racial classifications are dynamic and subject to constant re-examination. In short, the inexact and unstable nature of scientific racial classification makes the tool all too treacherous for a court seeking to determine the precise coverage of federal law.

More significantly, the scientific debate over the meaning of race is simply irrelevant to the determination of the protection of a statute addressed to a social phenomenon. As this case demonstrates, it is not scientifically authenticated views but rather distorted social perceptions that lie at the root of racial violence. "The social definition and not the biological facts actually determines the status of an individual and his place in interracial relations.... The scientific concept of race is *totally inapplicable at the very spots where we recognize 'race problems.'*" We cannot be blind to the fact that "to most people, a race is any group of people whom they choose to describe as a race." In construing statutes designed to eliminate racial prejudice, we must confront the reality that the perceptions of individuals, rather than the measurements of science, define the scope of racial discrimination. To limit § 1982 to discrimination against scientifically established racial groups would deprive the remedy of its force in an artificial and disingenuous manner.

Perhaps in recognition of the inadequacies of a scientific approach to the scope of § 1982, several courts have employed a "common perception" test to determine the coverage of the statute. The majority implies that § 1982 might apply here if the misperception at work were a common or widely shared view but rejects the application of this test because "the position of Jews in this society [is not] analogous to that of Mexican Americans or others commonly considered to be non-white." Thus, while recognizing the role of misperceptions in racial discrimination, the majority apparently requires that they be broadly held for § 1982 to apply. There are several reasons why any such approach must be rejected on these facts.

First, the majority's assertion of the common perception of Jews is totally unsupported. The level and persistence of racial violence against Jews, as discussed above, certainly suggests that the misperceptions here are shared by too sizeable a number of individuals. One anthropologist has observed that "Jews are nearly always referred to in popular parlance as a 'race.' This is done not only by the so-called 'man in the street' but also by many scientists, medical men, philosophers, politicians, historians, and the members of many other professions." Thus, there exists a real question about the breadth of the views at work in this case. If the majority insists that misperceptions be broad based for § 1982 to apply, plaintiffs should at least be given the opportunity to show the scope of the belief that they are members of a distinct race.

In any event, the scope and breadth of illegitimate views is not controlling where, as here, plaintiffs seek to demonstrate that these particular defendants held, and were motivated by, racial misperceptions. The very purpose of the Civil Rights Acts was to ensure that the most bigoted people are not permitted to translate their impulses into tangible harms. Protection against the acts of racial prejudice is necessary whether the views are widely held or idiosyncratic. Where, as here, plaintiffs are prepared to show defendants were motivated by racial beliefs, however misguided, there is no reason for a court to require more. Many courts have recognized that proof of racial motivation, without more, is sufficient to bring an action within § 1981 or § 1982. The fact that courts may sometimes find it convenient to look to common perceptions to determine racial status should not preclude plaintiffs from showing that defendants here operated on the basis of racial misperceptions, however misguided or idiosyncratic.

Permitting the subjective belief of defendants to give a claim the "racial character" necessary to bring it within the civil rights statutes thus not only ensures adequate coverage but also avoids in many cases the difficult and troubling task of drawing racial lines. Even if courts were well equipped to make racial determinations without engaging in "precisely the kind of stereotyping which the civil rights statutes were designed to prevent," the undertaking presents a potential for continued harm and prejudice so great that it should be avoided wherever possible. It is an understatement to note that attempts to place individuals in distinct racial groups frequently serve only to facilitate continued discrimination and postpone the day when all individuals will be addressed as such. It is regrettable that the majority has adopted an approach that demands judicial draftsmanship of an officially recognized and protected list of races.[43] It is doubly regrettable that it adopts this approach in a case where the racial nature of the acts is clear and compelling.

---

43. It is only the majority's approach that establishes a need for racial distinctions here. In McDonald v. Santa Fe Trail Transportation Co., 427 U.S. 273, 295 (1976), the Supreme Court examined the legislative history of the Civil Rights Act of 1866 and rejected the view that the act applied only to non-Whites. There is thus no need to draw racial lines to determine those who are potential beneficiaries of the protection offered by § 1982. This task is imposed only by the majority's requirement that plaintiffs demonstrate the reality of the racial class in which defendants place them.

Racial Antisemitism Is Not Racism Because Jews Are Not a Race

1. *The discriminator's perception.* The Congregation's argument is an example of what Marcus calls a "subjectivist" approach to anti-discrimination law, including as applied to Jews. This approach, he explains:

> focus[es] on the perpetrator, asking whether the discriminator targeted Jewish victims based on racial biases or misperceptions. Under this subjectivist method, one who targets Jews based on notions of Jewish racial inferiority discriminates "because ... of race" even if history, scientific evidence, and common usage indicate that Jews do not form a race. The subjectivist approach also can be described as a theory of imputed group membership ... because it permits persons to claim those group traits which are imputed to them by their oppressors, whether their oppressors' perceptions are accurate or not.[44]

2. *The Congregation maintains.* As Judge Hall notes, "the Congregation maintains that Jews are not members of a racially distinct group and do not wish to be so considered." Should the Congregation have strengthened their claim by arguing that Jews, while not in fact a race, should nonetheless be treated as a distinct racial group for the purposes of § 1982? How would such treatment be justified? If it would have strengthened their case, why didn't they argue this?

3. Manzanares *and* Shaare Tefila. Did Judge Hall think *Manzanares* was correctly decided? If not, why did he proceed to distinguish between that case and *Shaare Tefila*? Assuming Judge Hall thought *Manzanares* was correctly decided, how does he distinguish the two cases? What, in his view, (a) justifies extending §1981's coverage to Latinos while (b) not extending §1982's coverage to Jews? Separately, how would Judge Seth have decided *Shaare Tefila*?

4. *Arise out of nothing more.* Judge Hall asserts that if the court supported the Congregation's § 1982 claim, courts would be obliged to "permit charges of racial discrimination to arise out of nothing more than the subjective, irrational perceptions of defendants." What is the *something more* that would have permitted the Congregation's claim to succeed?

5. *Arise out of something less?* Judge Hall notes that § 1982 does not address discrimination based on religion. Is this, in his view, the crucial distinction between Latinos and Jews? If Jews were simply a marginalized non-racial ethnic group unconnected to a specific religion, would they be entitled to coverage alongside Latinos? On some reckonings, Jews are a religious group. In Judge Hall's view, are Jews disqualified from § 1982's coverage because they are also a religious group?

6. *A slippery slope?* In *Wald v. Intl. Broth. of Teamsters*, 1980 WL 306 (C.D. Cal. Oct. 10, 1980), the court rejected a Jewish employee's claim that the anti-Jewish discrimination he experienced violated § 1981. The court declined to follow *Manzanares.*

44. Kenneth L. Marcus, Jewish Identity and Civil Rights in America 154 (2010).

> The reading which the [*Manzanares*] court gives to § 1981 leaves many questions unanswered. The court does not seek to explain why religion or sex-based discrimination does not violate § 1981, although under the terms of its broad analysis such [discrimination] clearly involved "group" distinctions. The court also does not deal with the fact that the analysis, standing alone, would include many types of group distinctions that have never been considered within protection of the law.

Is this critique persuasive? Can § 1981 be applied to Jews without applying it to religion-based discrimination more generally, such as anti-Catholic or anti-Protestant discrimination?

7. *Jews as White ethnics.* Using a common perception approach, the court in *Budinsky v. Corning Glass Works*, 425 F. Supp. 786, 788 (W. D. Pa. 1977) rejected a Slavic plaintiff's § 1981 claim. In dictum, the court disapproved the statute's extension to Jews and persons of Italian descent:

> These groups are not so commonly identified as "races" nor so frequently subject to that "racial" discrimination which is the specific and exclusive target of § 1981. Members of these groups ... do not properly fall within the coverage of the statute.

On what basis does the *Budinsky* court base its claims that Jews are neither commonly identified as a race nor sufficiently subject to anti-Jewish discrimination? Would he categorically exclude Jews from § 1981's coverage, regardless of racial perceptions and anti-Jewish discrimination? Or is there a tipping point and, if so, how more widely must the perception that Jews are a race be held before he would extend § 1981's coverage to Jews, and how much more discrimination must Jews experience?

Can a principled distinction be drawn between Jews on the one hand and Slavic and Italian Americans on the other that would permit the extension of § 1981 to the former but not to the latter? Is the non-Jew/Jew binary a more consequential axis of discrimination than the non-Slavic/Slavic and non-Italian/Italian binaries?

8. *Other remedies available?* In rejecting the Slavic plaintiff's § 1981 claim, the *Budinsky* court "start[ed] from the fundamental premise that plaintiff Budinsky has a full and complete remedy available under Title VII" of the Civil Rights Act of 1964, which prohibits discrimination based on national origin. The critical question, in its view, was "whether the federal courts need or should open the door to a new remedial alternative in the area of employment discrimination where Congress already has provided a specific, far-reaching remedy in Title VII. I think that question must be answered in the negative."

In *Manzanares*, the Latino plaintiff sought relief only under § 1981. It is unclear why the plaintiff did not seek relief under Title VII for national origin discrimination. Judge Seth acknowledged that the plaintiff had the option of doing so but stated that the potential availability of a Title VII action did not affect his § 1981 analysis. Should Judge Seth, like the *Budinsky* court, have denied the Latino plaintiff's claim on the grounds that he had an adequate alternative remedy? This prompts the question: should § 1981 be construed broadly to cover groups not protected by other civil rights statutes?

9. *The base/bases of anti-Jewish discrimination.* Judge Richard Posner has noted "the dual character of anti-Semitism."

> There is religious anti-Semitism, typified by the attitude of the medieval Roman Catholic Church, and racial anti-Semitism, typified by Hitler. The one objects to Jews because of their religion, the other objects to Jews because they are descended from Jews, even if they are converts to other faiths.[45]

Does Judge Hall's ruling implicitly deny the existence of racial antisemitism? Assuming it does not, are there sound reasons for courts to treat antisemitism and anti-Jewish discrimination as an exclusively religious phenomenon for § 1982 purposes?

10. *Jewish by religion.* According to a 2020 survey by Pew Research, only 10 percent of American Jews say being Jewish is only a matter of religion:

> U.S. Jews do not have a single, uniform answer to what being Jewish means. When asked whether being Jewish is mainly a matter of religion, ancestry, culture or some combination of those things, Jews respond in a wide variety of ways, with just one-in-ten saying it is only a matter of religion.
>
> Many American Jews prioritize cultural components of Judaism over religious ones. Most Jewish adults say that remembering the Holocaust, leading a moral and ethical life, working for justice and equality in society, and being intellectually curious are "essential" to what it means to them to be Jewish. Far fewer say that observing Jewish law is an essential part of their Jewish identity. Indeed, more consider "having a good sense of humor" to be essential to being Jewish than consider following halakha (traditional Jewish law) essential (34 [percent] vs. 15 [percent]).
>
> Orthodox Jews are a striking exception to many of these overall findings. They are among the most highly religious groups in U.S. society—along with White evangelicals and Black Protestants—in terms of the share who say religion is very important in their lives.[46]

Does the fact that most Jews do not identify being Jewish as solely or mainly a religious matter affect the claim that anti-Jewish discrimination is a religious phenomenon?

Antisemitism vs. Irish Sectarianism

1. *Jews and the Irish.* Judge Murnaghan would not extend § 1982's scope to Irish Catholics and Irish Protestants. He makes an analogy—non-Jews/Jews :: Irish Catholics/Irish Protestants :: Irish Protestants/Irish Catholics. Why does Judge Murnaghan group Jews, Irish Catholics, and Irish Protestants together in his § 1982 analysis? Can

---

45. Bachman v. St. Monica's Congregation, 902 F.2d 1259, 1260–61 (7th Cir. 1990).

46. Pew Rsch. Ctr., Jewish Americans in 2020 56 (2021), https://www.pewresearch.org/religion/2021/05/11/the-size-of-the-u-s-jewish-population/.

you meaningfully distinguish between (a) anti-Jewish discrimination by non-Jews and (b) anti-Protestant discrimination by Irish Catholics and vice versa? Does this distinction change the § 1982 analysis? Which is more persuasive: Judge Murnaghan's analogy or Judge Hall's refusal to extend *Manzanares* to anti-Jewish discrimination?

2. *A hard case?* Judge Murnaghan refers to the legal maxim that "hard cases make bad law." As originally used:

> [The maxim] concerned cases in which the law had a hard impact on some person whose situation aroused sympathy. In such cases there was an inevitable, and often strong, temptation to offer a strained interpretation of the law to avoid the hard effect in the individual case. The slogan "hard cases make bad law" amounted to an exhortation to refrain from bending the law on account of exceptional individual hardship....
>
> "Hard case" has over the past few decades changed its meaning, under the influence of Ronald Dworkin, who suggests (in effect) that such cases provide occasions to make good law. A hard case is now understood as a case where some difficulty of interpreting the law has arisen, where there are strong arguments for each of the rival understandings or interpretations of the law put forward by or on behalf of the parties.[47]

Judge Murnaghan uses "hard case" in a negative sense: it would change the law in a negative way by requiring unintended bad outcomes in future cases. What bad outcomes does he fear if § 1982 is extended to Jews? Was he mistaken—was *Shaare Tefila* a hard case in the Dworkinian sense?

Racial Antisemitism Is Racism for Remedial Purposes

1. *The affirmative reach of § 1982.* Judge Wilkinson claims that the majority does not provide "so much as a hint as to the affirmative reach of § 1982," that is, it does not provide criteria for determining which groups fall within § 1982's scope and which fall outside of it. Is that correct? What principle does he provide for setting its limits?

2. Would Judge Wilkinson find a § 1982 claim where the plaintiff alleged that the defendant (a) discriminated against her because she belongs to group X and (b) he perceives group X to be a distinct racial group, where: (c) group X does not exist or have an objective reality, but is in fact based on "nothing more than the subjective, irrational perceptions of defendants"? Consider the case of Aryans and Amazonians. Does the analysis change if X equals Jews?

3. If § 1982 were extended to Jews, should it apply to (a) potentially any act of anti-Jewish discrimination or (b) only those acts of anti-Jewish discrimination motivated by the belief that Jews are a distinct race—a potentially difficult standard to satisfy? Note that a Latina can raise a § 1982 claim for anti-Latino discrimination without having

---

47. Neil MacCormick, Rhetoric and the Rule of Law: A Theory of Legal Reasoning 49–50 (2005).

to prove that the defendant believes Latinos are a distinct race. On the Congregation's theory, would Jews' § 1982 claims be held to a higher standard than Latinos' claims? If so, why would they argue that?

4. *Religion-based discrimination.* Judge Wilkinson states that "not every wrong against a Jewish citizen would be actionable" under a civil rights law that did not prohibit religious discrimination. Which acts of anti-Jewish discrimination should not be actionable under § 1982?

5. *Racialism versus racism.* In Judge Wilkinson's view, the defendants' misconceptions of Jews were "evil" in two senses: first, they falsely believe that Jews are a distinct race, and second, they falsely believe that Jews are an inferior race.

It may be fruitful to distinguish between racialism and racism. Racialism denotes "beliefs that members of a particular racial or ethnic group possess innate characteristics or qualities."[48] This term may perhaps be distinguished from "racism," which denotes "prejudice, antagonism, or discrimination by an individual, institution, or society against a person or people on the basis of ... their membership [in] a particular racial or ethnic group."[49] In theory, a person can be a racialist without being a racist; he may believe that all races are equal in the sight of God. A racist, in contrast, believes not only that races exist, but that some are superior to others. Note that the Oxford English Dictionary defines "racialist" as one meaning of "racist" with the former being "largely superseded" by the latter.[50] Is non-racist racialism a viable construct?

6. *Line-drawing problems.* Judge Wilkinson expresses concern that extending § 1982's protections on a group-by-group basis (e.g., African Americans, then Latinos, then Jews) might harm the cause of equality by reinvigorating categories and constructs we seek to leave behind. In Martha Minow's formulation, line-drawing issues in civil rights statutes present the "dilemma of difference":

> We may recreate difference either by noticing it or by ignoring it. Decisions about employment, benefits, and treatment in society should not turn on an individual's race, gender, religion, or membership in any other group about which some have deprecating or hostile attitudes. Yet refusing to acknowledge these differences may make them continue to matter in a world constructed with some groups, but not others, in mind. If women's biological differences from men justify special benefits for women in the workplace, are women thereby helped or hurt? Are negative stereotypes reinforced, and does that matter? Focusing on differences poses the risk of recreating them. Especially when used by decisionmakers who award benefits and distribute burdens, traits of difference can carry meanings uncontrolled and unwelcomed by those to

---

48. *Racist,* Oxford Eng. Dictionary, https://doi.org/10.1093/OED/8744131157 (last visited Sept. 17, 2024).

49. *Racism,* Oxford Eng. Dictionary, https://doi.org/10.1093/OED/1101660185 (last visited Sept. 17, 2024).

50. *Racialist,* Oxford Eng. Dictionary, https://doi.org/10.1093/OED/8021459503 (last visited Sept. 17, 2024).

> whom they are assigned. Yet denying those differences undermines the value they may have to those who cherish them as part of their own identity.

Minnow saw this dilemma on display in *Shaare Tefila:*

> The difference dilemma appeared on the face of the [Congregation's] complaint: the petitioners argued that Jews are not a racially distinct group, and yet they claimed that Jews should be entitled to protection against racial discrimination because others treat them as though they were distinct. The petitioners thus demonstrated their reluctance to have a difference identified in a way that they themselves could not control, while simultaneously expressing their desire for protection against having that difference assigned to them by others. To gain this protection, the petitioners had to identify themselves through the very category they rejected as a definition of themselves.[51]

Marcus identifies trade-offs for groups seeking protection under civil rights statutes: "While there are clearly some group advantages that now inhere in governmental recognition of racial distinctiveness, there are also social disadvantages in that same recognition."[52]

How does Judge Wilkinson attempt to resolve this dilemma? Does he succeed?

Naomi W. Cohen,
Shaare Tefila Congregation v. Cobb:
A New Departure in American Jewish Defense?[53]

3 Jewish History 95–108 (1988)

In 1986, when Shaare Tefila prepared to appeal to the Supreme Court for review, the national defense agencies—the Anti-Defamation League, the American Jewish Congress, the American Jewish Committee, the National Jewish Community Relations Advisory Council—considered the advisability of participation. These organizations had serious reservations. From the point of view of the Jewish Establishment, Shaare Tefila's initial foray into the federal courts was tantamount to a wildcat action. The three major agencies—the Congress, the Committee, and the ADL—questioned the advisability of the approach, arguing that state laws on vandalism were the proper recourse. More important, why run the risk of both stirring up additional hatred by overblowing the actual episode and linking the issue of race, in whatever fashion, to Jews? After all, even before Hitler took racist dogma to its logical conclusions, race had long been the *bête noire* of modern Jews seeking integration within the polity. Largely because of the implications of raising the race issue, the Anti-Defamation League refused to participate when the suit was before the lower courts.

---

51. Martha Minow, *Justice Engendered*, 101 Harv. L. Rev. 10, 20 (1987).

52. Marcus, *supra* note 44, at 153.

53. Reprinted by permission of Springer Nature.

The "Big 3" were also dubious of the motives and methods of the congregation's legal representatives, the Jewish Advocacy Center. The center, founded in 1982 by several Washington lawyers, offered to bring lawsuits against individuals or organizations guilty of anti-Semitic acts. Its announced purpose was to collect monetary damages for the victims and thereby discourage antisemites. The center sought out the victims and, by not charging for its services, persuaded them to file the suits.... The center and its request for assistance were summarily dismissed by the older organizations. Professional jealousy may have been involved in their response to an upstart organization, but weightier arguments were mustered to explain the opposition. The new agency was "superfluous"; the possibility of winning sizable damages was "remote"; the center's perception of anti-Semitic episodes was exaggerated; and its "alarmist" stand "elevates the temperature and brings out the nuts." The fact that the center was responsible for suggesting a federal civil suit to Shaare Tefila probably made the case even less palatable to the established agencies.

Despite the misgivings of the professionals, other pressures forced the defense organizations to weigh the merits of filing *amicus* briefs with the Supreme Court. To concerned Jews within the wider community, and even to lay members of the defense agencies, going the federal route was attractive. Federal civil rights legislation protected Jews from religious discrimination in employment, housing, and public accommodations, but these laws did not consider vandalism of a synagogue a violation. Statistics showed no improvement with respect to episodes of anti-Semitic vandalism and the violent actions of anti-Semitic hate groups and opening the Civil War racial statutes to Jews held out the promise of federal jurisdiction over a wider range of discrimination cases. Furthermore, the remedies, that is, relief and damages, available under these laws outweighed the remedies available under others. Since the approach itself—for non-Blacks to invoke the protection of sections 1981 and 1982 of the Code—had been tried, the move for a federal suit could not be interpreted as a radical *Jewish* action. In sum, here was an opportune time for an attempt to broaden the dimensions of security by resorting to law already on the books.

The desire for federal jurisdiction also bared a deep emotional need. To the post-Holocaust generation of Jews, vandalism of a synagogue transcended the garden variety of torts; this was a hate crime whose perpetrators linked it directly to Nazi teachings. Widespread outrage on the part of American Jews stemmed not from fear but from anger; communal pride demanded that antisemitism and not mere vandalism be punished, preferably in *a federal* forum. As the attorneys for Shaare Tefila argued: "Unlike a criminal prosecution for trespass ... under state ... law, a federal civil rights action tells the perpetrators that it is the racist character of the acts—and the resulting injury to individual dignity—that society deplores, not just damage to property." The symbolic gesture of the federal government's denunciation of anti-Semitism seemed all important. One member of the Executive Committee of the American Jewish Congress argued: "After having lived through Hitler it was unthinkable that we would stay out of the case."

The National Jewish Community Relations Council decided not to participate. In a vote that passed with only one dissent, the member organizations held to the view "that there ought not to be the suggestion that the Jewish community in any way gives sanction to the notion that Jews constitute a race." They agreed that state remedies were sufficient, and that any expansion of the civil rights statutes should be sought through legislative rather than judicial action.

The American Jewish Congress, despite its record as the feistiest and most daring agency with respect to litigation, also passed. Its legal committee shied away from the *Al-Khazraji* decision; there, the court's definition of those covered by the civil rights statutes—"membership in a group that is ethnically and physiognomically distinctive"—held the potential of greater danger than relief. The dissenting opinion in the *Shaare Tefila* case agreed that Jews did not constitute a race, but that the need to prove the subjective racist intent of the bigots was a peculiarly difficult task.

The Anti-Defamation League, the first of the agencies to change its policy on plunging into racial waters, latched on to the dissenting opinion of Judge Wilkinson. It filed a brief in support of the congregation's petition to the Supreme Court for review of the circuit court's decision. Two months later the agency filed its second brief, an *amicus curiae*.

The usually conservative American Jewish Committee followed suit. Its sharply divided legal committee was polled twice; the second vote was fourteen to twelve in favor of filing an *amicus* brief. Since the legal committee preferred a consensus of at least sixty percent of its members before entering a case, it submitted the question to its parent body, the National Affairs Commission, which, after considerable discussion, voted decisively to file. One member of the lay legal committee, a senior partner at Cravath, Swaine & Moore, who argued for an *amicus* brief before the national affairs commission, also participated actively in the research and composition of the brief.

It should be noted that the major agencies considered the matter sufficiently important to refer the question of participation to the policy-making bodies that outranked their legal committees. The Executive Committee of the Congress debated the issue at two meetings, and in a close vote of seven to six, made the final decision not to participate. As noted, the National Affairs Commission of the Committee, responding to the considerations that a synagogue was a litigant and that the affair had "elicited extraordinary interest within the Jewish community," decided for its legal committee. In 1984, at the Anti-Defamation League, the legal committee made the initial decision to stay out, but, in 1986, the Executive Committee reviewed the policy of not linking Jews with racial statutes and reversed its decision.

In the final version of the *amicus* brief, since the Supreme Court decided to hear the two cases in tandem, the Anti-Defamation League and American Jewish Committee spoke out for Al-Khazraji as well as Shaare Tefila. The brief attracted other groups—among them the Lawyers' Committee for Civil Rights under Law, the National Association for the Advancement of Colored People, and the American Civil Liberties Union. Jewish agencies have always welcomed such alliances with non-Jews, for joint ventures lend credence to the claim that Jewish interests are general rather than parochial. Not surprisingly, two Jewish organizations representing survivors of the Holocaust added their names on behalf of Shaare Tefila as well.

The joint brief, which urged reversal of the Fourth Circuit Court's decision, argued several major points:

1. The racial motivation and character of the discrimination, rather than the racial status of the plaintiff, was the focus of the Civil Rights Act of 1866. The language of the statute was broad; it offered protection to "all persons" and in no way limited the intended beneficiaries to certain races. Indeed, the Court itself ruled that way in 1976, when it held that the law could be invoked by non-Whites. The Fourth Circuit, by looking only at the plaintiff's race, had erred.
2. The intent of the Congressmen in 1866, attested to by Congressional debates, was to protect all citizens of all races, not just Blacks. Conforming to the general understanding of the word "race" in the mid-nineteenth century, they, like all Americans, used the term loosely, often in the modern sense of ethnic group. Jews were labeled a race in the nineteenth century not only by bigots but by neutral Christians as well. Since the Court had held that interpretation of a statute had to follow the popular vocabulary of its time, the Court in this instance should act according to the intent of the lawmakers.
3. The Fourth Circuit held that the racist views of the vandals were unfounded on scientific grounds and were thus beyond the applicability of the law. This decision served to excuse the defendants. In essence, it said that racial misconduct against Jews lacked validity and could therefore not be punished.
4. Jews are not a race, but anti-Semitic persecution throughout much of Jewish history rested on precisely that misperception. To require proof of actual membership in a race would deny the protection of the law to Jewish (and Arab) victims of discrimination no different in kind from that suffered by non-White racial minorities.
5. There is no consensus on the meaning of race, and it would be "impossible and unseemly" for the Court to attempt such a definition. A three-pronged test could be used to determine whether a litigant was the victim of *racial* discrimination:

    > The factors to be considered should include the plaintiff's allegations concerning the racial or racist motivations of the defendant. In addition, the court should weigh the plaintiff's allegations regarding his own race or skin color. Equally important factors are the extent to which the plaintiff belongs to an identifiable group that is commonly or historically regarded by bigots or lay persons as constituting a "race," as the term is understood in a broad sense.

In the annals of American Jewish defense, the *Shaare Tefila* brief, like the decision of the ADL and the American Jewish Committee to become involved, signified a departure from traditional patterns. Since 1945, when the defense organizations undertook to expand their role in litigation, the two religious clauses of the First Amendment—"Congress shall make no law respecting an establishment of religion or prohibiting the free exercise thereof"—had been the primary base for shoring up Jewish security. This approach derived logically from the fact that the United States refused to draw distinctions among various groups of citizens on grounds other than religion. It accorded as well with Jewish reasoning. Despite the different ways in which American Jews identified themselves, they believed that Christian religious teachings were the foundations of Jew-hatred, and that the persecution suffered by Jews throughout the history of the Christian world—at least until the time of Hitler—was religiously inspired. Hence, American Jews felt most threatened by any gesture that could be construed as an entering wedge to the recognition of a Christian state. It therefore followed that church-state was the all-important area in which to build fences around American law. To be sure, broadening the dimensions of religious freedom and equality did not offer protection against popular anti-Semitic eruptions. But nineteenth-century American Jews believed in the ultimate triumph of "enlightened public opinion," and twentieth-century Jews pinned their faith on the liberal consensus.

In the *Shaare Tefila* case, a qualitatively new dimension appeared: Jews sought the protection of *racial laws*. Jews knew consciously that they could be opening a can of worms. To argue before the Supreme Court that Jews were not a race although the bigots perceived them as such, was providing the most respectable of all possible forums for the airing of racial theories and definitions. In effect, it raised anew the issue of the legitimacy of racist categories. Even if the Court found for Shaare Tefila, it might conceivably leave the implication that Jews were indeed a race. As the legal director of the American Jewish Congress had warned his executive committee, newspaper headlines reading "Court Finds Jews Are a Race" could be imagined. The battle could be won, but the war that American Jewish leaders had been waging since racism became a pseudo-science in the last quarter of the nineteenth century would flare up anew. And, if the Court found for Shaare Tefila by broadening the sweep of the Civil Rights Act to include common ancestry, the extension, Justice Sandra Day O'Connor suggested when the Court heard oral arguments, might logically lead to a national-origins test.

Why the Jews took the chance and argued as they did merits closer examination. Clearly, as native-born and affluent Americans, members of the community felt more confident than ever before. The lessons of the Holocaust—that a common destiny linked all Jews and that only circumstance had spared American Jews from the gas chambers; that "enlightened public opinion" had not deterred Hitler; that accommodationism carried to an extreme was despised as weakness—had left their mark. The existence of a Jewish state further lessened American Jewish timidity.

Jews were also more realistic about the American scene. They had watched the old alliances, particularly those of Jews and liberals, grow tired, if not die. If the old allies were no longer loyal and new alliances had to be forged, Jews, like the politically active ethnic groups around them, had to strengthen their independence. Not only had the liberal consensus evaporated, but the reality was that racism, even in America, had not disappeared. Jews now tacitly acknowledged that fighting racism meant getting down into the gutter and wrestling with it directly. (The establishment of the Jewish Advocacy Center and its activities testified to this more activist mood in the community.) A court victory might not eradicate racist thought, but it could deter further racist acts.

In no way does this mean to suggest that American Jews changed their spots overnight. There was certainly no thought of going outside the law, the desire for *federal* attention was not new, and the organizational debates proved that Jews had not thrown caution to the winds. They were not pioneers in seeking redress under the racial statutes but had waited until other white groups tested the waters. They refused to enter the case until they heard encouraging words from the lower courts. When they prepared their brief, they welcomed the support of non-Jewish groups and willingly allied themselves with an Arab. But the very decision to fight antisemitism under a racial statute was qualitatively different.

Perhaps the most striking aspect of the case was the Jews' tacit invitation to the Supreme Court to define Jewishness in terms other than religious. To be sure, the brief denied several times that Jews were a race, and it ignored the label of "ethnic group." Nevertheless, the Jewish agencies had allied themselves with Professor Al-Khazraji, whose brief argued that the issue was common ancestry. Moreover, they knew the weakness of building a case solely on the grounds of the racist motivations of the vandals. Their suggested three-pronged test by which the courts could determine the applicability of the racial laws admitted the relevance of other factors, viz., the plaintiff's own allegations regarding his race, and the extent to which he belonged to "an identifiable group" commonly or historically regarded as a race. These factors indicated a readiness to accept definitions broader than the conventional religious one.

Being tagged with a common ancestry or as a group with identifiable ethnic characteristics did not offend American Jews in the 1980s. Both they and the government had come a long way in fifty years. From 1899 through the 1930s, the Bureau of Immigration had classified "Hebrews" as a separate race; in 1909, in the first *amicus curiae* brief filed by American Jews, this practice was unsuccessfully contested. The immigration laws of the 1920s that were predicated on national origins and inspired by racist ideology generated similar resentment and dismay. Worried about their image and security, many leading Jews bitterly fought political Zionism until the 1930s because it belied the religious, and therefore safe, definition of a Jew. To be called more than a religion in popular or Congressional parlance carried the stigma of "inferior" or "un-American," and conjured up the specter of dual loyalty.

Jewish views in the 1980s derived from the factors mentioned above and at least as much from the sense of the changed climate of opinion within society. America had never exacted a price from the Jews for equal political rights. But, since the early days of the Republic, statesmen had argued that there was no room in the country for distinct and separate nationalities or peoples; *hyphenate* was often a pejorative term. Like other immigrant groups, most Jews accepted the canon that only religious differences could legitimately resist Americanization. Some Jews went further. In 1918, Isaac Bernheim proposed a *church* of American Israelites. Other Jews, stopping short of outright conversion, suggested a merger of Jews with Unitarians. In contemporary America, however, where pluralism has gained public respectability and where "ethnic" no longer stands diametrically opposed to "American," Jews feel sufficiently comfortable to emerge from behind the religious curtain and assert their peoplehood. The two strands—the benign attitude of society and a new confidence on the part of Jews—converged in the *Shaare Tefila* case to modify, at least partially, the face that American Jews had worn publicly for two centuries. (Just before the final decision was reached, Dean Norman Redlich of the American Jewish Congress admitted that it was a mistake for the Congress to have stayed out.)

One side effect of the case that might lead further is the increased emphasis that Jews and their organizations placed on the need for federal legislation outlawing hate crimes, or crimes committed against religious practices or property. Here, too, the remedy sought was federal, but through new laws rather than litigation.

The importance of the case was lost on the press. Newspapers that commented on the decision usually highlighted the fact that in this matter, Jews and Arabs had cooperated. The essential significance of the *Shaare Tefila* case, however—the willingness of Jews to admit before the law that they are a people as well as members of a religion—should not be ignored. To what extent the precedent will be followed by the Jewish defense agencies before the courts remains to be seen.

Jewish Advocacy in the Shadow of Antisemitism

1. *Joint amicus brief.* What were the main arguments presented in the joint amicus brief filed by the Anti-Defamation League and American Jewish Committee? How closely did these arguments track Judge Wilkinson's? How well did these arguments address Judge Hall's and Judge Murnaghan's points?

2. *Laws versus litigation.* Compare the advantages and disadvantages of combatting antisemitism through new laws versus litigation.

3. *Pulling punches.* When, if ever, should Jews refrain from pursuing an available legal remedy out of fear of reinforcing antisemitic stereotypes or provoking an antisemitic "backlash" in response to their legal self-defense?

Transcript of Oral Argument, *Shaare Tefila Congregation v. Cobb*

(1987)

Patricia A. Brannan, Counsel for Congregation

[After losing before the court of appeals, the Congregation filed a petition for a writ of certiorari to the Supreme Court, which granted it. At oral argument, the Congregation was represented by Patricia A. Brannan.]

Figure 1.2. Members of the U.S. Supreme Court. This photograph, taken on February 25, 1987, shows the Supreme Court Justices in their official positions. Seated, from left: Associate Justice Thurgood Marshall, Associate Justice William J. Brennan, Jr., Chief Justice William H. Rehnquist, Associate Justice Bryon R. White, Associate Justice Harry A. Blackmun. Standing, from left: Associate Justice Sandra Day O'Connor, Associate Justice Lewis F. Powell, Jr., Associate Justice John Paul Stevens, Associate Justice Antonin Scalia. Public domain.

John Paul Stevens

Do you think at the time the statute was passed that the people who voted for the statute thought that Jews were racially distinct or not?

Patricia A. Brannan

I believe that they did, under the common understanding of the word "race" at that time.... For our purposes, we don't believe that that even would matter. That what really matters, if persons who discriminate against Jews, Arabs or other minorities now, who do that because they view them as racially distinct, that that conduct should be covered. After all—

John Paul Stevens

Maybe it should. But you don't contend that at the time the statute was passed, that the authors of the statute might well have used the term "race" in a way that would have treated the Jews as a separate race?

Patricia A. Brannan

We believe that they did use that term at that—

John Paul Stevens

But you don't rely on that fact? . . .

Antonin Scalia

So long as they [the discriminators] are intelligent enough to know that they [Jews] are not a distinct racial group, it would be okay; they could paint the same things on the synagogue so long as they know that the Jews are not a separate race? . . . That is the position you are urging us to take, though, isn't it?

Patricia A. Brannan

No. I don't think it turns only on admissions. In this case, if the Respondents denied up and down that they had a racial belief about Jews, I think—

Antonin Scalia

They in fact didn't. I'm not saying they just admit . . . they in fact didn't. They in fact know that Jews are not a separate race. But they still set out to defame and cause injury to Jews. Do you think that that would not be covered, so long as the individual is not doing it because he thinks Jews are a separate race?

Patricia A. Brannan

Well, I have some difficulty, I suppose, with the notion of, you know, "they don't think," because given the content of the message that they put up on the walls of Shaare Tefila, it really evokes a racist history.

Antonin Scalia

Don't change my hypothetical. I am giving you a hypothetical in which the individual knows Jews are not a separate race and paints the same things as were painted here on the synagogue. Now, under your theory if I understand it correctly, that would not be actionable?

Patricia A. Brannan

Under my theory, I guess I can't reconcile them knowing that Jews are racially distinct and still invoking the Holocaust.

Antonin Scalia

Make believe, all right?

Patricia A. Brannan

All right.

Antonin Scalia

Accept my hypothetical. Under your theory it would not be actionable; isn't that right?

Patricia A. Brannan

If we could know completely what was in their minds, it would not be actionable. . . .

Sandra Day O'Connor

Well, what in the legislative history supports that very unusual approach to the statute, and perhaps unworkable approach?... There may be some support in the legislative history for treating Jews as a separate race or treating Germans as a separate race. But I don't see anything in the legislative history that would make it turn on the relative sophistication of the person doing the discriminating, which you are urging. The view of the discriminator ... I mean, that's what gets you into a very peculiar approach here. And is there anything in the legislative history to support that?

Patricia A. Brannan

Well, Justice O'Connor, we think it isn't so much the sophistication as the intent of the discriminator....

Antonin Scalia

But why isn't it enough if the intent is to discriminate against a race, as race was understood when the statute was enacted? You are not just insisting that the intent be to discriminate against a race, but you are insisting that the intent be to discriminate against a race because it is a race, not because we have been at war with Germans for 200 years, but because Germans are a separate race. Now, why do you have to add in that qualification under the statute? Isn't it enough that you are discriminating against a race? Isn't that all the statutory language would require?

Patricia A. Brannan

Yes, but the difference, I think, between the last part of what you said and what we are arguing, Justice Scalia, is the motivation of the actor must be racially discriminatory. That is the thing that we are emphasizing.

Antonin Scalia

Why? Where is that in the statute?...

Byron R. White

If these people had just vandalized the synagogue without painting anything, swastikas or anything like that, they had just trashed the place, would you be here?

Patricia A. Brannan

It would be a much more difficult case.

Byron R. White

You would then have to have some other evidence that they did it on a racial basis?

Patricia A. Brannan

Exactly.

Byron R. White

But if it turned out that they ... as Justice Scalia suggested, if it turned out that as a matter of fact they knew that Jews were not a different race, they claimed that they just didn't like Jews, you wouldn't be here then?

Patricia A. Brannan

Exactly, if there weren't some evidence. Here the character of what was painted is the strongest evidence....

Byron R. White

You don't want to urge in this Court, I take it, that Jews are a different race?

Patricia A. Brannan

No, not at all, Justice White....

Byron R. White

Well do you think it would be error if we read the legislative history to say, Congress thought that Jews were a different race and therefore the statute covers it? Would we be in error?

Patricia A. Brannan

No, I don't, although we would certainly urge the Court to make clear that of course Jews or any other group now bringing a claim would not have to prove some racial distinctness. That was really what was suggested by the Fourth Circuit majority, that there is an extra burden beyond racial motivation on the plaintiff to show that they are non-White or racially distinct, although it is unclear, racially distinct from whom. That, we believe, was the crux of the error and that particular aspect of that opinion, we believe should be reversed and made clear by the Court, whether or not the Court accepts the racial motivation theory that we have put forward or the respondents' approach that is more closely tied to the meaning of race in 1866....

Antonin Scalia

Very strange.... It seems to me you are only getting at the ill-educated discriminator, right?

Patricia A. Brannan

Well, perhaps, Justice Scalia, it's a question of ignorance, not education. I think that there are perhaps those in much more sophisticated places with a string of degrees who may be surprised to hear a congregation arguing before the Supreme Court that Jews are not a race....

One of the additional difficulties with th[e Fourth Circuit's] test is that it simply is not practicable and sensible for the district courts to be trying to figure out who is racially distinct or non-White.... Racially distinct from whom?...

In terms, of course, of its language about the Jewish plaintiffs in *Shaare Tefila* being non-White, we think perhaps it goes without saying that it would be completely inappropriate exercise for the district courts to undertake trying to figure out who is White and non-White in some objective, anthropological or scientific test, that that simply would not be an appropriate approach for the courts to take.

For all of these reasons we respectfully ask this Court to reverse and to hold that all victims of racially motivated deprivations of the rights enumerated in the Civil Rights Acts of 1866 may state a cause of action under Sections 1981 and 1982.

Deborah T. Garren, Counsel for Defendants

Deborah T. Garren

Your Honor, I am not attempting to suggest that the Court define scientific categories of race.... There are certain groups in our society that are commonly identified as non-White. Those groups would be entitled to protection, and if an individual is subjected to discrimination because he is perceived to be a member of such a group, then he would be covered.

Lewis F. Powell, Jr.

That is a matter of perception?

Deborah T. Garren

It is a perception only of an individual's membership in a group that is commonly identified as non-White. And that is something that the jury could determine, in other words, whether or not that individual was acted against because he was non-White.

Lewis F. Powell, Jr.

Does that bring you close to the position of your opposition here today?

Deborah T. Garren

No, I think it does not, because the petitioner argues that the perceptions of the discriminator, without reference to groups, are determinative. In other words, under the petitioner's argument, to take an extreme example, if a group of anti-gay people decided that homosexuals were racially different than others and discriminated against them on that basis, I think carrying the petitioners' argument to its logical conclusion, that claim would be covered by the statute. The same might be true for handicapped individuals. Suppose some deviant organization in our society decided that handicapped people were different racially and acted against them on that basis, I believe that claim also would be covered under the petitioners' theory for coverage of this statute. So, it is something different. It's an effort to bring the statute into the 20th century and to recognize racial groups in a way with reference to society's perceptions.

Thurgood Marshall

Where do you want to go to find this ... if you are part Scandinavian, part Indian, part South African, part Japanese? What are you? What book do you find—

Deborah T. Garren

Again, Your Honor, I am not saying that anyone has to make that determination. I am saying that there only has to be a decision by a jury whether you are discriminated against because you are identified as non-White....

Thurgood Marshall

How did he become identified as a non-White person?

Deborah T. Garren

Well, I think one obvious way in which he would be identified as a non-White person would be by reference to immutable physical characteristics such as skin color, which we traditionally understand—

Thurgood Marshall

I would like to have seen you identify my father. He was White with blond hair and blue eyes.

Deborah T. Garren

In that case, sir, I don't think he would have a cause of action for race discrimination.

Thurgood Marshall

Oh, but he did. He was a Negro.... What do you do with Sammy Davis? [Laughter]

Deborah T. Garren

Sammy Davis might certainly have a cause of action for race discrimination. He would not have a cause of action based on his religion....

Deborah T. Garren

It's simply a matter of what the statute was intended to address. It was not, I would argue, a statute to root out all forms of invidious discrimination or bigotry in our society. This Court has held that it does not address sex discrimination, religious discrimination, national origin discriminations standing alone, and all of those categories would be pulled in, arguably, under the petitioners' theory.

Harry A. Blackmun

Are you taking the position, however, that the statute is applicable only to Blacks?

Deborah T. Garren

No, sir, I am not.

Harry A. Blackmun

So, if they were Chinese you would say the statute is applicable?

Deborah T. Garren

That is correct. That group would be—

Harry A. Blackmun

And yet, when the statute was enacted, the concern was with the freed men, was it not?

Deborah T. Garren

Well, if one looks to the actual concern of the legislators in passing this statute, I think one would have to realize that it was passed in an effort to protect and extend the rights of the newly freed slaves. And this Court has indicated, therefore, that Blacks are protected, and has subsequently indicated that Whites as well are protected.

The additional step that you must take, not in my case, I would argue, because in this case Jewish petitioners have indicated that they do not have a racial identity but in the case that follows mine [*St. Francis Coll. v. Al-Khazraji*], there is a need to make an effort to define race.

I would argue that the petitioners just throw that out the window and say, we don't need to define it; we don't need to determine what groups are protected by this statute; we'll determine the statute's coverage by reference to each individual's deviant ideas, without any reference to protected groups in our society.

John Paul Stevens

May I ask, Ms. Garren ... years ago, and of course it's still prevalent in some areas, there was prejudice against Jews. That was known in our society. There was a lot of anti-Semitism. How would you characterize that prejudice?... You wouldn't call it racial prejudice?

Deborah T. Garren

Prejudice that is based on their religion.

John Paul Stevens

Do you think it was based entirely on their religion?

Deborah T. Garren

That is the characteristic that defines them. There is no racial characteristic that in fact defines people of the Jewish faith. It is a religion.

John Paul Stevens

Do you think that would be the proper characterization in Germany when it was so virulent?

Deborah T. Garren

No, sir, but again that was the deviant perception of a couple of organizations in the society that had run rampant. It wasn't a common perception in the society. They weren't commonly identified.

John Paul Stevens

Do you think the origin of the prejudice in this country was entirely religious?

Deborah T. Garren

Of the prejudice against Jewish people?

John Paul Stevens

Yes.

Deborah T. Garren

I think I am not qualified to comment on that, but I have every reason to believe that religion in part motivated that prejudice because that is what in fact defines the group.

Antonin Scalia

It didn't extend to Jews who were atheists, nonbelievers? Do you really think that was the case?

Deborah T. Garren

I'm not sure I understand your question, Justice Scalia.

Antonin Scalia

I mean, do you think that the prejudice that existed against Jews in this country was only against believing Jews, and so long as the Jew said, I really no longer believe in the religious tenets of Judaism, the prejudice no longer existed, and that person would have been able to get into all sort of country clubs and what not?

Deborah T. Garren

No, sir, but I do think that the discriminators identify the group by their religious beliefs. They may not know in each individual instance whether that Jewish person follows his faith or not.

Antonin Scalia

You want us to use modern concepts of taxonomy in order to apply this statute?

Deborah T. Garren

No, I don't think I do, Your Honor.

Antonin Scalia

Why?

Deborah T. Garren

I don't think I do. I am not suggesting that you attempt to define racial categories in a taxonomical fashion, or any kind of scientific way, because I do think there are incredible difficulties with doing that. I am saying that—

Antonin Scalia

Modern perceptions [are] what you want us to use?

Deborah T. Garren

Common identification of a group as non-White in our society, and that's an approach that the lower courts have taken without fail in attempting to grapple with these cases. And none of those lower courts have included Jewish people within the rubric of [this approach]....

Thurgood Marshall

Just because certain Jews are White in complexion doesn't take away the rights of them as Jews.

Deborah T. Garren

Those are rights against religious discrimination.... I would say this is religious discrimination and is not encompassed within this race discrimination statute.

Thurgood Marshall

That's the only thing the swastika means.

Deborah T. Garren

A synagogue was desecrated.

Thurgood Marshall

"Death to the Jews." That's what the swastika means.

Deborah T. Garren

I appreciate what Nazis believed and I also think that that is not a belief that is common to society.

Thurgood Marshall

I didn't say Nazis. I said anybody that uses the swastika means, "Death to the Jews." German, American, or whoever he is, you don't use the swastika.

Deborah T. Garren

Well, I think even the petitioners in this case would agree that a claim would not be covered if the swastika wasn't used to indicate that Jews are racially inferior. That's what results from their standard.

Thurgood Marshall

It means that you should die.

Deborah T. Garren

Pardon?

Thurgood Marshall

It means that you should die.

Deborah T. Garren

These are horrible views. The question is whether or not we should determine that—

Thurgood Marshall

The word is Holocaust. That's what the swastika means....

Antonin Scalia

Ms. Garren, you rely on the fact that it was a synagogue to show that it was ... religious rather than racial. But actually, they just went across the street to the synagogue after they had initially spray-painted a Drug Fair, which is not notably religious. [Laughter]

Deborah T. Garren

That's correct.

Antonin Scalia

And they sprayed the Drug Fair with the words, "White Power" and "Aryan Brotherhood." And then after that they happened to see a synagogue and they go over and do what they did to the synagogue.

Deborah T. Garren

That's correct.

Antonin Scalia

That doesn't strike me as predominantly religious, the whole episode.

Deborah T. Garren

No one has denied, at least for purposes of this appeal, that these defendants acted out of a belief that Jews are racially inferior and that the symbols they painted suggested that.

Antonin Scalia

Well, then I don't understand ... why you raise the fact that it was a synagogue and saying that that proves something about the case. I don't see that it does....

What if we concluded that the theory of these people was scientifically foolish but not necessarily socially foolish? There are a lot of people who might use the term "Jewish" to refer to what they think is a racial group, a stock.

Deborah T. Garren

I think that the petitioners would disagree that there is any kind of common perception....

Antonin Scalia

Has that been conceded away too, that there's no common perception? I don't recall any ... I do recall them forcefully arguing that ... Jews are not scientifically a race, but I don't recall their arguing that there is no general social perception that to be a Jew is only a religious thing.

Deborah T. Garren

I think that they have never indicated that there is a common perception in our society today that Jews are racially distinct either....

John Paul Stevens

Well, how do you define race, then? If you don't do it by reference to scientific standards, what are the standards for defining whether two people are in different races or not?

Deborah T. Garren

The approach that, in fact, anthropologists take in many instances is by reference to culture and by reference to common perceptions in society.

John Paul Stevens

Well, if you look at culture, I suppose a pretty strong argument could be made that the Jewish have a very special culture of their own.

Deborah T. Garren

I do not believe a strong argument could be made that the Jewish people are commonly identified as racially different. That's what I am referring to when I say that cultural—

John Paul Stevens

What I am trying to get at is, how does one decide whether two people are in the same or different races?

Deborah T. Garren

You look at the individual, first of all, and you evaluate whether that individual is identified as White or is identified as non-White in our society, in some sense.

John Paul Stevens

So, now we've got two races, White and non-White? We're down to two, is that it?

Deborah T. Garren

There are various groups that would fall in the non-White category. This isn't an effort to get at defining what race means.

Sandra Day O'Connor

In your view, would Hispanics ... how about Hispanics and Arabs. Would they fit in your category?

Deborah T. Garren

I think it's quite conceivable that Hispanics would be a group that is commonly identified as non-White in our society. Several of the lower circuit courts have held that and have approached the statute in precisely the way that I am suggesting that you approach it.

Sandra Day O'Connor

And how about Muslims or Arabs?

Deborah T. Garren

"Muslims" is a religious term, I believe. Again, it would require the courts to evaluate whether there is a common identification of that group as racially distinct, or non-White in our society. For my individual reaction—I think that those groups would be included within the categories that are protected because in many instances individuals that are in those groups have dark skin, for example. And there can be no doubt that if an individual is discriminated against because he is Black and has dark skin, or a large number of members of that group are Black and have dark skin, they would have a cause of action under this statute....

Assessing the Parties' Oral Arguments

1. The Justices posed several key questions to Ms. Brannan during her oral argument. Assess the questions and Brannan's responses.

a. Justice Stevens asked if Brannan believed that at the time § 1982 was passed, people thought Jews were racially distinct. Brannan argued that it wasn't critical to the Congregation's § 1982 whether the 1866 Congress believed Jews were a distinct race. Why not? Did the Justices agree?

b. Chief Justice Rehnquist asked how to determine if discrimination between different European nationalities (e.g., French vs. German) would be considered racially motivated.

c. Justice Scalia asked when discrimination against Germans as Germans would be covered under § 1982.

d. Justice O'Connor asked if Brannan was essentially equating race with national origin discrimination.

e. Several Justices, including Scalia and O'Connor, asked Brannan why the discriminator's belief about whether a group constitutes a distinct race should matter for determining if § 1982 applies.

f. Justice White asked if Brannan would have a case if the synagogue was vandalized without any racial symbols or messages.

2. *Fighting the hypothetical.* Justice Scalia presented a hypothetical where someone discriminates against Jews while knowing that Jews are not a separate race, but still paints the same offensive symbols on a synagogue. He asked if this would be actionable under Brannan's theory. Why and how did Brannan "fight the hypothetical?" How did she ultimately respond?

3. Some of the key points of disagreement between Brannan and Garren concerning § 1982's application or non-application to Jews encompass the following questions:

a. What role does the discriminator's racial perception of and intent towards the targeted group (even if factually incorrect) play in the analysis?

b. Assuming the discriminator's racial perception and intent alone do not suffice to establish a § 1982 action, what is the required correspondence between the discriminator's perception about the targeted group and the reality concerning the targeted group?

c. Are Jews objectively a distinct race?

d. Did Congress consider Jews a distinct race in 1866?

e. Were Jews commonly identified as a distinct race in 1866?

f. Are Jews commonly identified as a distinct race today?

g. Is discrimination against Jews religious discrimination?

4. *Nazi racial ideology.* According to Garren, the view that Jews are a race was present in Nazi Germany but "was the deviant perception of a couple of organizations in the society that had run rampant" and "wasn't a common perception in the society." Is this a form of Holocaust distortion or minimization? Assuming Garren was aware of Nazi racial ideology's grip on German society, what might have prompted her to deny this? How would this fact, if conceded, have affected her argument? Under what set of circumstances, in her view, would Jews be a protected class under § 1982?

5. The Justices posed several key questions and comments to Garren during her oral argument. Assess the questions and comments and Garren's responses.

a. Justice O'Connor asked about evidence in the legislative history that Congress intended to treat race broadly to cover groups like Gypsies, Chinese, and Germans when enacting § 1982.

b. Justice Stevens asked how Garren would characterize historical prejudice against Jews in America.

c. Justice Scalia questioned Garren's assertion that anti-Jewish prejudice was only religious. In Garren's view, what is the relevance of the fact that defendants defaced a synagogue? In Scalia's view, what is the relevance of the fact that defendants also defaced a nearby drug store?

d. Justice Marshall posed hypotheticals about mixed-race individuals and how Garren's theory would categorize them.

e. Justice Powell asked how Garren's approach would handle the reality of intermarriage and mixed-race individuals in America's heterogeneous society.

f. Justice Scalia challenged Garren's focus on modern perceptions of race rather than historical understandings when the statute was enacted.

g. Justice Marshall questioned Garren about the meaning of swastikas and whether their use indicated racial rather than just religious discrimination.

h. Justice Marshall asserted that "just because certain Jews are White in complexion doesn't take away the rights of them as Jews." Does this assertion beg the question of whether Jews do in fact and/or should have rights as Jews in the first place, most notably, the right to bring §1982 claims? Assess Garren's response.

i. In Garren's view, did the Congregation undermine its § 1982 claim by contending that Jews are not a biological race? Did the Congregation also concede that there is no common perception that Jews are a distinct race? What light does the oral argument shed on the question of whether Jews are commonly identified as non-White? Had the Congregation asserted this, would that have changed the result?

j. Justice O'Connor asked Ms. Garren whether § 1982 might cover Latinos and Arabs and Ms. Garren responded that it did, might, and/or should. How did she distinguish the cases of Latinos and Arabs from Jews? Garren suggests that Latinos and Arabs would be included "because in many instances individuals that are in those groups have dark skin...." What percentage of Jews' skins would need to be darker in order to qualify for § 1982 coverage?

6. *McDonald.* According to Garren, for what proposition does *McDonald* stand? Is this interpretation sound?

7. Assuming § 1982 applies to Jews, would it provide relief to all anti-Jewish discrimination that interferes with Jews' property rights? Most notably, should it be limited to anti-Jewish discrimination motivated by racial antisemitism but not religious discrimination? What criteria should courts use to distinguish between discrimination motivated by racial as opposed to religious antisemitism or, for that matter, other forms of antisemitism?

Shaare Tefila Congregation v. Cobb

481 U.S. 615 (1987)

[The Congregation appealed the Fourth Circuit's ruling to the Supreme Court, which granted their petition for a writ of certiorari and reversed the Fourth Circuit's judgment. In a unanimous opinion, the Court found for Shaare Tefila.]

JUSTICE WHITE delivered the opinion of the Court.

Section 1982 guarantees all citizens of the United States, "the same right ... as is enjoyed by white citizens ... to inherit, purchase, lease, sell, hold, and convey real and personal property." The section forbids both official and private racially discriminatory interference with property rights. Petitioners' allegation was that they were deprived of the right to hold property in violation of § 1982 because the defendants were motivated by racial prejudice. They unsuccessfully argued in the District Court and Court of Appeals that Jews are not a racially distinct group, but that defendants' conduct is actionable because they viewed Jews as racially distinct and were motivated by racial prejudice. The Court of Appeals held that § 1982 was not "intended to apply to situations in which a plaintiff is not a member of a racially distinct group but is merely *perceived* to be so by defendants." (emphasis in original). The Court of Appeals believed that "because discrimination against Jews is not racial discrimination," the District Court was correct in dismissing the § 1982 claim.

We agree with the Court of Appeals that a charge of racial discrimination within the meaning of § 1982 cannot be made out by alleging only that the defendants were motivated by racial animus; it is necessary as well to allege that defendants' animus was directed towards the kind of group that Congress intended to protect when it passed the statute. To hold otherwise would unacceptably extend the reach of the statute.

We agree with petitioners, however, that the Court of Appeals erred in holding that Jews cannot state a § 1982 claim against other white defendants. That view rested on the notion that because Jews today are not thought to be members of a separate race, they cannot make out a claim of racial discrimination within the meaning of § 1982. That construction of the section we have today rejected in *Saint Francis College v. Al-Khazraji*. Our opinion in that case observed that definitions of race when § 1982 was passed were not the same as they are today and concluded that the section was "intended to protect from discrimination identifiable classes of persons who are subjected to intentional discrimination solely because of their ancestry or ethnic characteristics."

As *Saint Francis* makes clear, the question before us is not whether Jews are considered to be a separate race by today's standards, but whether, at the time § 1982 was adopted, Jews constituted a group of people that Congress intended to protect. It is evident from the legislative history of the section reviewed in *Saint Francis College* ... that Jews and Arabs were among the peoples then considered to be distinct races and hence within the protection of the statute. Jews are not foreclosed from stating a cause of action against other members of what today is considered to be part of the Caucasian race.

St. Francis Coll. v. Al-Khazraji

481 U.S. 604 (1987)

[This is the companion case to *Shaare Tefila*. St. Francis College denied tenure to Majid Ghaidan Al-Khazraji, an Iraqi American philosophy professor. Al-Khazraji brought a § 1981 claim in district court, alleging that the college denied him tenure because of his Arab ancestry in violation of 42 USC. § 1981. The college argued that Arabs are taxonomically Caucasian and therefore cannot raise a § 1981 claim alleging discrimination against him in favor of other Caucasians. The district court granted summary judgment for the college upon finding that § 1981, while prohibiting racial discrimination, does not reach discrimination claims based on Arab ancestry. The court of appeals reversed the judgment, holding that § 1981 did not automatically bar allegations of discrimination between persons taxonomically classified as Caucasian. It would have permitted the plaintiff to prove that he was subjected to racially motivated discrimination within the meaning of § 1982. After granting the college's petition for a writ of certiorari, the Supreme Court found for Professor Al-Khazraji and affirmed the court of appeals' judgment.]

Justice White delivered the opinion of the Court.

All those who might be deemed Caucasian today were not thought to be of the same race at the time § 1981 became law.

In the middle years of the 19th century, dictionaries commonly referred to race as a "continued series of descendants from a parent who is called the *stock*" (1830), "the lineage of a family" (1841), or "descendants of a common ancestor" (1871).... It was not until the 20th century that dictionaries began referring to the Caucasian, Mongolian, and Negro races (1911), or to race as involving divisions of mankind based upon different physical characteristics. (1916). Even so, modern dictionaries still include among the definitions of race "a family, tribe, people, or nation belonging to the same stock" (1971).... Encyclopedias of the 19th century also described race in terms of ethnic groups, which is a narrower concept of race than petitioners urge. Encyclopedia Americana in 1858, for example, referred to various races such as Finns, gypsies, Basques, and Hebrews. The 1863 version of the New American Cyclopaedia divided the Arabs into a number of subsidiary races, represented the Hebrews as of the Semitic race, and identified numerous other groups as constituting races, including Swedes,

Norwegians, Germans, Greeks, Finns, Italians, [referring to mixture of different races], Spanish, Mongolians, Russians, and the like. The Ninth edition of the Encyclopedia Britannica also referred to Arabs, Jews, and other ethnic groups such as Germans, Hungarians, and Greeks, as separate races.

These dictionary and encyclopedic sources are somewhat diverse, but it is clear that they do not support the claim that for the purposes of § 1981, Arabs, Englishmen, Germans, and certain other ethnic groups are to be considered a single race. We would expect the legislative history of § 1981, which ... had its source in the Civil Rights Act of 1866 ... to reflect this common understanding, which it surely does. The debates are replete with references to the Scandinavian races, as well as the Chinese, Latin, Spanish, and Anglo-Saxon races. Jews, Mexicans, Blacks, and Mongolians were similarly categorized. Gypsies were referred to as a race. Likewise, the Germans:

> Who will say that Ohio can pass a law enacting that no man of the German race ... shall ever own any property in Ohio, or shall ever make a contract in Ohio, or ever inherit property in Ohio, or ever come into Ohio to live, or even to work? If Ohio may pass such a law and exclude a German citizen ... because he is of the German nationality or race, then may every other State do so.

There was a reference to the Caucasian race, but it appears to have been referring to people of European ancestry.

Based on the history of § 1981, we have little trouble in concluding that Congress intended to protect from discrimination identifiable classes of persons who are subjected to intentional discrimination solely because of their ancestry or ethnic characteristics. Such discrimination is racial discrimination that Congress intended § 1981 to forbid, whether or not it would be classified as racial in terms of modern scientific theory. The Court of Appeals was thus quite right in holding that § 1981, "at a minimum," reaches discrimination against an individual "because he or she is genetically part of an ethnically and physiognomically distinctive sub-grouping of homo sapiens." It is clear from our holding, however, that a distinctive physiognomy is not essential to qualify for § 1981 protection. If respondent on remand can prove that he was subjected to intentional discrimination based on the fact that he was born an Arab, rather than solely on the place or nation of his origin, or his religion, he will have made out a case under § 1981.

JUSTICE BRENNAN, concurring.

Pernicious distinctions among individuals based solely on their ancestry are antithetical to the doctrine of equality upon which this Nation is founded. Today the Court upholds Congress's desire to rid the Nation of such arbitrary and invidious discrimination, and I concur in its opinion and judgment. I write separately only to point out that the line between discrimination based on "ancestry or ethnic characteristics," and discrimination based on "place or nation of ... origin" is not a bright one. It is true that one's ancestry—the ethnic group from which an individual and his or her ancestors are descended—is not necessarily the same as one's national origin—the country "where a person was *born*, or, more broadly, the country from which his or her ancestors came."

Espinoza v. Farah Manufacturing Co. (1973). Often, however, the two are identical as a factual matter: one was born in the nation whose primary stock is one's own ethnic group. Moreover, national origin claims have been treated as ancestry or ethnicity claims in some circumstances. For example, in the Title VII context, the terms overlap as a legal matter. *See* 29 CFR § 1606.1 (1986) (national origin discrimination "includ[es], but [is] not limited to, the denial of equal employment opportunity because of an individual's, or his or her ancestor's, place of origin; *or* because an individual has the physical, cultural, or linguistic characteristics of a national origin group"); *Espinoza* (the deletion of the word ancestry from the final version of § 703 of Title VII of the Civil Rights Act of 1964 "was not intended as a material change ... suggesting that the terms 'national origin' and 'ancestry' were considered synonymous"). I therefore read the Court's opinion to state only that discrimination based on *birthplace alone* is insufficient to state a claim under § 1981.

The Legal Legacy of *Shaare Tefila*

1. *Rule of the case.* For what propositions do *Shaare Tefila* and *Al-Khazraji* stand?

a. Sections 1981 and 1982 protect Jews as a class because the statute's drafters specifically intended the statute to cover Jews.[54]

b. Sections 1981 and 1982 protect Jews as a class because Jews were widely perceived to be a distinct racial group as the concept of "race" was defined and understood at the time of the statute's enactment.[55]

c. Sections 1981 and 1982 protect Jews as a class because they are the kind of group whom the statute's drafters generally intended the statute to cover, namely, "identifiable classes of persons who are subjected to intentional discrimination solely because of their ancestry or ethnic characteristics."

d. Sections 1981 and 1982 do not cover groups whose members were considered White in 1866, even if those groups are not regarded as White today.

e. Jews are not too White, rich, powerful, privileged, etc. for §§ 1981 and 1982, whose protections are not contingent on the protected group having a relatively low socio-economic status.

f. It serves §§ 1981 and 1982's remedial purposes to protect Jews as a class for reasons that pertain today, e.g., because they are commonly regarded as a distinct racial group and experience discrimination for this reason. However, for prudential reasons, §§ 1981 and 1982 will be construed to apply to Jews on grounds that require a finding that today's Jews are a distinct racial group.

---

54. This approach, known as *original intent*, holds that "a legal instrument should be interpreted to effectuate the intent of those who prepared it or made it legally binding." *Originalism*, Black's Law Dictionary (12th ed. 2024).

55. This approach, known as *original public meaning*, holds that "a legal text should be interpreted through the historical ascertainment of the meaning that it would have conveyed to a fully informed observer at the time when the text first took effect." *Id.*

g. It is unthinkable for §§ 1981 and 1982 *not* to apply to Jews. The doctrinal basis for its application is an afterthought.

h. Sections 1981 and 1982 only protect Jews from anti-Jewish discrimination motivated by racial antisemitism.

i. Sections 1981 and 1982 protect Jews from anti-Jewish discrimination regardless of whether such discrimination is motivated by racial or religious antisemitism.

j. Other civil rights statutes that prohibit racial discrimination but not religious discrimination, including Title VI of the Civil Rights Act of 1964, should be construed to cover Jews only if the drafters of those other statutes regarded Jews as a distinct race.

k. Other civil rights statutes that prohibit racial discrimination but not religious discrimination, including Title VI of the Civil Rights Act of 1964, should cover Jews regardless of whether their drafters regarded Jews as a distinct race.

l. Where (a) a group of people may be defined as either a race or a religion, and (b) a racial definition would protect their rights more effectively under a race-based anti-discrimination statute, then (c) the Court should construe the group in racial terms for that statute's purposes.

2. *From argument to opinion.* Compare the Justices' analysis of *Shaare Tefila* at Oral Argument with Justice White's analysis in the Court's opinion. How do they differ? How do you account for their differences?

3. *Frozen.* In *Al-Khazraji*, Justice White writes, "all those who might be deemed Caucasian today were not thought to be of the same race at the time § 1981 became law." Are §§ 1981 and 1982's coverage frozen as of 1866? Consider Martha Minow's observation:

> The Court's reliance on contemporaneous encyclopedias and dictionaries confined its analysis to a kind of static historicism that would deny protection to a group discovered after 1866 or thought in 1866 to be Caucasian, but not so understood in 1987, or at any other time. Moreover, the reliance on dictionaries and encyclopedias for this kind of static result is curious precisely because those sources are amended regularly, to reflect changing and evolving meanings ascribed by society.[56]

4. Marcus criticizes *Shaare Tefila* because it "put[s] the onus on victims of discrimination to prove their racial *bona fides*," and to "defend, before a skeptical authority, their group identity in the face of an alleged perpetrator who is given a legal incentive to challenge the victim's claim to membership" in the protected class.[57] Assuming this is correct, should the Supreme Court have grounded its decision on some other basis? What would that basis be?

---

56. Minow, *supra* note 51.

57. Marcus, *supra* note 44, at 152, 154.

5. For what propositions does Justice Brennan's concurrence stand:

a. In some cases, discrimination based on national origin may also constitute discrimination based on ancestry or ethnicity, and vice versa.

b. Where (a) a remedial statute prohibits national origin discrimination but does not explicitly prohibit discrimination based on ancestry or ethnicity; and (b) the statute's remedial purposes will be served by prohibiting ancestry/ethnicity-based discrimination, then (c) the category of national origin discrimination will be construed to include ancestry/ethnicity-based discrimination,

6. Is *Shaare Tefila* the Magna Carta for American Jews?

7. Al-Khazraji *and Latinos*. Shortly after the Supreme Court decided *Al-Khazraji*, the Second Circuit cited the case for the proposition "that 'race' for the purposes of § 1981 comprehends ethnicity," and drew the inference that anti-Latino discrimination constitutes racial discrimination under the statute.[58]

Robert Katz, *How Antisemitism Infects the Law*

ABA Human Rights (Dec. 9, 2024)

The Shaare Tefila Congregation had a straightforward path to victory: to allege that Jews should be a protected group under Section 1982 on grounds that Jews today—although not a biological race—are widely perceived or socially constructed as one. Yet rather than make a solid argument they feared would hearten racial anti-Semites, the congregation's lawyers advanced a weaker alternative that was ultimately unsuccessful: that the vandals violated the statute insofar as they perceived Jews to be an inferior race, thereby making their actions "racially motivated." In other words, discrimination against perceived members of a notional, fictional, or imaginary race is impermissible racial discrimination.

By putting the focus on the discriminators' racial beliefs about Jews, the congregation hoped that the courts would affirm their Section 1982 claim without finding contemporary Jews are a racial group—even on a narrow legal basis for remedial purposes.

The district court, court of appeals, and Supreme Court rejected the Shaare Tefila Congregation's argument. The argument led to odd outcomes: on the congregation's theory, Section 1982 would apply only to "ignorant antisemites," that is, those who labor under the false belief that Jews are a race. By contrast, if a swastika-spraying vandal knows that Jews are not a race, Section 1982 would not apply.

---

58. Albert v. Carovano, 851 F.2d 561, 572 (2d Cir. 1988); *see also* Lopez v. S.B. Thomas, Inc., 831 F.2d 1184, 1188 (2d Cir. 1987) ("There can be no question that [§ 1981's ban on racial discrimination] includes persons . . . who are of Puerto Rican descent").

The congregation's argument also provided no criteria for determining which notional races are covered by Section 1982. Suppose a person thinks that blue-eyed persons are an inferior race and violates a blue-eyed person's property rights. Can the blue-eyed victim bring a Section 1982 action?

It is a testament to the power of antisemitism that civil rights advocates advanced the weaker argument because they feared that the stronger argument would fuel antisemitism. It is yet another indicator of the threat antisemitism poses to the integrity of our legal system, which relies on each side to present the strongest possible arguments for their position.

Ultimately, the U.S. Supreme Court saved the congregation's Section 1982 claim by supplying the legal missing link they were too inhibited to advance, namely, the claim that Jews are a protected group under Section 1982. The Supreme Court justified its ruling on the originalist and somewhat strained grounds that Jews were perceived to be a race when the Civil Rights Act of 1866 was enacted. I suspect that for some Justices at least, the relevant question was not, "Were Jews considered a race in 1866?" but rather, "Would extending Section 1982's protections to Jews today advance the statute's remedial purposes?"

The *Shaare Tefila* opinion is masterful *because* of its doctrinal disingenuousness, not despite it. Its artful elision enabled it to reach the correct result and do so in a manner that was sensitive to the congregation's concerns about racializing American Jews today.[59]

C. Racial vs. Religious Antisemitism

William Kaplowitz, *We Need Inquire Further: Normative Stereotypes, Hasidic Jews, and the Civil Rights Act of 1866*

12 Mich. J. Race & L. 537 (2007)

Jews Are Complicated: Jews Are Both an Ethnicity and a Religion and Have Faced Religious and Racial Anti-Semitism

While the Supreme Court has held that Jews are a distinct race for purposes of The Civil Rights Act of 1866, Jews are more than a distinct race; Jews are also members of a shared religion.... In most cases, Jewish religion and Jewish ancestry overlap.

Given this two-dimensional religious and racial identity, Jews have also historically been subjected to two distinctive types of anti-Semitism: racial anti-Semitism based on Jewish ancestry, and religious anti-Semitism, based on Jewish beliefs and behaviors.

---

59. Robert Katz, *How Antisemitism Infects the Law*, Am. Bar. Ass'n (Dec. 9, 2024), https://www.americanbar.org/groups/crsj/publications/human_rights_magazine_home/combating-antisemitism/how-antisemitism-infects-the-law/.

Racial anti-Semitism has been a more recent phenomenon, typified by the Nazis and the 1935 passage of their Nuremberg Laws, which classified Germans into Jewish and non-Jewish persons based on principles of heredity. The history of, and main distinctions between, these two types of hatred are lucidly explained by Jay Weinstein and Nico Stehr:

> It has been widely observed that [the ancestral anti-Semitism enshrined in the Nuremberg laws] represents a significant departure from traditional forms of anti-Semitism. For nearly two millennia the Jews of Europe had been viewed as 'different' (marginals, outsiders, and in many instances pariahs) because they refused to accept Christ as their Messiah and, according to Church doctrine, belatedly revoked in 1968 [sic], because they were responsible for the Saviour's death. Although these beliefs and the exclusionary practices based on them made life difficult for Jews, they also allowed for the possibility of exculpation through conversion. Moreover, since even a Jewish mother and father could produce a Christian child, the religion of one's parents was not necessarily grounds for exclusion, persecution or execution. 'The world without Jews' envisioned by European Christians prior to World War I was one in which all former Jews will have joined the faith—or, as in Karl Marx's secularized formulation, will have stopped behaving 'like Jews.'

As Weinstein and Stehr emphasize, racial anti-Semitism, as per the Nazis, targets Jews because of their ancestry. As a result, there is no action that a Jew can take to protect herself. On the other hand, religious anti-Semitism, as per the Catholic Church or even Marx, targets Jews because of their religious affiliation with Judaism, following of Jewish doctrine, and Jewish practices. This hatred, however, can be appeased if a Jew chooses to believe and behave differently. More generally and drastically, racial anti-Semitism can only be satisfied when there are no more people with Jewish blood in their veins. Religious anti-Semitism can be satisfied when there are no more adherents to Judaism.

The Civil Rights Act Purports to Reach Only Racial Anti-Semitism

When a Jew brings a claim under The Act alleging that she was discriminated against for being Jewish, the courts ... must determine whether the plaintiff's claim is really one of racial discrimination. If it is instead a claim of religious discrimination, it should not be cognizable under The Act.... Put differently, The Act reaches only racial animus.

In the 1970s and 1980s, the number of Orthodox (predominantly Hasidic) Jews residing in Ramapo, New York—an unincorporated township—rose substantially. In fact, by 1986, Orthodox Jews constituted approximately 23,000 out of the 94,000 residents of Ramapo.89 The total Jewish population of the township was much higher.

Many non-Jewish and non-Orthodox residents of Ramapo reacted to this growth with hostility. These residents formed the Airmont Civic Association in order to incorporate their area of Ramapo as the village of Airmont and, consequently, gain control of the local zoning process. Because Orthodox Jews do not drive on the Sabbath, home synagogues were essential to the expansion of Hasidic neighborhoods away from established synagogues. The Village of Airmont could therefore contain the expansion of Hasidic neighborhoods by enacting zoning laws that prevented the establishment of home synagogues in new housing developments. This anti-Hasidic animus was the express impetus for the incorporation movement. As one village trustee allegedly stated at a public meeting, "We all know that the purpose is to keep those Orthodox from Brooklyn out of here." Other speakers declared that they would not stand for a Hasidic community in their backyard, and some "forecast a grim picture of a Hasidic belt" stretching across part of upstate New York.

There is nothing to suggest that the Village of Airmont was established out of opposition to a general increase in the Jewish population, especially as many non-observant Jews already resided in the area. Instead, the incorporation movement was driven purely by opposition to the influx of Hasidic or Orthodox Jews, specifically. Hasidic and Orthodox Jews were described as "'foreigners and interlopers,' 'ignorant and uneducated,' and 'an insult to' the community." They were also allegedly referred to as "a bunch of people who insist on living in the past," and "a tent-dwelling society." Jews and non-Jews alike participated in this anti-Hasidic hostility, and this was not the first time that other Jews had tried to prevent Hasidic Jews from entering their community. In a nearly identical zoning dispute litigated in 1979, there were thirty-seven named defendants: thirty-three of them, or 89 percent, were Jewish.

After his petition to establish a home synagogue was denied, Rabbi LeBlanc-Sternberg sued the trustees of the Village of Airmont and the Town of Ramapo under § 1982, alleging that the defendants violated the Hasidim's right to use and enjoy property. In reply, the defendants asserted that "their alleged discriminatory acts were addressed solely to the plaintiffs' affiliation as Orthodox Jews. They suggest that the complaint is framed in terms which claim religious-based discrimination in that any discrimination was directed toward the plaintiffs' lifestyle as dictated by the tenets of plaintiffs' religion." This characterization of the complaints is clearly accurate, based on the newspaper and trial record. The defendants further argued that since § 1982 does not cover religious discrimination, the plaintiffs' claims should be dismissed.

The Court agreed with the defendants that the plaintiffs' complaint alleged religious discrimination. Nonetheless, the court ruled that the plaintiffs' claims were cognizable under the Act. The court reasoned as follows:

> The complaint does assert that the plaintiffs suffered discrimination because they were Orthodox Jews. However, that makes no difference. Sections 1981 and 1982 were "intended to protect from discrimination identifiable classes of persons who are subjected to intentional discrimination solely because of their ancestry or ethnic characteristics." Because Jewish culture, ancestry, and ethnic identity are intricately bound up with Judaic religious beliefs, racial and religious discrimination against Jews cannot be as easily distinguished as defendants would have it. Moreover, the Supreme Court has explicitly stated that Jews are entitled to the protections of §§ 1981 and 1982 because Jews were

> considered to be a separate race in 1870 when those statutes became law. We need not inquire any further. When confronted with Hasidic Jews who, the court acknowledged, claimed that they were discriminated against for their religious practice, the court said that it could not distinguish between religious and ancestral anti-Semitism, and there was no need to try.

This is nonsense. While there may be some cases in which religious and racial anti-Semitism are hard to distinguish, this was not one of them.... To the extent that any of the defendants in LeBlanc-Sternberg were themselves Jewish—as seems highly likely given the similarity to the 1979 case—the requirement that the plaintiff and defendant be of different races would have immediately blocked the plaintiff's claims as to those defendants.

Perhaps even more curious than LeBlanc-Sternberg is the strange case of Yishai Singer. Jesse Hernandez was a Hispanic teacher for the Denver Public Schools from 1986 to 1994. In 1989–1990, he converted to Judaism, became a Hasid, and changed his name to Yishai Singer. In 1994, Singer submitted a letter of resignation to the district in which he stated, "I have been subjected to a hostile work environment for members of the Jewish religion and for Hispanics. I cannot tolerate any more anti-Semitic or racist conduct."

Singer's specific allegations of hostility were almost all related to his religion. As the court noted, Singer believed his principal was hostile to him "because Singer is a Chassidic Jew." Singer alleged many incidents of hostility towards his Orthodox beliefs and Hasidic dress, but none of these reflected racial animus towards Jewish ancestry (which, as a convert, Singer lacked in the first place). For example, Singer alleged that the principal "continually made anti-Semitic remarks about his Chassidic clothing and appearance, criticizing his kippah/yarmulke, long black coat, side locks of hair and long beard." This anti-Hasidic animus was directed not only at Singer's dress and appearance but also at his Orthodox religious convictions:

> [The principal] made anti-Semitic remarks to him regarding the eating of pork, and intentionally interfered with his Sabbath observance.... [The principal] used profane language when disciplining him, which ... [the principal] knew to offend his religious sensibilities.... Despite his request, he was not provided with a kosher meal at a luncheon he was required to attend.... [The principal] pressured him to violate his religious beliefs by ordering him to attend graduation ceremonies where women would be singing.... Singer himself seems to have conceptualized this all as religious discrimination: He stated that "he frequently accused [his superior] of religious harassment," and claimed that he was discriminated against for being of the Jewish religion. At a basic logical level it could not be any other way—as a convert, Singer is Jewish, but he is not of Jewish ancestry. Therefore any discrimination that he experienced for being Jewish could not be racial anti-Semitism, based on Jewish parentage, but would instead be discrimination based on his Jewish beliefs and practices—religious anti-Semitism.

The school district and Singer's principal brought motions for summary judgment. The school district's motion asserted that, for technical reasons based on the interaction of 42 U.S.C. § 1983 and § 1981, the district could not be liable to Singer under The Act. The court agreed. Singer's principal argued that The Act "does not apply to religious discrimination and the claim should be dismissed insofar as it is based on such discrimination."

Singer argued that *Shaare Tefila* was a sufficient basis for his claim, stating that since "Jews are a distinct race for civil rights purposes ... discrimination against him on the basis of his being Jewish is actionable under § 1981." The court accepted Singer's logic and ruled against the principal. The court reasoned that "since Singer is claiming he was discriminated against as a Jew, a distinct racial group for the purposes of § 1981, Defendants are not entitled to judgment on the basis that he is claiming religious discrimination."

There are two things that are deeply surprising about the holding in *Singer*. First, because Singer had no Jewish ancestry, he could not claim that he faced discrimination based on his Jewish ancestry. Because racial discrimination under The Civil Rights Act is equivalent to ancestral discrimination, Singer's lack of Jewish ancestry should have been fatal to his claim.... Second, the discriminatory incidents upon which Singer based his claim were ... expressions of religious animus, which has long been beyond the scope of The Act.

Do Anti-Racism Laws Address Religious Antisemitism?

1. *Does* Shaare Tefila *apply? Shaare Tefila* does not expressly address the question of whether §§ 1981 and 1982 protect Jews who experience discrimination for reasons that are closely connected to their adherence to Judaism, e.g., by virtue of their observance of one or more of Judaism's 613 commandments or mitzvot,[60] or their espousal of Judaism's beliefs. Does *Shaare Tefila* require the outcomes in either *LeBlanc-Sternberg* or *Singer*, i.e., is it controlling authority? Does *Shaare Tefila* lend support to these outcomes, even if it does not require them? Are either of these cases' outcomes inconsistent with *Shaare Tefila*? In each case, should the court have inquired further into whether the defendants discriminated against the Jewish plaintiffs because of their Jewish ancestry and/or ethnicity (for §§ 1981 and 1982 purposes) or their practice of Judaism?

2. *The rule of the cases.* For what propositions might *LeBlanc-Sternberg* and/or *Singer* stand?

a. As a matter of law, *Shaare Tefila* requires courts to apply §§ 1981 and 1982 to anti-Jewish discrimination based on a plaintiff's Judaism.

b. As a matter of law, *Shaare Tefila* bars courts from applying §§ 1981 and 1982 to anti-Jewish discrimination based on a plaintiff's Judaism.

60. *The 613 Commandments*, Jewish Virtual Libr., https://www.jewishvirtuallibrary.org/commandments-the-613 (last visited Dec. 29, 2024).

c. As a matter of prudence, courts should (all things being equal) construe §§ 1981 and 1982 to bar anti-Jewish discrimination that is arguably based on plaintiff's Judaism, because the distinction between religious and racial antisemitism is too difficult for courts to parse.

d. Section 1981 prohibits anti-Jewish discrimination, including discrimination against converts to Judaism who have no Jewish ancestry and/or are not ethnically Jewish.

3. *Hasidic Jews and the Amish.* In *King v. Twp. of E. Lampeter* (E.D. Pa. 1998), the Amish plaintiffs, citing *LeBlanc-Sternberg*, alleged that the defendants had discriminated against them as members of "the Amish ethnic culture" in violation of § 1981. The court rejected their claim:

> We have been unable to locate any cases in which the Amish have been found to be a distinctly identifiable ethnic or racial group. The emergence of an independent, separate ethnic identity out of such a distinct religious group may well be possible. Nevertheless, Plaintiffs have presented no evidence which would support such a finding, and we are not prepared to hold in this case that a distinctly Amish ethnic group can be identified apart from the Amish religious identity. While there is a large population of "non-practicing" Jews in America, there is no proof of a similar population of "non-practicing" Amish. Therefore, in this case, we believe that the Amish are most accurately described as a religious group, rather than a distinct racial or ethnic minority, and as such, do not fall within the scope of § 1981.[61]

Was this case correctly decided? Did the court draw a principled distinction between Jews and Amish? Does it treat Amish persons unfairly vis-à-vis Jews in general, or vis-à-vis the Hasidic plaintiffs in *LeBlanc-Sternberg*? In a similar vein, Molly E. Swartz argues that § 1981 would not cover Mormons alleging that they were fired as a result of their Mormon religious observance.[62]

4. *Discrimination against non-observant Jews.* In *Kratz v. Coll. of Staten Is.* (E.D.N.Y. 2000), Kratz brought a § 1981 claim alleging that he was discriminated against because he was a non-observant Jew. The court dismissed his claim:

> Kratz does not claim that he was discriminated against because he is of Jewish descent. Quite on the contrary, Kratz asserts that people of Jewish ancestry are favored in the hiring process provided that they are religiously observant. Indeed, the core allegation of his complaint is religious discrimination for being a non-observant Jew.[63]

---

61. King v. Twp. of E. Lampeter, 17 F. Supp. 2d 394, 417–418 (E.D. Pa. 1998), *aff'd*, 182 F.3d 903 (3d Cir. 1999).

62. Molly E. Swartz, *By Birth or by Choice? The Intersection of Racial and Religious Discrimination in School Admissions*, 13 U. Pa. J. Const. L. 229, 254 (2010).

63. Kratz v. Coll. of Staten Island, No. 96-CV-0680, 2000 WL 516888 (E.D.N.Y. Mar. 15, 2000).

Is Kratz's § 1981 claim stronger than, weaker than, or equally as compelling as Rabbi LeBlanc-Sternberg's or Singer's? Are the outcomes of these cases unfair to non-Orthodox Jews?

5. *Double dipping?* Assume the legal system creates a new two-track system of remedial statutes, one based on race, ancestry, and ethnicity and the other based on religion. Should a member of an ethnoreligious group like Jews or Sikhs alleging discrimination to both tracks? Consider Molly E. Swartz's argument:

> In the interests of consistency and fairness, courts should examine anti-Jewish discrimination to ensure that all victims of religious and racial discrimination are treated similarly. By allowing Jews to bring race-based claims and refusing to inquire into the nature of the discrimination (racial or religious) against Jews, courts effectively provide Jews with a unique level of protection from discrimination....
>
> By providing Jews with race-based protections, courts give Jews greater protection than other victims of religious discrimination. This kind of disparate treatment belies the fairness that forms the basis of the American legal system because courts have differentiated between religious and racial discrimination when dealing with other groups.[64]

6. *Reinforce antisemitic stereotypes?* Swartz further argues that dual religious and racial civil rights protection for Jews is not only unfair to non-Jews, but also dangerous to Jews:

> Allowing Jewish victims of religious discrimination to assert race-based discrimination claims could trigger "backlash against 'special rights' and 'special treatment'" afforded to Jewish victims of religious discrimination, leading to a fortification of anti-Semitic animus.

To whom is this warning addressed? To courts? This would yield a canon of construction: as between two interpretations of the 1866 Act concerning Jews, courts should choose the construction that will result in less antisemitic backlash. Is it addressed to Jews? Does she mean that Jews and Jewish advocacy groups should refrain on prudential grounds from pursuing all lawful recourse for anti-Jewish discrimination, where doing so may provoke an antisemitic backlash, even if it exposes Jews to more anti-Jewish discrimination? If Jews know what's good for them, they won't overreach.

Why, in any event, might such advocacy provoke an antisemitic backlash? Is it because it would confirm antisemitic beliefs that Jews are greedy, opportunistic, willing to game the system to get more than their fair share due to a heightened sense of entitlement? Is concern over inflaming anti-Jewish bias a valid reason for Jews to pass up legal opportunities to combat anti-Jewish discrimination? Or is it simply a sad truth that they must come to terms with?

---

64. Swartz, *supra* note 61, at 255–56.

Is this argument for sub-par advocacy and self-silencing specific to Jews? There are other ethnoreligious groups whose identities also blur the line between religion and race or ethnicity. Assume that Sikh plaintiffs and advocacy groups can safely "double dip" civil rights laws (raise religious discrimination claims under the rubric of racial discrimination) without fear of provoking an anti-Sikh backlash. Is it unfair to Jews vis-à-vis Sikhs that Sikhs don't fear defending their rights to the full extent of the law? Should courts grant such access to Sikhs but not Jews on prudential grounds, since safety concerns arising from such access for Sikhs are absent?

Jewish Demography

1. *How many Jews in the world?* There are approximately 14 million Jewish people in the world. Yet, according to ADL global cross-country surveys, 18 percent of adult respondents believe that the total worldwide population of Jews exceeds 700 million. People who overestimate the world's Jewish population by this amount are more likely to harbor antisemitic attitudes.[65]

2. *How many Jews in the US?* In a 2020 survey of Jewish Americans, the Pew Research Center categorized respondents into three categories:[66]

a. *Jews* (5.8 million). This category consists of Jews by religion (4.2 million) and Jews of no religion (1.5 million). The "Jews of no religion" grouping consists of adults who, when asked about their present religion, say they (a) are atheist, agnostic or have no religion in particular; (b) had a Jewish parent or were raised Jewish; and (c) consider themselves Jewish in some way aside from religion, such as ethnically, culturally, or because of their family background.

b. *Jewish background* (2.8 million). This category consists of adults who had at least one Jewish parent or a Jewish upbringing. The majority of people in this category, 1.9 million, identify with another religion, such as Christianity. Another 700,000 have no religion and do not consider themselves Jewish in any way.

c. *Jewish affinity* (1.4 million). This category consists of adults who, although they lack a Jewish parent or upbringing and do not identify as Jewish by religion, consider themselves Jewish in some other way. About two-thirds of such adults identify with a religion other than Judaism, usually Christianity.

3. *Racial diversity among Jews.* According to a 2020 Brandeis University survey, 89 percent of Jewish adults are non-Latino Whites, 6 percent of Jewish adults are Latinos, and 5 percent are other non-Latinos, a group that includes all other racial groups

---

65. *Did you Know?*, The Anti-Defamation League, https://global100.adl.org/did-you-know (last visited Nov. 25, 2024).

66. Pew Rsch. Ctr., Jewish Americans in 2020 50 (2021), https://www.pewresearch.org/religion/2021/05/11/the-size-of-the-u-s-jewish-population/.

(Black, Asian, Pacific Islander, etc.) as well as all who identify with multiple groups, and those who identify with no groups at all.[67] American Jews say they are Ashkenazi.[68]

Does the fact that American Jews are predominantly non-Latino/Hispanic Caucasian demand that they be treated as "white citizens" under § 1982? Does this fact preclude a ruling that Jews are a subset of "all citizens" (a distinct non-racial group) under the statute, comparable to Latinos and African Americans?

4. *Genetic studies of Jewish populations.* Two leading genetic studies found that "most of the Jewish communities are interrelated to various degrees, are genetically closer to each other than to their non-Jewish hosts and have genetic ties to the Middle East."[69] Insofar as persons of Jewish ancestry have significant genetic commonalities, does this strengthen Jews' claims to § 1982 coverage? In Kenneth L. Marcus's view, studies of Jewish genetics suggest that:

> The 'racial' aspect of population groups is not a wholly social construct.... To the extent that biological attributes have any significance in the legal determination as to the demarcation of genetically distinct population groups, the latest data suggest that Jews should be included if anyone is.[70]

A Snapshot of Antisemitism

1. *Anti-Jewish discrimination.* In 2023, the ADL tabulated 8,873 antisemitic incidents across the United States—more incidents than in the previous three years combined. This represents a 140 percent increase from the 3,698 incidents recorded in 2022 and is the highest number on record since the ADL began tracking antisemitic incidents in 1979.[71]

According to a 2024 survey by the Pew Research Center, "an overwhelming majority of U.S. Jews (94 percent) say there is at least some discrimination against Jews in our society, including 72 percent who say there is a lot."[72]

---

67. Leonard Saxe et al., Brandeis Steinhardt Soc. Rsch. Inst., American Jewish Population Estimates 2020 Summary & Highlights 19 (2021), https://ajpp.brandeis.edu/us_jewish_population_2020.

68. *Race, Ethnicity, Heritage and Immigration among U.S. Jews*, Pew Rsch. Ctr. (May 11, 2021), https://www.pewresearch.org/religion/2021/05/11/race-ethnicity-heritage-and-immigration-among-u-s-jews/.

69. Noa Sophie Kohler, *What Are Jews: Interrogating Genetic Studies and the Reification of Race*, 101 J. Anthropological Sci. 185, 188–89 (2023); *see also* Gil Atzmon et al., *Abraham's Children in the Genome Era: Major Jewish Diaspora Populations Comprise Distinct Genetic Clusters with Shared Middle Eastern Ancestry*, 86 Am. J. Hum. Genetics 850 (2010); *see also* Doron M. Behar et al., *The Genome-Wide Structure of the Jewish People*, 466 Nature 238 (2010).

70. Marcus, *supra* note 44, at 152, 154.

71. *Audit of Antisemitic Incidents 2023,* The Anti-Defamation League (Apr. 16, 2024), https://www.adl.org/resources/report/audit-antisemitic-incidents-2023.

72. Becka A. Alper et al., *Rising Numbers of Americans Say Jews and Muslims Face a Lot of Discrimination,* Pew Rsch. Ctr. (Apr. 2, 2024), https://www.pewresearch.org/2024/04/02/rising-numbers-of-americans-say-jews-and-muslims-face-a-lot-of-discrimination/.

2. *Anti-Jewish stereotypes.* In a 2022 ADL survey, 4,007 American adults were asked to rate the truthfulness of fourteen statements describing different traditional anti-Jewish tropes. See Figure 1.3 below.

3. *Jewish conspiracy theories.* Professors Cass R. Sunstein and Adrian Vermeule define a conspiracy theory as "an effort to explain some event or practice by reference to the machinations of powerful people, who attempt to conceal their role (at least until their aims are accomplished)."[73] Jonathan Fox and Lev Topor report that the most reliable predictor of anti-Jewish discrimination by governments and society alike is the proportion of the population that believes in conspiracy theories about Jewish power and control.[74] Examples of Jewish conspiracy theories include claims that:[75]

a. Jews are pulling strings behind the scenes with the goal of controlling the world or a particular locale.

b. Jews manipulate the media behind the scenes to control information and world events.

c. Jews control world finances and the economy.

d. Jews or Israel causes various negative events which suit their own sinister purposes, such as 9/11, the historic slave trade, and training U.S. police to kill ethnic minorities.

e. Jews use the blood of gentiles, typically children's blood, in religious rituals, such as to bake matzahs for Passover.

f. Jews cause illnesses such as the historic bubonic plague, AIDS in African American babies, and COVID-19.

g. Jews killed Jesus.[76]

h. Jews seek to extinguish the "white race" in the U.S. by orchestrating the immigration of non-Whites into the U.S. This notion, called the "Great Replacement Theory," was reflected in the slogan chanted by White supremacists in Charlottesville, Virginia in August 2017—"Jews will not replace us"—and was the animating belief of White supremacist Robert Bowers, who killed 11 people at the Tree of Life synagogue in Pittsburgh, Pennsylvania in October 2018.[77]

---

73. Cass R. Sunstein & Adrian Vermeule, *Conspiracy Theories: Causes and Cures*, 17 J. of Pol. Phil. 202, 205 (2009).

74. Jonathan Fox & Lev Topor, Why Do People Discriminate against Jews? 173 (2021).

75. *Id.* at 118–119.

76. But note that the Quran holds that Jesus was raised alive to heaven and a look-alike was crucified in his place and that Jews, believing he had been crucified, boasted that they killed him. Quran, An-Nisa. 4:157–158, https://quran.com/4 (last visited Nov. 15, 2024).

77. *You Will Not Replace Us*, The Anti-Defamation League, https://www.adl.org/resources/hate-symbol/you-will-not-replace-us (last visited Oct. 5, 2024).

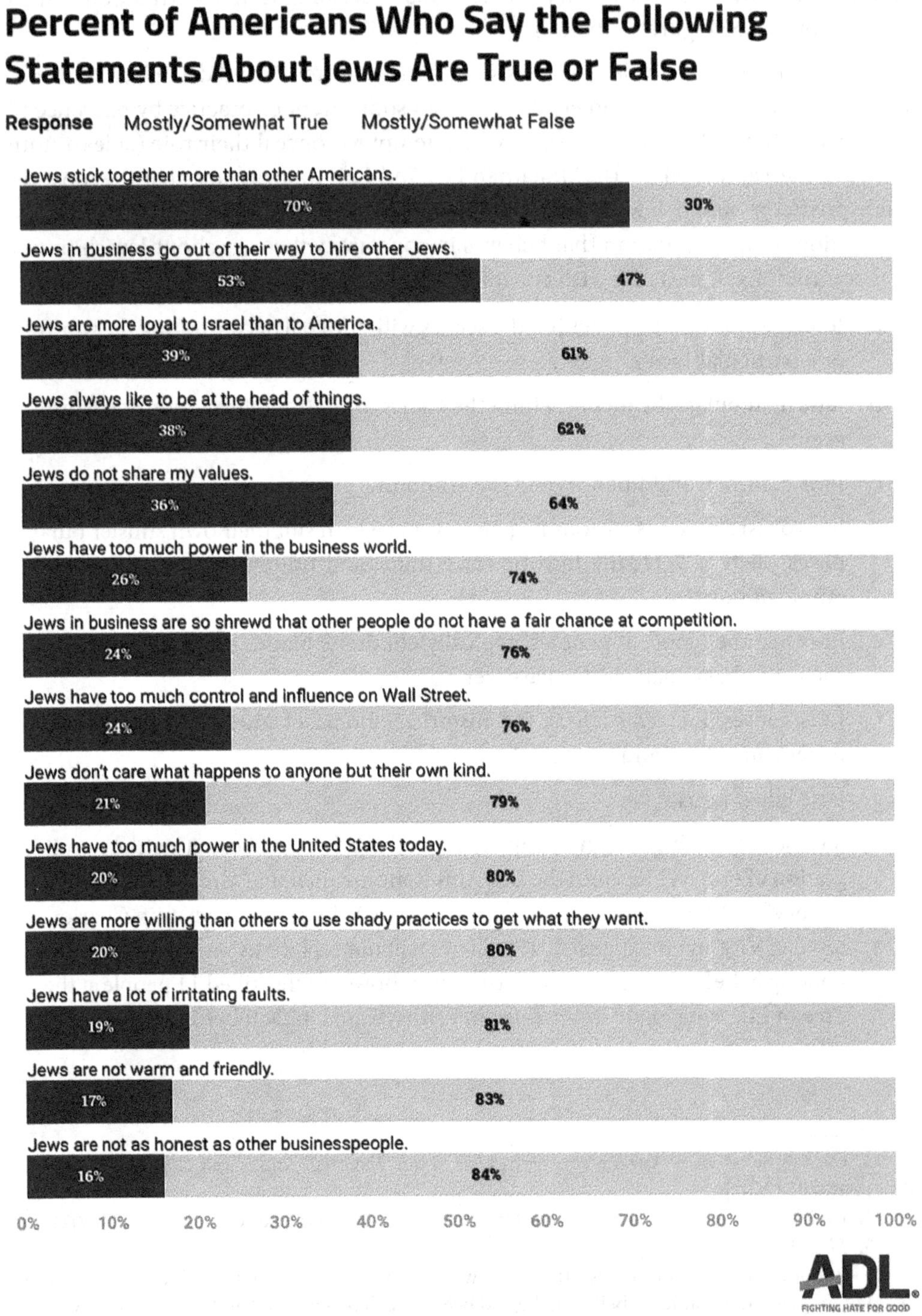

Figure 1.3. *Antisemitic Attitudes in America: Topline Findings*, The Anti-Defamation League (Jan. 12, 2023), https://www.adl.org/resources/report/antisemitic-attitudes-america-topline-findings.

Fox and Topor argue that belief in Jewish conspiracy theories can be fueled by religion-based antisemitism and anti-Zionist forms of antisemitism. Also dangerous are tropes that blame Jews for their troubles, such as "people hate Jews because of the way Jews behave."[78]

4. *Global antisemitism.* The ADL further reports that an estimated 26 percent of the total adult population in the 100 surveyed countries—1.09 billion people—harbor antisemitic attitudes, including 74 percent of the population in the Middle East and North Africa, 34 percent in Eastern Europe, 24 percent in Western Europe, and 10 percent in the U.S. People in predominantly English-speaking countries are half as likely to hold antisemitic views (13 percent) as the overall global population surveyed. 49 percent of surveyed Muslims harbor such attitudes, as do 24 percent of Christians and 19 percent of Hindus. 74 percent of ADL survey respondents have never met a Jewish person.[79]

5. *Check before traveling.* According to ADL surveys completed in 2014, the least antisemitic places in the world (as judged by the percentage of the population holding negative views toward Jews) are Laos (0.2 percent), Philippines (3 percent), Sweden (4 percent), Netherlands (5 percent), Vietnam (6 percent), the U.K. (8 percent), Denmark (9 percent), the U.S. (10 percent), Tanzania (12 percent), and Thailand (13 percent). The most antisemitic places in the world are West Bank and Gaza (93 percent), Iraq (92 percent), Yemen (88 percent), Algeria (87 percent), Libya (87 percent), Tunisia (86 percent), Kuwait (82 percent), Bahrain (81 percent), Jordan (81 percent), and Morocco (80 percent).[80] The least antisemitic Middle Eastern country is Iran (56 percent). The most antisemitic countries outside of the Middle East and North Africa are Greece (69 percent), Malaysia (61 percent), and Armenia (58 percent).[81]

---

78. *Id.*

79. *ADL Poll of Over 100 Countries Finds More Than One-Quarter of Those Surveyed Infected with Anti-Semitic Attitudes,* The Anti-Defamation League (May 13, 2024), https://www.adl.org/resources/press-release/adl-poll-over-100-countries-finds-more-one-quarter-those-surveyed-infected.

80. *Id.*

81. The Anti-Defamation League, *supra* note 64.

Chapter 2

Jews as Off-White

In Chapter One, we saw Judge Hall, in his opinion for the Fourth Circuit's ruling in *Shaare Tefila Congregation v. Cobb*, reject the Congregation's argument that anti-Jewish discrimination constituted racial discrimination under 42 U.S.C. § 1982. Judge Hall pronounced "We do not find the position of Jews in this society to be analogous to that of Mexican Americans or others commonly considered to be non-whites." We also saw the National Jewish Community Relations Council (NJCRC) refusing to support the Congregation's claim, declaring "that there ought not to be the suggestion that the Jewish community in any way gives sanction to the notion that Jews constitute a race." Each for their own reasons, Judge Hall and the NJCRC agree that Jews are White, or at least *not* non-White, for § 1982 purposes. It is a fascinating convergence.

This chapter continues the exploration of Jewish identity and Whiteness, supplementing legal analysis with social and historical perspectives. In "The Jewish Racial Question," Kenneth L. Marcus surveys different responses to "Are Jews White?" In a podcast from the "Adventures in Jewish Studies" series, scholars trace the social history of Ashkenazi American Jews and their relationship to Whiteness. In "White Jews: An Intersectional Approach," Professor David Schraub shows how an intersectional approach to Jewishness and Whiteness can uncover nuances in the Jewish experience that might otherwise remain hidden. The last item is a photo of "Religious Liberty" (1876), a marble sculpture by Sir Moses Jacob Ezekiel (1844–1917), which sheds light on how American Jews of that era wished Jewish identity to be perceived.

What impact, if any, do this chapter's readings have on your assessment of whether and how civil rights statutes should apply to Jews? Should their application to Jews depend on whether Jews are White or non-White in the relevant sense? What is that relevant sense anyway?

A. Are American Jews White?

Kenneth L. Marcus, *The Jewish Racial Question*

Jewish Identity and Civil Rights in America (2010)

Here and now, in twenty-first-century America, are Jews White? The putative Whiteness of American Jews is a highly contested question that has generated an astonishing range of mutually contradictory responses. Commentators variously argue, to provide just a few examples, that Jews are obviously White, that they are definitely not White, that they are "off-White," that they are sometimes off-White and sometimes White, that they recently became White, that they have occupied many different locations on the Whiteness scale, that their shiftiness on the Whiteness scale is a significant source of anxiety to others, that they are still negotiating a costly process in which they have become mostly but perhaps incompletely White, and that they should take ownership of their socially constructed status as Whites because it is the only position plausibly available to them, but they should do so in solidarity with non-White people. In general, the more sophisticated contemporary commentators agree that the Whiteness and non-Whiteness of American Jews largely has been a social construct and that, however read, Jewish non-Whiteness has entailed both social power and social disadvantage in varying mixtures at different periods.

The question of Jewish racial construction may appear obvious to those who observe that many American Jews appear White, are perceived as White, and experienced themselves as White. As Melanie Kaye/Kantrowitz poignantly observes, many light-skinned Ashkenazic Jews do not face various forms of disadvantage frequently experienced in communities of color: along the city streets and state highways, where Black and Brown people pass and are routinely stopped, harassed, sometimes tortured and killed, these Jews pass freely. In stores, no one immediately pegs them as shoplifters. Encountering these Jews in apartment building lobbies or elevators, no one assumes they don't belong.

At the same time, Kaye/Kantrowitz acknowledges that this distinction cannot be pushed too far, because some Jews do share in experiences of persecution, which must also be explained. She does so by noting the specific locations and marks that separate those Jews who are most likely to suffer from contemporary bigotry: "Hate violence against these Jews manifests, almost always, in Jewish spaces—that's how they are identified—or to Jews who visibly mark themselves, meaning, usually, orthodox men." Empirically, this observation is confirmed by the Stephen Roth Institute's finding that in 2007 most antisemitic physical attacks were perpetrated against "Jews on their way to or from Jewish facilities, and bore symbols of their religious identity."

This observation categorically fails to address what Kaye/Kantrowitz calls "the other Jews, the ones who don't look White," such as some "Mizrachi Jews from the Middle East, Latino/as from Latin America, Beta Israel from Ethiopia, Cochins from India, Chinese Jews from China ... Jews by choice ... and biracial and multiracial Jews." These groups arguably are "invisible, marginalized, not even imagined" in the narrative of obvious Jewish Whiteness. In fact, however, these groups represent a much larger share of the American Jewish experience than is typically recognized. The Institute for Jewish & Community Research estimates that at least 20 percent of the American Jewish community consists of African, African American, Hispanic, Asian, Native American, Sephardic, Mizrachi, biracial, and multiracial Jews.

The shortcomings of the mainstream narrative about Jewish "Whiteness" are not limited to the ambiguous position that it leaves for these categories of Jews. In fact, that narrative cannot entirely cover even those Jews who seem most obviously White. Kaye/Kantrowitz illustrates this point well:

> Even the Jew who looks white on New York City's Upper West or Lower East Side may look quite the opposite in Maine or Colorado. Besides, what happens

> when you speak your (Jewish-sounding) name, or when your (less-white-looking) parent or child or lover meets you at work? What happens to your whiteness when you enter a Jewish space: a synagogue, Judaica bookstore, klezmer performance, or Jewish community center?

Kaye/Kantrowitz provides what she calls the "correct" answer to the question of Jewish Whiteness: "Jews are a multiracial, multiethnic people, and, anyway what's white?"... As Kaye/Kantrowitz acknowledges, however, this response seldom satisfies her interlocutors, who respond with an annoyed insistence: "Yeah, but White Jews: are Jews White?" By this, of course, the questioner refers to those light-skinned Ashkenazic Jews who look White. At this point Kaye/Kantrowitz can only throw her hands up in despair, asking further unsatisfying questions: "Isn't Whiteness, like race itself, a historical invention? What does Whiteness confer or deprive, ensure or endanger?"

Katya Gibel Azoulay, who occupies a peculiar vantage point on this issue as a Black Jewish Israeli-American African Studies scholar, has argued that "anyone familiar with twentieth century anti-Semitism, particularly in Europe and the United States, should question the presumption that Jewishness and whiteness are coterminous, particularly when it is recalled that until recently Jews were identified as a race.... White-skinned Jews, perhaps; Caucasian and Jewish is an oxymoron." Indeed, Azoulay maintains that "the tendency of most—though not all—American Jews to refer to themselves alternatively as 'white' and as 'Jewish' witnesses a collective amnesia of the roots of the Jewish people in the East." This, in turn, has facilitated the imagination of Palestinians as "people of color," whereas Ashkenazi Jews have been seen more as White Europeans than as one branch of a multicultural people whose diversity reflects diasporic migrations and admixtures. Politically, this is facilitated by the "misrepresentation of Israel as a colonial intrusion into the brown Arab and Muslim Middle East." Azoulay points out that a quick trip to Israel will "dispel the myth of white Jewish Israelis versus brown Muslim and Christian Palestinians—despite the persistence of social discrimination and cultural elitism that cuts across party lines."

B. A Social and Racial History of Ashkenazi Jews in America

Adventures in Jewish Studies Podcast, "Are Jews White?"

Association for Jewish Studies (Sept. 4, 2019)[1]

[The Association for Jewish Studies (AJS) produces a podcast series called "Adventures in Jewish Studies." In the podcast episode, "Are Jews White?" from this series, several experts discuss the complex relationship between Jewish identity and whiteness in America. Below is the transcript of that discussion.

1. This podcast was downloaded using Apple Podcasts. For information about the Association for Jewish Studies, see *About the AJS*, Ass'n for Jewish Stud., https://www.associationforjewishstudies.org/about-ajs (last visited Dec. 13, 2024).

The podcast was moderated by Dr. Jeremy Shere, the Founder and CEO of Connversa, a communications firm. Participants included Lila Corwin Berman, professor of history at Temple University; Eric Goldstein, professor of history and Jewish studies at Emory University and author of the book, *The Price of Whiteness: Jews, Race, and American Identity*; Ilana Kaufman, director of the Jews of Color Field Building Initiative; and Dr. Judith Rosenbaum, executive director of the Jewish Women's Archive.]

Jeremy Shere

On the evening of August 11th, 2017, hundreds of White nationalist neo-Nazis and others associated with the far right gathered in Charlottesville, Virginia, to protest the removal of a statue of Confederate general Robert E. Lee from a local park. Carrying flags with Nazi and Confederate symbols and brandishing torches, the protesters marched toward the park, chanting.

[Sound of people chanting]

In case it's hard to make out, the marchers are chanting, "Jews will not replace us." Now, like most people, you were probably horrified by this brazen display of bigotry, antisemitism, and racial hatred. But for American Jews—at least for those born after World War II—the scene in Charlottesville was also surreal, as though a Nazi rally from an old black-and-white newsreel had sprung to life in full color in the present. Jews will not replace us? Who exactly is the "us"?

Eric Goldstein

The "us" is obviously some definition of White society that doesn't include the Jews. It's a narrower definition of Whiteness from which they are casting the Jews out—which is not unique in American history, but it is a departure from a kind of longer tradition of including Jews and other groups within the White category.

Jeremy Shere

I think that rings true, especially for American Ashkenazi Jews of my generation, who grew up in the '70s and '80s, and who, for the most part, consider themselves to be fully accepted members of mainstream White American society. And this way of thinking is often reinforced by some on the progressive left, who ... often lump Jews of European background in with the White mainstream.

Judith Rosenbaum

Jewishness encompasses many different things. It can be an ethnicity. It can be a religion. It can be cultural. Some people understand it racially. So, instead of people saying, well, obviously there's a lot of intersectionality baked into Jewish identities, instead there's a way in which Jews are often, in intersectional conversations, just placed into the category of White, and anything else about their identities is dismissed or stripped away.

Jeremy Shere

But if you're a Jew, or if you identify as Jewish, it might not seem so simple. First, and most obviously, not all Jews are of European background. If you're a Sephardic

Jew and you trace your ancestry to the Jews who lived in Spain and Portugal and were expelled in 1492, or if you're a Mizrahi Jew with roots in Arab lands, then you may very well not see yourself as White, or as having benefited nearly as much by dint of being considered part of the White majority. But even if you are an Ashkenazi Jew and do benefit from being part of the White majority—well, maybe you don't see yourself as only, or simply, White. Maybe you feel that your Jewishness marks you as different, or perhaps you define yourself as a member of a Jewish minority whose collective identity has been shaped by centuries of antisemitism. And almost certainly, your grandparents, maybe even your parents, tell you about a time in the not-too-distant American past, when the socioeconomic status of Jews was less certain, and Jews were not yet fully acculturated into and accepted by the White, Anglo-Saxon American mainstream.

Now, before we dive into that history, I want to acknowledge a few things. First, the title of this episode, "Are Jews White?" is, in some sense, a deliberate provocation. Because as we've just seen, the answer is obviously no, not all Jews in the United States or elsewhere are White, are seen as White, or see themselves that way.

But we also need to recognize that by White, we're not talking only about skin tone or physical features. We're also talking about Whiteness as access to social, economic, educational, and other resources and opportunities that, until fairly recently, were available more or less exclusively to members of the White Anglo-Saxon majority in America, and to which Ashkenazi American Jews, especially, have most fully laid claim.

And so, exploring how and why American Jews became accepted members of the Anglo-Saxon establishment, and the anxieties and sense of deep ambivalence that accompanied them in that journey, means exploring the social history of Ashkenazi American Jews, a story unique in American Jewish history.

By the last few decades of the 19th century, many American Jews whose families had come to the United States, mostly from Central and Western Europe, particularly German Jews, were fairly well integrated into White Anglo-Saxon society.

Lila Corwin Berman

You do have, at least, the slice of the Jewish population that's living in the United States, that's gained some real socioeconomic comfort, that has integrated into a lot of the kinds of business and cultural and political spaces, the civic life of the United States.

Jeremy Shere

And as she suggests, while not all American Jews in those days were so fully acculturated, many were. In fact, by the late 1800s, Jews began to socialize with non-Jews and marry into non-Jewish families to such an extent that some Jewish leaders began to worry that American Jewry would assimilate completely and disappear.

To preserve Jews as a cohesive group, some prominent Jews highlighted the distinctiveness of Judaism and Jewish ritual, and some used the language of race as a way of expressing Jewish difference.

Eric Goldstein

Usually when Jews described themselves as a race, it was a way of praising their background, praising their heritage, making certain claims about the contributions that they had made.

Jeremy Shere

For example, in the late 1880s, prominent banker Jacob Schiff helped fund the Semitic Museum at Harvard to document the history and cultural contributions of the ancient ancestors of the Jews. Around the same time, another prominent Jew, Reform rabbi David Einhorn, used racial language to argue against intermarriage.

Eric Goldstein

He believed that Jews were innately religious and that they had this task of spreading ethical monotheism to the world, and he saw intermarriage as a threat to that mission. And he says intermarriage, in his words, was "a nail in the coffin" of the Jewish race with its lofty mission.

Jeremy Shere

Now, to be clear, not all Jewish leaders or American Jews generally thought or talked about themselves in racial terms. Many Jews of the period characterized Jewish difference in religious terms only. But the notion that Jews constituted a distinct race was not uncommon, both among Jews and Gentiles. "Race" was a newly coined scientific term used to explain perceived biological differences among people from various countries and regions of the world. African Americans belonged, in the nomenclature of the time, to the Negro race, the Chinese constituted a race, as did the Irish, and nearly every other group.

But the new science was also used as a way of ranking racial groups, with the White race at the top. And so, as Corwin Berman notes, when Jews described their difference in racial terms, they did so in part because they felt secure enough in their social status.

Lila Corwin Berman

And so, I think that does afford some sense of comfort, to be able to then say, how can we still maintain a sense of what it means to be Jewish, while still firmly committing ourselves to being Americans? And I think that this kind of language of racial pride is attractive because, first of all, other groups are using that kind of language. It's a very imperial, colonial type of language. And that particular kind of language doesn't seem to be necessarily marginalizing those Jews who are using it. It's often being used in ways that are different from anything that would validate antisemitic tropes, which are also being used at the same time.

Jeremy Shere

That sense of comfort began to fade toward the end of the 19th century and the early years of the 20th century, as hundreds of thousands of Jewish and other immigrants from Eastern and Southern Europe poured into the United States. Unlike the Jews from Central Europe who'd arrived decades earlier and had made significant strides in joining the ranks of White society, the newcomers appeared alarmingly foreign. Most were desperately poor and lived in overcrowded Jewish enclaves in big cities, such as New York's Lower East Side. Religious Jews wore beards and sidelocks. Nearly all spoke Yiddish and brought with them Old World customs and manners. But at the same time, Jews were also seen as emblematic of new and troubling modern trends.

Eric Goldstein

They were seen as a people that was particularly urban, that were concentrated in mercantile fields that were related to capitalism. And so, because of their particular history and their social and economic profile, they were a convenient group to use to think about this larger set of problems. So, they're both more visible, more numerous, and then they provide this mechanism for thinking about some of the struggles that American society was going through at that time.

Jeremy Shere

The central problem for the White Anglo-Saxon majority was that the massive waves of immigration and changes associated with modernization were perceived as a threat to their sense of stability and self-confidence. And because Jews came to represent some of the most troubling aspects of modernization, they came under a special kind of scrutiny.

Eric Goldstein

Sometimes there's a move to compare them to African Americans. It's not unlike what the people in Charlottesville were doing. If White Americans traditionally had found a sense of stability and confidence in the idea that their society was divided into the stable categories of Black and White, and if Jews could kind of be worked into that system, then that system could be preserved, and their sense of confidence that they could meet these challenges of the modern age could be preserved.

Jeremy Shere

And so, to a certain extent, Jews felt pressure to distinguish themselves from African Americans, a pressure also felt by other immigrant groups.

Lila Corwin Berman

In the case of Jews who came to the United States, particularly if we're talking now about the early 20th century, that same kind of dynamic is important. To say that—one way that we might say that we fit in is by saying, look, at least we're not this group that is seen as still very, very marginal to being able to have access to resources and privilege in the United States.

Jeremy Shere

This was certainly the case in the South, where Jews felt extra pressure to endorse racist stereotypes of African Americans. For example, when in 1906, Booker T. Washington compared the lynching of Blacks in the American South with pogroms against Jews in Russia, an editorial in the *New Orleans Jewish Ledger* opined that "to compare the Jew, who occupies the highest pinnacle of human superiority and intellectual attainment, with the Negro, who forms the mud at its base, is something only a Negro with more than the usual vanity and impudence of his race could attempt."

The case of Leo Frank,[2] a Jewish factory foreman in Atlanta who was convicted of murdering a 13-year-old female employee in 1913 and lynched, two years later, when a court declined to administer the death sentence, fed Jewish fears of being placed in the same category as African Americans.

Eric Goldstein

It was a great threat to Jewish confidence that they could successfully integrate and that they would be accepted as part of the White population, because it was such a departure from the normal acceptance that Jews had felt, being welcomed as part of the White majority, among themselves.

Jeremy Shere

Many Jews struggled with how to maintain that acceptance without giving up everything that made them distinctly Jewish. Intermarriage remained a major sticking point.

Lila Corwin Berman

It becomes so important precisely because it seems like it would lend itself so easily to being evidence in favor of a theory that either, if Jews start to marry non-Jews, once and for all, we know that Jews are not racially different from non-Jews—or if they don't, that seems to be indicative of the fact that they are.

Jeremy Shere

The debate among Jews about whether to identify strictly in religious terms or to cling to the notion of Jews as a unique race took on a new urgency in the early 1900s.

Simon Wolf, one of the first Jewish lobbyists for the B'nai Birth and other Jewish organizations in Washington, DC, testified before Congress in 1909 that Jews were only a religious group and that therefore the census bureau should not start counting Jews as a race, as it had proposed to do. But many of the Jewish scholars Wolf called on to support his argument contradicted him.

Eric Goldstein

That of course, Jews are [a] race, and he was criticized in the Jewish press for denying what many Jews considered the obvious nature of Jews as what they called a race, a collective that was tied together by biological and historical ties.

Jeremy Shere

So, while publicly, many Jews of the period minimized Jewish difference and tried to stay clear of racial language, in private many felt that they were held together by a common racial heritage. The sense of unease with modern life that many Americans felt during the first decade of the 20th century morphed into something closer to social

---

2. *See* ADL Education, *Remembering Leo Frank*, The Anti-Defamation League (Aug. 12, 2015), https://www.adl.org/resources/backgrounder/remembering-leo-frank; *see also* Douglas O. Linder, *The Trial of Leo Frank: An Account*, Famous Trials, https://www.famous-trials.com/leo-frank/27-home (last visited Dec. 13, 2024).

panic after World War I. The horrifying death and destruction of the war, combined with the rise of Soviet Communism and widespread instability throughout Europe, gave the Anglo-Saxon majority a sense that their civilization had been wrecked and infiltrated by foreign elements, most prominently Jews, who had stubbornly refused to assimilate completely into the dominant culture, even as they gained prominence in many areas of American life. And so, the Jew became the focus of a stream of books, articles, and editorials concerned with what many European Enlightenment thinkers defined as "the Jewish problem."

Lila Corwin Berman

The problem was, what about a group like Jews? What about a group that seems to have such strong kinds of loyalties to one another, that seems to be perceived as so strongly different from other people? Can even that group fit into this Enlightenment liberal idea of individual citizenship and the nation-state?

So, the "Jewish problem" is an extension of that same-long standing question about, at the end of the day, can this American democratic experiment extend itself so fully that even groups that seem really quite different from the imagined center of the United States—that even those groups can participate fully in what it means to be American?

Jeremy Shere

There was no simple answer to that question, partly because Jews didn't fit easily into the racial hierarchy that played such a central role in shaping how the Anglo-Saxon majority thought about what it meant to be a real American.

Eric Goldstein

It partially had to do with the fact that it was harder and harder in this period, because of Jews' rising social status, but also because they were still very distinctive and segregated socially from the mainstream White population. They could no longer easily be compared to African Americans, because their social status was so different, but they also couldn't easily be seen as kind of a group that would simply vanish into White society. So, they started to be described as a kind of special problem that needed to be focused on and worked out.

Jeremy Shere

Attempts to solve the "Jewish problem" gave rise to the harshest period of antisemitism in American history, in the early 1920s. To prevent Jews from becoming too prominent, many of the country's best universities—Harvard, Columbia, Yale, and other Ivy league schools—created quotas to limit Jewish enrollment around the same time. Automobile magnate Henry Ford republished the antisemitic text, *The Protocols of the Elders of Zion.*

Lila Corwin Berman

He republishes it in his company town newspaper, the *Dearborn Independent,* that has a broad circulation. And this sense of really saying that here's this group of people that's getting a lot of the opportunities and resources from the United States, but when it comes down to it, we don't believe they're fully vested in the American experiment.

And so, it ends up that if they're not fully vested in it, if they're not fully committed to it, then they are really sapping the resources for their own aims and not for the good of the whole.

Jeremy Shere

The advent of the Great Depression at the end of the 1920s only intensified anti-Jewish sentiment. Tens of millions of Americans tuned into the weekly radio addresses of Charles Coughlin, a Roman Catholic priest who often laced his fiery speeches with antisemitic language.

This type of overheated rhetoric was not universally supported by the Anglo-Saxon majority, but liberal elites mainly spoke out against antisemitism as a barrier to White unity, and they mostly blamed antisemitism on Jews' failure to assimilate.

Jews responded to the rise in antisemitism and increasing pressure to assimilate in a variety of ways. One strategy involved asserting the Whiteness of Jews, for example, by staging blackface minstrelsy shows at Jewish social clubs.

Lila Corwin Berman

What's interesting, I think, about Jews putting on blackface is it's Jews stepping into a place of power and authority to put it on and take it off, which is actually not the kind of power and authority that most Jews had in the United States. In many cases, Jews were prey to whatever the perception of them might have been by non-Jews. You know that they, in fact, weren't Christian. That they were different in this and that and the other way, that they were objects of suspicion.

Jeremy Shere

In other words, if only Whites could put on blackface, then Jewish blackface performance was a way for Jews to define themselves as White. The most famous Jewish blackface performance was by Al Jolson in the first "talkie" motion picture, *The Jazz Singer*, which came out in 1927. Blackface was a demeaning, racist caricature of African Americans, but Yiddish journalists who reviewed the movie downplayed its racism, focusing instead on how Jolson's performance suggested an affinity between Jews and Blacks.

Eric Goldstein

There's a culminating scene in the movie where he's torn between making his blackface performance and going to be the cantor in the synagogue, because his father is unable to be there. And he looks in the mirror and it's only when he has on the blackface that he's able to connect with his sense of himself as Jewish. And so, there's a way in which the blackface both makes this Jewish performer White, but it also is a vehicle for getting in touch with his emotions about Jewishness, that he doesn't feel comfortable accessing as a person trying to fit into White society in real life.

Jeremy Shere

By the early 1930s, the strain of economic insecurity, combined with the rise of the Nazi regime in Germany, and fears that Nazi ideology might spread to the United States, in some ways did foster greater Jewish identification with African Americans.

For example, Jews expressed unequivocal support for the Scottsboro boys, nine black teenagers who were falsely accused of raping two White women near Scottsboro, Alabama in 1931.

But at the same time, Jews also felt increasing pressure to position themselves above African Americans in the social pecking order. In the Bronx, in New York City, and also in Chicago, Jewish housewives attended so-called "street corner slave markets," where destitute, often starving African American women hired themselves out as domestic servants for as little as 15 cents an hour.

Eric Goldstein

So, it really points out the middling place that Jews held in American society, where their framework, their goal, was to fit in and be accepted within a white elite society. In the 1930s, most Jews would have seen themselves as outsiders and people scratching to get into American society. And yet from the African American perspective, already at that time, Jews who had stores in African American neighborhoods, or these housewives who were hiring African American domestic servants at very cheap, exploitative prices, were seen as part of a white power structure already.

Jeremy Shere

A common strategy used by Jews during this period was to redefine the concept of the Jewish race in a way that highlighted how Jewish traits were a boon to White civilization. Jews might have been a distinct race, but they were one that deserved inclusion among the family of White races.

Eric Goldstein

In using the language of race, they would specifically try to use it in a way that was different than the way it was used in reference to African Americans. In other words, they would argue that Jews were White and yet they had certain character traits, certain innate sensibilities and psychological traits, for example, that made them unique and different. So, they tried to spin it into a positive thing that did not threaten their acceptance as White.

Jeremy Shere

In the aftermath of World War II, America became a more open, inclusive place for minority groups of European origin. The full integration of Jews and Catholics into the American armed forces went a long way toward establishing them as members of the White, Anglo-Saxon majority. Plus, in the wake of the defeat of the Nazis and their ideology of race and racial superiority, racial science fell out of favor.

Lila Corwin Berman

How this played out in Nazi Germany was bracing and made it become pretty unacceptable in the United States to think about racial classification in this way. So, it was a massive intellectual shift. There are historians who've really shown how in the period of just about a decade, scientific racism becomes pretty much discredited in the American scientific community and other European minority groups.

Jeremy Shere

The decline of scientific racism helped to pave the way for social integration. During the '20s and '30s, Jews may have become Americanized in their cultural behavior, but socially they were segregated. That changed after the war.

Eric Goldstein

You see a lot of those barriers declining after World War II. So, Jews are socially integrating into the larger society.

Jeremy Shere

By the late '50s and on into the '60s, American society may have become more welcoming to Jews, Catholics, and other European minority groups, but racism was still prevalent. African Americans, especially, continued to endure segregation in nearly all aspects of life, and, especially in the South, lacked many of even the most basic rights.

Some Jews supported the civil rights movement, most famously Rabbi Abraham Joshua Heschel, who marched alongside Martin Luther King in Selma in 1965. A handful of Southern rabbis openly supported Black civil rights. And a significant percentage of Northerners who rode freedom buses south to register Black voters were Jews.

But most Jews in the North and South were still in the process of blending in and cementing their place as part of the majority. And so, they were still wary of challenging the racial status quo, as Judith Rosenbaum notes. It wasn't until the latter half of the 1960s that American Jews felt secure enough and had enough social standing to more openly and forcefully support civil rights for African Americans.

Judith Rosenbaum

For many of the Jews who were involved, it did come out of a sense of identification, a sense both of identification with African Americans and a sense of fairness. And a sense also, I will say, of entitlement and power. Like you have to have a certain amount of sense that I believe that I can change the world and that I have a right to be heard, and I have a right to speak up. And often those things come along with education that I'm privileged enough that I'm able to take these risks.

Jeremy Shere

But the more militant elements of the civil rights movement, such as the Black Panthers, the Nation of Islam, and other Black nationalist groups, were tricky for Jews who supported civil rights. For many Black nationalist leaders, Jews were simply part of the White majority and so part of the problem. Still, many young Jews were inspired by Black nationalism, feminism, and other social and political movements to proudly assert their Jewishness in ways that often borrowed from African American politics and culture, and that are still with us today.

Eric Goldstein

It's no longer something to be afraid of. And they abandoned the tendency of their parents to always want to fit in and be the same. And increasingly in American Jewish society, as they become more and more accepted, their concern and their focus shifts not to, how can we fit in and be the same, but how can we preserve and assert our sense of difference?

For example, if you look at the Soviet Jewry movement, they have the March on Washington and you have young Jews in the Jewish Renewal wearing colorful *kippot* and wearing their hair in a very curly fashion—you know, the idea of the "Jewfro"—all of these are inspired by the kinds of cultural assertiveness that you see in African American movements.

Jeremy Shere

And so, we come full circle to today, when we find ourselves in a strange moment in American Jewish history, a moment when most Ashkenazi Jews in the United States benefit from being fully integrated into mainstream society, but also a time when antisemitism is on the rise across the political spectrum.

And as we saw in Charlottesville and in the horrific massacre at the Tree of Life synagogue in Pittsburgh, when Jews remain the targets of those who want to return to a notion of White America, in which Jews are not included. Thankfully, we also live at a time when White nationalists and White pride racists feel marginalized and despised by the mainstream, while the Jews they fear occupy positions of privilege and are as fully integrated into American society as they have ever been in any country outside Israel.

One measure of the sense of security of American Jews is the extent to which many young liberals Jews are mobilized around issues of racial justice.

Eric Goldstein

In Jewish organizations, Jews are coming to terms with the idea that Jews have White privilege. You didn't see that 10 or 15 years ago. And I see Jewish organizations like HIAS, for example, organizing around refugee issues, and Jews are a visible group within movements for racial justice and actively associating their own history with the plight of groups who are the victims of White nationalism today.

Jeremy Shere

Increasingly, members of some of those groups are also Jews and are changing the racial makeup of American Jewry in significant ways.

Ilana Kaufman

We're talking about Jewish people in the United States who are also Latinx, Native, multi-racial, Black, African American, Asian Pacific Islander.

Jeremy Shere

This is Ilana Kaufman and as she notes, these Jews face many of the same types of discrimination and prejudice the Jews of the 1920s and '30s faced, not only from American society at large, but from the Jewish communities to which they aspire to belong. And so, American Jews who enjoy the privileges of being part of White society, she says, have an obligation to not just welcome Jews of color, but to truly appreciate their struggle.

Ilana Kaufman

It means that those Jews who've appreciated and experienced the privileges of Whiteness have a burden and an invitation to be more conscious about their relationship with their own race, their relationship with people who have races that are different than them, and to really understand racism in the United States, power and privilege in the United States, and how their own White identity gets informed, not only by internal pressures of this country around race, but also informed by the experiences of those who are people of color in the United States relative to their own White Jewish experience.

Jeremy Shere

Ashkenazi American Jews may benefit from being considered White, but despite their success and acceptance, Jews remain a distinct group in America, part of the mainstream, and yet still apart from it.

Eric Goldstein

You have liberal spokespeople pointing to the Holocaust and the Jewish refugee issue of the '30s as a talking point, in terms of describing the urgency of the situation at the border. And at the same time, you have the Trump administration pointing to Israel and the barrier on the West Bank as an example of why we need a wall on the southern border. And it's so interesting that Jews are still this kind of liminal group that disturbs and confounds an easy racial divide.

Further Considerations: *Are Jews White?* Podcast

1. How, according to the various discussants, has the concept of Jewish "Whiteness" in America evolved over time, and what factors have driven these changes?

2. How did the influx of Eastern European Jewish immigrants in the late 19th and early 20th centuries impact perceptions of Jewish Whiteness in America?

3. In what ways did Jews attempt to assert their Whiteness in early 20th century America? How did Jewish racial identity intersect with class status?

4. How did World War II and its aftermath affect perceptions of Jewish racial identity?

5. How have antisemitic conspiracy theories affected Jewish efforts to assimilate into White American society?

6. In what ways did Jewish racial identity differ regionally within the United States?

7. How has the increasing diversity within the American Jewish community affected contemporary discussions of Jewish Whiteness?

C. An Intersectional Approach to Jews and Whiteness

David Schraub, *White Jews: An Intersectional Approach*[3]

43 Ass'n for Jewish Stud. Rev. 379 (2019)

Intersectional Methods and Intersectional Gaps: Relating Whiteness and Jewishness

Today, intersectionality is sometimes deployed whenever a scholar or activist wishes to evoke multiple axes of identity-based discrimination. In its initial formulation by Kimberlé Williams Crenshaw, however, "intersectionality" sought to tackle a much more specific problem. The issue was not just that, for example, racial oppression and gender oppression were often held out as separate inquiries. It was that even an inquiry that incorporated both an analysis of racial and gender oppression might still fail to adequately encompass the experiences of (say) Black women, to the extent that "racial oppression" was viewed through the lens of Black *men*, and gender oppression through the vantage of *White* women. Where that is the case, Crenshaw observes, the exclusion of Black women is not solved "simply by including Black women within an already established analytical structure. Because the intersectional experience is greater than the sum of racism and sexism, any analysis that does not take intersectionality into account cannot sufficiently address the particular manner in which Black women are subordinated." The core of the intersectional insight is that the experience that lies at the *intersection* of race and sex is not simply the combination of what are taken to be the "simpliciter" cases of race and sex, precisely because the "simpliciter" case is in actuality a discretely White (for women) or male (for Blacks) experience.

Hence, intersectionality is not a matter of building coalitions between groups combatting various forms of identity-based oppression: antiracist groups should also oppose sexism, homophobia, antisemitism, Islamophobia, and so on. This practice, sometimes dubbed the "additive" approach, simply ladles different marginalized identities on top of one another in the hopes that their summation will sufficiently include all persons in the full panoply of their diverse identities....

One of the key benefits of intersectional approaches is that they encourage us to look into how the function and operation of our identity categories change when placed, as they always are, in dynamic relation with one another. Crenshaw's observation that, for example, Black female oppression is "greater than the sum of race and sex" is applicable across a wide range of cases. Avtar Brah and Ann Phoenix provide a more general formulation of intersectionality, associating it with "the complex, irreducible, varied, and variable effects which ensue when multiple axes of differentiation—economic, political, cultural, psychic, subjective and experiential—intersect in historically specific contexts." This aspect of intersectionality explains why I draw on it in a case that is—in more ways than one—unorthodox....

---

3. Reprinted with permission of the University of Pennsylvania Press.

Whiteness can operate differently in conjunction with different social categories, "doing" different things to, say, a recent East European immigrant, a working-class Irishman, an upper-class WASP, or a Jewish college student. Through this lens, we can begin to answer [Cynthia] Levine-Rasky's penetrating set of questions: "What does whiteness 'do' for Jews? How does it confer or deprive them of power or privilege? What does it ensure or endanger?"

White + Jew ≠ "White Jew"

An example can help further illuminate the problem I wish to explore. In 2016, as the Stanford Student Council debated a resolution condemning antisemitism, one senator objected to a particular clause identifying claims that "Jews [control] the media, economy, government and other societal institutions" as a form of antisemitism. The senator argued, "[The clause] says: 'Jews controlling the media, economy, government and other societal institutions' [is] a feature of anti-Semitism that we theoretically shouldn't challenge. I think that that's kind of irresponsible foraying into another politically contentious conversation. Questioning these potential power dynamics, I think, is not anti-Semitism. I think it's a very valid discussion."

The senator's comments were widely condemned as antisemitic or an apologetic for antisemitism; he ultimately withdrew his bid for reelection.

I agree that the statement in question was antisemitic in nature. And perhaps its utterance can be explained simply by there being some people who possess antisemitic attitudes. Yet I think one can reconstruct the thinking behind the senator's statement in a way that explains how—at least not knowing the particular history of the trope of Jewish hyperpower—one might have not instinctively recognized the problem. The line of argument would go as follows:

> It is standard practice in opposing White supremacy to note the power and significant control White people, as compared to people of color, have in institutions like the media, economy, government, and other social bodies. So how can it be that the same argument made all the time with respect to White people generally—and acknowledged to be valid and progressive in that case—suddenly becomes a form of bigotry when applied to a particular *subset* of White people (i.e., the Jews)? Indeed, we frequently see White people try to deny they possess this power and instead take on the role of the victim; how is this any different?

If we view the issue through the lens of Whiteness, the need to question distributions of power—who has it, how is it exercised—is unremarkable, even essential. Under this framework, the objectors' claim of bigotry or bias looks worse than inapposite, it looks familiar. It echoes larger efforts to dismiss or deny the real power and privileges White people, as a class, possess in important societal institutions.

Contrast the framing that emerges if we looked at the matter from a Jewish lens:

> It is a standard form of antisemitism and anti-Jewish bigotry to argue that Jews have power and control over institutions like the media, economy, govern-

> ment, and other social bodies—power they exercise to the exclusion of and detriment of non-Jews. So why should such claims suddenly cease to be antisemitic simply because they cloak themselves in the garb of "antiracism" or "progressivism"? Indeed, historically speaking, there is no oddity in such a connection; antisemitism of this form has not just occasionally but frequently manifested precisely in this way—leftist self-identification and all.

Adopting the Jewish perspective, we encounter a familiarity of a different kind. Antisemitic tropes focusing on Jewish domination and control are standard-issue, and there is nothing uncommon in their being clothed in progressive language. Nor is there anything unfamiliar in dismissing Jewish objections to such stereotypes by labeling them further proof of Jewish power and censorial instincts.

Hopefully, this illustrates the sense of talking past one another that seems to explain at least part of this affair. The senator is talking about Jews no differently, he thinks, from how he talks about other members of the White community. How can it be that the argument shifts from valid to illicit simply because the subject is Jews? Meanwhile, the Jewish objectors think that the senator is talking about them in a way no different from any other antisemite. How could the same argument gain legitimacy simply because the senator thought his approach was antiracist in nature?

More importantly, it is clear that one cannot fully understand what was happening in this case if one insists on holding "Jewish" and "White" apart from one another. The incompatible narratives emerge because they seek to analyze the "Jewish" and "White" dimensions of the issue separately. One cannot simply add the two analyses back together at the end; the result would be gibberish. It is evident, rather, that something specific happened at the point of intersection. Discourses of White power and privilege—valid as far as they go—acted as a sort of accelerant for prejudiced tropes of Jewish power and privilege. The Whiteness of the Jewish figure served to cleanse, even validate, arguments that otherwise would reek in their antisemitic familiarity.

Tropes of Jewishness; Tropes of Whiteness

The above example illustrates that Whiteness and Jewishness do not simply sit side by side as social categories. Rather, Whiteness seems to be *doing* something to Jewishness. "White Jews" are not "White" and then also "Jews." Jewish Whiteness seems to inflect, in serious and fundamental ways, the understanding of what it means to be Jewish—or what Jewish experience could possibly be. At the extreme, it subsumes Jewishness entirely—Jewishness cannot be understood but through the interpretive frames offered by Whiteness.

Why does this happen? What is it about Jewishness that appears to make it particularly vulnerable to this sort of elision? "Why," as Jessica Greenebaum asked, "is this oppression different from all others (or not)?" And what are the impacts of the "White Jew" concept on actual Jewish persons (of any racial background)? Part of the difficulty is that Jewishness crosses over and blurs categories that theorists—particularly non-intersectional ones—often wish to keep separate. It is simultaneously national, racial, ethnic, and religious in character, but not reducible to any of these. As Albert Memmi, the renowned Tunisian Jewish anticolonialist writer, wryly observed, it is the "sociologists' lack of imagination" that renders them unable to latch on to the peculiarity of the Jewish case and instead sees them grasping about for a more familiar box in which to place Jews.

Yet there are answers to be had upon a close look at the relationship between tropes about Whiteness and tropes about Jewishness. Viewed apart from one another, we can talk about Whiteness in a particular way and Jewishness in another way, without ever coming to grips with how these respective discourses interact. By placing them in a dynamic relationship, it becomes evident how Whiteness and Jewishness operate upon each other in particular and often troublesome ways.

Start with Whiteness. Identified with control, privilege, dominance, and exclusivity, "Whiteness," writes Abby Ferber, "is a privileged status. To be White is to have greater access to rewards and valued resources simply because of one's group membership." ...

Turn now to Jewishness. While perceptions about Jews are varied and diverse, antisemitism frequently manifests particularly as a putative criticism of Jewish power. In her influential pamphlet *The Past Didn't Go Anywhere*, April Rosenblum identifies several themes common to antisemitic narratives, including:

- Jews are mysterious, or act secretly behind the scenes;
- Jews have abnormal or supernatural amounts of power;
- Jews are disloyal to, or seek the destruction of, the society they live in;
- Jews are disproportionately the cause of harm in the world;
- Jews are unlike the rest of humanity (at best); or inherently evil, or tied to the devil (at worst);
- Jews are wealthy or greedy;
- Jews are the "brains" behind the action.

What these themes all share is their presentation of the Jew as distinctively empowered compared to humanity in general. In the antisemitic imagination, Jews are hated specifically because they are presumed to be dominant. "Anti-Semites," writes Phoebe Maltz Bovy, "weren't—aren't—just people who think they're better than Jews. They're people who think they're being *oppressed* by Jews." As Moishe Postone thus observed, "Anti-Semitism, consequently, can appear to be antihegemonic ... the expression of a movement of the little people against an intangible, global form of domination."

The antisemite views the Jew as an omnipresent, world-spanning character—distinguished by his or her unrivaled ability to act, control, dominate, or take over. As Frantz Fanon observed, "Jews are feared because of their potential to appropriate. 'They' are everywhere. The banks, the stock exchanges, and the government are infested with them. They control everything. Soon the country will belong to them." This power is distinguished by being both extraordinary (they *control everything*, nothing is outside the Jewish grasp) and illicit (they gained such control through trickery, deceit, or other underhanded or illegitimate means). Viewed through Ahmed's frame of what is "within reach," the answer given by the antisemite regarding the Jews is "everything." Jews are marked by their exceptional, even superhuman, capacities—there is nothing they can't do, no institution or community that is insulated from their tendrils.

Narratives of ill-gotten Jewish power convert basic Jewish political participation into a "Kosher conspiracy." It is presumed that Jews are persistent and perpetual winners in the political game, such that the proper orientation towards Jews in society is to rein in their exceptional influence and leverage. To the extent Jews are even recognized as marginalized, they are taken as a model of legislative and social protection—the outgroup that's in. Other groups seek the bounty that Jews are assumed to already possess. So, for example, Didi Herman documents the use of the Jewish case as justification for expanding the Race Relations Act (the United Kingdom's major antidiscrimination law) to other out-groups such as Sikhs and Muslims. Shouldn't they enjoy the same protections as Jews? And surely the answer is yes—but what was overlooked was that Jews had *never* actually won a reported case under the Race Relations Act against a non-Jewish defendant. The image of the Jew as modeling protection completely overwrote a reality of continued vulnerability.

The point here is not that Jews are somehow distinct from other minority groups in receiving often-inadequate protection from formal or informal legal sources. That, of course, is an experience quite common to political out-groups. What may well be distinctive is that, in seeking out these protections, Jews lose even as—or perhaps because—they are thought of as winners.

What Does Whiteness Do to Jewishness?

1. Jewish Power

We can finally zero in on Levine-Rasky's question: What does Whiteness *do* to Jewishness? In its critical manifestation, Whiteness as a lens of analysis is designed to elevate or accentuate certain aspects of experience that might otherwise go unnoticed. A middle-class, Christian, suburban man thinks of himself, and is thought of as, "just a person." He does not see himself, and society does not portray him as particularly powerful, privileged, or influential. He works for what he gets, sometimes struggles or faces hardships "like anyone else," and otherwise is presented as simply "normal." The goal of Whiteness studies is not necessarily to fully falsify these stories as much as it is to provide a counterweight. It emphasizes opportunities that the man as White receives, or treatment that he gets, or spaces he can move in that others do not or cannot. Peggy McIntosh's "Invisible Knapsack" is an effort to draw out the privileges of Whiteness as a *contrast* to a deracinated, individualistic perspective that is blind to these particular sets of racialized advantages.

But in the Jewish case, something different happens. Jews are *not* seen as "normal," everyday persons. As discussed above, the prevailing view of Jews—the view that *subordinates* Jews—is precisely that they are "particularly powerful, or privileged, or influential." And so, when the Whiteness frame—which by design draws attention to these attributes—is overlaid upon the White Jew (as a body or a concept), it serves not as a counterweight but as an accelerant. The hope in applying the Whiteness frame to a gentile White is to unsettle received understandings of the White experience—to make people see things they had not seen before. By contrast, the effect of applying Whiteness to Jewishness is confirmatory: "I always thought that Jews had all this power and privilege—and see how right I was!"

Bryan Cheyette, commenting on the absence of antisemitism in many academic works dealing with oppression, attributes the gap to Jewishness being folded into an untextured Whiteness that operates indiscriminately upon Jews and non-Jews alike. "Where," he asks, "within this supposed 'common culture' does 'the Jew'—other than as an aspect of dominant 'white' oppression—fit?" And the problem is worse than he lets on: Jews are not just another flavor of White. They *epitomize* Whiteness, they exemplify its vices as "the iciest of the ice people." Jewishness is perceived as "a form of almost hyper-Whiteness," its ultimate avatar. Pushed to its limit, "Jewish simply displaces White." Jews, as *inherently* avaricious, deceitful, domineering, and possessive, stand in for those Whites who are irredeemably supremacist in orientation; we end White supremacy at the point where Whites stop acting like Jews.

It is no accident, then, that the latest Far Right gambit to enlist people of color into antisemitic projects is to promote the idea of "Jewish privilege" as the true and ultimate manifestation of "White privilege."[4] ...

2. Jewish Hegemony

Thus far, the key trope linking Jewishness and Whiteness has been power, and power as a very visible thing—Jews are actively thought of and recognized as powerful. But Whiteness as a *hegemonic* concept also speaks of power as frequently cloaked or invisible, disguised as normal....

This aspect of Whiteness, too, intersects with Jewishness in ways that demand unpacking. It is not for nothing that Evelyn Beck's pathbreaking article on the exclusion of Jews in feminist movements was titled "The Politics of Jewish Invisibility." Writing in 1988, Beck observed that while there were many Jewish women writing as feminists, very few feminist works spoke specifically to or about Jewish themes—including those that held themselves out as multicultural in orientation.... On that note, there is a plethora of articles exploring why Jews seem not to be included in the "multicultural" pantheon, and nearly all suggest part of the reason is the perception of Jews as "White." ...

Why is it that "Whiteness" serves to obscure Jewishness in this way? Consider two possibilities for how we might account for an absence of distinctively "Jewish" contributions or discourses. The first account says they are excluded—they are not desired,

4. Antisemitic flyers posted at the University of Illinois at Chicago made this link explicit: "Ending white privilege starts with ending Jewish privilege." Stephen Gossett, *Anti-Semitic Flyers Found on UIC Campus for Second Time in a Week*, CHICAGOIST (Mar. 20, 2017), http://chicagoist.com/2017/03/20/more_anti-semitic_flyers_found_on_u.php.

or not recognized, or not valued. But the second account holds that they are already included—they exist as part of the implicit background of dominant, hegemonic conversation. Jewishness is seen as adding nothing to a multicultural conversation; it is already implicitly included as part of the hegemonic "White" conversation. As one Jewish feminist related being told (at a conference that featured presentations by Black, Latina, and Irish Catholic women), "Jewish women are just White middle-class women." Consequently, her interlocutor went on, "There is nothing that differentiates them from the ruling majority. There is no reason to treat them as a specialized minority or to devote any of our time to their particular experience." To demand significant time and attention be devoted to the Jewish case is little different from demanding still more resources and consideration be accorded to White people—that is, an insistence from those who already have so much that they should be given yet more. In turn, the belief that this will be the reaction when Jews attempt to put "Jewish issues" on a multicultural or intersectional agenda is a major reason why many Jews are deeply reticent to do so.

In short, the politics of Jewish invisibility is predicated on a presumption of Jewish omnipresence. Jews are not heard from because everyone assumes they have already heard from Jews—heard enough, perhaps heard too much, perhaps it is time to allow others to talk. Because Jews are thought to be everywhere, the possibility that there is in fact a gap or quietude around Jews becomes almost inconceivable. After all, if there is one thing Jews *are not*, it's "quiet." . . .

That Israel is viewed either as a subspecies of European colonialism or as a European cultural vanguard, rather than something at least arguably sui generis, is reflective of the broader view of Jews as basically White. . . .

Jewishness Outside of Kyriarchy

The problem should now be evident. The Whiteness frame looks at its subjects and asks that we see their power, their privilege, their enhanced societal standing. So far so good—it is important to unpack all of these things. But stereotypes of Jewishness sound many of the same notes: they too look at Jews and point out their putative power, privilege, and domination of social spaces. The issue is not that (some) Jews do have power or privilege along certain dimensions in American or Western society—for example, insofar as they are White, or male, or heterosexual, or economically well-off. But in those cases, the power that they have is as Whites, or men, or straight, or wealthy—it is not by virtue of being Jewish that they hold these benefits.

Normally, acknowledging multiple distinct axes of oppression yields the unremarkable conclusion that the same person can be advantaged along one dimension while marginalized along another. A White woman may be privileged through her race while subordinated through her sex; vice versa for a Black man. And in theory, antisemitism and racism could operate the same way—the White Jew reaps the benefits of White supremacy while being oppressed by antisemitism, and likewise the non-White non-Jew stands superior over the Jew along the axis of antisemitism even as she suffers under

White supremacy....[5] The concept of kyriarchy—that dimensions of power and marginalization are cross-cutting, such that all of us simultaneously stand in both positions across various social identities and locations—would seem an easy fit.

Yet the kyriarchical frame is definitively not how we talk about "White Jews." Antisemitism is cast as an intramural divide *within* White populations, something that alters or degrades the status of Jews vis-à-vis *other Whites*. Harold Cruse made this point explicit: antisemitism may be a problem for Jews, but it is, he contended, "a problem for [Jews] to settle with other whites with whom they share political, economic, and cultural power." It is not seen as impacting Jewish standing qua Jews compared to non-Jews as a whole. Indeed, the rare attempts to make this kyriarchical observation are beset with anxiety—as when Brenda Cossman and Marlee Kline laboriously articulate what they are *not* saying when they *are* saying that Jews continue to face antisemitism. (We are not saying Jews are *more* oppressed than others, we are not saying Jews are oppressed *identically* to others, we are not saying that Jews do not necessarily possess advantages as White or wealthy or well-educated, nor are we saying that all Jews necessarily *do* possess those advantages.) It is a preemptive defense against the assumption that discourse about antisemitism is in reality a "burst of victim-competition" where Jews "will deny both responsibility for racism and privileges derived from it."

For many White Jews, the upshot of all of this is the denial of antisemitism's status as a unique and distinctive axis of marginalization, one that neither displaces nor is displaced by racism. Instead, writers act as if the operative question about *antisemitism* is whether Jews are properly labeled *White*. If they are not, or if they were in eras when they were not, then Jewish claims of marginalization make sense. But if/when Jews are White, they lose access to claims of ever being outsiders *even as Jews*. In effect, Whiteness absorbs Jewishness, removing it from the kyriarchical field and cordoning it off from any sort of system-wide reckoning of privilege and marginalization. All that is left of antisemitism, under this view, is a sort of internal jockeying for position among White people. Additionally, this framing has important marginalizing effects on non-White Jews, both as Jews and as non-Whites. "The Whitening of Jews," writes Lewis Gordon, meant "that large groups of nonwhite Jews simply disappeared, or at least disappeared *as Jews*."... Corey Balsam goes so far as to say that "the simple attribute of being Jewish functions to whiten Sephardic and other non-white Jews"—putting them in a position of relative power by virtue of their Jewishness. All Jews are "White Jews" in this sense—non-White Jews are deemed White *in their Jewishness*; Jewish problems are assumed to be White problems regardless of which particular Jew is the one experiencing them....

5. One need not think that the "advantages" conferred to non-Jews under conditions of antisemitism cancel out the advantages conferred to Whites through White supremacy to accept this formulation—indeed, in the American case, it is clear that racial oppression is far more extensive than antisemitic marginalization.

Conclusion: Is Gal Gadot White?

Why any Jew would be invested in identifying Gal Gadot [*Wonder Woman* star] as non-White—and, more broadly, why many Jews possessing pale skin, whose immediate ancestors lived in or immigrated from Europe, and who are in most day-to-day interactions (particularly with state actors) racially perceived as White, nonetheless passionately resist the label. One answer is that doing so serves to elide Jewish enjoyment of White privilege. And that may well be a sizeable part of the explanation. But Tamar Herman offers up another angle to the story that is quite illustrative. Forthrightly agreeing that Gal Gadot is White, she nonetheless declares that "Gadot isn't just another white woman on screen, and it's dismissive to say so." Herman's essay speaks movingly of how important and meaningful it was to have someone so openly and distinctively *Jewish* on screen in this sort of role—it genuinely mattered that someone *like her* was on screen, in a way that it would not if she were "just another white woman." Those correctly insisting on Gadot's Whiteness, Herman suggests, sometimes acted as if that meant she did not count as a representational victory of *any* sort—even as a Jew, and in particular, a noticeably accented non-American Jew. It seems plausible that at least some of the Jewish writers arguing that Gadot was not White were reacting to the sense that the "White Jew" concept impedes, even obliterates, the recognition of a distinctive Jewish qua Jewish experience. Contesting their Whiteness is a means for White Jews to create space to talk about their Jewishness.

One need not find this decision to be analytically sound or ethically warranted to think that it is reacting to genuine social phenomena. Yet if complete denial of Jewish Whiteness ends up obscuring the ways in which White Jews enjoy and have in some cases helped propagate White privilege as against their non-White peers (Jewish and not), that only underlines the need for an alternative approach that affirms the legitimacy of Jewish articulations of Jewish experience as existing in relation with, but not displacing, a nuanced and complex understanding of Jewish Whiteness for those Jews who are of European descent. Accepting that, in their relations with African Americans and other people of color in America, White Jews are indeed White should not be taken to negate the existence or importance of antisemitism as a distinctive axis of marginalization—one that cannot always be fully disassociated or disentangled from Whiteness as a social concept. In this way, grasping how Whiteness and Jewishness intersect not only can further illuminate certain mechanics of antisemitism, but also can facilitate Jewish acknowledgment of the ways and contexts in which they *are* White and *do* benefit from White privilege....

Without careful attention to the particular social location that exists where Whiteness and Jewishness intersect, the Whiteness frame can reinscribe—even accentuate—deep antisemitic tropes of Jewish power, hegemony, and dominion.

Further Considerations: An Intersectional Approach

1. Does Schraub's position require denying that "White" or Ashkenazi Jews are, in at least some important respects, White?

2. How can one harmonize Schraub's analysis of (a) how Whiteness sometimes accelerates antisemitic tropes with (b) his belief that White Jews are White in certain contexts and benefit from White privilege?

3. What is Jewish "hyper-Whiteness"? How does the association of Jews with power function as an antisemitic trope within critiques of Whiteness?

4. How does Schraub's intersectional approach illuminate aspects of Jewish experience that might otherwise remain obscure?

5. How can Jews be both privileged and marginalized?

6. In Schraub's view, how does antisemitism function as a distinct "axis of marginalization"?

7. In what ways does Schraub suggest that labeling Jews as White erases their specificity as a minority group?

8. How does anti-Jewish discrimination differ from other forms of discrimination against marginalized groups?

9. How does Schraub's analysis challenge or complicate traditional narratives of Jewish assimilation and "becoming White" in America, such as those discussed in the podcast? Building on the podcast's discussion of Jewish strategies for asserting Whiteness, how does Schraub's analysis shed new light on the long-term consequences of Jewish efforts to assert Whiteness?

10. How might Schraub's account of Jewish Whiteness influence contemporary civil rights discourse?

11. Had the various judges and justices in *Manzanares* and *Shaare Tefila* read Schraub's article, how might it have affected their analyses?

D. A Monument to Jewish Identity

Moses Jacob Ezekiel, "Religious Liberty" (Sculpture, 1876)

Nat'l Museum of Am. Jewish Hist., Philadelphia, Pa

Moses Jacob Ezekiel, an American Jewish artist, sculpted "Religious Liberty" for an exhibition held in Philadelphia in 1876 to celebrate the 100th anniversary of the signing of the Declaration of Independence. It now stands in Philadelphia in front of the National Museum of American Jewish History, which describes the statue as follows:

> The highly-classical, allegorical marble presents *Liberty* as a ten-foot woman, wearing a coat of mail partly covered by a toga. *Liberty* dons a Phrygian cap, the *pilleus libertatis* bestowed on freed slaves, with a border of thirteen golden-colored stars representing the original colonies. In her hand is a laurel wreath of victory, which also rests on fasces, a bundle of birch rods tied together with a ribbon, as a symbol of power and unified strength. The fasces are covered by an open book, meant to signal the U.S. Constitution. *Liberty* extends her right

> arm protectively over an idealized, nude young boy standing at her right. Meant to personify Faith, the boy grasps a flaming lamp, and he raises his other hand up to heaven. At *Liberty*'s feet is an eagle, a well-recognized emblem of America, that attacks a serpent signifying Intolerance. The eagle's sharp, oversized talons grip the serpent's body, flipped on its back, as the bird attempts to quash its foe. The group stands on a pedestal bearing the inscription "Religious Liberty, Dedicated to the People of the United States by the Order B'nai B'rith and Israelites of America."

A rabbi spoke at the unveiling. His remarks "carefully mentioned God but avoided Hebrew language and Hebrew prayers. He emphasized the importance of religious freedom as a universal ideal that benefited all Americans, not just Jews."[6]

Further Considerations: Ezekiel's "Religious Liberty"

1. Does "Religious Liberty" depict Jews as a racial group? If so, what race?
2. Does "Religious Liberty" depict Jews as a religious group? If so, what religion?

---

6. Weitzman Nat'l Museum of Am. Jewish Hist., An Enduring Monument: Moses Jacob Ezekiel's "Religious Liberty" (1876), https://theweitzman.org/exhibitions/enduring-monument/ (last visited Jan. 8, 2025).

Figure 2.1. "Religious Liberty" by Moses Jacob Ezekiel. Courtesy of National Museum of American Jewish History, Philadelphia, PA.

Chapter 3

Jews as Ethnic

In Chapter One, we saw U.S. courts construe §§ 1981 and 1982, which bar racial discrimination, to protect Latinos, Jews, and Arabs under the rubric of race and the White/non-White binary. U.K. anti-discrimination law, the subject of this chapter, has gradually come to protect Jews under the rubric of ethnicity rather than race.

The U.K.'s landmark anti-discrimination statute, the Race Relations Act 1976 ("the 1976 Act"), facially resembles the U.S. approach in that it prohibits discrimination based on "racial grounds" or "racial group." The critical difference is that the 1976 Act explicitly defines "racial group" to include groups characterized by "ethnic origins." This broader definition would seem to encompass Jews in their capacity as an ethnic group. In practice, however, the legal path towards extending such coverage proved to be more arduous.

This chapter traces the U.K. courts' evolving approach to the 1976 Act and its application to Jews. It looks at a single case, *Mandla v. Dowell Lee,* and how two different courts interpreted the statute. In Section A, "Jews as an Ethnoracial Group," Lord Denning of the Court of Appeal defines "ethnic" as "ethnoracial" and posits Jews as the exemplary and best known such group. In Section B, "Jews as an Ethnoreligious Group," the House of Lords develops a sociological definition of an ethnic group, one that includes Jews but is not limited to them. As will be seen, an ethnic group approach to applying anti-discrimination laws to Jews has certain advantages over a racial or racial-like approach.

A. Jews as an Ethnoracial Group

The drafters of the 1976 Act understood it as prohibiting anti-Jewish discrimination. The unanswered legal question was: on what basis or in what capacity? Did the 1976 Act protect Jews (a) as members of a group defined by common ancestry and genetic distinctiveness—the classic "racial group," or (b) as members of an "ethnic group," however defined? In turn, how courts defined Jewish identity under the 1976 Act informed the courts' decision to extend or not extent its coverage to groups such as Sikhs.

The issue of the 1976 Act's application to Jews arose indirectly through an English case involving a private school's discrimination against a Sikh boy. Sikhism is a monotheistic religion that originated in the Punjab region of the Indian subcontinent around the end of the 15th century. Anti-Jewish and anti-Sikh discrimination are related because Sikhs, like Jews, are not a distinct racial group.

Sikhs who wear a turban and do not cut their hair are known as "orthodox" Sikhs. Sikhs who do not are known as "Sahajdhari," a Punjabi word meaning "slow adopters." While most Sikhs are of Punjabi descent, converts to Sikhism come from various backgrounds. The case was brought by Mandla, an orthodox Sikh teenager who sought admission to Park Grove School, a private boys' school with a strict uniform policy. The school was attended by several "slow adopter" Sikh students who complied with this policy. The headmaster refused to admit Mandla unless he removed his turban and cut his hair as required by the uniform policy. Challenging this refusal, Mandla claimed that Sikhs were a "racial group" under the 1976 Act because they could be defined by reference to their "ethnic origins" and were thus protected from "racial group" discrimination in this context. Critically, Mandla did *not* claim that Sikhs were a "racial group" by reference to their color, race, nationality, or national origins, even though he could have argued this because of the statutory definition of "racial group."

Mandla sought a declaration that the headmaster had discriminated against him in violation of the 1976 Act. The English courts were tasked with deciding whether Sikhs constituted a "racial group" and if so, whether by virtue of their race or their ethnicity.

The trial court dismissed Mandla's claim. In *Mandla v. Dowell Lee* (1982), the Court of Appeal, per Lord Denning, affirmed the trial court's decision. He interpreted "racial group" to mean a group possessing "a racial characteristic." He held that Sikhs are primarily a religious group without distinct racial characteristics and thus not a "racial group" under the 1976 Act. He therefore refused to extend the 1976 Act's protections to Sikhs. In dicta,[1] Lord Denning contrasted Sikhs with Jews, whom he believed to be a "racial group" under the 1976 Act.

On appeal, the House of Lords, in an opinion by Lord Fraser, overturned Lord Denning's ruling and applied the 1976 Act to Sikhs and, by implication, to Jews.

Mandla v. Dowell Lee

Court of Appeal of England and Wales

[1982] 3 All ER 1108

LORD DENNING MR delivered the opinion of the House of Lords.

The Law

The case raises this point of great interest: What is a "racial group" within the Race Relations Act 1976? If the Sikhs are a "racial group," no one is allowed to discriminate

1. Dictum (plural, dicta) is short for *obiter dictum* [Latin: "something said in passing"]. It is a judicial comment made while delivering a judicial opinion, but one that is not necessary for the resolution of the specific legal issue before the court. While *obiter dicta* do not have the same precedential value as the *ratio decidendi* (the essential reasoning behind the decision), they are sometimes cited and discussed in legal literature and subsequent cases.

against any of their members in the important fields of education and employment and so forth.... But, if they are not a "racial group," discrimination is perfectly lawful. So everything depends on whether they are a "racial group" or not.

The statute in section 3(1) [of the Act] contains a definition of a "racial group." It means a "group of persons defined by reference to colour, race, nationality or ethnic or national origins." That definition is very carefully framed. Most interesting is that it does not include religion or politics or culture. You can discriminate for or against Roman Catholics as much as you like without being in breach of the law. You can discriminate for or against Communists as much as you please, without being in breach of the law. You can discriminate for or against the "hippies" as much as you like, without being in breach of the law. But you must not discriminate against a man because of his colour or of his race or of his nationality, or of "his ethnic or national origins." It is not suggested that the Sikhs are a group defined by reference to colour or race or nationality. Nor was much stress laid on national origins. But it is said—most persuasively by [counsel for the plaintiffs]—that the Sikhs are a group of persons "defined by reference to ethnic origins." It is so important that I will consider each word of that phrase.

"Ethnic"

The word "ethnic" is derived from the Greek word "εθνος" which meant simply "nation."[2] It was used by the 72 Palestinian Jews who translated the Old Testament from Hebrew into Greek (in the Septuagint[3]). They used it to denote the non-Israelitish nations, that is, the Gentiles "ταεθυη."[4] When the word "ethnic" was first used in England, it was used to denote peoples who were not Christian or Jewish. This was the meaning attached to it in the great *Oxford English Dictionary* itself in 1890.[5]

But in 1934 in the *Concise Oxford Dictionary*, it was given an entirely different meaning. It was given as: "pertaining to race, ethnological." And "ethnological" was

2. Editor's note: ἔθνος, a singular noun, can be transliterated as *ethnos* and translated as "a nation," "a people," or "a tribe."

3. Editor's note: The Septuagint is the Greek version of the Hebrew Bible made for Greek-speaking Jews in Egypt in the 3rd and 2nd centuries B.C.E. It is called the Septuagint after the number of translators it is said to have required (*septuaginta* is Greek for "seventy").

4. Editor's note: τα εθυη can be transliterated *ta ethnē*. The Hebrew word *goy* is a singular noun that means "nation" but can also refer to a non-Jew, also sometimes pejoratively. The plural of is *goyim*; it often refers to foreign nations, Gentiles, but can also be used to refer to non-Jews in general, sometimes pejoratively. The Septuagint translates the Hebrew word *goyim* as *ta ethnē*.

5. Editor's note: The *Oxford English Dictionary* (OED) was a ten-volume work published between 1884 and 1928. Its definitions were based on actual evidence of words in use as taken from printed sources and traced each word's historical development. Two supplements were designed to update the original OED; the first was published in 1933 and the second in 1972. Then there was the "Shorter OED," first published in 1933, which is an abridged version of the OED and includes both historical and contemporary usage. The "Concise OED," first published in 1911, is a single-volume dictionary that covers contemporary usage. *History of the OED*, Oxford Eng. Dictionary, https://www.oed.com/information/about-the-oed/history-of-the-oed/?tl=true (last visited Oct. 18, 2024).

given as meaning: "corresponding to a division of races."[6] That is the meaning which I—acquiring my vocabulary in 1934[7]—have always myself attached to the word "ethnic." It is, to my mind, the correct meaning. It means "pertaining to race."

But then in 1972 there was appended a second supplement of the *Oxford English Dictionary*. It gives a very much wider meaning than that which I am used to. It was relied upon by [counsel for the plaintiffs]:

> Also, pertaining to or having common racial, cultural, religious or linguistic characteristics, especially designating a racial *or other group* within a larger system; hence (U.S. colloquial), foreign, exotic.[8]

As an example of this new meaning, the second supplement refers to a book by Huxley & Haddon called *We Europeans* (1935). It mentions "the non-committal terms *ethnic group*"[9] and refers to the "special type of *ethnic* grouping of which the Jews form the best-known example" (emphasis added).[10] This reference to the Jews gives a clue to the meaning of ethnic.

Why are "the Jews" given as the best-known example of "ethnic grouping"? What is their special characteristic which distinguishes them from non-Jews? To my mind it is a racial characteristic. The *Shorter Oxford Dictionary* describes a Jew as "a person of Hebrew race." Some help too can be found in our law books, especially from *Clayton v. Ramsden* (1942 and 1943) and *Re Tuck's Settlement Trust* (1978).[11] If a man desires that his daughter should only marry "a Jew" and cuts her out of his will if she should marry a man who is not "a Jew," he will find that the court will hold the condition void for uncertainty. The reason is because "a Jew" may mean a dozen different things. It may mean a man of the Jewish faith. Even if he was a convert from Christianity, he would be of the Jewish faith. Or it may mean a man of Jewish parentage, even though

---

6. Editor's note: OED describes the word "ethnology" as "now somewhat dated" and defines it as "the branch of knowledge concerned with human society and culture, and its development; = social anthropology n., cultural anthropology n." *Ethnology*, Oxford Eng. Dictionary (Mar. 2024), https://doi.org/10.1093/OED/4814914800.

7. Editor's note: In 1934, Lord Denning (1899–1999) was 34 years old and working as a barrister in London. *Tom Denning, Baron Denning*, wikipedia.org, https://en.wikipedia.org/wiki/Tom_Denning,_Baron_Denning (last visited Nov. 26, 2024).

8. Editor's note: Compare with the 2023 edition of OED (defining "ethnic" (adj) 3.a. as "of or relating to peoples with regard to their (actual or perceived) common descent. Now usually: of or relating to national or cultural origin or tradition.... Of a population group: regarded as having a common descent, or a common national or cultural tradition"). *Ethnic*, Oxford Eng. Dictionary (July 2023), https://doi.org/10.1093/OED/1011146976.

9. Editor's note: The entire passage OED quotes from *We Europeans* (1935) reads as follows: "*Nowhere does a human group now exist which corresponds closely to a systematic sub-species in animals....* For existing populations, the noncommittal term ethnic group should be used" (emphasis added). Does the systemic categorization of animals into subspecies correspond to systemic categorization of humans into racial groups?

10. Editor's note: The 2023 OED does not include this reference. Its sole reference to Jews is as follows: "the Jews are an ethnic unit, although one which has little regard for spatial considerations." Carleton Stevens Coon, Races of Europe 444 (1939).

11. These cases will be discussed in detail in Chapter Five, "Jews as Racist."

he may be a convert to Christianity. It may suffice if his grandfather was a Jew and his grandmother was not. The Jewish blood may have become very thin by intermarriage with Christians, but still many would call him "a Jew." All this leads me to think that, when it is said of the Jews that they are an "ethnic group," it means that the group as a whole share a common characteristic which is a racial characteristic. It is that they are descended, however remotely, from a Jewish ancestor. When we spoke of the "Jewish regiments" which were formed and fought so well during the war, we had in mind those who were of Jewish descent or parentage.[12] When Hitler and the Nazis so fiendishly exterminated "the Jews," it was because of their racial characteristics and not because of their religion.

There is nothing in their culture of language or literature to mark out Jews in England from others. The Jews in England share all of these characteristics equally with the rest of us. Apart from religion, the one characteristic which is different is a racial characteristic.

"Origins"

The statute uses the word "ethnic" in the context of "origins." This carries the same thought. I turn once again to the *Shorter Oxford Dictionary*. Where the word "origin" is used of a person it means "descent, parentage." I turn also to the speech of Lord Cross in *Ealing London Borough v. Race Relations Board* [1972]:

> To me it suggests a connection subsisting at the time of birth.... The connection will normally arise because the parents or one of the parents of the individual in question are or is identified by descent....

So, the word "origin" connotes a group which has a common racial characteristic.

"Ethnic Origins"

If I am right in thinking that the phrase "ethnic origins" denotes a group with a common racial characteristic, the question arises: why is it used at all? The answer is given by Lord Cross in the *Ealing London Borough* case [1972]:

> The reason why the words "ethnic or national origins" were added to the words "racial grounds" which alone appear in the long title was, I imagine, to prevent argument over the exact meaning of the word "race."

In other words, there might be much argument whether one group or other was of the same "race" as another, but there was thought to be less whether it was a different "ethnic group."

"Racial Group"

This brings me back to the definition in the statute of a "racial group." It means "a group of persons defined by reference to colour, race, nationality or ethnic or national origins."

---

12. Editor's note: The Jewish Legion was a military formation of Jewish volunteers in World War I who fought in the British Army. *The Jewish Legion*, Jewish Virtual Libr., https://www.jewishvirtuallibrary.org/jewish-legion (last visited Dec. 16, 2024).

The word "defined" shows that the group must be distinguished from another group by some definable characteristic. English, Scots, or Welsh football teams are to be distinguished by their national origins. The Scottish clans are not distinguishable from one another either by their ethnic or national origins, but only by their clannish or tribal differences. French Canadians are distinguished from other Canadians by their ethnic or national origins. Jews are not to be distinguished by their national origins. The wandering Jew has no nation. He is a wanderer over the face of the earth.[13] The one definable characteristic of the Jews is a racial characteristic. I have no doubt that, in using the words "ethnic origins," Parliament had in mind primarily the Jews. There must be no discrimination against the Jews in England. Anti-Semitism must not be allowed. It has produced great evils elsewhere. It must not be allowed here.

But the words "ethnic origins" have a wider significance than the Jews. The question before us today is whether they include the Sikhs.

The Sikhs

The word "Sikh" is derived from the Sanskrit "Shishya," which means "disciple." Sikhs are the disciples or followers of Guru Nanak, who was born on 5 April, 1469. There are about 14m[illion] Sikhs, most of whom live in the part of the Punjab which is in India....

There is no difference in language which distinguishes the Sikhs from the other peoples in India. They speak Punjabi or Hindi or Urdu, or whatever the vernacular may be. There is no difference in blood which distinguishes them either. The people of India are largely the product of successive invasions that have swept into the country. They have intermingled to such an extent that it is impossible now to separate one strain from the other. The Sikhs do not recognise any distinction of race between them and the other peoples of India. They freely receive converts from Hinduism, or vice versa. Not only from outside, but even within the same family. The outstanding distinction between the Sikhs and the other peoples of India is in their religion, Sikhism, and its accompanying culture.

It is plain to me that the Sikhs, as a group, cannot be distinguished from others in the Punjab by reference to any racial characteristic whatever. They are only to be distinguished by their religion and culture. That is not an ethnic difference at all.

Conclusion

Sikhs are not a racial group. They cannot be defined by reference to their ethnic or national origins. No doubt they are a distinct community, just as many other religious and cultural communities. But that is not good enough. It does not enable them to complain of discrimination against them....

---

13. The "Wandering Jew" is an antisemitic legend about a Jew who mistreated Jesus as he carried the cross to the crucifixion and, as a result, was cursed to wander the earth until the Second Coming. *See* Jeremy Gillick, *Jewish Word | The Wandering Jew*, MOMENT (Sept. 23, 2019), https://momentmag.com/jewish-word-the-wandering-jew/; GEORGE K. ANDERSON, THE LEGEND OF THE WANDERING JEW (1965).

Jews as an Ethnoracial Group

1. *Converts.* Lord Denning is aware that a person may become a Jew through conversion. Even so, he concludes that Jews "as a whole share a common ... racial characteristic." Why is that? In what sense is a convert to Judaism "Jewish" in any sense other than religion?

2. *Religious versus racial discrimination against Jews.* During Parliamentary debate over the 1976 Act, several Members of Parliament expressed concern that anti-Semites would use the omission of religious discrimination to escape its coverage on grounds that their discrimination was based on Judaism rather than Jewishness. Sir Barnett Janner, a Jewish MP, asked for clarification that the 1976 Act would cover Jews *qua* Jews, without regard to the basis of the discrimination:

> I ask my right hon. Friend to consider the question again to see whether it could be widened, though not, of course, so as to enter the realm of contentions on religious matters. Everyone understands that, and everyone can speak strongly about whether the Law of Moses is right, whether the Mohammedan Law is right, and so on. That is another matter, and it has not been the issue in the thousands of years during which the Jew has been persecuted because he is a Jew.
>
> My own co-religionists, or fellow Jews, are concerned about the possibility of that type of argument being used against the intention of the Bill, and I hope that, by the time the Bill goes through, we shall have a clear understanding about it, at least to the extent of making abundantly plain and confirming that it covers offences against Jewish persons.[14]

In a similar vein, Mr. Bernard Floud, MP, said:

> I do not see how the Bill can be effective unless we specifically deal with religious discrimination. If we do not, we will find that religion can be used as a loophole for evading provisions about race, not only as regards Jews, but as regards Muslims or Hindus. That will certainly be attempted in order to get round the Bill's provisions. I believe sincerely that if we are to deal with race discrimination—and I am in favour of doing so—as part of it we have to deal with religious discrimination.[15]

Sir Dingle Foot, Her Majesty's Solicitor General for England and Wales, responded that it was not necessary to include religious discrimination in the 1976 Act because in his view, anti-Jewish discrimination was almost always based on racial rather than religious grounds:

> I appreciate that my hon. Friend seeks to distinguish the case of the Jews who, he says, may be subject to attack both on racial and on religious grounds. With great respect, I found that distinction rather unreal. I agree—we all agree—that

14. HC Deb (3 May 1965) (711) col. 960.
15. *Id.* at col. 970.

> nothing is more loathsome and more contemptible than expressions of anti-Semitism. But those expressions are not, at any rate in 99 cases out of 100, based on theological considerations. When there are attacks upon the Jews ... they are not directed merely against those who observe the Mosaic law. They are directed against Jews as a race. For these reasons it seemed to the Government both unnecessary and undesirable to include reference to religion.[16]

3. *Basis of Jews' coverage.* Several MPs, with varying motivations, were concerned as to whether the 1976 Act would even apply to Jews and, if so, under what heading. Mr. Anthony Buck expressed his frustration as follows:

> What an ill-digested Bill this is. Cannot the right hon. and learned Gentleman think of a better definition ... to tell us precisely how the Jews are brought into the Bill? Is it by race? Is it by the words "ethnic," "race," or "colour"? What definitions are to be put on those words? In an intervention in the right hon. and learned Gentleman's speech, I sought to point out that the word "ethnic" is a difficult word to define. In the *Longer Oxford Dictionary*, one finds a definition which takes the matter no further than the question of race or national origins, but if one goes to certain international dictionaries, one finds a broader definition.
>
> What does the word mean? What does the Government think that it means? What do they think Clause 1 means? This is a very ill-prepared Bill. It is quite extraordinary, when one realizes that what concerns most of us more than anything else is the possibility of anti-Semitism, that it should not have been made absolutely clear that Judaism and anti-Semitism is caught [by the Act].[17]

Rt. Hn. Sir Frank Soskice, the Home Secretary, asserted that the 1976 Act would cover Jews under one or more headings:

> It is certainly the intention of the Government that people of Jewish faith should be covered.... [A] person of Jewish faith, if not regarded as caught by the word "racial" would undoubtedly be caught by the word "ethnic," but if not caught by the word "ethnic" would certainly be caught by the word "national." ... He would certainly have an origin which many people would describe as ethnic if not a racial origin.[18]

The Home Secretary's point was that Jews would be covered. As to the specific alternative basis for such coverage—"racial," "ethnic," "national," or "national origin"—this seems to be of secondary importance, if not ultimately irrelevant.

4. *Exemplar of protected group.* Some U.K. drafters of the 1976 Act might have viewed Jews as the exemplary group to be protected. To what extent did this shape how U.K. courts interpreted the 1976 Act's application to other groups? Was the statute applied to other groups only insofar as they could be meaningfully analogized to Jews? What

16. *Id.* at col. 1043.
17. *Id.* at col. 1030.
18. *Id.* at col. 933.

are the limits of that approach? Compare this approach to U.S. law. Richard Delgado, Juan F. Perea, and Jean Stefancic's describe the "Black-White binary paradigm of race" as "plac[ing] two groups, blacks and whites, at the center and deems their relations constitutive of that concept. Other groups enter into the analysis only insofar as they succeed in analogizing their situation to that of one of the two main groups."[19] Concerning Jews, this paradigm has difficulty acknowledging that antisemitism possesses, in Schraub's words, "a unique and distinctive axis of marginalization."

5. *U.K. versus U.S. civil rights statutes.* Compare and contrast the basis for Jews' coverage under U.K. versus U.S. civil rights statutes that do not prohibit religious discrimination, at least not explicitly. In the UK, a single statute is at issue, the 1976 Act, containing multiple categories into which Jews might be fit, some more laboriously than others. In the U.S., there are multiple civil rights statutes that do not include religious discrimination—most notably the Civil Rights Act of 1866 and Titles VI of the Civil Rights Act of 1964. Is it problematic for the basis of Jews' coverage to vary with the civil rights statute at issue, e.g., "race" under the 1866 Act, "national origin" under Title VI, and "religion" under Title VII?

6. *How are Jews different?* Lord Denning asserts that the "special characteristic" which distinguishes Jews from non-Jews is a common "racial" characteristic. At the same time, he states that the term "'a Jew' may mean a dozen different things." What in his view are some of these different things? Is one or more of them non-racial? If "a Jew" can mean so many different things, how does Lord Denning distill "race" as its essential meaning? Why not "ethnic" origins?

7. *In what sense a race?* Does Lord Denning assert that: (a) Jews are in fact a race, biologically or scientifically speaking? (b) Jews are commonly perceived as a race, but are not actually a race? He states that Hitler and the Nazis sought to exterminate Jews "because of their racial characteristics." Does Lord Denning think this shows that Jews are in fact a race, or that the Nazis were deluded about Jews' racial identity?

8. *Why are Jews covered?* How does Lord Denning define a group defined by reference to "ethnic origins"—a.k.a., an ethnic group—under the 1976 Act? In his view, what is the difference between an "ethnic group" and a "racial group" under the 1976 Act? In his view, are Jews an "ethnic group" or a "racial group" under the 1976 Act? Is this a distinction without a difference?

9. *Jews defined by national origin?* For Lord Denning, the defining characteristic of English, Scots, Welsh, and French Canadians are their national origins. Why, in Lord Denning's view, are Jews not defined by national origin, for example, by the Jewish people's historic origins in the Land of Israel? "Jews are not to be distinguished by their national origins. The wandering Jew has no nation. He is a wanderer over the face of the earth." Can Jews be defined by reference to their national origins?

---

19. Richard Delgado et al., Latinos and the Law: Cases and Materials 3 (2d ed. 2009).

10. *Jews and French Canadians.* Consider the case of French Canadians, also known as Québécois, the majority of whom reside in the Canadian province of Québec.[20] Québécois are descendants of French persons who settled in Canada between 1534 and 1763. Assume Québécois living in the U.K. are protected under The Equality Act 2010, the successor of the Race Relations Act 1976, based on their ethnic or national origins. Posit the following factors. Which support or counter the view that Jews living in the U.K., like Québécois in the U.K., should be protected under the 1976 Act by reference to their national origins?

a. Most U.K. Québécois consider France their ancestral homeland; most U.K. Jews consider the Land of Israel their ancestral homeland.

b. Most Québécois have lived outside of France for over 260 years. Most of the world's Jews have lived outside the Land of Israel for much longer.

c. The ancestors of most U.K. Québécois lived in only two places before moving to the U.K.: France and Canada. The ancestors of most U.K. Jews likely lived in more places before moving to the U.K.

d. France was an independent state when the Québécois emigrated to what is now Canada. There was no independent Jewish state when most Jews left the Land of Israel.

e. France has remained an independent state since the Québécois's departure, except during WWII. There was no independent Jewish state in the Land of Israel from the Roman times until 1948.

f. The majority of Québécois live in Quebec, whereas most Jews live outside the Land of Israel.

g. Although most Québécois are Catholic, they share this religion with many others. Judaism, by contrast, is uniquely identified with Jews.

h. The native language of most Québécois is French, their ancestral language, whereas the native language of most Jews is not Hebrew.

i. Non-Jews can become Jewish through conversion; there is no formal conversion process to become Québécois.

11. *Remedial racialism.* Recall the possible distinction between *racialism*, the belief that there are races, and *racism*, the belief that some races are superior to others. Is Lord Denning a non-racist remedial racialist, at least concerning Jews? Although he considers Jews a distinct race, he also condemns antisemitism and supports anti-discrimination laws to protect Jews.

12. *Perceptions change.* Assume that: (a) when the 1976 Act was enacted, Parliament and most people in the U.K. perceived Jews as a race; and (b) in 1982, when this case was decided, a majority perceived that Jews are defined by their ethnic origins rather than their race. Would that have altered Lord Denning's analysis of the 1976 Act and

---

20. In Chapter Seven, we'll examine *Ortenberg v. Plamondon*, a case involving French Canadian antisemitism.

its application to Jews? Would it suffice that Jews were regarded as a race in 1976, even if they were not so considered in 1982? Compare his analysis with the Supreme Court's analysis in *Shaare Tefila*.

13. *Lord Denning.* Lord Denning, unlike other members of the judiciary, always did his own research on the relevant law prior to deciding a case. English courts generally rely purely on the lawyers in the case to provide all the law and facts they need to decide it. English judges, unlike American judges, do not have clerks to assist with research. Lord Denning was of the view that leaving the research to the lawyers in the case could prejudice the litigant who had hired the less experienced or the least competent lawyer.

It's very likely that Lord Denning had consulted *Hansard*, the official report of all Parliamentary debates, and discovered that: (a) the 1976 Act was intended to protect Jews, and (b) such protection was discussed in Parliament in relation to the word "ethnic." Ultimately, however, the meaning of the word "ethnic" was left for the judiciary to work out. The government's response to questions concerning its meaning was simply to state that it was intended to avoid any ambiguity over the meaning of the word "race"; in other words, "ethnic" was meant to catch anyone it might be argued was not a "race" but was still "distinguished by skin colour."[21] It seems that the term was not being used as one of art, but merely as a means of avoiding contentious debates about biological race.[22]

14. *"Ethnic origins" has wider significance.* Lord Denning claims, first, that "ethnic origins" casts a wider net than just Jews; alternatively, it is a genus of which Jews are a species or a member. The racial characteristic is presumably necessary to be an ethnic group. What additional characteristics distinguish an ethnic group from simply a racial group? Which of these additional characteristics are necessary to make an ethnic group and which are sufficient? Are there other necessary conditions to qualify as an ethnic group? Are there other characteristics that members of ethnic groups typically share—history, culture, language, etc.—that are relevant to determining their ethnic status but are not necessary conditions? Stated differently, is there a menu of additional characteristics where a group's possession of some of these suffices to make it an ethnic group? Posit with Lord Denning that Jews are "the best-known example of 'ethnic grouping.'" What are some of the lesser-known examples? Why are or aren't Sikhs one such example?

15. *Historic reasons for including Jews.* From the mid-1960s onwards, the legislative debates also included references to Nazi Germany and the mass killings of European Jews, suggesting that Jews were never far from some politicians' minds when discussing racism. One MP presented an exposition on German anti-Jewish policies, another referred to the "gas chambers of Auschwitz," while a third said: "This House must never forget that about six million Jews were put to death as a result of Hitler."[23]

---

21. *Id.* at col. 932.
22. *Id.*
23. *Id.* at cols. 956–1005.

16. *Contemporary necessity*? Politicians on both sides of the question—did the 1976 Act cover Jews?—referred to the Holocaust to support their position. Opponents pointed to the Holocaust to argue that antisemitism was virtually unheard of in England at the time and was therefore no excuse for introducing freedom-infringing legislation like the Race Relations Act.[24] Other MPs argued that, on the contrary, antisemitic incidents in England, both in the recent past and currently, were on the rise, justifying the legislation partly on that basis.[25]

17. *Must not be allowed here*. Lord Denning claims that when Parliament included the ban on race-based discrimination under the 1976 Act, it "had in mind primarily the Jews." He further asserts that "anti-Semitism must not be allowed," perhaps suggesting his belief that the 1976 Act must be construed to apply to Jews, separate and apart from whether Parliament intended it to. Why did Lord Denning believe that the 1976 Act must apply to Jews? Consider the "absurdity doctrine," a canon of construction which states "that a provision in a legal instrument may be either disregarded or judicially corrected as an error (especially when the correction is textually simple) if failing to do so would result in a disposition that no reasonable person could approve."

18. *Mandel v. Dowell Lee*. Mandel is an Orthodox Jewish teenager. He seeks admission to a Christian-run private high school that is attended by several Jewish students who do not wear *kippot* (yarmulkes). The headmaster of the school refuses to admit Mandel unless he removes his *kippah*. He refuses and sues the school under the 1976 Act, arguing that Jews are a "racial group" defined by reference to their ethnic origins. Will his suit succeed? What if Mandel is a non-Orthodox Jew who wears a *kippah* out of Jewish pride rather than Jewish belief? A different result?

19. *Lord Denning on Jews on juries*. The year he retired from the bench, Lord Denning published a book expressing concern over Jewish and Black people serving on juries. Concerning Jews, he wrote:

> The Jews are a race apart. In Israel they are separate from the Gentiles. They have their own language, their own religion, their own culture. They seek to remain separate from the rest of the world. In England they take care to remain separate from the rest of us. They gather together in their own communities. They have their own schools. They have their own synagogues and eat only their own food. If a Jew is on trial, it is his own race who try him. If he is on a jury, it is his own race he has to deal with. Jews try Jews and Gentiles try Gentiles. That is the way they have always done it.[26]

In Lord Denning's view, what characteristics define (in whole or in part) the Jewish race? What might he propose the legal system do when a Jew sues a non-Jew and vice versa?

---

24. Mr. Henry Brooke, MP: "I believe that there is less outward evidence of anti-Semitic feeling here than almost anywhere in the world." *Id.* at col. 963.

25. *Id.* at col. 965.

26. Lord Baron Alfred Denning, What Next in the Law (1982).

20. *Disraeli.* Benjamin Disraeli (1804–1881) twice served as the Prime Minister of the United Kingdom (1868, 1874–1880). Disraeli, the child of two Jewish parents and the descendant of Jews who fled the Spanish Inquisition, was baptized into the Church of England at the age of 12. At the time of his conversion, Jews were prohibited from serving in Parliament unless they swore allegiance to the British monarchy on the New Testament and "on the true faith of a Christian." This was not changed until Parliament passed the Jewish Relief Act of 1858, which, inter alia, removed the phrase "on the true faith of a Christian" and permitted Jews to swear on the Hebrew Bible. It's possible that Disraeli's parents wanted him to avoid the legal disabilities on Jews then in place. Despite his conversion to Christianity, Disraeli faced antisemitic comments and caricatures throughout his career. Disraeli described himself as Jewish in seemingly racial terms in an 1857 speech to the House of Commons in support of the Jewish Relief Act, saying, "I am not a Jew by religion—I am a Christian, but I am of Jewish race, and I am proud of my race." Would Disraeli be protected under the 1976 Act? Sections 1981 and 1982?

Sikhs Are Not Ethnic Because They're Not Ethnoracial

1. *Are Sikhs a race?* Lord Denning finds that Sikhs have no distinguishing characteristic from Hindus or other Punjabis. Therefore, they cannot be "defined by reference to their ethnic origins," in turn defining the term "ethnic" in non-racial terms. The Commission for Racial Equality (CRE), an official body that pursued the claim on behalf of Mandla and represented him, might have done better had they argued that Mandla was a member of a "racial group" because he could be "defined by reference to his colour" or "by reference to his nationality" under the 1976 Act. There are dicta to this effect in Kerr L.J.'s judgment.

2. *Why define "ethnic" as ethnoracial?* The 1976 Act does not define the term "ethnic." There is no consensus on its meaning. Lord Denning had an interpretive choice: He could have defined the term narrowly by limiting it to ethnoracial groups, or he could have defined the term broadly to include ethnic groups whose members are not racially distinct. Why did he choose to do the former? Are there important reasons to exclude multi-racial ethnic groups from the 1976 Act's protection? Stated differently, would it hurt to include multi-racial ethnic groups like Sikhs? Are there important reasons to include such groups? What legislative purposes are served by excluding Sikhs from the 1976 Act's protection?

3. *Conversion.* Under Jewish law, a person who converts to Judaism is a Jew. Because Judaism does not recognize out-conversion, a Jew who converts to another religion remains a Jew under Jewish law. Under Sikh law, a person who converts to Sikhism is a Sikh, but a Sikh who converts to another religion ceases to be Sikh. How does this affect Lord Denning's analysis of Jews under the 1976 Act?

4. *U.K. Census.* Neither Sikhs nor Jews can identify themselves as belonging to an "ethnic group" in the U.K. census, only as a "religious one," despite being the paradigmatic "ethnic" groups for the purposes of the 1976 Act. This is also true for the

purposes of "diversity and equality monitoring" forms in hospitals, universities, and employment.[27] No scholars appear to have written on this subject.

B. Jews as an Ethnoreligious Group

Mandla v. Dowell Lee

House of Lords of the United Kingdom of
Great Britain and Northern Ireland
1 All ER 1062 [1983]

[Mandla appealed the Court of Appeal's decision to the Appeal Committee of the House of Lords ("House of Lords"), then the highest court in the land. The House of Lords, per Lord Fraser of Tullybelton, held that the Sikhs were defined by their "ethnic origins" under the 1976 Act and thus protected by it. It defined "ethnic" in holistic and sociological terms without requiring a racial component and thus enabled its application to Jews without a determination that they are a distinct race.]

Lord Fraser of Tullybelton delivered the opinion of the House of Lords.

"Ethnic Origins"

It is not suggested that Sikhs are a group defined by reference to colour, race, nationality or national origins. In none of these respects are they distinguishable from many other groups, especially those living, like most Sikhs, in the Punjab. The argument turns entirely on whether they are a group defined by "ethnic origins." It is therefore necessary to ascertain the sense in which the word "ethnic" is used in the 1976 Act. We were referred to various dictionary definitions. The *Oxford English Dictionary* (1897 edition) gives two meanings of "ethnic." The first is "pertaining to nations not Christian or Jewish, gentile, heathen, pagan." That clearly cannot be its meaning in the 1976 Act, because it is inconceivable that Parliament would have legislated against racial discrimination intending that the protection should not apply either to Christians or (above all) to Jews.... The second meaning given in the *Oxford English Dictionary* (1897 edition) was "pertaining to race peculiar to a race or nation ethnological." A slightly shorter form of that meaning (omitting "peculiar to a race or nation") was given by the *Concise Oxford Dictionary* in 1934 and was expressly accepted by Lord Denning MR as the correct meaning for the present purpose. The respondent, who appeared on his own behalf, submitted that that was the relevant meaning of "ethnic" in the 1976 Act, and that it did not apply to Sikhs because they were essentially a religious group, and they shared their racial characteristics with other religious groups, including Hindus and Muslims, living in the Punjab.

---

27. *See Religion, England and Wales: Census 2021*, Off. For Nat'l Stat. (Nov. 29, 2022), https://www.ons.gov.uk/peoplepopulationandcommunity/culturalidentity/religion/bulletins/religionenglandandwales/census2021.

My Lords, I recognise that "ethnic" conveys a flavour of race but it cannot, in my opinion, have been used in the 1976 Act in a strict racial or biological sense. For one thing, it would be absurd to suppose that Parliament can have intended that membership of a particular racial group should depend on scientific proof that a person possessed the relevant distinctive biological characteristics (assuming that such characteristics exist). The practical difficulties of such proof would be prohibitive, and it is clear that Parliament must have used the word in some more popular sense. For another thing, the briefest glance at the evidence in this case is enough to show that, within the human race, there are very few, if any, distinctions which are scientifically recognised as racial. I respectfully agree with the view of Lord Simon ... in *Ealing L.B.C. v. Race Relations Board* [1972] when he said:

> Moreover, "racial" is not a term of art, either legal or, I surmise, scientific. I apprehend that anthropologists would dispute how far the word "race" is biologically at all relevant to the species amusingly called homo sapiens.

A few lines lower down ... Lord Simon said:

> This is rubbery and elusive language—understandably when the draftsman is dealing with so unprecise a concept as "race" in its popular sense and endeavouring to leave no loophole for evasion.

I turn, therefore, to the third and wider meaning which is given in the 1972 *Supplement to the Oxford English Dictionary* ["the 1972 definition"]. It is as follows: "pertaining to or having common racial, cultural, religious, or linguistic characteristics, esp. designating a racial or other group within a larger system...." Counsel for the appellants, while not accepting the third (1972) meaning as directly applicable for the present purpose, relied on it to this extent, that it [this third meaning] introduces a reference to cultural and other characteristics, and is not limited to racial characteristics. The 1972 meaning is, in my opinion, too loose and vague to be accepted as it stands. It is capable of being read as implying that any one of the adjectives, "racial, cultural, religious or linguistic," would be enough to constitute an ethnic group. That cannot be the sense in which "ethnic" is used in the 1976 Act, as that Act is not concerned at all with discrimination on religious grounds. Similarly, it cannot have been used to mean simply any "racial or other group." If that were the meaning of "ethnic," it would add nothing to the word group, and would lead to a result which would be unacceptably wide. But in seeking for the true meaning of "ethnic" in the statute, we are not tied to the precise definition in any dictionary. The value of the 1972 definition is, in my view, that it shows that ethnic has come to be commonly used in a sense appreciably wider than the strictly racial or biological. That appears to me to be consistent with the ordinary experience of those who read newspapers at the present day. In my opinion, the word "ethnic" still retains a racial flavour but it is used nowadays in an extended sense to include other characteristics which may be commonly thought of as being associated with common racial origin.

For a group to constitute an ethnic group in the sense of the 1976 Act, it must, in my opinion, regard itself, and be regarded by others, as a distinct community by virtue of certain characteristics. Some of these characteristics are essential; others are not essential but one or more of them will commonly be found and will help to distinguish the group from the surrounding community. The conditions which appear to me to be essential are these: (1) a long-shared history, of which the group is conscious as distinguishing it from other groups, and the memory of which it keeps alive; (2) a cultural tradition of its own, including family and social customs and manners, often but not necessarily associated with religious observance. In addition to those two essential characteristics, the following characteristics are, in my opinion, relevant: (3) either a common geographical origin, or descent from a small number of common ancestors; (4) a common language, not necessarily peculiar to the group; (5) a common literature peculiar to the group; (6) a common religion different from that of neighbouring groups or from the general community surrounding it; (7) being a minority or being an oppressed or a dominant group within a larger community, for example a conquered people (say, the inhabitants of England shortly after the Norman conquest) and their conquerors might both be ethnic groups.

A group defined by reference to enough of these characteristics would be capable of including converts, for example, persons who marry into the group, and of excluding apostates. Provided a person who joins the group feels himself or herself to be a member of it, and is accepted by other members, then he is, for the purpose of the 1976 Act, a member. That appears to be consistent with the words ... "references to a person's racial group refer to any racial group into which he falls." In my opinion, it is possible for a person to fall into a particular racial group either by birth or by adherence, and it makes no difference, so far as the 1976 Act is concerned, by which route he finds his way into the group.... A person may treat another relatively unfavourably "on racial grounds" because he regards that other as being of a particular race, or belonging to a particular racial group, even if his belief is, from a scientific point of view, completely erroneous....

My Lords, I have attempted so far to explain the reasons why, in my opinion, the word "ethnic" in the 1976 Act should be construed relatively widely, in what was referred to by counsel for the appellants as a broad, cultural/historic sense. The conclusion at which I have arrived by construction of the 1976 Act itself is greatly strengthened by consideration of the decision of the Court of Appeal in New Zealand in *King-Ansell v. Police* [1979]. That case was discovered by the industry of the appellants' counsel, but unfortunately not until after the Court of Appeal in England had decided the case now under appeal. If it had been before the Court of Appeal, it might well have affected their decision. In that case the appellant had been convicted by a magistrate of an offence under the New Zealand Race Relations Act 1971, the offence consisting of publishing a pamphlet with intent to incite ill-will against Jews, "on the ground of their ethnic origins." The question of law arising on the appeal concerned the meaning to be given to the words "ethnic ... origins of that group of persons" in § 25(1) of the Act. The decision of the Court of Appeal was that Jews in New Zealand did form a group with common ethnic origins within the meaning of the Act. The structure of the New

Zealand Act differs considerably from that of the 1976 Act, but the offence created by §25 of the New Zealand Act (viz inciting ill-will against any group of persons on the ground of their "colour, race, or ethnic or national origins") raises the same question of construction as the present appeal, in a context which is identical, except that the New Zealand Act does not mention "nationality," and the 1976 Act does. The reasoning of all members of the New Zealand court was substantially similar, and it can, I think, be sufficiently indicated by quoting the following short passages. The first is from the judgment of Woodhouse J where, after referring to the meaning given by the [1972 Supplement] to the *Oxford English Dictionary*, he says:

> The distinguishing features of an ethnic group or of the ethnic origins of a group would usually depend upon a combination, present together, of characteristics of the kind indicated in the Supplement. In any case it would be a mistake to regard this or any other dictionary meaning as though it had to be imported word for word into a statutory definition and construed accordingly. However, subject to those qualifications, I think that for the purposes of construing the expression "ethnic origins" the 1972 Supplement is a helpful guide and I accept it.

Richardson J said:

> The real test is whether the individuals or the group regard themselves and are regarded by others in the community as having a particular historical identity in terms of their colour or their racial, national or ethnic origins. That must be based on a belief shared by members of the group.

And the same judge said:

> A group is identifiable in terms of its ethnic origins if it is a segment of the population distinguished from others by a sufficient combination of shared customs, beliefs, traditions and characteristics derived from a common or presumed common past, even if not drawn from what in biological terms is a common racial stock. It is that combination which gives them an historically determined social identity in their own eyes and in the eyes of those outside the group, they have a distinct social identity based not simply on group cohesion and solidarity but also on their belief as to their historical antecedents.

My Lords, that last passage sums up in a way on which I could not hope to improve the views which I have been endeavouring to express. It is important that courts in English-speaking countries should, if possible, construe the words which we are considering in the same way where they occur in the same context, and I am happy to say that I find no difficulty at all in agreeing with the construction favoured by the New Zealand Court of Appeal....

The result is, in my opinion, that Sikhs are a group defined by a reference to ethnic origins for the purpose of the 1976 Act, although they are not biologically distinguishable from the other peoples living in the Punjab.

Sikhs and Jews Are Ethnoreligious Groups within the Broader Category of Ethnic Groups

1. *Lessons.* Do U.K. legislators and courts know something about protecting Jewish equality and civil rights that their U.S. counterparts do not, and vice versa? What lessons does the U.K. experience offer us?

2. *How distinct?* At the end of the day, U.K. and U.S. courts extended race-based anti-discrimination law (loosely defined) to protect Jews. How profound, then, are the differences between these two bodies of law?

3. *Would it have made a difference?* In *King Ansell v. Police* [1979], a New Zealand case, the court took a sociological approach to ethnicity and, indeed, heard testimony from a sociologist on the matter. Mandla did not raise *King Ansell v. Police* [1979], the New Zealand case, until after the Court of Appeal had handed down its ruling. Lord Fraser suggests that if the Court of Appeal had been aware of it, "it might well have affected their decision." What do you think?

4. *Characteristics.* What are the essential characteristics for a group to constitute an ethnic group under the 1976 Act? Is race one of them? What are relevant but not essential characteristics? If a group is not a race, is the threshold for coverage higher?

5. *Converts.* Under what circumstances would the 1976 Act protect a convert to a protected group? Should a group that accepts converts be held to a higher or lower standard to qualify as an ethnic group under the 1976 Act? Note that in Judaism, apostates are regarded as halakhically Jewish (meaning, according to Jewish law). How does that affect the analysis of Jews as an ethnic group? Of *Bonadona*?

6. *Apostates.* Under what circumstances would the 1976 Act protect an apostate from a protected group? Consider *Bonadona v. Louisiana College*, 1:18-cv-00224 (W.D. La. 2019), in which the plaintiff, who converted from Judaism to Christianity, was denied employment due to his Jewish heritage. The plaintiff alleged racial discrimination under Title VII but did not allege religious discrimination. (Title VII prohibits both.) The Court ruled that the plaintiff failed to establish a prima facie case of racial discrimination because Jews are not considered a separate race for Title VII purposes (note that they are for § 1981 purposes). It ruled this way even though the plaintiff presented direct evidence that the defendants did not hire him based on his Jewish descent. Would this plaintiff state a claim under the 1976 Act?

7. *Discrimination by perception.* Under English anti-discrimination law now enshrined in the Equality Act 2010, which superseded the Race Relations Act 1976, someone can be held to have discriminated against another because he *perceives* her to be a member of a racial group, even if she is not, in fact, a member of that racial group. This is discrimination based on the erroneous perception of the victim belonging to a protected group.[28]

---

28. Equality Act 2010, c. 15, § 13(1) (UK).

8. *Basis for protection.* Lord Fraser states that "it is inconceivable that Parliament would have legislated against racial discrimination intending that the protection should not apply either to Christians or (above all) to Jews." Why inconceivable? What role do Jews play in Lord Fraser's analysis as compared to Lord Denning's? For example, do they serve as the exemplar of some category against which other groups are measured? In Lord Fraser's analysis, what is the basis of Jews' protection under the 1976 Act? Which characteristics of ethnic groups apply to Jews?

Mandla v. Dowell Lee is cited as the authority for the principle that Jews are legally protected as a "racial group" as well as a "religious group" under English law. As it so happens, the actual status of Jews as a "racial group" under the 1976 Act has never been adjudicated and no English legal decision has ever explained how, and why, Jews fit into the 1976 Act's categories.

9. *How does it resonate?* Whose account of group identity, Lord Fraser's or Lord Denning's, aligns more closely with how most Jews view their Jewishness?

10. *Dominant and oppressive groups.* In determining whether a group is "ethnic," Lord Fraser considered the characteristic of "being a minority or being an oppressed or a dominant group within a larger community, for example a conquered people (say, the inhabitants of England shortly after the Norman conquest) and their conquerors might both be ethnic groups." Why would being a dominant and oppressive group be a factor in favor of its designation as an "ethnic" group under the 1976 Act? Under §§ 1981 and 1982?

11. *English-speaking countries.* Is it important that U.S. courts construe the words in civil rights statutes the same way they occur and in the same context as in U.K. and Commonwealth countries? What canon of construction does Lord Fraser propose? What would it mean for U.S. courts to follow such a canon in this case?

12. *Ethnoreligious groups.* Consider the concept of "ethnoreligious" groups as a subset of ethnic groups. The term denotes a community in which ethnic and religious identities are deeply intertwined. According to Victoria Arakelova,[29] key characteristics of ethnoreligious groups include:

a. Shared history and ancestry: Members often trace their lineage back to a common ancestor or group of ancestors.

b. Endogamy: Marriage within the group is encouraged or expected to maintain cultural and religious identity.[30]

c. Distinct customs and traditions: The group has unique cultural practices, often tied to religious observances.

---

29. Victoria Arakelova, *Ethno-Religious Communities: To the Problem of Identity Markers*, 14 Iran & the Caucasus (2010) 1, https://www.academia.edu/3764877/Ethno_Religious_Communities_Identity_markers.

30. We'll consider a series of cases concerning endogamy in Chapter 5, "Jews as Racist," in the section titled, "Are Jewish Clauses Racist?"

d. Language or dialect: In some cases, ethnoreligious groups have their own language or dialect that is closely associated with their identity.

e. Self-identification and recognition by others: Members see themselves as part of a distinct ethnic and religious community and are recognized as such by outsiders.[31]

How well does the ethnoreligious conception apply to Jews?

13. *Other cases.* Consider these other cases that addressed the question of whether a minority group was an ethnic group under the Race Relations Act 1976: (a) in the *Commission for Racial Equality v. Dalton*, [1989] 2 WLR17, the Court of Appeal found that "gypsies" constituted an ethnic group under the 1976 Act; (b) in *Crown Suppliers (PSA) v. Dawkins*, [1991] 22 LS Gaz R 36, the Court of Appeal found that Rastafarians did not qualify as an ethnic group under the 1976 Act because they did not have a "long shared history" which separated them ethnically from native or diasporic Jamaicans; (c) in *BBC Scotland v. Souster*, [2001] IRLR 150 CS, the Scottish Court of Session held that English (or Scottish) persons could be protected under the 1976 Act on the grounds of "national origins" but not on the grounds of "ethnic group." Both the Scottish and the English lack the "distinctiveness of community" to qualify as "ethnic"; and (d) in *R v. White*, [2001] 1 WLR 1352, it was held that the word "African" did not denote sufficient distinctiveness to qualify for the term "ethnic group" but that it did qualify as a "race."

Sources

NICHOLAS BAMFORTH ET AL., DISCRIMINATION LAW: THEORY AND CONTEXT (1st ed. 2008).

Helen Benyon & Nigel Love, *Mandla and the Meaning of "Racial Group,"* 100 L.Q. REV. 120–36 (1984).

Davina Cooper & Didi Herman, *Jews and Other Uncertainties: Race, Faith, and English Law*, 19 LEGAL STUD. 339–66 (1999).

Didi Herman, *"An Unfortunate Coincidence": Jews and Jewishness in Twentieth-Century English Judicial Discourse*, 33 J. OF L. AND SOC'Y 277–301 (2006).

Clement Labi, *The Fate of the Jews as an Ethnoreligious Group*, 6 J. OF CONTEMP. ANTISEMITISM 69–74 (2023).

Anthony Lester, *The Politics of the Race Relations Act 1976, in* MUHAMMAD ANWAR ET AL., FROM LEGISLATION TO INTEGRATION: RACE RELATIONS IN BRITAIN 24–39 (2000).

ROBERT MILES & MALCOLM BROWN, RACISM (2d ed. 2003).

31. In Chapter 4, "Jews as Jewish," we'll examine the proverbial "Who is a Jew?" question, in which various Jewish authorities—Halakhah, the State of Israel, and the Reform Movement—define a person's Jewish status for various purposes.

Benjamin T. Phillips & Shaul Kelner, *Reconceptualizing Religious Change: Ethno-Apostasy and Change in Religion Among American Jews*, 67 SOCIO. OF RELIGION 507–543 (2006).

Joseph Ruane & Jennifer Todd, *Ethnicity and Religion: Redefining the Research Agenda*, 9 ETHNOPOLITICS 1–8 (2010).

Part Two

Jewish Identity

Chapter 4

Jews as Jewish

The previous chapters examined how non-Jewish actors define Jews for discrete purposes: protecting or excluding them from race-based anti-discrimination statutes, situating them in racial and social hierarchies, and regulating their participation in social justice spaces. The focus of the current chapter is internal: it explores how various Jewish actors have defined Jewish identity and Jewish projects. These actors include Halakhah (Jewish law), U.S. Reform rabbis, U.S. secular Jewish leaders, and Israel's Supreme Court. The purposes include regulating participation in Jewish religious and national life and promoting the Jewish people's self-determination and continued existence.

Section A, "The Definition of 'Jew' Under the Law of Return," examines the 1962 Israeli Supreme Court case, *Rufeisen v. Minister of the Interior* (also called the "Brother Daniel Case"). The case interpreted the Law of Return, which guarantees entry to Israel for any "Jew," a term the statute did not define. The central question was whether the statutory definition of "Jew" should incorporate the halakhic definition of a Jew, which includes converts to Christianity, or define it more narrowly to exclude such converts.

The next section, "Jewish Status in Reform Judaism," explores how U.S. Reform rabbis redefined "Jew" for the purposes of regulating membership in the Reform movement. Like the Israeli Supreme Court, Reform rabbis departed from the halakhic definition, in this case by expanding it to include the children of Jewish fathers and non-Jewish mothers.

The last section, "Zionism as a Jewish American Project," presents Louis Brandeis's 1915 defense of Zionism, written when he was the leader of the U.S. Zionist movement. It also explores opposition and ambivalence to Zionism among some American Jews in the early 20th century.

A. The Definition of "Jew" Under the Law of Return

The State of Israel was established on May 14, 1948, on the eve of the termination of the British Mandate. Immediately upon its establishment, the fledgling state adopted the existing Mandatory law which consisted of English common law and equity, some Ottoman civil law, and the Millet System, in which matters of personal status were under the sole jurisdiction of the religious courts of the various religious denominations in the Ottoman Empire. Mandatory law, however, introduced judicial review by the secular courts of religious court decisions found to be *ultra vires*, or in contravention of natural justice. The Millet System in relation to Jews was codified by the Israeli parliament, known as the Knesset, in the Rabbinical Courts Jurisdiction (Marriage and Divorce) Law in 1953, which provided that "matters of marriage and divorce of Jews in Israel, being nationals or residents of Israel, shall be under the exclusive jurisdiction of the Rabbinical Courts, and ... shall be performed in Israel in accordance with Jewish Law (Halakhah)."

Halakhah is traditional Jewish law, which goes back to the fourth century BCE and continues to influence the lives of Jewish people to the present day, especially Orthodox Jews. Its primary literary source is the Torah ("Five Books of Moses"), the juristic development of which has given rise to a voluminous literature spanning the centuries. The most significant products of Halakhah are the Talmud (fifth century); the Mishneh Torah (twelfth century), the code written by Moses Maimonides ("Rambam") (1138–1204), the greatest Jewish philosopher of the Middle Ages; and the Shulhan Arukh (16th century), the standard legal code of Judaism written by Rabbi Joseph ben Ephraim Caro (1488–1575), the foremost systematizer of Halakhah.

Rabbinical courts (Bet Din) have been in existence since ancient times, and Israeli rabbinical courts continue to apply Halakhah.[1] Similar legislation governs the personal status of the Muslim, Druze, and Christian communities. All other areas of Israeli law are governed by secular law as applied in the secular court system. The law applied by secular Israeli courts originated in the Mandatory period, but over the years, it has developed into a sophisticated body of home-grown law, together with many rules and principles absorbed from other legal systems.

The secular and religious legal systems in Israel are generally self-contained, but there is a limited interaction between the two areas. In addition to the limited judicial review of religious court decisions, secular Israeli courts have adopted a practice of selectively applying halakhic law when it provides a good solution to a legal problem. Such a solution, however, must comply with the standards of substantive democracy and the legal culture of the State (Foundations of Law Act, 1980). The language of secular Israeli law is Hebrew, as is that of Halakhah (a mixture of Hebrew and Aramaic); hence much of the terminology of the former is derived from the latter. Halakhah also provides legal definitions for terms relating to the Jewish religion that are incorporated into secular law.

In 1950, the Knesset enacted the Law of Return (1950), Section 3(a) of which provides that: "[a] Jew who has come to Israel and ... has expressed a desire to settle in Israel may ... receive an *oleh's* [immigrant's] certificate." The statute does not define the word "Jew." The Law does, however, authorize the Minister of the Interior to withhold the right of return from Jews deemed to be "engaged in an activity directed against the Jewish people"; to be "likely to endanger the public health or the security of the state"; or to be persons "with a criminal past, likely to endanger public welfare." Under the

1. *See Halakhah*, *in* 7 Encyclopaedia Judaica 1156–66 (2d ed. 2007); Daniel Sinclair, *Halakhah and Israel*, *in* Modern Judaism: An Oxford Guide 352–62 (Nicholas de Lange & Miri Freud-Kandel eds., 2005).

1952 Nationality Law, every Jewish immigrant is granted automatic citizenship. Non-Jews may become naturalized Israelis after five years of residence if they qualify for citizenship under the Law.

The case below involves Shmuel Oswald Rufeisen (a.k.a., "Brother Daniel"), a man who was born Jewish and sought to immigrate to Israel under the Law of Return. His application was complicated by the fact that he had converted to Catholicism and later become a Carmelite monk. He claimed that, his conversion notwithstanding, he was a "Jew" within the meaning of the Law of Return. He pointed to the facts that he had worked on behalf of the Jewish people, posed no danger to the public health, and did not fall within any other statutory category warranting denial. The Minister of the Interior denied his application and Rufeisen appealed to the Israeli Supreme Court sitting as the High Court of Justice; in this capacity, it has original jurisdiction to hear petitions against the legality of government decisions.

By a 4–1 vote, the Court denied Rufeisen's petition. Justice Moshe Silberg delivered the opinion of the Court with Justices Landau and Berinson writing concurring opinions. Justice Berinson also summarized the facts of the case. Justice Cohn wrote the lone dissenting opinion.

Rufeisen v. Minister of the Interior (Brother Daniel Case)

HCJ 72/62,16 PD 2428 (1962)

Justice Berinson summarized the facts of the case.

The petitioner was born in Poland in the year 1922, his parents were Jews, and he was reared as a Jew. As a youth he was active in the Zionist Youth Movement "Akiva" and after completing his secondary school studies in 1939 he underwent two years' training in pioneering in Vilna, preparatory to immigrating to this country. At the outbreak of the German-Russian war in June 1941 he was caught by the Gestapo and imprisoned. He managed, however, to escape and succeeded in obtaining a certificate that he was a German Christian and as such became in due course secretary and interpreter at the German police station in Mir, the district capital. There he established contact with the Jews of the town and the neighbourhood and used to inform them of German designs and plans of action against the Jews. When he learnt that the Germans were about to liquidate the Jewish ghetto, he reported this to the local Jews to whom he also supplied arms. Acting on this information many of the Jews who were in the ghetto escaped to the forests. Some 150 of them managed to survive and joined the ranks of the partisans. Most of the survivors are now living in Israel. As the result, however, of some Jew disclosing to the Germans that the petitioner was exposing their plans to the Jews, he was questioned by his superiors and thereupon revealed his true colours and with Jewish pride confessed that he was helping the Jews because he himself was a Jew. The petitioner was imprisoned but escaped once more successfully and found refuge in a convent where he stayed for a long time. When able to do so he left the convent and

Figure 4.1. Oswald Rufeisen. Undated. Courtesy of Yad Vashem Photo Archive.

Figure 4.2. Three Justices of the Israeli Supreme Court: Zvi Berinson, Moshe Silberg, and Haim Herman Cohn (June 1965). Wikimedia Commons.

joined the Russian partisans but the partisans, suspecting him of being a German spy, condemned him to death. Miraculously he escaped execution when one of the Jews of Mir whom he had saved suddenly appeared and testified as to his true identity. He was finally awarded a Russian decoration for his services with the partisans.

Whilst in the convent in 1942 the petitioner embraced Christianity and in 1945, at the end of the war, he became a priest and entered the Order of the Carmelites. He chose this Order deliberately, he says, because he knew that it had a Chapter in this country which he could join in due course. During our own War of Liberation and several times thereafter he sought permission of his superiors to immigrate to Israel and in the year 1958 such permission was finally granted to him. After the Israeli consul in Warsaw had informed him that he could obtain an entry visa to Israel, he applied to the Polish authorities for a passport and for permission to travel to Israel to remain there permanently. I wish to quote this application in full because it clearly shows that even after he became a Christian he never ceased both by inner conviction and in external manifestation to regard himself as a national Jew bound heart and soul to the Jewish people:

> I, the undersigned, the Rev. Oswald Rufeisen, known in the Monastic Order as Brother Daniel, hereby respectfully apply for permission to travel to Israel for permanent residence and also for a passport. I base this application on the ground of my belonging to the Jewish people, which I have continued to do although I embraced the Catholic faith in 1942 and joined a monastic order in 1945. I have made this fact clear whenever it has been raised with me officially as, for instance, when I received my military papers and identity card. I chose an Order which has a Chapter in Israel, having regard to the fact that I would receive the leave of my superiors to travel to the land for which I have yearned since my childhood when I was a member of a Zionist Youth Organization. My national allegiance is known to the Church.

The Polish authorities agreed to comply with the request of the petitioner only after he had waived his Polish citizenship, and they issued to him a travel document of the type that is only issued to Jews immigrating to Israel and leaving Poland permanently. This means that as far as the land of his birth is concerned the petitioner has immigrated to Israel as a Jew who has severed his links with Poland without leaving himself a way of return. On his arrival in this country, he applied for an immigration certificate [under the Law of Return] and for registration in his identity card as a Jew. His application, however, was refused on the basis of the Government's decision of July 20, 1958, which provides on the question of Jewish nationality as follows:

> Anyone declaring in good faith that he is a Jew and who does not profess any other religion shall be registered as a Jew.

A personal appeal to the Minister of the Interior was also of no avail. Mr. Bar Yehuda, who was then the Minister, wrote to the petitioner and explained his personal point of view as follows:

> The mere declaration bona fide that he [the applicant] belongs to the Jewish people should (in the Minister's opinion) be sufficient in the State of Israel for registration of the declarant as a Jew, and this without further reference to the question of his religion, in regard to which it is not for the secular authorities to make any decision.... All that I have read and heard about you is undoubtedly sufficient in my opinion to justify your right to claim recognition as a member of the Jewish people even though, because of your special position, I am not sure that it would be possible for you to become integrated organically into the body of the nation. But the Government has decided otherwise.

Hence Mr. Bar Yehuda says at the beginning of his letter that as a Minister of the State of Israel:

> He is not free to act according to his own understanding and inclination alone. He must act within the limits of the existing Laws even if he struggles to secure their change or amendment.

Justice Silberg delivered the opinion of the Court.

1. From the outset of this most unusual case I have been faced with a great psychological difficulty. Paradoxically enough this is due to the deep sympathy and great sense of obligation which we as Jews feel for the petitioner, Oswald Rufeisen, known since his conversion as Brother Daniel. The petitioner is a man who during the dark years of the Holocaust in Europe risked his lifetimes without number in rescuing his brother Jews by daring feats of courage from the very jaws of the Nazi German beasts. Can he be denied the burning desire of his life to be completely identified with the people which he loves and to become a citizen of the land of his dreams, not as a stranger coming from without but as a Jew returning home?

But this sense of profound sympathy and obligation must not be permitted to mislead us and to justify our profaning the concept of "Jew" both in name and in meaning.

I have pondered deeply upon this question and have considered it in all its aspects. I have reached the conclusion that what Brother Daniel is asking us to do is to erase the historical and sanctified significance of the term "Jew" and to deny all the spiritual values for which our people gave their lives in different periods of our long dispersion. To grant his request would dim the lustre and darken the glory of the martyrs who sanctified the Holy Name [by being killed rather than convert to Christianity] in the Middle Ages beyond recognition; our history would lose its unbroken continuity and our people begin numbering its days from the Emancipation which followed the French Revolution. A sacrifice such as this no one is entitled to ask of us, even one so meritorious as the petitioner before this court.

2. The question of law before us is very simply the meaning of the expression "Jew" as used in the Law of Return, 1950. Does it also include a Jew who has changed his religion and been baptised as a Christian but who still feels and regards himself as a Jew in spite of his conversion?

3. At this point I do not propose to decide this question or to give it an unequivocal answer. I wish to examine first the various alternatives which it involves. But I will say at once that were I to agree with the second or alternative submission of counsel for the petitioner, that the expression "Jew" as used in the Law of Return bears the identical religious connotation which it bears in the Rabbinical Courts Jurisdiction (Marriage and Divorce) Law, 1953, I would then propose making the order *nisi* absolute and ordering the Minister of the Interior to grant the petitioner an immigration certificate under section 3(a) of the Law of Return. I would do so however strange and anomalous it may seem that a man who has renounced one creed in favour of another should rely on the doctrines of the faith he has abandoned, and in spite of my deep aversion for an argument so inconsistent and confused.

According to the prevailing opinion in Jewish law, so it seems to me, a Jew who is converted or becomes an apostate continues to be treated as a Jew for all purposes save perhaps as to certain "marginal" laws which have no real importance with regard to the central problem....

Mr. Bar Niv, the State Attorney, submitted on behalf of the respondent that even according to religious law a convert to another faith is not considered fully a Jew; is only partly Jewish. This is evidenced, says Mr. Bar Niv, by the fact that he is not regarded as a Jew for purposes of inheritance or the law prohibiting the taking of interest, nor is he to be counted as one of a *minyan* (the quorum of ten male adults required for public prayer).

I cannot accept this argument.

Firstly, in point of principle, Jewishness is a status and status is indivisible. I have never heard of anyone having the status of a half Jew, or of a third or a fourth of a Jew....

The Jewish religion, like all other religions, is by its very nature total and complete. It can never regard itself as shared with any other faith. The second Commandment "Thou shalt have no other gods before me", expresses this exclusiveness in full sharpness and in terms of ancient origin....

4. As I said at the beginning of the last section, were I of the opinion that the term "Jew" in the Law of Return is identical in meaning with the same term in the Rabbinical Courts Jurisdiction (Marriage and Divorce) Law, that is to say, a Jew *according to the rules of Jewish law*, I would grant the application of the petitioner and make the order *nisi* absolute. The difficulty is, however, that the term "Jew" is not employed in the same sense in both of these Laws. In the Rabbinical Courts Jurisdiction (Marriage and Divorce) Law, it bears a religious connotation according to its precise meaning in Jewish law, whereas in the Law of Return the term has a secular meaning, as it is usually understood in common parlance—and this I emphasize—by the ordinary simple Jew.

The reason for this is so clear that it need hardly be mentioned. The Rabbinical Courts Jurisdiction (Marriage and Divorce) Law was enacted for the purpose of extending rabbinical jurisdiction. It is an open secret that the extension of this jurisdiction was sought and granted in order to broaden the application of Jewish religious law to Jews. Hence the further question who is a Jew for the purposes of this Law must be answered according to Jewish law. If it were to be answered on the basis of other considerations, extrinsic, secular or outside the framework of Jewish law, then the law applicable would no longer be Jewish religious law.

It is otherwise with the Law of Return. For all its immense historical importance, this Law is a secular Law, and in the absence of definition either in the statute itself or in the decided cases, we must interpret its terms according to their ordinary meaning, taking into consideration, when departing from the ordinary sense, the legislative purpose behind its provisions. And because the Law of Return is an Israeli statute, originally enacted in Hebrew and not translated, the term "Jew" must be interpreted in the sense that it is understood by Jews, for they are nearest to the subject matter of the Law, and who better than they know the essential content of the term "Jew"?

Once more the question must be asked, what is the ordinary Jewish meaning of the term "Jew," and does it include a Jew who has become a Christian?

5. The answer to this question is, in my opinion, sharp and clear—a Jew who has become a Christian is *not* deemed a "Jew."

It is not my purpose to preach religion nor to present any particular point of view as to the most desirable course for the future development of the Jewish people. I know full well that opinion in Israel as to what is and what should be is divided into all the various shades of the spiritual rainbow—from the extreme orthodox to the total agnostic. But there is one thing that is shared by *all* Jews who live in Israel (save a mere handful) and that is that we do not cut ourselves off from our historic past nor deny our ancestral heritage. We continue to drink from the original fountains. The shape has changed, the channels have been altered, but we have not sealed the wells for without them we would be but "as the poor that are cast out". Only the simple believe or think that we are creating here a *new* culture; for this it is much too late. A people which is almost as old as the human race cannot start *ab ova*, and our new culture in this land—at the highest—is merely a *new version* of the culture of the past.

Whether he is religious, non-religious or anti-religious, the Jew living in Israel is bound, willingly or unwillingly, by an umbilical cord to historical Judaism from which he draws his language and its idiom, whose festivals are his own to celebrate, and whose great thinkers and spiritual heroes—not the least of whom are the martyrs of 1096 and those who perished at the stake in Spain—nourish his national pride. Would a Jew who has become a Christian find his place in all this? What can all this national sentiment mean to him? Would he not see in a different light and appraise by other standards our draining to the dregs the bitter cup from which we drank so deeply in those dark Middle Ages? Certainly, Brother Daniel will love Israel. This he has proved beyond all doubt. But such love will be from without—the love of a distant brother. He will not be a true inherent part of this Jewish world. His settling in Israel in the midst of the Jewish community and his sincere affection for it cannot take the place of absolute inner identification which is absent.

In order to avoid all mistake or misunderstanding, let me say this: we have no quarrel here with the Catholic Church, and far be it from us to identify the modern Church of John XXIII with that of the medieval Papacy.[2] Most certainly we do not seek to hold Daniel, the convert, responsible for the sins of Nicholas Donin or of Pablo Christiani, apostates of the thirteenth century. We are sure that he will harbour no hatred towards Israel. He will seek to maintain a mutually correct relationship. He will observe the rule of "molest not my annointed, and harm not my prophets". But the personal decency, the humanity of Brother Daniel, is not in issue here. The question is whether he may assume the name of "Jew." To this question I must reply in the negative.

6. Counsel for the petitioner has urged before us that to refuse to recognize his client as a Jew is to make of Israel a theocratic state.

This argument is completely unfounded and I reject it utterly. Israel is not a theocratic state because, as the present case demonstrates, the life of its citizens is regulated by the law and not by religion. As I have shown above, if the *religious* categories of Jewish law applied, the petitioner would indeed be regarded as a Jew.

7. As emerges from the literature cited to us by the State Attorney, the deeply rooted belief that "Jew" and "Christian" are contradictory terms is shared alike by simple people and scholars. In fact the matter is so clear to them that they do not even bother to explain it....

JUSTICE LANDAU, concurring.

The question before us is what did the Legislature intend when it used the term "Jew" in that Law.

The State of Israel was established by Zionists on the principles of Zionism, and the Law of Return itself gives expression to the fulfillment of one of the basic principles of Zionism. It is therefore legitimate to seek guidance not only from the Jew in the street but also from the fathers of Zionism as to the construction of this Law in the case of a Jew who has changed his faith. The State Attorney indeed was right in drawing our attention to the letter which Herzl wrote on September 12, 1897 to Dr. Bodenheimer.... This letter concerned a Jew named De Jong who had become a Christian and had applied to be accepted as a member of the Zionist Organization. To this Herzl answers very simply as follows:

> Mr. De Jong being a Christian cannot join the [Zionist] Organization. We would be grateful to him if he assisted us as a non-member.

Now let us see what Ahad Ha'am had to say on this question for modern Zionism is a synthesis of his thought and Herzl's vision....

> Jewish nationalism without any trace of those elements which for thousands of years had been the very life breath of the nation and had given it its special

---

2. Editor's note: St. Pope John XIII later convened the Second Vatican Council, (1962–65), also known as Vatican II, which issued *Nostra Aetate* in 1965 (*see infra* Chapter 14, "Antisemitism Is Antithetical to Christianity").

> place in the cultural evolution of mankind—such a grotesque creature can be imagined only by one who is very far removed from the spirit of our people.

[Ahad Ha'am was asked to respond to the claim that] "one can be a good Jew and at the same time experience some religious emotion at the Christian legend of the son of God who was sent to mankind in order to redeem with his blood the sins of the generations." To this Ahad Ha'am retorts:

> National consciousness "freed" from the past of the nation is an "absurdity" such as has been unheard of in any nation or tongue. No one can free himself from the natural conditions of his being unless simultaneously he "frees" himself from continuing to exist. Can the tree free itself from its roots buried deep in the soil which deprive it of freedom of movement?…

Is it necessary to mention the Declaration of the Establishment of the State of Israel, which opens with a description of "the historic and traditional attachment" of the Jewish people to the land of Israel where was shaped "the spiritual, religious and political identity" of a people who have "never ceased to pray and hope for their return to it and for the restoration in it of their political freedom"? It is in that spirit that the Law of Return was enacted, a Law for sons returning home. The meaning of this Law cannot be severed from the sources of the past from which its content is derived, and in these sources nationalism and religion are inseparably interwoven.

A Jew who, by changing his religion, cuts himself off from the national past of his people ceases thereby to be a Jew in the national sense to which the Law of Return gives expression.… By changing his religion he has erected a barrier between himself and his brother Jews.…

Justice Berinson, concurring.

Vast changes have taken place in the life of the Jewish people. It has been overwhelmed by the holocaust of the Nazis who set out to kill, exterminate and obliterate the whole of the Jewish people without distinction between believers and agnostics, orthodox and heretics. The State of Israel was established and we became a sovereign nation in our own land enjoying an international status like other nations. Had the petitioner fallen into the hands of the Nazis after embracing Christianity his religion would not have saved him from their murderous claws and he would have fallen victim to them as a *Jew*. Now that the State of Israel has been created and the petitioner comes knocking at its gates, will it refuse to recognise him as a Jew?…

Can it be that the petitioner who has embraced another creed but has remained attached to his people, is no longer a Jew? Had he declared that he believed in Buddhism which does not require a change of religion and lived as a Buddhist monk, he would apparently have been recognized as a Jew. Thus, as a Buddhist monk yes, but as a Christian monk no!

Even Ahad Ha'am, the father of modern spiritual Zionism, who traced his Zionist convictions to Jewish spiritual nationalism and considered the Jewish religion an inseparable part of our national past, did not believe that a Jew would have to be excluded from the Jewish fold because of his refusal to accept the spiritual values of the nation and because "of the truly great chasm which lies between such a man and the others, be they religious or otherwise." In one of his articles, Ahad Ha'am recalls the question put to him very frankly by some Jew who asked:

> What would you call a Jew who is devoted to his people, its literature and all its spiritual treasures; who longs for its renaissance in the ancestral home and yearns for its liberty, but who at the same time is a free thinker in the widest and most general meaning of the word; who sees beauty and order in nature everywhere and at all times but refuses recognition to Him who is the author and regulator of it all and certainly to Him who gave the Law unto His people with all the consequences thereof—is such a man one of us or not? Can we exclude such a man from the generality of the Jewish people and say to him, "Leave our camp"?

To this Ahad Ha'am answers:

> From all the particulars given by the questioner, this Jew is "one of us," that is to say, a loyal son of his people and of its spiritual heritage, not only like the multitude who have faith but in some sense more than they.

He goes on to explain in detail why a non-believing Jew, such as this, is more Jewish from the national point of view than the Jew of religious faith. Towards the end of the article Ahad Ha'am deals with a "third kind of Jew," those whom a deep chasm divides from the rest, the believers and the non-believers, those who:

> have wiped out the past as if it did not exist and consider the nation to have come into being only on the day they were born and began to give voice. For history they have neither feeling nor use. Their aspiration is not for the revival of their people as it was of old but for the creation of a new people, a strange people out of the scattered fragments of the old materials. They love the sons of their people, their brothers in misfortune, but they neither know nor love themselves, or value the historical soul or spiritual treasures of the people.

But even these Ahad Ha'am did not think of expelling from the Jewish camp, only that they should not be allowed to lead the people along the path they have chosen for themselves:

> Against Jews such as these we must arm ourselves with all our strength. Not for the purpose of "detaching them from the rest of the people and telling them to depart from our camp"! Heaven forbid! Whoever has come into our camp is our brother and must not be told to go! But not all who come may be allowed to lead it along the path of their own choice.

Such was the view of Ahad Ha'am, a view consistent with Jewish religious ruling which holds that "A Jew who sins nevertheless remains a Jew" and though he change his religion does not cease to be part of the Jewish people.

The people themselves, however, because of a well-developed sense of self-preservation, have decided otherwise, have behaved differently throughout the centuries. For them a Jew who has embraced another religion has withdrawn himself not only from the Jewish faith but also from the Jewish nation and has no place in the Jewish community.... In the contemplation of the Jewish people, a Jew and a Christian cannot reside in one person and certainly not a Jew who is a Catholic priest—to them that would be a contradiction in terms.

I believe that the Law of Return was enacted wholly in this spirit and in using the word "Jew" therein the Knesset intended it to be understood in its popular meaning as explained above....

A fresh wind is blowing even in the world of religious creeds.... Who could have imagined that the day would dawn when Jewish religious leaders would attend a meeting in a Christian church to consult with their gentile colleagues on common public problems? But this kind of thing is only at its beginning and has not yet become part of the consciousness of the people. It will still take a long time, so it seems, before convictions will change and that deeply rooted feeling against Christianity for the wrongs it did to the Jewish people, the pages of whose history are soaked with the blood of martyrs who died in order to sanctify the Holy Name, will disappear. Until that day dawns the petitioner cannot be recognized as a Jew under the Law of Return. I agree therefore that the order *nisi* be discharged.

JUSTICE COHN, dissenting.

I cannot agree that ... it is imperative or permissible to deprive the petitioner of his rights as a Jew.

It is true that the history of our people throughout its dispersion is soaked with the innocent blood of thousands and tens of thousands of martyrs who were racked and tortured, slain and burnt by the Catholic Church and its retinues for their fidelity to the God of Israel. Even the recent outrages of the Nazi holocaust cannot erase the memory of earlier ones, the martyrdom of the Jewish people under the Roman Empire and in the course of the Crusades, the Inquisition and the European pogroms. The war of the Church against the Jews was total war, and if it could not compass their spiritual annihilation, it meant to destroy them physically. The fact that the Church was intent as it were upon the glory of the Divinity has made no difference to the Jews throughout the ages and given them no comfort.

If I have correctly understood my learned colleague, Silberg J., he is of the opinion that the historic continuity of the Jewish people from those terrible times till the present day can never permit us to regard anyone as a Jew who has entered into the covenant of the Catholic Church and joined one of its orders. Although the Church has both in theory and in practice ceased to be our mortal enemy, it can no more deny its past than we can deny ours, and a Jewish Catholic will forever remain a contradiction in terms.

I myself do not postulate an "historical continuity" such as this. If history is continuous and uninterrupted from the start, this does not mean that it does not change, progress and evolve. On the contrary, changes of times and ideas, evolution of concepts and cultural values, and continuous improvement of ways of life and of law—all these are in the very nature of the process of history. To me historical continuity means continuing to *build* on the foundations of the past, adding brick to brick, renewing and developing—and not remaining stagnant.

Never has there been such a revolutionary event in the history of the Jewish people, scattered and dispersed amongst the nations, as the establishment of the State of Israel. In the Diaspora we were a minority, tolerated or persecuted, but in our own State we are an independent nation like all other nations. In place of our former status as a minority, whether religious, ethnic, national or racial, we have created for ourselves in our own State "the status of a fully-privileged member of the comity of nations" (as it is expressed in the Declaration of the Establishment of the State of Israel). This revolution is not merely of a political character; it renders imperative a revision of the values which we have imbibed in our long exile. All this is commonplace and self-evident and what I am saying is nothing new.

At the gates of the homeland which (according to the said Declaration) "the State will open wide to every Jew," the petitioner now knocks and declares: "I am a Jew, let me in." And the Minister of the Interior, who is charged with implementing the Law of Return, refuses to listen because of the gown that the petitioner wears as a Catholic priest, the cross that hangs from his neck and his self-declaration that his creed is that of the Gentiles. Had he folded his gown, hidden his cross and concealed his creed, the gates would have been opened wide without protest. But he chose to come as he is, openly and without guile, and he finds the gates locked.

It is difficult not to recall those Jews who, loyal to their ancestral faith, donned the outward garb of the Christian religion so that they might continue to dwell in the lands beloved to them and harvest the fruit of their toils. How loudly they cried: "We are Christians, open up the gates." But had they revealed their true selves, their devotion to the religion of Israel, all gates would have been closed before them.

Times have changed and the wheel has turned full circle. There comes now to the State of Israel a man who regards Israel as his mother land and craves to find fulfilment within its borders, but his religion is Christian. Shall we therefore close the gates? Does the turning wheel of history indeed demand that we deal out measure for measure? Should the State of Israel, "based on freedom, justice and peace as envisaged by the prophets of Israel," act towards its inhabitants and those who return as did the evil rulers of some Catholic kingdoms in the past?

This was the vision of the prophets of Israel: "Open ye the gates that the righteous gentile which keepeth the truth may enter in" (Isaiah xxvi, 2). Isaiah speaks of the righteous gentile, and not of priests, levites or the people of Israel. Almighty God does not disqualify anyone; all are acceptable to Him; the gates are always open and whoever wishes may enter (*Sifra, Aharei Mot; Shmot Raba*, ch. 17)....

I accept that part of the decision of the Government that anyone declaring in good faith that he is a Jew is to be regarded as a Jew for the purposes of the Law of Return, but

I cannot accept the proviso thereto which restricts its effectiveness to those cases where the declarant has no other religion. I have already pointed out that the tests provided by religious law cannot apply to the Law of Return and it is unnecessary to add that the tests employed by the English courts in determining who is a Jew, cited to us by the State Attorney, cannot apply either. In the absence of an objective test provided by the Law itself, there is no alternative, in my opinion, but to assume that the Legislature intended to content itself with the subjective test, that is to say, that the right to return to Israel belongs to any person who declares that he is a Jew returning to his homeland and wishes to settle there.... Had it been desired to limit the application of the Law only to Jews not practising any other but the Jewish religion or only those who believe in the God of Israel, or had any other similar religious qualification been intended, the Legislature could and should have said so in clear language. Since it did not do so, the Law must be construed and applied as it stands literally, without attributing to the term "Jew" any religious significance or qualification.

I am not unaware of the fact that the decision of the Government was taken in connection with the implementation of the Registration of Inhabitants Ordinance, 1949, and not the Law of Return. Among the particulars that have to be included under sec. 4(f) of the Ordinance in the Register of Inhabitants are "Citizenship, Nationality, Religion," and the bracketing together of these three particulars would appear to indicate that a man may be Jewish by nationality but not by religion. The petition before us is not only to affirm the right of the applicant as a Jew under the Law of Return but also to enable him to obtain an identity card under section 7 of the Registration of Inhabitants Ordinance, in which will be specified in the column dealing with nationality that he is a Jew. It was in accordance with this section that the order *nisi* was issued. Seemingly the respondent too considers that, as far as the petitioner is concerned, the implementation of the Law of Return is interrelated and connected with that of the Registration of Inhabitants Ordinance. However that may be, he has applied the Government's decision relating to the Registration of Inhabitants Ordinance to the petitioner's application under the Law of Return. And indeed it seems to me that no distinction can be drawn between these two statutes as far as the question before us is concerned, and that the decision of the Government cannot be upheld in regard also to the implementation of the Registration of Inhabitants Ordinance.

That the test to be employed under the Registration of Inhabitants Ordinance in regard to a person's nationality and religion is subjective and not objective is also shown by the fact that the duty to register under the Ordinance lies upon the inhabitant and not upon the registration officer; and the inhabitant discharges his obligation when he informs the registration officer of his nationality and religion, in the same way as he discharges it by informing the officer of his address. The direction in the Ordinance to register a person's nationality or religion does not oblige or authorise the registration officer to enquire into, investigate and decide from a religious or any other point of view the nationality or religion of the person seeking registration. Although the officer is entitled under sec. 6 of the Ordinance to demand documentary or other proof from the applicant, he must only use this power in those cases where he has reason to suspect that the applicant has not made his declaration in good faith but for ulterior purposes. The registration officer is neither a secular judge nor a religious authority; he is merely a registrar and he registers only that which the citizen required to register tells him. Registration in the Register of Inhabitants that some person is Jewish by nationality and Christian by religion merely proves that that person has requested the registration officer to register his nationality as Jewish and his religion as Christian. In other words, registration is nothing more than evidence of a declaration made before the registrar. It is unnecessary to add that such a declaration and the registration effected pursuant thereto cannot bind any judicial or administrative authority before which the actual question of what are the nationality and religion of the particular applicant may arise.

It follows that the decision of the Government which purports to limit the freedom of a person to declare his nationality and his religion as he sees fit and as his conscience commands him, when fulfilling his duty to register under the Ordinance, is contrary both to the language and to the spirit of the statute, and for the purposes of the registration itself this limitation also has no binding force.

Since the declaration of the petitioner that he is a Jew was accepted as having been made in good faith—and in view of the material available to the Minister of the Interior and to us, it could not have been accepted otherwise—the petitioner is entitled to an immigration certificate under the Law of Return, and to be registered as a Jewish national in the Register of Inhabitants.

The Halakhic Definition of Jewish Status

1. *A Jew according to Halakhah.* The two ways in which Jewish status in Halakhah is determined are birth to a Jewish mother—the matrilineal principle—and conversion to Judaism. The Talmud (Kiddushin 68b) derives the matrilineal principle from an analysis of the biblical verse forbidding the Israelites who entered the land of Canaan from intermarrying with the local inhabitants: "neither shall you intermarry with them; your daughter you shall not give to his son, nor his daughter shall you take to your son. For he will turn away your son from following Me that they may serve other gods" (Deuteronomy 7:3–4). The "son" (in this case grandson) whom the Bible is concerned to protect from idolatrous influence is the son of the Israelite daughter married to the gentile. The Bible expresses no similar concern regarding the offspring of the Israelite son married to a gentile woman. In the light of this omission, the Talmud argues that the lack of concern in this scenario is because the child of an Israelite man and a gentile woman is no longer an Israelite but a gentile; hence, there is no need to protect him from idolatrous influence. Maimonides codifies the matrilineal principle in his Mishneh Torah (Laws of Forbidden Intercourse 12:7) and it is established Halakhah to the present day. From a historical perspective, however, it is likely that the

matrilineal principle developed over time and became binding Halakhah only in the third century.[3]

2. *Conversion to Judaism.* The halakhic position regarding conversion to Judaism is more complex. In addition to the two technical requirements of circumcision for males, and immersion in a ritual bath for both sexes, candidates for conversion must also undertake to observe the precepts of Jewish law and have no motive other than the sincere desire to affiliate religiously with the Jewish people (Yevamot 46a–47b; Keritut 9a; Yevamot 24b; Maimonides, Laws of Forbidden Intercourse 13; Shulhan Arukh, Yoreh Deah 268).

In the present secular age, very few conversions would pass muster if the candidates for conversion were subject to intense scrutiny regarding their acceptance of Halakhah and the purity of their motivation for becoming Jewish. There is, indeed, a significant divergence of views in relation to these requirements among both modern and conservative Orthodox authorities. The more conservative of them opt for maximum scrutiny and are prepared to retroactively annul technically valid conversions if it transpires that the candidates were insincere in their commitment to a halakhic lifestyle or concealed an ulterior motive. More liberal authorities, especially those in the State of Israel, are prepared to finesse the non-technical requirements, thus making halakhic conversion available to a much larger pool of candidates.[4]

In the 1970s, a special Rabbinical Conversion Court was established in Israel to make halakhic conversions easier for non-Jews living in the State, but its legitimacy has been attacked from time to time by panels of rabbinical judges belonging to the conservative school within the general rabbinical courts system, and on each occasion special measures have been required to prevent long-standing converts being subjected to retroactive annulment of their conversions.

3. *Jewish status is unalienable.* As far as the negative component, namely the abandonment of Jewish status, is concerned, the Talmudic position is that Jewish status is unalienable. The example given by the Talmud to illustrate this principle is that of a convert to Judaism who later rejects his new faith and reverts to his old ways. Nevertheless, says the Talmud, he retains his Jewish status, and his Jewish marriage is still considered valid (Yevamot 47b: Maimonides, Laws of Marriage 4:15; Shulhan Arukh, Even Ha'ezer no. 44). The same principle governs the halakhic status of Jewish apostates, who, although they have rejected the Jewish faith, are still considered Jews, albeit seriously sinful ones (*meshumad*), and are subject to various sanctions. They, like gentiles may be charged interest on loans; they may suffer discrimination in relation to inheritance law; their testimony may not be accepted by a Rabbinical Court, and they

---

3. Shaye J. D. Cohen, *The Origins of the Matrilineal Principle in Rabbinic Law*, 10 Am. Jewish Stud. Rev. 19 (1985).

4. Daniel Sinclair, *Trends in Rabbinic Policy in Relation to Insincere Conversions in Post-Emancipation Responsa*, 16 Dine Isr. 47 (1991–1992).

may not complete a prayer quorum (*minyan*) or perform ritual slaughter. Their Jewish status is, however, not impugned.[5]

4. *Rashi on out-converts.* Some halakhic authorities in the post-Talmudic era were in favor of depriving an apostate of his Jewish legal personal status in hard cases such as that of the apostate *levir*. Rabbi Shlomo Yitzchaki (Rashi) (1040–1105), the preeminent biblical commentator of the Middle Ages, closed off this option in his seminal responsum on the issue written in the wake of the First Crusade in 1095, when large numbers of Jews living in the Holy Roman Empire were forced to choose between baptism or death. Rashi ruled that an apostate Jew never loses his Jewish status and cited as his source the Talmudic dictum that "although Israel has sinned it is still called Israel" (*Sanhedrin* 44a glossing Joshua 7:11). The case before Rashi involved a levirate release (*halitzah*), a biblical ceremony required to permit the widow of a childless man to remarry someone other than his brother (Deuteronomy 25:5–10). In this case, the brother (known as the *levir*) had become an apostate, and his participation in the *halitzah* ceremony was practically impossible. Rashi ignored the handful of earlier precedents to the effect that apostasy may very well nullify the *levir*'s Jewish status and insisted that *halitzah* was necessary even though the widow would be deprived of her chance to remarry (Resp. Rashi no. 173).

The historian Jacob Katz, in partial reliance upon the technically non-normative status of the dictum "although Israel has sinned, it is still called Israel," opines that Rashi's definitive ruling was a response to forced baptism. By simply closing off any debate as to the ongoing Jewish status of a medieval apostate who generally only underwent baptism in order to save his life and that of his family, Rashi declared that baptism was halakhically ineffective and paved the way for a full return of forcefully baptized Jews to their ancestral fold.[6] Mainstream Halakhah, therefore, imposes certain sanctions upon the apostate, but he remains a Jew by definition, and his legal personal status is unaffected by his conversion to another faith.

5. *A halakhic argument for denying Jewish status to out-converts?* It is noteworthy that in the *Rufeisen* case, Justice Landau cited Jacob Katz in his decision and makes the point that the Supreme Court's decision to reject Brother Daniel's application may not be such an egregious breach of Halakhah as might appear at first sight, since Rashi's ruling that closed off any other option was geared to the very specific context of forced baptism. Speculating along those lines, Justice Elon in *Beresford v. Minister of the Interior* (H.C. 265/87) emphasized the halakhic sanctions imposed upon an apostate and sought to compare them to the citizenship rights granted under the Law of Return. Indeed, he later went as far as to opine that "[a] rabbinical court, too, if it had to decide on the matter, would not apply the rights in the Law of Return to a Jew who has become

---

5. *Apostasy*, *in* The Oxford Dictionary of the Jewish Religion 57 (R. J. Zwi Werblowsky & Geoffrey eds., 1997).

6. Jacob Katz, Exclusiveness and Tolerance 67–76 (1961); Gerald Blidstein, *Who is not a Jew—The Medieval Discussion*, 11 Isr. L. Rev. 369 (1976).

an apostate."[7] This is, however, all in the realm of speculation, and it is highly unlikely that a rabbinical court in Israel would directly question the validity of Rashi's precedent in the context of Jewish status.

A Secular Definition of Jewish Status Prior to *Rufeisen*

1. *Letting the courts sort it out.* In the early years of the State of Israel, control of the Knesset was in the hands of the secular Labor Party, with the Jewish religious parties often providing the government with its coalition majority. As far as defining Jewish status in the proposed Law of Return was concerned, the ruling secular majority found it difficult to accept the distinction made by Halakhah between a child born to a Jewish mother and one born to a Jewish father. There was also a strong desire—highly understandable in the wake of events during the Holocaust—to grant the right of Israeli citizenship to people coming to Israel who had suffered as Jews; who had been defined as Jews by non-Jewish authorities or who considered themselves to be Jewish but were not members of the Jewish faith according to Halakhah. At the same time, defining the term "Jew" in the Law of Return in a non-halakhic manner would be seriously opposed by the Jewish religious parties, and would lead to their leaving the governing coalition. In 1950, therefore, the Knesset decided to leave the word "Jew" undefined in the Law to avoid a coalition crisis.

2. *Religion versus nationality.* A similar approach had been adopted for the same reasons in relation to the 1949 Residents Register Ordinance (today the Population Registry Law, 1965) which required all residents in the State of Israel to fill in two boxes: one for religion and the other for nationality. In addition, every resident was to be issued an identity card in accordance with the particulars recorded in the Register. National security was cited as the main reason for keeping the Register, and for requiring every male resident to carry his identity card on his person during a time of emergency.

The Ministry of the Interior oversaw the registration process, and decisions on the definition of Jewish nationality were made on an ad hoc basis in accordance with the minister's views on the subject. In April 1958, Yisrael Bar-Yehuda, the first avowedly secular minister of the interior, published a set of guidelines whereby "a person who declares in good faith that he is Jewish should be registered as a Jew." The guidelines also instructed the Ministry to accept a parental declaration regarding the Jewish status of their child, notwithstanding any halakhic ruling to the contrary.

In June of that year, the government intervened, changing the guidelines to exclude any Jew who professed another religion from registering as a Jewish national. It was based on that intervention that Brother Daniel's application in 1962 for an immigration certificate under the Law of Return, and for registration as a Jew in the Register,

---

7. Jewish Law Association Studies XI: Law, Judicial Policy and Jewish Identity in the State of Israel 35 (Daniel Sinclair ed., 2000); *see also* Aharon Lichtenstein, *Brother Daniel and Jewish Fraternity*, 12 Judaism 261 (1963).

was refused by Bar-Yehuda's Ministry of the Interior, notwithstanding the minister's personal preference for granting the application.

Not surprisingly, Bar-Yehuda's published guidelines raised the hackles of the religious parties in the Knesset, and later that summer they left the governing coalition, thereby provoking a political crisis. The prime minister, David Ben-Gurion, was able to resolve it only by promising to approach leading scholars in Israel and the Diaspora with a request for their opinions on the issue of "Who is a Jew?" and to submit their conclusions to a special committee, with a view to incorporating them into Israeli law. A letter to the scholars was sent out in October 1958, and thirty-seven out of fifty responders pronounced in favor of Halakhah, namely, that a Jew is someone born to a Jewish mother or a convert to Judaism.

In January 1960, the minister of the interior issued new registration guidelines in accordance with Halakhah which included the requirement of a halakhic conversion. Children of a Jewish father and a non-Jewish mother were to be registered in accordance with their mother's religion and nationality. There was also an option to record the parents' religion and leave the nationality box blank. These guidelines were never submitted to the Knesset for ratification, and unlike the original ones, the justices in *Rufeisen* did not refer to them.[8] The reason for keeping these guidelines under wraps was undoubtedly the lesson learned from the publication of Bar-Yehuda's guidelines: when it came to pronouncements regarding Jewish status, non-disclosure was the best policy.

3. *An easy case or a hard case?* The facts of Brother Daniel's case presented a unique opportunity for achieving public consensus regarding the adoption of an official secular definition of Jewish status in Israeli law. The reason for this was that in 1962, even the most ardent champion of the halakhic definition of Jewish status was likely to balk at the prospect of recognizing a Carmelite monk as a Jew for the purpose of immigration to the Jewish State and registration as a Jewish national, no matter what Halakhah might have to say on the subject.

Justice Silberg's Non-Halakhic Definition of Jewish Status

1. *A secular interpretation.* As the most halakhically erudite judge on the bench, Justice Silberg was on relatively safe ground when he distinguished between the meaning of the word "Jew" in the 1953 Rabbinical Courts (Marriage and Divorce) Law and its meaning in the context of the Law of Return. According to Silberg, there was no doubt that in the former piece of legislation, the word was to be interpreted in accordance with Halakhah, whereas in the latter, it was to be understood as a non-halakhic term, and its meaning was to be found in the secular canons of ordinary usage and legislative purpose. In the light of the crisis provoked by the publication of Bar-Yehuda's guidelines, it is evident that Silberg's confident dismissal of the halakhic identity criterion

8. A. Rubinstein, *The State of Israel as a Jewish State*, *in* LAW, JUDICIAL POLICY AND JEWISH IDENTITY IN THE STATE OF ISRAEL 17–22 (2000).

in the present case was driven by the dramatic facts of the case rather than any solid jurisprudential justification. Whatever its reasoning, *Rufeisen* paved the way for the Supreme Court to articulate a secular definition of Jewish status for purposes of citizenship and registration.

2. *Jewish status linked to Jewish past.* Writing for the majority, Silberg emphasized that any definition of secular Jewish status of Israeli Jews must retain a link with Jewish history and culture. The Jewish past may not be jettisoned, and for the purposes of Israeli law, Jewish status can only be attributed to a Jew who has not broken the umbilical cord connecting the Jewish people with its past. Moreover, Silberg would require an "absolute inner identification" with Jewish history and culture. Clearly, this cannot be the case in relation to a Catholic monk, notwithstanding his Jewish birth and upbringing, identification with the Zionist cause, bravery during the Holocaust, and ongoing identification with the Jewish people and State following his conversion to Catholicism. Silberg added that scholars and simple people alike subscribe to the belief that "Jew" and "Christian" are polar opposites. He also made the point that the Supreme Court's decision is totally free of any animosity towards the Catholic Church, despite its past oppression of the Jewish people.

3. What is the basis for Silberg's decision not to interpret "Jew" in the Law of Return according to Halakhah?

Justice Landau's Zionist Interpretation of "Jew"

1. *Jewish status interpreted according to Zionist principles.* Justice Landau agreed with Silberg that Jewish status in the Law of Return cannot be severed from the sources of the past, and in these sources nationalism and religion are inseparably interwoven. A Jew who, by changing his religion, cuts himself off from the national past of his people, ceases thereby to be a Jew in the national sense to which the Law of Return gives expression. Landau cited various secular precedents to support this position, including the ruling by Theodore Herzl (1860–1904), the founder of modern Zionism, that a Jew who converted to Christianity cannot become an official member of the Zionist Movement. He also cited the seminal Zionist ideologue Ahad Ha'am (1856–1927), and Israel's Declaration of Independence in support of the proposition that a national Jew in Israel cannot be a Christian. He too cited "the man in the street" in support of the inherent contradiction between the terms "Jew" and "Christian." He also mentioned the fact that preservation of the link between Israel and the Diaspora turned to a great extent on the existence of a shared Jewish status.

2. Like Justice Silberg, Justice Landau also adverts to the halakhic definition of "Jew," but his analysis with regard to the Jewish status of apostates diverged somewhat from that of Justice Silberg. How did it diverge and what explanation can you offer for the divergence? Do the two Justices differ with regard to the *normative* halakhic position governing Jewish status?

3. Justice Landau referred to Ahad Ha'am's theory of cultural Zionism in support of his ruling. Ahad Ha'am was the *nom de plume* of Asher Zvi Ginzberg (1856–1927), who was born into a Hassidic family in the Ukraine and received a traditional Jewish education. "Ahad Ha'am" means "one of the people," but is also an allusion to royalty (see: Rashi on Genesis 26:10). By dint of his own efforts, he acquired an extensive secular education and eventually forsook traditional Judaism entirely. He is the founder of cultural Zionism as opposed to the political form espoused by Theodor Herzl, and in his many writings he emphasized the need for the future Jewish state to embody the cultural values of the Jewish people, and not only to provide a place of refuge for the persecuted Jewish nation. How did Justice Landau use Ahad Ha'am to demonstrate that basic religious attachment is necessary for a Zionistic definition of Jewish identity?

Justice Berinson and the Ordinary Meaning of "Jew"

1. *Ordinary meaning.* Justice Berinson made no attempt to conceal his sympathy for Brother Daniel's cause and agreed fundamentally with Bar-Yehuda's subjective approach to determining secular Jewish status both in relation to registration and citizenship. He nonetheless felt legally constrained to rule against Brother Daniel's suit. He believed that the term "Jew" in the Law must be interpreted in terms of "common parlance" and "popular usage," and from that perspective, a "Jew" could not be a Christian. He cited the Hebrew word for an apostate, *meshumad*—which carries a highly pejorative meaning in Jewish folk culture, attended as it is by various mourning customs associated with the apostasy of a family member—to buttress his legal interpretation of the word "Jew" both in terms of the language of the law and legislative intent.

2. *Christian-Jewish rapprochement.* Berinson also referred to the antipathy towards the Catholic Church on the part of many Jews as a factor in shaping the common man's approach to the case at hand. He did, however, add that in light of the growing ecumenical movement and the burgeoning dialogue between Christianity and Judaism, things might change in the future. Berinson expressed skepticism about crafting a secular definition of "Jew" on the basis of Zionist thinkers.

3. *Ahad Ha'am.* How did Justice Berinson use Ahad Ha'am to bolster his personal view that Jewish status ought to be granted to Brother Daniel? Justice Landau also relied on Ahad Ha'am but arrived at the entirely opposite conclusion. Which view is closer to the truth? Justice Berinson claimed that Ahad Ha'am's approach was consistent with the halakhic ruling that "a Jew who sins nevertheless remains a Jew." Is this a fair statement?

4. How did Justice Berinson justify retreating from his personal view in favor of Brother Daniel's application, to which he devoted three quarters of his judgment, and concluding that a Jew who changed his religion could not be considered a Jew under the Law of Return? Is the justification convincing?

5. Both Justice Silberg and Justice Landau emphasized the fact that their decision to reject Brother Daniel's application to enter Israel as a Jew under the Law of Return was

not to be construed as a form of revenge against the Catholic Church for its centuries of persecution of the Jewish people. Rather it was based on the "ordinary meaning of the word Jew" (Silberg) and the opinion of "the Jew on the street" (Landau). At the end of his judgment, Justice Berinson made the observation that the popular Jewish view of the Church was the "deeply rooted feeling against Christianity for the wrongs it did to the Jewish people, the pages of whose history are soaked with the blood of martyrs who died in order to sanctify the Holy Name." In his view, changing this perception of Christianity and replacing it in the popular conscience with a more benign view would take a long time.

Does Justice Berinson's comment mean that in effect, defining Jewish status on the basis of popular opinion does, in fact, give expression to anti-Christian sentiment? If so, does this undercut the entire basis for the claim by Justice Silberg and Justice Landau that their decision had nothing to do with the perceived guilt of the Catholic Church for its centuries-old persecution of the Jewish people? Is there anything in Justice Berinson's background that would account for his aspiration with regard to changing the negative Jewish sentiment of his time towards Christianity?

Justice Cohn's Subjective Interpretation of "Jew"

1. *A dynamic interpretation.* In his minority opinion, Justice Cohn agreed with his colleagues that the secular interpretation of Jewish status in the Law of Return must not cut Israeli society off from its historic past or ancestral heritage, but he rejected the idea that the past in question was to be understood as Halakhah or as popular or scholarly conceptions of Jewish identity. Rather, Jewish status should be the contemporary application of the visions of the ancient prophets of Israel. There was a dynamic, progressive element in these visions, and it was that element that should prevail in the crafting of the definition of Jewish status in the modern Jewish State.

2. *What would the prophets say?* In Cohn's view, the prophets were all in favor of opening the gates of Israel in as inclusive a manner as possible (Isaiah 26:2), and the modern State should not shut its doors in the same oppressive way as that in which the Catholic kingdoms of the past persecuted the Jews. Nor should it encourage duplicity by rewarding those who conceal their religious identity, as Jews were forced to do in the past.

3. *A subjective test.* The best way of achieving this goal was to adopt a purely subjective test, namely, a declaration by the applicant under the Law that he or she is a Jew, which was the Bar-Yehuda directive prior to the government intervention disqualifying a Jew who had become the member of another faith from entering Israel under the Law of Return. Cohn felt that religion should not be a factor in determining secular Jewish status, which ought to be a purely subjective matter. Taking his cue from registration procedure, Cohn argued that application for Jewish nationality was a matter for the applicant: the registration clerk need only to establish that the application was made in good faith and then record the applicant's statement as to nationality. Religion was irrelevant, and since there was no doubt that Brother Daniel's application was

made in good faith, his request for Israeli citizenship under the Law of Return ought to have been granted.

4. Justice Cohn rejected the historical-cultural definition of Jewish status adopted by Justice Silberg and Justice Landau on the grounds that it enshrined a "historic continuity of the Jewish people from those terrible times till the present day which can never permit us to regard anyone as a Jew who has entered into the covenant of the Catholic Church and joined one of its orders." Justice Cohn sought to replace this suffering-based approach to defining Jewish identity with a universalistic and inclusive definition based upon the "open gate" policy enshrined in prophetic writings. Do you agree with his approach? Does the verse in Isaiah 26:2 about the righteous gentile cited by Justice Cohn in support of his position in favor of Brother Daniel actually provide such support?

5. Is Justice Cohn's claim that no distinction can be made between the Registration of Inhabitants Ordinance and the Law of Return with respect to the definition of Jewish status a convincing one? Note the fact that in the later case of *Shalit v. Minister of the Interior* (1969), several of the Justices in the Supreme Court believed the two laws were to be treated differently. Do you agree?

Rufeisen's Aftermath and the Creation of a Hybrid Definition of Jewish Status

1. Shalit v. Minister of the Interior *(1969)*. The secular definition of Jewish status in Israeli law crafted by the Justices in the Rufeisen case did not remain uncontroversial for very long, and in 1968, the Supreme Court of Israel found itself debating the issue once more in *Shalit v. Minister of the Interior*, P.D. 23 (2) 477. The petitioner in that case was an Israeli Jew married to a non-Jewish woman. He wanted to register his children as Jewish nationals and to leave the religious affiliation box on the registration form blank. The clerk at the Ministry of the Interior refused to accede to his request and wrote "no registration" in the nationality box, and "Jewish father, non-Jewish mother" in the religion box, in accordance with the Minister's directives. Shalit then petitioned the Supreme Court sitting as the High Court of Justice to change the registration to comply with his request.

The majority of the nine Supreme Court justices in the case decided to grant the petition, basing themselves upon the secular character of the word "Jew" as established in *Rufeisen*, and in light of the fact that the issue before the Supreme Court was simply registration, and not the right to citizenship under the Law of Return. That being the case, the majority was prepared to adopt the purely subjective definition of Jewish status advocated by Cohn in *Rufeisen*, provided that the registrant's statement of Jewish identity was made in good faith.

The minority of four justices split into two camps. One camp argued that in light of the controversial nature of defining Jewish identity in Israeli society, the better course for the Supreme Court was to avoid taking a stand and to leave the matter to the minister of the interior and the immigration authorities. Indeed, the desire of the Supreme Court to have the legislature solve the problems arising out of the complex nature of Jewish identity in the Jewish State has been a consistent theme in this area of the law, beginning with the *Rufeisen* case itself. The second camp, which included Silberg, insisted on applying the halakhic definition of Jewish status in the nationality box in the registration form. Silberg explained that he was not prepared to "drive a wedge between Jewish nationality and its religious foundations, since by so doing our political claim to the Land of Israel would be undermined." He sought to distinguish between the present case and *Rufeisen* in that in *Rufeisen*, the question before the Supreme Court was the determination of the Jewish status of an apostate who had become a Catholic monk, whereas in *Shalit*, the Supreme Court here was being asked to actively strip Jewish nationality of all religious content—something he was absolutely not prepared to do.

2. Rufeisen *enacted into law.* The inevitable governmental crisis in the wake of *Shalit* was not long in coming, resulting in the amendment of the Law of Return in 1970. In section 4(b), the new Law adopted the halakhic definition of Jewish status, i.e., birth to a Jewish mother or conversion to Judaism, but limited it, in accordance with *Rufeisen*, to a Jew who has not converted to another religion. In section 4 (a), the new Law granted the rights of an immigrant (*oleh*) to "a child and a grandchild of a Jew (as defined in section 4 (b), the spouse of a Jew, the spouse of a child of a Jew and the spouse of a grandchild of a Jew, except for a person who has voluntarily changed his religion."

3. Beresford v. Minister of the Interior *(1993).* The two unresolved issues in the new Law, i.e., the definition of membership to "another religion" and the conversion to Judaism component of Jewish status began to tax the Supreme Court quite shortly after its passage. In *Beresford v. Minister of the Interior*, P.D. 43(4) 793, the issue before the Supreme Court of Israel was the Jewish status, under the Law of Return, of Messianic Jews who believe in Jesus but have not been baptized into the Christian faith. On both halakhic and secular grounds, the Supreme Court rejected Beresford's argument that as a believer in Jesus, he was not a member of another faith for the purposes of the Law of Return.

4. *Non-Orthodox conversions.* The conversion issue bedevils Israeli law to this day, and a slew of Supreme Court cases and various pieces of Knesset legislation have yet to provide a satisfactory resolution to the question of the status of non-Orthodox conversions with respect to Jewish status under the Law of Return.

Biographies of Israeli Supreme Court Justices

1. *Moshe Silberg* (1900–1975). Silberg was a Lithuanian-born Talmudic scholar who played a crucial role in integrating Halakhah into the Israeli legal system. As an expert in both Jewish and Israeli law, Silberg was undoubtedly the most qualified Supreme Court justice in the *Rufeisen* case to rule on the definition of Jewishness in Halakhah and to differentiate between the term "Jew" in relation to personal status matters and its meaning in the Law of Return. The crafting of a secular definition of the word "Jew"

for a Jewish State composed of a large number of non-religious Jews might also be regarded as a prime example of the accommodation of Halakhah to the needs of the modern State of Israel.

2. *Moshe Landau* (1912–2011). Landau's mainstream secular Zionist ideology influenced him to adopt a nationalist approach to defining the term "Jew" in the Law of Return, while at the same time not discounting the religious aspect of Jewish identity. This was essential, given that Diaspora Jews identified themselves in terms of being part of the Jewish creed, even if its observance of that creed was entirely of a nominal nature.

3. *Zvi Berinson* (1907–2001). Berinson's decision in the *Rufeisen* case is striking in that over three quarters of it is devoted to a position which he ultimately rejected. In terms of his democratic ideology, he would have preferred to have recognized Brother Daniel as a Jew, but he felt constrained by both popular opinion and official declarations by political representatives of the State not to do so. He did, however, express a hope that in the future, the social climate would change, and Brother Daniel could be granted the right of return.

4. *Haim Herman Cohn* (1911–2002): Cohn was a staunch champion of human rights throughout his career, beginning with his decision as attorney general not to prosecute homosexuals, and continuing with judicial decisions in favor of allowing Arab parties opposed to the existence of the State of Israel (i.e., anti-Zionist) to participate in Israeli elections, and affirming the right of Brother Daniel to become an Israeli citizen under the Law of Return. In *Rufeisen*, Cohn favored a progressive approach to Jewish status, free of the shackles of past prejudice and shaped by what, in his view, was the universalistic and inclusive approach of the prophets of Israel, with the subjective declaration of the applicant for citizenship as the sole criterion for the legal determination of Jewish status: religion did not play any part in this definition. Not surprisingly, he generally found himself in the minority.

5. *Miriam Ben-Porat* (1918–2012). Appointed to the Supreme Court in 1977, Ben-Porat became the first woman to hold a permanent seat, serving as the Court's vice president from 1983 until her retirement in 1988. Born in Russia, she emigrated to Israel in 1936 and was one of the first women to study law at the Hebrew University. She later served as State Comptroller and received the Israel Prize for her contributions to society and the State.[9]

6. *Salim Joubran* (1947–). Appointed to the Supreme Court in 2004, Joubran became the first Arab to hold a permanent seat. He was born in Haifa to a Christian family of Maronite Lebanese origin, studied law at the Hebrew University, and served on the Haifa Magistrates Court and the Haifa District Court. Joubran is also involved in var-

9. Galia Eliahou, *Miriam Ben-Porat*, THE SHALVI/HYMAN ENCYC. OF JEWISH WOMEN, https://jwa.org/encyclopedia/article/ben-porat-miriam (last updated July 16, 2024); *see also* Cardozo L., *Ben-Porat, Miriam*, VERSA OPS. OF THE SUP. CT. OF ISR., https://versa.cardozo.yu.edu/justices/ben-porat-miriam (last visited Oct. 25, 2024).

ious Jewish-Arab organizations, promoting coexistence and understanding between communities.[10]

7. *Khaled Kabub* (1958–). Appointed to the Supreme Court in 2022, Kabub became its first Muslim member. He was born in Haifa and received degrees in history, Islam, and law from Tel Aviv University, as well as a master's in commercial law. He previously served on the Netanya Magistrate's Court and the Tel Aviv District Court, and taught courses in corporations and economics. Kabub is regarded as an outstanding jurist in economic, civil, and criminal fields.[11]

Sources

Gerald Blidstein, *Who Is Not a Jew? The Medieval Discussion*, 11 Isr. L. Rev. 369–390 (1976).

Shaye J. D. Cohen, *The Origins of the Matrilineal Principle in Rabbinic Law*, Am. Jewish Stud. Rev. 19–53 (1985).

Bernard. S. Jackson, *Brother Daniel: The Construction of Jewish Identity in the Israeli Supreme Court*, 6 Int. J. for the Semiotics of L. 115–146 (1993).

Jacob Katz, Exclusiveness and Tolerance (1961).

Oscar Kraines, The Impossible Dilemma: Who Is a Jew in the State of Israel? (1976).

Aharon Lichtenstein, *Brother Daniel and the Jewish Fraternity*, 12 Judaism 260–280 (1963).

Baruch Litvin and Sidney B. Hoenig, Who Is a Jew? (2012).

Daniel Sinclair, *Jewish Law in the State of Israel*, *in* An Introduction to the Sources and History of Jewish Law 1–16 (N.S. Hecht et al. eds., 1996).

Daniel Sinclair, *Introduction*, *in* 11 Jewish Law Association Studies: Law, Judicial Policy and Jewish Identity in the State of Israel 1–16 (Daniel B. Sinclair ed., 2000).

Daniel Sinclair, *Trends in Rabbinic Policy in Relation to Insincere Conversions in Post-Emancipation Responsa*, 16 Dine Isr. 47–70 (1991–1992).

Ralph Slovenko, *Brother Daniel and Jewish Identity*, 9 St. Louis U.L.J. 1–28 (1964).

---

10. Cardozo L., *Joubran, Salim*, VERSA Ops. of the Sup. Ct. of Isr., https://versa.cardozo.yu.edu/justices/joubran-salim (last visited Oct. 25, 2024); *see also* Salim Joubran, *State and Religion in Israel: A Perspective by an Arab Christian Citizen and Judge*, Justice 4–8 (2013); *see* also The Declaration of the Establishment of the State of Israel (Isr. 1948). ("WE APPEAL—in the very midst of the onslaught launched against us now for months—to the Arab inhabitants of the State of Israel to preserve peace and participate in the upbuilding of the State on the basis of full and equal citizenship and due representation in all its provisional and permanent institutions.")

11. Cardozo L., *Kabub, Khaled*, VERSA Ops. of the Sup. Ct. of Isr., https://versa.cardozo.yu.edu/justices/kabub-khaled (last visited Oct. 25, 2024); *see also Khaled Kabub*, Wikipedia, https://en.wikipedia.org/wiki/Khaled_Kabub (last visited Oct. 25, 2024).

Solomon Zeitlin, *The Jews—Race, Nation or Religion?*, 26 Jewish Q. Rev. 337–343 (1935–1936).

B. Jewish Status in Reform Judaism

Reform Judaism, sometimes called Liberal or Progressive Judaism, is the largest organized Jewish religious movement in the United States. It has a tripartite organizational structure:

1) The Union for Reform Judaism (URJ), established in 1873 as the Union of American Hebrew Congregations (UAHC), is the federation of Reform synagogues in the U.S. and Canada.
2) The Hebrew Union College-Jewish Institute of Religion, founded in 1875, is the seminary that educates rabbis, cantors, and educators for the movement.
3) The Central Conference of American Rabbis (CCAR), established in 1889, is the organization of Reform rabbis in North America.

The three largest modern Jewish religious movements (also referred to as branches, streams, or denominations) known as Orthodox, Conservative, and Reform all emerged in Germany in the 1840s.[12] The founders of all three movements were of the first generation of Jews raised with relatively equal rights as citizens, including the opportunity to attend university. While many traditional Jews shunned some or all secular education, becoming today's so-called "ultra-Orthodox" or Haredi community, others, including a number of rabbis, seized the opportunity for a modern education and consequently came to question some elements of their inherited tradition. The central question they struggled with was this: To what extent are the Written Torah (the Pentateuch) and the Oral Torah (Mishnah, Talmud, codes, and the rest of the rabbinic canon) divinely revealed and eternally valid, and to what extent are they merely human products reflecting the views and circumstances of the people who produced them, and mutable as social conditions and intellectual perspectives change? What was at stake was whether, and to what extent, Halakhah could or should be altered to render the Jewish way of life less incongruous with modern life. The crucial difference between the founders of Reform and the founders of the other movements was the rejection by the former of the binding authority of Halakhah.

In 1978, several thousand laypeople, delegates from Reform synagogues across North America, gathered for the UAHC Biennial Assembly. Among the most pressing concerns for these delegates was the rate of interfaith marriage, rising rapidly for over a decade at that point, and consequently, the presence of a growing number of children with one Jewish parent. In a major address to the assembly, UAHC President Rabbi

12. Reconstructionist Judaism originated in the early 20th century in the U.S. *Judaism: Reconstructionist Judaism*, Jewish Virtual Libr., https://www.jewishvirtuallibrary.org/reconstructionist-judaism (last visited Dec. 17, 2024). Humanistic Judaism emerged in the U.S. in the 1960s. *Judaism: Humanistic Judaism*, Jewish Virtual Libr., https://www.jewishvirtuallibrary.org/humanistic-judaism (last visited Dec. 17, 2024).

Alexander Schindler proposed a plan of organized outreach to intermarried families to draw them into the Jewish community. Most controversially, he called for a special committee of the CCAR to find a way to declare the children of Jewish fathers and non-Jewish mothers to be Jews. The rabbinic body accordingly created the ad hoc Committee on Patrilineal Descent to study the idea. Five years later, it presented this resolution ("the Resolution") to the CCAR convention, which adopted it.

Central Conference of American Rabbis, *The Status of Children of Mixed Marriages*

(March 15, 1983)

The purpose of this document is to establish the Jewish status of the children of mixed marriages in the Reform Jewish community of North America.

One of the most pressing human issues for the North American Jewish community is mixed marriage, with all its attendant implications. For our purpose, mixed marriage is defined as a union between a Jew and a non-Jew. A non-Jew who joins the Jewish people through conversion is recognized as a Jew in every respect. We deal here only with the Jewish identity of children of which one parent is Jewish and the other parent is non-Jewish.

This issue arises from the social forces set in motion by the Enlightenment and the Emancipation. They are the roots of our current struggle with mixed marriage. "Social change so drastic and far reaching could not but affect on several levels the psychology of being Jewish.... The result of Emancipation was to make Jewish identity a private commitment rather than a legal status, leaving it a complex mix of destiny and choice" (Robert Seltzer, *Jewish People, Jewish Thought*, p. 544).

Since the Napoleonic Assembly of Notables of 1806, the Jewish community has struggled with the tension between modernity and tradition. This tension is now a major challenge, and it is within this specific context that the Reform Movement chooses to respond. Wherever there is ground to do so, our response seeks to establish Jewish identity of the children of mixed marriages.

According to the Halakhah as interpreted by traditional Jews over many centuries, the offspring of a Jewish mother and a non-Jewish father is recognized as a Jew, while the offspring of a non-Jewish mother and a Jewish father is considered a non-Jew. To become a Jew, the child of a non-Jewish mother and a Jewish father must undergo conversion.

As a Reform community, the process of determining an appropriate response has taken us to an examination of the tradition, our own earlier responses, and the most current considerations. In doing so, we seek to be sensitive to the human dimensions of this issue.

Both the biblical and the rabbinical traditions take for granted that ordinarily the paternal line is decisive in the tracing of descent within the Jewish people. The biblical genealogies in Genesis and elsewhere in the Bible attest to this point. In intertribal marriage in ancient Israel, paternal descent was decisive. Numbers 1:2, etc., says: "By their families, by their fathers' houses" (*lemishpechotam leveit avotam*), which for the Rabbis means, "The line [literally: 'family'] of the father is recognized; the line of the mother is not" (*Mishpachat av keruya mishpacha; mishpachat em einah keruya mishpacha*; Bava Batra 109b, Yevamot 54b; cf. *Yad*, Nachalot 1.6).

In the rabbinic tradition, this tradition remains in force. The offspring of a male *Kohen* who marries a Levite or Israelite is considered a *Kohen*, and the child of an Israelite who marries a *Kohenet* is an Israelite. Thus: *yichus*, lineage, regards the male line as dominant. This ruling is stated succinctly in Mishna Kiddushin 3.12 that when *kiddushin* (marriage) is licit and no transgression (*ein avera*) is involved, the line follows the father. Furthermore, the most important *parental* responsibility to teach Torah rested with the father (Kiddushin 29a; cf. *Shulchan Aruch*, Yoreh De-a 245.1).

When, in the tradition, the marriage was considered not to be licit, the child of that marriage followed the status of the mother (Mishna Kiddushin 3.12, *havalad kemotah*). The decision of our ancestors thus to link the child inseparably to the mother, which makes the child of a Jewish mother Jewish and the child of a non-Jewish mother non-Jewish, regardless of the father, was based upon the fact that the woman with her child had no recourse but to return to her own people. A Jewish woman could not marry a non-Jewish man (cf. Shulchan Aruch, Even Ha-ezer 4.19, *la tafsei kiddushin*). A Jewish man could not marry a non-Jewish woman. The only recourse in rabbinic law for the woman in either case was to return to her own community and people.

Since Emancipation, Jews have faced the problem of mixed marriage and the status of the offspring of mixed marriage. The Reform Movement responded to the issue. In 1947 the CCAR adopted a proposal made by the Committee on Mixed Marriage and Intermarriage:

> With regard to infants, the declaration of the parents to raise them as Jews shall be deemed sufficient for conversion. This could apply, for example, to adopted children. This decision is in line with the traditional procedure in which, according to the Talmud, the parents bring young children (the Talmud speaks of children earlier than the age of three) to be converted, and the Talmud comments that although an infant cannot give its consent, it is permissible to benefit somebody without his consent (or presence). On the same page the Talmud also speaks of a father bringing his children for conversion and says that the children will be satisfied with the action of their father. If the parents therefore will make a declaration to the rabbi that it is their intention to raise the child as a Jew, the child may, for the sake of impressive formality, be recorded in the Cradle-Roll of the religious school and thus be considered converted.
>
> Children of religious school age should likewise not be required to undergo a special ceremony of conversion but should receive instruction as regular students in the school. The ceremony of Confirmation at the end of the school course shall be considered in lieu of a conversion ceremony. Children older

> than confirmation age should not be converted without their own consent. The Talmudic law likewise gives the child who is converted in infancy by the court the right to reject the conversion when it becomes of religious age. Therefore, the child above religious school age, if he or she consents sincerely to conversion, should receive regular instruction for that purpose and be converted in the regular conversion ceremony. (*CCAR Yearbook*, Vol. 57)

This issue was again addressed in the 1961 edition of the *Rabbi's Manual*:

> Jewish law recognizes a person as Jewish if his mother was Jewish, even though the father was not a Jew. One born of such mixed parentage may be admitted to membership in the synagogue and enter into a marital relationship with a Jew, provided he has not been reared in or formally admitted into some other faith. The child of a Jewish father and a non-Jewish mother, according to traditional law, is a Gentile; such a person would have to be formally converted in order to marry a Jew or become a synagogue member.
>
> Reform Judaism, however, accepts such a child as Jewish without a formal conversion, if he attends a Jewish school and follows a course of studies leading to Confirmation. Such procedure is regarded as sufficient evidence that the parents and the child himself intend that he shall live as a Jew. (*Rabbi's Manual*, p. 112)

We face today an unprecedented situation due to the changed conditions in which decisions concerning the status of the child of a mixed marriage are to be made.

There are tens of thousands of mixed marriages. In a vast majority of these cases the non-Jewish extended family is a functioning part of the child's world and may be decisive in shaping the life of the child. It can no longer be assumed *a priori*, therefore, that the child of a Jewish mother will be Jewish any more than that the child of a non-Jewish mother will not be.

This leads us to the conclusion that the same requirements must be applied to establish the status of a child of a mixed marriage, regardless of whether the mother or the father is Jewish.

Therefore:

The Central Conference of American Rabbis declares that the child of one Jewish parent is under the presumption of Jewish descent. This presumption of the Jewish status of the offspring of any mixed marriage is to be established through appropriate and timely public and formal acts of identification with the Jewish faith and people. The performance of these *mitzvot* serves to commit those who participate in them, both parent and child, to Jewish life.

Depending on circumstance,[13] *mitzvot* leading toward a positive and exclusive Jewish identity will include entry into the covenant, acquisition of a Hebrew name,

13. According to the age or setting, parents should consult a rabbi to determine the specific *mitzvot* which are necessary.

Torah study, Bar/Bat Mitzvah, and *Kabbalat Torah* (Confirmation).[14] For those beyond childhood claiming Jewish identity, other public acts or declarations may be added or substituted after consultation with their rabbi.

Jewish Status of Children of Mixed Marriages in Reform Judaism (Patrilineal Descent)

1. *To establish the Jewish status of the children of mixed marriages.* By employing this phrase, the Resolution already indicates its departure from traditional Halakhah. There is no halakhic problem here, only a practical one: under the 1947 tradition, the Reform process of a child's conversion requires a number of acts over a span of sixteen years—from birth through Confirmation. What if some of them were skipped?

2. *Mixed marriage.* The Halakhah has no mechanism for formalizing a relationship between a Jew and a non-Jew. With the advent of civil marriage and the extension of citizenship to Jews, individual Reform rabbis began improvising ceremonies for religiously mixed couples. If the marriage was valid civilly, the couple was regarded as married—regardless of whether there was *kiddushin* or not.

3. *Social forces.* The Resolution asserts that the issue presented "arises from the social forces set in motion by the Enlightenment and the Emancipation." The Resolution does not address whether the proposed change constitutes the *only* way to resolve this issue.

4. *Patrilineal descent is normative.* The Resolution correctly notes that "both the biblical and the rabbinical traditions take for granted that ordinarily the paternal line is decisive in the tracing of descent *within* the Jewish people" (emphasis added). The transmission of Jewish status vis-à-vis non-Jews is another matter entirely.

5. *Mother has no recourse but to return.* The Resolution claims that the matrilineal principle was based upon the fact that a mother who intermarried "had no recourse but to return to her own people" with her child. Yet neither the Resolution nor subsequent responsa provides evidence to support this claim. The Resolution presumes that it would have been impossible for the man and woman to live together as a married couple, and that she would have had no option but to return to her family, and that the child would have necessarily gone with her, and that *because of that social reality*, the rabbis decided to classify the child of their union as a gentile. This is terrible social history. It is true that there was no way for the Jewish father and the non-Jewish mother to be married according to Halakhah. But it is highly doubtful that when the Mishnaic laws regarding lineage were formulated, in the Greco-Roman period, most Jews actually lived their lives according to rabbinic law. The couple could have chosen to marry

14. A full description of these and other *mitzvot* can be found in *Sha'arei Mitzvah*. [Editor's note. In 1979 the CCAR published *Gates of Mitzvah: A Guide to the Jewish Life Cycle*, here referenced by its alternate Hebrew title. The first guide to Reform ritual practice to appear as an official publication of the CCAR, its chapter on Birth, Childhood, and Education included a subsection headed "Raising and Educating a Jewish Child."

under Roman law, or some local law; the woman might have been a concubine. Yes, of course, much later, when rabbinic Judaism became the norm among Jews (except for the Karaites), it would have been impossible for the couple to live together, unless she converted, and they were properly married. But to attribute the Halakhah regarding lineage and status to the halakhic impossibility of the couple having *kiddushin* ignores the fact that when the Mishnah was redacted, around 200 CE, many—perhaps most—Jews were not living according to rabbinic law.

6. *No guarantee the child will be Jewish.* The Resolution states that in most intermarriages, the non-Jewish spouse's "extended family is a functioning part of the child's world and may be decisive in shaping the life of the child." For this reason, it claims, "it can no longer be assumed *a priori*, therefore, that the child of a Jewish mother will be Jewish any more than that the child of a non-Jewish mother will not be." Yet, why is this the case? All of this is only relevant because Reform guidelines for conversion had already tossed out the means to create a hard-and-fast status by virtue of conversion rituals. If the Jewish father and non-Jewish mother simply had a *b'rit milah* for their 8-day-old son and, as soon as the pediatrician cleared their son or daughter to put their head underwater, took the baby to the *mikveh*, the child's Jewish status would be clear. That would not address the issue of whether that Jewish child was being raised and educated as a Jew; but the problem the Resolution was intended to address was, in large part, a problem of the movement's own making.

7. *Egalitarian descent.* The Resolution provides that "the same requirements must be applied to establish the status of a child of a mixed marriage, regardless of whether the mother or the father is Jewish." The argument placing children of Jewish women and non-Jewish women on the same footing cloaks itself in virtue by appealing to the ideal of equality between the sexes. It was a timely argument certain to appeal to its audience. Rabbi Schindler first proposed this change in 1978, only six years after HUC-JIR ordained its first female rabbi. By 1978 there were a total of seven women in the CCAR, with approximately twenty-five women enrolled as rabbinic students, and the ideal of gender equality was coming hard up against the reality of sexism in the rabbinate and in congregational hiring committees. This proposal thus seized the moral high ground.

More practically, in the 1970s and early 1980s, Jewish men were still more than twice as likely as Jewish women to marry non-Jews. The result was many children with last names like O'Brien or DiNapoli whose Jewish status was unimpeachable, while the Jewish status of a larger number of children with last names like Cohen or Goldstein was doubtful unless and until they went to religious school through Confirmation. Many Reform Jews saw this as an arbitrary holdover from a more backward era and agreed that it needed to be updated.

8. *Jewish status of child with one Jewish parent is a defeasible fee simple interest.* The Resolution's operative language provides that the: (a) the child of one Jewish parent, be it the mother or the father, is under the *presumption* of Jewish status; (b) the presumption of Jewish status becomes conclusive or irrebuttable when the child performs "appropriate and timely public and formal acts of identification with the Jewish faith

and people." In the event a presumptively Jewish child does not perform such acts, do they forfeit their Jewish status? Concerning an adult with one Jewish parent who did not perform the requisite acts of identification, must they convert to Judaism to obtain Jewish status under Reform Judaism?

For children of non-Jewish mothers, there is really no change here from the 1947 guidelines. However, for children of Jewish mothers, this is a massive repudiation of both Halakhah and earlier Reform practice, which provided that the child of a Jewish mother is conclusively or irrefutably Jewish. This Resolution clearly says that the child of a Jewish mother and a non-Jewish father is not a Jew unless they are raised as such. Where a child has two Jewish parents, the presumption of Jewish status appears to be conclusive, even if the child does not perform the requisite acts of identification.

9. *Depending on circumstance.* Formal acts of identification would include the acquisition of a Hebrew name, a bar/bat mitzvah, and so forth. The enumerated rituals and acts are almost the same as those named in 1947, though updated a bit (the "Cradle Roll" had fallen out of fashion, and to make Confirmation sound less like the Protestant ritual the 19th century Reformers copied, it had been given a Hebrew name). The innocuous phrase "depending on circumstances" and the reference to consulting the rabbi reflected the reality that many intermarried families had not decided to raise their children as Jews. If the Outreach program succeeded in bringing them into the synagogue, their children might have already missed *b'rit milah* and most of the years of religious school. Individual rabbis would have to work with each individual family to determine what was necessary for their child to be considered a Jew.

10. *Jews by birth under Halakhah.* A born Jew who was not raised as such, or who was raised in another religious tradition, and then comes to formally affiliate with the Jewish community (e.g., by joining a synagogue or planning a Jewish marriage) may be asked to undergo *divrei ⊠averut*, a formal reaffirmation of Jewish status. This is generally understood to include *tevilah* (ritual immersion in the *mikveh*), though without the blessing (ritual formula) referring to accepting proselytes. Beyond that, the process depends on the background of the individual since the purpose is to assure both the individual and the community that this person is not just a Jew in name only. The practice appears to have originated for the sake of *conversos* returning to Judaism. *Conversos* (also known as New Christians or Marranos) were those Jews of Spain and Portugal who converted to Christianity under physical or social duress in the 14th and 15th centuries, and their descendants. *Conversos* generally married among themselves, meaning that over multiple generations, they retained their Jewish lineage. However, returning to Judaism openly depended on the possibility of emigration to a non-Catholic country where Jews had legal residence. *Conversos* who succeeded in doing so, often after several generations of being denied access to any Jewish learning, and could show an unbroken ancestry of matrilineal descent, were Jews according to Halakhah, but were psychologically like non-Jews. Returning male *conversos* also underwent *brit milah*.

11. *Adult male converts under Halakhah.* A male who has been medically circumcised requires *hatafat dam b'rit* (taking the drop of blood of the covenant). All the

prayers and blessings for the ritual are recited, but a pinprick is made at the line where the foreskin was removed, sufficient to draw a single drop of blood.

A male born to a Jewish woman but who is only medically circumcised, or is not circumcised at all, is still a Jew. His parents did not fulfill their halakhic duty to "bring him into the covenant of our father Abraham," as the *mitzvah* (commandment) of circumcision is called. When he reaches the age of majority (*bar mitzvah*) it is now his obligation to fulfill it; but if he does not, it does not impinge on his status as a Jew. However, in an observant Jewish community, intentional failure to observe any of the *mitzvot* means that that person is not an upstanding citizen, and there will be social consequences.

12. *Adult converts in the pre-Resolution Reform Movement.* The "reorientation" of Reform Judaism toward reclaiming rituals that had been abandoned in the 19th century sped up in the 1960s and 1970s, thanks to a Zeitgeist that valued "authenticity" and minority ethnic and cultural identities. By the 1980s, at least a large plurality, and perhaps a majority, of CCAR members were encouraging or even requiring *milah* and *tevilah* for conversion. However, enough opposition remained that the CCAR did not make them a requirement.

13. *Ritual required for Reform conversion.* The "reorientation" of Reform toward reclaiming rituals that had been abandoned in the 19th century sped up in the 1960s and 1970s, thanks to a *Zeitgeist* that valued "authenticity" and minority ethnic and cultural identities. By the 1980s at least a large plurality, and perhaps a majority, of CCAR members were encouraging or even requiring *milah* and *tevilah* for conversion. However, enough opposition remained that the CCAR itself did not make them a requirement.

The Resolution's Reception

1. *Outreach to intermarried families.* The patrilineal decision did help the outreach campaign of the 1980s and 1990s draw intermarried families into synagogue life. However, it gave rise to a new set of questions and problems. What, exactly, constitutes "raising a Jewish child"? What if the child is being sent to religious school but was also baptized, or also attends a Christian Sunday school or church services? What if the child is being raised as a Jew but the family celebrates both Christian and Jewish holidays at home? What if the parents have been remiss—they ignored the rituals around birth, do not have an observant home, and did not send the child to religious school—and the child is now approaching the age of bar/bat mitzvah and wants to celebrate that coming-of-age custom? Forty years after the decision, most of these issues have been addressed. A body of Reform responsa exists that, while remaining sensitive to the nuances of individual cases, articulates some general principles: the child must have one biological Jewish parent; a child who is receiving any instruction in, or participating in any ritual of, another religious tradition does not meet the standard of an "exclusive" Jewish identity; and parents who wait years to give their child some Jewish education should expect that the child will require a formal conversion.

2. *Rejected by Canadian Reform rabbis.* Although the patrilineal decision was quite popular among U.S. Reform Jews, it was unpopular in Canada, where Reform is far less radical. The Canadian Reform rabbis issued their own dissenting statement, employing much of the same language as the CCAR Resolution, but reasserting the pre-1983 Reform position that the child of a Jewish mother is a Jew by birth and the child of a non-Jewish mother requires conversion. Liberal Judaism, the British equivalent of U.S.-style Reform, also accepts patrilineality, but Reform Jews in all other countries, including Israel, do not accept it.

3. *Confirmed split with Orthodox.* Not surprisingly, the patrilineal decision has been vehemently criticized by the Conservative, Orthodox, and ultra-Orthodox rabbinates. However, since the Orthodox and ultra-Orthodox have never regarded Reform Judaism as a legitimate form of Judaism, they already do not regard any Reform conversions as valid. The patrilineal decision merely added one more reason for ultra-Orthodox and Orthodox Jews to assert that the Reformers have split the Jewish people by creating hundreds of thousands of so-called Jews whom "real" Jews cannot consider as potential marriage partners, because their Jewish lineage and/or status is suspect. This sounds terrible, but the practical consequences are almost nil. A marriage between a Reform Jew and an ultra-Orthodox Jew could only take place under very limited circumstances, i.e., if the Reform Jew has become ultra-Orthodox in belief and practice, in which case, that individual has necessarily accepted the stringent ultra-Orthodox Halakhah on *yichus* (lineage) and would conform to its requirements and to the community's custom of an arranged marriage to a suitable partner; or (2) the ultra-Orthodox Jew has left their community, and either is willing to operate within the parameters of the Reform approach to Halakhah or doesn't care what their partner's Jewish status is. Modern Orthodox Jews would insist that anyone marrying into their family be either the child of a Jewish mother or—with rare exceptions—be converted under Orthodox auspices.

4. *Conservative rabbis and patrilineal Jews.* The patrilineal decision complicated matters for Conservative rabbis. The Conservative movement has never stopped requiring *milah* and *tevilah* for conversion, but the boundary between Reform and Conservative Jews in the U.S. is quite porous. Does a Conservative rabbi have an obligation to ascertain whether a new member of their congregation is a "patrilineal" Jew, or a Reform convert whose rabbi did not require the traditional rituals? Officially, yes; but in practice, many Conservative rabbis choose not to ask, relying on any one of several halakhic principles about when to simply accept someone's words at face value.

5. *Patrilineal Jews under the Law of Return.* A patrilineal Jew qualifies as a Jew under the Law of Return for the purpose of immigrating to Israel. However, the Ministry of the Interior, which is responsible for issuing identity cards to Israeli citizens, makes it as difficult as possible for all non-Orthodox converts to receive status as Jews under Israeli law.

The Resolution's Legal and Historical Context

1. *Enlightenment and Emancipation.* This Resolution roots itself in a historical reality brought about by the intellectual revolution of the 18th century Enlightenment and its profound consequences for the Jews, i.e., their admission to civil and political equality. Histories of the Jews refer to this latter as the Emancipation.

Prior to the French Revolution, *Jew* was a legal status in all Christian and Muslim states where Jews were allowed to reside. Jewish communities possessed the right to varying degrees of internal self-government, but were also subject to severe restrictions on where they could live and what occupations they could engage in. The *kehillah*, the organized Jewish community in each location, administered its own affairs according to a combination of Talmudic law and customary practice evolved over centuries. Rabbis, selected by the *kehillah* but confirmed by the government, served as the judicial authorities for the *kehillah*. Individually or as conveners of three-person courts, they had jurisdiction over contracts and torts where both parties were Jews, as well as taxation, marriage, divorce, inheritance, conversions (if allowed by the state), and, of course, all matters of ritual.

Beginning with France in 1791, Jews were emancipated from the legal disabilities under which they had lived, but the corollary was the revocation of state support for the legal structure rooted in Halakhah by which Jewish communities governed themselves. Emancipation, as the Resolution notes, instantly turned Jewishness into a matter of voluntary religious commitment. If *law* necessitates some power of enforcement, then Halakhah ceased to be law.

2. *The "Assembly of Notables."* After Emancipation, it was still necessary to clarify the relationship between the state and Jewish practice with respect to family and personal status. In marriage, divorce, and inheritance, which prevailed—religious practice or civil law?

Napoleon emancipated the Jews everywhere he conquered, but he shared the general suspicion of their fitness for, and openness to, equality. He convened representatives of the empire's Jews to answer twelve questions concerning the relationship between rabbinic law and state law and between "Jews" and "Frenchmen," including these:

a. Is divorce allowed by the Jewish religion? Is divorce valid when not pronounced by courts of justice by virtue of laws in contradiction with those of the French Code?

b. Can a Jewess marry a Christian, and a Jew a Christian woman? Or does the law allow the Jews to marry only among themselves?

c. In the eyes of Jews, are Frenchmen considered their brethren? Or are they considered strangers?

d. Do Jews born in France, and treated by the law as French citizens, consider France their country? Are they bound to defend it? Are they bound to obey the laws and to conform to the dispositions of the civil code?

e. What police jurisdiction do rabbis exercise among the Jews? What judicial power do they enjoy among them?[15]

The clear implication was that permanent emancipation would depend on satisfactory responses to the questions, i.e., responses that placed the jurisdiction of the state above the jurisdiction of the rabbis and that expressed a desire for Jewish integration into the larger population.

The Notables' response assured the emperor that "in the eyes of every Israelite, without exception, submission to the prince is the first of duties," and that "at the epoch when they were admitted to the rank of citizens, the Rabbis and the principal Jewish leaders appeared before the municipalities of their respective places of abode, and took an oath to conform, in everything to the laws, and to acknowledge no other rules in all civil matters." They declared flatly that "the Rabbis exercise no manner of Police Jurisdiction among the Jews." Yes, they had, in the past, to the extent allowed by the civil authorities, but:

> The attributes and even the existence of these tribunals have, to this day, always depended on the will of governments under which the Jews have lived, and on the degree of tolerance they have enjoyed. Since the Revolution those rabbinical tribunals are totally suppressed in France, and in Italy. The Jews, raised to the rank of citizens, have conformed in every thing to the laws of the state; and, accordingly, the functions of Rabbis, wherever any are established, are limited to preaching morality in the temples, blessing marriages, and pronouncing divorces.[16]

The Resolution casts the answers of the Assembly of Notables as emblematic of "the social forces set in motion by the Enlightenment and the Emancipation," thus blaming not the choices of countless individual Jews, but the social reality in which Jews and non-Jews mix freely, for "our current struggle with mixed marriage."

3. *The emergence of new forms of Judaism.* Between 1791 and 1871, Jews acquired equal, or nearly equal, rights in most European Christian-majority countries as well as in the Ottoman Empire, while persecution elsewhere, most notably of the world's largest Jewish community in Tsarist Russia, intensified. Unrelated to political equality, however, was the falling away from traditional belief and practice by many, or even most Jews, following the intellectual currents unleashed by the Enlightenment. Some Jews converted, unwilling to accept even the slightest legal disability to maintain a religious faith they rejected; others simply disconnected from Jewish communal life. Many, especially in Eastern Europe, abandoned religious belief but developed a strong secular cultural and national Jewish identity.

In Western and Central Europe, emancipated Jews were generally a small minority among relatively homogeneous national majorities, proudly referring to themselves as

---

15. Paul Mendes-Flohr & Jehuda Reinharz, The Jew in the Modern World: A Documentary History 152–54 (3d ed. 2011).

16. *Id.*

"Frenchmen of the religion of Israel" or "Germans of the Mosaic persuasion." Most of these Jews sought some middle ground between abandoning the religion they loved and continuing to believe and practice it in ways that appeared intellectually absurd in the modern context, and they eagerly adopted the new, reformist approaches to Judaism articulated by rabbis who called their schools of thought Neo-Orthodox (or Modern Orthodox), Reform, and Positive-Historical (Conservative, as it became known).

Neo-Orthodoxy held that both the Written Torah and the Oral Torah were of divine origin and therefore eternally valid and binding, but that over the centuries, harmful attitudes and practices had crept into Judaism that had distorted it. Neo-Orthodoxy rejected the extreme ultra-Orthodox resistance to change, which extended to declaring that Halakhah forbade wearing modern dress, speaking the vernacular, obtaining a university education, attending the theater, and so forth. The Positive-Historical school agreed that the Written Torah was divinely revealed but asserted that the Oral Torah was a human creation. The rabbis had developed it over the centuries so that Jews could live their lives according to the commandments of the Torah, and since it was the historical vehicle of living the covenant with God, it was obligatory. However, as a human product, Halakhah changed as circumstances demanded. In this era also, therefore, the rabbinic authorities could make changes to Halakhah so that the values of Judaism and actual life did not become distant from each other.

The Reform Movement not only rejected the binding authority of Halakhah but also reconceptualized the nature of the Torah and its commandments (*mitzvot*; sing.: *mitzvah*). It drew a distinction between the ethical commandments and the ritual commandments of the Torah. God intended the ethical obligations to stand for all time; the ritual ones, however, were merely utilitarian—a system that enabled the people of Israel, both in its ancient homeland and in the centuries of exile, to maintain their separate and distinct identity in order to preserve the precious ethical teachings that the rest of the world did not yet understand. Ethics were the kernel; rituals were the shell that preserved it. Ethics were eternal; the "ceremonial law" was time-bound, historically determined, and in need of alteration when it outlived its usefulness.

4. *Reform Judaism in the United States, a.k.a., "American Judaism."* In 1881, there were approximately a quarter million Jews in the U.S.; the vast majority had come as part of the mid-century wave of migration from the German lands and Austria-Hungary. Although most tried at first to maintain a traditional religious life, their knowledge and commitment were limited, and they rapidly became quite acculturated, particularly as many prospered after the Civil War. At the same time, there was a small influx of rabbis from the same regions. In the old world, even after Jews acquired civil equality, governments generally continued to recognize them as an organized religious body (*Israëlitische Kultusgemeinde*), and rabbinic appointments therefore needed to be acceptable to the Jewish community as a whole. Reformers who were too radical to be appointed in Europe came to the U.S., where their presence led to an American Reform far more radical than its continental counterpart. Some Jews, especially earlier in the century, resisted the liturgical changes these rabbis wanted to make, but most were

happy that their new rabbi spoke their language and did not expect them to return to traditional practices they had abandoned, and they reveled in building elegant "temples" where the service did not appear too alien to their gentile friends and business colleagues, or to their own acculturated sensibilities.

Crucially, these Reform rabbis were convinced that their new form of Judaism was not an alternative to traditional Judaism but its successor—the next stage into which Judaism would inevitably evolve as Jews became free and equal citizens of states that were progressing from ignorance and tyranny into enlightenment and republican forms of government. As America was the forefront of this social and political process, so this next phase of Judaism would be known as "American Judaism." New World Reform went much further in its rejection of traditional Jewish law than Old World Reform ever did.

5. *The "Russianization" of American Reform.* Between 1881 and 1924, about 2.5 million Jews arrived in the U.S. from Eastern Europe. Very few were firmly committed to ultra-Orthodoxy; traditional rabbis viewed America as a place where it was impossible to live a genuinely traditional life and preached against immigrating there. Most of these immigrants attended traditional-style synagogues on holy days and observed the dietary laws at least to some extent but went to their factory jobs or ran their small businesses six days a week. Observing the Sabbath (Friday sundown through Saturday evening) in a fully traditional manner was a luxury few could afford. However, most of them arrived here already more invested in Jewish cultural and political life than in religious life, establishing branches of the socialist General Jewish Labor Bund ("the Bund") and similar groups, as well as Zionist groups of all ideological shades. They spoke Yiddish, the vernacular of East European Jews derived from medieval German, and they were bound together by a powerful sense of ethnic and cultural identity, referred to as *Yiddishkeit*, "Jewishness."

A small number of rabbis and knowledgeable laypeople among these immigrants were actually committed to one or the other of the new Jewish religious movements. Imitating the existing tripartite Reform organizational structure, adherents of Modern Orthodoxy established the Union of Orthodox Jewish Congregations of America (1898), Yeshiva University (1915), and the Rabbinical Council of America (1923). Adherents of the Positive-Historical school renamed themselves Conservatives and did the same, establishing the Jewish Theological Seminary of America (1902), the United Synagogue of America (1913, now the United Synagogue for Conservative Judaism), and the Rabbinical Assembly (1918).

Few Russian Jewish immigrants found their place in Reform temples, which in those years were places devoid of *Yiddishkeit*, more like Unitarian churches than traditional synagogues. However, after 1900, the Reform seminary's entering classes were overwhelmingly made up of Russian immigrants—many drawn there rather than to the Conservative seminary by the opportunity to obtain a free college education while completing the rabbinic curriculum. The interwar years then saw a demographic shift within the Reform rabbinate, reinforced by a rise in Russian immigrant congregants, who saw joining a Reform temple as a mark of successful upward mobility. The result was a Reform movement that stopped distancing itself from traditional observance and began reclaiming abandoned practices. That trend accelerated in the postwar decades with an influx of second-generation Russian Jews. Both Conservative and Reform congregations multiplied in the burgeoning suburbs, and both movements' complacency was shattered in the 1960s and 1970s as their youth rebelled against everything their synagogues appeared to stand for—including endogamy.

6. *Intermarriage prior to Emancipation.* From 339 CE, when the Roman Emperor Constantius I prohibited marriages between Christians and Jews, until 1791, when Jews were granted French citizenship, instances of marriage between Jews and non-Jews (excluding converts, who are Jews) were few and far between. Halakhah has no mechanism for formalizing such relationships. The absence of civil marriage and the reality of religion as the organizing principle in both the Christian and Muslim realms, where nearly all Jews lived, made the performance or recognition of such marriages impossible from all sides.

7. *Intermarriage in the U.S.* Emancipation eliminated the legal obstacles to civil marriage, while the decline in antisemitism, Jews' greater acculturation and social integration in successive native-born generations, the modern erosion of religious belief, and social norms of marrying for love and compatibility have increasingly normalized marriages between Jews and non-Jews. Sociologists and demographers disagree vehemently among themselves regarding methodologies for accurately determining the rate of mixed marriage in the American Jewish community, but there is broad agreement that prior to 1960, somewhere between 5 and 10 percent of Jews were marrying non-Jews; that this number began to rise sharply in the 1970s; and that today it is somewhere between 35 and 45 percent. While rates are highest among Jews with no formal religious affiliation, rates of intermarriage are higher among Reform Jews than among Conservative or Orthodox Jews.

As a small minority (currently between 2 and 3 percent of the U.S. population, depending on who counts as a Jew) whose identity is conveyed by birth and then maintained through a distinctive way of life involving both ritual and education for children, Jews are unanimous in perceiving intermarriage as a challenge to their cohesiveness, their generational continuity, and their very survival as a people. Rabbi Schindler's 1978 call for organized efforts to draw intermarried households into the Jewish community was thus a response to a situation that virtually all Jews perceived as a crisis.

8. *Conversion in traditional Judaism.* The religion of ancient Israel had no formal process of "conversion." When the Torah refers to a *ger*, "stranger," it means a non-Israelite who lives permanently among the Israelites—a non-citizen, who was obligated to adhere to some Israelite laws, and had the privilege of participating in some rites. Negotiating the relationship between *ethnic* Jewishness and *religious* Jewishness was a complex process that extended over centuries, but well before the destruction of the Second Temple in 70 CE, *ger* was understood to mean "proselyte," i.e., one who

wishes to join the community of Israel by committing not only to the God of Israel, but to the way of life ordained for Israel in the Sinai covenant, i.e., becoming a *ben b'rit*, a "member of the covenant."

A Talmudic passage details the conversion process, which is carried out under the auspices of a three-person rabbinic court (Bet Din): ascertaining that the *ger* is motivated by spiritual seeking and not for any ulterior motive; ensuring that the *ger* is prepared to take on the difficult lot of the Jewish people and the demands of its way of life; teaching the *ger* the practicalities of living a Jewish life, but without too much burdensome and discouraging detail; and then finally formalizing their entry into the community of Israel through *milah* (ritual circumcision for males and immersion in a *mikveh* (ritual pool) for males and females (B. Yevamot 47a–b; Shul⊠an Arukh Yoreh De'ah 268:1–2).

If the parent of a minor child, i.e., a boy younger than thirteen or a girl younger than twelve, asks the Bet Din to convert the child, the Bet Din does so on the principle of *zakhin le-adam shelo be-fanav*, "we may benefit someone without their consent" (B. Ketubot 11a; Shul⊠an Arukh Yoreh De'ah 268:7).

9. *Reform conversion.* In 1892, the CCAR overwhelmingly approved, by a vote of 25–5, a resolution eliminating the need for any conversion ritual whatsoever. Any rabbi, together with two "associates," could now "accept into the sacred covenant of Israel ... any honorable and intelligent person, who desires such affiliation, without any initiatory rite, ceremony, or observance whatever; provided such person be sufficiently acquainted with the faith, doctrine and religious usages of Israel." The convert was to pledge verbally and in writing to commit himself or herself to worship God alone; to be governed in life by God's laws; and to adhere to "the sacred cause and mission of Israel."[17]

In 1914, the CCAR rejected the draft of a new conversion ceremony requiring the convert to promise a *b'rit milah* for any future male children, though they changed their minds three years later, probably helped by the growing advocacy of circumcision by the medical profession.

But if instruction and a verbal pledge was now sufficient for an adult, this posed a dilemma with respect to children. If the child in question is a newborn, this entails arranging for a *mohel* (ritual circumciser) to perform the *b'rit milah* on the eighth day, and then when the infant, male or female, is old enough to put their heads safely under water, the Bet Din arranges to be present at the *mikveh* and a parent immerses the baby, while either they or a member of the Bet Din recites the required blessing. Without the rituals, the conversion process is entirely intellectual. How could any child have the necessary mental capacity?

The answer is in the 1947 "Report on Mixed Marriage and Intermarriage," adopted at that year's CCAR convention, and quoted extensively in the 1983 Resolution. The rule there is that *the child of a non-Jewish mother becomes a Jew by raising it as a*

---

17. *Yearbook*, CENT. CONF. OF AM. RABBIS 36–37 (1891–92).

Jew—performing the *b'rit milah* for a son, holding the customary naming ceremony, enrolling the child in religious school, and educating the child all the way through to Confirmation. The 1947 Report was simply describing what Reform rabbis were already doing; by adopting it formally, the CCAR raised *de facto* practice to *de jure* Reform practice.

10. *Patrilineal descent: a "legal" solution to a non-legal problem.* Given that Reform Judaism already recognized being raised as a Jew as equal to conversion for the children of non-Jewish mothers, why was this not sufficient in 1978? Why were intermarried families and their extended Jewish families not availing themselves of this option? Why did the North American Reform movement choose, instead, to make a radical change in the halakhic definition of who is a Jew?

There are three interrelated answers to these questions, and none has anything to do with Halakhah per se. The first is attitudes toward intermarriage. Jews are essentially a large and geographically dispersed tribe with a distinctive way of life. Endogamy eliminates most challenges to maintaining and perpetuating that way of life. Membership in the tribe is conferred by birth to a Jewish mother or by formal initiation (conversion). Both cultural and biological continuity are predicated on endogamy. Halakhah does not even have a mechanism for formalizing a union between a Jew and a non-Jew. But outside of the ultra-Orthodox segment of the Jewish people, modern Jews are free to meet and choose to marry whom they please. As intermarriage rates for U.S. Jews rose beginning in the 1960s, rabbis came under pressure to officiate at mixed marriages. Most refused, not always as tactfully as they could; but tactful or not, many couples and Jewish parents felt this as a rejection or as a personal criticism, not as a justified response to a breach of communal norms and chose to stay away from synagogue life.

The second is attitudes toward conversion. Many people in the Greco-Roman world converted to Judaism, but these conversions ceased when the Christianized Roman Empire made it a capital crime for a Christian to convert to Judaism. That prohibition persisted everywhere Christianity—Catholic, Orthodox, or Protestant—held status as the state religion, until the modern era. Similarly, in Muslim realms it was a capital crime for a Muslim to convert to Judaism. In the face of the hostility of the dominant religions, Jews developed a resistance to accepting converts. Furthermore, Russian Jews brought with them to the U.S. a historical memory of centuries of persecution, recent experiences of pogroms perpetrated by peasant mobs, and a tendency to identify more strongly as ethnic Jews than as religious ones. The parents of the Baby Boomer generation retained an almost visceral distrust of *goyim* (the Yiddish pejorative for non-Jews) and, as religious skeptics themselves, did not really believe that conversion could turn someone into a Jew.[18] Many non-Jewish fiancées who were willing to convert before marriage were put off by in-laws who didn't think a *shiksa* (the Yiddish pejorative for a non-Jewish woman) who had studied with the rabbi and was now going to light Shab-

18. The wife of this section's contributor, a convert, encountered this skepticism when she was in a New York kosher deli in the 1980s; a waiter gestured to the Star of David necklace she wore and said, "Who are you kidding? You've got the map of Ireland all over your face."

bat candles and fast on Yom Kippur—observances the parents themselves may well have ignored—could really be a Jew when she still gagged at a serving of chopped liver and had not seen *Fiddler on the Roof* at least a dozen times. Faced with these mixed messages, many intermarried couples opted to forego the non-Jewish wife's conversion and to stay away from the synagogue—until it was time to think about how to raise the children, or until their son began to approach the age of bar mitzvah. The Reform movement's policy of equating a child's Jewish education with conversion fell apart when parents gave no sign that they intended to raise their child as a Jew until the child was nine or ten or twelve years old, when parents grudgingly agreed to send their child to a year of lessons to prepare him for bar mitzvah.

Finally, the Russian Jewish migration also brought with it a strong streak of anticlericalism, rooted in the intracommunal struggle between ultra-Orthodox and secularists of the 19th century. Suburbanizing American Jews built and joined Conservative and Reform synagogues because America allowed its citizens to cultivate religious difference but not ethnic difference; but "Who does that rabbi think he is, to tell me what to do?" was a commonly heard sentiment in those same synagogues. People do not like having to abide by the rules of any system they don't buy into, and Jews who are not religiously observant do not like being told that there is something wrong with the way they live their lives as Jews. One heard a great deal of "who does that rabbi think he is, to tell me my kid/grandkid is not Jewish?" in the 1970s and 1980s. Thus, the idea of "patrilineal descent" had enormous appeal.

11. *Pre-modern Judaism.* Prior to the encounter with modernity, Jews (excepting Karaites and isolated groups such as the Beta Israel of Ethiopia) constituted a classic text-centered community, i.e., a community in which agreement on a common text defines the boundaries of the community and makes it cohesive.

> The shared text may be a source of conflicting beliefs and practices, but the community recognizes that it alone must be used to justify them all.... It is a procedural agreement that all practices, beliefs, or institutions, whatever they may be, are to be justified in reference to the text, as an interpretation of the text. In a text-centered community ... interpretation becomes the main and central form of justification. Legal practice is similarly bounded by such procedural agreement. Courts can produce radically opposing rulings; what binds them together is agreement about the text that is the ground for the rulings.[19]

The text at the center of the Jewish community was the Torah, both written and oral. Jewish life was lived within the "four cubits of Halakhah," the laws of the Torah as expounded in the Talmud and the literary edifice of commentaries, codes, responsa, and so forth, erected upon it.

12. *Challenge of modernity.* Rabbinic authority rested upon two legs: popular acceptance of rabbis as the authoritative scholars and expositors of Halakhah and the legitimate deciders in questions and disputes resolved based on Halakhah; and the rabbis'

19. Moshe Halbertal, People of the Book 8 (1997).

power to enforce their decisions by virtue of the authority vested in them by the state. In addition to destroying the political system under which Jews constituted a separate legal community in which rabbis held enforcement powers, the Enlightenment also undermined the belief in Torah as divine revelation and the belief that the rabbis were its authoritative expositors because they were the successors of Moses, whom God appointed as the Torah's first expositor at Mt. Sinai. Most European Jews welcomed their new rights as equal citizens and did not object to the demise of the *kehillah* system. But the rabbis who remained untouched by any currents of modern thought were so strenuously opposed to any change in Halakhah, however slight, intended to facilitate the participation of observant Jews in modern life, that it is easy to understand how those who saw a need for change had no choice but to create an alternative nexus of rabbinic authority.

13. *The early Reformers.* The early Reformers were a mix of "evolutionaries," so to speak, and revolutionaries. Rabbi Samuel Holdheim famously spoke for the revolutionaries when he proclaimed that "the Talmud speaks out of the consciousness of its age and for that time it *was* right; I speak out of the higher consciousness of my age and for this age I *am* right."[20] The evolutionaries, however, were committed to engaging with the Halakhah as the indispensable historical framework of Jewish life, but *without* having to adhere to codified precedent. They felt free to disregard principles such as *Halakhah ke-vatrei*, "the law is according to the most recent authorities," which served only to reinforce what they saw as the extreme conservatism and rigidity of the early modern rabbinate. In place of the traditional rabbinic legal hermeneutics, they applied the insights of modern critical scholarship, particularly the study of history, to biblical and rabbinic texts. The history of Halakhah, properly understood, would guide them in deciding which parts of it should be retained, which parts modified, and which parts entirely discarded to create a Judaism that retained the essence of its religiosity but was now unfrozen and properly caught up to modern civilization.

14. *Reform rabbinical parliament.* On both sides of the Atlantic, Reform rabbis gathered on several occasions to propose, study, debate, and adopt changes to Halakhah in the areas that mattered to their people, who were now acculturated citizens of their respective states: synagogue liturgy, life cycle practices, and holiday observances. These early rabbinic gatherings were also innovative with respect to *process*. Participants referred to them as conferences, councils, and even synods, reflecting their growing sense of being a distinct segment of the rabbinate with a distinctive approach to Jewish law and life. When Rabbi Isaac Mayer Wise, the organizational genius behind Reform Judaism in North America, created the CCAR, he envisioned it as the rabbinic body with authority to make decisions about Jewish law and practice for the Jews of North America. Thus, a majority vote of the members of the CCAR was now how matters of Jewish ritual practice would be decided. At its first conference in 1890, the new organization voted to print in their Yearbook the decisions of all the preceding European

20. Michael A. Meyer, Response to Modernity: A History of the Reform Movement in Judaism 83 (1988).

and American Reform rabbinical conferences as a *de facto* way of accepting them as precedent. At its 1891 conference, the rabbis heard two scholarly papers arguing for and against ritual circumcision for adult male proselytes. These and several shorter opinions on the same question were published in the Yearbook; attendees at the 1892 conference voted 25–5 in favor of a resolution eliminating the need for any ritual whatsoever in conversion. At these 19th century rabbinical conferences, parliamentary procedure—resolutions approved by a body of rabbis—thus became the normative manner of making decisions regarding Jewish ritual practice. This was an innovation upon which no one stopped to reflect.

Furthermore, these resolutions effectively replaced the genre of rabbinic literature that has historically been the vehicle for addressing change—responsa. For more than a millennium, questions about how to respond to new situations in a halakhically appropriate manner have been resolved by submitting a question to a rabbi known for scholarship and judicial acumen, who sends back a judicial opinion based on his evaluation of the relevant sources. The earliest reformers had justified their changes in this manner. But "the absence of [responsa] literature by the 1890s reveals that Reform Judaism ultimately came to abjure law as a defining characteristic of the movement and marks its departure from the classical legal canon of rabbinic civilisation.... It was a Reform ... that was no longer tied to 'the authority of precedent' to sanction its actions."[21]

15. *Reform responsa and renewed interest in halakhic engagement.* Between 1890 and 1914, the CCAR attempted to impose some order and uniformity upon the chaotic and variegated practice of American Reform congregations. At least on a pragmatic level, unity of praxis would reflect unity of purpose and a shared vision of Reform Judaism. Nevertheless, there remained an implicit tension between a concept of Judaism in which ritual was not a proper subject of religious law, and the need to reach agreement on what constituted appropriate Reform praxis. That tension led the CCAR to create a Responsa Committee in 1906. Its mandate was to contribute to the Yearbook "appropriate answers" to "certain questions that might, from time to time, be submitted concerning Jewish customs and traditions"[22] However, it was agreed—these responsa would be merely advisory, for anyone who wanted them. They would not carry the weight of a CCAR resolution, which constituted a collective decision of the Reform rabbinate.

However, since the 1960s, the significance of the Responsa Committee has increased dramatically in the eyes of Reform rabbis and laypeople. A great deal of the credit for that goes to Rabbi Solomon B. Freehof (1892–1990), who chaired the committee for almost three decades and published seven volumes of Reform responsa. Freehof was insistent that Reform Judaism could not ignore Halakhah because if it failed to take it into account, it would be inauthentic. "Judaism is a religion which was formed by law and has lived by law. It is clear that Reform Judaism must come to an understanding

21. David Ellenson, *A Disputed Precedent: The Prague Organ in 19th Century Central European Legal Literature and Polemics*, 40 Leo Baeck Inst. Y.B. 263 (1995).

22. *Yearbook*, 16 Cent. Conf. of Am. Rabbis 58 (1906).

with the law or at least must define clearly its own relationship to it."[23] He went on to define that relationship succinctly: "The law is authoritative enough to influence us, but not so completely as to control us. The rabbinic law is our guidance but not our governance."[24]

Orthodoxy had always asserted that Reform was an inauthentic and illegitimate form of Judaism, but two postwar developments led to an intensification of that hostility. One was the new ultra-Orthodox presence in the U.S., including some prominent rabbis, after the Holocaust. The other was the establishment of the State of Israel and the power the state gave to the Orthodox Chief Rabbinate by giving it a monopoly on Jewish religious life there. The hostility escalated further in 1972, when the Reform movement began ordaining female rabbis; the 1983 patrilineal decision provoked even greater condemnation.

Meanwhile, however, the theological outlook of most Reform rabbis had been changing. In place of classical Reform's hyper-rationalism, twentieth century religious thought paid more attention to the non-rational elements of religion. Ritual could be meaningful without having to be "edifying." Mainstream Reform thought moved away from the sharp distinction between essential "ethics" and utilitarian "ritual," and toward a more traditional view of Torah as an organic whole, embodying the Sinai covenant. Consensus emerged among the Reform rabbinic leadership that Reform needs to engage with Halakhah. The CCAR holds, therefore, that its departures from traditional Halakhah are in keeping with halakhic *process* even if they depart from traditional halakhic *rulings*, because they are reasoned continuations of the classic rabbinic process of reading and interpreting Torah to meet the needs of the present. As Rabbi Mark Washofsky, Responsa Committee chair from 1994–2017, puts it:

> An "authentically" Jewish religious practice is one that is grounded in the tradition, a practice that speaks to us from the historical experience of our people. And by "tradition" ... we mean the halachic tradition, because halachah is the discourse of Jewish practice.... Halachah is the textual language through which the Jews have worked out their answers to the question "What does God, speaking through the medium of Torah, want us to do?" Therefore, if we want to know how the "Jewish tradition" addresses *any* question of ritual or ethical practice, then we have no choice but to consult and study the halachic literature."[25]

To consult and study it—yes; to adhere to precedent solely because it is precedent—no. The Resolution shows how biblical and halakhic precedent can be cited correctly, and yet dramatically non-halakhic conclusions can be reached.

---

23. Soloman Bennett Freehof, *Reform Judaism and the halacha, in Yearbook*, 56 Cent. Conf. of Am. Rabbis 290 (1906).

24. Soloman Bennett Freehof, Reform Responsa 22 (1960).

25. Mark Washofsky, Reading Reform Responsa: Jewish Tradition, Reform Rabbis, and Today's Issues 13 (2024).

Sources

Central Conference of American Rabbis Yearbook.

David Ellenson, *A Disputed Precedent: The Prague Organ in 19th Century Central European Legal Literature and Polemics*, 40 Leo Baeck Inst. Y.B. 251–64 (1995).

Encyclopedia Judaica (2d ed. 2007).

Soloman Bennett Freehof, *Reform Judaism and the Halacha* (1946) in *Yearbook*, 56 Cent. Conf. of Am. Rabbis 290 (1906).

Soloman Bennett Freehof, Reform Responsa 22 (1960).

Moshe Halbertal, People of the Book 8 (1997).

Walter Jacob, Contemporary American Reform Responsa (1987).

Dana Evan Kaplan, American Reform Judaism: An Introduction (2003).

Paul Mendes-Flohr & Jehuda Reinharz, The Jew in the Modern World: A Documentary History 152–54 (3rd ed. 2011).

Michael A. Meyer, Response to Modernity: A History of the Reform Movement in Judaism (1988).

Mark Washofsky, Reading Reform Responsa: Jewish Tradition, Reform Rabbis, and Today's Issues (2024).

Mark Washofsky, Jewish Living: A Guide to Contemporary Reform Practice (2010).

Additional Readings on the Relationship Between Reform Judaism and Halakhah

The Reform Jewish Quarterly: Halachah and Reform Judaism, 67 CCAR J. (2020).

Joan Friedman, "Guidance, Not Governance": Rabbi Solomon B. Freehof and Reform Responsa (2013).

Dynamic Jewish Law: Progressive Halakhah—Essence and Application (Walter Jacob & Moshe Zemer eds., 2001).

Re-Examining Progressive Halakhah (Walter Jacob & Moshe Zemer eds., 2002).

Moshe Zemer, Evolving Halakhah: A Progressive Approach to Traditional Jewish Law (2003).

C. Zionism as a Jewish American Project

Louis Dembitz Brandeis (1856–1941) was the first Jewish justice on the U.S. Supreme Court (1916–1939) and one of the most influential justices in U.S. history.[26] He was described as "the most prestigious Jew in the world"[27]—indeed, "the Greatest Jew in the World since Jesus Christ."[28] He is also regarded as "the maker of American Zionism," serving from 1914–1916 as Chairman of the leading American Zionist organization, and he continued to serve in an informal leadership role afterwards. Brandeis's leadership transformed American Zionism by dramatically increasing membership, fundraising, and organizational efficiency.[29] Jonathan Sarna explains that Brandeis's "success in promoting the Zionist movement in America owed more to his persona and mystique, his charm, prestige, fluency, sincerity and passion, the thrill of being part of a movement that he headed."[30]

The following essay is Brandeis's most comprehensive statement on Zionism.[31] It is a sort of "Brandeis brief" for the proposition that, in his words, "the Jews require a state of their own for their continued existence."[32] In it he responds to some American Jews' fears that Zionism reinforced the stereotype that Jews have divided loyalties and are untrustworthy citizens. Brandeis's "intellectual breakthrough" were the ideas that Jewish nationalism and American patriotism were mutually reinforcing, and that American Jews could support the Zionist project but without feeling obliged to emigrate to the Land of Israel.[33]

Louis D. Brandeis, *The Jewish Problem: How to Solve It*

Zionist Essays Publications Committee
New York 1915

What the Problem Is.

For us the Jewish Problem means this: How can we secure for Jews, wherever they may live, the same rights and opportunities enjoyed by non-Jews? How can we secure for the world the full contribution which Jews can make, if unhampered by artificial limitations?

---

26. Jonathan D. Sarna, *The Jewish Legacy of Louis D. Brandeis*, 81 Am. Jewish Hist. 346–364 (1994).

27. Jeffrey Rosen, Louis D. Brandeis: American Prophet 171 (2016).

28. Sarna, *supra* note 26.

29. *Id.* at 354.

30. Louis D. Brandeis, Brandeis on Zionism: A Collection of Addresses and Statements by Louis D. Brandeis 35 (1999).

31. Rosen, *supra* note 27 at 160.

32. *Id.* at 186.

33. *Id.* at 151.

Figure 4.3. This photograph shows a dignified Louis D. Brandeis in formal attire, resting on a chair, and holding a book. It is dated November 9, 1913 (public domain).

The problem has two aspects: That of the individual Jew—and that of Jews collectively. Obviously, no individual should be subjected anywhere, by reason of the fact that he is a Jew, to a denial of any common right or opportunity enjoyed by non-Jews. But Jews collectively should likewise enjoy the same right and opportunity to live and develop as do other groups of people. This right of development on the part of the group is essential to the full enjoyment of rights by the individual. For the individual is dependent for his development (and his happiness) in large part upon the development of the group of which he forms a part. We can scarcely conceive of an individual German or Frenchman living and developing without some relation to the contemporary

Figure 4.4. Sheet Music, "Marching on to Zion" (Zionist Bureau for New England) 1915). "Dedicated to my dear friend Louis D. Brandeis Esq., who has made the revival of Zionism possible. Samuel H. Borofsky." Courtesy of Robert D. Farber University Archives & Special Collections, Brandeis University.

German or French life and culture. And since death is not a solution of the problem of life, the solution of the Jewish Problem necessarily involves the continued existence of the Jews as Jews....

Nations and Nationality.

The difference between a nation and a nationality is clear; but it is not always observed. Likeness between members is the essence of nationality; but the members of a nation may be very different. A nation may be composed of many nationalities, as some of the most successful nations are. An instance of this is the British nation, with its division into English, Scotch, Welsh, and Irish at home; with the French in Canada; and, throughout the Empire, scores of other nationalities.... The unity of a nationality is a fact of nature. The unity into a nation is largely the work of man. The false doctrine that nation and nationality must be made co-extensive is the cause of some of our greatest tragedies. It is, in large part, the cause also of the present war.... As a nation may thrive though composed of many nationalities, so a nationality may thrive though forming parts of several nations. The essential in either case is recognition of the equal rights of each nationality.

Jewish Nationality.

W. Allison Philips recently defined nationality as "an extensive aggregate of persons, conscious of a community of sentiments, experiences, or qualities which make them feel themselves a distinct people." And he adds:

> If we examine the composition of the several nationalities we find these elements: Race, language, religion, common habitat, common conditions, mode of life and manners, political association. The elements are, however, never all present at the same time, and none of them is essential.... A common habitat and common conditions are doubtless powerful influences at times in determining nationality; but what part do they play in that of the Jews or the Greeks, or the Irish in dispersion?

See how this high authority assumes without question that the Jews are, despite their dispersion, a distinct nationality; and he groups us with the Greeks or the Irish—two other peoples of marked individuality. Can it be doubted that we Jews—aggregating 14,000,000 people—are "an extensive aggregate of persons;" that we are "conscious of a community of sentiments, experiences and qualities which make us *feel* ourselves a distinct people," whether we admit it or not?

It is no answer to this evidence of nationality to declare that the Jews are not an absolutely pure race. There has, of course, been some intermixture of foreign blood in the 3000 years which constitute our historic period. But, owing to persecution and prejudice, the intermarriages with non-Jews which occurred, have resulted merely in taking away many from the Jewish community. Intermarriage has brought few additions. Therefore the percentage of foreign blood in the Jews of today is very low. Probably no important European race is as pure.

But common race is only one of the elements which determine nationality. Conscious community of sentiments, common experiences, common qualities are equally, perhaps more, important. Religion, traditions and customs bound us together though scattered throughout the world. The similarity of experiences tended to produce similarity of qualities and community of sentiments. Common suffering so intensified the feeling of brotherhood as to overcome largely all the influences making for diversification. The segregation of the Jews was so general, so complete, and so long continued as to intensify our "peculiarities" and make them almost ineradicable.

Assertion of Jewish Nationality.

We recognize that with each child the aim of education should be to develop his own individuality, not to make him an imitator, not to assimilate him to others. Shall we fail to recognize this truth when applied to whole peoples? And what people in the world has shown greater individuality than the Jews? Has any a nobler past? Does any possess common ideas better worth expressing? Has any marked traits worthier of development? Of all the peoples in the world those of two tiny states stand preeminent as contributors to our present civilization—the Greeks and the Jews. The Jews gave to the world its three greatest religions, reverence for law, and the highest conceptions of morality. Never before has the value of our contribution been so generally recognized. Our teaching of brotherhood and righteousness has, under the name of democracy and social justice, become the twentieth century striving of America and of western Europe. Our conception of law is embodied in the American constitutions which proclaim this to be a "government of laws and not of men." And for the triumph of our other great teaching—the doctrine of peace, this cruel war is paving the way.

While every other people is striving for development by asserting its nationality, and a great war is making clear the value of small nations, shall we voluntarily yield to anti-Semitism, and instead of solving our "problem" end it by ignoble suicide? Surely this is no time for Jews to despair. Let us make clear to the world that we too are a nationality clamoring for equal rights, to life and to self-expression. That this should be our course has been recently expressed by high non-Jewish authority. Thus Seton-Watson, speaking of the probable results of the war, said:

> There are good grounds for hoping that it (the war) will also give a new and healthy impetus to Jewish national policy, grant freer play to their splendid qualities, and enable them to shake off the false shame which has led men who ought to be proud of their Jewish race to assume so many alien disguises and to accuse of anti-Semitism those who refuse to be deceived by mere appearances. It is high time that the Jews should realize that few things do more to foster anti-Semitic feeling than this very tendency to sail under false colors and conceal their true identity. The Zionists and the orthodox Jewish Nationalists have long ago won the respect and admiration of the world. No race has ever defied assimilation so stubbornly and so successfully; and the modern

tendency of individual Jews to repudiate what is one of their chief glories suggests an almost comic resolve to fight against the course of nature.

Zionism.

Standing upon this broad foundation of nationality, Zionism aims to give it full development. Let us bear clearly in mind what Zionism is, or rather what it is not.

It is not a movement to remove all the Jews of the world compulsorily to Palestine. In the first place there are 14,000,000 Jews,[34] and Palestine would not accommodate more than one-fifth of that number. In the second place, it is not a movement to compel anyone to go to Palestine. It is essentially a movement to give to the Jew more, not less freedoms—it aims to enable the Jews to exercise the same rights now exercised by practically every other people in the world. To live at their option either in the land of their fathers or in some other country; a right which members of small nations as well as of large—which Irish, Greek, Bulgarian, Serbian, or Belgian—may now exercise as fully as German or English.

Zionism seeks to establish in Palestine, for such Jews as choose to go and remain there, and for their descendants, a legally secured home, where they may live together and lead a Jewish life; where they may expect ultimately to constitute a majority of the population, and may look forward to what we should call home rule. The Zionists seek to establish this home in Palestine because they are convinced that the undying longing of Jews for Palestine is a fact of deepest significance; that it is a manifestation in the struggle for existence by an ancient people which had established its right to live—a people whose three thousand years of civilization has produced a faith, culture, and individuality which enable them to contribute largely in the future, as they had in the past, to the advance of civilization; and that it is not a right merely, but a duty of the Jewish nationality to survive and develop. They believe that there only can Jewish life be fully protected from the forces of disintegration; that there alone can the Jewish spirit reach its full and natural development; and that by securing for those Jews who wish to settle in Palestine the opportunity to do so, not only those Jews, but all other Jews will be benefited and that the long perplexing Jewish Problem will, at last, find solution....

Since the destruction of the Temple, nearly two thousand years ago, the longing for Palestine has been ever present with the Jew. It was the hope of a return to the land of his fathers that buoyed up the Jew amidst persecution, and for the realization of which the devout ever prayed. Until a generation ago this was a hope merely—a wish piously prayed for, but not worked for. The Zionist movement is idealistic, but it is also essentially practical. It seeks to realize that hope; to make the dream of a Jewish life in a Jewish land come true as other great dreams of the world have been realized—by men working with devotion, intelligence, and self-sacrifice. It was thus that the dream

---

34. Editor's note: According to the ADL, there are an estimated 13,700,000 Jews in the world. According to an ADL global survey, 18 percent of respondents believe that the total worldwide Jewish population exceeds 700 million people. People who overestimate the world's Jewish population by this amount are more likely to harbor antisemitic attitudes. *Did you know?*, The Anti-Defamation League, https://global100.adl.org/did-you-know (last visited Nov. 25, 2024).

of Italian independence and unity, after centuries of vain hope, came true through the efforts of Mazzini, Garibaldi and Cavour; that the dream of Greek, of Bulgarian and of Serbian independence became facts: that the dream of home rule in Ireland has just been realized....

Zionism and Patriotism.

Let no American imagine that Zionism is inconsistent with Patriotism. Multiple loyalties are objectionable only if they are inconsistent. A man is a better citizen of the United States for being also a loyal citizen of his state, and of his city; for being loyal to his family, and to his profession or trade; for being loyal to his college or his lodge. Every Irish American who contributed towards advancing home rule was a better man and a better American for the sacrifice he made. Every American Jew who aids in advancing the Jewish settlement in Palestine, though he feels that neither he nor his descendants will ever live there, will likewise be a better man and better American for doing so.

Note what Seton-Watson says:

> America is full of nationalities which, while accepting with enthusiasm their new American citizenship, nevertheless look to some centre in the old world as the source and inspiration of their national culture and traditions. The most typical instance is the feeling of the American Jew for Palestine which may well become a focus for his *declasse* kinsmen in other parts of the world.

There is no inconsistency between loyalty to America and loyalty to Jewry. The Jewish spirit, the product of our religion and experiences, is essentially modern and essentially American. Not since the destruction of the Temple have the Jews in spirit and in ideals been so fully in harmony with the noblest aspirations of the country in which they lived.

America's fundamental law seeks to make real the brotherhood of man. That brotherhood became the Jewish fundamental law more than twenty-five hundred years ago. America's insistent demand in the twentieth century is for social justice. That also has been the Jews' striving for ages. Their affliction as well as their religion has prepared the Jews for effective democracy. Persecution broadened their sympathies; it trained them in patient endurance, in self-control, and in sacrifice. It made them think as well as suffer. It deepened the passion for righteousness.

Indeed, loyalty to America demands rather that each American Jew become a Zionist. For only through the ennobling effect of its strivings can we develop the best in us and give to this country the full benefit of our great inheritance. The Jewish spirit, so long preserved, the character developed by so many centuries of sacrifice, should be preserved and developed further, so that in America as elsewhere the sons of the race may in future live lives and do deeds worthy of their ancestors.

America's Demand.

But we have also an immediate and more pressing duty in the performance of which Zionism alone seems capable of affording effective aid. We must protect America and ourselves from demoralization, which has to some extent already set in among American Jews. The cause of this demoralization is clear. It results, in large part, from the fact that in our land of liberty all the restraints by which the Jews were protected in their Ghettos were removed and a new generation left without necessary moral and spiritual support. And is it not equally clear what the only possible remedy is? It is the laborious task of inculcating self-respect—a task which can be accomplished only by restoring the ties of the Jew to the noble past of his race, and by making him realize the possibilities of a no less glorious future. The sole bulwark against demoralization is to develop in each new generation of Jews in America the sense of "Noblesse oblige." That spirit can be developed in those who regard their race as destined to live and to live with a bright future. That spirit can best be developed by actively participating in some way in furthering the ideals of the Jewish renaissance; and this can be done effectively only through furthering the Zionist movement....

And the Zionist movement has brought like inspiration to the Jews in the Diaspora, as Steed has shown in this striking passage from "The Hapsburg Monarchy":

> To minds like these Zionism came with the force of an evangel. To be a Jew and to be proud of it; to glory in the power and pertinacity of the race, its traditions, its triumphs, its sufferings, its resistance to persecution; to look the world frankly in the face and to enjoy the luxury of moral and intellectual honesty; to feel pride in belonging to the people that gave Christendom its divinities, that taught half the world monotheism, whose ideas have permeated civilization as never the ideas of a race before it, whose genius fashioned the whole mechanism of modern commerce, and whose artists, actors, singers and writers have filled a larger place in the cultured universe than those of any other people. This, or something like this, was the train of thought fired in youthful Jewish minds by the Zionist spark. Its effect upon the Jewish students of Austrian universities was immediate and striking. Until then they had been despised and often ill-treated. They had wormed their way into appointments and into the free professions by dint of pliancy, mock humility, mental acuteness, and clandestine protection. If struck or spat upon by 'Aryan' students, they rarely ventured to return the blow or the insult. But Zionism gave them courage. They formed associations and learned athletic drill and fencing. Insult was requited with insult, and presently the best fencers of the fighting German corps found that Zionist students could gash cheeks quite as effectually as any Teuton, and that the Jews were in a fair way to become the best swordsmen of the university. Today the purple cap of the Zionist is as respected as that of any academical association.
>
> This moral influence of Zionism is not confined to university students. It is quite as noticeable among the mass of the younger Jews outside, who also find in it a reason to raise their heads, and, taking their stand upon the past, to gaze straightforwardly into the future.

Our Duty.

Since the Jewish Problem is single and universal, the Jews of every country should strive for its solution. But the duty resting upon us of America is especially insistent. We number about 3,000,000, which is more than one-fifth of all the Jews in the world—a number larger than that comprised within any other country, except the Russian Empire. We are representative of all the Jews in the world; for we are composed of immigrants, or descendants of immigrants coming from every other country, or district. We include persons from every section of society, and of every shade of religious belief. We are ourselves free from civil or political disabilities; and are relatively prosperous. Our fellow Americans are infused with a high and generous spirit, which ensures approval of our struggle to ennoble, liberate, and otherwise improve the condition of an important part of the human race; and their innate manliness makes them sympathize particularly with our efforts at self-help. America's detachment from the old world problem relieves us from suspicions and embarrassments frequently attending the activities of Jews of rival European countries. And a conflict between American interests or ambitions and Jewish aims is not conceivable. Our loyalty to America can never be questioned.

Let us therefore lead—earnestly, courageously and joyously in the struggle for liberation. Let us all recognize that we Jews are a distinct nationality of which every Jew, whatever his country, his station or shade of belief is necessarily a member. Let us insist that the struggle for liberty shall not cease until equality of opportunity is accorded to nationalities as to individuals. Let us insist that full equality of opportunity cannot be obtained by Jews until we, like members of other nationalities shall have the option of living elsewhere or of returning to the land of our forefathers.

Organization.

The whole world longs for the solution of the Jewish Problem. We have but to lead the way, and we may be sure of ample cooperation from non-Jews. In order to lead the way, we need not arms, but men; men with those qualities for which Jews should be peculiarly fitted by reason of their religion and life: men of courage, of high intelligence, of faith and public spirit, of indomitable will and ready self-sacrifice; men who will both think and do; who will devote high abilities to shaping our course, and to overcoming the many obstacles which must from time to time arise. And we need other, many, many other men—officers commissioned and non-commissioned, and common soldiers in the cause of liberty, who will give of their effort and resources, as occasion may demand, in unfailing and ever strengthening support of the measures which may be adopted. Organization, thorough and complete, can alone develop such leaders and the necessary support.

Organize, Organize, Organize—until every Jew in America must stand up and be counted—counted with us—or prove himself wittingly or unwittingly, of the few who are against their own people.

Brandeis's Jewish American Zionism

1. *The Jewish problem.* OED defines "the Jewish problem" (used interchangeably with "the Jewish question") as "a question or debate about the appropriate status, rights, and treatment of Jewish people within a nation state or in society in general." It describes the term as "historical" or "offensive" and "often [used] in anti-Semitic contexts."[35] How does Justice Brandeis define the Jewish Problem? What are the overlaps and discontinuities between a global "Jewish Problem" and the specific problems confronting American Jews? How does he think (his formulation of) Zionism helps solve his formulation of either problem?

2. *Nationality and nation.* What is Brandeis's view on the relationship between nationality and nation? What are the key elements that define Jewish nationality? In what circumstances and on what basis are Jews and others entitled to legal personhood?

3. *Zionism.* The OED defines Zionism as "originally: a movement among Jewish people for the re-establishment of a Jewish nation in Palestine. Later: a movement for the development and protection of the state of Israel. Also: advocacy of or support for this."[36] How does Brandeis describe the aims and goals of Zionism? Which stream or streams of Zionism inform Justice Brandeis's essay?

4. *Multiple loyalties.* What is Brandeis's argument regarding the compatibility of Zionism and American patriotism? Consider Brandeis's views on multiple loyalties through the lens of First Amendment rights, particularly freedom of association and expression.

5. *Demoralization.* In what sense did Brandeis think Jews in general and American Jews in particular were demoralized? How did he think Zionism could uplift them?

6. *Judaism.* What's the relationship between Brandeis's analysis and Judaism? How do his ideas about preserving Jewish culture and identity relate to current legal debates on religious freedom and accommodation?

7. *Non Jews and Zionism.* How might various groups of non-Jewish Americans in the early 20th century have responded to Brandeis's arguments? How might responses differ today?

8. *Brother Daniel.* How might Brandeis have decided *Rufeisen v. Minister of the Interior* (1962)?

9. *Multiculturalism.* Consider Brandeis's ideas about Jewish identity and assimilation as they relate to multiculturalism.

10. *Group-based rights.* Brandeis writes that "Jews collectively should likewise enjoy the same right and opportunity to live and develop as do other groups of people." Is there a connection between the recognition of Jewish self-determination under international law and the extension of civil rights statutes' coverage to Jews? What legal

---

35. *Jewish question*, Oxford Eng. Dictionary, https://doi.org/10.1093/OED/4783894721 (last visited Dec. 4, 2024).

36. *Zionism*, Oxford Eng. Dictionary (2023), https://doi.org/10.1093/OED/6544780727.

basis or bases for extending coverage—race, religion, national origin, etc.—might Brandeis support?

11. *Brandeis's* Whitney *concurrence.* Consider this passage from Justice Brandeis's concurrence in *Whitney v. California* (1927), which Professor Vincent Blasi describes as "what may be the most important judicial opinion ever written on the subject of freedom of speech."[37]

> Those who won our independence believed that the final end of the State was to make men free to develop their faculties, and that, in its government, the deliberative forces should prevail over the arbitrary. They valued liberty both as an end, and as a means. They believed liberty to be the secret of happiness, and courage to be the secret of liberty. They believed that freedom to think as you will and to speak as you think are means indispensable to the discovery and spread of political truth; that, without free speech and assembly, discussion would be futile; that, with them, discussion affords ordinarily adequate protection against the dissemination of noxious doctrine; that the greatest menace to freedom is an inert people; that public discussion is a political duty, and that this should be a fundamental principle of the American government. They recognized the risks to which all human institutions are subject. But they knew that order cannot be secured merely through fear of punishment for its infraction; that it is hazardous to discourage thought, hope and imagination; that fear breeds repression; that repression breeds hate; that hate menaces stable government; that the path of safety lies in the opportunity to discuss freely supposed grievances and proposed remedies, and that the fitting remedy for evil counsels is good ones. Believing in the power of reason as applied through public discussion, they eschewed silence coerced by law—the argument of force in its worst form. Recognizing the occasional tyrannies of governing majorities, they amended the Constitution so that free speech and assembly should be guaranteed.

Are there affinities between Brandeis's *Whitney* concurrence and his defense of Zionism? Consider connections concerning self-development, participation, courage, discussion, pluralism, conformity, reason, liberty, and minorities. Are there circumstances in which restricting (i.e., repressing) hate speech could counter hate? Are there reasons specific to antisemitism that limit the efficacy of anti-antisemitic speech to remedy antisemitic speech?

12. *Relevance*? How relevant do you think Brandeis's arguments about Jewish nationality and Zionism are in today's context? How does Brandeis's vision of Zionism compare to the realities of the modern state of Israel?

---

37. Vincent Blasi, *The First Amendment and the Ideal of Civic Courage: The Brandeis Opinion in Whitney v. California*, 29 Wm. & Mary L. Rev. 653, 660 (1988).

13. *Blind spot.* Jeffrey Rosen argues that Brandeis's blind spot was his failure to anticipate or to understand Arab nationalism and appreciate its power.[38] How does Brandeis address, directly or indirectly, the potential conflict between the Zionist project and the indigenous Arab population in Palestine? What solution might he have favored to the ongoing conflict?

Matthew Silver, *Louis Brandeis and Louis Marshall vs. Anti-Zionists* (2024)

In 1906–1907, Louis Marshall, a New York City attorney and later the most prominent Jewish communal leader in the U.S., became embroiled in a controversy about Zionism. This generated out of a debate at the Jewish Theological Seminary (JTS), a major religious institution for American Jewry, affiliated with its Conservative stream, whose reorganization Marshall championed in this period. Marshall's mentor-colleague, the powerful banker Jacob Schiff, advocated a strong anti-Zionist position, arguing that Jewish nationalist activity in the United States would encourage many Americans to impugn the patriotic loyalty of American Jews. The educational/administrative leader at JTS, Solomon Schechter, disagreed, and this distinguished scholar-rabbi's challenge to Schiff, a key JTS funder, instigated debate, and forced American Jews to clarify their orientations toward organized Zionism, which had been formally founded in Europe just a decade before by Theodor Herzl.

Anti-Zionism in America included, perhaps surprisingly, many American Jews, particularly from the Reform movement, who worried that Jewish nationalism would compromise their hard-won socioeconomic status in the United States. On an ideological level, Reform Judaism asserted that Jewishness in the modern world is a religious, rather than national, identity, and hence conferences of leading Reform rabbis, dating back to the mid-1880s (that is, years before Herzl formally organized Jewish nationalism) issued statements condemning Zionism.

This anti-Zionist position had several variations, and combined ideology and social anxiety. Its core, as exemplified by arguments issued by Schiff, was the double loyalty issue whereby American Jews worried that if they worked for Jewish settlement in Turkish-controlled (later, British-controlled) Palestine, others would assert that they had diluted loyalty and were not fully American. Of course, anti-Semites and other gentile Americans exploited this "double loyalty" line of thought—for instance, a generation after this 1906 turning point, Ford's *Dearborn Independent* reformatting of the *Protocols* asserted, mendaciously, that Zionists were leading players in an international Jewish conspiracy.

---

38. Rosen, *supra* note 27 at 175.

Before WWI, no less than they were compelled to confront gentile Americans on the Zionist issue, American Jews were compelled to confront their own, often-conflicted, attitudes about Jewish nationalism. A growing part of the American Jewish community in this period was composed of immigrants from Eastern Europe, that is, persons who had often faced vicious forms of antisemitism in their former homes, who spoke a "Jewish" language (Yiddish), and who were used to living mostly among other Jews—for these, and related, reasons, these Jewish immigrants had strong inclinations in favor of Zionist ideology and activity. On the other hand, as Jewish immigrants who were heavily invested in gaining a notch of socioeconomic security in the United States, they were highly sensitive about loyalty issues. They had especially acute reasons to worry about "double loyalty" accusations connected to Zionism.

These are the circumstances in which Louis Brandeis's 1915 essay, "The Jewish Problem and How to Solve It," can be read as a kind of legal brief in a public trial prosecution of anti-Zionism. Brandeis draws a few distinctions, such as one between "nation" and "nationality," which might be regarded, in 1915 and also 110 years later, as semantic hair-splitting; but the main purpose of his words can be read between the lines, particularly when we keep in mind the conflicted view of his Jewish listeners/readers, many of them pro-Zionist immigrants who were kept in check by double loyalty concerns.

Brandeis's argument is that American-based activity for Zionism will *enhance* Jews' credibility and viability as American citizens, rather than compromising it. Part of this argument was the assumption that Americans who display pride in their ethnonational ancestry will be more confident, emotionally healthy citizens who are better appreciated by their neighbors. Aphoristically, Brandeis proclaimed that being a better American meant being a better Jew, and that being a better Jew meant being a Zionist.

Another part of this argument brief against anti-Zionism, one which appears only in embryonic form in this essay, is a "cultural pluralist" position holding that America's sociopolitical system, as envisioned by its constitutional founders, inherently values ethnonational diversity. This position (later known as multiculturalism) was more fully espoused the same year in a landmark essay written by a university philosophy professor, Horace Kallen. A Zionist, Kallen collaborated closely with Brandeis, who became in this period a uniquely successful organizational leader of American Zionism, concurrent with his appointment as a Supreme Court Justice.

While Brandeis became a Zionist, as the term came to be defined in the American setting, Marshall attacked anti-Zionism on the basis of another, third, ideological position. Neither an anti-Zionist nor an organized Zionist, Marshall and the American Jewish Committee (AJC) developed what became known as the "non-Zionist" position. Its supporters distanced themselves from the political objectives of organized Zionism, meaning that they took exception to Jewish nationalism's agenda of creating a sovereign Jewish state. Their reservations largely stemmed from familiar "double loyalty" concerns; but these non-Zionists also realized that the overall aim of security for Jews, wherever they lived, would never really be served by a situation in which Zionists and anti-Zionists openly maligned one another, as seemed to be happening in

1906–1907, when the American Jewish community's prominent philanthropist, Schiff, openly quarreled with its prominent scholar-theologian, Schechter.

In addition, as has been the case with Jews for centuries, these non-Zionists had powerful religious and sentimental attachments to the ancestral, "Eretz Israel" homeland of the Jews. Despite reservations about "political" Zionism, many of these non-Zionists, including Marshall, were deeply inspired by the accomplishments of Zionist pioneers who were in this period establishing new agricultural communes in Ottoman Palestine.

In practical terms, the non-Zionists were often quite active in philanthropy and lobbying endeavors in the support of educational, social and religious projects and programs involving Jews in Ottoman Palestine. To phrase this in contemporary terms, the non-Zionists were passionately pro-Israel, even though they had reservations about the political policies and intentions of the organized Zionist leadership of pre-1948 Israel.[39] In fact, in the 1920s, Marshall became an important collaborator with the World Zionist Organization's leader, Chaim Weizmann. As a non-Zionist, Marshall represented American Jewry as a whole in constructive negotiations with Weizmann, which culminated in an arrangement by which American Jews, and other overseas Jews, became delegates on the Jewish Agency, which functioned before Israeli statehood in 1948 as the governing body for Jews who lived in British Mandatory Palestine.

Palestine, in the late stages of WWI, passed from Turkish to British control, and became committed to support for a "Jewish National Home" in the country. This was thanks to Weizmann's signature accomplishment, Britain's issuance of the "Balfour Declaration" in November 1917.

In America, this landmark development for Zionism kept hundreds of thousands of Jews in a state of suspense. In New York City and elsewhere, the masses of Jewish immigrants, who were favorably disposed to Zionism, celebrated the Balfour Declaration announcement, but they were also wary that American Jewry's veteran leaders, anti-Zionists like Schiff, who harbored legitimate double loyalty concerns, might publicly oppose Britain's new policy of support for a Jewish National Home.

This is why the Marshall-written brief, the AJC statement on the Balfour Declaration (April 1918), is a critical document in the case against anti-Zionism. Under Marshall's leadership, the AJC clearly announced that non-Zionism, rather than anti-Zionism, was, or ought to be, the representative American Jewish position regarding Jewish nationalism. In other words, Marshall and the Committee announced that while many

39. Editor's note: David Baddiel has a different take on what it means to be a non-Zionist today:

> My position on Israel is: I don't care about it more than any other country, and to assume I do is racist. To assume that I have to have a strong position either way on Israel is racist. Because I am a British person—a Jew, yes, but my Jewish identity is about Groucho Marx, and Larry David, and Sarah Silverman, and Philip Roth, and Seinfeld, and Saul Bellow, and pickled herring, and north London seders, and my mother being a refugee from the Nazis, and wearing a yarmulke at my Jewish primary school—and none of that has anything to do with a Middle Eastern country three thousand miles away.

David Baddiel, Jews Don't Count: How Identity Politics Failed One Particular Identity 93–94 (2021).

American Jews had concerns about Zionism's political objectives, they were nonetheless sympathetic toward what Jewish nationalism was accomplishing in Palestine, as it passed on to British Mandatory control.

A careful reading of this document shows that Marshall and other non-Zionists firmly affirmed that their understanding of Jewish experience in Eretz Israel differed from how Zionism conceptualized it. The basis of Jewish settlement in the country, the statement proclaimed, was not a political nationalist program but rather "religious or historic associations." Nonetheless, the document emphatically rejected anti-Zionism as a viable position for American Jews. In words that envisioned and enabled a wealth of future American Jewish activities on behalf of Israel, Marshall, wrote that the AJC greeted the Balfour Declaration "with profound appreciation."

Sources

MATTHEW MARK SILVER, LOUIS MARSHALL AND THE RISE OF JEWISH ETHNICITY IN AMERICA: A BIOGRAPHY (2013).

MATTHEW MARK SILVER, ZIONISM AND THE MELTING POT: PREACHERS, PIONEERS, AND MODERN JEWISH POLITICS (2020).

JEWISH PUBLICATION SOC'Y, 1 LOUIS MARSHALL: CHAMPION OF LIBERTY: SELECTED PAPERS AND ADDRESSES (Reznikoff, Charles, ed. 1957).

Varieties of Zionism[40]

1. *Diaspora Zionism* sees Zionism as providing, in the words of Henrietta Szold, American Zionist and founder of Hadassah, "a center from which Jewish culture and inspiration will flow," and provide Diaspora Jews—and above all American Jews—with a source of "spiritual nourishment from a center dominated wholly by Jewish traditions and the Jewish ideals of universal peace and universal brotherhood."[41]

2. *Political Zionism*, championed by Theodor Herzl, "emphasizes the need for a Jewish state to rescue the Jewish people." In Herzl's formulation, Zionism had both a negative and a positive agenda. The negative agenda was to defend Jews from antisemitism: he wrote that "we shall live at last as free people on our own soil, and in our own homes peacefully die." The second agenda was to provide Jews with a project to exercise collective agency and self-fulfillment: "the world will be liberated by our freedom, enriched by our wealth, magnified by our greatness."[42]

3. *Labor Zionism*, epitomized by kibbutzim, "focus[ed] on farming, unions, socialist structures, secular egalitarianism, and state-building," and envisioned Jewish national liberation through Jewish-specific participation in international proletarian revolution.

---

40. Gil Troy, *Zionism: A Response to Antisemitism? in* THE ROUTLEDGE HISTORY OF ANTISEMITISM 390–397 (Mark Weitzman et al. eds, 2023).

41. *Id.*

42. *Id.* at 390.

4. *Religious Zionism* sees Zionism as a holy endeavor emanating from the Hebrew Bible and the divine plan for the Jewish people's redemption.

5. *Cultural Zionism*, championed by Ahad Ha'am, drew upon the Jewish people's spiritual and cultural heritage, which it defined more broadly than traditional Judaism.

6. *Revisionist Zionism* focused on the creation and maintenance of a Jewish state and deemphasized what it saw as excursions into socialism, Judaism, and Jewish culture. Ze'ev Jabotinsky, its premier exponent, wrote that:

> The phenomenon called Zionism may include all kinds of dreams—a "model community," Hebrew culture, perhaps even a second edition of the Bible—but all this longing for wonderful toys of velvet and silver is nothing in comparison with that tangible momentum of irresistible distress and need by which we are propelled and borne.

7. *Identity Zionism.* Historian Gil Troy champions what he calls "Identity Zionism," which he describes as a "patchwork quilt" that weaves together the other streams:

> True, the State is established—but it is not yet perfected. True, challenges of delegitimization, terrorism, and the quest for peace loom. But Identity Zionism embraces Zionism, and Jewish peoplehood, as collective, rooted, identity-building platforms in an increasingly alienated, individuated world. . . .[43]

8. *Zionism and the Justices.* Which stream or streams of Zionism inform the opinions of Justices Silberg, Landau, Berinson, and Cohn, and Justice Brandeis in his 1915 essay?

43. *Id.* at 396.

Chapter 5

Jews as Racist

In the previous chapter, we heard Jewish actors discuss Jewish matters on Jewish terms—an internal perspective. In this chapter, we hear a particular external perspective, one that accuses Jews and Jewish collectivities of engaging in racist conduct and endeavors due to reasons that may inhere in Jews and/or Judaism. This accusation has appeared in some U.S. and U.K. court opinions and a resolution adopted by the United Nations General Assembly.

A degree of endogamy has proved essential to the Jewish people's continued existence. To encourage endogamy, some Jews require their descendants to marry Jews to receive their inheritances. When inserted into wills and trusts, these restrictions are known as "Jewish Clauses." In Section A, "Are Jewish Clauses Racist?" considers five cases, two American and three English, that touch on the question of whether Jewish Clauses are racist towards non-Jews.

Section B, "Are Halakhically-Based Admissions Policies Racist?" examines the case *R(E) v. Governing Body of JFS* (2010), decided by the UK Supreme Court. It involved an Orthodox Jewish day school in England which, in accordance with its halakhically-based admissions policy, rejected a child whose mother was not Jewish and who had not converted to Judaism according to Halakhah. The rejected applicant challenged the school's policy under the Race Relations Act 1976, and most justices deemed it racially discriminatory. A lower court judge compared it to Apartheid.

Section C, "Is Zionism Racist?" concerns Resolution 3379, adopted by the U.N. General Assembly on November 10, 1975, which declared that "Zionism is a form of racism." The U.S. voted against it and Daniel Patrick Moynihan, the U.S. Ambassador to the U.N., delivered the U.S. response, which is set forth below. The section then examines the allegation, made by the Association of American University Professors (AAUP), that unspecified persons—including "well-funded political organizations"—characterize "pro-Palestinian speech or critiques of the Israeli state as invariably antisemitic." In "No One Believes that Any Criticism of Israel is Invariably Antisemitic," Professor David Schraub analyzes this allegation and its implications for scholars who study antisemitism.

A. Are Jewish Clauses Racist?

Jewish Clauses, which can vary from document to document, raise several legal questions: (1) Are they constitutional—most critically, do they violate the Equal Protection Clause? This determination turns on whether Jewish Clauses are racially discriminatory and, if so, whether their judicial enforcement unduly enlists the state's aid in effecting the discrimination. (2) Are the terms of a specific Jewish Clause so unreasonable as to violate public policy? (3) Is a specific Jewish Clause's conception of "Jew" or "Jewish" sufficiently clear for judges to understand it? (4) Do the Jewish Clause's provisions enable courts to readily ascertain whether a would-be spouse is a "Jew" or "Jewish"?

Judicial interpretation of Jewish Clauses can reveal judicial attitudes about who Jews are and what they're like. In trusts and estates law, is a person's Jewish status based on race, ethnicity, or religion? Are these categories legally tractable? Should public policy favor Jewish survival or oppose it as racist?

Shapira v. Union Nat. Bank

315 N.E.2d 825 (Ohio Ct. Com. Pl. 1974)

JUDGE HENDERSON.

This is an action for a declaratory judgment and the construction of the will of David Shapira, M.D. [deceased]....

The portions of the will in controversy are as follows....

> My son Daniel Jacob Shapira should receive his share of the bequest only, if he is married at the time of my death to a Jewish girl whose both parents were Jewish.... In the event, however, that my said son Daniel Jacob is unmarried within the seven (7) years after my death to a Jewish girl whose both parents were Jewish, or if he is married to a non-Jewish girl, then his share of my estate ... should go to The State of Israel, absolutely.

Daniel Jacob Shapira, the plaintiff, alleges that the condition upon his inheritance is unconstitutional, contrary to public policy, and unenforceable because of its unreasonableness, and that he should be given his bequest free of the restriction. Daniel is 21 years of age, unmarried and a student at Youngstown State University.

The provision in controversy is an executory device or legacy, under which vesting of the estate of Daniel Jacob Shapira or the State of Israel is not intended to take place necessarily at the death of the testator, but rather conditionally, at a time not later than seven years after the testator's death.

Constitutionality

Plaintiff's argument that the condition in question violates constitutional safeguards is based upon the premise that the right to marry is protected by the Fourteenth Amendment to the Constitution of the United States. *Loving v. Virginia* (1967)....

It appears clear, as plaintiff contends, that the right to marry is constitutionally protected from restrictive state legislative action. Plaintiff submits, then, that under the doctrine of *Shelley v. Kraemer* (1948), the constitutional protection of the Fourteenth Amendment is extended from direct state legislative action to the enforcement by state judicial proceedings of private provisions restricting the right to marry. Plaintiff contends that a judgment of this court upholding the condition restricting marriage would, under *Shelley v. Kraemer,* constitute state action prohibited by the Fourteenth Amendment as much as a state statute.

In *Shelley v. Kraemer,* the United States Supreme Court held that the action of the states to which the Fourteenth Amendment has reference includes action of state courts and state judicial officials. Prior to this decision the court had invalidated city ordinances which denied blacks the right to live in white neighborhoods. In *Shelley v. Kraemer,* owners of neighboring properties sought to enjoin blacks from occupying properties which they had bought, but which were subjected to privately executed restrictions against use or occupation by any persons except those of the Caucasian race. Chief Justice Vinson noted... "these are cases in which the purposes of the agreements were secured only by judicial enforcement by state courts of the restrictive terms of the agreements."

In the case at bar, this court is not being asked to enforce any restriction upon Daniel Jacob Shapira's constitutional right to marry. Rather, this court is being asked to enforce the testator's restriction upon his son's inheritance. If the facts and circumstances of this case were such that the aid of this court were sought to enjoin Daniel's marrying a non-Jewish girl, then the doctrine of *Shelley v. Kraemer* would be applicable, but not, it is believed, upon the facts as they are.

Counsel for plaintiff asserts, however, that his position with respect to the applicability of *Shelley v. Kraemer* to this case is fortified by two later decisions of the United States Supreme Court: *Evans v. Newton* (1966), 382 U.S. 296 and *Pennsylvania v. Board of Directors of City Trusts of the City of Philadelphia* (1957), 353 U.S. 230.

Evans v. Newton involved land willed in trust to the mayor and city council of Macon, Georgia, as a park for white people only, and to be controlled by a white board of managers. To avoid the city's having to enforce racial segregation in the park, the city officials resigned as trustees and private individuals were installed. The court held that such successor trustees, even though private individuals, became agencies or instrumentalities of the state and subject to the Fourteenth Amendment by reason of their exercising powers or carrying on functions governmental in nature. The following comment of Justice Douglas seems revealing: "If a testator wanted to leave a school or center for the use of one race only and in no way implicated the State in the supervision, control, or management of that facility, we assume arguendo that no constitutional difficulty would be encountered." The case of *Pennsylvania v. Board,* as the full title, above, suggests, is a case in which money was left by will to the city of Philadelphia in trust for a college to admit poor white male orphans. The court held that the board which operated the college was an agency of the state of Pennsylvania, and that, therefore, its refusal to admit the plaintiffs because they were negroes [*sic*] was discrimination by the state forbidden by the Fourteenth Amendment.

So, in neither *Evans v. Newton* nor *Pennsylvania v. Board* was the doctrine of the earlier *Shelley v. Kraemer* applied or extended. Both involved restrictive actions by state governing agencies, in one case with respect to a park, in the other case with respect to a college. Although both the park and the college were founded upon testamentary gifts, the state action struck down by the court was not the judicial completion of the gifts, but rather the subsequent enforcement of the racial restrictions by the public management.

Basically, the right to receive property by will is a creature of the law, and is not a natural right or one guaranteed or protected by either the Ohio or the United States constitution.... This would seem to demonstrate that, from a constitutional standpoint, a testator may restrict a child's inheritance. The court concludes, therefore, that the upholding and enforcement of the provisions of Dr. Shapira's will conditioning the bequests to his sons upon their marrying Jewish girls does not offend the Constitution of Ohio or of the United States.

Public Policy

The condition that Daniel's share should be "turned over to him if he should marry a Jewish girl whose both parents were Jewish" constitutes a partial restraint upon marriage. If the condition were that the beneficiary not marry anyone, the restraint would be general or total, and, at least in the case of a first marriage, would be held to be contrary to public policy and void. A partial restraint of marriage which imposes only reasonable restrictions is valid, and not contrary to public policy. The great weight of authority in the United States is that gifts conditioned upon the beneficiary's marrying within a particular religious class or faith are reasonable....

There can be no question about the soundness of plaintiff's position that the public policy of Ohio favors freedom of religion.... However, the controversial condition in the case at bar is a partial restraint upon marriage and not a covenant to restrain the freedom of religious practice; and, of course, this court is not being asked to hold the plaintiff in contempt for failing to marry a Jewish girl of Jewish parentage....

Counsel for the plaintiff asserts that the number of eligible Jewish females in this county would be an extremely small minority of the total population especially as compared with the comparatively much greater number in New York, whence have come many of the cases comprising the weight of authority upholding the validity of such clauses. There are no census figures in evidence. While this court could probably take judicial notice of the fact that the Jewish community is a minor, though important segment of our total local population, nevertheless the court is by no means justified in judicial knowledge that there is an insufficient number of eligible young ladies of Jewish parentage in this area from which Daniel would have a reasonable latitude of choice. And of course, Daniel is not at all confined in his choice to residents of this county....

> In the opinion of this court, the provision made by the testator for the benefit of the State of Israel upon breach or failure of the condition is most significant.... It demonstrates the depth of the testator's conviction. His purpose was not merely a negative one designed to punish his son for not carrying out his wishes. His unmistakable testamentary plan was that his possessions be used to encourage the preservation of the Jewish faith and blood, hopefully through his sons, but, if not, then through the State of Israel. Whether this judgment was wise is not for this court to determine. But it is the duty of this court to honor the testator's intention within the limitations of law and of public policy. The prerogative granted to a testator by the laws of this state to dispose of his estate according to his conscience is entitled to as much judicial protection and enforcement as the prerogative of a beneficiary to receive an inheritance.
>
> It is the conclusion of this court that public policy should not and does not preclude the fulfillment of Dr. Shapira's purpose, and that in accordance with the weight of authority in this country, the conditions contained in his will are reasonable restrictions upon marriage, and valid.

Jewish Clauses and Jewish Survival

1. *Freedom of disposition.* The Restatement (Third) of Property provides that "the organizing principle of the American law of donative transfers is freedom of disposition," and that "property owners have the nearly unrestricted right to dispose of their property as they please."[1] In determining the meaning of a gift's terms, "the controlling consideration ... is the donor's intention."[2] As a result, "the donor's intention is given effect to the maximum extent allowed by law."[3]

Even so, the testator's freedom to condition gifts is not unlimited. The Restatement (Third) of Trusts provides that:

> Although one is free to give property to another or to withhold it, it does not follow that one may give in trust with whatever terms or conditions one may wish to attach. This is particularly so of provisions that the law views as exerting a socially undesirable influence on the exercise or nonexercise of fundamental rights that significantly affect the personal lives of beneficiaries and often of others as well.[4]

---

1. Restatement (Third) of Prop.: Wills and Donative Transfers § 10.1 cmt. a (Am. L. Inst. 2003). The Restatements are scholarly works published by the American Law Institute, an independent organization of legal scholars, judges, and expert practitioners. The Restatements attempt to both synthesize the prevailing common law and propose changes to it. By themselves, Restatements are not law: they are instead a secondary source intended to guide judges how to apply and develop the law. Judges can choose to follow or ignore them as they think best.
2. *Id.* § 10.1.
3. *Id.*
4. Restatement (Third) of Trusts § 29 (Am. L. Inst. 2003).

Daniel argues that Dr. Shapira's exercise of his freedom of disposition via the Jewish Clause must be set aside because it violates his fundamental and constitutionally protected right to marry and because it unduly affects his personal life.

2. *Why marry Jewish?* Why would Dr. Shapira want Daniel to marry someone Jewish? Perhaps he believed that by marrying someone Jewish, Daniel was more likely to have a happy marriage, well-adjusted children, a robustly Jewish family life, and pass on Jewish heritage to the next generation.[5]

3. *Two Jewish parents.* In Orthodox Judaism, a person whose mother is Jewish when the person is born is Jewish, as is a person who converts to Judaism. Dr. Shapira undoubtedly knew this. By requiring the wife to be born Jewish and have two Jewish parents, Dr. Shapira ruled out a spouse who converted to Judaism or whose parents converted to Judaism after she was born. (Note that Dr. Shapira does not rule out a spouse whose parents converted to Judaism before the woman was born.) Why might Dr. Shapira have added these requirements? Note that the court uses the term "Jewish parentage" to refer specifically to the spouse's parents, as opposed to Jewish ancestry defined more broadly.

4. *A "Jewish" girl.* Although Dr. Shapira specifies that anyone Daniel marries would have to be born Jewish and have two Jewish parents, his will does not define the term "Jewish" or what would constitute a Jewish person. There are several possibilities. Dr. Shapira might have meant someone whose parents (a) were halakhically Jewish, i.e., Jewish according to Orthodox Jewish law, which requires being born to a halakhically Jewish mother; (b) were Jewish according to Reform Judaism, which could apply to someone with a non-Jewish mother and a Jewish father; (c) self-identified as Jewish, even if they were not Jewish according to either Orthodox or Reform Judaism; or (d) some other criteria. If and when Daniel presents a spouse whom he claims is Jewish, the court will have to sort this matter out. Do you envy the court its task? What are some different ways this could play out?

5. *Void for vagueness?* Rather than having to define "Jewish," Judge Henderson could simply have voided the Jewish Clause as vague, i.e., "couched in general or indefinite terms; not definitely or precisely expressed; deficient in details or particulars."[6] This would permit Daniel to take the gift free of the condition. Because it is vague, the clause

---

5. Doron Kornbluth, *Why Marry Jewish?* OHR SOMAYACH (Feb. 2004), https://ohr.edu/1480. According to Kornbluth:

> When one marries another Jewish person, the chances of a family's Jewishness lasting increase exponentially. In the vast, vast majority of intermarried families, Jewishness simply doesn't last. Even amongst [intermarried] families where the kids are being raised as "Jews only," 79% celebrate Christmas in some form. Only 11% of the children of intermarriage would be "very upset" if their kids did not regard themselves as Jews. Less than 10% of the children of intermarriage themselves marry Jews.

6. *Vague*, OXFORD ENG. DICTIONARY, https://doi.org/10.1093/OED/1009237772 (last visited Jan. 1, 2025); *see also*, *Vague*, BLACK'S LAW DICTIONARY (12th ed. 2024) (defining "vague" as "1. Imprecise or unclear by reason of abstractness; not sharply outlined; indistinct; uncertain. 2. Of language describing a distribution around a central norm, as opposed to a neatly bounded class; broadly indefinite; not clearly or concretely expressed. 3. Characterized by haziness of thought."

is arguably unfair to Daniel because it does not give him proper notice of the criteria for assessing a spouse's Jewishness. It may also be difficult for a court to ascertain its meaning and/or apply it.

6. *Seven years.* Dr. Shapira's will gave Daniel seven years to find a wife who met the will's conditions.[7] Rather than seeking to have the condition stricken and obtain the gift outright, why didn't he wait seven years to see if he could find a suitable wife in that time? If seven years weren't enough, what were Daniel's options?

7. *Gift over.* What role did Dr. Shapira's gift over to the State of Israel play in Judge Henderson's analysis?

8. *Race-based restraints on marriage.* The Restatement (Second) of Property asserts that "If a restraint designed to prevent the marriage of the transferee to a person of another race is judicially enforced, the enforcement may constitute state action resulting in a denial of the equal protection of the law."[8] Daniel did not argue that the Jewish Clause was racially discriminatory. Would that argument have merit? Judge Henderson asserted that Dr. Shapira was concerned about the "preservation" of Jewish "blood."[9] What role did blood preservation or purity (if that's what Judge Henderson meant) play in his analysis? Was Dr. Shapira a racialist, racist, and/or Jewish supremacist towards non-Jews? Assume that Daniel married someone whose parents were Lutherans of Swedish ancestry who converted to Judaism before the spouse's birth, retaining of course their Swedish ancestry, thereby satisfying the terms of Dr. Shapira's gift. In what sense would such a gift preserve Jewish "blood"? Does a convert to Judaism thereby acquire Jewish ancestry? How might Judge Henderson's characterization of Dr. Shapira's motive be restated?

9. *Acquired Jewish ancestry.* Many converts to Judaism acquire a Hebrew name, with men taking the name Abraham and women taking the name Ruth or Sarah, daughter of Abraham. The Jewish Virtual Library explains this practice as follows:

> Two reasons are offered for naming converts Avraham. First, the Bible (Genesis 17:5) speaks of Abraham as being "the father of a multitude of nations," and since proselytes come from diverse peoples and backgrounds, it is appropriate that they be called the sons and daughters of Abraham.
>
> A second explanation, offered in the Midrash, runs as follows: Since the Children of Israel are called G-d's "friends," as it is written, "the seed of Abra-

---

7. Professor Robert Sitkoff suggests that the donative transfer should have been set up as a trust, thereby allowing the estate to close rather than be left open for seven years. JESSE DUKEMINIER & ROBERT H. SITKOFF, WILLS, TRUSTS, AND ESTATES 1–3 (11th ed., professor materials, 2021).

8. RESTATEMENT (SECOND) OF PROP.: DONATIVE TRANSFERS § 6.2 (AM. L. INST. 1983); *see also* RESTATEMENT (THIRD) OF TRUSTS § 29 (AM. L. INST. 2003) ("the temper of society will reject restraints involving race as contrary to public policy") (quoting Gareth H. Jones of Cambridge University, *The Dead Hand and the Law of Trusts*, in DEATH, TAXES AND FAMILY PROPERTY 119 (1977)).

9. *See Blood*, OXFORD ENG. DICTIONARY, https://doi.org/10.1093/OED/1014922293 (last visited Sep. 2024) ("Ties of birth or heredity, esp. those connecting a person to his or her parents or ancestors; family background, lineage, descent; (also more widely) nationality, ethnicity, race."). OXFORD ENG. DICTIONARY, https://doi.org/10.1093/OED/1014922293 (last visited Sep. 2024).

> ham My [G-d's] friend" (Isaiah 41:8), and since proselytes are called G-d's "friends," as it is written, "G-d is the friend of the proselyte" (Deuteronomy 10:18), it was concluded that Abraham has a special relationship to proselytes. In Jewish tradition, Abraham becomes known as "the father of proselytes" because once non-Jews have converted to Judaism, their legal connection with their former non-Jewish families is, for the most part, severed, and the family of Abraham is now their family. The Talmud calls them, "newborn babies"[10] (Yevamot 22a).

In Judaism, converts may be said to acquire Jewish ancestry. In what sense does it preserve Jewish "blood"—Judge Henderson's word—for Daniel to a marry a Jewish woman whose Swedish Lutheran parents converted to Judaism before she was born?

10. *The Lieberman solution.* Professor Robert Sitkoff relates how Senator Joseph Lieberman handled a similar situation:

> Senator Joseph Lieberman, the unsuccessful Democratic candidate for Vice President in 2000, declined to enforce a religious restriction as the executor of his uncle's estate. The restriction would have disinherited two of his cousins for marrying persons who were not born Jewish. Instead, he brokered a deal whereby the spouses of the disinherited cousins converted to Judaism and the cousins' shares were restored. Lieberman said that his uncle "knew who he was making the executor.... He knew that these were my cousins and that I love them, and that by my nature I'm not as hard as the will was. He knew what I would do." Did Lieberman betray his uncle's trust or carry out his uncle's intent?[11]

11. *Postscript on Daniel.* Professor Sitkoff reports that:

> In 1994, [the late Professor Jesse Dukeminier] asked the lawyer who represented Daniel Shapira for information about the aftermath of the litigation. The lawyer contacted Mr. Shapira, who declined to give any information. It was a bitter experience, he said, one that he wanted to forget. Was this what Dr. Shapira had intended as his posthumous legacy?[12]

12. *Why marry a Jewish ally?* In her 1947 novel, *Gentleman's Agreement,* Laura Z. Hobson makes the case that non-Jewish allies against antisemitism should marry like-minded individuals.[13] The 1947 film based on Hobson's novel starred Gregory Peck playing Phil Green, a non-Jewish ally.[14] Dave Goldberg, a Jewish friend of Phil's,

---

10. *Issues in Jewish Ethics: Conversion to Judaism,* Jewish Virtual Libr., https://www.jewishvirtuallibrary.org/conversion-to-judaism (last visited Oct. 23, 2024).

11. Jesse Dukeminier & Robert H. Sitkoff, Wills, Trusts, and Estates (11th ed. 2021).

12. *Id.* at 11.

13. Laura Z. Hobson, Gentleman's Agreement (1947).

14. The film won eight Academy Awards, including the award for Best Picture and Best Actor in a Leading Role (Peck). *Gentleman's Agreement Awards,* IMDB, https://www.imdb.com/title/tt0039416/awards/ (last visited Dec. 16, 2024).

explains to Kathy—Phil's soft-on-antisemitism fiancée—why she and Phil might not be well-suited for each other.

Dave

Phil will fight. He can fight. He always will fight.

Kathy

And if I just sit by and feel sick, then I'm not a fit wife for him. It was always on those deeper issues that we had our quarrels. Always.

Dave

A man wants his wife to be more than just a companion, Kathy, more than his beloved girl ... more than even the mother of his children. He wants a sidekick, a buddy ... to go through the rough spots with. And well, she has to feel that the same things are the rough spots ... or they're always out of line with each other.[15]

Assume an ally against antisemitism wants their child to marry an ally. How might that person draft a will or trust to increase the likelihood of that happening?

Does Judicial Enforcement of Jewish Clauses Implicate the State in Racial Discrimination?

1. *The right to marry.* In *Loving v. Virginia*, 388 U.S. 1 (1967), the U.S. Supreme Court held that Virginia's anti-miscegenation statute, which banned interracial marriages, violated the Due Process Clause of the Fourteenth Amendment, which protects the right to marry, regardless of race or ethnicity, as fundamental. The Court, per Chief Justice Earl Warren, stated that, "The freedom to marry has long been recognized as one of the vital personal rights essential to the orderly pursuit of happiness by free men. ..." *Id.* at 12. The Supreme Court confirmed this right in *Obergefell v. Hodges*, 576 U.S. 644 (2015), which invalidated bans on same-sex marriage. Delivering the opinion of the Court, Justice Kennedy wrote that "the right to personal choice regarding marriage is inherent in the concept of individual autonomy." The right to marry is thus a fundamental right protected by the Due Process Clause of the Fourteenth Amendment, which provides that no State shall "deprive any person of life, liberty, or property, without due process of law." *Id.* at 664.

2. *State action.* The Equal Protection Clause of the Fourteenth Amendment provides that "no State shall ... deny to any person within its jurisdiction the equal protection of the laws." The Equal Protection Clause thus restricts only "state action," defined as "anything done by a government; especially in constitutional law, an intrusion on a person's rights (especially civil rights). ..." Historically, "state action" did not apply, without more, to the acts of private individuals.

15. Scripts, https://www.scripts.com/script-pdf/8852 (last visited Dec. 16, 2024).

How does the court distinguish *Shelley* from *Evans v. Newton* and *Pennsylvania v. Board*? What are the policy concerns that inform *Shelley*? Are these present in the other two cases? Are these concerns present where, as in *Shapira*, judicial enforcement of inheritance conditions indirectly influence a would-be beneficiary's marital choices?

3. *Judicial enforcement can be "state action."* In *Shelley v. Kraemer*, 334 U.S. 1 (1948), the Court held that judicial enforcement of an anti-Black restrictive covenant violated the Equal Protection Clause. What are the limits to the principle? Under *Shelley*, does the Equal Protection Clause constitutionalize all judicial enforcement of private arrangements? Presumably, the state could not condition gifts on whether an individual marries a Jewish person. Does judicial enforcement of such a condition constitute "state action"? How airtight is the constitutional distinction between: (a) a court enforcing a will provision disinheriting Daniel for marrying a non-Jew? and (b) a court granting Dr. Shapira's request for an order enjoining Daniel from marrying a non-Jew? In both cases, Dr. Shapira enlists the court's aid in restricting Daniel's ability to marry the person of his choice. How does Judge Henderson address this concern?

4. *Restrictive covenants.* Can the marriage restriction Dr. Shapira imposes on Daniel's inheritance be meaningfully compared to and/or distinguished from a racially restrictive covenant, separate and apart from the issue of whether state action is present?

5. *Dr. Shapira's free exercise.* Judge Henderson notes that the Jewish clause manifested Dr. Shapira's desire "that his possessions be used to encourage the preservation of the Jewish faith and blood." Would judicial non-enforcement of the Jewish clause interfere with Dr. Shapira's religious exercise?

Are Jewish Clauses Unreasonable? Do They Violate Public Policy?

1. *Public policy.* Public policy denotes "the collective rules, principles, or approaches to problems that affect the commonwealth or (especially) promote the general good; specifically, principles and standards regarded by the legislature or by the courts as being of fundamental concern to the state and the whole of society."[16] Public policy favors freedom in the choice of a mate.[17]

2. *Restraint on marriage.* A restraint on marriage is a condition in a disposition intended to curtail the beneficiary's choice of marriage partner.[18] Courts will invoke public policy to invalidate restraints on first marriages that unreasonably limit the transferee's opportunity to marry. The unreasonableness of a limit is defined in terms of the likelihood that a permitted marriage will actually occur.[19] In *Maddox v. Maddox's*

---

16. *Public Policy*, Black's Law Dictionary (12th ed. 2024).

17. Restatement (Second) of Prop.: Donative Transfers § 6.2 cmt. a (Am. L. Inst. 1983).

18. *Restraint of Marriage*, *in* A Dictionary of Law (10th ed. 2022), https://www-oxfordreference-com.proxy.ulib.uits.iu.edu/view/10.1093/acref/9780192897497.001.0001/acref-9780192897497-e-3403.

19. Restatement (Second) of Prop.: Donative Transfers § 6.2 cmt. f (Am. L. Inst. 1983).

Administrator, 52 Va. (11 Grat.) 804 (1854), the court held that a gift to a woman conditioned on her marrying a Quaker was void as unreasonable, noting that less than six eligible Quakers lived in the vicinity.

Did Dr. Shapira unduly limit Daniel's choice of spouse? (Keep in mind that it did not suffice for the woman to be Jewish; *both* her parents had to be Jewish.) Would it be unreasonable to expect him to move to a city with a larger Jewish population? Have the costs of finding a Jewish spouse changed since 1974?

3. *Daniel's religious exercise.* Does the Jewish Clause violate public policy by unreasonably interfering with Daniel's freedom of religious practice?[20] That would be the case if the Jewish Clause conditioned Daniel's gift on his adherence to the beliefs and practices of Judaism.[21] Yet, such inducements must operate directly on the beneficiary. Daniel, of course, is free to go to synagogue and so forth, regardless of his choice of spouse. But is that where the bulk of Jewish living occurs? For example, if he marries a Christian, he's more likely to be hanging ornaments on Christmas Eve. If he marries a Jewish person, he's more likely to be eating Chinese food on Christmas. Judge Henderson did not address the cultural and ethnic dimensions of Jewish life.

4. *Apostate.* If Daniel converted to Christianity, would this change the analysis? The Restatement provides that "if marriage within the [membership of a designated religious faith] would be so contrary to the [transferee's] beliefs that it is unlikely that such marriage will ever occur, the restraint is general and invalid."[22] As a Christian convert, how likely would Daniel be to marry a Jew?

In re Estate of Feinberg

891 N.E.2d 549 (Ill. App. Ct. 2008), rev'd, 919 N.E.2d 888 (2009)

[Max Feinberg included a Jewish Clause in a trust he created to benefit his grandchildren. The executor of Mr. Feinberg's estate refused to distribute the trust's benefits to any of his grandchildren who married non-Jews. The grandchildren challenged the Jewish Clause, which the trial court invalidated as against public policy. *In re Feinberg* (Ill Cir Ct, Cook County 2006), the executor appealed the decision to the Appellate Court of Illinois, whose ruling, set forth below, affirmed the trial court's opinion. The Illinois Supreme Court reversed the Appellate Court's decision on technical grounds.]

Justice Cunningham delivered the opinion of the Court.

Max's trust contained the following provision, which the parties refer to as the Jewish clause:

---

20. Note that such provisions are invalid as against "public policy," as opposed to infringements on constitutionally protected religious freedom. Restatement (Third) of Trusts § 29 (Am. L. Inst. 2003).

21. *Id.* cmt. k (stating that a trust provision is "ordinarily invalid if its enforcement would tend to restrain the religious freedom of the beneficiary by offering a financial inducement to embrace or reject a particular faith or set of beliefs concerning religion.").

22. Restatement (Second) of Prop.: Donative Transfers § 6.2 (Am. L. Inst. 1983).

> A descendant of mine other than a child of mine who marries outside the Jewish faith (unless the spouse of such descendant has converted or converts within one year of the marriage to the Jewish faith) and his or her descendants shall be deemed to be deceased for all purposes of this instrument as of the date of such marriage....

The Restatement (Third) of Trusts provides that trust provisions which are contrary to public policy are void. It gives as a specific example a provision that all of a beneficiary's rights to a trust would terminate if he married a person who was not of a specified religion:

> A trust provision is ordinarily invalid if it tends seriously to interfere with or inhibit the exercise of freedom to marry ... by limiting the beneficiary's selection of a spouse....
>
> The marriage condition terminates all of [beneficiary] N's rights if, before termination of the trust, he "should marry a person who is not of R Religion," with the same gift over to C College. The condition is an invalid restraint on marriage; the trust and N's rights will be given effect as if the marriage condition and the gift over to C College had been omitted from the terms of the trust.[23]

We hold that under Illinois law and under the Restatement (Third) of Trusts, the provision in the case before us is invalid because it seriously interferes with and limits the right of individuals to marry a person of their own choosing. The provision's clear intent was to influence the marriage decisions of Max's grandchildren based on a religious criterion and thus to discourage marriage by the grandchildren other than to those of the Jewish faith. This provision violated public policy.... As there is clearly a nonconstitutional basis on which to resolve this issue, we need not determine whether the provision is also a violation of the state and federal constitutions.

Affirmed and remanded.

Presiding Justice Quinn, specially concurring.

I completely concur with Justice Cunningham's majority opinion. I write separately to express the bases of my disagreement with Justice Greiman's dissent.... The dissent asserts that "Max and Erla had a dream," and that they "seek to preserve their 4,000-year-old heritage by providing that upon their death, a grandchild who married outside of the Jewish faith shall be deemed to have predeceased the testators." Unfortunately, this noble defense of "the Jewish Clause" is refuted by the appellants [trustees of Max and Edna's trust] themselves.... "If a Feinberg grandchild were to convert to Catholicism there is no restriction on that grandchild receiving his or her distribution under the Max Trust B."

---

23. Restatement of Trusts § 29, Explanatory Notes, Comment j, Illustration 3, at 62–64 (3d ed. 2003).

While the dissent frames the issue as being whether Max and Erla could make testamentary dispositions "to preserve their 4,000-year-old heritage," the position it espouses could just as well result in the courts being required to enforce the worst bigotry imaginable ... [citing cases upholding conditions not to marry "Papists" or "Scots"]. Logically, the dissent would uphold the "Jewish Clause" in the instant case if it had provided that any of Max and Erla's grandchildren would lose their bequests if they had married someone who was Jewish or Black or a member of any other group Max did not like....

In *Shelley v. Kraemer* (1948), the Supreme Court relied on the fourteenth amendment in striking down privately executed restrictive covenants prohibiting real property from being used or occupied by any persons except those of the Caucasian race. In doing so, Chief Justice Vinson noted, "These are cases in which the purposes of the agreements were secured only by judicial enforcement by state courts of the restrictive terms of the agreements." *Shelley* v. Kraemer ... I am aware that the Shapira court rejected the applicability of *Shelley* to cases such as the instant one, holding:

> In the case at bar, this court is not being asked to enforce any restriction upon Daniel Jacob Shapira's constitutional right to marry. Rather, this court is being asked to enforce the testator's restriction upon his son's inheritance.

However, I believe that this rationale may be a distinction without a difference....

One of the decisions relied upon by the dissent illustrates the difficulties which face courts in attempting to enforce certain "partial restraints." In *In re Kempf's Will*, 252 A.D. 28, 297 N.Y.S. 307 (1937) the court interpreted the following testamentary condition:

> The bequest of a legacy on condition that the beneficiary "shall be brought up and educated in the faith of and according to the Roman Catholic Religion, otherwise this paragraph of this, my last will and testament, shall cease and be void and of no effect."

The court held that the beneficiary failed to comply with this condition even though he had been baptized as a Catholic, attended Catholic Sunday school, and attended mass at various Roman Catholic churches with "reasonable regularity" for years. The beneficiary had missed attending his first communion due to illness and never received communion. The court found that this failure violated the testamentary condition and, therefore, the bequest to the beneficiary was denied.

In the instant case, the appellees question what would occur if one of the grandchildren initially married a non-Jew but subsequently married a Jew. Under the "Jewish Clause" the grandchild would be deemed to be deceased as of the date of the first marriage. The question arises as to whether the grandchild would be "resurrected" upon marrying the Jewish spouse. While the question is only theoretical, it is a very likely scenario. I believe that courts are ill-suited to decide this issue or the issue presented in *Kempf*....

As quoted in the dissent, "It is generally held in this country that partial restraints on marriage are valid unless unreasonable..." While the Restatement (First) and (Second) of Trusts explained that restraints such as the instant "Jewish Clause" were once considered reasonable, the Restatement (Third) of Trusts now provides that they are no longer reasonable. While many jurists, notably the Justices of the United States Supreme Court who adhere to the principle of following the "original intent" of the framers of the constitution believe in a static jurisprudence, the authors of the Restatements do not. I believe the Restatement (Third) of Trusts § 29 (2003) is correct and I concur in affirming the circuit court's well-reasoned decision.

JUSTICE GREIMAN, dissenting.

Max and Erla Feinberg seek to preserve their 4,000-year-old heritage by providing that upon their death, a grandchild who married outside the Jewish faith shall be deemed to have predeceased the testators, but if they have complied with the restrictions, are to immediately receive their legacy....

Gifts which are conditioned upon children being brought up and educated in the faith of and according to the Roman Catholic religion have been held as valid. In *In re Kempf's Will*, 297 N.Y.S. 307 (1937), the New York Supreme Court, after observing the federal constitution's first amendment, stated:

> These constitutional guarantees of religious freedom are limitations upon the power of government, not upon the right of an individual to make such testamentary disposition of his property as he may desire provided always that positive law or public policy is not contravened. We find nothing in the condition here in question which deprives the petitioner of freedom of conscience as to his religion; nor is it against public policy.... Having chosen to make the petitioner an object of his bounty, the testator had the right to burden his gift with conditions.

The concurring opinion reaches out to *Shelley v. Kraemer*, where the United States Supreme Court held that restrictive covenants prohibiting real property from being used or occupied by any persons except those of the Caucasian race were invalid. In *Shelley*, the covenants were placed upon the real estate by grantors that had no relationship whatsoever with subsequent grantees or grantors. The covenants could affect the transfer of real property from grantors to grantees, neither of which had any relationship with the original creator of the restriction, and would continue for decades, generations and perhaps forever. In the case at bar, we have a man and woman placing restrictions on a gift to their grandchildren and those gifts do not touch upon strangers in the distant future.

Moreover, in *Shelley*, the court understood its limitations and provided that its holding would only provide authority for enforcement by state courts allowing them to refuse to enforce restrictive covenants that violate the equal protection clause of the fourteenth amendment, stating: "That Amendment erects no shield against merely private conduct, however discriminatory or wrongful."

The concurring opinion further suggests there are difficulties which face courts in attempting to enforce certain partial restraints. Indeed, there are. For example, in matters where there is a question as to whether the beneficiary has "been brought up and educated in the Roman Catholic religion or whether he attended Catholic Sunday school and attended mass at various Roman Catholic churches with 'reasonable regularity' for years," the court would be required to inquire as to whether the legatee heir performed various religious rites. However, that is not the case here, where there is no suggestion that the spouses of the grandchildren are Jewish....

Accordingly, the great weight of authority as to cases which have considered this subject have held such provisions as it appears in the case at bar to be reasonable and not contrary to the state's public policy. The majority places us in the minority of jurisdictions that have considered this issue.

Max and Erla had a dream with respect to the provisions of their will and if you will it, it is no dream.[24]

Jewish Clauses and "the Worst Bigotry Imaginable"

1. *A re-restatement.* The traditional rule, outlined in the Restatement (Second) of Property (1983), provides that restraints on marriage to a member of a designated religious faith are valid unless they unreasonably restrict the beneficiary's ability to marry.[25] Based on scant discussion and no authority, the Restatement (Third) of Trusts, issued between 2003–2012, would courts have invalidated such a marriage condition?

2. *We hold under the Restatement.* Judge Cunningham asserts that "we hold under Illinois law and under the Restatement (Third) of Trusts" that the condition was invalid. The assertion is peculiar because courts are tasked with deciding cases under the controlling law—in this case, Illinois law and federal law. By themselves, Restatements have no legal force, nor are they co-equal sources of law: they only extend to jurisdictions whose judges find them persuasive and elect to follow them. The proper framing would have been: "Finding the Restatement to be persuasive on such-and-such a point, we hereby adopt it on that point." Assuming this is what Judge Cunningham thought he was doing, he failed to explain *why* he found the Restatement persuasive on this point, nor does he cite authority for the "public policy" he claims the condition violated.

3. *Different results.* What accounts for the different results in *Shapira* and *Feinberg*? What did the two courts disagree about? What factors did one court consider that the other did not, and vice versa?

4. *Refuted?* Justice Quinn claims that Justice Greiman's position is "refuted" by the fact that the condition would not apply to any grandchild who apostatized. Revisit the discussion above concerning Daniel's hypothetical apostasy. Where's the refutation?

---

24. Judge Greiman here quotes Theodor Herzl, the founder of modern political Zionism, from his 1902 book, *Altneuland* (translated as "Old New Land"). Note that Judge Grieman, like Dr. Shapira and Judge Henderson, perceived a connection between the Jewish continuity project and the Zionist project.

25. Restatement (Second) of Prop.: Donative Transfers § 6.2 (Am. L. Inst. 1983).

5. *The worst bigotry imaginable.* In Justice Quinn's view, Justice Greiman's dissent has dangerous implications. Specifically, the position Justice Greiman articulates:

> could just as well result in the courts being required to enforce the worst bigotry imaginable.... Logically, the dissent would uphold the "Jewish Clause" in the instant case if it had provided that any of Max and Erla's grandchildren would lose their bequests if they had married someone who was Jewish or black or a member of any other group Max did not like....

Can you identify a principle that would (a) permit a court to enforce a Jewish parent's gift conditioned on the child marrying a Jewish person? and (b) invalidate a Jew-hater's gift conditioned on the child *not* marrying a Jew, a.k.a., a "Klansman Clause"? Is there a principle that would permit the court to enforce an African American Clause but not a Klansman Clause? A gift conditioned on the child marrying an African American spouse? Are these the same principles?

6. *A "noble defense."* The Oxford English Dictionary (OED) defines "noble" as "characterized by moral superiority or dignity; elevated, lofty."[26] When used sarcastically, the word "noble" serves to mock someone's words or actions and suggest that the person is hypocritical, self-serving, self-righteous, and so forth. Does Judge Cunningham use "noble" sarcastically? If so, what would warrant that? What would be his point?

7. *A distinction without a difference?* Justice Quinn asserts that *Shapira* cannot be meaningfully distinguished from *Shelley* such that Dr. Shapira's condition must be invalidated? Is he right?

8. *Max's religious exercise.* Does the court interfere with Max's religious exercise by invalidating the Jewish Clause? According to several Orthodox advocacy groups, Max's Jewish Clause was "an act of religious conviction."

> For a Jew to condition a bequest on his or her descendants not marrying outside the faith is an act of religious conviction. A core component of Jewish religious law and tradition is that one of the most significant duties of any Jewish parent or grandparent is to teach Jewish religious law to his or her descendants and to transmit his or her heritage to subsequent generations. By contrast, Jewish religious law prohibits intermarriage and treats it as an abandonment of the faith—recognizing that the descendants of an intermarried couple are either unlikely to maintain their Jewish identity or will not even be Jewish at all....
>
> Max's attachment to his religious heritage was informed by his experiences with anti-Semitism. His parents fled from Russia in the beginning of the twentieth century in order to avoid widespread pogroms against Jews. When he was a teenager, he was aware of Ku Klux Klan marches in Chicago, as well as the anti-Semitic broadcasts of Father Coughlin during the 1930s. As a young adult, Max learned, along with the rest of the world, of the Holocaust.

---

26. *Noble*, Oxford Eng. Dictionary, https://doi.org/10.1093/OED/2762579915 (last visited Jan. 1, 2025).

> Max worried that his Jewish heritage would not be passed down to succeeding generations because of the rising rate of intermarriage. After becoming aware that more than fifty percent of Jews were intermarrying, he told his family that he feared "potential extinction of the Jewish people." Max acted on his desire to perpetuate his Jewish heritage and to encourage his grandchildren to marry into the faith by including the Religious Preference Clause to incentivize his grandchildren to marry only Jewish spouses.

9. After Mr. Feinberg's death, his widow, Erla, modified the will's terms so that it rewarded a grandchild's past decision to marry a Jewish partner, and thus did not influence or interfere with their future choice of spouse. This obviated the concern that the gift interfered with their choice of spouses. So modified, the trust was distinguishable from the Restatement: in its hypothetical, N's vested interest was terminated in the event he married a person who is not of the specified religion. It is thus an open question whether Dr. Shapira's Jewish Clause, which sought to influence Daniel's future choice of spouse, violates Illinois public policy.

10. *Gifts conditioned on a Jewish upbringing.* In *In re Lesser's Estate*, 158 Misc 895 (N.Y. Sur. Ct. 1936), a court upheld a gift to the testator's grandchildren on condition that they be raised Jewish. The gift would be paid on each grandchild's twenty-first birthday:

> provided these children are given a normal Jewish, liberal education including an ability to read Hebrew, up to and including at least their fourteenth year: and, further, provided that the Jewish dietary laws are observed by their parents.... If these conditions are not complied with to the complete satisfaction of my executor or his successor or successors, then the funds herein bequeathed are to go to the Federation for the Support of Jewish Philanthropic Societies of New York City.

The court observed that "there is nothing any more contrary to our policy in the requirement of a testator that his beneficiary should espouse and be trained in a certain religious faith, than in a stipulation that he shall marry one of a certain belief, which has been sustained." In other words, if courts permit a testator to induce a child to marry a Jewish person, he can induce them to raise their children Jewish. *In re Lesser's Estate*, 158 Misc. 895, 901 (Sur. Ct. N.Y. County 1936). In the court's view, public policy favors gifts that promote the perpetuation of Judaism.

> It is in the interest of the state that uprightness and morality be fostered and any person who would fully adhere to the tenets of any of the standard religions of the world would closely approximate a model of rectitude. It is a psychological principle that inner grace, if not necessarily a concomitant, is frequently a promoted consequence of outward manifestation. It follows that strict adherence by these children, during their formative years, to the teachings and observances of one of the greatest of present-day religions which had its beginnings before the dawn of secular history, cannot reasonably be considered other than as beneficial to the individuals themselves, and thus, indirectly, to the state.

In re Lesser's Estate, 158 Misc 895, 901 [Sur. Ct. 1936].

11. *Are Jewish Clauses judicially manageable?* Citing *In re Kempf's Will*, 297 N.Y.S. 307 (1937), Justice Quinn worries that if courts are called upon to enforce a Jewish Clause—for example, to decide whether a person is Jewish—they will be at sea. How do you assess his concern and Justice Grieman's response?

12. *Shelley v. Kraemer.* Justice Quinn argues that the Equal Protection Clause applies equally to judicial enforcement of restrictive covenants and gift restrictions. In Judge Henderson's and Justice Grieman's view, the Clause should apply to the former but not the latter. Who has the better argument?

Gentlemen's Agreements

1. *No non-gentiles. Harris v. Sunset Islands Prop. Owners, Inc.*, 116 So. 2d 622 (Fla. 1959) involved the case of B.J. Harris, a Jewish man who purchased a lot in Sunset Islands, a development in Dade County, Florida. The lot was subject to a restrictive covenant that it could not be sold "to any person not of the Caucasian race, or who is not a Gentile, or who has been convicted of a felony...." Sunset Islands sued to remove Harris from the development, and the Dade County Circuit Court ordered Harris to sell the property and leave. On appeal, the Supreme Court of Florida, citing *Shelley v. Kraemer*, reversed this ruling on the grounds that judicial enforcement of the covenant "denied to the appellants the equal protection of the laws and in so doing inspired state action proscribed by the Fourteenth Amendment." The Supreme Court criticized the lower court's failure to grapple with *Shelley*.

> The rule of *Shelley v. Kraemer* ... has become so thoroughly grounded in the decisions of the state courts around the country as well as in the courts of the federal system that only a total blindness to the compelling and controlling aspects of the decision would enable us to avoid it.[27]

2. *Did* Loving *and* Shelley *bar anti-Jewish restrictive covenants?* In *Loving*, the Supreme Court declared that "the clear and central purpose of the Fourteenth Amendment was to eliminate all official state sources of invidious racial discrimination in the States." 388 U.S. at 10. This would preclude restrictive covenants concerning Asians, Native Americans, and other archetypal non-white races. Should Jews, though not a race, be treated as a race under *Shelley* and the Equal Protection Clause? The *Harris* court did not address this question.

3. *Jewish race stipulated.* In another Florida case, a restrictive covenant prohibited the sale of property "by any person of the Semitic branch of the Caucasian race." *Steuer v. Glevis*, 243 So 2d 453, 453 (Fla. Dist. Ct. App. 1971). In their lawsuit, the Jewish plaintiffs in turn identified themselves as "members of the Semitic branch of the Caucasian race." Citing *Shelley* and *Harris*, the court held that "the race restriction clause

27. Harris v. Sunset Islands Property Owners, Inc., 116 So. 2d 622, 625 (Fla. 1959).

objected to by the plaintiffs is void." The court appears to have viewed the parties' racial perception of Jews as a stipulated fact. Why might each party have agreed to it?

4. *Are Jewish racial restrictions void as uncertain?* The court might have voided the restriction as uncertain: if there's no such thing as a Jewish race, or even a "Semitic branch of the Caucasian race," then it is nonsensical to ask whether a person belongs to it. See, e.g., *Re Noble & Wolf*, [1949] Ont R 503 [1949] 4 DLR 375, revd [1951] Can SC 64, [1951] 1 DLR 321 (invalidating as uncertain restrictive covenant barring sale "to any person of the Jewish, Hebrew, Semitic, Negro or coloured race or blood"); *In Re Wren* [1945] Ont R 778, [1945] 4 DLR 674 (invalidating as uncertain a restrictive covenant that land was "not to be sold to Jews or persons of objectionable nationality").

5. *Jewish advocacy groups.* In a consolidated amicus brief filed in *Shelley*, the American Jewish Committee (AJC), Anti-Defamation League (ADL), and other Jewish groups argued that judicial enforcement of the restrictive covenant in that case violated the Equal Protection Clause. Its legal argument was trained at *anti-Black* discrimination and did not go beyond it. At the same time, the brief drew attention to restrictive covenants that discriminated against groups other than African Americans, including some, like Jews, who are *not* defined by race, and argued that they were un-American:

> The racial restrictive covenant is an instrument of bigotry giving aid and comfort to racial and religious prejudice. Implicit in such a covenant is the anti-democratic and false racist doctrine that undesirable social traits are an attribute not of the individual but of a racial or religious group. Such covenants classify an individual not on the basis of his behavior, but on the basis of his racial origin. They would deny the free choice of a home to a Carver, Cardozo, or Lin Yutang merely because of color or religion. They ascribe social objectionability to unborn generations.
>
> Slums and overcrowding are the inescapable concomitants of restrictive covenants and racial segregation. Death, disease, and crime are the notorious spawn of overcrowding. Inter-group stresses and tensions which threaten our democratic state arise inevitably when racial or religious groups find themselves isolated within the community and forced to live in circumscribed segregated areas. Clearly, the growing fusion of interest of America's varied racial, religious, and ethnic groups, the free interchange of varying cultural viewpoints, the development of mutual tolerance and confidence among our citizens—requisites for the strengthening and fulfillment of our democracy—are dangerously impeded by restrictive covenants. It is not surprising that the President's Committee on Civil Rights found that "segregation is an obstacle to establishing harmonious relationships among groups" and recommended vigorous action to outlaw restrictive covenants.
>
> Although Negroes have suffered most from the widespread use of restrictive covenants, many other groups including Mexicans, Spanish Americans, Orientals, Armenians, Hindus, Syrians, Turks, Jews, and Catholics have found such covenants barring them from many residential areas in many cities. In a

> recent case in California, a full-blooded American Indian was ordered by the court to vacate his home because of a limitation upon occupancy to Caucasians only. In a Maryland suburb of Washington, D. C., a group of homeowners, seeking to enforce a restrictive covenant against Jews, petitioned the Maryland court for a decree directing a non-Jewish wife to oust her Jewish husband from their jointly owned home. This is the reductio ad absurdum to which racial restrictive covenants lead.[28]

While the racially restrictive covenant is definitionally an instrument of racial prejudice, it provides a template for instruments giving effect to other forms of prejudice, including religious, ethnic, ancestry, and national origin. Yet the brief does not attempt to provide a doctrinal basis for extending the Equal Protection Clause's reach beyond racially restrictive covenants. In practice, however, invalidating the former served to discourage their use against Jews and other non-racial groups.

On what doctrinal basis might a court extend *Shelley* to anti-Jewish restrictive covenants? Are there principled reasons for courts not to extend *Shelley* to such covenants?

Re Samuel, Jacobs v. Ramsden

Court of Appeal of England and Wales
[1941] All ER 196

[Mr. Samuel, a Jewish testator, wished to leave his assets to his daughter, Edna, while at the same time ensuring that his property did not descend to non-Jews. To this end, he inserted a Jewish Clause into his will which provided that his daughter would forfeit her inheritance if she married a man "who is not of Jewish parentage and of the Jewish faith." After marrying a Christian Englishman, Edna challenged the provision. The trial court, per Judge Bennett, ruled that the provision was void for uncertainty, thereby permitting Edna to take the gift outright. Samuel's estate appealed this ruling. The Court of Appeal, per Lord Greene, reversed the trial court's ruling and upheld the gift condition.[29]]

Lord Greene MR delivered the opinion of the Court.[30]

The testator in this case did what many testators do, or attempt to do—namely, direct the lives of his children from the grave. Such a thing is distasteful to many people, and I can understand the court's desire to escape from such a result if the language used

---

28. Brief for Am. Jewish Comm. et al. as Amici Curiae, *Shelley v. Kraemer*, 334 US1 (1948) (No. 72) 1947 WL 44160, at *3–4.

29. Peter Butt, *Testamentary Conditions in Restraint of Religion*, 8 Sydney. L. Rev. 400, 400 (1977).

30. Editor's note: MR stands for Master of the Rolls, a judge of the Court of Appeal and the President of its Civil Division. The Master of the Rolls is second in judicial importance to the Lord Chief Justice, the head of the judicial branch in England and Wales. The Master of Rolls is responsible for the deployment and organization of the work of the judges of the division and presides in one of its courts and was originally responsible for the safekeeping of charters, patents, and records of important court judgments written on parchment rolls. *Master of the Rolls*, Cts. & Tribunals Judiciary, https://www.judiciary.uk/about-the-judiciary/who-are-the-judiciary/judges/profile-mor/ (last visited

and the law applicable so permit. In the present case, Bennett J held that the provision in question in the testator's will was void for uncertainty, and that, accordingly, the forfeiture clause did not operate. That clause was expressed in the following terms....

> I declare that if my ... daughter Edna Samuel shall at any time after my death contract a marriage with a person who is not of Jewish parentage and of the Jewish faith then [all gifts] in favour of ... my ... daughter ... shall cease....

The rest I need not read. The principles upon which forfeiture clauses are to be constructed are well-known, and I need not repeat them. It is manifest that, if a testator uses words which are insufficient to describe the conception in his mind with such distinctness as to enable practical action to be based upon them, the words must be too vague to be enforced. Words, for instance, which import conceptions involving degree or relativity may well be too vague, such as "large" or "small" or "tall." ...

In the present case, there are two questions which fall to be considered in discussing the construction of the clause.[31] The first question is what is meant by the words "Jewish parentage." ...

It appears to me that they refer to religion, and not to race.... It was contended that the words were capable of construction, and that they referred to race, and not to religion. It may very well be that, if, on the true construction of the words, they did refer to race, they might be too vague.... It is obvious, from the requirements which he lays down for the husband himself, that it is religion of which he is thinking, and it is the Jewish religion into which he wishes his daughter to marry. That, I think, gives a clue to his intention when he goes back a generation and deals with the parents of the proposed husband. It is reasonably clear that a testator actuated by motives of that kind would not wish his daughter to marry a mere proselyte, who perhaps for the very purpose of satisfying the condition had gone through the ceremony of being admitted to the Jewish faith. In order to avoid such a result, he lays down a further condition, the effect of which in popular language is to ensure that the husband shall not merely belong to the Jewish faith at the date of the marriage but shall have been born into it by reason of the fact that his parents were of that faith. I think that the argument is strengthened when it is remembered that the testator must have known that the question of what is meant by "Jewish race" is one of the greatest difficulty, and one which in practice must necessarily involve all sorts of questions and leave all sorts of matters in doubt. That, I think, is a legitimate consideration to bear in mind in selecting from the language of the testator the construction which he intended, because it must not be assumed that the testator was doing something ... the difficulties of which he was ignorant. There are two other matters with regard to the expression "Jewish parentage." The first is whether it refers to both parents or only to one, and the second is to what point of time it refers. With regard to both those questions, I feel no doubt.

Oct. 23, 2024); *see also*, *Lady Chief Justice*, CTS. & TRIBUNALS JUDICIARY, https://www.judiciary.uk/about-the-judiciary/who-are-the-judiciary/judges/lord-chief-justice/ (last visited Oct. 23, 2024).

31. That is, questions the court *must* consider to resolve the case, i.e., those that have fallen into its lap.

It seems to me that the ordinary meaning of the language in a context of this kind is that it refers to both parents and refers to the time when they became parents—that is to say, to the birth of the husband. I find no difficulty about that, and it seems to me that, on that construction, the testator was laying down a good working test to enable him to achieve the result which he obviously intended. No test, of course, can be watertight, and it might be that a husband who satisfied this condition would not have been the sort of husband whom the testator wished for his daughter. In practice, however, one would have thought that this was as good a working test as any in order to ensure that the husband of his daughter—namely, the daughter with whom we are concerned—should be so confirmed in the Jewish faith as to be not merely himself a member of it but born of parents who likewise held it....

On the footing that the words "of Jewish parentage" bear the meaning which I attribute to them, two arguments were addressed to us. First of all, it was said that there is an insuperable difficulty in ascertaining the necessary facts with regard to the parents of the husband. It was said that many Jews, both now and in earlier times, have moved about the world, that their parentage may often be unknown, that the religious beliefs of their parents may also be unknown, and that it may be impossible to establish the facts. It is to be noticed that that has really nothing to do with the question of uncertainty, because we are proceeding upon the footing that the language is certain. The argument is really directed, not to uncertainty, but to difficulties of proving facts, and, in my opinion, the mere difficulty of proving facts is not of itself sufficient to render a clause of this kind too vague.... In practice, I cannot help thinking that these questions must be approached with a certain measure of common sense. In the case of a Jew, I should have thought that it ought not to be difficult to ascertain the religion of his parents.

The next argument was directed to the alleged vagueness of the expression "of the Jewish faith," and that argument, of course, applies both to the case of the parents and to that of the husband, once the reference to the parents is construed in the way in which I have construed it. It is said that the phrase "of the Jewish faith" leaves it uncertain what tenets of that faith must be held, what degree of observance is required, and what degree of fervour in the holding of beliefs is necessary, to enable a husband to satisfy the condition.

In my judgment, an expression of this kind in such a context as this is not to be construed by reference to sectarian disputes or theological arguments, or to degrees of zeal in performance of religious duties or attendance at religious ceremonies. A much more practical test appears to me to be required. *Prima facie*, I should have thought without hesitation that the question falls to be answered out of the mouth of the person in question. Religious faith is a matter so serious that it is to be assumed that, in the normal case, a person who is asked whether or not he is a Jew by religion, or whether he belongs to any other religion, will give a perfectly conscientious answer. Counsel for the first and second respondents drew an alarming picture of this lady surrounded, like Penelope, by a crowd of suitors but condemned to perpetual spinsterhood because she would be unable to know whether or not marriage with any one of them would enable her to enjoy the advantages of a romantic union without forfeiting the solid benefits of a settled income. I should have thought that the lady, in such a situation, could resolve the question very simply by asking the gentlemen of her choice whether or not he was of the Jewish faith, and, if he answered "Yes," I should have thought that, *prima facie*, that was enough. At any rate, of one thing I feel certain—namely, that the correctness or otherwise of his confession of faith would not fall to be ascertained by calling in a rabbi to cross-examine him with regard to the tenets of the faith with a view to finding out whether he was an Orthodox Jew, a Reform Jew or a liberal Jew, or by inquiring into the precise degree of conviction or fervour with which he held certain specified tenets of the Jewish faith, or the frequency or sincerity of his observance of religious ceremonial or religious occasions. To find out whether or not a person who was born a Jew and alleged that he was a Jew had in point of fact repudiated his religion would be a matter which could be established by evidence without much difficulty, but, if a man, when asked a serious question of that kind, whether in the drawing-room or in the witness-box, answered, "I am a Jew by faith," that, I should have thought, was the most cogent evidence that it was to that religion that his adherence was devoted, be it zealous or lukewarm, be it wide enough to cover every strict and orthodox tenet of the faith or of a looser or more easy-going description....

I should mention here a distinction which it was attempted to make between the words "faith" and "religion" in a clause of this kind. It was said that "faith" involves and means, and means only, the spiritual convictions of the person in question. "Religion," on the other hand, it is said, imports not merely that, but also the element of ceremonial observance. It is to be noticed that on that argument a condition which used the word "religion" should be more vague than one which used the word "faith," because in each case the question of spiritual conviction and belief would fall to be considered, and, in the case of religion, the additional element of ceremonial observance would fall to be considered. I make that observation in view of the fact that in some of the reported cases the word "religion" has appeared, and, upon that argument, those cases were decided on a completely wrong view of the principles applicable to matters of this kind. In my judgment, there is no difference in such a context as this between the word "faith" and the word "religion." When testators frame clauses of this kind, they are not concerned with distinctions of that description. They intend the clause to be a practical working affair, and one to be construed without reference to the more subtle, and no doubt more accurate, conceptions of theologians....

Appeal allowed.

A "Good Working Test" for Determining Who Is a Jew

1. *Deadhand control.* "Deadhand control" denotes "the convergence of various legal doctrines that allow a decedent's control of wealth to influence the conduct of a living beneficiary."[32] Such measures, which include conditional gifts, are often used "to ensure

32. *Deadhand Control*, Black's Law Dictionary (12th ed. 2024).

that property remains in the hands of a particular family or organization."[33] As Lord Greene notes, many people find it "distasteful" for testators to attempt to control their children's lives and choice of spouse from beyond the grave.[34] Yet courts are tasked with "balancing" the testator's freedom of disposition and deadhand control. Lord Greene chastises judges who, on the grounds of preference or ideology, rush to subordinate freedom of disposition to weaken deadhand control. Such judges are inclined to void otherwise manageable terms as vague even where the meaning of the allegedly vague terms is ascertainable.

2. *Ambiguous versus vague.* A vague term is "imprecise or unclear by reason of abstractness" or because it is "not sharply outlined."[35] If a term is vague, it can be difficult to ascertain the testator's meaning. An ambiguous term, by contrast, is "open to more than one plausible interpretation."[36] A testator may use a term with multiple possible meanings, each of which is precise, clear, and sharply outlined. The interpretative question is which available meaning did the testator intend?

3. *Jewish parentage.* In Lord Greene's view, the Jewish Clause's use of the term "Jewish parentage" is ambiguous in two ways. First, it could refer to either: (a) the Jewish status of the spouse's parents, or (b) "the Jewish race." He chose the former meaning. Second, concerning the spouse's parents, "Jewish parentage" could refer to either (a) one parent; or (b) both parents. He chose the latter. In each case, why did he construe the term the way he did?

Judge Henderson referred to Dr. Shapira's two-Jewish-parent requirement as "Jewish parentage," which accords with Lord Greene's construction of Mr. Samuel's "Jewish parentage" as requiring two Jewish parents. In other words, parental identity denotes parentage and vice versa. This corresponds to the OED's definition of "parentage" as "the identity of one's parents."[37]

4. *Jewish religion or race.* In construing the term "Jewish parentage," Lord Greene notes that "it may very well be that, if, on the true construction of the words, they did refer to race, they might be too vague." His implicit choice is between (a) a manageable construction—were the spouse's parents Jewish in the religious sense? and (b) a potentially unmanageable construction—were the parents racially Jewish? Lord Greene also explains why he thinks Mr. Samuels meant "Jewish parentage" to refer to religion rather than race. Do Lord Greene's reasons persuade you? This reasoning points to a canon of construction: between two interpretations of a gift term, assume the testator intended the manageable (valid) one over the unmanageable (invalid) one.

---

33. *Id.*

34. See, e.g., Jeffrey G. Sherman, *Posthumous Meddling: An Instrumental Theory of Testamentary Restraints on Conjugal and Religious Choices*, 1999 U. Ill. L. Rev. 1273 (1999) (arguing against the enforcement of testamentary conditions that restrict the personal choices of legatees, particularly regarding marriage and religion).

35. *Vague*, Black's Law Dictionary (12th ed. 2024).

36. *Ambiguous*, Black's Law Dictionary (12th ed. 2024).

37. *Parentage*, Oxford Eng. Dictionary, https://doi.org/10.1093/OED/5854162348 (last visited Jan. 1, 2025).

5. *When were the parents Jewish?* In *Shapira*, Judge Henderson was not called upon to construe Dr. Shapira's requirement that an acceptable spouse is one "whose both parents *were* Jewish." Here, Lord Greene "feels no doubt" that the husband's parents are required to have been Jewish at the time of his birth. This leaves open the possibility that the parents converted to Judaism.

6. *Converts.* In Lord Greene's view, why might Mr. Samuel prefer a spouse with two Jewish parents over "a mere proselyte"? Is he onto something? Do the same reasons apply to Dr. Shapria's preference for two Jewish parents?

7. *A good working test.* Lord Greene lays down what he believes to be "a good working test" for identifying a spouse who meets Mr. Samuel's criteria. What is this test? Do you agree that it is workable in theory? In practice? Where might it encounter difficulty in application? How does Lord Greene think these difficulties could be managed?

8. *No rabbi.* Under oath, a spouse is asked, "are you a Jew by faith?" and answers, "Yes." How does Lord Greene think his answer should be evaluated? In the abstract, who is more qualified to ascertain whether the spouse is "of the Jewish faith"—a rabbi or a jury consisting mainly or exclusively of non-Jews? In the present context, to whom would Lord Greene entrust the determination and why?

9. *Secular Jews.* Assume Edna marries a halakhically Jewish man who considers himself to be Jewish ethnically, culturally, or by family background, but who does not identify with Judaism as a religion, i.e., a "secular" Jew. If he is asked under oath "are you a Jew by faith," how should he answer?

It is common for persons to self-identify as Jewish without identifying with Judaism as a religion, as indicated by the recent Pew Research survey:

> Overall, about a quarter of U.S. Jewish adults (27%) do not identify with the Jewish religion: They consider themselves to be Jewish ethnically, culturally or by family background and have a Jewish parent or were raised Jewish, but they answer a question about their current religion by describing themselves as atheist, agnostic or "nothing in particular" rather than as Jewish. Among Jewish adults under 30, four-in-ten describe themselves this way....
>
> More than eight-in-ten U.S. Jews say that they feel at least some sense of belonging to the Jewish people, and three-quarters say that "being Jewish" is either very or somewhat important to them.[38]

10. *Birthright Israel.* Birthright Israel is a nonprofit organization that arranges for eligible people of Jewish identity to visit Israel at reduced rates. It is supported by the Birthright Israel Foundation, whose mission is "to help give Jewish young adults the gift of a transformational and educational trip to Israel" and thereby help "secure a Jewish tomorrow." https://birthrightisrael.foundation/. To be eligible for such a trip, a young adult must (1) "Identify as Jewish," (2) be "recognized as [Jewish] by their local

---

38. Pew Rsch. Ctr., Jewish Americans in 2020 8, 20 (2021), https://www.pewresearch.org/wp-content/uploads/sites/20/2021/05/PF_05.11.21_Jewish.Americans.pdf.

community or by one of the recognized denominations of Judaism; and (3)(a) "have at least one Jewish birth parent" or (b) have completed Jewish conversion through a recognized Jewish denomination." Given the donors' purposes, are these conditions under or over-inclusive? How easy are they to apply? Would they supply a "good working test" for judges tasked with identifying who is a Jew under a Jewish Clause?

Clayton v. Ramsden

House of Lords
[1943] A.C. 320

[Edna Clayton appealed the Court of Appeal's ruling to the Appellate Committee of the House of Lords, then the court of last resort in the English legal system. Five Lords were empaneled and all found in Edna's favor, reversing the ruling of Lord Greene. Lord Romer delivered the opinion of the House of Lords; Lords Atkin, Russell of Killowen, and Wright wrote concurring opinions.]

Lord Romer delivered the opinion of the House of Lords.

The appellant Edna Violet Clayton was married to the appellant Harold Clayton who admittedly was not of Jewish parentage or of the Jewish faith on any reasonably possible construction of those words....

My Lords, the first question to be determined on the appeal is what is the meaning of the words "of Jewish parentage." Do they refer to race or religion? This is no doubt a difficult question to answer, but the difficulty of answering it does not render the forfeiture clause void for uncertainty. It is the duty of the court to solve the problem if it be possible to do so and for my own part I do not find it impossible. In my opinion on the true construction of this will the words refer to race and not to religion or faith, which I agree with Lord Greene MR, are for the present purpose synonymous terms. In the first place the testator in stating the qualifications that must be possessed by a husband of his daughter Edna seems to be drawing a clear distinction between parentage and faith. If he had intended that the husband should be and his parents should have been of the Jewish faith, he could so easily have said so. I cannot think that he would have used the language in which this clause is in fact expressed. In the next place it seems to me to be much more probable that, when stating the qualifications to be possessed by a husband of his daughter, the testator, while stipulating that he should be of the Jewish faith, should concern himself in addition with the racial descent of the husband rather than with the religion of the husband's father and mother. Finally, one of the meanings of the word "parentage," and I am disposed to think its primary meaning when coupled with a word indicating nationality such as Jewish, English, French or the like, is race or descent.

What then did the testator mean by the stipulation that the daughter's husband was to be of Jewish race or descent? It cannot reasonably be supposed that the husband was to show an unbroken line of descent from the patriarch Jacob. If the daughter were compelled to wait for such a husband, she would remain a spinster all her life and the condition would be void as amounting to a total restraint on marriage. It seems far more probable that the testator meant no more than that the husband should be of Hebraic blood. But what degree of Hebraic blood would a permissible husband have to possess? Would it be sufficient if one only of his parents were of Hebraic blood? If not, would it be sufficient if both were? If not, would it be sufficient if in addition it were shown that one grandparent was of Hebraic blood or must it be shown that this was true of all his grandparents? Or must the husband trace his Hebraic blood still further back? These are questions to which no answer has been furnished by the testator. It is, therefore, impossible for the court to see from the beginning precisely or distinctly upon the happening of what event it is that Mrs. Clayton's vested interests under the will were to determine, and the condition is void for uncertainty.

My Lords, this is sufficient to dispose of the appeal. If one of the two qualifications required in a permissible husband is expressed in so uncertain terms that it is impossible to say of any particular individual whether he does or does not possess it, the whole condition is void. For it is a composite qualification that is required and, if it cannot be said of an individual that he possesses part of the composite qualification, it is obvious that he cannot be said to possess the whole. It is impossible merely because the condition as to Jewish parentage fails for uncertainty to split up the forfeiture clause in such a way as to permit, for example, marriage with a husband whose ancestors have been Christian for many generations but who on the eve of the marriage has embraced the Jewish faith in the fullest sense of those words. Such a thing would be quite contrary to the testator's intention. His intention cannot be given effect to because he has not chosen to express it in sufficiently unambiguous terms. But that does not justify the court in making a new will for him and treating him as if he had expressed a different intention altogether.

Even if the clause could be read as though it merely provided for a forfeiture in the event of the daughter being married to a man not of the Jewish faith, I am of opinion that it would still be void for uncertainty. For how is it to be ascertained whether a man is of the Jewish faith? It will have been observed from what I have already said that in the Court of Appeal they answered this question by saying that whether a man was or was not of the Jewish faith was a mere question of fact to be determined on evidence and that the assertion by the man that he was of that faith was well-nigh conclusive. I should agree entirely with the Court of Appeal as to this if only I knew what was the meaning of the words "of the Jewish faith." Until I know that, I do not know to what the evidence is to be directed. There are, of course, an enormous number of people who accept every tenet of and observe every rule of practice and conduct prescribed by the Jewish religion. As to them there can be no doubt that they are of the Jewish faith. But there must obviously be others who do not accept all those tenets and are lax in the observance of some of those rules of practice and of conduct and the extent to which the tenets are accepted and the rules are observed will vary in different individuals. Now, I do not doubt that each of these last mentioned individuals, if questioned, would say and say in all honesty, that he was of the Jewish faith. On the other hand, I do not doubt that one who accepted all the tenets and observed all the rules would assert that some of the individuals I have mentioned were certainly not of the Jewish faith. It would surely depend on the extent to which the particular individual accepted the tenets and observed the rules.

My Lords, I cannot avoid the conclusion that the question whether a man is of the Jewish faith is a question of degree. The testator has, however, failed to give any indication what degree of faith in the daughter's husband will avoid and what degree will bring about a forfeiture of her interest in his estate. In these circumstances the condition requiring that a husband shall be of the Jewish faith would, even if standing alone, be void for uncertainty.

Lord Russell of Killowen, concurring.

I now turn to consider the words "of Jewish parentage." The first doubt which is obviously inherent in them is whether they refer to race or religion or both....

In my opinion, on construction, the words, "of Jewish parentage" refer to race. Other elements of doubt surround the words. Must both parents be of the Jewish race, or would one alone and which, suffice? I confess myself unable to find any context which provides an answer; but the answer may well be that, in the absence of a context to the contrary, the true construction is that both parents must be of the Jewish race. But at this point the real difficulty begins, viz, the question of degree. The testator has given no information or clue as to what percentage or proportion of Jewish blood in the husband will satisfy the requirement that he should be of Jewish parentage. The daughter could never, before marrying the man of her choice, be certain that he came up to the requisite standard of Jewish parentage, nor could a court enlighten her beforehand. The standard is unknown and incapable of ascertainment. It is this uncertainty of degree which prevents the divesting event from being seen precisely and distinctly from the beginning and which makes this condition void for uncertainty. The uncertainty attaching to the requirement of Jewish parentage avoids the whole condition subsequent, with the result that no defeasance takes place.

In these circumstances it is unnecessary to express an opinion upon the certainty of the words "of the Jewish faith"; but had it been necessary, I should have felt a difficulty in holding that their meaning was clear or certain. It seems to me that (apart from the difficulty which arises from the existence of the three varieties of Judaism referred to by Lord Greene MR) the testator has given no indication of the degree of attachment or adherence to the faith which he requires on the part of his daughter's husband. The requirement that a person shall be of the Jewish faith seems to me too vague to enable it to be said with certainty that a particular individual complies with the requirement.

Lord Wright, concurring.

The first question is whether the defeasance [of the gift] depends on one composite condition, so that if either limb is not sufficiently clear and distinct, the whole condition is void. In my opinion that is the true construction. The defeasance clause which is one and indivisible is void as a whole if one limb is void. In the language of the condition subsequent "not of Jewish parentage and of the Jewish faith," the word "and" is I think conclusive, even apart from material considerations which support that view. It is then necessary to consider each limb of the composite condition separately. In my opinion the former limb fails to pass the test of clearness and distinctness. I am prepared to accept that it refers to both parents and not merely to one; but I think it refers to race, not to faith. These may be regarded as being matters of ambiguity in construction capable of being resolved by the court. But it is a different problem to determine what is the degree of racial purity in fact required by the condition. In that respect the clause falls short of clearness and distinctness. On reading it, the court or other party interested is left in complete doubt what degree of racial purity will satisfy the condition. Is it to be 100 per cent or will 75 per cent or 50 per cent be sufficient? The words of the clause do not enable any definite answer to be given. Lord Greene MR construed the clause as referring to religion, not to race. But if they were to be construed as referring to race "they might," he said, "be too vague." On the construction which I adopt they are, I think, too vague. It is not that the language is ambiguous, so much as imperfect and incomplete. The court would have to amplify and add to it before it could be held to denote any definite set of facts. That would be to rewrite the testator's will in that respect and be beyond the competence of the court and still more of the party interested. That limb of the composite condition is therefore void and, it follows, so is the whole condition.

This conclusion renders it unnecessary to express a final opinion on the words "of the Jewish faith." As at present advised, I do not think they are of insufficient clearness and distinctness. I am not impressed by the contention that they refer to a state of mind or of religious conviction which is incapable of proof. States of mind are capable of proof like other matters of fact: courts of law and equity have to decide questions of fraudulent intent or the like.... I do not see why "Jewish faith" should not connote a specific fact equally with "Christian faith." The latter is an all-embracing term which includes many possible varieties: Roman Catholic, Anglican, Presbyterian, Lutheran and others. There are many mansions but they are all included in one house. I should not be disposed to regard "Christian faith" as a phrase lacking in clearness and distinctness. I see no reason in principle why "Jewish faith" is not sufficiently clear and distinct to identify a specific set of facts to which it may be applied. But I do not pursue these questionings. The view I have expressed on the words "Jewish parentage" is sufficient to decide the appeal with the result that in my judgment the whole condition is void...

Lord Atkin, concurring.

For my own part I view with disfavour the power of testators to control from their grave the choice in marriage of their beneficiaries and should not be dismayed if the power were to disappear.

Do Jews Use Jewish Clauses to Preserve Their Racial Purity?

1. *"The Jewish race" as an available legal construction.* Lords Romer, Russell of Killowen, and Wright all agree that "of Jewish parentage" is ambiguous and could refer either to the parents' religion or to "the Jewish race." In other words, "of the Jewish race" is an available legal construction of the term "of Jewish parentage."

2. *Who is of the Jewish race?* What possible criteria or tests do the Lords consider in ascertaining whether someone is of the Jewish race? Does one seem more suitable than the others? Are any satisfactory? Could any be reformed to make them satisfactory?

3. *A "Jewish" son-in-law.* Which son-in-law would Mr. Samuel have preferred? (a) A Christian Anglo-Saxon man whose parents converted to Judaism before his birth, or (b) A man who was born Jewish and of Jewish stock who converted to Christianity. Why does Lord Romer think that Mr. Samuel "should concern himself ... with the racial descent of the husband rather than with the religion of the husband's father and mother"? His assumption makes sense if you believe that Jews are in fact a race and possess an instinct for racial self-preservation and concern for the purity of their race.

4. *Imputed irrationality.* Why do the Lords think that by "Jewish parentage," Mr. Samuel meant "Jewish race," even though a reasonable and knowledgeable person—starting with Lord Greene—could predict that courts would void this restriction as vague?

5. *Presumption against intestacy.* What canon of construction does the Lords' analyses suggest? Where the meaning of a gift condition is ambiguous and susceptive of two meanings—one vague and the other clear—the court should select the vague meaning and then void the condition if: (a) the donor specifically intended the vague meaning, even where (b) the clear meaning would yield a result that the donor would have preferred over a voided vague term. Consider the words of Lord Esher, M.R. in *Re Harrison Estate* (1885), 30 Ch.D. 290 at 393–4:

> There is one rule of construction, which to my mind is a golden rule, viz., that when a testator has executed a will in solemn form you must assume that he did not intend to make it a solemn farce—that he did not intend to die intestate when he has gone through the form of making a will. You ought, if possible, to read the will so as to lead to a testacy, not an intestacy. This is a golden rule.

The Lords' construction of Mr. Samuel's Jewish Clause effectively rendered the testator intestate concerning the gift to Edna. What justified that?

6. *Favors Jewish converts to Christianity.* The Lords' ruling reduces the risk that Jewish converts to Christianity will be cut off by their parents. This result is consistent with English public policy as expressed, inter alia, by the 1702 Act of Parliament, which obligated Jewish parents to maintain and provide for any child who converted to Protestantism. The 1702 Act ratified the public policy announced by the Third Lateran Council (1179 C.E.) which declared that Jewish converts to Christianity "are in no way to be excluded from their possessions, since the condition of converts ought

to be better than before their conversion." In such cases, the Council enjoined secular rules "to restore fully to these converts the share of their inheritance and goods." This same policy was performed on the stage in *The Merchant of Venice*, in which Venetian law permits a Jewish convert to Christianity to benefit from her father's wealth upon her conversion.

7. *If only I knew.* What might account for Lord Romer's difficulty in understanding the meaning of the words "of the Jewish faith"? Assume Mr. Samuel's will only required Edna's husband to be "of the Jewish faith." Would the gift condition fail? Would Lords Romer or Russell of Killowen invalidate as conceptually uncertain a gift conditioned on the beneficiary's spouse being "of the Christian faith"? Lord Atkin simply stated that he disfavored posthumous meddling in a beneficiary's choice of spouse. Assuming Lord Atkin found a "Christian faith" condition to be conceptually certain, would he invalidate it nonetheless as deadhand control? Assuming English courts enforce "Christian faith" conditions, should they enforce "Jewish faith" conditions only insofar as "Jewish faith" can be analogized to "Christian faith," or Judaism to Christianity?

8. *How antisemitism deranged the House of Lords' reasoning.* Professor Robert Katz offers this interpretation of this case:

> The House of Lords found the term "Jewish parentage" ambiguous—it found it could refer to either the parents' religion or their "race." Which son-in-law would Mr. Samuel have preferred: a man of Jewish "blood" who converted to Christianity or a man of Gentile blood who converted to Judaism?
>
> The House of Lords deemed that Mr. Samuel preferred a son-in-law who was "racially" Jewish; it reasoned that Jews instinctively seek to preserve the blood purity of their race. The House of Lords then ruled that the non-existent blood purity condition it inserted into the will was void for vagueness: Mr. Samuel had not specified the quantum of Jewish blood he wanted his son-in-law to possess. This allowed Edna to inherit an unrestricted gift and marry a Christian man.
>
> The *Clayton* case is a testament to antisemitism's power to impair cognition. The House of Lords's opinion posited nonsensical canons of construction by interpreting an uncontroversial and enforceable term as having an unenforceable alternative meaning and concluding that the donor intended the unenforceable alternative meaning. It established a perverse precedent seemingly applicable only to Jews. Where a group can be legally defined by reference to either race or religion and where a racial definition would be more injurious to the group, the group should be defined (injuriously) by race. Lastly, *Clayton*'s outcome failed to honor the donor's intent, violating the central principle of donative transfer law. *Clayton*, the product of antisemitic thinking, is an embarrassment to the legal profession.[39]

39. Robert Katz, *How Antisemitism Infects the Law*, AM. BAR ASS'N (Dec. 9, 2024), https://www.americanbar.org/groups/crsj/publications/human_rights_magazine_home/combating-antisemitism/

9. *Drafting problem.* If you were Mr. Samuel's attorney, how would you have advised him? What was he trying to accomplish? What enforceable language would enable him to achieve some approximation of his goals?

Re Tuck's Settlement Trusts

Court of Appeals (England and Wales)

[1977] EWCA Civ 11

[In 1911, Sir Adolf Tuck included a Jewish Clause in a trust that conditioned gifts to his male descendants, which included a baronetcy, on their marrying women of "Jewish blood" and of "the Jewish faith." Sir Bruce Tuck, Sir Adolf Tuck's grandson, married a woman who was not Jewish. The trustees sought the court's guidance on whether the Jewish Clause was void for uncertainty. The first court, the Chancery Division of the High Court, held that the trust was valid. Sir Bruce Tuck appealed the decision to the Court of Appeals which, per Lord Denning MR, upheld the Jewish Clause. Lord Russell wrote a concurring opinion.]

Lord Denning MR delivered the opinion of the Court.

In 1910 Sir Adolph Tuck was made a baronet.[40] He was rightly proud of this dignity. It was hereditary and on his death, would pass to his successors in the male line of descent.

Being a Jew himself, he was anxious to ensure that his successors to the title should all be of Jewish blood and Jewish faith. To do this he wanted his son to marry a wife who was Jewish; and his grandson likewise to marry a Jewish wife; and so on. So in 1912 he made a settlement by which he sought to ensure that each baronet in succession should marry an "approved wife." He put money in trust for "the Baronet for the time being if and when and so long as he shall be of the Jewish faith and be married to an approved wife." In the settlement, this was the definition of "an approved wife": "'An approved wife' means a wife of Jewish blood by one or both of her parents and who has been brought up in and has never departed from and at the date of her marriage continues to worship according to the Jewish faith." Then he added this significant clause: "as to which facts in case of dispute or doubt, the decision of the Chief Rabbi in London of either the Portuguese or Anglo-German Community (known respectively as the Sephardim and the Ashkenazim Communities) shall be conclusive."

Sir Adolph himself died on 3rd July, 1926, leaving two sons and three daughters. He was succeeded by his eldest son, Sir William Tuck. He married an approved wife and had a son and daughter. Sir William died on 12th May, 1954, and was succeeded by his

how-antisemitism-infects-the-law/.

40. Editor's note: A baronet, styled as "Sir," is the lowest hereditary title in the British peerage system. Sir Adolph Tuck (1854–1926) was created a baronet by King George V in 1910 in recognition of his contributions to British industry and society, including his Jewish philanthropy. *See Baronet*, Britannica, https://www.britannica.com/topic/baronet (last visited Dec. 16, 2024); *see also William Reginald Tuck (1883–1954)*, WikiTree, https://www.wikitree.com/wiki/Tuck-244 (last updated Oct. 3, 2023).

son, Sir Bruce Tuck. Sir Bruce married first an approved wife and had two sons.[41] But in 1964 there was a divorce. In 1968 he married a lady who was not an approved wife.

Now a question arises whether the settlement is valid or not. If it is valid, the fund will go to Sir Bruce Tuck and his two sons. If it is invalid, it will go to Sir Adolph's estate.

Mr. Dillon, Q.C.[42] [attorney for Sir Bruce Tuck] submitted that the definition of "approved wife" was so uncertain as to be void for uncertainty; that this uncertainty could not be cured by referring the matter to the Chief Rabbi; and that in consequence all the provisions in the settlement referring to an "approved wife" must be disregarded.

If this argument is correct, it means that the intentions of the settlor, Sir Adolph, have been completely defeated by the ingenuity of the lawyers: first, in discovering the uncertainty; and, secondly, in refusing to allow it to be cured by reference to the Chief Rabbi. I will deal with these two points in order.

In making his submissions, Mr. Dillon, Q. C. used two phrases which have begun to fascinate Chancery lawyers. They are "conceptual uncertainty" and "evidential uncertainty." After a little probing, I began to understand a little about them. "Conceptual uncertainty" arises where a testator or settlor makes a bequest or gift upon a condition in which he has not expressed himself clearly enough. He has used words which are too vague and indistinct for a court to apply. They are not sufficiently precise. So, the court discards the condition as meaningless. It makes it of no effect....

"Evidential uncertainty" arises where the testator or settlor, in making the condition, has expressed himself clearly enough. The words are sufficiently precise. But the court has difficulty in applying them in any given situation because of the uncertainty of the facts. It has to resort to extrinsic evidence to discover the facts, for instance to ascertain those whom the testator or settlor intended to benefit and those whom he did not. Evidential uncertainty never renders the condition meaningless. The Court never discards it on that account. It applies the condition as best it can on the evidence available.

I must confess that I find the dichotomy most unfortunate. It has led the courts to discordant decisions. On the one hand, a condition that a person shall "not be of

41. Editor's note: It is unclear whether Sir Bruce's first wife, Louise Renfro, was in fact an "approved wife." Her parents were buried in a Christian cemetery and she and Sir Bruce named their second son Christopher. (Christopher later inherited the baronetcy.) The efficacy of Sir Tuck's Jewish Clause is thus open to question. *See A Genealogical Survey of the Peerage of Britain as Well as the Royal Families of Europe*, THE PEERAGE (last visited Oct. 23,2024); *see also Lula Catherine Townsend Renfro*, FIND A GRAVE, https://www.findagrave.com/memorial/99058177/lula-catherine-renfro (last visited Oct. 23, 2024); *see also Sir Bruce Tuck, 3rd Baronet 1926–2020*, PEERAGE NEWS (Jan. 30, 2020); *see also* FIND A GRAVE, https://www.findagrave.com/memorial/99058177/lula-catherine-renfro#view-photo=69166744 (last visited Oct. 23, 2024); *see also Miss Louise Renfro Will Wed Bruce Tuck of London*, SAN ANGELO WKLY. STANDARD, Feb. 25, 1949 (society page) (on file with author). The marriage between her and Sir Bruce produced their second son Christopher, who became the fourth baronet in 2020. THE PEERAGE, *supra*.

42. Editor's note: In English law, "Q.C." stands for "Queen's Counsel," an honorific given to outstanding lawyers. *Becoming a KC*, THE L. SOC'Y (Jan. 11, 2022), https://www.lawsociety.org.uk/topics/advocacy/becoming-a-kc.

Jewish parentage" has been held by the House of Lords to be void for conceptual uncertainty ... see *Clayton v. Ramsden* [1943] A.C. 320 ... [on grounds] that the testator had given no information or clue as to what percentage or proportion of Jewish blood would satisfy the requirement. Is it to be 100 per cent, or will 75 per cent or 50 per cent be sufficient? The words do not enable any definite answer to be given.

On this reasoning the condition in the Tuck settlement that an "approved wife" should be "of Jewish blood" would seem to be afflicted with conceptual uncertainty.

On the other hand, a condition that a person shall be "of the Jewish faith" has produced diverse views. Four out of five Law Lords thought that it was void for conceptual uncertainty.... *Clayton v. Ramsden* [1943]. Lord Wright thought it was sufficiently clear and distinct to be able to be applied.... I should range myself with Lord Wright. His view is supported by reference to the cases on other religions. Thus, a condition that a person should be or not be "of the Roman Catholic faith" is not open to objection on the ground of uncertainty ... nor a condition that he shall or shall not be an "adherent of the doctrine of the Church of England" ... nor a condition that he shall be "of the Lutheran religion...." The reason being in each case that evidence can be given of the tenets of that religion or faith so as to see if the person is or is not an adherent of it.

On this reasoning the condition in the Tuck settlement about "Jewish faith" would seem to be valid and not voided for conceptual uncertainty....

I deplore ... these dichotomies, for a simple reason and a good reason. They serve in every case to defeat the intention of the testator or settlor. The courts say: "We are not going to give effect to his intentions—because he has not expressed himself with sufficient distinctness or clearness." That assertion gives rise to argument without end as to whether his words were sufficiently clear and distinct....

The Chief Rabbi's Clause

How is any testator or settlor to overcome these legal difficulties? And all the costs, expense and time expended in resolving them? Sir Adolph Tuck in this settlement said: "Let any dispute or doubt be decided by the Chief Rabbi." That seemed to him a good solution, and it seems to me a good solution. The Chief Rabbi should be able to decide—better than anyone else—whether a wife was "of Jewish blood" and had been brought up "according to the Jewish faith." But Mr. Dillon, Q. C. said that that was not an admissible solution. He submitted that, in a case where there was conceptual uncertainty (where the words were not clear enough for the court) it followed inexorably that they were not clear enough for a Rabbi either....

The testator may even today think that the Courts of Law are not really the most suitable means of deciding the dispute or doubt. He would be quite right. As this very case shows, the courts may get bogged down in distinctions between conceptual uncertainty and evidential uncertainty.... The testator may want to cut out all that cackle and let someone decide it who really will understand what the testator is talking about; and thus save an expensive journey to the lawyers and the courts. For my part, I would not blame him. I would give effect to his intentions. Take this very case: Who better to decide these questions of "Jewish blood" and "Jewish faith" than a Chief Rabbi? The settlor mentions two Chief Rabbis. It is not necessary to ask both of them. Either one will suffice. I suggest that his decision would be much more acceptable to all concerned than the decision of a Court of Law. I would let him decide it.

Conclusion

So it comes to this: If there is any conceptual uncertainty in the provisions of this settlement, it is cured by the Chief Rabbi clause.... If the Chief Rabbi clause is inoperative, then I would so construe the settlement as to hold that there is no conceptual uncertainty.

Lord Russell, concurring.

What, it was asked, is involved in the concept "of Jewish blood"? Now one thing appears to me plain as a matter of construction of this settlement that the Settlor did not intend by the phrase 100 percent Jewish blood; for he in the recital expects and hopes that successive Baronets shall be born of parents both of whom shall be of Jewish blood. But the approved wife (mother of the next Baronet) need not have any Jewish blood from one of her parents. He envisages therefore the possibility of there being only *some* Jewish blood in the parents of a Baronet. Every Baronet must of course have some Jewish blood by male descent from the settlor: but that could be increasingly diluted through the generations by marriages to wives of whom it could not be said that their blood was wholly Jewish. I therefore consider that marriage to a wife of Jewish blood means a wife with some Jewish blood. It was argued that the Settlor could not conceivably have intended or envisaged a woman with some very small proportion of Jewish blood by descent: but I think here the second requirement that she "has been brought up in and has never departed from and at the date of her marriage continues to worship according to the Jewish faith" may well have been considered by the Settlor, as a practical matter, a sufficient safeguard against undue dilution of Jewish blood in the Baronetcy: for though it is theoretically possible that a girl should be brought up in the Jewish faith when her parents between them could only produce one remote ancestor with Jewish blood, it is almost inconceivable. It was also contended that if any amount of Jewish blood, however small, would qualify a wife as an approved wife it might be impossible to establish that it existed, but if that were so, the fulfilment of the qualifying or precedent condition would not be established. If I am right in construing the requirement in this case as only that the approved wife should have *some* Jewish blood, there are not the problems met with in a case in which it is required simply that X should be "of Jewish blood" or "of Jewish parentage."

Mr. Dillon for the appellants accepted that if he could not succeed in his attack based on uncertainty in the requirement of Jewish blood in an approved wife, he could not succeed on the basis of uncertainty in the various requirements of adherence to the Jewish faith.... In this I think he was right.... No doubt there are variations in rites, practices, and for ought I know, beliefs among the different groups of Jews who practice their religious faith. But I would not wish to destroy a settlement and defeat a settlor's intentions on the supposition that adherence to the Jewish faith is an unintelligible concept, any more than had the reference been to Christianity however diverse have become attitudes to the latter....

It was argued by the Respondents that this solved any question of uncertainty: for the Appellants it was argued that if the concept was uncertain this could not be a solution; if it was too uncertain for the court, it was too uncertain for the Rabbis, who could not make a trust for the Settlor, or could not oust the jurisdiction of the court to decide. I do not propose to rule upon this. No problem may arise in the spheres allotted to the Rabbis. None has arisen yet.

Rabbis, Not Courts, Should Interpret Jewish Clauses

1. *What would Lord Denning do?* How would Lord Denning have decided *Clayton*? How would Lords Greene, Romer, Russell of Killowen, and Wright each have decided *Tuck's*?

2. *A wife of Jewish blood by one or both of her parents.* Is "of the Jewish race" an available construction of the language? How is it to be determined whether one or both parents are "of Jewish blood"? Are we back to where we started in *Clayton*? Does Lord Denning assert that "of Jewish blood" is conceptually certain? If it is not conceptually uncertain, how can this condition be enforced?

3. *According to the Jewish faith.* Why does Lord Denning think this term, "according to the Jewish faith," is conceptually certain? How would it be determined in each case whether the spouse adheres to "the Jewish faith"? Even if conceptually certain, does the requirement fail for evidentiary reasons or "evidential uncertainty"?

4. *The Chief Rabbi Clause.* Lord Denning states, "if there is any conceptual uncertainty in the provisions of this settlement, it is cured by the Chief Rabbi clause." How is that possible? Does Lord Denning define conceptual uncertainty relative to a specific party? The terms "Jewish blood" and "Jewish faith" may be conceptually uncertain to members of England's Christian nobility, but conceptually certain to a rabbi or other Jewish person. Does this solve the uncertainty problem? What if the son appeals the rabbi's determination back to the House of Lords? By what standards will the Lords review the rabbi's determination? By declaring "Jewish faith" as uncertain from the outset, the Lords could avoid this situation. If there were no Chief Rabbi Clause, would the condition fail?

5. Why might the enforceability of Jewish Clauses vary across different jurisdictions and time periods?

6. Consider the potential unintended consequences of enforcing or striking down Jewish Clauses. How might these decisions impact family dynamics, religious communities, and broader social cohesion?

7. *Practitioner's note.* If you were advising a client who wanted to include a Jewish Clause in their will, what alternative approaches might you suggest to achieve their goals while minimizing legal risks?

B. Are Halakhically-Based Admissions Policies Racist?

This section explores how the Supreme Court of the United Kingdom—which in October 2009 replaced the House of Lords as the highest court in the land—applied the 1976 Race Relations Act to remedy alleged racial discrimination within the Jewish community. It discusses *R (E) v. Governing Body of JFS*, [2010] IRLR 136, SC (The JFS Case), which involved an Orthodox Jewish school that denied admission to a child who was not Jewish by Orthodox standards (the child's mother, who was not born Jewish, had converted to Judaism under non-Orthodox auspices). The Supreme Court found that this denial discriminated against the child because, on its reading, the mother was not ethnically Jewish, as opposed to the child not being halakhically Jewish. It held that this denial constituted impermissible racial discrimination under the 1976 Act, notwithstanding the Judaic basis of the admission policy. The ruling suggested that Orthodox Judaism's criterion for Jewish identity is racist. The Court of Appeal made this suggestion explicit by comparing the Orthodox school's preference for halakhically Jewish students to an Apartheid-era Dutch Reformed Church's preference for Whites over Blacks.

One of the most comprehensive judicial engagements with Jewishness in English case law was in the latter case of *R (E) v. Governing Body of JFS*. The High Court,[43] the Court of Appeal,[44] and the Supreme Court all asserted that there was no question that the group "Jews" was protected by the 1976 Act. They either relied on *Mandla* for this assertion or treated it as a matter of common sense. Questions that the *Mandla* case left open that the JFS courts had to grapple with were whether, given that ethnicity and religion are two separate things, one could be Jewish by religion and not by ethnicity, or Jewish by ethnicity and not by religion. *Mandla's* failure to resolve any of the complex issues to do with Jewish identity was apparent in the confusing judicial narratives about Jewishness in The JFS Case. The issue in the case was whether a school policy that only admitted children who were Jewish because their mother was Jewish, was a "religious" policy, or a "racial policy." The answer to this question was crucial to deciding whether the policy breached the Race Relations Act 1976, and yet *Mandla* provided no help at all.[45]

R (E) v. Governing Body of JFS (The JFS Case)

1. *Context.* The Jewish Free School (JFS) is a Jewish faith school in London that, until the Supreme Court decision in this case, relied on the Office of the Chief Rabbi (OCR) of Britain to determine who was Jewish for the purposes of its school admissions policy. In keeping with Halakhah or Orthodox Jewish law, the OCR recognizes

43. R (E) v. Governing Body of JFS [2008] ELR 445.

44. R (E) v. Governing Body of JFS [2009] 4 ALL ER 375.

45. Didi Herman, *'An Unfortunate Coincidence': Jews and Jewishness in Twentieth-century English Judicial Discourse*, 33 J. of L. & Soc'y 277–301 (2006).

Jewish status through matrilineal descent. This means that the mother of an applicant had to be Jewish, and this could be a) by birth or b) by conversion through an appropriate conversion process. The OCR does not recognize any conversion process other than its own Orthodox conversion carried out under the auspices of the London Beth Din. The Beth Din has functioned as the central Jewish religious authority in Britain since the early eighteenth century.

2. *Facts.* A pupil applied for admission to the JFS. His Italian Catholic mother had converted to Judaism under the auspices of the Reform synagogue. The OCR does not recognize the Reform synagogue's conversion process. This meant that it did not recognize the pupil applicant's mother or the pupil applicant as Jewish according to Jewish law and neither, therefore, did the JFS for the purposes of its admissions policy. Consequently, the JFS denied the pupil a place at the school. Note that schools officially designated as having a "religious character" were permitted to discriminate on religious grounds under the 1976 Act and are still permitted to do so under the Equality Act 2006.[46]

3. *Legal argument.* The pupil's father argued that the determination of Jewish status through matrilineal descent amounted to race discrimination under the 1976 Act. In other words, the mother and her son were being discriminated against because they were not genetically Jewish in the eyes of the school.

The school and the Secretary of State for Education argued that the reason for the non-admission was religious and not racial; this meant that the school had a legal right to engage in religious discrimination. The JFS did not dispute that the mother and son could be Jewish ethnically; the school's position was that, as the mother's conversion was not recognized by the Orthodox branch of Judaism to which the school belonged, the son could not be considered Jewish under Jewish law as interpreted by the OCR. If the mother had obtained a conversion through a recognized Orthodox synagogue, that would have sufficed. The Office of the Schools Adjudicator, an independent body set up to hear appeals against schools regarding admissions decisions, which reports to the Secretary of State for Education, agreed with the school. The father then launched an action for judicial review.

4. *Judicial Review.* This is an action brought before the High Court to challenge the decisions or acts of a public body. The claim is that the public body in question has not acted lawfully. The High Court acts as an administrative court and it reviews the decision and the decision-making process of the public body in question. There are three main grounds for an action of judicial review: illegality, procedural unfairness, and irrationality.

5. *The High Court decision.* The High Court upheld the school's position. The judge, Munby J., found that *Seide v. Gillett Industries Ltd.* (1980) was authority for the fact that (a) Jews were an ethnic group under the 1976 Act and (b) ethnicity and religion were two separate things. Munby reasoned that a person could be Jewish by religion rather

46. Equality Act 2006, c. 3, § 50 (U.K.).

than by ethnicity and vice versa. While ethnicity involved some element of biological descent, the reverse was not necessarily the case—a determination of descent did not necessarily involve a racial or ethnic categorization. He found that the case was one of Jewish "status"—"descent" being used to determine a child's Jewish status for the purposes of an admissions policy, not their race or ethnicity. According to Munby J., determining this status was a purely religious exercise: was this child Jewish according to Orthodox Jewish law? The discrimination was thus religious and therefore allowed under legal provisions for faith schools. Munby J. recognized that judicial meddling in religious law would not be appropriate. He said:

> The fact that ... religion is the true focus here, is illustrated ... by the very fact that at the heart of all the three cases I am considering is a dispute—a quintessentially religious dispute—about the validity of the conversion of the applicant child's mother.... A dispute about what constitutes a valid conversion is simply not a matter which engages the 1976 Act at all; it is a question of religious doctrine on which the secular courts should be wary to tread.[47]

6. *The Court of Appeal decision.* The pupil's father appealed from the High Court to the Civil Division of the Court of Appeal, presided over by three judges. A unanimous Court of Appeal overturned the High Court's decision. With little reasoning, commentary, or reference to the conversion question, the Court found that: (1) citing *Mandla* as authority, Jews constituted a racial group under the 1976 Act and any discriminatory treatment based on a person's Jewish, or non-Jewish, status was *per se* discriminatory; (2) the school clearly engaged in a racially discriminatory act against a person it defined as "not Jewish"; and (3) such an act could not be justified on any account. The Court then proclaimed that any test of "Jewishness" used by JFS must be religious and not racial.

> The refusal of JFS to admit M [the boy] was accordingly, in our judgment, less favourable treatment of him on racial grounds. This does not mean ... that no Jewish faith school can ever give preference to Jewish children. It means that, as one would expect, eligibility must depend on faith, however defined, and not on ethnicity.[48]

7. *Comparison to Apartheid.* Lord Justice Sedley in the Court of Appeal drew a parallel between the JFS admissions policy and Apartheid South Africa, arguing that it was no defense to the school's "racial" discrimination that it was based on sincerely held beliefs about what does or does not constitute a valid conversion to Judaism.

> M was refused admission to JFS because his mother, and therefore he, was not regarded as Jewish. The school has been perfectly open in giving this as the ground of non-admission. There are of course theological reasons *why* M is not regarded as Jewish, but they are not the ground of non-admission: they are the motive for adopting it.

47. R (E) v. Governing Body of JFS [2008] ELR 445, para. 171.
48. Governing Body of JFS [2009] 4 ALL ER 375, CA, para. 33, per Sedley LJ.

> If it were otherwise, a person who honestly believed, as the Dutch Reformed Church of South Africa until recently believed, that God had made black people inferior and had destined them to live separately from whites, would be able to discriminate openly without breaking the law. The reason why it is not so is that the ground of any such discrimination would be that the victim was black; its religious motive would be immaterial.[49]

Lord Justice Sedley's analogy seems to run as follows: (1)(a) Orthodox Judaism's beliefs about what constitutes a valid conversion to Judaism can result in (b) Orthodox institutions discriminating in favor of persons who converted under Orthodox auspices vis-à-vis persons who did not convert under Orthodox auspices. (2) So too, (a) the Dutch Reformed Church's belief that Whites were racially superior to Blacks could justify (b) Church discrimination in favor of Whites vis-à-vis Blacks. Do you find this analogy persuasive?

8. *The Supreme Court decision.* JFS appealed the decision of the Court of Appeal to the Supreme Court. This court was created by the Constitutional Reform Act 2005 to replace the House of Lords. Nine judges presided over the appeal. Five of the nine judges found that the JFS had engaged in direct racial discrimination. Two found there was indirect racial discrimination. Two found there was no discrimination.

Is Halakhah Racist?

1. *Majority reasoning in the Supreme Court.* The reasoning of the majority was as follows:

a. There was no question that the group "Jews" was protected by the 1976 Act. They either relied on *Mandla* for this assertion or treated it as a matter of common sense.

b. The matrilineal test was a racial test as well as a religious test as it was based fundamentally on examining the genetic descent of the mother.

c. Several of the judges decided that the group "Orthodox Jews" was a sub-ethnicity of the group "Jews," and that another sub-ethnicity consisted of those Jews whose mother was not "born Jewish." Thus, through the imposition of the matrilineal test in a school admissions policy, they reasoned that one sub-ethnicity was engaged in racial discrimination against another.

d. The claim that the discrimination was religious and not racial was a red herring. Like Sedley LJ in the Court of Appeal, they stated that religion was simply a *motive* for the test. What mattered were "simply the factual criteria applied by the discriminator."

2. *The issue of the mother's conversion.* As part of this line or reasoning, the majority of the Court insisted that the arguments about conversion were a diversion. It did not matter that anyone could convert—what mattered was that a racial test was in place; if

49. Governing Body of JFS [2009] 4 ALL ER 375, CA, paras. 29 & 30, per Sedley LJ.

the boy's mother had been "born" Jewish, he would have been admitted to the school. Lady Hale declared:

> M was rejected because of his mother's ethnic origins, which were Italian and Roman Catholic. The fact that the Office of the Chief Rabbi would have overlooked his mother's Italian origins, had she converted to Judaism in a procedure which they would recognise, makes no difference to this fundamental fact. M was rejected, not because of who he is, but because of who his mother is.[50]

3. "*Justification*" *under the 1976 Act.* All five majority judges said that even if there had been no *direct* discrimination, then the school had committed racial discrimination *indirectly* as there was no justification for the school's admissions policy. "Indirect discrimination" was introduced by the 1976 Act, § 1(1)(b), which later became § 1(1A). Indirect discrimination is where there is a policy, requirement, or practice that applies to everybody in the same way but disadvantages a group of people who are members of a particular racial group. So, for example, a requirement that employees work on Saturdays could amount to indirect discrimination against Jews, who observe the Sabbath on that day. Once a prima facie case of indirect discrimination is made out, the burden of proof moves to the defendant to show that the discriminatory policy, requirement, or practice is objectively justified; in other words, to show that it was proportionate to some legitimate aim.

4. *Indirect racial discrimination under the 1976 Act.* Lords Hope and Walker disagreed with the reasoning of the majority on the question of direct discrimination; they both concurred in finding the school responsible for indirect discrimination:

> I would hold that, by applying the oversubscription criteria to M in a way that put him at a particular disadvantage when compared with others not of the same ethnicity by reason of matrilineal descent, JFS discriminated against him in breach of § 1(1A) of the Race Relations Act 1976.[51]

Lord Walker concurred.

> I respectfully agree with Lord Hope that this was a case of indirect, but not direct discrimination on grounds of ethnic origins contrary to § 1 of the Race Relations Act 1976 as amended.[52]

5. *Dissenting judgments.* Lords Roger and Brown issued strong dissenting judgments. They found that religion was the *reason why* and not simply the *motive for* the difference in treatment. They insisted that the element of conversion in Judaism was crucial to the determination of the case, and not a red herring. In essence, they fully agreed with how Munby J had decided the case in the High Court—this matter was fundamentally about a religious dispute within the Jewish community over the recognition of non-Orthodox conversions. Racial discrimination had nothing to do with it. Lord Roger declared:

---

50. R (E) v. Governing Body of JFS [2010] IRLR 136, SC, para. 66.

51. *Id.* at para. 215 per Lord Hope DP.

52. *Id.* at para. 235 per Lord Walker.

> The majority's decision leads to such extraordinary results, and produces such manifest discrimination against Jewish schools in comparison with other faith schools, that one can't help feeling something has gone wrong.... Lady Hale says that M was rejected because of his mother's ethnic origins which were Italian and Roman Catholic. I respectfully disagree. His mother could have been as Italian in origin as Sophia Loren and as Roman Catholic as the Pope for all that the governors cared: the only thing that mattered was that she had not converted to Judaism under Orthodox auspices.[53]

Viewing Halakhah Through Christian Lenses

1. *Impact of the Supreme Court decision.* In striking down the "matrilineal" test as racial, Lady Hale remarked that "the Christian church will admit children regardless of who their parents are" (*id.*, para. 68). As a result of the Supreme Court decision, the JFS has had to adopt an admissions policy that requires a "Certificate of Religious Practice" in lieu of the matrilineal test.

Note that under Jewish law, a person's level of religious observance is irrelevant to their status as a Jew. The Certificate of Religious Practice helps the more hardline Orthodox Jews who insist on the importance of theological belief and religious observance, and it marginalizes the ties that non-religious Jews have with Jewish history and culture, by making it more difficult for their children to be admitted to JFS because they will not be sufficiently observant and the JFS tends to be over-subscribed.

2. *Dissenting.* Justice Lord Brown, who is Jewish, objected to the imposition upon the school of Christian ideas about worship:

> To impose a religious practice test, besides being felt by many to be invasive, difficult to measure and open to abuse, would be contrary to the positive desire of schools like JFS to admit non-observant as well as observant children. Ironically, moreover, to impose such a test would narrow, rather than widen, the character of the school's intake so as to make it appear more, rather than less, discriminatory.
>
> Jewish schools in future, if oversubscribed, must decide on preference by reference only to outward manifestations of religious practice. The Court of Appeal's judgment insists on a non-Jewish definition of who is Jewish ... ignoring whether the child is or is not Jewish defined by Orthodox Jewish law. That outcome I would not contemplate with equanimity.[54]

Did the majority judgments result in a "Christianization" of the JFS?

3. *Consistent with Mandla v. Dowell Lee?* One effect of the Supreme Court's judgment is to turn the JFS into an exclusively religious school, making a child's "ethnic ties" with Jewishness irrelevant. It thus seems to render *Mandla* irrelevant here because

53. *Id.* at paras. 226, 228.
54. *Id.* at paras. 248, 253, 258.

there is no question of protecting a Jewish person from discrimination based on their *ethnicity.*

4. *Orientalizing processes in the Supreme Court's majority opinion.* "Orientalizing" is a process whereby Jews and Jewishness are looked at from the point of view of a patronizing Western superiority, rationality, and sense of a developed culture and society. Professor Didi Herman states that the orientalist tone of the majority's opinion in the *JFS* case is clear from the remarks made by Lady Hale and Lord Mance, especially when they are combined with how Lord Phillips chooses to begin his opening judgment.[55] Consider these judicial remarks:

a. As indicated above, Lady Hale observed, "the Christian Church will admit children regardless of who their parents are."[56] Herman argues that in comparing Judaism with Christianity, Lady Hale was suggesting that Christianity is about equality, but Judaism is not. This, Herman claims, promotes "Christian universalism" and "orientalizes" Jews and Jewishness.

b. Lord Mance found that the matrilineal test of Jewishness contravened the 1976 Act:

> To treat individual applicants to a school less favourably than others, because of the happenstance of their respective ancestries, is not to treat them as individuals, but as members in a group defined in a manner unrelated to their individual attributes.... To treat as determinative the view of others, which an applicant may not share, that a child is not Jewish by reason of his ancestry, is to give effect not to the individuality or interests of the applicant, but to the viewpoint, religiously and deeply held though it be, of the school applying the less favourable treatment. That does not seem to me either consistent with the scheme or appropriate in the context of legislation designed to protect individuals from discrimination. I accept that parental responsibility and choice relating to a child can determine the extent to which children are treated as having certain attributes, e.g., membership of a particular religion in the case of Christian baptism. But neither parental birth nor the fact that a mother has not converted to Orthodox Judaism at a time prior to a child's birth can be regarded as within the concept of parental responsibility and choice.[57]
>
> For the reasons I have given, the Court of Appeal in my view reached the correct conclusion, when it held that as a matter of law the admissions policy followed by JFS was inherently discriminatory, contrary to § 1(1)(a) of the 1976 Act, although the policy was adopted by the school for the most benign, religious motives.[58]

55. Didi Herman, An Unfortunate Coincidence: Jews, Jewishness and English Law 163–165 (2010).

56. R (E) v. Governing Body of JFS [2010] IRLR 136, SC, para. 69.

57. *Id.* at para. 90.

58. *Id.* at para. 92.

c. Lord Phillips opened the Supreme Court judgment with the passage from Deuteronomy where God instructs the Jewish people to destroy others and certainly to never marry them:

> The seventh chapter of Deuteronomy records the following instructions given by Moses to the people of Israel, after delivering the Ten Commandments at Mount Sinai:
>
> 1. When the Lord thy God shall bring thee into the land whither thou goest to possess it, and hath cast out many nations before thee, the Hittites, and the Girgashites, and the Amorites, and the Canaanites, and the Perizzites, and the Hivites, and the Jebusites, seven nations greater and mightier than thou;
>
> 2. And when the Lord thy God shall deliver them before thee; thou shalt smite them, and utterly destroy them; thou shalt make no covenant with them, nor show mercy unto them.
>
> 3. Neither shalt thou make marriages with them; thy daughter thou shalt not give unto his son, nor his daughter shalt thou take unto thy son.
>
> 4. For they will turn away thy son from following me, that they may serve other gods: so will the anger of the Lord be kindled against you, and destroy thee suddenly.[59]

Do these judicial remarks orientalize Jews and Jewishness? Stated differently, do they implicitly universalize Christianity and posit it as the epitome of fairness and freedom when compared to the insular, even backward, Jewish world?

5. *Racializing processes in the Supreme Court's majority opinion.* Didi Herman also argues that the judges in the majority engaged in the "racialization" of Jews. Racialization is a process whereby racial identities are systematically constructed by means of racial descriptors. For example, Lady Hale declared:

> M was rejected because of his mother's ethnic origins, which were Italian and Roman Catholic. The fact that the Office of the Chief Rabbi would have overlooked his mother's Italian origins, had she converted to Judaism in a procedure which they would recognise, makes no difference to this fundamental fact.[60]

This illustrates Lady Hale's view that a person cannot be both Jewish and Italian. Lord Hope seems to subscribe to this view also, as indicated by his description of the boy's parents: "M's father is of Jewish ethnic origin. M's mother is Italian by birth and ethnic origin."[61] Similarly, this line of thought is further evident in Lord Mance's remarks suggesting that a "Cohen" and an "English woman" are two different species.[62]

---

59. *Id.* at para. 1.
60. *Id.* at para. 66.
61. *Id.* at para. 166.
62. *Id.* at para. 87.

For Lord Mance, it appears that a "Cohen" is clearly not "English," and an "English woman" is clearly not Jewish. These kinds of sentiments resonate with the blood approach to Jewish identity.

Sources

James Gould, *Book Reviews: Litigating Religions: An Essay on Human Rights, Courts, and Beliefs*, 21 ECCLESIASTICAL L.J. 236–238 (2019).

Didi Herman, AN UNFORTUNATE COINCIDENCE: JEWS, JEWISHNESS AND ENGLISH LAW 163–170 (2010).

Gwyneth Pitt, *Keeping the Faith: Trends and Tensions in Religion or Belief Discrimination*, 40 INDUS. L.J. 384 (2011).

J. H. H. Weiler,[63]
Discrimination and Identity in London: The Jewish Free School Case

JEWISH REVIEW OF BOOKS (Spring 2010)

It is not every day that the Chief Rabbi of Britain, Sir Jonathan Sacks, is found by the Supreme Court of the United Kingdom to be guilty of racial discrimination, but that is what happened in the recent Jewish Free School (JFS) Case.

The facts of the case are as simple as the underlying legal, religious, and cultural issues are complex. The Jewish Free School, founded in 1732, is Europe's largest Jewish secondary school and one of the best schools in London. Moreover, as a state-funded school, it is literally free. As a matter of policy, JFS gives preference to Jews in its admissions decisions. Since the number of Jewish applications consistently exceeds the places available, non-Jews are, in effect, excluded. No one contests the right of JFS to do this. By law, Catholic schools can give preference to Catholics, Muslim schools to Muslims, and so on. The law also allows such schools to determine eligibility by reference to religious "membership or practice." But there is no exemption for discrimination on grounds of race.

The legal limits of JFS's policy were recently tested when a twelve-year-old boy, identified in court documents as "M," applied for admission to the school. M's mother, who is Italian Catholic by birth, converted to Judaism through a non-Orthodox rabbinic court. At the time of his application, M was living with his father and although the two of them were members of a Masorti synagogue, M was denied admission because Chief Rabbi Sacks, whose authority is recognized by JFS, did not recognize the conversion of his mother as valid, rendering M not Jewish, by extension.

---

63. J.H.H. Weiler is University Professor and Joseph Straus Professor of Law at New York University School of Law, as well as the European Union Jean Monnet Chaired Professor; Director of the Jean Monnet Center for International and Regional Economic Law and Justice; and Co-Director of the Tikvah Center for Law & Jewish Civilization.

In determining whether M was Jewish, the Chief Rabbi, as head of the United Synagogue, applied the criterion of "membership in the Jewish people" rather than that of "the practice of Judaism." Membership was determined by traditional norms: someone born to a Jewish mother or converted according to halakha. Since Rabbi Sacks and the United Synagogue do not recognize the halakhic authority of Masorti Rabbinic courts, M was treated as if he were a non-Jewish applicant, his family's practice of Judaism notwithstanding. A lower court upheld the school's right to do deny M a place, but this decision was reversed on appeal and came before the Supreme Court.

In the eyes of the Majority, this exclusion amounted to prohibited racial discrimination.

Five Law Lords found direct discrimination, which, under British Law, can never be justified or excused. Two Law Lords found indirect racial discrimination which can be justified or excused, but which was not so justified in this case. Only two found for the School and the United Synagogue. So how did the Majority reach its conclusion?

English law includes "ethnic origins" as a proxy for race, which is understood to be "appreciably wider than the strictly racial or biological." Several criteria determine ethnicity: shared history, cultural tradition, common geographical origins, descent from a small number of common ancestors, a common language, a common literature, a common religion, being a minority within a larger community, and so on.

> A group defined by reference to enough of these characteristics would be capable of including converts, for example, persons who marry into the group.... Provided a person who joins the group feels himself or herself to be a member of it, as is accepted by other members, then he is [for the purposes of the law prohibiting racial discrimination,] such a member.

The Majority found that on these anthropological criteria, the Jewish people are an ethnic group.

Now, one should not condemn the British courts for construing race anthropologically and giving a non-religious definition to Jewishness. In the first place, it is consistent with the purpose of Britain's Race Relations Act. Anti-Semites are distinctly uninterested in halakhic definitions of Jewishness, and we would not want someone who was discriminated against as a Jew to face a legal defense that—according to Orthodox standards—she was not actually Jewish, ergo it wasn't really discrimination. Second, we do not want the legislature or the courts to be in the business of setting religious criteria for Jewishness. But we should note that a gap exists between this anthropological definition of Jewishness and a religious definition. It is possible that someone would be anthropologically Jewish but religiously not. (Many such Jews were gassed at Auschwitz.)

Lady Hale, in a lucid and succinct opinion, captures the core of the Majority's reasoning:

> There is no doubt that the Jewish people are an ethnic group.... It is just as unlawful to treat one person more favourably on the ground of his ethnic or-

> igin as it is to treat another person less favourably. There can be no doubt that, if an employer were to take exactly the same criterion as that used by the ... Chief Rabbi and refuse to employ a person because the Chief Rabbi would regard him as halachically Jewish, the employer would be treating that person less favourably on grounds of his ethnic origin....

M was treated less favorably because he did not come under the Chief Rabbi's definition of Jewishness, as the son of a Jewish mother. In the eyes of the Majority that definition was an ethnic and hence racial determination. The Jewish Free School was guilty of racial discrimination. Or was it?

In order to highlight the problems with the Supreme Court's decision, let us imagine that both of M's parents were Italian by birth, or for that matter Chinese. M would then be ethnically Italian or Chinese. But had his mother undergone a halakhically incontestable conversion, M would be fully Jewish, according to Rabbi Sacks and JFS—race, genes, and ethnicity notwithstanding. This is the traditional Jewish position, and there is nothing racist about it. Thus, an M with the same "racial" or "ethnic" makeup would be considered Jewish had his mother satisfied the *religious* requirements of conversion.

As an internal Jewish matter, the wisdom of the Chief Rabbi and JFS's decision to exclude students such as M calls for serious reflection. But even from the perspective of the non-Orthodox denominations, whose conversions the Chief Rabbi does not recognize, the result of the case should be alarming. All Jewish denominations accept the proposition that Jewish identity is determined by either descent or conversion, though they differ on the precise rules. Indeed, the Masorti movement accepts the same Jewish legal tradition, but interprets it more liberally. A Reform school could also face an M who felt Jewish but was not so by Reform criteria, say because neither of his parents had converted, as noted by Rabbi Bayfield, head of England's Reform Movement in a statement cited in the Court's decision.

The Majority has conflated the secular anthropological criterion of ethnicity, which is the province of the civil authorities, with the religious criterion, which is the province of religious authorities.

Was the Chief Rabbi concerned with ethnicity as the Majority held? To the Minority, it was clear that his concerns were not even remotely ethnic or racial. Thus, Lord Rodger in dissent:

> Faced with a boy whose mother had converted under Orthodox auspices, the governors would have considered him for admission without pausing for a single second to enquire whether he or his mother came from Rome, Brooklyn, Siberia, or Buenos Aires, whether she had once been a Roman Catholic or a Muslim, or whether he or she came from a close-knit Jewish community or had chosen to assimilate and disappear into secular society. In other words, the "ethnic origins" of the child or his mother ... would not have played any part in the governors' decision to admit him ... the only ground for treating M less favourably than the comparator [i.e. a son of an Halakhically converted

woman] is the difference in their respective mothers' conversions—a religious, not a racial ground.

This is cogent but it should be noted that it is this very example given by Lord Rodger which seems to animate the Majority, too. Although never explicitly articulated, the following argument seems to underlie the Court's decision: How is it possible that the Jewish Free School and the Chief Rabbi can consider someone eligible who is an atheist, uninterested in Judaism, believes in none of its propositions, and whose main reason for going to JFS is that it is excellent and free, while rejecting a candidate such as M, who is a deeply religious, committed, and knowledgeable Jew, albeit non-Orthodox? Since the first applicant is, by definition, not religious, preferential treatment of him over M must be due to racial discrimination.

What is wrong with the above implicit reasoning? Well, nothing except that it is underwritten by a profoundly Christian understanding of religion and religious membership. It is shaped by the fundamental Christian idea of the New Covenant in which the "old" covenantal boundaries of Israelite peoplehood were dissolved, and a universal salvific message was extended to all *individuals* regardless of the people to whom they belonged. To quote Paul, "There is neither Jew nor Greek, there is neither bond nor free, there is neither male nor female: for ye are all one in Christ Jesus." On this view, you are Christian if and only if you believe in Christ. This idea of religion as a matter of doctrinal conviction has shaped the Western sensibility as to what religious membership means. It is to be respected. But it is not the Jewish understanding of religious belonging. In fact, it originated in a rejection of Judaism. (Paul also spoke of being circumcised in the heart rather than the flesh.) One can, as a Jewish religious proposition, belong to the Jewish people even if you have lost your faith.

What is troubling about the Majority is its sheer incomprehension and consequent intolerance of a religion whose self-understanding is different than that of Christianity. Their anthropological reading of ethnicity is suitable in the circumstances for which the Race Relations Act was intended. But when the law makes an exception for religion and the religion in question is Judaism, it should be understood on its own terms, not on Christian (or, more precisely, Protestant) terms.

But, one might protest, even if one accepted the self-understanding of the religion in question, that acceptance cannot be absolute. We would not allow child sacrifice, even if religiously mandated. What, then, if I continue to hold that the Jewish self-understanding and definition of membership—descent and conversion—just are discriminatory? In fact, this is the unstated conclusion of the Majority's decision, and it is deeply troubling. For the most troubling discrimination I see here is the one against Jewish institutions applying religious criteria of membership. Lady Hale speaks of the Jewish "people." The Jewish religious definition of peoplehood—descent and conversion—is no different from all of the secular definitions with which I am familiar. You are French, or Italian, or German, or Irish, or Australian or, yes, British, if you are born to a parent or parents belonging legally to that people (descent) or if you legally naturalize (conversion). Some countries add place of birth, but practically none exclude the two first criteria.

Among the rights of being British is eligibility for election to Parliament. Imagine a different M, born and bred in Britain, speaking English and feeling entirely patriotic, but, alas, the son of non-British parents whose naturalizations were invalid by extant British rules. "I am afraid, Sir," the British election officer will say, "that until such time as you legally naturalize, you may not stand for election, which is a right reserved to Britons." "Even to Britons," M might protest, "who never set foot in this country, who hate it, who disparage it, who want to abolish the Monarchy?" "I am afraid so," would be the inevitable answer of the election officer in Britain and in virtually every other country.

If the majority of the Law Lords of the Supreme Court in the JFS case accept the peoplehood of the Jews, why would they hold the Jewish religious definition of membership to be discriminatory when it is similar to the secular universal practice among all other peoples?

C. Is Zionism Racist?

The U.N. Charter empowers the General Assembly (GA) to issue non-legally binding recommendations on various matters within its purview.[64] On November 10, 1975, the U.N. General Assembly adopted Resolution 3379, which declared that "Zionism is a form of racism and racial discrimination." Resolution 3379 also cited earlier denunciations of Zionism "as a threat to world peace" and a "racist and imperialist ideology."[65] Resolution 3379 accelerated the use of "Zionist" as a term of abuse and "a catch-all word for nefarious behavior."[66]

72 countries voted in favor of Resolution 3379, led by the Soviet Union and its bloc. (For many years, the Soviet Union actively promoted the "Zionism is racism" equation to promote alliances with anti-Zionist countries.[67]) Other supporters included members of the Arab League, Muslim-majority countries, many African countries, as well

64. U.N. Charter arts. 10–14.

65. Evelyn Sommer, *Fighting Delegitimization: The United Nation's "Zionism Is Racism" Resolution, a Case Study*, World Jewish Cong., https://www.worldjewishcongress.org/en/85th-anniversary/fighting-delegitimization-the-united-nations-zionism-is-racism-resolution-a-case-study (last visited Dec. 16, 2024).

66. *Id.* GA resolutions may have special force insofar as they declare or determine general international law principles. This was not the case with GA Resolution 3379, which made a specific determination about Zionism. L. Libr. of Cong., Legal Effect of United Nations Resolutions Under International and Domestic Law 4 (2015), https://tile.loc.gov/storage-services/service/ll/llglrd/2019669646/2019669646.pdf.

67. *Soviet Anti-Zionism*, Wikipedia, https://en.wikipedia.org/wiki/Soviet_anti-Zionism (last visited Dec. 16, 2024); *see also* Ctr. for Antisemitism Rsch., *Contemporary Anti-Zionism's Connections to Soviet Propaganda*, The Anti-Defamation League (Feb. 22, 2023), https://www.adl.org/resources/article/contemporary-anti-zionisms-connections-soviet-propaganda; Avner Yeshurun, *The Soviet Origins of Left-Wing Anti-Zionism*, Jewish News Syndicate (June 8, 2022), https://www.jns.org/the-soviet-origins-of-left-wing-anti-zionism/.

as Brazil, Mexico, and Portugal. 35 countries voted against it, including the U.S. and Germany. 32 countries abstained, including Argentina and Japan.[68]

The U.S. was represented at the GA by Daniel Patrick Moynihan, then U.S. Ambassador to the U.N., a former Harvard professor, future long-serving U.S. Senator from New York, a devout Catholic, and one of the preeminent scholar-statesmen in U.S. history.[69]

Daniel Patrick Moynihan, *We Have Drained the Word "Racism" of Its Meaning*[70]

Before the United Nations General Assembly
November 10, 1975[71]

The United States rises to declare before the General Assembly of the United Nations, and before the world, that it does not acknowledge, it will not abide by, it will never acquiesce in this infamous act.

Not three weeks ago, the United States Representative in the Social, Humanitarian, and Cultural Committee—and what—with what irony those terms ring on our ears today—pleaded in measured and fully considered terms for the United Nations not to do this thing. It was, he said, "obscene." It is something more today, for the furtiveness with which this obscenity first appeared among us has been replaced by a shameless openness.

There will be time enough to contemplate the harm this act will have done the United Nations. Historians will do that for us, and it is sufficient for the moment only to note one foreboding fact: A great evil has been loosed upon the world. The abomination of antisemitism—as this year's Nobel Peace Laureate Andrei Sakharov observed

---

68. The following 35 countries voted against Resolution 3379: Australia, Austria, Bahamas, Barbados, Belgium, Canada, Central African Republic, Costa Rica, Denmark, Dominican Republic, El Salvador, Fiji. Finland, France, West Germany, Haiti, Honduras, Iceland, Ireland, Israel, Italy, Ivory Coast, Liberia, Luxembourg, Malawi, Netherlands, New Zealand, Nicaragua, Norway, Panama, Swaziland, Sweden, United Kingdom, United States, and Uruguay. Countries abstaining included many in Latin America as well as Greece and Japan.

69. Moynihan (1927–2003) served as U.S. Senator from New York from 1977–2001. Prior to becoming U.S. ambassador to the U.N., Moynihan served as U.S. ambassador to India and held cabinet or sub-cabinet positions under four presidents: John F. Kennedy, Lyndon B. Johnson, Richard M. Nixon, and Gerald R. Ford. He also served as a professor of education and government at Harvard University and was an accomplished scholar and public intellectual. In 2000, Senator Moynihan received the Presidential Medal of Freedom. In 2021, New York Penn Station's interior was named Moynihan Train Hall in recognition of his efforts to expand and improve Penn Station. *Daniel Patrick Moynihan*, The Moynihan Ctr., https://moynihancenter.ccny.cuny.edu/about/daniel-patrick-moynihan/ (last visited Dec. 16, 2024); *see also Daniel Patrick Moynihan*, Am. Acad. of Pol. & Soc. Sci, https://www.aapss.org/fellows/fellow/daniel-patrick-moynihan/ (last visited Dec. 16, 2024); *see also Zionism Is Not Racism: Moynihan Defends Israel*, Tikvah (Dec. 20, 2021) https://tikvahfund.org/collegiate-forum/zionism-is-not-racism-moynihan-defends-israel/.

70. *Daniel Patrick Moynihan Response to the Passing of United Nations Resolution 3379*, Am. Rhetoric, https://www.americanrhetoric.com/speeches/danielpatrickmoynihanun3379.htm (last visited Dec. 15, 2024).

71. 107 Cong. Rec. S8341 (2001), https://www.gpo.gov/fdsys/pkg/CREC-2001-07-27/pdf/CREC-2001-07-27-pt1-PgS8341-3.pdf.

Figure 5.1. U.S. Ambassador to the U.N. Daniel Patrick Moynihan delivering historic speech to the U.N. General Assembly condemning its "Zionism as racism" resolution as an "abomination." November 10, 1975. U.N. Photo.

in Moscow just a few days ago—the abomination of anti-Semitism has been given the appearance of international sanction. The General Assembly today grants symbolic amnesty—and more—to the murderers of the six million European Jews. Evil enough in itself, but more ominous by far is the realization that now presses upon us—the realization that if there were no General Assembly, this could never have happened.

As this day will live in infamy, it behooves those who sought to avert it to declare their thoughts so that historians will know that we fought here, that we were not small in number—not this time—and that while we lost, we fought with full knowledge of what indeed would be lost....

Nor should any historian of the event, nor yet any who have participated in it, suppose that we have fought only as governments, as chancelleries, and on an issue well removed from the concerns of our respective peoples. Others will speak for their nations, as others have. I will speak for mine....

One after another, the great private institutions of American life pronounced anathema on this evil thing—and most particularly the Christian churches have done so....

The proposition to be sanctioned by a resolution of the General Assembly is that "Zionism is a form of racism and racial discrimination." Now this is a lie. But it is a lie which the United Nations has now declared to be a truth—and so the actual truth must be restated.

The first point to be made ... is that the United Nations has declared Zionism to be racism without ever having defined racism. "Sentence first—verdict afterwards," as the Queen of Hearts said. But this is not Wonderland, but a real world, where there are real consequences to folly and venality. Just on Friday, the President of the General Assembly, speaking on behalf of Luxembourg, warned not only of the trouble which would follow from the adoption of this resolution but of its essential irresponsibility—for, he noted, Members have wholly different ideas as to what they are condemning. "It seems to me," he said—and to his lasting honor he said it when there was still time—"It seems to me that before a body like this takes a decision they should agree very clearly on what they are approving or condemning, and it takes more time." . . .

If, as the distinguished delegate [from the USSR] declared, Racism is a form of Nazism—and if, as this resolution declares, Zionism is a form of racism—then we have step to step taken ourselves to the point of proclaiming—the United Nations is solemnly proclaiming—that Zionism is a form of Nazism.

What we have here is a lie—a political lie of a variety well known to the twentieth century and scarcely exceeded in all that annal of untruth and outrage. The lie is that Zionism is a form of racism. The overwhelmingly clear truth is that it is not.

The word "racism" is a creation of the English language, and relatively new to it. . . . The term derives from relatively new doctrines—all of them discredited—concerning the human population of the world to the effect that there are significant biological differences among clearly identifiable groups, and that these differences establish, in effect, different levels of humanity. Racism, as defined by Webster's Third New International Dictionary, is, (and I quote), "The assumption that . . . traits and capacities are determined by biological race and that races differ decisively from one another," (unquote). It further involves (quote), "a belief in the inherent superiority of a particular race and its right to domination over others," (again unquote).

This meaning is clear. It is equally clear that this assumption, this belief, has always been altogether alien to the political and religious movement known as Zionism. As a strictly political movement, Zionism was established only in 1897, although there's a clearly legitimate sense in which its origins are indeed ancient. For example, many branches of Christianity have always held that from the standpoint of the biblical prophets, Israel would be reborn one day.

But the—the modern Zionist movement arose in Europe in the context of a general upsurge of national consciousness and aspiration that overtook most of the peoples of Central and Eastern Europe after 1848, and that in time spread to all of Africa and Asia. It was, to those persons of the Jewish religion, a Jewish form of what today is called a national liberation movement. Probably, a majority of those persons who became active Zionists and sought to emigrate to Palestine were born within the confines of Czarist Russia, and it was only natural for Soviet Foreign Minister Andrei Gromyko to deplore, as he did in 1948, in the 299th meeting of the Security Council, the act by Israel's neighbors of (and I quote) "sending their troops into Palestine and carrying out military operations aimed"—in Mr. Gromyko's words—"at the suppression of the national liberation movement in Palestine."[72]

---

72. Extended quotation:
It is very difficult not to agree that the military operation in Palestine, in which eight states, the majority of which are members of the United Nations, are more or less involved, constitutes a threat to peace. . . . The USSR delegation can but express surprise at the position adopted by the Arab states in the Palestine question, and particularly at the fact that those states—or

Now it was the singular nature—if, I am not mistaken, it was the unique nature—of this national liberation movement that in contrast with the movements that preceded it, those of that time, and those that have come since, it defined its members in terms not of birth, but of belief. That is to say, it was not a movement of the Irish to free Ireland, or of the Polish to free Poland, not a movement of the Algerians to free Algeria, nor of Indians to free India. It was not a movement of persons connected by historic membership in a genetic pool of the kind that enables us to speak loosely but not meaninglessly of, say, the Chinese people; nor yet of diverse groups occupying the same territory which enables us to speak of the American people with no greater indignity to truth.

To the contrary, Zionists defined themselves merely as Jews and declared to be Jewish anyone born of a Jewish mother or—and *this is the absolutely crucial fact*—anyone who converted to Judaism—which is to say, in the terms of International Convention on the Elimination of All Forms of Racial Discrimination, adopted by the 20th General Assembly, anyone—regardless of (quote) "race, colour, descent, or national or ethnic origin...."[73]

The state of Israel, which in time was the creation of the Zionist Movement, has been extraordinary in nothing so much as the range of (what are called sometimes) "racial stocks" from which it has drawn its citizenry. There are black Jews, brown Jews, white Jews, Jews from the Orient, and Jews from the West. Most such persons could be said to have been "born" Jews, just as most Presbyterians and most Hindus are "born" to their faith. But there are many Jews who are just converts. And with a consistency in the matter which surely attests to the importance of this issue to that religious and political culture, Israeli courts have held that a Jew who converts to another religion is no longer a Jew. In the meantime, the population of Israel also includes large numbers of non-Jews, among them Arabs both of the Muslim and Christian religions, and of Christians and others of national origins. Many of these persons are citizens of Israel, and those who are not can become citizens by legal procedures very much like those which obtain in a typical nation of Western Europe.

---

some of them, at least—have resorted to such action as sending their troops into Palestine and carrying out military operations aimed at the suppression of the national liberation movement in Palestine.

[Source: https://doczz.es/doc/97496/the-case-for-israel] [Record of 3rd Year U.N. Security Council Meeting, 21 May 1948 at: https://documents-dds-ny.un.org/doc/UNDOC/GEN/NL4/817/33/PDF/NL481733.pdf?OpenElement] (alteration in original).

73. The full definition of "racial discrimination" as stated in Article I reads: "... any distinction, exclusion, restriction or preference based on race, colour, descent, or national or ethnic origin which has the purpose or effect of nullifying or impairing the recognition, enjoyment or exercise, on an equal footing, of human rights and fundamental freedoms in the political, economic, social, cultural or any other field of public life." (alteration in original).

Now I should wish to be understood—wish to be understood that I am here making one point and one point only, which is: Whatever else Zionism may be, it is not and cannot be "a form of racism." In logic, the State of Israel could be or could become many things, theoretically, including many things undesirable, but it could not be and could not become racist unless it ceased to be Zionist.

Indeed, the idea that the Jews are a "race" (quote, unquote) was invented not by Jews but by those who hated Jews. The idea of Jews as a race was invented by nineteenth century anti-Semites such as Houston Steward Chamberlain[74] and Edouard Drumont,[75] who saw that in an increasingly secular age, which is to say an age which made for fewer distinctions between people based on religion, the old religious grounds for anti-Semitism were losing force. New justifications were needed for excluding and persecuting Jews, and so the idea of Jews as a race rather than as a religion was born. It was a contemptible idea at the beginning, and no civilized person would be associated with it. To think that it is an idea now endorsed by the United Nations is to reflect on what civilization has come to.

It is precisely [a] concern for civilization, for civilized values that are or should be precious to all mankind, that arouses us at this moment to such special passion. What we have at stake here is not merely the honor and the legitimacy of the State of Israel—although a challenge to the legitimacy of any Member nation ought always to arouse the vigilance of all Members of the United Nations—for a yet more important matter is at issue, which is the integrity of that whole body of moral and legal precepts which we know as human rights.

The terrible lie that has been told here today will have terrible consequences. Not only will people begin to say, indeed they have already begun to say that the United Nations is a place where lies are told, but far more serious, grave and perhaps irreparable harm will be done to the cause of human rights. The harm will arise first because it will strip from racism the precise and abhorrent meaning that it still precariously holds

74. Editor's note: Houston Steward Chamberlain (1855–1927) "was a British-born Germanophile political philosopher, whose advocacy of the racial and cultural superiority of the so-called Aryan element in European culture influenced pan-German and German nationalist thought, particularly Adolf Hitler's National Socialist movement." *Houston Stewart Chamberlain*, BRITANNICA, https://www.britannica.com/biography/Houston-Stewart-Chamberlain (last visited Dec. 16, 2024).

75. Editor's note: Édouard Adolphe Drumont (1844–1917) was a French journalist, author and politician, most often remembered for his antisemitic ideology and animus. He was the founder in 1892 and editor of the newspaper *La Libre Parole*. His work played a major role in catalyzing the Dreyfus Affair. According to Wikipedia, Drumond was a pioneer in the development of modern antisemitism:

> After spending years of research, he synthesized three major types of antisemitism. The first type was traditional Catholic attitudes toward the alien "Christ killers" augmented by vehement antipathy toward the French Revolution. The second type was hostility toward capitalism. The third type was so-called scientific racism, based on the argument that races have fixed characteristics, and asserting that Jews have negative characteristics.

Édouard Drumont, WIKIPEDIA, https://en.wikipedia.org/wiki/%C3%89douard_Drumont (last visited Dec. 16, 2024).

today. How will the people of the world feel about racism and the need to struggle against it, when they are told that it is an idea as broad as to include the Jewish national liberation movement?

As the lie spreads, it will do harm in a second way. Many of the members of the United Nations owe their independence in no small part to the notion of human rights, as it has spread from the domestic sphere to the international sphere and exercised its influence over the old colonial powers. We are now coming into a time when that independence is likely to be threatened again. There will be new forces, some of them arising now, new prophets and new despots, who will justify their actions with the help of just such distortions of words as we have sanctioned here today. Today we have drained the word "racism" of its meaning. Tomorrow, terms like "national self-determination" and "national honor" will be perverted in the same way to serve the purposes of conquest and exploitation. And when these claims begin to be made—as they already have begun to be made—it is the small nations of the world whose integrity will suffer. And how will the small nations of the world defend themselves? And on what grounds will others be moved to defend and protect them, when the language of human rights, the only language by which the small can be defended, is no longer believed and no longer has a power of its own?

There is this danger, and then a final danger which is the most serious of all—which is that the damage we now do to the idea of human rights and the language of human rights could well be irreversible.

The idea of human rights as we know it today is not an idea which has always existed in human affairs. It is an idea which appeared at a specific time in the world, and under very special circumstances. It appeared when European philosophers of the seventeenth century began to argue that man was a being whose existence was independent from that of the State, and that he need join a political community only if he did not lose by that association more than he gained. From this very specific political philosophy stemmed the idea of political rights, of claims that the individual could justly make against the State. It was because the individual was seen as so separate from the State that he could make legitimate demands upon it.

That was the philosophy from which the idea of domestic and international rights sprang. But most of the world does not hold with that philosophy now. Most of the world believes in newer modes of political thought, in philosophies that do not accept the individual as distinct from and prior to the State, in philosophies that therefore do not provide any justification for the idea of human rights and philosophies that have no words by which to explain their value. If we destroy the words that were given to us by past centuries, we will not have words to replace them, for philosophy today has no such words.

But there are those of us who have not forsaken these older words, still so new to much of the world; not forsaken them now, not forsaken them—not here, not anywhere, not ever.

Aftermath of U.N. General Assembly Resolution 3379

1. *Amnesty?* In what sense, in Ambassador Moynihan's view, did Resolution 3379 grant "symbolic amnesty" to the perpetrators of the Holocaust?

2. *The Jews = Nazis trope.* What is problematic about this comparison? Consider scholar Lesley Klaff's discussion of the phenomenon of "Holocaust Inversion," which she describes as:

> An inversion of reality (the Israelis are cast as the "new" Nazis and the Palestinians as the "new" Jews), and an inversion of morality (the Holocaust is presented as a moral lesson for, or even a moral indictment of "the Jews"). More: those who object to these inversions are told ... that they are acting in bad faith, only being concerned to deflect criticism of Israel. In short, the Holocaust, an event accurately described ... as a "rupture in civilisation," organised by a regime that, as the political philosopher Leo Strauss observed, "had no other clear principle except murderous hatred of the Jews," is now being used, instrumentally, as a means to express animosity towards the homeland of the Jews. "The victims have become perpetrators" is being heard more and more. That is Holocaust Inversion.[76]

3. *A festival of hate.* Professor Gil Troy describes the U.N.'s 2001 World Conference against Racism in Durban, South Africa as "one of modern Jewish history's lowest moments." Others described it "as a carnival of antisemitic expression that drove Jewish participants to tears each night and had them fearing for their physical safety." Many conference attendees linked Zionism to racism, genocide, war crimes, crimes against humanity, ethnic cleansing, and Apartheid. Irwin Cotler, former minister of justice and attorney general of Canada, writes that:

> The indictment of Israel as an apartheid state was born in Durban. It was triggered in Durban. Durban became the tipping point for the demonological antisemitism that we see today, where Israel is blamed for all the evils of the world, that Israel and the Jewish people are the enemy of good, the embodiment of all those evils.[77]

---

76. Lesley Klaff, *Holocaust Inversion and Contemporary Antisemitism*, FATHOM (2014), https://fathomjournal.org/holocaust-inversion-and-contemporary-antisemitism/.

77. Ron Kampeas, *20 Years Ago, the U.N. Durban Conference Aimed to Combat Racism. It Devolved into a 'Festival of Hate' Against Jews.*, JEWISH TELEGRAPHIC AGENCY (Sept. 9, 2021), https://www.jta.org/2021/09/09/politics/20-years-ago-the-un-durban-conference-aimed-to-combat-racism-it-devolved-into-a-festival-of-hate-against-jews.

American Association of University Professors (AAUP), *Polarizing Times Demand Robust Academic Freedom*

(November 15, 2023)

In the aftermath of the events of October 7, 2023, powerful campus outsiders—including donors, legislators, and well-funded political organizations—have escalated demands that institutions crack down on what can be said or expressed on campus....

The AAUP rejects the characterization of pro-Palestinian speech or critiques of the Israeli state as invariably antisemitic. As institutional leaders combat discrimination and uphold principles of community, they should not lose sight of how proponents of overly broad definitions of antisemitism and proponents of eliminating teaching about the history of racial and other violence share a desire to mobilize the government to enforce particular, emaciated accounts of history, harm, and injury. These efforts to control what is thought, said, taught, and researched are antithetical to the educational mission of a university and the democratic values upon which it rests....

[T]he AAUP condemns the climate of intimidation that now attempts to silence people who express unpopular views on the current conflict in the Middle East.... [78]

David Schraub, *No One Believes That Any Criticism of Israel Is Invariably Antisemitic*

Fathom (December 2023)

Over the past few weeks, as the initial shock of Hamas's October 7 attack on Israel wore off and a new shock regarding Israel's bruising response set in, colleges around the country have been wracked by renewed controversies regarding the contours of antisemitism. Many Jewish students, alumni, and faculty members have contended that certain instances of protest and advocacy against Israeli actions in the Gaza Strip have crossed the line into antisemitism. Many Palestinians on campus and their allies have been equally fervent in rejecting the charge, contending that the claims of antisemitism are actually attempts to target free speech and legitimate criticism of Israel.

Last week, in a statement released this week discussing challenges to academic freedom posed by the current conflict in Israel and Gaza, the American Association of University Professors waded into this debate by stating that it 'rejects the characterization of pro-Palestinian speech or critiques of the Israeli state as invariably antisemitic.' This language—'invariably antisemitic'—appears advised, and echoes a common theme purveyed in public discourse about the intersection of antisemitism and Israel. A few weeks earlier, a group of 'Jewish writers, artists, and activists' drafted an open letter published in N+1 Magazine titled "A dangerous conflation" which opened by 'disavow[ing] the widespread narrative that any criticism of Israel is inherently an-

78. *Polarizing Times Demand Robust Academic Freedom*, Am. Ass'n of Univ. Professors (Nov. 15, 2023), https://www.aaup.org/news/polarizing-times-demand-robust-academic-freedom.

tisemitic.' And indeed, this framing—attacking the view that any criticism of Israel is inherently antisemitic—predates the current round of hostilities: an open letter from Independent Jewish Voices in Canada in 2021 complained that the widely-used IHRA antisemitism definition 'is being used worldwide as a tool to assert that criticism of Israel is inherently antisemitic.'

These letters and press releases are speaking an incontestable truth. Criticism of Israel is not inherently or invariably antisemitic. But some truths are so obvious that they loop back around into falsity. And the AAUP, in adopting this framing, actually endangers essential academic freedom values for both scholars of antisemitism as well as Jewish academic community members, who have to be free to make good faith contentions that *some* events, practices, arguments, and ideologies concerning Israel *are* indeed antisemitic. Just as with claims about racism, sexism, Islamophobia, colonialism, and similar sins, we can expect that many of these allegations will be contentious and some of them may turn out to be unsustainable. But that does not remove them from the ambit of open academic discussion.

To be sure, the position that critiques of the Israeli state are 'invariably' antisemitic is one that is impossible to adhere to in good faith. But that impossibility is so obvious that it raises the immediate question of whether anyone actually is making such a claim? When I read a sentence objecting to the 'narrative'—indeed, a '*widespread* narrative,' a narrative supposedly so commonplace it demands intervention from the AAUP—that *any* criticism of Israel is *inherently* or *invariably* antisemitic, my first thought is to wonder who exactly the writers are arguing against? Who is so foolish, so blinkered, that they actually believe that *any* criticism of Israel is *invariably* antisemitic?

No matter where one looks along the political spectrum, falsifying examples abound. It was only months ago that we witnessed historic protests, in Israel and around the world, vocally condemning the Israeli government's proposed efforts to neuter the state's judiciary—criticism of Israel that even where disagreed with was rarely if ever called antisemitic. The hammerlock Israel's ultra-Orthodox rabbinate holds over large swaths of civil society, and the ensuing discrimination against non-Orthodox Jews, has long been a source of denunciation by liberal Jews in the diaspora. And many people, Jewish and not, have bitterly indicted the Netanyahu government's response to Hamas's attack for fecklessness and incompetence—raining down death and destruction on Gaza with seemingly little plan other that trying to delay his own political reckoning for as long as possible. In my case, even as I conceded that Israel was left with few good options in the wake of Hamas's 10/7 attacks, I nonetheless declared that 'this dilemma is certainly beyond the capacities of the pathetic rabble of fascists and lickspittles that comprises Netanyahu's coalition.' Vituperative language—and yet, I was not accused of antisemitism.

Now of course, it is fair to say that these 'criticisms of Israel' are not the ones that the letter writers had in mind when they complained of criticism of Israel being characterized as antisemitic. They were not thinking of criticisms of Israel's domestic policy arrangements, they were not thinking about religious liberty issues afflicting non-

Orthodox Jews, and they certainly were not thinking of criticism of Israel's wartime behavior (however passionately expressed) that nonetheless holds sympathy for Israel's genuine security dilemmas. They were envisioning meatier fare. But this is precisely the point: it is *not* the case the *any* criticism of Israel is called *inherently* antisemitic. Rather, *specific* criticisms in *specific* contexts are called antisemitic for *specific* reasons. These reasons may, of course, be well- or ill-taken. But even the most poorly-reasoned assertion of antisemitism almost certainly does not rely on a fallacy quite so blatant as a belief that *any* criticism of Israel is *inherently* antisemitic.

This may seem like splitting hairs. It isn't. Rather, it identifies a dangerous conflation of its own. By framing accusations of antisemitism as generally being predicated on flagrantly absurd premises, the letter writers can skip past the more demanding work of actually responding to the specific claims being made. And precisely because the refutation 'criticism of Israel is not inherently antisemitic' literally responds to no one, it can be wielded against anyone and everyone. *All* contentions of antisemitism tied to claims about Israel can be dismissed through this reply—the well-reasoned, the ill-founded, and everything in between.

Put differently, the statement 'criticism of Israel is not inherently antisemitic' is obviously true, but the statement that any non-trivial number of individuals *believe* that 'criticism of Israel is inherently antisemitic' is obviously false. But this falsity permits the valence of our discourse about antisemitism to be reframed. The problem is no longer antisemitism itself, but rather the way 'antisemitism,' as a concept, is allegedly abused to victimize innocent bystanders.

As an academic who studies antisemitism as a central area of research, it was deeply disheartening to see the AAUP in particular miss the threat that their framing poses to my ability to pursue my scholarship freely, given that by necessity my research will regularly entail making claims about antisemitism that others might not agree with. Any professor, but especially any Jewish professor, who researches antisemitism is well familiar with the reflexive skepticism that our field of study is often greeted with—the almost instinctual demand for assurance that we're not one of 'those people' who calls anything and everything antisemitic. 'Anything and everything,' in this context, means 'anything that I don't already think is antisemitic.' And so if I depart from their preconceived notions, the conclusion they draw is not that I'm making a contribution to an academic debate that they are not yet prepared to agree with, it's that I'm engaged in a project of intentional political slander and defamation.

When I, as part of my scholarly research, make a claim that a given practice or ideology or assertion is antisemitic, I do not expect my audience to give me unquestioning deference or blind acquiescence. I do expect that my audience will not assume I'm making a transparently bad faith argument to score cheap political points. But the AAUP has in effect constructed my entire scholarly agenda not as a form of academic research but as a threat to it. Antisemitism, under their view, is not something we debate; it's something that's used to close off debate. And again, because there is nobody (in academia or out) who *actually* takes the absurd stance that 'critiques of the Israeli state [are] invariably antisemitic,' the AAUP's concerns can only be directed towards those who believe that critiques of the Israeli state can ever be antisemitic. Whether by design or not, the AAUP has placed every academic who seeks to make assertions of antisemitism under a pall of suspicion.

When discussions of antisemitism are treated as something that stands outside the normal patterns of academic life—not a scholarly claim, but a threat to scholarship—the result can only be a shutting down of legitimate, even essential avenues of research and debate. Consider a recent presentation by philosopher Ruadhán Flynn at the University of Vienna, 'On Palestine, Antisemitism, and Academic Silence.' Flynn framed his talk around the same trope the AAUP did: the notion that 'anyone making any criticism of the actions of the Israeli government will be accused of antisemitism,' and the concurrent desire to reject the position that 'any and all criticism of Israeli state policies or actions is necessarily an expression of antisemitism.' But Flynn was not, unsurprisingly, actually speaking about *any* criticism of Israel, but rather two considerably more specific criticisms of Israel—the claim that it is an apartheid state, and the claim that it commits genocide.

To both claims, Flynn says that one can disagree in good faith as to whether either the apartheid claim or the genocide claim are true or not. 'Let's have that conversation,' he urges. However, he says, neither of them can be said to be antisemitic. As it happens, it turns out that most American Jews agree with Flynn on both scores: even before the latest round of hostilities, while solid majorities of American Jews disagree that Israel either is an apartheid state or is committing a genocide, most did not think either claim was antisemitic (this stood in contrast to the position that Israel has no right to exist, which overwhelmingly *was* viewed as antisemitic).

But as an antisemitism scholar, I'm not sure there's *nothing* that can validly be said relating the charge of, say, genocide to inferences of antisemitism. The allegation that Israel is committing genocide long predates the events of the past month, and in the past I've argued that the ubiquity of the 'genocide' claim at least in part is traceable to frustration that Jews get to 'claim' the Holocaust and can use it to contest default hegemonic narratives of gentile supremacy and Jewish subordination.

To be sure, the terrain has changed over the past month, and so I will absolutely concede one can disagree with this analysis' applicability to present affairs. As Flynn says, 'let's have that conversation.' But while I may be wrong about the connection between 'antisemitism' and genocide allegations (either in 2016 when I initially made my argument, or as overtaken by events in 2023), if I am, it is not because I am so foolish as to believe that 'any criticism of Israel is inherently antisemitic.'

The larger point here is that the issue of antisemitism is *part* of the conversation, it is not something that can be surgically excised from it. The late Critical Race Theory scholar Jerome McCristal Culp, Jr. made this same point in response to liberal critics who were willing to have debates over issues like affirmative action and racial inequity so long as charges of 'racism' were taken off the table: he labeled this insistence as one demanding 'a coerced argument … that concedes the key intellectual contest.' It's one thing to say it's not inherently racist to criticize, e.g., affirmative action programs. It's another thing to say we can even intelligibly discuss affirmative action programs if the issue of 'racism' is artificially removed from consideration. Put simply, those of us who research and write on antisemitism cannot do our jobs if our job is constructed as a form of illegitimate cheating or illiberal academic censorship. Academic freedom includes, and must include, the freedom to call things antisemitic *even when other people think we're wrong to do so.*

And in many ways, the austere confines of scholarly research is the arena in which Jews are least vulnerable. At least there, norms of academic freedom and research ethics still stand as at least a partial bulwark against the silencing of speech about antisemitism—even if these norms are sometimes honored in the breach. In other contexts, where we're more reliant on general social bonds of trust and good faith, the proliferation of the narrative that antisemitism claims are regularly a bad faith ploy to silence legitimate criticism of Israel can exert terrible pressure on Jews who are trying in good faith to articulate their own experiences and defend their dignity both on campus and in the wider world. A colleague of mine at another university, for instance, recently spoke of a situation where she had to remove a student from class for repeated antisemitic disruptions. The incident had nothing to do with Israel—the student refused to engage with assigned readings in favor of old-school, far-right declarations about supposed Jewish control of the media, Hollywood, finance, and so on. But my (untenured) colleague was nonetheless beset with anxiety—if the story got out of 'Jewish professor removes student from class for "antisemitism,"' how many people would just assume it was a case of blunt censorship on behalf of Israel? What would happen if the student did try to give his remarks just a little more of a fig leaf ('Zionist' control instead of 'Jewish' control)? One would hope that her colleagues in academia would trust her professional judgment and her ability to distinguish between a student making a controversial argument and naked antisemitic trolling. But the unrelenting narrative that just assumes that when Jews speak of antisemitism there's a decent chance they're maliciously trying to shield Israel from all criticism gives her worries genuine weight.

Students are in an even more vulnerable position. I've felt very lucky that my home institution, while certainly experiencing its share of tensions, has not witnessed any of the major blow-ups that have made national headlines. But even without the high-profile incidents of assault or terrorist threats, there remains a more subtle yet pervasive problem—Jewish students feel dismissed. They want to have an open conversation about what's going on in the world and with their families, to speak of and sort through sufferings of Israelis and Palestinians, and they're finding that their contributions are ignored if not actively derided.

The students I've talked to are decidedly not all-in rah-rah supporters of the Israeli government. They do not believe that 'any' criticism of Israel is antisemitic; they typically have a laundry list of their own criticisms they're happy to share. But what they report back to me is that if they try to forward *any* claims about antisemitism, if they even advance the possibility that some of their fellows' rhetoric or practices or behaviors (up to and including outright praise for Hamas' massacre of Israeli civilians) could potentially be antisemitic, they're immediately shut down—and the preferred rhetorical move to justify the shutdown is none other than the venerable 'criticism of Israel is not inherently antisemitic.' This declaration is not, it turns out, the last resort deployed only against the most unreasonable and inveterate far-right Zionists. It is rather the move of first resort, the initial response and too often the only response to any claim made about antisemitism, regardless of its merits.

The brute fact is that 'one cannot simultaneously purport to oppose antisemitism and assert that Jews are usually lying about their own experiences with antisemitism. That circle will never be successfully squared.' This is antisemitism in its *epistemic* dimension—the pervasive, unrelenting, uncompromising insistence that Jews speaking about our own experience are deluded, deceitful, or outright running a scam. Where this view pervades, our orientation towards antisemitism claims should not be one of open receptivity and fair-minded consideration, but rather wary alert to ensure that these likely bogus charges don't claim more innocent victims.

To be clear, not all claims about antisemitism are good claims. And we might suspect that certain contexts—to name a few: highly charged social controversies, violent geopolitical conflicts, young students whose political beliefs are yet to be fully developed—may be more prone to generating bad claims than others. One can certainly sympathize with the frustration of people who are faced with allegations of antisemitism when they earnestly believe the claim is meritless. But it is worth stressing just how *normal* that all is. In civil society and certainly on university campuses, there are many cases where things are called racist that many people sincerely do not believe are racist. The same is true for claims about sexism, and colonialism, and Islamophobia, and any number of analogous oppressions. Ideally, the way we respond to that conflict is by doing our best to consider the claim with charity and curiosity, with an open-mind and also with rigor. We ought not reflexively accept the claim as automatically true, nor should we instantly dismiss it as necessarily false. And at the end of our conversation, sometimes we'll conclude the claim has merit, sometimes we won't; sometimes, disagreements may simply remain intractable. But what we should not do is simply declare, in advance, that these claims somehow stand outside the walls of what is permissible to enter into the arena of intellectual consideration. Antisemitism claims deserve the same treatment.

And as difficult as it is, I do believe these conversations can occur. I teach a law school seminar on theories of anti-discrimination—a topic that unavoidably covers hot-button, fraught, and deeply contested issues of tremendous social import. At the start of the semester, I lay out two ground rules for discussion. First, I say that it is impossible to have a class on anti-discrimination where people are *forbidden* from calling things, e.g., racist. And that means that it's possible that some arguments you, the students, make or positions you hold may be called racist. That's not impermissible. We have to allow that. But the second rule is that a claim of racism does not end a conversation, it begins one. Just like any other assertion or argument that might be proffered in class, a claim of racism is just that—a claim, to be analyzed, debated, and dissected in full. And that means it's possible that some arguments you, the students, make asserting that something is racist will be contested and pushed back on. 'Racism' is not a trump card. It sits inside, not outside, of the normal boundaries of scholarly discussion.

Even as the perceived campus climate for having robust and open discussions on racism and other like oppressions has decayed, I've been exceptionally pleased with the caliber and quality of the discussions I've had in my seminars. Students, it turns out, are fully capable of having these hard conversations fruitfully. And I see no reason why antisemitism should be different. We can have hard, contested conversations about antisemitism. But in order to begin, we must be free to call things antisemitic.

Straw Man Arguments

1. *How do straw man arguments work?* Schraub's argument might be restated as follows. Where:

a. A, a scholar of antisemitism, makes a serious argument (X) that *some* criticisms of Israel are antisemitic, such as claims that Israel harvests the organs of Palestinian children; and

b. B falsely claims that A makes a non-serious argument (Y) that any and all criticism of Israel is antisemitic; and

c. Lurking in the background is the unstated non-serious argument (Z) that criticism of Israel is *never* antisemitic; then

d. Y is a "straw man argument," which OED defines as:

> In an argument, debate, etc.: an intentionally weak or misrepresented proposition, set up because it is easier to defeat than, or deflects attention away from, an opponent's real argument, giving the superficial impression that the original charge has been refuted or defeated.[79]

2. *What work do straw man arguments do?* This straw man argument serves several functions:

a. It enables B to avoid engaging X, A's serious argument.

b. It enables B to avoid having to defend Z, a non-serious argument.

c. It gives the appearance of discrediting X, A's serious argument, by casting it as indistinguishable from Y, the non-serious argument that B falsely ascribed to A.

In Schraub's view, the AAUA's argument serves to discredit scholarship on antisemitism, including law and antisemitism, by preemptively dismissing its foundational inquiry into what is or isn't antisemitic.

---

79. *Straw man*, Oxford Eng. Dictionary, https://doi.org/10.1093/OED/8212493808 (last visited Dec. 2023).

3. *Non-antisemitic critiques of the Israeli state.* What examples does Schraub provide to demonstrate that not all criticism of Israel is antisemitic or labeled as such?

4. *Paradox.* How does Schraub explain the paradox of the statement "criticism of Israel is not invariably antisemitic" being both true and potentially harmful? What role does the straw man argument play in his critique of antisemitic discourse?

5. *Conversation starter.* Schraub argues that claims of antisemitism should "begin conversations, not end them." What would this look like in practice?

6. *Impact of reflexive dismissal.* How does the reflexive dismissal of antisemitism claims affect the work of scholars who research antisemitism?

Chapter 6

Jews as Diabolical

This chapter's first two sections, "Jews as Heretical" and "Jews as Sub-Human," examine the legal frameworks established by the Spanish Inquisition and Nazi Germany, respectively, to persecute and destroy, spiritually or physically, Jews within their jurisdictions. This persecution extended to persons whom these regimes designated as Jews even though the victims themselves did not identify as Jewish or profess Judaism. It then presents a table comparing Canonical and Nazi measures designed to persecute Jews.

A. Jews as Heretical

Juana González, wife of Lope de Herrera, lived with her husband and family in Guadalupe, Castile, southwest of Madrid. Juana probably had been born a Christian to parents of Jewish ancestry. Seven years before this case, Pope Sixtus IV authorized the Spanish state to create a judicial entity to investigate and try Jewish converts to Christianity and their descendants, collectively known as *conversos*, for heresy. In the first decade of its activity, there were no fixed tribunals or districts. Instead, ad hoc tribunals were established in various cities for periods ranging from a few months to a few years.

In 1485, a tribunal of this entity, known as the Spanish Inquisition, was established in Guadalupe. One of its first steps was to publish an "edict of grace" stating that individuals who appeared and confessed would be reconciled to the Church. Juana, like many others, did this. These confessions often served as sources of information for later trials, and this is what happened to Juana. The inquisitors determined that Juana's confession was "false and insincere" and accused her of being a "Judaizing heretic and apostate," which she allegedly manifested through various statements and activities.

Suspicions about the veracity of Juana's defense during her trial led the inquisitors to threaten her with torture and, under threat of torture, she admitted to learning two Jewish prayers and sharing one of them with another person, also a *converso*. The inquisitors ruled that the prosecutor's initial charges of heretical actions were uncorroborated and absolved her of those charges, but for learning and sharing Jewish prayers, she was sentenced to perpetual exile.

The Trial of Juana González for Judaizing[1]

Tribunal of the Holy Office of the Inquisition
Guadalupe, Castile, sentenced November 19, 1485

Initial Confession and Reconciliation During Grace Period

Very Reverend and Lord Fathers:

I, Juana González, wife of Lope de Herrera, appear before Your Reverences with great pain in my soul and penitence in my heart and greatly shame-faced to say and bear witness to my sins that I have committed in offense of Our Lord Jesus Christ, whom I embrace, and against his Holy Catholic faith, repenting myself of them and I ask pardon of your Holy Piety and ask of Your Reverences penitence.

I say, Lords, my guilt that before I was married, in the house of my father I saw my mother order that the oil lamps be cleaned and order them to be lit Friday evenings, and that they not spin on Saturdays either and thus I saw it in their house, and even after I married. Sometimes and even at times those similar nights they didn't do anything and also at times my husband. I beg penitence; and I consented to it in my home. I ask penitence.

I say, Lords, my guilt that also my mother fasted some days and didn't begin to eat until night, and also fasted the Great Fast [Yom Kippur] and one day would stew for eating in [illegible] and that they would eat. I beg pardon for the ones and the others, and I also did it in their house and sometimes even after being married and I consented to it, and I saw my husband do it for reasons of ceremony. I ask penitence....

Accusation and Beginning of Trial

Very Reverend and Virtuous Lords:

I, the lawyer Diego Fernández de Zamora, prosecuting attorney [*promotor fiscal*][2] of this Holy Inquisition, accuse Juana González, wife of Lope de Herrera, who is herself present, citizen of this town of Guadalupe, who lived in possession and in the name of a Christian, and thus she called herself and enjoyed the privileges and immunities conceded to all those of the Christian religion, is a Judaizing heretic and apostate following the law of Moses in offense and injury of God and of our Holy Catholic faith, furthered when she said in her false reconciliation: asking for alms for the *conversos* saying *çedaca* [*tzedakah* (Hebrew:): mercy, alms] like the Jews say; and not praying the Pater Noster or Ave Maria when she is in church, but says "give me, Lord, what you promised me," as the Jews say; and circumcising and consenting and permitting her son to be circumcised and after this to have reconciled. She burned her pots in the fire

1. Trial translated in full in Gretchen D. Starr-LeBeau, In the Shadow of the Virgin: Inquisitors, Friars, and Conversos in Guadalupe, Spain (2008). The original document is at the National Historical Archive, Madrid, Inquisition section, legajo 154, expediente 20.

2. Editor's note: The *promotor fiscal* was a trained lawyer and an official of the inquisitorial tribunal. He oversaw an initial investigation before an accusation was made, could compel witnesses to speak, and continued to investigate as the trial continued. He functioned as a prosecutor.

because lard had been cooked in them, which she did last July 4 to observe the ceremony of the law of Moses and in this law it is prohibited and especially condemned to eat such meat for any person who observes and holds to that law ... and other things and cases that further were said by her in her so-called confession that I will protest and allege in the progress of this trial. For which I ask you and require, Reverend Lords, that for such heresy and false penitence and [illegible] you pronounce and declare her to have incurred a sentence of excommunication and confiscation and loss of all her goods and in all the other penalties and censures for these offenses both canonical and civil imposed against such persons, relaxing her and ordering her relaxed to the secular arm and justice.[3]

Initial Defense Statement

And after this on this day the Reverend Lord inquisitors ordered me, the notary, to go to the prison where Juana González was held. And there I read her the accusation so that she could respond to each item specifically. And ... Juana González responded to each item in the following way: [to the accusation] that she asked alms saying *çedaca*: she acknowledged that she never knew that was anything, except that she asked alms for the poor Christians and for the *conversos* without Judaizing intention, nor saying *çedaca*.... And that the truth is that being in church and having a son ill at around six months that she said among other prayers, "Lord, give me what you promised me and give health to this son." And that she had Masses said for his health. Because she never said with Judaizing intention, "Lord, give me what you promised me," except as a Christian ... and that she always ate lard and eats it now, and that she never [illegible] God with Judaizing intention; she would do it except to clean her pots like Christians do. And that she reconciled.

Witnesses

[The defense presented witnesses who testified that Juana's sons were not circumcised, that Juana said the Pater Noster and Ave Maria, that she had used fire to clean dirty pots on multiple occasions, and that she was known to eat lard. They also testified that she seemed to them to be a good Christian and was widely regarded as such. The prosecution presented a witness who testified that "she heard tell from some peasants" that Juana had circumcised a son.]

Defense Statement Responding to Prosecution Witnesses[4]

Very Reverend and Virtuous Lords:

I, Juan de Texeda, solicitor of Juana González wife of Lope de Herrera.... Your Reverences will find that the prosecutor has not proven his accusation. It contains four accusations:

---

3. Editor's note: Being "relaxed" means being handed over to the secular authorities for execution. Church authorities could not carry out a death sentence.

4. Editor's note: The accused were not permitted to know the names of the prosecution witnesses, and they were not permitted to read the anonymized prosecution testimony until after they closed their initial defense. The secrecy of prosecution witnesses was mandated by Queen Isabel at the be-

The first saying that she asked alms for the *conversos* and saying *çedaca* like the Jews say. About this he deposes the fourth witness presented for the prosecutor whose speech and deposition does not make a pronouncement against my party. The one does not because she is alone and singular;[5] the other because she does not say that the alms were collected for the *conversos* as is contained in his accusation. The other does not apply to my party because she reconciled to many other greater and graver things and thus in consequence this was seen to have been reconciled if it would have been done; but my party says that she never said *çedaca* nor *zanquzda* nor did she know it or hear it until this accusation. So that this first accusation was not proven.

The second accusation (that she did not pray the Pater Noster nor the Ave Maria when she was in church but that she used to say, "Lord, give me what you promised me," etc.), about this he deposes the fifth witness presented for the prosecutor, and there is no other that says such, and so her speech is denied cur dictum uniq. [because it is unique], etc. And Juana said it is true that she had said it, because Our Lord has promised sinners in that very hour in which they converted to Him and they asked mercy, he would hear them. And so Juana, because one son had died and another had been killed, and she had another ill to the death, repented her sins and asked God's mercy, that He would give mercy to her son, saying, "Lord, You promised well to give this to me and heal this son of mine." And so understood the witness and the deposition of the witness. It does not pertain to my party....

Prosecutor's Closing Statement

Very Reverend Lords:

I the prosecution attorney, Diego Fernández ... will be found to have well and completely proven my intention for that which is contained in my accusation and the witnesses presented by me well deposed and like they should be in law....

Conclusion of Presentation of Witnesses and Decision to Torture

On 26 October the Lords Inquisitors ... said that they concluded with the parties; they followed to give sentence on the third day and from there until when they had free.[6]

On the tenth of November 1485, seen by the Reverend Lords Inquisitors together with the other jurists to see the trials of the heretics they alleged.... And for other indications and causes that moved them to order her put to the question of torture. And to the bailiff Anton de Castillo to bring her then to the house, where they were accustomed to give the tortures and putting Juana González at the door of the house she

ginning of the Spanish Inquisition out of fear that accused people might seek revenge against their accusers.

5. Editor's note: To prove an accusation, prosecutors needed at least two eyewitnesses. The solicitor defending Juana is arguing that this testimony is insufficient to convict.

6. Editor's note: Five days after closing statements from the prosecutor and solicitor for the defense, the inquisitors are stating that the testimony portion of the trial is closed and that they will issue a sentence in three days. In fact, as in this trial, there were often much longer gaps between actions by the inquisitors.

was required to say the truth, and if not, they would give her torture. And never did she wish to say anything until they began to tie her arms [and then she admitted to learning two Jewish prayers and sharing one of them with someone else]. And her hands being tied, she said about the pots she had burned, that it was true what the witness had said it was because of the lard that had fallen in them. And also, the spoon. And also, the alms were according to this accusation and deposition of the witnesses saying *çedaca*, and she had asked it for three old women, two Old Christians and one *conversa*. Also, she said Lope de Herrera her [deceased] husband is a great Jew because many times she had words with him saying to him that she did not want two laws in her house and this because her husband kept the law of Moses. And how much her husband knew and did of the law of Moses, which he would show but he is dead. And being put on the *escalera*[7] before giving her any water she said she held the law of Moses before she reconciled, not believing the Messiah promised in the law to have come, nor less that the crucified Christ was in the consecrated Host that is raised on the altar, nor less that the Virgin Mary was a virgin before or during the birth, nor after the birth. Nor less did she believe that Christ had been received as the Son of God, that the Passion was to save us other sinners, that He is God.

... Also, she said that she kept all the Sabbaths until two or three years ago and that she reconciled after this. Then she asked that they untie her and let her go. And she had told the whole truth of what she knew and had done. And then she was untied and released from the *escalera* with protestation that if what she said proved true, and also if she confessed, where they would not continue the torture, and that the torture was considered not given.

On 16 November, Juana González wife of Lope de Herrera was brought by the bailiff Anton de Castillo before the Lord Doctor Inquisitor, at which time the confession she had given [under torture] was read to her. [She confirmed some elements of her statement under torture and denied others.]

Determination and Sentencing

WE FIND the accusation attempted by the prosecutor against Juana González not proved nor was proven as according to law ... to the end that we absolve her of the accusation....[8] This trial redounded to infamy and suspicion against Juana González, and also because she confessed that she knew the prayer that begins "of the covering" and others that begin "*cados*" and that this she had shown to Ínez Sánchez: In pain and penitence of all this ... we exile her perpetually from this town and its surrounding countryside to ten leagues, and that within nine days she comply with the exile....[9]

7. Editor's note: *Escalera* is Spanish for "ladder" or "stairs." The *escalera* torture was waterboarding.

8. Editor's note: The inquisitors determined that the prosecutor had not proven his initial accusations; the solicitor successfully demonstrated that the witnesses provided uncorroborated testimony.

9. Editor's note: Confession was sufficient to prove an accusation without corroboration, and the inquisitors sentenced Juana based on the statements she made under threat of torture. Execution was an uncommon sentence.

The Spanish Inquisition Was Legally Meticulous

1. *The accusation.* Juana is not accused of being Jewish; nor is she simply accused of being a heretic. Instead, she is accused of having falsely, incompletely confessed to heretical behavior in a previous legal statement. The prosecutor (*promotor fiscal*) charges Juana with hiding additional heretical behavior. This implies to the prosecutor that her initial confession and reconciliation were not genuine.

2. *Proving heresy.* Heresy is an incorrect belief that is intentionally held (despite knowing that the church understands it to be incorrect) and that is shared with others. Any prosecution for heresy therefore must demonstrate that the accused knowingly and publicly held incorrect beliefs. The charges the accuser makes (using a Jewish term for alms, cleaning pots in a manner consistent with keeping kosher, avoiding pork products, etc.) all occurred in the presence of others; that is, they were public acts.

> How does the prosecutor attempt to prove heresy (a mental state without an obvious victim) in a legal context? What are the behaviors or practices that the prosecutor cites as evidence? What is the relationship between the initial confession and the later accusation?

3. *Incomplete confession.* The accused's alleged failure to make a full confession is important evidence for two reasons. First, it suggests that the accused knew that her actions were heretical. Second, it implies that the confession was false or insincere, which challenges the validity of the confession. Also, at a practical level, prosecutors in the Spanish Inquisition routinely used confessions as a starting point for further accusations. They indicated a network of family and friends to pursue, and as with Juana, any unconfessed behavior (or any behavior deemed heretical that occurred after the confession) were grounds for an accusation.

4. *Fama.* Prosecutions based in Roman law required someone to make an accusation, but since there was no victim to serve as an accuser, inquisitors from the Middle Ages relied upon the reputation, or *fama*, of the accused to serve as the accuser. *Fama* was an important concept in early modern law generally, and the defense witnesses were careful to affirm Juana's good reputation, or *fama*, in their testimony.

5. *Witnesses.* What restrictions and stipulations were placed on witnesses? Defense attorneys labored under severe restrictions and stipulations concerning witnesses. Their witnesses could only respond to a list of pre-arranged questions common to all defense witnesses. They could not make open-ended statements. Prosecution witnesses were permitted to make a statement with few restrictions. The testimony of both prosecution and defense witnesses was taken down by notaries and provided in writing to the opposing side. Names were removed from prosecution witness statements so that the accused could not retaliate against them. And once statements were taken, both the prosecution and the defense were required to rely on these sworn statements. Witnesses could not be cross-examined or questioned a second time.

6. *Defense strategies.* The Spanish Inquisition permitted defense attorneys to employ three different defense strategies. First, they could make an argument of innocence based on character references for the accused (called *abonos*). Character witnesses were more persuasive if they were Old Christians, that is, not descended from Jewish converts. But character witnesses could be Old or New Christians. Second, the attorneys could provide witness statements contradicting prosecution testimony (*indirectas*). Third, they could challenge a witness for holding capital enmity against the accused (*tachas*). Because defendants did not know who had testified against them, they had to generate a list of people who held capital enmity in the hope that they were included among the prosecution witnesses. If enmity was proven in a subsidiary investigation, that prosecution testimony was stricken from the record. Juana's attorney, Juan de Texeda, was relying on *abonos* and *indirectas*.

7. *Alms for* conversos. Asking alms specifically and only for *conversos* meant that charitable activity was not intended to support Christians generally, and therefore appeared to be an attempt to provide Jewish charity rather than Christian charity, that is, to practice Judaism.

8. *Saying* çedaca *like the Jews say.* Juana's only explanation for this legally was denial. If proven, this would have been clear proof of heresy, because it met both qualifications for heresy: first, knowingly holding a belief contrary to Christianity; and second, sharing that belief publicly.

9. *She had her son circumcised.* Since all of Juana's children predeceased her, there was no way to confirm or refute this accusation physically. As a result, the inquisitors were dependent upon typical modes of proof, that is, two eyewitnesses.

10. *"Give me, Lord, what you promised me," as the Jews say.* Charges of Judaizing could take many forms, from attempts to engage in normative Jewish practices, to avoiding normative Christian practices, to statements of religious skepticism/toleration that might be made by Christians whether or not they had Jewish ancestry (for example, voicing the belief that Jews and Muslims could be saved in their religion just as Christians could be saved through Christianity). Any atypical statement, such as this one, could be interpreted to have Judaizing intent. But since the nature of the statement is ambiguous and not self-evidently Jewish, Juana attempts to defend herself by asserting a Christian meaning for her plea to God.

11. *Burning pots in the fire.* This is one method accepted in normative Judaism for ritually cleaning cookware after it has been contaminated with non-kosher food, such as lard (pork fat). It was not a typical way for Spanish Christians to clean their pots, and, therefore, was considered to show an effort to cook and eat according to Jewish law.

12. *Torture.* Throughout most of the history of the Spanish Inquisition, inquisitors and other officials of the tribunal, such as theological experts, voted on whether a defendant should be tortured. Torture was a way to gain legally legitimate testimony (a confession) when existing evidence was inconclusive, when there was a significant disagreement between prosecution and defense testimony, and when the defendant ad-

amantly refused to admit wrongdoing. After 1625, all decisions to torture a defendant were automatically reviewed by the Supreme Council of the Inquisition (*Suprema*). After the first few decades of the Spanish Inquisition, torture was rare.

> A series of rules governed the use of torture. Inquisitors recognized that a tortured person might say anything to end the torture, so there were several stages of questioning a witness before torturing them. First, witnesses were taken to the door of the torture chamber and asked to confess. If, like Juana, they did not, then they were brought inside and shown the torture implements and asked again. If the accused still did not speak, then they were tied to the torture device and asked again—itself a humiliating and painful process. This was when Juana spoke.
>
> After these stages, if the accused still did not speak, then the torturer began the official torture session. Afterward, the accused was returned to the inquisitorial prison. The tortured person also had to ratify their testimony at least twenty-four hours after the torture session. In many cases, as with Juana, the tortured person retracted some elements of their testimony and confirmed others. A prisoner of the Spanish Inquisition was only permitted to be tortured once (unlike in secular courts). By stating that the torture would be considered not to have happened if she confessed, the inquisitors were reserving the right to torture her again later in the trial.

How did inquisitors decide to torture Juana González? What evidence is there of constraints on judicial torture in the Spanish Inquisition? How would the decision to use torture relate to the laws of evidence (requiring two eyewitnesses or a confession) and the rules governing prosecution and defense testimony?

13. *Dutiful wife and daughter.* Women often defended themselves by blaming their behavior on their parents or husbands, that is, those who had authority over them. This allowed them to describe themselves as "good, obedient women," fulfill inquisitors' gendered expectations, and avoid blame.

14. *Implicate others.* Inquisitorial penitents were asked to name people who had taught them heretical beliefs or people with whom they had participated in heretical acts. In many cases, people tended to blame relatives or others who were deceased, absent, or otherwise safe from prosecution. The accused might have hoped to gain leniency from implicating others, if their compliance was understood as a sign of genuine contrition; but for inquisitors, the primary goal of gaining additional names was to identify more potential heretics.

15. *Sentencing.* Death sentences and prison sentences were uncommon in the Spanish Inquisition. More common were physical penalties (flogging, lightly administered), spiritual penalties (fasting, prayers, public humiliation by wearing tunics identifying their guilt), and in the early years of the Inquisition, exile. About ten percent of those tried by the Spanish Inquisition were not found guilty.

The Spanish Inquisition in Context

1. *The Spanish Inquisition as an agency of the Spanish state.* Although it was formally established under the Pope's authority, this authorization was a one-time event and irreversible; the Pope lacked the authority to terminate it unilaterally. The Spanish government created the apparatus; appointed the agency head, the Inquisitor General, and other officials; held ultimate control over its operations and policies; and funded its operations (by confiscating property of convicted persons). Only the state could abolish it, which it did for the last time in 1834.

2. *Religious explanations for the Inquisition.* Individuals past and present have made many arguments for why Isabella and Ferdinand began the Spanish Inquisition and, shortly thereafter, in 1492, expelled the Jews from their united kingdoms. Part of their motivation was religious. They saw themselves as having a special role in history as the year 1500 approached and millenarian expectations rose. Furthermore, the indeterminate and mutable beliefs and practices of converted Jews and their descendants challenged the religious environment and the potential salvation of everyone in their kingdoms. Similar concerns led to the forced expulsion of all Muslims from Spain a few years later.

3. *Political explanations for the Inquisition.* At the same time, the Inquisition also had political advantages for some people. When it was founded, some critics labeled it a "money grab" (*sacadineros*) on the part of the monarchs because of the seizure of goods belonging to those found guilty. Also, both Ferdinand's and especially Isabella's kingdoms were emerging from a period of political conflict and (in Isabella's Castile) civil war. The earliest tribunals of the Spanish Inquisition were held in places where there were powerful nobles and deep-seated resistance to Isabella's authority. Over time, many people across Spanish society found that bringing denunciations to the Spanish Inquisition provided an opportunity to punish their enemies.

4. *Jewish resistance to the Inquisition.* The Spanish Inquisition was not universally popular when it was founded. There was resistance from elites and non-elites, and from Old Christians and New Christians (Jews and Muslims were not under the Inquisition's authority). Some of this resistance was on theological grounds, while others objected to the political power it provided Isabella and Ferdinand. Evidence of ongoing resistance and discontent with the Inquisition continued for centuries. The King began to limit its power in the 18th century, and the Spanish Inquisition ended in the 19th century. Resistance to the Inquisition, therefore, was not primarily Jewish.

5. *What happened to Spain's Jews who left rather than convert to Christianity?* Spain's Jewish community was definitively ordered to convert or be expelled in 1492, barely a decade after the Inquisition held its first cases. One scholar plausibly estimates that over half the Jewish population of the Spanish Kingdoms (Aragon and Castile) left, but many of those returned and converted, while the rest of the Jewish population converted rather than leave their homes. Total net emigration was perhaps 40,000–50,000

people. Initially, Jews relocated to nearby areas, such as the kingdoms of Navarre and Portugal, and cities in southern France, the Italian peninsula, and North Africa. Under pressure from the Spanish monarchs, the Portuguese King mandated the forced conversion of all Jews in Portugal in 1497, and Navarre expelled its Jews in 1499. As a result, many Jews who had fled to these locations returned to Spain and converted, which gave them the right to reclaim the property they had left behind. Other Jews fled to North Africa, but anti-Jewish violence there also drove some Jews back to Spain.[10] Others carried forward a large Iberian Jewish diaspora which spread around the world; but this occurred in stages. Some moved on to the Netherlands, German territories, and the Ottoman Empire. Ultimately, the Sephardic diaspora extended around the Mediterranean, and with the Dutch, around the world.

6. *How did the Spanish Inquisition define Jews and Judaism?* The Inquisition was not explicitly interested in defining Jews; its interest was in identifying, prosecuting, and reforming heretics. In practice, inquisitors defined secret Jews and Judaizing practices. Their definition had a biological component; Jews and Judaizing Christian heretics were the children of Jews or the descendants of Jews (inquisitors did not distinguish between matrilineal and patrilineal descent). Inquisitors also defined Judaism through practices they deemed "Judaizing," which they publicized in sermons. In fact, some *conversos* used these lists to help them learn how to practice Judaism in secret as adults. Some of these were normative Jewish practices (fasting on the Day of Atonement, known as Yom Kippur, or the Great Fast in Spanish), while others were not conventionally Jewish but indicated Judaizing intent (praying to St. Esther). Public synagogue worship, which centered around men, was not available to *conversos*, who were technically Christian. As a result, secret, Judaizing practices tended to focus on domestic practices that were the responsibility of women, such as keeping kosher and observing the Sabbath in the home.

7. *How did Jews at the time define Jewish belief?* Jewish philosopher Moses ben Maimon (Maimonides, or the Rambam) (1138–1204), was born in Córdoba, Spain, which he fled after Muslim leaders threatened Jews and Christians with conversion to Islam or death. Maimonides has been described as "the most influential Jewish thinker of the Middle Ages, and quite possibly of all time." The Rambam identified thirteen principles or articles of faith he considered binding on every Jew:

(1) the existence of God

(2) the absolute unity of God

(3) the incorporeality of God

(4) the eternity of God

(5) that God alone is to be worshipped

(6) that God communicates to prophets

10. Henry Kamen, *The Mediterranean and the Expulsion of the Spanish Jews in 1492*, 119 Past & Present 30 (1988).

(7) that Moses is the greatest prophet
(8) that the Torah was given by God
(9) that the Torah is immutable
(10) that there is divine providence
(11) that there is divine punishment and reward
(12) that there will be a Messiah; and
(13) that the dead will be resurrected.[11]

8. Conversos' *religious convictions.* In earlier generations, scholars wanted to identify *conversos* collectively or individually as either devout Christians or devout Jews. In recent years, however, scholars have shifted their approach. There is a consensus that individuals' beliefs shifted over time, or even by context. Some were certainly devout Catholics, and others fled to the Netherlands, Italy, or the Ottoman Empire, recommitted or converted to Judaism, and learned to live as "New Jews" (as opposed to their earlier designation as "New Christians"). Some *conversos* identified themselves as Jewish, but their beliefs and practices were influenced by Christian assumptions and theology and included nonstandard practices, which is not surprising given that they grew up in a Christian environment.[12]

Discrimination Against Persons of Jewish Ancestry

1. Conversos *as targets.* A *converso* was someone who had at least one ancestor (counting back four generations) who was a convert from Judaism to Christianity, or the descendant of such a convert. By 1492, the Spanish Crown required all Jews to convert to Christianity or to emigrate. By 1526, all Muslims in Spain had been forced to convert to Christianity. Thereafter, Spanish residents and residents in their colonial territories were expected to adhere to normative Catholic doctrine and practices. There were a few limited exceptions to this rule for citizens from some Protestant countries whose governments established specific immunity rulings; and for a period, indigenous peoples in the Americas were exempt from prosecution for heresy.

In its earliest decades, the Spanish Inquisition targeted Jewish converts and their descendants almost exclusively, thus subjecting all *conversos* to heightened state scrutiny. After the first few decades, the Inquisition expanded its list of targets, but descendants of Jewish converts continued to face periods of intensified investigation and hostility. The Portuguese Inquisition, by contrast, maintained its primary focus on people of Jewish ancestry throughout its existence.

---

11. Moses Maimonides (Rambam) (1138–1204), Jewish Virtual Libr., https://www.jewishvirtuallibrary.org/moses-maimonides-rambam (last visited January 11, 2025). Kenneth Seeskin, *Maimonides*, Stan. Encyclopedia of Phil. Archive (Feb. 4, 2021), https://plato.stanford.edu/archives/spr2021/entries/maimonides/.

12. Nathan Wachtel, The Faith of Remembrance: Marrano Labyrinths (2013).

Figure 6.1. Monument to Maimonides, Córdoba, Spain. The monument was unveiled in 1964. A plaque was posted in 1985 to commemorate the 850th anniversary of the Rambam's birth.

The Spanish Inquisition operated on the basis of evidentiary principles specific to persons of Jewish ancestry—e.g., certain behaviors of a *converso* were construed differently than the same behavior by Old Christians. In fact, some evidence of Judaizing heresy (for example, avoiding pork and lard) were not in themselves considered heretical behaviors (Christians are not obligated to eat pork). These evidentiary principles in the tribunal had consequences for all *conversos*, including those not tried, because they had to avoid behavior that might not be presumed to manifest heresy in Old Christians. As a result, *conversos* were subjected to different levels of surveillance and investigation than Old Christians.

By the 16th century, Spain identified a state interest in maintaining correct Catholic practice among all its citizens. But to what extent did "correct Catholic practice" entail active participation in standard Catholic practices? Or, to what extent did "correct Catholic practice" entail avoiding practices that were not forbidden to Catholics but that suggested adherence to Judaism? And how might this distinction have resulted in legal inequality for *conversos*?

2. *Ascertainment of Jewish ancestry.* To carry out its work, the Inquisition had to define who was and who was not a *converso*. This was necessary to identify the persons to scrutinize for "Judaizing," and thus justify using *converso*-specific principles for evaluating evidence. Within a few decades of this trial, inquisitors also began asking the accused to present a detailed genealogy, listing relatives and identifying anyone who had been accused of Judaizing by the Inquisition in the past, in case the accused had *converso* ancestors. A person's reputation or *fama* could also provide evidence of Jewish ancestry. The negative reputation of families convicted by the Inquisition was maintained by hanging a person's penitential garments (*sanbenitos*) on the walls of the local parish church, so everyone could see them. The Portuguese Inquisition, by contract, did not record genealogies and depended on reputation and purity of blood certificates to determine Jewish ancestry.

3. *Blood purity laws.* Around the time of this trial, some secular and religious authorities started to establish "purity of blood" laws requiring candidates for local political offices and some monastic orders to present a genealogy that proved they had no Jewish or *converso* ancestors going back four generations. The Spanish Inquisition was not involved in proposing or policing purity of blood laws in general, though once these laws became commonplace, lay assistants who worked for the Inquisition needed to prove purity of blood to work for the Inquisition. Purity of blood laws were initially controversial in Spain because they overtly challenged Christian theological beliefs that saw all Christians of any background as equal in their Christianity; but eventually, they were adopted by most religious groups, political offices, and for emigration to the Americas. Some religious orders were more unwilling than others to embrace this practice. The Jeronymite Order, a local Spanish religious order with many *converso* friars, decided to institute purity of blood requirements for entry over many years, without informing their *converso* brethren. Two orders founded by *conversos*, St. Ignatius Loyola's Jesuits and St. Teresa of Avila's Discalced Carmelites, reluctantly adopted purity of blood requirements for admission to their orders after long fights—retroactively banning their own founders decades after their deaths.

4. *Disputing Jewish ancestry.* In theory, someone charged with Judaizing could refute the accusation that they were of Jewish descent, but if a person's reputation or *fama* linked them with Jewish ancestry, the inquisitors accepted that identification through

reputation unless there was specific evidence to the contrary. On the other hand, if a family had successfully been investigated for purity of blood and held the relevant certificate, this could exonerate the descendant of a claim of Jewish ancestry. Participating in Judaizing practices also resulted in an assumption of Jewish ancestry.

5. *Losing* converso *status*. There were a handful of ways that a person of Jewish ancestry could lose their status as a *converso*. Some individuals falsified their genealogies to avoid the stigma of *converso* status and enable them to emigrate to the Americas. Less commonly, wealthy *conversos* paid to have the Crown award them noble status, which legally erased their status as *conversos*. However, the Crown sometimes revoked noble status years later, pushing those individuals back to the status of *conversos*. Emigration out of Spanish territory was insufficient to erase one's status as a *converso*. In Italian cities such as Venice, local officials recognized that individuals from Spain or Portugal who arrived and identified themselves as Jews were likely baptized Christians and therefore heretics if they did not observe Christianity. Occasional large payments from the Venetian Jewish community mitigated this. On the other hand, the religiously diverse Netherlands did not concern itself with the baptismal status of immigrants who identified as Jewish. In any case, some *conversos* continued to travel in and out of Iberia on business, even after emigrating, and their *converso* status followed them back and forth across the border, even if its impacts were minimal outside of Iberia.

6. *The Spanish Inquisition as an incubator of Judaizing practices*. Scholars have argued that the inquisitorial system unintentionally helped preserve the very Judaizing practices it was designed to stamp out, both by publishing and disseminating information about specific Judaizing practices, and by indirectly encouraging a distinct *converso* social identity. Judaizers who made impassioned statements of their beliefs at the scaffold or the pyre impressed their listeners of all religious persuasions. Yet by the late eighteenth century, *conversos* were ultimately assimilated into Spanish society, while descendants of Muslim converts to Christianity (called *moriscos*) were not and were expelled as a group in the early 17th century.[13]

Sources

James S. Amelang, Parallel Histories: Muslims and Jews in Inquisitorial Spain (2013).

John F. Chuchiak IV, The Inquisition in New Spain, 1536–1820: A Documentary History (2012).

Lu Ann Homza, Spanish Inquisition, 1484–1614: An Anthology of Sources (2006).

Henry Kamen, *The Mediterranean and the Expulsion of the Spanish Jews in 1492*, 119 Past & Present 30 (1988).

Gretchen D. Starr-LeBeau, In the Shadow of the Virgin: Inquisitors, Friars, and Conversos in Guadalupe, Spain (2003).

13. James S. Amelang, Parallel Histories: Muslims and Jews in Inquisitorial Spain (2013).

Gretchen D. Starr-LeBeau, Seven Myths of the Spanish Inquisition (2023).
Nathan Wachtel, The Faith of Remembrance: Marrano Labyrinths (2013).

B. Jews as Sub-Human

German Jewish men experienced legal emancipation in Germany following the unification of Germany and culminating with the creation of the German Empire in 1871 under Otto von Bismarck. Jews accounted for less than one percent of the entire German population and were especially represented in the urban middle class and in the free professions such as lawyers or medical doctors. Even though they were full citizens and there was no antisemitic discrimination on legal grounds, many German Jews still suffered antisemitism and encountered "glass ceilings" regarding access to employment in the state sector, especially the civil service, the military, or the justice system. Only if Jews converted to Christianity did avenues in government professions open up. Day-to-day antisemitism was also a common phenomenon in Central Europe as well as in the United States, such as the exclusion of Jews from vacation resorts, hotels, and tourist destinations.

In 1919, following Germany's defeat in World War I, two significant events occurred in Germany. The first was the establishment of the liberal democratic Weimar Republic. The Weimar constitution (*Weimarer Reichsverfassung*) contained a catalogue of fundamental human rights and enshrined the principle of equality of all citizens before the law. Even prior to the Weimar Republic, most German Jews considered themselves German citizens of the Mosaic Belief. The Zionist movement remained small in Germany compared to other Central and Eastern European Countries. Jews in Germany were at this stage not singled out as a particular ethno-racial group but considered one of the religious communities present in German society, which was overwhelmingly Christian and, in the biggest state, Prussia, predominantly Protestant. Only after World War I did racial antisemitism influenced by social Darwinist ideas start to grow in German society. Jews' status as Jews was increasingly seen as based on "racial" grounds rather than religious ones, thus reducing the utility of conversion to Christianity as a means of escaping antisemitism. Nonetheless, in the 1920s, there were no formal, legal measures explicitly hindering German Jews in their professional advancement, and it was also possible to challenge—albeit not always successfully—manifestations of antisemitism in the political arena and in courts of law. 1919 also saw the founding of the National Socialist German Workers' Party (Nationalsozialistische Deutsche Arbeiterpartei, NSDAP), more commonly known as the Nazi Party. It was one out of many right-wing splinter parties that embraced bio-nationalistic ideas (*völkische Weltanschauung*) demanding the "removal" of "foreign elements" and calling for a "unity of all ethnic Germans" (*Volksgemeinschaft*). In 1920, a year after its founding, the Nazi party in its manifesto promised its members a "racial state"[14] and formulated its antisemitic policy:

---

14. *Cf.* Michael Burleigh & Wolfgang Wippermann, The Racial State: Germany 1933–1945 (1991).

> Only national comrades can be citizens. Only those of German blood can be national comrades, regardless of their religious denomination. Therefore, no Jew can be a national comrade. Those who are not citizens will live in Germany only as guests and must be subject to immigration legislation. Only citizens can have the right to vote on the leadership and laws of the state. We therefore demand that public office, of any kind, whether in the Reich, a state, or a municipality, be held only by citizens.[15]

Nazis Come to Power

After Hitler came to power on January 30, 1933, the Nazis largely dismembered the liberal Weimar constitution and recentered it around the rule of the Nazi Party and its ***Führer*** (the "Führer's principle"). Critically, the Nazi regime did not formally suspend or abrogate the Weimar constitution. Rather, the regime enacted certain laws that served as the basic foundational laws of the Reich (*Reichsgrundgesetze*), most notably the Nuremberg Laws defining the civic status of Jews and prohibiting intermarrying and extramarital intercourse between Jewish and non-Jewish Germans. Creating special ethno-racial laws for Jews and defining them legally as an out-group, meaning a group of the population that had been defined to stand "outside" the so-called legal community (*Rechtsgemeinschaft*) after 1933, was therefore a rupture with the liberal legal tradition in Germany since 1871 and presented a new "quality" in the history of persecution of Jews in modern Europe. The Nazi regime's process of depriving German Jews of their legal rights and their lives, culminating in the Holocaust, took less than ten years, starting right after Adolf Hitler acceded to power in 1933. The development of the disenfranchisement and persecution of Jews did not happen in a linear way, though, nor were the Nazis' antisemitic policies enforced only from the top down. Party activists used so-called "spontaneous street violence" in a deliberate manner to exercise pressure on supposedly less radical state actors to push them to adopt and implement anti-Jewish laws and measures. The "formalization" of antisemitic persecution through direct state actions was deemed necessary, as public participation in violence against Jews did not reach the levels intended by Nazi propaganda. Apparently, major parts of German society still needed to be persuaded of the "legitimacy" of anti-Jewish measures. The legalization and formalization of such measures might have contributed to the German population's acceptance of anti-Jewish discrimination as "formal," "legal," and "orderly." As in every modern political system based on the division of responsibilities and labor, legal forms and definitions were also deemed more efficient as a means to permeate and transform German society in order to work towards the establishment of a racial state.

Formalized discrimination resorting to traditional legal and administrative means to shape and implement antisemitic policy was not openly violent, but possibly even more coercive and effective when it came to demoralizing Jewish Germans: seizing their property, taxing them into bankruptcy, pushing them out of the labor market, and

---

15. Translation from quote in: Wilhelm Stuckart, *Staatsangehörigkeit und Reichsgestaltung*, 5 Reich Volksordnung Lebensraum 57, 66 (1943).

driving them out of the country. It had the advantage of being considered "legitimate action" by the majority of the German population as well as many foreign governments. As acts of the state, such laws were conceived and enforced by the ministerial bureaucracy and by the state administration on the regional and local level.

Reich Citizenship Act

On September 15, 1935, the German Parliament or Reichstag passed the Reich Citizenship Act (*Reichsbürgergesetz*),[16] which created a two-tiered system of citizenship in the Reich. The Reich Citizenship Act consisted of only three paragraphs: Article 1 stated that "a citizen is someone who belongs to the "protective association" (*Schutzverband*) of the German Reich and is "specially bound to it." Article 2 of the Act made a distinction between mere nationals and "political citizens" of the Reich. Only "citizens of German or related blood" could be the political citizens of the Reich and therefore "holders of full political rights in accordance with the law." They also had to prove through their behavior that they were "willing or able" to serve "the German people and Reich faithfully." Article 3 authorized the Reich and Prussian Interior Ministry (the "Ministry"), in agreement with the Office of the Deputy of the Führer ("SdF") to lay down the "legal and administrative provisions necessary to enforce and amend this law," i.e., to make the important definitional decision on who should be considered a "holder of political rights" and therefore a "citizen of the Reich."

The uncertainty surrounding the scope of the Nuremberg Laws increased pressure on the implementing bodies to find a solution to the definitional question. For the Ministry's officials, it was therefore of paramount importance to enforce a definition of the concept of Jews that was "practicable" in terms of administrative law and law on civil status (*Personenstand*). The Office of the Deputy of the Führer (SdF) mostly wanted to "class" so-called "half-Jews" as Jews. The Ministry and SdF agreed that, besides "German-blooded" individuals and Jews, "Jewish *Mischlinge*" should also remain in a third category, with fewer rights—divided into "quarter- and half-Jews"—whose members would, in several areas of life, be treated worse than German-blooded individuals but better than persons deemed full Jews. The *Mischlinge* would be restricted in their ability to practice professions and hold roles such as officials, officers, lawyers, doctors, or farmers of inherited agricultural estates. The "main aim" was "to make the mixed races disappear as quickly as possible."[17]

Eventually, the definitional uncertainties in the Reich Citizenship Act's categories were addressed by the First Regulation on the Reich Citizenship Act of 14 November 1933 (the "First Regulation").[18] Under Article 2 (2) of the regulation, a *Mischling* was

---

16. Reichsbürgergesetz [Reich Citizenship Act], Sept. 15, 1935, REICHSGESETZBLATT, Teil I [RGBL I], at 1146.

17. *Cf.* Wilhelm Stuckart, Home State Sec., Presentation on Grundsätzliches zu den Ausführungsbestimmungen zum Reichsbürgergesetz und zum Blutschutzgesetz, *in* Federal Archives Berlin-Lichterfelde, R 1501/5514, 45–55, 46 (Nov. 2, 1935). In almost identical words, also see the notes on Gegenüberstellung der Fassung Dr. Wagner und der Fassung MdI, loc. 56 et seq. (Nov. 2, 1935).

18. RGBL I 1935 at 1333.

defined as one who descended from one or two fully Jewish grandparents in terms of race, unless they were considered a Jew in accordance with Article 5, Sec. 2. A grandparent was deemed a full-blooded Jew if he or she had belonged to the Jewish religious community. The core provision of the regulation was Article 5, which defined who was a Jew and/or who should be considered as such:

1. A Jew is anyone who is descended from at least three grandparents who are racially full Jews.
2. A Jew is also one who is descended from two full Jewish parents, if
   (a) He belonged to the Jewish religious community at the time this law was issued, or joined the community later.
   (b) He was married to a Jewish person at the time the law was issued, or married one subsequently.
   (c) He was the offspring of a marriage with a Jew, in the sense of Section 1, which was contracted after the Law for the Protection of German Blood and German Honor became effective.
   (d) He was the offspring of an extramarital relationship with a Jew, according to Section I, and would be born out of wedlock after July 31, 1936.

Mischlinge were to be considered "provisional citizens of the Reich." A "Jew" could not be a citizen of the Reich in accordance with Article 4 (1). Although they remained German nationals, Jews had no political voting power and could not hold public office.

Racial classification was, in principle, based on the religious affiliation of an individual's grandparents. The criteria for affiliation with the Jewish community specifically included involvement in the customary ritual ceremonies, inclusion on the list of the Jewish synagogue community, or the payment of Jewish religious taxes. Accordingly, it was "immediately" and irrefutably legally assumed that one grandparent was "fully Jewish ... if they had belonged to the Jewish religious community," which was relatively easy to determine using marriage certificates. This way, the difficult assessment of the "race of great-grandparents" or "even more remote generations" could be omitted.[19] Nazi civil servants hoped that "fabricated claims, or claims that could never be verified, made by subjects of descent examinations" that many of their ancestors were indeed of the Jewish religion but were not of Jewish blood could be avoided.[20] Stricter provisions exceeding the scope of the Jewish concept laid down by the NSDAP and its divisions

---

19. *Cf.* Wilhelm Stuckart & Hans Globke, Reichsbürgergesetz vom 15. September 1935. Gesetz zum Schutze des deutschen Blutes und der deutschen Ehre vom 15. September 1935. Gesetz zum Schutze der Erbgesundheit des deutschen Volkes (Ehegesundheitsgesetz) vom 18. Oktober 1935. nebst allen Ausführungsvorschriften und den einschlägigen Gesetzen und Verordnungen 63 n. 6 (1936). (The "disadvantages inherent in this solution" had to be taken into account "to enable the provisions to be handled practically, quickly and securely.")

20. *Cf.* Bernhard Lösener & Friedrich A. Knost, Nürnberger Gesetze 52 n. 5 (The criteria for affiliation with the Jewish religion specifically included involvement in the customary ritual ceremonies, inclusion on the list of the Jewish synagogue community, or the payment of Jewish religious taxes.). *Cf.* Stuckart & Globke, *supra* note 19, at 64, 99 et seq.

were not affected by Article 6 of the regulation. However, Article 6 (2) stated that other further-reaching provisions required approval by the Reich and Prussian Ministry for the Interior and the SdF, or they would be rendered ineffective. Article 7 of the first regulation of the Reich Citizenship Act allowed for the possibility of Hitler granting exemptions from classification as a Jew, *Geltungsjude* and Jewish *Mischling* as a matter of political expediency.

In the following years, up until summer 1939, new regulations on the Reich Citizenship Act were issued, further limiting the professional and economic activities of Jewish citizens. The second regulation excluded "non-Aryan" doctors from public and charitable hospitals. The third regulation defined which businesses were deemed "Jewish." The fourth regulation revoked Jewish doctors' licenses to practice. The fifth and sixth regulations revoked Jewish lawyers' licenses to practice. The eighth regulation revoked the licenses of Jewish dentists, veterinary surgeons, and pharmacists to practice their professions.

Blood Protection Act

Also on September 15, 1935, the Reichstag enacted the "Act on the Protection of German Blood and German Honor" (*Gesetz zum Schutze des deutschen Blutes und der deutschen Ehre*),[21] also known as the "Blood Protection Act" (*Blutschutzgesetz*). This Act was intended to secure a "solution to the Jewish question" in the future, together with "purity of the blood." This was signified in the preamble:

> Entirely convinced that the purity of German blood is essential to the further existence of the German people and inspired by the uncompromising determination to safeguard the future of the German nation, the Reichstag has unanimously resolved upon the following law....

In conjunction with the name of the law, the preamble was considered a "guideline for the interpretation of individual provisions," as it indicated the "methodological meaning and aim of the law."[22] With reference to the aim of the law expressed in the prologue, to "protect German blood and German honor," punishment was justified in situations in which it was otherwise uncertain or even precluded based on the wording.[23]

The Blood Protection Act prohibited marriage (Article 1) and extramarital intercourse (Article 2) between Jews and non-Jewish Germans, and declared marriages entered into in spite of this invalid, even if they had been entered into abroad to bypass the law (Article 1 (1) (2)), a.k.a., "evasive marriage." The offense that was considered significant in practice according to the Blood Protection Act was "extramarital intercourse between Jews and citizens of German or related blood," which was banned by Article 2 of the Act. The first implementing regulation on the Blood Protection Act extended the ban on extramarital intercourse to include intercourse between Jews and

---

21. RGBl I 1935 at 1333.

22. *Cf.* Gerhard Werle, Justiz-Strafrecht und polizeiliche Verbrechensbekämpfung im Dritten Reich 180 et seq. (1989).

23. *Id.*

Mischling citizens with only one "fully Jewish grandparent," who in this respect were sufficiently non-Jewish and equal to citizens of German blood.

The Blood Protection Act punished only men who married or had extramarital intercourse (not women), threatening them with imprisonment for up to fifteen years. Regarding the "overall protection of blood and honor" that the Act was aimed at, the actual protection of the particular partners involved played no role. Article 3 of the Blood Protection Act prohibited Jews from "employing female citizens of German or related blood under 45 years old in their households," whereby the protection of domestic workers against "racially perverse sexual threats" was intended. Article 4 (1) of the Blood Protection Act prohibited Jews from "flying the flag of the Reich and nation and displaying the Reich colors"; Article 4 (2) permitted Jews to "display the Jewish colors" and brought the "exercise of this authority ... under state protection."

The personal scope of application of the Nuremberg Laws had to be laid down in law by way of implementing regulations issued by the Reich (and Prussian) Ministry of the Interior in agreement with the Deputy of the Führer, the Nazi-Party Ministry. This would enable registrars and public prosecutors to apply the new laws based on the basis of features that were clearly identifiable.

The laws concerned nothing less than the fundamental question of where the racial state would draw the line between so-called citizens and therefore also "holders of rights," i.e., participants in the rights of civil law, and the "others," the so-called "foreign peoples," who were not part of the "community of the people and legal community" (*Volks- und Rechtsgemeinschaft*) and only retained an inferior legal status with lesser rights. These were questions that, according to estimations at that time, affected approximately 1.5 million people and therefore almost 2 percent of the population of the Reich, who were classified as "full Jews" or so-called *Mischlinge*, as well as their spouses and/or sexual partners. The ban on the employment of "Aryan" domestic workers was scheduled to come into force on January 1, 1936, and the Reich and Prussian Ministry of the Interior expected it to lead to the dismissal of approximately 60,000 maids—and thus to have considerable repercussions for labor market policy. It was also apparent that the necessary exemptions and the associated application processes would entail a significant amount of bureaucracy.

The Appearance of Legality

The implementation of Nazi laws was entrusted to the administrative state and the judiciary, long famous for its professionality and efficiency. The upper echelons of these institutions were in large part staffed with conservative civil servants and judges, who had been skeptical or even openly hostile towards the democratic and egalitarian constitutional order of the Weimar Republic. Many welcomed the establishment of an authoritarian state in 1933, which bore more resemblance to pre-World War I imperial Germany.

The Nuremberg Laws created the appearance of legality for the persecution of the Jewish population and was the basis for a legion of other laws and regulations which subsequently also shaped the disenfranchisement process in other areas of life. The definition of Jews laid down in the legislation remained relevant for defining the victims of all disenfranchisement and extermination actions introduced and carried out in the territory of the Reich in the subsequent period.

Contemporary literature and the Supreme Senate of the Reichsgericht (*Großer Senat*), a.k.a., the supreme court of the German Reich, gave a rapturous welcome to new laws as so-called "constitutional laws of the NSDAP state," a "starting point for all German law" and the "core" of the "constitutional rights" of the German people."[24] From then on, "people and race" were considered "fundamental terms in the NSDAP constitution" which superseded the principle of equality before the law.[25]

Although the German Reich therefore ultimately decided to break with the liberal principle of equality before the law in 1935, many contemporaries viewed the Nuremberg Laws, which were issued following a wave of antisemitic riots and uncertainty since the spring of that year, with a certain relief. Instead of the antisemitic mobs often directed by local party offices, whose aggression resulted in pogrom-like attacks and the public denunciation of so-called "racial defilers" (*Rassenschänder*) in many German locales, the regulatory hand of the state now seemed to appear, creating clear regulations for a "legal ... solution to the Jewish question."

For his part, Hitler referred to the Nuremberg Laws as a mere "attempt at statutory regulation of a problem" and "in the event of further failure," threatened to deal with the "Jewish problem ... by way of a law devolving its solution to the NSDAP."

How was it possible that the liberal pre-Nazi system was so quickly adjusted to the demands of the Nazis? After 1933, most existing pre-Nazi laws were simply reinterpreted or adjusted and complemented by new laws to pursue the Nazis' political goals. Anti-Jewish policy and laws were based mostly on new Nazi legislation. This was often done by the same lawyers who had worked during the Weimar Republic or the German Empire.

Ernst Fraenkel, a German Jewish lawyer and émigré, characterized the Nazi State aptly as a "dual state," a state of violent measures or actions "outside the law" and—still—a state of norms, which employed "traditional" administrative and legal means characteristic of a system ruled by law.[26] Political scientist Franz Leopold Neuman, also a German Jewish lawyer and émigré, characterized the Party and the State as a state of exceptions and a state of norms, amalgamated into an indiscernible monster,

24. Reichsgericht [RG] [Federal Court of Justice] Feb. 23, 1938, 72 Entscheidungen des Reichsgerichts in Strafsachen [RGSt] 91, 96.

25. Cf. Roland Freisler, *Ein Jahr Blutschutzrechtsprechung in Deutschland*, *in* Deutsches Strafrecht 3 385–397, 389 (1936).

26. Ernst Fraenkel, The Dual State: A contribution to the theory of Dictatorship (1941).

a murderous state which started to persecute, deport, and murder minorities defined on eugenic and racial grounds.[27]

Judgment on the Jewish Status of a *Mischling*[28]

Reich Administrative Court (*Reichsverwaltungsgericht*)
June 5, 1941

The plaintiff challenged a police decision, which obliged him to carry a *Kennkarte für Juden* [identity card for Jews] although only his maternal grandparents had been classified as "Jewish" but he had been a member of the Jewish Community when the Reich Citizenship Law came into force on September 15, 1935 (§ 5a of the First Regulation on the Implementation of the law) and would thus be considered a so-called *Geltungsjude* ["full Jew"]. In the First Regulation to the Reich Citizenship Law, the group of later so-called *Geltungsjuden* is defined in Sec. 5(2):

> A Jew shall also be deemed to be the Jewish *Mischling* descended from two Jewish grandparents,
>
> (a) who ... belongs to the Jewish religious community ...
>
> (b) who was married to a Jew at the time of the enactment of the law ...
>
> (c) who comes from a marriage with a Jew ... which was concluded after ... September 15, 1935
>
> (d) who comes from extramarital intercourse with a Jew ... and was born out of wedlock after July 31, 1936.

The plaintiff had terminated his membership in the Jewish Community only on April 26, 1938, and stated that he did not consider himself Jewish as he was not circumcised and did not pay contributions to a Synagogue. The RVG finds that he was to be considered Jewish nonetheless. Not his subjective but the "external facts" were to be taken into account in order to assess his affiliation with the Jewish Community.

Sec. 1 of the Third Decree on the Compulsory Identification Card of July 23, 1938; Article 5 of the First Regulation on the Reich Citizenship Law (*RBürgerG*) of November 14, 1935. Jewish *Mischling*. Membership in the Jewish religious community. The "affiliation" with the Jewish religious community according to Sec. 5 of the First Regulation to the Civil Code of November 14, 1935, is not to be understood as a legally effective "membership." Rather, it is decisive whether certain facts exist, on the basis

---

27. *Cf.* Franz L. Neumann, Behemoth. Struktur und Praxis des Nationalsozialismus 1933–1944 (2018).

28. Dr. Hans-Christian Jasch translated the case and other German texts. This contribution is based on elements from two of his texts. *See* Hans-Christian Jasch, *Rassengesetzgebung im Dritten Reich*, *in* Die Nürnberger Gesetze—80 Jahre danach Vorgeschichte, Entstehung, Auswirkungen 165–203 (2017), pp. 165–203; *see also* Hans-Christian Jasch, *Antisemitic Policy in the Early Years of the Third Reich*, *in* I The Cambridge History of the Holocaust: Contexts, Origins, Comparisons, Entanglements, Cambridge 351–372 (forthcoming Sept. 2025).

Figure 6.2. Chart with the title: *Die Nürnberger Gesetze* [Nuremberg Race Laws]. The chart has columns explaining the *Deutschbluetiger* [German-bloods] *Mischling 2. Grades* [second-degree half-breeds], *Mischling 1. Grades* [first-degree half-breeds], and *Jude* [Jew]. Courtesy United States Holocaust Memorial Museum, courtesy of Hillel at Kent State.

of his own actions, or at least with his acquiescence, in which his connection with the Jewish religious community is outwardly apparent.

The plaintiff has German citizenship and is descended on his mother's side from two fully Jewish grandparents. The police order [administrative act] of October 1940, the *Polizeipräsident* [police president] obliged him to apply for an identification card for Jews.

The District Administrative Court dismissed the action brought by the plaintiff after an unsuccessful appeal. The action brought by the plaintiff against this decision is not successful.

The District Administrative Court has to be agreed with insofar as—for the decision of this legal dispute—it depends on whether or not the plaintiff belonged to the Jewish religious community on the day of the enactment of the *RBürgerG*, September 15, 1935, in accordance with Sec. 5, paragraph 2a of the First Regulation to the *RBürgerG*. When interpreting Sec. 5, para. 2a, it was to be assumed, in accordance with the case law of the Reich's Supreme Court (cf. RGSt. 73, 98, 99), that "belonging" to the Jewish religious community within the meaning of this provision does not constitute a legally effective "membership," but is to be understood as a concept of a special kind, which is to be developed for the purpose of racial legislation. This purpose is to bring about a blood-related separation between Germandom and Judaism (Stuckart-Gobke,

Kommentare zur Deutschen Rassengesetzgebung ["Commentary on German Racial Legislation"], p. 15).

> The inner attitude of the *Mischling* to the Jewish religion cannot be decisive in this respect, because it is not possible to precisely establish this inner attitude, since it is difficult or often not at all accessible to prove it. On the other hand, the conclusion that there is a special bond with the Jewish religious community is not immediately justified if the *Mischling* has been included in the lists of the Jewish religious community without his—or his legal representative's—will, but has himself never openly manifested and recognized his membership in this community. The decisive factor is whether due to his own actions or at least with the toleration of the *Mischling* there are certain facts in which his connection with the Jewish religious community emerges externally.

If one bases the assessment of the present case on these legal points of view, the court must also agree that the plaintiff's affiliation with the Jewish religious community on the deadline, September 15, 1935, is proven. As the plaintiff himself has declared himself as a member of the Jewish religion on the occasion of the police interrogations of September 1914 and February 6, 1920, furthermore in his registrations in the police records of March 19, 1926, and February 6, 1928, and in his signing off from the police records of February 6, 1928, at the acknowledgement of banns before the contraction of his marriage on March 6, 1928, and also at his civil registration [*Personenstandsaufnahme*] of October 10, 1935; only after the deadline, namely on April 26, 1938, he declared his leaving of the Jewish community in front of the district court, thus sufficient external facts have been created from which his affiliation to the Jewish religious community on September 15, 1935 can be inferred, especially since it is a matter of the plaintiff's own actions and not merely of circumstances tolerated by him.

The plaintiff argues in contrast that his non-affiliation to the Jewish religious community follows from the fact that he is not circumcised, not registered in the lists of the synagogue congregations, did not attend Jewish school, and did not pay any taxes to the synagogue congregation. However, the fact that the District Administrative Court attached no decisive weight to these circumstances was not objectionable. Since circumcision, registration in the lists of the synagogue congregation, attendance at a Jewish school, and payment of dues to a synagogue congregation are not conceptual prerequisites for membership of the Jewish religious community within the meaning of Sec. 5 para. 2 of the First Regulation to the *RBürgerG.*, it was thus not mandatory to conclude from their absence that the plaintiff does not belong to the Jewish religious community. The findings of the District Administrative Court, made in a free evaluation of the evidence and weighing all the circumstances, that the plaintiff belonged to this religious community, therefore does not reveal an error of law on the part of the District Administrative Court and can therefore not be successfully challenged in the appeal by the aforementioned argument of the plaintiff (Sec. 94 *Landesverwaltungsgesetz*).

The objection of the plaintiff that the witnesses named by him to testify for his inner development and his inner attitude were not heard by the District Administrative

Court is incorrect. There was no need to hear these witnesses, since, as stated above, his inner attitude was not decisive for the question of whether the plaintiff belonged to the Jewish religious community, but the administrative court need only take evidence to the extent that the assertion put in evidence is relevant to the decision.

The plaintiff is thus considered a Jew and, in accordance with the 3rd Decree on the compulsory identification card of July 23, 1938, Sec. 1, is obligated to apply for the issuance of an identification card with reference to his status as a Jew.

The Nazi Racial State Was Legally Meticulous

1. *Reich Administrative Court.* The Reich's Administrative Court had been created by "Führer's decree" of April 3, 1941, to replace several special administrative courts at the Reich's (federal) level and the Higher administrative Court of Prussia (*Oberverwaltungsgericht*) established in 1875. It was the highest administrative court of the Reich and one of its tasks was to harmonize the judicature of the various special administrative courts and the administrative law and judicature of the German states.

2. *Exemplary character.* The decision presented here was issued on June 5, 1941. Due to its "exemplary character" relating to the highly relevant "Jewish Question," it was published in the legal journal *Deutsches Recht*, which published articles and selected court decisions. The journal was the central organ of the National Socialist Lawyers' federation published under the direction of Hans Frank, Hitler's governor in occupied Poland (*Reichsrechtsführer; literally* "Law leader of the Reich").

3. *Legalistic character*. The case testifies to the legalistic character of the racial state established by the Nazis in Germany after 1933. Although the Nazi regime was fundamentally lawless, the Nazis paid attention to legal forms and used legal tools extensively to implement their criminal policies, in particular, when it came to discriminating against Jews and other disfavored minorities.

4. *Presumption of* Mischling *status rebutted.* A person with three or four Jewish grandparents was conclusively Jewish and designated a *Volljude* ("full Jew"). The plaintiff, as a person with two Jewish grandparents, was presumptively a first-degree *Mischling (Mischling ersten Grades*, literally "first-degree half-breed"). (Compare a first-degree *Mischling* to a person with a single Jewish grandparent, i.e., a second-degree *Mischling* (*Mischling zweiten Grades* ("second-degree half-breed"). Under certain circumstances, a first-degree *Mischling* could be recategorized as a Jew, notwithstanding the fact that they had only two Jewish grandparents. This could occur, most notably, if the first-degree *Mischling* "belong[ed] to the Jewish religious community" as of September 15, 1935, the day the Reich Citizenship Law was enacted. Such a person would be legally categorized as a Jew (*Geltungsjude* or "equivalent Jew"), which was the legal equivalent to a full-Jew or *Volljude*. The plaintiff's position is challenging because, according to the opinion, he did not terminate his membership until April 26, 1938. It is unclear whether and in what sense the plaintiff was a member of the Jewish religious community as of September 15, 1935. Rather than terminating actual membership on April 26, 1938, perhaps he was formalizing his long-standing *non*-membership.

5. *Contesting membership.* In the plaintiff's view, he should be deemed *not* to have belonged to the Jewish religious community as of September 15, 1935. This claim might have both a subjective and objective component. Subjectively, he did not consider himself as Jewish as of that date, as evidenced by the facts that (a) he was not circumcised; (b) he was not a dues-paying member of a synagogue as of September 15, 1935; (c) he was not registered in the lists of the synagogue congregations; and (d) he did not attend Jewish school. Objectively, he might be claiming that he did not belong to a synagogue as of September 15, 1935, because, let's posit, he was not a dues-paying member of a synagogue as of that date, nor was he registered on any synagogue list.

6. *Membership versus affiliation.* Assume the plaintiff was not a member of a synagogue, dues-paying or otherwise, as of September 15, 1935, nor was he registered on any synagogue's list. Could the court nonetheless find that he was sufficiently connected or "affiliated" with the Jewish religious community in some other sense? What is "affiliation" with the Jewish religious community as opposed to "membership"? What is the evidence of his affiliation?

7. *External facts.* Did the "external facts" establish that the plaintiff was a member of the Jewish religious community as of September 15, 1935, and/or affiliated with it? Assume that prior to September 15, 1935, the plaintiff had taken some official step to either (a) terminate his membership in the Jewish religious community (assuming he was a synagogue member as of that date) or (b) formalize his long-standing non-membership. A different result?

Nazi Leaders Debate Whether to Exterminate *Mischlinge*

1. *Disagreement within regime.* Different parties within the Nazi regime disagreed over how to classify *Mischlinge*: This was not least apparent from the discussion at the Wannsee Conference[29] on January 20, 1942, which also addressed the unanswered domestic policy question of a "final solution," i.e., the question of *Mischlinge* and "mixed marriages" in particular. "Point IV" of the minutes of the outcome of the conference stated: "In the course of the final solution, the Nuremberg Laws will, in a sense, form the basis whereby the solution to the issues of mixed marriages and 'Mischling' is a prerequisite for the complete resolution of the problem."

2. *"Hardline" position.* The head of the security police and the security service of the SS, Reinhard Heydrich, sought to include this group of approximately 70,000 to 100,000 individuals within the "Great German Reich" pre-1938 Germany plus annexed Austria, Czechoslovakia's Sudetenland, parts of Poland, etc.), and many more within the rest of occupied Europe, in the deportations; only in exceptional cases would individuals be allowed to remain within the Reich, and then only if sterilized. The preparation for the conference undertaken by Bernhard Lösener, the head of unit for Jewish Affairs in the Reich Ministry of Interior, for his superior state secretary Wilhelm

29. The Wannsee Conference itself is depicted in detail in the permanent exhibition at the Education and Memorial Site and has been analyzed in numerous publications.

Stuckart on December 4, 1941,[30] makes clear that there had already been differences in opinion in this regard between representatives of the Reich Main Security Office (*Reichssicherheitshauptamt*) and party representatives since spring 1941. The head of the NSDAP Office of Racial Policy (*Rassenpolitisches Amt*), Walther Groß, had demanded "full territorial expulsion," i.e., the expulsion of "half-Jews" and "full Jews" from Europe, as early as spring 1941. Judaism was "subjected to a historic mortal death" and he believed "with regard to the historic emergence of Jews in Europe … that their end has irrevocably come."[31]

3. *"Softline" position.* Stuckart instead proposed during the meeting in Wannsee "proceeding to compulsory sterilization" to "solve the issue of mixed marriages and *Mischlinge*." To simplify the problem of mixed marriages, other options would have to be considered, with the aim of the legislator saying something like: "These marriages are dissolved." The objection raised by Stuckart—that "the practical implementation" of these "possible solutions to the question of mixed marriages and *Mischlinge* in this form would entail endless administration"—is clearer considering this. From the Reich Ministry of Interior's perspective, extending the group of those affected was not just dubious in terms of war economy; it also feared that "dissolving the boundaries of the category of victims" in this way would cause unrest amongst the population. In fact, most *Mischlinge* and partners of "mixed marriages" were spared deportation, at least if residing in the Old Reich.

Nazi Lawyers Flourished During and After the War

1. *Wilhelm Stuckart.* The example of Wilhelm Stuckart shows that there were civil servants in key positions who sought to implement Nazi ideology with the same ideological conviction as their peers in the Party and the SS. Their defense of traditional legal methods and institutions did not necessarily imply that they were less radical or fanatical than their comrades in the party institutions. On the contrary, men like Stuckart were aware of the advantages and efficiencies which could be achieved using a legalistic approach to implement measures of structural violence. Young, high-flying lawyers in the public administration like Stuckart were needed to translate anti-Jewish intentions into law. The regime could count on their loyalty, diligence, legal expertise, administrative experience, and imagination.[32]

2. *Post-war role of Nazi lawyers and civil servants.* Despite the efforts of the U.S. military prosecution at Nuremberg to draw attention to the role of high-ranking civil

---

30. Proposal for Meeting with Appendices, Bernhard Lösener, *in* Federal Archives Germany R 1501/5519, 238–247, 477–495 (Dec. 4, 1941) (the meeting was scheduled for December 9, 1941, and postponed to January 20, 1942).

31. Walther Groß, *Die rassenpolitischen Voraussetzungen zur Lösung der Judenfrage*, 12 DEUTSCHES RECHT. ZENTRALORGAN DES NS-RECHTSWAHRERBUNDES A, 2, 2, 8 (1942). The article was republished here, first being published at the beginning of 1941 in Weltkampf at 52–63.

32. *Cf.* Hans-Christian Jasch, *Civil Service Lawyers and the Holocaust: The Case of Wilhelm Stuckart*, in THE LAW IN NAZI GERMANY: IDEOLOGY, OPPORTUNISM, AND THE PERVERSION OF JUSTICE 37–61, (Alan E. Steinweis & Robert D. Rachlin eds., 2013).

servants and their complicity in the genocide, in particular in the last of the Nuremberg trials, the Ministries Trial (*Wilhelmstrassenprozess*), many were able to continue their careers in post-war Federal Republic of Germany (a.k.a., "West Germany"). Eager to protect themselves against prosecution, they formed powerful networks, which successfully lobbied against the continuation of denazification and cuts in their salaries or pensions. They benefited from the general political climate, which called for "normalization" and forgetfulness in order to rebuild an effective and stabilizing administration in divided Cold War Germany. Even former émigrés or survivors, who took offices in the new administration, like Walter Strauss, the state secretary in the post-war Justice Department, who had been protected by a "mixed marriage" as discussed at the Wannsee Conference, sometimes closed their eyes to the "re-nazification" of the civil service, in part because they genuinely believed in the potential for change, in part because they were pressured, and in part because they thought that old expertise was needed to build the new system.

Continuity in the civil service after 1945 was also a consequence of the half-hearted efforts of the German administration and judiciary to investigate the criminal involvement of various professional groups, especially so-called "desk perpetrators" in the Holocaust. Continuity of personnel in the post-war judiciary did not differ much from the situation in the civil service. In many cases, the old generation of judges and prosecutors continued to stay in their posts to serve the new emerging West German democracy. It took nearly a generation for changes to set in and for the "old guard" to be replaced by younger lawyers not complicit with Nazism. It is therefore hardly surprising that the first West German attempts at criminal prosecution in the 1950s and 1960s were largely limited to rank and file policemen who had shot Jewish families in German-occupied Eastern Europe—as was the case in the *Einsatzgruppen* trial in Ulm in 1958/9—or to guards in Nazi extermination camps—as was the case in the Auschwitz trial in Frankfurt from 1963 onwards or the Majdanek trial in Düsseldorf in 1977. The so-called "desk perpetrators" (*Schreibtischtäter*), i.e., the perpetrators in the civil services or in the judiciary, largely benefitted from impunity.

3. *Hans Maria Globke.* Hans Maria Globke (1898–1973), a legal expert in the Reich Ministry of the Interior, co-authored with Stuckart a "Commentary on German Racial Legislation" (*Kommentare zur Deutschen Rassengesetzgebung*),[33] discussed in the *Mischling* judgement. Globke played a major role in rebuilding the administration of the future NATO member and outpost of the West in the Cold War. Globke's post-war career included serving as a top aide and confidant to Chancellor Konrad Adenauer in West Germany. He was involved in negotiations and policies that accompanied the Luxembourg agreement on paying reparations to Israel and the Claims Conference in 1952 and eventually led to the establishment of diplomatic relations with Israel in 1965. Globke had also been a trusted informer of the U.S. intelligence service (CIA). Men like Globke nearly managed to escape even historical scrutiny by influencing, and in part silencing, contemporary historical research.

---

33. *Cf.* STUCKART & GLOBKE, *supra* note 19.

Jewish Associations in Nazi Germany

1. *Reich Representation of Jews in Germany.* On September 17, 1933, in response to the repressive policy of the NSDAP regime, German Jews created the Reich Representation of Jews in Germany (*Reichsvertretung der deutschen Juden* or "Reich Representation") under the leadership of Leo Baeck (1873–1956), a Reform rabbi and theologian and the spiritual leader of German Jewry during the Nazi period. On September 24, 1935, the *Reichsvertretung* responded somewhat optimistically to the Nuremberg Laws and expressed hope that they could resemble something of a framework for socially and culturally secure Jewish life in Germany:

> The laws passed by the Reichstag in Nuremberg affected the Jews in the worst possible way. However, they should create a platform on which tolerable relations between the German and Jewish people are possible ... for tolerable relationships, there must be hope that the Jews and Jewish communities in Germany will be given the possibility of a moral, economic existence, by ending their defamation and boycotting.[34]

2. *Reich Association of Jews.* On July 4, 1939, the NSDAP administration created a mandatory operational unification under state control, the "Reich Association of Jews" (*Reichsvereinigung der Juden* or "Reich Association"), which compulsorily incorporated the infrastructure of all Jewish organizations and communities that were still in existence. All people in the German Reich classified as Jews became mandatory members of the "Reich Association." Although there was some continuity between the "Reich Representation" and "Reich Association," the new organization was actually under the full control of the Nazi authorities. It was subject to direct regulation by the Reich Ministry for the Interior and was forced to follow its instructions, which included seizing Jewish assets and preparing Jews for deportation. In 1943, the "Reich Association" was dissolved, its assets were seized, and the last remaining members were deported to concentration camps.

Sources

Harold J. Berman, Law and Revolution: The Formation of the Western Legal Tradition (1983).

Hans Petter Graver, Judicial Independence Under Authoritarian Rule: An Institutional Approach to the Legal Tradition of the West, 10 Hague J. Rule L. 317 (2018).

34. The statement is printed in Raul Hillberg, I Die: Vernichtung der europäischen Juden 499 et seq. (1990). Even though it must clearly be taken into account here that the *Reichsvereinigung* saw itself as being exposed to a climate of pressure and threats, at first the Nuremberg Laws appeared to contemporaries to be a form of regulation that mitigated the pogrom mood fueled by the NSDAP in 1935 through "reification" and rejected special local regulations for Jews.

Lothar Gruchmann, Justiz im Dritten Reich 1933–1940: Anpassung und Unterwerfung in der Ära Gürtner (3d ed. 2001).

Hans-Christian Jasch, *Civil Service Lawyers and the Holocaust: The Case of Wilhelm Stuckart*, in The Law in Nazi Germany: Ideology, Opportunism, and the Perversion of Justice 37 (Alan E. Steinweis & Robert D. Rachlin eds., 2013).

Hans-Christian Jasch, Staatssekretär Wilhelm Stuckart und die Judenpolitik: Der Mythos von der sauberen Verwaltung (2012).

Hans-Christian Jasch, *Staatssekretär Dr. Wilhelm Stuckart. Der Vertreter des Reichsministeriums des Innern auf der Wannsee-Konferenz und sein Prozess* in Nürnberg, 7 Einsicht 28, 28–38 (2012).

Hans-Christian Jasch, Zur Rolle der Innenverwaltung im Dritten Reich bei der Vorbereitung und Organisation des Genozids an den Europäischen Juden: Der Fall des Dr. Wilhelm Stuckart (1902–1953), 43 Die Verwaltung 217, 217–271, http://ejournals.duncker-humblot.de/toc/verw/43/2. (2010).

Hans-Christian Jasch et al., Die Nürnberger Gesetze—80 Jahre danach Vorgeschichte, Entstehung, Auswirkungen et al., Public Administration and the Holocaust (2017).

Hans-Christian Jasch et al., German Justice System and Holocaust Crimes After 1945 (2017).

Hans-Christian Jasch & Wolf Kaiser, Der Holocaust vor deutschen Gerichten Amnestieren Verdrängen Bestrafen.

Hans-Christian Jasch et al., Amateur War Photography During the German Attack on Poland (2017).

Hans-Christian Jasch & Christoph Kreuzmüller, eds., The Participants: The Men of the Wannsee Conference (2017).

Hans-Christian Jasch & Stephan Lehnstaedt, eds., Verfolgen und Aufklären—Crimes Uncovered: Die erste Generation der Holocaustforschung—The First Generation of Holocaust Researchers (2019).

Hans-Christian Jasch, *Staat und Verwaltung im „Dritten Reich". Der mordende Staat, seine Form und Entwicklung, in* [2 Gesellschaft, Staat und Verbrechen] Der Nationalsozialismus. Herrschaft und Gewalt 92–131 (2022).

Hans-Christian Jasch, *Antisemitic Policy in the Early Years of the Third Reich, in* I The Cambridge History of the Holocaust: Contexts, Origins, Comparisons, Entanglements, Cambridge 351–372 (forthcoming Sept. 2025).

H.W. Koch, In the Name of the Volk: Political Justice in Hitler's Germany (1989).

Herlinde Pauer-Studer & Julian Fink, Rechtfertigung des Unrechts: das Rechtstheorie im Nationalsozialismus (2014).

Stanley L. Paulson, *Lon L. Fuller, Gustav Radbruch, and the "Positivist" Theses*, 13 L. & Phil. 313 (1994).

C. Canonical vs. Nazi Anti-Jewish Measures

Table 6.1 Comparison Between Canonical Laws and Nazi Measures Against Jews[35]

Canonical Law	Nazi Measure
Prohibition of intermarriage and sexual intercourse between Christians and Jews (Synod of Elvira, 306 CE)	Law of protection of German blood and honor (September 15, 1935)
Christians and Jews not allowed to eat together (Synod of Elvira, 306)	Jews barred from dining cars (December 30, 1939)
Jews may not hold public office (Synod of Clermont, 535)	Law for the re-establishment of the professional Civil Service (April 7, 1933)
Jews may not employ Christian servants or possess Christian slaves (3rd Synod of Orleans, 538)	Law of protection of German blood and honor (September 15, 1935)
Jews barred from the streets during passion week (3rd Synod of Orleans, 538)	Decree authorizing local authorities to bar Jews from the streets on certain days (December 3, 1938)
Burning of the Talmud and other books (12th Synod of Toledo, 681)	Book burning in Nazi Germany (such as the German Student's Union—DST in 1930s)
Christians may not patronize Jewish doctors (Trulanic Synod, 692)	Jewish doctors may treat only Jewish parents (July 25, 1938)
Christians may not live in Jewish homes (Synod of Narbonne, 1050)	Concentration of Jews in houses directive by Göring (December 28, 1938)
Jews must pay same Church tax as Christians (Synod of Gerona, 1078)	Jews must pay a special income tax in lieu of donations to the Nazi Party (December 24, 1940)
Jews may not be plaintiffs or witnesses against Christians in courts (3rd Lateran Council, 1179)	Proposal by Nazi party Chancellery that Jews may not institute civil suits (September 9, 1942)
Jews may not withhold inheritance from descendants who accepted Christianity (3rd Lateran Council, Canon 26, 1179)	Decree empowering the Justice Ministry to void wills offending the "second Judgement of the people" (July 31, 1938)
The marking of Jewish clothes with a badge (4th Lateran Council, Canon 68, 1215)	Decree requiring Jews wear yellow star (September 1, 1941)
Prohibition of construction of new synagogues (Council of Oxford, 1222)	Destruction of synagogues in the entire Reich (November 11, 1938)
Christians may not attend Jewish ceremonies (Synod of Vienna, 1267)	Friendly relationships with Jews prohibited (October 24, 1941)
Compulsory ghettos (Synod of Breslau, 1267)	Compulsory ghettos ordered by Heydrich (September 21, 1939)

35. JONATHAN FOX & LEV TOPOR, WHY DO PEOPLE DISCRIMINATE AGAINST JEWS? 72 (2021).

Christians may not sell or rent real estate to Jews (Synod of Ofen, 1279)	Decree providing for compulsory sale of Jewish real estate (December 3, 1938)
Christian conversion to Judaism or a baptized Jew returning to the Jewish religion defined as heresy (Synod of Mainz, 1310)	Christian conversion to Judaism places the convert in jeopardy of being treated as a Jew (June 26, 1942)
Jews may not act as agents in the conclusion of contracts between Christians, especially marriage contracts (Council of Basel, Sessio XIX, 1434)	Decree liquidating Jewish real estate agencies, brokerage agencies, and marriage agencies catering to non-Jews (July 6, 1938)
Jews may not obtain academic degrees (Council of Basel, Sessio XIX, 1434)	Law against overcrowding German schools and universities (RGB 1, 225, April 25, 1933)

Part Three

Antisemitic Speech

Chapter 7

Defamation

The defamation of groups is generally not actionable under the common law unless the defamatory speech touches an ascertainable member of the group. In this way, common law defamation law provides anti-Semites with near-absolute immunity to collectively defame Jews. This chapter considers three rare lawsuits that successfully used defamation law to counter antisemitic speech. These lawsuits occurred in three Commonwealth jurisdictions during the twentieth century: *Ortenberg v. Plamondon* (Quebec 1915), *Levy v. von Moltke* (South Africa 1934), and *Irving v. Lipstadt* (England 2000).

The first section, "Contesting the Blood Libel," examines a Quebec case in which Jewish plaintiffs found creative ways to overcome the anti-Semites' defamation law immunity. In *Ortenberg*, the court held the defendant liable for defamation because he had failed to prove his accusations against Jews, including the Blood Libel, and also because Quebec City's Jewish community was legally not too large.

In *Levy*, the subject of "Debunking the *Protocols*," the court held defendants liable for defamation on grounds, in part, that the Jewish conspiracy they alleged did not exist and, perforce, the Jewish plaintiff was not part of it. In *Irving*, the subject of "Debunking Holocaust Denial," Holocaust denier David Irving sued historian Deborah Lipstadt after she described him as a Holocaust denier. The court ruled in favor of Lipstadt and Penguin Books, her publisher, on grounds that her description of Irving was true—he had indeed deliberately distorted evidence about the Holocaust to conform to his antisemitic viewpoints.

Each of these cases' implications go beyond the specifics of common law defamation law. The events following the *Ortenberg* trial demonstrate the difficulties with enacting hate speech laws. *Levy* was groundbreaking because it was the first time that the *Protocols of the Elders of Zion*[1] was adjudicated as a forgery in a court of law. Finally, the *Irving* judgment provided a legal definition of antisemitism and determined that it is a form of racism.

1. According to the Holocaust Encyclopedia: "*The Protocols of the Elders of Zion* is an antisemitic book used to promote hatred of Jews. It was first published in 1903. The *Protocols* contains conspiracy theories about alleged global Jewish power. It is the most widespread antisemitic publication of modern times." *An Antisemitic Conspiracy: The Protocols of the Elders of Zion*, Holocaust Encyc., https://encyclopedia.ushmm.org/content/en/article/protocols-of-the-elders-of-zion (last visited Dec. 17, 2024).

A. Contesting the Blood Libel

On March 30, 1910, at the Canadian Association of Catholic Youth in Quebec City, Jacques Édouard Plamondon, an ultramontane[2] and prominent civil law notary,[3] delivered a public lecture titled *Le Juif* ("The Jew"). The speech included canards concerning the "Talmudic Jew" and accused Jews of committing ritual murder. It also encouraged the boycotting of Jewish businesses in Quebec City. The following day, the speech was published in the local Roman Catholic newspaper, *La Libre Parole*, by its publisher, René Leduc. Shortly thereafter, mobs attacked Jewish homes, Jewish-owned businesses, and a synagogue.[4]

Benjamin Ortenberg, a local Jewish merchant whose business had been targeted, and Louis Lasarovitz, the president of a local synagogue, sued both Plamondon and Leduc for defamation and damages of £500. In 1913, the case was heard by the Superior Court of Quebec, the court of original general jurisdiction. This court, per Judge Malouin, dismissed the claim on grounds that the defendants' speech did not specifically refer to the plaintiff. Ortenberg appealed to the Quebec Court of Appeal, then called the Quebec Court of King's Bench, with Lasarovitz withdrawing from the litigation. The defendant-respondents launched multiple defenses: (a) the lecture did not refer to the plaintiff-appellants; (b) the substance of the lecture was true; and (c) the lecture merely repeated, in good faith and in the public interest, past literature and commentary (including, putatively, the Hebrew Bible).[5]

A panel of five judges heard the appeal: they delivered a unanimous decision in Ortenberg's favor but reduced his damages award from £500 to £50. Judge Carroll delivered the opinion of the Court. In a concurring opinion, Judge Cross wrote that he would have granted Ortenberg's request for £500 in damages. Neither judge addressed the truth or falsehood of the defendants' anti-Jewish propaganda.

This case has been described as "the most controversial and well-publicized libel trial in the province [of Quebec]."[6] Legal scholar Joseph Tanenhaus described *Ortenberg*

---

2. The Canadian Encyclopedia describes Ultramontanism as:

> A school of thought of the Catholic Church which promoted supreme papal authority in matters of spirituality and governance. Ultramontanism rejected modern ideals in favour of the supremacy of Catholicism and the Catholic Church in public life. This school of thought was particularly influent in the French-Canadian society during the 19th century and the beginning of the 20th century.

Nive Voisine, *Ultramontanism*, The Canadian Encyc. (Oct. 26, 2020), https://www.thecanadianencyclopedia.ca/en/article/ultramontanism.

3. In civil law jurisdictions, a notary public "is a public official who serves as a public witness of facts transacted by private parties ... and also serves as impartial legal advisor for the parties involved." *Notary Public*, Black's Law Dictionary (12th ed. 2024).

4. Five youths were convicted for perpetrating violence.

5. It is not entirely clear whether: (a) the public interest element raised by the respondents concerned a part of their "fair comment" defense; (b) whether there was an independent "public interest" defense; or (c) whether it really was a part of the "truth" defense.

6. Joseph Kary, *The Constitutionalization of Quebec Libel Law, 1848–2004*, 42 Osgoode Hall L.J. 229, 258 (2004).

as a "case which does not seem to fit in the suggested pigeonholes" of group libel law and as having weak precedential value despite being "frequently cited."[7]

Ortenberg v. Plamondon

Quebec Court of King's Bench
24 B.R. 69 (1915)

JUDGE CARROLL delivered the opinion of the Court.

The appellant, Ortenberg, a merchant of St. Rochs, belonging to the Jewish race and religion, complains that the respondent Plamondon, in a lecture delivered by him, attacked the Jew in general and the Jews of Quebec and the plaintiff in particular. Leduc, the other respondent, printed the lecture.

Ortenberg says that the lecture in question attacks him in his honour and his well-being; as a result of this lecture, he was insulted and assailed, and has lost a portion of his trade, and he asks for £500 damages.

The respondent pleads that he did not attack the plaintiff personally, but the Jewish race, and its methods, and that he had in mind the "Jew" collectively; that the accusations are true and in the public interest and had for object to put the Christian population of the Province of Quebec on its guard against the Jewish invasion. In addition, he says that the lecture contains, in substance, but the accusations made against Jews in the Old and New Testaments, in numerous works published on the Jewish peril during the past fifty years at least, and in the press; that the facts related are of public notoriety, legitimate matter for polemical discussion, like all other social, political or religious questions.

The plaintiff inscribed in law against certain paragraphs of the plea. This inscription was reserved for the trial judge, and, in the present state of the record, it is, perhaps, useless to decide if this inscription was well or ill-founded.

The judgment dismissed the action for the reason contained in the following considérant—

> Considering that, according to law, if the writing complained of contains no defamatory allegation or imputation against any person but confines itself solely to a discussion more or less violent and impassioned, of philosophic, social or religious opinions against a corporation, a religious sect, or an association, there is no defamation.

The principle is well-established and there is no doubt that had the Court of first instance believed that the plaintiff was sufficiently designated, the respondents would have been condemned.

The object of the speaker is seen at the commencement of the lecture:

---

7. Joseph Tanenhaus, *Group Libel: Who Controls the United States?*, 35 CORNELL L. REV. 261, 265 (1950).

> Although from the pulpit our revered pastor told us long ago that the Jew is not only a stranger but an enemy in our midst, yet few people believe that this fellow with the timorous and cringing look constitutes a real danger.

Plamondon tells us that his lecture is an attack against the Jews of the entire world, comprising those resident in Quebec; that he excepts none; that the accusations comprise all the Jews, with no intention, however, of attacking any one in particular; that is the gist of his deposition.

The lecture itself may be resumed in these words—

> It is stated that the Talmud[8] teaches Jews that our Lord Jesus Christ is an idol, begotten in vice, and in adultery; that his followers are therefore idolators; that the Goyim[9] (the non-Jew, and particularly the Christian) is an animal; that he who returns to a non-Jew a lost article commits a sin because he adds to the power of the impious; that our learned Rabbis, (it is a Rabbi who speaks) were right in teaching that an Israelite is permitted to practise usury towards the Christian (Goy); that if a Christian needs money, a Jew may willfully deceive him; he may compound usurious interest until the amount is so high that the Christian is unable to pay without selling his goods; that it is permitted to abuse the wife of the unfaithful, that is, a non-Jewess;[10] that he who causes the blood of the impious to flow, that is to say, of non-Jews, offers a sacrifice to God;[11] that the best among Christians should be strangled; that a Jew who has the power ought, under any pretext whatever, to publicly put heretics to death;

---

8. Editor's note: The OED defines "Talmud" as:

> In the wide sense, The body of Jewish civil and ceremonial traditionary law, consisting of the Mishnah n. or binding precepts of the elders, additional to and developed from the Pentateuch, and the later Gemara n. or commentary upon these, forming a complement, explanatory, illustrative, and discursive, to the Mishnah. The term was originally applied to the Gemara, of which two recensions exist, known respectively as the Jerusalem (or Palestinian) and the Babylonian Talmud; to the latter of which the name is in strictest use confined. The precepts of the Mishnah were collected and codified about 200 [C.E.] the redaction of the Jerusalem Talmud had reached almost its present form by 408 [C.E.]; that of the Babylonian Talmud extended from 400 to 500 [C.E.].

Talmud, Oxford Eng. Dictionary, https://doi.org/10.1093/OED/1091310459 (last visited Sept. 2024).

9. Editor's note: In Jewish usage: a non-Jew, a Gentile. *Goy*, Oxford Eng. Dictionary, https://doi.org/10.1093/OED/5692817595 (last visited Sept. 2024). In Hebrew and in Yiddish the term is often used disparagingly. "The Goyim Know" is an antisemitic catchphrase "intended to be understood as spoken by a panicked Jew responding to some occurrence that would ostensibly reveal Jewish manipulations or deceit to non-Jews." *The Goyim Know/Shut It Down*, The Anti-Defamation League, https://www.adl.org/resources/hate-symbol/goyim-knowshut-it-down (last visited Dec. 17, 2024).

10. Editor's note: It is a long-standing antisemitic trope, sometimes called the "Lust Libel," that Jews are sexual deviants and perverts. Jonah Cohen, *The Lust Libel: Sexual Antisemitism in History and Contemporary Culture*, fathom (Nov. 2022), https://fathomjournal.org/the-lust-libel-sexual-antisemitism-in-history-and-contemporary-culture/.

11. Editor's note: This is known as the "Blood Libel," defined as "the (unfounded) accusation that Jewish people use the blood of Christians in religious rituals, especially in the preparation of Passover bread." *Blood Libel*, Oxford Eng. Dictionary, https://doi.org/10.1093/OED/5636062764 (last visited Sept. 2024). It will be discussed at length in Chapter 14. *See* discussion *infra* chapter 14.

> that a Jew accused of murdering a man (a Christian) may swear that he has not killed a man, making the mental reservation that it is merely an "animal that he has killed."

The lecturer continued:

> Are not these precepts of the Talmud, taught, explained and commanded to the Jew by his spiritual advisers, the Rabbis in the synagogues, edifying? For us poor Goyim, rape, adultery,[12] theft, usury, murder and false swearing are abominable crimes which our religion rejects and prohibits. If we commit them we are afflicted with remorse and sadness. To a Jew these heinous crimes are considered such virtuous acts that his religion teaches and commands him to practice them, and he retains in his mind as pleasant a memory of them as if he had performed a good deed. You ought to begin to see that the Jew is a man in a class by himself, and *that his presence in our midst is not desirable.*

The lecturer then went on to cite certain traits and characteristics attributed to the Jewish race, and accused the race of being guilty of ritual murder, and he continued:

> The few facts which I have related to you are taken, it is true, from countries other than ours. But the Jew, bear in mind, is the same in all places, and that which he has done elsewhere he will certainly do here, the day he believes himself sufficiently strong to attempt it. Has he not already shown among us his tendency towards oppression, and his irresistible desire to attack our religion?

After quoting an article ... on "Sunday Labour and the Jews," the lecturer made the following comment:

> Even in St. Roche ... there is a factory at 115 ½ or 117 St. Joseph Street where parties, worthy of belief, have told me with righteous indignation, regular labour is performed every Sunday in the year.
>
> This is the first encroachment of the Jew among us; are we going to be so blind, so weak, as to submit without protesting?
>
> Will you continue, ladies, to purchase from these Jews garments made on Sunday in contempt of our holy religion, which they now silently treat with scorn, awaiting the time when they can show their hand publicly without danger?
>
> Will you continue, gentlemen, to rent, or what is still worse, to sell your houses to these people, thus permitting them to obtain a foothold among you, and assist them to realize their fond dream of enslaving us?

I do not intend to enter into a discussion of the theories and opinions of l'Abbé Lamarque,[13] and other authors upon whom the lecturer relies. Suffice it to say that for

12. Editor's note: That is, the Lust Libel.

13. Editor's note: Maximilien de Lamarque, The Talmudic Jew: A Brief Summary of the Dangerous Beliefs and Practices of Jewry Presented for the Consideration of All Christians (1888).

the purposes of the present case, it has not been proven that the Talmud teaches that murder, adultery, theft, and other crimes, if practised against Christians, become for Jews virtuous acts. Abbés d'Amour, Grandbois, and Nadeau, who were heard, state clearly that they base their opinions upon reliable authors, but not one of them has read the text of Talmud, nor can he read it because he has not sufficient knowledge of the language in which the work is written.[14]

The accusation, to my mind, resolves itself to this: The Jew is obliged to obey the teachings of the Talmud; the Talmud teaches that these crimes are not crimes towards Christians. The Jew is the same everywhere, and after having mentioned all the abominations attributed to the Jewish race, the lecturer said:

> Do you begin to understand that the Jew is a being living by himself and that his presence in our midst is undesirable; that which the Jew has done elsewhere, he will do here as soon as he is able?

After stating that the lecture was not a personal attack, the respondent declares that what he said applies to Quebec; that he makes no exception to any Jew in Quebec, of all the accusations charged against the Jewish race.

Among those who heard the lecturer were certain urchins who, a few days afterwards, threw a stone, smashing a window of the house belonging to the appellant, who was also insulted on the street, and, in addition, his business suffered.

Without doubt, attacks against a race, no matter how violent they may be, cannot give rise to an action in damages; writers may state everything they think against a collectivity of people, with this restriction, however, that if any one of the individuals of such collectivity is aimed at specially by the defamation, and suffers damage, he is entitled to an action at law. If the collectivity is numerous there is no right of action, because the injury in that case is not deemed to indicate any one person. Whether the collectivity is or is not sufficiently numerous to give the right to an action is a question of fact left to the discretion and wisdom of the courts.

The object of this lecture was certainly to put the public on guard against the Jews of Quebec, numbering 75 families, in a total population of 80,000 souls.

By imputing to this restricted collectivity all the crimes of the Jewish race, they are sufficiently indicated and I adopt as well-founded the following judgment of the Tribunal Civil de la Seine, *Corinaldi and others v. Feuillebois Renaud*—

> When a defamatory or injurious imputation indicates a number of persons sufficiently considerable not to cause to any of them personal wrong, individual action belongs to none of these persons, the defamatory matter being in such case so general and vague that it is in a way indiscernible: but it is otherwise when the number in the collectivity is sufficiently restricted that the defamation or injury, without indicating them particularly, attacks them person-

14. Editor's note: Unlearned witnesses for the defense.

> ally: in that case, each one of them must be given the right to exercise for himself, on his own account, an action for defamation.

In the case at present under review, it is said:

> The Jews in other countries have been guilty of murder, rape, adultery and theft against Christians; the Jew is the same everywhere; what he has done elsewhere, he will do here when he becomes sufficiently strong to attempt.

The Jewish collectivity of Quebec is composed of 75 families, as I have already stated, in a population of 80,000 souls. This is not the case of a wrong against an entire class so large that the injury is lost in its numbers....

In a word, the question at issue may be resumed as follows: Is the attack directed by the respondent against the Jew a general attack against the Jewish race, its methods, its doctrines, its activities—an impersonal attack, or, are the persons forming the Jewish community of Quebec sufficiently designated in this lecture? I am of opinion that they are sufficiently designated, that the plaintiff was included in this slander, that he has been injured in his sentiments and in his well-being, and that he ought to obtain judgment....

Let it be clearly understood: the respondent is not condemned because he attacked the Jewish race or religion, nor for having repeated the accusations which historians and pamphleteers have made against Jews in general, nor because he denounced with reason Sunday labour; but he is condemned for having attributed to all and each of the 75 Jewish families of Quebec the wish to commit the abominable crimes of which their race is accused, when they have obtained sufficient strength to so commit these offences.

In that, there is personal defamation.

The respondent says in his factum:—

> Naturally nothing should be done to awaken hatred, and for the Christian it is a duty not to molest Jews. Besides, they have nothing to complain of, seeing that they have equal rights here, which the Province of Quebec has conferred on them in 1832.[15]

Assuredly, no other country better understands or permits the freer enjoyment of liberty than this Province, and if civil liberty, conferred upon Jews has been a benefit to then, does not the respondent fear that he will make them lose sight of this great blessing by covering them with opprobrium, for, according to the high sentiment of Sainte-Beuve: *"S'il y a des bienfaits qui obligent, il y a des injures qui aliénent a jamais et qui délient."*[16]

---

15. Editor's note: In 1832, the British Parliament passed an Act granting Jews in Quebec (then called "Lower Canada") equal civil and political rights. David B. Green, *This Day in Jewish History | 1832: Canada's Jews Get Civil Rights*, HAARETZ (June 5, 2013), https://www.haaretz.com/jewish/2013-06-05/ty-article/.premium/1832-canadas-jews-get-civil-rights/0000017f-ef83-d8a1-a5ff-ff8b30a30000.

16. Editor's note: "If there are blessings that oblige, there are insults that alienate forever and unbind."

I am of opinion that the respondent was in good faith.[17] He felt he was performing a public duty, but he has injured the plaintiff. The costs are heavy. He will be condemned to £50, but he must pay all the costs. Leduc is condemned to pay £25 with costs.

Judgment of the Superior Court reversed, with costs.

JUDGE CROSS, concurring in the judgment.

This is an action taken by the appellant to recover damages for defamation alleged to have been done by the respondent in a public lecture delivered to the people of St. Roch's, in the City of Quebec.

It is set out in the action that the appellant plaintiff is of the Jewish faith, that the respondent's statements at the lecture were to the effect that the teachings of the Jewish Talmud is wicked in certain specified respects, such as that Christ-worship is idolatry, that usury and trade oppression against Christians is commendable, that the choking of persons not of the faithful and the shedding of the blood of Christians is permissible.[18]

It is alleged that the assertion that the Talmud contains such teachings is false and malicious and was made to render the plaintiff and others of his faith odious, and that appeal was made to the persons at the meeting to have no dealings with the Jews: that these statements are of a nature to hurt the appellant's business: that in consequence of them, the appellant has been violently attacked by people in Quebec, and that the appellant is entitled to recover damages.

The defence pleaded to the effect that the lecture speaks for itself; that the defendant does not know the plaintiff at all; that the Talmud does contain the teachings mentioned; that what was said at the lecture is true; that nothing was said about the plaintiff individually; that there is and has always been irreconcilable antagonism between Christians and Jews; that Christians regard Jews as a social pest; that the lecture merely repeated in good faith and in the public interest "the accusations recorded against the Jews in both Testaments" [etc.] ...

It has been found by the Superior Court, as a matter of fact, that the defendant in his lecture only called in question the Jewish race, its religious doctrines and social practices, and did not attack the plaintiff. If that finding of fact be accurate, it may well be that the judgment dismissing the action was a right conclusion in law.

It will be seen, so far as grounds of action are concerned, that the appellant did not set out in his declaration special damage in the way of exposure to loss of business and of actual personal ill-treatment.

It is proved that the anti-Jewish sentiment which followed upon the delivery of the lecture was such that persons who had dealt with the appellant shunned him, that his business fell off noticeably, and that he was insulted by youths in the street as *le Juif*, and the shutter of his dwelling was broken by a stone thrown by the youths.

---

17. Editor's note: To act in good faith is to "behav[e] honestly and frankly, without any intent to defraud or to seek an unconscionable advantage." *Acting in Good Faith*, BLACK'S LAW DICTIONARY (12th ed. 2024). In what sense did Plamondon act in good faith?

18. Editor's note: That is, the Blood Libel.

Those effects will be found to have been what might have been expected when it is considered that there are only about seventy-five Jewish householders in Quebec, that the appellant is a dealer in clothing at St. Roch's in Quebec, near where the lecture was delivered; that he, in fact, lived across the street from the respondent's own dwelling-house, so that a crowd of youths might applaud in front of the respondent's house and jeer in front of the appellant's house without changing place.

I do not grasp what the respondent means by saying in his plea that he did not know the appellant at all.

The lecture consists largely of quotations from books or pamphlets of more or less known writers, wherein the Jew is described in terms such as to make him an object of detestation from almost every possible point of view. After having made a number of such quotations, the respondent summarised thus: "The thief of our goods, the corrupter of our women,[19] the murderer of Christian children,[20] the Jew is also a revolutionary, where he finds ample scope for his usual perfidy."

So far, it may be that the lecture might be considered as a mere pronouncement upon *la question juive*, that is, an opinion upon a general question of a racial, or religious, or social kind, upon which there could be no ground for recovery for personal defamation.

It is, however, to be observed that, towards the end of his lecture, the respondent made reference to the matter of non-observance of the Sabbath. He said that there was a garment-making shop at No. 151 1/2 or 117 St. Joseph Street, wherein Sunday work was habitually carried on, and added in conclusion: "This is the first encroachment of the Jew among us; are we going to be so blind, so weak, as to submit without protesting? [etc.]"...

I have already indicated what effect that sort of thing might have been expected to have, and what effect it, in fact, did have upon the appellant. He was subjected to affront in public and his business was damaged.

I cannot agree that the respondent's utterances amount merely to a non-actionable denunciation of controversion of a race, or religion at large. They were that and, as regards the appellant, they were more. They were an invitation and incitement to a boycott of the handful of Jewish traders in the City of Quebec. The invitation to boycott was accepted and acted upon.

The respondent is answerable in reparation of the wrong which he thus caused to the appellant. [citing libel cases]....

Those are cases of libel. I, however, consider that it would be a mistake to test the appellant's right of recovery in this action by rules applicable only to actions of defamation or libel. The declaration in this case discloses a wider cause of action, namely that

19. Editor's note: That is, the Lust Libel.
20. Editor's note: Again, the Blood Libel.

of an action in damages for words maliciously spoken as I find described in a modern treatise as follows:

> It is a general rule an action will lie against any one who has without just cause or excuse published words which are untrue, if their publication has caused the plaintiff pecuniary loss. This is so, although the words are not defamatory, i.e., although they do not injure the reputation of the plaintiff, either personally or in the way of his profession or trade, so that no action of libel or slander will lie.... The action will not be one of defamation; it is an action on the case for maliciously acting in such a way as to inflict loss on the plaintiff.

The respondent pleaded that the statements made in his lecture are true, but he has failed to prove the ground of defence. He is in the position of having maliciously caused damage to the appellant. It is merely a case of applying art[icle] 1053.

I would maintain the appeal and give judgment for damages in the appellant's favour.

The Elements of Common Law Defamation

1. *Defamation*. A defamatory statement "tends... to harm the reputation of another as to lower him in the estimation of the community or to deter third persons from associating or dealing with him."[21] Accordingly, defamation "is the tort which protects reputation.... [Its] core concern ... [is]: the deterring and remedying of unwarranted harm to reputation."[22] Today, the right to be protected against defamation is understood to derive from "our basic concept of the essential dignity and worth of every human being—a concept at the root of any decent system of ordered liberty." *Rosenblatt v. Baer*, 383 U.S. 75, 92 (1966) (Justice Stewart, concurring). In *Reynolds v. Times Newspapers Ltd.*, [2001] 2 A.C. 127, Lord Nicholls explained that the right to protect one's reputation is not only a private good, but a public one as well:

> Reputation is an integral and important part of the dignity of the individual... [but] protection of reputation is [also] conducive to the public good. It is in the public interest that the reputation of public figures should not be debased falsely. In the political field, in order to make an informed choice, the electorate needs to be able to identify the good as well as the bad.

2. *Traditional Canadian defamation law.* Under traditional Canadian law, the usual common-law approach to defamation applies.[23] A plaintiff in a defamation action is required to prove three things to succeed in their claim: (a) that the impugned words were defamatory, in the sense that they would tend to lower the plaintiff's reputation in the eyes of a reasonable person; (b) that the words in fact referred to the plaintiff; and (c) that the words were published, meaning that they were communicated to at

---

21. Restatement (First) of Torts § 558 (Am. L. Inst. 1938).
22. Clerk and Lindsell on Torts (Andrew Tettenborn ed., 24th ed. 2023).
23. Rodney A. Smolla, 1 Law of Defamation § 1:9.75 (2d ed. 1999).

least one person other than the plaintiff.[24] If these conditions are met, the plaintiff prevails unless the defendant can establish a positive defense. Because the plaintiff is not required to show that the defendant intended to do harm, or even that the defendant was careless, defamation law in Canada has traditionally been a tort of strict liability.

3. *Comparison to U.S. defamation law.* Although U.S. defamation law historically presumed the falsity of defamatory statements,[25] *New York Times Co. v. Sullivan*, 376 U.S. 254 (1964), and subsequent decisions have eroded the practical significance of this element,[26] resulting in a requirement for the plaintiff to show fault on behalf of the defendant. Specifically, the plaintiff must demonstrate that the defendant acted "negligently, recklessly or with knowledge with regard to the falsity and defamatory character of the communication."[27] When the statement refers to a "public figure"—"someone who has achieved great fame or notoriety or who has voluntarily become involved in a public controversy"[28]—the plaintiff must show that "the defendant knew of the falsity of the communication or acted in reckless disregard of it."[29] Accordingly, traditional Canadian defamation law is more plaintiff friendly than that in the U.S.[30]

4. *A claim made under the civil code.* Quebec has a bijuridicial legal system: while matters of public law are governed by common law, private legal matters fall within the purview of a civil law system. Consequently, Ortenberg's (and Lasarovitz's) action was brought under the Quebec Civil Code's general civil liability condition (see Judge Cross's judgment above)[31]—Article 1053: "Every person capable of discerning right from wrong is responsible for the damage caused by his fault to another, whether by positive act, imprudence, neglect, or want of skill." Which approach to defamation is preferable?

5. *Actionable "per se": Must there be proof of tangible loss?* A key characteristic of the traditional common law approach to defamation is that to succeed in obtaining damages for libel, there is no need to demonstrate suffering of tangible loss by the plaintiff—it is actionable "per se."[32] This traditionally contrasts with slander, which requires the proof of "special damage"[33]—generally meaning "a specific and quantifiable

---

24. Grant v. Torstar Corp., 2009 CarswellOnt 7956 (Can. S.C.C.) (WL).

25. SMOLLA, *supra* note 23, at § 1:8; RESTATEMENT (SECOND) OF TORTS § 581A (AM. L. INST. 1977).

26. RESTATEMENT (SECOND) OF TORTS § 652D special note (AM. L. INST. 1977).

27. *Id.* at § 613.

28. *Public Figure*, BLACK'S LAW DICTIONARY (12th ed. 2024).

29. RESTATEMENT (SECOND) OF TORTS § 613 cmt. f. (AM. L. INST. 1977).

30. Canada rejected incorporating the *Sullivan* approach to defamation in the landmark case of Hill v. Church of Scientology of Toronto, 1995 CarswellOnt 396 (Can. S.C.C.) (WL).

31. *See also* David Fraser, *"Our judges in Quebec will give us fair play": Jews, Law, and Blood Libel in Canada, with some remarks on blood libel in the United States*, Paper at the Cardozo Law School Conference: A Thousand Years of Infamy 19 (Nov. 2013).

32. CHRISTIAN WITTING, STREET ON TORTS 792 (16th ed. 2021).

33. Although English law does provide that "special damage" need not be proved in cases of slander if "the words impute either a crime for which the claimant can be made to suffer physically by way of punishment, or where they are calculated to disparage the claimant in any office, profession,

financial loss."[34] Clearly, in this case, libel is not actionable "per se"—the Civil Code requires that "damage" be demonstrated. According to Judges Carroll and Cross, which of the defendants' many defamatory statements caused the plaintiffs (or Quebec's Jewish community) demonstrable damages, and which did not?

6. *Slander or libel?* Plamondon defamed Jews by giving a lecture. Leduc did so by publishing Plamondon's lecture. Judge Carroll's judgment states that the former was slander, while the latter was libel. Was Judge Carroll correct?

Consider the following propositions:

a. "Slander consists of a defamatory imputation in some non-permanent form by spoken words, or other sounds, or by gestures."[35]

b. "Defamation in permanent form is libel.... Libel generally indicates something printed or written, but it includes also anything in a more or less permanent form, such as a painting or picture, effigy, caricature, advertisement, talking film, or any disparaging object."[36]

c. "If the defendant makes an oral statement that is intended to be and is reduced to writing—e.g., dictation to a stenographer or a telephone call to a news reporter in the expectation that what is said on the phone will be published in the paper—the defamation is libel, not slander."[37]

d. Because Plamondon had strong ties to the newspaper, he likely intended or expected the *Libre Parole* to publish his lecture.[38]

7. *Why distinguish slander from libel?* As noted above, the tort of defamation is split in two: slander and libel. The need to distinguish between the two derives from the idea that libelous statements tend to cause greater harm than slanderous ones, and this is reflected by the greater difficulty in proving slander—there is a need to establish "special damage." In critiquing the term "hate speech laws," Jeremy Waldron writes as follows:[39]

> If we say we are interested in restrictions on hate speech, we convey the idea that the law is proposing to interfere with the spoken word, with conversation, and perhaps with vocabulary, with our use of racial or ethnic slurs or epithets stammered out, as Justice Jackson once put it, "when the spirits are high and the flagons are low." Speech, in the sense of the spoken word, can certainly be

---

calling, trade, or business held or carried on by him at the time of publication." CLERK AND LINDSELL ON TORTS, *supra* note 22.

34. *Id.* at § 21-54. There has also been recent debate, in English law, following the passage of the Defamation Act 2013 (U.K.), concerning whether § 1(1) of that statute is consistent with the traditional common law position that libel is actionable "per se." WITTING, *supra* note 32, at 899.

35. CLERK AND LINDSELL ON TORTS, *supra* note 22, at § 21-08.

36. *Id.* at § 21-47.

37. SMOLLA, *supra* note 23, at § 1:12.

38. Fraser, *supra* note 31, at 28.

39. Jeremy Waldron, *Dignity and Defamation: The Visibility of Hate*, 123 HARV. L. REV. 1596, 1600–1601 (2010).

> wounding. But I believe that the expressions of hatred that should concern us include most prominently those that are printed, published, pasted up, or posted, or in some other form become part of the visible environment in which our lives have to be lived. No doubt a speech can resonate long after the spoken word has died away, but to my mind it is the enduring presence of the published word that is particularly damaging.

Which caused more immediate and short-term harm to Quebec City's Jews—Plamondon's lecture or Leduc's publication of the lecture? Which caused more lasting harm?

8. *Advocating boycott.* In contrast to Quebec law, in the U.S. if a speaker's call for a boycott is politically motivated and related to a public issue, then such advocacy is generally legally protected free speech, and such advocates cannot be held liable for economic loss caused by such advocacy.[40]

9. *Doxing*[41] *and criminal libel.* In his lecture, Plamondon advanced that "even in St. Roche [neighborhood], there is a factory at 115 ½ or 117 St. Joseph Street where ... regular labour is performed every Sunday in the year." In both *Rex v. Osborn*, 2 Barn K.B. 138, 94 Eng. Rep. R. 406 (K.B. 1732) and *Ortenberg*, an antisemitic publication provoked anti-Jewish violence. Unlike in *Osborn*, however, the Quebec authorities did not prosecute Plamondon for common law criminal libel, defined as "a malicious libel that is designed to expose a person to hatred, contempt, or ridicule and that may subject the author to criminal sanctions."[42] Should they have?

10. *Avoiding a jury.* The plaintiffs purposefully limited their claim for damages against the defendants to £500. This is not because it quantified the amount of material and moral loss they suffered, but because if they had claimed more than £500, the defendants could have chosen a trial by jury. In Roman Catholic Quebec City, a Jewish plaintiff confronting the antisemitic outbursts of a well-known and highly respected member of the Church and the legal profession "would not have had the ghost of a chance with a Jury."[43] In other words, the plaintiffs purposefully limited their claim for damages because they were afraid of the prejudices jurors might hold.

Group Defamation Is Generally Not Actionable

1. *Group libel:* Group libel defames a group of people, including but not limited to groups defined by race, gender, national origin, religion, and so forth. It could, in theory, cover any group. Group defamation defames individual group members by ascribing negative common traits to each. Group libel may be described as "blanket" when it defames the group as a whole without identifying any particular member,

---

40. NAACP v. Claiborne Hardware Co., 458 U.S. 886 (1982).

41. Doxing (or doxxing) is the intentional online exposure of an individual's identity, private information, or personal details without their consent. *Doxing*, eSafety Comm'r, https://www.esafety.gov.au/industry/tech-trends-and-challenges/doxing (last updated Aug. 27, 2024).

42. *Libel*, Black's Law Dictionary (12th ed. 2024).

43. Fraser, *supra* note 31, at 20.

either by name or inference. It may be described as "targeted" or "tethered" when it singles out a particular member or group members for verbal abuse by tethering them to evils ascribed to the whole group. Although the state can prosecute blanket group libel, it generally does not create a civil action for individual group members.

> As a general rule, no action lies for the publication of defamatory words concerning a large group or class of persons.... No individual member of the group can recover for such broad and general defamation. The words are not reasonably understood to have any personal application to any individual unless there are circumstances that give them such an application. The extreme example is the statement of David that "All men are liars," which in a sense defames all mankind and yet could not reasonably be taken to have any personal reference to each member of the human race. On the same basis, the statement that "All lawyers are shysters," or that all of a great many persons engaged in a particular trade or business or those of a particular race or creed are dishonest cannot ordinarily be taken to have personal reference to any of the class.[44]

2. *Size.* A defamed group member's ability to bring a suit turns in part on the size of the group. The Restatement (Second) of Torts stipulates that:[45]

> One who publishes defamatory matter concerning a group or class of persons is subject to liability to an individual member of it if, but only if, (a) the group or class is so small that the matter can reasonably be understood to refer to the member, or (b) the circumstances of publication reasonably give rise to the conclusion that there is particular reference to the member.

3. *How many is not too many?* Justice Carroll found that the relevant defamed parties were not too numerous to sustain a libel action. The defamatory language picked out the Jews of Quebec City, which only comprised 75 families—Quebec City Jews could be reasonably identified and were not too numerous to recover. Yet, in the later Quebec case of *Abugov v. Arcand*, Cour Supérieure Montréal No 106465, September 13, 1932, CJC, which has a very similar fact pattern to *Ortenberg*, the case was thrown out for lack of reference to the plaintiff. One major difference in the facts of the cases is that Abugov lived in Lachine—an area of Greater Montreal where tens of thousands of Jews lived.

4. *Truth in the trial court.* The trial court dismissed the action on grounds that the defendants "had neither named the plaintiffs nor attacked them in particular," adding that "having arrived at this conclusion it is useless for me to study the other questions raised." For some Jewish commentators, the trial judge's dismissal meant that it would not address the question most affecting their safety—whether defendants' statements were true: "Are the Jews what Plamondon says they are, or are they not?" "By dismissing the action," the commentator continued, the trial court "has justified

---

44. Restatement (Second) of Torts § 564A (Am. L. Inst. 1977).

45. *Id.*

these treacherous accusations ... and gave them judicial approval." Is that correct? By dismissing the action on narrow (and perhaps correct) legal grounds, did the court leave untouched the claim that Judaism taught Jews to think and do terrible things? Is that how reasonable laypeople might interpret the dismissal? Should that likely perception have affected how the judges wrote their opinions? Compare the Quebec courts' approach to the South African court's approach in *Levy v. von Moltke*.

The commentator's point is not legal, i.e., that Plamondon had specifically tethered Quebec City's Jews or some subset thereof to group defamation. Rather, it is that the court passed up an opportunity to debunk that defamation, the true threat to Quebec Jews' safety. What could the court have done to make Jews safer within the available doctrinal categories, and without transgressing the rule of law?

5. *Tethered group defamation:* Tethered group libel is explicit when it explicitly identifies an individual as a member of the group, e.g., "David Cohen, a Jew, possesses all the negative traits of his race—he's greedy, devious, dishonest, loud, pushy, obnoxious, etc." It is implicit when it ascribes to an individual member traits perceived to belong to group members as a whole, but does not identify the group by name, for example, "David Cohen is greedy, devious, dishonest, loud, pushy, obnoxious, etc." Such statements use coded language whose meaning everyone knows, also known as "dog whistles."[46]

6. *To whom was the defamation tethered?* The Plamondon majority and concurrence appear to define the targeted people differently. Judge Carroll, writing for the majority, views the targets as every member of Quebec City's Jewish community. Judge Cross's concurrence views the targets as the Jewish merchants who operate on Sunday. How does this affect their analysis?

A Missed Opportunity to Debunk the Blood Libel

1. *The defense of "justification" or "truth."* Plamondon claimed that his statements were true.[47] In common law jurisdictions, this is known as the affirmative defense of "Justification."[48] In Smolla's words, "truth justifies the defamation"[49]—the truth justifies the statement. In both Canadian and U.S. law, the truth of a defamatory publication completely precludes recovery.[50] How does this defense work in practice?

---

46. A statement or expression which in addition to its ostensible meaning has a further, typically less publicly acceptable interpretation or connotation intended to be understood only by a specific target audience. *Dog Whistle*, Oxford Eng. Dictionary, https://doi.org/10.1093/OED/6895433502 (last visited July 2023).

47. In fact, some were: some Jewish merchants conducted business on Sunday, and lawfully too.

48. Although, in English law, following the passage of § 3 Defamation Act 2013 (U.K.), the defense is now known straightforwardly as "Truth."

49. Smolla, *supra* note 23, at § 1:9.75.

50. Restatement (Second) of Torts § 581A (Am. L. Inst. 1977). ("One who publishes a defamatory statement of fact is not subject to liability for defamation if the statement is true.")

> Canada follows the traditional common-law rule, placing on the defendant the burden of proving the truth of a defamatory statement, as part of the defendant's affirmative defense of "justification" or "truth." ...
>
> Proving falsity is not part of the plaintiff's burden, for the falsity of the defamatory statement is presumed as a matter of law.... In the traditional parlance of the common law, the "onus" is thus on the defendant to establish substantial truth, not on the plaintiff to establish substantial falsehood.[51]

2. *The central role of expert witnesses when a truth defense is raised.* Plamondon contended that his statements concerning the blood libel were true. In response, the plaintiffs called Rabbi Abramovitz of the Shaar Hashomayim synagogue in Montreal to the stand as their expert witness. David Fraser details his testimony as follows:[52]

> The plaintiffs in their case, and the defendants in their rebuttal, each played out the traditional juridical narrative—one side attempting to establish, by way of Abramowitz's expert testimony, that the accusation was untrue ... after establishing his [Abramowitz's] academic and theological credentials, and his familiarity with the Talmud, and this then allowed the rabbi to carefully detail the significance and content of Talmudic teachings. Jacobs led him through testimony that demolished each of Plamondon's assertions concerning Jewish perfidy. On the specifics of the blood libel in particular, Abramowitz stated without qualification or hesitation that there had never been a Jewish ritual calling for the spilling of the blood of Christians. He gave a lengthy statement about the history of the blood libel from the Middle Ages, and more significantly, he highlighted for the Court the number of Papal Bulls[53] and episcopal statements, and declarations from other prominent Roman Catholic theologians denouncing the ritual murder Accusation.

3. *The anti-Semite's treatment of a Jewish expert witness.* Plamondon, while being cross-examined by Ortenberg's lawyer, objected to Abramowitz's expert testimony on the ground that "Abramowitz 'is a Jew' whose testimony against a Gentile, as the Talmud itself proved, would be a lie."[54] Should Jewish litigants rely on non-Jewish expert witnesses, especially when the subject matter concerns antisemitism? Keep this question in mind when assessing the strategies of other Jewish litigants in this chapter, and when reading David H. Schraub, "The Epistemic Dimension of Antisemitism" (2022), in Chapter 12.

4. *Ortenberg: A pyrrhic victory*? Fraser describes Ortenberg's success in the case as a "win" in quotes.[55] He does so because the judges merely found that Plamondon had failed to sustain a Truth defense. That is, the judges did not speak in categorical terms

---

51. Smolla, *supra* note 23, at § 1:9.75.

52. Fraser, *supra* note 31, at 16–22.

53. *See, e.g.*, Pope Innocent IV, Lachrymabilem Judaeorum. July 5, 1247. This and other Roman Catholic Church pronouncements on the Blood Libel are discussed in Chapter 14, *infra*.

54. Fraser, *supra* note 31, at 25.

55. *Id.* at 36.

and hold that "ritual murder accusations ... [are] inherently gross falsehoods."[56] Thus, the judges technically left the door open for future anti-Semites to successfully mount the truth defense.

Canadian Jewry's Response to Antisemitism Pre-WWII

1. *Camel's back*: Fraser writes that despite the Jews' formal legal equality:

> For several years [prior to Plamondon's speech], Quebec's Jews had been subjected to increasingly vehement attacks from the ultramontane Francophone elite of the province. Again and again, prominent members of the Roman Catholic clergy and laity had singled out the province's growing Jewish population with increasing vitriol. Plamondon's speech and the ensuing violence against Jewish individuals and their property, and against the community's synagogue, served for the Jews of Quebec City and their co-religionists in Montreal, as a clear indication of an ever worsening situation.[57]

In short, Plamondon's speech was the final straw that spurred Quebec's Jews to take legal action.

2. *Sandwiched between French ultramontane Catholicism and Anglophone Protestantism.* In the early 20th Century, the demography of Quebec was composed of two main groups:

> An Anglophone Protestant minority constituted the industrial, commercial, and financial elite of the province. [And a] ... Francophone, Roman Catholic [majority] was excluded from effective economic power.[58]

Importantly:

> Jews were obviously neither Protestant nor Roman Catholic. They were, for the most part, with the influx of the 1890s and 1900s, neither Anglophone nor Francophone. While for a variety of reasons the vast majority of Quebec Jews chose to align themselves with the Anglophone Protestant minority for educational and economic purposes, they never really sat at all comfortably in a formal and informal constitutional matrix in which the dominant mythology of "Canada," of being "Canadian," or "Canadien," existed as the key discursive matrix of national (and increasingly nationalist) ideologies centered in the ideals of two founding nations ... Quebec's Jews often found themselves between the rock of Anglophone Protestant antisemitism and Francophone Roman Catholic Jew-hatred.[59]

---

56. *Id.*
57. *Id.* at 9.
58. *Id.*
59. *Id.* at 10.

3. *Hate speech statutes.* In addition to litigation, the Quebec Jewish community sought legislative means to combat antisemitism. In 1924, Sam Jacobs, Ortenberg's lawyer and the first Jewish MP in Canada,

> introduced a bill to amend the Criminal Code by outlawing the publication of false, defamatory, and seditious matter which is intended to produce such feelings of ill-will and hostility among different classes of the community that a breach of the peace is likely to follow, or lawful business pursuits are likely to be interfered with.... The proposed Jacobs' amendment would have combined elements of criminal and seditious libel, making a serious attack on the Jewish (or other) community a per se threat to public order and a criminal offence. It would have made calls for an anti-Jewish boycott of the Achat Chez Nous type more problematic and possibly a crime if "lawful business pursuits" were interfered with.

This bill did not pass.[60] In 1931, Peter Bercovitch and Joseph Cohen, Jewish members of the Quebec legislature, proposed a group defamation bill. It provided that:

> The repeated publication of a defamatory libel, without legal justification or excuse, against any nationality, race, or creed, likely to expose persons belonging to such nationality or race or professing such creed, to hatred, contempt or ridicule, shall give rise, without prejudice to any other recourse, in favour of any person belonging to such nationality or race or professing such creed, to the remedies hereinafter provided.[61]

This bill also did not pass.

Although these bills did not explicitly refer to Jews, "everyone was fully aware of the 'Jewish' background of the proposal, and this was enough to sink it."[62] Jewish groups could not assemble a broad coalition of support.

B. Debunking the *Protocols*

Reverend Abraham Levy, a graduate of Jews' College in England, was the Minister of the Port Elizabeth Hebrew Congregation, Western Road Synagogue. In 1934, he sued three members of the "Greyshirts" fascist organization[63] for defamation: von Moltke—the leader of the organization's East Providential branch; Olivier—the owner, editor, and publisher of the Greyshirts' newspaper, *Die Rapport*; and Inch—the

60. David Fraser, Nazi Antisemitism and Jewish Legal Self-Defense 122 (2023).

61. Act respecting the publication of defamatory libel, 1st session, 18th Legislature, 22 Geo. V., 1931–32.

62. Fraser, *supra* note 60.

63. The Greyshirts were a political movement, established in 1932–33, which

> modelled [itself] on the Nazi SA in terms of ideology, organization, and tactics. Their uniform was inspired by the German SA ... [and] they became the most well-organized, visible, and potentially violent and dangerous anti-Jewish group [in South Africa]. They drew their [2,000-man-strong] membership from disaffected working-class young men ... largely motivated by antisemitic propaganda and Afrikaner nationalism. Their aim was the creation of

leader of the Port Elizabethan subsidiary of von Moltke's organization. Levy sought an injunction and damages of £2000 from each of them, on the basis that they had each contributed to the publication of a defamatory document that resembled the *Protocols of the Elders of Zion.*[64] The document had apparently been signed by someone titled "Rabbi" and stolen by Inch from the Western Road Synagogue which, Levy contended, implied that he had authorized, agreed with, and counselled the contents of the document. Levy further claimed that the document implied that he was a member of a faith that conspired and counselled on such matters.

The document was read aloud by von Moltke at a well-attended public meeting, and it was subsequently published in *Die Rapport* by Olivier. In response to the claim, the Greyshirts advanced two main lines of defense: first, that the document did not refer to Abraham Levy, in part because he lacked the technical qualifications to be a rabbi; and second, that, in any event, the statements they had made were true and for the public benefit. However, during the hearing, and after Levy had finished his case, the defendants withdrew their second defense and substituted it with a defense of "good faith."

The trial was heard before the Supreme Court of the Eastern Province, South Africa, with two judges sitting in the case: Judge-President Graham and Judge Gutsche. The Court declared that: (i) the document was defamatory; (ii) it referred to Levy; (iii) Inch's story of stealing the document from the synagogue was completely concocted; (iv) the document itself was a fabrication and almost certainly compiled by the Greyshirts themselves; and (v) the original *Protocols* itself was a forgery. Given that the defendants withdrew their "true and for the public benefit" defense, declarations (iii)–(v) were made *obiter dicta* (incidental).

The court awarded the sums of £1,000 against Inch, £750 as damages against von Moltke, and £25 against Olivier, plus costs to the plaintiffs. The court made permanent its temporary injunction that ordered the defendants to stop printing or publishing the document. Following a subsequent criminal trial for distributing a forged document, perjury, and theft, Inch was sentenced to six years and three months' imprisonment.[65]

> a National Socialist regime in the union of South Africa ... [however, they did differ] from German National Socialism ... by mixing Nazi ideology with the distinct mission of forming a Christian country.

Fraser, *supra* note 60, at 66–67.

64. According to the Holocaust Encyclopedia: "*The Protocols of the Elders of Zion* is an antisemitic book used to promote hatred of Jews. It was first published in 1903. The Protocols contains conspiracy theories about alleged global Jewish power. It is the most widespread antisemitic publication of modern times." *An Antisemitic Conspiracy: The Protocols of the Elders of Zion*, Holocaust Encyc., https://encyclopedia.ushmm.org/content/en/article/protocols-of-the-elders-of-zion (last updated Nov. 26, 2024).

65. Harry Schneiderman & Melvin M. Fagen, *Review of the Year 5695*, 37 Am. Jewish Y.B. 172 (Sept. 1935–1936).

Levy v. Von Moltke

Supreme Court of the Eastern Province, South Africa (1934)

JUDGE-PRESIDENT GRAHAM delivered the opinion of the court.

Introduction

In these actions the Plaintiff [Reverend Abraham Levy] claims from each Defendant the sum of £2000 as damages on account of defamation.... The Plaintiff is the Minister in charge of the "Port Elizabeth Hebrew Congregation, Western Road Synagogue." He does not possess the academical degree or technical qualifications of a Rabbi but, as will appear, is spoken of and known amongst the general public as the "Rabbi" of that congregation. The Defendant [Johannes von Strauss] von Moltke is the leader in the Eastern Province of an organisation styled the "South African Gentile National Socialist Movement" whose object is to combat and destroy the alleged "perversive influence of the Jews in economics, culture, religion, ethics and statecraft and to reestablish European Aryan control in South Africa for the welfare of the Christian peoples of South Africa." The Defendant [David Hermanus] Olivier is the owner, editor, and publisher of "*Die Rapport*," [The Truth].... [T]he organ of the "South African Gentile National Socialist Movement".... The Defendant [Harry Victor] Inch [a part-time refrigerator plant attendant], is the leader in the Eastern Province of the "South African Grey Shirt Movement," which is a body subsidiary to the "South African Gentile National Socialist Movement." Its precise scope and functions have not been disclosed, but it is said to be, or to provide, the "Bodyguard" of the other movement, and its purpose is "to combat the pernicious influence of the Jewish race."

"The Document"

The alleged defamatory words are contained in a document which throughout these proceedings was referred to as "The document."... [At the top of the document] are badly formed Hebraic characters handwritten in red ink signifying "Fit for Passover," and under these words are similar characters making up the words which mean "The Book of Memorial or Remembrance" or "The Book of Chronicles." On the left side, similarly written, are Hebrew words meaning "Holy Congregation." The document is in these terms:

LECTURE NO. 2

SUBJECTS—"OUR PLAN OF ATTACK."

> As I have explained to you in previous meetings, our attitude to Christianity is one of great interest to the High Circle of The Jewish Citizens of Port Elizabeth. As you all know the divisions in the Christian Church were of our construction. It was our ancestors that urged Luther and the other reformers to break from the Mother Church. i.e. The Roman Catholic Church, for our own private purposes, which would hasten the fulfilment [*sic*] of our World Imperialism.... The R.C.C. has been unconscious for countless centuries, but it is beginning to stir to life again.... We must destroy it. It is interfering with our World Socialism....

We are confident in our success.... We who control, financially and even politically behind the scenes....

We stand for World Communism, for Dictatorship of the Proletariat. Our Imperialism or "PAX JUDAEICA" is one for the downfall of Western Civilisation and its replacement by the Eastern or Japanese System. We have seen the progress of the USS.R. since 1917 when our Agents, Lenin, Stalin &c. murdered the Tsar. The Pope is a religious Imperialist, and that interferes with our world Plan. As we have got control over Russia, so we will also control the Union [of South Africa], and so achieve our object in the destruction of the British Empire. It is our plan to give South Africa to the Natives....

The following papers financed through us are the *Express* (Mr. Barlow editing with our approval), *The Socialist Review*, [and] the *Anti-Nazi*.... We will fool the public.... We will make them digest as much silly rot as their decayed and filthy minds are capable of understanding....

On your very life take care of these instructions, do not mention a word to not even your own what is contained in these pages. You know our law. You know the Result. The propaganda that will shortly arrive from Moscow, that will be in our safe keeping in the Syn. West. RD will be handed to trusted members of the local and Cape Trade Unions....

ISSUED BY THE SELECT HIGH CIRCLE OF THE ANTI-NAZI PROPAGANDA VIGILANCE COMMITTEE C.X.V.O. 3838 AND AUTHORISED FOR USE BY THE TRUSTEE AND THE SIX COUNCIL MEMBERS ONLY.

"RABBI."

The Document's Meaning

It is claimed by the Defendant [von Moltke] that this document was stolen by Inch from the Western Road Synagogue.... The Plaintiff asserts that it is a false or forged document and that it was at no time lawfully brought into the Synagogue and denies that Inch stole it therefrom....

The [document] means and was intended to mean that the members of the Jewish Faith should keep silent with regard to the aforesaid designs and await propaganda from Moscow to help in the before-mentioned subversive activities and that this propaganda would be sent to and distributed by the Western Road Synagogue of which the Plaintiff was the Minister in charge. That the final words in capital letters mean and were intended to mean that the document, the course of conduct and all allegations in the document were approved of by Plaintiff as the Rabbi of the said Synagogue. It was further meant and understood that Plaintiff was a member of a Faith that counselled all the aforesaid matters including the commission of the crimes set out in the document and that the document was found in the Synagogue of which Plaintiff was the Minister and that Plaintiff authorised, agreed to and counselled the doing of all the things therein set out and that Plaintiff was accordingly a man who counselled blasphemy, religious hatred and the commission of crime and generally was a man destitute of all scruple or character.

The Defendants Did Not Publish the Defamatory Statements for the Plaintiff

In the action against von Moltke, it was alleged that on April 4, 1934, at a public meeting in the Feather Market Hall at Port Elizabeth, and on March 27, 1934 at a public meeting at Aberdeen, he published the contents of the document by reading it to the meeting and by falsely alleging that it had been obtained by theft from the Western Road Synagogue of which, as has been said, the Plaintiff is the Minister. In his plea, the Defendant admitted the publications. He denied that the Plaintiff was known or referred to as "Rabbi" in Port Elizabeth or elsewhere, and denied that the words complained of were meant or could be understood to refer to the Plaintiff inasmuch as they were directed against the Jewish race as a whole.... In the alternative he pleaded that the words were true in substance and in fact and for the public benefit. During the hearing, after the Plaintiff had closed his case, on the 21st July this plea of justification was withdrawn and an amended plea was filed to the effect that if the words complained of did refer to the Plaintiff, the Defendant, honestly and reasonably believing the document to be what it purported to be, lawfully published it in good faith without any intention or reasonable expectation of injuring the Plaintiff and with due reasonable care.

The Document Is a Forgery and Inch's Story was Concocted

In the action against Olivier it was alleged that he published in "Die Rapport" ... the document ... alleging that it had been procured by theft from the Western Road Synagogue of which the Plaintiff was the Minister....

We are satisfied from the evidence of the Plaintiff and his witnesses that there were no such documents as described by Inch in the Synagogue....

We are convinced that these documents bear the unmistakable imprint of having been compiled by a member or members of the Grey Shirt movement....

In arriving at this conclusion we have not overlooked the evidence of Mr. Beamish,[66] witness for defence who stated that he was definitely of the opinion that all three documents were of an Asiatic character and could not have been concocted by [von Moltke].... He was asked:

> (Q.) Have you any reason to believe that Western civilisation is in a sorry plight?
>
> (A.) I have every reason, because I have ears and eyes.
>
> (Q.) What do you mean by that?
>
> (A.) I mean that I defy anyone to name any Government in the whole of Europe to-day that is not absolutely controlled by the Jews.

He is asked about Russia, and stated 90 per cent. of the Soviet Government are Jews.

---

66. Editor's note: Henry Hamilton Beamish (1873–1948) was a prominent British antisemitic activist and leader of several racist, far-right, anti-Jewish organizations in the early 20th century. Along with many others, he published the *Protocols*. *Henry Hamilton Beamish*, Wikipedia, https://en.wikipedia.org/wiki/Henry_Hamilton_Beamish (last visited Dec. 17, 2024).

In cross-examination he stated he was a firm believer in the Protocols of the Elders of Zion, and that he could "prove every one of them." He stated that in every country the aristocracy, i.e., the landowners, are rapidly disappearing. He was satisfied that Mr. Lloyd George had introduced his land taxation measures because all the political parties throughout the world are controlled by Jews.

He is asked:

(Q.) We are told that the Jews are getting control of most of the land in South Africa?

(A.) I don't want to discuss it in this country because it is so palpable.

He is referred to Protocol (9), and states that the youth of all countries are being inculcated by false principles, "done through the terrible cinemas, theatres, jazz-music, the so-called architecture of Epstein, novels ... and of course the press. I go so far as to say there is not a single newspaper in this country that is not controlled by Jews ... it is not done by means of ownership but by means of advertisements." He states that religion is rapidly disappearing throughout the world. And asked:

(Q.) Who is behind that?

(A.) My old friends again, the Jews.

When asked about *the document,* he states it is merely a part of the plot which has been in existence for a large number of years, and is now being rapidly brought into effect. He stated he belonged to "a secret organisation finding out all these things, he does not go by his own name, there is danger over this matter." The last Spanish Revolution "was engineered by the 'Crypto' Jews, the descendants of Jews who have been kept in 'cold storage' for all these years, ever since the 15th century, and have now come out."

He is asked:

(Q.) By whom was the Cromwellian revolution worked?

(A.) The Jews of course.

The Jews, he states, also were at the back of the conquest of England by William the Conqueror. The Jameson Raid was "engineered by Alfred Beit." He states he is able to prove the Russo-Japanese War, the Boer War and the late World War, were all results of Jewish intrigues. He believes the Jews' aim is to destroy the Christian Church and religion and to judaize the civilised world. He states he opened Henry Ford's eyes to "the Jewish menace. I taught him." The Jewish Board of Deputies in England is "the super-Parliament of Great Britain, and you have one in this country too." He again refers to the manner in which he "taught Hitler." "I said to him 'How do you propose to deal with the Jews?' He said 'I have made up my mind.'—He said 'We are going to send all our Jews to the Allies' and I said 'I think they thoroughly deserve it.' But I said 'That won't cure the disease, if you have a mad dog and you tie him up in your back yard that does not get rid of the mad dog' and then Hitler became more reasonable." He added that this conversation took place in 1921. He is definitely of opinion that the Jews are in control in South Africa, and can prove it; and when reminded there are only two Jewish members in Parliament he replies: "That has nothing to do with it, only one mosquito gives you malaria." ... Asked if he thought "the propaganda" referred to in *the document* would be harboured in the Synagogue, with the knowledge of the Minister in charge, or Rabbi, he replied: "I don't know anything about the Synagogue, or where it is. All I know is that although we have heard there is no political atmosphere about a Synagogue, these plots are hatched in some place, and they may use these buildings for political purposes." ... He is satisfied that the Book of Deuteronomy foretold the conquest of England by the Jews, and their possession of the gold mines in South Africa, the establishment of the League of Nations, and the war debts incurred by England. Masonic institutions are under Jew control, and the French revolution was also due to Jews. He admits that in his book "The Jews' Who's Who" he alleges that in 1648 the Jews in England offered Oliver Cromwell £500,000 to purchase St. Paul's Cathedral to be converted into a Synagogue, and states he derived this information "from the Archives in the British Museum where the Protocols are filed. All the Prime Ministers of England are under Jewish influence."

(Q.) Is Lloyd George still in Jewish hands?

(A.) Never anything else.

(Q.) Mr. Clines?

(A.) The Labour Party, yes, all parties.[67]

He also thinks a great many of the learned professions are under Jewish influence. He is unaware of any institution in England which is not under Jewish influence "except the Church to a minor extent." All political parties in all parts of the world with the exception of Germany and Italy "in part" are under Jewish influence. "The trouble in India is fomented by the Jews," and there is "not the slightest doubt that Gandhi is under Jewish influence." ...

It is difficult to accept evidence of this character seriously ... [Beamish] has been unable to produce a vestige of relevant evidence in support of his charges....

It may at first sight appear improbable that anyone possessed of ordinary intelligence would have been so foolish as to devise a plot which could be so readily exposed, for even the most foolish conspirators usually take measures to avoid detection. But in this instance the action of the author or authors of the plot is easily accounted for; it was never anticipated that the story told by Inch to account for his possession of the three documents would ever be investigated in a Court of law. So long as no names were mentioned as authors of the document the plotters thought they were secure. Von Moltke stated he had been so advised by a lawyer whom he consulted prior to his first meeting at Aberdeen. Both the Defendants, Inch and von Moltke, plead that the attacks made by them were on a class and not upon any individual. Secure in this belief Inch

---

67. Editor's note: For a contemporary refutation of this claim, *see* EQUAL. AND HUM. RTS. COMM'N, INVESTIGATION INTO ANTISEMITISM IN THE LABOUR PARTY (Oct. 2020), https://www.equalityhumanrights.com/sites/default/files/investigation-into-antisemitism-in-the-labour-party.pdf (identifying inadequate processes for handling antisemitism complaints across the Labour Party).

handed the document to von Moltke who took immediate steps to publish it before large audiences and circulated it widely in the Aberdeen organ of the movement....

To enable the movement to gain ground something more than mere anti-Jewish propaganda was necessary. The South African people are a liberty-loving race, tolerant in their religious beliefs; "Jew baiting," until the formation of the Grey Shirt movement in Port Elizabeth, has hitherto been unknown in this country and von Moltke must have realised that to induce the masses to adopt what has been described as the "Hitler Movement" would require convincing evidence against the Jews....

The *Protocols* Are a Forgery

A great deal of evidence was called in the cases of all the Defendants with the object of proving the existence of a so-called world plot organised by the Jews, with the object, as stated by the witness Beamish, "to destroy the Christian Church and religion generally and to Judaize the civilised world." ... We think it right to say a few words upon the subject, inasmuch as the document alleged to have been found in the Western Road Synagogue implied that Plaintiff was associated with the plot. The Defendants have failed to produce a vestige of proof to establish the existence of this plot. They rely on a long series of opinions of persons who are admittedly hostile to the Jewish religion, and whose opinions are based upon the assertions of previous writers who give no authority of any value in support of their conclusions.

That the Jewish race has undergone persecution from the earliest days of their history is common knowledge, and this is relied upon as indicating the existence of the plot, the contention being that if there was no plot there would have been no persecution, overlooking the fact that religious persecutions are not confined to the Jewish race. The same authorities and arguments which were used to justify the persecution of the Jews in the Middle Ages were used by the Defendants' witnesses in the present case, coupled with the contention that what are known as *The Protocols of the Elders of Zion* definitely brought home the existence of this great conspiracy. It was alleged that the *Protocols* were secretly promulgated by Dr. Herzl at the first Zionist Congress in 1897 held at Basle; but the evidence of Mr. Nahum Sokolow, the leader of the Zionist movement, whose testimony we accept without hesitation, conclusively shows that no such document was ever referred to or mentioned in any way at that Congress. Mr. Sokolow stated he attended the Congress. The proceedings were open to the public; he was a member of all the Committees, and he was largely concerned in drawing up the agenda. Many Christian students attended the Congress, and there was no secrecy of any sort in connection with the meetings. Mr. Sokolow further stated that he first heard of the existence of the *Protocols* in 1920 whilst he was on a visit to Paris. He returned to London, where he first saw and read them. He states he then endeavoured to trace the history of the document, and eventually the officials of the British Museum discovered a pamphlet published in the reign of Napoleon III, appearing under the heading of Anti-Napoleonic pamphlets in the Museum catalogue.

This was the French edition of the *Protocols*. He states he personally, in the presence of Mr. Price, compared this document with the *Protocols*, and it was found that the

Protocols were a clumsy plagiarism. Mr. Sokolow states that Mr. Price subsequently published articles in the London *Times* in August 1921 containing the passages in the original Anti-Napoleonic pamphlet, which had been used by the author of the *Protocols*, and Mr. Sokolow states that having seen the two documents he is in a position to vouch for the accuracy of the statements contained in Mr. Price's articles. A copy of Mr. Price's articles was put in, and it will be seen that the Anti-Napoleonic pamphlet contains no references to the Jewish race, but was a veiled attack on the Emperor and his policy. The author of this literary forgery was one Maurice Joly, and shortly after the publication of this pamphlet he was arrested by the Emperor's police and sentenced to fifteen months' imprisonment. It would thus appear that the *Protocols* are an impudent forgery, obviously published for the purpose of anti-Jewish propaganda.

The Document Referred to the Plaintiff

From the pleadings as previously set out, two main questions immediately arise for consideration. Can the innuendoes be sustained, i.e., are the words capable of bearing the meaning ascribed to them? [The court found that they did.] If so, do they refer to the Plaintiff, that is, has he been so marked or identified that he is entitled to sue?

... All these innuendoes [in the forged document], if applied to a particular person, are defamatory and actionable. Whether the portion in capital letters can bear the meaning as is alleged, that the Plaintiff as Rabbi of the said Synagogue approved of the document and all its contents is an important feature of the case and will be considered when dealing with the further question as to whether the Plaintiff is entitled to sue....

The Defendants conten[d] that on a reasonable construction of the document the Plaintiff has failed to establish that he has been "hit" by the libel. They say that in fact he is not a "Rabbi" and if he were, there is nothing to connect him with the "Rabbi" referred to in the document....

... [W]hatever may be the academical and technical difference between a Rabbi and Jewish Minister or Priest any reference in the document to the "Rabbi" when associated with the Western Road Synagogue may reasonably be taken to refer to the Plaintiff.

It is abundantly clear that the persons who heard the document read or themselves perused it came to the conclusion that the "Rabbi" of the document was the Plaintiff.

Because we, sitting as Judges as well as Jurors, were of opinion, for the reasons already given, that the document was capable of bearing the innuendoes placed upon it and because we thought that it might reasonably refer to the Plaintiff, the evidence of the persons who heard or read it was admitted to show that in their minds it was aimed at and hit the Plaintiff. As has been pointed out, that evidence appears to us to be conclusive. And "it is not necessary that all the world should understand the libel, it is sufficient if those who know the Plaintiff can make out that he is the person meant..."

As has been said the first defence is that the words complained of were directed against the Jewish race as a whole, and were not meant and could not have been understood to refer to the plaintiff. Now it is an elementary principle ... under English law that the defamatory words must refer to some ascertained person.... Where whole nations or classes or professions are defamed and no particular person is directly or indirectly indicated, the defamatory statement is aimed too widely and hits no one and has therefore no legal effect. But where the words refer to all the members of a particular number, group or class—that is to definite persons though included under a general term—such as "all the officers of this Regiment" or "all the members of that Jury," each one of that particular group or class can sue.... In America this principle has received a wide application. The defendant in a lecture delivered in the City of Quebec violently assailed and abused the Jewish race, its religious doctrines and social practices, the object being to put the public of Quebec on guard against the Jews of Quebec who numbered only 75 families in a total population of 80,000 souls. It was held that though not assailed individually, the plaintiff being one of the "restricted collectively" of the Jews of Quebec was entitled to maintain an action of defamation against the defendant, the Jews of Quebec being sufficiently designated as the object of defendant's attack. *Ortenburg v. Plomondon omd Ors.* [*sic*] ... Though in the present case there is no evidence as to how many Jews there are in, and what is the total population of, Port Elizabeth, that case bears a close resemblance to this case and would be an authority for holding that the Rabbi, Trustee and six Council Members of the Western Road Synagogue belong to a "restricted collectivity" and that each could maintain an action provided that in terms of the document they can be reasonably associated with that Synagogue. To be "ascertained" the person defamed need not necessarily be referred to by name or precise description. If from the circumstances his identity is ascertainable he is an ascertained person and is entitled to bring an action.... So too in our law and in the English law when the plaintiff is not "ascertained" or referred to by name or unambiguous description, but in terms of the defamatory statement is ascertainable the plaintiff "is always entitled to call witnesses to show that, though he has not been specially named, his friends thought the libel referred to him."...

Whilst there is no evidence to show that the Plaintiff has suffered any *patrimonial* damage,[68] it is beyond doubt that he has suffered greatly in his reputation, and that the defamatory article has caused him great mental anguish owing to the insult he has suffered.... The Plaintiff stated in cross-examination, and we accept his evidence unreservedly, that the publication of the document excited a great deal of feeling in Port Elizabeth, and that he found it made a great difference in his relationship with his non-Jewish friends in that City. We can well understand this. The Plaintiff has been the Minister in charge of the Western Road Synagogue for 21 years, a Member of the School Board for 18 years, and Chairman of the Educational Committee for four years, a Member of the Board of the Port Elizabeth Museum for many years, a Member of the Committee of the Grey School, of the Committee of the Port Elizabeth Library, and he occupied a seat on the Committee of the Child Welfare Society. The majority

68. Editor's note: In tort law, "patrimonial damages" refer to measurable financial or economic losses suffered by the plaintiff as a result of the defendant's wrongful conduct. *South African Law of Delict*, Wikipedia, https://en.wikipedia.org/wiki/South_African_law_of_delict#:~:text=patrimonial%20damages%2C%20including%20medical%20costs,other%20causes%2C%20notable%20unjustified%20enrichment (last visited Dec. 17, 2024).

of his fellow-members on these various public institutions are, I think we can assume, Christians, and the contents of this "blood-curdling document" ... must inevitably have caused serious damage to the Plaintiff's reputation....

To say of a Jewish Minister of Religion that he has the custody of and approves of the contents of a document containing words which are not only in themselves obscene but would be regarded as blasphemous by any Christians is a slander of the gravest nature....

Group Defamation and the Conspiracy Libel

1. *Elements of a South African defamation action.* The South African position on defamation, which generally follows the traditional common law position,[69] is that the plaintiff prevails unless the defendant can establish a positive defense. In two 1996 opinions, however, the South African supreme court made it more difficult for plaintiffs to prevail where the defamatory speech involved "political activity."[70] A defamation plaintiff in South Africa can seek injunctive relief as well as the usual remedy of damages.[71]

2. *A typology of group libel actions.* Joseph Tanenhaus offered the following formulation of the principles of group libel law:[72]

a. Defamation of a large group gives rise to no civil action on the part of an individual member of the group unless he can show special application of the defamatory matter to himself.

b. Defamation of a small group gives rise to civil action on the part of each individual member of the group.

   1. If the defamatory language applies to each and every member as an individual and not solely to the group as a collectivity, or

   2. If the group is so small that the language of necessity applies to each and every member.[73]

c. Defamation of part of a group, whether large or small, gives rise to no civil action on the part of an individual member unless he is sufficiently identified to permit an action under A, or the part small enough to allow an action under

---

69. In reality, it is a blend of English common law and Roman-Dutch law.

70. *See* Holomisa v. Argus Newspapers Ltd 1996 (2) SA 588 (W); *see also* Bogoshi v. National Media Ltd & Others 1996 (3) SA 78 (W).

71. This is termed an "interdict." *Defamation Law in South Africa*, DMV, https://www.dmvinc.co.za/defamation-in-south-african-law/ (last visited Dec. 17, 2024).

72. Joseph Tanenhaus, *Group Libel: Who Controls the United States?*, 35 Cornell L. Rev. 261, 261 (1950).

73. That is why "where proceedings were pending against 17 persons, it was held that one of them could sue a third party who said of them all that 'these defendants helped to murder HF.'" Witting, *supra* note 32, at 521.

B (2). On occasion, courts have employed "class" to designate the larger collectivities falling into category A, and "group" to the smaller of category B.

3. *A restricted collectivity?* The judge states that the "Rabbi, Trustee and six Council Members of the Western Road Synagogue belong to a 'restricted collectivity'" and so had standing to bring a claim, notwithstanding the generalist statements of the Greyshirts in the document: on what basis does the judge reach this conclusion? Via route A or B? If A, how could the Trustee and six Council Members of the Western Road Synagogue demonstrate special application of the defamatory material to themselves?

How does Judge Graham's designation of the restricted class in *Levy* compare with Judges Carroll and Cross's designation in *Plamondon*? How large was the class in each? What accounts for the various judges' analyses as to whether the libel, which included group libel, was actionable?

4. *The Conspiracy Libel.* What is the difference between the claim that: (a) Jews conspire to control the world, and (b) a specific Jewish person is part of this wider Jewish conspiracy? Is the latter actionable, notwithstanding its element of group libel?

A conspiracy is an "agreement by two or more persons to commit an unlawful act, coupled with an intent to achieve the agreement's objective, and action or conduct that furthers the agreement; a combination for an unlawful purpose." Conspiracy is a separate offense from the crime that is the object of the conspiracy. Is it defamatory to accuse someone of belonging to a group of criminal conspirators, separate and apart from whether that individual personally engages in criminal activity? The allegation of a conspiracy puts both parties into ambiguous territory. The libelee, in the absence of group defamation laws, would need to prove only that they did not belong to a conspiratorial group. This makes life easier for a plaintiff, because it is close to impossible to prove the conspiracy is fiction. The libeler would deploy this strategy to avoid having to defend against a group defamation claim and thus restrict the case to the nefarious quality of this particular Jew. What would constitute a false allegation of being involved in a conspiracy? Wouldn't such an allegation give rise to a "conspiracy" libel cause of action, and then the publisher would bear the burden of proving the truth as a defense?

5. *Ascertainment: Who must be able to make the link?* The judge says that "to be 'ascertained' the person defamed need not necessarily be referred to by name or precise description." In which case, what is the test for ascertainment? What must the conditions be for such an inference to be made? The judge suggests that it would be sufficient if "his friends thought the libel referred to him"; is this conceptually identical with Street on Torts' position that what is required is "for ordinary sensible people with knowledge of the facts [to] reasonably ... believe that the statement referred to the claimant"?[74]

6. *Ascertaining Abraham Levy.* Despite the facts that: (i) the document does not explicitly mention Levy's name; and (ii) the Greyshirts' defense includes the claim that

74. WITTING, *supra* note 32, at 520.

Levy lacked the technical qualifications to be a "Rabbi," the following facts enabled Levy to show that the document referred to him:

(a) Von Moltke averred that the document was stolen from the Western Road Synagogue.

(b) The allegation was made that the document was signed "Rabbi."

(c) Reverend Levy gave evidence that the terms "Rabbi" and "Reverend" are often considered synonymous in the non-Jewish world.

(d) Levy had been the "Minister" of the Western Road Synagogue for around 21 years.

(e) Many witnesses testified that they believed that the document was authored by Levy when read aloud.

Which fact, though, do you think was most important? Did the case ultimately hinge on (c)?

7. *Individual libel claims and the dangers of a "hollow victory."* To win his private defamation suit, all that Levy needed to demonstrate was "that he was not the author of the Document and that it was never in his Synagogue";[75] the question of "whether an international Jewish conspiracy exists" was superfluous.[76] It is for this reason that Lawrence cautions against using individual libel actions as a vehicle to try and counter general antisemitic libels—they run the risk of *decontextualization*:

> Once the group aspects are taken out, what we are left with is a libel claim by one individual. Then, only evidence that is directly and specifically relevant to that individual charge is admissible in court. The very courtroom itself seems smaller as soon as you say that. The entire context becomes smaller. Inevitably, the case becomes de-contextualized.... This narrowing of the issues cannot help but lose a large element of the life-blood of the case, which was, after all, about the anti-Semitic calumny that had underpinned the entire charge.[77]

His ultimate fear is that, as a result of this decontextualization that flows from the legal processes and procedures, a private "acquittal" transforms into a "group conviction," resulting in a "hollow victory." As an analogy, Lawrence provides trials concerning blood libels:

> The acquittal in the blood libel trial runs the risk of being an acquittal only of the individual charge that the accused himself did not engage in the behaviour asserted in the libel. What the acquittal actually means is that the blood libel generally is accurate, but inapplicable in this particular case.[78]

75. Lisa Miranda Sarzin, Seeking Truth and Challenging Prejudice: Confronting Race hatred Through the South African Greyshirt Case of Levy v. Von Moltke 123 (2017), https://opus.lib.uts.edu.au/bitstream/10453/120342/2/02whole.pdf.

76. *Id.*

77. Lawrence McNamara, Reputation and Defamation 40 (2007).

78. *Id.* at 41.

8. *Widening the scope.* As Sarzin remarks, the distinctive element of the Levy trial is that the "decontextualization" trap was avoided, which "makes the Greyshirt case all the more remarkable. Despite the narrow legal frame of individual defamation ... Reverend Levy and his legal team were able to enlarge rather than narrow the material issues in dispute."[79] How, though, did they accomplish this? Sarzin points towards two key factors: good lawyers for the plaintiffs and self-representation by the defendants.

9. *Astute drafting by Levy's legal team.* Levy's attorney's might have treated the case like a typical individual defamation lawsuit by proving that Reverend Levy did not do the things defendants claimed he did. Instead, they enlarged the scope of the case to address beyond what was absolutely necessary to win so that the judgment would cover "the broader social issues"[80]—namely, whether an international Jewish conspiracy existed. They characterized defendants' statements as an attack on Judaism, especially the claim that the "Plaintiff was a *member of a faith* that counselled all the aforesaid matters including the commission of the crimes therein set out." The court approved this characterization, tasking the defendants to prove that Judaism was itself an international conspiracy. As plaintiff, Levy did not bear the burden of disproving the existence of a conspiracy. Given the rising antisemitism in South Africa, South African Jews may have deemed it necessary to go on the offensive.

10. *Fools as clients.* Because the defendants represented themselves, the normal legal submissions were transformed into a:

> speech or a monologue ... [where the defendants'] rhetorical flow would have only been interrupted by questions from the judges or by objections from the Plaintiff's barrister. This enabled von Moltke, in particular, to treat the courtroom as a vehicle for his oratory and for propounding the views he expressed at Greyshirt meetings, which attacked Jews in general. While a defence barrister may have limited the issues to those strictly necessary for the legal proceedings, von Moltke, Inch and Olivier felt no such constraints ... expand[ing] the issues within the court.[81]

Using a Defamation Action to Debunk the Protocols

1. *But he said it first.* The court disregarded defendants' evidence consisting of the "assertions of previous writers who give no authority of any value in support of their conclusions." This underscores a key feature of the truth defense: merely relying on some other person's word to establish a statement's truth is insufficient—the authority itself must be shown to be true,[82] e.g., relying on Beamish's word that a Jewish conspiracy exists is insufficient.

---

79. Sarzin, *supra* note 75, at 94.
80. *Id.* at 107.
81. *Id.* at 100.
82. Restatement (Second) of Torts § 581A cmt. e (Am. L. Inst. 1977).

2. *Three kinds of facts.* As Sarzin notes, three kinds of facts were at issue during the trial:

(a) Facts to demonstrate that the document referred to Levy

(b) Facts pertaining to fabrication and concoction

(c) Facts confuting the fundamental truth claims advanced by the Greyshirts

Each of these categories of fact served their own distinct purpose:

(1) Facts like (a) were necessary for Levy to discharge his burden as a plaintiff.

(2) Facts like (b) had to be assessed while the defendants asserted a truth for public benefit defense. After all, the defendants had to prove that the document was actually signed off by Levy (once it had been accepted that it referred to him). In showing this claim to be false, Levy demonstrated that: (i) the document was fabricated; and (ii) Inch's story for how he came into possession of it was concocted.

(3) Facts like (c), which concerned questions such as whether the *Protocols* was a forgery and whether Judaism is anti-Christian, also had to be assessed while the defendants advanced a "truth for public benefit" defense. However, this was only because Levy's lawyers had managed to incorporate "Levy being part of a worldwide Jewish conspiracy"[83] within the meaning of the defamatory statements about him. Accordingly, not only did the defendants have to show that Levy was part of a conspiracy, but that it was a *Jewish* conspiracy.

Once the defendants withdrew their defense of "truth for the public benefit," facts of kind (b) and (c) were no longer relevant to the outcome of the case (judicial comments referring to them became *obiter*).

3. *The critical role of expert witnesses.* Expert witnesses were crucial in convincing the court that the document was a fabrication. In particular, the court found the testimony of Professor Frank Dingemans, one of the founders of Rhodes University in Grahamstown and an expert in Hebrew, Dutch, and Christian philology, to be "devastating." His testimony focused on the form and content of the document. He explained that "the writings in and on the document indicated that they had been composed by someone with little or no knowledge of Hebrew."[84] Fraser also remarks that "it was perhaps most important that Dingemans was not Jewish. The defendants attacked any testimony given by Rabbi Levy or any representative of South African or international Jewry like Sokolow. It was foundationally flawed and lacking any credibility because they were Jews."

4. *Is the Court an effective forum for the discovery of truth?* Sarzin concludes that:

> An analysis of the facts that the Plaintiff was able to put before the court demonstrates the effectiveness of a courtroom (and judicial process and pro-

83. Technically, they managed to secure the following meaning: The "plaintiff was a *member of a faith* that counselled all the aforesaid matters including the commission of the crimes therein set out."

84. Fraser, *supra* note 60, at 81.

cedure) to create the time and space necessary for an objective, forensic and logical examination of facts. The Greyshirt trial lasted from the 10th to the 24th of July 1934, involved 12 days in Court, about 50 witnesses and generated 772 pages of typed transcript.[85]

5. *A good faith defense?* Once the defendants withdrew their defense of "truth for the public benefit," they substituted it with a defense of "honestly and reasonably believing the document to be what it purported to be in good faith without any intention or reasonable expectation of injuring the Plaintiff and with due reasonable care." Does this defense amount to one of 'fair comment' or 'honest opinion'? How would it fare under U.S. law?[86] Could it have any grounds in U.S. law where the plaintiff must show that the defendant acted with some fault in publishing the defamatory statement?[87]

Injunctive Relief for Defamation

1. *Injunctive relief.* In some common law jurisdictions, including South Africa in 1934, courts have the authority to issue injunctions to prevent someone from further disseminating statements adjudicated as defamatory. According to the JTA, the court's injunction "dealt a severe blow to the antisemitic movement and to the aspirations of their leaders. These Nazi officials had placed much reliance on the contents of the documents as propaganda material."[88]

2. *Injunctive relief not available under U.S. law.* The First Amendment bars U.S. courts from enjoining the publication of defamatory statements, a.k.a., a prior restraint, except under extraordinary circumstances. *Near v. Minnesota* (1931); *New York Times Co. v. United States* (1971).

---

85. SARZIN, *supra* note 75, at 110. As Sarzin further recognizes: "Evans makes a similar point in relation to the *Irving v. Penguin U.K. and Deborah Lipstadt* trial in which he was a key expert witness." *Id.* Evans, in his book *Lying About Hitler*, propounded:

> In many respects the High Court turned out to be a good place to settle the historical and methodological points at issue in the Irving case. There were for a start, none of the usual constraints of time and space that limit what can be said or written in other arenas of debate ... we could pursue every point, no matter how minor, for hours on end, until we had exhausted the subject or the judge was satisfied that everything had been said that was necessary and asked us to move on.... [Moreover], we simply wrote as much as we needed to fulfil the commissions we had been given, which in Robert Jan Van Pelt's case was over 600 pages and in mine over 700.

RICHARD J. EVANS, LYING ABOUT HITLER 96 (2002).

86. *See, e.g.*, RESTATEMENT (SECOND) OF TORTS § 613 (AM. L. INST. 1977).

87. *See id.*

88. *See South Africa Nazis Routed Completely in Defamation Suit*, JEWISH TELEGRAPHIC AGENCY (Aug. 5, 1934), https://www.jta.org/archive/see-south-africa-nazis-routed-completely-in-defamation-suit.

South African Jewry's Response to Rising Antisemitism

1. *Antisemitism in early-20th-century South Africa.* In the 1930s, South Africa presented a perfect storm for an outbreak of antisemitism, including a growing nativist nostalgia, entrenchment of racial worldviews, and an economic depression.[89] In this setting, Jews became "easy targets within ... the more specific set of debates relating to curbs on immigration."[90] For example, in 1930, the South African "legislature passed the Immigration Quota Act, effectively putting a stop to Jewish immigration from Eastern Europe and imposing severe restrictions on all other entry."[91]

2. *Levy trial: Galvanizing a united front?* "When the Greyshirts first commenced their virulent antisemitic propaganda, there was division within the Jewish community as to how best to respond."[92] While the quietist Board of Deputies, the Jewish communal organization in South Africa, did not speak out against Greyshirt propaganda,[93] Schauder, a leading voice in the Jewish community (and one-time mayor of Port Elizabeth) advocated a more proactive approach.[94] However, once tacking on the Greyshirts in court became a real possibility, such division dissipated, South African Jews embraced legal action as the appropriate strategy.[95]

3. *Why was Court an attractive forum for confronting the Greyshirts*? First, *trust*—the Jewish community felt that the courts were neutral and independent arbiters where truth would be objectively pursued. As Spiegelman writes, there is confidence that "the principal purpose of legal proceedings is to identify the true factual circumstances ... subject only to the fairness of the process and consistency with other public values"[96] (Spigelman 2011, p. 750). Second, *legitimacy*—a court decision would come with the authority of the law, which most non-Jews would be inclined to respect. Third, *non-violence*—it provided a means for Jews to resist the Greyshirts without situating themselves on the wrong side of the law.[97]

4. *Ramifications.* Did the defeat of the Greyshirts in court lead to Fascist backsliding in South Africa? Sarzin thinks so: "Although unprovable, the case may have been significant in arresting the progress of Greyshirt dogma in South Africa and preventing fascism from gaining greater and more widespread purchase on South African soil."[98]

---

89. Fraser, *supra* note 60, at 61–62.
90. *Id.* at 61.
91. *Id.* at 63.
92. Sarzin, *supra* note 75, at 137.
93. Fraser, *supra* note 60, at 70.
94. *Id.*
95. Sarzin, *supra* note 75, at 90.
96. James Spigelman, *Truth and the Law*, 85 Australian L. J. 746, 750 (2016).
97. Sarzin, *supra* note 75, at 105.
98. *Id.* at 134.

C. Debunking Holocaust Denial

Deborah Lipstadt is a professor of Modern Jewish and Holocaust Studies at Emory University. From 2022–24, Lipstadt served as the Special Envoy to Monitor and Combat Antisemitism, with the rank of Ambassador, and guided U.S. foreign policy to counter antisemitism throughout the world.[99]

In 1993, Professor Lipstadt published a book titled, *Denying the Holocaust: The Growing Assault on Truth and Memory*, which investigates the genealogy of Holocaust denial and its growth following since the end of WWII. The book included several passages discussing David Irving, an alleged historian, and his relationship with Holocaust denial. Irving complained that the passages were defamatory in nature; it represented him to be a Hitler and Nazi apologist, a Holocaust denier, a distorter of history where he bent the historical record to further his neo-fascist agenda and ideology, an ally of racists and anti-Semites, and a discredited historian. In 1995, Irving wrote a letter to Penguin Books, Lipstadt's publisher, demanding the book be removed from circulation; the publisher refused this request. In September 1996, Irving sued Lipstadt and Penguin Books for defamation. The trial, in which Irving represented himself, was conducted between January and March 2000 in the English and Welsh High Court at the Royal Courts of Justice in London.[100] The defendants conceded that Irving was broadly correct regarding what the book claimed about him but contended that its claims were truthful. The judgment, written by Mr. Justice Gray[101] and spanning 335 pages, was handed down in April of 2000, and found in favor of the defendants. The judge also found Irving to be an anti-Semite and a racist. Irving then sought permission to appeal Mr. Justice Gray's judgment; this was denied on the papers and then denied again at an

---

99. *Ambassador Deborah Lipstadt*, U.S. DEPT. OF STATE, https://www.state.gov/biographies/deborah-lipstadt/ (last visited Dec. 17, 2024).

100. The High Court's main function is as a trial court for civil claims worth over a certain value and which, either due to their financial value, complexity or public interest, ought to be heard before a High Court judge (although it also operates as an appellate court for: (i) smaller civil claims that were initially heard in a County Court; and (ii) criminal cases which where the initial trial was heard before a Magistrate's Court). The default position is that civil claims are to be heard before a judge (usual practice is for there to be only a single judge) rather than a jury—there is no right to have one's civil claim heard before a jury; whether it will be heard before a jury is at the discretion of the court (Senior Courts Act 1981, § 69(3) (U.K.); County Courts Act 1984, § 66(3) (U.K.)). Prior to the Defamation Act 2013, the existence of a qualified right to a jury in defamation claims was the exception, not the rule (the other instances where there was, and still exists, a qualified right to a jury trial, are: malicious prosecution; false imprisonment; and fraud; *see* Senior Courts Act 1981, § 69(1) (U.K.)).

101. Sir Charles Gray (1942–2022) was appointed as a judge of the High Court in the Queen's Bench Division in 1998 and remained in that post until his retirement in 2002. He was called to the bar at Lincoln's Inn in 1966 and appointed to the prestigious position of Queen's Counsel (QC) (a.k.a., he "took silk") in 1984. He was "known for his immense charm" and as "possibly the leading libel lawyer of his generation." *See Sir Charles Gray, Brilliant QC and Judge Renowned for His Judgment in the Irving Holocaust Denial Trial and Many Other Cases—Obituary*, THE TELEGRAPH (Mar. 7, 2022), https://www.telegraph.co.uk/obituaries/2022/03/07/sir-charles-gray-brilliant-qc-judge-renowned-judgment-irving/.

oral hearing before the English and Welsh Court of Appeal in June 2001. The Court of Appeal upheld the refusal.[102]

Irving v. Penguin Books Ltd and Deborah Lipstadt

England and Wales High Court
[2000] EWHC QB 115

Mr. Justice Gray delivered the opinion of the court.

A Summary of the Main Issues

1.2. The essential issues in the action can be summarised as follows: Irving complains that certain passages in the Defendants' book accuse him of being a Nazi apologist and an admirer of Hitler, who has resorted to the distortion of facts and to the manipulation of documents in support of his contention that the Holocaust did not take place. He contends that the Defendants' book is part of a concerted attempt to ruin his reputation as an historian, and he seeks damages accordingly. The Defendants, whilst they do not accept the interpretation which Irving places on the passages complained of, assert that it is true that Irving is discredited as an historian by reason of his denial of the Holocaust and by reason of his persistent distortion of the historical record so as to depict Hitler in a favourable light. The Defendants maintain that the claim for damages for libel must in consequence fail....

1.3. It is important that I stress at the outset of this judgment that I do not regard it as being any part of my function as the trial judge to make findings of fact as to what did and what did not occur during the Nazi regime in Germany. The need for [rehearsing historical data] arises because I must evaluate the criticisms of or the attack upon [Irving's] conduct as an historian in the light of the available historical evidence. But it is not for me to form, still less to express, a judgement about what happened. That is a task for historians.... [There is a] distinction between my judicial role in resolving the issues arising between these parties and the role of the historian seeking to provide an accurate narrative of past events.

2.15. The passages complained of in their context and read collectively bear the following meanings all of which are defamatory of him:

i. that Irving is an apologist for and partisan of Hitler, who has resorted to the distortion of evidence; the manipulation and skewing of documents; the misrepresentation of data and the application of double standards to the evidence, in order to serve his own purpose of exonerating Hitler and portraying him as sympathetic towards the Jews;

ii. that Irving is one of the most dangerous spokespersons for Holocaust denial, who has on numerous occasions denied that the Nazis embarked upon the deliberate planned extermination of Jews and has alleged that it is a Jewish deception that

102. This was on the grounds that: "it [was] not arguable that an appeal against the judge's verdict would succeed," Irving v. Penguin Books Ltd [2001] EWCA Civ 1197, at 101.

gas chambers were used by the Nazis at Auschwitz as a means of carrying out such extermination;

iii. that Irving, in denying that the Holocaust happened, has misstated evidence; misquoted sources; falsified statistics; misconstrued information and bent historical evidence so that it conforms to his neo-fascist political agenda and ideological beliefs;

iv. that Irving has allied himself with representatives of a variety of extremist and antisemitic groups and individuals and on one occasion agreed to participate in a conference at which representatives of terrorist organisations were due to speak;

v. that Irving, in breach of an agreement which he had made and without permission, removed and transported abroad certain microfiches of Goebbels's diaries, thereby exposing them to a real risk of damage.

vi. that Irving is discredited as an historian....

The Law of Defamation and the Defense of Justification

2.9. ... The burden rests on Irving to establish that, as a matter of probability, the passages of which he complains are defamatory of him, that is, that the ordinary reasonable reader of *Denying the Holocaust* would think the worse of him as a result of reading those passages....

3.1. Where the publication of defamatory words is proved and no substantive defence has been established, English law presumes that damage will have been done to the reputation of the person defamed....

3.2. ... The book accuses Irving, amongst other things, of deliberate perversion of the historical evidence....

4.7. The burden of proving the defence of justification rests upon the publishers. Defamatory words are presumed under English law to be untrue. It is not incumbent on defendants to prove the truth of every detail of the defamatory words published: what has to be proved is the substantial truth of the defamatory imputations published about the claimant. As it is sometimes expressed, what must be proved is the truth of the sting of the defamatory charges made.

4.8. It may, accordingly, be necessary, in a case like the present where a number of defamatory imputations are the subject of complaint, to consider whether such imputations (if any) as the Defendants have failed to prove to be true materially injure the reputation of the claimant in the light of those imputations against him which have been proved to be true.

4.9. ... Irving, however, points out that there are imputations which the Defendants made in the book which they have not sought to prove to be true. The principal such imputation is that Irving agreed to participate in a conference at which representatives of violent and extremist groups such as Hezbollah were due to speak. Irving contends that this defamatory imputation is so serious that the Defendants' failure to prove it or even to attempt to prove it is fatal to their plea of justification....

Irving Is a Holocaust Denier

8.2. It is necessary, in order to decide whether he is justifiably described by Lipstadt as a "Holocaust denier" to define precisely what is meant by that term....

8.3. Evans [Sir. Richard Evans, a historian who served as an expert for the defense] testified that a characteristic of Holocaust denial is that it involves a politically motivated falsification of history.

8.4. In the opinion of Evans, the views expressed by Holocaust deniers include the following: (i) that Jews were not killed in gas chambers or at least not on any significant scale; (ii) that the Nazis had no policy and made no systematic attempt to exterminate European Jewry and that such deaths as did occur were the consequence of individual excesses unauthorised at senior level; (iii) that the number of Jews murdered did not run into millions and that the true death toll was far lower; (iv) that the Holocaust is largely or entirely a myth invented during the war by Allied propagandists and sustained after the war by Jews in order to obtain financial support for the newly-created state of Israel.

8.5. According to Evans, whilst the expression of those views is typical, Holocaust deniers do not necessarily subscribe to all of them and the views of some deniers may be more extreme than others....

13.95. It appears to me to be incontrovertible that Irving qualifies as a Holocaust denier. Not only has he denied the existence of gas chambers at Auschwitz and asserted that no Jew was gassed there, he has done so on frequent occasions and sometimes in the most offensive terms....

13.98. I have already made findings that the evidence supports the following propositions: that the shooting of the Jews in the East was systematic and directed from Berlin with the knowledge and approval of Hitler; that there were gas chambers at several of the Operation Reinhard camps and that (as Irving during the trial admitted) hundreds of thousands of Jews were killed in them and that there were gas chambers at Auschwitz, where hundreds of thousands more Jews were gassed to death. It follows that it is my conclusion that Irving's denials of these propositions were contrary to the evidence....

Irving Is an Antisemite and a Racist

9.1. No allegation of racism or of antisemitism is levelled against Irving by Lipstadt in *Denying the Holocaust*. Nonetheless, the Defendants maintained that they were entitled to adduce evidence in support of such allegations against Irving because, if true, they support the case that Irving has been guilty of deliberately falsifying the historical record for racist reasons of his own....

9.9. In regard to his attitude towards Jews, Irving asserted that there is no reason why the Jews should be immune from criticism, but that is not to be equated with antisemitism. It is not antisemitic to make a statement hostile to Jews if the statement is justified....

10.3. The question is whether and, if so, to what extent Irving associates or has associated himself with such groups and individuals [neo-Nazis and fascists]. The question arises for two reasons. The first is that Lipstadt in *Denying the Holocaust* links Irving to various extremist organisations.... The second reason is that, according to the Defendants, the existence of an association between Irving and right-wing extremist groups or individuals supports their case that the reason for his falsification of the historical record is that he is himself a right-wing ideologue....

13.101. It appears to me to be undeniable that ... Irving is antisemitic. His words are directed against Jews, either individually or collectively, in the sense that they are by turns hostile, critical, offensive and derisory in their references to semitic people,[103] their characteristics and appearances. A few examples will suffice: Irving has made claims that the Jews deserve to be disliked; that they brought the Holocaust on themselves; that Jewish financiers are crooked; that Jews generate antisemitism by their greed and mendacity; that it is bad luck for Mr. Wiesel to be called "Weasel"; that Jews are amongst the scum of humanity; that Jews scurry and hide furtively, unable to stand the light of day; that Simon Wiesenthal has a hideous, leering evil face; and so on....

13.106. I have concluded that the allegation that Irving is a racist is also established for broadly analogous reasons. This is unsurprising for antisemitism is a form of racism....

13.115. I also have no doubt that Irving was aware of their political views [far-right individuals]. His association with such individuals indicates in my judgement that Irving shares many of their political beliefs....

Irving Deliberately Falsified the Historical Record

13.24. An objective historian is obliged to be even-handed in his approach to historical evidence: he cannot pick and choose without adequate reason....

13.136. The passages in *Denying the Holocaust* of which Irving complains include as an important part of their defamatory sting the meaning that he has *deliberately* falsified and distorted the historical evidence because he is an apologist for and a partisan of Hitler and on that account is intent on exonerating him....

13.138. The Defendants must, as they accept, go further [than proving falsification] if they are to succeed in their plea of justification: they must establish that the misrepresentation by Irving of the historical record was deliberate in the sense that Irving was motivated by a desire borne of his own ideological beliefs to present Hitler in a favourable light. Irving's case is that, if (which he denied but which I have found) he has misrepresented the evidence, such misrepresentation was innocent in the sense that it arose through simple mistake or misapprehension....

13.140. Historians are human: they make mistakes, misread and misconstrue documents and overlook material evidence. I have found that, in numerous respects, Irving

103. Editor's note: Mr. Justice Gray appears to use the words "Jews" and "semitic people" interchangeably.

has misstated historical evidence; adopted positions which run counter to the weight of the evidence; given credence to unreliable evidence and disregarded or dismissed credible evidence. It appears to me that an analysis of those instances may shed light on the question whether Irving's misrepresentation of the historical evidence was deliberate....

13.142. In my opinion, there is force in the opinion expressed by Evans that all Irving's historiographical "errors" converge, in the sense that they all tend to exonerate Hitler and to reflect Irving's partisanship for the Nazi leader. If indeed they were genuine errors or mistakes, one would not expect to find this consistency. I accept the Defendants' contention that this convergence is a cogent reason for supposing that the evidence has been deliberately slanted by Irving....

13.143. It is material to take account of the nature or quality of what Irving claims to have been mistakes or misapprehensions on his part. Certain of Irving's misrepresentations of the historical evidence might appear to be simple mistakes on his part.... But there are other occasions where Irving's treatment of the historical evidence is so perverse and egregious that it is difficult to accept that it is inadvertence on his part. Examples include Irving's rejection of the evidence for the existence of gas chambers at Auschwitz; his claim that Hitler lost interest in antisemitism on coming to power; his account of Hitler's meeting with Horthy in April 1943;[104] his wholesale dismissal of the testimony of Marie Vaillant-Couturier,[105] and his continued reliance on the forged Tagesbefehl No. 47 which purportedly gave the number of casualties in Dresden.[106]...

104. Editor's note: Admiral Miklós Horthy (1868–1957) was the leader of the Hungarian government in April 1943. On April 16–17, 1943, Horthy had meetings with Hitler to discuss the future of the 750,000 Jews resident in Hungary. Hitler pressured Horthy to identify and deport these Hungarian Jews, but Horthy resisted—he wanted to deal with Hungary's so-called "Jewish Problem" by means other than extermination (although he had permitted the deportation of over 20,000 "foreign national" Jews to Nazi-occupied Ukraine; almost all the deportees perished). Hungary's refusal to hand over their Jews to the Nazis resulted in the eventual invasion of Hungary and the murder of at least 450,000 Hungarian Jews at Auschwitz. The key thing in contention, in this trial, was that Irving failed to accurately represent the hardening of Hitler's position towards the Jews of Hungary between the meetings of the 16th and 17th of April 1943. The defense argued that Irving, in his book, *Hitler's War* (second edition: 1991), transposed a remark that Hitler made on April 16 to Horthy and attached it to the end of a statement he made on April 17, also to Horthy, in order to sanitize its appearance and to minimize the categorical nature of Hitler's genocidal intentions with regards to Hungarian Jews.

105. Editor's note: Marie Vaillant-Couturier was a non-Jewish French resistance fighter, a member of the French Communist Party, and a survivor of Auschwitz where she was held prisoner between 1942–45. She gave testimony at the Nuremberg Trials detailing the horrific conditions of the camp, the sterilization programs that operated there, as well as the murdering of babies that were born to pregnant women who entered the camp. Irving, when making a speech in Toronto in 1988, distorted a comment made by one of the Nuremberg judges concerning her testimony; his misrepresentation served to unjustifiably and untenably discredit her.

106. In February 1945, the German city of Dresden was subject to a series of ferocious bombing raids by Allied forces. The majority of historians believe that around 25,000–30,000 Germans died in these attacks. Irving, however, contended that the true figure was around 250,000. Irving's inflated numbers were based on a document called "*Tagesbefehl* No. 47"; Irving was aware (or, at least, certainly ought to have been aware) that this document was a forgery, yet he brazenly continued to rely on it anyway. Irving's inflation of the casualties at Dresden was part of his general attempt to try and draw moral equivalence between the Allies and the Nazis.

13.163. I find myself unable to accept Irving's contention that his falsification of the historical record is the product of innocent error or misinterpretation or incompetence on his part.... It appears to me that the correct and inevitable inference must be that for the most part, the falsification of the historical record was deliberate and that Irving was motivated by a desire to present events in a manner consistent with his own ideological beliefs even if that involved distortion and manipulation of historical evidence....

The Defense of Justification Succeeds

13.165. My overall finding in relation to the plea of justification is that the Defendants have proved the substantial truth of the imputations, most of which relate to Irving's conduct as an historian.... My finding is that the defamatory meanings set out in paragraph 2.15 above at (i), (ii), (iii) and the first part of (iv) are substantially justified.

13.166. But there are certain defamatory imputations which I have found to be defamatory of Irving but which have not been proved to be true. The Defendants made no attempt to prove the truth of Lipstadt's claim that Irving was scheduled to speak at an anti-Zionist conference in Sweden in 1992, which was also to be attended by various representatives of terrorist organisations such as Hezbollah and Hammas. Nor did they seek to justify Lipstadt's claim that Irving has a self-portrait by Hitler hanging over his desk.... The question which I have to ask myself is whether the consequence of the Defendants' failure to prove the truth of these matters is that the defence of justification fails in its entirety.

13.167. The charges which I have found to be substantially true include the charges that Irving has for his own ideological reasons persistently and deliberately misrepresented and manipulated historical evidence; that for the same reasons he has portrayed Hitler in an unwarrantedly favourable light, principally in relation to his attitude towards and responsibility for the treatment of the Jews; that he is an active Holocaust denier; that he is antisemitic and racist and that he associates with right wing extremists who promote neo-Nazism. In my judgment, the charges against Irving which have been proved to be true are of sufficient gravity for it be clear that the failure to prove the truth of the matters set out in paragraph 13.165 above does not have any material effect on Irving's reputation.

13.168. In the result therefore the defence of justification succeeds.

14.1. It follows that there must be judgment for the Defendants.

English Defamation Law

1. *Plaintiff-friendly nature of English defamation law.* To prove defamation, English law requires the plaintiff to establish that the defendant's statement is: (a) defamatory; (b) refers to them; and (c) has been published to someone other than the plaintiff.[107] If

107. Clerk and Lindsell on Torts, *supra* note 22, at §§ 21-01–13. Following the passage of the Defamation Act 2013, the plaintiff must now also show, per § 1(1), that the statement "caused or is

these conditions are met, the plaintiff prevails unless the defendant can make out a positive defense. These include, among others, establishing that the defamatory statement is substantially true,[108] that it is honest opinion,[109] or that it is in the public interest.[110] Once the plaintiff has shown the words to be defamatory in nature, there is no burden on them to show that the words are untrue.[111] Thus, in the trade-off between protecting individuals' reputations and the right to freedom of expression, English law squarely sides with the former; this is the result of "protections for [individuals' reputations] ... [being] embodied in defences to a claim for defamation rather than in the definition of the wrong of defamation."[112] It was unsurprising then that Irving opted to bring his claim in England instead of the U.S.—especially given that he would have likely qualified as a "public figure" per *New York Times Co. v. Sullivan* (1964).

2. *Determining defamatory meaning.* To be defamatory, Lipstadt's passages, according to Justice Gray at 2.9, must have lowered Irving's estimation in the eyes of the "ordinary reasonable reader." Who, though, does "ordinary" refer to: (a) the average representative of those who read the publication in question? Or (b) the median person in society? Interestingly, English authority is divided on this point: *Jeynes v. News Magazines Ltd.*, [2008] EWCA Civ 130, suggests an approach focusing on readership, while *Monroe v. Hopkins* [2017] 4 WLR 68, suggests that the demands of pluralism and freedom of expression require the "ordinary reader" to be reflective of the median person in society. If the position in *Jeynes* is correct, and further supposing that Lipstadt had published her statements in a journal read primarily by specialists in the Third Reich, then how would that have affected Irving's ability to show the passages to be defamatory given that, by the 1990s, historians who specialized in the Third Reich had little time for him?[113]

3. *The truth defense and its complexities.* The old common law defense of "justification"[114] required the defendant to show that their defamatory statements were substantially true. To succeed with this defense, the defendant need not have cared nor known

---

likely to cause serious harm to the reputation of the claimant."

108. At the time of the Irving trial, this was known as the defense of "justification." The defense is now labelled "truth" per § 2 of the Defamation Act 2013; they are substantively identical.

109. This defense, per § 3 Defamation Act 2013, replaced the old defense of "fair comment." "Honest Opinion" is a simpler defense and "malice" no longer plays a role in the defense.

110. This used to be called the "*Reynolds* defence"; this was abolished and replaced by the statutory defense of "publication on matter of public interest" per § 4 of the Defamation Act 2013. It should, though, be noted, that: "the rationale for each of the defences [the *Reynolds* and the statutory defence are] ... indeed not materially different and the principles which underpinned the Reynolds defence are indeed relevant to the interpretation of the statutory defence" (per Lord Wilson in Serafin v. Malkiewicz [2020] UKSC 23, at 68). Defenses of qualified and absolute privilege, as well as a defense relating to an "offer of amends" can also be made out.

111. Clerk and Lindsell on Torts, *supra* note 22, at § 21-09; see [4.7] in the *Irving* judgment above.

112. Peter Cane, The Anatomy of Tort Law 137 (1997).

113. Evans, *supra* note 85, at 10.

114. It has now been replaced by the essentially identical statutory defense of "truth" per § 2 of the Defamation Act 2013.

whether the statement was true (at the time of making it) and could even have made it with malice.[115] While Justice Gray correctly formulated the defense in these terms at 4.7, at 13.164, when discussing the defense, he made no reference to truth and instead required that the "imputations published ... in the meanings which I have found them to bear, [were] *substantially justified*." That is, he seems to say that the defense turns on demonstrating that the statement was *justified* in the epistemic sense, not that it was *true*.[116]

4. *Balancing defamatory statements.* The court found that Lipstadt did not justify her assertion that Irving was scheduled to attend an event where various representatives of Hezbollah and Hamas were present. Recall that a defendant will not be held liable for unsupported defamatory statements provided that they "do not materially injure the [plaintiff's] reputation having regard to the truth" of the other justified statements. Did Justice Gray (and the Court of Appeal[117]) correctly discount this unjustified assertion in light of everything else the defendants did prove? Or was this further statement so grievous that it should have completely defeated the justification defense? That is, does the assertion that a person had a planned rendezvous with terrorists harm that person's reputation in a distinct way (perhaps because it insinuates that they are a national security threat) from the finding that they are an anti-Semite or a racist? Also, how sharp is the distinction between being *scheduled to attend* an event whose attendees included terrorists, compared to that of being *affiliated* with terrorists?[118]

5. *Public interest considerations.* The old common law *Reynolds* defense[119] required the defendant to show that:

(a) There [was] a real public interest in the matter about which the material was published.

(b) It [was] reasonable to include the material complained of as part of the overall story.

---

115. Jenny Steele, Tort Law: Text, Cases, and Materials 812 (5th ed. 2022). There is one exception to malice being irrelevant: the Rehabilitation of Offenders Act 1974 § 8 (U.K.) provides that a defense of "truth" will be vitiated if: (a) the defamatory statement refers to an individual who has a "spent" conviction; (b) the statement implies that the individual is guilty of said offence; and (c) the statement was made with malice.

116. Justification and truth are not to be confused. A belief is justified when one has sufficient reason for believing it to be true, but that need not mean that the belief is, in fact, true. Accordingly, the judge made a slight conceptual mistake here.

117. Irving v. Penguin Books Ltd [2001] EWCA Civ 1197, Pill LJ at 100.

118. In any event, Irving's point would have even less prospect of succeeding under current English defamation law, since such a statement would have to pose further "serious harm" to his reputation per § 1 Defamation Act 2013.

119. The name comes from the case: Reynolds v. Times Newspapers Ltd, [2001] 2 A.C. 127, where the House of Lords "reviewed the law relating to qualified privilege in respect of publications in the media, and established a new variant of qualified privilege in which less emphasis was placed on the traditional, reciprocal duty and interest test, and more on the question of whether the publication was on a matter of public interest and whether it was the product of responsible journalism." Clerk and Lindsell on Torts, *supra* note 22, at § 24-148. Section 4 Defamation Act 2013 abolished the *Reynold's* defense and replaced it with a slightly different defense of "publication on matters of public interest."

(c) The steps taken to gather and publish the information [were] responsible and fair (i.e., responsible journalism).[120]

Why did the defendants decide not to plead this defense, at least as an alternative? There are three possible reasons: the first concerns *legal principles*—at the time of the Irving trial, the *Reynolds defense* had only recently been developed, and its scope seemed to only extend to instances involving journalists (although perhaps the defense could have argued that Lipstadt's works qualified as journalism).[121] The second concerns *case management*—understandably, there was a desire to minimize the limelight on Irving, and if the defense had argued that the matter was one of public interest, then that would have served to justify greater media attention on the case and thereby allowed Irving the publicity he craved. The third concerns *ethical convictions*—by solely advancing a truth defense, it was a way of saying to Irving: "you complain that we accuse you of being an anti-Semite. Well, you are right. That's exactly how we characterize you—and with full conviction that we are correct to do so."

6. *Judge vs. trials in defamation cases.* Prior to the Defamation Act 2013, the default position in English law was that defamation trials were to be heard before a jury. Yet, in this case, the trial was heard before a judge. Why did the defense seek a judge rather than a jury?

There seem to be three main reasons: (a) it would take longer; (b) the defense would not get a reasoned judgment; and (c) it increased the risk of losing—a jury would likely be more easily swayed by Irving's bluster and overwhelmed by the complex evidence. Compare these to the reasons why the *Ortenberg* plaintiffs decided not to seek a jury trial.

Were there drawbacks to a bench trial?

The court in any event could deny a jury trial. Section 69 of The Senior Courts Act 1981 provides that if the court is "of opinion that the trial requires any prolonged examination of documents or accounts or any scientific or local investigation which cannot conveniently be made with a jury," then a jury will be replaced with a judge at trial. The role of Julius, the defendant's solicitor,[122] was crucial in convincing the court of such an opinion; Julius exploited Irving's vanity and convinced him that only a judge

---

120. Clerk and Lindsell on Torts, *supra* note 22, at § 24-148.

121. Lord Nicholls, while formulating the defense, repeatedly mentioned that the rationale behind the defense concerned protecting "press freedom" (*see Reynolds v. Times Newspapers Ltd*, [2001] 2 A.C. 127 p. 202). It was only until *Charman v. Orion*, [2007] EWCA Civ 972 that the scope of the defense was explicitly acknowledged to extend to other mediums, such as books. It should be noted that the new statutory defense outlined in § 4 Defamation Act 2013 does clearly apply to any medium of publishing, *see* Economou v. Freitas, [2019] EMLR 7.

122. In the English legal profession, there are two main kinds of lawyers: solicitors and barristers. Solicitors are generally the first point of call for a client when they need legal advice, and tend to work for law firms. Solicitors also often take part in non-contentious transactional work. All barristers, on the other hand, are litigators, and only barristers tend to have rights of audience (although "solicitor-advocates" are a growing phenomenon)—i.e., only barristers tend to have the right to present their client's case orally at court. The majority of barristers are also self-employed and are often instructed when very complex questions of law arise.

could adequately come to grips with the complexities of his work.[123] If it had been a jury trial, how would that have affected the defense's approach to the case?

The Historiography of Holocaust Deniers vs. the Historicity of the Holocaust

1. *Scope of the trial: The Holocaust vs. Irving's historiography?*[124] Mr. Justice Gray at 1.3 was keen to emphasize that he did not see his function involving the "findings of fact as to what did and what did not occur during the Nazi regime in Germany." Rather, it was Irving's historiography, i.e., his historical methodology, that was on trial—not the actual facts concerning the Holocaust. Julius, the plaintiff's solicitor, took a similar view: "They [the defendants] had proved the truth of their allegations not by proving the truth of the Holocaust (which was never in issue) but by proving the truth of Irving's manipulation of the historical record (which became the issue in the case)."[125]

Does the distinction between the actual facts of the Holocaust and Irving's historiography hold up? Consider the following: First, to demonstrate that Irving adopted positions that no objective historian could, and so treated evidence in a way incompatible with how an objective and fair-minded historian would, the defendants sought to show that the evidence for certain elements of the Holocaust (e.g., the existence of gas chambers) was "overwhelming." In the view of historian Richard Evans, one of the defendants' experts, "this did amount to proving, insofar as historians could prove anything, that it had actually happened."[126] Second, a prerequisite for demonstrating that someone distorted the historical record, is to demonstrate what the correct historical record *is*. Is it surprising that the judge, at 13.98, went on to make findings of fact regarding the Holocaust—despite his insistence that it was not his role to do so?

2. *Defining an "objective, fair-minded historian."* The gravamen of the Irving trial turned on the court's assessment of Irving's historiography. To assess this, Mr. Justice Gray, "drawing on Evans's report ... created an 'objective historian' standard."[127] But, as Evans notes, the use of this standard gives rise to a set of preconceived questions: Is there even such a thing as historical objectivity? How far do historians' "interpretations depend on a selective reading of the evidence, and where does selectivity end and bias begin?... [And] are not the archives full of preselected material anyway?"[128] Does being

123. Deborah Lipstadt, *Irving v. Penguin U.K. and Deborah Lipstadt: Building a Defense Strategy, An Essay*, 27 NOVA L. REV. 243, 257 (2007).

124. Many commentators proclaimed that "the Holocaust was on trial." *See* Jonathan Freedland, *Court 73—Where History Is on Trial*, THE GUARDIAN (Feb. 5, 2000), https://www.theguardian.com/books/2000/feb/05/uk.irving.

125. ANTHONY JULIUS, TRIALS OF THE DIASPORA (1st ed. 2010).

126. EVANS, *supra* note 85, at 38.

127. This seems an elaboration of the "reasonable person" standard, which in English law is known as the "man on the Clapham omnibus" standard.

128. EVANS, *supra* note 85, at 249–250.

an "objective historian" ultimately require subordinating one's political beliefs to the discovery of the truth?[129]

Mr. Justice Gray never explicitly answered these questions or specified the qualities that such a historian should have. Even so, the properties that, in his view, an objective historian holds can be extracted from his criticisms of Irving:[130]

> (1) She must treat sources with appropriate reservations; (2) she must not dismiss counterevidence without scholarly consideration; (3) she must be even-handed in her treatment of evidence and eschew "cherry-picking"; (4) she must clearly indicate any speculation; (5) she must not mistranslate documents or mislead by omitting parts of documents; (6) she must weigh the authenticity of all accounts, not merely those that contradict her favored view; and (7) she must take the motives of historical actors into consideration.[131]

3. *Proving motivation through associations.* The defendants sought to show an association between Irving and right-wing extremists in order to support their contention that he shared their political beliefs, and thereby had a motive for falsifying the historical record. Did his associations make the falsification claim more likely to be true? Had the case been tried in the U.S., would his associations have been relevant to the question of whether he deliberately denied the Holocaust? Note the Supreme Court's discussion in *Mitchell* of *Dawson v. Delaware* (1992) and *Barclay v. Florida* (1983). In *Dawson*, the Court ruled that a White defendant's association with a White supremacist group was irrelevant to the question of whether he killed a White victim. In *Barclay*, the Court ruled that a Black defendant's membership in a Black extremist group that advocated a "race war" was relevant to the question of whether his murder of a White man was racially motivated. Which ruling is more on point?

4. *Distinguishing incompetence from deliberate falsification.* The defense not only had to establish that Irving was not an objective historian, but that he had manipulated the historical record *deliberately* to further his own political ends. Mere incompetence did not suffice. The defense latched onto three main points to demonstrate this intention. First, they illustrated that "Irving's historiographical 'errors' *converge*, in the sense that they all tend to exonerate Hitler and to reflect Irving's partisanship for the Nazi leader" (13.142). Second, they homed in on the *nature* of the mistakes that Irving made. They managed to show that, at times, "Irving's treatment of the historical evidence [was] so perverse and egregious that it is difficult to accept that it [was] inadvertence on his part" (13.143). Third, by demonstrating his links to the far right and his own antisemitism, an explanation could be provided for *why* he had made those deliberate contortions.

129. *Id.* at 35.

130. *See* Irving v. Penguin Books Ltd [2001] EWCA Civ 1197, at 13.13, 5.34–5.47, 13.17, 5.40–5.72, 13.24–13.25, 5.111–5.122, 13.22, 5.90–5.110, 13.31, 3.117–13.125, 11.6–11.48, 3.42–13.45, 5.199–5.214.

131. Wendie Ellen Schneider, *Past Imperfect*, 10 YALE L.J., 1531, 1535 (2001).

5. *The expert witness strategy in historical trials.* Reports by expert witnesses formed the bedrock of the defendants' case on Irving's historiography: "Almost every aspect of the assessment of Irving's work reached in the final judgment derived ultimately from the expert reports and the way Irving had dealt with them in court."[132] There were two key elements to the defendants' strategy regarding the experts:

First, there was a rigorous three-way conceptual division of work:

(a) The defendants presented experts who demonstrated that Irving got the history *wrong*; this involved an evaluation of the evidence for many of Irving's contentions about the Holocaust: Christopher Browning, "an eminent specialist in the history of the extermination and the policies that led to it,"[133] wrote a report on the evidence for the extermination of the Jews on a wide scale; Robert Jan Van Pelt, an expert on Auschwitz, provided a report on the evidence for the existence and use of gas chambers at Auschwitz; Peter Longerich, an expert on Nazi policy towards the Jews between 1933–45, compiled a report on the evidence for Hitler's antisemitism and the killings' systematic nature.

(b) The defendants presented experts who demonstrated *how* he got the history wrong; these included Richard Evans, professor of history at Cambridge University, who compiled a report of over 700 pages analyzing Irving's historiography and his various distortions and manipulations.

(c) The defendants presented experts who demonstrated his motivation to get the history wrong—i.e., *why* he got the history wrong; Hajo Funke, a professor of politics at the Free University of Berlin, wrote a report detailing Irving's affiliations with the far-right and neo-Nazis.

Second, the defendants' solicitors were selective vis-à-vis the *characteristics* of the experts. They picked experts that: (a) were mostly not Jewish; and (b) came from a variety of countries. This helped to support the idea that Holocaust scholarship "was [not] mainly carried out by one particular ethnic group or nationality" and so reduced the kickback that Irving could create.[134]

There are many stereotypes about Jews being clannish, only caring about what happens to other Jews, Jewish lawyers as shysters, and so forth. Should Jewish advocates take these stereotypes into account in making litigation decisions? Consider again the *Ortenberg* case: Could the treatment of Rabbi Abramowitz's testimony have shaped Lipstadt's counsel's decision to mainly avoid Jewish expert witnesses? To what extent did Lipstadt's lawyers' approach towards the characteristics of their expert witnesses mirror that of Rabbi Levy's counsel's in *Levy*? Do non-Jewish allies fear that, given stereotypes about Jews as manipulators and shadowy power brokers, they will be cast as Jews' puppets and hirelings?

---

132. Evans, *supra* note 85, at 192.

133. *Id.* at 29.

134. *Id.*

6. *The decision not to call Holocaust survivors.* The defendants made an active decision not to call Holocaust survivors as witnesses when pleading their defense. There were both *moral* and *strategic* reasons behind this decision. Regarding the former, Lipstadt remarks:

> [We] did not believe it ethical to place elderly survivors in a position to be harassed and challenged by a Holocaust denier. Though we did not doubt that they could withstand his challenges to their testimony, we did not feel it right to impose this burden on them.[135]

This fear was compounded by the treatment survivors had received in *R v. Zundel*, [1992] 2 S.C.R. 731, an earlier Holocaust denial trial in Canada in which Irving was an expert witness.[136] Regarding the latter, strategic reasons: "to have called survivors would have been to suggest that we needed the 'eyewitnesses' or 'witnesses of fact' to prove that there indeed was a Holocaust."[137] The defendants believed this would have eroded the distinction between the trial being about the Holocaust and Irving's historiography of it resulting in a widening of the frame of the trial—this also worked in tandem with the strategy to shift the limelight away from Irving himself and towards his work.

7. *Comparing litigation strategies:* Irving *vs.* Levy *trials.* Whilst Lipstadt and her defense lawyers sought to *minimize* the scope of the case (they repeatedly emphasized that Irving's historiography was on trial, not the Holocaust),[138] Levy sought to *maximize* the scope of his case beyond what was absolutely necessary to win such that the judgment would cover 'the broader social issues'[139]—in particular, the Conspiracy Libel. There are perhaps three reasons for this variance in approach: (i) Levy had the benefit of being the claimant, and so the burden of proof for proving the truth of the defamatory statements did not fall on him, unlike for Lipstadt; (ii) the wider sociopolitical context—South African Jewry were experiencing comparatively greater hostility and so there was greater need to go on the offensive; and (iii) Lipstadt and her team sought to limit Irving's publicity.

8. *Judicial notice of historical facts.*[140] Mr. Mel Mermelstein, an Auschwitz survivor, sued the *Institute of Historical Review*, a journal devoted to Holocaust denial to which Irving was connected, when they reneged on their offer to pay $50,000 to anyone who could prove that Jews were gassed at Auschwitz. Mermelstein's cause of action sounded

---

135. Lipstadt, *supra* note 123, at 251.

136. *Id.* at 254.

137. *Id.* at 251.

138. *See* Julius, *supra* note 125, at xxviii.

139. Sarzin, *supra* note 75, at 107.

140. Under the rubric of "judicial notice," American courts may accept, "for the purposes of convenience and without requiring a party's proof, ... a well-known and indisputable fact." For example, a court may take judicial notice of the fact that water freezes at 32 degrees Fahrenheit. *Judicial Notice*, Black's Law Dictionary (12th ed. 2024).

in contract law and tort law, including the intentional infliction of emotional distress.[141] The court took judicial notice of the historicity of the Holocaust and that Jews were gassed at Auschwitz without any further proof.[142] The case was subsequently settled when the Institute agreed to pay the £50,000 plus £100,000 for Mermelstein's pain and suffering caused by the revoked offer.[143]

Using a Defamation Action to Debunk Holocaust Denial

1. *The spectrum of Holocaust denial.* Evans makes the insightful point that there is a spectrum of Holocaust denial, with there being on one end "soft denial" and on the other "hard denial"[144]—the judge alludes to this at 8.5. Evans claims that Irving underwent an evolution: prior to the *Zundel* trial in 1988, Irving was in the former camp rather than the latter, being highly skeptical of Hitler's role in the Holocaust (in essence exonerating him) yet "accepting that the Nazis had systematically killed Jews in large numbers."[145] Suppose that by the time of the trial, Irving had maintained this position: do you think the judge would have found in favor of the defendants in making out their claim that Irving was a Holocaust denier? Might there be a difference between what academia is willing to accept as Holocaust denial compared to the law? That is, is the defamatory sting of "denier" solely limited to "hard core" denial?

2. *Tactics of Holocaust deniers.* Irving exhibited a repeating pattern in his approach towards the Holocaust: (a) there were running themes in his treatment of evidence: he would frequently take "the euphemistic language of Nazism at face value, but casting doubt on any source that avoided euphemisms and spoke directly and in unvarnished terms about murder and extermination";[146] and (b) to try and retain some credibility as a historian, after making a broad denialist remark concerning the Holocaust, he would qualify it in an attempt to create some kind of alibi that he was not a denialist whatsoever.[147] For example, although he denied the use of extermination camps by the Nazis, he was willing to say that gas chambers were used on an experimental basis.[148]

3. *Evaluating evidence in Holocaust denial cases.*[149] Holocaust denial is ultimately a descriptive position that denies that the Nazis' treatment of Jews in World War II had the properties we conventionally ascribe to it. Whether the Holocaust actually happened or not, is not, therefore, directly relevant to whether one is a Holocaust denier. For even if the Holocaust had not occurred, if Irving rejected that the Holocaust

141. Gerald Tishler, *When Academic Freedom and Freedom of Speech Confront Holocaust Denial and Group Libel: Comparative Perspectives*, 8 B.C. Third World L.J. 65, 78 (1988).

142. *Id.* at 79.

143. *See, e.g.*, *Lawsuit Over Proof of Holocaust Ends with Payment to Survivor*, N.Y. Times, July 25, 1985, at Al2.

144. Evans, *supra* note 85, at 112.

145. *Id.*

146. *Id.* at 127.

147. *Id.* at 122.

148. *Id.*

149. *See* Irving v. Penguin Books Ltd [2001] EWCA Civ 1197, at 13.98.

had the features we usually ascribe to it (such as six million Jews dying, the use of gas chambers, etc.), then he would still count as a Holocaust denier—but his denial would have involved elements of truth. Accordingly, it is not entirely clear why the judge felt the conceptual need to assess the strength of the evidence for the Holocaust in this section. Lipstadt should still have been able to show that her statement that Irving is a Holocaust denier was substantively true, regardless of the facts of the Holocaust. The recognition of such facts certainly is relevant in assessing whether Irving was an objective historian—but that concerns a different charge to the one under consideration: whether he is a Holocaust denier.

4. *The paradox of Holocaust denial for anti-Semites.* For the anti-Semite, there is a tension at the heart of Holocaust denial. On the one hand, the Holocaust "should have satiated the appetite of the most murderous antisemites for Jewish death." On the other, accepting its occurrence would rebut "once and for all the principal antisemitic fantasy of malign Jewish power."[150] Denial, though, is the favored course for the anti-Semite, for it adopts the methods of the Nazis in a different medium; "Denial is an attempt at extermination on paper; it attempts to revive the dead in order to strike at the living."[151] It is an instance of what Schraub calls "epistemic antisemitism," which marginalizing Jews in "their capacities as knowers—as testifiers, communicators, exponents, or purveyors of knowledge."[152] While Holocaust denial certainly represents the extreme manifestation of this type of antisemitism, its traits, such as skepticism of the authenticity of Jewish experience, are very much still present and rear their heads in different contexts—a case in point is the dismissal of antisemitic complaints by agents in the British Labour Party during the Corbyn years as "smears" and "fakes."[153]

A Judicial Definition of Antisemitism

1. *Judicial definition of antisemitism.* Mr. Justice Gray expounded his understanding of antisemitism at 13.101 as the following: "Words ... directed against Jews, either individually or collectively, in the sense that they are by turns hostile, critical, offensive and derisory in their references to semitic people, their characteristics and appearance."[154] Compare this to the IHRA definition of antisemitism: "Antisemitism is a certain perception of Jews, which may be expressed as hatred toward Jews."

In the IHRA definition, antisemitism is identified with the *mental state* of the perpetrator—it is a "certain perception"; rhetorical or physical acts against Jews are *expressions* of that antisemitism, but they are not technically what antisemitism *is*. Just as

150. Julius, *supra* note 125, at 64.

151. *Id.* at xxix.

152. David Schraub, *The Epistemic Dimension of Antisemitism*, 15 J. of Jewish Identities 153, 153 (2022).

153. Equal. and Hum. Rts. Comm'n, Investigation into antisemitism in the Labour Party 28 (Oct. 2020), https://www.equalityhumanrights.com/sites/default/files/investigation-into-antisemitism-in-the-labour-party.pdf.

154. The judge technically is not providing a definition here. Instead, he is giving a condition(s) which is/are *sufficient* for antisemitism; he has not adumbrated a set of necessary conditions.

smiling is an expression of "happiness," but is not technically what "happiness" *is*. That is, antisemitism, per IHRA, is a state of mind, whereas Mr. Justice Gray's understanding makes no reference to the perpetrators' state of mind. Rather, antisemitism is identified with affairs outside the mind, such as *words*, and the properties of those words.

Both these definitions seem inadequate.

Regarding IHRA, its main issue is that it seems to preclude the possibility of institutional antisemitism, where it does not acknowledge an individual state of mind that is hostile to Jews, but the overall *effect* of the current structure of an institution is that it is injurious to Jews (in other words, indirect discrimination). There would be antisemitism even if no one possessed prejudicial beliefs about Jews.

Regarding Mr. Justice Gray's understanding, it blindsides the notion that a mental state may be sufficient for antisemitism, for, at its extreme, one can surely be an anti-Semite by harboring prejudicial beliefs towards Jews, without ever actually expressing them through words or conduct.

Perhaps it is best to *merge* these different understandings of antisemitism. Does Julius's proposed two-fold definition of antisemitism perform this adequately? It comprises: (a) "beliefs about Jews or Jewish projects that are both false and hostile"; and (b), "the injurious things said to or about Jews or their projects or done to them, in consequence of those beliefs."[155]

2. *Proving someone is an anti-Semite in court.* We have seen how the court *defined* antisemitism, but what evidence did it rely on to reach the conclusion that Irving was an anti-Semite? At 13.101, Mr. Justice Gray provides various examples of antisemitic statements made by Irving:

> Irving has made claims that the Jews deserve to be disliked; that they brought the Holocaust on themselves; that Jewish financiers are crooked; that Jews generate antisemitism by their greed and mendacity; that it is bad luck for Mr. Wiesel to be called "Weasel"; that Jews are amongst the scum of humanity; that Jews scurry and hide furtively, unable to stand the light of day; that Simon Wiesenthal has a hideous, leering evil face; and so on.

3. *Defenses against charges of antisemitism.* Given the statements above, how did Irving try to deny that he was antisemitic? Irving advanced two arguments in his defense.

The first argument, outlined at 9.10, runs as follows:

(1) If an individual merely makes statements *explaining why* antisemitism exists, then they are not antisemitic.

(2) I [Irving] only made statements explaining why antisemitism exists.

Therefore,

(3) I [Irving] am not antisemitic.

---

155. Julius, *supra* note 125, at 65.

Although this argument is valid, it is not sound[156]—in particular, item (2) is the issue. For Irving's "explanations" for antisemitism were themselves derisory, hostile, and false in nature—they were not merely explanatory. Irving proclaimed that Jews "provoke the antisemitism by their own actions ... [and cites] examples, including claims for huge compensation from the Germans for the Holocaust and dishonesty on the part of Jewish financiers."

His second argument was the following:

(4) If someone makes a statement about Jews that is true, then they cannot be antisemitic regardless of the statement's other properties (e.g., it being hostile, etc.)

(5) All my [Irving's] statements made about Jews are true.

Therefore,

(6) I [Irving] am not antisemitic.

Interestingly, Mr. Justice Gray stated, at 13.104, that he had "more sympathy" for this argument of Irving's that "Jews are not immune from his criticism." Nonetheless, there are two issues with Irving's argument. The first, and most problematic one, is that (5) is false—Irving made many unsubstantiated and patently false claims about Jews; he would make sweeping statements about Jews as a whole, treating them as a monolith where each particular Jew instantiates some common property—for example, that "Jews deserve to be disliked."

The second issue involves disputing the veracity of (4), but this objection is less clearcut. The thrust behind this retort is that the IHRA definition makes no reference to the truth or falsity of one's perception of Jews, merely that it must be "hostile" in nature. In which case, it is entirely possible that one may be antisemitic, or make antisemitic comments, even if they are not true. However, Julius's definition requires the "injurious statements" to be made in "consequence" of *false* beliefs. But if Irving's belief mirrors the content expressed in his statement (something that is very likely), and the statement turns out to be true, then his belief must be true, too. Which, according to Julius's definition, therefore insulates him from a charge of antisemitism on this front.

4. *The relevance of antisemitism in historical falsification cases.* What was the purpose of demonstrating that Irving was an anti-Semite? As the judge notes at 9.1, Lipstadt in her book, *Denying the Holocaust*, did not actually state that Irving was an anti-Semite. In the trial, however, the defense expressly pleaded Irving's antisemitism.[157] Was Irving's alleged antisemitism relevant to the question of whether he deliberately falsified the historical record concerning the Holocaust? Did it go to show that there was a motive behind his distortions of the historical record? Did it thereby reinforce the contention that such distortions were not mere incompetence but were deliberate?

156. An argument is valid in cases where there is no possible way that, if all the premises were true, the conclusion could be false. A sound argument is one which is valid *and* all of its premises are true.

157. *See* Irving v. Penguin Books Ltd [2001] EWCA Civ 1197, 9.1.

5. *Is antisemitism a form of racism?* At 13.106, the judge seems to have no qualms with classifying antisemitism as a form of racism. Issues that might arise with this include: (a) this seems to require Jews to be a race; and (b) it is difficult to classify Jews as a race since one can *become* Jewish via conversion[158]—whereas race seems immutable, one is either born a certain race or they are not. Are there ways around this objection? Would it be useful to parallel the racial skeptic's position in accepting that "anti-X racism" may exist if "race X" is non-referential?[159] Or could it be of any help to adopt a social constructionist view of race where "intersubjectivity creates a certain kind of objectivity"?[160] Compare this view with Judge Seth's approach in *Manzanares* in Chapter 1. Sections 1981 and 1982 of Civil Rights Act of 1866 were intended to combat race-based discrimination and, implicitly, the racism that motivates it. Insofar as *Manzanares* and *Shaare Tefila* treat Latinos and Jews, respectively, as racial groups for the purposes of §§ 1981 and 1982, does it implicitly treat anti-Latino animus and antisemitism as forms of racism?

Legal Strategies for Combatting Antisemitism

1. *Collaboration between Jews and allies in legal battles.* The *Irving* trial is an example of Jews and allies using available legal tools to advance Jewish safety and equality. Julius hailed the *Irving* trial as an instance where "Jews and non-Jews of good will came together in defense of the historical truth of the Holocaust, and thereby repelled the attack of an antisemite. It was an act of resistance. And though it was merely one among countless others, it had its own, distinctive merit."[161] What, though, made the resistance here so *distinctive*? Was it that the non-Jewish allies came from such a variety of backgrounds (the expert witnesses instructed by the defense were of many different nationalities and religions)? Was it each party's deep commitment to the cause? Or was it that "there was a sense that battle had been joined with an antisemite in which, for once, the oppressor did not have the upper hand"?[162]

2. *What principle did the litigation vindicate?* Although Julius remarked that all the parties came together in "good will," there was a discordance among the defendants regarding their motivation for taking on the case. For Lipstadt, it was primarily "fidelity to the memory of the Jewish dead" that motivated her, while Penguin Books' stance, as Julius notes, "was determined by considerations of freedom of speech."[163] How closely did these motivations align? After the trial, Penguin donated the proceeds of their sales

158. Yair Rosenberg, *Are Jews a Race?* The Atlantic (Feb. 1, 2022), https://www.theatlantic.com/newsletters/archive/2022/02/are-jews-a-race-whoopi-goldberg-holocaust/676814/.

159. Alyssa Ney, Metaphysics: An Introduction 276 (2014); *see also* K. Anthony Appiah, *Race, Culture, Identity: Misunderstood Connections, in* Color Conscious: The Political Morality of Race 30 (1996).

160. Charles W. Mills, Blackness Visible: Essays on Philosophy and Race 48 (1998).

161. Anthony Julius, 7 Encyclopaedia Judaica 32 (Fred Skolnik & Michael Berenbaum eds., 2nd ed. 2007).

162. Julius, *supra* note 125, at xxix.

163. *Id.*

of the judgment to a cancer hospital. Julius felt that in failing to donate the money to a specifically Jewish cause, he, and perhaps the wider Jewish community, has been "snub[bed]"[164]—that Penguin Books, in essence, rejected what he perceived as the particularly Jewish nature of the case. Did this, in some sense, tarnish the nature of their allyship? To what extent is Jewish legal self-defense a particularistic cause or a universal cause? If a universal cause, did Penguin Books correctly identify the universal principle the case vindicated? How would you have distributed the proceeds of the sale?

It should be noted that in *Mermelstein*, the defendants settled the case by paying Mr. Mermelstein $150,000, which he donated to a Holocaust education foundation.[165]

3. *Categorizing lawyers in sensitive cases.* Shaffer and Cochran[166] conceive of four different categories of lawyers based on the values they instantiate.[167]

(a) The lawyer as "godfather." This lawyer's sole purpose consists in winning, and the frame of reference of that winning is financial. If the client seems to desire something other than victory, then this lawyer will often reinterpret their wants to that of winning on a pecuniary level—they impose their own conception of success on the client. They are, in some sense, ethically blind.

(b) The lawyer as "hired gun." This lawyer abstains from paternalistic behavior: they do not impose their own understanding of success on the client. "Client autonomy" is the basis of the relationship between this lawyer and the client. This is a lawyer who primarily counsels rather than steers.

(c) The lawyer as "guru." Here, the client will be advised to do what the lawyer thinks is right—but what is "right" need not be defined narrowly as winning on a financial metric; other moral or social values can come into play. This lawyer will often make both moral and practical decisions on behalf of their client in the name of "client rectitude."

(d) The lawyer as "friend." This lawyer's goals combine those of the other three types: winning, autonomy, and doing what is right all matter. However, the client is also seen as a friend—a collaborator in the good. There is an Aristotelian ingredient to this: friendship is a means of acquiring self-knowledge and understanding.[168]

4. *The unique role of Jewish lawyers in antisemitism cases.* Can Julius, the plaintiff's solicitor, who was Jewish, be neatly placed into any of these categories? Take into account the following:

---

164. *Id*.

165. Tishler, *supra* note 141, at 71 n.4.

166. Thomas L. Shaffer & Robert F. Cochran Jr., Clients, and Moral Responsibility 3 (2nd ed. 2009).

167. *Id.*

168. *See* Aristotle, Magna Moralia 1213a20–1213b (1915): "If, then, it is pleasant to know oneself, and it is not possible to know this without having someone else for a friend, the self-sufficing man will require friendship in order to know himself."

(a) Julius felt that Lipstadt and he were involved in a collective "great undertaking" in fighting Irving, a fight "characterized by both piety and resistance."[169]

(b) Combatting antisemitism, whether in an academic or legal domain, was "an expression of his deepest intellectual and moral commitments."[170]

(c) Lipstadt was directed by Julius, against her natural instincts and in "blunt fashion," not to speak to the press, "period."[171] This was to prevent Irving receiving the publicity he craved.

169. Julius, *supra* note 125, at xxix.
170. Lipstadt, *supra* note 123, at 249.
171. *Id.* at 259.

Chapter 8

Hate Speech

In Commonwealth countries, antisemitic speech can be actionable as group defamation, even if only occasionally. In the United States, by contrast, antisemitic speech is constitutionally protected and therefore non-actionable. In all jurisdictions, however, effective non-litigation responses to antisemitic speech may be available.

Section A of this chapter, "Non-Litigation Responses to Antisemitic Speech," concerns Henry Ford's publication of anti-Jewish propaganda and how some American Jewish leaders responded to Ford's activities. Section B, "Antisemitic Speech Is Protected Speech," examines a 1978 attempt by neo-Nazis to march through Skokie, Illinois, and official efforts to block the march. Professor R. George Wright describes this case as U.S. law's most significant constitutional response to antisemitic hate speech. Section C, "Casually Antisemitic Speech," examines speech containing antisemitic elements that is made in an offhand or seemingly innocuous manner but that nonetheless propagates antisemitic stereotypes and contributes to their normalization. It looks at an example of such speech from an unexpected source—the U.S. Equal Employment Opportunity Commission (EEOC).

A. Non-Litigation Responses to Antisemitic Speech

The *Dearborn Independent* was a weekly newspaper published in Dearborn, Michigan, from 1919 to 1927, with an average weekly circulation of approximately 700,000 at its peak in 1925. It was owned and controlled by Henry Ford, the founder of the Ford Motor Company. Between 1920 and 1922, the newspaper published a series of antisemitic articles titled "The International Jew," which were later published in book form under the same name. These articles falsely alleged that Jews controlled the world's finances and worked in concert to take control of the levers of global power. They relied heavily on *The Protocols of the Elders of Zion*, a tract written by a Russian pro-tsarist journalist and first published in 1905. The *Protocols* allege that Jews conspire to infiltrate governments, finance, and journalism in order to achieve total world control. After obtaining a copy in 1919, Ford decided to publish an Americanized version in the *Dearborn Independent*.

In 1924 and 1925, the newspaper renewed its campaign by publishing a series of articles attacking Aaron Sapiro, a Jewish lawyer from California and leader of the movement to organize farmers into collectives. The headline of its first article read, "Exploiting Farm Organizations: Jewish Monopoly Traps Operate Under Guise of Co-operative Marketing Associations." These articles accused Sapiro of defrauding farmers as part of a larger Jewish conspiracy to control the economy.

In 1925, Sapiro filed a lawsuit for libel against Henry Ford and the *Dearborn Independent*, seeking $1 million in damages, in the U.S. District Court for the Eastern District of Michigan. He alleged that the defendants had falsely defamed him by accusing him of legal malpractice. His complaint did not state group defamation as a cause of action, nor did Sapiro see himself primarily as acting on behalf of all Jews. At the same time, Sapiro's complaint listed defamatory statements made about his role in a supposed Jewish conspiracy, and his retraction request referenced the resultant harm to Jews as a class. For their part, national newspapers characterized the lawsuit as akin to a group libel action on behalf of all Jews, with Sapiro acting like a class representative.

When Sapiro stated his intention to call Ford as a witness, the *New York Graphic* published an article headlined, "The Jews Try Ford!" The trial court, per Presiding Judge Fred Raymond, struck out the complaint's allegations concerning the defendants' defamatory statements about Jews. He ruled "that Mr. Ford's ideas with regard to the Jewish race formed no part of the case built up by Mr. Sapiro." Sapiro was thus barred from suing for attacks made on "his people." The judge did not elaborate upon his ruling, so the defense explained it outside the courtroom: "You can't libel a race." The trial proceeded as an individual libel action, with Sapiro contesting the allegations that he had committed legal malpractice. It ended in a mistrial.

To avoid a second trial, Ford sent an emissary to Louis Marshall, the foremost Jewish leader in the U.S. at that time.[1] Without consulting Sapiro, Marshall wrote a statement that Ford signed, apologizing to Jews. It did not explicitly mention Sapiro. Marshall, in turn, wrote a statement thanking Ford for the apology. Ford's statement and Marshall's response were widely circulated. Soon afterward, Sapiro settled his lawsuit with Ford for his court costs and attorney's fees. The sum, $140,000, was huge in those days, but much less than the litigation had cost him. Ford also promised Sapiro and Marshall to shut down the *Dearborn Independent*, which published its last issue in December 1927.

Henry Ford, *Statement Regarding Charges Against Jews Made in His Publications, the* Dearborn Independent *and a Series of Pamphlets Entitled the "International Jew"*

Dearborn, Mich., June 30, 1927

[This statement, written by Louis Marshall for Henry Ford's signature, was published in the *Dearborn Independent* and other leading U.S. newspapers. It is followed by the letter Marshall wrote in response to Ford's statement. Many newspapers published the two letters together on July 7, 1927. Marshall subsequently issued a statement explaining his role in Ford's letter, also set forth below.]

1. We encountered Louis Marshall in Chapter 4.C., "Zionism as a Jewish American Project."

5

The Ford International Weekly

THE DEARBORN INDEPENDENT

By the Year One Dollar | Dearborn, Michigan, May 22, 1920 | Single Copy Five Cents

The International Jew: The World's Problem

"Among the distinguishing mental and moral traits of the Jews may be mentioned: distaste for hard or violent physical labor; a strong family sense and philoprogenitiveness; a marked religious instinct; the courage of the prophet and martyr rather than of the pioneer and soldier; remarkable power to survive in adverse environments, combined with great ability to retain racial solidarity; capacity for exploitation, both individual and social; shrewdness and astuteness in speculation and money matters generally; an Oriental love of display and a full appreciation of the power and pleasure of social position; a very high average of intellectual ability."

—The New International Encyclopedia.

THE Jew is again being singled out for critical attention throughout the world. His emergence in the financial, political and social spheres has been so complete and spectacular since the war that his place, power and purpose in the world are being given a new scrutiny, much of it unfriendly. Persecution is not a new experience to the Jew, but intensive scrutiny of his nature and super-nationality is. He has suffered for more than 2,000 years from what may be called the instinctive anti-semitism of the other races, but this antagonism has never been intelligent nor has it been able to make itself intelligible. Nowadays, however, the Jew is being placed, as it were, under the microscope of economic observation that the reasons for his power, the reasons for his separateness, the reasons for his suffering may be defined and understood.

In Russia he is charged with being the source of Bolshevism, an accusation which is serious or not according to the circle in which it is made; we in America, hearing the fervid eloquence and perceiving the prophetic ardor of young Jewish apostles of social and industrial reform, can calmly estimate how it may be. In Germany he is charged with being the cause of the Empire's collapse and a very considerable literature has sprung up, bearing with it a mass of circumstantial evidence that gives the thinker pause. In England he is charged with being the real world ruler, who rules as a super-nation over the nations, rules by the power of gold, and who plays nation against nation for his own purposes, remaining himself discreetly in the background. In America it is pointed out to what extent the elder Jews of wealth and the younger Jews of ambition swarmed through the war organizations—principally those departments which dealt with the commercial and industrial business of war, and also the extent to which they have clung to the advantage which their experience as agents of the government gave them.

IN SIMPLE words, the question of the Jews has come to the fore, but like other questions which lend themselves to prejudice, efforts will be made to hush it up as impolitic for open discussion. If, however, experience has taught us anything it is that questions thus suppressed will sooner or later break out in undesirable and unprofitable forms.

The Jew is the world's enigma. Poor in his masses, he yet controls the world's finances. Scattered abroad without country or government, he yet presents a unity of race continuity which no other people has achieved. Living under legal disabilities in almost every land, he has become the power behind many a throne. There are ancient prophecies to the effect that the Jew will return to his own land and from that center rule the world, though not until he has undergone an assault by the united nations of mankind.

The single description which will include a larger percentage of Jews than members of any other race is this: he is in business. It may be only gathering rags and selling them, but he is in business. From the sale of old clothes to the control of international trade and finance, the Jew is supremely gifted for business. More than any other race he exhibits a decided aversion to industrial employment, which he balances by an equally decided adaptability to trade. The Gentile boy works his way up, taking employment in the productive or technical departments; but the Jewish boy prefers to begin as messenger, salesman or clerk—anything—so long as it is connected with the commercial side of the business. An early Prussian census illustrates this characteristic: of a total population of 269,400, the Jews comprised six per cent or 16,164. Of these, 12,000 were traders and 4,164 were workmen. Of the Gentile population, the other 94 per cent, or 153,236 people, there were only 17,000 traders.

A MODERN census would show a large professional and literary class added to the traders, but no diminution of the percentage of traders and not much if any increase in the number of wage toilers. In America alone most of the big business, the trusts and the banks, the natural resources and the chief agricultural products, especially tobacco, cotton and sugar, are in the control of Jewish financiers or their agents. Jewish journalists are a large and powerful group here. "Large numbers of department stores are held by Jewish firms," says the Jewish Encyclopedia, and many if not most of them are run under Gentile names. Jews are the largest and most numerous landlords of residence property in the country. They are supreme in the theatrical world. They absolutely control the circulations of publications throughout the country. Fewer than any race whose presence among us is noticeable, they receive daily an amount of favorable publicity which would be impossible did they not have the facilities for creating and distributing it themselves. Werner Sombart, in his "Jew and Modern Capitalism" says, "If the conditions in America continue to develop along the same lines as in the last generation, if the immigration statistics and the proportion of births among all the nationalities remain the same, our imagination may picture the United States of fifty or a hundred years hence as a land inhabited only by Slavs, Negroes and Jews, wherein the Jews will naturally occupy the position of

Figure 8.1. Front cover, *Dearborn Independent*, May 22, 1920, on file with Victoria Saker Woeste.

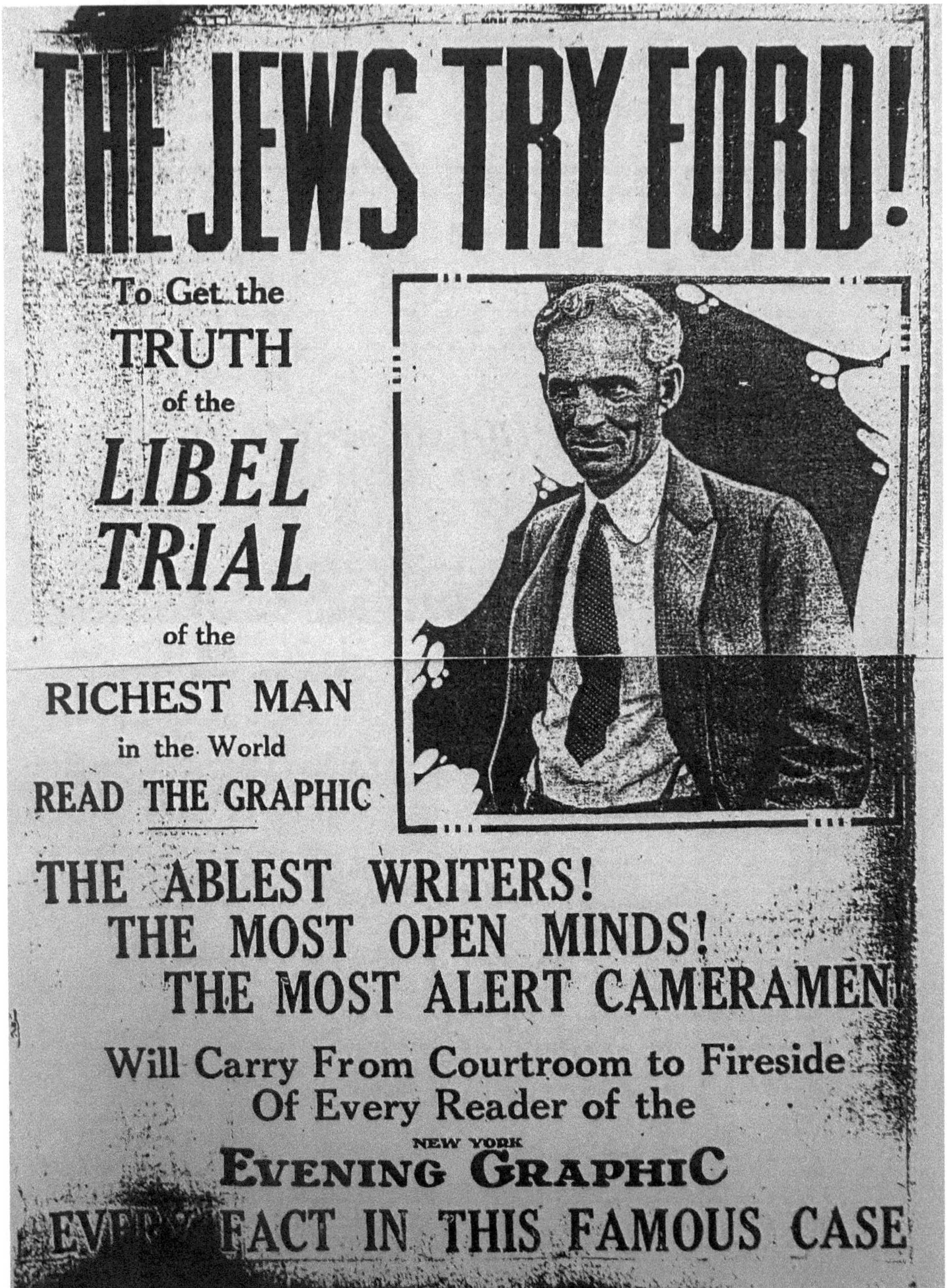

THE JEWS TRY FORD!

To Get the
TRUTH
of the
LIBEL
TRIAL
of the
RICHEST MAN
in the World
READ THE GRAPHIC

THE ABLEST WRITERS!
THE MOST OPEN MINDS!
THE MOST ALERT CAMERAMEN!

Will Carry From Courtroom to Fireside
Of Every Reader of the
NEW YORK
EVENING GRAPHIC
EVERY FACT IN THIS FAMOUS CASE

Figure 8.2. Front cover, *New York Evening Graphic*, March 1927. From the William Henry Gallagher Papers, collection of Patricia Gallagher Wooton, on file with Victoria Saker Woeste.

For some time past I have given consideration to the series of articles concerning Jews which since 1920 have appeared in the *Dearborn Independent*. Some of them have been reprinted in pamphlet form under the title "The International Jew." Although both publications are my property, it goes without saying that in the multitude of my activities it has been impossible for me to devote personal attention to their management or to keep informed as to their contents. It has therefore inevitably followed that the conduct and policies of these publications had to be delegated to men whom I placed in charge of them and upon whom I relied implicitly.

To my great regret I have learned that Jews generally, and particularly those of this country, not only resent these publications as promoting antisemitism, but regard me as their enemy. Trusted friends with whom I have conferred recently have assured me in all sincerity that in their opinion the character of the charges and insinuations made against the Jews, both individually and collectively, contained in many of the articles which have been circulated periodically in the *Dearborn Independent* and have been reprinted in the pamphlets mentioned, justifies the righteous indignation entertained by Jews everywhere toward me because of the mental anguish occasioned by the unprovoked reflections made upon them.

This has led me to direct my personal attention to this subject, in order to ascertain the exact nature of these articles. As a result of this survey I confess that I am deeply mortified that this journal, which is intended to be constructive and not destructive, has been made the medium for resurrecting exploded fictions, for giving currency to the so-called *Protocols of the Wise Men of Zion*, which have been demonstrated, as I learn, to be gross forgeries, and for contending that the Jews have been engaged in a conspiracy to control the capital and the industries of the world, besides laying at their door many offenses against decency, public order and good morals.

Had I appreciated even the general nature, to say nothing of the details, of these utterances, I would have forbidden their circulation without a moment's hesitation, because I am fully aware of the virtues of the Jewish people as a whole, of what they and their ancestors have done for civilization and for mankind and toward the development of commerce and industry, of their sobriety and diligence, their benevolence and their unselfish interest in the public welfare. Of course there are black sheep in every flock, as there are among men of all races, creeds and nationalities who are at times evildoers. It is wrong, however, to judge a people by a few individuals, and I therefore join in condemning unreservedly all wholesale denunciations and attacks.

Those who know me can bear witness that it is not in my nature to inflict insult upon and to occasion pain to anybody, and that it has been my effort to free myself from prejudice. Because of that I frankly confess that I have been greatly shocked as a result of my study and examination of the files of the *Dearborn Independent* and of the pamphlets entitled "The International Jew." I deem it to be my duty as an honorable man to make amends for the wrong done to the Jews as fellow-men and brothers, by asking their forgiveness for the harm that I have unintentionally committed, by retracting so far as lies within my power the offensive charges laid at their door by these publications, and by giving them the unqualified assurance that henceforth they may look to me for friendship and good will.

It is needless to add that the pamphlets which have been distributed throughout the country and in foreign lands will be withdrawn from circulation, that in every way possible I will make it known that they have my unqualified disapproval, and that henceforth the *Dearborn Independent* will be conducted under such auspices that articles reflecting upon the Jews will never again appear in its columns.

Finally, let me add that this statement is made on my own initiative and wholly in the interest of right and justice and in accordance with what I regard as my solemn duty as a man and as a citizen.

Louis Marshall, *Reply to Mr. Ford*

July 5, 1927

Dear Sir:

I am in receipt of... your statement regarding the long series of vituperative articles which since May, 1920, has appeared in the *Dearborn Independent* and which contain the most violent attacks upon the Jews. You now declare that after an examination of those articles you feel shocked and mortified because of the harm which they have done, and you ask for forgiveness....

We could not at first credit the information that the *Dearborn Independent* had permitted itself to be made the vehicle for disseminating exploded falsehoods and the vilest concoctions of vicious minds, invented by adventurers who had barely found asylum here when they attempted to introduce the exotic growths of antisemitism.

Happily such excrescences could not flourish on American soil. Happily the enlightened press of this country treated them with contempt and as unworthy of notice.

What seemed most mysterious was the fact that you whom we had never wronged and whom we had looked upon as a kindly man, should have lent yourself to such a campaign of vilification apparently carried on with your sanction.

The statement which you have sent me gives us assurance of your retraction of the offensive charges, of your proposed change of policies in the conduct of the *Dearborn Independent*, of your future friendship and good will, of your desire to make amends, and what is to be expected from any man of honor, you couple these assurances with a request for pardon. So far as my influence can further that end, it will be exerted... because essentially the spirit of forgiveness is a Jewish trait.

It is my sincere hope that never again shall such a recrudescence of ancient superstition manifest itself upon our horizon.

Louis Marshall, *An Explanatory Statement*

New York, July 14, 1927

About a month ago, Earl J. Davis of Detroit, Mich., former Assistant District Attorney of the United States, and Joseph A. Palma of New York came to my office, introduced by former Congressman Nathan D. Perlman, who... came as representatives of

Figure 8.3. Louis Marshall (1856–1929). Lawyer and President of the American Jewish Committee (1912–1929). Photographed c.1900. Courtesy of Granger Historical Picture Library.

Figure 8.4. Henry Ford receiving the Grand Cross of the German Eagle from Nazi officials, 1938. Courtesy of Getty Images.

Henry Ford, and asserted that ... he desired to know what could be done to put an end to the strained relations on the part of the Jews toward him.

Thereupon, I reviewed the history of these defamations and of their reprints known as "The International Jew," commented upon their gross injustice, and the injury they had occasioned both here and abroad, and pointed out that the Jews everywhere have been grievously wounded by these libels.... There must be a complete retraction of all of the false charges made, a full apology and request for forgiveness, a discontinuance of the attacks which had been indulged in these publications, the withdrawal of the pamphlets constituting "The International Jew," and a pledge that like publications would never again be made....

A Case Study in Non-Litigation Relief for Group Defamation

1. *Ford's implausible deniability.* It strains credulity to accept the idea that Ford did not know what his employees were publishing in the newspaper he owned and controlled. Most everything that was published under Ford's name during the 1920s was ghost-written—his autobiography and commentary on politics, culture, and society—so in that respect, it is not surprising that Ford accepted the statement Marshall wrote for him. The apology gave Ford a face-saving exit from the litigation and enabled him to avoid confessing to libeling Sapiro.

2. *Impact of Ford's letter on Sapiro's lawsuit.* Ford's letter does not apologize for his claim that Sapiro committed legal malpractice, nor for the antisemitic invective he lodged against Sapiro—only for his attacks on the Jewish people. Ford's letter refers to "black sheep in every flock." Was Sapiro one of the black sheep Ford was referring to? Note that Sapiro's lawsuit against Ford was still pending when he issued this letter. In his letter, Ford claimed to have had no knowledge of the antisemitic articles in the *Dearborn Independent*. This contradicted Sapiro's claim, essential to his cause of action, that Ford orchestrated the publication, a claim that witnesses substantiated at trial. What legal significance, if any, did Ford's claims of ignorance have? For example, could Ford have introduced his letter at trial to rebut the evidence that he was aware of the defamatory statements against Sapiro? What practical impact might the letter have had on Sapiro's litigation? Would it have increased or decreased the pressure on Ford to settle the Sapiro lawsuit, and on what terms?

3. *Assessing Marshall's role.* Marshall likely knew that Ford's apology would have an impact on Sapiro's lawsuit against Ford. Marshall justified his role in Ford's apology as serving "the destinies and honor of hundreds of thousands infinitely more important than anybody's lawsuit" (Marshall had a law partner who had a Ford libel client of his own in pending litigation at this time. Though contemporary ethics rules required Marshall not to adversely affect the interests of his firm's client, Marshall proceeded.) Marshall ensured that Ford apologized for group libel but not for individual libel. Should Marshall have done better by Sapiro, whose lawsuit forced Ford to make the

concession to group libel? Which was more important legally: the individual libel suit Sapiro was almost certain to win (which would have established Ford's responsibility for the newspaper), or the group libel apology that was legally unenforceable?

4. *Postscript on* The Dearborn Independent. The newspaper published its last issue in December 1927, following Ford's promise to Marshall that he would shut it down, a condition that was reiterated in Sapiro's settlement agreement. But equally relevant to this outcome was the opposition of Ford's wife and son to the antisemitic content of the newspaper. They threatened to sell their stock in the Dearborn Publishing Company if the newspaper continued to malign Jews.

5. *Postscript on* The International Jew. Marshall failed in his attempts to push Ford to withdraw the book from circulation. Ford refused to compensate publishers in the U.S., Europe, and South America for canceling their print runs. The book was translated into over a dozen languages and continued to circulate during and after World War II, now with Ford himself falsely credited as the author. *The International Jew* and the *Protocols of the Elders of Zion* constitute the canon of the international antisemitic movement and are easily found on the internet's many hate sites. Documentary films have been released depicting the events described in the *Protocols*. More recently, copies of the *Protocols* have been discovered among possessions of shooters who attacked synagogues in Pittsburgh, Pennsylvania, and Poway, California, in the late 2010s. Could anything else have been done to take these books out of circulation or, failing that, to lessen their impact?

6. *"I regard Henry Ford as my inspiration."* In 1931, Adolf Hitler told a *Detroit News* reporter that, "I regard Henry Ford as my inspiration," and that he kept a life-size portrait of Ford next to his desk. In July 1938, four months after the German annexation of Austria, Ford accepted the highest medal that Nazi Germany could bestow on a foreigner, the Grand Cross of the German Eagle. When the Nazis nationalized the Ford manufacturing plant in Berlin, Ford and his son cooperated with the militarization of the factory that then supplied Germany's war effort. In addition, the Ford Motor Company sought compensation for its loss of the plant after the war, while refusing to pay reparations to Jews and others who were forced to work at the plant.

Sources

Cyrus Adler, "Louis Marshall: A Biographical Sketch." American Jewish Year Book 32 (1930–1931): 21–55.

Selected Letters, ed. Ira Robinson. 2 vols. Philadelphia and New York: Jewish Publication Society of America, 1985.

Allan Nevins and Frank Ernest Hill, Ford: Expansion and Challenge, 1915–1933. New York: Scribner, 1957.

"Ford Wins Ruling Barring Race Issue from Sapiro Suit: Court Holds Defense of Jewish Race Immaterial to Plaintiff's Case," New York Times, March 17, 1927, p. 1.

GEOFFREY STONE, PERILOUS TIMES: FREE SPEECH IN WARTIME FROM THE SEDITION ACT OF 1798 TO THE WAR ON TERROR. New York: Norton, 2004.

PHILLIPA STRUM, WHEN THE NAZIS CAME TO SKOKIE: FREEDOM FOR SPEECH WE HATE. Lawrence: University Press of Kansas, 1999.

Jeremy Waldron, "Dignity and Defamation: The Visibility of Hate." 123 HARVARD L. REV. (2010), 1596–1657.

SAMUEL WALKER, HATE SPEECH: THE HISTORY OF AN AMERICAN CONTROVERSY. Lincoln: University of Nebraska Press, 1994.

MAX WALLACE, AMERICAN AXIS: HENRY FORD, CHARLES LINDBERGH, AND THE RISE OF THE THIRD REICH. New York: St. Martin's Press, 2003.

STEVEN WATTS, THE PEOPLE'S TYCOON: HENRY FORD AND THE AMERICAN CENTURY. New York: Knopf, 2005.

VICTORIA SAKER WOESTE, HENRY FORD'S WAR ON JEWS AND THE LEGAL BATTLE AGAINST HATE SPEECH. Stanford: Stanford University Press, 2012.

Matthew Silver, *The Legal Battles of Louis Marshall: Marshall v. Ford (1920–1927)*

The saga of Henry Ford's attacks on Jews begins with the arrival of the antisemitic forgery, *The Protocols of the Elders of Zion*, in the U.S. in February 1918, several months before the end of WWI. Despite its unfounded accusations about an international Jewish conspiracy, the *Protocols* won some backing, as though it were an actual document, among some powerful Americans, and the document was presented to a Senate subcommittee.

The antisemitic forgery posed problems for American Jewish leaders in several ways. As seen by Louis Marshall, a New York City attorney who became after WWI the most prominent Jewish communal leader in the U.S. following the death of his patron and colleague, the banker Jacob Schiff, the *Protocols* forgery was a damaging menace on several fronts.

These can be listed. First, international efforts for Jewish rights, particularly in Eastern Europe. After WWI, Marshall led a delegation in Paris that secured a minority rights treaty for Jews in newly created Poland. The damage caused by the *Protocols* in this sphere is that the forgery tarnished such international Jewish advocacy by misleadingly suggesting that it was part of a global conspiracy. Second, Capitol Hill advocacy for open immigration opportunities, for Jewish immigrants and other newcomers (masses of Jews suffered from antisemitic depredation in the Ukraine and other areas after WWI and sought resettlement in the U.S.). Third, the *Protocols* forgery became widely disseminated when, in 1920, Henry Ford threw the enormous weight of his industrial enterprises behind it, reformatting and circulating the *Protocols* in a journal called the *Dearborn Independent* that was distributed around the U.S. by Ford Motor dealers.

Combatting Ford's antisemitism, Marshall and others faced a phenomenon that tolled serious damage to Jewish interests in the U.S. and overseas during the first half of the 1920s. These damages are unquantifiable, and Jewish setbacks in these decades had multiple causes, but the antisemitic lies spread by Henry Ford, probably America's most popular hero in this period, had devastating consequences. The Dillingham Commission legislative process over the 1921–1924 period which culminated in the shutting of doors to immigrants from Eastern and Southern Europe exploited stereotypes about Jews and others which were fanned by media outlets like the *Dearborn Independent.* Had America's immigration doors remained open in this period, the dimensions of the Holocaust would have been reduced, to some extent. Also, the *Dearborn Independent*'s antisemitic aspersions about global conspiracies discouraged leaders like Marshall, and England's Lucien Wolf, from persisting with rights advocacy lobbying of the sort done by the Marshall-led Jewish delegation at the 1919 Paris Peace Conference. This meant that nobody in the international arena would represent Poland's three million Jews, when that country's regime brazenly ignored its treaty obligations toward minorities.

In addition to compensation for the sheer insult felt by American Jews as a result of Ford's *Dearborn Independent* campaign, Marshall's work for relief should be seen in this broad context, whose tributaries flow into the Holocaust. Directly or indirectly, Henry Ford's antisemitism lessened America's role as a haven for Jewish immigrant refugees, and it also enhanced the vulnerability of East European Jews, hamstringing the ability of American Jewish leaders like Marshall, and organizations like the WWI-formed Joint Distribution Committee, to work on their behalf.

In opposition to Ford, Marshall represented the American Jewish Committee (AJC), the country's longest-standing defense agency for Jews, which was directed by a cadre of Jewish lawyers and businessmen. This organization was sometimes criticized for not being representative of the American Jewish community as a whole; but Marshall's defense work and lobbying in the 1920s came unusually close to having across-the-board backing in Jewish America. His work on immigration and Polish Jewish minority rights, for instance, had the backing not just of the elite-spirited AJC, but also of the broad-based American Jewish Congress, an organization created during WWI at the initiative of the American Zionist movement, headed by Louis Brandeis (Marshall's overseas lobbying at the Paris Peace Conference had "electoral" backing never known before or since in American Jewish life, since it was sanctioned by the American Jewish Congress, whose delegates were chosen in a nation-wide election where 300,000 American Jews cast ballots). So, in a broad sense, the "client" in Marshall's efforts against Ford can be seen as the American Jewish community.

Marshall attempted a number of tactics and techniques in efforts to expose the *Protocols*' forgery and cause *Dearborn Independent*'s campaign to desist. At his suggestions, the AJC commissioned Herman Bernstein, an independent journalist, to expose the *Protocols* forgery. Also, Marshall sponsored a lobbying effort with President Harding and forged a coalition of American Jewish organized groups for united action against Ford.

Marshall was originally not convinced about the viability of court defamation action in a situation like Ford's antisemitism, but this defamation suit approach picked up momentum in the mid-1920s. Beyond Sapiro's "million dollar" suit against Ford, two other defamation actions (one by the journalist, Bernstein) were brought against the automobile manufacturer; and so, in 1927, the accumulated momentum of this litigation, as well as Ford's suddenly vulnerable management situation when his company made a risky and expensive transition from the Model T to the Model A, provided Marshall leverage to win relief, for American Jews, from Ford.

This happened in mid-1927 when, unexpectedly, the automobile manufacturer indicated to Marshall that he was prepared to offer a retraction. In his statement, which was actually drafted by Marshall, Ford promised to "make amends for the wrong done to the Jews" by the *Dearborn Independent* publications, affirmed his "retraction" of their "lies" and asked for "forgiveness." Marshall accurately assessed this letter as a "staggering blow for the anti-Semites," but also hinted that some measure of the damage caused by Ford was irreversible. For instance, he warned that in Central and Eastern Europe, the libels disseminated by the car manufacturer could prove deadly to "desperate and harried Jews."

Frederick M. Lawrence, The Protocols of the Elders of Zion: *Group Defamation Trials in Civil Courts and the "Court" of Public Opinion*[2]

(2007)

Our task is to discuss ways in which assertions of truth and falsity can be made in the academy and in our public civic institutions. Our particular task is to consider these complex questions in the context of the *Protocols of the Elders of Zion* ("the *Protocols*")....

It is a time for vigilance, perhaps not overkill, but certainly vigilance. But permit me, by way of only that transition, to begin with an uplifting story. This story concerns one of the most remarkable moments, one of the most powerful and uplifting moments, in the history of the treatment and reaction to American anti-Semitism. The climactic event of the story went by very quietly; you might easily have missed it. The lead-up to the story, however, did not go by quietly at all. The story beings with a notorious speech by Khalid Abdul Mohammad, one of the main leaders of the Nation of Islam,

---

2. Frederick M. Lawrence, *The Protocols of the Elders of Zion: Group Defamation Trials in Civil Courts and the 'Court' of Public Opinion*, *in* From the Protocols of the Elders of Zion to Holocaust Denial Trials: Challenging the Media, the Law and the Academy (2007), https://ssrn.com/abstract=799024. Frederick M. Lawrence is an American lawyer, civil rights scholar, and secretary and CEO of the Phi Beta Kappa Society. He previously served as president of Brandeis University, dean of the George Washington University Law School, and a visiting professor and senior research scholar at Yale Law School. Lawrence delivered these remarks at a conference held at Northeastern University in Boston on May 1–2, 2001.

MINISTER LOUIS FARRAKHAN AND THE NATION OF ISLAM CLAIM THEY ARE MOVING TOWARD MODERATION AND INCREASED TOLERANCE.

YOU DECIDE.

Excerpts from remarks by Khalid Abdul Mohammad, Nation of Islam National Spokesman, at Kean College, NJ, 11/29/93:

Brothers and sisters – the so-called Jew, and I must say so-called Jew, because you're not the true Jew. You are Johnny-come-lately-Jew, who just crawled out of the caves and hills of Europe just a little over 4,000 years ago. You're not from the original people. You are a European strain of people who crawled around on your all fours in the caves and hills of Europe, eatin' Juniper roots and eatin' each other.

Who are the slumlords in the black community? The so-called Jew... Who is it sucking our blood in the black community? A white imposter Arab and a white imposter Jew. Right in the black community, sucking our blood on a daily and consistent basis. They sell us pork and they don't even eat it themselves. A meat case full of rotten pork meat, and the imposter Arab and the imposter white Jew, neither of them eat it themselves. A wall full of liquor keeping our people drunk and out of their head, and filled with the swill of the swine, affecting their minds. They're the blood suckers of the black nation and the black community. Professor Griff was right, when he spoke here... and when he spoke in the general vicinity of Jersey and New York, and when he spoke at Columbia Jew-niversity (sic) over in Jew (sic) York City. He was right.

The DeBeers mines, Oppenheimer, our people, our brothers and sisters in South Africa, hundreds of them lose their lives. Sometimes thousands in those mines. Miles underground, mining diamonds for white Jews. That's why you call yourself Mr. Reubenstein, Mr. Goldstein, Mr. Silverstein. Because you been stealing rubies and gold and silver all over the earth. That's why we can't even wear a ring or a bracelet or a necklace without calling it Jew-elry. We say it real quick and call it jewelry, but it's not jewelry, it's Jew-elry, 'cause you're the rogue that's stealing all over the face of the planet earth.

You see everybody always talk about Hitler exterminating 6 million Jews. That's right. But don't nobody ever ask what did they do to Hitler? What did they do to them folks? They went in there, in Germany, the way they do everywhere they go, and they supplanted, they usurped, they turned around and a German, in his own country, would almost have to go to a Jew to get money. They had undermined the very fabric of the society. Now he was an arrogant no-good devil bastard, Hitler, no question about it. He was wickedly great. Yes, he was. He used his greatness for evil and wickedness. But they are wickedly great too, brother. Everywhere they go, and they always do it and hide their head.

We don't owe the white man nothin' in South Africa. He's killed millions of our women, our children, our babies, our elders. We don't owe him nothing in South Africa. If we want to be merciful at all, when we gain enough power from God Almighty to take our freedom and independence from him, we give him 24 hours to get out of town, by sundown. That's all. If he won't get out of town by sundown, we kill everything white that ain't right (inaudible) in South Africa. We kill the women, we kill the children, we kill the babies. We kill the blind, we kill the crippled, (inaudible), we kill 'em all. We kill the faggot, we kill the lesbian, we kill them all. You say why kill the babies in South Africa? Because they gonna grow up one day to oppress our babies, so we kill the babies. Why kill the women? They, they...because they lay on their back, they are the military or the army's manufacturing center. They lay on their back and reinforcements roll out from between their legs. So we kill the women too. You'll kill the elders too? Kill the old ones too. Goddamit, if they in a wheelchair, push 'em off a cliff in Cape Town. Push 'em off a cliff in Cape Town, or Johannesburg, or (inaudible), or Port Sheppston or Darbin, how the hell you think they got old. They old oppressing black people. I said kill the blind, kill the crippled, kill the crazy. Goddamit, and when you get through killing 'em all, go to the goddam graveyard and dig up the grave and kill 'em, goddam, again. 'Cause they didn't die hard enough. They didn't die hard enough. And if you've killed 'em all and you don't have the strength to dig 'em up, then take your gun and shoot in the goddam grave. Kill 'em again. Kill 'em again, 'cause they didn't die hard enough.

We found out that the Federal Reserve ain't really owned by the Federal Government... But it ain't owned by the Federal Government. The Federal Reserve is owned by, you just touched on it a little while ago. (Jews.) It's owned by the Jews.

Brother. I don't care who sits in the seat at the White House. You can believe that the Jews control that seat that they sit in from behind the scenes. They control the finance, and not only that, they influence the policy-making.

No white Jews ever in bondage in Egypt for 400 years. You're not the chosen people of God. Stop telling that lie. Let's go a little further with this. Many of you put out the textbooks. Many of you control the libraries. Lie-braries. NBC, ABC, CBS, you don't see nothin', or makes sure we don't see. Warner Brothers, Paramount, huh? Hollywood, period.

But [they] also are most influential in newspaper, magazine, print media and electronic media.

These people have had a secret relationship with us. They have our entertainers in their hip pocket. In the palm of their hand, I should say. They have our athletes in the palm of their hand.

Many of our politicians are in the palm of the white man's hand, but in particular, in the palm of the Jewish white man's hand.

The Jews have told us, the so-called Jews have told us, ve (sic) ve, ve suffer like you. Ve, ve, ve, ve marched with Dr. Martin Luther King, Jr. Ve, ve, ve were in Selma, Alabama. Ve, ve were in Montgomery, Alabama. Ve, ve, were on the front line of the civil rights marches. Ve have always supported you. But let's take a look at it. The Jews, the so-called Jews, what they have actually done, brothers and sisters, is used us as cannon fodder.

Go to the Vatican in Rome, when the old, no-good Pope, you know that cracker. Somebody need to raise that dress up and see what's really under there.

The Anti-Defamation League is the world's leading organization fighting anti-Semitism through programs and services that counteract hatred, prejudice and bigotry.

Melvin Salberg, National Chairman   Abraham H. Foxman, National Director

Anti-Defamation League of B'nai B'rith, 823 United Nations Plaza, New York, NY 10017

ADL Anti-Defamation League®

Figure 8.5. Advertisement taken by the ADL in the *New York Times,* 1993.

a man who repeated all of the vulgarities that have been spewed about Judaism with which we have all become too familiar, vulgarities of Judaism being a "gutter religion," and about Jewish behavior and Jewish activities within the United States and in the International community. The uplifting and remarkable moment was the response of the Anti-Defamation League (ADL). A full-page advertisement was taken in *The New York Times* that merely repeated the speech, verbatim. The advertisement repeated the speech and at the bottom of the page printed "the Anti-Defamation League—founded in 1913, is the world's leading organization fighting anti-Semitism through programs and services that counteract hatred, prejudice and bigotry." This was truly a remarkable moment, a breathtaking moment. ADL acted on the assumption that no rebuttal of Abdul Mohammad's statements was necessary, and that the mere exposing of the falsehood would be sufficient to assert the truth.

When Stephen Bronner talks about the *Protocols* having been "proved to be a forgery," he says, "it is indisputable." But proven to whom? Proven how? That is the critical concern for this essay. How do we prove it? Stephen proves it to me in his book. But to whom generally does one prove this assertion, and by what measure may we judge the proof to be satisfactory, let alone indisputable? Who wants to listen? And how do we go about proving it? All of these questions, for the purposes of this volume, become the question of how best to respond to the *Protocols*. The specific context I will address is the sustained affirmation and assertion of the *Protocols*, through the 1920s, in a series of articles in Henry Ford's newspaper, the *Dearborn Independent*. How do we prove that the arguments contained in the *Protocols* are wrong? Do we do what ADL did in the 1990s? Merely repeat it? Do we rebut the arguments or combat them? In short, how does one prove it to be false?

What I would like to do is to sketch out the three formal means in which responses to the *Protocols* might have been made, and in which truth and falsity might have been weighed. I will consider the benefits and risks of each, the cost of each, and then I will suggest a different way in fact in which it might actually have played out, that is, in which truth and falsity could be weighed. Two ways of responding, which I will get to shortly, involve actual litigation: individual libel and group libel. The means of response with which I begin is that of Congressional investigation.

The option of seeking a Congressional investigation was explored in the aftermath—actually not even in the aftermath, but beginning in the very time during which the *Dearborn Independent* continued to produce articles based on the falsehoods of the *Protocols*. The AJC and ADL, two of the leading American Jewish organizations of the time, considered launching efforts to bring about a Congressional investigation of the *Independent* and of Ford. Congressional investigations have certain advantages over litigation. For example, there are significantly looser limits on the admissibility of evidence for consideration by a Congressional Committee at an investigation than for formal admissibility of evidence by a court at a trial. The issues for a Congressional investigation may be broad and, relative to the courtroom, there are few limitations on what may be considered "relevant," a word that lawyers live with on a daily basis, certainly so in the courtroom. "Relevance" to a Congressional Committee is generally as broad as the committee wishes it to be.

There is, however, also an underside to this advantage. The broad interpretation of relevance and admissibility in a Congressional investigation affects not only the party seeking the investigation and hoping to introduce evidence to Congress, but every other aspect of the investigation as well. If the party seeking the investigation is not bound by rules of evidence, neither is anyone else.... It was largely for this reason that Louis Marshall of the AJC was opposed to pursuing the strategy of seeking Congressional investigations. He feared that the record would be filled with the stuff and nonsense of his enemies, or, as he put it, such an investigation "would enable our enemies to shovel into the record all kinds of stupid and inane charges."

In a sense, the process of a politicized search for—and we cannot avoid the use of quotation marks here—"truth," shows us that in an ironic, almost absurd way, the search for the truth represented by a Congressional investigation is overtly postmodern. There is an abandonment of any sense of objective truth, and in its place, there is an assertion of normative positions advanced by each side.... There is a role for Congressional investigations, and there are ways in which they may even work quite well. But as a search for the "truth," Congressional investigations are perhaps a very dangerous approach, and ultimately not an approach that the American Jewish community was interested in pursuing during the 1920s as a response to Henry Ford and the *Dearborn Independent*.

What about litigation, and specifically, what about libel suits? The individual libel suit is the one that is best known to us. That is the standard defamation or slander case brought by an individual asserting that he or she has had a reputation slandered and harmed by the defendant. Group libel, on behalf of an entire group or ethnic community, asserts that the group collectively has been attacked and harmed in some sense. The *Dearborn Independent* accused Aaron Sapiro, a San Francisco attorney, and certain other Jews of using farm cooperatives to seize control of American agriculture. Sapiro brought allegations against the *Dearborn Independent* for slander both on his own behalf individually and on behalf of the Jewish community collectively, or, as he described it, "myself and my race." All of those group allegations ultimately were dismissed by the trial judge, leaving only the individual claims involving Sapiro himself.

The dismissal of the group claims in Aaron Sapiro's case against the *Independent* is highly relevant for our inquiry. The Sapiro defamation case was a notorious case in its time. Each age has had its great trials that have become the focus of the general public.

Some of these, such as the Lindbergh baby kidnapping trial or the Sacco and Vanzetti trial, are still well known. Others, such as Aaron Sapiro's defamation case, are all but lost to us now. The Sapiro defamation case preoccupied the Jewish community. Even beyond the Jewish community at the time, many in the general public followed this case to see what would happen in court. Nevertheless, once the group aspects are taken out, what we are left with is a libel claim by one individual. Then only evidence that is directly and specifically relevant to that individual charge is admissible in court. The very courtroom itself seems smaller as soon as we say that. The entire context becomes smaller. Inevitably, the case becomes de-contextualized. It is about Aaron Sapiro's individual libel claim. This narrowing of the issues cannot help but lose a large element of the lifeblood of the case, which was, after all, about the anti-Semitic calumny that had underpinned the entire charge.

Also inevitably, the case concludes at best with a hollow victory. The greatest victory that Aaron Sapiro could win was a verdict based on a finding that he had not used farm cooperatives illegally to try to seize control of American agriculture. The blood libel case . . . is analogous. In the blood libel case, an acquittal is actually a conviction, a win is a kind of loss. In a much more trivial way, one is reminded of the old joke of the "defender" who tells his friend that "someone said you weren't fit to sleep with the pigs, and I defended you by saying that, 'You are too fit to sleep with the pigs.'" Or perhaps better, one is reminded of the classic leading question concerning when one "stopped beating his wife." The general leading question contains the implication of proof as to the general crime; the specific defense cannot completely remove the general taint. The acquittal in the blood libel trial runs the risk of being an acquittal only of the individual charge that the accused himself did not engage in the behavior asserted in the blood libel. So, what does the acquittal actually mean? It means that the blood libel generally is accurate, but inapplicable in this particular case. Sapiro's victory would mean that he himself did not try to seize control of American agriculture, but this would leave untouched—or worse, implicitly validated—the allegation that American Jews, albeit American Jews other than Aaron Sapiro, were engaged in such behavior. The individual acquittal becomes the group conviction.

In the individual libel case, it becomes impossible to get at the heart of the fundamental truth claims. Precisely because the truth claims and the falsity claims that are advanced and evaluated in the courtroom are necessarily limited to the individual case, these claims are de-contextualized. The individual defamation suit is not without its place and not without its purpose. Obviously, the individual suit plays an important role in restoring the individual victim's reputation. But ultimately, the individual libel suit cannot be a way of testing the truth and falsity of the group claims, or of what I have called the fundamental truth claims. Sapiro's reputation may be restored by the verdict of an individual libel suit, but the truth and falsity of the *Protocols* cannot be evaluated in this manner.

Group defamation suits would appear to provide a context for weighing the truth or falsity of claims such as those contained in the *Protocols*. But the very concept of group libel raises serious issues of free expression, concerns that were true at the time of the *Dearborn Independent* controversy and have only become more so since that time given the evolution of free speech doctrine.[3]

A full evaluation of group libel doctrine and its constitutional ramifications cannot be adequately explored here. For now, however, let me make the following cautionary

3. The Supreme Court upheld a group libel statute in *Beauharnais v. Illinois*, 343 U.S. 250, 258–63 (1952) ("We are precluded from saying that speech concededly punishable when immediately directed at individuals cannot be outlawed if directed at groups with whose position and esteem in society the affiliated individual may be inextricably involved."). Nonetheless, "it has become a commonplace of constitutional law discussions that the case is no longer good law." Lee Bollinger, *Rethinking Group Libel*, in Group Defamation and Freedom of Speech 243 (Monroe H. Freedman & Eric M. Freedman, eds., 1995). *Beauharnais* was undercut by, for example, Brandenburg v. Ohio 395 U.S. 444, 447 (1969) ("Constitutional guarantees of free speech and free press do not permit a State to forbid or proscribe advocacy of the use of force or of law violation except where such advocacy is directed to inciting or producing imminent lawless action and is likely to incite or produce such action."). *See* R.A.V. v. City of St. Paul, 505 U.S. 377, 382–392 (1992) (continuing vitality of *Beauharnais* has been questioned given *New York Times v. Sullivan* requirement of actual malice, but has not been explicitly overruled).

notes about group libel. Among its core values, free expression doctrine protects the right to have, hold, and express personal opinions and beliefs.[4] Either in a procedural context or a broader constitutional context, issues of truth and falsehood cannot help but conflate with issues of opinion and belief and thus implicate core free expression values. As a procedural matter, the question in a defamation suit, at least a suit involving a public figure, is not so much whether what the defendant said was true or false, but did the defendant know it was false or act with reckless disregard for the truth.[5] All of this focuses, and must focus, on the mind of the actor. Necessarily, this takes us away from truth and falsehood per se and to issues of opinion and belief.

If we shift from the narrow procedural questions concerning the specific elements that must be proven, to a more constitutional, theoretical context, questions of group libel and opinions concerning ethnic groups and religious groups cannot help but run squarely into questions of free expression. I am reminded of Robert Hughes's essay concerning the controversial exhibition of photographs by Robert Mapplethorpe in the early 1990s. Sometimes lawyers need non-lawyers to call our attention to profound truths concerning the legal system. Hughes observed that the questions concerning the exhibition of Mapplethorpe's photographs had become largely constitutionalized, taking the form of whether or not the exhibit of this work is constitutionally protected. The debate, therefore, is centered around whether, as a matter of constitutional right, a museum may exhibit this work, or whether a city may, as Cincinnati, Ohio did, shut such an exhibition down. When, however, we focus on these questions of constitutional limits of expression and municipal authority to regulate expression, we preclude asking a more important question: as a matter of art criticism and aesthetics, not constitutional doctrine and theory, is this art any good? Some of it may be terrific, some of it may be okay, and, one might argue, if given the opportunity, that some of it is terrible. But we cannot even have that discussion if we remain preoccupied solely with the constitutional questions.

When we are caught up in these constitutional questions, as we must be about the right to say certain things and to express certain opinions, we lose the context in which to have the vital discussion of whether the assertion under consideration is any good as history, or any good as philosophy, or good as art, or good as literature. Where do we have the context in which Stephen Bronner gets to say, "it's indisputable that the *Protocols* is wrong?" Probably not in a group libel case.

So what did happen to the *Dearborn Independent*? The case against Henry Ford and the *Dearborn Independent* was tried, in a sense, before the "court of public opinion," a terribly hackneyed expression, but, I think, very helpful here. When we think about the "court" of public opinion, it permits us to think of it as another kind of quasi-judicial proceeding. So, although I do not wish to overuse the metaphor, I am going to use it

---

4. *See* Thomas I. Emerson, The System of Freedom of Expression 3 (1980); Palko v. Connecticut, 302 U.S. 319 (1937) ("Freedom of thought and speech ... is the matrix, the indispensable condition, of nearly every other form of freedom.").

5. *See* New York Times Co. v. Sullivan, 376 U.S. 254 (1964).

because it will help us to understand the context of broad-based public debate as an example of another kind of forum, or "court," in which a form of litigation may occur.

How is a case litigated in the court of public opinion? The case of the promulgation of the *Protocols* in the *Dearborn Independent* is illustrative. The case against Ford and the *Independent* was litigated, first and foremost, by a counter-leaflet that was put together by the American-Jewish community, called "The Protocols, Bolshevism and the Jews," and addressed to the American public. This remarkable leaflet was essentially a legal brief addressed to the court of public opinion. The American-Jewish community also organized a boycott of Ford, as well as a petition of prominent Americans, including Presidents Taft and Wilson, that was highly critical of Ford.[6] The sustained effort had a negative impact on Ford economically and, of perhaps even greater significance to Ford, a negative impact on his own political ambitions. The association of the *Independent* with the *Protocols* became an embarrassment from which Ford had to disassociate himself.

We should contrast the success of this "litigation" in the court of American public opinion with the European context of the same time. In Europe of the 1920s, the *Protocols* continued to be published, and to have an extraordinary and tragic impact. Why is it that the court of public opinion worked in the 1920s in America in a way that it did not in Germany? For that matter, why did the court of public opinion to which the Anti-Defamation League presented its response to Khalid Abdul Mohammad in the United States in the 1990s work differently from either that of the United States or Europe in the 1920s? Let me address these questions with two observations about how we might think about the court of public opinion, that is, two additional questions that we must ask. The first question asks whether we are talking about a matter of broad-based group issues that will, in fact, capture the public attention. If not, we would not expect the court of public opinion to give us any satisfaction as a way of thinking about truth or falsity of claims or issues; in such instances, individual libel cases may be the only answer. It will give us partial answers, but perhaps those are the only answers we can obtain, however imperfect and de-contextualized. If, however, we have an issue that will focus public attention, then perhaps we can think about an address to the general public and to a national community, and perhaps we can think about bringing the case to the court of public opinion.

The second question is much more amorphous, but I dare say much more important as well. This question concerns the normative context of the society into which the argument is made. As my late teacher, Robert Cover, wrote, "We inhabit a nomos,"[7] an unavoidably normative social context. It is into this nomos that the argument must

---

6. Other notable signatories included Charles A. Beard, William Jennings Bryan, Robert Frost, Paul D. Cravath, W.E.B. Du Bois, Clarence Darrow, and the presidents of Princeton, Brown and Columbia Universities: John Grier Hibben, W.H.P. Faunce, and Nicholas Murray Butler, respectively.

7. Robert M. Cover, *The Supreme Court, 1982 Term—Foreword: Nomos and Narrative*, 97 HARV. L. REV. 4 (1983). ("We inhabit a *nomos*—a normative universe. We constantly create and maintain a world of right and wrong, of lawful and unlawful, of valid and void.... In this normative world, law and narrative are inseparably related. Every prescription is insistent in its demand to be located in

be placed and within the context of this nomos that the argument must be made. In the 1920s in America, the court of public opinion could be turned to, but it required a counter-leaflet, it required a kind of direct argument. In the court of public opinion in the America of the 1990s, the Anti-Defamation League operated under the assumption that the defamatory allegations themselves were sufficient to make the argument of rebuttal. Repeating the falsehood was sufficient to assert the truth.

Let me end with the story of a correspondence between Mahatma Gandhi and Martin Buber during the 1930s. Gandhi, not sympathetic to Zionism as a program, argued that the proper response to rising Nazism was passive resistance.[8] Buber reminded Gandhi, in essence, that whereas Gandhi was dealing with the British, Buber was dealing with Nazis.[9] Non-violent resistance against the British in India was an entirely different proposition from non-violent resistance against Nazis in Central and Eastern Europe, and ultimately Western Europe. When you are dealing with Nazis, you cannot act as if you are dealing with the British. And when you are dealing with the British, it is not the same thing as dealing with Americans. And Americans in the 1920s talking about Jews is not the same thing as Americans in the 1920s talking about Blacks, which is not the same thing as Americans in the 1990s talking about Jews, which is not the same thing as Americans talking about Blacks in the 1990s, either.

To understand the nature of a particular court of public opinion, to grasp its rules and contemplate a litigation strategy before it, requires that we understand the social context from which that court arises. Such an inquiry will help us in turn to understand the extent of that court's "jurisdiction," that is, the type of issues that may be brought before the court and indeed whether, in a particular time or place, the court exists at all. Only when there is a less prejudicial social climate, can the kind of truth-falsity discussions we are considering have any hope of being adjudicated in the court of public opinion, that is, adjudicated in any way that may provide the parties and the society with a full and meaningful "remedy."

---

discourse—to be supplied with history and destiny, beginning and end, explanation and purpose. And every narrative is insistent in its demand for its prescriptive point, its moral.")

8. The statement was published on November 26, 1938, in the weekly, *Harijan*. *See* Martin Buber, The Letters of Martin Buber: A life of dialogue 476 (Nahum N. Glatzer and Paul-Mendes-Flohr, eds., Richard Winston Et a., trans.) (1991)

9. *Id.* at 476–486. ("Now, do you know or do you not know, Mahatma, what a concentration camp is like and what goes on there?... Indians were despised and despicably treated in South Africa. But they were not deprived of rights, they were not outlawed, they were not hostages to a hoped-for change in the behavior of foreign powers.... Of what significance is it to point to a certain something in common when such differences are overlooked?")

B. Antisemitic Speech as Protected Speech

The National Socialist Party of America (NSPA) was a Chicago-based organization founded in 1970 by Frank Collin.[10] In early 1977, Collin announced that the NSPA would hold demonstrations in Jewish suburbs of Chicago. He distributed a flyer that read as follows:

> WE ARE COMING!
> [graphic of swastika]
>
> Many White Americans who have followed our Movement over the years have been distressed that we have confined our activities to Chicago's far south side and southern suburbs. Recent articles in the Lerner newspapers have expressed the fears of the Jewish community, especially the Jewish Defense League, that we may soon concentrate our efforts in their areas. Traditionally, we have always had the best support in Marquette Park and in suburbs like Park Forest. But a new factor has entered the picture. Namely, the Chicago Park District and the courts. They have both enforced what amounts to a complete ban of our right to free speech in public. And, since we have been so banned, we have decided to relocate in areas heavily populated by the real enemy—the Jews!
>
> An old maxim goes: "Where one finds the most, there also shall one find the most Jew-haters." We [*sic*] this basic truth in mind, we are now planning a number of street demonstrations and even speeches in Evanston, Skokie, Lincolnwood, North Shore, Morton Grove, etc. This leaflet is but the first of a number now being prepared for eventual mass-distribution. A beautiful, full-color poster ... is already in the works. The poster shows three rabbis involved in the ritual murder of an innocent Gentile boy during the hate-fest of Purim. Our propaganda will deal at large with exposé after exposé of the Talmud, the *Protocols of Zion*, and revealing quotes, many never before presented anywhere, from loose-lipped Hebes. In short, our successful opposition to the Black Invasion of Southwest Chicago will now be turned on the culprits who started it all: the Jews! ALL BECAUSE WE HAVE BEEN DENIED OUR RIGHT TO SPEAK IN MARQUETTE [*sic*] PARK! We are therefore compelled to seek new group [*sic*] for support. And we shall find it: in the Aryan American masses of the Jewized suburbs, who have had enough of political manipulation, economic thievery and forced integration!
>
> HEIL HITLER!
>
> The Nationalist Socialist Party of America[11]

---

10. Collin's father, nee Max Simon Cohn, was a German-born Jewish Holocaust survivor and his mother was Catholic. *Frank Collin*, WIKIPEDIA, https://en.wikipedia.org/wiki/Frank_Collin (last visited Dec. 17, 2024).

11. Complaint at Exhibit A, Goldstein v. Collin, No.77-4367, (Cir. Ct. of Cook Cnty. filed June 27, 1977), https://skokiehistory.omeka.net/items/show/67.

On May 1, 1977, Collin announced that the NSPA planned to hold their first demonstration in the Village of Skokie, a Chicago suburb with a large Jewish population (about 60%), including several thousand Holocaust survivors. NSPA members intended to wear brown shirted Nazi-like uniforms and swastikas.[12]

On May 2, 1977, Skokie enacted several ordinances relating to public assemblies and parades. Most notably, Ordinance 994 required would-be organizers of large assemblies (i.e., more than 50 persons) to obtain $350,000 in liability insurance. Ordinance 994 also prohibited assemblies from "portray[ing] criminality, depravity or lack of virtue in, or incite violence, hatred, abuse or hostility toward a person or group of persons by reason of reference to religious, racial, ethnic, national or regional affiliation." In the same vein, Ordinance 995 prohibited "the dissemination of any materials within the Village of Skokie which promotes and incites hatred against persons by reason of their race, national origin, or religion, and is intended to do so." Ordinance 996 provided that "no person shall engage in any march, walk or public demonstration as a member or on behalf of any political party while wearing a military-style uniform."

On June 27, 1977, the Village denied Collin and the NSPA's permit application on grounds that it violated Ordinance 996. Collin and the NSPA filed suit, attacking the constitutionality of all three ordinances. After a federal district court invalidated the ordinances as facially unconstitutional, the Village appealed to the U.S. Court of Appeals for the Seventh Circuit. In a 2–1 decision, the Seventh Circuit, per Judge Pell, affirmed the district court's decision. Judge Harlington Wood, Jr., filed a concurring opinion. Judge Sprecher dissented from the majority's ruling that the insurance requirement was unconstitutional. The Village then asked the Supreme Court to stay the Seventh Circuit's ruling, which the Court denied.[13]

Also on June 27, 1977, a class action lawsuit against Collin was brought in state court by Sol Goldstein, a Holocaust survivor who lived in Skokie, on behalf of himself and similar Skokie residents. Goldstein, who had fought with the partisans in the forests near Vilna, Lithuania, related that:

> The Nazis murdered his mother by throwing her into a well with fifty other women and covering them with gravel. He witnessed selections for forced labor and concentration camps. His wife's parents and five brothers and sisters were murdered by the Nazis.

This lawsuit, litigated by attorneys connected to the ADL, sought an injunction to restrain the NSPA "from intentionally inflicting severe emotional distress upon class

12. State courts granted the Village's request for a preliminary injunction against the demonstration, an injunction which the U.S. Supreme Court ultimately stayed. Nat'l Socialist Party of Am. v. Vill. of Skokie, 432 U.S. 43 (1977). ("Petitioners claim that the outstanding injunction will deprive them of rights protected by the First Amendment during the period of appellate review which, in the normal course, may take a year or more to complete. If a State seeks to impose a restraint of this kind, it must provide strict procedural safeguards. Absent such review, the State must instead allow a stay.") State courts subsequently reversed the injunctions. Vill. of Skokie v. NSPA, 366 N.E.2d 347 (1977) (reversing the injunction in part), 373 N.E.2d 21 (1978) (reversing the injunction in its entirety).

13. Smith v. Collin, 436 U.S. 953 (1978).

members." The complaint included an affidavit by Dr. Lawrence Z. Freedman, M.D., a professor of psychiatry at the University of Chicago.[14] His affidavit included the following:

> 2. During the period in which Adolf Hitler was the head of government in Germany, the Jews in that country and those which its armies subsequently conquered lived under a reign of terror. The Jews lived in dread of outrage or death: the total lack of security for the individual and his inability to know when he would be the target of terrorism, isolation and death.
>
> 3. Clinical studies have demonstrated that profound trauma inflicted upon individuals and groups from causes which cannot be avoided and from which there is no escape suffer from depression, withdrawal and intense anxiety—in short, terror.
>
> 4. Even when the circumstances which created these pathological states are removed, the traumatized individual remains sensitized and vulnerable to signs and symbols, as well as to the substance of their recurrences.
>
> 5. It is my opinion that exposure to such symbols as swastikas, Nazi-like uniforms and the marching of men in para-military style could inflict serious recurrences of the psychic assault previously suffered by these people. This form of psychological assault has been called by some experts "menticide." It is a significant and possibly dangerous attack on the sensibilities of a highly vulnerable population. The sense of harmful assault is greatly reinforced when such a reenactment is forced upon persons within the very community in which they live.
>
> 6. The severe emotional distress which will be suffered by survivors of the Holocaust as a result of exposure to this reenactment of behavior they witnessed in conjunction with their experiences during the Holocaust includes
>
> a. an overwhelming sense of anxiety,
>
> b. feelings of terror, shame or guilt,
>
> c. withdrawal manifested by an inner blunting of emotions, as well as withdrawal from ordinary contact with society, and alienation from family and friends,
>
> d. a paralyzing sense of helplessness and an incapacity to deal with day-to-day problems,
>
> e. an urge to respond pathologically to the reenactment experience,

---

14. Dr. Freedman (1919–2004) was an internationally recognized authority on the psychiatry of aggression, violence, crime, and terrorism and the interaction between psychiatry and law. He helped draft portions of the Model Penal Code, adopted by the American Law Institute in 1962, dealing with the relationship between mental illness and legal responsibility. *Renowned Forensic Psychiatrist Lawrence Z. Freedman, 1919–2004*, The Univ. of Chicago Med (Oct. 20, 2004), https://www.uchicagomedicine.org/forefront/news/renowned-forensic-psychiatrist-lawrence-z-freedman-1919-2004.

> f. emotional turmoil and anguish in assessing a response to the reenactment,
>
> g. experiencing of psychosomatic symptoms of physical ailments and pain suffered during the holocaust.

In the end, the march in Skokie never took place:

> On June 22, Collin cancelled the march. He explained that he had used the threat of a march in Skokie as a means to win the right to demonstrate in Chicago, a right he had won while the Skokie litigation was proceeding. On July 9, 1978, the party held an hour-long rally in Chicago at which four hundred riot-helmeted policemen protected the twenty-five Nazi demonstrators. There were seventy-two arrests and some rock and bottle throwing, but no serious violence.[15]

Collin v. Smith (*The Skokie Affair*)

578 F.2d 1197 (7th Cir. 1978)

Circuit Judge Pell delivered the opinion of the court.

Plaintiff-appellee, the National Socialist Party of America (NSPA) is a political group described by its leader, plaintiff-appellee Frank Collin, as a Nazi party. Among NSPA's more controversial and generally unacceptable beliefs are that black persons are biologically inferior to white persons, and should be expatriated to Africa as soon as possible; that American Jews have "inordinate ... political and financial power" in the world and are "in the forefront of the international Communist revolution." NSPA members affect a uniform reminiscent of those worn by members of the German Nazi Party during the Third Reich,[16] and display a swastika thereon and on a red, white, and black flag they frequently carry ...

[Ordinance 994] is a comprehensive permit system for all parades or public assemblies of more than 50 persons. It requires permit applicants to obtain $300,000 in public liability insurance and $50,000 in property damage insurance.

The insurance requirements of 994 were invalidated [by the district court] as insuperable obstacles to free speech in Skokie, and [a subsection of 994] when used to deny permits on the basis of anticipated violations of 995 or 996) were adjudged impermissible prior restraints.

On its appeal, the Village concedes the invalidity of the insurance requirements as applied to these plaintiffs and of the uniform prohibition of 996.

---

15. Stone et al., The First Amendment 67 (7th ed. 2024).

16. In Collin's words:

We wear brown shirts with a dark brown tie, a swastika pin on the tie, a leather shoulder strap, a black belt with buckle, dark brown trousers, black engineer boots, and either a steel helmet or a cloth cap, depending on the situation, plus a swastika arm band on the left arm and an American flag patch on the right arm.

I.

The conflict underlying this litigation has commanded substantial public attention, and engendered considerable and understandable emotion. We would hopefully surprise no one by confessing personal views that NSPA's beliefs and goals are repugnant to the core values held generally by residents of this country, and, indeed, to much of what we cherish in civilization. As judges sworn to defend the Constitution, however, we cannot decide this or any case on that basis. Ideological tyranny, no matter how worthy its motivation, is forbidden as much to appointed judges as to elected legislators.

The record in this case contains the testimony of a survivor of the Nazi holocaust in Europe. Shortly before oral argument in this case, a lengthy and highly publicized citizenship revocation trial of an alleged Nazi war criminal was held in a federal court in Chicago,[17] and in the week immediately after argument here, a four-part "docudrama" on the holocaust was nationally televised and widely observed.[18] We cannot then be unmindful of the horrors associated with the Nazi regime of the Third Reich, with which to some real and apparently intentional degree appellees associate themselves.[19] Nor does the record allow us to ignore the certainty that appellees know full well that, in light of their views and the historical associations they would bring with them to Skokie, many people would find their demonstration extremely mentally and emotionally disturbing, or the suspicion that such a result may be relished by appellees.

But our task here is to decide whether the First Amendment protects the activity in which appellees wish to engage, not to render moral judgment on their views or tactics. No authorities need be cited to establish the proposition, which the Village does not dispute, that First Amendment rights are truly precious and fundamental to our national life. Nor is this truth without relevance to the saddening historical images this case inevitably arouses. It is, after all, in part the fact that our constitutional system protects minorities unpopular at a particular time or place from governmental harassment and intimidation, that distinguishes life in this country from life under the Third Reich....

Before undertaking specific analysis of the clash between the Village ordinances and appellees' desires to demonstrate in Skokie, it will be helpful to establish some general

17. Editor's note: *See* "John Demjanjuk: Prosecution of a Nazi Collaborator," Holocaust Encyc., https://encyclopedia.ushmm.org/content/en/article/john-demjanjuk-prosecution-of-a-nazi-collaborator (last visited Dec. 17, 2024); *see also* Robert D. McFadden, *John Demjanjuk, 91, Dogged by Charges of Atrocities as Nazi Camp Guard, Dies*, N.Y. Times (Mar. 17, 2012), https://www.nytimes.com/2012/03/18/world/europe/john-demjanjuk-nazi-guard-dies-at-91.html.

18. Editor's note: *Holocaust Miniseries*, Wikipedia, https://en.wikipedia.org/wiki/Holocaust_(miniseries)# (last visited Dec. 17, 2024); *see also* Toby Axelrod, *40 Years Ago, an American Miniseries Changed the Way Germans Thought about Their History. Now 'Holocaust' is Being Shown There Again.*, Jewish Telegraphic Agency (Jan. 23, 2019, 12:38 PM), https://www.jta.org/2019/01/23/global/40-years-later-the-holocaust-miniseries-returns-to-germany.

19. Collin testified, however, that NSPA did not advocate genocide as a solution to the "Jewish problem," but was content to expose to the American people what his group conceived that problem to be.

principles of pertinence to the decision required of us. Putting to one side for the moment the question of whether the content of appellees' views and symbols makes a constitutional difference here, we find we are unable to deny that the activities in which the appellees wish to engage are within the ambit of the First Amendment.

The activities in which the appellees wish to engage are within the ambit of the First Amendment....

Indeed, an orderly and peaceful demonstration, with placards, in the vicinity of a seat of government, is "an exercise of (the) basic constitutional rights of (speech, assembly, and petition) in their most pristine and classic form."

No doubt, the Nazi demonstration could be subjected to reasonable regulation of its time, place, and manner. Although much of the permit system of 994 is of that nature, the provisions attacked here are not. No objection is raised by the Village, in ordinances or in their proofs and arguments in this case, to the suggested time, place, or manner of the demonstration, except the general assertion that in the place of Skokie, in these times, *given the content of appellees' views and symbols*, the demonstration and its symbols and speech should be prohibited.[20] Because the ordinances turn on the content of the demonstration, they are necessarily not time, place, or manner regulations.

Legislating against the content of First Amendment activity, however, launches the government on a slippery and precarious path:

> Above all else, the First Amendment means that government has no power to restrict expression because of its message, its ideas, its subject matter, or its content. To permit the continued building of our politics and culture, and to assure self-fulfillment for each individual, our people are guaranteed the right to express any thought, free from government censorship. The essence of this forbidden censorship is content control. Any restriction on expressive activity because of its content would completely undercut the "profound national commitment to the principle that debate on public issues should be uninhibited, robust, and wide-open."

This is not to say, of course, that content legislation is *per se* invalid. [There are] the established exceptions to such a rule, namely obscenity, fighting words, and, as limited by constitutional requirements, libel. Likewise, in very narrow circumstances, a government may proscribe content on the basis of imminent danger of a grave substantive evil. But analysis of content restrictions must begin with a healthy respect for the truth that they are the most direct threat to the vitality of First Amendment rights.

20. Thus these are not appropriately narrow ordinances, criminalizing, e.g., the invasion of residential neighborhoods by sound trucks blaring racial epithets or other messages, or the menacing by uniformed bullies of a survivor of the holocaust, or anyone else, on the street, or at his or her residence, and we decline to treat them viscerally as if such were their scope. Logically, we consider only whether these ordinances can prohibit the type of conduct and content this case involves.

II.

We first consider ordinance 995, prohibiting the dissemination of materials which would promote hatred towards persons on the basis of their heritage. The Village would apparently apply this provision to NSPA's display of swastikas, their uniforms, and, perhaps, to the content of their placards.

The ordinance cannot be sustained on the basis of some of the more obvious exceptions to the rule against content control. While some would no doubt be willing to label appellees' views and symbols obscene, the constitutional rule that obscenity is unprotected applies only to material with erotic content. Furthermore, although the Village introduced evidence in the district court tending to prove that some individuals, at least, might have difficulty restraining their reactions to the Nazi demonstration, the Village tells us that it does not rely on a fear of responsive violence to justify the ordinance, and does not even suggest that there will be any physical violence if the march is held.[21] This confession takes this case out of the scope of *Brandenburg v. Ohio*. The Village does not argue otherwise.

The concession also eliminates any argument based on the fighting words doctrine of *Chaplinsky v. New Hampshire* (1942). The Court in *Chaplinsky* affirmed a conviction under a statute that, as authoritatively construed, applied only to words with a direct tendency to cause violence by the persons to whom, individually, the words were addressed. A conviction for less than words that at least tend to incite an immediate breach of the peace cannot be justified under *Chaplinsky*.[22] . . .

Four basic arguments are advanced by the Village to justify the content restrictions of 995. First, it is said that the content criminalized by 995 is "totally lacking in social content," and that it consists of "false statements of fact" in which there is "no constitutional value." We disagree that, if applied to the proposed demonstration, the ordinance can be said to be limited to "statements of fact," false or otherwise. No handbills are to be distributed; no speeches are planned. To the degree that the symbols in question can be said to assert anything specific, it must be the Nazi ideology, which cannot be treated as a mere false "fact."

We may agree with the district court that:

> If any philosophy should be regarded as completely unacceptable to civilized society, that of plaintiffs, who, while disavowing on the witness stand any advocacy of genocide, have nevertheless deliberately identified themselves with a regime whose record of brutality and barbarism is unmatched in modern history, would be a good place to start.

But there can be no legitimate start down such a road.

---

21. The Village understandably offers no guarantee that there will not be violence, but commendably advises us that if a final order in this case requires it to permit the march, it will make every effort to protect the demonstrators (and the Village) from responsive violence.

22. Because the ordinance does not even refer to such a breach, the ordinance would inevitably fall, if *Chaplinsky* were its basis, because of overbreadth and vagueness.

> Under the First Amendment there is no such thing as a false idea. However pernicious an opinion may seem, we depend for its correction not on the conscience of judges and juries but on the competition of other ideas.

In the words of Justice Jackson, "every person must be his own watchman for truth, because the forefathers did not trust any government to separate the true from the false for us." The asserted falseness of Nazi dogma, and, indeed, its general repudiation, simply do not justify its suppression.

The Village's second argument, and the one on which principal reliance is placed, centers on *Beauharnais v. Illinois* (1952). There a conviction was upheld under a statute prohibiting, in language substantially (and perhaps not unintentionally) similar[23] to that used in the ordinance here, the dissemination of materials promoting racial or religious hatred. The closely divided Court stated that the criminal punishment of libel of an *individual* raised no constitutional problems, relying on *Chaplinsky v. New Hampshire* (1942). That being so, the Court reasoned that the state could constitutionally extend the prohibition to utterances aimed at groups.

In our opinion *Beauharnais* does not support ordinance 995, for two independent reasons. First, the rationale of that decision turns quite plainly on the strong tendency of the prohibited utterances to cause violence and disorder.... The [Supreme] Court also pointed out that the tendency to induce breach of the peace was the traditional justification for the criminal libel laws which had always been thought to be immune from the First Amendment. After stating the issue (whether Illinois could extend criminal libel to groups) the Court turned to Illinois' history of racial strife "and its frequent obligato of extreme racial and religious propaganda," and concluded that the Illinois legislature could reasonably connect the strife and the propaganda and criminalize the latter to prevent the former.

The danger in these times from the coercive activities of those who in the delusion of racial or religious conceit *would incite violence and breaches of the peace* in order to deprive others of their equal right to the exercise of their liberties, is emphasized by events familiar to all. These and other transgressions of (the limits to First Amendment rights) the States appropriately may punish.

It may be questioned whether the *tendency to induce violence* approach sanctioned implicitly in *Beauharnais* would pass constitutional muster today. Assuming that it would, however, it does not support ordinance 995, because the Village ... does not assert appellees' possible violence, an audience's possible responsive violence, or possible violence against third parties by those incited by appellees, as justifications for 995. Ordinance 995 would apparently be applied in the absence of any such threat. The rationale of *Beauharnais*, then, simply does not apply here.

The Village asserts that *Beauharnais* implicitly sanctions prohibiting the use of First Amendment rights to invoke racial or religious hatred *even without reference to fears*

---

23. The actual language in *Beauharnais* invoked specifically the depiction of criminality, depravity, unchastity, or lack of virtue in target groups.

of violence. In the light of our discussion of *Beauharnais* premises, we do not find the case susceptible of this interpretation. Even if it were, however, we agree with the district court that decisions in the quarter-century since *Beauharnais* have abrogated the *Chaplinsky* dictum, made one of the premises of *Beauharnais*, that the punishment of libel "has never been thought to raise any Constitutional problem." *New York Times Co. v. Sullivan*, (1964) [is] indisputable evidence that libel does indeed now raise serious and knotty First Amendment problems, sufficient as a matter of constitutional law to require the substantial rewriting of both criminal and civil state libel laws.

[We doubt] that *Beauharnais* remains good law at all after the constitutional libel cases. We agree at least this far: If 995 is to be sustained, it must be done on the basis of the Village's interest asserted, and the conduct to which 995 applies, not on the basis of blind obeisance to uncertain implications from an opinion issued years before the Supreme Court itself rewrote the rules....

The Village's fourth argument is that the Nazi march, involving as it does the display of uniforms and swastikas, will create a substantive evil that it has a right to prohibit: the infliction of psychic trauma on resident Holocaust survivors and other Jewish residents.[24] The Village points out that Illinois recognizes the "new tort" of intentional infliction of severe emotional distress, the coverage of which may well include personally directed racial slurs. Assuming that specific individuals could proceed in tort under this theory to recover damages provably occasioned by the proposed march, and that a First Amendment defense would not bar the action,[25] it is nonetheless quite a different matter to criminalize protected First Amendment conduct in anticipation of such results.

It would be grossly insensitive to deny, as we do not, that the proposed demonstration would seriously disturb, emotionally and mentally, at least some, and probably many of the Village's residents. The problem with engrafting an exception on the First Amendment for such situations is that they are indistinguishable in principle from speech that "invite(s) dispute ... induces a condition of unrest, creates dissatisfaction with conditions as they are, or even stirs people to anger." Yet these are among the "high purposes" of the First Amendment. It is perfectly clear that a state may not "make criminal the peaceful expression of unpopular views." Likewise, "mere public intolerance or animosity cannot be the basis for abridgement of these constitutional freedoms." Where, as here, a crime is made of a silent march, attended only by symbols and not by extrinsic conduct offensive in itself:

> Any shock effect ... must be attributed to the content of the ideas expressed. It is firmly settled that under our Constitution the public expression of ideas may

---

24. Ironically the witnessing of the television show "Holocaust" might seem to have the same trauma producing possibilities. The extent to which the residents of Skokie may have willingly exposed themselves to the painful reminders of this production might have been pertinent to the psychic trauma issue if the airing had occurred prior to the district court evidentiary hearing.

25. These questions, of course, are not before us, and we intimate no views thereon, one way or the other.

not be prohibited merely because the ideas are themselves offensive to some of their hearers.

It is said that the proposed march is not speech, or even "speech plus," but rather an invasion, intensely menacing no matter how peacefully conducted. The Village's expert psychiatric witness, in fact, testified that the effect of the march would be much the same regardless of whether uniforms and swastikas were displayed, due to the intrusion of self-proclaimed Nazis into what he characterized as predominately Jewish "turf." There is room under the First Amendment for the government to protect targeted listeners from offensive speech, but only when the speaker intrudes on the privacy of the home, or a captive audience cannot practically avoid exposure. The Supreme Court has consistently stressed that "we are often 'captives' outside the sanctuary of the home and subject to objectionable speech." The ability of government, consonant with the Constitution, to shut off discourse solely to protect others from hearing it is, in other words, dependent upon a showing that substantial privacy interests are being invaded in an essentially intolerable manner. *Any broader view of this authority would effectively empower a majority to silence dissidents simply as a matter of personal predilections.*

This case does not involve intrusion into people's homes. There need be no captive audience, as Village residents may, if they wish, simply avoid the Village Hall for thirty minutes on a Sunday afternoon,[26] which no doubt would be their normal course of conduct on a day when the Village Hall was not open in the regular course of business. Absent such intrusion or captivity, there is no justifiable substantial privacy interest to save 995 from constitutional infirmity, when it attempts, by fiat, to declare the entire Village, at all times, a privacy zone that may be sanitized from the offensiveness of Nazi ideology and symbols.

We conclude that 995 may not be applied to criminalize the conduct of the proposed demonstration. Because it is susceptible to such an application, we also conclude that it suffers from substantial overbreadth, even if some of the purposes 995 is said to serve might constitutionally be protectible by an appropriate and narrower ordinance. The latter conclusion is also supported by the fact that the ordinance could conceivably be applied to criminalize dissemination of *The Merchant of Venice* or a vigorous discussion of the merits of reverse racial discrimination in Skokie. Although there is reason to think, as the district court concluded, that the ordinance is fatally vague as well, because it turns in part on subjective reactions to prohibited conduct, we do not deem it necessary to rest our decision on that ground.

IV.

As we have indicated, the Village has conceded that 996 is unconstitutional. We agree, and affirm the district court in this respect as well.

---

26. We appreciate that, as the Village's expert psychiatrist testified, avoidance might also be psychologically unsatisfying to some of the Village's residents. Nonetheless, the choice will be theirs, and it meaningfully undercuts the invasion of privacy justification for 995.

The Village has also conceded that the insurance requirements of 994 cannot be applied to appellees' proposed demonstration

Appellees proved in the district court that they could not obtain the requisite insurance, and also that, in the opinion of their expert, insurance would typically be unavailable to those very controversial groups as to which the Village's interest in having insurance would presumably be the greatest. This expert testimony comports with the teachings of common sense

Judge Sprecher would uphold the "facially neutral" insurance requirement. It is true that the requirement does not turn on the content of a proposed demonstration, except in the sense that controversial groups will likely be unable to obtain insurance, as here. (That several less controversial groups were able to do so, of course, proves nothing.) But it is most assuredly not facially neutral towards First Amendment activity....

Even if the *O'Brien*'s test[27] could somehow be applied here, the use of the insurance requirement to prohibit the proposed demonstration would fail. First, it is difficult, following even a casual examination of the chronological exegesis of the ordinances, particularly in light of the religious complexion of the Village, to think other than that the governmental interest here was directly related to the suppression of these plaintiffs' First Amendment rights. Second, the governmental interest advanced by the dissent could more narrowly be served by criminalizing, as has no doubt already been done, the conduct (by appellees or others) directly producing any feared injury to persons or property and by marshalling local, county, and state police to prevent violations. Instead, the Village has flatly prohibited First Amendment activity, not itself directly productive of the feared injury, by those too controversial to obtain commercial insurance....

The preparation and issuance of this opinion has not been an easy task, or one which we have relished. Recognizing the implication that often seems to follow overprotestation, we nevertheless feel compelled once again to express our repugnance at the doctrines which the appellees desire to profess publicly. Indeed, it is a source of extreme regret that after several thousand years of attempting to strengthen the often thin coating of civilization with which humankind has attempted to hide brutal animal-like instincts, there would still be those who would resort to hatred and vilification of fellow human beings because of their racial background or their religious beliefs, or for that matter, because of any reason at all.

Retaining meaning in civil rights, particularly those many of the founding fathers believed sufficiently important as to delay the approval of the Constitution until they

27. Editor's note: In *United States v. O'Brien*, 391 U.S. 367 (1968), the Supreme Court created a four-part test (a.k.a., the "O'Brien test") for determining whether expressive conduct or symbolic speech merits First Amendment protection:

> We think it clear that a government regulation is sufficiently justified if it is within the constitutional power of the Government; if it furthers an important or substantial governmental interest; if the governmental interest is unrelated to the suppression of free expression; and if the incidental restriction on alleged First Amendment freedoms is no greater than is essential to the furtherance of that interest.

Id. at 377.

could be included in the Bill of Rights, seldom seems to be accomplished by the easy cases, however, and it was not so here.

Although we would have thought it unnecessary to say so, it apparently deserves emphasis in the light of the dissent's reference to this court apologizing as to the result, that our regret at the use appellees plan to make of their rights is not in any sense an apology for upholding the First Amendment. The result we have reached is dictated by the fundamental proposition that if these civil rights are to remain vital for all, they must protect not only those society deems acceptable, but also those whose ideas it quite justifiably rejects and despises.

Circuit Judge Harlington Wood, Jr., concurring.

Agreeing with Judge Pell's analysis of the law, I join in affirming the judgment of the district court and add only a few footnotes.

I would in addition adopt the finding of the district court that Ordinances 995 and 996 are unconstitutionally vague and overbroad as criminal statutes.

Since there is ample warning of the proposed event, this situation is not equivalent to the sudden and unfounded cry of "fire" in a crowded and unsuspecting theatre to which it is sometimes analogized.

Recognition of the full scope of freedom of speech does not compel anyone to listen, or if listening to believe.

It may also be well to remember that often "words die away, and flow off like water leaving no taste, no color, no smell, not a trace." Any exception, however, to the First Amendment which we might be tempted to fashion for these particular persuasive circumstances would not "die away." It would remain a dangerous and unmanageable precedent in our free and open society.

Circuit Judge Sprecher, dissenting in part.

The basic situation in this case—the efforts of avowed and uniformed Hitlerian Nazis to demonstrate without municipal regulations in the streets of a predominantly Jewish village housing some 7,000 Jewish survivors of World War II and their families—conjures up a unique amalgam of complex First Amendment concepts such as prior restraint, group libel, fighting words and hostile audiences, incitement to riot, and shouting "fire" in a crowded theater. Seldom before has a federal court been faced with a situation raising such powerful cross-pressures as have been created in this case. For instance, the fact that it now seems to be instilled in Jewish culture to confront threatened oppression with active resistance and aggressive retaliation differentiates this case factually from *Terminiello v. Chicago* (1949).

The prophetic words of Mr. Justice Holmes ... become more pertinent with the passage of time:

> Great cases like hard cases make bad law. For great cases are called great, not by reason of their real importance in shaping the law of the future, but because of some accident of immediate overwhelming interest which appeals to the

> feelings and distorts the judgment. These immediate interests exercise a kind of hydraulic pressure....

It is, therefore, with some hesitancy and much concern that I approach the instant case. My wariness is enhanced by the fact that each court dealing with these precise problems (the Illinois Supreme Court, the District Court and this Court) feels the need to apologize for its result.

II.

[Judge Sprecher argues that the insurance requirement for public assemblies in the Village of Skokie is a content-neutral reasonable regulation of the time, place, and manner of protected speech, designed to further significant governmental interests in protecting property and ensuring public safety.]

III.

Up to this point, the analysis assumed the validity of two premises. The first is that the activities which plaintiffs proposed to engage in are protected by the First Amendment. The second is that it is impermissible for a government to consider in any way the content of the activities or speech when regulating the time, place or manner in which that activity takes place. A closer examination of each of these assumptions fortifies the conclusion that the insurance ordinance is constitutional not only on its face, but also as applied to the facts of this case.

We must first examine whether plaintiffs' proposed conduct falls within the scope of the First Amendment. We are dealing with a proposed march through a predominantly Jewish community. The plaintiffs would wear Nazi-style uniforms and swastika armbands or emblems and carry written signs. No speeches were to be made.[28] Plaintiffs' handbills had been distributed in the Village and a number of Skokie residents with Jewish surnames had received "offensive and threatening telephone calls." The portent of this action and the proposed march could not be lost on anyone familiar with the methods of Hitler's Nazis in Germany.[29]

---

28. We note that, even assuming that plaintiffs' activities can be found to fall in a class protected by the First Amendment, such activity is not "pure speech" and is thereby properly subject to more concern and regulation by municipalities. [Editor's note: A proper balancing of the public interest with the expression of ideas in this manner therefore must take place.].

29. Hitler summed up the strategy of the mass demonstration as used by both Fascism and Communism: "We should not work in secret conventicles, but in mighty mass demonstrations, and it is not by dagger and poison or pistol that the road can be cleared for the movement but By the *conquest of the streets*. We must teach (them) that the future *master of the streets* is National Socialism, just as it will some day be the master of the state." [*Mein Kampf.*] First laughed at as an extravagant figure of speech, the battle for the streets became a tragic reality when an organized *Sturmabteilung* began to give practical effect to its slogan that "possession of the streets is the key to power in the state."

The present obstacle to mastery of the streets by either radical or reactionary mob movements is not the opposing minority. It is the authority of local governments which represent the free choice of democratic and law-abiding elements, of all shades of opinion, but who, whatever their differences, submit them to free elections which register the results of their free discussion. The fascist and communist groups, on the contrary, resort to these terror tactics to confuse, bully and discredit those freely chosen governments. Violent and noisy shows of strength discourage participation of moderates in

Under these circumstances, the appearance of plaintiffs' group in Skokie may be so extremely offensive and of such little social utility as to be beyond the protection of the First Amendment.[30] In this sense the present case does not differ greatly from *Chaplinsky v. New Hampshire* (1942), where the Court upheld the conviction of a Jehovah's Witness for calling complainant a "God damned racketeer" and "a damned fascist." The analysis the Court used there applies with equal force here to the activities proposed by plaintiffs:

> Allowing the broadest scope to the language and purpose of the Fourteenth Amendment, it is well understood that the right of free speech is not absolute at all times and under all circumstances. [*Chaplinsky*]

Another basis on which to conclude that plaintiffs' proposed conduct falls outside the protection of the First Amendment is that under the circumstances it constitutes a pernicious form of group libel. In *Beauharnais v. Illinois* (1952), the Court upheld a statute which is strikingly similar to those attacked here....

Nor do we need to back away from this analysis merely because the Supreme Court has substantially modified the law of libel insofar as it relates to public officials or public figures as opposed to the minor backtracking concerning libel of private individuals. Moreover, although Beauharnais is said to have been scarcely noted since 1952, neither has it been overruled.

It appears to me that plaintiffs' proposed activities, under the circumstances presented here, might reasonably be viewed as not within the area of constitutionally protected activity. At least the question seems close enough to warrant serious concern and analysis within the factual situation presented. Plaintiffs' proposed actions in this case arguably "are no essential part of any exposition of ideas, and are of such slight social value as a step to truth that any benefit that may be derived from them is clearly outweighed by the social interest in order and morality." *Chaplinsky*. This conclusion supports a finding at the very least of the validity of the challenged insurance ordinance.

---

discussions so fraught with violence, and real discussion dries up and disappears. And people lose faith in the democratic process when they see public authority flouted and impotent and begin to think the time has come when they must choose sides in a false and terrible dilemma such as ... "Christian Nationalism or World Communism—Which?"

This drive by totalitarian groups to undermine the prestige and effectiveness of local democratic governments is advanced whenever either of them can win from this Court a ruling which paralyzes the power of these officials. This is such a case.

30. It is not clear from Supreme Court opinions exactly what it means to say that such activity is "not protected." On the one hand, it seems to mean that this speech is not treated as being for First Amendment purposes and, therefore, First Amendment principles do not apply. Other cases imply that, although First Amendment principles apply to such speech initially, the fact that the activity falls within certain designated categories (e.g., libel, fighting words) means that there exists a sufficient basis for regulating that speech. Regardless of what it means to say that some activity is "not protected" by the First Amendment, it is clear that the restrictions on government regulation in such circumstances is less stringent.

IV.

Concerning the assumption that the content of speech or conduct is an impermissible consideration when regulation of those activities are proposed, we note that regulation of First Amendment activities never has been and never can be "content blind." As early as 1919, the Supreme Court in *Schenck v. United States* (1919) declared through Mr. Justice Holmes:

> The question in every case is whether the words used are used in such circumstances and are of such a nature as to create a clear and present danger that they will bring about the substantive evils that Congress has a right to prevent. It is a question of proximity and degree.

There is no dispute that speech may not be suppressed merely because it offends its listeners. At some point, however, considerations of a neutral desire to maintain the public peace and general welfare come into play in determining whether activities should be allowed. Where the activity is, as here, by its nature and by the circumstances, a threat to a reasonable attempt to maintain the public order, it cannot claim to go unregulated under the auspices that content may not properly be considered.

Such considerations apply with added force where the municipality does not seek to prevent the conduct proposed, but simply proposes to protect against the consequences of such activity. The insurance ordinance at issue here merely attempts to provide this protection. The Village should not be required to ignore the dangers that are presented by plaintiffs' conduct. We noted at the outset that the Supreme Court has recently recognized that "even within the area of protected speech, a difference in content may require a different governmental response. In my opinion, the response of the Village of Skokie in enacting the insurance ordinance was constitutionally permissible.

For the reasons discussed above, I would reverse the decision of the district court declaring the insurance requirement of the ordinance unconstitutional.

Was *Collin v. Smith* a Hard Case?

1. *A hard case?* Did the Seventh Circuit decide this case correctly? Is this a hard case? If so, is it a hard case because: (1) the equities of the situation tempt courts to stretch or even disregard an otherwise uncontested principle of law; or (2) due to the contested nature of the applicable law, the case presents courts with the opportunity to make new and better law?

2. *Slippery slopes.* Judge Pell writes, "It is, after all, in part the fact that our constitutional system protects minorities unpopular at a particular time or place from governmental harassment and intimidation, that distinguishes life in this country from life under the Third Reich." Judge Pell argues that any content-based restriction on speech "launches the government on a slippery and precarious path." Can a liberal democracy enact certain forms of hate speech regulation without slouching towards Germany? Had the Weimar Republic been less tolerant of the Nazis, might the Third Reich and the Holocaust have been averted? Judge Pell compares a law prohibiting the

march with a law criminalizing dissemination of *The Merchant of Venice.* Can you draw a principled distinction between the two, one that might permit the former without compelling the latter?

The First Amendment Protects Hate Speech

1. *Why protect speech?* Why should the government be barred from regulating speech based on its content? Consider Dean Chemerinsky's survey of four theories for protecting freedom of speech as a fundamental right:

(a) *Self-governance.* To further self-governance, most notably by protecting the ability of citizens to debate public issues, criticize public officials, and so forth. The Supreme Court has described protection of such speech—also known as "political speech"—as "the central meaning of the First Amendment." *New York Times v. Sullivan.*

(b) *Discovering the truth.* To aid the discovery of truth via "the marketplace of ideas," following Justice Oliver Wendell Holmes, Jr.'s claim that "the best test of truth is the power of the thought to get itself accepted in the competition of the market...."[31]

(c) *Advancing autonomy.* This rationale defends the protection of speech as "an essential aspect of personhood and autonomy."[32] Some people engage in speech acts as a means of self-expression, separate from whether they expect their speech to aid self-governance or further the search for truth.

(d) *Promoting tolerance.*[33] Where the government protects unpopular or distasteful speech, it requires listeners to exercise self-restraint—a liberal virtue—which may, in turn, cultivate citizens' capacity for tolerance in other contexts.

Dean Chemerinsky further explains that these theories "are not mutually exclusive, although the choice of a theory can influence views on many specific issues."[34] How does protecting the neo-Nazis' speech enable self-governance, advance the pursuit of truth, facilitate self-fulfillment, and/or cultivate tolerance?

2. *Brandeis's* Whitney *concurrence.* Re-read Justice Brandeis's concurring opinion in *Whitney v. California* (1927) in Chapter 4, where he explains the value of protecting speech. Which rationales for such protection does Brandeis invoke and how?

3. *Content-based regulation of speech.* Judge Pell describes content-based restrictions on speech as "the most direct threat to the vitality of First Amendment rights," echoing the foundational principle that, with limited exceptions, "the First Amendment means that government has no power to restrict expression because of its message, its ideas,

31. Abrams v. United States, 250 U.S. 616, 630 (1919) (Holmes, J., dissenting).

32. Erwin Chemerinsky, The First Amendment 8 (3d ed. 2024).

33. *Id.* at 5.

34. *Id.* at 5–9.

its subject matter, or its content."[35] The limited exceptions apply to "low-value speech" deemed not to meaningfully advance what Judge Pell calls the "'high purposes' of the First Amendment." The idea that "low value" speech receives little to no First Amendment protection originates in *Chaplinsky v. New Hampshire* (1942):

> It is well understood that the right of free speech is not absolute at all times and under all circumstances. There are certain well-defined and narrowly limited classes of speech, the prevention and punishment of which have never been thought to raise any Constitutional problem. These include the lewd and obscene, the profane, the libelous, and the insulting or 'fighting' words—those which [1] *by their very utterance inflict injury* or [2] *tend to incite an immediate breach of the peace.* It has been well observed that such utterances are no essential part of any exposition of ideas, and are of such slight social value as a step to truth that any benefit that may be derived from them is clearly outweighed by the social interest in order and morality.[36]

4. *Very utterance.* In Professor Rodney A. Smolla's view, the above passage articulates two regulatory approaches to speech. The first is based on whether the speech is potentially harmful, for example, because it is likely to incite imminent lawless action. The second is based on whether the speech is inherently or intrinsically harmful, including to society's "moral fabric." In Smolla's view, this approach suggests that:

> It may be appropriate for society to prohibit and punish certain expression because the expression itself is inherently harmful. The words themselves are "bullets" that inflict injury. No extraneous proof of injury, no additional assessment of causation or imminence or likelihood of damage is required to justify laws that penalize their utterance. Doctrinal formulations such as "clear and present danger" or "directed to the incitement of imminent lawless action and likely to produce such action" or "strict scrutiny" are essentially irrelevant under this approach, for there is no need to connect the offending speech to any external harm. The words by their utterance are deemed to inflict injury.[37]

These two approaches, argues Smolla, reflect a "competing vision of the national identity as a 'marketplace' or a 'moral place.'"[38] How does the court justify overlooking *Chaplinsky*'s "very utterance" prong? How could it?

5. Ortenberg v. Plamondon *revisited.* If Plamondon was prosecuted for his speech, would it be unprotected as fighting words tending to incite an immediate breach of the peace? Would his words be a good test case for denying protection for words which by their very utterance inflict injury?

---

35. Police Dept. of Chicago v. Mosley, 408 U.S. 92, 95 (1972).

36. Chaplinsky v State of New Hampshire, 315 U.S. 568, 571–72 (1942).

37. Rodney A. Smolla, *Words "Which by Their Very Utterance Inflict Injury": The Evolving Treatment of Inherently Dangerous Speech in Free Speech Law and Theory*, 36 PEPP. L. REV. 317, 357 (2009).

38. *Id.* at 360.

Hate Speech and Group Protection

1. *Hate speech.* "Hate speech" may be defined as "speech whose sole purpose is to demean people on the basis of race, ethnicity, gender, religion, age, disability, or some other similar ground, especially when the communication is likely to provoke violence."[39] Can antisemitic expression (i.e., anti-Jewish hate speech) be meaningfully distinguished from political discourse that merely "invites dispute" or "stirs people to anger"? Can it be constitutionally distinguished?

2. Beauharnais v. Illinois *(1952). Beauharnais* involved an Illinois group-libel-like law that criminalized publications that portrayed "depravity, criminality, unchastity, or lack of virtue of a class of citizens, of any race, color, creed or religion" which exposes them "to contempt, derision, or obloquy *or* which is productive of breach of the peace or riots."[40] The Supreme Court, per Justice Frankfurter, ruled that the law was valid. Frankfurter analogized this criminalized speech to ordinary libel.

> If an utterance directed at an individual may be the object of criminal sanctions, we cannot deny to a State power to punish the same utterance directed at a defined group, unless we can say that this is a willful and purposeless restriction unrelated to the peace and well-being of the State.
>
> Illinois did not have to look beyond her own borders or await the tragic experience of the last three decades to conclude that willful purveyors of falsehood concerning racial and religious groups promote strife and tend powerfully to obstruct the manifold adjustments required for free, ordered life in a metropolitan, polyglot community....

Justice Frankfurter also argued that the Court should defer to the Illinois legislature's determination as to the best means to a given end.

> It is not within our competence to confirm or deny claims of social scientists as to the dependence of the individual on the position of his racial or religious group in the community. It would, however, be arrant dogmatism, quite outside the scope of our authority in passing on the powers of a State, for us to deny that the Illinois legislature may warrantably believe that a man's job and

---

39. *Speech*, BLACK'S LAW DICTIONARY (12th ed. 2024). Oxford English Dictionary (OED) defines "hate speech" as "speech (or sometimes written material) inciting ... hatred or intolerance ... especially towards a particular social group on the basis of ethnicity, religious beliefs, sexuality, etc." *Hate Speech*, OXFORD ENG. DICTIONARY, https://doi.org/10.1093/OED/2283136643 (last visited Mar. 2024). OED also defines a "hate speech" in the singular sense, i.e., as "a speech or address inciting hatred or intolerance, esp. towards a particular social group on the basis of ethnicity, religious beliefs, sexuality, etc." *Id.* OED reports the term first used in the singular sense ("*a* hate speech") to describe Hitler's September 26, 1938 speech demanding that Czechoslovakia hand over the Sudetenland to Germany: "Hitler's single hate speech did more to alienate the world from Germany than anything he has done." *Id.* Hitler's hate speech apparently did little to alienate British Prime Minister Neville Chamberlain and French Prime Minister Édouard Daladier, both of whom had already agreed to Hitler's demand to occupy the Sudetenland. *Sudetenland*, WIKIPEDIA, https://en.wikipedia.org/wiki/Sudetenland (last visited Dec. 17, 2024).

40. Beauharnais v. Ill., 343 U.S. 250, 251 (1952) (emphasis added).

> his educational opportunities and the dignity accorded him may depend as much on the reputation of the racial and religious group to which he willy-nilly belongs, as on his own merits.
>
> We are precluded from saying that speech concededly punishable when immediately directed at individuals cannot be outlawed if directed at groups with whose position and esteem in society the affiliated individual may be inextricably involved.

3. The Village modeled its ordinance after the one in *Beauharnais* and cited the decision as authority for its ordinances' validity. On what basis did Judge Pell reject the Village's reliance on *Beauharnais*?

4. *No hate speech exception to the First Amendment.* In Professors Smolla and Nimmer's view, *Beauharnais* proposed "a special 'hate speech exception' to modern First Amendment principles."[41] They conclude, like Judge Pell, that modern First Amendment jurisprudence recognizes no such exception.[42]

The key case in point is *R.A.V. v. City of St. Paul* (1992), which involved a First Amendment challenge to an ordinance in St. Paul, Minnesota. That ordinance made it a misdemeanor to place:

> on public or private property, a symbol, object, appellation, characterization or graffiti, including but not limited to, a burning cross or Nazi swastika, which one knows or has reasonable grounds to know arouses anger, alarm, or resentment in others on the basis of race, color, creed, religion, or gender.

The defendant had been convicted of violating the ordinance by burning a cross inside an African American family's yard. On appeal, St. Paul defended the statute on the grounds that it applied only to low-value "fighting words" and, as such, the government could regulate it without raising First Amendment problems. The Supreme Court, per Justice Scalia, invalidated the statute as discriminating against speech that (a) invoked race, creed, color, religion, or gender (i.e., content-based or subject matter-based), and (b) preached intolerance rather than tolerance on these grounds (i.e., viewpoint-based). In so deciding, argue Smolla and Nimmer, "the Supreme Court essentially laid to rest any prospect that 'hate speech' would be treated as an independent First Amendment category in which reduced levels of constitutional protection would be applied.[43]

---

41. Rodney A. Smolla & Melville B. Nimmer, 1 Smolla and Nimmer on Freedom of Speech § 12:7 (1994).

42. *Id.* at § 12:4.

43. *Id.*

Speech-Protective Doctrines, Neutral Regulations, and Hostile Audiences

1. *Overbreadth and vagueness.* Because the Village does not allege that the neo-Nazis' speech would tend to incite an immediate breach of the peace, they forgo reliance on that prong of *Chaplinsky*. Absent such reliance, writes Judge Pell, "the ordinance would inevitably fall . . . because of overbreadth and vagueness." Under the overbreadth doctrine, "if a statute is so broadly written that it deters free expression, then it can be struck down on its face because of its chilling effect—even if it also prohibits acts that may legitimately be forbidden."[44] The vagueness doctrine, based on the Due Process Clause and rule of law principles, "requir[es] that a criminal statute state explicitly and definitely what acts are prohibited or restricted, so as to provide fair warning and preclude arbitrary enforcement."[45] Both doctrines are speech protective.

2. *Prior restraint or a reasonable regulation of time, place, and manner?* Judge Sprecher argued that the insurance requirement was a content-neutral reasonable regulation of the time, place, and manner. The First Amendment prohibits "prior restraints," defined as a state-imposed restraint on expression prior to its actual expression,[46] a principle established in *Near v. Minnesota*, 283 U.S. 697 (1931). It especially refers to state actions to "prevent a communication from reaching the public," as by requiring a license or permit to speak or by obtaining an injunction.[47] At the same time, the First Amendment permits the state to place reasonable and content-neutral restrictions on when, where, or how expressive activity may occur, such that the same rules apply regardless of the content of speech. Did the insurance requirement meet these criteria?

3. *Speech that provokes a hostile audience reaction.* Judge Pell reports that the Village did not invoke the risk of hostile audience response to justify Ordinance 995, which prohibited the dissemination of materials promoting hatred against persons because of their race, national origin, or religion.

4. *Instilled in Jewish culture.* Judge Sprecher indicated that "it now seems to be instilled in Jewish culture to confront threatened oppression with active resistance and aggressive retaliation. . . ." In a similar vein, Judge Bell stated that "we appreciate that . . . avoidance"—namely, staying away from the march—might also be psychologically unsatisfying to some of the Village's residents." Why might Judge Sprecher, who is Jewish, feel the need to ascribe this characteristic to Jewish culture? What, in his view, is the legal upshot of this alleged characteristic for this case? How might it relate to *Chaplinsky* and the "fighting words" doctrine, which denies protection to speech that "tend[s] to incite an immediate breach of the peace"?

---

44. *Overbreadth Doctrine*, Black's Law Dictionary (12th ed. 2024).
45. *Vagueness Doctrine*, Black's Law Dictionary (12th ed. 2024).
46. *Prior Restraint*, Black's Law Dictionary (12th ed. 2024).
47. *Id.*

Speech that Inflicts Emotional Distress

1. *Infliction of emotional distress.* Does "hate speech" inflict harm by its very utterance? Judge Pell surmises that the neo-Nazis knew that many Skokie residents will "find their demonstration extremely mentally and emotionally disturbing," and that they in fact reveled in the prospect of this result. Consider whether hate speech victims can seek recourse under the tort of "intentional infliction of severe emotional distress." While the second Skokie case, brought by Sol Goldstein with ADL support, was unsuccessful, this tort claim was theoretically available. The Restatement (Second) of Torts § 46(1) (1965) provides that:

> one who by extreme and outrageous conduct intentionally or recklessly causes severe emotional distress to another is subject to liability for such emotional distress, and if bodily harm to the other results from it, for such bodily harm.

The Restatement further provides that "the actor is never liable ... where he has done no more than to insist upon his legal rights in a permissible way, even though he is well aware that such insistence is certain to cause emotional distress." Should Skokie residents have been able to recover from the neo-Nazis under this tort?[48]

Attorney Tasnim Motala argues that while racial insults cause unique dignitary, psychological, and societal harms, legal responses have been inadequate. She argues that recognizing racial insults as intentional infliction of emotional distress (IIED) would reflect society's existing intolerance for racism and provide a needed and, in her view, a constitutionally permissible legal remedy.

2. *Snyder v. Phelps* (2011). Members of the Westboro Baptist Church picketed near the funeral of a Marine killed in Iraq with signs such as "God Hates Fags," "Thank God for IEDs," and "America is Doomed."[49] The Marine's father sued the Church for IIED. The Supreme Court ruled 8–1 that the First Amendment protected Westboro's speech on the grounds that it addressed matters of public concern (here, the U.S.'s political and moral conduct, homosexuality in the military, and so forth), the picketing was conducted in a public place, and the father was not a captive audience. The Court set aside the plaintiff's IIED claim, notwithstanding the adjudicated outrageousness of Westboro's conduct:

> The jury here was instructed that it could hold Westboro liable for intentional infliction of emotional distress based on a finding that Westboro's picketing was "outrageous." "Outrageousness," however, is a highly malleable standard with "an inherent subjectiveness about it which would allow a jury to impose liability on the basis of the jurors' tastes or views, or perhaps on the basis of their dislike of a particular expression." In a case such as this, a jury is "unlike-

48. Restatement (Second) of Torts § 46 cmt. g (Am. L. Inst. 1977).

49. Other placards read "God Hates the USA/Thank God for 9/11," "Don't Pray for the USA," "Fag Troops," "Semper Fi Fags," "Maryland Taliban," "Fags Doom Nations," "Not Blessed Just **1217 Cursed," "Thank God for Dead Soldiers," "Pope in Hell," "Priests Rape Boys," "You're Going to Hell," and "God Hates You." Snyder v. Phelps, 562 U.S. 443, 454 (2011).

> ly to be neutral with respect to the content of [the] speech," posing "a real danger of becoming an instrument for the suppression of... 'vehement, caustic, and sometimes unpleasant' expression. Such a risk is unacceptable; "in public debate [we] must tolerate insulting, and even outrageous, speech in order to provide adequate 'breathing space' to the freedoms protected by the First Amendment." What Westboro said, in the whole context of how and where it chose to say it, is entitled to "special protection" under the First Amendment, and that protection cannot be overcome by a jury finding that the picketing was outrageous.

Professor Russell Weaver describes *Snyder v. Phelps* as:

> broadly consistent with U.S. First Amendment jurisprudence. While the views of Westboro Baptist Church, as well its tactics, may be offensive to many (most?) people, the Westboro protestors had a constitutional right to express those views, and the government is denied the power to censure those views.[50]

A. Abbot Rosen,[51] *Not the Work of a Day*

Anti-Defamation League of the B'nai B'rith Oral Memoirs

In April 1977, there was a meeting in a synagogue in Skokie to consider what to do about the threat of Nazism coming to Skokie. The argument was that this is the way it had started in Germany in 1924. The ADL knew that the National Socialist Party of America consisted of 15 pimply-faced youths, who at the very most could march 15 minutes before the village hall of Skokie in their ragtag Nazi-type uniforms, and that moment would be the end of Nazism in Skokie.

In this meeting in the synagogue, in April of 1977, the Anti-Defamation League, as represented by myself, argued and pleaded with these people, in the terms which I just expressed. "We understand what's going on but this is a deliberate provocation of you; don't fall into their trap; don't make this mistake." In that meeting, survivors came forward, rolling up their sleeves and showing Rosen, the "apparachik," if you will, the bureaucratic Jew, who knew so much about anti-Semitism, but never had experienced anti-Semitism, what it was all about. In the face of numbers on the arm, which had been tattooed in concentration camps, all reason disappeared. The Nazis will not advance into Skokie, that was a decision of that community on that particular

---

50. Russell L. Weaver, Understanding the First Amendment § 3.04 (8th ed. 2023).

51. A. Abbot Rosen (1915– 2002) served as Director of the ADL's Midwest Region from 1948 to 1986. Upon his passing, the Illinois Senate passed a resolution declaring that "Mr. Rosen's unwavering leadership and judgement throughout the crisis were greatly needed for it was a time of high tension and passion." He served as legal advisor to the U.N. special committee that drafted the Genocide Convention. In 1947, President Harry S. Truman appointed him as the first Chief of the U.S. Department of Justice Civil Rights Section. *See* S. Res. 314, 92d Gen. Assemb., 2002 Sess. (Ill.), https://www.ilga.gov/legislation/legisnet92/srgroups/sr/920SR0314LV.html; *see also Abbot Rosen Dies, Headed ADL in Chicago,* The Ind. Jewish Post & Op., Jan 30, 2002 at 12, https://newspapers.library.in.gov/?a=d&d=-JPOST20020130-01.1.12&e=-------en-20--1--txt-txIN-------.

occasion.... It became apparent very soon that the community itself, privately, was not going to permit the Nazis to demonstrate unmolested. So, the village of Skokie, being astute and sensitive to public opinion, began to get up a series of ordinances to bar the Nazis from coming to Skokie.

The ADL, having its first responsibility to the welfare of the Jewish community, and representing the Jewish community, which was its client, so to speak, then decided to shift gears. Our advice having been rejected, we then brought our own lawsuit in the name of Sol Goldstein, a survivor of the Holocaust and the leader of the survivors in Skokie—vocally and intellectually. The suit was in the Circuit Court of Cook County, a case entitled *Goldstein v. Collin*, and was based on the theory of mental assault. We said that, in essence, the purpose of this demonstration in Skokie was not to assert a political idea, which the Nazis were entitled to do, as repugnant as the idea might be, but was to inflict mental harm, mental anguish, upon these survivors. In other words, it was as if they were going to hit them mentally over the heads with baseball bats. This was their purpose, and the village had it within its authority, and the courts had it within their authority, to enjoin such behavior. The issue was now joined in the courts. The press and the media recognized, in what appeared to be a small encounter, all the elements of the classic morality tale. What happened, for well over a year was that the world's press—not this nation's alone, but the world's press—focused upon Nazis coming to Skokie and this band of survivors of the Holocaust, trying to stop the Nazis from coming to Skokie....

The American Civil Liberties Union took a position on the litigation diametrically opposed to ours. The issue to them was that free speech was involved. So that on the one hand, you have the ACLU and on the other hand you have the survivors in the village of Skokie. As it turned out, the Nazis were mere artifacts in all of this. Nobody really seemed to care about the Nazis anymore. The ACLU represented evil, if you will, against the others representing good. This went on for well over a year with debates all over the country—television programs and so forth. Finally—a happy resolution! The American Civil Liberties Union made that point in public debate which was useful from a tactical standpoint as well as in terms of the issues involved. We were not opposed to free speech. We were opposed to harassment and assault.

The ACLU in this period was taking a tremendous beating from their members, Their membership rolls dissolved very rapidly; there were tremendous numbers of resignations. The ACLU finally came to me one day and ... suggested that we use a little influence on some public officials in Chicago to get a permit for a demonstration for Collin in Chicago. The Skokie demonstration might be called off. They had had it. I met, at that time, a group of Jewish community leaders and told them of the conversation with the ACLU and the decision was an easy and ready one, namely, that we would in no way do business with Frank Collin and the National Socialist Party of America and that we would take our chances on a demonstration in Skokie. However, the Nazis did receive their permit for a Chicago meeting and announced that it was no longer, in their terms, necessary to come to Skokie. This ended, for all practical purposes, the great threat of Nazism in Skokie.

R. George Wright,[52] *Free Speech and Antisemitism: Collin v. Smith Today*

The *Skokie*-based *Collin v. Smith* litigation[53] resulted in our law's most significant constitutional response to antisemitic hate speech.... The argument herein is that our understanding of freedom of speech, and of its value and limits, has significantly evolved over the decades since *Collin v. Smith*. Relatedly, our collective understanding of the harms and injuries inflicted by antisemitic speech has, at the deepest level, been significantly changing as well. In both of these respects, the *Collin v. Smith* litigation has only increased in importance over time....

I. The Key Cases in The *Collin v. Smith* Litigation

A reading of *Chaplinsky*, in the Skokie context, suggests that the Illinois Supreme Court completely overlooked the most profoundly relevant aspect of *Chaplinsky*. The *Chaplinsky* Court, after all, did not limit fighting words to those words that "tend to incite an immediate breach of the peace." There is, instead, an apparently separate and independent form of "fighting words," however misleadingly labeled. In particular, the *Chaplinsky* Court also allowed, separately, for the prohibition of "[words] which by their very utterance inflict injury."

It is this prong of the "fighting words" doctrine, left undiscussed by the court in *Village of Skokie*, that seems the more deeply relevant and important. We must think carefully about the nature of the injury inflicted by Nazi speeches, signs, emblems, and insignia, and by the organized Nazi presence in Skokie....

The Illinois Supreme Court throughout adopts an abstract, disembodied, distanced tone that manifests not an admirably detached judicial impartiality, but a failure to meaningfully distinguish among crucially different circumstances....[54]

The problem here is that antisemitism that evokes the experience of the Shoah, individually and collectively, is not merely "offensive" in the sense in which we might think of a vulgar comedy monologue, a crude denunciation of the military draft, or even a public act of personal disrespect in general. Referring to distinctively Nazi symbols and language as "offensive," or even as "highly offensive," amounts to what the philosopher Gilbert Ryle referred to as a "category mistake."[55]

---

52. Wright, R. George. "Free Speech and Antisemitism: Collin v. Smith Today." (September 8, 2021). Available at SSRN: https://ssrn.com/abstract=3919752. Wright is Lawrence A. Jegen III Professor of Law at Indiana University's Robert H. McKinney School of Law. He has authored more than one hundred full-length professional publications and six books, including SELLING WORDS (1997) and DOES THE LAW MORALLY BIND THE POOR? (1996).

53. For our purposes, the most essential case opinions are: *Vill. of Skokie v. Nat'l Socialist Party of Am.*, 373 N.E.2d 21 (Ill. 1978) (per curiam); *Collin v. Smith*, 447 F. Supp. 676 (N.D. Ill. 1978); and then, chronologically last but of greatest authority, *Collin v. Smith*, 578 F.2d 1197 (7th Cir. 1978), *cert. denied*, 439 U.S. 916 (1978).

54. *See, e.g., Skokie*, 373 N.E.2d at 24. ("That the air may at times seem filled with verbal cacophony is, in this sense not a sign of weakness but of strength.")

55. *See* Ofra Magidor, *Category Mistakes*, STAN. ENCYC. PHIL. (July 5, 2019), https://plato.stanford.edu/entries/category-mistakes/.

The overall tendency in the *Skokie* cases is to treat the proposed demonstration as raising a personal "fighting words" issue, with the emphasis being on the breach of the peace, or violent physical response, prong. This is, again, hardly the most insightful or most valuable approach to the *Skokie* cases....

Crucially, we should instead consider what kinds of "injuries" may be inflicted in *Skokie*-like cases, and how those kinds of "injuries" should be constitutionally distinguished and addressed....

The problem here is that the Seventh Circuit in *Collin* opts for a mental model of what is actually taking place in the case that grossly distorts the most crucial realities. The Seventh Circuit adopts here what we might call an otherwise widely appropriate "forensic" view of First Amendment circumstances.[56] At the core of this "forensic" view is the idea of a broad, ongoing, community practice involving the cooperative, competitive, and indeed often fractious mutual discursive exchange of data and opinions.

On this "forensic" model of speech, the logical move is, in accordance with John Stuart Mill's argument, to assume the generally protected status of presumably false and widely rejected Nazi dogma. On this model, the familiar state law tort of the intentional infliction of severe emotional distress raises interesting complications, but any such tort must then be constrained by "forensic" free speech rules.[57]

On the Seventh Circuit's model, the problem with distinguishing *Skokie*-like contexts from other contexts is that all of the cases involve speech that "invite[s] dispute ... induces a condition of unrest, creates dissatisfaction with conditions as they are, or even stirs people to anger." ...

All of these categories abstract away from, and implicitly deny, essential elements of the *Skokie* context.[58]

II. *Collin v. Smith* in Light of Our Shifting Understanding of the Underlying Reasons For Protecting Speech

Today, no less than as of the time of the *Collin v. Smith* litigation, the underlying justifications for constitutionally protecting speech are commonly thought to be plural.[59] As of 1970, for example, the scholar Thomas Emerson identified pursuing truth and knowledge, promoting self-fulfillment or autonomy, and facilitating meaningful democratic participation as crucial values thought to underlie freedom of speech.

Among the most fundamental and ultimately most indispensable of these values has been that of the optimal pursuit of truth. But it is fair to say that for broad cultural

56. *See* R. George Wright, *Civil Disobedience Today: Some Basic Problems and Possibilities*, 51 Mem. L. Rev. 197, 218–21 (2020).

57. *See Collin*, 578 F.2d at 1203. See also, more authoritatively, the military funeral protest case of *Snyder v. Phelps*, 562 U.S. 443, 456–58 (2011) (citing the satiric cartoon case of *Hustler Magazine v. Falwell*, 485 U.S. 46, 55 (1988)).

58. For background, see generally, R. George Wright, *Freedom of Speech as a Cultural Holdover*, 40 Pace L. Rev. 235 (2020).

59. *See generally* Thomas I. Emerson, The System of Freedom of Expression 6–7 (1970) (listing several underlying justifications for protecting speech).

reasons, the depth, extent, and the very meaning of the pursuit of truth, as a free speech justification and elsewhere, has noticeably evolved since the time of *Collin v. Smith*. In particular, the idea of truth, and of the meaningful pursuit thereof, is now of clearly diminished status.

Certainly, various forms and depths of truth-skepticism in free speech contexts were available even at the time of *Collin v. Smith*. But the relevant cultural trends and schools of thought have moved in that direction across the intervening decades. As the metaphysical depth and meaning of "truth" for free speech purposes have gradually eroded, the idea of a "post-truth" culture has gained purchase.

Thus, claims as to truth and falsity in political conflict in general are now more frequently thought of as contested social constructs, or as veiled assertions of power, than formerly. Political claims are thus interrogated, rather than examined for any degree of objective insight. At best, truth claims are not merely classically tentative or provisional, but inherently and inescapably linked to some particular adopted perspective.

This trend toward the evacuation of any objective standards for appraising the truth of political and other claims reflects far broader considerations than can be attributed to any movement or school of thought. A leading contemporary philosopher, Professor Simon Blackburn, has argued that "almost all the trends in the last generation of serious philosophy lent aid and comfort to the 'anything goes' climate ... [and] any hope for a genuine vindication of knowledge and rationality went into retreat." ...

Of course, the value of the pursuit of truth by itself hardly exhausts the logic of protecting freedom of speech. But it seems unlikely in the extreme that any diminution in the status and coherence of the idea of truth itself can be prevented from similarly affecting any other value that is thought to justify protecting freedom of speech. In this sense, any sensible reason for promoting free speech is inescapably dependent upon current understandings of what the truth can amount to.

In fact, other crucial justifications of free speech have undergone related transformations. The idea of developing meaningful autonomy through free speech illustrates this trend. Classically, we have had available to us the idea of autonomy in a metaphysically robust, undiluted, non-attenuated sense. Autonomy in this sense requires a belief that considerations of reason can be meaningful and effective as exercises of freedom in choosing among actions, apart from deterministic or merely random material causes.

Any such metaphysically ambitious understanding of autonomy—and of the possibilities opened thereby—is increasingly thought to be implausible, and thus somehow unavailable....

Of course, we can still talk of "autonomy" in some merely attenuated, minimalist, reductive, or fictionalist sense. Thus, in the free speech law context, we might today think of autonomy as something like the ability to successfully pursue some life-path we happen to endorse regardless of how causally we came to adopt and endorse that life-path in the first place. The logic of some sort of gradual transition from a robust Kantian dignity and autonomy to a metaphysically less ambitious concern for, ultimately, an autonomy perhaps merely comprising arbitrary pleasures and pains[60] may increasingly take hold.[61]

Whether we choose to construe autonomy as largely some sort of a calculus of endorsed or unendorsed pleasures and pains or not, any gradual dilution of the idea of autonomy, in the relevant classic sense, tends to similarly dilute the case for freedom of speech on such grounds....

Importantly, the evolution of values such as autonomy and the pursuit of truth since *Collin v. Smith* does not affect merely the free speech elements of the case. Unavoidably, the attenuation of our sense of what truth, autonomy, and dignity can amount to importantly affects the other side of all such cases.

III. *Collin v. Smith* in Light of Our Shifting Understanding of the Very Nature of Antisemitic Speech Injuries

In large measure, the costs of antisemitic speech, as in *Collin v. Smith*, involve psychological trauma or other related injury. Such harms are often treated by the courts as forms of pain or suffering, and the emotions related thereto.[62] ...

Inescapably, experiences of pain, suffering, trauma, psychological injury, and the associated emotions are of various sorts. Equally important for our purposes, however, is that these phenomena may differ, in any instance, quite substantially in the nature, depth, and character of what we might call their metaphysical presuppositions. Not all such injuries are qualitatively on a par.

Thus, in the simplest Benthamite cases, pain and suffering do not presuppose much in the way of chains of reasoning, or of any metaphysical ambition.... But pain and suffering, of whatever sort, typically involve some more or less elaborate process of reasoning on the part of the sufferer. At a minimum, for example, we may distinguish between being inadvertently tripped, and being deliberately tripped.[63] The injuries in these two circumstances are significantly different.

---

60. For a classic taxonomy, see JEREMY BENTHAM, AN INTRODUCTION TO THE PRINCIPLES OF MORALS AND LEGISLATION ch. IV. (1781) (ebook), http://www.utilitarianism.com/jeremy-bentham/index.html.

61. Bentham's approach to pains tends to be methodologically individualist, or aggregative, as distinct from recognizing a harm, injury, or pain that is essentially joint, collective, or deeply communitarian in nature, as presumably characterizes some reactions to antisemitic speech.

62. *See, e.g.*, Donald A. Downs, *Skokie Revisited: Hate Group Speech and the First Amendment*, 60 NOTRE DAME L. REV. 629, 634 (1985) (referring to "assaultive speech ... meant to inflict an emotional injury"); David Goldberger, *Skokie: The First Amendment Under Attack by Its Friends*, 29 MERCER L. REV. 761, 764 (1978) (referring to the anticipation of being "emotionally harmed by the Nazis' appearance in Skokie because it would trigger memories of their terrible war experiences" and thus "inflict emotional trauma"); Mark A. Rabinowitz, *Nazis in Skokie: Fighting Words or Heckler's Veto?*, 28 DEPAUL L. REV. 259, 260 (1979) (focusing on "the recognition that a person's emotional well-being is worthy of greater protection").

63. Thus "as Holmes observed, even a dog knows the difference between being tripped over and being kicked." W. PAGE KEETON ET AL., PROSSER AND KEETON ON TORTS 33 (5th ed. 1984).

More elaborately, though, pain and suffering and their related emotions may well be affected by, for example, the perceived nature of the relationship between perpetrator and victim. Perceived betrayal, or ingratitude, for example, attending a physical injury may well affect the victim's response.[64] And the sense of ingratitude must logically depend upon some more or less elaborate chain of reasoning, any step of which, crucially, may be either justified or unjustified.

Even more importantly, the reactions of hate speech victims are conditioned not only by the literal assertions made by their tormentors, but by what we might call the metaphysical depth of the speech in question. Mere expressions of subjective distaste do not carry the same weight as condemnation that is supposedly mandated by some objective fundamental principle.

A Post-Truth Analysis of *Collin v. Smith*

1. *Correct?* In Professor Wright's view, did the Seventh Circuit decide this case correctly? Is the question beside the point? Correct or not, what does he think is wrong with it?

2. *The distinctive nature of antisemitic harm.* What specific harms does Wright identify as flowing from antisemitic speech? How do these harms differ from other forms of speech-based injury? Why does Wright argue these harms cannot be reduced to mere offense or emotional distress? How do collective memory and historical trauma factor into these harms?

3. *The fighting words doctrine.* Why did courts focus primarily on the "breach of peace" prong rather than "infliction of injury" of *Chaplinsky*'s fighting words doctrine? How might courts develop a workable legal standard based on the "infliction of injury" prong? What challenges exist in translating psychological and dignitary harms into legal doctrine?[65]

4. *Doctrinal inadequacy.* Why, in Wright's view, do traditional First Amendment frameworks fail to capture antisemitic speech's nature? How do concepts like "marketplace of ideas" and "offensive speech" mischaracterize the harm? What assumptions underlie these doctrinal frameworks? What aspects of antisemitic speech fall outside these traditional categories?

5. *The forensic model and its limitations.* In the marketplace of ideas metaphor, the truth (or at least the better ideas) emerge through fair competition with one another. Was this ever true, and if so, is it true today? What is different and distinctive about Wright's model of free speech? Which is more protective than the forensic model of false or offensive speech? How does each approach the issue of antisemitic speech? What is "partial forensic disarmament"?

---

64. *See, e.g.*, William Shakespeare, King Lear act 1, sc. 4 (1606). ("How sharper than a serpent's tooth it is to have a thankless child.")

65. *See* Rodney A. Smolla, *Words "Which by Their Very Utterance Inflict Injury": The Evolving Treatment of Inherently Dangerous Speech in Free Speech Law and Theory*, 36 Pepp. L. Rev. 317 (2009).

6. *Truth and metaphysics in free speech law.* How has the concept of "truth" in free speech discourse evolved since *Collin v. Smith*? What are the implications of "post-truth" culture for hate speech regulation? How does the erosion of metaphysical concepts affect legal analysis? What alternative frameworks might better address contemporary challenges?

7. *The evolution of autonomy.* What is the shift from "metaphysically robust" to "attenuated" autonomy? How does this shift affect traditional free speech justifications? What are the implications for balancing individual rights against collective harms?

8. *Practical implications.* Were the Skokie cases wrongly decided? How might courts better balance free speech protection with preventing antisemitic harm? What doctrinal reforms might better address hate speech while respecting First Amendment values? How can, might, and/or should courts approach similar cases today, given our evolved understanding?

James Loeffler,[66]
An Abandoned Weapon in the Fight Against Hate Speech[67]

The Atlantic (June 16, 2019)

A 1952 Supreme Court ruling gave civil rights groups a way to combat anti-Semitism and other prejudices—but in the years since, it's largely gone unused.

"Jews will not replace us." When 300 neo-Nazis marched with flaming torches through the central quad of the University of Virginia on a late Friday evening in August 2017, their message was clear. The college's response, in contrast, was a study in confusion. As a public institution, wrote then-President Teresa Sullivan, the university "must abide by state and federal law" regarding the First Amendment rights of free speech and freedom of assembly. Short of barring the "torch-bearing protesters" as an imminent threat to safety, university officials' hands were tied. National Jewish organizations such as the Anti-Defamation League and the American Jewish Committee concurred, denouncing the shocking display of hatred but urging the public to let the "protesters" voice their "protected speech."

Yet after the violent weekend that led to one death and multiple casualties, UVA lawyers unearthed a decades-old state law still on the books that banned the burning of objects on private or public property "with the intent of intimidating any person or group of persons." It turned out that the Virginia General Assembly had dealt with this very problem back in the early 1950s, when the Ku Klux Klan tried to launch a new campaign in the state. The legal means to prevent this racist and anti-Semitic

66. James Loeffler is the Jay Berkowitz Professor of Jewish History at the University of Virginia, where he directs the Jewish Studies Program. He is the author of Rooted Cosmopolitans: Jews and Human Rights in the Twentieth Century (2018). *Loeffler*, Inst. of the Human. & Glob. Cultures, https://ihgc.as.virginia.edu/loeffler (last updated Nov. 26, 2024).

67. From The Atlantic. © 2019 The Atlantic Monthly Group, LLC. All rights reserved. Used under license.

menace without violating the First Amendment had existed. No one had remembered to look for it.

An overlooked law written for a danger assumed to be long past. A domestic extremist movement masquerading as a political cause. An unswerving fealty to the First Amendment blinding lawyers to the violent danger staring them in the face. This lonely epilogue to Charlottesville is a fitting symbol for the current crisis facing the American civil rights movement. White supremacists have twisted the law itself into a weapon with which to launch a frontal attack on American liberalism.

That this brazen attack took place on a campus where I teach Jewish history, including the long Jewish struggle on behalf of human rights, only underscored another historical irony. Anti-Semitism has returned with a vengeance, yet American Jews have forgotten how to fight it.

From Charlottesville to Squirrel Hill, Pennsylvania, to Poway, California, American anti-Semitism has repeatedly demonstrated its deadly propensity for violence. The common link is a social mediascape in which anti-Semitic and racist ideas and memes freely circulate, intensifying as they do so. Yet most American Jews feel powerless to fight anti-Semitism, trapped in a simplistic understanding of the First Amendment. Separate church and state, they believe, defends freedom of expression, and fights for equal treatment and a race-blind society, and over time anti-Semitism and other hatreds will dissipate. So the logic goes. Many Jewish lawyers pride themselves on their defense of civil liberties, safeguarding the expression of even unpopular views, from politics to pornography. Some proudly defend the rights of neo-Nazis and other anti-Semitic bigots.

That principled approach has its virtues. Yet in our day and age, this civil-libertarian orthodoxy has left society reliant on the fuzzier tools of tolerance education, public shaming, and private litigation to fight anti-Semitism. As a result, the press often replaces the courts as the forum for judging harmful words. Civil rights lawyering is reduced to an exercise in punishing violent hate crimes after the fact, rather than preventing them beforehand. And worst of all, free speech and hate speech are imagined as two disconnected islands of contradictory ideologies, separated by an unbridgeable sea of constitutional law, rather than interrelated categories whose shared history stretches back to the opening years of the 20th century.

Just like Virginia's forgotten anti-Ku Klux Klan law, there is more to the story of American Jews and civil rights than a stalwart faith in the ennobling virtues of free speech. Across the first half of the 20th century, Jewish lawyers stretched civil rights law wider and deeper than the pursuit of absolute individual equality in order to prevent both verbal and physical attacks on Jews and other vulnerable minorities. They employed the novel legal approach of group libel. Their efforts formed part of the larger Jewish drive to defend civil liberties and seek political inclusion. They yielded striking legal innovations, including a bevy of state laws to shut down the most extreme peddlers of racism and anti-Semitism. Those laws even produced an important Supreme Court precedent, *Beauharnais v. Illinois*, which has never been overturned and remains relevant to contemporary civil rights questions.

Yet even though the courts deemed group libel a legitimate way to stop hate speech without violating the First Amendment, over time American Jewish civil rights groups edged away from their own achievement. Instead, they began to focus on the First Amendment as the ultimate counter-majoritarian instrument of self-defense against hatred. Exposing extremism would suffice to stop its spread. The teeming marketplace of ideas would crowd out the few malevolent Judeophobes and racists. Curbing present-day incitement risked future government censorship. The price of American freedom was some marginal discomfort inflicted by extremists, who were best managed through the tools of mainstream liberalism.

Today, as American society grapples with a deadly resurgence of anti-Semitism, it is well worth recovering the lost history of Jewish civil rights. For just as the roots of contemporary hatred stretch far back into the American past, so too does the forgotten record of the law's struggle against it. Charlottesville is not only a reminder of the persistence of the past. It is a summons to reckon with American Jewish history's timely legal lessons for today.

* * *

In August 1790, the newly elected President George Washington wrote a short note to the Jews of Newport, Rhode Island. Thanking them for their message of congratulations, he went on to praise the "Children of the Stock of Abraham who dwell in this land." "The Government of the United States, which gives to bigotry no sanction, to persecution no assistance," Washington memorably wrote, "requires only that they who live under its protection, should demean themselves as good citizens."

Over time, the Newport letter came to symbolize the larger promise of religious liberty in the new American republic. Right now, these very words adorn the facade of the National Museum of American Jewish History in Philadelphia. In contrast to Europe, where ancient prejudices trailed Jews ominously into modern times, the new country announced its ideal of strict religious neutrality. The United States would privilege no one religion, for as Washington proclaimed, "All possess alike liberty of conscience and immunities of citizenship."

Today American Jews treasure Washington's letter like a precious birthright. Few realize that the stirring words were actually scripted for him by the Jewish community itself. Most of the ideas and much of the language were copied verbatim from the initial letter sent to Washington by Moses Seixas, a leader of Newport's Jewish community. Yet even more striking than the language Washington cribbed is what he chose to omit from his letter. By describing Jews as entitled to civil equality despite their non-Christian status, and only at risk of discrimination for their religious beliefs, Washington effectively established a legal precedent. There would be no European-style corporate group identity or racial stigma attached to Jewishness in America. By law, American Jews would be implicitly treated as white Americans of a different religious faith.

That liberal vision, of Jews flourishing as individual citizens living in voluntary communities, neatly matched the egalitarian ideals of the young republic. It worked well in a country where Jews remained a negligible percentage of the population, and where there were virtually no Jews of color. In Washington's day, the 1790 census counted a mere 1,500 Jews, most of whom came from Sephardic backgrounds in western Europe, amounting to 0.05 percent of the total American population.[68] A century later, despite another wave of immigration, this time from German-speaking Central Europe, the number had risen only to 0.5 percent.

Then, in the late 19th century, millions of Yiddish-speaking eastern-European Jews began to pour into American society. Their arrival coincided with the post-Reconstruction rise of modern American nativism, Jim Crow laws, and a new current of racial anti-Semitism. Suddenly, formal religious equality was not enough to stop active discrimination from WASP elites in the urban North, or rippling threats of violence from Southern Ku Klux Klan members. New kinds of anti-Semitic mass media and populist demagogues targeted wealthier, acculturated Jews and their unwashed immigrant cousins alike. They blamed successful Jewish entrepreneurs for the ills of capitalism and poorer newcomers for their racial deviancy. Almost overnight, America decided that Jews might not count as fully white after all.

* * *

In May 1907, the management of the Marlborough-Blenheim Hotel in Atlantic City, New Jersey, turned away the family of a Jewish widow from Baltimore named Bertha Rayner Frank with a curt line: "We don't entertain Hebrews." In response, Louis Marshall, a renowned constitutional lawyer and the president of a newly established Jewish civil rights organization, the American Jewish Committee, proposed an anti-discrimination law for New York State. When finally passed in 1913, the New York Civil Rights Act banned denial of service to people at restaurants, hotels, and all manner of other commercial venues based on race, color, or creed. Yet in a twist, it also prohibited any advertising that even mentioned denying accommodations to certain groups. Now it was a legally punishable offense to discriminate in deed or to defame in words.

That same year, the Anti-Defamation League launched as a second Jewish civil-rights organization. Its stated mission was "to stop, by appeals to reason and conscience and, if necessary, by appeals to law, the defamation of the Jewish people." Over the next decade, at the behest of Jewish civil rights groups, six more states followed New York's lead, drafting laws that outlawed advertising and other published expressions of discrimination directed at a specific group. At root, these laws relied on a concept of group defamation, or, as it was alternately known, group libel. For hundreds of years, English common law had recognized the individual citizen's right to sue for personal libel. Now state legislatures began to experiment with civil rights statutes that allowed for the prosecution of individuals who defamed or injured the reputation or property of members of a minority group. Marshall even helped sponsor a draft federal law before World War I to ban the dissemination of hate literature by U.S. mail.

---

68. Editor's note: As discussed in Chapter 1, it is an open question as to whether Sephardic Jews are Hispanic or Latino.

Targeting defamatory speech against a group was a bold step to protect the freedom of Jews, African Americans, and other minorities. Much of this work went hand in hand with the new African American civil rights activism of groups such as the NAACP, which numbered among its senior leadership many Jewish lawyers and rabbis. Just like anti-lynching laws, group-libel statutes moved the law beyond the protection of formal equality for individuals, to an equity-based model that acknowledged group differences in society. The ideal of blind justice would not suffice when it came to a racialized society in which minorities were targeted disproportionately and distinctively—sometimes with the law's consent.

Yet the assertive drive for positive group protection also stirred up anxieties among Jewish leaders. Some feared that anti-bias laws might not only run afoul of the First Amendment rights to freedom of speech and assembly but actually compromise the legal and political security of Jews as individual citizens. Separating Jews out as a minority group risked reinforcing anti-Semitic stereotypes. Worse still, such a move might give the American government license to treat Jews as a potentially unassimilable national or racial minority as in Europe. That fear derived from a disturbing reality. The turn-of-the-century restrictive American immigration laws banned nonwhite racial minorities, threatening to close the doors to millions of Jews fleeing extreme poverty and increasingly violent anti-Semitism in eastern Europe.

Then, in 1920, America's most famous business tycoon, Henry Ford, began publishing a nakedly anti-Semitic newspaper with a national distribution, *The Dearborn Independent*. Ford promoted a variety of malicious stereotypes about Judeo-Bolshevik power, fanned fears of Jewish racial impurity, and portrayed jazz and baseball as Hebraic conspiracies to pollute American society. He even republished the Russian anti-Semitic conspiracy tract, *The Protocols of the Elders of Zion*.

Ford's hate speech seemed tailor-made for the kind of group-libel law already in effect in states across the country. Yet bitter divisions quickly emerged among Jewish civil rights leaders over how to respond, as Victoria Saker Woeste showed in her 2012 book, *Henry Ford's War on Jews and the Legal Battle Against Hate Speech*. In 1924, Ford's newspaper launched a series of articles to expose "Jewish exploitation" in the American cooperative farming industry, particularly targeting the California lawyer and cooperative activist, Aaron Sapiro. Enraged by the patent falsehoods and anti-Semitic attacks, Sapiro sued in federal court in Detroit for libel.

Sapiro's lawsuit attracted the attention of other Jewish civil rights leaders, chief among them Marshall. By the early 1920s, Marshall had argued several cases for the NAACP at the Supreme Court, mediated labor conflicts between Jewish workers and factory owners in New York City, and pioneered environmental conservation in upstate New York. But he balked at the idea of suing Ford for libel of any kind. Marshall feared such a move would trigger more anti-Semitism and mark Jews as a racial minority. In a pretrial ruling, the judge had found that Sapiro could not sue for group libel, because Michigan had not passed a group libel statute. When Sapiro's personal libel lawsuit was then dismissed on a technicality after a secret smear campaign by

Ford, Marshall breathed a sigh of relief. He seized on the moment to negotiate a public apology in which Ford claimed (falsely) that he had not known his underlings were spreading anti-Semitic calumnies.

Having pioneered the progressive idea of outlawing hatred in the 1910s, a decade later now, Marshall swung toward an uncompromising defense of individual free expression. Immigration fears no longer mattered, since the worst had just come to pass. In 1921 and 1924, Congress had imposed sweeping restrictions that excluded eastern-European Jews, along with many other races deemed inferior, from entering the country. Now Marshall feared that in a climate of rising nativism and conservative populism, political progressives might lose out if speech were to be overly regulated in a modern democracy.

Similar reasoning led Marshall's fellow Jewish lawyer and great rival Louis Brandeis, the first Jewish Supreme Court justice, to write his 1927 opinion in *Whitney v. California*. In a ruling upholding the conviction of a California woman charged with espousing communism, Brandeis offered an eloquent defense of the moral virtues of the First Amendment. The solution to offensive speech of all kinds, he wrote, was to "expose through discussion the falsehood and fallacies, to avert the evil by the process of education, [such that] the remedy to be applied is more speech, not enforced silence."

Neither Ford's pseudo-apology nor Brandeis's soaring rhetoric, though, did much to stop the surge of anti-Semitism in American society in the late 1920s and 1930s. Racial populists such as Father Charles Coughlin began to use the new medium of radio to seek out national audiences. Propagandists mastered the art of cheap publishing on a national scale. The most famous of these new hate-merchants was Robert Edward Edmondson, the founder of the Pan-Aryan League and the premier anti-Semitic pamphleteer of his day.

Over the course of the 1930s, Edmondson published hundreds of booklets and newspaper articles, denouncing "Jewish anti-Americanism and Talmudic communism," "the communistic Jew deal," and the "invisible government" for destroying American business, media, government, and entertainment. He also repeatedly smeared non-Jews such as Secretary of Labor Frances Perkins, who he falsely claimed was in reality one "Rachel Lazanski" of "Russian Jewish origin" impersonating a New England WASP.

In 1936, Congressman Samuel Dickstein of New York demanded legal action. Mayor Fiorello La Guardia responded by invoking his power as chief magistrate of the city of New York to issue a summons for criminal libel, and then asking the New York County district attorney to take a personal role in the case, suggesting he charge Edmondson with "false, malicious, scandalous, and defamatory libel of and concerning all persons of the Jewish religion." La Guardia dismissed his critics: "The right of free speech is based on the recognition that those who indulge in it or who claim it as a right must be prepared to be held responsible for their utterances or their writings if they transgress. The remedy is not by suppression or curtailment of speech or writing, but by invoking the law of criminal libel if the statement is not truthful or the motive unlawful."

American Jews responded to Edmondson's indictment with great enthusiasm. The Yiddish-language *Jewish Daily Forward* opined, "The entire population of New York, regardless of race or religion, wholeheartedly welcomes Mayor La Guardia's swift action against the fanatics and juvenile-delinquents, who spread ... social poison, wild race-hatreds, anti-Jewish calumnies, and antisemitism ... that incite unlawful acts." Rabbi Stephen S. Wise, the leader of the American Jewish Congress and a co-founder of the NAACP, showered La Guardia with praise for the "grand thing" he had accomplished. Wise mocked the murmurs of hesitation among the more anxious of his own people, the "sh-sh Jews who, instead of rejoicing over what you have done, are chiefly fearful lest, as they put it, Edmondson has his day in court—as if he had not had it already, through the publication of millions of pamphlets!"

Edmondson's lawyer defended his client's writings as "patriotic politico-economic educational analyses, issued under the Constitutional guarantee of free speech and free press." His client never meant to criticize Jews in the United States or elsewhere, his lawyer insisted, only the true enemies of the American people: "Socialist Jews, Communist Jews, Bolshevist Jews, and Mongol Jews." There was no case for group defamation, only an instance of legitimate political criticism of the wrong kinds of Jews. To ensure a fair trial, however, he insisted that the judge empanel an all-Aryan jury.

Edmondson never got his all-Aryan jury, or any jury for that matter. The case did not go to trial. Despite their initial eagerness to prosecute, the Jewish civil rights groups, including Wise's own American Jewish Congress, the American Jewish Committee, and the National Council of Jewish Women, all summarily retreated as the trial approached. All three submitted amicus briefs petitioning the judge to dismiss the case on the grounds that applying criminal libel in defense of any group was a mistake. In the words of Wise's own organization, to sanction Edmondson would only make him a "'martyr' to the great cause of civil rights ... and freedom of speech and of the press." Better to let an anti-Semite speak his erroneous truth than expand the role of the law in the fight against anti-Semitism. The judge acquiesced and threw out the case. If the injured party itself disavowed the injury, he reasoned, how could it be called a crime?

* * *

The outbreak of World War II and the emerging news of the Nazi Holocaust shocked American Jews out of this pattern of ambivalence vis-à-vis group libel. In 1943, Wise's American Jewish Congress successfully campaigned for a Massachusetts statute criminalizing the publication of "false written or printed material with intent to maliciously promote hatred of any group of persons in the commonwealth because of race, color or religion." To spearhead its legal efforts, it hired Alexander Pekelis, an Italian Jewish refugee law professor and prominent early scholar of fascism.

Fleeing Italy for the United States in 1940, Pekelis quickly emerged as a leading practitioner of the "legal realism" school of jurisprudence that emphasized law's dynamic interaction with society. In the same New Deal spirit, Pekelis viewed law as a constructive tool for modern social reform. Across the early 1940s, he pushed forward a number of ideas for how to combine "individual protection and group action" to stop anti-Semitism. Time and again, he stressed that modern economics had changed the way people thought about law for workers and organized labor. The right to organize workers was necessary because of the power of businesses in the marketplace. Now law could do the same for members of minority groups, who were both individuals and members of a vulnerable segment of society. In a 1945 essay in *The New Republic*, he wrote:

> People singled out for attack as a group have the right to defend themselves as a group. This principle has led, in industrial relations, to collective bargaining and has provided a defense against conspiracy charges. The same principle can lead to equally important results in the field of ethnic relations. For instance, the enforcement of antidiscrimination laws should not be left to individual initiative only, but minority organizations should be given the power, analogous to that enjoyed by the unions under the National Labor Relations Act, to file charges of unfair practices.

That same year, Pekelis petitioned the Federal Communications Commission to deny an FM radio station a license to the *New York Daily News* on the grounds of its "consistent bias and hostility ... in its editorial and news columns against Jews and Negroes" and "its readiness to publish irresponsible and defamatory news items." During World War II, he charged, the *Daily News* had all but adopted the Nazi line on Jewish malfeasance and warmongering. Far from violating the First Amendment, denying bigotry a media platform would "result in a fuller protection of the basic aims of free speech and free press."

Pekelis's argument was echoed in an influential series of early 1940s articles by another law professor, David Riesman. He cast his proposal in terms of the larger struggle of liberalism. "Defamation and the law of defamation have become weapons in the political struggle between democracy and fascism," he wrote. Why not extend that principle to social groups? "It is only through strengthening the protection of the groups to which an individual belongs that his own values and his own reputation can be adequately safeguarded," he insisted. "The isolated person is as helpless in the face of systematic defamation by opposing groups ... as in the face of concerted economic power." Relying on the general theory of torts (civil damages), Riesman proposed to give Jews and other minority groups a necessary legal remedy.

The chief obstacle to such a legal move, according to Riesman, was not the legal fine print or free-speech concerns, but "the American heritage of middle-class individualistic liberalism," which obscured the need for group protections. "Our thinking is still in terms of the 'individual' and the 'state,' and our law of defamation, such as it is, is conceived of only as a protection against individual injury, as the law of assault and battery is a protection for individual life and limb." Where there was a political will, as in the case of labor unions, it was possible to construct legal protections for groups in society. The same could be done for Jews and other minorities.

By the end of the 1940s, eight states had enacted statutes to criminalize different forms of group libel. Meanwhile, in 1949, Senator Jacob Javits of New York and Representative Arthur Klein sponsored a bill to create a federal group libel statute. A legal revolution seemed in the offing. Yet behind all these new laws lurked a question that had dogged similar efforts since the 1910s: Were group libel statutes even constitutional?

* * *

In July 1951, the ACLU petitioned the Supreme Court to hear the appeal of an anti-Semitic, racist pamphleteer in Chicago convicted of violating an Illinois group libel law. The defendant, Joseph Beauharnais, the president of the White Circle League of America, had published a pamphlet opposing the "the further encroachment, harassment and invasion of white people, their property, neighborhoods and persons, by the Negro." The great dangers of crime and communism, "which is rife among the Negroes," he wrote, justified the need for the white race "to assert its natural rights to self-preservation."

The news that the ACLU would defend Beauharnais broke during the very same week as the Cicero race riot, when a mob of 4,000 white Chicagoans attacked an apartment building that housed a single African American family. In a letter to his ACLU friends, the NAACP's Walter White questioned the logic of their decision, especially given the fact that Beauharnais had just reportedly led the mob violence in Cicero: "You will remember, of course, Mr. Justice Holmes's famous edict that the right of free speech does not include the right to shout fire in a crowded theatre."

Other letter writers did not mince words. "Exactly what, in the name of an all-merciful God, do you gentlemen think you are accomplishing [by defending] ... the Chicago monster?" asked Isidor Shaffer of Queens. The ACLU executive director's reply to both men was a study in condescension: "This is one of those hard choices that people who believe in *all* civil liberties for *everybody* are frequently forced to make—in a conflict between free expression and respect for the human dignity of a minority group. In asking you to join us in choosing free expression, we realize that such a choice costs you far more than it costs us."

The price tag on principle also proved too costly for the Supreme Court. In a close 5–4 verdict, the justices ruled in *Beauharnais v. Illinois* that the Illinois law was constitutional. Writing for the majority, the court's sole Jewish justice, Felix Frankfurter, himself a co-founder of the ACLU, laid out the opinion's reasoning:

> If an utterance directed at an individual may be the object of criminal sanctions, we cannot deny to a State power to punish the same utterance directed at a defined group.... Long ago this Court recognized that the economic rights of an individual may depend for the effectiveness of their enforcement on rights in the group, even though not formally corporate, to which he belongs. Such group protection on behalf of the individual may, for all we know, be a need not confined to the part that a trade union plays in effectuating rights abstractly recognized as belonging to its members.

A notable dissent came from Justice Robert Jackson, fresh from his tour as the chief U.S. prosecutor at the Nuremberg trials. "Group libel statutes represent a commendable desire to reduce sinister abuses of our freedoms of expression—abuses which I have had occasion to learn can tear apart a society, brutalize its dominant elements, and persecute, even to extermination, its minorities," he wrote, adding charitably, "Such efforts, if properly applied, do not justify frenetic forebodings of crushed liberty." Yet in the end, Jackson worried, such laws would "present most difficult policy and technical problems" of enforcement. Minority groups also had to acknowledge the double-edged sword: "No group interest in any particular prosecution should forget that the shoe may be on the other foot in some prosecution tomorrow."

Frankfurter dismissed Jackson's concerns about the logistical challenges and the potential abuse of the statute for censorship. This was merely "the price to be paid for the trial-and-error inherent in legislative efforts to deal with obstinate social issues." When all was said and done, it would be foolish to avoid reasonable legal efforts "to curb false or malicious defamation of racial and religious groups, made in public places and by means calculated to have a powerful emotional impact on those to whom it was presented."

Frankfurter's majority opinion might have ushered in a new era of expanded civil-rights efforts to stamp out anti-Semitism and white supremacy in American society. Though not without its critics at the time, *Beauharnais* offered a powerful tool to complement the array of other state-level legal efforts to ban discrimination in housing, employment, and education. Moreover, given that the civil rights struggle had begun to play out on the national political landscape, this law provided a means to check a new wave of Ku Klux Klan and other white supremacist mobilization. Immediately following the verdict, for instance, an alarmed Gerald L. K. Smith, the notorious Christian nationalist crusade leader, wrote to the ACLU, worried that the "terrible decision handed down by the Supreme Court" might yet put his movement out of business. Though he was aware that the ACLU was full of Jewish lawyers, he still counted on its help for his cause: "I do know that it requires a philosophical Jew to defend my right of free speech."

Smith needn't have worried about his freedom of expression; many Jewish civil rights lawyers were on his side. Across the board, Jewish civil rights organizations greeted *Beauharnais* with silence. Fearful of the rising tide of McCarthyism, all of the major Jewish organizations declined to seize the opportunity it presented. They opted to stress their all-American bona fides and push liberalism in a different direction, rather than emphasize their minority needs. They wagered that civil libertarianism coupled with formal desegregation would suffice to secure racial and religious equality.

In 1954, Jewish organizations vigorously supported the NAACP in the *Brown v. Board of Education* case to strike down federal racial segregation. They followed with other state-level anti-discrimination legal initiatives and a vigorous push against religious discrimination by insisting on the larger legal separation of church and state and against school prayer. But one by one, in the 1960s, all the Jewish civil rights organizations formally renounced their support for group libel as a legal strategy in favor of individual equal protection. Instead, they embraced the landmark 1964 Civil Rights Act, which forbids all discrimination on the basis of race, religion, color, sex, or national origin.

A rising faith in free speech, equal protection, and due process as the best antidotes for racism and anti-Semitism formed the quintessence of postwar American Jewish civil rights work. There was a compelling logic to this approach at the time. Eliminate prejudice as a whole, treat everyone as individuals, handle hate speech as an individual pathology best fought in the classroom and church pew rather than the courtroom, and anti-Semitism would vanish together with American racism. Fulfilling liberalism's promise meant making American justice race-blind and faith-blind, not creating new protected categories for what one Jewish activist called "imaginary groups in American society."

Alongside this philosophical faith in mid-century liberalism, American Jews recognized tactically that defending free speech in maximalist terms could help block the rearguard actions of white supremacy. In 1962, a Montgomery, Alabama, police official sued *The New York Times* for libel, claiming that he had been unfairly maligned in a paid advertisement by civil rights groups that accused local police of racial bias. The Supreme Court's 1964 decision in *New York Times v. Sullivan* produced the most famous affirmation of the freedom of the press. It solidified as a core tenet of liberal faith the assumption that unfettered free speech would always serve the cause of civil rights more effectively than troublesome hate speech laws.

But white supremacists and neo-Nazis also took note. Though *Sullivan* in theory left *Beauharnais* undisturbed, it signaled to new groups such as George Lincoln Rockwell's American Nazi Party and the National Socialist Party of America that they had little to fear from the courts. Worse still, it inspired a cynical new tactic on the part of these groups, which began using their freedom of speech to directly target their victims.

* * *

In 1977, the National Socialist Party of America declared its intention to march, dressed in military-style uniforms displaying the swastika, through a Chicago suburb full of Jewish Holocaust survivors. Town authorities went to court to ban the march. After both the local and state courts acceded to that request, the ACLU appealed to the U.S. Supreme Court, prompting one of its most famous free-speech rulings. The ACLU dispatched two Jewish lawyers, David Goldberger and Aryeh Neier, himself a child Holocaust survivor, to argue on behalf of neo-Nazi First Amendment rights.

Just as in earlier decades, Jewish civil rights organizations found themselves internally divided on their response. In the end, the American Jewish Committee, American Jewish Congress, and Anti-Defamation League all reversed their 1960s policy. Each submitted briefs calling, to various degrees, for modest prior restraints on the neo-Nazi provocation. Still, they focused narrowly on the use of incendiary symbols and the event's location. "The flaunting of the swastika or a Nazi uniform," said the American Jewish Congress official Naomi Levine, "is not an expression of a constitutionally protected idea ... [but] a provocative and insulting symbol which by its very nature inflicts injury and tends to incite an immediate breach of peace."

The tactics of these Jewish groups reflected a desire to reconcile their proud tradition of civil libertarianism with an anguished awareness that violent anti-Semitism had not disappeared from society. The old tools still applied; they just should be used with utmost discretion. This time, however, the Supreme Court chose to view hate speech not as group defamation or inciteful "fighting words" but simply as insults to Jewish feelings: The "public expression of ideas may not be prohibited merely because the ideas are themselves offensive to some of their hearers."

Skokie marked the beginning of a new free speech orthodoxy in American civil-rights jurisprudence. Over the course of the 1980s and 1990s, nearly all of the state group libel statutes still on the books were repealed. A wave of progressive hate speech codes floated in colleges and universities were consistently ruled illegal by courts. Other related anti-bias criminal statutes were deemed unconstitutional. After Skokie, courts began a march toward maximalist views of free speech.

American Jewish civil rights groups, meanwhile, struggled to balance their proud fidelity to the First Amendment with a growing unease at the persistence of anti-Semitism. Neo-Nazi hate groups remained active, and politicians such as David Duke suggested the potential for such ideology to seep into mainstream electoral politics. The far left revealed its own brand of anti-Semitism as well, centered principally on classic tropes of exaggerated global Jewish financial and political power, along with a venomous anti-Zionism that often bled into anti-Semitism. Still other versions came directly from the Reverend Louis Farrakhan and the Nation of Islam, which targeted Jews in grossly anti-Semitic terms as racial enemies, even to the point of finding common cause with white supremacists.

These and other controversies, many centered on college campuses, tested the limits of Jewish faith in free speech as an absolute good. In search of a solution, Jewish civil rights groups opted to privatize the battle against anti-Semitism. Across the 1980s and 1990s, they conducted private intelligence surveillance on extremists and promoted educational initiatives to combat extremism and anti-Semitism. The soft instruments of public awareness campaigns, tolerance training, and informal advocacy replaced the harder force of legal action.

The privatization of Jewish civil rights produced one other strategy: individual civil lawsuits to bankrupt hate groups. In 1971, a white southern businessman and lawyer named Morris Dees Jr. joined with his Jewish law partner Joseph Levin and the African American activist Julian Bond to launch the Southern Poverty Law Center. Their novel approach was to use civil tort law to combat racism and anti-Semitism. In 1979, the SPLC sued several Ku Klux Klan and neo-Nazi groups for civil damages for racist attacks on individuals, winning multimillion-dollar jury verdicts. A new idea was born. Rather than task the government with silencing extremists, private citizens could simply take matters into their own hands by pursuing their material assets after the fact. The effect would be the same. Putting hate groups out of business would ensure that they could not speak freely anymore.

During the 1980s and 1990s, the SPLC grew into a multimillion-dollar nonprofit behemoth. It took advantage of a war chest filled via direct-mail fundraising and its own private intelligence work to launch a series of successful high-profile lawsuits on behalf of victims of domestic terrorism and violent hate crimes. That approach scored some wins. But it removed the burden of litigation from the government—as well as the responsibility to prevent transparently ideological abuses of free speech.

The reliance on private torts to do the work of public justice led over time to a technocratic, free market approach to combatting extremism. Anti-Semitism and racism became economic problems to be solved through seizing assets after the fact rather than checking hate speech before it could inflict its damage. Most crucially, the regnant free speech orthodoxy has proved increasingly ineffective in the face of a newly empowered alt-right that makes sophisticated use of digital publishing, social media, and public spectacle to market its own ideology. The whack-a-mole approach to defunding hate is unlikely to achieve the same effect as comprehensive public legal statutes. Nor will politicians' demands for Facebook, Twitter, and other social-media companies to police their own users serve as effectively as constitutional laws that draw a clear line between legitimate expression and hate speech....

* * *

Protecting American Jews today may require revisiting legal ideas that were repeatedly proposed and abandoned by earlier generations of Jewish lawyers in their quest for civil rights. Group libel laws hold the potential to protect Jews and other minorities from incitement and other dangerous speech that poses a new threat. They can fill the space between free speech and hate speech with a comprehensive, uniform set of laws to settle controversies otherwise reduced to media circuses and political polemics.

American Jews long ago pioneered new legal tools to combat hate from spreading through the national media, stop its entry into mainstream politics, and check its threat to minority communities. They, too, faced a world of disruptive media, populist politics, and global anti-Semitic currents. Those ideas and experiments remain available today as options to confront rising anti-Semitism and other forms of hatred across the political spectrum.

To access those legal instruments, however, will require accepting some hard truths about the place of Jews in American society and exploding some myths about the First Amendment. Progressives must accept that Jews face real threats and deserve legal protection. Conservatives must come to terms with the fact that not all offensive political speech about Zionism and Israel is anti-Semitism.[69] Moreover, the best way to ban discriminatory behavior is not by singling out American Jews or the state of Israel for special protection, but by drafting laws that address all forms of bias equally. And everyone needs to think again about the proper balance between free speech and hate speech in American civil rights law.

We live in an era in which what was once thought impossible has become possible. Generations of constitutional lawyers assumed that the right of free speech could never be applied to private corporations. Then came the Supreme Court *Citizens United v.*

69. Editor's note: Recall that in Chapter 5, David Schraub argued that some anti-Zionists must come to terms with the fact that *some* speech about Zionism and Israel is in fact antisemitic.

FEC decision. For decades, *Roe v. Wade* was considered settled law. Now conservatives have set their sights on overturning it. For nearly a century, law professors decried President Franklin D. Roosevelt's 1937 attempt to "pack the Court" by expanding the size of the Supreme Court. Now progressive lawyers have begun to refloat this radical idea as a legal solution to the larger ills of American politics. All of these developments should remind us that constitutional law is a fundamentally open-ended project subject to ceaseless debate and constant reinterpretation.

When it comes to civil rights, the arc of the moral universe does not bend toward justice all by itself; humans bend it. Their hands can shape law only in the directions that their minds can imagine. That mental exercise begins with historical retrospection. If we look backwards with opened eyes, law's forgotten past can suggest new ways to rethink its present and reenvision its future.

Is Hate Speech Over-Protected?

1. *Newport letter.* How did George Washington's 1790 letter to the Newport Jews shape the legal treatment of Jewish identity in America, according to Loeffler? What were the long-term implications of this framework?

2. *Loeffler on Marshall.* What is Loeffler's assessment of Louis Marshall's advocacy on behalf of American Jews? Does it change your assessment of Marshall? How did Marshall navigate the tension between free speech principles and protecting Jews and other marginalized groups from the harms of hate speech?

3. *Turning points.* In what sense were the Henry Ford case and the Skokie case turning points in Jewish advocacy, according to Loeffler? How did these cases shape the approach of Jewish civil rights organizations to combating hate speech?

4. *The* Beauharnais *precedent.* Why was the *Beauharnais v. Illinois* ruling significant? How does it challenge the conventional interpretation of the First Amendment? Why did Jewish advocacy groups largely choose not to utilize this precedent? Could *Beauharnais* be revived in contemporary law, or is it beyond revival?

5. *Alternative history.* What alternative history does Loeffler envision if Jewish advocacy groups had embraced *Beauharnais*? What new era of Jewish civil rights might it have ushered in? Would it have worked?

6. *Realists.* How did legal realists like Alexander Pekelis and David Riesman approach group protections? How did their ideas differ from the prevailing legal thought of their time?

7. *Public versus private.* What public and private enforcement approaches to combating hate speech and antisemitism does Loeffler discuss? What is his assessment of their efficacy?

8. *Online hate speech.* As we consider the next chapter on "Online Hate Speech," how might the concept of group defamation be adapted or reimagined to combat hate and extremism on social media platforms, based on Loeffler's historical analysis?

C. Covertly Antisemitic Speech

The U.S. Equal Employment Opportunity Commission (EEOC) is an independent federal agency that enforces federal anti-discrimination laws concerning employment. These include, most notably, Title VII of the Civil Rights Act of 1964 (Title VII), 42 U.S.C. §§2000e et seq., which prohibits employment discrimination based on race, color, religion, sex, and national origin. The EEOC issues guidance expressing official agency policy and explaining how the EEO laws and regulations apply to specific workplace situations.

In January 2021, the EEOC published Section 12 of the *Compliance Manual on Religious Discrimination*, which addresses Title VII's prohibition against religious discrimination in employment. This document contains the following passage with three examples intended to illustrate religious discrimination.

EEOC Compliance Manual on Religious Discrimination, *Employment Decisions Based on Religion*

§12-I-A.1 (2021)

An otherwise qualified applicant is not hired because he is a self-described evangelical Christian. A qualified non-Jewish employee is denied promotion because the supervisor wishes to give a preference based on religion to a fellow Jewish employee. An employer terminates an employee based on his disclosure to the employer that he has recently converted to the Baha'i Faith. Each of these is an example of an employment decision based on the religious belief or practice of the applicant or employee, and therefore is discrimination based on "religion" within the meaning of Title VII.[70]

1. *Jews are clannish.* Professor Robert Katz offers the following critique of this passage:

> The second example in this passage, intentionally or not, reflects the antisemitic trope that Jews are clannish. This stereotype is widely held: According to a 2022 Anti-Defamation League (ADL) survey, 53 percent of respondents agreed with the statement that "Jews in business go out of their way to hire other Jews."
>
> Two parties are responsible for this example: those who wrote it and those who approved it. The writers presumably started with a simple, non-antisemitic fact pattern that mirrored the Christian and Baha'i examples: "An otherwise qualified applicant is not hired because he is Jewish." The Christian and Baha'i examples do not provide fact patterns that reinforce stereotypes.

70. U.S. Equal Opportunity Emp. Comm'n, OLC Control No. EEOC-CVG-2021-3, Section 12: Religious Discrimination (2021), https://www.eeoc.gov/laws/guidance/section-12-religious-discrimination#h_9593682596821610748647076.

Figure 8.6. EEOC Seal.

The writers might have similarly provided the "Jewish" example. They instead chose to modify the example in certain telling ways. For example, they made the victim a non-Jew and the victimizer a Jew. They depicted the Jew as engaged in illegal activity, playing into a stereotype that Jews are devious and dishonest. They gave the Jew the power to control the fate of the non-Jew. They depicted the Jew as disloyal to the employer, who desired to promote the most qualified person.

While it seems unlikely the EEOC intended to lend credence to antisemitic stereotypes that Jews are dishonest, devious, disloyal, malevolent, controlling, and give unfair advantages to fellow Jews, the example can clearly be interpreted that way. Asserting or implying that Jews possess these odious qualities is a form of group defamation or hate speech.

The people who approved the manual's publication with this passage also should have known better. Even if this language reflects unintentional or unconscious anti-Jewish bias, it demonstrates the ease with which such bias can infect otherwise sound legal minds. The fact that this appears in an EEOC publication magnifies the problem. If there is any agency that should know better it is the EEOC, an agency charged with fighting discrimination.[71]

71. Robert Katz, *How Antisemitism Infects the Law*, Am. Bar. Ass'n (Dec. 9, 2024), https://www.americanbar.org/groups/crsj/publications/human_rights_magazine_home/combating-antisemitism/how-antisemitism-infects-the-law/.

2. *Racial antisemitism. In Clayton v. Ramsden* (Chapter 5.A.), the House of Lords provided an explicitly biological explanation for Jews' alleged clannishness, namely, Jews are driven by racial instinct to look after their own. Is the EEOC racist?

3. *Religious antisemitism.* Concerning the EEOC's Jewish example, antisemitism scholar Lesley Klaff writes:

> The Jew is cast as the 'discriminator.' ... There is also the antisemitic stereotype of Jews as clannish, tribal, and self-serving. Informing the characterization of the 'Jew-as-discriminator' and the stereotype of the 'Jew-as-tribal' and 'self-serving', is an implicit comparison of Judaism with Christianity, which views the latter as intrinsically about universalism, and Judaism as not. This racializes Jews as a people who treats non-Jews less favourably than they treat themselves.... [T]his racializing process involves the "orientalising" of Jews. This considers the 'law of the Jews' to be archaic and discriminatory and the 'law of the Christians' to be modern, just, and protective of individual rights.... In other words, Christian values are about fairness, equality, and individual rights, whereas Jewish values are about advancing Jewish interests.... Of course, all this happens at an unconscious level in the antisemite and in many ways is endemic to Western Christian thinking. We see it in the idea of Jewish particularism and Christian universalism.... It's all a relic of Christian antisemitism.[72]

4. *The racism that sneaks past you.* Author David Baddiel describes antisemitism as:

> a racism that often shows itself in codes and tropes and assumptions. It is, as one antiracist tweeter said, after being shocked at how unwittingly snared he had been by some of the traps outlined in this book, "the racism that sneaks past you." *Jews Don't Count* is to some extent a primer to prevent that sneakiness, to spot the traps in advance: perhaps even to see when you yourself... have fallen into them.[73]

Relatedly, Katz writes that "antisemitism can warp the work of lawyers—even intelligent and well-intentioned professionals—by loosening the inhibitions for engaging in antisemitic speech."[74]

5. "*Every Jew noticed that.*" In a televised debate, U.K. politician Jeremy Corbyn pronounced the last name of Jeffrey Epstein, the pedophile sex-trafficker, as "Epshteen." David Baddiel reports that Corbyn's expression "was taken, by some, as unconsciously highlighting the Jewishness of a very unsavory character. In other words, some Jews perceived Corbyn's expression, while not explicitly naming Jews, as latently antisemitic." In response, Baddiel posted on Twitter "Every Jew noticed that." Some non-Jews angrily responded, "How dare you call Corbyn an antisemite!" Baddiel retorts

---

72. E-mail from Lesley D. Klaff to Robert Katz (Nov. 3, 2024, 9:02 AM) (on file with author).

73. David Baddiel, Jews Don't Count: How Identity Politics Failed One Particular Identity xiii–xiv (2021).

74. Katz, *supra* note 70.

that he was making a different point: Corbyn's speech registered as antisemitic with Jews—separate and apart from whether Corbyn intentionally or subconsciously intended his speech to be antisemitic.[75] Baddiel writes:

> We live in a culture now where impact is more important than intent; where how things are taken is more significant than how they are meant....
>
> It is a progressive article of faith ... that those who experience racism need to listen, to learn, to accept and not challenge, when others speak about their experiences.[76]

6. *What did they know and when did they know it?* Assume (a) prior to the Manual's publication, EEOC officials were not consciously aware that the Jewish example was antisemitic; (b) at some point after the publication, EEOC was made consciously aware of the Jewish example's antisemitic content; and (c) despite such awareness, the EEOC does not withdraw the Jewish example. How much time must elapse before the EEOC, by intentionally declining to remove antisemitic expression from its publications, fully owns such expression—even if the initial defamation was not intentional?

7. *A comparator?* Has the EEOC ever propagated stereotypes about another group it is tasked with protecting, presumably unintentionally? If so, how did respond once being made aware of this? If it has never defamed another group, only Jews, this itself is worthy of remark. Does the EEOC have a compelling non-antisemitic interest in using an antisemitic example? Has it chosen the least antisemitic means available to advance that interest?

8. *Recourse.* What avenues of recourse, legal, political, or otherwise, are available to pressure or compel the EEOC to withdraw its antisemitic speech? Do you know how to reach your Senator or Congressperson? Were you aware that several congressional committees have oversight responsibility of the EEOC, it is funded through congressional appropriations, and its leaders are appointed by the President and confirmed by the Senate?

9. *Self-silencing.* Presumably one or more Jewish attorneys either inside or outside the EEOC read the passage, detected its antisemitic content, and didn't complain to the EEOC. Why didn't they?

10. *Training allies.* Why is the passage's antisemitic content visible to some non-Jews but invisible to others? How might more allies be trained to detect it?

75. BADDIEL, *supra* note 72, at 39–40.

76. *Id.*, at 40–41.

Chapter 9

Online Hate Speech

Social media serves as an effective means of propagating messages, including group defamation and hate speech. One commentator notes that "defamatory messages can be sent to countless numbers of users by merely pressing a button from a private home computer, such as by sending email messages or through bulletin board or other website postings."[1] In one instance, 714 antisemitic posts were viewed over 7.3 million times.[2]

Jews may experience more antisemitism on social media than in any other venue.[3] Religion is one of the top reasons Jews experience online harassment.[4] Sixty-two percent of American Jews have reported encountering antisemitism online or on social media within the last year. This content takes a personal toll: twenty-two percent of American Jews who experienced antisemitism online reported that the incident made them feel physically threatened.[5] Forty-one percent altered their online behavior to avoid being recognized as Jews.[6] Online antisemitic content surged after Hamas's October 7, 2023, attack on Israel. CyberWell documented a doubling of antisemitic in the weeks following the attack compared to previous periods.[7] ADL reported an "eruption

---

1. Jay M. Zitter, *Liability of Internet Service Provider for Internet or E-mail Defamation*, 84 A.L.R. 5th 169 (2000).

2. *Failure to Protect*, Ctr. for Countering Digit. Hate (July 30, 2021), https://counterhate.com/research/failure-to-protect/.

3. *Antisemitism Online and on Social Media Runs Rampant*, Am. Jewish Comm. (Feb. 18, 2024), https://www.ajc.org/news/antisemitism-online-and-on-social-media-runs-rampant; *New AJC Report; 46% of American Jews Altered Behavior Out of Fear of Antisemitism*, Am. Jewish Comm. (Feb. 13, 2024), https://www.ajc.org/news/new-ajc-report-46-of-american-jews-altered-behavior-out-of-fear-of-antisemitism.

An AJC 2023 survey reported that "among all Jewish adults who experienced antisemitic content online at least once in the past 12 months, 51% say they experienced antisemitism on Facebook, 47% say they experienced it on X (formerly known as Twitter), 27% on Instagram, 24% on YouTube, and 18% on TikTok. Another one in ten (11%) say they experienced antisemitism via online gaming platforms." *Antisemitism Online and on Social Media Runs Rampant*, *supra*.

4. *See Online Hate and Harassment: The American Experience 2024*, The Anti-Defamation League (June 11, 2024), https://www.adl.org/resources/report/online-hate-and-harassment-american-experience-2024.

5. *The State of Antisemitism in America 2023*, Am. Jewish Comm., https://www.ajc.org/AntisemitismReport2023#prioritybox (last visited Nov. 15, 2024).

6. The Anti-Defamation League, Online Hate and Harassment: The American Experience 2024 5 (2024), https://www.adl.org/sites/default/files/documents/2024-06/online-hate-and-harassment-the-american-experience-v2024.pdf.

7. Brooke Sarah Borden, *Antisemitism Online Directly Increases Real-World Violence, Study Finds*, The Jerusalem Post (Nov. 18, 2023, 3:17 PM), https://www.jpost.com/diaspora/antisemitism/article-773895. The ADL recorded a nearly 919% increase in antisemitic content on X and 28% on Facebook.

of antisemitism" on social media after October 7, with a 434 percent increase in violent antisemitic posts on platforms like X and Telegram on the day of the attack. Trending keywords included "Jew," "money," "TheNoticing," "Jews killed Jesus," "Jewish control," "Synagogue of Satan," "Zionist-occupied government," and "Protocols of the Elders of Zion."[8] There was a 1,600 percent surge in the hashtag #HitlerWasRight.[9]

Online hate speech may contribute to offline violence against Jews. Consider its role in the mass shooting at Pittsburgh's Tree of Life Synagogue on October 27, 2018, which resulted in the deaths of eleven people and was the deadliest attack on the Jewish community in American history.[10] The AJC reports that:

> In the days leading up to the [Tree of Life] attack, the shooter posted anti-immigrant polemics and antisemitic conspiracy theories on Gab, his favored social media service. The shooter's Gab profile featured the tagline, "Jews are the children of Satan" alongside the numbers "14:88," a coded reference to white supremacist slogans from Hitler's Europe. His posts displayed clear antisemitic hatred: "Kikes are enemy number one. Dealing with anything after will be a relative piece of cake. I will not fire on someone who is shooting my enemy."
>
> Subsequent analysis showed that much of the graphic and violent content on the Pittsburgh shooter's account was reposted from elsewhere, including from accounts maintained by Neo-Nazi groups. The gunman was able to develop and find encouragement for his antisemitic murders through conspiracy theories and violent imagery that was ubiquitous on Gab.
>
> After a sustained period steeped in anti-Jewish hatred and blood libels, the shooter's last message before committing the mass shooting at Tree of Life Synagogue read: "HIAS likes to bring invaders in that kill our people. I can't sit by and watch my people get slaughtered. Screw your optics, I'm going in." (HIAS refers to the Hebrew Immigrant Aid Society, which now seeks to help predominantly non-Jewish immigrants seek refuge on new shores.)[11]

This chapter explores online hate speech regulation, including self-regulation by social platforms.[12] Section A considers the challenges of applying common law defa-

---

Ctr. for Tech. and Soc'y, *Online Antisemitism Increased after Hamas Attack*, THE ANTI-DEFAMATION LEAGUE (Nov. 9, 2023), https://www.adl.org/resources/article/online-antisemitism-increased-after-hamas-attack.

8. Borden, *supra* note 7.

9. *Id.*

10. Emily Shapiro, *Pittsburgh Synagogue Shooter Sentenced to Death, Families Open up About 'Relief'*, ABC NEWS (Aug. 3, 2023, 1:00 PM), https://abcnews.go.com/US/pittsburgh-synagogue-mass-shooting-jury-reaches-verdict-death/story?id=101220141.

11. Brief of Am. Jewish Comm. as Amicus Curiae Supporting Respondents at 4–5, Moody v. NetChoice, LLC, 144 S. Ct. 2383 (2024) (No. 22-277), 2023 WL 8652852.

12. Whatever social media platforms are doing to combat online antisemitism, they could presumably do more. In 2021, platforms failed to act on 84 percent of posts containing antisemitism reported to them. CTR. FOR COUNTERING DIGIT. HATE, *supra* note 2.

mation law to speech published online. Section B explores the transformative impact of Section 230 of the Communications Decency Act of 1996, which largely immunized platforms from liability for user-generated content. Section C investigates platform self-regulation efforts, particularly Meta's evolving policies on hate speech. Section D analyzes the creation and function of Meta's Oversight Board, examining a case study on Holocaust denial content. Section E explores recent legislative attempts to increase platform transparency and accountability. Finally, Section F examines challenges to state laws attempting to prevent perceived platform bias in content moderation.

A. Applying Defamation Law to Platform Regulation

Stratton Oakmont, Inc. v. Prodigy Servs. Co.

1995 WL 323710 (N.Y. Sup. Ct., Nassau Cnty. 1995)[13]

The plaintiff brought a defamation action against a social media platform for alleged defamatory statements posted on its platform. Defamation law distinguishes between the "publishers" of defamatory speech and its "distributors," with the former being held to a stricter liability standard. This case presented the question of how to categorize the company. The plaintiff argued that the defendant should be deemed a "publisher" and the trial court, per Justice Ain, agreed. This case, decided one year before Section 230's enactment, typified the common law approach to online defamation.

JUSTICE STUART L. AIN.

At issue in this case are statements about Plaintiffs made by an unidentified bulletin board user or "poster" on PRODIGY's "Money Talk" computer bulletin board.... These statements included the following:

> (a) STRATTON OAKMONT, INC. ("STRATTON"), a securities investment banking firm, and DANIEL PORUSH, STRATTON's president, committed criminal and fraudulent acts in connection with the initial public offering of stock of Solomon-Page Ltd.
>
> (b) the Solomon-Page offering was a "major criminal fraud" and "100% criminal fraud."
>
> (d) STRATTON was a "cult of brokers who either lie for a living or get fired."

Plaintiffs commenced this action against PRODIGY, the owner and operator of the computer network on which the statements appeared, and the unidentified party who posted the aforementioned statements. The second amended complaint alleges ...

---

13. In New York State, the term "Supreme Court" refers to the trial-level courts of general jurisdiction, whose judges are referred to as "justices." New York State's highest court is the "Court of Appeals," and its judges are called "judges." New York can do this because it is New York.

claims for *per se* libel.... Plaintiffs seek partial summary judgment on ... whether PRODIGY may be considered a "publisher" of the aforementioned statements....

PRODIGY's computer network has at least two million subscribers who communicate with each other and with the general subscriber population on PRODIGY's bulletin boards. "Money Talk," the board on which the aforementioned statements appeared, is allegedly the leading and most widely read financial computer bulletin board in the United States, where members can post statements regarding stocks, investments, and other financial matters. PRODIGY contracts with bulletin Board Leaders, who, among other things, participate in board discussions and undertake promotional efforts to encourage usage and increase users....

Plaintiffs base their claim that PRODIGY is a publisher in large measure on PRODIGY's stated policy ... that it was a family oriented computer network....

First, PRODIGY held itself out to the public and its members as controlling the content of its computer bulletin boards. Second, PRODIGY implemented this control through its automatic software screening program, and the Guidelines which Board Leaders are required to enforce. By actively utilizing technology and manpower to delete notes from its computer bulletin boards on the basis of offensiveness and "bad taste," for example, PRODIGY is clearly making decisions as to content ... and such decisions constitute editorial control....

Based on the foregoing, this Court is compelled to conclude that for the purposes of Plaintiffs' claims in this action, PRODIGY is a publisher rather than a distributor.

Lawsuits for Online Defamation

1. *Common law publisher.* Under the common law of defamation, false defamatory content is not actionable unless "published," that is, it is communicated to a third person.[14] The quintessential publisher is a traditional media outlet that exercises editorial control over content, such as a newspaper, book publisher, or a radio or television broadcaster.[15] A publisher can be held liable for intentionally or negligently publishing defamatory content, including those that republish a third party's defamatory comment with the requisite knowledge of its defamatory character.[16]

2. *Common law distributor.* The common law distinguishes between a "publisher" or "republisher" of defamatory content and a "distributor," which consists of a news dealer, vendor, bookstore, or library. A distributor is deemed to act as a mere conduit of content without exercising editorial control and often transmits far more content than it could be expected to review. A distributor is not liable for what they transmit unless they knew or had reason to know of its defamatory character.[17]

---

14. Restatement (Second) of Torts § 577 (Am. L. Inst. 1977).
15. *Id.*; cmt. k; Rodney A. Smolla, Law of Defamation § 4:92 (2d ed. 1999).
16. *Supra* note 14, at § 578.
17. *Id.* § 581.

3. *Duty to remove defamatory content.* In some instances, an outlet could be held liable for failing to remove a defamatory statement posted on their platform. The Restatement (Second) Torts illustrates this situation as follows:

> A writes on the wall of the men's washroom in B's tavern a statement that C is an unchaste woman. B fails to discover the writing for an hour. After he discovers it, he fails to remove it for another hour, although he has ample opportunity to do so. During the second hour the writing is read by several men. B is subject to liability for the continued publication of the libel during the second hour, although not for the original publication.[18]

The rule is that "one who knows that defamatory matter is exhibited upon land or chattels in his possession or under his control and intentionally and unreasonably fails to remove it, becomes subject to liability for the continued publication."[19] Critically, a distributor has no absolute duty to police or inquire whether defamatory matter is being posted to its outlet. Its duty to remove defamatory content, moreover, is contingent and based on reasonableness:

> He is required only to exercise reasonable care to abate the defamation, and he need not take steps that are unreasonable if the burden of the measures outweighs the harm to the plaintiff. In extreme cases, as when, for example, the defamatory matter might be carved in stone in letters a foot deep, it is possible that the defendant may not be required to take any action at all. But when, by measures not unduly difficult or onerous, he may easily remove the defamation, he may be found liable if he intentionally fails to remove it.[20]

4. *Was* Stratton Oakmont *correctly categorized*? Did the *Stratton Oakmont* court correctly categorize PRODIGY as a "publisher" concerning the alleged defamatory statements? Is it more accurately characterized as a "distributor?" What are the social consequences, positive or negative, of the categorization? Are there special reasons unique to social media platforms for subjecting them to a lower liability standard, or none?

5. *Compare to* Cubby, Inc. v. CompuServe Inc.[21] In this case, the court held that the computer network CompuServe was not liable for allegedly defamatory material contained in a publication "Rumorville" uploaded to its platform. The court noted that "Rumorville" was written by an independent contractor, and that CompuServe had no opportunity to review its contents before uploading it. The court found that CompuServe's product was "in essence, an electronic for-profit library" that carried a vast number of publications, and that CompuServe had "little or no editorial control" over the contents of those publications:

---

18. *Id.* § 577 cmt. p, illus. 15.
19. *Id.* § 577 cmt. p.
20. *Id.*
21. 776 F. Supp. 135 (S.D.N.Y. 1991).

> A computerized database is the functional equivalent of a more traditional news vendor, and the inconsistent application of a lower standard of liability to an electronic news distributor such as CompuServe than that which is applied to a public library, bookstore, or newsstand would impose an undue burden on the free flow of information.

In short, the court found that CompuServe was more akin to a common law distributor than a publisher and thus held to a lower standard of liability. On this basis, the court ruled that plaintiffs' liability claim failed because it pleaded no basis for finding that CompuServe knew or had reason to know of the allegedly defamatory nature of Rumorville's statements. Can *Stratton Oakmont* and *Cubby* be meaningfully distinguished?

6. *Defamation using TV broadcasts.* The categorization of defamatory statements as either libel (written) or slander (spoken) has legal consequences: libel can give rise to both civil actions and criminal prosecution (criminal libel), whereas slander gives rise to civil suits only, i.e., there is no "criminal slander." With the advent of TV broadcasting, the new medium in its time, courts had to decide whether defamation using TV constituted libel or slander. The Restatement (Second) of Torts deemed it libel, a less speech-protective category than slander.[22] The Re-staters justified this position on policy and interest-balancing grounds.

> The wide dissemination that results from broadcasting over radio and television, together with the prestige and potential effect upon the public mind of a standardized means of publication that many people tend automatically to accept as conveying truth, are such as to put the broadcaster upon the same footing as the publisher of a newspaper.[23]

7. *You are there.* In 1939, NBC launched the first regularly scheduled television service in the U.S. Between 1946 and 1951, the number of TV sets in the U.S. grew from around 6,000 to 12 million. Assume the year is 1951 and you are the first judge called upon to decide whether defamatory statements disseminated by TV broadcasters should be deemed libel—thereby subjecting TV broadcasters to more liability (or less immunity), or slander—thereby subjecting them to less liability (or more immunity). How would you decide? If you were *currently* on the bench and called upon to resolve the same question, how would you decide?

---

22. *Id.* Restatement (Second) of Torts § 568A.

23. *Id.* cmt. a.

B. Platform Regulation under Section 230 of the Communications Decency Act of 1996

Zeran v. America Online, Inc.

129 F.3d 327 (4th Cir. 1997)

Stratton Oakmont put a spotlight on the issue of how social media platforms should be regulated. It raised concerns among platforms about their liability for content, concerns exacerbated by the growing volume of posts and videos being uploaded and their limited capacity to review them. Just one year after the opinion, Congress enacted Section 230 of the Communications Decency Act (CDA) of 1996, which immunized platforms from "publisher" liability for third-party content. Professor Jeff Kosseff argues that Section 230 was a "direct and swift response" to *Stratton Oakmont*.[24]

Section 230 left open the question of whether platforms are common law "distributors" and thus subject to distributor (if not publisher) liability. *Zeran v. America Online, Inc.*, one of the first significant cases to interpret Section 230, answered this question in the negative. The plaintiff claimed that America Online (AOL) had violated its distributor duties by failing to promptly remove defamatory messages posted by an unidentified third party on an AOL bulletin board. The district court ruled that Section 230 barred the plaintiff's claims and dismissed them. The Court of Appeals, per Chief Judge Wilkinson, affirmed.[25] This case illustrates how Section 230 supplanted the common law approach to harmful online speech and did so at a crucial juncture in the online world's development.

Chief Circuit Judge Wilkinson delivered the opinion of the Court.

Kenneth Zeran brought this action against America Online, Inc. ("AOL"), arguing that AOL unreasonably delayed in removing defamatory messages posted by an unidentified third party, refused to post retractions of those messages, and failed to screen for similar postings thereafter. The district court granted judgment for AOL on the grounds that the Communications Decency Act of 1996 ("CDA")—47 USC. § 230—bars Zeran's claims. Zeran appeals, arguing that § 230 leaves intact liability for interactive computer service providers who possess notice of defamatory material posted through their services.... Section 230, however, plainly immunizes computer service providers like AOL from liability for information that originates with third parties.... Accordingly, we affirm the judgment of the district court.

"The Internet is an international network of interconnected computers," currently used by approximately 40 million people worldwide. One of the many means by which individuals access the internet is through an interactive computer service. These ser-

24. Jeff Kosseff, The Twenty-Six Words That Created the Internet 55 (2019).

25. Recall that Chief Judge Wilkinson filed the dissenting opinion to the Fourth Circuit's ruling, denying the Shaare Tefila Congregation's § 1982 claim. *See* Shaare Tefila Congregation v. Cobb, 785 F.2d 523 (4th Cir. 1986), *rev'd*, 481 U.S. 615 (1987).

vices offer not only a connection to the internet as a whole but also allow their subscribers to access information communicated and stored only on each computer service's individual proprietary network. AOL is just such an interactive computer service. Much of the information transmitted over its network originates with the company's millions of subscribers. They may transmit information privately via electronic mail, or they may communicate publicly by posting messages on AOL bulletin boards, where the messages may be read by any AOL subscriber....

On April 25, 1995, an unidentified person posted a message on an AOL bulletin board advertising "Naughty Oklahoma T-Shirts." The posting described the sale of shirts featuring offensive and tasteless slogans related to the April 19, 1995, bombing of the Alfred P. Murrah Federal Building in Oklahoma City. Those interested in purchasing the shirts were instructed to call "Ken" at Zeran's home phone number in Seattle, Washington. As a result of this anonymously perpetrated prank, Zeran received a high volume of calls, composed primarily of angry and derogatory messages, but also including death threats. Zeran could not change his phone number because he relied on its availability to the public in running his business out of his home. Later that day, Zeran called AOL and informed a company representative of his predicament. The employee assured Zeran that the posting would be removed from AOL's bulletin board but explained that as a matter of policy, AOL would not post a retraction....

On April 26, the next day, an unknown person posted another message advertising additional shirts with new tasteless slogans related to the Oklahoma City bombing. Again, interested buyers were told to call Zeran's phone number, to ask for "Ken," and to "please call back if busy" due to high demand. The angry, threatening phone calls intensified. Over the next four days, an unidentified party continued to post messages on AOL's bulletin board, advertising additional items including bumper stickers and key chains with still more offensive slogans. During this period, Zeran called AOL repeatedly and was told by company representatives that the individual account from which the messages were posted would soon be closed. Zeran also reported his case to Seattle FBI agents. By April 30, Zeran was receiving an abusive phone call approximately every two minutes.

Meanwhile, an announcer for Oklahoma City radio station KRXO received a copy of the first AOL posting. On May 1, the announcer related the message's contents on the air, attributed them to "Ken" at Zeran's phone number, and urged the listening audience to call the number. After this radio broadcast, Zeran was inundated with death threats and other violent calls from Oklahoma City residents. Over the next few days, Zeran talked to both KRXO and AOL representatives. He also spoke to his local police, who subsequently surveilled his home to protect his safety. By May 14, after an Oklahoma City newspaper published a story exposing the shirt advertisements as a hoax and after KRXO made an on-air apology, the number of calls to Zeran's residence finally subsided to fifteen per day....

II. A

Because § 230 was successfully advanced by AOL in the district court as a defense to Zeran's claims, we shall briefly examine its operation here. Zeran seeks to hold AOL liable for defamatory speech initiated by a third party. He argued to the district court that once he notified AOL of the unidentified third party's hoax, AOL had a duty to remove the defamatory posting promptly, to notify its subscribers of the message's false nature, and to effectively screen future defamatory material. Section 230 entered this litigation as an affirmative defense pled by AOL. The company claimed that Congress immunized interactive computer service providers from claims based on information posted by a third party.

The relevant portion of § 230 states: "No provider or user of an interactive computer service shall be treated as the publisher or speaker of any information provided by another information content provider." 47 USC. § 230(c)(1). By its plain language, § 230 creates a federal immunity to any cause of action that would make service providers liable for information originating with a third party user of the service. Specifically, § 230 precludes courts from entertaining claims that would place a computer service provider in a publisher's role. Thus, lawsuits seeking to hold a service provider liable for its exercise of a publisher's traditional editorial functions—such as deciding whether to publish, withdraw, postpone, or alter content—are barred.

The purpose of this statutory immunity is not difficult to discern. Congress recognized the threat that tort-based lawsuits pose to freedom of speech in the new and burgeoning Internet medium. The imposition of tort liability on service providers for the communications of others represented, for Congress, simply another form of intrusive government regulation of speech. Section 230 was enacted, in part, to maintain the robust nature of Internet communication and, accordingly, to keep government interference in the medium to a minimum. In specific statutory findings, Congress recognized the Internet and interactive computer services as offering "a forum for a true diversity of political discourse, unique opportunities for cultural development, and myriad avenues for intellectual activity." § 230(a)(3). It also found that the Internet and interactive computer services "have flourished, to the benefit of all Americans, *with a minimum of government regulation*." § 230(a)(4). Congress further stated that it is "the policy of the United States ... to preserve the vibrant and competitive free market that presently exists for the Internet and other interactive computer services, *unfettered by Federal or State regulation*." § 230(b)(2).

None of this means, of course, that the original culpable party who posts defamatory messages would escape accountability. While Congress acted to keep government regulation of the Internet to a minimum, it also found it to be the policy of the United States "to ensure vigorous enforcement of Federal criminal laws to deter and punish trafficking in obscenity, stalking, and harassment by means of computer." § 230(b)(5). Congress made a policy choice, however, not to deter harmful online speech through the separate route of imposing tort liability on companies that serve as intermediaries for other parties' potentially injurious messages.

Congress's purpose in providing the § 230 immunity was thus evident. Interactive computer services have millions of users. The amount of information communicated via interactive computer services is therefore staggering. The specter of tort liability in an area of such prolific speech would have an obvious chilling effect. It would be impossible for service providers to screen each of their millions of postings for possible problems. Faced with potential liability for each message republished by their services, interactive computer service providers might choose to severely restrict the number and type of messages posted. Congress considered the weight of the speech interests implicated and chose to immunize service providers to avoid any such restrictive effect.

Another important purpose of § 230 was to encourage service providers to self-regulate the dissemination of offensive material over their services. In this respect, § 230 responded to a New York state court decision, *Stratton Oakmont, Inc. v. Prodigy Servs. Co.*, 1995 WL 323710 (1995). There, the plaintiffs sued Prodigy—an interactive computer service like AOL—for defamatory comments made by an unidentified party on one of Prodigy's bulletin boards. The court held Prodigy to the strict liability standard normally applied to original publishers of defamatory statements, rejecting Prodigy's claims that it should be held only to the lower "knowledge" standard usually reserved for distributors. The court reasoned that Prodigy acted more like an original publisher than a distributor both because it advertised its practice of controlling content on its service and because it actively screened and edited messages posted on its bulletin boards.

Congress enacted § 230 to remove the disincentives to self-regulation created by the *Stratton Oakmont* decision. Under that court's holding, computer service providers who regulated the dissemination of offensive material on their services risked subjecting themselves to liability, because such regulation cast the service provider in the role of a publisher. Fearing that the specter of liability would therefore deter service providers from blocking and screening offensive material, Congress enacted § 230's broad immunity "to remove disincentives for the development and utilization of blocking and filtering technologies that empower parents to restrict their children's access to objectionable or inappropriate online material." 47 USC. § 230(b)(4). In line with this purpose, § 230 forbids the imposition of publisher liability on a service provider for the exercise of its editorial and self-regulatory functions.

B

Zeran argues, however, that the § 230 immunity eliminates only publisher liability, leaving distributor liability intact. Publishers can be held liable for defamatory statements contained in their works, even absent proof that they had specific knowledge of the statement's inclusion. According to Zeran, interactive computer service providers like AOL are normally considered instead to be distributors, like traditional news vendors or book sellers. Distributors cannot be held liable for defamatory statements contained in the materials they distribute unless it is proven at a minimum that they have actual knowledge of the defamatory statements upon which liability is predicated....

Because of the difference between these two forms of liability, Zeran contends that the term "distributor" carries a legally distinct meaning from the term "publisher." Accordingly, he asserts that Congress's use of only the term "publisher "in § 230 indicates a purpose to immunize service providers only from publisher liability. He argues that distributors are left unprotected by § 230 and, therefore, his suit should be permitted to proceed against AOL. We disagree. Assuming *arguendo* that Zeran has satisfied the requirements for imposition of distributor liability, this theory of liability is merely a subset, or a species, of publisher liability, and is therefore also foreclosed by § 230....

Our view that Zeran's complaint treats AOL as a publisher is reinforced because AOL is cast in the same position as the party who originally posted the offensive messages. According to Zeran's logic, AOL is legally at fault because it communicated to third parties an allegedly defamatory statement. This is precisely the theory under which the original poster of the offensive messages would be found liable. If the original party is considered a publisher of the offensive messages, Zeran certainly cannot attach liability to AOL under the same theory without conceding that AOL too must be treated as a publisher of the statements.

Zeran next contends that interpreting § 230 to impose liability on service providers with knowledge of defamatory content on their services is consistent with the statutory purposes outlined in Part IIA. Zeran fails, however, to understand the practical implications of notice liability in the interactive computer service context. Liability upon notice would defeat the dual purposes advanced by § 230 of the CDA. Like the strict liability imposed by the *Stratton Oakmont* court, liability upon notice reinforces service providers' incentives to restrict speech and abstain from self-regulation.

If computer service providers were subject to distributor liability, they would face potential liability each time they receive notice of a potentially defamatory statement—from any party, concerning any message....

Whenever one was displeased with the speech of another party conducted over an interactive computer service, the offended party could simply "notify" the relevant service provider, claiming the information to be legally defamatory. Considering the vast amount of speech communicated through interactive computer services, these notices could produce an impossible burden for service providers, who would be faced with ceaseless choices of suppressing controversial speech or sustaining prohibitive liability. Because the probable effects of distributor liability on the vigor of Internet speech and on service provider self-regulation are directly contrary to § 230's statutory purposes, we will not assume that Congress intended to leave liability upon notice intact....

Section 230 Rejects a Defamation Law Approach to Platform Regulation

1. *Findings.* Congress's legislative findings indicate that they were interested in promoting the "free development of the internet" while also providing support for industry efforts to implement technology that could filter and block problematic content. This extended to restricting children's access to inappropriate online material.[26]

2. *The publisher/distributor distinction. Zeran* and subsequent cases essentially removed any distinction between publishers and distributors for social media platforms,

---

26. Valerie c. Brannon & Eric N. Holmes, Cong. Rsch. Serv., R46751, Section 230: An Overview 2 (2024).

while still allowing them to exercise editorial control. Is it fair to say that platforms are publishers of all their content, especially when they do not materially contribute to most of the content posted on their sites? How much contribution is required to turn the third party's speech into the platform's speech, such as organization, application of algorithms, formatting, and word limitations?[27]

3. *Statutory interpretation.* According to the *Zeran* court, Section 230(c)(1) "plainly immunizes computer service providers ... from liability for information that originates with third parties." Is that your reading as well? Is the court's interpretive approach more accurately characterized as purposive? Rodney Smolla argues that such a reading cannot be grounded on legislative intent. In his view, courts have expanded Section 230's reach "far beyond any plausible mooring to what Congress had in mind when it passed the statute...."[28]

4. *Common law background.* In *Grace v. eBay Inc.* (Cal. Ct. App. 2004), an unfollowed opinion, the state court rejected the claim that Section 230 abrogated common law distributor liability for platforms:

> Section 230(c)(1) states that a provider or user of an interactive computer service may not "be treated as the publisher or speaker" of information provided by another person. To understand the intended effect of this provision on the common law of libel requires an understanding of the common law of libel. We presume that Congress was aware of common law principles and intended those principles to apply absent some indication to the contrary. In such cases, Congress does not write upon a clean slate. In order to abrogate a common-law principle, the statute must "speak directly" to the question addressed by the common law.
>
> Section 230(c)(1) does not state that a provider or user of an interactive computer service may not be treated as a "distributor" or "transmitter" of information provided by another person, but only that a provider or user may not "be treated as the publisher or speaker." In light of the common law distinction between liability as a primary publisher and liability as a distributor, we conclude that section 230(c)(1) does not clearly and directly address distributor liability and therefore does not preclude distributor liability.[29]

5. *Defamation law as government regulation.* The *Zeran* court described defamation suits against providers as a form of government regulation. This characterization tests

---

27. *See* Jones v. Dirty World Ent. Recordings LLC, 755 F.3d 398, 411 (6th Cir. 2014) (articulating a "material contribution test" to discern whether a party is immune under Section 230); *see also* Twitter, Inc. v. Taamneh, 598 U.S. 471 (2023); *see also* Gonzalez v. Google LLC, 598 U.S. 617 (2023).

28. Rodney A. Smolla, Law of Defamation § 4:92 (2d ed. 1999).

29. *Compare* Grace v. eBay Inc., 16 Cal. Rptr. 3d 192, 198 (Cal. Ct. App.), *rev. granted and superseded by* 99 P.3d 2 (Cal.), *appeal dismissed*, 101 P.3d 509 (Cal. 2004), *with* Gentry v. eBay, Inc., 121 Cal. Rptr. 2d 703 (Cal. Ct. App. 2002), *and* Kathleen R. v. City of Livermore, 104 Cal. Rptr. 2d 772 (Cal. Ct. App. 2001).

the distinction between "public law" and "private law."[30] Defamation law, traditionally a branch of private law, is government regulation insofar as the state maintains a legal system that interprets and applies defamation law to decide cases and enforce remedies. By enforcing defamation law, the state encourages parties to act with reasonable care to avoid harming other parties' reputations, an outcome generally perceived as serving the public interest. Characterizing defamation suits as government regulation recalls *Shelley v. Kraemer*'s holding that judicial enforcement of restrictive covenants is "state action" for Equal Protection purposes. This approach leaves intact voluntary "self-regulation" wherein non-state actors can make non-judicially enforceable arrangements, for example, to discriminate based on race or to regulate speech based on content. Defamation law continues to apply to speech disseminated via "offline" media such as newspapers, books, television, and radio.

C. Challenges to Broad Immunity for Platforms

Force v. Facebook, Inc.

934 F.3d 53 (2d Cir. 2019)

[The plaintiffs were victims of Hamas attacks in Israel. They sued Facebook under the civil remedies provision of the Anti-Terrorism Act (ATA) related to Hamas's acts. The district court found that Section 230(c)(1) immunized Facebook's conduct and so barred plaintiffs' claims. Plaintiffs appealed to the Court of Appeals which, per Judge Droney, affirmed the district court's ruling. In an important dissent, Robert A. Katzmann, Chief Judge of the Second Circuit, argued for limiting Section 230 immunity concerning recommendations generated by a platform's algorithms. Note that Section 230 did not immunize platforms from being held legally responsible for information that they have developed.[31]]

CIRCUIT JUDGE DRONEY delivered the opinion of the Court.

The principal question presented in this appeal is whether 47 USC. § 230(c)(1), a provision enacted by the Communications Decency Act of 1996 ["CDA"], shields Facebook, Inc., from civil liability as to Plaintiffs federal antiterrorism claims. Plaintiffs include the U.S. citizen victims, and relatives and representatives of the estates of those victims, of certain terrorist attacks committed by Hamas in Israel. They contend that Facebook unlawfully provided Hamas, a U.S. designated foreign terrorist organization, with a communications platform that enabled those attacks....

---

30. Public law denotes "the body of law dealing with the relations between private individuals and the government, and with the structure and operation of the government itself," and includes constitutional law, criminal law, and administrative law. *Public Law*, BLACK'S LAW DICTIONARY (11th ed. 2019). Private law denotes "the body of law dealing with private persons and their property and relationships," and includes the law of contracts, torts, wills, and trusts. *Private Law*, BLACK'S LAW DICTIONARY (11th ed. 2019).

31. BRANNON & HOLMES, *supra* note 25.

[Plaintiffs] argue that Facebook does not act as the publisher of Hamas's content within the meaning of Section 230(c)(1) because it uses algorithms to suggest content to users, resulting in "matchmaking." For example, plaintiffs allege that Facebook's "newsfeed" uses algorithms that predict and show the third-party content that is most likely to interest and engage users. Facebook's algorithms also provide "friend suggestions," based on analysis of users' existing social connections on Facebook and other behavioral and demographic data. And Facebook's advertising algorithms and "remarketing" technology allow advertisers to target ads to its users who are likely most interested in those ads.

We disagree with plaintiffs' contention that Facebook's use of algorithms renders it a non-publisher. First, we find no basis in the ordinary meaning of "publisher," the other text of Section 230, or decisions interpreting Section 230, for concluding that an interactive computer service is not the "publisher" of third-party information when it uses tools such as algorithms that are designed to match that information with a consumer's interests....

Indeed, arranging and distributing third-party information inherently forms "connections" and "matches" among speakers, content, and viewers of content, whether in interactive internet forums or in more traditional media. That is an essential result of publishing. Accepting plaintiffs' argument would eviscerate Section 230(c)(1); a defendant's interactive computer service would be ineligible for Section 230(c)(1) immunity by virtue of simply organizing and displaying content exclusively provided by third parties.

Plaintiffs' "matchmaking" argument would also deny immunity for the editorial decisions regarding third-party content that interactive computer services have made since the early days of the Internet. The services have always decided, for example, where on their sites (or other digital property) particular third-party content should reside and to whom it should be shown. Placing certain third-party content on a homepage, for example, tends to recommend that content to users more than if it were located elsewhere on a website. Internet services have also long been able to target the third-party content displayed to users based on, among other things, users' geolocation, language of choice, and registration information. And, of course, the services must also decide what type and format of third-party content they will display, whether that be a chat forum for classic car lovers, a platform for blogging, a feed of recent articles from news sources frequently visited by the user, a map or directory of local businesses, or a dating service to find romantic partners. All of these decisions, like the decision to host third-party content in the first place, result in "connections" or "matches" of information and individuals, which would have not occurred but for the internet services' particular editorial choices regarding the display of third-party content. We, again, are unaware of case law denying Section 230(c)(1) immunity because of the "matchmaking" results of such editorial decisions.

Seen in this context, plaintiffs' argument that Facebook's algorithms uniquely form "connections" or "matchmaking" is wrong. That, again, has been a fundamental result of publishing third-party content on the Internet since its beginning. Like the decision to place third-party content on a homepage, for example, Facebook's algorithms might cause more such "matches" than other editorial decisions. But that is not a basis to exclude the use of algorithms from the scope of what it means to be a "publisher" under Section 230(c)(1). The matches also might—as compared to those resulting from other editorial decisions—present users with targeted content of even more interest to them, just as an English speaker, for example, may be best matched with English-language content. But it would turn Section 230(c)(1) upside down to hold that Congress intended that when publishers of third-party content become especially adept at performing the functions of publishers, they are no longer immunized from civil liability....

Chief Judge Katzmann, dissenting in part.

Our precedent does not grant publishers CDA immunity for the full range of activities in which they might engage. Rather, it "bars lawsuits seeking to hold a service provider liable for its exercise of a publisher's traditional editorial functions—such as deciding whether to publish, withdraw, postpone or alter content...." For instance, a claim against a newspaper based on the content of a classified ad (or the decision to publish or withdraw that ad) would fail under the CDA not because newspapers traditionally publish classified ads, but rather because such a claim would necessarily treat the newspaper as the publisher of the ad-maker's content. Similarly, the newspaper does not act as an "information content provider"—and thus maintains its CDA protection—when it decides to run a classified ad because it neither "creates" nor "develops" the information in the ad.

This case is different. Looking beyond Facebook's "broad statements of immunity" and relying "rather on a careful exegesis of the statutory language," the CDA does not protect Facebook's friend- and content-suggestion algorithms. A combination of two factors, in my view, confirms that claims based on these algorithms do not inherently treat Facebook as the publisher of third-party content. First, Facebook uses the algorithms to create and communicate its own message: that it thinks you, the reader—you, specifically—will like this content. And second, Facebook's suggestions contribute to the creation of real-world social networks. The result of at least some suggestions is not just that the user consumes a third party's content. Sometimes, Facebook's suggestions allegedly lead the user to become part of a unique global community, the creation and maintenance of which goes far beyond and differs in kind from traditional editorial functions....

While the majority and I disagree about whether § 230 immunizes interactive computer services from liability for all these activities or only some, it is pellucid that Congress did not have any of them in mind when it enacted the CDA. The text and legislative history of the statute shout to the rafters Congress's focus on reducing children's access to adult material. Congress could not have anticipated the pernicious spread of hate and violence that the rise of social media likely has since fomented. Nor could Congress have divined the role that social media providers themselves would play in this tale. Mounting evidence suggests that providers designed their algorithms to drive users toward content and people the users agreed with—and that they have done it too well, nudging susceptible souls ever further down dark paths. By contrast, when the CDA became law, the closest extant ancestor to Facebook (and it was still several branches lower on the evolutionary tree) was the chatroom or message forum, which acted as a digital bulletin board and did nothing proactive to forge off-site connections.

Whether, and to what extent, Congress should allow liability for tech companies that encourage terrorism, propaganda, and extremism is a question for legislators, not judges. Over the past two decades "the Internet has outgrown its swaddling clothes," and it is fair to ask whether the rules that governed its infancy should still oversee its adulthood. It is undeniable that the Internet and social media have had many positive effects worth preserving and promoting, such as facilitating open communication, dialogue, and education. At the same time, as outlined above, social media can be manipulated by evildoers who pose real threats to our democratic society. A healthy debate has begun both in the legal academy and in the policy community about changing the scope of § 230. Perhaps Congress will clarify what I believe the text of the provision already states: that the creation of social networks reaches beyond the publishing functions that § 230 protects. Perhaps Congress will engage in a broader rethinking of the scope of CDA immunity. Or perhaps Congress will decide that the current regime best balances the interests involved. In the meantime, however, I cannot join my colleagues' decision to immunize Facebook's friend- and content-suggestion algorithms from judicial scrutiny. I therefore must in part respectfully dissent....

Some Problems with Broad Immunity for Platforms

1. *Internet exceptionalism.* Stuart Minor Benjamin observes that Section 230 was written only for the internet; "offline" platforms continue to be liable for defamatory postings in some cases. Benjamin refers to this as "internet exceptionalism."[32] Congress could presumably extend the same immunity to newspapers for letters to the editor or advertisements, creating "online/offline equivalence." Should it? Did the *Zeran* court balance the burden on providers to remove defamatory content and the harms of non-removal to defamed parties? Did it find that the former outweighed the latter such that it would be unreasonable to require platforms to remove such content? Benjamin observes that "AOL did not claim it could not take down the offending posts more quickly or prevent new posts from occurring." Do these reasons apply to newspapers and TV?

2. *Proposals to amend Section 230.* The broad immunity granted to internet platforms is not without its downsides. As legal scholar Danielle Keats Citron has noted, Section 230 has helped spur considerable harm to internet users, as "platforms lack sufficient incentive to combat online abuse because they generate significant profits from our likes, clicks, and shares," while victims of online abuse are unable to "sue

32. Stuart Minor Benjamin et al., Internet and Telecommunications Regulation 777 (2d ed. 2023).

sites ... [for] their suffering." In this vein, scholars have proposed several measures to reform Section 230, including:

(a) Revise the "under-filtering provision" of § 230(c)(1) to be "conditioned on a duty of care when claims involve intimate privacy violations, cyber stalking, or cyber harassment."

(b) Assign liability for websites that "deliberately encourage, solicit, or maintain intimate privacy violations, cyber stalking, or cyber harassment."

(c) Clarify that Section 230 applies only to speech by "replac[ing] the word 'information' in (c)(1) with the word 'speech.'" This change would "put all parties ... on notice that the classification of content as speech is not a given, but a fact to be demonstrated." Only where "content" is "speech" is the party immune from liability.

(d) Condition immunity on "reasonable content moderation." This would mean that platforms are immune from liability only if they can demonstrate that their "content-moderation practices writ large are reasonable."[33]

3. *Self-regulation.* As the popularity of the internet grew, and grew rapidly, the guidelines that platforms created to help decide what content was permissible, and what content was not, assumed increased importance. Over time, the social impact of online speech began to compete and sometimes overtake "offline "speech in public forums. And contrary to the First Amendment rules that opened the door to antisemitic and other hate speech in classic open public forums, with limited restrictions, speech online was not taking place in an open forum. Rather, it was taking place in privately-owned online spaces. This issue raised questions about how those concerned with antisemitism in those spaces should respond. What should they be seeking from social media platforms? What should a responsible social media platform's guidelines look like? How should they be enforced?

4. *Pushback.* Section 230(c)(2), addressing civil liability, provides in part that "no provider or user of an interactive computer service shall be held liable on account of any action voluntarily taken in good faith to restrict access to or availability of material that the provider or user considers to be obscene, lewd, lascivious, filthy, excessively violent, harassing, or otherwise objectionable, whether or not such material is constitutionally protected. ..." With the protection Section 230 offered, more websites that allowed comments from users began establishing rules to govern what would be permissible. They could do so, as private entities, and they had incentives to do so because a growing number of comments were offensive to them and/or to their users. Thanks to Section 230, they were now broadly protected in two ways. In most circumstances

33. *See* Danielle Keats Citron, *How to Fix Section 230*, 103 B.U. L. Rev. 713 (2023); *see also* Lauren Feiner, *Lawmakers Want to Carve Out Intimate AI Deepfakes from Section 230 Immunity*, The Verge (July 30, 2024, 11:47 AM), https://www.theverge.com/2024/7/30/24209514/intimate-privacy-protection-act-ai-deepfakes-section-230; *see generally Section 230 Legislative Tracker*, Lawfare, https://www.lawfaremedia.org/resources/section-230-tracker (last updated Sept. 19, 2023).

they would not be liable if they allowed something that someone found objectionable, nor would they be liable if they removed something that should have been allowed.

5. *Continuing liability for platform-generated content?* Does Section 230 immunize platforms from liability arising from their own speech or that of their agents or employees? *See, e.g.*, *Enigma Software Grp. USA, LLC v. Bleeping Comput. LLC*, 194 F. Supp. 3d 263 (S.D.N.Y. 2016) (holding that software developer adequately stated a defamation claim against defendant consumer support website whose staff member made false, defamatory statements of fact about developer's software); *Huon v. Denton*, 841 F.3d 733 (7th Cir. 2016) (holding that Section 230(c)(1) did not bar internet platform's alleged conduct in employing individuals who authored and posted defamatory comments).

6. *First Amendment-based public policies.* There is a backdoor way of importing First Amendment values into platform regulations even if the First Amendment doesn't apply: courts can interpret statutes to advance First Amendment-based public policies, as in *Zeran*.

7. *Algorithms.* To keep up traffic and keep viewers on their sites longer, many platforms have developed algorithms that match or recommend content to users likely to be interested in that content, perhaps with insufficient attention to the nature of the content they are recommending. For those concerned about antisemitic and other offensive content, these algorithms are a significant concern because they tend to draw users already open to such content in ever more deeply.[34]

8. *Justice Thomas takes note.* Justice Thomas commented on Judge Katzman's opinion in an opinion on the denial of *certiorari* in *Malwarebytes, Inc. v. Enigma Software Grp. USA* (2020). "Paring back the sweeping immunity of Section 230," wrote Justice Thomas, "would not necessarily render defendants liable for online misconduct. It simply would give plaintiffs a chance to raise their claims in the first place." Justice Thomas added that "extending Section 230 immunity beyond the natural reading of the text can have serious consequences." Who would or should take the next step to consider the questions Judge Katzman raised—the courts or Congress?

---

34. *See* Tammy Qiu, *A Psychiatrist's Perspective on Social Media Algorithms and Mental Health*, Stan. Univ. Hum.-Centered A.I. (Sept. 14, 2021), https://hai.stanford.edu/news/psychiatrists-perspective-social-media-algorithms-and-mental-health; *see also* Alfonso Pellegrino et al., *Research Trends in Social Media Addiction and Problematic Social Media Use: A Bibliometric Analysis*, 13 Frontiers in Psychiatry 1 (2022).

D. Platform Self-Regulation

Meta Transparency Center, *Facebook Community Standards—Hateful Conduct*

(Current Version as of January 7, 2025)

[META, formerly known as Facebook, Inc., has developed and published on its platform Community Standards that specify what speech may be propagated on its products and services. These standards, which have evolved over time, are designed to create a safe environment for users by prohibiting content that attacks people based on protected characteristics.[35] As of January 2025, there are 27 different topics addressed in these Standards, ranging from coordinating harm and promoting crime, to adult sexual exploitation, privacy violations, and third-party intellectual property infringement. The following excerpt is from Meta's standard regarding hateful conduct.]

We believe that people use their voice and connect more freely when they don't feel attacked on the basis of who they are. That is why we don't allow hateful content on Facebook, Instagram, or Threads....

We define hateful conduct as direct attacks against people—rather than concepts or institutions—on the basis of what we call protected characteristics (PCs): race, ethnicity, national origin, disability, religious affiliation, caste, sexual orientation, sex, gender identity, and serious disease. Additionally, we consider age a protected characteristic when referenced along with another protected characteristic. We also protect refugees, migrants, immigrants, and asylum seekers from the most severe attacks, though we do allow commentary on and criticism of immigration policies. Similarly, we provide some protections for non-protected characteristics, such as occupation, when they are referenced along with a protected characteristic. Sometimes, based on local nuance, we consider certain words or phrases as frequently used proxies for protected characteristics.

We remove dehumanizing speech, allegations of serious immorality or criminality, and slurs. We also remove harmful stereotypes, which we define as dehumanizing comparisons that have historically been used to attack, intimidate, or exclude specific groups, and that are often linked with offline violence. Finally, we remove serious insults, expressions of contempt or disgust, cursing, and calls for exclusion or segregation when targeting people based on protected characteristics ...

We recognize that people sometimes share content that includes slurs or someone else's hate speech in order to condemn the speech or raise awareness of it. In other

35. *See Hate Speech*, META, https://transparency.meta.com/policies/community-standards/hate-speech/ (last visited Nov. 15, 2024); *see also Community Standards*, META, https://transparency.meta.com/policies/community-standards/ (last visited Nov. 15, 2024); *see generally Meta Platforms*, WIKIPEDIA, https://en.wikipedia.org/wiki/Meta_Platforms (last visited Nov. 15, 2024); *see generally, Learn About Who We Are*, META, https://about.meta.com/company-info/ (last visited Nov. 15, 2024) (select "Who we are"; then select "Learn about who we are").

cases, speech, including slurs, that might otherwise violate our standards is used self-referentially or in an empowering way. We allow this type of speech where the speaker's intention is clear. Where intention is unclear, we may remove content.

People sometimes use sex- or gender-exclusive language when discussing access to spaces often limited by sex or gender, such as access to bathrooms, specific schools, specific military, law enforcement, or teaching roles, and health or support groups. Other times, they call for exclusion or use insulting language in the context of discussing political or religious topics, such as when discussing transgender rights, immigration, or homosexuality. Finally, sometimes people curse at a gender in the context of a romantic break-up.

Challenges in Moderating Content

1. *Unanswered questions.* How does Meta address essential questions concerning hateful conduct, including: (1) defining hateful conduct; (2) understanding context; (3) assessing intent; (4) determining appropriate enforcement; and (5) addressing mistakes and continuing to improve?

2. *Considering the overall context.* Social media platforms face challenges in moderating content that isn't clearly antisemitic. Context matters when addressing potentially offensive quotes, lyrics, or satire. Note that Meta relies on both humans and artificial intelligence to moderate content.[36]

E. Platform Censorship of Holocaust Denial

In 2018, Facebook founder Mark Zuckerberg expressed a permissive view on free speech, saying that the company "wasn't in the business of removing content just because it was factually wrong." To do otherwise, he suggested, was un-American:

> Some people argue internet platforms should allow all expression protected by the First Amendment, even though the First Amendment explicitly doesn't apply to companies. I'm proud that our values at Facebook are inspired by the American tradition, which is more supportive of free expression than anywhere else.

Concerning Holocaust denial, Zuckerberg responded that:

> I'm Jewish, and there's a set of people who deny that the Holocaust happened. I find that deeply offensive. But at the end of the day, I don't believe that our platform should take that down because I think there are things that different people get wrong.

---

36. *Case Study: Facebook*, New Am., https://www.newamerica.org/oti/reports/everything-moderation-analysis-how-internet-platforms-are-using-artificial-intelligence-moderate-user-generated-content/case-study-facebook/ (last visited Sept. 6, 2024).

Crucially, he said that "I don't think [Holocaust deniers are] intentionally getting it wrong." Several Jewish figures criticized Zuckerberg's statements, including Professor Deborah Lipstadt and the Anti-Defamation League's CEO, Jonathan Greenblatt. Lipstadt stated:

> I do not believe that non-governmental entities, such as Facebook, should be posting denial claims, Freedom of the press means the press should be free of governmental control. It does not mean that the press or social media platforms have to provide space for deniers. [Holocaust denial is] not a "mistaken" notion of history. It is a deliberate distortion, made in the name of hatred. Simply put: Denial is a form of antisemitism and racism.

Greenblatt called on Facebook to regard Holocaust denial as a violation of its community guidelines. In a related development, in 2020, the ADL, NAACP, Color of Change, and other civil rights groups called upon advertisers to stop buying advertisements on Facebook in July 2020 to protest its lax hate speech policy. More than 1,000 companies, including North Face, Patagonia, Unilever, Eddie Bauer, and Starbucks, participated in this campaign, called "Stop Hate for Profit."

On October 12, 2020, Facebook revised its Hate Speech Community Standard to explicitly prohibit content that denied or distorted the Holocaust. Zuckerberg explained:

> I've struggled with the tension between standing for free expression and the harm caused by minimizing or denying the horror of the Holocaust. My own thinking has evolved as I've seen data showing an increase in anti-Semitic violence, as have our wider policies on hate speech.[37]

In 2020, Meta launched the Facebook Oversight Board to serve as the platform's "Supreme Court" regarding content. According to Mark Zuckerberg, the Board is composed of "independent folks who don't work for Facebook" and "ultimately make the

---

37. Billy Perrigo, *Facebook Has Finally Banned Holocaust Denial. Critics Ask What Took Them So Long*, TIME (Oct. 12, 2020, 2:47 PM), https://time.com/5899201/facebook-holocaust-denial/. *But see* Ben Sales, *Mark Zuckerburg Says Facebook Won't Delete Holocaust Denial Posts*, Jewish Telegraphic Agency (July 18, 2018, 3:48 PM), https://www.jta.org/2018/07/18/united-states/heres-mark-zuckerberg-deals-holocaust-deniers-facebook; *but see* The Anti-Defamation League (@ADL), X (July 18, 2018, 4:00 PM), https://x.com/ADL/status/1019673174986969089?ref_src=twsrc%5Etfw%7Ctwcamp%5Etweetembed%7Ctwterm%5E1019673174986969089%7Ctwgr%5E23eb7cd733c05fd57c5b2a8187f5821b1bd69a72%7Ctwcon%5Es1_&ref_url=https%3A%2F%2Ftime.com%2F5342383%2Fmark-zuckerberg-holocaust-denial%2F; *but see* Ben Sales, *Sacha Baron Cohen Makes Nazi Analogy to Slam Mark Zuckerburg's Facebook Policy*, Jewish Telegraphic Agency (Oct. 18, 2019, 4:10 PM), https://www.jta.org/quick-reads/sacha-baron-cohen-makes-nazi-analogy-to-slam-mark-zuckerbergs-facebook-policy; *but see* Ben Sales, *Protesting Hate Speech, ADL and NAACP Call On Companies to Stop Running Facebook Ads in July*, Jewish Telegraphic Agency (June 17, 2020, 6:00 AM), https://www.jta.org/2020/06/17/united-states/protesting-hate-speech-adl-and-naacp-call-on-companies-to-stop-running-facebook-ads-in-july; *but see* Ben Sales, *How the ADL Went from Working with Facebook to Leading a Boycott Against It*, Jewish Telegraphic Agency (July 1, 2020, 5:32 PM), https://www.jta.org/2020/07/01/united-states/how-the-adl-went-from-working-with-facebook-to-leading-a-boycott-against-it; *but see* Stop Hate for Profit, https://www.stophateforprofit.org/.

final judgment call on what should be acceptable speech in a community that reflects the social norms and values of people all around the world."[38] This case, heard by the Oversight Board, involved an Instagram user who posted a meme containing false claims about the Holocaust. Several users subsequently reported them for violating Meta's Hate Speech policy, but Meta decided to leave the content up. The Oversight Board overturned that decision.

Meta Oversight Board,
Oversight Board Overturns Meta's Original Decision in Holocaust Denial Case

Oversight Bd. (Jan. 23, 2024)[39]

Summary

The Oversight Board has overturned Meta's original decision to leave up an Instagram post containing false and distorted claims about the Holocaust. The Board finds that the content violated Meta's Hate Speech Community Standard, which bans Holocaust denial. This prohibition is consistent with Meta's human rights responsibilities. The Board is concerned about Meta's failure to remove this content and has questions about the effectiveness of the company's enforcement. The Board recommends Meta take steps to ensure it is systematically measuring the accuracy of its enforcement of Holocaust denial content, at a more granular level.

About the Case

On September 8, 2020, an Instagram user posted a meme of Squidward—a cartoon character from the television series *SpongeBob SquarePants*. This includes a speech bubble titled, "Fun Facts About the Holocaust," which contains false and distorted claims about the Holocaust. The claims, in English, question the number of victims of the Holocaust, suggesting it is not possible that six million Jewish people could have been murdered based on supposed population numbers the user quotes for before and after the Second World War. The post also questions the existence of crematoria at

38. Kate Klonick, *The Facebook Oversight Board: Creating an Independent Institution to Adjudicate Online Free Expression*, 129 Yale L.J. 2418 (2020); *see also* Mark Zuckerberg, *A Blueprint for Content Governance and Enforcement*, Facebook, https://www.facebook.com/notes/751449002072082/?hc_location=ufi (last updated May 5, 2021); *see also* Kate Klonick, *The New Governors: The People, Rules, and Processes Governing Online Speech*, 131 Harv. L. Rev. 1598 (2018); *see also* Ezra Klein, *Mark Zuckerberg on Facebook's Hardest Year, and What Comes Next*, Vox (Apr. 2, 2018, 6:00 AM), https://www.vox.com/2018/4/2/17185052/mark-zuckerberg-facebook-interview-fake-news-bots-cambridge; *see also* Kate Klonick, *Inside the Making of Facebook's Supreme Court*, The New Yorker (Feb. 12, 2021), https://www.newyorker.com/tech/annals-of-technology/inside-the-making-of-facebooks-supreme-court.

39. This is the Oversight Board's summary of its decision. *See* Holocaust Denial, Case No. 2023-022-IG-UA (Oversight Board Oct. 2024), https://www.oversightboard.com/wp-content/uploads/2024/10/364381166094702.pdf (last accessed Jan. 8, 2025).

Auschwitz by claiming the chimneys were built after the war, and that world leaders at the time did not acknowledge the Holocaust in their memoirs.

On October 12, 2020, several weeks after the content was posted, Meta revised its Hate Speech Community Standard to explicitly prohibit Holocaust denial or distortion.

Since the content was posted in September 2020, users reported it six times for violating Meta's Hate Speech policy. Four of these reports were reviewed by Meta's automated systems that either assessed the content as non-violating or automatically closed the reports due to the company's COVID-19 automation policies. These policies, introduced at the beginning of the pandemic in 2020, automatically closed certain review jobs to reduce the volume of reports being sent to human reviewers, while keeping open potentially "high-risk" reports.

Two of the six reports from users led to human reviewers assessing the content as non-violating. A user who reported the post in May 2023, after Meta announced it would no longer allow Holocaust denial, appealed the company's decision to leave the content up. However, this was also automatically closed due to Meta's COVID-19 automation policies, which were still in force in May 2023. They then appealed to the Oversight Board.

Key Findings

The Board finds that this content violates Meta's Hate Speech Community Standard, which prohibits Holocaust denial on Facebook and Instagram. Experts consulted by the Board confirmed that all the post's claims about the Holocaust were either blatantly untrue or misrepresented historical facts. The Board finds that Meta's policy banning Holocaust denial is consistent with its human rights responsibilities. Additionally, the Board is concerned that Meta did not remove this content even after the company changed its policies to explicitly prohibit Holocaust denial, despite human and automated reviews.

As part of this decision, the Board commissioned an assessment of Holocaust denial content on Meta's platforms, which revealed use of the Squidward meme format to spread various types of antisemitic narratives. While the assessment showed a marked decline since October 2020 in content using terms like "Holohoax," it found that there are gaps in Meta's removal of Holocaust denial content. The assessment showed that content denying the Holocaust can still be found on Meta's platforms, potentially because some users try to evade enforcement in alternative ways, such as by replacing vowels in words with symbols, or creating implicit narratives about Holocaust denial using memes and cartoons.

It is important to understand Holocaust denial as an element of antisemitism, which is discriminatory in its consequences.

The Board has questions about the effectiveness and accuracy of Meta's moderation systems in removing Holocaust denial content from its platforms. Meta's human reviewers are not provided the opportunity to label enforcement data in a granular way (i.e., violating content is labelled as "hate speech" rather than "Holocaust denial"). Based on insight gained from questions posed to Meta in this and previous cases, the Board understands these challenges are technically surmountable, if resource intensive. Meta should build systems to label enforcement data at a more granular level, especially in view of the real-world consequences of Holocaust denial. This would potentially improve its accuracy in moderating content that denies the Holocaust by providing better training materials for classifiers and human reviewers. As Meta increases its reliance on artificial intelligence to moderate content, the Board is interested in how the development of such systems can be shaped to prioritize more accurate enforcement of hate speech at a granular policy level.

The Board is also concerned that, as of May 2023, Meta was still applying its COVID-19 automation policies. In response to questions from the Board, Meta revealed that it automatically closed the user's appeal against its decision to leave this content on Instagram in May 2023, more than three years after the pandemic began and shortly after both the World Health Organization and United States declared that COVID-19 was no longer a "public health emergency of international concern." There was a pressing need for Meta to prioritize the removal of hate speech and it is concerning that measures introduced as a pandemic contingency could endure long after circumstances reasonably justified them.

The Oversight Board's Decision

The Oversight Board overturns Meta's original decision to leave up the content. The Board recommends that Meta:

(a) Take technical steps to ensure that it is sufficiently and systematically measuring the accuracy of its enforcement of Holocaust denial content [policy], to include gathering more granular details.

(b) Publicly confirm whether it has fully ended all COVID-19 automation policies put in place during the pandemic.

Oversight Board Review

1. How does the Oversight Board's decision-making process compare to judicial review in the American legal system? Can a Board appointed by Meta truly act independently?

2. How should platforms like Meta balance the tension between protecting free speech and preventing the spread of harmful or false content, such as Holocaust denial?

3. Can the evolution of Meta's stance on Holocaust denial be seen as a reflection of broader societal shifts, or is it more about responding to external pressures, e.g., from advertisers and civil rights groups?

F. Regulation to Promote Transparency and Counter Bias

California Assembly Bill 587, *Content Moderation Requirements for Internet Terms of Service*

Cal. Bus. & Prof. Code, §§ 22675–22681 (West 2024)

Several states, including, Texas, and Florida, have enacted laws aimed at increasing transparency in content moderation practices on social media platforms. California Assembly Bill 587 (AB 587), a.k.a., the "Social Media Transparency and Accountability Act," requires platforms to publicly share their rules for moderating content, how violations are flagged, and data on flagged content.

22675. For purposes of this chapter, the following definitions apply....

(f) "Terms of service" means a policy or set of policies adopted by a social media company that specifies, at least, the user behavior and activities that are permitted on the internet-based service owned or operated by the social media company, and the user behavior and activities that may subject the user or an item of content to being actioned. This may include, but is not limited to, a terms of service document or agreement, rules or content moderation guidelines, community guidelines, acceptable uses, and other policies and established practices that outline these policies.

22676.

(a) A social media company [earning more than $100 million] shall post terms of service for each social media platform owned or operated by the company in a manner reasonably designed to inform all users of the social media platform of the existence and contents of the terms of service.

(b) The terms of service posted pursuant to subdivision (a) shall include all of the following:

(1) Contact information for the purpose of allowing users to ask the social media company questions about the terms of service.

(2) A description of the process that users must follow to flag content, groups, or other users that they believe violate the terms of service, and the social media company's commitments on response and resolution time.

(3) A list of potential actions the social media company may take against an item of content or a user, including, but not limited to, removal, demonetization, deprioritization, or banning....

22677.

(a) On a quarterly basis, a social media company shall submit to the Attorney General a terms of service report [including] ...

(3) A statement of whether the current version of the terms of service defines each of the following categories of content, and, if so, the definitions of those categories, including any subcategories:

(A) Hate speech or racism

(B) Extremism or radicalization

(C) Disinformation or misinformation

(D) Harassment

(E) Foreign political interference

(4) A detailed description of content moderation practices used by the social media company for that platform, including, but not limited to, all of the following:

(A) Any existing policies intended to address the categories of content described in paragraph (3).

(B) How automated content moderation systems enforce terms of service of the social media platform and when these systems involve human review.

(C) How the social media company responds to user reports of violations of the terms of service.

(D) How the social media company would remove individual pieces of content, users, or groups that violate the terms of service, or take broader action against individual users or against groups of users that violate the terms of service.

(5) (A) Information on content that was flagged by the social media company as content belonging to any of the categories described in paragraph (3),

22678. (a) (1) A social media company that violates the provisions of this chapter shall be liable for a civil penalty not to exceed fifteen thousand dollars ($15,000) per violation per day and may be enjoined in any court of competent jurisdiction....

Moody v. NetChoice, LLC

144 S. Ct. 2383 (2024)

In 2021, the Texas legislature enacted HB 20, legislation "relating to censorship of or certain other interference with digital expression," which prohibits large social media platforms from moderating content based on the user's or speaker's viewpoint. It also requires, inter alia, platforms to disclose how they moderate and promote content and explain how they enforce their policies. NetChoice, a trade association representing online and e-commerce businesses, challenged the law as a facially unconstitutional violation of their First Amendment rights, which the law burdened by compelling them to host and disseminate content they disagree with and by interfering with their editorial discretion and content moderation practices. Also in 2021, Florida enacted a similar law, S.B. 7072, a.k.a., the "Stop Social Media Censorship Act," which NetChoice also challenged.

In both cases, the district court entered preliminary injunctions blocking the laws' enforcement. Texas appealed to the U.S. Court of Appeals for the Fifth Circuit, which reversed the district court's injunction. The Fifth Circuit rejected the idea that large corporations have a "freewheeling" First Amendment right to censor what people say. It reasoned that the Texas law does not regulate the platforms' speech but protects other people's speech and regulates the platforms' conduct. Florida appealed to the U.S. Court of Appeals for the Eleventh Circuit, which upheld the injunction on grounds that the law was unlikely to survive First Amendment scrutiny. In each case, the losing party petitioned the Supreme Court for *certiorari*. The Supreme Court agreed to hear the cases to resolve the split between the Fifth and Eleventh Circuits, and the two cases were argued together.

The Court, per Justice Kagan, did not reach the First Amendment question on the merits. Rather, it found that the courts of appeal misapplied the law concerning facial challenges to statutes. It vacated the lower courts' decisions and remanded the cases. Justice Alito, with Justice Thomas and Justice Gorsuch, filed an opinion concurring in the judgment.

Justice Kagan delivered the opinion of the Court.

Despite the relative novelty of the technology before us, the main problem in this case—and the inquiry it calls for—is not new. At bottom, Texas's law requires the platforms to carry and promote user speech that they would rather discard or downplay. The platforms object that the law thus forces them to alter the content of their expression—a particular edited compilation of third-party speech. That controversy sounds a familiar note. We have repeatedly faced the question whether ordering a party to provide a forum for someone else's views implicates the First Amendment. And we have repeatedly held that it does so if, though only if, the regulated party is engaged in its own expressive activity, which the mandated access would alter or disrupt. So too we have held, when applying that principle, that expressive activity includes presenting a curated compilation of speech originally created by others....

Consider three general points to wrap up.

First, the First Amendment offers protection when an entity engaged in compiling and curating others' speech into an expressive product of its own is directed to accommodate messages it would prefer to exclude. Second, none of that changes just because a compiler includes most items and excludes just a few. It "is enough" for the compiler to exclude the handful of messages it most "disfavor[s]." Third, the government cannot get its way just by asserting an interest in better balancing the marketplace of ideas. In case after case, the Court has barred the government from forcing a private speaker to present views it wished to spurn in order to rejigger the expressive realm....

Texas is not likely to succeed in enforcing its law against the platforms' application of their content-moderation policies to their main feeds....

Texas has never been shy, and always been consistent, about its interest: The objective is to correct the mix of viewpoints that major platforms present. But a State may not interfere with private actors' speech to advance its own vision of ideological balance.... A State cannot prohibit speech to rebalance the speech market. That unadorned interest is not "unrelated to the suppression of free expression." And Texas may not pursue it consistent with the First Amendment....

To give government that power is to enable it to control the expression of ideas, promoting those it favors and suppressing those it does not. And that is what the First Amendment protects all of us from....

JUSTICE ALITO, with JUSTICE THOMAS and JUSTICE GORSUCH, concurring in the judgment.

Because not all compilers express a message of their own, not all compilations are protected by the First Amendment. Instead, the First Amendment protects only those compilations that are "inherently expressive" in their own right, meaning that they select and present speech created by other persons in order "to spread [the compiler's] own message." If a compilation is inherently expressive, then the compiler may have the right to refuse to accommodate a particular speaker or message. But if a compilation is not inherently expressive, then the government can require the compiler to host a message or speaker because the accommodation does not amount to compelled speech....

The majority's discussion also rests on wholly conclusory assumptions that lack record support. For example, the majority paints an attractive, though simplistic, picture of what Facebook's News Feed and YouTube's homepage do behind the scenes. Taking NetChoice at its word, the majority says that the platforms' use of algorithms to enforce their community standards is *per se* expressive. But the platforms have refused to disclose how these algorithms were created and how they actually work. And the majority fails to give any serious consideration to key arguments pressed by the States. Most notable is the majority's conspicuous failure to address the States' contention that platforms like YouTube and Facebook—which constitute the 21st century equivalent of the old "public square"—should be viewed as common carriers....

Transparency Reports

1. *Upheld.* In X Corp. v. Bonta (E.D. Cal. 2023), a federal district court rejected a challenge by X (formerly Twitter) to A.B. 587's constitutionality, find that "while the reporting requirement does appear to place a substantial compliance burden on social media companies, it does not appear that the requirement is unjustified or unduly burdensome within the concept of First Amendment law."[40]

2. *Less than pellucid.* In a February 2024 Report, the ADL described transparency reports as:

> Key to allowing civil society and governments to determine whether there are gaps between platforms' guidelines for curbing hate, and how those guidelines

---

40. X Corp. v. Bonta, No. 23-cv-01939 AC, 2023 U.S. Dist. LEXIS 230575, at *5 (E.D. Cal. Dec. 28, 2023), *rev'd*, No. 24-271, 2024 U.S. App. LEXIS 22456 (9th Cir. Sept. 4, 2024).

are enforced. And understanding effective and ineffective policy and enforcement tactics, as well as general trends and issues, can also inform lawmakers' ability to push for effective regulation.

In the same report, it described the transparency practices of leading platforms as "anything but transparent."

> Most of these platforms only publish partial information about how much hate content they remove or action in some way. To make matters worse, these reports are often hard to locate, void of meaningful information, and only provide patchy insights into how platforms address hate, harassment, and antisemitism. Furthermore, there is no way to independently verify transparency reports, meaning that users, researchers, and civil society must take companies at their word.[41]

How well does California's law address the ADL's concerns? What are its likely effects?

3. *Pool of potential regulators.* Consider various actors who might prompt social media platforms to issue more transparent transparency reports: platforms, states, Congress, independent third parties. What role should each play?

The Expressive Nature of Algorithmic Recommendations

1. *Algorithmic recommendations.* The Congressional Research Service writes that:

> A key feature of many websites and online services is the use of algorithm-based systems to select content that may be of interest to the website's users (recommendation systems or recommender systems). These systems rely on a variety of inputs, including those that are explicitly directed by a user (such as a search term or a user's decision to "follow" another user account) as well as inputs derived from user behavior or sitewide trends....[42]

2. *Are algorithms expressive?* How does the Court's understanding of social media algorithms impact its ruling? Is this understanding sufficient given the complexity of these technologies? Should the Court have requested more technical information about how these algorithms work before making its decision? How does Justice Alito's argument about "inherently expressive" compilations differ from the majority's view? What are the potential implications of this distinction?

3. Section 230 case law has developed based on statutory text that is mostly unchanged from the law's enactment in 1996. How might Section 230 be amended to alter or limit its applicability to algorithmic recommendations? How might amendments

---

41. Ctr. for Tech. & Soc'y, *Platform Transparency Reports—Just How Transparent?*, The Anti-Defamation League (Feb. 14, 2024), https://www.adl.org/resources/blog/platform-transparency-reports-just-how-transparent.

42. Eric N. Holmes, Cong. Rsch. Serv., R47753, Liability for Algorithmic Recommendations (2023).

to Section 230 alter judicial applications of existing case law and the scope of any amendments? Would altering Section 230's protections impermissibly abridge speech?

4. *Constitutional hurdles.* Internet scholar Daphne Keller has identified "six constitutional hurdles for platform speech regulation":

(a) Congress can't ban constitutionally protected speech.

(b) Laws that restrict only illegal speech, but foreseeably cause platforms to restrict legal speech, can violate the First Amendment.

(c) Laws requiring platforms to remove speech and laws requiring them to reduce its "reach" both trigger First Amendment scrutiny.

(d) Laws explicitly or implicitly requiring platforms to monitor and police their users raise multiple constitutional issues.

(e) Laws designed to regulate conduct are a bad fit for regulating online speech, but Congress has reason to use them anyway.

(f) Congress probably can't avoid First Amendment restrictions by merely incentivizing, instead of requiring, platforms to take down lawful speech.[43]

Are these "hurdles" helpful in considering how Section 230 might be revised to address the challenges posed by algorithmic amplification?

---

43. Daphne Keller, *Six Constitutional Hurdles for Platform Speech Regulation*, STAN. CTR. FOR INTERNET & SOC'Y (Jan. 22, 2021, 8:49 AM), https://cyberlaw.stanford.edu/blog/2021/01/six-constitutional-hurdles-platform-speech-regulation/.

Chapter 10

Comparative Hate Speech

This chapter examines how three legal systems outside the United States have regulated antisemitic speech. Section A of this chapter, "Incitement to Genocide," presents *United States v. Streicher* (1946), the trial of Nazi propagandist Julius Streicher before the International Military Tribunal (IMT) at Nuremberg. Streicher was charged and convicted of crimes against humanity for his role in inciting hatred against Jews through his antisemitic newspaper, *Der Stürmer*.

Section B presents *R. v. Keegstra* (1990), in which the Canadian Supreme Court upheld a Canadian law banning the willful promotion of hatred, and the conviction of a high school teacher who taught antisemitic ideas to his students. The Court's opinion, written by Chief Justice Dickson, discusses U.S. free speech law and provides a nuanced explanation of how the Canadian legal system balances freedom of expression with the need to protect vulnerable groups from the harms of hate propaganda.

Section C presents the *Wunsiedel Decision* (2009), in which Germany's highest constitutional court upheld a law prohibiting speech that glorifies the Nazi regime—even when such speech does not threaten imminent lawless action—for reasons specific to the Federal Republic of Germany's relationship to Germany's Nazi past.

A. Incitement to Genocide

Julius Streicher (1885–1946), an early member of the Nazi Party, was the leading organizer of the Nazi regime's first official Reich-wide boycott of Jewish businesses in 1933, and the founder, publisher, and editor-in-chief of the antisemitic newspaper, *Der Stürmer*. Streicher used *Der Stürmer* as a forum for spreading anti-Jewish propaganda since its founding in 1923 and through the events of the Holocaust.

In 1945, the four major Allied nations—the U.S., the U.K., France, and the Soviet Union—established the International Military Tribunal (IMT) at Nuremberg to hold Nazi leaders and enablers individually accountable for their actions in prosecuting the war and committing atrocities. The IMT chose 24 defendants, including Hermann Göring[1] and Rudolf Hess, to represent a cross-section of Nazi diplomatic, economic,

1. Göring, the lead defendant in the Nuremberg trials, was one of Hitler's closest associates and his designated successor. In 1922, Hitler appointed him to be the first leader of the Storm Troopers (SA or *Sturmabteilung*), the Nazi Party's paramilitary organization. He participated with Hitler in the failed Beer Hall Putsch against the German government on November 9, 1923, and was seriously wounded. He later served as Reichstag president and facilitated Hitler's appointment as chancellor on January 30, 1933. Göring served as commander-in-chief of the Luftwaffe; created the Hermann Göring Works

Preis 30 Pfennig

Ritualmord-Nummer

Der Stürmer

tsches Wochenblatt zum Kampfe um die Wahrheit

HERAUSGEBER: JULIUS STREICHER

Sonder-Nummer 1 | Nürnberg, im Mai 1934 | 12. Jahr 1934

Jüdischer Mordplan

gegen die nichtjüdische Menschheit aufgedeckt

Das Mördervolk

Die Juden stehen in der ganzen Welt in einem furchtbaren Verdacht. Wer ihn nicht kennt, der kennt die Judenfrage nicht. Wer die Juden nur ansieht, wie Heinrich Heine (Chaim Bückeburg) sie beschreibt: „Ein Volk, das zu seinem Unterhalt mit Wechseln und alten Hosen handelt und dessen Uniform die langen Nasen sind," der ist auf falschem Wege. Wer aber weiß, welch eine ungeheuerliche Anklage schon seit Anbeginn gegen die Juden erhoben wird, dem erscheint dieses Volk in einem anderen Lichte. Er sieht in ihnen nicht nur ein eigenartiges, seltsam anmutendes Volk, er sieht in ihnen Verbrecher und Mörder und Teufel in Menschengestalt. Und es überkommt ihn gegen dieses Volk ein heiliger Zorn und Haß.

Der Verdacht, in dem die Juden stehen, ist der des Menschenmordes. Sie werden bezichtigt, nichtjüdische Kinder und nichtjüdische Erwachsene an sich zu locken, sie zu schlachten und ihnen das Blut abzuzapfen. Sie werden bezichtigt, dieses Blut in die Mazzen (ungesäuertes Brot) zu verbacken und auch sonstige abergläubische Zauberei damit zu treiben. Sie werden bezichtigt, ihre Opfer, besonders die Kinder, dabei furchtbar zu martern und zu foltern. Und während dieses Folterns Drohungen, Flüche und Verwünschungen gegen die Nichtjuden auszustoßen. Dieser planmäßig betriebene Menschenmord hat eine besondere Bezeichnung, er heißt

Ritualmord.

Das Wissen vom jüdischen Ritualmord ist schon Jahrtausende alt. Es ist so alt wie die Juden selbst. Die Nichtjuden haben es von Generation zu Generation übertragen. Es ist uns durch Schriften überliefert. Es ist aber auch in der breiten Volksmasse vorhanden. In den verstecktesten Bauerndörfern stößt man auf dieses Wissen. Der Ahne sprach von ihm zu seinem Enkel. Und dieser wieder trug es weiter auf Kinder und Kindeskinder. So vererbte es sich bis zum heutigen Tag.

Es ist auch in den anderen Völkern vorhanden. Wo irgendwo in der Welt eine Leiche gefunden wird, die die Anzeichen des Ritualmordes trägt, erhebt sich sofort laut und groß die Anklage. Sie richtet sich überall nur gegen die Juden. Hunderte und aberhunderte von Völkern, Stämmen und Rassen bewohnen den Erdball. Niemand denkt daran, sie des planmäßigen Kindermordes zu beschuldigen und sie als Mördervolk zu bezeichnen. Den Juden allein wird diese Anklage aus allen Völkern entgegengeschleudert. Und viele große Männer haben

Judenopfer

Durch die Jahrtausende vergoß der Jud, geheimem Ritus folgend, Menschenblut
Der Teufel sitzt uns heute noch im Nacken, es liegt an Euch die Teufelsbrut zu packen

Die Juden sind unser Unglück!

Figure 10.1. Front page of *Der Stürmer*, 1934.

(*Reichswerke Hermann Göring*), a state-owned steel producer that compelled more than half a million forced laborers to work in its factories and mines; facilitated the Anschluss, Germany's annexation of Austria in March 1938; facilitated Germany's acquisition of Czechoslovakia's Sudetenland in September 1938; and ordered the development of the "Final Solution to the Jewish Question," the Nazis' plan for exterminating all the Jews in Europe. The IMT found Göring guilty of conspiracy to commit crimes against peace, war crimes, and crimes against humanity. The court sentenced him to death by political, and military leadership. (Adolf Hitler, Heinrich Himmler,[2] and Joseph Goebbels[3] could not be tried because they had committed suicide.)

On October 18, 1945, IMT prosecutors indicted Streicher for crimes against humanity, defined as:

> Murder, extermination, enslavement, deportation, and other inhumane acts committed against any civilian population, before or during the war, or persecutions on political, racial, or religious grounds in execution of or in connection with any crime within the jurisdiction of the Tribunal, whether or not in violation of domestic law of the country where perpetrated.[4]

Streicher was also indicted for crimes against peace, defined as "planning, preparation, initiation or waging of a war of aggression, or a war in violation of international treaties, agreements or assurances, or participation in a common plan or conspiracy for the accomplishment of any of the foregoing."[5]

The U.S. appointed former U.S. Attorney General Francis Biddle to serve as one of the four judges. Robert H. Jackson, Associate Justice of the Supreme Court, served as Chief Prosecutor for the U.S.

In his opening statement before the IMT, Justice Jackson stated that:

> The privilege of opening the first trial in history for crimes against the peace of the world imposes a grave responsibility. The wrongs which we seek to condemn and punish have been so calculated, so malignant and so devastating, that civilization cannot tolerate their being ignored, because it cannot survive their being repeated. That four great nations, flushed with victory and stung with injury, stay the hands of vengeance and voluntarily submit their captive

---

hanging. On the night before his execution, Göring committed suicide by taking cyanide. *Herman Göring*, Holocaust Encyc., https://encyclopedia.ushmm.org/content/en/article/hermann-goering (last updated Nov. 22, 2024).

2. Himmler (1900–1945) was the Reich Leader (*Reichsführer*) of the SS (*Schutzstaffel*; Protection Squadrons), the Nazi Regime's guardian of "racial purity" and responsible for carrying out the "Final Solution," and founder of the Gestapo (*Geheime Staatspolizei*; Secret State Police). Captured by British forces after the war, he committed suicide by taking cyanide. *See The Man Behind Hitler Heinrich Himmler (1900–1945)*, Pub. Broad. Serv., https://www.pbs.org/wgbh/americanexperience/features/goebbels-himmler/ (last visited Dec. 17, 2024); *see also Heinrich Himmler*, Wikipedia, https://en.wikipedia.org/wiki/Heinrich_Himmler (last visited Dec. 17, 2024).

3. Goebbels was Reich Minister for Propaganda and Public Enlightenment. He was a chief instigator of Kristallnacht ("Night of Crystal" or "Night of Broken Glass"), the Nazi-organized pogrom across Germany on November 9–10, 1938, so-named because of the shards of broken glass that lined German streets afterward. Goebbels escaped capture by committing suicide. *Joseph Goebbels*, Holocaust Encyc., https://encyclopedia.ushmm.org/content/en/article/joseph-goebbels-1 (last updated Dec. 18, 2019); *Kristallnacht*, Holocaust Encyc., https://encyclopedia.ushmm.org/content/en/article/kristallnacht (last updated Oct. 18, 2019).

4. *The Nuremberg Trial and the Tokyo War Crime Trials (1945–1948)*, Off. of the Historian, https://history.state.gov/milestones/1945-1952/nuremberg (last visited Jan. 2, 2025).

5. *Id.*

> enemies to the judgement of the law, is one of the most significant tributes that Power ever has paid to Reason....
>
> We must never forget that the record on which we judge these defendants today is the record on which history will judge us tomorrow. We must summon such detachment and intellectual integrity to our task that this Trial will commend itself to posterity as fulfilling humanity's aspirations to do justice.[6]

In addition to advocating for fair trials, Jackson sought to use the proceedings to document the history of the Nazi regime and its crimes. The charge of crimes against humanity provided a legal basis for documenting the inhumanity of the Nazi regime and its enablers, like Streicher.

The prosecutors argued that Streicher committed crimes against humanity by:

> Us[ing] the foregoing positions, his personal influence, and his close connection with the Führer in such a manner that: He promoted the accession to power of the Nazi conspirators and the consolidation of their control over Germany ... he authorized, directed, and participated in the Crimes against Humanity ... including particularly the incitement of the persecution of the Jews.

Professor Gregory S. Gordon argues that "the gravamen of the case against Streicher was his incendiary rhetoric against the Jews." In his view, the prosecutors' decision to try Streicher was surprising, given the fact that he was not directly involved in carrying out physical acts of violence or extermination.

> Streicher's role in the life of the Third Reich was reduced to publishing *Der Stürmer.* And that makes his presence in the IMT dock even more surprising. Why? At war's end, he attempted to go into hiding but was found and arrested "by American soldiers in Austria, near Berchtesgaden." Given Streicher's notoriety as a *media* personality, not to mention his marginal status as a Nazi leader, one could easily imagine his First Amendment-focused captors concluding that a Streicher prosecution would represent too much of an incursion on free speech prerogatives. But the other Allies were able to prevail upon the Americans to include Streicher in the IMT indictment given his newspaper's impact on crimes against peace.

In a similar vein, historian Donald Bloxham argues that:

> Much of the evidence on the antisemitic propagandist Julius Streicher concerned the pre-war period. He was primarily included in the trial in a sort of early attempt at prosecuting incitement to racial hatred, for his pornographic, racist publications. As the only defendant indicted exclusively for his anti-Jewish influence, Streicher was also alone in being charged with the peculiar

6. Robert H. Jackson, U.S. Chief of Couns., Opening Statement Before the Int'l Mil. Tribunal, Nov. 21, 1945, https://www.roberthjackson.org/speech-and-writing/opening-statement-before-the-international-military-tribunal/.

> combination of conspiracy and crimes against humanity. His presence suggests that the Allies recognized the need to account on some level for the virulence of the Nazi hatred of Jews, though—clearly under American influence—within the context of the plan for aggressive warfare.

The Tribunal found Streicher guilty of crimes against humanity for spreading anti-Jewish propaganda and inciting anti-Jewish violence through *Der Stürmer*. Critical to the prosecution's case was the fact that Streicher continued his incitement activities even after he had knowledge that the Nazi regime was in the process of exterminating Jews. Streicher was sentenced to death and executed by hanging on October 16, 1946.

Professor Gordon argues that Streicher's conviction "left an indelible imprint on the law of incitement." This is partly due to the efforts of Raphael Lemkin (1900–1959), a Polish-Jewish lawyer who studied the Ottoman destruction of Armenians during World War I and later coined the term "genocide" to describe this phenomenon. He escaped to the U.S. after Nazi Germany invaded Poland. Forty-nine members of his family, including his parents, perished in the Holocaust. In his words:

> By "genocide" we mean the destruction of a nation or of an ethnic group. This new word, coined by the author to denote an old practice in its modern development, is made from the ancient Greek word *genos* (race, tribe) and the Latin *cide* (killing).... Generally speaking, genocide does not necessarily mean the immediate destruction of a nation, except when accomplished by mass killings of all members of a nation. It is intended rather to signify a coordinated plan of different actions aiming at the destruction of essential foundations of the life of national groups, with the aim of annihilating the groups themselves. Genocide is directed against the national group as an entity, and the actions involved are directed against individuals, not in their individual capacity, but as members of the national group.

Following World War II, Lemkin campaigned to have genocide recognized as an international crime. On December 9, 1948, the United Nations approved the Convention on the Prevention and Punishment of Genocide. Article III(c) of the Conventions criminalizes "direct and public incitement to commit genocide," an offense implicit in the concept of "crimes against humanity" as applied to Streicher. "Direct incitement," explains the Legal Information Institute:

> refers to when someone directly and publicly encourages others to commit genocide. It has to be a clear and direct call to action, rather than a vague or indirect suggestion. The level of directness is judged based on the context and audience it was intended for. Even if the incitement is not obvious to outsiders, it can still be considered direct as long as the intended audience immediately understands the message. The level of directness must be clear and unambiguous in its intended context.

At the Tribunal, Streicher was cross-examined by Lieutenant Colonel John Mervyn Griffith-Jones, Junior Counsel for the British prosecuting team. As the following excerpt from the trial attests, Griffth-Jones "exhibited the common law art of cross-examination at its best," and exposed Streicher as "a coarse, garrulous, repulsive fanatic whom even Nazi loyalists found embarrassing."[7]

United States v. Streicher

Transcript of Cross-Examination of Julius Streicher
Trial of the Major War Criminals Before the International Military Tribunal
Nuremberg, April 29, 1946

Lt. Col. Griffith-Jones

I want to make myself quite clear to you in what I am suggesting. I am suggesting that from 1939 onwards you set out to incite the German people to murder and to accept the fact of the murder of the Jewish race. Do you understand that?

Streicher

That is not true.

Lt. Col. Griffith-Jones

No doubt you will say it isn't true. I just wanted you to be quite clear on what my suggestion is going to be. I want you to look now at a bundle, which will be given to you, of extracts from *Der Stürmer*.

> The Jewish problem is not yet solved, nor will it be solved when one day the last Jew will have left Germany. Only when world Jewry has been annihilated, will it have been solved.

Is that what you were working for when you say you were working for the international solution to this problem, an annihilation of world Jewry?

Streicher

If that is how you understand "annihilation."

Lt. Col. Griffith-Jones

The German word used there is *vernichtet*, is it not? Look at your copy. *Vernichtet* that means "to annihilate."[8]

Streicher

Today when you look back, you could interpret it like that, but not at that time....

Lt. Col. Griffith-Jones

Do I understand you to say now, to have said in your evidence, that you never knew that Jews were being exterminated in thousands and millions in the Eastern territories? Did you never know that?

---

7. *Mervyn Griffith-Jones*, SPARTACUS EDUC., https://spartacus-educational.com/Mervyn_Griffith-Jones.htm (last visited Dec. 17, 2024).

8. Editor's note: Langenscheidt defines *vernichtet* as destroy, annihilate, wipe out, demolish, flatten, exterminate, extirpate, eradicate, kill, ruin, shatter, wreck, and crush. *See Vernichtet*, LANGENSCHEIDT, https://en.langenscheidt.com/german-english/search?term=+vernichtet&q_cat=%2Fgerman-english%2F (last visited Nov. 13, 2024).

Streicher

No.

Lt. Col. Griffith-Jones

As I understood your evidence about the *Israelitisches Wochenblatt*[9] this morning you said this, as I have written it down:

> Sometimes that journal contained hints that everything was not in order. Later in 1943 an article appeared stating that masses of Jews were disappearing but the article did not quote any figures and did not mention anything about murders.

Are you really saying that those copies of the *Israelitisches Wochenblatt*, which you and your editors were reading, contained nothing except for a hint of disappearance with no mention of figures or murder? Is that what you are telling this Tribunal?

Streicher

Yes, I stick to that, certainly.

Lt. Col. Griffith-Jones

Now, I want you, if you will, to take this bundle and keep it in front of you. It is a bundle of extracts from the *Israelitisches Wochenblatt* from July 1941 until the end of the war. The Tribunal will be able to see what a fanatic for the truth really tells.... In November 1941:

> Very bad news comes from the Ukraine. Thousands of Jewish dead are being mourned, among whom are many of the Galician Jews who were expelled from Hungary.

Did you read that?

Streicher

That might be possible. It says "thousands," thousands are being mourned. That is no proof that millions were killed. There are no details as to how they came to their end.

Lt. Col. Griffith-Jones

If that is the explanation you want us to accept we will leave it.... I just want you to see what you were writing after having heard, or after having read, or anyway after those copies of the *Israelitisches Wochenblatt* had been published. This is a leading article by yourself.

> If the danger of the reproduction of that curse of God in the Jewish blood is finally to come to an end, then there is only one way open—the extermination of that people whose father is the devil.

9. Editor's note: *Israelitisches Wochenblatt* ("Israelite Weekly Journal") was a Jewish weekly paper unaffiliated with any religious or political positions. It published a range of articles of general interest to the Jews of Germany.

And is the word that you use for extermination there *Ausrottung*, rooting out, extirpation? Can you tell me, is that "extermination"? Does that mean murder of Jews? What else can it mean?[10]

Streicher

It depends on the whole context....

Lt. Col. Griffith-Jones

Now just see what your Chief Editor[11] ... has got to say first of all:

> But the ghetto too, which has today been re-established in nearly all European countries, is only an interim solution, for mankind once awakened will not merely solve the ghetto question but the Jewish question in its totality. A time will come when the present demands of the Jews will be fulfilled. The ghetto will have disappeared—and with it, Jewry.

What is he referring to, if he isn't referring to the mass killing, murder, of the Jewish race?

Streicher

That was a statement of his opinion, his conviction.

Lt. Col. Griffith-Jones

Very well. I am sure we have heard your explanation. Let's see what you have to say about your own article on the same date....

> When, with the outbreak of the second World War, world Jewry again began to manifest themselves as warmongers, Adolf Hitler announced to the world from the platform of the German Reichstag that the World War conjured up by world Jewry would result in the self-destruction of Jewry. This prophecy was the first big warning. It was met with derision from the Jews, as were all the subsequent warnings.... But now, in the fourth year of this war, world Jewry is beginning in its retrospective considerations to understand that the destiny of Jewry is finding its fulfillment at the hands of German National Socialism.

What do you mean by saying "World Jewry is finding its fulfillment at the hands of National Socialism"? How did you mean that National Socialism was finding the fulfillment of Jewry's destiny?

Streicher

National Socialism could not fulfill the fate, that is to say, find the solution, since the Führer intervened with the hand of destiny. That was not a solution. During an

---

10. Editor's note: Landenscheidt defines *ausrottung* as extermination, eradication, stamping out, rooting out, extirpation. *See Ausrottung*, LANGENSCHEIDT, https://en.langenscheidt.com/german-english/ausrottung (last visited Nov. 13, 2024).

11. Editor's note: Ernst Hiemer (1900–1974). *See Ernst Hiemer*, WIKIPEDIA, https://en.wikipedia.org/wiki/Ernst_Hiemer (last visited Dec. 17, 2024).

interrogation I pointed out that I who personally wanted a total solution, was, right from the beginning, against trying to solve the Jewish problem by means of pogroms. If I said that the destiny of Jewry was to be fulfilled by National Socialism, then I wanted to say that through National Socialism the world would gain the knowledge and the realization that the Jewish problem must be solved internationally.

Lt. Col. Griffith-Jones

Let's just go on.... We are not discussing war now. We are discussing the extermination, the mass murder of Jews, by the National Socialists. That is what we are discussing. Let me read on:

> When Adolf Hitler stepped before the German people 20 years ago to submit to them the National Socialist demands which pointed the way into the future, he also made the promise which was to have the gravest repercussions; that of freeing the world from its Jewish tormentors. How wonderful it is to know that this great man and leader is following up this promise with practical action. It will be the greatest deed in the history of mankind.

Do you say that you are not putting forward propaganda for the policy of mass extermination which the Nazi Government had set out to do?

Streicher

We too had freedom of the press like democratic countries. Every author knew of the forecast, which perhaps later on turned out to be a fact, and could write about it. That is what I did....

Lt. Col. Griffith-Jones

What I do not understand is what you meant when you said this morning that the *Israelitisches Wochenblatt* made no mention of murders and gave no figures. You didn't say that the figures were unbelievable; you told this Tribunal, on your oath, that the newspaper contained nothing except the hints of disappearance, with no mention of figures.

I just want you to examine for the last time whether or not you are speaking the truth in telling the Tribunal that you did not know what was happening. You quote in that article from the Swiss newspaper, the *Israelitisches Wochenblatt*, of the 27th August 1943. I start now from that line in the middle:

> The Swiss Jewish newspaper goes on to say, "The Jews of Europe, with the exception of those in England and of insignificant Jewish communities in the few neutral countries, have disappeared, so to speak. The Jewish reservoir of the East that was able to counterbalance the force of assimilation in the West no longer exists."

That is the end of your quotation from the newspaper, and you go on to say:

> This is not a Jewish lie; it is really true that the Jews have, "so to speak," disappeared from Europe and that the "Jewish reservoir of the East" from which the Jewish pestilence spread for centuries among the European nations has ceased to exist. If the Swiss newspaper wishes to affirm that the Jews did not expect

> this kind of development when they plunged the nations into the second World War, this is to be believed; but already at the beginning of the war the Führer of the German Nation prophesied the events that have taken place. He said that the Second World War would swallow those who had conjured it.

Now, are you really saying that when that article was written you did not know how to interpret the word "disappearance," the disappearance of the Jews from the East? Are you really telling the Tribunal that?

Streicher

Yes, the word "disappear" after all does not mean extermination *en masse*. This deals with a quotation from the *Israelitisches Wochenblatt* and is a repeated quotation of what the Führer had prophesied.

Lt. Col. Griffith-Jones

Well, now, would you look at the article from which you quote there.... Now—there you go on, "The Jewish reservoir of the East"—the original goes on—"three million dead, the same number outlawed; many thousands, all over the world, mentally and physically broken."

Are you telling this Tribunal now that on the 27th of August, or when you read that article of the 27th of August, you didn't know that Jews were being murdered in the East and that you had not read of those things in the *Israelitisches Wochenblatt*?

Streicher

Whether I had read it or not, I would not have believed it, that three million Jews had been killed. That is something I would not have believed, and that is why I left it out, at any rate....

Lt. Col. Griffith-Jones

You say you didn't believe it. Is that what you say now, that you must have read it—must you not?

Streicher

Yes.

Lt. Col. Griffith-Jones

But you just didn't believe it; is that right?

Streicher

No, I did not believe it.

Lt. Col. Griffith-Jones

Even if you didn't believe it, when you were reading this newspaper more or less regularly, when your cameraman had been to the ghettos in the East, did you think it right to go on, week after week, in your newspaper crying for the extermination, murder, of the Jews?

Streicher

That is not correct. It is not true that murder was demanded week after week.... I state here that if I had known what had in fact happened in the East, then I would not have used these quotations at all.

Lt. Col. Griffith-Jones

But, Defendant, you must have known then, must you not, after reading that article, after sending your cameraman, after the United Nations published their declaration, after Hitler's prophecies had been made again and again in his proclamations, after you said his prophecy had been fulfilled? You really say you didn't know?... Now we had just dealt with the *Israelititsches Wochenblatt* issue for 27 August, the copy that you quoted from....

It is quite clear that there were plenty of figures for you, quoted in this *Israelitisches Wochenblatt* over the period that we are discussing. Plenty of figures, it now turns out, doesn't it?... I just want to put one or two further articles of your own to you. You remember what I am suggesting, that you are inciting the German people to murder. We know now that at least you had read one article in the *Israelitisches Wochenblatt* where murder is mentioned. I just want to see what you go on to publish in your own paper after that date.

Would you look at Page 47-A. This is an article by yourself on 6 January 1944. This is after you had been living on your estate for some time.

> After the National Socialist uprising in Germany, a development began in Europe, too, from which one can expect that it will free this continent for all time of the Jewish disintegrator and exploiter of nations; and, over and above this, that the German example will, after a victorious termination of the second World War, bring about the destruction of the Jewish world tormentor on the other continents as well.

What example was the German nation setting to the other nations of the world? What example do you mean there?

Streicher

This article corroborates what I have been saying all along. I spoke of an international solution of the Jewish question. I was convinced that if Germany had won this war or had been victorious over Bolshevism, then the world would have agreed that an understanding should be reached with the other nations for an international solution of the Jewish question. If I wrote here about destruction, it is not to be understood as destruction by mass killing; as I have said, that is an expression....

Lt. Col. Griffith-Jones

You have not yet told us what is this international solution that you are advocating by talking about extermination; if it is not murder, what is it? What is the solution?

Streicher

I have already said that I founded the Anti-Semitic Union, and through this Anti-Semitic Union we wanted to create movements among the nations which should, above and beyond governments, act in such a way that an international possibility would be created, such as has been represented today here in this Trial—thus I conceived it, to form an international congress center which would solve the Jewish question by the creation of a Jewish state and thereby destroy the power of the Jews within the nations.

Lt. Col. Griffith-Jones

That is your answer—that you were advocating a Jewish state? Is that all that this comes to? Is it simply that you were advocating a Jewish national home? Is that what you have been talking about in all these extracts that we have read? Is that the solution which you are advocating?

Streicher

Well, I do not know what you want with that question. Of course, that is the solution.

Lt. Col. Griffith-Jones

Very well. Let us just go on now. Turn to Page 48-A now, will you? This is 24 January 1944:

> Whoever does what a Jew does is a scoundrel, a criminal, and he who repeats and wishes to copy him deserves the same fate—annihilation, death.

Are you still advocating a national Jewish home?

Streicher

Yes, that has nothing to do with the big political plan. If you take every statement by a writer, every statement from a daily newspaper, as an example, and want to prove a political aim by it, then you miss the point. You have to distinguish between a newspaper article and a great political aim.

Lt. Col. Griffith-Jones

Very well, let us just turn now to the next page, 2 March 1944:

> Eternal night must come over the born criminal race of Jews so that eternal day may bless awakening non-Jewish mankind.

Were they going to have eternal night in their national Jewish state? Is that what you wanted?

Streicher

That is an anti-Semitic play of words. Again it has nothing to do with the great political aim.

Lt. Col. Griffith-Jones

It may be an anti-Semitic play of words, but the only meaning it can have is murder. Is that not true?

Streicher

No.

Lt. Col. Griffith-Jones

Will you turn to the next page, 25 May 1944; and I remind you that these are all after you must have read of the murder in *Israelitisches Wochenblatt.* I quote the second paragraph:

> How can we overcome this danger and restore humanity to health? Just as the individual human being is able to defend himself against contagious diseases only if he proclaims war against the cause of the disease, the germ, so the world can be restored to health only when the most terrible germ of all times, the Jew, has been removed. It is of no avail to battle against the outward symptoms of the world disease without rendering the morbific agents innocuous. The disease will break out again sooner or later. The cause and the carrier of the disease, the germ, will see to that. But if the nations are to be restored to health and are to remain healthy in the future, then the germ of the Jewish world plague must be destroyed, root and branch.

Is that what you mean? Are you saying there when you say, "must be destroyed root and branch"—did you mean to say, "ought to be given a Jewish national state"?

Streicher

Yes, it is a far cry from such a statement in an article to the act, or to the will, to commit mass murder.

Lt. Col. Griffith-Jones

Turn over to the 10th of August.

> When it loses this struggle, Judaism will be ruined, then the Jew will be extinguished. Then will Judaism be annihilated down to the last man.

Are we to read from these words: Provide the Jews with a Jewish national state?

Streicher

That is a vision of the future. I would like to call it an expression of a prophetic vision. But it is not incitement to kill 5 million Jews. That is an opinion, a matter of belief, of conviction.

Lt. Col. Griffith-Jones

It is the prophetic vision of what you wanted, is it not—of what you have been advocating now for the last 4 years—the beginning of the war? Isn't that what it is?

Streicher

Mr. Prosecutor, I cannot tell you today what I may have been thinking years ago at a certain moment when writing an article. But still I admit that when I saw lying before me on the table declarations from the Jewish front, many declarations saying, "the German nation has to be destroyed; bomb the cities, do not spare women, children, or old men"—if one has declarations like these in front of one, it is possible that things will come from one's pen such as I have often written.

Lt. Col. Griffith-Jones

You know, do you not, now, even if you do not believe the full figures, that millions of Jews have been murdered since the beginning of the war? Do you know that? You have heard the evidence, have you not?...

Streicher

Yes, I have to say, evidence for me is only the testament of the Führer. There he states that the mass executions took place upon his orders. That I believe. Now I believe it.

Lt. Col. Griffith-Jones

Do you think that it would have been possible to carry out the extermination of six million Jews in 1921? Do you think the German people would have stood for it? Do you think it would have been possible under any regime in 1921 to have carried out the murder of six million men, women, and children of the Jewish race?

Streicher

Whether that would have been possible with the knowledge of the people—no, it would not have been possible. The prosecutor himself has said here that since 1937 the Party had full control over the people. Now even if the people had known this, according to the opinion of the Prosecution, they could not have done anything against that dictatorship because of that control. But the people did not know it. That is my belief, my conviction, and my knowledge.

Lt. Col. Griffith-Jones

Was it possible to exterminate people in that way only after some 20 years of incitement and propaganda by you and other Nazis? Is that what made that possible?

Streicher

I deny that the population was incited. It was enlightened, and sometimes a harsh word may have been directed against the other side as an answer. It was enlightenment, not incitement. And if we want to keep our place before history I have to state again and again that the German people did not want any killings, whether individually or *en masse*....

Lt. Col. Griffith-Jones

I am going to remind you of what you said yesterday. I read from the transcript: You speak of a Jewish question at the time—that is 1923:

> I would like to say that the public distinguished Jews only by their religion; to speak about a Jewish problem then would have been nonsense.

Was that because there was no Jewish problem then, and that the Jewish problem had only been created by you and the Nazi regime?

Streicher

It was my aim, and I reached that goal in part: If the laws which in the future should make impossible sexual intercourse between different races, that is to say if that should become law—then it would make the public realize that to be a Jew is not a point of religion but of people and race. I helped to create that basis. But mass killings were not the result of the enlightenment, or as the Prosecution say, incitement. Mass killings were the last acts of will of a great man of history who was probably desperate because he saw that he would not win.

Lt. Col. Griffith-Jones

I have no further questions.

United States v. Streicher

Judgement of the International Military Tribunal
Issued October 1, 1946

Crimes Against Peace—Count 1

Streicher was a staunch Nazi and supporter of Hitler's main policies. There is no evidence to show that he was ever within Hitler's inner circle of advisers; nor during his career was he closely connected with the formulation of the policies which led to war. He was never present, for example, at any of the important conferences when Hitler explained his decisions to his leaders. Although he was a Gauleiter there is no evidence to prove that he had knowledge of those policies. In the opinion of the Tribunal, the evidence fails to establish his connection with the Common Plan or conspiracy to wage aggressive war as that conspiracy has been elsewhere defined in this Judgment.

Crimes Against Humanity—Count 4

For his twenty-five years of speaking, writing, and preaching hatred of the Jews, Streicher was widely known as "Jew-Baiter Number One." In his speeches and articles, week after week, month after month, he infected the German mind with the virus of anti-Semitism and incited the German people to active persecution. Each issue of *Der Stürmer*, which reached a circulation of 600,000 in 1935, was filled with such articles, often lewd and disgusting....

But it was not only in Germany that this defendant advocated his doctrines. As early as 1938 he began to call for the annihilation of the Jewish race. Twenty-three different articles of *Der Stürmer* between 1938 and 1941 were produced in evidence, in which extermination "root and branch" was preached. Typical of his teachings was a leading article in September, 1938, which termed the Jew a germ and a pest, not a human being, but "a parasite, an enemy, an evildoer, a disseminator of diseases who must be destroyed in the interest of mankind." Other articles urged that only when world Jewry had been annihilated would the Jewish problem have been solved, and predicted that fifty years hence the Jewish graves "will proclaim that this people of murderers and criminals has after all met its deserved fate." Streicher, in February, 1940, published a letter from one of *Der Stürmer*'s readers which compared Jews with swarms of locusts which must be exterminated completely. Such was the poison Streicher injected into the minds of thousands of Germans which caused them to follow the National Socialist policy of Jewish persecution and extermination. A leading article of *Der Stürmer* in May, 1939, shows clearly his aim:

> A punitive expedition must come against the Jews in Russia. A punitive expedition which will provide the same fate for them that every murderer and criminal must expect. Death sentence and execution. The Jews in Russia must be killed. They must be exterminated root and branch.

As the war in the early stages proved successful in acquiring more and more territory for the Reich, Streicher even intensified his efforts to incite the Germans against the Jews. In the record are twenty-six articles from *Der Stürmer*, published between August, 1941, and September, 1944, twelve by Streicher's own hand, which demanded annihilation and extermination in unequivocal terms. He wrote and published on 25th December, 1941:

> If the danger of the reproduction of that curse of God in the Jewish blood is finally to come to an end, then there is only one way—the extermination of that people whose father is the devil.

And in February, 1944, his own article stated:

> Whoever does what a Jew does is a scoundrel, a criminal. And he who repeats and wishes to copy him deserves the same fate—annihilation, death.

With knowledge of the extermination of the Jews in the occupied Eastern territory, this defendant continued to write and publish his propaganda of death. Testifying in this Trial, he vehemently denied any knowledge of mass executions of Jews. But the evidence makes it clear that he continually received current information on the progress of the "final solution." His press photographer was sent to visit the ghettos of the East in the spring of 1943, the time of the destruction of the Warsaw ghetto. The Jewish newspaper, *Israelitisches Wochenblatt*, which Streicher received and read, carried in each issue accounts of Jewish atrocities in the East, and gave figures on the number of Jews who had been deported and killed.... Streicher quoted verbatim an article from the *Israelitisches Wochenblatt*, which stated that the Jews had virtually disappeared from Europe, and commented "This is not a Jewish lie." In December, 1942, referring to an article in the London Times about the atrocities, aiming at extermination, Streicher said that Hitler had given warning that the Second World War would lead to the destruction of Jewry. In January, 1943, he wrote and published an article which said that Hitler's prophecy was being fulfilled, that world Jewry was being extirpated, and that it was wonderful to know that Hitler was freeing the world of its Jewish tormentors....

Streicher's incitement to murder and extermination, at the time when Jews in the East were being killed under the most horrible conditions, clearly constitutes persecution on political and racial grounds in connection with War Crimes, as defined by the Charter, and constitutes a Crime Against Humanity.

The Tribunal finds that Streicher is not guilty on Count One, but that he is guilty on Count Four. •

Sources

Coining a Word and Championing a Cause: The Story of Raphael Lemkin, U.S. Holocaust Mem'l Museum, https://encyclopedia.ushmm.org/content/en/article/coining-a-word-and-championing-a-cause-the-story-of-raphael-lemkin (last visited Nov. 13, 2024).

Convention on the Prevention and Punishment of the Crime of Genocide art. III(c), Dec. 9, 1948, 78 U.N.T.S. 277.

Exec. Order No. 9547, 10 Fed. Reg. 4961 (May 8,1945).

Genocide, Cornell L. Sch. Legal Info. Inst., https://www.law.cornell.edu/wex/genocide (last visited Nov. 13, 2024).

Gregory S. Gordon, *The Propaganda Prosecutions at Nuremberg: The Origin of Atrocity Speech Law and the Touchstone for Normative Evolution*, 39 Loy. L.A. Int'l & Comp. L. Rev. 209 (2017).

Whitney R. Harris, *Justice Jackson at Nuremberg*, 20 Int'l Law. 867, 875 (1986).

International Military Tribunal at Nuremberg, U.S. Holocaust Mem'l Museum, https://encyclopedia.ushmm.org/content/en/article/international-military-tribunal-at-nuremberg (last visited Nov. 13, 2024).

Julius Streicher, U.S. Holocaust Mem'l Museum, https://encyclopedia.ushmm.org/content/en/article/julius-streicher (last visited Nov. 13, 2024).

David Luban, *The Legacies of Nuremberg*, 54 Soc. Res. 779 (1987).

U.S. Prosecutor Jackson, U.S. Holocaust Mem'l Museum, https://encyclopedia.ushmm.org/content/en/film/us-prosecutor-jackson (last visited Nov. 13, 2024).

B. Willful Promotion of Hatred

James Keegstra was a high school teacher and mayor of the town of Eckville, Alberta, a small town with a population of approximately 800 people. Keegstra taught his students that Jews are the root of all evil. According to Keegstra, Jews were responsible for the Russian Revolution and both world wars; they control the banking system, media, Hollywood, universities, most publishers, most churches, and almost all political leaders; and the Holocaust was a hoax perpetrated for economic gain and to establish the State of Israel.

Keegstra introduced his anti-Jewish teachings around 1971 and taught them unimpeded for a decade. He was removed from his teaching position in December 1982. In January 1984, Keegstra was charged with one count of willful promotion of hatred against an identifiable group under Section 319(2) of the Criminal Code of Canada.[12]

12. R.S.C. 1985, c 46 (*Criminal Code*). Unlike the United States, in Canada the federal government has exclusive jurisdiction over the criminal law. Accordingly, the *Criminal Code* is a federal statute that applies across the country.

Enacted in 1970, this provision had rarely been used and no one had been successfully prosecuted for this offense.

At trial, the prosecution's case consisted primarily of the evidence of Keegstra's students, including their classroom notes, essays, and exams. In his defense, Keegstra introduced almost 150 books, articles, and other materials into evidence that he purportedly relied on for his beliefs. Included among these were excerpts from the Talmud which Keegstra claimed authorized Jews to engage in pedophilia and sodomy and to kill and rob non-Jews.

The jury found Keegstra guilty, and the judge sentenced him to a $5,000 fine and no jail time. (After the sentence was rendered, the jury's foreman asked how he could contribute to Keegstra's fine.) Keegstra appealed his conviction. The central issue on appeal was whether the offense of willful promotion of hatred infringed the right to freedom of expression, guaranteed by Section 2(b) of the Canadian Charter of Rights and Freedoms (the "Charter"), a document analogous to the United States Bill of Rights. An important subsidiary question was whether, even if the law infringed on the right to freedom of expression, it could be "saved" under Section 1 of the Charter, pursuant to which legislation must be upheld so long as the infringement amounted to a "reasonable limit prescribed by law as can be demonstrably justified in a free and democratic society."

The Court of Appeal of Alberta agreed with Keegstra that the provision was unconstitutional and acquitted him. The government then obtained leave to appeal to the Supreme Court of Canada. In an opinion written by Chief Justice Dickson, the Supreme Court in a 4–3 decision sided with the prosecution, overturned the Court of Appeal, and upheld the offense of willful promotion of hatred. Justice McLachlin filed a dissenting opinion, joined by Justice Sopinka.

R. v. Keegstra[13]

Supreme Court of Canada
[1990] 3 S.C.R. 697

Chief Justice Dickson delivered the opinion of the Court.

This appeal ... raises a delicate and highly controversial issue as to the constitutional validity of s. 319(2) of the Criminal Code, R.S.C., 1985, c. C-46, a legislative provision which prohibits the willful promotion of hatred, other than in private conversation, towards any section of the public distinguished by colour, race, religion or ethnic origin. In particular, the Court must decide whether this section infringes the guarantee of freedom of expression found in s. 2(b) of the Canadian Charter of Rights and Freedoms in a manner that cannot be justified under s. 1 of the Charter....

---

13. "R" stands for *Regina*, Latin for "the Queen," signaling that the case was brought by the State. Following the death of Queen Elizabeth II and ascension of King Charles III in 2022, the letter "R" now signifies *Rex*, meaning the King.

V. The History of Hate Propaganda Crimes in Canada

In Canada, the post-war mood saw an attempt to include anti-hate propaganda provisions in the 1953 revision of the Criminal Code, but most influential in changing the criminal law in order to prohibit hate propaganda was the appointment by Justice Minister Guy Favreau of ... the Special Committee on Hate Propaganda in Canada, usually referred to as the Cohen Committee.[14] ... This was a particularly strong Committee, and in 1966 it released the unanimous Report of the Special Committee on Hate Propaganda in Canada....

The recurrent theme running throughout the [Cohen Committee's] Report is the need to prevent the dissemination of hate propaganda without unduly infringing the freedom of expression, a theme which led the Committee to recommend a number of amendments to the Criminal Code. These amendments were made, essentially along the lines suggested by the Committee, and covered the advocation of genocide (s. 318), the public incitement of hatred likely to lead to a breach of peace (s. 319(1)) and the provision challenged in this appeal and presently found in s. 319(2) of the Code, namely, the willful promotion of hatred....

VI. Section 2(b) of the Charter—Freedom of Expression

[Section 2 of the Canadian Charter of Rights and Freedoms reads in part:

"Everyone has the following fundamental freedoms ...

b) freedom of thought, belief, opinion and expression, including freedom of the press and other media of communication"

Having briefly set out the history of attempts to prohibit hate propaganda, I can now address the constitutional questions arising for decision in this appeal. The first of these concerns is whether the Charter guarantee of freedom of expression is infringed by s 319(2) of the Criminal Code. In other words, does the coverage of s. 2(b) extend to the public and willful promotion of hatred against an identifiable group. Before looking to the specific facts of this appeal, however, I would like to comment upon the nature of the s. 2(b) guarantee. Obviously, one's conception of the freedom of expression provides a crucial backdrop to any s. 2(b) inquiry; the values promoted by the freedom help not only to define the ambit of s. 2(b), but also come to the forefront

14. Editor's note: The committee was named after its chair, Maxwell Abraham Cohen (1910–1998). This committee was established in response to the rise of anti-Jewish and anti-Black hate propaganda and other forms of racism in Canada during the 1960s. Cohen was the first full-time Jewish professor at the McGill Faculty of Law and went on to serve as the Dean of Law and Dean of McGill University. He heavily influenced the drafting of the Canadian Charter of Rights and Freedoms. He was a leader in the Canadian Zionist Federation, which represents Canada in the World Zionist Organization. *See* William Edward Kaplan, *Maxwell Cohen*, The Canadian Encyc. (Dec. 14, 2013), https://www.thecanadianencyclopedia.ca/en/article/maxwell-cohen; *see also Trailblazers in Law and Beyond*, Bicentennial, https://200.mcgill.ca/faculties/faculty-of-law/trailblazers-in-law-and-beyond/ (last visited Dec. 17, 2024); *see also* Philip Rosen, 85-6E, Hate Propaganda (2000), https://publications.gc.ca/Collection-R/LoPBdP/CIR/856-e.htm.

when discussing how competing interests might co-exist with the freedom under s. 1 of the Charter....

The term "expression" as used in s. 2(b) of the Charter embraces all content of expression irrespective of the particular meaning or message sought to be conveyed....

In my view, through s. 319(2) Parliament seeks to prohibit communications which convey meaning, namely, those communications which are intended to promote hatred against identifiable groups....

I thus conclude on the issue of s. 2(b) by finding that s. 319(2) of the Criminal Code constitutes an infringement of the Charter guarantee of freedom of expression, and turn to examine whether such an infringement is justifiable under s. 1 as a reasonable limit in a free and democratic society.

VII. Section 1 Analysis of Section 319(2)

A. *General Approach to Section 1*

Though the language of s. 1 appears earlier in these reasons, it is appropriate to repeat its words:

> The Canadian Charter of Rights and Freedoms guarantees the rights and freedoms set out in it subject only to such reasonable limits prescribed by law as can be demonstrably justified in a free and democratic society.

[Chief Justice Dickson then set out the framework for assessing whether a constitutional infringement is a reasonable limit pursuant to Section 1.... The first question in the Section 1 analysis is whether the impugned state action has an objective of pressing and substantial concern in a free and democratic society. The second inquiry is whether that objective is proportional to the impugned measure. This, in turn, involves three sub-questions: (1) Is there a rational connection between the law and its objective? (2) Does the law minimally impair the Charter right in question? and (3) Do the beneficial effects of the law outweigh the law's negative impact on the Charter right at issue? If the government fails at any of these steps, the infringement is not justified, and the law must be struck down.]

The analytical framework of *Oakes* has been continually reaffirmed by this Court, yet it is dangerously misleading to conceive of s. 1 as a rigid and technical provision, offering nothing more than a last chance for the state to justify incursions into the realm of fundamental rights. From a crudely practical standpoint, Charter litigants sometimes may perceive s. 1 in this manner, but in the body of our nation's constitutional law it plays an immeasurably richer role, one of great magnitude and sophistication.... In the words of s. 1 are brought together the fundamental values and aspirations of Canadian society....

[Before turning to Section 1 in more detail, Chief Justice Dickson discussed the relevance of American jurisprudence to the Canadian right to freedom of expression.]

B. *The Use of American Constitutional Jurisprudence*

Having discussed the unique and unifying role of s. 1, I think it appropriate to address a tangential matter, yet one nonetheless crucial to the disposition of this appeal:

the relationship between Canadian and American approaches to the constitutional protection of free expression, most notably in the realm of hate propaganda. Those who attack the constitutionality of s. 319(2) draw heavily on the tenor of First Amendment jurisprudence in weighing the competing freedoms and interests in this appeal, a reliance which is understandable given the prevalent opinion that the criminalization of hate propaganda violates the Bill of Rights (see, e.g., L. H. Tribe, *American Constitutional Law* (2nd ed. 1988), at p. 861, n. 2; K. Greenawalt, "Insults and Epithets: Are They Protected Speech?" (1990), 42 *Rutgers L. Rev.* 287, at p. 304). In response to the emphasis placed upon this jurisprudence, I find it helpful to summarize the American position and to determine the extent to which it should influence the s. 1 analysis in the circumstances of this appeal.

A myriad of sources—both judicial and academic—offer reviews of First Amendment jurisprudence as it pertains to hate propaganda. Central to most discussions is the 1952 case of *Beauharnais v. Illinois*, 343 U.S. 250, where the Supreme Court of the United States upheld as constitutional a criminal statute forbidding certain types of group defamation. Though never overruled, *Beauharnais* appears to have been weakened by later pronouncements of the Supreme Court (see, e.g., *New York Times Co. v. Sullivan* (1964); *Brandenburg v. Ohio* (1969); and *Cohen v. California* (1971)). The trend reflected in many of these pronouncements is to protect offensive, public invective as long as the speaker has not knowingly lied and there exists no clear and present danger of violence or insurrection....

The question that concerns us in this appeal is not, of course, what the law is or should be in the United States. But it is important to be explicit as to the reasons why or why not American experience may be useful in the s. 1 analysis of s. 319(2) of the Criminal Code. In the United States, a collection of fundamental rights has been constitutionally protected for over two hundred years. The resulting practical and theoretical experience is immense, and should not be overlooked by Canadian courts. On the other hand, we must examine American constitutional law with a critical eye....

Canada and the United States are not alike in every way, nor have the documents entrenching human rights in our two countries arisen in the same context. It is only common sense to recognize that, just as similarities will justify borrowing from the American experience, differences may require that Canada's constitutional vision depart from that endorsed in the United States....

Though I have found the American experience tremendously helpful in coming to my own conclusions regarding this appeal, and by no means reject the whole of the First Amendment doctrine, in a number of respects I am thus dubious as to the applicability of this doctrine in the context of a challenge to hate propaganda legislation....

Applying the Charter to the legislation challenged in this appeal reveals important differences between Canadian and American constitutional perspectives. I have already discussed in some detail the special role of s. 1 in determining the protective scope of Charter rights and freedoms. Section 1 has no equivalent in the United States, a fact previously alluded to by this Court in selectively utilizing American constitutional jurisprudence. Of course, American experience should never be rejected simply because the Charter contains a balancing provision, for it is well known that American courts have fashioned compromises between conflicting interests despite what appears to be the absolute guarantee of constitutional rights. Where s. 1 operates to accentuate a uniquely Canadian vision of a free and democratic society, however, we must not hesitate to depart from the path taken in the United States. Far from requiring a less solicitous protection of Charter rights and freedoms, such independence of vision protects these rights and freedoms in a different way. As will be seen below, in my view ... the special role given equality and multiculturalism in the Canadian Constitution necessitate a departure from the view, reasonably prevalent in America at present, that the suppression of hate propaganda is incompatible with the guarantee of free expression....

[Chief Justice Dickson then squarely addressed Section 1 and the test from *R. v. Oakes*.]

C. *Objective of Section 319(2)*

I now turn to the specific requirements of the *Oakes* approach in deciding whether the infringement of s. 2(b) occasioned by s. 319(2) is justifiable in a free and democratic society. According to *Oakes*, the first aspect of the s. 1 analysis is to examine the objective of the impugned legislation. Only if the objective relates to concerns which are pressing and substantial in a free and democratic society can the legislative limit on a right or freedom hope to be permissible under the Charter....

The presence of hate propaganda in Canada is sufficiently substantial to warrant concern. Disquiet caused by the existence of such material is not simply the product of its offensiveness, however, but stems from the very real harm which it causes. Essentially, there are two sorts of injury caused by hate propaganda. First, there is harm done to members of the target group. It is indisputable that the emotional damage caused by words may be of grave psychological and social consequence.... Words and writings that willfully promote hatred can constitute a serious attack on persons belonging to a racial or religious group, and in this regard the Cohen Committee noted that these persons are humiliated and degraded.

In my opinion, a response of humiliation and degradation from an individual targeted by hate propaganda is to be expected. A person's sense of human dignity and belonging to the community at large is closely linked to the concern and respect accorded the groups to which he or she belongs. The derision, hostility and abuse encouraged by hate propaganda therefore have a severely negative impact on the individual's sense of self-worth and acceptance. This impact may cause target group members to take drastic measures in reaction, perhaps avoiding activities which bring them into contact with non-group members or adopting attitudes and postures directed towards blending in with the majority. Such consequences bear heavily in a nation that prides itself on tolerance and the fostering of human dignity through, among other things, respect for the many racial, religious and cultural groups in our society.

A second harmful effect of hate propaganda which is of pressing and substantial concern is its influence upon society at large. The Cohen Committee noted that individuals can be persuaded to believe "almost anything" if information or ideas are communicated using the right technique and in the proper circumstances....

It is thus not inconceivable that the active dissemination of hate propaganda can attract individuals to its cause, and in the process create serious discord between various cultural groups in society. Moreover, the alteration of views held by the recipients of hate propaganda may occur subtly, and is not always attendant upon conscious acceptance of the communicated ideas. Even if the message of hate propaganda is outwardly rejected, there is evidence that its premise of racial or religious inferiority may persist in a recipient's mind as an idea that holds some truth, an incipient effect not to be entirely discounted.

The threat to the self-dignity of target group members is thus matched by the possibility that prejudiced messages will gain some credence, with the attendant result of discrimination, and perhaps even violence, against minority groups in Canadian society. With these dangers in mind, the Cohen Committee made clear in its conclusions that the presence of hate propaganda existed as a baleful and pernicious element, and hence a serious problem, in Canada....

(iv) Conclusion Respecting Objective of Section 319(2)

In my opinion, it would be impossible to deny that Parliament's objective in enacting s. 319(2) is of the utmost importance. Parliament has recognized the substantial harm that can flow from hate propaganda, and in trying to prevent the pain suffered by target group members and to reduce racial, ethnic and religious tension in Canada has decided to suppress the willful promotion of hatred against identifiable groups. The nature of Parliament's objective is supported not only by the work of numerous study groups, but also by our collective historical knowledge of the potentially catastrophic effects of the promotion of hatred [citation omitted]. Additionally, the international commitment to eradicate hate propaganda and the stress placed upon equality and multiculturalism in the Charter strongly buttress the importance of this objective. I consequently find that the first part of the test under s. 1 of the Charter is easily satisfied and that a powerfully convincing legislative objective exists such as to justify some limit on freedom of expression.

D. *Proportionality*

The second branch of the *Oakes* test—proportionality—poses the most challenging questions with respect to the validity of s. 319(2) as a reasonable limit on freedom of expression in a free and democratic society. It is therefore not surprising to find most commentators, as well as the litigants in the case at bar, agreeing that the objective of the provision is of great importance, but to observe considerable disagreement when it comes to deciding whether the means chosen to further the objective are proportional to the ends....

(i) Relation of the Expression at Stake to Free Expression Values

In discussing the nature of the government objective, I have commented at length upon the way in which the suppression of hate propaganda furthers values basic to a free and democratic society. I have said little, however, regarding the extent to which these same values, including the freedom of expression, are furthered by *permitting* the exposition of such expressive activity. This lacuna is explicable when one realizes that the interpretation of s. 2(b) under [controlling precedent] gives protection to a very wide range of expression. Content is irrelevant to this interpretation, the result of a high value being placed upon freedom of expression in the abstract. This approach to s. 2(b) often operates to leave unexamined the extent to which the expression *at stake in a particular case* promotes freedom of expression principles. In my opinion, however, the s. 1 analysis of a limit upon s. 2(b) cannot ignore the nature of the expressive activity which the state seeks to restrict. While we must guard carefully against judging expression according to its popularity, it is equally destructive of free expression values, as well as the other values which underlie a free and democratic society, to treat all expression as equally crucial to those principles at the core of s. 2(b)....

Let me begin by saying that, in my opinion, there can be no real disagreement about the subject matter of the messages and teachings communicated by the respondent, Mr. Keegstra: it is deeply offensive, hurtful and damaging to target group members, misleading to his listeners, and antithetical to the furtherance of tolerance and understanding in society. Furthermore, as will be clear when I come to discuss in detail the interpretation of s. 319(2), there is no doubt that all expression fitting within the terms of the offense can be similarly described. To say merely that expression is offensive and disturbing, however, fails to address satisfactorily the question of whether, and to what extent, the expressive activity prohibited by s. 319(2) promotes the values underlying the freedom of expression. It is to this difficult and complex question that I now turn.

From the outset, I wish to make clear that in my opinion the expression prohibited by s. 319(2) is not closely linked to the rationale underlying s. 2(b).... I am of the opinion that expression intended to promote the hatred of identifiable groups is of limited importance when measured against free expression values....

The suppression of hate propaganda undeniably muzzles the participation of a few individuals in the democratic process, and hence detracts somewhat from free expression values, but the degree of this limitation is not substantial. I am aware that the use of strong language in political and social debate—indeed, perhaps even language intended to promote hatred—is an unavoidable part of the democratic process. Moreover, I recognize that hate propaganda is expression of a type which would generally be categorized as "political," thus putatively placing it at the very heart of the principle extolling freedom of expression as vital to the democratic process. Nonetheless, expression can work to undermine our commitment to democracy where employed to propagate ideas anathemic to democratic values. Hate propaganda works in just such a way, arguing as it does for a society in which the democratic process is subverted and individuals are denied respect and dignity simply because of racial or religious characteristics. This brand of expressive activity is thus wholly inimical to the democratic aspirations of the free expression guarantee.

Indeed, one may quite plausibly contend that it is through rejecting hate propaganda that the state can best encourage the protection of values central to freedom of expression, while simultaneously demonstrating dislike for the vision forwarded by hate-mongers. In this regard, the reaction to various types of expression by a democratic government may be perceived as meaningful expression on behalf of the vast majority of citizens. I do not wish to be construed as saying that an infringement of s. 2(b) can be justified under s. 1 merely because it is the product of a democratic process; the Charter will not permit even the democratically elected legislature to restrict the rights and freedoms crucial to a free and democratic society. What I do wish to emphasize, however, is that one must be careful not to accept blindly that the suppression of expression must always and unremittingly detract from values central to freedom of expression.

I am very reluctant to attach anything but the highest importance to expression relevant to political matters. But given the unparalleled vigour with which hate propaganda repudiates and undermines democratic values, and in particular its condemnation of the view that all citizens need be treated with equal respect and dignity so as to make participation in the political process meaningful, I am unable to see the protection of such expression as integral to the democratic ideal so central to the s. 2(b) rationale.... In my view, hate propaganda should not be accorded the greatest of weight in the s. 1 analysis....

Hate propaganda contributes little to the aspirations of Canadians or Canada in either the quest for truth, the promotion of individual self-development or the protection and fostering of a vibrant democracy where the participation of all individuals is accepted and encouraged. While I cannot conclude that hate propaganda deserves only marginal protection under the s. 1 analysis, I can take cognizance of the fact that limitations upon hate propaganda are directed at a special category of expression which strays some distance from the spirit of s. 2(b), and hence conclude that restrictions on expression of this kind might be easier to justify than other infringements of s. 2(b)....

Having made some preliminary comments as to the nature of the expression at stake in this appeal, it is now possible to ask whether s. 319(2) is an acceptably proportional response to Parliament's valid objective. As stated above, the proportionality aspect of the Oakes test requires the Court to decide whether the impugned state action: i) is rationally connected to the objective; ii) minimally impairs the Charter right or freedom at issue; and iii) does not produce effects of such severity so as to make the impairment unjustifiable. I will now address these segments of the proportionality inquiry, beginning with the question of whether a rational connection exists between s. 319(2) and the legislative objective.

(ii) Rational Connection

Section 319(2) makes the willful promotion of hatred against identifiable groups an indictable offense,[15] indicating Parliament's serious concern about the effects of such activity. Those who would uphold the provision argue that the criminal prohibition of

---

15. Editor's note: Indictable offenses under Canadian law are analogous to felonies under American law.

hate propaganda obviously bears a rational connection to the legitimate Parliamentary objective of protecting target group members and fostering harmonious social relations in a community dedicated to equality and multiculturalism. I agree, for in my opinion it would be difficult to deny that the suppression of hate propaganda reduces the harm such expression does to individuals who belong to identifiable groups and to relations between various cultural and religious groups in Canadian society....

In sum, having found that the purpose of the challenged legislation is valid, I also find that the means chosen to further this purpose are rational in both theory and operation, and therefore conclude that the first branch of the proportionality test has been met. Accordingly, I move now to the issue of whether s. 319(2) minimally impairs the s. 2(b) guarantee of freedom of expression.

(iii) Minimal Impairment of the Section 2(b) Freedom

It ... must be shown that s. 319(2) is a measured and appropriate response to the phenomenon of hate propaganda, and that it does not overly circumscribe the s. 2(b) guarantee.

The main argument of those who would strike down s. 319(2) is that it creates a real possibility of punishing expression that is not hate propaganda. It is thus submitted that the legislation is overbroad, its terms so wide as to include expression which does not relate to Parliament's objective, and also unduly vague, in that a lack of clarity and precision in its words prevents individuals from discerning its meaning with any accuracy. In either instance, it is said that the effect of s. 319(2) is to limit the expression of merely unpopular or unconventional communications. Such communications may present no risk of causing the harm which Parliament seeks to prevent, and will perhaps be closely associated with the core values of s. 2(b). This overbreadth and vagueness could consequently allow the state to employ s. 319(2) to infringe excessively the freedom of expression or, what is more likely, could have a chilling effect whereby persons potentially within s. 319(2) would exercise self-censorship. Accordingly, those attacking the validity of s. 319(2) contend that vigorous debate on important political and social issues, so highly valued in a society that prizes a diversity of ideas, is unacceptably suppressed by the provision.

The question to be answered, then, is whether s. 319(2) indeed fails to distinguish between low value expression that is squarely within the focus of Parliament's valid objective and that which does not invoke the need for the severe response of criminal sanction. In order to answer this question, and thus to determine whether s. 319(2) minimally impairs the freedom of expression, the nature and impact of specific features of the provision must be examined in some detail. These features relate to both the terms of the offense and the available defenses enumerated in s. 319(3), and I find it convenient to utilize this slightly arbitrary division for the purposes of the following discussion. As well, in examining this aspect of the proportionality test I will comment upon the relevance of alternative modes of combatting the harm caused by hate propaganda.

a. Terms of Section 319(2)

In assessing the constitutionality of s. 319(2), especially as concerns arguments of overbreadth and vagueness, an immediate observation is that statements made "in private conversation" are not included in the criminalized expression. The provision thus does not prohibit views expressed with an intention to promote hatred if made privately, indicating Parliament's concern not to intrude upon the privacy of the individual....

Is s. 319(2) nevertheless overbroad because it captures *all* public expression intended to promote hatred? It would appear not, for the harm which the government seeks to prevent is not restricted to certain mediums and/or locations. To attempt to distinguish between various forms and fora would therefore be incongruent with Parliament's legitimate objective.

A second important element of s. 319(2) is its requirement that the promotion of hatred be "willful." The nature of this mental element was explored ... in *R. v. Buzzanga and Durocher* (1979).... This mental element is satisfied only where an accused subjectively desires the promotion of hatred or foresees such a consequence as certain or substantially certain to result from an act done in order to achieve some other purpose....

The meaning of "hatred" remains to be elucidated.... Noting the purpose of s. 319(2), in my opinion the term "hatred" connotes emotion of an intense and extreme nature that is clearly associated with vilification and detestation....

Hatred is predicated on destruction, and hatred against identifiable groups therefore thrives on insensitivity, bigotry and destruction of both the target group and of the values of our society. Hatred in this sense is a most extreme emotion that belies reason; an emotion that, if exercised against members of an identifiable group, implies that those individuals are to be despised, scorned, denied respect and made subject to ill-treatment on the basis of group affiliation.

Those who argue that s. 319(2) should be struck down submit that it is impossible to define with care and precision a term like "hatred". Yet, as I have stated, the sense in which "hatred" is used in s. 319(2) does not denote a wide range of diverse emotions, but is circumscribed so as to cover only the most intense form of dislike....

b. The Defenses to Section 319(2)

The factors mentioned above suggest that s. 319(2) does not unduly restrict the s. 2(*b*) guarantee. The terms of the offense, as I have defined them, rather indicate that s. 319(2) possesses definitional limits which act as safeguards to ensure that it will capture only expressive activity which is openly hostile to Parliament's objective, and will thus attack only the harm at which the prohibition is targeted. The specific defenses provided are further glosses on the purview of the offense, and I repeat them here.

319(3) No person shall be convicted of an offense under subsection (2)

(a) if he establishes that the statements communicated were true;

(b) if, in good faith, he expressed or attempted to establish by argument an opinion on a religious subject;

> (c) if the statements were relevant to any subject of public interest, the discussion of which was for the public benefit, and if on reasonable grounds he believed them to be true; or
>
> (d) if, in good faith, he intended to point out, for the purpose of removal, matters producing or tending to produce feelings of hatred toward an identifiable group in Canada.

A careful reading of the s. 319(3) defenses shows them to take in examples of expressive activity that generally would not fall within the "willful promotion of hatred" as I have defined the phrase. Thus the three defenses which include elements of good faith or honest belief—namely, s. 319(3)(b), (c) and (d)—would seem to operate to negate directly the *mens rea* in the offense, for only rarely will one who intends to promote hatred be acting in good faith or upon honest belief. These defenses are hence intended to aid in making the scope of the willful promotion of hatred more explicit; individuals engaging in the type of expression described are thus given a strong signal that their activity will not be swept into the ambit of the offense. The result is that what danger exists that s. 319(2) is overbroad or unduly vague, or will be perceived as such, is significantly reduced. To the extent that s. 319(3) provides justification for the accused who would otherwise fall within the parameters of the offense of willfully promoting hatred, it reflects a commitment to the idea that an individual's freedom of expression will not be curtailed in borderline cases. The line between the rough and tumble of public debate and brutal, negative and damaging attacks upon identifiable groups is hence adjusted in order to give some leeway to freedom of expression....

c. Alternative Modes of Furthering Parliament's Objective

One of the strongest arguments supporting the contention that s. 319(2) unacceptably impairs the s. 2(b) guarantee posits that a criminal sanction is not necessary to meet Parliament's objective. Thus ... it is said that non-criminal responses can more effectively combat the harm caused by hate propaganda. Most generally, it is said that discriminatory ideas can best be met with information and education programmes extolling the merits of tolerance and cooperation between racial and religious groups....

Given the stigma and punishment associated with a criminal conviction and the presence of other modes of government response in the fight against intolerance, it is proper to ask whether s. 319(2) can be said to impair minimally the freedom of expression. With respect to the efficacy of criminal legislation in advancing the goals of equality and multicultural tolerance in Canada, I agree that the role of s. 319(2) will be limited. It is important, in my opinion, not to hold any illusions about the ability of this one provision to rid our society of hate propaganda and its associated harms. Indeed, to become overly complacent, forgetting that there are a great many ways in which to address the problem of racial and religious intolerance, could be dangerous. Obviously, a variety of measures need be employed in the quest to achieve such lofty and important goals....

Though the fostering of tolerant attitudes among Canadians will be best achieved through a combination of diverse measures, the harm done through hate propaganda may require that especially stringent responses be taken to suppress and prohibit a modicum of expressive activity. At the moment, for example, the state has the option of responding to hate propaganda by acting under either the Criminal Code or human rights provisions. In my view, having both avenues of redress at the state's disposal is justified in a free and democratic society. I see no reason to assume that the state will always utilize the most severe tool at hand, namely, the criminal law, to prevent the dissemination of hate propaganda. Where use of the sanction provided by s. 319(2) is imprudent, employing human rights legislation may be the more attractive route to take, but there may equally be circumstances in which the more confrontational response of criminal prosecution is best suited to punish a recalcitrant hatemonger. To send out a strong message of condemnation, both reinforcing the values underlying s. 319(2) and deterring the few individuals who would harm target group members and the larger community by intentionally communicating hate propaganda, will occasionally require use of the criminal law.

d. Conclusion as to Minimal Impairment

I thus conclude that s. 319(2) of the Criminal Code does not unduly impair the freedom of expression, and it remains only to examine whether its effects nonetheless present so grave a limitation upon the s. 2(b) guarantee so as to outweigh the benefits to be gained from a measure otherwise proportional to an important legislative objective.

(iv) Effects of the Limitation

The third branch of the proportionality test entails a weighing of the importance of the state objective against the effect of limits imposed upon a Charter right or guarantee. Even if the purpose of the limiting measure is substantial and the first two components of the proportionality test are satisfied, the deleterious effects of a limit may be too great to permit the infringement of the right or guarantee in issue....

It is ... apposite to stress yet again the enormous importance of the objective fueling s. 319(2), an objective of such magnitude as to support even the severe response of criminal prohibition. Few concerns can be as central to the concept of a free and democratic society as the dissipation of racism, and the especially strong value which Canadian society attaches to this goal must never be forgotten in assessing the effects of an impugned legislative measure. When the purpose of s. 319(2) is thus recognized, I have little trouble in finding that its effects, involving as they do the restriction of expression largely removed from the heart of free expression values, are not of such a deleterious nature as to outweigh any advantage gleaned from the limitation of s. 2(b).

E. Analysis of Section 319(2) Under Section 1 of the Charter: Conclusion

I find that the infringement of the respondent's freedom of expression as guaranteed by s. 2(b) should be upheld as a reasonable limit prescribed by law in a free and democratic society. Furthering an immensely important objective and directed at expression distant from the core of free expression values, s. 319(2) satisfies each of the components of the proportionality inquiry. I thus disagree with the Alberta Court of Appeal's conclusion that this criminal prohibition of hate propaganda violates the Charter, and would allow the appeal in this respect.

[Chief Justice Dickson proceeded to address a separate issue, rejecting Keegstra's argument that the reverse onus applicable to the defense of truth was an unjustifiable infringement of the presumption of innocence under Charter Section 11(d). The Supreme Court of Canada thus allowed the appeal and remitted the case back to the Court of Appeal of Alberta "to resolve those issues left unexamined by reason of its decision to strike down the impugned provisions."

Future Chief Justice Beverly McLachlin authored a lengthy dissent. Although she acknowledged that the "evil of hate propaganda is beyond doubt," Justice McLachlin (as she then was) deemed the criminalization of hate speech a disproportionate and ineffective response to the objective of preventing the promotion of hatred against identifiable groups. In so concluding, Justice McLachlin drew heavily on the protective approach to freedom of expression taken by the U.S. Supreme Court. Justice McLachlin also would have declared the reverse onus applicable to the defense of truth an unjustifiable limit on the presumption of innocence.]

Canada's Hate Speech Trilogy

1. *Overview*. The *Keegstra* case was heard by the Supreme Court of Canada in the same week as two other cases that raised issues pertaining to freedom of expression and harmful speech: *R. v. Andrews* [1990] and *Canada (Human Rights Commission) v. Taylor* [1990]. The decisions in all three matters were released on the same day.[16] *Andrews*, like *Keegstra*, concerned the constitutionality of the offense of willful promotion of hatred. The accused in that case were members of a White nationalist political organization who had distributed a newsletter that promoted hatred against Blacks and Jews. *Taylor* dealt with the constitutionality of a provision under Canada's human rights legislation that prohibited telephonic communications likely to expose members of an identifiable group to hatred or contempt.[17] The Supreme Court sided with the government and upheld the relevant legislation in all three cases as a justifiable limit on freedom of expression. The vote in each case was 4–3, with the same judges lining up on each side. Justice McLachlin authored the dissenting judgment in all three cases.

2. *R. v. Zundel*, [1992] 2 S.C.R. 731, which also dealt with freedom of expression, was decided by the Supreme Court of Canada two years after *Keegstra*. The accused in that case, Ernst Zundel, was a prominent Holocaust denier who lived in Toronto. Although some members of the Jewish community lobbied the government to charge Zundel with willful promotion of hatred, the attorney general of Ontario refused to consent

---

16. R. v. Andrews, [1990] 3 S.C.R. 870; Canada (Human Rights Commission) v. Taylor, [1990] 3 S.C.R. 892.

17. *Canadian Human Rights Act*, R.S.C. 1985, c H-6, s 13(1). The federal government repealed this provision in 2013. The purpose of human rights legislation in Canada, broadly speaking, is to prevent and alleviate discrimination against vulnerable groups. Human rights legislation prescribes civil rather than criminal penalties.

to a prosecution.[18] Frustrated by the attorney general's inaction, a Holocaust survivor named Sabina Citron commenced a private prosecution against Zundel for an offense called "spreading false news." The government then took over the case.

Zundel's trial, like Keegstra's, took place in 1985. As with Keegstra, the trial garnered considerable media coverage across Canada, taking a tremendous emotional toll on the Jewish community. To make matters worse, the prosecution called several Holocaust survivors for the purpose of proving the falsity of Zundel's claims; these Holocaust survivors were then subjected to merciless cross-examination by Zundel's attorney.

Zundel was convicted and sentenced to fifteen months in jail. Although a second trial was necessitated because of certain legal errors made by the trial judge in the first trial, Zundel was convicted again, and the matter ultimately reached the Supreme Court of Canada.

The sole issue in the Supreme Court was whether the offense of spreading false news was a justifiable infringement on freedom of expression under Section 2(b) of the Charter. The decision was once again 4–3, but this time the majority sided with the accused and struck down the relevant law. Justice McLachlin wrote the majority's reasons. She described the crime of spreading false news as overly broad and presenting too great a threat to freedom of expression. Justice McLachlin noted that the offense of willful promotion of hatred was a more targeted provision and could have been used instead. The dissenting judges, as with the majority in *Keegstra*, focused on the harms of hate speech, including its impact on vulnerable groups like the Jewish community. Notably, Chief Justice Dickson did not participate in *Zundel*, as he retired in 1990.

Canadian Jewry's Response to Antisemitism Post-WWII

1. *Population*. According to the 2021 Canadian census, about 335,000 Canadians identify as Jewish out of a total population of approximately 37 million (0.9%).[19] Canada's Jewish population has hovered around 1% of the total population for the last fifty years.[20] Canada is currently home to the fourth-largest Jewish community in the world.[21]

2. *Holocaust survivors*. A relatively large portion of the Canadian-Jewish community is descended from Holocaust survivors. Canada took in approximately 30,000 to 35,000 Holocaust survivors after the Second World War. As a result, by 1961, approximately

---

18. Recall that no charges may be brought for advocating genocide or willful promotion of hatred without the consent of the attorney general of the relevant province.

19. *Census of Population*, Statistics Canada, www.12.statcan.gc.ca (last visited Oct. 15, 2024).

20. Allan Levine, Seeking the Fabled City: The Canadian Jewish Experience 365 (2018).

21. *Countries with the Largest Jewish Population 2022*, Statista, https://www.statista.com/statistics/1351079/jewish-pop-by-country/ (last visited Oct. 15, 2024). With 171,000 Jews, Argentina has the sixth largest Jewish community in the world and the third largest in the Western Hemisphere. *Vital Statistics: Jewish Population of the World*, Jewish Virtual Libr., https://www.jewishvirtuallibrary.org/jewish-population-of-the-world (last visited Dec. 17, 2024).

13 to 15 percent of the Canadian-Jewish community consisted of Holocaust survivors and their descendants. This is far greater than the ratio of Holocaust survivors among American Jews during the same period (approximately 4 percent). Commencing in the 1960s, Holocaust survivors began to have a dramatic impact on the political and social dynamic of the Canadian-Jewish community.[22]

3. *Jewish advocacy groups*. Prior to 2011, the two major Jewish advocacy organizations in Canada were the Canadian Jewish Congress and B'nai B'rith Canada, both of which intervened in the *Keegstra* case on the government's side.[23] In 2011, the Canadian Jewish Congress ceased operations and was incorporated into the Centre for Israel and Jewish Affairs.[24]

Criminalization of Hate Speech in Canada

1. *Jewish role*. Prior to 1970, the Criminal Code of Canada contained no provisions specifically outlawing hate speech. Chief Justice Dickson notes briefly in *Keegstra* that there was an attempt to include hate speech provisions as part of wholesale revision to the *Criminal Code* in 1953. In fact, efforts to criminalize hate speech in Canada go back even further and were spearheaded by the Jewish community. In 1937, motivated by a rise in Nazi sympathizers, the Canadian Jewish Congress asked the government to make libelous accusations against minority groups a criminal offense, but the government dismissed the idea.[25] In 1953, during hearings in Canada's Parliament that preceded the Criminal Code revision, a Canadian Jewish Congress delegation requested that the government criminalize incitement to violence against groups.[26] The government once again took no action. In the 1960s, Jewish groups renewed their efforts to have hate speech criminalized. This time, advocacy was driven largely by Holocaust survivors, who were alarmed by the emergence of neo-Nazi groups in Canada and in the United States.[27] These efforts bore fruit with the creation of the Cohen Committee.

2. *The Cohen Committee*. Chief Justice Dickson's judgment contains several references to The Special Committee on Hate Propaganda in Canada, commonly referred to as the "Cohen Committee." The Cohen Committee was created by the Canadian government in 1965 to study possible legal measures against hate speech. The Com-

22. Franklin Bialystok, Delayed Impact: The Holocaust and the Canadian Jewish Community 73 (2000).

23. Specifically, the intervenor was the League for Human Rights of B'nai Brith Canada, which is similar to the ADL operating specifically in Canada. *B'nai Brith Advocacy*, B'nai Brith Canada, https://www.bnaibrith.ca/league-for-human-rights/ (last visited Dec. 17, 2024).

24. Andy Levy-Ajzenkopf, *Congress Era Over as CIJA Reboot Starts*, Can. Jewish News, Aug 25, 2011, at 13.

25. Letter from H.M. Caiserman to W.L. Mackenzie King (Aug. 25, 1937), Montreal, Alex Dworkin Canadian Jewish Archives [CJA], CJC ZA 1937 Box 1, File 16; *see also* Letter from W.L. Mackenzie King, to E. Lapointe (Sept. 10, 1937), CJA, CJC ZA 1937 Box 1, File 16.

26. House of Commons, Special Committee on Bill No. 93, *Evidence*, 21-7, vol 1, No. 2, Mar. 3, 1953, at 57.

27. Kenneth Grad, *A Gesture of Criminal Law: Jews and the Criminalization of Hate Speech in Canada*, 59 Osgoode Hall L.J. 375, 388–404 (Spring 2022).

mittee took its name from its chairman, Maxwell Cohen, then dean of the Faculty of Law at McGill University in Montreal, and Canada's first Jewish law school dean.[28] The Committee's membership included Pierre-Elliott Trudeau, then a professor at the Faculty of Law of the Université de Montréal, who went on to become Canada's Prime Minister in 1968.[29]

3. *Passage of legislation in 1970.* The Canadian government released the Cohen Committee's Report in April 1966, which recommended the criminalization of hate speech. Several months later, the government introduced legislation virtually identical to what the Cohen Committee had recommended. The government proposed three new criminal offenses: (1) advocacy or promotion of genocide; (2) incitement of violence or hatred against an identifiable group through public communication, where such incitement was likely to lead to a breach of the peace; and (3) willful promotion of hatred or contempt against an identifiable group. The legislation provoked considerable debate. The most controversial provision was the offense of willful promotion of hatred, because of its broad applicability, including the absence of any requirement that the impugned speech pose any risk of violence or public disorder. However, the bill was supported by Jewish and other minority groups and championed by new Prime Minister Trudeau upon his election in 1968. It was passed in April 1970.[30]

4. *Use of legislation after enactment.* The hate speech provisions were seldom used after their enactment. With respect to willful promotion of hatred, the first prosecution did not come until 1977 in the case of *R. v. Buzzanga and Durocher*. In that case, the accused were convicted at trial, but the conviction was overturned by the Court of Appeal for Ontario.[31] The government then declined to re-prosecute. As a result, at the time that Keegstra was charged with willful promotion of hatred, there had never been a successful prosecution for this offense.

5. *Generally.* The core of Canada's hate speech laws remains the three provisions enacted by Canada's Parliament in 1970: advocating genocide, public incitement of hatred, and willful promotion of hatred. The content of these provisions remains largely the same as when they were first introduced, with some amendments noted below. These laws are infrequently utilized and, when used, the conviction rate is lower than the average for other criminal offenses in Canada.[32] According to legal scholar William

---

28. Sheldon Kirshner, *Cohen Feels at Home in Academia, Government*, CAN. JEWISH NEWS, Mar 12, 1981, at 5; *see also* Ronald St John MacDonald, *Maxwell Cohen at Eighty: International Lawyer, Educator, and Judge*, 27 CAN. YEARBOOK INT'L L. 3, 31.

29. Pierre-Elliott Trudeau was the father of Justin Trudeau, who is, as of this writing, the prime minister of Canada. *See Pierre Elliott Trudeau,* BRITANNICA, https://www.britannica.com/biography/Pierre-Elliott-Trudeau (last updated Dec. 17, 2024).

30. Grad, *supra* note 27 at 413–424.

31. R v. Buzzanga and Durocher, [1979] O.J. No. 4345, 1979 CarswellOnt 1502, at para. 46.

32. See Grad, *supra* note 2727, at 377, n. 3, and the statistics and sources cited therein.

Kaplan, "If number of prosecutions and convictions is the standard used for assessment, the legislation has clearly failed."[33]

6. *Advocating genocide.* The crime of advocating genocide is now contained in Section 318 of the Criminal Code, which reads in relevant part: "Every person who advocates or promotes genocide is guilty of an ... offense." "Genocide" is defined in Section 318(2) as (a) the killing of members of an identifiable group or (b) deliberately inflicting conditions of life calculated to bring about an identifiable group's destruction. The maximum punishment for this offense is five years imprisonment.

7. *Public incitement of hatred.* The crime of public incitement of hatred is now contained in Section 319(1) of the Criminal Code, which reads in relevant part: "Every one who, by communicating statements in any public place, incites hatred against any identifiable group where such incitement is likely to lead to a breach of the peace is guilty of [an offense]."

8. *Willful promotion of hatred.* The crime of willful promotion of hatred is found in Section 319(2) of the Criminal Code, which reads in relevant part: "Every one who, by communicating statements, other than in private conversation, willfully promotes hatred against any identifiable group is guilty of [an offense]." The maximum penalty for this offense is two years imprisonment.

9. *Defenses.* The offense of willful promotion of hatred is subject to several broad defenses, contained in Criminal Code Section 319(3). The existence of these defenses significantly reduces the risk that the offense of willful promotion of hatred will be invalidated as overbroad or unduly vague.

(a) *Truth.* The accused cannot be convicted if their statements were true. In contrast to the other defenses, which must be disproved by the prosecution beyond a reasonable doubt, the onus of establishing the defense of truth is placed on the accused on a balance of probabilities. In *Keegstra*, the majority of the Supreme Court upheld this reverse onus as a reasonable limit on the Charter right to be presumed innocent until proven guilty (Section 11(d)).

(b) *Good faith opinion on matter of religion.* The accused cannot be convicted "if, in good faith, the person expressed or attempted to establish by an argument an opinion on a religious subject or an opinion based on a belief in a religious text."

(c) *Matter of public interest.* The accused cannot be convicted if the impugned "statements were relevant to any subject of public interest, the discussion of which was for the public benefit, and if on reasonable grounds he believed them to be true."

(d) *Pointed out for purpose of removal.* The accused cannot be convicted if "in good faith, he intended to point out, for the purpose of removal, matters

33. William Kaplan, *Maxwell Cohen and the Report of the Special Committee on Hate Propaganda*, *in* LAW, POLICY, AND INTERNATIONAL JUSTICE: ESSAYS IN HONOUR OF MAXWELL COHEN 243, 266 (William Kaplan & Donald McRae, eds., 1993).

producing or tending to produce feelings of hatred toward an identifiable group in Canada."

10. *Definition of willful.* To have acted willfully, the accused must have subjectively desired the promotion of hatred or foreseen such a consequence as certain or substantially certain to result from an act done in order to achieve some other purpose.

11. *Definition of hatred.* Chief Justice Dickson also defines hatred narrowly, as "connot[ing] emotion of an intense and extreme nature that is clearly associated with vilification and detestation." This formulation has stood the test of time. Indeed, the government of Canada recently proposed enshrining this definition of hatred in the Criminal Code as part of a legislative package called the Online Harms Act, discussed below.

12. *Definition of identifiable group.* The hate speech offenses all refer to crimes committed against identifiable groups. The term "identifiable group" is defined in the legislation as "any section of the public distinguished by colour, race, religion, national or ethnic origin, age, sex, sexual orientation, gender identity or expression, or mental or physical disability."[34] The list of identifiable groups has expanded over time; the original version of this provision referred only to colour, race, religion, and ethnic origin.

13. *Consent of attorney general required.* No charges may be brought for advocating genocide or willful promotion of hatred without the consent of the attorney general of the relevant province.[35] This is an unusual requirement, not applicable to most criminal offenses in Canada. It was inserted to alleviate concern over misuse of the hate speech laws.[36]

14. *Willful promotion of antisemitism.* In 2022, the Canadian government enacted a new criminal offense called "willful promotion of antisemitism." This offense proscribes the willful promotion of antisemitism by condoning, denying or downplaying the Holocaust.[37] The provision was introduced in response to rising antisemitism in Canada.[38] It appears only one person has thus far been charged under this legislation.[39]

15. *Online Harms Act.* In February 2024, the Canadian government introduced new legislation, called the Online Harms Act, that would increase regulation of speech particularly on social media. As part of this legislative package, the government plans to increase the maximum penalties available for existing hate speech crimes. The maximum punishment for willful promotion of hatred, public incitement of hatred, and willful promotion of antisemitism would be increased from two years to five years

---

34. R.S.C. 1985, c 46 s 318(4) (*Criminal Code*).

35. *Id.* at ss 318(3), 319(6).

36. Grad, *supra* note 27, 415–16, 421–22.

37. *Criminal Code, supra* note 34 s 319(2.1).

38. Marie Woolf, *Holocaust Denial—and Downplaying the Nazis' Murder of Jews—to be Outlawed*, CAN. PRESS, Apr. 8, 2022.

39. Stephanie Taylor, *Canada Criminalized 'Condoning, Denying or Downplaying' the Holocaust: Is It Working?* CTV NEWS (Nov. 19, 2023), ctvnews.ca/canada/canada-criminalized-condoning-denying-or-downplaying-the-holocaust-is-it-working-1.6651817; *see also RCMP Arrest Rivière-du-Loup Man Suspected of Promoting Hate*, MONTREAL GAZETTE (Dec. 13, 2024), montrealgazette.com/news/provincial-news/article571103.html.

imprisonment. The maximum penalty for advocating genocide would be raised from five years to life imprisonment. Additionally, the Online Harms Act would add a definition of "hatred" in the Criminal Code, virtually identical to the definition provided in Keegstra.[40] The Online Harms Act is opposed by the Conservative Party, the main opposition to Prime Minister Justin Trudeau's governing Liberals, and it is unclear whether it will be passed prior to the next federal election in October 2025.[41]

16. *Residential school denialism.* Another bill introduced in Canada's Parliament in September 2024 proposes to criminalize the promotion of hatred against Indigenous Peoples by condoning, justifying, or downplaying the historical and lasting impact of residential schools. The residential schools, which operated from 1883 to 1997, were government-run institutions that aimed to assimilate Indigenous youth into Canadian society; abuse was rampant and at least six thousand children died as a result.[42]

The Canadian Approach to Freedom of Expression

1. *Introduction to the Charter.* The Canadian Charter of Rights and Freedoms,[43] akin to the United States Bill of Rights, is a constitutional document that protects the basic rights and freedoms of Canadians, including freedom of expression. Courts are empowered to strike down any legislation inconsistent with the Charter's provisions. Unlike the Bill of Rights, the Charter is of relatively recent vintage, having been enacted in 1982.

2. *Charter Section 1.* Also, unlike the Bill of Rights, the rights and freedoms guaranteed by the Charter are subject to such reasonable limits prescribed by law as can be demonstrably justified in a free and democratic society, as set out in Charter Section 1. This means that when a court finds legislation has contravened one of the Charter's rights and freedoms, the court must go on to assess whether the legislature can justify this contravention as a reasonable limit. As described in the majority's judgment in *Keegstra*, this reconciliation of individual rights against the goals of the state is assessed under a four-part analysis (taken from the earlier decision in *R. v. Oakes*), which weighs the legitimacy of the government's objective and the proportionality between the means chosen to achieve that objective and the burden on the claimant's rights.

3. *Charter Section 2(b).* Section 2(b) of the Charter enshrines the "freedom of thought, belief, opinion and expression, including freedom of the press and other media of communication."

---

40. H. of Commons B C-63, 44th Parliament, 1st Sess. (Can. 2021), parl.ca/LegisInfo/en/bill/44-1/c-63.

41. Stephanie Taylor, *Poilievre Promises to Scrap Online Harms Act After Budget Watchdog Projects $200M cost*, Can. Press, July 4, 2024, ca.news.yahoo.com/creating-proposed-online-harms-regulators-134135238.html.

42. Olivia Stefanovich, *Bill Before Parliament Would Outlaw Residential School 'Denialism,'* CBC News (Sept. 26, 2024), cbc.ca/news/politics/ndp-mp-private-members-bill-residential-school-denialism-1.7334916.

43. Part I of the *Constitution Act, 1982*, being Schedule B to the *Canada Act 1982* (UK), 1982, c 11 (Charter).

4. *Jewish community concerns.* Prior to the Charter's enactment, members of the Canadian Jewish community, including Maxwell Cohen, wanted the government to specifically carve out hate speech from protection under Section 2(b).[44] The government declined. However, then Minister of Justice Jean Chrétien (later Prime Minister of Canada from 1993–2003) wrote to Cohen assuring him that the legislation would survive a constitutional challenge.[45]

5. *Hate speech presumptively protected expression.* In *Keegstra*, all members of the Supreme Court agreed that hate speech constitutes expression within the ambit of Section 2(b) of the Charter. In so doing, the Court set down a very broad approach to freedom of expression, ruling that all communications that convey meaning or attempt to convey meaning, irrespective of the meaning sought to be conveyed, are protected. Accordingly, the entire Court was of the view that the offence of willful promotion of hatred infringed on the right to freedom of expression. As we have seen, the division between the majority and dissenting judgments centered on whether this infringement was a reasonable limit. In finding that it was, Chief Justice Dickson states that hate speech is of limited value and should be accorded little weight in the balancing exercise under Section 1.

U.S. vs. Canadian Approaches to Hate Speech

1. *Use of U.S. law in Keegstra.* Both the majority and dissenting judgments in *Keegstra* draw on American jurisprudence interpreting the First Amendment, which is generally regarded as precluding the criminalization of speech absent imminent lawless action.[46] As commented upon by Chief Justice Dickson, those who opposed the criminalization of hate speech in Canada, including the dissenting judges in *Keegstra*, argued that Canada should adopt an American-style approach.

2. *The Canadian position.* Instead, the majority chose a different path, explicitly separating Canada from the more protective American approach to freedom of expression. Chief Justice Dickson cites the need to "examine American constitutional law with a critical eye." One important difference noted by the majority is the existence in Canada of Section 1 of the Charter, which permits reasonable infringements on basic rights like freedom of expression. Section 1, according to the majority, "operates to accentuate a uniquely Canadian vision of a free and democratic society." Furthermore, the majority emphasizes "the special role given equality and multiculturalism in the Canadian Constitution." In a paean to this multiculturalist vision, Chief Justice Dickson justifies hate speech legislation as essential to uplifting the dignity of vulnerable groups:

---

44. Minutes of CJC National Executive Meeting at 4–5 (Apr. 5, 1981), Winnipeg, Provincial Archives of Manitoba (Abraham J. Arnold Fonds, P5104/2); *see also CJC Reiterates Stand on Hate Propaganda*, Can. Jewish News, Apr. 9, 1981, at 7.

45. Letter from Jean Chrétien to Maxwell Cohen (May 1, 1981) (Abraham J. Arnold Fonds, P5104/2).

46. Brandenburg v. Ohio, 395 U.S. 444, 447 (1969).

> Disquiet caused by the existence of such material is not simply the product of its offensiveness ... but stems from the very real harm that it causes.... In my opinion, a response of humiliation and degradation from an individual targeted by hate propaganda is to be expected.... The derision, hostility and abuse encouraged by hate propaganda therefore have a severely negative impact on the individual's sense of self-worth and acceptance.... Such consequences bear heavily in a nation that prides itself on tolerance and the fostering of human dignity through, among other things, respect for the many racial, religious and cultural groups in our society.[47]

3. *Continued divergence between Canadian and American approaches*. Divergence between Canadian and American approaches to hate speech has continued to grow since *Keegstra*. In a series of decisions rendered by the Supreme Court of the United States subsequent to *Keegstra*'s release in 1990, the U.S. Supreme Court has repeatedly evidenced its hostility to speech regulation.[48] The Supreme Court of Canada, in contrast, has provided the Canadian government with wide latitude to regulate speech. For example, in the landmark decision in *Saskatchewan (Human Rights Commission) v. Whatcott*, [2013], the Supreme Court of Canada unanimously upheld the key components of human rights legislation in the province of Saskatchewan that prohibits harmful expression directed toward protected groups. Then Chief Justice McLachlin, who had vigorously dissented in all three of the trilogy cases in 1990 and wrote the majority decision in *R. v. Zundel*, concurred in *Whatcott*.

The Impact of *Keegstra* on Canadian Jewry

1. *Lead-up to prosecution*. Because no Jews lived in Eckville, Alberta, James Keegstra largely escaped notice from the Jewish community until he was dismissed from his teaching position in December 1982.[49] The decision to charge Keegstra was made by the Alberta government without significant pressure from the Jewish community. Many Jews opposed the prosecution, fearing that a trial would only serve to provide Keegstra with a larger platform for his hateful views. The *Jewish Star*, Alberta's leading Jewish newspaper, called the Keegstra prosecution a "fruitless endeavour" that reflected "the anger and insecurity" of Canadian Jews.[50]

2. *Community trauma*. The legal victory in the *Keegstra* case came at a steep price. Media coverage of the trial was extensive, visiting trauma throughout the Jewish community. Keegstra's ridiculous claims about the Holocaust enraged and tormented Ho-

47. R. v. Keegstra, [1990] 3 S.C.R. 697.

48. *See* R.A.V. v. City of St. Paul, 505 U.S. 377 (1992); *see also* Virginia v. Black, 538 U.S. 343 (2003); *see also* Snyder v. Phelps, 562 U.S. 443 (2011); *see also* Matal v. Tam, 582 U.S. 218 (2017).

49. David Bercuson & Douglas Wertheimer, A Trust Betrayed: The Keegstra Affair 127–28 (1985).

50. *Listen to the High Court*, Jewish Star (Calgary ed.), June 10, 1988, at 4.

locaust survivors.[51] Jewish (and non-Jewish) people who attended the trial found it very difficult to listen to the defense evidence. One Jewish observer approached Keegstra during a break in the trial and called him a "sick and pitiful man." A police officer had to separate the two men.[52]

3. *Postscript.* Despite some reservations over the wisdom of prosecution, Jewish groups celebrated the Supreme Court's decision in *Keegstra*, including the sensitive manner in which Chief Justice Dickson recognized the harms of hate speech and the need to protect vulnerable communities.[53] But the Court's decision was not the end of Keegstra's legal proceedings. The Supreme Court remitted the case back to the Court of Appeal of Alberta to deal with separate legal issues, apart from the constitutionality of the hate speech law, that the Court of Appeal had declined to address. The Court of Appeal then quashed Keegstra's conviction and ordered a new trial.[54] At his second trial, Keegstra was convicted again; however, this time the trial judge imposed only a $3,000 fine.[55] The case ultimately reached the Supreme Court of Canada once more, with the Court unanimously upholding the conviction in a brief decision.[56]

Should Hate Speech Be Criminalized?

1. *Scope of debate.* Whether hate speech should be criminalized within a liberal democratic legal order committed to freedom of expression is a difficult and complex question. The prevailing opinion among the U.S. Supreme Court justices and many American commentators is that regulating hate speech carries too great of a risk to the free exchange of ideas necessary for democracy to function.[57] Others disagree. For example, Professor Jeremy Waldron has argued that hate speech inflicts reputational damage on vulnerable groups, thereby undermining their group dignity and sense of inclusion. Waldron has advocated for the United States to adopt hate speech laws similar to Canada's.[58]

2. *Impact of hate speech prosecutions.* There is significant empirical evidence to support Waldron's position that hate speech undermines the group dignity of its targets.[59] However, the Canadian experience may point to some pitfalls associated with criminalization of such speech. For one, the *Keegstra* case suggests that hate speech trials

---

51. Howard Solomon, *Keegstra Slurs Meant Anguish for Jews*, Calgary Herald, July 21, 1985, at B6.

52. Paul Lungen, *Psychologist in Alberta Protesting Loss of Job*, Can. Jewish News, Jan. 2, 1986, at 3.

53. Paul Lungen, *High Court Backs Anti-Hate Law*, Can. Jewish News, Dec. 20, 1990, at 1.

54. R. v. Keegstra, 1991 ABCA 97.

55. Patrick Nagle, *Keegstra Threatens Another Appeal*, Calgary Herald, July 11, 1992, at A1.

56. R. v. Keegstra, [1996] 1 S.C.R. 458.

57. *See, e.g.*, Anthony Lewis, Freedom for the Thought That We Hate: A Biography of the First Amendment (2007).

58. Jeremy Waldron, The Harm in Hate Speech (2012).

59. Evelyn Kallen, Human Rights for Human Beings: Ethnicity and Human Rights in Canada 57–60 (2020) (ebook).

extract a steep emotional toll from targeted groups by providing hatemongers with a wider audience for their harmful expression. Indeed, two studies published after the *Keegstra* trial suggested that the legal proceedings had undermined Canadian Jews' sense of inclusion.[60]

3. *Symbolism.* In Waldron's defense, it must be acknowledged that the mere existence of hate speech laws—regardless of whether or how often they are utilized—may send an important symbol to minority groups that the state views them with dignity and respect. But one difficulty with this position is that the laws' existence may create pressure to use them, and if the state fails to do so, the vulnerable group may draw the opposite conclusion: that the government does not care enough about the victim community to implement the tools at its disposal. In fact, this is arguably what has happened in Canada, where lack of prosecutions for hate speech offenses is being interpreted by minority groups (including the Jewish community) as evidence that the government is not truly concerned about their welfare despite the alarming increase in racist speech.[61]

4. *Objectives of criminal sanction.* When thinking about the criminal law's purposes—what the criminal law is designed to achieve—the best place to look is sentencing and punishment. The primary objectives of punishment in the United States are deterrence, retribution, incapacitation, and rehabilitation.[62] The Canadian experience suggests hate speech prosecutions may be a poor fit for these goals.

(a) *Deterrence.* The underlying assumption of deterrence theory is that the threat or example of punishment will discourage crime. Deterrence is typically said to work on two levels: individual and general. Individual deterrence theorizes that criminal punishment will discourage the specific offender from repeating their criminal behavior. General deterrence assumes that punishing the offender will discourage others from engaging in the same conduct.

Hate speech prosecutions do not well serve individual deterrence. Debunking misinformation and conspiracy theories like Holocaust denial does little to change—and may further entrench—the views of its proponents. Nor do hate speech trials seem to advance general deterrence. For purposes of maximizing general deterrence, certainty of punishment has a far greater impact than severity of punishment. As such, punishing a few offenders to set an example for the rest may not work. Instead, to achieve meaningful deterrence, it is necessary to apprehend people with relative

---

60. Evelyn Kallen & Lawrence Lam, *Target for Hate: the Impact of the Zundel and Keegstra Trials on a Jewish-Canadian Audience*, 25 Can. Ethnic Stud. 9, 17 (1993); *see also* Gabriel Weimann & Conrad Winn, Hate on Trial: The Zundel Affair, the Media, and Public Opinion in Canada 37 (1986).

61. Chris Selley, *'Very Narrow': Here's Why 'Hate Crimes' Are Rarely Charged and Almost Never Prosecuted in Canada*, Nat'l Post (June 17, 2024), nationalpost.com/opinion/why-hate-crimes-are-rarely-charged-and-almost-never-prosecuted-in-canada.

62. *See* 18 U.S.C. § 3553(a)(2); *see also* United States v. Blarek, 7 F. Supp. 2d 192, 199 (E.D.N.Y. 1998).

certainty. The difficulty with hate speech crimes is that it is essentially impossible to apprehend perpetrators with regularity. Thanks to the Internet, this problem has gotten exponentially worse since the time of Keegstra's criminal proceedings. Judicial and police resources are finite; hate speech is almost infinite.

(b) *Retribution.* Retributive theory justifies punishment as a means for expressing society's moral outrage or for restoring the moral imbalance caused by the offense.[63] Retribution is reliant on publicization; communicating to victims and society that the offender has received their just deserts promotes confidence in the justice system.

One reason why a retributive theory of punishment may be a poor fit for hatemonger trials is because publicization is often precisely what the hatemonger wants. It is reasonable to assume that someone convicted of a different offense—murder or sexual assault, for example—will perceive publicization of their punishment as shameful. Few people want to be publicly labeled a murderer or a rapist. But the hatemonger seems different. Purveyors of hate speech may welcome publicity and revel in their notoriety. Indeed, Keegstra was unashamed of his public label as a hatemonger. Keegstra's persecution merely reinforced his worldview that there existed an international Jewish conspiracy, and that he had been ensnared in it.[64] Conversely, publicizing is often precisely what the victim community does *not* want. As we have seen, the attendant publicity from the Keegstra prosecution visited significant trauma on the victim group.

(c) *Incapacitation.* Incapacitation rests on the premise that those incarcerated are rendered physically incapable of committing another offense. However, an offender's hateful speech may be impossible to eradicate—living its own life, as it were, primarily on the Internet—even if the offender is temporarily incapacitated. Once uploaded online, harmful expression can spread throughout the globe in a matter of hours and continue to circulate even if the initial content is taken down. Accordingly, separating the offender from society may do little to stop hate speech.

(d) *Rehabilitation.* Rehabilitation assumes that offenders can be treated and cured of their criminal tendencies. Yet the Keegstra case may suggest that rehabilitation of a hatemonger will not be achieved by subjecting the offender to a criminal prosecution, which is apt to retrench their views.

5. *Search for truth.* A central goal of the criminal trial is to discover the truth. Yet there is good reason to doubt that criminalizing hate speech advances the search for truth. Establishing the contours of highly complex historical events is beyond the ken

63. Graham v. Florida, 560 U.S. 48, 71.

64. Kathryn Warden, *Jim Keegstra: Persecution Reinforces His Beliefs*, Calgary Herald, June 3, 1983, at A5.

of the adversarial criminal trial, which is not a suitable replacement for diligent and good-faith historical research. Furthermore, the ever-present risk of acquittal creates the possibility that a not-guilty verdict will be interpreted as the court's approval for the historical accounting put forward by the defense, thereby undermining the careful work of historians. Establishing the facts of historical events that are disputed or denied may be better served through amnesty, not prosecution. This is the reason why truth and reconciliation commissions, effectively utilized in numerous instances (including recently in Canada[65]) to excavate the historical and social contexts that gave rise to past human rights violations, have offered amnesty as a tool to incentivize an honest accounting from the perpetrators and to stimulate healing and forgiveness. What do you think?

C. Glorification of the Nazi Regime

After the death of Rudolf Hess[66] in 1987, a Nazi leader and convicted war criminal, German neo-Nazis met yearly in Wunsiedel, the Bavarian town where Hess was once interred, for an open-air commemoration of him and a procession to his grave.

The local chief administrative office (*Landratsamt*) banned the event for violating § 130.4 of the German Criminal Code. Section 130.4 provides that:

> Whosoever publicly or in a meeting disturbs the public peace in a manner that violates the dignity of the victims by approving of, glorifying, or justifying the National Socialist rule of arbitrary force shall be liable to imprisonment of not more than three years or a fine.

The planned theme of that year's procession was "His honour meant more to him than freedom." The *Landratsamt* concluded that the elevation of Rudolf Hess as an individual would have been perceived as tacit approval of the National Socialist Regime in all its manifestations. (The City of Wunsiedel ultimately exhumed Hess's remains, cremated them, and scattered the ashes in an unidentified lake.)

---

65. *Canada's Residential Schools: the Final Report of the Truth and Reconciliation Commission of Canada*, Gov't of Can., https://publications.gc.ca/site/eng/9.807830/publication.html (last updated Apr. 4, 2013).

66. Hess was Deputy Führer of the Nazi Party from 1933 to 1941. On September 15, 1935, Hess signed, on Hitler's behalf, the Nuremberg Laws. He ended his Nazi career on May 10, 1941, when he secretly flew solo to Scotland on a self-styled mission to negotiate a peace between Great Britain and Germany. He was arrested upon arrival and held as a prisoner of war. The IMT convicted Hess of crimes against peace and of conspiracy with other German leaders to commit crimes; it sentenced him to life imprisonment. Hess died on August 17, 1987, at the age of 93, found hanged in his cell, after four decades as the sole inmate at Berlin's Spandau Prison. His grave in Wunsiedel became a pilgrimage site for neo-Nazis. *See Rudolf Hess*, Britannica, https://www.britannica.com/biography/Rudolf-Hess (last visited Dec. 17, 2024); *see also Rudolph Hess*, Jewish Virtual Libr., https://www.jewishvirtuallibrary.org/rudolf-hess-2 (last visited Dec. 17, 2024); *see also Rudolph Hess*, Wikipedia, https://en.wikipedia.org/wiki/Rudolf_Hess (last visited Dec. 17, 2024).

The petitioners alleged that § 130.4 was speech protected by Article 5.1, sentence 1 of the Basic Law (*Grundgesetz*), Germany's constitutional document. Article 5.1 provides that:

> Every person shall have the right freely to express and disseminate his opinions in speech, writing, and pictures, and to inform himself without hindrance from generally accessible sources.

Petitioners further argued that § 130.4 violated Article 5.2 of the Basic Law, which provides that free speech rights "shall find their limits in the provisions of general laws...." In other words, Article 5.2 prohibits the state from restricting speech based on its officially disfavoured content or viewpoint.

After multiple denials below, the case reached the Federal Constitutional Court (*Bundesverfassungsgericht*), Germany's highest constitutional court. The Court ruled that § 130.4 was compatible with the Basic Law for reasons specific to Germany's historical experience with Nazism. This was so even though § 130.4 was constitutionally valid, and despite the fact that it punished speech based upon its viewpoint, namely, because it approves, glorifies, or justifies the Nazi regime.

The Wunsiedel Decision: Judgment of 4 November 2009

Federal Constitutional Court of Germany (*Bundesverfassungsgericht*)
1 BvR 2150/08[67]

Before JUDGES BRYDE, EICHBERGER, GAIER, HOHMANN-DENNHARDT, KIRCHOF, MASING, and PAPIER.

I.

Section 130.4 Encroaches on a Protected Area of the Basic Law

Article 5.1, sentence 1 of the Basic Law guarantees to every person the right to express and disseminate his or her opinion freely.... [Opinions] enjoy the protection of the fundamental right irrespective of whether the statement is well-founded or groundless, emotional or rational, evaluated as valuable or valueless, dangerous or harmless.... Nor are citizens legally obliged to personally share the values on which the Constitution is based. The Basic Law is built on the expectation that citizens accept and realize the general values of the Constitution but does not force loyalty to those values....

Opinions aiming to fundamentally change the political system regardless of whether and how far they can be implemented within the system of the Basic Law are hence also protected by Article 5.1 of the Basic Law. The Basic Law trusts free debate as the most effective weapon against the dissemination of totalitarian and inhumane ideologies. Accordingly, even the expression of National Socialist ideas questioning the

67. This text was translated by the publisher at *Order of 4 November, 2009*, BUNDESVERFASSUNGSGERICHT [FED. CONST. CT.], https://www.bundesverfassungsgericht.de/SharedDocs/Entscheidungen/EN/2009/11/rs20091104_1bvr215008en.html (last visited Dec. 17, 2024).

existing legal system are not necessarily unprotected by Article 5.1 of the Basic Law. Within the free system of the Basic Law, it is primarily the civil commitment to free political debate, state education, and upbringing in schools ... that are entrusted with countering its dangers.

Since 130.4 of the Criminal Code links to the approval, glorification, and justification of the National Socialist rule of arbitrary force and penalizes it subject to further preconditions, the provision encroaches on the area protected by freedom of opinion.

II.

The Encroachment on Freedom of Opinion Is Justified

1. § 130.4 of the Criminal Code is not a general law within the meaning of Article 5.2 of the Basic Law.

a) According to Article 5.2 of the Basic Law, freedom of opinion finds its limits in the provisions of the general laws. These are to be understood as including laws which do not prohibit an opinion as such, which are not directed against the utterance of the opinion as such, but which serve to protect a legal interest which is to be protected per se without regard to a specific opinion.... This legal interest must be protected in the legal system generally, and hence regardless of whether it can be violated by expressions of opinion or by other means....

b) A law is not general if a content-related restriction of opinion is not worded in a sufficiently open manner and, from the outset, only targets specific convictions, stances, or ideologies. Laws for the protection of legal interests are only general if, when considered as a whole, they prove to be consistent and abstract in terms of the legal interest and are formulated without taking into account specific existing views....

c) On this basis, § 130.4 of the Criminal Code is not a general law. Admittedly, the provision serves the public peace and thus the protection of a legal interest that is also protected in many other ways in the legal system. However, § 130.4 of the Criminal Code does not formulate this protection in a general way that is open in terms of content, but rather refers only to expressions of opinion that express a certain attitude towards National Socialism. The provision is not intended to protect victims of violence in general and deliberately does not focus on the approval, glorification, and justification of the violence and arbitrary rule of totalitarian regimes as a whole, but is limited to statements relating solely to National Socialism. The history of the provision's origin also makes it clear that it was understood as a response to public gatherings and marches by right-wing extremists who make reference to the Nazi era in their rallies—not least directed against the annual memorial services for Rudolf Hess. It is in this respect the legislator's reaction to specific political opinions in the battle of public opinion that are considered particularly dangerous.

2. Even though it is not a general [viewpoint-neutral] law, § 130.4 of the Criminal Code is compatible with Article 5.1 and 5.2 of the Basic Law....

a) Concerning the requirement of the general nature of laws which impose restrictions on opinions according to Article 5.2 of the Basic Law, the law recognizes an exception for statutory provisions which aim to prevent a propagandistic affirmation of the National Socialist rule.... The inhuman regime of this period, which brought immeasurable suffering, death, and suppression to Europe and the world, is uniquely antithetical to the identity of the constitutional system of the Federal Republic of Germany.... The Allied Powers, who participated in establishing the German constitution, were centrally concerned with the deliberate discarding of the tyrannical regime of National Socialism.... They were particularly concerned about the Parliamentary Council[68] ... and the internal structure of the Basic Law (see only Article 1,[69] Article 20,[70] and Article 79.3[71]). The Basic Law in particular can be largely interpreted as an antithesis to the totalitarianism of the National Socialist regime, and from its structure through to its many details, seeks to learn from historical experience and to rule out a repeat of such injustice once and for all. [The court explains that defeating National Socialism once and for all was the Allies' central goal]....

Against this background, the propagandistic approval of the historical National Socialist dictatorship, with all the terrible things that actually happened for which it was responsible, has effects that go far beyond the general tensions of the public battle of opinions and cannot be grasped on the basis of the general rules regarding the limits of freedom of expression alone. In Germany, advocating this rule is an attack on the identity of the polity internally, with the potential to threaten peace. In this regard, it

---

68. Editor's note: The Parliamentary Council was the constitutional convention convened by the Allied Powers to draft the Basic Law. It consisted of representatives elected by the state (*Land*) parliaments. The Parliamentary Council approved the Basic Law on May 8, 1949. *The Basic Law*, BUNDESVERFASSUNGSGERICHT [FED. CONST. CT.], https://www.bundesverfassungsgericht.de/EN/BasicLawLegalBasis/TheBasicLaw/thebasiclaw_node.html (last visited Dec. 17, 2024).

69. Editor's note: Article 1. Human dignity—Human rights—Legally binding force of basic rights:
(1) Human dignity shall be inviolable. To respect and protect it shall be the duty of all state authority.
(2) The German people therefore acknowledge inviolable and inalienable human rights as the basis of every community, of peace and of justice in the world. Available at *Basic Law for the Federal Republic of Germany*, FED. MINISTRY OF JUST., https://www.gesetze-im-internet.de/englisch_gg/englisch_gg.html (last visited Dec. 17, 2024).

70. Editor's note: Article 20. Constitutional principles—Right of resistance:
(1) The Federal Republic of Germany is a democratic and social federal state.
(2) All state authority is derived from the people. It shall be exercised by the people through elections and other votes and through specific legislative, executive, and judicial bodies.
(3) The legislature shall be bound by the constitutional order, the executive, and the judiciary by law and justice.
(4) All Germans shall have the right to resist any person seeking to abolish this constitutional order if no other remedy is available. Available at *Basic Law for the Federal Republic of Germany*, FED. MINISTRY OF JUST., https://www.gesetze-im-internet.de/englisch_gg/englisch_gg.html (last visited Dec. 17, 2024).

71. Editor's note: Article 79. Amendment of the Basic Law:
(3) Amendments to this Basic Law affecting the division of the Federation into *Länder*, their participation in principle in the legislative process, or the principles laid down in Articles 1 and 20 shall be inadmissible. Available at *Basic Law for the Federal Republic of Germany*, FED. MINISTRY OF JUST., https://www.gesetze-im-internet.de/englisch_gg/englisch_gg.html (last visited Dec. 17, 2024).

is not comparable with other expressions of opinion, and ultimately it can also trigger profound disquiet abroad. To do justice to this historically rooted special situation, Article 5.2 of the Basic Law cannot invalidate these special provisions.... Section 130.4 of the Criminal Code is ... not unconstitutional because it is a special provision which has as its sole subject-matter the evaluation of the National Socialist rule of arbitrary force.

b) The fact that Article 5.1 and 5.2 of the Basic Law is open to such special provisions that relate to statements on National Socialism in the years between 1933 and 1945 does not detract from the substantive content of freedom of expression. In particular, the Basic Law does not have a general anti-National Socialist fundamental principle ... which would permit a ban of the dissemination of right-wing radical or even National Socialist ideas with regard to the intellectual impact of its content.... The Basic Law goes as far as granting freedom of opinion to the enemies of freedom, trusting in the power of the public debate carried on in freedom. The Parliamentary Council also acknowledged this towards National Socialism, which had only recently been overcome.[72] In Article 9.2, Article 18,[73] and Article 21.2[74] of the Basic Law, it stipulated that the dissemination of anti-constitutional ideas as such does not, in itself, limit free political debate; that could only be accomplished by an actively combative, aggressive stance towards the fundamental freedoms of the democratic system....

III.

Section 130.4 of the Criminal Code satisfies the requirements of the principle of proportionality. The provision pursues a legitimate purpose with the protection of the public peace, to achieve which it is suitable, necessary and appropriate....

---

72. Editor's note: Article 9. Freedom of association:
(2) Associations whose aims or activities contravene the criminal laws or that are directed against the constitutional order or the concept of international understanding shall be prohibited. Available at *Basic Law for the Federal Republic of Germany*, FED. MINISTRY OF JUST.,https://www.gesetze-im-internet.de/englisch_gg/englisch_gg.html (last visited Dec. 17, 2024).

73. Editor's note: Article 18. Forfeiture of basic rights:
Whoever abuses the freedom of expression, in particular the freedom of the press, freedom of teaching, the freedom of assembly, the freedom of association, the privacy of correspondence, posts and telecommunications, the rights of property, or the right of asylum in order to combat the free democratic basic order shall forfeit these basic rights. This forfeiture and its extent shall be declared by the Federal Constitutional Court. Available at *Basic Law for the Federal Republic of Germany*, FED. MINISTRY OF JUST., https://www.gesetze-im-internet.de/englisch_gg/englisch_gg.html (last visited Dec. 17, 2024).

74. Editor's note: Article 21. Political parties:
(2) Parties that, by reason of their aims or the behaviour of their adherents, seek to undermine or abolish the free democratic basic order or to endanger the existence of the Federal Republic of Germany shall be unconstitutional. Available at *Basic Law for the Federal Republic of Germany*, FED. MINISTRY OF JUST., https://www.gesetze-im-internet.de/englisch_gg/englisch_gg.html (last visited Dec. 17, 2024).

IV.

The Court finds that § 130.4 of the Criminal Code also does not breach Article 3.3 sentence 1[75] (ban on placing at a disadvantage because of political views) which protects against encroachments which link solely to merely "holding" a political view....

V.

Section 130.4 of the Criminal Code is also compatible with Article 103.2 of the Basic Law.[76]

Section 130.4 is also constitutionally unobjectionable at the level of the application of the law.... For the question whether the statement remains solely at the intellectual level or crosses the threshold to constituting a risk to legal interests, it is crucial whether the statement creates only distant threats or whether their realization is already set in motion with the statement. The more the ideas intended with the propagation of an ideology reveal their impact only as an abstract consequence of an ideal construct, the more unambiguously they remain in the intellectual domain, which is protected as a matter of principle. The more, however, they become tangible through the nature of the statement in concrete, direct terms, the more they pose an imminent threat to specific persons, groups of individuals, or real situations, the sooner they can be attributed to the real domain. A merely symbolic presentation of convictions, teachings, or ways of attaining a sort of salvation will be more likely to be attributed to the intellectual domain than if violations of rights are, for instance, imagined in the shape of historic events in concrete, direct terms and are depicted as desirable....

The court deduces from this that § 130.4 requires (1) that the condonation covered with this provision is recognizably related to National Socialism as a historically real rule of arbitrary force, (2) the speech's approval, glorification, and justification [of the Nazi regime] can be inferred from the meaning it carries in itself, but the speaker must recognizably have actively approved its message; and (3) that the meaning of the statement has been correctly understood. According to these standards, the impugned ruling is not constitutionally objectionable.

An Anti-Nazi Fundamental Principle?

1. *An anti-Nazi principle?* The Court claims that Germany's Basic Law does not "have a general anti-National Socialist fundamental principle ... which would permit a ban of the dissemination of right-wing radical or even National Socialist ideas"? How

---

75. Editor's note: Article 3. Equality before the law:
(3) No person shall be favoured or disfavoured because of sex, parentage, race, language, homeland and origin, faith, or religious or political opinions. Available at *Basic Law for the Federal Republic of Germany*, Fed. Ministry of Just., https://www.gesetze-im-internet.de/englisch_gg/englisch_gg.html (last visited Dec. 17, 2024).
76. Editor's note: Article 103. Fair trial:
(2) An act may be punished only if it was defined by a law as a criminal offense before the act was committed. Available at *Basic Law for the Federal Republic of Germany*, Fed. Ministry of Just., https://www.gesetze-im-internet.de/englisch_gg/englisch_gg.html (last visited Dec. 17, 2024).

would you characterize the principle or principles that drive or inform the Wunsiedel Decision? Insofar as the legal system has such a principle, how far does the Court's opinion extend it? What principled limits does the Court impose on its reach? How does the German legal system incorporate safeguards against Nazi ideology and protect democratic principles?

2. *Disquiet abroad and a potential threat to peace.* In exchange for peace, the Allied Powers required the new German state to guarantee that Nazism would never return. France, the U.K., and the U.S. required the new German state to be a liberal democracy. What is the relationship between (a) speech glorifying the Nazi regime; and (b) the German state's fidelity to the terms whereby it came into existence?

3. *Understood by whom?* Section 130.4 is constitutional as applied if "the meaning of the statement has been correctly understood." Does this mean the speaker must understand the import of their speech? Does it mean the state must correctly determine whether the speech glorifies the Nazi regime?

4. *A second-degree hate speech crime?* Assume a German resident engages in speech that:

(a) He does not understand as glorifying the Nazi regime;

(b) He does not intend to glorify the Nazi regime; and

(c) There is substantial and unjustifiable risk that Jews will perceive his speech as motivated by antisemitism; and

(d) He engages in the speech with conscious disregard for this risk.

On these facts, should German authorities prosecute this speaker for violating § 130.4? Here consider Frederick Lawrence's proposal for a "second-degree (reckless) bias crime," which occurs when an offender:

> commits any crime against a person or property in this state's criminal code (the "parallel crime") with conscious disregard for the substantial and unjustifiable risk that his conduct will be perceived by the individual victim or victim target group to have been motivated in substantial part by ill will, hatred, or animus due to the real or perceived race, color, religion [or other protected characteristic] of the victim.

5. *Power of free debate.* The court states that "the Basic Law trusts in the power of the free debate as the most effective weapon against the dissemination of totalitarian, inhumane ideologies." Does the Court share the Basic Law's trust?

6. *Civic education.* What is the value in producing citizens less likely to question the Basic Law's authority? How does the Court propose this be achieved?

7. *Militant democracy.* Militant democracy is a concept developed by Karl Loewenstein in 1937. It refers to the idea of a democratic regime that is willing to adopt preemptive, prima facie illiberal measures to prevent those aiming at subverting democracy with democratic means from destroying the democratic regime.[77] Is the Court's

77. Jan Werner Müller, Militant Democracy (2012).

decision meant to implement this concept? Does this opinion suggest that Germany is a militant democracy?

8. Compare the *Wunsiedel Decision* to *Keegstra, Beauharnais, Ortenberg v. Plamondon, Levy v. von Moltke,* and *Irving v. Penguin.*

Does Germany Have a Special Duty to Protect Jews?

1. *Germany and Jewish safety.* Philosopher Leo Strauss described the Nazi regime as "the only regime ... which had no other clear principle except murderous hatred of the Jews."[78] Insofar as the Basic Law posits an anti-Nazi principle, does it necessarily commit Germany to protecting the safety of the Jewish people?

On November 9, 2023, Nancy Faeser, Germany's Federal Minister of the Interior, stated that "it is our shared duty to protect Jewish people in Germany. Antisemitism—no matter its source—is an attack on human dignity. Fighting antisemitism is a task for all of society!"[79] Faeser was expressing the German government's policy that "protecting Jewish people is a priority. Commitment to the existence of the State of Israel and to fostering and protecting Jewish life in Germany are central tenets of German policy."[80]

2. *Germany and Zionism.* Consider the following description of Germany's relationship to the State of Israel by Deutsche Welle ("German wave"), Germany's official international broadcaster:

> For Germany, the past is always present. Its genocide of European Jews and other groups during the Nazi era have a profound impact on its existence today, influencing its policymaking and shaping its view of the world.
>
> When it comes to Israel, which the Zionist movement founded as the Jewish state just three years after Germany's systematic murder of six million Jews in the Holocaust, the German state sees a "special responsibility." Its commitment to Israel is more than just a policy goal; it is a fundamental part of present-day Germany's very existence.
>
> That makes Israel's security and existence Germany's *Staatsräson* (reason of state). Former Chancellor Angela Merkel used the term when addressing the Knesset, Israel's parliament, in 2008. Her successor, Olaf Scholz, has repeated it several times since Hamas's terrorist attacks on Saturday, October 7 killed some 1,300 Israelis, the overwhelming majority of whom are civilians.
>
> "At this moment, there is only one place for Germany. That is the side of Israel," Scholz said in an address to the Bundestag, Germany's parliament, on

78. Leo Strauss, Preface to Spinoza's Critique of Religion 6 (E.M. Sinclair trans., 1965).

79. *Protecting Jewish Life in* Germany, Fed. Ministry of the Interior & Cmty., https://www.bmi.bund.de/SharedDocs/schwerpunkte/EN/gegen-antisemitismus-en/gg-as-artikel-en.html (last visited Dec. 17, 2024).

80. *Id.*

Thursday. "That's what we mean when we say, 'Israel's security is Germany's reason of state.'"[81]

3. *Vom Fluss zum Meer.* A German court fined a 22-year-old protester 600 euros (about $650) for chanting the slogan "From the river to the sea, Palestine will be free" at a Berlin rally in October 2023, in violation of Criminal Code § 86a (use of symbols of unconstitutional and terrorist organizations) and § 86 (dissemination of propaganda material of unconstitutional and terrorist organizations). The judge ruled that in the context, the phrase could only be understood as a denial of Israel's right to exist and an endorsement of Hamas's October 7 attacks. German courts are split on the question and the ruling is being appealed.[82]

Memory Laws

1. *Memory laws.* Section 130.4 of the Criminal Code is an example of a "memory law," i.e., a legal provision that inscribes a certain state-official interpretation of the past into law. By prohibiting the approval, glorification, and justification of the Nazi regime, the law excludes questioning the official view that the Nazi rule was a horrific regime that brought about immeasurable suffering, death, and suppression and should never be repeated.

Why might German legislators seek to prescribe the way Germans remember the past? Which crimes and periods should such laws emphasize, and why? In the court's view, what legal value did the Germany legislature aim to protect with § 130.4? What role did common goods such as democracy, social peace, and public order play? What role did the victims of Nazi atrocities play? Are memory laws a means to protect their personal rights, human dignity, and/or collective memory?

2. *Memorable choices.* Memory laws enact their choices of which historical crimes or periods to remember. Compare and contrast § 130.4 with changing U.S. official holidays such as Columbus Day, increasingly supplanted by Indigenous Peoples' Day;[83] the consolidation of Washington's and Lincoln's birthdays into Presidents' Day; the adoption of Martin Luther King Jr. Day in 1983; the adoption of Juneteenth National Independence Day (June 19th) in 2021.

---

81. William Noah Glucroft, *Germany's Unique Relationship with Israel*, DW (Oct. 15, 2023), https://www.dw.com/en/israel-and-germanys-reason-of-state-its-complicated/a-67094861#:~:text=When%20it%20comes%20to%20Israel,fundamental%20part%20of%20present%2Dday.

82. Sarah Maslin Nir, *German Court Fines Protester for 'River to Sea' Chant*, N.Y. Times (Aug. 6, 2024), https://www.nytimes.com/2024/08/06/world/europe/germany-river-to-sea-chant-fine.html; *see also* Benjamin Weinthal, *Berlin Criminalizes Slogan 'From the River to the Sea, Palestine Will be Free,'* 124 News (Nov. 9, 2023), https://www.i24news.tv/en/news/international/europe/1699528989-berlin-criminalizes-slogan-from-the-river-to-the-sea-palestine-will-be-free; *see also "From the River to the Sea: Berlin Court Convicts Activist Over Chant,"* The Berliner (Aug. 7, 2024), https://www.the-berliner.com/english-news-berlin/from-the-river-to-the-sea-palestine-israel-berlin-court-convicts-activist-over-chant/.

83. Drew Desilver, *Working on Columbus Day or Indigenous People's Day? It Depends on Where Your Job Is*, Pew Rsch. Ctr. (Oct. 5, 2023), https://www.pewresearch.org/short-reads/2023/10/05/working-on-columbus-day-or-indigenous-peoples-day-it-depends-on-where-your-job-is/.

3. *Speech denying the Armenian genocide.* The European Court of Human Rights, in its Grand Chamber decision, *Perinçek v. Switzerland,*[84] held that Switzerland violated Mr. Perinçek's freedom of expression under Article 10 of the European Convention on Human Rights by sentencing him for denying the genocide committed by the Ottoman Empire against Armenians. The Grand Chamber argued that unlike in cases of criminalization of Holocaust denial by Germany, Austria, Belgium, and France, there was no direct link between Switzerland and the events in the Ottoman Empire in 1915, and that the lapse of time between the denial and the events was considerably longer than in the case of Holocaust denial. Is this persuasive? In the Chamber's view, what is the requisite linkage between a jurisdiction and the historical fact that jurisdiction seeks to assert by prosecuting someone who denies it? Does this approach yield intelligible principles to govern the Chamber's review of such prosecution?

4. The EU Framework Decision on combatting certain forms and expressions of racism and xenophobia by means of criminal law[85] provides that all states must ensure that the following intentional conduct is punishable:

> Publicly condoning, denying or grossly trivialising crimes of genocide, crimes against humanity and war crimes as defined in Articles 6, 7 and 8 of the Statute of the International Criminal Court, directed against a group of persons or a member of such a group defined by reference to race, colour, religion, descent or national or ethnic origin when the conduct is carried out in a manner likely to incite to violence or hatred against such a group or a member of such a group.[86]

EU member states have been very reluctant to implement the framework decision. Did the EU legislator go too far in seeking to harmonize memory laws at the EU level, rather than leaving such decisions to domestic legislators? European memories about the Second World War and its aftermath diverge in emphasis, with Western Europe focusing on the Holocaust and Nazi crimes and Eastern Europe focusing on suffering at the hands of both Nazi Germany and the Soviet Union.

5. *Holocaust (mis)remembrance?* In 2018, Poland amended its national memory laws to make it a crime to publicly claim that Poland had any responsibility for or complicity in the Holocaust.[87] This law led to a controversy between the Polish and Israeli governments over the role that ethnic Poles played in the Holocaust.[88]

---

84. 27510/08 Eur. Ct. H.R. (2015).

85. Council Framework Decision 2008/913/JHA of November 28, 2008 on combating certain forms and expressions of racism and xenophobia by means of criminal law, 2008 O.J. (L 328).

86. *Id.* at art. 1.1(c).

87. Act of January 26, 2018 Amending the Act on the Institute of National Remembrance—Commission for the Prosecution of Crimes against the Polish Nation, the Act on War Graves and Cemeteries, the Act on Museums and the Act on the Responsibility of Collective Entities for Acts Prohibited Under Penalty (Dz.U. 2018, item 369) (Pol.).

88. Natanya Katz, Competitive Victimhood and Moral Authority: Israeli Diplomatic Strategy in Response to Poland's 2018 Holocaust Memory Law (2025) (Capstone thesis, Indiana University Bloomington) (on file with author).

Part Four

Anti-Jewish Activity

Chapter 11

Hate Crimes

This chapter examines hate crime law in the United States, with a focus on their role in combating antisemitism. Section A, "The Role of Jewish Advocates in the Leo Frank Affair," examines the tragic case of Leo Frank, a Jewish factory superintendent lynched in Georgia in 1915, and the response of Jewish advocates to this affair. Section B, "Hate Crimes Statute Protects Jews," analyzes the case of *United States v. Nelson*, which held that the Thirteenth Amendment authorizes Congress to enact a hate crimes statute that protects Jews. Section C, "Hate Crimes Statute Does Not Violate the First Amendment," analyzes the landmark decision of *Wisconsin v. Mitchell*, which ruled that a hate crimes statute did not violate the perpetrator's freedom of speech. Section D, "Hate Crimes Law in Practice," examines a flawed state hate crimes statute and reviews recent cases involving hate crimes against Jews. Section E, "Does German Hate Crimes Law Under-Protect Jews from Anti-Zionist Violence?," examines a recent German case in which a court determined that defendants' attack on a synagogue was not a hate crime because it was motivated by opposition to Israel rather than animus towards Jews.

A. The Role of Jewish Advocates in the Leo Frank Affair

Matthew Silver, *The Leo Frank Affair: Louis Marshall and the ADL vs. the KKK*[1]

The 1920s is remembered colorfully in America as the prosperous "Roaring Twenties" decade, but historians like John Higham stressed how Ku Klux Klan racism and Nativist anti-immigration activity mounted in this period (Higham called the era the "Tribal Twenties"). For many vulnerable immigrants and minority group members, the issue of legal due process and fair trial procedure raised acute concerns.

From the Jewish standpoint, the links between anti-defamation work and fair trial advocacy became palpable in this period: in the same period in 1927, when American Jews were elated as Marshall received Henry Ford's retraction, many in the community were troubled by the execution of two Italian immigrant anarchists, Nicola Sacco and Bartolomeo Vanzetti. Many distinguished American Jewish jurists, such as Louis

1. This essay is based on research by Professor Matthew Silver, author of Louis Marshall and the Rise of Jewish Ethnicity in America: A Biography (2013).

Figure 11.1. Leo Frank and Lucille Frank, his wife, during Frank's 1913 trial for the murder of 13-year-old Mary Phagan, in a courtroom in Atlanta, Georgia. Courtesy of Alamy.

Brandeis's colleague and student, Felix Frankfurter, had lobbied against this death penalty sentence, arguing that the two accused men had not received a fair trial.

A key precedent for the Sacco and Vanzetti controversy occurred on the eve of WWI, in Georgia, when an American Jewish manager of a pencil factory, Leo Frank, was unfairly accused in a murder trial that was accompanied by a swell of public ac-

Figure 11.2. Lynching of Leo Frank, Marietta, Georgia, August 17, 1915. Courtesy of Library of Congress.

rimony. Subsequently, commentators on this affair established that Frank was unjustly accused; and, at the time, for American Jews, the trial evoked harsh memories of "blood libel" trials in Europe (referring to the infamous, unjust conviction of a Jewish French army officer in the late 19th century, Marshall privately called the Frank case a "second Dreyfus affair").

The sequences in the Frank case were dramatic and complicated. They culminated in a gruesome turn of events: after the wrongful conviction, Frank's death sentence was lessened to a life term by Georgia Governor John Slaton, but in August 1915, a lynch mob dragged Frank out of his cell and murdered him near Marietta.

The anti-Semitic agitation against Frank spurred racist groups to reorganize, and scholars associate this Atlanta affair with the rebirth of the KKK. From the Jewish point of view, the affair's unsatisfactory conclusion inspired proposals for reorganization of activity specifically designed to counter antisemitism. In fact, the birth of another American Jewish defense agency, the Anti-Defamation League, can be linked to the Frank affair.

For the American Jewish Committee (AJC), President Louis Marshall directed the latter stages of Frank's defense, which can be regarded as a success at least in the sense that the death sentence was commuted. The Frank case had obvious defamatory aspects. In this connection, Marshall and the AJC deployed tactics comparable to work undertaken in the Henry Ford defamation affair. They attempted a mix of public relations lobbying (featuring a well-known figure in this field, Albert Lasker), and, out of the public limelight, they engaged talks with politicians, jurists and others in Atlanta.

The specific, novel aspect of Marshall's work for Frank relates to the issue of fair trial process. Marshall faced pressure to appear in the courtroom during the Frank trial, but he judged that it was an inherently unfair venue where an American Jewish activist's presence would harm Frank's chances ("the fact that I am a New Yorker, and a Jew, would not help the case there," he opined). However, once the Frank case went on appeal, leaving the Atlanta courtroom and reaching the Supreme Court, Marshall became publicly affiliated with it. In his April 1915 appeal to the Supreme Court, Marshall focused on the fair venue aspect, arguing that Frank could never have received a fair trial. He described Frank's trial as a "judicial lynching, where the mob triumphantly intervened and was permitted to control and dominate the instrumentalities of judicial procedure."

Marshall's appeal was rejected by the Court, on a 7 to 2 vote, but it nonetheless set a precedent on behalf of fair trial process. The two dissenters, Oliver Wendell Holmes and Charles Evans Hughes, maintained that "mob law does not become due process of law by securing the assent of a terrorized jury." This dissent, in 1923, formed the basis of a Supreme Court ruling (*Moore v. Dempsey*) strengthening standards for fair trial rights. Though it was too late for Leo Frank, this ruling retroactively warranted the key argument developed by Marshall in the Frank case on behalf of American Jewish interests. Moreover, Marshall understood how this *Moore v. Dempsey* ruling also reduced the vulnerability of other minority groups. In March 1923, he wrote to NAACP leader Walter White, praising the Court's ruling, saying that it left him "exceedingly grateful."

B. Hate Crimes Statute Protects Jews

The case of *United States v. Nelson* arose from tragic events in 1991 in Crown Heights, New York, following an accident involving a driver in an Orthodox rabbi's motorcade. The accident injured two African American children, one of whom, Gavin Cato, later died of his injuries. The incident escalated when Charles Price, a defendant, incited a milling crowd by claiming that a visibly Jewish ambulance crew was unwilling to help the two children because they were not Jewish, but African American. After the crowd marched into a Jewish neighborhood amid shouts of "get the Jews," 16-year-old defendant Lemrick Nelson stabbed Yankel Rosenbaum, a demonstrably Jewish 29-year-old man. Rosenbaum later died of his wounds.

Federal prosecutors charged Price and Nelson with violating 18 U.S.C. § 245 "federally protected activities." Section 245 makes it a federal crime for a person (even if acting in a purely private capacity) to injure someone else because of the victim's race or religion and because the victim was enjoying a public facility provided by any state or local government. Nelson and Price were convicted in federal district court for attacking Rosenbaum while using a public street. Nelson was sentenced to 235 months and Price to 262 months.

On appeal, Price and Nelson challenged the validity of § 245 on grounds that Congress lacked the constitutional authority to criminalize private violence motivated by the victim's religion, especially if the victim is a Jew. The court of appeals, per Judge Guido Calabresi, upheld the constitutionality of § 245 as applied to Jews based on the Thirteenth Amendment, which was originally aimed at African American slavery. Judge Calabresi specifically found that Jews are protected under the Thirteenth Amendment through two paths: (1) the historical understanding of Jews as a "race" when the Thirteenth Amendment was ratified and (2) the direct protection the Amendment affords religious groups, as religious-based subjugation is consistent with historical forms of slavery. The connection between private violence and slavery was crucial to the ruling—the court noted that slavery fundamentally involved "the master's constant power to use private violence against the slave" and this practice continued after emancipation, to prevent freed people from exercising their rights in public spaces. However, the court of appeals vacated the convictions due to errors in jury selection and remanded for a new trial.

United States v. Nelson

277 F.3d 164 (2d Cir 2002)

Circuit Judge Calabresi.

Lemrick Nelson, Jr. ("Nelson") and Charles Price ("Price") appeal their convictions and sentences, under 18 U.S.C. § 245(b)(2)(B) for willfully injuring, intimidating, and interfering with Yankel Rosenbaum ("Rosenbaum"), by force and threat of force, because of Rosenbaum's Jewish religion and because Rosenbaum was enjoying use of a Brooklyn city street. Nelson's and Price's primary contentions on appeal are ... that § 245(b)(2)(B), as applied to them, is unconstitutional because it reaches conduct that lies beyond Congress's powers of regulation. We conclude that § 245(b)(2)(B) is constitutional as applied to Nelson and Price....

I

Background

Shortly after eight o'clock in the evening on August 19, 1991, a station wagon struck two children in the Crown Heights area of Brooklyn, New York. The driver of the car was Jewish, and both children were African American. A crowd soon gathered at the scene of the accident. As some of its members attempted to aid the injured children, others began to attack the driver of the car.

The first ambulance to reach the scene was from a Jewish hospital and was readily identifiable as such by Hebrew writing on its sides.[2] The driver of the car that had hit

---

2. Editor's note: Rosenbaum was retrieved by Hatzalah (Hebrew for "rescue" or "relief"), a volunteer ambulance service and the largest nonprofit ambulance service in the U.S. whose mission is to provide emergency medical treatment and transportation to the public, regardless of race, religion, ethnicity, or ability to pay. Phillip Gourevitch, *The Crown Heights Riots & Its Aftermath*, Commentary, https://www.commentary.org/articles/philip-gourevitch/the-crown-heights-riot-its-aftermath/ (last visited Nov. 20, 2024). *See also* Chevra Hatzalah, https://hatzalah.org/ (last visited Nov. 20, 2024). The Hebrew writing on Hatzalah's ambulances reads "Chevra Hatzalah" (Hebrew for "rescue squad").

the children was treated by personnel from this ambulance, and, at the direction of police officers who had arrived, the ambulance quickly left the scene in order to protect the injured Jewish driver from the angry crowd. Shortly after the ambulance from the Jewish hospital departed, two New York City ambulances arrived at the accident site. Their crews gave medical assistance to the two injured African American children, and took them to the hospital. Both children had been seriously hurt; one ultimately died.

In the meantime, a crowd of several hundred people (watched over by between seventy and one hundred police officers) had formed in the neighborhood of the accident. Some members of the crowd complained about Jews and the preferential treatment that Jews allegedly received. They cited, as an example of this favored treatment, the fact that the Jewish driver had received medical attention before the African American children even though the children were more seriously injured. Some members of the crowd began to throw objects.

At about eleven o'clock, a bald, African American man later identified as defendant Price began addressing the crowd. Price's speech ... was angry and aggressive and included ... the following statements:

"If it was a black man that did this they would have been gone to jail instead of being pulled inside of an ambulance for safekeeping."

"We can't take this anymore. They're killing our children. The Jews get everything they want. The police are protecting them."

"What are we going to do about this? Are we going to take this anymore?"

"Let's get the Jews" and "Eye for an eye. No justice no peace."

In response to Price's exhortations, many people in the crowd began to yell, "Get the Jews." Toward the end of his speech, Price shouted something to the effect of "Let's go to Kingston Avenue and get the Jews."[3] Thereupon, a large part of the crowd, including Price and defendant Nelson (who had been in the crowd and had heard Price's speech) proceeded towards Kingston Avenue.

Witnesses testified that prior to Price's speech, the crowd was neither unified nor particularly out of control, but that after he spoke, it became transformed into an explosive mass. It also became violent, throwing objects and setting two cars on fire, attacking a Jewish couple who may have had a baby with them, and assaulting a second Jewish man as he exited a building on Kingston Avenue. As the crowd proceeded past Kingston Avenue and onto the next block (Brooklyn Avenue), it spotted Yankel Rosenbaum ("Rosenbaum"), a bearded man in Orthodox Jewish dress. A member of the crowd, possibly Price, yelled "get 'em" and "there goes one." Someone else in the crowd was also heard to shout "get the Jew, kill the Jew."

On being targeted, Rosenbaum sought to escape the mob, running across Brooklyn Avenue and then across President Street. The crowd, however, caught up with him. A group of between ten and fifteen people, including Nelson, then began beating him,

---

3. Kingston Avenue is a predominantly Jewish commercial street.

knocking him to the ground, and striking him repeatedly. Eventually, a police car approached the scene, causing the attacking group to scatter. Nelson attempted to flee with the rest of the crowd, but ... Rosenbaum grabbed hold of Nelson's T-shirt and prevented him from making good his escape. After trying unsuccessfully, by other means, to induce Rosenbaum to let him go, Nelson ... stabbed Rosenbaum and fled.

Nelson was seen running away by the police and was subsequently caught; when searched, he was found to have a bloody knife in his possession. Although Nelson initially denied committing the stabbing, Rosenbaum, (before going to the hospital) identified Nelson out of a lineup of four African American males, and angrily asked him "why did you stab me?" Testing conducted later, moreover, revealed that the blood on the knife found on Nelson (and also blood found on Nelson's trouser pocket) matched Rosenbaum's DNA and was inconsistent with Nelson's own DNA.[4]

After receiving what the government concedes was inadequate medical care, Rosenbaum died from the stab-wounds he had sustained. Nelson was thereupon tried in New York State court on a variety of charges, including second degree murder in connection with the death of Rosenbaum. In October 1992, a jury acquitted Nelson of all charges.

Following Nelson's acquittal in New York State court, Nelson and Price (collectively the "defendants") were indicted on federal charges. Nelson was charged with violating 18 U.S.C. § 245, which states, in pertinent part, that:

> Whoever, whether or not acting under color of law, by force or threat of force willfully injures, intimidates or interferes with, or attempts to injure, intimidate or interfere with ... (2) any person because of his race, color, religion or national origin and because he is or has been ... (B) participating in or enjoying any benefit, service, privilege, program, facility or activity provided or administered by any State or subdivision thereof ... shall be fined under this title, or imprisoned not more than one year, or both; and ... if such acts include the use, attempted use, or threatened use of a dangerous weapon ... and if death results from the acts ... shall be fined under this title or imprisoned for any term of years or for life, or both, or may be sentenced to death.

18 U.S.C. § 245(b)(2)(B). Price was charged both with violating § 245(b)(2)(B) directly and with aiding and abetting Nelson's violation of § 245(b)(2)(B), in violation of 18 U.S.C. § 2.[5]

---

4. After he had been arrested and had received his *Miranda* warnings, Nelson admitted to police detective Edward Brown that he had stabbed Rosenbaum. Nevertheless, when asked whether he had stabbed Rosenbaum because Rosenbaum was Jewish, Nelson continued to deny this motive, saying "no, I was just high from the beer," and "no, that's not why I did it. I just got caught up in the excitement."

5. Editor's note: 18 U.S.C. § 2 provides:

(a) Whoever commits an offense against the United States or aids, abets, counsels, commands, induces or procures its commission, is punishable as a principal.

(b) Whoever willfully causes an act to be done which if directly performed by him or another would be an offense against the United States, is punishable as a principal.

The federal indictment against Nelson and Price principally alleged that the defendants

> by force and threat of force did willfully injure, intimidate and interfere with, and attempt to injure, intimidate and interfere with, Yankel Rosenbaum, an Orthodox Jew, because of his religion and because he was enjoying facilities provided and administered by a subdivision of the State of New York, namely, the public streets provided and administered by the City of New York, and bodily injury to and the death of Yankel Rosenbaum did result.

II

Discussion

A. 18 USC § 245(B)(2)(B).

Nelson and Price ... claim that § 245(b)(2)(B) represents, at least as applied to them, an improper exercise of congressional power beyond the authority given to the federal government by the Constitution....

1. The Constitutionality of 18 U.S.C. § 245(b)(2)(B).

We believe that § 245(b)(2)(B) falls comfortably within Congress's powers under the Thirteenth Amendment as that Amendment has authoritatively been interpreted.

A. The Scope of the Thirteenth Amendment.

The Thirteenth Amendment to the United States Constitution provides:

> Section 1. Neither slavery nor involuntary servitude, except as a punishment for a crime whereof the party shall have been duly convicted, shall exist within the United States, or any place subject to their jurisdiction.
>
> Section 2. Congress shall have power to enforce this article by appropriate legislation. U.S. Const. amend. XIII.

In the case at bar, the government asserts that this constitutional provision authorizes the application of § 245(b)(2)(B) to make a federal crime of concededly private, bias-motivated violence against a person because of that person's Jewishness and because that person was enjoying the use of a city street. In considering this contention, we focus on each of the two Sections of the Thirteenth Amendment in turn. We bear in mind, however, that much of the doctrine surrounding the Amendment implicates both sections, so that our *seriatim* approach is more expository than substantive.

In contrast to Section One of the Fourteenth Amendment, which famously includes the language "No State shall,"[6] ... Section One of the Thirteenth Amendment eliminates

---

6. Editor's note: The Fourteenth Amendment provides:

All persons born or naturalized in the United States, and subject to the jurisdiction thereof, are citizens of the United States and of the State wherein they reside. No State shall make or enforce any law which shall abridge the privileges or immunities of citizens of the United States; nor shall any State deprive any person of life, liberty, or property, without due process of law; nor deny to any person within its jurisdiction the equal protection of the laws.

U.S. Const. amend. XIV, § 1.

slavery and involuntary servitude generally, and without any reference to the source of the imposition of slavery or servitude. Accordingly, it has been recognized from the Amendment's enactment that Congress's powers under the Thirteenth Amendment are not limited by any analogue to the State Action Doctrine that was early deemed to restrict the Fourteenth Amendment. The Thirteenth Amendment, unlike the Fourteenth, in and of itself reaches purely private conduct.

Thus it has long been settled that the Thirteenth Amendment "is not a mere prohibition of State laws establishing or upholding slavery, but an absolute declaration that slavery or involuntary servitude shall not exist in any part of the United States." And accordingly, "under the Thirteenth Amendment the legislation, so far as necessary or proper to eradicate all forms and incidents of slavery and involuntary servitude, may be direct and primary, operating upon the acts of individuals, whether sanctioned by state legislation or not." The fact that § 245(b)(2)(B) is applied in this case to reach purely private conduct therefore does not—regardless of what might be the rule in the context of the Fourteenth Amendment—present any obstacle to that statute's being upheld as a proper exercise of Congress's power under the Thirteenth Amendment.

Although the Thirteenth Amendment, which was ratified in 1865, was enacted in the historical context of American slavery, which applied almost exclusively to African Americans, the interpretation of the Amendment itself has not been so limited. The text of the Amendment nowhere identifies or otherwise singles out those whose servitude the Amendment had specifically been enacted to address. And the Supreme Court early on held that although "negro slavery alone was in the mind of the Congress which proposed the thirteenth article, it forbids any other kind of slavery, now or hereafter," and would apply equally to "Mexican peonage or the Chinese coolie labor system."[7] *The Slaughter-House Cases* (1873). The Court, moreover, re-affirmed this sentiment roughly thirty years later, explaining that the Thirteenth Amendment "is the denunciation of a condition, and not a declaration in favor of a particular people. It reaches every race and every individual, and if in any respect it commits one race to the nation, it commits every race and every individual thereof. Slavery or involuntary servitude of the Chinese, of the Italian, of the Anglo Saxon, are as much within its compass as slavery or involuntary servitude of the African." Hodges v. United States (1906). There can, therefore, be no doubt that the Thirteenth Amendment's prohibitions extend, at the least, to all race-based slavery or servitude.

Furthermore, "race" as used in Thirteenth Amendment jurisprudence is a term of art, whose meaning is not limited by today's usage.[8] The fact that Jews (the group to which the government seeks, through the application of § 245(b)(2)(B) against Nelson and Price, to extend the protections of the Thirteenth Amendment) are today

7. *See also Civil Rights Cases*, 109 U.S. at 33, 3 S.Ct 18 (Harlan, J., dissenting) ("The terms of the thirteenth amendment are absolute and universal. They embrace every race which then was, or might thereafter be, within the United States.").

8. Of course, as the Supreme Court itself has noted, the modern usage may well itself be a fiction, in the sense that it groups people into what are no more than socially constructed categories....

generally not considered a distinct race, therefore, does not rule out Jews from the shelter of the Thirteenth Amendment. Indeed, the Supreme Court's case law firmly and clearly rules that Jews count as a "race" under certain civil rights statutes enacted pursuant to Congress's power under the Thirteenth Amendment. *See St. Francis Coll. v. Al-Khazraji* (1987); *Shaare Tefila Congregation v. Cobb* (1987).... These cases not only extend the protections of Reconstruction Era civil rights statutes, now codified at 42 U.S.C. §§ 1981 and 1982, to Jews understood as a "race," they also implicitly rule that the Thirteenth Amendment, the source of congressional power upon which the Court found that these statutes relied, protects Jews as a race.

In establishing this conclusion, it will be useful to begin by describing §§ 1981 and 1982. Title 42, Section 1981 of the United States Code has its origins in the Civil Rights Act of 1866.... Like the Thirteenth Amendment, the text of § 1981 does not expressly mention the race of the person benefitted by the statute, and, as it has done with the Thirteenth Amendment, the Supreme Court has construed the section to forbid any "racial" discrimination in the making of private as well as public contracts. Section 1982 similarly has its origins in the 1866 Act.... Because the Fourteenth Amendment was not ratified until 1868, both § 1981 and § 1982 must, in their initial 1866 instantiations, have been enacted pursuant to the Thirteenth Amendment, which was adopted in 1865. And, because both sections reach purely private action, it remains the Thirteenth Amendment that must continue to play a dominant role in supporting their constitutionality today.... It follows that the scope of the "races" protected by the Thirteenth Amendment cannot be narrower than the scope of "races" these statutes themselves protect.

St. Francis College and *Shaare Tefila* make clear that §§ 1981 and 1982 (and consequently the Thirteenth Amendment) extend to protect the Jewish "race." ... The Supreme Court expressly held that when 42 U.S.C. § 1982 was adopted, "Jews constituted a group of people that Congress intended to protect," and that "it is evident from the legislative history of the section reviewed in *Saint Francis College* ... that Jews and Arabs were among the peoples then considered to be distinct races and hence within the protection of the statute." *Shaare Tefila.*

As noted above, these arguments apply, *a fortiori*, to the Thirteenth Amendment itself. For it is on the authority of the Thirteenth Amendment that the applications of these civil rights statutes developed in *St. Francis College* and *Shaare Tefila* depend. Accordingly, we find that Jews were among the "races" intended to be protected from slavery and involuntary servitude by the Thirteenth Amendment, and that Congress may today protect Jews pursuant to that Amendment.[9]

---

9. The defendants try to defeat this conclusion by arguing that, whatever race meant in 1866, the 1968 Congress that included the language "because of his race, color, religion or national origin" in 18 U.S.C. § 245(b)(2)(B) gave the word "race" its modern usage and, consistent with this usage, aimed to protect Jews not as a race but as a religion. The defendants imply that because Congress, in enacting 18 U.S.C. § 245(b)(2)(B), intended to protect Jews as a religion and not as a race, and that because Congress's powers under the Thirteenth Amendment do not extend to protecting religions, the constitutionality of 18 U.S.C. § 245(b)(2)(B) as it was adopted cannot be upheld under the Thirteenth

Finally, there is strong precedent to support the conclusion that the Thirteenth Amendment extends its protections to religions directly, and thus to members of the Jewish religion, without the detour through historically changing conceptions of "race" that we have just taken. Certainly there is nothing in the conceptual or linguistic structure of the prohibition of "slavery" and "involuntary servitude"—which appears in the Thirteenth Amendment, it is worth noting once again, unadorned by the adjective "racial"—that limits the banning of these evils only when they are imposed along racial lines. The most basic feature of "slavery" or "involuntary servitude"—the subjugation of one person to another by coercive means[10]—remains the same regardless of whether a person is subjugated on grounds of race or for some other reason. Indeed, one need look no further than Thucydides' famous Melian Dialogue to recognize that over much of the course of human history, slavery has been imposed, without regard to race, as the policy of a conquering nation over a conquered. *See* Thucydides, *The Peloponnesian War* book v para. 85–116. Certainly religion- rather than race-based slavery is consistent with both the status of the slave and with how that condition has been imposed historically. Over much of the course of human history, slavery has been imposed, without regard to race, as the policy of a conquering nation over a conquered.... Certainly religion—rather than race-based slavery—is consistent with both the status of the slave and with how that condition has been imposed historically.

Although *St. Francis College* casts its argument in terms of historical understandings of the meaning of the word "race," the conclusion of the Court in that case—that § 1981 and, by implication, the Thirteenth Amendment, "protect from discrimination identifiable classes of persons who are subjected to intentional discrimination solely because of their ancestry or ethnic characteristics," *St. Francis Coll.*—reads much more broadly than it would were the opinion limiting its sweep to the historicized concept of "race." As a result, Chasidic Jews (like Rosenbaum[11]) would fall within the coverage of

---

Amendment. And that that is so even if Congress could, under that Amendment, have protected Jews as a race had it chosen to do so.

But quite apart from the fact that this argument fails because the Thirteenth Amendment extends its protections against slavery to religions as well as to races, the argument confuses the category of persons that Congress may protect under the Thirteenth Amendment with the heading under which Congress acts in protecting such persons. And, especially where words—that is headings—change their meanings over time, it is the former, rather than the latter, that determines whether Congress has acted within or exceeded its constitutional powers. (citations omitted). Congress' power to enforce the Thirteenth Amendment by enacting § 241 and § 1584 is clear and undisputed. The scope of conduct prohibited by these statutes is therefore a matter of statutory construction. (citations omitted). Congress is authorized to protect Jews under the Thirteenth Amendment because that Amendment's framers understood Jews to come within its purview; and once Congress enjoys this authority, Congress may exercise its power for whatever reason and under whatever heading it chooses.

10. There is a dispute about whether any form of coercion, if sufficiently powerful, may reduce a person to actual slavery or involuntary servitude, or whether only physical or legal coercion may do so. This question about the precise limits of the concept of actual slavery is irrelevant to the case before us, however, since our case involves not actual slavery but rather the badges and incidents of slavery.

11. Editor's note: Yankel Rosenbaum was, in fact, Orthodox rather than Hasidic. For more on the differences between the two, see *The Jewish Denominations*, My Jewish Learning, https://www.myjewishlearning.com/article/the-jewish-denominations/ (last visited Nov. 20, 2024).

this phrase even if, as a historical matter, Jews had never been considered specifically a distinct *race*.

That the protections of the Thirteenth Amendment extend to private actions, and that Jews are entitled to the full measure of these protections, does not, however, settle the question now before us. It remains to be determined whether these protections (bestowed upon Jews or any other groups) suffice to authorize the congressional exercise of power at issue here—§ 245(b)(2)(B)'s criminalization of violence applied against a person on account of (a) his race (religion), and (b) his use of a public street. If the Thirteenth Amendment included only Section One, this would present an unsettled question. Although it has been agreed from the outset that "by its own unaided force and effect [the Thirteenth Amendment] abolished slavery, and established universal freedom the Supreme Court has "left open the question whether § 1 of the Amendment by its own terms did anything more than abolish [actual] slavery."

B. The Power of Congress Under Section Two of the Thirteenth Amendment

Congress's powers under Section Two of the Thirteenth Amendment extend beyond the prohibition on actual slavery and servitude expressed in Section One. Congress, through its enforcement power under Section Two of the Thirteenth Amendment is empowered to control conduct that does not come close to violating Section One directly. The question before us is whether, in light of this jurisprudence, § 245(b)(2)(B), as applied in the case at bar, lies within this expansive enforcement power. We must, in other words, ask whether Congress could rationally have determined that the acts of violence covered by § 245(b)(2)(B) impose a badge or incident of servitude on their victims.

C. The Meaning and Significance Under the Thirteenth Amendment of the Language of Section 245(b)(2)(B).

The critical feature of § 245(b)(2)(B) for purposes of this constitutional analysis is that it does not seek to reach most force-based injuries, intimidations, or interferences and by no means attempts to create a general, undifferentiated federal law of criminal assault....

Acts of violence or force committed against members of a hated class of people with the intent to exact retribution for and create dissuasion against their use of public facilities have a long and intimate historical association with slavery and its cognate institutions. Thus there is widespread agreement among scholars of slavery that slavery in general (across cultural and historical periods) centrally involves the master's constant power to use private violence against the slave, and that "slavery is preeminently a relationship of power and dominion originating in and sustained by violence." Moreover, the peculiar institution of American slavery unquestionably did not depart from this general rule....

Significantly, this practice of race-based private violence both continued beyond the demise of the institution of chattel slavery and was closely connected to the prevention of former slaves' exercise of their newly obtained civil and other rights (rights that slavery had previously denied them), thereby presenting "a spectacle of slavery unwilling to die Thus "violence against blacks reached staggering proportions in the immediate aftermath of the [Civil War]," and such violence was specifically directed at the exercise, by black Americans, of the rights and habits of free persons.

As these studies suggest, there exist indubitable connections (a) between slavery and private violence directed against despised and enslaved groups and, more specifically, (b) between American slavery and private violence and (c) between post-Civil War efforts to return freed slaves to a subjugated status and private violence directed at interfering with and discouraging the freed slaves' exercise of civil rights in public places. It is in the shadow of these connections, and citing to Justice Douglas's characterization of slavery as "unwilling to die," that the Eighth Circuit (the only Circuit previously to address the question of § 245(b)(2)(B)'s constitutionality under the Thirteenth Amendment), concluded "[n]or can there be doubt that interfering with a person's use of a public [facility] because he is black is a badge of slavery."

On the basis of the foregoing analysis, we similarly conclude that § 245(b)(2)(B)'s prohibition against private violence motivated by the victim's race, religion, etc., *and* because of the victim's use of a public facility, etc., falls comfortably within Congress's "power under the Thirteenth Amendment rationally to determine what are the badges and the incidents of slavery, and [its] authority to translate that determination into effective legislation. Accordingly, we find that § 245(b)(2)(B), as applied in the case at bar, is a constitutional exercise of Congress's power under the Thirteenth Amendment....

III

Conclusion

We hold that 18 U.S.C. § 245(b)(2)(B)—as applied to religiously or racially motivated attacks against Jews—is a constitutional exercise of the Congress's power under the Thirteenth Amendment.

Hate Crimes Statute for Federally Protected Activities

1. *Chaney, Goodman, and Schwerner.* Congress enacted § 45(b)(2)(B) partly in response to the murders of three civil rights workers on June 21, 1964, near Philadelphia, Mississippi, during the "Freedom Summer" of 1964. The victims were James Earl Chaney, an African American from Mississippi, and Andrew Goodman and Michael Henry Schwerner, two Jews from New York. (The 1988 film *Mississippi Burning* was based on the FBI investigation of their murders.) It was enacted as part of the broader Civil Rights Act of 1968, which was a landmark law in the United States signed by President Lyndon B. Johnson. Section 245(b)(2)(B) enabled federal prosecutors to charge hate crimes perpetrators with conspiracy to violate a victim's civil rights, even though the underlying offense of murder, etc., could only be prosecuted under state law.[12]

12. Federal prosecutors charged 18 individuals under 18 U.S.C. §§ 242, 371. Section 242 makes it a crime for someone acting under color of law to willfully deprive a person of a federally protected right. It is not necessary that the offense be motivated by racial bias or by any other animus. Section 371 makes it a crime to conspire to commit offense against the United States. *See, e.g.*, Investigation of the 1964 Murders of Michael Schwerner, James Chaney, and Andrew Goodman, File No. DJ 144-41-686, U.S. Dep't. of Just. (June 21, 1964), https://www.justice.gov/crt/case-document/micheal-schwerner-james-chaney-andrew-goodman; *see also Murders of Chaney, Goodman, and Schwerner*, WIKIPEDIA,

Figure 11.3. Dr. Martin Luther King, Jr. (1929–1968), holding photographs of three civil rights workers who were murdered by the Ku Klux Klan: Andrew Goodman, James Earl Chaney, and Michael Henry Schwerner. Everett Collection, Inc./Alamy Stock Photo.

2. Section 245(b)(2)(B) includes "race" and "religion" as protected categories. Which would be easier for the state to prove: that Nelson's attack on Rosenbaum was motivated by animus (a) to his ethnicity/ancestry or (b) to his religion, i.e., religious beliefs and practices? Here consider:

a. Rosenbaum's beard and Orthodox dress. These definitively signified that he belonged to a particular religion. They were a less reliable indicator, however, of his ethnicity/ancestry, because he or his parents, etc., could have converted to Judaism. Does this cut in favor of applying the statute to protect Jews as a religious group?

b. The language used by the mob. Did it focus on Rosenbaum's ethnicity/ancestry or his religion?

c. How much did Nelson know about Rosenbaum's religious beliefs and practices? For example, what's the likelihood that he attacked Rosenbaum out of animus for Judaism?

3. Assume Jews were generally not considered a race when the Civil Rights Act of 1968 was enacted. Does this mean that § 245(b)(2)(B) only applies to Jews as members of a religious group?

4. Was Price's speech to the crowd protected by the First Amendment? *See Brandenburg v. Ohio*, 395 U.S. 444 (1969) (speech loses First Amendment protection if it "is directed to inciting or producing imminent lawless action and is likely to incite or produce such action.").

The Thirteenth Amendment Authorizes Hate Crimes Statutes that Protect Jews

1. *Authority based on race.* Judge Calabresi ruled that the Thirteenth Amendment protects races other than African Americans from "badges and incidents of slavery" and that Jews are a race for Thirteenth Amendment purposes.

2. *Authority based on religion.* Judge Calabresi also stated that the Thirteenth Amendment protects religious groups, and that Jews are a religious group for Thirteenth Amendment purposes. He wrote, "the Thirteenth Amendment extends its protections to religions *directly*, and thus to members of the Jewish religion, *without the detour* through historically changing conceptions of 'race.'"

What do you make of Judge Calabresi's religious argument? It might be narrowly construed to claim that the Thirteenth Amendment protects only religious groups considered to be "races" when the Thirteenth Amendment was enacted. Is such a construction redundant? Consider the broader construction that the Thirteenth Amendment

---

https://en.wikipedia.org/wiki/Murders_of_Chaney,_Goodman,_and_Schwerner (last visited Nov. 20, 2024); *see also Murder in Mississippi*, PBS, https://www.pbs.org/wgbh/americanexperience/features/freedomsummer-murder/ (last visited Nov. 20, 2024).

directly protects all religions and/or religious groups. Which construction is more persuasive, judicially manageable, etc.? Under the broader construction, which forms of religious discrimination constitute a badge of slavery, and what is the limiting principle for determining which religious groups are protected?

3. Judge Calabresi claimed that the Thirteenth Amendment authorized Congress to enact §§ 1981 and 1982. What, according to the Supreme Court's opinions in *St. Francis Coll.* and *Shaare Tefila*, is the constitutional basis of these statutes? Is *Nelson* controlled by *St. Francis Coll.* and *Shaare Tefila* and, if so, to what extent? If the Thirteenth Amendment does not authorize Congress to enact Section 245(b)(2)(B), can it authorize it to enact §§ 1981 and 1982?

4. Assume most anti-Jewish discrimination today is based on ancestry/ethnicity rather than perceptions of Jews as a race. In Judge Calabresi's view, would §§ 1981 and 1982 apply to Jews?

5. *Judging the judges.* Compare Judge Calabresi's opinion with Justice White's in *Shaare Tefila*. Which is more gratifying? Which is more persuasive? What theories of statutory interpretation do they enlist to support their rulings? Which opinion is more narrowly tailored to the task at hand?

6. *Mindful.* In a footnote, Judge Calabresi expressed sensitivity, writing:

> We are mindful of the irony that attaches to applying the Thirteenth Amendment in this case. In doing so, we employ a constitutional provision enacted with the emancipation of black slaves in mind to uphold a criminal law as applied against black men who, the jury found, acted with racial motivations, but in circumstances in which they were, at least partly, responding to perceived discrimination against them. We make no effort to dissolve this irony, noting only that the post-Civil War amendments' specific historical focus on black Americans and the amendments' generally egalitarian language are all too often in tension.

7. *The Matthew Shepard and James Byrd, Jr. Hate Crimes Prevention Act* (The Shepard-Byrd Act). The Shepard-Byrd Act, 18 U.S.C. § 249(a)(1), provides:

> Whoever ... willfully causes bodily injury to any person ... because of the actual or perceived race, color, religion, or national origin of any person—
>
> (A) shall be imprisoned not more than 10 years, fined ... or both;
>
> (B) shall be imprisoned for any term of years or ... both, if
>
> (1) death results from the offense; or
>
> (2) the offense includes kidnapping or an attempt to kidnap, aggravated sexual abuse or an attempt to commit aggravated sexual abuse, or an attempt to kill.

According to then Attorney General Eric H. Holder, Jr., Congress could enact the Shepard-Byrd Act's § 249(a)(1) pursuant to its Thirteenth Amendment authority to eradicate badges and incidents of slavery. Section 249(a)(1) has withstood several constitutional challenges.[13]

8. *Different proof requirements.* Critically, § 245(b)(2)(B) and the Shepard-Byrd Act's § 249(a)(1) have different proof requirements for motivation. § 245(b)(2)(B) requires the prosecution to prove that the defendant acted (a) because of the victim's race, color, religion or national origin; and (b) because the victim was participating in or enjoying a benefit, etc., provided by a state or subdivision. Under the Shepard-Byrd Act's § 249(a)(1), by contrast, the prosecution need only prove the defendant acted because of the victim's actual or perceived race, color, religion, or national origin. In the *Nelson* case, brought under § 245(b)(2)(B), the government had to prove both that the defendants targeted Rosenbaum because he was Jewish *and* because he was using a public street, the federally protected activity. This distinction helps explain why Congress later passed the Shepard-Byrd Act's § 249(a)(1) with its simpler proof requirement focusing solely on bias motivation.[14]

The Psychology of Prejudice, Stereotyping, and Discrimination

1. *A proud Jew. A tough Jew.* Yankel Rosenbaum (1962–1991) was a graduate student and PhD candidate from Melbourne, Australia. His friends described him as "a proud Jew" and "a tough Jew" and someone who spoke his mind. They expected "that Yankel would have taken it to his attackers and not shied away from a confrontation." Rosenbaum had come to New York to conduct research into shtetls, that is, the small, rural Jewish towns and villages in pre-World War II Eastern Europe.[15] A friend observed "the bitter irony that he was essentially the victim of a pogrom in a modern recreation or transplantation of the very shtetl he studied." Sharing a "bond in grief," Yankel Rosembaum's brother and Gavin Cato's father became friends.[16]

---

13. In United States v. Diggins, 36 F.4th 302, 309 (1st Cir. 2022), the court upheld 18 U.S.C. § 249(a)(1) as "a constitutional exercise of Congress's power under the Thirteenth Amendment." *See also* United States v. Earnest, 536 F. Supp. 3d 688, 716 (S.D. Cal. 2021) (analyzing § 249(a)(1) under the Thirteenth Amendment and holding that "Congress rationally determined that race-based violence is a badge and incident of slavery and that eliminating it is crucial to eliminating the remnants of slavery"); *see also* United States v. Bowers, 495 F. Supp. 3d 362, 370 (W.D. Pa. 2020) (holding that "§ 249(a)(1) includes protection for Jewish people in that they were considered a distinct race when the Thirteenth Amendment was applied"); *see also* United States v. Beebe, 807 F. Supp. 2d 1045 (D.N.M. 2011) (finding that section 249(a)(1) does not violate the Tenth Amendment or the Fifth Amendment's Equal Protection Clause), *aff'd*, 722 F.3d 1193 (10th Cir. 2013); United States v. Maybee, No. 11-30006, 2011 WL 2784446, at *6 (W.D. Ark. July 15, 2011) (holding that § 249(a)(1) "is constitutional as applied under the Thirteenth Amendment"), *aff'd*, 687 F.3d 1026 (8th Cir. 2012).

14. Civil Rights Division, *The Matthew Shepard and James Byrd, Jr., Hate Crimes Prevention Act of 2009*, U.S. DEP'T OF JUST., https://www.justice.gov/crt/matthew-shepard-and-james-byrd-jr-hate-crimes-prevention-act-2009-0 (last updated May 30, 2023).

15. *Shtetl*, OXFORD ENG. DICTIONARY, https://doi.org/10.1093/OED/5200875690 (last visited Nov. 20, 2024).

16. Peter Kohn, *Yankel Remembered 25 Years On*, AUSTRALIAN JEWISH NEWS (Aug 25, 2016, 12:00 AM), https://www.australianjewishnews.com/yankel-remembered-25-years/; *see also* David Werdi-

2. *Heuristics.* To understand why Rosenbaum was murdered, we need to know more about biases and how they operate. Key concepts include heuristics, confirmation bias, and group attribution bias. A heuristic is a mental shortcut or rule of thumb that our brains use to make decisions quickly without having all the relevant information.[17] This can be an evolutionary advantage: when a lion roars, people who start running are more likely to pass their genes along than people who pause to wonder if the lion is caged, friendly, injured, etc. A useful heuristic allows us to make a decision that has a high enough probability of being correct without having to think everything through.

3. *Confirmation bias.* Confirmation bias is "the tendency to seek or [favor] new information which supports one's existing theories or beliefs, while avoiding or rejecting that which disrupts them."[18] Biased interpretation is a confirmation bias in which people tend to interpret data and information in a way that supports their prior opinion, and are thus inclined to stick to that interpretation even when presented with new data.[19] Researcher Dayva Segal identifies several theories as to why people tend to have confirmation bias:

a. *Helps to process information.* Some people believe that confirmation bias helps you *sort efficiently through the large amount of information you see every day.*

b. *Builds confidence.* Other experts think that people seek out information to support their opinions to preserve or build their self-esteem. Finding information that *supports their ideas makes them feel more confident.*

c. *Reduces mental conflict.* Another theory about why people use confirmation bias is that it reduces the risk of mental conflict, also called cognitive dissonance. When someone holds or has information about two opposite ideas, they may experience psychological stress. Confirmation bias may lower the risk of feeling the negative emotions from this stress.[20]

4. *Group attribution bias.* This type of confirmation bias occurs when a person:

> attributes the behavior of another person not simply to individual characteristics, but also to characteristics associated with the group to which the other

---

ger, *Yankel Rosenbaum—20 Years On*, David Werdiger (Sept. 2011) https://davidwerdiger.com/blog/death-mourning/yankel-rosenbaum-20-years-on/; *see also* Mary Murphy, *9 Minutes That Triggered the Crown Heights Riots 30 Years Ago*, PIX11 (Aug. 19, 2021, 5:44 PM), https://pix11.com/news/local-news/brooklyn/crown-heights-riots-30-years-later-august-2021/.

17. *Heuristics*, Conceptually, https://conceptually.org/concepts/heuristics (last visited Nov. 20, 2024). The word "heuristics" derives from the Greek *heuriskein* ("to discover"). Michael McDonough, *Heuristic*, Britannica, https://www.britannica.com/topic/heuristic-reasoning (last updated Nov. 12, 2024).

18. *Confirmation Bias*, Oxford Eng. Dictionary, https://doi.org/10.1093/OED/2139286550 (last visited Nov. 20, 2024).

19. Dayva Segal, *What Is Confirmation Bias?* WebMD (Sept. 15, 2023), https://www.webmd.com/balance/what-is-confirmation-bias.

20. *Id.*

person belongs. Moreover, the group membership of the perceiver, or attributor, can also affect the intergroup attribution process.[21]

Researchers presented Bengali Muslims with a scenario in which a passerby helped a child who fell off his bike. If told that the Good Samaritan was Muslim, Muslim participants tended to attribute the passerby's behavior "to causes rated as internal, stable, uncontrollable by others, and global," i.e., related to being a Muslim. If the passerby was Hindu, by contrast, participants tended to attribute the Hindu's behavior "to causes rated as external, unstable, controllable by others, and specific," i.e., unrelated to being Hindu. If the passerby failed to help the child, the participants' perceptions were reversed: if the Bad Samaritan was Hindu, their behavior was perceived as related to his being Hindu; if Muslim, the causes were deemed unrelated to being a Muslim.[22]

5. *Cross-categorization.* Two social psychologists, Rhiannon Turner and Miles Hewstone, report that group attribution bias can be reduced through "cross-categorization":

> *Cross-categorization* ... involves crossing a dichotomous categorization with a second categorization. In the case of Hindus and Muslims in Bangladesh, for example, it is possible to introduce a second categorization, the distinction between Bangladeshi and Indian nationality. This cross-categorization creates four groups. For a Bangladeshi Muslim, the double ingroup refers to those who share both group memberships (other Bangladeshi Muslims), the partial ingroups are those who share one group membership (Bangladeshi Hindus and Indian Muslims), and the double outgroup refers to those who share neither group membership (Indian Hindus). People tend to favor double ingroup members and show the greatest discrimination against the double outgroup. Intergroup bias against partial ingroup members, however, is reduced compared to the double outgroup. Thus, seeing an outgroup member as being an ingroup member on a second dimension has benefits for intergroup relations. Research on intergroup attribution biases mirrors these findings. Bangladeshi Muslim study participants made the most positive attributions about a Bangladeshi Muslim protagonist and the most negative attributions about an Indian Hindu protagonist. Attributions made about Bangladeshi Hindus and Indian Muslims were, however, significantly more positive than those made about Indian Hindus.

6. *Historically burdened bias.* Turner and Hewstone also discuss *historically burdened* confirmation bias:

> Research has also considered whether there are biases in attributions made for the historical actions of entire outgroups. (Non-German) Jewish and (non-Jewish) German participants were asked why they thought Germans

---

21. Rhiannon N. Turner & Miles Hewstone, *Attribution Biases, in* ENCYCLOPEDIA OF GROUP PROCESSES & INTERGROUP RELATIONS 43–46, 44 (John M. Levine & Michael A. Hogg. ed., 2009), https://study.sagepub.com/sites/default/files/reference8.2.pdf.

22. *Id.*

mistreated Jewish people during the Second World War. Jewish participants were more likely to attribute the behavior of the Germans to internal characteristics such as German aggression than were German participants.[23]

7. *A hypothetical.* Consider the following scenario. An accident occurs in which three people are injured: one adult, A, and two children, B and C. An ambulance arrives and retrieves A. Soon after, a second ambulance arrives and retrieves B and C. Consider the following explanations for these events.[24]

a. A's injuries were more severe;
b. B's and C's injuries were more severe and the first ambulance didn't have the expertise to handle them.
c. The second ambulance had been called specifically for B and C and was en route to the scene when the first ambulance arrived.*
d. The first ambulance was better equipped for adults and/or the second ambulance was better equipped for children.
e. Keeping the two children together in one ambulance provided them with emotional support and aided in reuniting them with their families;*
f. A pediatric hospital was just a few blocks away but the hospital for adults was much further.
g. For safety reasons, the police ordered the first ambulance driver to retrieve A and leave.*
h. Assuming (a) the first ambulance's drivers and A are members of group X (in this case, Jews); and (b) B and C are members of group Y (in this case, African Americans); then (c) the drivers retrieved A because they—like other members of group X—only care about members of group X.

Nicholas L. Georgakopoulos,[25] *An Economic Analysis of Hate Crime*

The economic analysis of crime has a foundational paradox. Crimes should not occur. No rational individual should accept the enormous tort liability that accompanies any crime. Granted, the incentives of tort law are easily weakened by poverty: judgement-proof individuals do not fear tort liability (now that debtor's prisons are no longer). Thus, at the foundation of criminal law lies a failure of both tort law and the incentives of criminal law.

---

23. *Id.* at 44.

24. The asterisked options were the actual motivations for the Jewish affiliated ambulance's actions in *Nelson*.

25. Nicholas L. Georgakopoulos is Harold R. Woodard Professor of Law at Indiana University Robert H. McKinney School of Law. His scholarship explores the intersection of business and uncertainty. He is the author of PRINCIPLES AND METHODS OF LAW AND ECONOMICS (2005).

The next paradoxical layer of analysis is that intentional wrongs cannot be over-deterred. Since no battery and no larceny should occur, then, shouldn't the criminal penalty for those who fail to heed the incentives of tort law be the death penalty? The problem with imposing the death penalty for lesser crimes is marginal deterrence. Someone who commits a discoverable lesser crime would have no incentive to not commit more crimes and more serious ones. Given imperfect detection and prosecution, then, lesser crimes deserve smaller penalties.

Against this backdrop of a general failure of rationality, the economic analysis of hate crimes looks at the question of enhancing penalties because the victim belongs to a group against which the perpetrator has hatred. Why should this hatred be treated differently than the hatred an ordinary criminal has for their victim?

The leading economic analysis of the issue focuses on the interaction between groups in society.[26] Society benefits from interactions. Each exchange, from an economic perspective, produces gains for both sides (otherwise it would not occur). When a group fears interacting with outsiders, society loses the benefit of the exchanges that would have occurred. Crimes motivated by group hatred are worse for society than crimes motivated by individual hatred because they make all members of the group avoid interacting with outsiders. This justifies enhancing the penalty from an economic perspective.

One body of law and economics scholarship looks at the Jim Crow South and how the dominant group managed to perpetuate the oppression of Blacks despite this economic force toward integration and finds that the dominant group would punish its members who would interact with Blacks![27] For example, the son of Justice Black, an Alabaman who joined the Supreme Court's desegregation decisions, was a lawyer in Birmingham after having graduated second in his class from Yale Law School. After the desegregation decisions he had to leave Alabama. A similar story is depicted in the film *Song of the South* (2020), an autobiographical account of a white high schooler in 1961 whom racists warned not to become involved with the civil rights movement by burning a cross in his yard.

The Economic Costs of Hate Crimes

1. *The economic costs of hate crimes.* Kenneth Stern, director of the Bard Center for the Study of Hate, observes that "if we don't quantify the cost of a societal problem, it's less likely that we'll do something to address it."[28] According to Professor Michael E.

---

26. Dhammika Dharmapala & Nuno Garoupa, *Penalty Enhancement for Hate Crimes: An Economic Analysis*, 6 Am. L. & Econ. Rev. 185 *passim* (2004).

27. Richard H. McAdams, *Cooperation and Conflict: The Economics of Group Status Production and Race Discrimination*, 108 Harv. L. Rev. 1003 *passim* (1995).

28. Michael E. Martell, Bard Ctr. for the Study of Hate, Economic Costs of Hate Crimes 3 (2023), https://bcsh.bard.edu/files/2023/03/BCSH-Economic-Cost-of-Hate_3-13-23_Online-.pdf.

Martell, hate crimes cause the U.S. and its residents to incur costs of at least $3.4 billion. Martell breaks down these costs into several categories:

2. Tangible Costs

a. Direct victim costs: These include medical care expenses, lost earnings, and property loss/damage

b. Societal costs:

   (1) Macro costs: Resources allocated to policing, hate crime prevention, legal proceedings, and incarceration

   (2) Micro costs: Opportunity costs associated with perpetrators' actions, such as lost productivity

c. Intangible Costs. These are harder to quantify but include:

   (1) Victim and victim-adjacent costs: Pain and suffering, decreased quality of life, and psychological distress experienced by victims and their families

   (2) Community impact: Fear rippling through a community, potentially leading to decreased economic activity and social cohesion.[29]

3. *Cost unaccounted for.* Professor Martell notes that his methodology does not capture the costs that hate crimes impose on targeted groups.

> We also note that the intended targets of hate crimes are populations, not individuals. The crime-costing methodology here does not incorporate the notion that, in the aftermath of a hate crime (such as the increased assaults on Muslims and Sikhs after the 9/11 attacks, or the more recent assaults on Asian Americans and Jews), the psychological and moral costs of this crime were felt by the targeted groups (and their allies) everywhere. These costs include people being nervous about enjoying the services associated with the venue that was attacked, or people being fearful of going to similar venues elsewhere. The intangible costs of hate crimes—the pain, fear, suffering, and decreased quality of life—should be determined for communities and not just individuals.[30]

C. Hate Crimes Statute Does Not Violate the First Amendment

Wisconsin v. Mitchell (1993) is a landmark Supreme Court case that addressed the constitutionality of a hate crime law and its relationship to the First Amendment. The case centered on Wisconsin's penalty enhancement statute, which allowed for increased sentences when a crime was committed with bias motivation.

The case arose from an incident in which Todd Mitchell, an African American man, was convicted of aggravated battery for his role in an attack on a white boy. The offense

29. *Id.* at 8–9.
30. *Id.* at 13.

carried a maximum sentence of two years. The jury separately found that Mitchell had selected the victim because of his race, i.e., the attack was racially motivated. The state's bias crimes law provided for an enhanced maximum sentence from two years to four years where the batterer "intentionally selected" the victim "because of" their race, a protected class. The trial court therefore enhanced Mitchell's sentence from a maximum of two years to four years.

The state court of appeals affirmed this judgment. The state supreme court reversed the judgment, reasoning that the bias crimes law violated the First Amendment. A unanimous Supreme Court, per Chief Justice Rehnquist, upheld the statute, ruling that Mitchell's First Amendment rights were not violated by the application of the Wisconsin penalty enhancement provision in sentencing him.[31]

Wisconsin v. Mitchell

508 U.S. 476 (1993)

Chief Justice Rehnquist delivered the opinion of the Court.

Respondent Todd Mitchell's sentence for aggravated battery was enhanced because he intentionally selected his victim on account of the victim's race. The question presented in this case is whether this penalty enhancement is prohibited by the First and Fourteenth Amendments. We hold that it is not.

On the evening of October 7, 1989, a group of young black men and boys, including Mitchell, gathered at an apartment complex in Kenosha, Wisconsin. Several members of the group discussed a scene from the motion picture *Mississippi Burning*, in which a white man beat a young black boy who was praying. The group moved outside and Mitchell asked them: "Do you all feel hyped up to move on some white people?" Shortly thereafter, a young white boy approached the group on the opposite side of the street where they were standing. As the boy walked by, Mitchell said: "You all want to fuck somebody up? There goes a white boy; go get him." Mitchell counted to three and pointed in the boy's direction. The group ran towards the boy, beat him severely, and stole his tennis shoes. The boy was rendered unconscious and remained in a coma for four days.

After a jury trial in the Circuit Court for Kenosha County, Mitchell was convicted of aggravated battery. That offense ordinarily carries a maximum sentence of two years' imprisonment. But because the jury found that Mitchell had intentionally selected his victim because of the boy's race, the maximum sentence for Mitchell's offense was increased to seven years under § 939.645. That provision enhances the maximum penalty for an offense whenever the defendant "intentionally selects the person against whom the crime ... is committed ... because of the race, religion, color, disability, sexual orientation, national origin or ancestry of that person. ..." § 939.645(1)(b). The Circuit Court sentenced Mitchell to four years' imprisonment for the aggravated battery.

31. Frederick M. Lawrence, Punishing Hate: Bias Crimes Under American Law 30 (1999).

[Reversing Mitchell's conviction and sentence,] the [Wisconsin] Supreme Court held that the statute "violates the First Amendment directly by punishing what the legislature has deemed to be offensive thought." It rejected the State's contention "that the statute punishes only the `conduct' of intentional selection of a victim." According to the court, "the statute punishes the `because of' aspect of the defendant's selection, the *reason* the defendant selected the victim, the *motive* behind the selection.» And under *R.A.V. v. St. Paul* (1992), "the Wisconsin legislature cannot criminalize bigoted thought with which it disagrees."

The Supreme Court also held that the penalty enhancement statute was unconstitutionally overbroad. It reasoned that, in order to prove that a defendant intentionally selected his victim because of the victim's protected status, the State would often have to introduce evidence of the defendant's prior speech, such as racial epithets he may have uttered before the commission of the offense. This evidentiary use of protected speech, the court thought, would have a "chilling effect" on those who feared the possibility of prosecution for offenses subject to penalty enhancement. Finally, the court distinguished antidiscrimination laws, which have long been held constitutional, on the ground that the Wisconsin statute punishes the "subjective mental process" of selecting a victim because of his protected status, whereas antidiscrimination laws prohibit "objective acts of discrimination."

We granted *certiorari* because of the importance of the question presented and the existence of a conflict of authority among state high courts on the constitutionality of statutes similar to Wisconsin's penalty enhancement provision.[32] ... We reverse.

Mitchell argues that we are bound by the Wisconsin Supreme Court's conclusion that the statute punishes bigoted thought and not conduct. There is no doubt that we are bound by a state court's construction of a state statute.... But here the Wisconsin Supreme Court did not, strictly speaking, construe the Wisconsin statute in the sense of defining the meaning of a particular statutory word or phrase. Rather, it merely characterized the "practical effect" of the statute for First Amendment purposes. This assessment does not bind us. Once any ambiguities as to the meaning of the statute are resolved, we may form our own judgment as to its operative effect.

The State argues that the statute does not punish bigoted thought, as the Supreme Court of Wisconsin said, but instead punishes only conduct. While this argument is literally correct, it does not dispose of Mitchell's First Amendment challenge. To be sure, our cases reject the "view that an apparently limitless variety of conduct can be la-

32. Several states have enacted penalty-enhancement provisions similar to the Wisconsin statute at issue in this case. The state high courts are divided over the constitutionality of penalty-enhancement statutes and analogous statutes covering bias-motivated offenses. In 1990, Congress enacted the Hate Crimes Statistics Act, Pub. L. 101-275, § 1(b)(1), 104 Stat. 140, codified at 28 U.S.C. § 534 (note) (1988 ed., Supp. III), directing the Attorney General to compile data "about crimes that manifest evidence of prejudice based on race, religion, sexual orientation, or ethnicity." Pursuant to the Act, the Federal Bureau of Investigation reported in January 1993, that 4,558 bias-motivated offenses were committed in 1991, including 1,614 incidents of intimidation, 1,301 incidents of vandalism, 796 simple assaults, 773 aggravated assaults, and 12 murders.

beled 'speech' whenever the person engaging in the conduct intends thereby to express an idea." Thus, a physical assault is not by any stretch of the imagination expressive conduct protected by the First Amendment.

But the fact remains that under the Wisconsin statute the same criminal conduct may be more heavily punished if the victim is selected because of his race or other protected status than if no such motive obtained. Thus, although the statute punishes criminal conduct, it enhances the maximum penalty for conduct motivated by a discriminatory point of view more severely than the same conduct engaged in for some other reason or for no reason at all. Because the only reason for the enhancement is the defendant's discriminatory motive for selecting his victim, Mitchell argues (and the Wisconsin Supreme Court held) that the statute violates the First Amendment by punishing offenders' bigoted beliefs.

Traditionally, sentencing judges have considered a wide variety of factors in addition to evidence bearing on guilt in determining what sentence to impose on a convicted defendant.... The defendant's motive for committing the offense is one important factor. Thus, in many States the commission of a murder, or other capital offense, for pecuniary gain is a separate aggravating circumstance under the capital sentencing statute.

But it is equally true that a defendant's abstract beliefs, however obnoxious to most people, may not be taken into consideration by a sentencing judge. *Dawson v. Delaware* (1992). In *Dawson*, the State introduced evidence at a capital sentencing hearing that the defendant was a member of a white supremacist prison gang. Because "the evidence proved nothing more than [the defendant's] abstract beliefs," we held that its admission violated the defendant's First Amendment rights.[33] In so holding, however, we emphasized that "the Constitution does not erect a *per se* barrier to the admission of evidence concerning one›s beliefs and associations at sentencing simply because those beliefs and associations are protected by the First Amendment.» Thus, in *Barclay v. Florida* (1983) (plurality opinion), we allowed the sentencing judge to take into account the defendant's racial animus towards his victim. The evidence in that case showed that the defendant's membership in the Black Liberation Army and desire to provoke a "race war" were related to the murder of a white man for which he was convicted. Because "the elements of racial hatred in [the] murder" were relevant to several aggravating factors, we held that the trial judge permissibly took this evidence into account in sentencing the defendant to death.

Mitchell suggests that *Dawson* and *Barclay* are inapposite because they did not involve application of a penalty enhancement provision. But in *Barclay* we held that it was permissible for the sentencing court to consider the defendant's racial animus in determining whether he should be sentenced to death, surely the most severe enhancement of all. And the fact that the Wisconsin Legislature has decided, as a general matter, that bias motivated offenses warrant greater maximum penalties across the

33. Editor's note: The *Dawson* Court found that evidence as to the defendant's membership in a white supremacist prison gang was irrelevant given that the victim was, like Dawson, white, so that elements of racial hatred were not involved in the killing.

board does not alter the result here. For the primary responsibility for fixing criminal penalties lies with the legislature.

Mitchell argues that the Wisconsin penalty enhancement statute is invalid because it punishes the defendant's discriminatory motive, or reason, for acting. But motive plays the same role under the Wisconsin statute as it does under federal and state antidiscrimination laws, which we have previously upheld against constitutional challenge. Title VII of the Civil Rights Act of 1964, for example, makes it unlawful for an employer to discriminate against an employee "*because of* such individual's race, color, religion, sex, or national origin." 42 U.S.C. § 2000e 2(a)(1) In *Hishon*, we rejected the argument that Title VI infringed employers' First Amendment rights. And more recently, in *R.A.V. v. St. Paul*, we cited Title VII (as well as 18 U.S.C. § 242 and 42 U.S.C. §§ 1981 and 1982) as an example of a permissible content neutral regulation of conduct.

Nothing in our decision last Term in *R.A.V.* compels a different result here. That case involved a First Amendment challenge to a municipal ordinance prohibiting the use of "'fighting words' that insult, or provoke violence, `on the basis of race, color, creed, religion or gender.'" Because the ordinance only proscribed a class of "fighting words" deemed particularly offensive by the city—i.e., those "that contain ... messages of 'bias motivated' hatred,"—we held that it violated the rule against content-based discrimination. But whereas the ordinance struck down in *R.A.V.* was explicitly directed at expression (i.e., "speech" or "messages"), the statute in this case is aimed at conduct unprotected by the First Amendment.

Moreover, the Wisconsin statute singles out for enhancement bias inspired conduct because this conduct is thought to inflict greater individual and societal harm. For example, according to the State and its *amici*, bias motivated crimes are more likely to provoke retaliatory crimes, inflict distinct emotional harms on their victims, and incite community unrest. See, e.g., Brief for the Anti-Defamation League et al. as Amici Curiae.... The State's desire to redress these perceived harms provides an adequate explanation for its penalty enhancement provision over and above mere disagreement with offenders' beliefs or biases. As Blackstone said long ago, "it is but reasonable that among crimes of different natures those should be most severely punished, which are the most destructive of the public safety and happiness."

Finally, there remains to be considered Mitchell's argument that the Wisconsin statute is unconstitutionally overbroad because of its "chilling effect" on free speech. Mitchell argues (and the Wisconsin Supreme Court agreed) that the statute is "overbroad" because evidence of the defendant's prior speech or associations may be used to prove that the defendant intentionally selected his victim on account of the victim's protected status. Consequently, the argument goes, the statute impermissibly chills free expression with respect to such matters by those concerned about the possibility of enhanced sentences if they should in the future commit a criminal offense covered by the statute. We find no merit in this contention.

The sort of chill envisioned here is far more attenuated and unlikely than that contemplated in traditional "overbreadth" cases. We must conjure up a vision of a

Wisconsin citizen suppressing his unpopular bigoted opinions for fear that if he later commits an offense covered by the statute, these opinions will be offered at trial to establish that he selected his victim on account of the victim's protected status, thus qualifying him for penalty enhancement. To stay within the realm of rationality, we must surely put to one side minor misdemeanor offenses covered by the statute, such as negligent operation of a motor vehicle; for it is difficult, if not impossible, to conceive of a situation where such offenses would be racially motivated. We are left, then, with the prospect of a citizen suppressing his bigoted beliefs for fear that evidence of such beliefs will be introduced against him at trial if he commits a more serious offense against person or property. This is simply too speculative a hypothesis to support Mitchell's overbreadth claim.

The First Amendment, moreover, does not prohibit the evidentiary use of speech to establish the elements of a crime or to prove motive or intent. Evidence of a defendant's previous declarations or statements is commonly admitted in criminal trials subject to evidentiary rules dealing with relevancy, reliability, and the like.

The Rationale for Hate Crimes Laws

1. *ADL model hate crimes legislation* (1981). The ADL played a pioneering role in developing and promoting hate crime legislation in the US. In 1981, the organization drafted a model hate crimes law with two components: a law providing for enhanced penalties for certain bias-motivated crimes; and a law prohibiting vandalism of places of worship, cemeteries, schools, and community centers. At least 45 states and the District of Columbia have since enacted laws based on or similar to the ADL model.[34]

2. *The prototypical hate crime.* Mitchell exemplifies the prototypical hate crime, which Frederick Lawrence identifies as consisting of:

a. multiple assailants
b. terrorizing an individual victim
c. whom they have never met before
d. solely because of the victim's group, and
e. causing the victim great physical harm

> "As opposed to the perpetrators of other crimes," explains Lawrence, "perpetrators of bias crimes are more likely to be strangers to their victims, having focused *exclusively* on race in selecting the victim." Lawrence iden-

34. Steven M. Freeman, *The Anti-Defamation League and the Evolution of Hate Crime Laws*, 27 Lewis & Clark L. Rev. 1037, 1042 (2024); *see also* Michael Lieberman & Steven M. Freeman, *Confronting Violent Bigotry: Hate Crime Laws and Legislation*, *in* 5 Hate Crimes 1–30 (2009); *see also Pioneering Hate Crime Legislation and Advocacy: ADL's Legacy of Addressing Violent Bigotry in America*, The Anti-Defamation League, https:/www.adl.org/sites/default/files/documents/assets/pdf/combating-hate/Hate-Crimes-2-pager.pdf (last visited Nov. 20, 2024); *see also* The Anti-Defamation League, *ADL (Anti-Defamation League) Model Legislation: A Primer for Action Legislation*, *in* Bias Crime: American Law Enforcement and Legal Responses 206–209 (1993).

tifies the "fungibility of victims" as an essential component of the bias crime.[35]

3. *The arithmetic of thought crime law.* Susan Gellman writes:

> The only substantive element of most hate crime statutes is that the defendant had a bias motive for committing the base offense. As motive consists solely of the defendant's thoughts, the additional penalty for motive amounts to a thought crime which offends the First Amendment.[36]

Gabriel S. Mendlow characterizes this position as follows:

> If a crime motivated by hatred or prejudice is punished more harshly than an otherwise identical crime not so motivated, then the difference in punishment necessarily amounts to separate punishment for the offender's hatred or prejudice.[37]

Had Mitchell not selected his victim because of his race, he would have faced up to two years for aggravated battery. Because of his race-based selection criteria, he faced up to five years under the Wisconsin statute, for a combined total of seven years. The court sentenced Mitchell to four years, or 48 months. How can those years be apportioned between the aggravated assault and the penalty enhancement? Per Gellman, we might surmise that 2/7 of Mitchell's four-year sentence represents his penalty for the aggravated assault, and 5/7 of the four years represents his thought crime. Does this add up?

4. *A subtractive fallacy?* Mendlow rejects an arithmetical account of penalty-enhancing laws:

> When the law provides that some aggravating factor increases the punishment for a given crime, one need not (and generally ought not) construe the additional quantum of punishment as separate punishment for the aggravating factor. In Michigan, offenders who commit a robbery can ordinarily be punished by up to fifteen years in prison, but if they "represent orally ... that ... [they are] in possession of a dangerous weapon," they can be punished by up to life in prison. Suppose you are sentenced to twenty-five years after committing a robbery in the course of which you claimed to have a gun. I submit that it would be exceedingly odd, even absurd, to say that your prison sentence represents punishment for two separate wrongs—fifteen years for the robbery and ten for the statement about the gun. Your statement surely doesn't warrant ten years in prison; in itself it might not warrant any punishment at all. But the "armed" robbery, a unitary wrong, could well warrant twenty-five years. Your statement increases the overall punishment by making the robbery a worse robbery, not by serving as a separate wrong that receives a separate punish-

35. Lawrence, *supra* note 31, at 39.

36. Susan Gellman, *Hate Crime Laws Are Thought Crime Laws*, 1993 Ann. Surv. Am. L. 509, 514–515.

37. Gabriel S. Mendlow, *Thoughts, Crimes, and Thought Crimes*, 118 Mich. L. Rev. 841, 871–872 (2020).

> ment. We would commit a kind of subtractive fallacy if we subtracted the fifteen-year maximum sentence for unarmed robbery from your twenty-five-year sentence for armed robbery and concluded that the law was imposing a ten-year punishment for your having claimed to be armed. Punishment for armed robbery can't be disaggregated into multiple punishments for the offense's multiple constituents.[38]

5. *Should bias crimes be punished more severely?* There are several arguments for punishing crimes motivated by group animus more severely than the same underlying offense committed without bias.

a. The perpetrators of such are intrinsically more blameworthy and thus deserve more punishment.
b. Additional punishment is required to deter bias crimes adequately.
c. Victims of bias crimes suffer more harm than victims of the same crime not motivated by group animus.
d. Bias crimes inflict more harm on the target community than on other members of society.
e. Bias crimes inflict more harm on society as a whole.
f. Such laws are necessary to express society's great disapproval of bias crimes.

Which arguments provide the most persuasive rationale for enacting such laws? For enforcing such a law? Which rationale provides the best criteria for setting the sentences of specific bias criminals? At what point does the magnitude of the penalty enhancement become disproportionate to the underlying offense? For example, if the penalty for simple vandalism is up to 30 days, is a 75-day penalty enhancement excessive? 125 days? One year? Five years?[39]

6. *Opportunistic thought crime law?* Does the statute effectively burden bigots more than non-bigots? Had Mitchell acted without a discriminatory mental state, he would have served no more than two years. In this sense, his bigotry caused the enhanced penalty. Did the legislature specifically intend to harm bigots for their bigotry as a free-standing goal, independent of any attempt to deter bias crimes? Consider these possibilities.

7. Assume the legislature's sole goal in enacting a bias crimes law was to harm bigots and experience gratification as they suffer for their bigotry. Its purpose is to generate *schadenfreude*.[40] The statute advances this goal by punishing conduct unique to bigots,

---

38. *Id.* at 872.

39. *See* Alexander Tsesis, *Contextualizing Bias Crimes: A Social and Theoretical Perspective*, 28 L. & Soc. Inquiry 315 *passim* (2003).

40. *Schadenfreude* is the "malicious enjoyment of the misfortunes of others." *Schadenfreude*, Oxford Eng. Dictionary, (last visited Nov. 22, 2024). Compare פּורימשפּילמאַכן (purim-shpil-makhn) (mock anti-Semites in a festive and elaborate manner) and אַנטיסעמיטן־פּלאָצן־נחת (antisemitn-platsn-nakhes) (pleasure derived from the downfall of an anti-Semite). Note from Julian Max Katz Rappaport to Robert Katz (on file with author).

as only bigots commit bias crimes. (No non-bigot suffers from the enactment of such a law.) The statute, in effect, seizes upon a bigot's commission of a bias crime as the *occasion* to make him suffer for his bigotry—like prosecuting Al Capone for tax evasion. Serendipitously, the statute also deters the commission of bias crimes.

a. The legislature specifically intended the statute to deter bias crimes *and* make bigots suffer for their bigotry.

b. The legislature specifically intended to deter bias crimes. Although it was aware the statute would harm some bigots by causing them to suffer for their bigotry, it did not specifically intend this result.

Which possibility seems most plausible? Does the legislature's intent affect the First Amendment analysis? Does what the legislature intended matter on any level? Insofar as a bias crimes law causes bigots to suffer for their bigotry, is this something to be deplored?

8. *The costs of being at odds with society.* Philosopher David Brax argues that hate crimes laws may deter such crimes by increasing "the cost of being at odds with the expressed values of society." One effect of such laws is to discourage bigotry by tapping into people's desire to conform.[41] Is that a bad thing?

9. *Chilling effect.* Chief Justice Rehnquist does not deny that the Wisconsin statute might deter some bigots from engaging in constitutionally protected (bigoted) speech in order to avoid creating evidence in a potential bias crimes prosecution. Instead, he concludes that the chilling effect is so slight or "speculative" as to be constitutionally insignificant. Might bias crime laws also chill speech beyond their reach, such as the speech of non-violent, law-abiding bigots? Do such laws put moral, social, or other non-legal pressure on such persons to avoid making bigoted statements? How would you feel if someone told you, accurately, that "if you are ever prosecuted for a bias crime, what you just said can and will be used against you in a court of law"?

10. *Anti-discrimination law.* Title VII permits an employer to take adverse action against an employee for almost any reason, or none, unless it discriminates against an employee because of their protected group.[42] The Wisconsin statute might be compared to Title VII in that both prohibit the intentional selection of an individual for adverse action based on their membership in a protected group.[43] Chief Justice Rehnquist found this comparison meaningful while the Wisconsin Supreme Court did not. Who had the better of the argument?

---

41. *See Hate Crime Economics*, David Brax (May 27, 2011), https://david.brax.nu/blog/hate-crime-economic/.

42. 42 U.S.C. § 2000e-2(a)(1) provides that

> It shall be an unlawful employment practice for an employer to fail or refuse to hire or to discharge any individual, or otherwise to discriminate against any individual with respect to his compensation, terms, conditions, or privileges of employment, because of such individual's race, color, religion, sex, or national origin.

43. *Hate Crime Laws: The ADL Approach*, The Anti-Defamation League (Nov. 2, 2019), https://www.adl.org/resources/tools-and-strategies/hate-crime-laws-adl-approach.

11. *Bigots and gay people.* In enacting the law, did the Wisconsin legislature thereby express its moral disapproval of bigotry and, by extension, its disapproval of bigotry in general and all who hold bigoted beliefs? Consider the Texas "homosexual conduct" law struck down in *Lawrence v. Texas* (2003).[44] That law made it illegal for people of the same sex, but not men and women, to engage in certain sex acts. The Supreme Court invalidated the law on the grounds that it violated the Due Process clauses. Justice O'Connor, who concurred in the judgment, would have struck down the law on the Equal Protection Clause, which requires state classifications of persons to be rationally related to a legitimate state interest. The Texas legislature penalized conduct that only same-sex oriented people engaged in, in order to express its disapproval of the mental attitude—same-sex attraction—that motivated this conduct. It put all members of this unpopular minority under the cloud of being presumptive criminals, and thus served to stigmatize them as a class.

Bigots are an unpopular minority whose defining characteristic can be so enduring as to seem immutable. Do bias crimes laws serve to stigmatize all bigots as prospective bias criminals? Do they invite comparisons to Texas's anti-sodomy law?

12. *The message behind bias crimes laws.* Is it legitimate for the state to express moral disapproval of bigotry through criminal law? Robin M. Valeri and Kevin Borgeson write that hate crimes may be understood as "message crimes" because of their intended impact on the victim's community and beyond. [45] By what other means, legal or non-legal, may the state send the counter-message that bigotry is wrong? How does their efficacy compare to bias crimes law?

13. *Justifications for imposing harsher sentences.* Professor Christopher Heath Wellman summarizes several arguments in favor of imposing harsher punishments for hate crimes. These include:

a. Hate crimes cause broader societal harm and tension.
b. They degrade not just the direct victim but also secondary victims from the targeted group. They send harmful messages that need to be countered by society.
c. Hate criminals may require more intense moral education.
d. The increased social cost of hate crimes justifies stronger deterrence.
e. Both the act (actus reus) and the mindset (mens rea) of hate criminals are considered more morally reprehensible.[46]

44. Lawrence v. Texas, 539 U.S. 558 (2003)

45. Robin Maria Valeri & Kevin Borgeson, Hate Crimes Typology, Motivations, and Victims 54 (2d ed. 2023).

46. Christopher Heath Wellman, *A Defense of Stiffer Penalties for Hate Crimes*, 21 Hypatia 62 *passim* (2006).

Mental State for a Hate Crime: Discriminatory Selection vs. Group Animus

1. On Monday, Thief T sees two people carrying backpacks. A is wearing a Mets hat and B is wearing a Red Sox hat. T flips a coin and says, "heads Mets fan; tails Red Sox fan." The coin turns up heads and T robs A, the Mets fan. On Tuesday, T again sees two people carrying backpacks. C is Black, and D is White. T flips a coin and says, "heads Black; tails White." The coin turns up heads and T robs C, the Black person. Were T's actions more blameworthy on Tuesday than Monday? If T is convicted for both robberies, should his sentence be aggravated for robbing C? Does it matter whether T is a white racist?

2. *Intentional selection.* The jury found that Mitchell had intentionally selected his victim because of the boy's race. The Wisconsin statute did not require the jury to ascertain *why* Mitchell selected the boy because of his race, i.e., his motive. Defending the statute, the Wisconsin attorney general asserted that "the statute would have applied to Todd Mitchell if his sole motivation in selecting a white victim had been to impress his friends and if Mitchell himself was otherwise indifferent as to the choice of his victim."[47] Did the attorney general accurately construe the statute? If so, should this construction be rejected?

Lawrence describes the Wisconsin statute as the archetypal "discriminatory selection" bias crimes law. (They are also known as "intentional selection" laws.) Under this model, "it is irrelevant why an offender selected his victim on the basis of race or group; it is sufficient that the offender did so." He notes "many cases of discriminatory victim selection are in fact also cases of racial animus—perhaps most, but not all."[48]

3. *Group animus laws.* Contrast intentional selection statutes with the "group animus" model, which focuses on whether a "defendant has acted out of hatred for the victim's racial group or the victim for being a member of that group."[49] *See, e.g.*, 18 Pa. Cons. Stat. § 2710 (penalty enhanced for offenses "motivated by hatred toward" the victim's protected group); Arizona Ariz. Rev. Stat. Ann. § 13–701(D)(15) (Penalty enhancement when the offender "committed the crime out of malice toward" victim's group); Ga. Code Ann. § 17-10-17 (2017) (penalty enhanced if "the defendant intentionally selected any victim ... because of bias or prejudice" towards the victim's group); Haw. Rev. Stat. § 706–662 (offender "intentionally selected a victim ... because of hostility toward the" victim's protected group).

4. *Mitchell and the two models.* For what proposition does *Mitchell* stand: that states may enhance sentences for offenders who: (a) select their victims out of animus for the victim's protected group; or (b) select their victims based on their membership in a protected group but are not motivated by animus towards that group? Does Chief

---

47. Lawrence, *supra* note 31, at 215 n.20.

48. *Id.* at 30.

49. *Id.* at 29.

Justice Rehnquist's opinion illuminate or elide the distinction between intentional selection and group animus statutes?

5. *Is the group animus model preferable?* Lawrence would restrict bias crimes law to offenders motivated by group animus. To illustrate his position, Lawrence considers a non-misogynistic purse snatcher who:

> preys exclusively upon women because he believes that he will better achieve his criminal goals by grabbing purses from women than by trying to pick wallets out of the pockets of men. The Purse Snatcher discriminatorily selects his victims on the basis of gender, but he has no animus toward women as a group, nor are his thefts motivated by any attitudes about women other than the manner in which they carry their valuables.[50]

Purse carriers and wallet carriers are not protected classes. The non-misogynistic purse snatcher's criminal goal is to steal purses, at which he excels, and he uses gender as a proxy for purse-carrying. His targeting of women seems instrumental and opportunistic. If more men carried purses than women, he would presumably target men. Is this a satisfactory account of why this purse snatcher is less blameworthy than an animus-motivated offender? Compare this character to a misogynistic purse snatcher who, though equally adept at snatching purses and wallets, targets purses because women tend to carry them, and favors purses because of their gender association.

Brawl Between Red Sox and Mets Fans at UMass Turns Racial

1. *Post-game violence at University of Massachusetts Amherst.* On October 27, 1986, the New York Mets defeated the Boston Red Sox, 8–5, winning the World Series. The Red Sox were widely perceived as "the white team" and the Mets as "the Black team."[51] Many UMass students watched the game on campus. After the game, fighting broke out among students as they poured out of their dorms.[52] It sparked an incident that

---

50. *Id.* at 173–74.

51. The Red Sox were the last team to integrate, not doing so until 1959 with Pumpsie Green, 12 years after Jackie Robinson. Delaney Colson, *#Shortstops: A Reluctant Trailblazer,* NAT'L BASEBALL HALL OF FAME, https://baseballhall.org/discover/Shortstops-A-reluctant-trailblazer#:~:text=Twelve%20years%20after%20Jackie%20Robinson,to%20sign%20anyone%20until%201959. (last visited Nov. 2, 2024). *See also* Gabriel Fernandez, *Boston Red Sox Release Statement Acknowledging Racism from Fans at Fenway Park Directed at Players,* CBS SPORTS (June 10, 2020, 6:33 PM), https://www.cbssports.com/mlb/news/boston-red-sox-release-statement-acknowledging-racism-from-fans-at-fenway-park-directed-at-players/; *see also* Chris Bengel, *Kevin Youkilis: Red Sox Teammates Were Victims of Racism by Boston Fans at Fenway Park,* CBS SPORTS (June 12, 2020, 1:36 PM), https://www.cbssports.com/mlb/news/kevin-youkilis-red-sox-teammates-were-victims-of-racism-by-boston-fans-at-fenway-park/.

52. Matthew L. Wald, *Racism Blamed for Brawl at U. of Massachusetts,* N.Y. TIMES, Feb. 6, at A12, https://www.nytimes.com/1987/02/06/us/racism-blamed-for-brawl-at-u-of-massachusetts.html.

involved from 1,200 to 3,000 students and left ten people injured, including a Black student who was beaten unconscious.[53]

At some point during the incident, which continued past midnight, groups of white students began assaulting random Black students, without inquiring if they were Mets fans. Many of the instigators were reportedly white members of the football team. In its report on the events that night, the Massachusetts Commission Against Discrimination wrote:

> No one present that night can explain quite why or how, but the focus of the crowd perceptibly shifted toward the Black students.... It seemed as though the crowd was unconsciously focusing on a surrogate target against which to take revenge for the Sox loss, and that surrogate target conveniently became black students.[54]

The Commission determined that the events were "primarily racially motivated."[55] UMass Chancellor Joseph Duffey gave a more nuanced account:

> What happened that night was not a totally racial event. People saw different things. If you were on the edge of the crowd you could see it as a fight or a brawl. If you were a black student chased and beaten, it was a racial event. If you were one of the white students chasing [Black] people, it was racial.

2. *White students' lived experience.* Chancellor Duffy suggests that there is no objective truth about what happened at UMass that night; it depends on your perspective. Consider the following possible mindsets of White student/Red Sox fans who assaulted Black students (and presumptive Mets fans):

a. Some were consciously motivated by racism.

b. Some were subconsciously motivated by racism, but believed their actions were motivated by team loyalty.

c. Some were motivated by team loyalty, not racism, and they had no reason to think that Black victims would perceive assaults as racially motivated.

d. Some students were motivated by team loyalty, not racism, but they had reason to think that Black victims would perceive the assaults as racially motivated.

3. *Black students' lived experience.* Consider the following possible mindsets of Black students assaulted by White students/Red Sox fans.

a. In some instances, victims believed they were being assaulted for their team affiliation. Some were correct and some were not, i.e., their assaulters were in fact motivated by racism.

b. In some instances, victims believed that the assaults were racially motivated. Some were correct and some were not, i.e., their assaulters objected to their team affiliation.

---

53. *Id.*
54. *Id.*
55. *Id.*

How do we describe an incident where (i) the victim perceives an assault as racially motivated and experiences it as such, but (ii) the attacker was neither consciously nor subconsciously motivated by racial animus? Should we chalk this up to the victim's hypersensitivity or paranoia? Was the victim's perception reasonable? Was the attacker unreasonably oblivious to the possibility that the victim would perceive the assault as racially motivated?

4. *Intentional selection?* Following the Red Sox' defeat, White student Y asked a group of fellow White students/Red Sox fans, "Do you feel hyped up to move on some Mets fans?" Leaving their dorm, they see P, a Black person whom they've never met and who is not wearing Mets regalia. Y says, "There's a Mets fan. Go get him!" Y and the group assault the Black student, rendering him unconscious. Did Y commit a bias crime under an intentional selection bias crimes law? Under a group animus model? Consider the following scenarios suggested by Lawrence.

a. Y consciously hates Black people and, by extension, the Mets, which he conceives of as a Black collectivity. He used the occasion of the Red Sox defeat to assault a Black person.

b. Y doesn't hate Black people, nor does he hate the Mets *because* of its perception as the "Black team." He hates the Mets because they beat the Red Sox and hates Mets fans for supporting their team. He selected a Black person because he wanted to assault Mets fans and used Blackness as a (perhaps reliable) proxy for Mets fandom. Had there been a more reliable predictor of Mets fandom—say, height (the Mets were the "tall team")—he would have targeted tall people.

c. Y is an unconscious racist who falsely believed he was motivated by a desire to attack Mets fans. In truth, he subconsciously equated Black people with Mets fans.

5. *A semi-conscious racist?* What if Y had an inkling that he was prejudiced against Blacks? Lawrence describes such a person as having:

> Some reason to know of his unconscious racism; for example, he knows that he feels exceedingly uncomfortable around people of races other than his own. Suppose he puts himself in a position where this unconscious racism is likely to come to the surface. He spends time at a bar frequented by a violent racist gang. On one occasion, a racist assault is committed by the gang. He joins in the attack, claiming afterwards that he shared the gang's purpose to assault, but not their racism.

Lawrence compares this person to a recidivist sleepwalker—someone "who knows that he is prone to cause harm to others while sleepwalking"—but "fails to take precaution" not to cause such harm.[56]

6. *Second-degree (reckless) bias crime?* Assume Y, the unconscious racist, lacked the requisite motivation for a group animus bias crime. Even so, did it occur to him that,

---

56. Lawrence, *supra* note 31, at 70.

in chasing down and attacking random Black people, his conduct might be perceived as motivated by group animus? Was he aware of the "bias crimes" optics of his activity? In such circumstances, should society expect him to alter his conduct based on such awareness? Should the law impose a new and distinct legal duty of care upon him and others?

Consider Lawrence's proposal for what he terms a "second-degree bias crime" based on recklessness:

a. A person is guilty of a second-degree bias crime if he commits any crime against a person or property in this state's criminal code (the "parallel crime") with conscious disregard for the substantial and unjustifiable risk that his conduct will be perceived by the individual victim or victim target group to have been motivated in substantial part by ill will, hatred, or animus due to the real or perceived race, color, religion [and other protected characteristic] of the victim.

b. "A second-degree bias crime is a felony and shall be punished by a term of imprisonment and/or fine that exceeds that of the relevant parallel crime by one level."[57]

7. *Teenager sprays swastika.* Consider two scenarios involving Z, a teenager who sprays swastikas on a building for the "thrill" of it and out of a desire to cause a great public upset, but without consciously intending to cause particular harm to Jews. Lawrence calls this person the "unknowingly offensive actor." How should his offense be characterized? An intentional selection bias crime? A group animus bias crime? A second-degree bias crime? Does the characterization change depending upon the building, e.g., a synagogue instead of a drug store?

8. *Alternatives to increased criminal penalties.* Alternative approaches to hate crimes, which are not mutually exclusive, include:

a. *Restorative justice.* Restorative justice programs entail facilitated meetings between victims, offenders, and sometimes community representatives. In these meetings, the victims typically share the impact of the crime on them and their community; the offenders take responsibility; and the participants develop a plan for the offender to make amends.

b. *Victim support.* Provide support for targeted communities, including victim compensation, mental health services, security grants, legal advocacy, and community education and outreach programs.[58]

c. *Education.* Reduce bigotry through education, including courses on antisemitism.

---

57. *Id.* at 171.

58. Stanford L. Sch. L. & Pol'y Lab, Exploring Alternative Approaches to Hate Crimes 24–34 (2021), https://law.stanford.edu/wp-content/uploads/2021/06/Alternative-to-Hate-Crimes-Report_v09-final.pdf.

D. Hate Crimes Law in Practice

Senate Bill 198 (2019):
Indiana's Hate Crime Statute

Ind. Code § 35-38-1-7.1(a)(12): Considerations in imposing sentence

In determining what sentence to impose for a crime, the court may consider the following aggravating circumstances.... The person committed the offense with bias due to the victim's or the group's real or perceived characteristic, trait, belief, practice, association, or other attribute the court chooses to consider, including but not limited to an attribute described in IC 10-13-3-1.

Ind. Code § 10-13-3-1: "Bias crime"

As used in this chapter, "bias crime" means an offense in which the person who commits the offense knowingly or intentionally: (1) selected the person who was injured; or (2) damaged or otherwise affected property; by the offense because of the color, creed, disability, national origin, race, religion, or sexual orientation of the injured person or of the owner or occupant of the affected property or because the injured person or owner or occupant of the affected property was associated with any other recognizable group or affiliation.

Ind. Code § 10-13-3-38

(a) A law enforcement agency shall collect information concerning bias crimes.

(b) At least two (2) times each year, a law enforcement agency shall submit information collected under subsection (a) to the Indiana central repository for criminal history information. Information shall be reported in the manner and form prescribed by the department.

Is This a True Hate Crimes Statute?

1. *A nothing burger?* Indiana judges have always had discretion to enhance a criminal defendant's sentence based on circumstances they deem relevant. This includes the ability to aggravate a sentence based on the racially motivated nature of a crime, even where the sentencing statute does not list racial motivation as an aggravating circumstance: the list is not exclusive. *See Witmer v. State*, 800 N.E.2d 571 (Ind. 2003). The law also does not require Indiana judges to enhance a defendant's sentence if certain circumstances are present, nor does it require them to consider these circumstances in setting the sentence. This is true even if a jury finds that the defendant's crime was motivated by bias against a group's members. SB 198 is best understood as a codification of the status quo. Assuming SB 198 has little if any legal value, could it be valuable in other respects?

2. *Checking it twice.* If SB 198 didn't change anything legally, why did the Indiana General Assembly bother to enact it? ADL advocacy was a driving force. Indiana Governor Eric J. Holcomb encouraged the General Assembly to enact a hate crimes

law that would remove it from the ADL's list of states without hate crimes law—a list that presently includes Arkansas, South Carolina, and Wyoming. This state of affairs, Holcomb claimed, was hurting Indiana's attempts to recruit businesses to the state. "There's no reason why we can't be on the same list as our competitors like Florida and Tennessee and Virginia and Texas," he said. "We need to get on the right list and off the list that's holding us potentially back."

3. *Not ADL-approved.* SB 198 did not persuade the ADL to remove it from the list of states without hate crimes laws. In the ADL's view:

> The law's deliberate failure to explicitly list gender identity, gender, and sex is unacceptable. And because of its uniquely and problematically broad language, we do not even consider it a hate crimes law. The fact that it includes such broad, undefined terms as "belief," "practice," and "association"—unconnected to personal characteristics, immutability and a history of targeted discrimination/violence—means that it could encompass virtually any crime targeting a person for virtually any reason, thus diluting the concept and undermining the intended purpose of a hate crimes law. This framing is a clear departure from the approach taken in any other hate crime law in America.60

Indiana legislators may have thought that the statute they enacted would get Indiana off of ADL's list. But after SB 198 passed, Governor Holcomb changed the bar by emphasizing the U.S. Department of Justice's determination that SB 198 constituted a hate crimes law. What does this experience teach us about the efficacy and limits of Jewish advocacy groups' power to persuade?

4. *Special treatment?* Some conservatives opposed the statute on grounds that "it would unfairly create specially protected classes of victims." Professor Wellman notes:

> [The objection] to meting out harsher punishments for hate crimes is that, like affirmative action, it creates special rights. That is, if people who hate minorities are punished more strenuously for indulging their hatred, then minorities are being given extra protection. Insofar as we construct special criminal laws to deter people from satisfying their desires to put down members of a minority group, there is a sense in which we are ascribing special rights to these minorities. But this seems unjust. As terrible as hate crimes are, we should not resort to unjust measures to combat them. Given that we are all equal, minorities have no right to see their enemies punished more, and thus laws that reserve an exalted status for minorities are illegitimate. While it is horrible that some groups have been oppressed, those who voice this objection suggest that the appropriate response is to work diligently to end the oppression, not to add a second wrong in the misguided hope of making things right.[59]

What are potential responses to this objection? To what extent do they track arguments in favor of affirmative action? Does it matter that in the landmark *Mitchell* case, the victim was White?

---

59. Wellman, *supra* note 46, at 71–72.

5. *Some assembly required.* SB 198 separates out the law's operative language (Ind. Code § 35-38-1-7.1) from the enumerated list of protected groups (Ind. Code § 10-13-3-1), referencing the latter in the former. Why is that? What political, legislative, or other purpose(s) does the separation serve?

6. *Underinclusive?* SB 198 omits gender and gender identity from the enumerated list of protected classes.[60] SB 198's defenders correctly observed that the law does not disturb a judge's discretion to punish crimes motivated by bias against such groups. According to former Indiana Supreme Court Justice Frank Sullivan, Jr., "You [the perpetrator] are subject to getting every bit severe of a sentence, every bit as much time as if your target was in a category in the bill."[61] Is that a satisfactory response? If SB 198 does not preclude aggravated sentences for bias crimes based on gender and gender identity, the same is true for bias crimes based on color, creed, disability, national origin, race, religion, or sexual orientation. Why did SB 198 include the latter but not the former? Why did it specify *any* group as protected? Would not the catch-all provision catch all these groups? Is a hate crime law that doesn't enumerate gender and gender identity better or worse than no law at all? Does the statute discriminate against transgender persons by not enumerating them?[62] Does it discriminate against blue-eyed people?

7. *Overinclusive?* What was the point of recognizing the court's authority to aggravate a sentence where "the person committed the offense with bias due to the victim's or the group's real or perceived characteristic, trait, belief, practice, association, or other attribute the court chooses to consider"? This would presumably include crimes committed against blue-eyed people motivated by animus against such people. The ADL expressed "serious concerns that an over-generalized bill ... could actually cause harm by being used to further marginalize communities of color and minority religious communities, the exact opposite of the bill's original intent." Why might that be? SB 198's defenders argued that this broad language was a feature, not a flaw; it was better than "trying to craft a list that could cover every conceivable trait that might cause someone to be a victim of a bias crime."

---

60. In 2022, the FBI reported a 32.9 percent jump in reported hate crimes based on gender identity. Delphine Luneau, *FBI's Annual Crime Report—Amid State of Emergency, Anti-LGBTQ+ Hate Crimes Hit Staggering Record Highs*, Hum. Rts. Campaign (Oct. 16, 2023), https://www.hrc.org/press-releases/fbis-annual-crime-report-amid-state-of-emergency-anti-lgbtq-hate-crimes-hit-staggering-record-highs.

61. Kayla Sullivan, *Is Indiana Off the List of States Without a Hate Crime Law?*, FOX59 (July 1, 2019, 6:41 PM), https://fox59.com/news/indycrime/is-indiana-off-the-list-of-states-without-a-hate-crime-law/.

62. On April 5, 2023, the Indiana General Assembly enacted Senate Enrolled Act 480, which prohibits transgender minors from receiving what the law labels as "gender transition procedures." S.E.A. 480, 123rd Gen. Assemb., 1st Reg. Sess. (Ind. 2023).

8. *Unconstitutionally vague?* The ACLU of Indiana criticized the statute's language as inviting legal challenges on grounds that it is "unconstitutional, violating due process and threatening to suppress free speech."[63] Are they right?

9. *No* Apprendi *problem. Apprendi v. New Jersey* (2000)[64] bars courts from aggravating sentences for crimes motivated by group animus unless the state proves beyond a reasonable doubt that the defendant was so motivated. An offender's intentional selection of a victim based on group membership is relevant insofar as it is probative of an underlying group animus. Indiana judges can generally enhance a sentence based on biased motive without the prosecution being required, as per *Apprendi*, to prove biased motive beyond a reasonable doubt. Indiana law sets maximum and minimum limits for each class of felony offenses and posits "advisory sentences" somewhere in between. Courts have discretion to depart from the advisory sentence up to the maximum or down to the minimum without any requirement that they find aggravating circumstances to exist.[65]

10. *Underreporting*. Hate crimes are traditionally one of the most underreported types of crime in the U.S. There are multiple cities with more than 500,000 people that report fewer than 10 hate crimes in a year. Because "data drives policy," official underreporting of hate crimes impairs the legal system's ability to combat them.[66] In recent years, the number of reported hate crimes in Indiana has increased, for example from 80 in 2019 to 180 in 2020. This may be due in part to efforts like the Indianapolis (Marion County) prosecutor's office creation of a hotline for reporting hate crimes.[67]

United States v. Sechriest, Government's Sentencing Memorandum

No. 22-cr-053
W.D. Tex. (Nov. 20, 2023)

[This document is a sentencing memorandum filed by the United States government in a federal hate crime case. It outlines the prosecution's argument for imposing a 120-month prison sentence followed by 3 years of supervised release on the defendant, Franklin Barrett Sechriest, for an arson attack on Congregation Beth Israel, a synagogue in Austin, Texas. Sechriest was charged with arson under 18 U.S.C. § 844(i)

---

63. *Current Hate Crimes Bill Omits Gender Identity and Threatens Free Speech*, The Am. C.L. Union Ind. (Mar. 25, 2019), https://www.aclu-in.org/en/press-releases/current-hate-crimes-bill-omits-gender-identity-and-threatens-free-speech.

64. Apprendi v. New Jersey, 530 U.S. 466

65. Frank Sullivan, Jr., *Selected Developments in Indiana Criminal Sentencing and Death Penalty Law (1993–2012)*, 49 Ind. L. Rev. 1349, 1350–1358 (2016).

66. Freeman, *supra* note 34, at 1044 (2024).

67. Katrina Pross, *Law Enforcement Says More People Are Reporting Hate Crimes than Ever Before*, WFYI (Oct. 14, 2021), https://www.wfyi.org/news/articles/law-enforcement-says-more-people-are-reporting-hate-crimes-than-ever-before; Katrina Pross, *Prosecutor's Office Launches Hate Crime Hotline*, WFYI (Aug. 24, 2021), https://www.wfyi.org/news/articles/prosecutors-office-launches-hate-crime-hotline.

and damage to religious property, a bias crime, under 18 U.S.C. § 247(c). Section 247(c) provides that:

> Whoever intentionally defaces, damages, or destroys any religious real property because of the race, color, or ethnic characteristics of any individual associated with that religious property, or attempts to do so, shall be punished [up to an additional three years' imprisonment].

The sentencing memorandum, signed by AUSA Matthew Devlin, illustrates how prosecutors build a case for enhanced sentencing in hate crime cases. It emphasizes the need for an upward variance due to the severity of the crime, the defendant's history of racially motivated violence, and the importance of deterring similar acts of antisemitic violence. Because the prosecution's case relies heavily on defendant's expression of antisemitic beliefs in his journal entries and other materials, it invites discussion of the intersection between protected speech and proving bias.]

TO THE HONORABLE JUDGE OF SAID COURT:

The United States urges the Court to impose a sentence of 120 months followed by a 3-year term of supervised release. An upward variance is necessary to reflect the seriousness of the Defendant's hateful, destructive attack on the Jewish community, to account for the characteristics of the Defendant and protect the community from the Defendant, who has committed other acts of racially-motivated violence and failed to show contrition, and to deter others from engaging in anti-Semitic and racist violence. A sentence of 120 months imprisonment would satisfy the purposes of sentencing as envisioned by the Sentencing Guidelines and 18 U.S.C. § 3553.[68]

...

III. FACTS OF DEFENDANT'S CASE

1. On October 31, 2021, Defendant SECHRIEST, by the use and attempted use of fire, intentionally and maliciously defaced, damaged, and destroyed, and attempted to deface, damage, and destroy, religious real property, namely, Congregation Beth Israel, a synagogue located in Austin, Texas, because of the race and ethnic characteristics of any individual associated with that religious property.

2. Congregation Beth Israel was at the time, and remains, a Reform Judaism synagogue serving Jewish families in Austin, Texas (hereinafter "the Synagogue"). Congregation Beth Israel was established in 1879 and is the oldest synagogue in Texas.

---

68. Editor's note: 18 U.S.C. § 3553. Section 3553(a) directs courts to consider several factors in determining the particular sentence to be imposed. These include:

(1) the nature and circumstances of the offense and the history and characteristics of the defendant;

(2) the need for the sentence imposed—

(A) to reflect the seriousness of the offense, to promote respect for the law, and to provide just punishment for the offense;

(B) to afford adequate deterrence to criminal conduct;

(C) to protect the public from further crimes of the defendant;

(D) to provide the defendant with needed educational or vocational training, medical care, or other correctional treatment in the most effective manner.

3. On October 31, 2021, video surveillance from the Synagogue's security system shows a dark SUV driving into the parking lot at around 9:00 pm. Defendant SECHRIEST, the driver and sole occupant of the vehicle, parked the SUV and got out. Defendant SECHRIEST was wearing green utility pants, a black shirt, and a mask. Shortly after he got out of the SUV, the vehicle began rolling backwards, so Defendant SECHRIEST jumped into the SUV to stop the car's backward motion. Defendant SECHRIEST then got out of the SUV a second time, leaving the driver's side door open, and walked around the front of the SUV towards the Synagogue's sanctuary with a green gas container in one hand and a roll of toilet paper in the other. He then walked back down the walkway toward the Synagogue's sanctuary entrance. Seconds later, Defendant SECHRIEST set fire to the Synagogue's sanctuary, then swiftly ran away and drove off in his SUV.

4. Shortly after the fire was set, the Austin Fire Department (AFD) responded to a 9-1-1 call and was on scene within 9 minutes. AFD arson investigators examined the scene and concluded that the fire was intentional and could have destroyed the Synagogue. They observed burn patterns consistent with the use of accelerants and ruled out all other ignition sources other than an open flame introduced by a person.

5. Additional surveillance video from the Synagogue, recorded three days earlier on the evening of October 28, 2021, showed Defendant SECHRIEST's dark SUV entering the Synagogue parking lot near the sanctuary. Defendant SECHRIEST, the driver and sole occupant of the vehicle, drove around to the front entrance of the Synagogue's Child Development Center (CDC). Surveillance footage of the area in front of the CDC shows Defendant SECHRIEST shining what appears to be a cellphone flashlight toward the entrance. The video also clearly shows the SUV's license plate number, which was used to identify the vehicle as a black Jeep Cherokee registered to Defendant SECHRIEST's mother.

6. On or about November 10, 2021, the FBI executed federal search warrants issued by the United States District Court for the Western District of Texas for Defendant SECHRIEST's residence in San Marcos, the Jeep Cherokee SUV, Defendant SECHRIEST's phone, and Defendant SECHRIEST's person. During the searches, agents discovered several items linking Defendant SECHRIEST to the Synagogue fire, including (1) green utility pants and boots matching the clothes Defendant was wearing as seen on the October 31 video surveillance footage; (2) an American Express card that was used at a local store to purchase a green gas container matching the container seen in the video; and (3) three large bottles of lighter fluid, three empty 33oz glass bottles, and storm proof matches, which were consistent with materials that could be used and combined to produce destructive devices known as Molotov cocktails.

7. In addition, during the execution of the search warrant for Defendant's residence, agents recovered from Defendant SECHRIEST's bedroom and the family dining room several journals belonging to Defendant SECHRIEST that contained numerous entries in his handwriting. In an entry from a journal found in Defendant SECHRIEST's bedroom and dated October 28, 2021 (the same date he was seen on surveillance footage

Figure 11.4. Decals in Sechriest's possession expressing antisemitic messages. *United States v. Sechriest*, Government's Sentencing Memorandum at 7 (photo).

casing the Synagogue), Defendant SECHRIEST had written the phrase "scout out a target." Another entry in the journal, dated October 31, 2021, states "I set a synagogue on fire" (Exhibit 1): [graphic of excerpt from journal]. Defendant SECHRIEST's journal entries in the first few days of November 2021 show that he was actively monitoring media reports to track the progress of the investigation into the Synagogue arson.

8. Defendant SECHRIEST intentionally targeted the Synagogue for damage and destruction because of the race and ethnic characteristics of individuals associated with the Synagogue, namely, Jewish people and people who worshiped at the Synagogue, and because of his hatred of Jews. Defendant SECHRIEST's journals are replete with virulent anti-Semitic statements and views. In one entry, Defendant SECHRIEST said he had to listen to "*a third-hand speech about the holocaust and 'hate'*" and that he "*had a long talk with mom about Jews controlling the media.*" He later wrote that he listened to another Holocaust survivor's speech and that "*They [Jews] do control the media.*" In a June 4, 2019 entry, Defendant SECHRIEST stated that he dressed like a neo-Nazi. On August 15, 2019, Defendant SECHRIEST wrote that he "*Learned why Jews cause ALL the suffering.*" In his journals, Defendant SECHRIEST claimed membership in white supremacist organizations, including the Asatru Folk Assembly (AFA), which preaches racist doctrines based on a belief in ethnic Germanic superiority. Defendant SECHRIEST also stated that he planned to get a ring with Thor's Hammer, a symbol often appropriated by neo-Nazi groups.

9. Defendant Sechriest also possessed several decals expressing anti-Semitic messages. One decal in particular expressed deep hatred for and threatening language about Jews. The decal featured images of a police officer, a doctor, and a person behind a pulpit or *bimah*, each with a Star of David on them, each with a red "X" over the face. Above the three figures, the sticker reads in bold and with capital letters, "*Would you KILL THEM ALL to seize your rights?*" and below the figures, between two red swastikas, it reads, "*The price of freedom is paid in BLOOD.*"

10. At the time of the fire, the real property of the Synagogue was used in interstate commerce and used in activities affecting interstate commerce. In particular, the Synagogue operates and maintains its CDC that runs preschool programs open to both members and non-members of the Synagogue. The CDC is structurally connected to the sanctuary portion of the Synagogue that was set on fire.

11. Defendant SECHRIEST intentionally defaced, damaged, and destroyed, and attempted to deface, damage, and destroy the Synagogue, religious real property, because of the race and ethnic characteristics of individuals associated with that religious property. Defendant SECHRIEST intentionally set fire to the Synagogue causing damage to the religious real property and personal property of the Synagogue....

Legal and Ethical Considerations in Hate Crime Sentencing

1. The government's Memo identified several factors that it claimed warranted an increased sentence under Section 3553(a):

a. In his journals, Defendant wrote about making Molotov cocktails and obtaining and using firearms.

b. "Defendant's hate-filled journal entries and other statements of hate are aggravating factors in and of themselves."

c. He wrote a "missive" against the Congregation and the ADL, exclaiming that they "can rot in hell for buying off my first lawyer"—conspiratorial thinking—and that the FBI, "egged on" by the ADL, would show no mercy to him.

d. He showed no remorse or regret for his conduct.

e. He caused great harm to the Jewish community.

f. There was a need to deter bias crimes.

g. There was a special need to deter anti-Jewish violence because of the increased incidence of antisemitic incidents in and around Austin and the "growing tide of antisemitism" more generally [19–20].

h. Which factors for enhancing Sechriest's sentence do you find more or less compelling than others? What punishment rationale underlies each cited factor?

2. *Indoctrinated to hate.* In *U.S. v. Sechriest*, the government's sentencing memo stated that at the time of the offense, "Defendant was attending Texas State, and was aca-

demically high-performing in high school, meaning he had the capacity to knowingly embrace his hateful, violent agenda." Jacobs and Potter ask whether indoctrinated hate criminals deserve lesser sentences.

> Should [hate crimes] offenders be held fully responsible for their prejudices? A prejudiced offender might plea that he is *less culpable* than a "cold-blooded" profit-motivated criminal, because he was indoctrinated by his parents and youthful peers. He might argue that he was brought up to believe that homosexuals, women, Jews, blacks, and/or others are inferior, evil, immoral, hostile, etc. He might even argue that his prejudice, for example, against homosexuals, was the result of religious training. According to this account, his prejudice was imposed, not chosen, and should make him a candidate for a lesser punishment, not a greater one.[69]

Should the indoctrinated antisemitic offender receive a more lenient sentence than a confirmed anti-Semite who comes to his antisemitism in the full light of his consciousness and conscience?

3. *Additional disturbing statements.* The government submitted excerpts from Sechriest's journal, with portions highlighted for the court's convenience, including:

a. "Listened to White power music"

b. "Be racist"

c. "Bash talmud"

d. "Solidify racist beliefs"

e. "Was (correctly) accused of Nazism"

f. "Learn Covid was caused by a (Jewish) American harvard [*sic*] proffessor [*sic*] smuggling bioweapons to the Chinese"

g. "Officially christen [*sic*] myself as a racist"

h. "I am a racist and do not want my mom getting ideas on curbing my radicalization process"

i. A complaint about the "insane prices" for "foreskin restoration gear."

4. *Public scrutiny of a lifetime.* As Gellman predicted, a person accused of committing a bias crime loses privacy.

> In addition to any words that a person may speak during, just prior to, or in association with the commission of one of the underlying offenses, all of his or her remarks upon earlier occasions, any books ever read, speakers ever listened to, or associations ever held could be introduced as evidence that he or she held racist views and was acting upon them at the time of the offense. Anyone charged with one of the underlying offenses could be charged with

69. James B. Jacobs & Kimberly Potter, Hate Crimes: Criminal Law and Identity Politics 81 (1998).

> [intentional selection] as well, and face the possibility of public scrutiny of a lifetime of everything from ethnic jokes to serious intellectual inquiry.[70]

Sechriest understandably regretted putting his bigoted thoughts to paper: "Above all I'm sorry for these awful journals. If I'd stopped writing like I'd wanted to I maybe could have made bail...."

Phyllis B. Gerstenfeld cites critics who argue "that to rest a hate crime conviction nearly exclusively on proof of constitutionally protected activities comes perilously close to punishing those activities themselves."[71] Does the government's use of Sechriest's journal and decal cross the line? What's the risk that the court will punish him for holding antisemitic beliefs, independent of his beliefs' relevance to his violation of Section 247(c)?

5. *Relevant?* Suppose Sechriest is charged with violating a group animus statute like Pennsylvania's, which enhances penalties for offenses "motivated by hatred toward" the victim's protected group.[72] He pleads not guilty, and his case goes to trial. The government submits the journal entries and the decal as evidence. The Federal Rules of Evidence provide that evidence is relevant if "it has any tendency to make a fact more or less probable than it would be without the evidence."[73] Which of the submitted items are relevant to the question of whether Sechriest's offense was "motivated by hatred" towards Jews?

6. *More prejudicial than probative?* Federal Rule of Evidence 403 provides that relevant evidence may be excluded if "its probative value is substantially outweighed by a danger of ... unfair prejudice...."[74] The term "'unfair prejudice' ... means an undue tendency to suggest decision on an improper basis, commonly, though not necessarily, an emotional one."[75]

> Evidence of an offender's bias "is usually offensive to many jury members," and creates a risk that "they would be so offended that they could not impartially consider the facts of the case."[76] What is an offender's attorney to do? Karl Menninger advises that:
>
> The defense attorney may choose at the beginning to acknowledge that the defendant's views may be distasteful or repugnant to members of the jury, but those views alone are not a crime, nor are they alone proof the defendant committed a hate crime. The jury should be asked to look beyond the defen-

70. Susan Gellman, *Sticks and Stones Can Put You in Jail, but Can Words Increase Your Sentence? Constitutional and Policy Dilemmas of Ethnic Intimidation Laws*, 39 UCLA L. Rev. 333, 360–361 (1991).

71. Phyllis B. Gerstenfeld, Hate Crimes: Causes, Controls and Controversies 50 (Jerry Westby et al. eds., 2d ed. 2011).

72. 18 Pa. Stat. and Cons. Stat § 2710 (West 2024).

73. Fed. R. Evid. 401.

74. Fed. R. Evid. 403.

75. Fed. R. Evid. 403, advisory committee's notes to 1972 proposed rules.

76. *Id.*

dant's beliefs, and determine whether there is proof beyond a reasonable doubt of all the elements of the crime.[77]

7. *Insane prices.* What to make of Sechriest's complaint about the "insane prices" for "foreskin restoration gear?" On one hand, Federal Rule of Evidence 403 permits relevant evidence to be excluded if the danger of confusing the issues substantially outweighs its probative value. On the other hand, the complaint may address a matter of public concern—are the prices too high? Professor Dan T. Coenen argues that the First Amendment considerations should restrict the prosecutorial use of defendants' speech on matters of public concern, even if such speech is relevant and more probative than prejudicial.[78] Note that the Federal Rules of Evidence do not rule speech admissible or inadmissible based on its content or viewpoint. Yet is the very question antisemitic and thus prejudicial to the hate crime victims?

8. *Hatred toward Jews versus antisemitic beliefs.* Some of the items in Sechriest's possession were direct expressions of hatred toward Jews, such as "*It's OK to hate them back.*" Others express biased beliefs *about* Jews, such "*They [Jews] do control the media,*" "*Jews cause ALL the suffering,*" and "*bash talmud.*" The distinction between hatred toward Jews and biased beliefs about Jews may be seen in IHRA's Working Definition: "Antisemitism is a certain perception of Jews, which may be expressed as hatred toward Jews." Such hatred is most clearly manifested by statements "calling for, aiding, or justifying the killing or harming of Jews in the name of a radical ideology or an extremist view of religion." Yet under IHRA's definition, hatred of Jews is only one expression of antisemitism. IHRA identifies certain perceptions as antisemitic, including: "the myth about a world Jewish conspiracy or of Jews controlling the media, economy, government or other societal institutions."

In theory, a person can hold certain negative beliefs about Jews without consciously hating Jews as a group or Jewish individuals. If this were not the case, then a sizable percentage of Americans would be regarded as hating Jews.

9. *Negative perceptions of Jews.* Assume that the items in Sechriest's possession contained no direct expressions of hatred towards Jews, only statements reflecting negative perceptions of Jews. Consider the statements in the ADL's survey, e.g., "Jews stick together more than other Americans." Suppose Sechriest's journal contained one or more of the statements. Which would be relevant to the question of whether Sechriest's attack on the synagogue was motivated by hatred toward Jews? Which are more probative of such hatred than others? How many such statements, and, with what variety, repetition, and so forth, would—combined with the circumstantial evidence of the arson itself—would prove that he was motivated by hatred towards Jews?

Suppose X sincerely believes that Jews control the media and that he does not hate Jews. Relying on this belief, he vandalizes the headquarters of a media company perceived as Jewish to protest such control, which he believes is unjust, harmful for

77. 57 AM. JUR. PROOF OF FACTS 3d *Hate Crimes and Liability for Bias-Motivated Acts* § 8 (2000).

78. Dan T. Coenen, *Free Speech and the Law of Evidence*, 68 DUKE L.J. 639 *passim* (2019).

society, and so forth. If he operated under the assumption that, say, Blacks or Asians controlled the media, he would have attacked the headquarters of a media company perceived as Black or Asian. Has he committed a bias crime? If not, should bias crimes law be revised to apply to crimes so motivated? How might that be accomplished?

X is a Holocaust denier, sincerely believes the Holocaust did not happen and that the does not hate Jews. If he vandalizes a Holocaust memorial in the public square, has he committed a hate crime? Suppose the Holocaust memorial that X vandalizes is located on the grounds of a Jewish Community Center (JCC). X vandalizes the memorial—not because it is located on property associated with Jews, but because that is where the memorial is located.

U.S. Department of Justice, *Hate Crimes Case Examples*

[The Department of Justice's webpage contains a selection of "representative" federal hate crimes case summaries. These include crimes specifically targeting Jews and Jewish institutions across multiple states that occurred between January 2023 and July 2024.[79] Hate crimes include death and bomb threats to synagogues, vandalizing synagogues, and antisemitic threats online. Common themes include Nazi symbols, references to Hitler and the Holocaust, and white supremacist language.]

Massachusetts | January 29, 2024 | Religion

A Massachusetts man was arrested and charged for leaving a threatening voicemail at a local synagogue, including antisemitic death threats and calls to bomb synagogues.

According to evidence, on the morning of January 25, 2024, the defendant called a synagogue in Attleboro, Massachusetts, and left a voicemail calling for violence and genocide against the Jewish community. The message included calls to bomb Jewish places of worship and to kill Jewish children. Shortly after leaving the voicemail, the defendant called another synagogue and a local Jewish-affiliated organization. He was arrested shortly after the calls were made.

Michigan | March 4, 2024 | Religion

A Michigan man was sentenced to one year in prison for making a series of violent threats to kill Jewish people.

In November 2023, the defendant pleaded guilty to sending messages on social media including references to Adolf Hitler, antisemitic language, and plans to engage in a mass shooting and to commit suicide. The defendant was sentenced to 12 months and one day in prison, with 3 years of supervised release.

79. To view the DOJ press releases on these cases or to subscribe for updated case summaries, go to the "Hate Crimes Case Examples" page. *Hate Crime Case Examples*, U.S. Dep't of Just., https://www.justice.gov/hatecrimes/hate-crimes-case-examples (last visited Nov. 22, 2024).

Oregon | March 7, 2024 | Religion

An Oregon man was charged with hate crimes for repeatedly spray-painting a synagogue with antisemitic graffiti.

According to evidence, the defendant spray-painted a synagogue in Eugene, Oregon on four separate occasions with graffiti, some of which used antisemitic symbols and phrases. In January 2024, the defendant was caught on tape preparing to swing a hammer at the glass doors of the temple. When he saw he was being recorded, he moved to a different area and spray-painted "White Power" on the outside of the building. Detectives searched the defendant's home and found evidence connecting him to three earlier cases of vandalism at the temple. He was arrested and charged with federal hate crimes in March.

California | March 13, 2024 | Race, National Origin

A rideshare driver in California was charged with attacking a passenger for her suspected Jewish heritage.

According to evidence, the defendant drove to pick up a rider from her house. When he arrived, he asked the rider if she was Jewish or Israeli and claimed he would not drive a Jewish or Israeli passenger. He then punched the passenger in the face. The defendant was arrested and charged with a federal hate crime.

Florida | March 14, 2024 | Race, Religion, National Origin

A Florida man was sentenced to six months in prison for leaving threatening messages at a Jewish organization in New York City. Evidence showed the defendant left a message on October 21, 2023, threatening to kill all Israelis and "cause mass genocide." The defendant pleaded guilty to the hate crime in December 2023.

Michigan | March 27, 2024 | Religion

A Michigan man was charged for spray-painting Nazi symbols on a Jewish house of worship.

According to evidence, in November 2023, the defendant spray-painted swastikas on the Chabad House of Kalamazoo and destroyed a large menorah in front of the house. The defendant vandalized the house because the Chabad organization hosts religious, cultural, and community activities including Jewish religious services. The defendant was arrested and faces charges for federal hate crimes.

New York | April 10, 2024 | Religion

A former student at Cornell University pleaded guilty to posting violent threats on social media targeted at Jewish students.

In October 2023, the defendant posted on a Cornell online discussion forum threatening to "shoot up" the cafeteria and "bomb" the Jewish student house. The defendant threatened to "stab" and "slit the throat" of any Jewish man he saw on campus, to rape and throw off a cliff any Jewish women he saw, and to behead any Jewish babies. In that same post, he threatened to "bring an assault rifle to campus and shoot all you pig jews." The defendant faces up to five years in prison.

Maine | April 18, 2024 | Religion

A Maine man was sentenced to a year in prison for posting violent threats directed at Jewish people on social media.

According to evidence, on September 8, 2021, the defendant posted on social media, "I'm going to kill jews with my ar15 tomorrow." FBI investigators searched his home and found about 1,700 rounds of ammunition that could be fired from an AR-15-style rifle and evidence of long-standing antisemitic beliefs. Investigators later found an AR-15-style rifle and more ammunition in a case that had been hidden in the woods behind his home.

Texas | April 23, 2024 | Religion

A Texas man was sentenced to more than two years in prison for sending a series of antisemitic death threats.

From December 2022 through January 2023, the defendant sent death threats over email to two former coworkers. The emails detailed how he planned to murder them and included photographs of pipe bombs, ammunition, and a firearm. The emails also included personal information about the victims and their families. These threats were part of a larger pattern of death threats sent to people in his life, as well as politicians, judges, and prosecutors. In these threats, the defendant consistently used violent, threatening language that targeted Jewish people. The defendant pleaded guilty two days into the trial.

North Carolina | May 2, 2024 | Race, National Origin

A North Carolina man was charged with mailing antisemitic threats to a rabbi in Georgia.

According to evidence, a rabbi in Macon, Georgia received a threatening postcard from the defendant at her home address in February of 2024. On one side of the postcard, there was a handwritten message: "Is there a child rape, torture, and murder tunnel under your house? We have the Zyklon B. Use Code "GASTHEJEWS" for 10% off!" The other side of the postcard had a drawing with the words "JEWS ARE RATS."

California | May 14, 2024 | Religion

A California man pleaded guilty to hate crimes and gun charges for shooting and wounding two Jewish men as they left religious services in February 2023.

According to evidence, the defendant shot the first victim as they were leaving services at the synagogue. The next day, the defendant shot another victim who was leaving services at a different synagogue in the same Los Angeles neighborhood. Evidence indicates that the defendant held antisemitic beliefs, and he targeted a predominately Jewish neighborhood after searching a popular business review app for a kosher market in the Pico-Robertson district of Los Angeles.

California | May 24, 2024 | Religion

A California woman was sentenced to 32 months in prison for sending a series of antisemitic threats over the phone to former executive director of Pittsburgh's Tree of Life Synagogue and his family.

According to evidence at trial, the defendant left over 240 messages over four years with the victim, his wife, and her adult child. These messages were filled with hateful antisemitic remarks and death threats to the family and all Jewish people. In several messages, she mentioned victims killed in the October 2018 massacre at Tree of Life Synagogue by name. Her threats left the family scared for their lives. The defendant was arrested in March 2023 and pleaded guilty to hate crimes in March 2024.

Michigan | June 4, 2024 | Race, Religion

A Michigan man was sentenced to 26 months in prison for conspiring with other members of a white supremacist group, The Base, to victimize Black and Jewish people, and for spray-painting a synagogue using swastikas and symbols associated with The Base.

Evidence presented at trial showed the defendant planned to destroy property associated with Black and Jewish Americans with other members of the Base. They called it "Operation Kristallnacht"—a term that means "Night of Broken Glass," and refers to events that took place on Nov. 9 and 10, 1938, when Nazis murdered Jews and burned and destroyed their homes, synagogues, schools and businesses. On Sept. 21, 2019, the defendant acted on the plan and spray-painted swastikas and neo-Nazi symbols on the outside walls of Temple Jacob in Hancock, Michigan. A jury found the defendant guilty in January 2024.

New Jersey | July 23, 2024 | Religion

A New Jersey man has been sentenced to 40 years in prison for a series of carjackings and violent assaults against Orthodox Jewish men on April 8, 2022.

According to evidence, the defendant stole two vehicles and violently assault and attempted to run down and murder three pedestrians with the stolen vehicles. All five victims were targeted for their outwardly religious dress and appearance, and each suffered severe injuries including several broken bones.

E. Does German Hate Crimes Law Under-Protect Jews from Anti-Zionist Violence?

The Thuringian Decision: Judgment of July 13, 2000

Thuringian Higher Regional Court
1 St 1-3/00 (Ger.)

1. *The Case.* This case involved three juvenile defendants who threw Molotov cocktails at a synagogue in the German state of Thuringia. Two were convicted of attempted aggravated arson and the third, their getaway driver, was charged with aiding and abetting this crime. The court found that the attackers committed the crime "out of antisemitic sentiments" and deliberately planned the event for April 20, 2000, Hitler's birthday "in order to incite like-minded people to commit similar acts." The court sentenced the attempted arsonists to between two and three years apiece and confiscated the getaway driver's car.

2. *The defendants' motives.* The court based its finding as to the defendants' motives on the following facts. They:
   a. Selected the synagogue because of its association with Jews
   b. Confessed that they "wanted to burn down the Jews' hut"
   c. Described Jews as "deceitful, false and exploitative"
   d. "Accused [Jews] of being so bold as to still demand money and support from Germany 60 years after the war, although as prisoners of war they should have expected to perish"
   e. Selected Hitler's birthday as a means of "showing the world that the spirit of Adolf Hitler was still alive, and that like-minded people should regard the deed as a beacon for the commission of similar criminal acts"
   f. Belonged to right-wing political parties
   g. Listened to music and read material with right-wing content (the worst being materials produced by right-wing groups in the U.S.)
   h. Wore short hair
   i. Wore clothing with right-wing extremist views
   j. Displayed swastikas in their bedrooms
   k. Confessed that the attack was "based purely on antisemitism!"
   l. Expressed slogans such as "Heil Hitler," "Sieg Heil," "Break Jewish tyranny," and "The Jews are our misfortune"
3. *Aggravating Factors.* In assessing the gravity of the defendants' crime, the court considered as aggravating factors:
   a. "The psychological effects of the attack on Jews inside and outside Germany," its tendency "to create a climate of fear and intimidation among the Jewish population," causing some Jews to "consider leaving Germany for security reasons out of fear of further similar attacks on Jewish institutions."
   b. The attack's impact was intensified by its occurrence on Hitler's birthday.
   c. The attack's impact on Jews posed a threat to Germany's "internal security."
   d. The attack's "painful effects on other sections of the population who uphold the principle of coming to terms with the past."
   e. "The great interest of the media and the public in the arson attack."
   f. "The loss of Germany's reputation abroad caused by such an act."
   g. The court enhanced the defendants' sentences, as well as ordering the confiscation of a defendant's car.

The Wuppertal Decision: Judgment of 5 February 2015

Wuppertal District Court (*Amtsgericht*)
84 Ls 50 Js 156/14–22/14 (Ger.)

[In the early hours of July 29, 2014, three Germans of Palestinian descent threw Molotov cocktails at a synagogue in Wuppertal, a city west of Berlin. The attack caused modest structural damage and no injuries. The district court, per an unnamed judge, found the defendants guilty of attempted aggravated arson. [80] The court sentenced two defendants to suspended sentences of 15 months and the third, deemed an adolescent, to a lesser sentence.]

[The prosecutor asked the court to increase the defendants' sentences on grounds that it was motivated by antisemitism.[81] A leader of Wuppertal's Jewish community asked, "Can there be a clearer indication for antisemitism than trying to burn down a synagogue?"[82] The question, it turned out, was not rhetorical. The court denied the prosecutor's request, instead accepting the defendants' claims that, first, they simply sought to draw attention to the Gaza conflict and second, they had nothing against Jews. The regional district court, per Judge Thomas Bittner, affirmed this judgment while slightly increasing the sentences on technical grounds. It did not disturb the district court's factual finding, which it claimed it was bound to accept, that the crime was not motivated by antisemitism. In Judge Bittner's view, mitigating factors for sentencing included the defendants' confessions, apologies, payment of restitution, and their consumption of drugs and alcohol. At the same time, the regional court stated:

> It had to be taken into account as an aggravating factor that the defendants had frightened a large number of people, namely members of the Jewish community, by committing the crime, even if ... it was also to their detriment that

---

80. Under German law, criminal trials are conducted without juries and German court opinions typically do not name the deciding judge. *See* William T. Sweigert, *The Legal System of the Federal Republic of Germany*, 11 Hastings L.J. 7 (1959).

81. Section 46(2) of the German Criminal Code provides

- When fixing the penalty the court weighs the circumstances which speak in favour of and those which speak against the offender. The following, in particular, may be taken into consideration:
- the offender's motives and objectives, in particular including racist, xenophobic, antisemitic or other motives evidencing contempt for humanity,
- the attitude reflected in the offence and the degree of force of will involved in its commission,
- the degree of the breach of the offender's duties,
- the modus operandi and the consequences caused by the offence to the extent that the offender is to blame for them,
- the offender's prior history, personal and financial circumstances, and
- the offender's conduct in the period following the offence, in particular efforts to make restitution for the harm caused as well as efforts at reconciliation with the victim.

Strafgesetzbuch [StGB] [Penal Code], § 46, para. 2, https://www.gesetze-im-internet.de/englisch_stgb/englisch_stgb.html (Ger.).

82. Benjamin Näegele, *Judge Rules Wuppertal Synagogue Firebombing Was Not Anti-Semitic, So What Happened?*, B'nai B'rith Int'l (Jan. 17, 2017), https://www.bnaibrith.org/judge-rules-wuppertal-synagogue-firebombing-was-not-anti-semitic-so-what-happened-html/.

> they displayed a not inconsiderable amount of criminal energy (cooperation based on division of labor, joint preparation and production of various Molotov cocktails to be used as incendiary devices, throwing five of these incendiary devices at once) in the act....]

[UNNAMED DISTRICT COURT JUDGE.]

Defendant F spent the night from 27 to 28 July 2014 in the apartment of defendant B. The following day, on the occasion of the end of Ramadan and the celebration of Eid, they started drinking alcohol in the afternoon at around 4 or 5 pm. They mainly drank mixed vodka drinks and later beer. As the evening progressed, they went outside and to M Street in W because of the nice weather. There they initially continued drinking alone until defendant B2, who had previously been on the phone with defendant F, spontaneously joined them. He too had already drunk a considerable amount of alcohol, including whisky, at home. At M Street, all three continued to consume mixed vodka drinks and beer and defendants B2 and B also smoked pot. During the day, defendants F and B had informed themselves about the state of the conflict between Israel and the Palestinians living in the Gaza Strip through news reports.[83] All three defendants have relatives in Palestine. They had no contact with them, at least temporarily, due to the smoldering conflict. On M Street, they discussed the conflict and finally came up with the idea of throwing incendiary devices at the Jewish synagogue in Wuppertal, although it could not be determined with certainty what their motive was. Putting their spontaneous plan into action, all three went together to the petrol station on G-Allee. They carried a 1.5 liter [plastic] bottle with them, which had previously contained a vodka-energy drink mixture and which they had emptied together.

Defendants F and B went to the gas station pump while defendant B2 stood nearby. Defendant B filled the empty [plastic] bottle with diesel and defendants B and F then went inside the gas station, where defendant F first paid for 1.54 liters of diesel and then a bottle of beer at 0:57 a.m. on 29 July 2014. All three defendants then went to the apartment of defendant B, I Street, in W.

Once there, they all three worked together to make incendiary devices, so-called "Molotov cocktails," by first filling six empty beer bottles of the brands Krombacher, Becks and Heineken with diesel fuel, then hanging a fuse in the form of a strip of cotton fabric in each of the bottles and wrapping the bottles with masking tape that had already been in the apartment, in particular to fix the fuse.

Afterwards, all three defendants went to the synagogue of the Jewish community in W, H Street, which was within walking distance. At the time, they had the idea of using the incendiary devices to set fire to the synagogue, but without endangering people, as they correctly assumed that there would be no more people in the synagogue at this time of day. At around 2:12 a.m., they threw a total of five incendiary devices towards the entrance area of the synagogue, where a window and the entrance door with glass

83. Editor's note: Israel launched Operation Protective Edge in the summer of 2014 to stop Hamas rocket attacks into Israeli territory.

inserts were located, while the sixth incendiary device slipped out of one of their hands and shattered before being thrown. The five incendiary devices that were thrown extinguished during the flight and hit the ground in the area of the staircase of the entrance area or on the façade, including in the area of the window and the immediate entrance area, where they shattered.

The shards of the broken bottles and the diesel caused stains, the professional removal of which cost a total of € 858.70....

The members of the Jewish community in W were very shocked by the crime, but community life was not affected. The defendant F apologized to the Jewish community in writing for the act he had committed.... All three defendants also apologized for their actions [in court].

The defendants each confessed to their own involvement in the crime and that of their co-defendants. Defendants F and B stated that the motive for their crime was to draw attention to the ongoing armed conflict between Israel and the Palestinians living in the Gaza Strip. Defendant B2 could not give a motive. All three stated that they had nothing against Jews.

The court followed the defendants' confessions and found them credible....

The court also questioned the motive of the defendants. The statements made by defendants F and B that they wanted to draw attention to the Israeli-Palestinian conflict at the time of the crime are supported by the fact that all three defendants come from Palestine and were no longer in contact with their relatives in Palestine at the time of the crime due to the ongoing conflict. In addition, pictures from the Facebook profile of defendant F also show that he is in favor of a Palestinian state.

However, anti-Semitism was also a possible motive for the crime. This was supported by the fact that the defendants, as Palestinians and members of the Muslim faith, had thrown incendiary devices at a Jewish synagogue. However, these admittedly serious indications alone did not allow the court to conclude with sufficient certainty that the crime was in any case motivated by anti-Semitism.

The results of the investigation did not reveal any other evidence that the defendants were antisemitic. The police searched the defendants' homes and questioned witnesses from their environment. This did not reveal any circumstances that could lead to the conclusion that the defendants have a fundamentally antisemitic attitude.

As a result, the court could not rule out with certainty that a purely political motivation, at least in the case of two of the three defendants, may indeed have been the reason for committing the crime. It must certainly be made clear that the Jewish population living in Germany, in particular the Jewish community in W, has nothing to do with the policies of the Israeli government and its conflict with the Palestinians living in the Gaza Strip. On the other hand, however, when considering all the circumstances and the personality of the accused, it must also be taken into account that it is by no means far-fetched that they did not draw this conclusion, but—also in the absence of any other object of crime that could be clearly attributed to the state of Israel on the night of the crime—chose a synagogue as a sign of Jewish life as the object of the crime in order to make clear their concern to draw attention to the conflict flaring up between Israel and the Palestinians.

The defendants are guilty of attempted aggravated arson committed jointly on 29.07.2014 at the expense of the synagogue of the Jewish community in W....

All the circumstances in favor of and against the defendants had to be weighed against each other when sentencing the defendants F and B2 and also when assessing the question of how the defendant B [deemed an adolescent] should be educated.

The first thing to be considered was the attitude of the accused, which was evident from the crime, and the intention of the accused in committing the crime. In doing so, it was not a general attitude of the defendants, such as a possible anti-Jewish attitude, that was to be taken into account, but the individual intentions behind the crime. Specifically, it had to be taken into account that the defendants showed particular recklessness towards the members of the Jewish community, for whom their synagogue has special symbolic significance and is an expression of the freedom of religion that they were once again able to exercise in Germany after years of persecution. At the same time, they behaved thoughtlessly, if not recklessly, towards the entire population, including non-Jews, who strive for a prosperous coexistence of Jewish and non-Jewish people and, in particular, never again want to allow crimes to occur that even have the appearance of antisemitism....

When sentencing the defendants F and B2 and when considering what is educationally appropriate with regard to defendant B, the behavior of the defendants after the crime was also to be taken into account, in particular their efforts to make amends for the damage and to reach a settlement with the injured parties.

All three defendants apologized for their actions and showed their insight and remorse for the injustice they had committed. Defendant F also apologized in writing to the Jewish community.

[The court sentenced defendants F and B2 to suspended sentences of 15 months "appropriate to the crime and guilt." The court also gave B a modest sentence, finding that] the defendant's motive alone and the recklessness expressed in the crime towards the Jewish population and the population as a whole were not sufficient to assume a particularly serious degree of guilt.

Antisemitic Violence vs. Anti-Zionist Violence

1. *Different treatment.* What accounts for the courts' differential treatment of the defendants in the *Thuringian* and *Wuppertal* decisions?

2. *Selection criteria.* What criteria, in the court's view, did defendants use to select their target?

3. *Instrumental selection.* Assume (a) they selected the target based solely on how much attention they believed it would draw to the Gaza situation, i.e., without considering its

impact on Wuppertal and Germany's Jews; and (b) rationally concluded that, of all the potential targets in Wuppertal, attacking the synagogue would most effectively accomplish this goal. Did the defendants commit a hate crime? Also assume that defendants do in fact hate Jews but would have chosen a non-Jewish target if thought it would draw more attention to the Gaza conflict. Does their anti-Jewish animus alter the analysis?

4. *Target rich Jews.* Thief T strategically targets Jewish victims, relying on statistical data that Jews have higher per capita incomes than non-Jews. Was T's theft a hate crime?

5. *Why a synagogue?* Why, in the court's view, did defendants decide to draw attention to the Gaza conflict by targeting a synagogue? Consider the following passage.

> It must certainly be made clear that the Jewish population living in Germany, in particular the Jewish community in W, has nothing to do with the policies of the Israeli government and its conflict with the Palestinians living in the Gaza Strip. On the other hand, however, when considering all the circumstances and the personality of the accused, it must also be taken into account that it is by no means far-fetched that they did not draw this conclusion but—also in the absence of any other object of crime that could be clearly attributed to the state of Israel on the night of the crime—chose a synagogue as a sign of Jewish life as the object of the crime in order to make clear their concern to draw attention to the conflict flaring up between Israel and the Palestinians.

The court here hints at the possibility that the defendants might hold German Jews responsible for Israel's actions and, presumably, targeted the synagogue to exact revenge. The court then rejects this possibility mid-sentence in favor of the instrumentalist explanation—targeting the synagogue was an effective means to draw attention to the Gaza conflict.

6. *Burden of proof.* Under *Apprendi v. New Jersey* (2000),[84] a perpetrator's sentence cannot be aggregated under a hate crimes law unless the state proves beyond a reasonable doubt that the defendant was motivated by bias. Indiana judges, by contrast, have some discretion to increase a sentence based on factors, include their assessment of the perpetrator's biased motives, without the factor being proved beyond a reasonable doubt. What burden of proof does the Wuppertal judge use? Which should he?

7. *Bound by the findings?* The court of appeals claimed it was bound by the lower court's finding that the defendants were not motivated by antisemitism. How so? The determination as to whether a crime was motivated by antisemitism would seem to require a legal definition of antisemitism—a question of law. How does German law define it? Did the lower court use the correct definition? Assuming the court used the correct definition, did it apply it correctly to the facts—a question of law applied to fact?

8. *Second-degree bias crime?* Assume the defendants were not motivated by anti-Jewish animus. Have they committed a "second-degree" bias crime?

---

84. Apprendi v. New Jersey, 530 U.S. 466 (2000).

9. *Legal criticisms.* Volker Beck, a Green Party member of the Bundestag, said that "the ignorance of the judiciary toward antisemitism is for many Jews in Germany especially alarming."[85] According to B'nai B'rith International, *Wuppertal* "refused to make the shockingly obvious connection between anti-Zionism and anti-Semitism" and represented the German judiciary's "surrender towards anti-Semitic hate crimes motivated by a disdain for the state of Israel."

10. *Community life not affected?* The blinkered court claimed that "the members of the Jewish community in X were greatly shocked by the crime, but community life was not affected." Other sources described the Jewish community members "in shock," "traumatized," and "horrified,"[86] *Wuppertal* was described as sending "a devastating and shocking signal to German Jews,"[87] "created a tremendous feeling of insecurity"[88] in Wuppertal, and "triggered anger and dismay … throughout European Jewry."[89]

The attack on the synagogue exacerbated many community members' long-standing concern for their security because they are Jewish. "For years now, our rabbis haven't worn their kippahs in public as they go through Wuppertal," according to a community leader, "Jews that do wear their kippah in public attempt to hide it by wearing a hat on top so that they don't have to hear insults from young Muslims, most of all."[90] The Wuppertal synagogue was already being protected by security guards, security cameras, a locked entrance, and bulletproof glass.[91] Following the attack, the police guarded the synagogue around the clock.[92] "I thought the time of packed suitcases was over forever," said Leonid Goldberg, the head of the Jewish Community in Wuppertal. "I am now wondering—when would be the right moment to pack them again."[93]

11. *Community life affected.* In *U.S. v. Sechriest* the government's memo described the impact of Sechriest's crime on the local Jewish community:

> Defendant's crimes were not only physically destructive but were also intended to cause, and did cause, severe emotional and psychological damage. De-

---

85. Benjamin Weinthal, *German Court Calls Synagogue Torching an Act to 'Criticize Israel,'* The Jerusalem Post, https://www.jpost.com/Diaspora/German-court-calls-synagogue-torching-an-act-to-criticize-Israel-478330 (Jan. 15, 2017, 6:05 AM).

86. Benjamin Näegele, *Judge Rules Wuppertal Synagogue Firebombing Was Not Anti-Semitic, So What Happened?*, B'nai B'rith Int'l (Jan. 17, 2017), https://www.bnaibrith.org/judge-rules-wuppertal-synagogue-firebombing-was-not-anti-semitic-so-what-happened-html/; Sarah Wildman, *German Court Rules that Firebombing a Synagogue is Not Anti-Semitic*, Vox (Jan. 13, 2017, 4:50 PM), https://www.vox.com/world/2017/1/13/14268994/synagogue-wuppertal-anti-semitism-anti-zionism-anti-israel.

87. Näegele, *supra* note 87.

88. Wildman, *supra* note 87.

89. Näegele, *supra* note 87.

90. *Id.*

91. *Id.*

92. Sven Pöhle, *'Pure Anti-Semitism' Behind Wuppertal Synagogue Attack*, Deutsche Welle (Jan. 27, 2015), https://www.dw.com/en/pure-anti-semitism-behind-synagogue-attack-says-wuppertal-jewish-leader/a-18216819.

93. Wildman, *supra* note 87.

fendant desecrated a Jewish place of worship. Defendant intended his crimes to terrorize the Jewish community, and he selected as his target the oldest synagogue in Texas, a choice that only magnified the impact of his crime.

Defendant's use of fire as his chosen means of destruction was particularly intimidating, insidious, and psychologically devastating. The harm caused by fire extends well beyond the physical damage. Fire often fully obliterates and consumes what it burns, leaving virtually no trace. In the context of Defendant's hate crime, there seems to be symbolic significance to that.

The many victim impact statements submitted to the Court reflect the emotional and psychological damage inflicted by Defendant's crimes. Defendant's crimes had a devastating impact on the CBI congregation and the larger Austin Jewish community.

Hate crimes that target religious institutions, such as CBI, aim right for the heart of a community, and have a heightened symbolic value in the eyes of perpetrators like the Defendant. As demonstrated by the Victim Impact Statements, these crimes also have a lasting impact on the communities they target because they destroy a place of safety and alter the pattern of life for the community for months and years.[94]

12. *State-sanctioned hate crime?* On November 9 and 10, 1938, the previous synagogue in Wuppertal was vandalized and subsequently destroyed as part of a state-sanctioned hate crime known as *Kristallnacht*, or the Night of Broken Glass.[95] In what sense, if any, did *Wuppertal* transform the synagogue attack into a state-laundered hate crime?

13. *Anti-Zionist versus antisemitic expression.* For what propositions does *Wuppertal* stand?

a. Perpetrators who intentionally attack Jewish targets without further expression are presumptively motivated by antisemitism.

b. If a perpetrator intentionally attacks a Jewish target, is there a presumption that they were motivated by antisemitism? Insofar as there is a presumption, is it rebuttable or irrebuttable? If rebuttable, is it rebutted where the perpetrator:

(1) Expressed anti-Zionist motivation; and

(2) Explicitly denied antisemitic motivation; and

(3) Had not previously expressed anti-Jewish animus?

14. Assume that the *Wuppertal* defendant's Facebook page expressed support for a Palestinian state *and* animus towards Jews. A different result? Would the answer depend on the ratio of pro-Palestinian expression to antisemitic expression? For example,

---

94. Gov't's Sent'g Memorandum, United States v. Sechriest, No. 22-cr-00053 (W.D. Tex. filed Nov. 20, 2023).

95. *Wuppertal, Germany*, Yad Vashem, https://collections.yadvashem.org/en/places/5449033 (last visited Nov. 23, 2024).

what if he made ten pro-Palestinian statements for every one antisemitic statement. Has he rebutted the presumption that his attack was motivated by antisemitism? One pro-Palestinian statement for every antisemitic one? One pro-Palestinian statement to every ten antisemitic ones, etc.? What is the tipping point?

15. *Nelson* versus *Wuppertal* defendants. Recall that Nelson, like the *Wuppertal* defendants, expressly denied that his attack was motivated by animus towards Jews, asserting instead that he was "high from the beer" and "got caught up in the excitement." Assume that Nelson, like the *Wuppertal* defendants, credibly alleged that his attack was intended to raise awareness about Gaza and had never previously expressed antisemitic views. Would a German and/or U.S. court have concluded that the attack was *not* motivated by antisemitism?

16. *IHRA definition of antisemitic crimes.* IHRA adopted the following non-legally binding working definition of antisemitism:

> Antisemitism is a certain perception of Jews, which may be expressed as hatred toward Jews. Rhetorical and physical manifestations of antisemitism are directed toward Jewish or non-Jewish individuals and/or their property, toward Jewish community institutions and religious facilities.

The IHRA definition states that "criminal acts are antisemitic when the targets of attacks . . . are selected because they are, or are perceived to be, Jewish or linked to Jews."[96] Does IHRA rely on an "intentional selection" or "group animus" model of a hate crime? Does it posit a rebuttable or irrebuttable presumption that attacks against Jewish targets are antisemitic?

17. Which of the following statements would, if posted on the defendants' social media accounts, be relevant to the question of whether they were motivated by hatred of Jews?

a. "Jews are responsible for wrongdoings committed by other Jews."

b. "Jews are collectively responsible for actions of the state of Israel."

c. "Islam justifies violence against Jews."

d. "The Holocaust is a myth."

e. "Jews invented the Holocaust to gain sympathy."

f. "The State of Israel is a racist endeavor."

g. "Israel should meet standards no other democracy is held to."

h. "Israeli policies are just like those of the Nazis."

18. *Antisemitic motivation as penalty-enhancing factor.* In 2021, the Bundestag (German Parliament) amended the criminal code's sentencing principles to require judges to consider a perpetrator's "antisemitic" motives and goals. This added a new category to the list of penalty-enhancing factors; these previously consisted of "racist, xenopho-

---

96. *Working Definition of Antisemitism*, INT'L HOLOCAUST REMEMBRANCE ALL., https://holocaustremembrance.com/resources/working-definition-antisemitism (last visited Nov. 23, 2024).

bic, or other motives evidencing contempt for humanity."[97] The report accompanying the bill stated:

> Particularly in view of the inhuman persecution and murder of millions of Jews during the National Socialist reign of violence and despotism, the Federal Republic of Germany bears a special responsibility and obligation to resolutely combat the resurgence of anti-Semitism and to protect its Jewish fellow citizens. This includes, in particular, the emphatic prosecution of anti-Semitic crimes.[98]

At least one critic complained that the amendment was superfluous because antisemitism was encompassed by "xenophobia" and/or "other motives evidencing contempt for humanity."[99] In response to this superfluous critique, the bill report explained:

> The German Criminal Code (StGB) does not yet take sufficient account of the social and forensic significance of anti-Semitically motivated acts—especially in times of rising numbers of cases. It is true that the general provision on sentencing in Section 46 StGB expressly allows for racist, xenophobic or other inhuman motives or goals of the perpetrator to be taken into account to increase the penalty. Anti-Semitic motives and goals can also be qualified as inhuman in this sense. However, in contrast to racist and xenophobic motives, which are also special forms of inhuman motives, they are not explicitly named and remain hidden behind the abstract generic term "inhuman." As a result, the relevance—also in practice—of anti-Semitic crimes, which together with racist and xenophobic crimes make up the statistically largest part of hate crime, is not adequately reflected in the law.[100]

---

97. *Extending the Scope of Section 46 of the Criminal Code*, FED. GOV'T COMM'R FOR JEWISH LIFE IN GER. & THE FIGHT AGAINST ANTISEMITISM, https://www.antisemitismusbeauftragter.de/Webs/BAS/EN/fight-against-antisemitism/initiatives/extending-criminal-code-46/extending-criminal-code-46-node.html (last visited Nov. 23, 2024).

98. Regierungsentwurf [Cabinet Draft], Deutscher Bundestag: Drucksachen [BT] 19/16399, https://dserver.bundestag.de/btd/19/163/1916399.pdf (Ger.).

99. Dr. iur. Oliver Harry Gerson, *Fauler (Wort-)Zauber im Strafzumessungsrecht—Plädoyer gegen die ausdrückliche Einfügung „antisemitischer Beweggründe" als Strafzumessungstatsache in § 46 Abs. 2 S. 2 (1.Gruppe) StGB* [*Lazy (Word) Magic in Sentencing Law: Plea Against the Explicit Inclusion of "Anti-Semitic Motives" as a Sentencing Factor in Section 46 (2) Sentence 2 (1st Group) StGB*], 2020 KRIMINALPOLITISCHE ZEITSCHRIFT 22, 22–31 (Ger.). Interestingly, Gerson did not argue that "racism" encompasses antisemitism:

> The classification of an antisemitic or anti-Jewish motivated act as "racist" is incorrect. Since Jews do not share any *biological* characteristics—and even the attempt to construct such a distinction is structurally anti-Semitic—there is no "racial" connection. The perpetrator's illusion of being able to recognize a biological determination is irrelevant.

Gerson, *supra*. Is his claim that the statement "antisemitism is a form of racism" is itself racist? How would the *Shaare Tefila* courts address this claim?

100. BT 19/16399 at 2.

A Provocation Defense to a Hate Crimes Charge?

1. *Does an offender's national and/or religious identity affect the court's analysis? Wuppertal* flagged "the fact that the defendants, as Palestinians and members of the Muslim faith, had thrown incendiary devices at a Jewish synagogue." Why did the court mention this detail? Did it mean to say that the defendants threw incendiary devices in their capacities as Palestinians and Muslims? As an expression of their Palestinian and Muslim identities? Because they were Palestinian and Muslim? They would not have done so but for the fact that they are Palestinian and Muslim? And so forth. If the defendants were anti-Israel Canadian Christians instead of anti-Israel Palestinian Muslims, would that have affected the court's analysis?

2. *Indoctrinated to hate?* According to a leader of Wuppertal's Jewish community, members are sometimes insulted in the street by "young Muslims." This leader claims:

> Their upbringing is to blame, as well as Turkish and Arab media. He says young Muslims have constant access to anti-Israeli and anti-Semitic coverage. As a result, anti-Semitism among young Muslims has grown strongly.

Assume that the defendants had, by virtue of their Palestinian and Muslim connections, more exposure to antisemitism when they were growing up than Canadian Christians did.[101] How might this affect the court's analysis?

3. *"Crimes of passion" and the provocation defense.* In American law, a murder charge may sometimes be reduced to voluntary manslaughter under the common law defense of "provocation," also known as a "crime of passion." The provocation defense applies where the defendant commits a murder in the "heat of passion" and sparked by special provoking circumstances that the law deems to be adequate justification.[102] The paradigmatic case consists of the husband who sees his wife in bed with another man and kills one or both in a jealous rage.[103] A Wisconsin statute defines the terms as follows:

> (a) "Adequate" means sufficient to cause complete lack of self-control in an ordinarily constituted person.

---

101. ADL surveys report that 93 percent of West Bank and Gaza residents harbor antisemitic attitudes, making it the most antisemitic location in the world, as do 75 percent of Muslims in the Middle East and North Africa and 49 percent of Muslims worldwide. *ADL Poll of Over 100 Countries Finds More Than One-Quarter of Those Surveyed Infected with Anti-Semitic Attitudes*, The Anti-Defamation League (May 13, 2014), https://www.adl.org/resources/press-release/adl-poll-over-100-countries-finds-more-one-quarter-those-surveyed-infected. Fourteen percent of Canadians harbor antisemitic attitudes, as do 24 percent of Christians worldwide. *Id.; Canada*, The Anti-Defamation League, https://global100.adl.org/country/canada/2014 (last visited Nov. 23, 2024); *see also West Bank and Gaza*, The Anti-Defamation League, https://global100.adl.org/country/west-bank-and-gaza/2014 (last visited Nov. 23, 2024); *see also Did You Know?*, The Anti-Defamation League, https://global100.adl.org/did-you-know (last visited Nov. 23, 2024); *see also About the Survey Methodology*, The Anti-Defamation League, https://global100.adl.org/about/ (last visited Nov. 23, 2024).

102. Paul H. Robinson et al., 1 Criminal Law Defenses § 102 (updated in 2024).

103. *See, e.g.*, State v. Thornton, 730 S.W.2d 309 (Tenn. 1987).

(b) "Provocation" means something which the defendant reasonably believes the intended victim has done which causes the defendant to lack self-control completely at the time of causing death.[104]

The provocation defense reflects society's judgment that certain murderous responses are less blameworthy than others, i.e., the offense is partially justified. It also reflects society's judgment that some criminal urges are on some level worthy of its respect, even if not per se praiseworthy. "The basic moral question," writes George P. Fletcher, "is distinguishing between those impulses to kill as to which we as society demand self-control, and those as to which we relax our inhibitions."[105]

4. *Partially justified homophobic murders.* Some jurisdictions recognize a provocation defense for certain murders of gay men. Consider the male defendant who murdered a gay male victim after the victim propositioned him. For a murder charge to be reduced to voluntary manslaughter, the defendant must establish that: (1) he is extremely homophobic; (2) he is so homophobic, in fact, that the victim's proposition drove him into an uncontrollable, murderous rage; and (3) it would be wrong and unreasonable for society to expect him not to kill the victim in this situation. Robert B. Mison describes the homophobic defense as "a judicial institutionalization of homophobia" that sends the message "that revulsion and hostility are natural reactions to homosexual behavior."[106]

5. *Bias crimes law and homophobic murders.* Where a murderer successfully invokes the homophobic defense, thereby reducing the charge to voluntary manslaughter, he may effectively evade a hate crimes law.[107] In the end, the homophobic murderer may be treated the same as a murderer who is not motivated by impermissible bias. The homophobic defense effectively creates an exemption for homophobes from bias crime law consequences.[108]

6. *Post-September 11 violence against Muslim, Arab, and South Asian Americans.* Following the September 11, 2001 terrorist attacks, there was a dramatic increase in bias-motivated violence committed against Muslim, Arab, and South Asian Ameri-

---

104. WIS. STAT. ANN. § 939.44 (West 2024).

105. GEORGE P. FLETCHER, RETHINKING CRIMINAL LAW 247 (Oxford Univ. Press 2000) (first printed 1978).

106. Robert B. Mison, *Homophobia in Manslaughter: The Homosexual Advance as Insufficient Provocation*, 80 CALIF. L. REV. 133, 133, 136 (1992); *see also* ROBINSON ET AL., *supra* note 103, at § 102.50; *see also* Patrick v. State, 104 So.3d 1046 (Fla. 2012) (rejecting the homophobic defense). The homophobic defense may be rejected where the defendant had reason to believe, based on his murderous reaction to a previous proposition from a gay man, that he might do so again. *See, e.g.*, People v. Cass, 965 N.E.2d 918 (N.Y. 2012). He is like the repeat sleepwalker. *See* LAWRENCE, *supra* note 31, at 70.

107. In other words, (1) the sentence for (a) a manslaughter conviction plus (b) hate crimes law penalty enhancement on the manslaughter may be the *same* as (2) the sentence for (a) a murder conviction (b) with no penalty enhancement.

108. *See* Scott D. McCoy, *The Homosexual-Advance Defense and Hate Crimes Statutes: Their Interaction and Conflict*, 22 CARDOZO L. REV. 629 *passim* (2001).

cans, as well as those perceived to belong to these groups.[109] Professor Muneer I. Ahmad argues that the perpetrators of these bias crimes were widely perceived as less culpable than perpetrators of bias crimes against members of other protected groups. Ahmad uses the metaphor of "crimes of passion" to illustrate what was distinctive about post-September 11 violence.

> Transposing the crime of passion metaphor to post-September 11 violence in this fashion, we can understand the perpetrators acting ... out of quintessentially heated blood. The terrorist attacks were assaults not just on property that the perpetrators of post-September 11 violence claimed as their own, but on their sense of honor, here expressed as resurgent nationalism. The perpetrators' attacks, then, have been understood as undertaken in the heat of passion to avenge the affront to their national honor, and because the provocation is one with which we sympathize, it mitigates our condemnation of the act.[110]
>
> The clearest evidence of the perpetrators' claimed motivations for their violence comes from their own statements. When Frank Roque, the killer of Balbir Singh Sodhi, was arrested, he stated, "I'm a patriot.... I'm a damn American all the way." A man who tried to run over a Pakistani woman with his car declared that she was "destroying my country." Mark Anthony Stroman, who killed Waqar Hasan and Vasudev Patel and shot a third South Asian man, said he did so out of revenge for the terrorist attacks. Brent Seever, who was convicted of shooting Ali Almansoop, a Yemeni immigrant who had lived in the United States for thirty years, told the police, "I was motivated by all this terroristic activity." Such statements were among the first to signal a much broader and sustained resurgence of patriotism in the aftermath of September 11. Describing this remarkable transmogrification of hate violence, Robert Chang wrote, "Hate crimes become redeployed as patriotic gestures, when belongingness is exercised through the negation or abjection of those people marked as truly different."
>
> Implicit in the violence of the post-September 11 perpetrator are claims of honor, loyalty, property, and violation. Notably, all four claims are strongly inflected by gender. While in the paradigmatic crime of passion the husband acts to redeem his besmirched honor, the perpetrator of post-September 11 violence strikes for the honor of the nation. Whereas the husband is presumptively loyal (in contradistinction to the adulterer), so, too, is the perpetrator of post-September 11 violence (in contradistinction to the terrorists). Just as the wife is viewed as the property of the husband, so does the post-September 11 perpetrator lay claim to the nation. And finally, the violation of the husband's

---

109. Amardeep Singh, HUM. RTS. WATCH, *We Are Not the Enemy* § 5 (2002), https://www.hrw.org/reports/2002/usahate/usa1102-04.htm.

110. Muneer I. Ahmad, *A Rage Shared by Law: Post-September 11 Racial Violence as Crimes of Passion*, 92 CALIF. L. REV. 1259, 1306–07 (2004).

wife by her lover parallels the violation of the feminized (and raced) nation by the terrorists, nineteen swarthy, foreign men.

7. *Retaliatory bias crimes.* Valeri and Borgeson define "retaliatory hate crimes" as crimes motivated by the desire for revenge for perceived or actual wrongs committed by the targeted group.[111] The retaliation, they write, "is random or indiscriminate, being directed against anyone and everyone associated with the offending group." …

8. *Antisemitic conspiracy theories about September 11.* Antisemitic conspiracy theories about September 11 appeared soon after the attacks and have since proliferated, especially with the rise of social media. These theories often blame Jews, Israel, or both for orchestrating or having prior knowledge of the attacks. The ADL describes these theories as "a continuation of centuries-old antisemitic tropes about Jews supposedly manipulating world events for their own benefit."[112] According to Franklin Foer, September 11 signaled the end of the "Golden Age" for American Jews, one characterized by relative safety and prosperity. "The Jewish vacation from history ended on September 11, 2001," writes Foer. "The terror attacks opened an era of perpetual crisis, which became fertile soil where the hatred of Jews took root."[113]

---

111. Valeri & Borgeson, *supra* note 45, at 46.

112. *Antisemitic Conspiracies About 9/11 Endure 20 Years Later*, The Anti-Defamation League (Sept. 9, 2021), https://www.adl.org/resources/report/antisemitic-conspiracies-about-911-endure-20-years-later; *see also 11 September 2001: The Conspiracy Theories Still Spreading After 20 Years*, BBC (Sept. 9, 2021), https://www.bbc.com/news/58469600; *see also* Simon Wiesenthal Ctr., September 11 Conspiracies: 20 Years Later 7–9 (2021), https://www.wiesenthal.com/assets/pdf/september-11-conspiracies-20.pdf.

113. Franklin Foer, *The Golden Age of American Jews Is Ending*, The Atlantic, April 2024, https://www.theatlantic.com/magazine/archive/2024/04/us-anti-semitism-jewish-american-safety/677469/.

Chapter 12

Campus Antisemitism

This chapter examines the harassment that Jewish students have experienced from non-Jewish students, faculty and administrators. It examines legal tools available for holding faculty and administrators accountable for expressing antisemitism and for tolerating a hostile environment for the Jewish students in their charge.

Section A, "Title VI Protects Jewish Students," presents *T.E. v. Pine Bush Central School District* (S.D.N.Y. 2014), a landmark case which established that Title VI of the Civil Rights Act of 1964 protects Jewish students from antisemitic harassment in schools, despite not explicitly mentioning religion-based discrimination. It examines the role that government agencies and Jewish advocacy groups played in extending Title VI's protections to Jewish students.

The second section examines the hostile anti-Jewish environment the University of Vermont (UVM) tolerated and which UVM administrators accelerated by questioning the credibility of Jewish students who reported their experiences of antisemitism, a form of antisemitism that Professor David Schraub describes as "epistemic."

The third section, "Anti-Zionist Harassment," deals with a UVM faculty member's anti-Zionist tweets that were treated as antisemitic despite not being patently antisemitic, where the faculty member also posted separate tweets that were patently antisemitic. The episode raises the larger question of when anti-Zionist expression that is not patently antisemitic is or should be treated as antisemitic. The section also discusses a student publication that adopted a policy to bar speakers who hold Zionist viewpoints.

The final section, "Free Speech and Antidiscrimination Law," explores the tension between combatting antisemitic harassment on campus and protecting the free speech rights of anti-Zionist activists.

A. Title VI Protects Jewish Students

The case of *T.E. v. Pine Bush Central School District*, presented below, involves Jewish students who endured severe antisemitic harassment over many years and across several schools within the Pine Bush Central School District in New York's Hudson Valley region. The harassment included physical assaults like students throwing coins at them, making explicit Holocaust "jokes," threats to "burn them in ovens," drawing swastikas throughout the schools, performing Hitler salutes, and making "Christ killer" accusations. Particularly disturbing were incidents where students repeatedly sang "white power" songs about "stomping the niggers and killing the Jews" in school cafeterias and on buses.

Despite being aware of these incidents, school officials' responses were more than inadequate—they actively discouraged reporting. When two students regularly reported antisemitic incidents, an administrator told them to "stop coming as often" and claimed they were "looking for trouble." When parents raised concerns about the systemic nature of the harassment, administrators insisted on handling incidents only on an "individual basis."

District Judge Kenneth M. Karas ruled that the harassment fell under Title VI's protections against discrimination based on race or national origin, finding that the antisemitic abuse was rooted in the students' "actual or perceived shared ancestry or ethnic characteristics, rather than solely on its members' religious practices." He found that a reasonable jury could conclude the district acted with deliberate indifference by failing to monitor the effectiveness of its limited interventions, implement tracking of bias-related incidents, or take meaningful steps to address the pervasive antisemitic culture.

The case ultimately settled with the district agreeing to pay $4.5 million to the affected students and commit to remedial actions. At the settlement hearing, Judge Karas thanked one of the students "for having the courage to come into court and saying the things you said."[1]

T.E. v. Pine Bush Cent. Sch. Dist.

58 F. Supp. 3d 332 (S.D.N.Y. 2014)

District Judge Kenneth M. Karas.

BACKGROUND

The harassment alleged by Plaintiffs in this case spans half a decade and three separate schools within PBCSD [Pine Bush Central School District].... Plaintiffs' allegations catalogue years of harassment at the hands of their fellow students, but a few key incidents, and the District's responses thereto, are informative for the purposes of the instant Motion.

1. *Plaintiff D.C.*

D.C. is a male student who claims to have suffered anti-Semitic harassment and to have been subject to physical and verbal threats during his enrollment in PBCSD from sixth through twelfth grade. He alleges that, throughout this time, other students physically and verbally threatened him by "pellet[ing]" change at him, telling him he "was going to be burned in an oven," and that "if [he] did anything [in response to this harassment,] that they knew where [he] lived." D.C. also witnessed "swastikas everywhere in the high school and in the middle school" that he testified "would be impossible" for

1. Joseph Berger, *Settlement Over Anti-Semitic Bullying at Pine Bush Central Schools Is Approved*, N.Y. Times (July 9, 2015), https://www.nytimes.com/2015/07/10/nyregion/settlement-over-anti-semitic-bullying-at-pine-bush-central-schools-is-approved.html.

teachers to miss. He further describes "fairly constant" harassment, during his years in PBCSD, during which time he was called "countless" names, including "dirty jew," "filthy jew," "stupid Jew," "fat Jew," "Jew faggot," "fucking Jew kike," "ashes," "dust," and "mocky fuck."

Mr. C., D.C.'s father, reported the slur ["F'ing Jew"] to [middle school principal] Boyle.... Boyle told Mr. C. that the incident would be handled on an individual basis, Mr. C. told Boyle that "this isn't an individual thing, this is systemic."... Boyle had no response to Mr. C.'s question about how the District would handle "all the other kids that [we]re making Jewish jokes," and also did not follow up with Mr. C. about addressing anti-Semitism in the school....

When D.C. was in seventh grade, students repeatedly sang and chanted a "song about stomping the niggers and killing the Jews and washing off their blood," in both the school cafeteria near D.C.'s table, and on D.C.'s bus. When students sang this "white power song" on D.C.'s bus, D.C. complained to the bus driver, but the white power chants continued—in fact, other students found out that D.C. had complained and the harassment "got worse."...

When D.C. was in ninth grade, another student "would constantly berate [D.C]," telling him that D.C.'s "ancestors died in the Holocaust," calling D.C. "ashes," and pantomiming the blowing of dust off his hands while telling D.C. that he was "just ashes." The same student would slap D.C. in the face as the student got off the bus and smirk at D.C. Other students joined in this harassment, slapping D.C. in the face and telling him, "Shut up, D., or I will burn you in an oven." The bus driver did nothing in response to this harassment, which continued throughout D.C.'s ninth grade year. D.C. also witnessed students in the school cafeteria and classrooms performing "Hitler salutes," both to each other and to D.C. D.C. testified that these students "didn't hide" their behavior and made "no attempt to conceal" it, and that D.C. "c[ouldn't] really imagine [adults in the school] missing it."...

D.C. witnessed "swastikas everywhere" and testified that they were so prominently displayed that "it would be impossible for [teachers or administrators] to miss the swastikas ..."

The harassment D.C. suffered throughout his time in the District made him feel unsafe, as though "[e]very day ... was the wors[t] day of [his] life" and led D.C. to contemplate suicide.... D.C. felt that "Mr. Boyle didn't really care or couldn't do anything about [the harassment]," and that "the system had apathy towards [D.C.], so [he] didn't know who to talk to and [D.C.] thought [he] was on [his] own." Furthermore, "after alerting the teachers in eighth grade and seeing their ... inability ... to correct the problem," D.C. felt "overwhelmed" and "did not report a lot of swastikas because [he] felt like [he] was fighting a losing battle and [that he] couldn't make a difference."

2. *Plaintiff T.E.*

A student on T.E.'s bus called her a "Jew" and gave the middle finger to T.E. and her mother. Mrs. E. reported the incident to ... [elementary school] Principal Fisch.... The student was given a 50-minute "recess detention," and his parents were called, but the student was not forced to apologize to T.E. or her mother, do any assignment, or be subject to suspension or after-school detention.

Two of T.E.'s classmates ... showed T.E. swastikas that were drawn in their planners. Mrs. E., T.E.'s mother, reported this incident to Fisch, who allegedly told her "what's the big deal, they didn't aim [the swastikas] towards [T.E.], they were just writing in their book." ... After Mrs. E. persisted, Fisch agreed to "talk with the kids." ... Fisch testified that he spoke with the offending students about "the significance of the swastika" and "what an offensive symbol it was to a particular group [including Jewish people]."

[In response to Mrs. E's report of swastikas in the classroom, middle school assistant principal] Winter responded by saying that "anti-Semitism is prevalent in the community ... and that it's rather hard to stop something that's inbred in the community."

T.E. witnessed on the bus in which one student had drawn a picture on his stomach and "said it is a Hasidic Jew, so let's shove pennies in his mouth...."

When T.E. was in eighth grade, she continued to hear anti-Semitic slurs "on almost a daily basis" and recalls that "people would use Jew like they would use the N word." ...

A student threw a coin at T.E. in the Crispell hallway.... T.E. told her mother that "if she had to go back to the school ever again, she was going to have a nervous breakdown." Mrs. E. took T.E. to Mobile Mental Health, to meet with a counselor "who said that ... [Crispell] was [not] a healthy place for her." T.E. subsequently left PBCSD and was home schooled.

3. *Plaintiff O.C.*

[Non-Jewish students harassed O.C. by, inter alia, throwing pennies at her and calling her "Christ killer." School officials' responses were generally ineffective.]

4. *District Response*

When T.E. and O.C. were in fifth grade at PBE, [elementary school principal] Fisch held an assembly to discuss the "bullying problem" in the fifth-grade class and sent a letter to students' parents informing them about the consequences of "any verified complaints about bullying behavior ... from any school related area including the bus." Fisch did not discuss anti-Semitism in the assembly....

When T.E. and O.C. were in seventh grade, Crispell held an assembly in which a Holocaust survivor addressed a group of seventh grade students.... Defendants do not dispute Plaintiffs' contention that "no one addressed anti-Semitism in Pine Bush [S]chools" at this assembly.

During their seventh-grade year, T.E. and O.C. regularly reported anti-Semitic harassment to [middle school assistant principal] Winter. The girls complained to Winter so frequently that he told them to "stop coming as often as [they] did," and that they "were looking for trouble." In response, T.E. and O.C. began writing down each incident of anti-Semitic harassment and "bring[ing] it to [Winter] at the end of the week," to which Winter responded that they "were now just looking for trouble and that [they] were causing [their] own problems." ...

In response [to the parents' complaints], Winter said that he would "deal with it on an individual basis." Mr. C. told Winter that "this isn't an individual problem, this is systemic, and ... a much broader problem and you cannot deal with it individually." ...

DISCUSSION

1. Jewish Identity and Title IV

Title VI prohibits a recipient of federal funds from discriminating based on race, color, or national origin. *See* 42 U.S.C. § 2000d. The United States Department of Education's regulations regarding Title VI further state that a recipient of federal funds may not, "on ground of race, color, or national origin ... restrict an individual in any way in the enjoyment of any advantage or privilege enjoyed by others receiving any service, financial aid, or other benefit under the program." 34 C.F.R. § 100.3(b)(1)(iv). Nor may a funding recipient, such as the District in this Action, "deny an individual an opportunity to participate in the program through the provision of services or otherwise, or afford him an opportunity to do so which is different from that afforded others under the program" on the basis of race, color, or national origin. *Id.* § 100.3(b)(1)(vi).

[Defendants] sheepishly raise the question of whether Plaintiffs may bring a Title VI claim on grounds of deliberate indifference to anti-Semitic harassment, stating that Defendants have found "no prior case holding that claims of discrimination based on the plaintiffs' identification as Jewish come within Title VI's protection." Defendants appear to correctly identify an area of legal ambiguity, at least to the extent that they suggest that there is a question as to whether religious bias alone can form the basis of a Title VI claim where it is not "deeply intertwined" with national origin. Moreover, some courts have held that "allegations of discrimination because one is Jewish ... do not by themselves state a claim for national origin discrimination." This Court, however, need not address these issues in the instant Action.

Regardless of whether religious bias alone can form the basis of a Title VI claim or anti-Semitism can provide a basis for national origin discrimination, courts have regularly found that anti-Semitic harassment and discrimination amount to racial discrimination. *See Shaare Tefila Congregation v. Cobb* (1987); *United States v. Nelson*, 277 F.3d 164, 177 (2d Cir. 2002); *Singer v. Denver Sch. Dist. No. 1* 959 F. Supp. 1325, 1331 (D. Colo. 1997).

Furthermore, the Office for Civil Rights has made clear that "anti-Semitic harassment can trigger responsibilities under Title VI ... when the harassment is based on the group's actual or perceived shared ancestry or ethnic characteristics, rather than solely on its members' religious practices." Such agency interpretations of ambiguities in an agency's own regulation merit "substantial deference," as the courts have "no reason to think that the agency's interpretations do not reflect its fair and considered judgment on the matter in question."[2]

2. *Cf.* Kenneth L. Marcus, *Jurisprudence of the New Anti-Semitism*, 44 Wake Forest L. Rev. 371, 388–89 (2009) (chronicling U.S. Department of Education's Office for Civil Rights letters dating back to 2004 that conclude "that Title VI covers harassment of students of Jewish heritage").

Plaintiffs' Amended Complaint asserts that Plaintiffs faced discrimination on the basis of national origin, specifically their "Jewish ancestry," rather than on the basis of their religious beliefs or observance. As summarized above, the harassment Plaintiffs allege did not concern Plaintiffs' religious beliefs or practices, but rather drew on hackneyed stereotypes, bigoted "jokes," and painful references to the Holocaust and Nazism. In short, the harassment alleged is rooted in Plaintiffs' actual or perceived national origin or race rather than just Plaintiffs' faith or religious practices. The Court finds that, regardless of whether they assert their claims on "national origin" or "race," Plaintiffs are within their rights to assert a claim under Title VI based on anti-Semitic discrimination.

2. Application to Plaintiffs' Case

A school district may be held civilly liable for its deliberate indifference to student-on-student harassment under Title VI. Such "liability only arises if a plaintiff establishes: (1) substantial control, (2) severe and discriminatory harassment, (3) actual knowledge, and (4) deliberate indifference."[3]

a. *Substantial Control*

[The school district had substantial control over the circumstances of the alleged harassment because the incidents occurred on school property, during school trips, or on district-hired buses, and the harassers were fellow students subject to the district's disciplinary authority.]

b. *Severe and Discriminatory Harassment*

These Plaintiffs' depositions catalogue numerous incidents for each Plaintiff that exceed the sort of "non-actionable 'simple acts of teasing and name-calling among school children.'"[4] ... A jury could reasonably conclude that Plaintiffs suffered "severe, pervasive, and objectively offensive" harassment.[5]

A jury could further conclude that Plaintiffs were improperly denied educational benefits as a result of this harassment. At minimum, Plaintiffs were "deprived of a supportive scholastic environment free of racism and harassment." In addition, Plaintiffs report being emotionally distressed by the harassment.... Given these facts, a jury could reasonably find that Plaintiffs suffered severe and discriminatory harassment that denied Plaintiffs educational benefits under Title VI.

---

3. Zeno v. Pine Plains Cent. Sch. Dist., 702 F.3d 655, 665 (2d Cir. 2012).

4. *Id.* at 667 (quoting Davis, 526 U.S. at 652, 119 S.Ct. 1661); *see also* DiStiso v. Cook, 691 F.3d 226, 242–43 (2d Cir.2012) (finding that allegations that a student's "classmates called the child racial epithets or disparaged his race ... by calling him 'nigger' [and] 'blackie,' and by suggesting that the boy's skin remained dirty even after washing" indisputably "raise[d] a question of severe harassment going beyond simple teasing and name-calling").

5. *Zeno*, 702 F.3d at 665 (internal quotation marks omitted); cf. HB v. Monroe Woodbury Cent. Sch. Dist., No. 11-CV-5881, 2012 WL 4477552, at *15 (S.D.N.Y. Sept. 27, 2012) (rejecting Plaintiffs' claims as insufficiently severe to support a Title VI violation because "the utterance of one comment by a student cannot be said to be so 'severe, pervasive and objectively offensive' that it effectively denied [the plaintiff] educational benefits" (internal quotation marks omitted)).

c. Actual Knowledge

[Court finds that administrators' awareness of specific incidents, complaints about other students' harassment, and pervasive anti-Semitic graffiti could establish the district's actual knowledge of harassment against the Jewish students.]

d. Deliberate Indifference

"Responses that are not reasonably calculated to end harassment are inadequate." [The court considers that] "five circumstances should have informed the district's continued response to student harassment of [the plaintiff]." First ... the District had knowledge that meting out discipline to the students who harassed Plaintiffs (to the extent there was such discipline) did not deter others from harassing D.C., O.C., and T.E.... Plaintiffs' parents stressed the "systemic" nature of the harassment that their children regularly faced. Second ... the uncontested facts suggest that harassment of Plaintiffs began at [elementary school], persisted through their time at [middle school], and ... continued throughout their time at [high school]. Third ... attempts at disciplining students for harassment did not appear to have had an effect.... Fourth ... there is no dispute that Plaintiffs here were harassed because they were Jewish. Last, [the District was] aware of other options and resources for countering anti-Semitic sentiment in the District—if only because Plaintiffs' parents told Defendants about them. (*See* ([Mr. C.] describing Mr. C.'s request to Steinberg "to invite in organizations like the [Anti-Defamation League] and NAACP" into the schools and require online classes for teachers.) In light of these considerations, the Court concludes that a jury could find that the District's response was unreasonable....

Here, the District argues that it took measures to combat anti-Semitism in its schools beyond that of the individual disciplining of offending students. PBE Principal Fisch held an assembly to address general bullying issues when T.E. and O.C. were in fifth grade, and later Crispell held a seminar in which a Holocaust survivor spoke to T.E. and O.C.'s seventh-grade class. The Parties dispute the extent to which the District engaged in any other programs to combat anti-Semitism, though Defendants argue that the District's anti-bullying efforts encouraged tolerance generally and "sometimes specifically mentioned anti-Semitism." In addition, District administrators met with Plaintiffs' parents and the students themselves to discuss the harassment and possible solutions, including transferring T.E. and O.C. to a middle school other than Crispell.

Some courts have concluded that general anti-bullying programs (among other actions) prevent a district from being found deliberately indifferent when such programs are used as part of a larger strategy that targets the harassment.

But conducting assemblies, even ones that specifically address the discrimination complained of, does not immunize a school district from liability, as the school district's response must be assessed "in light of the known circumstances." In *Zeno*, for example, despite evidence demonstrating that the school district disciplined the plaintiff's harassers immediately and held an assembly as an attempt to combat school-wide racial harassment, the court nonetheless found the district's response to have been unreasonable. In particular, the court affirmed judgment for the plaintiff on grounds that the jury had reasonably found the district's actions could not have plausibly changed the culture of bias or stopped the harassment and could find that the district ignored many signals that greater, more directed action was needed.

And so it is here. A reasonable jury could find that, while the District may have taken some steps to combat the culture of anti-Semitism in its schools, the handful of assemblies—which addressed only students in T.E. and O.C.'s grade—could not have plausibly changed the anti-Semitic sentiments of the student harassers, many of whom were not classmates of T.E. and O.C. These assemblies also did nothing to target anti-Semitism among the students who harassed D.C. A reasonable jury could find that the number of incidents of harassment against Plaintiffs and the fact that this harassment did not cease following the District's assemblies provided ample indication that additional efforts to change the anti-Semitic culture were required. Moreover, the administrators in question appear to have done nothing to attempt to address anti-Semitism in the District across schools, despite the fact that the incidents that occurred on the school bus involved students who were older than Plaintiffs and who did not attend the same school. Furthermore, taking Plaintiffs' evidence as true, a jury could find that the District also failed to raise awareness among the administration and faculty about the rampant harassment, and that the District failed to implement programs to assist in determining the sources and potential solutions to the culture of anti-Semitism among the District's students. A jury also could reasonably conclude that there were no broad measures put in place to address anti-Semitic graffiti, which appears to have been handled on a case-by-case basis, despite the fact that graffiti often reappeared shortly after it had been removed.

Furthermore, a jury could find that the District's response in instituting programs to target anti-Semitism was unreasonably delayed....

A reasonable jury could find not only that the District failed to adequately respond to specific incidents of reported harassment, but also that it failed to take steps as necessary to combat the atmosphere of anti-Semitism which permeated the District's schools. A jury could further find that the District failed to monitor the effectiveness of the measures it *did* take or implement measures that would enable the District to track bias-related harassment as distinct from non-bias-related bullying, thereby failing to take the ongoing, iterative steps needed to respond to a culture of bias, as required by Title VI. For these reasons, a jury could reasonably conclude that Defendants were deliberately indifferent in their response to the harassment suffered by D.C., O.C., and T.E.

The Legal Basis for Applying Title VI to Jewish Students

1. *Sheepishly.* Judge Karas states that the school district "sheepishly raise[s] the question of whether Plaintiffs may bring a Title VI claim on grounds of deliberate indifference to anti-Semitic harassment...."[6] Why "sheepishly," if the argument advanced their litigation aims? If sheepishly, why raise it at all? Is Judge Karas suggesting that

6. Why sheepishly? An argument is an argument. If bashful about it, why make it at all?

the school district should be ashamed to raise this argument, or that he would have preferred they didn't?

2. *And no religion, too.* While both Title VI (education) and Title VII (employment) of the Civil Rights Act of 1964 prohibit discrimination based on race, color, or national origin, only Title VII bars discrimination based on religion. (Title VI is like §§ 1981 and 1982 in this respect.) If the 1964 Act's drafters intended to include religion as a protected category, it appears that they knew how to do so.[7] Congress might have omitted religion-based discrimination so as to enable religious institutions to favor co-religionists in admissions and employment.[8] Some legislators might also have believed that religious discrimination in education was not widespread.[9]

3. *Race and/or national origin?* On what basis or bases does Judge Karas ground Title VI's application to Jews? There appear at least four possibilities: (a) it is based solely on race; (b) it is based solely on national origin; (c) it could be wholly based on either race or national origin, with each one sufficient but neither necessary; or (d) it is not wholly based on either race or national origin; rather, it is based on some combination or hybrid of race and national origin, with neither sufficient and both necessary. How would that work?

4. Shaare Tefila *as authority.* Does *Shaare Tefila* stand for the proposition that Jews are a racial group for Title VI purposes? Does it strengthen the case for this proposition without commanding it? Were Jews understood as a distinct race when the 1964 Act took effect? If not, is *Shaare Tefila* off point? The same questions can be asked of *U.S. v. Nelson,* 277 F.3d 164 (2d Cir. 2002), which held that § 245(b)(2)(B), enacted as part of the Civil Rights Act of 1968, protected Jews.

5. *Enforcement of Title VI.* In *Pine Bush*, the Jewish students are plaintiffs in a private lawsuit to enforce Title VI in federal court. The U.S. Department of Justice may also enforce Title VI in federal courts, although this is typically limited to school desegregation cases. The U.S. Department of Education's Office for Civil Rights ("OCR") can also investigate a school's compliance with Title VI and, if that is found wanting, cause them to lose their federal funding. Marcus describes OCR administrative action as "arguably the most critical pillar of civil rights enforcement at educational institutions."[10]

---

7. See *expressio unius est exclusio alterius*, "a canon of construction holding that to express or include one thing implies the exclusion of the other, or of the alternative. For example, the rule that 'each citizen is entitled to vote' implies that noncitizens are not entitled to vote." *Expressio Unius Est Exclusio Alterius*, Black's Law Dictionary (12th ed. 2024).

8. Kenneth L. Marcus, *Anti-Zionism As Racism: Campus Anti-Semitism and the Civil Rights Act of 1964*, 15 Wm. & Mary Bill Rts. J. 837, 878–83.

9. *Id.*

10. *Id.* at 857.

Applying Title VI to the Pine Bush School District

1. *Throwing pennies.* There is a long history of throwing change or pennies at Jews, which is rooted in the stereotype that Jews are greedy and avaricious, hoping to make themselves rich by any means.[11] The act of throwing change at Jews is a specifically antisemitic form of harassment and humiliation.

2. *Using "Jew" like the N word.* In certain contexts, the word "Jew" can carry a derogatory or offensive connotation. This is always the case when the word is used as a verb (to "jew down the price")[12] an adjective ("Jew lawyer"), or when spelled with a lowercase *j*. The phrase "T.E. is a Jew" is potentially offensive in a way that "T.E. is Jewish" is not.[13] OED defines "Jew" in the offensive sense as "a hostile or contemptuous term for a Jewish person, especially one regarded stereotypically as scheming or excessively concerned with making or saving money."[14]

3. *Institutional versus structural antisemitism.* The plaintiffs' parents described the anti-Jewish harassment in the school district as "systemic" rather than "an individual thing." Systemic antisemitism might be further broken down into institutional and structural antisemitism, respectively, akin to different forms of racism. Institutional racism inheres in:

> an infrastructure of rulings, ordinances or statutes promulgated by a sovereign government or authoritative entity, whereas such ordinances and statutes entitles one ethnic group in a society certain rights and privileges, while denying other groups in that society these same rights and privileges because of long-established cultural prejudices, religious prejudices, fears, myths, and xenophobias held by the entitled group.[15]

---

11. *See Greed,* THE ANTI-DEFAMATION LEAGUE, https://antisemitism.adl.org/greed/ (last visited Dec. 15, 2024); *see also* Oscar Rickett, *Jews, Money and Antisemitism: How the Hate Myth Was Born,* MIDDLE E. EYE (May 9, 2019, 3:58 PM), https://www.middleeasteye.net/discover/jews-money-antisemitism-hate-myth-was-born-jewish-museum-london.

12. Oxford English Dictionary defines "Jew" used as a verb as "to get or try to get the better of (a person) by charging too much or paying too little; to cheat or swindle." *Jew,* OXFORD ENG. DICTIONARY, https://doi.org/10.1093/OED/7143561626 (last visited June 2024).

13. *How Did "Jew" Become Pejorative?,* STACK EXCH. (JUNE 13, 2014), https://english.stackexchange.com/questions/43466/how-did-jew-become-pejorative.

14. *Jew,* OXFORD ENG. DICTIONARY, https://doi.org/10.1093/OED/5457641791 (last visited Sept. 2024).

15. United Nations Hum. Rts. Off. of the High Comm'r, *Systemic Racism vs. Institutional Racism,* UNITED NATIONS, https://www.ohchr.org/sites/default/files/Documents/Issues/Racism/smd.shahid.pdf (last visited Nov. 26, 2024). Institutional racism and structural racism are also known as (confusingly) "systemic racism" and "institutional racism," respectively. GEETA N. KAPUR, RACE, LAW, AND THE STRUGGLE FOR RACIAL EQUALITY IN THE U.S. 14–15 (1st ed. 2024). The term "systemic racism" can refer to either institutional or structural racism, or both. *See e.g., Systemic Racism,* OXFORD ENG. DICTIONARY, https://doi.org/10.1093/OED/3519067187 (last visited Nov. 26, 2024) (defining systemic racism as "discrimination or unequal treatment on the basis of membership of a particular racial or ethnic group (typically one that is a minority or marginalized), arising from systems, structures, or expectations that have become established within society or an institution.").

Structural racism denotes the cultural, social, and ideological context that perpetuates and normalizes racist attitudes, and:

> can be defined as the racial attitudes found in an ethnic group's traditions, beliefs, opinions, and myths that are firmly ingrained in the very fiber of the ethnic group's cultural paradigm, where such traditions, beliefs, opinions, and myths have been practiced and sustained for so long, that they are accepted as common facts, understood to be normal behavioral practices, whereas, such practices in effect marginalize and demonize the human worth of another ethnic group.[16]

The plaintiffs were confronted with two types of structural antisemitism: the culture of antisemitism in the school district and the pervasive antisemitism in the surrounding community. Assistant principal Winter aptly observed "that it's rather hard to stop something that's inbred in the community."

Consider the student who hears a religious leader sermonize that Jews collectively murdered Jesus.[17] It is not unforeseeable that the same student would call a Jewish student, "Christ Killer." What if anything can school districts do to combat antisemitism based on religious doctrine or scripture?[18]

4. *The harassment got worse.* Was Assistant Principal Winter wrong to advise T.E. and O.C. that they "were causing [their] own problems" by reporting antisemitic incidents to school authorities? Students told D.C. that "if [he] did anything [in response to this harassment,] that they knew where [he] lived." When D.C. later complained, things "got worse." What should the Jewish students have done? By reporting the harassment, they might, in fact, have made things worse for themselves in the short term. By collecting evidence about the administrators' response, however, these students made things "worse" for the school district (and perhaps for some administrators) in the form of bad publicity, a losing lawsuit, and so forth, and helped create good law in the form of Judge Karas's opinion.

5. *General anti-bullying programs.* Judge Karas distinguishes between "bias-related harassment" and "non-bias-related bullying," concluding that a program to combat the latter was an inadequate response to antisemitic harassment. Is antisemitic-specific training necessary for the same reason the law should punish bias-motivated crimes more severely than non-bias-motivated crimes?

6. As part of the settlement, the school district agreed, inter alia, to the following steps:

a. Mandatory training for teachers and staff members on how to recognize and report antisemitic harassment.

---

16. United Nations Hum. Rts. Off. of the High Comm'r, *supra* note 15.

17. *See Myth: Jews Killed Jesus*, The Anti-Defamation League, https://antisemitism.adl.org/deicide/ (last visited Dec. 15, 2024).

18. *See generally* Richard Moon, Putting Faith in Hate: When Religion Is the Source or Target of Hate Speech (2018).

b. A diversity and anti-bullying curriculum developed by the ADL.[19]

c. A policy against discrimination and bullying to ensure that they cover and prohibit antisemitic harassment and that such episodes be "promptly and thoroughly" investigated.

d. Meaningful, consistent, minimum consequences for antisemitic harassment that increase in severity for repeated instances .

7. *Unexpurgated.* Judge Karas's opinion included the hateful words other students directed at the plaintiffs:

> The Court recognizes that some of the language that Plaintiffs allege to have been directed against them is undeniably offensive and may be painful for some readers. Nonetheless, the Court does not see fit to censor or euphemize Plaintiffs' allegations in this Opinion. As Plaintiffs' counsel stated at oral argument, "the language matters in this case, and there's a way in which, by not articulating some of these things, they lose their force."[20]

Did Judge Karas's make the right decision?

8. *Deliberate indifference versus selective indifference.* To determine whether a school is deliberately indifferent to its Jewish students' distress, is it relevant to consider how they address the concerns of students who belong to other marginalized groups? According to Executive Order on Combating Anti-Semitism (December 11, 2019), "it shall be the policy of the executive branch to enforce Title VI against prohibited forms of discrimination rooted in anti-Semitism *as vigorously* as against all other forms of discrimination prohibited by Title VI."[21] What is the relationship between (a) a school's deliberate indifference to the harassment of its Jewish students; and (b) its relative indifference to the harassment of Jewish students as compared to a more proactive response to the harassment of students belonging to other marginalized groups? The latter would appear to be direct discrimination, a separate Title VI violation.

9. *Pollard v. Georgetown Sch. Dist.*, 132 F. Supp. 3d 208 (D. Mass. 2015). A Jewish middle school student's Title VI complaint contained a single allegation concerning Jewishness: "Fellow students have mocked J.H. for his religion and ethnicity with snide comments about Jews being massacred and stating that the Holocaust was unsuccessful because J.H.'s family survived." The court rejected the student's Title VI claim:

> Although the comments here were certainly objectively offensive, the factual allegations as presently alleged do not meet the high standard of severity or

---

19. *See, e.g.*, ADL Education, *Anti-Bias Curriculum Guides*, The Anti-Defamation League (Jan. 11, 2024), https://www.adl.org/resources/tools-and-strategies/anti-bias-curriculum-guides?gad_source=1&gclid=CjwKCAjwx4O4BhAnEiwA42SbVC8bQvX1rAhthY_2PBWUBT-prF8s-No5TI83_H5U5kK9uBalN5Lg6xoCQ4cQAvD_BwE&gclsrc=aw.ds.

20. T.E. V. Pine Bush Cent. Sch. Dist., 58 F. Supp. 3d 332, 339 n.5.

21. Exec. Order No. 13899, 84 Fed. Reg. 68779 (Dec. 11, 2019).

pervasiveness under well-developed case law, but Pollard may seek to amend as to same.[22]

10. *Kyrene School District #28.* In August 2022, OCR found that the Kyrene School District #28 in Arizona violated Title VI by failing to respond appropriately to at least nine students' harassment of a Jewish student in school and on social media. Most notably, other students called the girl a "dirty Jew," "stinky Jew," and "filthy Jew"; made jokes about the Holocaust; spoke or pretended to speak in German; and were marching/saluting like Nazi soldiers to the student and in her presence. They said, "I hear you are good at head because Jews are so good at gasping for air," asked her "How do you get a Jewish girl's number?" and demanded that she "lift her sleeve." The school district entered into a voluntary resolution agreement with OCR to review and revise its policies and procedures to address Title VI. [23]

11. *Park City School District in Utah.* On March 20, 2024, the Park City School District in Utah signed a resolution agreement to resolve OCR's investigation of alleged antisemitic harassment including slurs, threats, name-calling, jokes, gestures, symbols, and assaults at the school, an investigation that revealed evidence of 27 antisemitic incidents.[24] OCR found that the school district's responses were insufficient based on, inter alia, its failure to inform affected students about available support or keep records of its responses to reports, and the fact that most employees were unaware of the district's responses.

Kenneth L. Marcus,[25] The Landmark Case of *Shaare Tefila v. Cobb*

25 Federalist Soc'y Rev. 17 (2024)

On September 28, 2023, eight federal cabinet-level agencies formally clarified, for the first time, that Title VI of the Civil Rights of 1964 prohibits ethnic and ancestral discrimination against Jewish Americans and members of various other ethno-religious

22. Pollard v. Georgetown Sch. Dist., 132 F. Supp. 3d 208, 230–31 (D. Mass. 2015).

23. Michael D. Todd, U.S. Dep't of Educ., Off. of C.R., OCR Reference No. 08-19-1367, Kyrene School District (2022), https://www2.ed.gov/about/offices/list/ocr/docs/investigations/more/08191367-a.pdf.

24. J. Aaron Romine, U.S. Dep't of Educ., Off. of C.R., Park City Cases, Park City School District, (2024), https://www.ed.gov/sites/ed/files/about/offices/list/ocr/docs/investigations/more/08231193-a.pdf.

25. Marcus is Founder and Chairman of the Louis D. Brandeis Center for Human Rights Under Law. He served as Assistant U.S. Secretary of Education for Civil Rights in two U.S. administrations. He formulated the doctrine that Title VI protects Jews and members of other faiths when they are targeted due to their ancestry or ethnicity. The Brandeis Center and other Jewish advocacy groups have used this legal doctrine to advocate on behalf of the rights of Jewish students and employees at numerous institutions. *See* Vimal Patel, *The Man Who Helped Redefine Campus Antisemitism*, N.Y. Times (Mar. 24, 2024), https://www.nytimes.com/2024/03/24/us/politics/kenneth-marcus-college-antisemitism-complaints.html.

groups.[26] This move, and its underlying concept, dispelled any remaining doubt that Title VI—which prohibits discrimination on the basis of race, color, or national origin, but not religion—applies to ethnic groups that share a common religion. The White House announced that this move was taken to advance President Joseph Biden's National Strategy to Combat Anti-Semitism. In fact, the action was the culmination of a twenty-year effort, begun during the George W. Bush administration, to ensure that federal officials would extend uniform protections to such populations in a manner consistent with the U.S. Supreme Court's unanimous decision in the case of *Shaare Tefila v. Cobb*. Full disclosure: I have been a principal player in these efforts. Indeed, the notion that Title VI protects ethno-religious groups from discrimination based on ethnic or ancestral characteristics has been variously described as the "Marcus Policy" or "Marcus Doctrine" (although I will describe it below as the 2004 Policy).

Shaare Tefila does indeed provide an important perspective on the relationship between Jewish identity, religion, and race in American law. And yet it is also a landmark case in American civil rights law, not only because of the Biden Administration's action, but also because it has supported a large-scale revision in the way that Jewish Americans and other religious groups are treated under Title VI of the Civil Rights Act of 1964.

While not as widely known as it deserves to be, *Shaare Tefila* should be considered—together with its companion case, *St. Francis College v. Al-Khazraji*—the seminal case on the legal status of ethno-religious groups such as Jews and Sikhs under racial discrimination laws in the United States. *Shaare Tefila* established for the first time that ethno-religious group members could avail themselves of civil rights protections that were established to protect against race discrimination. In other words, ancestral groups that also share a common religion would not be treated differently (i.e., with fewer protections) than those that do not. During the period when [the Department of Education was debating whether Title VI covered Jews], *Shaare Tefila* provided crucial legal support for agency guidance regarding the protection of such groups....

Shaare Tefila's *Downstream Effects*

Sixteen years [after the Supreme Court decided *Shaare Tefila*], in 2004, a Sikh man went to the New York office of the U.S. Department of Education's Office for Civil Rights (OCR) and complained that his son, a New Jersey junior high school student, had been beaten up and called "Osama." He sought relief from OCR under Title VI of the Civil Rights Act of 1964. At the time, OCR's unwritten policy was to dismiss such cases on the grounds that Title VI, which bars discrimination on the basis of race, color, or national origin, but not religion, could not provide the protection being sought. This time, however, OCR's response would be different.

---

26. *Biden administration to take new actions against antisemitism*, Reuters, Sept. 28, 2023, https://www.reuters.com/article/usa-biden-antisemitism/biden-administration-to-take-new-actions-against-antisemitism. Editor's note: The eight agencies did not include the Departments of Justice and Education, which had already issued similar statements.

I had recently been appointed acting head of that agency, and I had asked my staff to be on the lookout for such cases. In the wake of September 11, 2001, I was aware of news reports indicating an uptick of discrimination against various Middle Eastern and North African minorities, as well as a surge in anti-Semitism incidents, both globally and also on U.S. college campuses. It was clear that some of these cases might be based on religious animus, but others were more likely related to ethnic or racial attitudes. In this case, there were many possible explanations for why a Sikh American youth might be subjected to such mistreatment, and some of them would clearly fall within the lawful jurisdiction of the agency. While Sikhism is a major religion, for example, members of the Sikh community also share various ethnic or ancestral characteristics, such as distinctive dress, music, culture, and geographic origins. I directed my staff to open an investigation and issued a series of memoranda explaining the basis for my decision.

On September 13, 2004, I issued informal guidance clarifying that discrimination on the basis of Sikh or Jewish identity is no less unlawful than discrimination based on membership in a group that shares ethnic but not religious attributes:

> Groups that face discrimination on the basis of shared ethnic characteristics may not be denied the protection of our civil rights laws on the ground that they also share a common faith. Similarly, the existence of facts indicative of religious discrimination does not divest OCR of jurisdiction to investigate and remedy allegations of race or ethnic discrimination.... Thus, for example, OCR aggressively investigates alleged race or ethnic harassment against Arab Muslim, Sikh and Jewish students.[27]

In this common-sense formulation, I did not find it necessary to cite *Shaare Tefila*, although I drew some of the language (e.g., "ethnic characteristics") directly from it. I was also aware, as Justices Stevens and Scalia suggested, that Jewishness is more than a religion, while anti-Semitism is more than a religious animus. As one commentator would later write of the 2004 Policy, "The logic behind the clarification is simple: much of the hatred embodied in anti-Semitism (and the same is true for Islamophobia) has nothing to do with specific religious practices, and everything to do with ancestral bias."[28]

[The 2004] policy faced numerous objections. Progressives argued that the civil rights laws should be used for disadvantaged minorities and that Jews had no need for it. Bureaucrats were often change-averse and suspicious that the policy would somehow be used to increase the role of religion in education. Some Jewish officials were

---

27. *See* Letter from Kenneth L. Marcus, Deputy Ass't Sec'y for Enforcement, Delegated the Auth. of Ass't Sec'y of Educ. for Civil Rights, U.S. Dep't of Educ., to Colleague, Title VI and Title IX Religious Discrimination in Schools and Colleges (Sept. 13, 2004), *available at* https://www2.ed.gov/about/offices/list/ocr/letters/religious-rights2004.pdf.

28. Mark Goldfeder, *Defining Antisemitism*, 52 SETON HALL L. REV. 119, 144 (2021), *available at* https://scholarship.shu.edu/cgi/viewcontent.cgi?article=1808&context=shlr.

reluctant to view Jews as victims. Even some conservatives objected, misunderstanding the legal basis for the policy.

The most serious objection was this: While the Supreme Court had held that Jews are protected by the Civil Rights Act of 1866 on the grounds that Congress at that time considered Jews to be a separate race, no congressmen in 1964 thought of Jews that way; at any rate, the legislative record contains no record of that. Thus, the reasoning supporting the decision in *Shaare Tefila* was inapplicable when later-passed civil rights laws were at issue. This objection is premised on the unworkable notion that terms like "race" and "national origin" have different meanings in each place that they appear in the U.S. Code, depending on the changing understandings of those terms over the years during which various civil rights laws were passed. Additionally, it ignores the Supreme Court's repeated holding that "race" has the same meaning in the Civil Rights Act of 1964 as in the Fourteenth Amendment and the 19th-century civil rights laws.[29] The basis for this principle is that the Civil Rights Act was not designed to create new rights with respect to race, but rather to create a new system for enforcing rights that had been established a century before.

Nevertheless, despite the clear holding of *Shaare Tefila v. Cobb*, federal officials refused to accept that Jews were protected under a statute that prohibited racial and national origin but not religious discrimination. The Commission, however, supported my view. On April 3, 2006, the Commission sent a shot across OCR's bow, issuing a statement (which I had drafted) that included this affirmation of the 2004 Policy:

> Many college campuses throughout the United States continue to experience incidents of anti-Semitism.... When severe, persistent, or pervasive, this behavior may constitute a hostile environment for students in violation of Title VI of the Civil Rights Act of 1964.[30]

In other words, the Civil Rights Commission confirmed the 2004 Policy that Title VI applies to some forms of anti-Semitism, even though the statute (like the one at issue in *Shaare Tefila*) does not mention religion. Since then, the 2004 Policy has been confirmed in court with respect to Title VI[31] and also Title VII.[32]

Over the next four years, we received increasing reports that OCR was nevertheless refusing to apply Title VI in anti-Semitism cases. In deposition testimony, OCR officials confirmed that this was the case. Senior OCR leadership privately believed—and later disclosed when questioned under oath—that anti-Semitism cases were purely

---

29. *See, e.g.*, Regents of University of California v. Bakke, 438 U.S. 265, 272 (1987). *See also* Gratz v. Bollinger, 539 U.S. 244, 275 (2003).

30. Findings and Recommendations of the United States Commission on Civil Rights Regarding Campus Anti-Semitism (Aug. 3, 2006), https://www.usccr.gov/files/pubs/docs/081506campusanti-brief07.pdf.

31. T.E. v. Pine Bush Cent. Sch. Dist., 58 F. Supp. 3d 332, 354–55 (S.D.N.Y. 2014). *See generally* Goldfeder, *Defining Antisemitism, supra* note 28, at 144–45.

32. *See, e.g.*, Vill. of Freeport v. Barrella, 814 F.3d 594, 607 (2d Cir. 2016) ("Hispanic" constitutes a race for purposes of Title VII). *But see* Bonadona v. La. Coll., No.18-cv-0224, 2018 WL 4353979, at *4 (W.D. La. July 13, 2018) (rejecting a Jewish Title VII race claim).

religious matters that should not be handled by their agency. In response, when I left the federal government, I led a coalition of Jewish organizations seeking to convince the Education and Justice Departments that Jews and other ethno-religious groups are indeed covered by the terms of Title VI, just as the Supreme Court had held that they are covered by earlier civil rights legislation. Those two departments responded favorably to our advocacy.

In 2010, Assistant Attorney General Thomas Perez affirmed this interpretation on behalf of the Department of Justice. In response to a request from Assistant Secretary of Education Russlynn Ali, who had succeeded to my position at OCR, Perez quoted the operative paragraph of my September 2004 letter (set forth above) and wrote, "We agree with that analysis."[33] Perez explained the rationale, drawing language from *Shaare Tefila*:

> Although Title VI does not prohibit discrimination on the basis of religion, discrimination against Jews, Muslims, Sikhs, and members of other religious groups violates Title VI when that discrimination is based on the group's actual or perceived shared ancestry or ethnic characteristics, rather than its members' religious practice. Title VI further prohibits discrimination against an individual where it is based on actual or perceived citizenship or residency in a country whose residents share a dominant religion or a distinct religious identity.[34]

OCR reiterated this position in 2010[35] and in subsequent communications.[36] Nevertheless, this extension of *Shaare Tefila* remained a creature only of informal agency guidance until 2019. Various efforts were made, without success, to codify the approach of my 2004 Dear Colleague Letter, but these efforts remained unsuccessful.

On December 11, 2019, President Donald Trump elevated the issue to the level of a government-wide decree. In his Executive Order 13899 on Combating Anti-Semitism, President Trump reiterated the substance and rationale of the 2004 Policy:

> While Title VI does not cover discrimination based on religion, individuals who face discrimination on the basis of race, color, or national origin do not lose protection under Title VI for also being a member of a group that shares common religious practices. Discrimination against Jews may give rise to a

---

33. Thomas E. Perez, Ass't Att'y Gen., Dep't of Justice, to Russlynn H. Ali, Ass't Sec'y of Educ., Office for Civil Rights, U.S. Dep't of Educ., Title VI and Coverage of Religiously Identifiable Groups (Sept. 8, 2010), *at* https://www.justice.gov/sites/default/files/crt/legacy/2011/05/04/090810_AAG_Perez_Letter_to_Ed_OCR_Title%20VI_and_Religiously_Identifiable_Groups.pdf.

34. *Id.*

35. *See* Russlyn H. Ali, Ass't Sec'y of Educ., Office for Civil Rights, U.S. Dep't of Educ., to Colleague (Oct. 26, 2010), *available at* https://www2.ed.gov/about/offices/list/ocr/letters/colleague-201010.pdf (not for reliance for certain purposes immaterial to the topic of this review).

36. *See, e.g.*, U.S. Department of Education, Office for Civil Rights, Combating Discrimination Against Jewish Students (Jan. 2017), https://www2.ed.gov/about/offices/list/ocr/docs/jewish-fact-sheet-201701.pdf.

> Title VI violation when the discrimination is based on an individual's race, color, or national origin.[37] . . .

President Trump's Executive Order 13899 remains in place, as do the 2004, 2010, and 2017 guidance documents. In May, the Biden National Anti-Semitism Strategy directed the Assistant Secretary of Education for Civil Rights to remind schools of "their legal obligation under Title VI . . . to address complaints of discrimination. . . ."[38] That same document directed eight agencies to produce fact sheets explaining that "Title VI . . . prohibits discrimination based on shared ancestry or ethnic characteristics, including certain forms of antisemitic, Islamophobic, and related forms of discrimination and bias, in federally funded programs and activities." This is precisely the dictate with which these agencies complied on September 28, 2023, an outcome made possible by the legal groundwork a courageous synagogue laid long ago.

The nearly twenty-year saga since the passage of the 2004 Policy, which owes much of its vitality to the *Shaare Tefila v. Cobb* case, demonstrates that this litigation has had a profound effect on the trajectory of the fight against anti-Semitism. This case . . . underlies the once-controversial notion, developed under the George W. Bush, Barack Obama, and Donald Trump administrations, and confirmed yet again under Joseph Biden's, that Jews and other ethno-racial groups must receive equal protection under statutes, like Title VI, that prohibit racial and national origin but not religious discrimination. It may be time to reappraise the importance of the *Shaare Tefila* case, and to recognize it as the landmark decision that it clearly was.

Are Jews Defined by Religion, Race, National Origin, Ancestry, or Ethnicity Under Title VI?

1. *Ethnic groups.* As between two groups defined by ancestry and/or ethnicity, a group should not be denied Title VI's protections simply because it is *also* partly defined by religion. So far so good. Yet what is the basis for extending Title VI to any ancestral or ethnic group, ethno-religious or otherwise, given that Title VI's scope is limited to "race, color, or national origin"? Recall how Judge Karas answered (or didn't) the question.

2. *Is Jewishness a national origin?* In *Lapine v. Edward Marshall Boehm, Inc.*, No. 89 C 8420, 1990 WL 43572 (N.D. Ill. 1990), the district court rejected the claim that anti-Jewish discrimination is a form of Title VII national origin discrimination:

> Plaintiff can point to no authority for the proposition that the characteristic of being "Jewish" indicates national origin. Judaism is indisputably a religion and

37. Donald J. Trump, E.O. 13899, *Combating Anti-Semitism* (Dec. 11, 2019), https://www.govinfo.gov/content/pkg/DCPD-201900859/pdf/DCPD-201900859.pdf. This order is probably best known for its application of the International Holocaust Remembrance Alliance's Working Definition of Anti-Semitism.

38. The White House, *The U.S. National Strategy to Counter Antisemitism* (May 2023), https://www.whitehouse.gov/wp-content/uploads/2023/05/U.S.-National-Strategy-to-Counter-Antisemitism.pdf.

> has been held to constitute a race as well. See *Shaare Tefila Congregation v. Cobb*. However, stating that one is Jewish gives no indication of that individual's country of origin. Nor does it indicate the country of origin of one's ancestors or suggest the physical or cultural characteristics of a national origin group. Indeed, Jews, like Catholics and Protestants, hail from a variety of different countries. Accordingly, applying the standards for national origin as set forth in *Espinoza v. Farah Mfg. Co.*, (1973), we do not find that plaintiff has stated a claim for discrimination based on national origin.[39]

Is Jewish identity more akin to "national origin" than Catholic and/or Protestant identity?

While rejecting the Jewish plaintiff's Title VII national origin claim, the *Lapine* court accepted the Title VII claim of religious discrimination. Would the result have been different if Title VII (like Title VI and §§ 1981 and 1982) barred discrimination based on national origin but not on religion? So as to provide the plaintiff with recourse for employment discrimination, should the court define Jewishness as a "national origin" for Title VII purposes?

In a 2007 article, Marcus expressed skepticism as to whether anti-Jewish discrimination could be construed as a form of national origin discrimination.

> As an intuitive matter, many policymakers would prefer to bar anti-Semitism as a form of national origin discrimination because that category appears, at first blush, to approach most closely the common understanding of Jews as an ethnic group. In fact, the legal basis for barring anti-Semitism as a form of national origin discrimination is much shakier than the ground for barring it as a form of racial discrimination.
>
> Although this area of the law is unsettled, at least one district court has held ... that Jews do not constitute a national origin group under Title VII,[40] but a couple of others have held that they do.[41] This reflects the current tension that exists, more generally, with respect to the scope of "national origin" protection. Some lower courts have extended "national origin" broadly to include, e.g., gypsies, Serbs, Cajuns, and Ukrainians at times when these groups have not held independent nations. Such courts have relied upon various ancestral or ethnic features to establish "nationality": physical characteristics, language, distinct culture, surnames, documented history of the group's existence, physiognomically distinct characteristics, and even predominant religion. Some of these traits could form the basis of an argument that American Jews form a national origin group. Similarly, the U.S. Equal Employment Opportunity

39. Lapine v. Edward Marshall Boehm, Inc., No. 89 C 8420, 1990 WL 43572, at *5 (N.D. Ill. Mar. 28, 1990).

40. *Id.* This unpublished opinion provides only a brief, perfunctory discussion of the issue and cannot be considered persuasive.

41. *See* Weiss v. United States, 595 F. Supp. 1050 (E.D. Va. 1984); *see also* Compston v. Borden, Inc., 424 F. Supp. 157 (S.D. Ohio 1976).

Commission has defined national origin discrimination to "includ[e], but not [be] limited to, the denial of equal employment opportunity because of an individual's, or his or her ancestor's, place of origin; or because an individual has the physical, cultural or linguistic characteristics of a national origin group." Such a broad construction of "national origin" could be used to prohibit anti-Semitism.

On the other hand, the single Supreme Court case to analyze "national origin" within the meaning of the 1964 Act, *Espinoza v. Farah Manufacturing Co.*, interpreted the term very narrowly. In *Espinoza*, the plaintiff alleged that the defendant clothing company's policy of restricting its hiring to United States citizens constituted national origin discrimination in violation of Title VII. The Court, noting the absence of significant legislative history on this issue, held that Title VII only protected U.S. citizens from discrimination. When specifically addressing the national origin issue, Justice Marshall noted that national origin "on its face refers to the country where a person was born, or, more broadly, the country from which his or her ancestors came."[42]

3. *A pragmatic approach.* Schraub reports that some Jews took offense to the "national origin" designation as calling into question American Jews' Americanness: "It was perceived as ... another way of telling American Jews, 'This is not your country.'"[43] In Schraub's view:

> The emphatic denials by some Jewish commentators that Jews should ever be conceived as a national grouping risk unraveling the entire basis for affording Jews Title VI protection in the first place.... Only some notion of legally cognizable Jewish nationhood (or race) brings Jews under Title VI's ambit....
>
> Jews are ... taking a very dangerous position here—insisting that we must withdraw from the protection of antidiscrimination law, because it might obliquely confirm the anti-Semite's suspicion that the Jew is different.

Should Jews contest the specific Title VI designation—racial versus national origin—so long as it yields the desired result? Compare some Jews' trepidation to being defined as a "national origin" group under Title VI with some other Jews' trepidation to being defined as a racial group under § 1982. Which designation might concern Jews more, and why? Which interpretation requires less wrangling to obtain?

Where does this leave us? Is Title VI's ban on racial discrimination the only principled basis for banning ancestry/ethnicity discrimination?

4. *Racial discrimination?* Can Title VI's ban on racial discrimination be reasonably construed as a ban on ancestral and/or ethnic discrimination? Marcus argues that *Shaare Tefila* provided "crucial legal support" for efforts to include Jews in Title VI's

---

42. Marcus, *supra* note 8, at 874–875.

43. David Schraub, *Why Trump's Executive Order on Anti-Semitism Touched Off a Firestorm*, THE ATLANTIC (Dec. 12, 2019) https://www.theatlantic.com/ideas/archive/2019/12/dilemma-jewish-identity/603493/.

purview. How crucial? In Marcus's view, does *Shaare Tefila* stand for the proposition that Jews are a racial group for Title VI purposes? If not, does it support that proposition or make it more plausible?

5. *Does the Equal Protection clause define "race" under Title VI?* When Title VI was enacted in 1964, most legislators likely did not view Jews as a distinct race. Marcus argues that the drafters of the 1964 Act's views concerning Jews should not control the meaning of "race" as used in Title VI. He would ground its meaning on the Fourteenth Amendment's Equal Protection Clause. He argues, first, that the Fourteenth Amendment was enacted to provide a constitutional foundation to §§ 1981 and 1982 of the Civil Rights Act of 1866 and that, second, Title VI was enacted to enforce the rights established under the Equal Protection Clause and, by extension, the 1866 Act. Stated differently, the drafters of the 1964 Act incorporated the Equal Protection Clause, and in this way incorporated the Clause drafters' idea of Jews with an identity. It simply does not matter what the drafters of the 1964 Act thought about Jewish identity. Does anti-Jewish discrimination by schools receiving federal funds constitute "state action" for Equal Protection purposes? If not, the Thirteenth Amendment, which requires no state action, may be the surer constitutional basis for applying Title VI to Jews.

6. *A penumbral category?* Marcus argues that the protected categories of race, color, national origin, and religion should be viewed as "a single undifferentiated totality rather than four discrete categories" and that "they represent the categories of disadvantaged otherness."[44] This penumbral category of "disadvantaged otherness" might authorize Title VI to ban discrimination based on religion without it being specifically named and without requiring courts to subsume Jews within one or more of the other named categories.

Assume a civil rights statute explicitly bars discrimination based on race, color, or religion. On Marcus's theory, should that statute be construed to bar national origin discrimination?

7. So, what, after all, is the legal basis for applying Title VI to multiracial ethnic groups, ethnoreligious or otherwise?

Kenneth L. Marcus, *Standing Up for Jewish Students*

Jerusalem Post (September 9, 2013)

For several years, the Jewish community has struggled with the right response to such incidents [of anti-Jewish harassment on campus] as they have escalated. There are, of course, brave students and faculty willing to stand up to this thuggish behavior.... But there is yet one more critical approach: Confronting this behavior for what it is—a violation of the civil rights of Jewish students.

44. Kenneth L. Marcus, Jewish Identity and Civil Rights in America 197–198 (2010).

This can be done by pursuing a claim before the U.S. Department of Education's Office for Civil Rights. In 2004, and again in 2010, OCR acknowledged that Jewish students have civil rights that must be protected. Since then, several Jewish advocates have filed complaints with OCR, trying to protect the rights of Jewish students.

It is fair to ask whether this effort is working.

In one sense, we have been disappointed [citing unsuccessful Title VI actions].

Seeing all these cases rejected has been frustrating and disappointing, but we are, in fact, comforted by knowing that we are having the effect we had set out to achieve.

First, we have given voice at the highest levels of the federal government to the concerns of Jewish students and faculty. These cases may have been rejected by a low-level regional staffer, but as long as we bring them, they will force federal officials to take seriously the conclusions reached by two successive administrations: that Jews deserve protections from ethnic disparagement in higher education settings.

Second, we have put universities on notice.

These cases—even when rejected—expose administrators to bad publicity. Just last week, I heard from a university chancellor who is eager to work with the Schusterman Center for Israel Studies at Brandeis University to avert the possibility of a civil rights complaint.

At many campuses, the prospect of litigation has made a difference.

If a university shows a failure to treat initial complaints seriously, it hurts them with donors, faculty, political leaders and prospective students. No university wants to be accused of creating an abusive environment.

Federal officials have noted the abusive habits of some faculty and students, and those findings have bruised the reputation of these campuses. This is important.

Third, by pursuing complaints through legal channels, we affirm that these are legal—not political—issues. In this respect, it doesn't matter whether Israel should or should not have a security barrier. It doesn't matter whether Israel should support Jewish housing beyond the Green Line. It doesn't matter even that there is such a thing as a Jewish state.

What matters is that universities should be places where Jews do not feel threatened by virtue of their shared ethnic heritage. We are shifting the debate.

Fourth, we are creating a very strong disincentive for outrageous behavior by students in particular. Israel-haters now publicly complain that these cases make it harder for them to recruit new adherents. Apparently, students are being told not to get mixed up in Jewbaiting,[45] rather to focus on their studies and get their degrees. Needless to say, getting caught up in a civil rights complaint is not a good way to build a resume or impress a future employer.

45. Editor's note: "The harassment, abuse, or intentional provocation of a Jewish person or Jewish people; the incitement or exploitation of anti-Semitic sentiment." *Jew-baiting*, Oxford Eng. Dictionary, https://doi.org/10.1093/OED/7575073003 (last visited Sept. 2024).

Finally, the only way to win these cases is to file them, even when we see some or most rejected. In my view, the findings of existing authorities are important but not final. Not all cases are going to meet the same fate.

Sadly, the outrages of anti-Semitism on campus make it likely that Jew-hatred will become even more extreme, and another incident will capture the attention of our legal team and federal investigators. When that happens, we will be ready.

After all, we cannot leave Jewish students undefended. When young people have the courage to step forward and assert their rights, we must stand behind them.

B. *Don't Roll Your Eyes*: Listen to Jews When They Perceive Antisemitism

Jewish Students at the University of Vermont, *Personal Reports*[46]

(September 9, 2022)

Student 1:

"As a survivor myself, I felt isolated. When I came back to campus this fall, I didn't hang my *mezuzah* on the wall outside my door because of fear of antisemitism."

Student 2:

"I wore a Jewish-identifying necklace every day until I began to feel unsafe at UVM due to antisemitic rhetoric on campus and on social media as well as personal antisemitic messages that I received. Antisemitism on campus has caused my mental health to decline and has caused multiple anxiety/panic attacks, and I no longer wear Jewish-identifying items, as I feel unsafe."

Student 3:

"If it were not for the immense support I have gotten from UVM Hillel staff and students, I would have left UVM a long time ago and never returned. I genuinely considered transferring over the summer, going as far as to meet with a college coach and re-open the Common App. I talk to my Jewish friends at colleges all over the New England area, and they are all appalled that I am still here. My mental health has suffered immensely, and the various antisemitic incidents on campus and online have left me suffering with feelings of loneliness, depression, and hopelessness. I am tired of feeling scared on my own college campus. I am tired of feeling anxious to wear my Star of Da-

46. *Personal Reports from UVM Students to Jewish on Campus*, Jewish on Campus (Sept. 13, 2022), https://www.jewishoncampus.org/media/personal-reports-from-uvm-students-to-jewish-on-campus. These reports were collected and posted by Jewish on Campus, whose stated mission is "to amplify the voices of Jewish students, strengthen Jewish identity, and combat hate to secure the future of the Jewish people." *Who We Are*, Jewish on Campus, https://www.jewishoncampus.org/about (last visited Dec. 15, 2024).

vid. I am tired of being scared to mention my Judaism or connection to Israel to people in my college classes, afraid that they will cut all contact with me if they find out who I truly am. I want to feel like I am a part of this college, but I feel more disconnected from each antisemitic incident that occurs. Jewish students on campus deserve better, and we deserve to feel safe."

Student 4:

"When people ask me what it's like to go to college, I always tell them it was a culture shock. But I don't mean living by myself or that Vermonters say 'creemees' instead of 'soft-serve.' I mean that I had to learn what it means to stop expressing my identity and to live in fear because I'm Jewish. I've heard my classmates yell slurs at other Jews, and I've seen them march through downtown chanting antisemitic things. I'm terrified of what would happen if they knew more about me. But what scares me the most is that I know there's nothing I can do about it, because every time I try to ask the administration to even denounce antisemitism, they dismiss me."

Student 5:

"Antisemitism at UVM has become so pervasive that I've become numb to it. When Israel is brought up in class and I automatically tense up, afraid to make any motion that suggests I have some sort of connection to the country, when I walk past posters every day that seek to exclude me as a Jew from otherwise inclusive spaces, when I am forced to choose all the time between my progressive identity and my Jewish identity, it hardly even fazes me anymore. This is simply the unfortunate reality of being a Jewish student at many colleges in the U.S. What I feel particularly makes UVM stand out negatively is the administration's complete apathy in the wake of numerous reported acts of antisemitism on campus. It's very upsetting to attend a university whose entire ethos is their image as a progressive and tolerant school when Jewish students have been trying to tell them for years now that this is not the case and have gone ignored."

Student 6:

"I could not concentrate on my finals last year. Everywhere I turned, people were posting and talking about Israel and how terrible Israelis were. Dealing with the misconceptions and rumors about my people while checking in on my close family who spent their days in bomb shelters took a toll on my well-being. I just sat in my room feeling too paralyzed to move for days even after my last final."

Common Themes in Jewish Students' Experiences of Antisemitism

1. *Harm to mental health and academic performance.* Students report significant negative effects on their mental well-being, including anxiety, panic attacks, depression, loneliness, hopelessness, and inability to concentrate on final exams. Students in the Pine Bush school district reported similar feelings.

2. *Safety concerns and identity suppression.* Students expressed feeling unsafe on campus, leading them to hide their Jewish identity by removing *mezuzahs* or Star of

David necklaces. Jewish students in the Pine Bush School District, whom others had known since kindergarten, did not have the option of hiding their Jewish identity.

3. *Exclusion from progressive spaces.* Jewish students expressed fear of claiming any connection to Israel in classes or social settings. This is new: Jewish students in the Pine Bush School District did not report this fear.

4. *Inadequate institutional response.* Several accounts expressed frustration with the university administration's lack of action or dismissal of their concerns regarding antisemitism on campus. Unlike at Pine Bush, however, no administrator suggested that the Jewish students were harming themselves or the school by reporting antisemitism. Question whether that is the case in the following document.

President Suresh V. Garimella, *Letter to the UVM Community*[47]

September 15, 2022

[On October 2, 2021, the Brandeis Center and Jewish on Campus (JOC) filed a complaint with OCR alleging that the University of Vermont (University) violated Title VI by tolerating a hostile environment for Jewish students.[48] This complaint included the students' testimonials as evidence. On September 13, 2022, the OCR announced it was opening a formal investigation into antisemitic harassment at the University. Two days later, Dr. Suresh Garimella, the president of UVM, released the letter (Letter) set forth below in response to the OCR's announcement.

On April 3, 2023, OCR sent UVM a letter with its findings. Following the OCR letter, University officials published an annotated version of Garimella's Letter which identified portions they deemed problematic. The underlined text indicates language these officials deemed "hostile or accusatory." The *italicized text* highlights statements they considered "inaccurate, misleading, or incomplete" based on the OCR's findings. They also added footnotes containing information deemed to be "corrective" of the Letter.]

Dear Members of the UVM Community,

This week's media coverage of an investigation by the U.S. Department of Education's Office for Civil Rights (OCR) into an anonymous third party's allegations that the university failed to adequately respond to complaints of anti-Jewish, biased behavior at UVM has painted our community in a patently false light.

47. *President Garimella's 9/15/22 Letter with Annotations*, The Dep't of Educ. Off. of C.R. Title VI Investigation of Antisemitism at UVM, https://dfeurzei.w3.uvm.edu/OCR/SG_statement/letter-text.php (last visited Dec. 15, 2024).

48. Letter from Alyza D. Lewin, President, & Denise Katz-Prober, Dir. Of Legal Initiative, The Louis D. Brandeis Ctr., to Suzanne Goldberg, Acting Assistant Sec., & Adrienne Mundy-Shephard, Acting Reg'l Dir. (Oct. 2, 2021), https://dfeurzei.w3.uvm.edu/OCR/OCR_complaint-redacted-2021-10-02.pdf.

While common wisdom dictates remaining patiently silent as we cooperate diligently with an agency's investigation, I simply cannot do so. These public allegations and our community's deeply held values call for a strong and immediate response....

The uninformed narrative published this week has been harmful to UVM. Equally importantly, it is harmful to our Jewish students, faculty, staff, and alumni.... Exploitation of fear and divisiveness by advancing false claims that UVM failed to respond to complaints of antisemitic behavior creates confusion and a sense of insecurity for the entire community.

I therefore would like to set the record straight regarding the OCR complaint by sharing the core elements of UVM's forthcoming response....

- UVM vigorously denies the false allegation of an insufficient response to complaints of threats and discrimination.
- The complaint alleges UVM failed to adequately respond to three specific incidents:

Allegation 1. The complaint alleges that the university did not adequately respond to student reports of antisemitism by a teaching assistant.

University response to the incident:

A university community member reported on September 6, 2021 that an undergraduate teaching assistant made antisemitic remarks and threatened to lower the grades of Jewish students on their personal social media accounts *prior to serving as a TA. The university took prompt action to ensure that the objectionable statements did not adversely impact students in the classroom and further, to perform a thorough review to ensure all grades were awarded on a non-discriminatory basis. No student reported to the university that this teaching assistant harassed or discriminated against them.*

Allegation 2. A group of university students threw rocks at the Hillel building.

University's response to the incident: On September 24, 2021, UVM Police responded to a report regarding students throwing small rocks at the Hillel building. The incident was reported to the university administration as an incident of hate and bias the following day. The investigation was immediate, and *it was quickly determined that the students who threw the small rocks at a window of the Hillel building were doing so to get the attention of a friend who was convalescing in the building while recovering from an illness, that the throwing stopped after they got a student's attention,*[49] and that there was no reported damage to the building. *There was no evidence of any threatening behavior or that the conduct was motivated by antisemitic bias.*[50] The university's review

49. Two witness statements were obtained regarding the incident. One student reported that the men asked her if she was Jewish and then threw rocks at her window, while another student said that the men were his friends and threw rocks at his window to get him to come outside. The student who knew those who threw the rocks did not feel comfortable sharing their names and was not pressed to report this information.

50. While there were contrasting narratives in the witness statements, it is not accurate to say that there was no evidence of antisemitic bias. President Garimella's statement related the story of only one

and response to the police and administrative reports was completed by September 28, 2021.

Allegation 3. Two UVM student organizations excluded students who "expressed support for Zionism" from membership in their organizations.

University response to the incident:

On September 30, 2021, students reported this conduct to university administration. The university investigated the report quickly and thoroughly[51] and determined that the groups who apparently made these statements were not recognized UVM student organizations. The unrecognized organizations received no university support and *were not bound by UVM's policies governing student organizations.*[52] To ensure an inclusive environment within recognized UVM student organizations, student leaders were reminded of university policies prohibiting discrimination on the basis of religion, national origin, or any other protected category.

It is important that our community know the truth about what happened, and how the university responded. Although the allegations were investigated and addressed, we recognize we can and should do more to support the success of our students....

Taking Jews Seriously

1. *Negative responses to the letter.* Twenty Jewish organizations issued a statement in response to the UVM president's letter:

> Instead of summoning the courage that other university leaders across the country have shown in acknowledging the problem or offering support for Jewish students who are fearful about identifying publicly as Jewish, the UVM President's statement doubles down and refuses to take responsibility.... All the more concerning is the inference that aggrieved Jewish students should not have sought recourse through a regular legal process that exists for the very purpose of investigating civil rights complaints, including those pertaining to antisemitism. As a consequence, the concerns of antisemitism are further delegitimized.[53]

---

witness statement while ignoring the witness statement that indicated this was an antisemitic incident.

51. Multiple reports were filed in May 2021 about anti-Zionist comments and exclusion by @ShareYourStoryUVM. However, the AAEO did not investigate these reports and did not document the reason for its decision not to do so. Instead, the matter was referred to the Bias Response Team.

52. During a meeting with the Provost, students identified the Revolutionary Socialist Union (RSU) as excluding Jewish/Zionist students. The RSU's draft constitution requires every member to pledge "no" to Zionism. The university administration concluded that since the RSU was not a registered student organization, the university had no jurisdiction over it.

53. *Jewish Orgs. Respond with Grave Alarm to UVM Pres' Denial of Antisemitism Allegations*, Jewish on Campus (Sept. 16, 2022), https://www.jewishoncampus.org/media/jewish-orgs-respond-with-grave-alarm-to-uvm-pres-denial-of-antisemitism-allegations. The signatories included AJC, Alums for Campus Fairness, CAMERA on Campus, Chabad on Campus at the University of Vermont, Club Z, Conference of Presidents of Major American Jewish Organizations, Hasbara Fellowships, Hillel International, ICC, Israel Peace Initiative, JewBelong, Jewish Federations of North America, Jewish Na-

Several university-affiliated groups also criticized the letter and called upon the president to apologize for causing distress to Jewish students and faculty.[54]

2. *OCR analysis of UVM President's response.* In its report on anti-Jewish harassment at UVM, the OCR expressed concern that:

> The President's initial letter to the UVM community in response to OCR's investigation may have perpetuated a hostile environment. As previously noted, the President "vigorously denied" what he characterized as "false allegation[s] of an insufficient response" to antisemitic incidents at the University shortly before OCR requested to interview the students who had complained about or were witnesses to the harassing incidents. OCR is concerned that the President's statements may have discouraged these students from speaking with OCR about their experiences. Likewise, OCR is concerned that the President's letter, including its explanatory statement that "No student reported to the university" any discrimination claims, may have discouraged both the students who in fact had reported to the Provost their concerns as well as University employees from further raising concerns either to OCR or to the University.

3. *Improved life for Jewish students.* Jewish life at the university improved after its settlement with the OCR. To wit:

a. Jewish students now report timely responses, most often within 24 hours, for complaints about antisemitism.

b. The university hosted several workshops on antisemitism, and several university leaders have undergone training in antisemitism.

c. The university convened a panel of scholars to discuss "the historical roots of the war in Israel and Gaza."

d. The president and provost issued affirming statements containing messages specific to the Jewish community.

e. The university updated its policies to prohibit bias and harassment based on shared ancestry, explicitly including antisemitism.[55]

---

tional Fund—USA, Jewish on Campus, The Louis D. Brandeis Center for Human Rights Under Law, Simon Wiesenthal Center, StandWithUs & StandWithUs Saidoff Legal Department, SSI, and ZOA.

54. The Dep't of Educ. Off. of C.R. Title VI Investigation of Antisemitism at UVM, https://dfeurzei.w3.uvm.edu/OCR/ (last visited Dec. 15, 2024). An online search reveals no apology from Dr. Garimella, now president of the University of Arizona (using search terms "apology and garimella and Vermont," Dec. 3, 2024). *See* Carolina Cuellar, *Quick Hiring of New UA President Left No Time for Public Scrutiny of His Record, Group Tells ABOR*, Ariz. Luminaria (Aug. 15, 2024), https://azluminaria.org/2024/08/15/quick-hiring-of-new-ua-president-left-no-time-for-public-scrutiny-of-his-record-group-tells-abor/.

55. Matt Vogel, *Matt Vogel: UVM's Remarkable Turnaround Has Improved Life for Jewish Students (vtdigger)*, Brandeis Ctr. (Feb. 20, 2024), https://brandeiscenter.com/matt-vogel-uvms-remarkable-turnaround-has-improved-life-for-jewish-students-vtdigger/. For a critical analysis of UVM's settlement with the U.S. Department of Education, see *University of Vermont's Settlement with Dep't of Education Refuses to Adopt IHRA Despite Pressure*, Palestine Legal (June 28, 2023), https://pales-

4. *Exclusionary clubs.* The university dropped its investigation of the two unofficial clubs after determining they were beyond its jurisdiction. In the OCR's view, what more should the University have done?

5. *Defamation claim.* If UVM brought a defamation action in response to the Jewish students' reports and subsequent events, would it have a colorable claim? The university would have to establish that the testimonials were (1) defamatory, (2) false, and (3) unprivileged.[56]

a. *Defamatory.* The Letter asserts that the students' allegations have "been harmful" to the University. This element is readily established. Defamatory statements about a corporation may be actionable if they "tend to prejudice it in the conduct of its business or to deter others from dealing with it. . . ."[57] Here consider prospective students who may avoid the university. Defamatory statements about a charitable organization may be actionable if the entity "depends upon financial support from the public, and the matter tends to interfere with its activities by prejudicing it in public estimation." Here consider the donors who will withhold gifts pending the investigation's outcome. The statement identifies as causing further harm the "confusion and a sense of insecurity . . . for the entire community."

b. *Falsity.* The letter refers to "false light," an "uninformed narrative," "false claims," "the false allegation," and the "truth." These characterizations of the allegations in the students' testimonials appear to be premature prior to the OCR's completion of its investigation.

c. *Privileged.* The students' statements were privileged by virtue of their connection to an official judicial-like proceeding.[58]

6. *Students as defendants.* If the university were to notionally sue for defamation, the testimonial authors would be the defendants. This would be consistent with the distinction the letter draws between (a) "members of the UVM community" and (b) the "anonymous third party," i.e., the testimonials' authors.

7. *Liars?* The letter implies that the testimonials gave rise to an "uninformed narrative" about the university's alleged failure to keep Jewish students safe. The class of Jewish students, of course, includes the Jewish students who wrote the testimonials. The OCR's decision to investigate the university was of course informed by these testimonies, i.e., "based on or influenced by knowledge or by an understanding of a particular situation."[59] The letter implies that the OCR's decision was misinformed, insofar

---

tinelegal.org/news/2023/6/28/university-of-vermonts-settlement-with-dept-of-education-refuses-to-adopt-ihra-despite-pressure.

56. Restatement (Second) of Torts § 559 (Am. L. Inst. 1977).

57. *Id.* § 561.

58. *Id.* § 588.

59. *Informed*, Oxford Eng. Dictionary, https://doi.org/10.1093/OED/4310088601 (last visited July 2023).

as the testimonials contained false or misleading ("false light") information.[60] If so, did the Jewish students *intentionally* supply the OCR with such information? In other words, are they liars?

8. *Confused?* Perhaps the Jewish students were confused about the information contained in their testimonials. Did someone gaslight them into thinking that the university was *not* protecting them? Stated differently, are these Jews credible witnesses of their own experiences of antisemitism?

9. *Epistemic antisemitism.* In the next article, Professor David Schraub argues that Jews are frequently undermined or dismissed in their ability to make claims, share knowledge, or have their experiences taken seriously, particularly regarding matters of antisemitism. He refers to this phenomenon as "epistemic antisemitism." This form of antisemitism can exist even without overt hatred or disdain for Jews, manifesting instead as viewing Jews as less credible than non-Jews in relating information about anti-Jewish oppression.

David Schraub,
The Epistemic Dimension of Antisemitism

15 J. Jewish Identities 153 (2022)

The subject of this essay is a variety of antisemitism I will term *epistemic antisemitism*. Epistemic antisemitism injures, wrongs, or marginalizes Jews in their capacities as knowers—testifiers, communicators, exponents or purveyors of knowledge. It is by no means the only form of antisemitism, nor (necessarily) the most important or foundational type. However, I do believe it is a distinct type and that it occupies an underappreciated niche in the ecology of antisemitism. In particular, epistemic antisemitism is particularly well-suited to insulate the broader structure of antisemitism from critique or challenge—and indeed, it plays a central role in obstructing collective Jewish political or social action generally.

To give a brief example: consider the widespread antisemitic trope that casts Jews as part of an elite conspiratorial cabal, running various social institutions (the banks, the media, Hollywood, or even all of global affairs) from the shadows. One common result of such a belief might be resentment or antipathy towards Jews (few believe that Jews run the world *and* that they're doing a good job at it). Such ill-will, in turn, marks out a common case of antisemitic sentiment. But there is another likely upshot of a belief in a Jewish conspiracy: a concurrent belief that Jews can't be trusted, that they're always plotting something or working the angles, that all of their public action is in service of a deeper game. A person who believes such things about Jews may be considerably less likely to take Jewish claims made to the public seriously. Even if she does not reject them out of hand, she may be extra-alert for a hidden agenda or secret meaning and may be unwilling to credit Jewish testimony (even—or especially—on matters where

60. *Misinformed*, Oxford Eng. Dictionary, https://doi.org/10.1093/OED/6914043653 (last visited July 2023).

Jews might be thought to possess first-hand knowledge) to the same degree she does other actors. These are distinctively *epistemic* wrongs—they obstruct Jews' ability to stand as equals in the space of knowledge-sharing. And while epistemic antisemitism frequently goes hand in hand with more traditional kinds, they need not be joined at the hip. A person who lacks any phenomenological sense of *hating* or *disdaining* Jews might still think of them as less credible or reliable, or at least needing to be watched carefully lest one be taken advantage of....

1. Taking Jews Seriously

So, what would it mean to "take Jews seriously"? Does it mean immediate and uncritical acceptance of any Jewish claim? No. It rather demands consciously adopting a posture of open receptivity towards Jewish claims about Jewish experience. Sociologist David Hirsh, one of the preeminent academic figures writing on the subject of contemporary antisemitism, draws a distinction between "those who are accused of employing antisemitic discourse and who respond in a measured and rational way to such accusations in a good faith effort to relate to the concern, and to refute it" and those who refuse outright "to engage with the issue of antisemitism."[61] The latter consider the entire topic to be off-limits—certainly as to themselves, often as to anyone but the most explicit neo-Nazi—and view it as a form of oppression or censorship to even be challenged on the matter. The former, even if they do not initially believe the discourse they employ is antisemitic, do not view as illicit the demand that they consider the possibility otherwise. They do not treat the conversation as frivolous or, worse, oppressive; they are willing to engage in the discussion, open to the potentiality that there might be a "there there." In practice, they may tamp down on or (at least temporarily) shunt aside instinctive reactions of cynicism, dismissiveness, or outrage. Louise Antony characterizes this as "a kind of epistemic affirmative action," urging that listeners "adopt the working hypothesis that when a woman, or any member of a stereotyped group says something anomalous, they should assume that it's they who don't understand, not that it is the woman who is nuts." Such a hypothesis can be defeated, but adopting it as a starting position commits one to a fair-minded posture of open receptivity to the claim that otherwise might be skipped.

The posture of open receptivity implies a fundamental humility, a lack of confidence that our immediate, pre-deliberative intuitions about a claim of oppression (whether antisemitism, misogyny, or something else) are so obviously conclusive that we need not look into the matter further....

The epistemic framework, in essence, suggests certain markers for when "disagreeing" with an antisemitism claim is really a form of preemptive dismissal of it. Examples include immediately pooh-poohing the claim as made in bad faith, ignoring the declared substance of the claim by asserting its true purpose is "silencing criticism of Israel," rolling one's eyes and asserting sarcastically that "everyone

---

61. David Hirsh, "Accusations of Malicious Intent in Debates about the Palestine-Israel Conflict and about Antisemitism: The Livingstone Formulation, 'Playing the Antisemitism Card' and Contesting the Boundaries of Antiracist Discourse," *Transversal* 1 (2010), 47–77, 47–48.

is a Nazi now," validating dismissal of a particular Jew's claim by reference to characteristics that supposedly inhere to Jewish claims generally (without establishing that the particular claimant is included), and refusing the possibility of good faith disagreement by sweepingly declaring all controversial claims one opposes "frivolous," "false," "smears," and other like terms. Simply put, a person who relates to the antisemitism claim openly receptive to the possibility that it might be true would not level these sorts of responses....

"Taking Jews seriously" means ... there is no wrong committed in asking people to treat antisemitism claims as live possibilities.

2. Why Might We Not Take Jews Seriously?

The attempt to justify declining to "take Jews seriously" on the grounds that Jews are merely a subset of the dominant class fails to adequately account for genuine areas of Jewish difference. Yet one must take care not to let this real failing become a warrant for a different sort of failing—the complete and wholesale denial that Jews can, in any context or any capacity (i.e., not qua Jews but qua White people or qua men or qua heterosexuals) possess any advantages. Ideally, a possible, albeit not guaranteed, salutary consequence of correcting this misapprehension and acknowledging Jewishness as an independent axis of differentiation not included under the umbrella of Whiteness or "Judeo-Christian" is that we may see some dissipating of the denial by some Jews that they ever or in any context might experience White privilege or the prerogatives of Whiteness. This sort of nuanced appraisal of Jewish positionality, however, can only emerge in an epistemic universe where Jews can make assertions of Jewish experience that are recognized as emanating from a genuinely distinctive Jewish social position that cannot simply be collapsed into broader categories of "Whiteness" or "Judeo-Christian."

The other argument against "taking Jews seriously" ... denies that there is any general failure to believe Jews when we claim antisemitism. Rather, these critics suggest that Jews are believed *too often*, and that this over-credence is *not* primarily a function of being conflated with Christianity and/or Whiteness but is specific to Jewish positionality. In contemporary society, and in large part "thanks" to the Holocaust, Jews enjoy a credibility excess and have become spoiled as a result. If the epistemic antisemitism frame sees a society generally unwilling to engage on the question of antisemitism and thereby blockading consideration of even many potentially valid claims, this perspective sees the opposite problem: Jews make antisemitism claims frivolously, and yet these claims are accepted virtually without question. We need to tamp down on false positives, not false negatives.

This is not simply a matter of litigating the veracity of any particular controversy over antisemitism. There is a broader move at issue: the delegitimization of the litigation itself. Some persons hold that they should be *generally* freed from the obligation to "take seriously" antisemitism claims; that is, to act as if the typical case of antisemitism brought before them might well be a valid one. These are the people for whom, in Columbia Professor Bruce Robbins's words, "The real issue here is anti-Semitism:

that is, accusing people of it."[62] Robbins presents a view where antisemitism claims are at least as much of an "issue" as antisemitism itself: they chill conversations, destroy careers, and ruin lives. And because it is the *claim* (not the eventual conclusion drawn following analysis) that chills, destroys, and ruins, it is the *claim-making* authority of the Jews alleging antisemitism that must ultimately be undermined.

Framed this way, the duty to "believe Jews" can be jettisoned because—let's not mince words—on the subject of antisemitism, Jews lie too frequently to be worthy of the privilege. Jews have intentionally and maliciously blurred the boundaries between, for example, "antisemitism" and "criticism of Israel" and now we are reaping what we have sown. If there is a move toward disbelief in the present moment, it is occurring not because of antisemitism, but because Jews have discredited ourselves by making so many bad antisemitism claims. We've cried wolf too many times; now we're not to be taken seriously.

It is important to be clear that this assertion—that Jews are *lying* and doing so *consistently*—is essential to this argument. It is not a rhetorical flourish; it is a *necessary* condition if the general presumption that Jews ought to be listened to and taken seriously on the subject of our own oppression is to be defeated. It would not be enough to demonstrate that there exist Jewish bad actors who truly have thrown out "antisemitism" charges in unsustainable ways. (Of course there are; all groups have their bad eggs.) Nor is it enough to show that some of what is being called antisemitic is, in fact, contestable and that there are differing views on the matter. The duty to take Jewish claims *seriously* does not demand awe-stricken acquiescence; it only requires that the allegations be treated as genuine and live possibilities whose truth potential we must be open to. It is an expected, not troublesome, feature of such discourse that there will not always be unanimity. If Jewish claims are not to be taken seriously as a general rule, it is the *systematic fictitiousness* of antisemitism claims that must be asserted. Purported instances of antisemitism must be maliciously false, not just disputed, and such maliciously false claims need to be the modal (or at least regular) case.

At this stage, one can anticipate an objection: Those who object to a default posture of "belief" towards Jewish antisemitism claims, the argument goes, are not adopting a blanket posture of disbelief either. They rather urge a posture of agnosticism—antisemitism claims should be adjudged on a case-by-case basis, the true claims being validated and the bad claims rejected. If they do dismiss certain cases, that dismissal occurs not because of a general antagonism towards antisemitism claims or Jews as claimants; it merely reflects the particular judgment in particular cases that these par-

62. Bruce Robbins, "Anti-Semitism at Fordham?" *Mondoweiss* (Jan. 7, 2015), https://mondoweiss.net/2015/01/anti-semitism-fordham/. Robbins's article primarily deals with a controversy at Fordham University involving a Jewish professor, Doron Ben-Atar, seeking departmental condemnation of the American Studies Association's endorsement of BDS. Ironically, given Robbins's thesis, it was Ben-Atar, not those he accused of antisemitism, who was the one subjected to university investigation—his complaints of antisemitism were alleged by some of his colleagues to constitute anti-Christian discrimination.

ticular, identified antisemitism claims do not hold water. Others, with more support, might fare better.

One problem with this rejoinder is that it largely relies upon the understanding of "belief"—uncritical acceptance—rejected above. If "belief" is a question of "taking seriously," of being willing to travel down the investigative path, then refusing to "believe" Jews does in practice amount to a posture of presumptive skepticism. As noted above, moving from hearing a given allegation to actually considering requires some measure of trust in order to prompt the commencement of investigative efforts. And so when people speak of withdrawing that trust or being warier regarding who is "'entitled' to speak, and to be listened to," they are not (just) casting doubt on a particular claim in a particular case but rather asserting principles seeking to limit how future, as yet undeveloped, cases need (not) be considered.

The sobering reality is that, when it comes to antisemitism, there is very little that is truly "uncontested." Recent high-profile cases have seen everything from firebombing a synagogue[63] to flatly saying "fucking Jews!" defended as not antisemitic but rather just "criticism of Israel." And this tendency extends also to contemporary right-wing antisemitism. The right does not accept that its paranoid fantasies about Soros-funded caravans and the "globalist" string-pullers are antisemitic—and in support of that denial you'll hear some very familiar defenses: "It's not antisemitic to criticize George Soros!"[64] "Don't conflate 'globalist' and Jewish!" "Jews need to stop calling everything they dislike 'antisemitism.'" They use that language not because they've "learned" it but because it was theirs all along—it is the general patrimony of antisemitism, equally available to right- and left-wing critics alike.

3. Reckoning with Epistemic Antisemitism

So what, then, is the alternative? When Littleton asserted feminism's heart to be the "act of taking women seriously,"[65] she was again not making the tritely false point that women could never make an unserious or unbelievable allegation. Rather, the importance of this obligation only becomes clear when viewed in systemic terms. Women and other members of marginalized groups are *routinely*—not idiosyncratically, not case-by-case—disbelieved and dismissed as valid claim-makers. We are *right* to dismiss women's claims regarding their own experience, for as we all know, women are too emotional and too stunted to know of what they say. We are *right* to dismiss Jewish claims regarding our own experience, for as we all know, Jews are too devious and too cunning (or, in a more "generous" light, too clouded by past trauma) to have their statements taken at face value.

---

63. Editor's note: This is a reference to *The Wuppertal Decision* (Germany 2015), discussed in Chapter 11.E.

64. Editor's note: *See, e.g.*, *Soros*, Am. Jewish Comm., https://www.ajc.org/translatehate/Soros (last visited Dec. 15, 2024); *see also, e.g.*, *The Antisemitism Lurking Behind George Soros Conspiracy Theories*, The Anti-Defamation League (Oct. 11, 2018), https://www.adl.org/resources/article/antisemitism-lurking-behind-george-soros-conspiracy-theories.

65. Christine A. Littleton, "Feminist Jurisprudence: The Difference Method Makes," *Stanford Law Review* 41 (Feb. 1989): 751–84, 764.

But for Jews, this doubled challenge is just the newest manifestation of age-old antisemitic tropes. Jews have always been *dis*believed precisely because we're assumed to be *over*believed. The right-wing *Culture Wars Magazine* expressed this view pithily when it said, "Jewish privilege entails being taken seriously while making absurd claims." Whether by cunning or corruption, the great power of the Jew, in the Gentile imagination, is to bend others to do our bidding. "Antisemitism" allegations are just one of our many tools to contort the truth, deployed liberally to browbeat non-Jews into submission to our tribal ends. As many others have stressed, antisemitism often has not cast the Jew as inferior but superior (in capacity and power, if not in morality or virtue). Disbelieving Jews has thus always been cast as an act of resistance to Jewish power and Jewish supremacy.

In the Jewish case, then, acknowledging the epistemic dimension of antisemitism begins by overturning much conventional wisdom. The conventional wisdom is that Jews make antisemitism claims almost constantly, with no compunction and with absolute confidence that when they do so they will be reflexively believed. The counternarrative is that Jews do *not* make antisemitism allegations cavalierly; in fact, there is tremendous pressure on Jews to keep quiet, and it is impressed upon Jews that our instincts on antisemitism are unreliable. Those allegations which are made are routinely not believed, and their subjects typically remain free from significant consequence. We do not live in a brave new world where Jews enjoy surplus credibility on antisemitism. We continue to live in the same old world where antisemitism claims, unless they're being wielded against one's enemies, are primarily viewed as a Jewish ploy or trick to gain power or manipulate for our own ends. And in that world, it is impossible to grasp or combat antisemitism as a complete ideology without understanding how it sets up *systemic* barriers designed to occlude and undermine Jewish deliberative participation.

The decay in testimonial self-confidence—the belief that Jews know of what we speak when the subject is antisemitism—quiets Jewish speakers. This decay is compounded by a glut of resources which justify the failure of non-Jewish listeners to take Jews seriously when we do speak. Necessary to the operation of antisemitism is a network of tropes, stereotypes, and presuppositions about Jewish deliberative practice, all of which unify around the central theme that Jewish testimonial offerings should not be given credence. Jews are devious and conspirators, we are running a long game for Soros or the Rothschilds, we are hypocrites and "Pharisees," Judeo-Bolsheviks or Judeo-Capitalists, we are Hasbara shills (the Hebrew word for "explanation," but generally taken to mean "propaganda"—query the symbolism of *that* elision) or outright operatives being run out of the Israeli embassy. What appears to be organic Jewish outrage or action is not truly so; Jews are merely reading from a script written by self-selected "communal leaders." When would-be allies come to our aid, it's not because they are truly in agreement with us but because they've been corruptly purchased. If Jews succeed, it's proof of how deeply the supposed powers-that-be are actually in the Jewish throne, and if we fail, it is an inspirational tale of the people shaking off the Jewish yoke.

And it must be emphasized that all Jews—no matter their politics—are victimized by the epistemic form of antisemitism. It is not something that can be evaded simply by adopting "better" politics (whether "better" means more progressive, more conservative, more Zionist, more anti-Zionist, or something else). It is true that certain Jewish critics of mainstream or consensus Jewish opinions on antisemitism are given credence even by those who deny any duty to defer to Jews generally. These Jews occupy the role of Arendt's "exceptional Jews": they are "Jews and yet presumably not *like* Jews" and gain paradoxical power-as-Jews by virtue of their contrast with Jews.[66] But this is a precarious position, and the credibility that these actors may have thought they'd won by being willing to criticize other Jews can be stripped just as easily the moment they cease being "exceptional." Even Jews who may have thought that they (unlike most of their peers) have proven themselves reliable interlocutors by being clear-eyed and forthright about the duplicitousness of their co-religionists will find that if they do try to argue something important to their allies is antisemitic, an appeal to their "exceptional" character as reason why they should be trusted will often find that they are derided and dismissed in much the same way as their fellows....

Where does this leave us? At the very least, it requires us to affirm what one would have hoped would be an unremarkable proposition: one cannot simultaneously purport to oppose antisemitism and assert that Jews are usually lying about their own experiences with antisemitism. That circle will never be successfully squared.

But more broadly, it is useful to remember that we do not stand on untrodden ground. The core set of temptations—to find reasons to dismiss Jews, to ignore them, to label them liars or cheats—is not, as it is sometimes implausibly asserted, something *only* Jews endure (in "progressive" circles or otherwise), but rather something that is a common affliction of marginalized groups laboring under epistemic injustices. Jews can be victimized by it and can also exploit it (as when White Jews refuse to meaningfully take up serious allegations that they enact and uphold racist practices and structures—both vis-à-vis non-Jews and Jews of Color). When Jews talk about defensiveness, dismissal, fragility, and related concepts in the context of antisemitism, they are not talking about anything particularly new or novel. Nor ought these concepts be thought of as zero-sum. To the contrary, the use of these frameworks in one circumstance helps solidify its credence in other cases, more tightly binding together communities who are working from similar toolkits and can lend one another resources, advice, and strategies. Recognizing epistemic injustice as a wrong in the Jewish case also emphasizes how it is a wrong when used to dismiss claims of sexual violence or when it is used to brush off claims of racism as "playing the race card"—and vice versa. One can find endless partisans ready to explain why the Jewish case is different from the others (to its benefit or detriment). That, too, is a temptation that should be resisted....

---

66. Hannah Arendt, *On the Origins of Totalitarianism* (Orlando: Harvest, 1994), 56.

Felicia Kornbluh, *On UVM President's Response to Charges of Antisemitism*

VTDIGGER, September 26, 2022[67]

Allow me to explain a few of the ways in which President Garimella's letter to the UVM community struck troubling chords, at least to this Jewish professor who also teaches, among other material, American Jewish history:

The president opened his letter with broad-brush assertions about the veracity of the claims that underlay the argument that students' civil rights were violated. These worked, he insisted, to paint UVM in a "patently false light," were made by an "anonymous third party," and made for an "uninformed narrative." …

One persistent rhetorical strategy of antisemites in Europe and the United States has been to say that there is no antisemitism—to discount and aggressively deny the observed and felt reality of Jews and their non-Jewish allies.

President Garimella continued in a similar mode, underlining his belief that the university always responds appropriately to allegations that the institution has not done enough to protect the rights of historically oppressed populations. "We denounce hateful actions," he wrote, "and respond briskly and decisively whenever those responsible are identified."

Unfortunately, in the light of an ongoing federal investigation that seeks to discover whether the university did or did not act appropriately when it learned of "hateful actions"—and in the face of reports by members of the university community that it did not—this landed for me like gaslighting. The point of gaslighting, in the case of antisemitism as well as in other arenas, is to get people who experience something disturbing to doubt their own interpretations of reality, as well as to intimidate and silence them so that they do not report what they know or attempt to change policies that promote or allow bias, discrimination or violence.

That line in particular concerned me because it seemed to be enacting a kind of legalistic verbal jujitsu, more political wordsmithing than heartfelt response to the pain of some UVM students. Perhaps it is technically true that the UVM administration habitually "denounce[s]" instances of antisemitism: Is that a sufficient way to discharge its legal responsibilities, or to care for the young people (and not-so-young people, like the faculty) whose thriving is the heart of the university's mission? Perhaps it is even true that the central administration is in the habit of "respond[ing] briskly and decisively whenever those responsible are identified." … Is that all the administration can do, or can be expected to do? Whose burden is it to identify "those responsible" if not officers of the university?

---

67. Felicia Kornbluh, *Felicia Kornbluh: On UVM President's Response to Charges of Antisemitism*, VTDIGGER (Sept. 26, 2022), https://vtdigger.org/2022/09/26/felicia-kornbluh-on-uvm-presidents-response-to-charges-of-antisemitism/. Dr. Felicia Kornbluh is professor of history at UVM, director of its Jewish Studies program, and former president of United Academics, UVM's faculty union.

Unfortunately, President Garimella's letter left this reader with the sense that he and his administration were aggrieved by the federal complaint and investigation. This, too, rang tones that are familiar from the history of world antisemitism and from revanchist politics in the modern United States. He identified the main problem at issue as the existence of a government effort to find out if civil rights have been violated at UVM, and, undergirding that effort, a set of student reports. It is this, he wrote, and not any insensitivity, bias or negligence on the part of people affiliated with the university, that "has been harmful to UVM" as well as to "our Jewish students, faculty, staff, and alumni."

American political history has taught us that the reaction to an allegation of misdeeds often matters more than any misdeeds themselves. In fact, institutional reactions have often been the most revealing aspects of important controversies—and have led ultimately to greater understanding and ameliorative action. In this instance, the insensitive response matters as much as the incidents under investigation. I can only hope that a serious reckoning with the missteps in that response will lead to understanding how prevalent antisemitism is at the University of Vermont and whether the university administration has appropriate mechanisms in place to address it.

Understanding and Addressing Epistemic Antisemitism

1. What does Schraub mean by "taking Jews seriously"? How does one do so?

2. How does Schraub differentiate between epistemic antisemitism and other forms of antisemitism?

3. Have you ever experienced epistemic antisemitism? Have you ever manifested it? Have you ever tried to combat it?

4. Consider the following claim: "powerful, well-funded Jews are controlling phenomenon X from behind the scenes." Is this statement always antisemitic or only antisemitic some of the time?

5. Consider the following claim: "powerful, well-funded forces consisting of A are controlling phenomenon X from behind the scenes." Assume it does not specify that Jews are A. Which of the following statements are true?

a. This claim is overtly antisemitic.

b. This claim is covertly antisemitic.

c. This claim is functionally indistinguishable from antisemitism in the sense that if A were replaced with "Jews," the claim would work just as well, if not better.

d. The claim, while not presently antisemitic, will inevitably morph into antisemitism.

e. None of the above.

6. *Exceptional Jews.* Are you an "exceptional Jew"? Would you like to be?

7. *Jewish agency.* Why does Schraub consider epistemic antisemitism particularly dangerous for collective Jewish action?

8. *Epistemic affirmative action.* What does Schraub mean by the term "epistemic affirmative action"? Can it be meaningfully compared to ordinary-sense affirmative action, which OED defines as "active measures taken by an employer, college, etc., to provide opportunities for members of minority groups, women, or other people regarded as having suffered from discrimination"?[68]

9. Consider two types of non-Jews: (a) those who are aware of their biases and misconceptions concerning Jews; or (b) those who are *not* aware of them. Schraub thinks that the former are more likely to take Jews seriously. Why?

10. *Epistemic injustice.* What connections does Schraub draw between epistemic antisemitism and epistemic injustice faced by other marginalized groups?

11. *Institutional epistemic antisemitism.* Schraub primarily analyzes epistemic antisemitism as a broader social and cultural phenomenon. In the UVM case, there were multiple levers of institutional involvement—university leadership, the university's internal processes, legal requirements and administrative oversight, etc. What can the UVM case teach us about what institutions do to address epistemic antisemitism?

12. *Exercise.* You've been appointed to your university's "Task Force to Combat Epistemic Antisemitism." What recommendations will it make?

C. Anti-Zionist Activity

U.S. Department of Education, Office of Civil Rights, *Letter to Suresh V. Garimella, University of Vermont President*

(April 3, 2023)

Summary of Evidence Obtained

Allegations Concerning the Teaching Assistant

[An undergraduate teaching assistant (TA) allegedly posted antisemitic remarks and threats on the TA's personal social media accounts. Alleged postings included the following:]

> [1] "its [*sic*] good and funny" "for me, a TA, to not give zionists credit for participation" and to give the students for whom she was a teaching assistant "-5 points for going on birthright," "-10 points for posting a pic with a tank in the Golan heights," and "-2 points just cuz I hate ur vibe in general";
>
> [2] "why do so many zionists work for the writing center[?]";
>
> [3] the word "Kristallnacht" above a picture of a damaged storefront with accompanying Hebrew text from another user;

68. *Affirmative Action*, Oxford Eng. Dictionary, https://doi.org/10.1093/OED/2023105587 (last visited June 2024).

> [4] "i get the indelible [*sic*] surge [*sic*] to cyber bully" when receiving "posts from UVM Zionist Instagram accounts";
>
> [5] "serotonin rush of bullying zionists on the public domain" . . .
>
> [7] "free trips, both sides discourse,"[69] and the statement "my family lives in tel aviv" should be "politically unthinkable, worthy of private and public condemnation, [and] likened to historical and contemporary segregationist movements"; and
>
> [8] "who stole the israeli flag on [redacted content]? i just wanna . . . tell you how cool and special and loved you are" and "defend [your] honour" for "anonymously doing good."
>
> [9] [Also reported was a] tweet by another student stating that "it'd be a shame if something happened to the israeli flag" off campus, noting that a student's Israeli flag at that location had been [stolen] shortly afterward. . . . As noted above, the Teaching Assistant subsequently tweeted in praise of this theft.

Analysis

While the University's policies and procedures do not require an identified victim in order for AAEO to investigate, the University declined to investigate the Teaching Assistant's conduct. That decision was made without interviewing the Teaching Assistant, whom they could have identified based on the social media handle names associated with her actual name and two accompanying photographs, students in her course, or staff in the writing center. Additionally, the University only considered a small subset of the allegedly discriminatory social media posts (including those sent from a different account but which the University may have connected to the Teaching Assistant upon a reasonably diligent inquiry) when reaching this determination.

While the University ultimately responded to the Teaching Assistant's conduct, it was done outside of the Discrimination Policy and not until four months after the [redacted content]'s complaints were filed. Further, while the Teaching Assistant wrote that she was a teaching assistant during the spring 2021 semester, it is not clear that the University fully investigated whether she had served as a teaching assistant prior to the fall of 2021. There is also no indication that the University informed any of the students who were affected by the Teaching Assistant's harassing statements that the University had taken steps to ameliorate any hostile environment and to ensure that the students' equal access to education would not be affected, including because the course professor independently evaluated the students' grades. . . .

---

69. This is likely a reference to Birthright Israel, a program that provides young Jews with free trips to Israel and whose stated mission is "to provide all young Jewish adults with opportunities for transformative and immersive shared experiences in Israel and a foundation for ongoing Jewish connection." *Our Story*, TAGLIT BIRTHRIGHT ISR., https://www.birthrightisrael.com/about-us (last visited Dec. 15, 2024).

[The University inadequately responded to allegations that (i) students threw rocks at the Hillel and (ii) two student organizations excluded students "who expressed support for Zionism" from membership in that organization.]

It does not appear that the University determined whether the cumulative effects of these incidents created a hostile environment based on students' shared ancestry (Jewish) or took action regarding the cumulative effects of the incidents until after the commencement of OCR's investigation of this matter.

Anti-Zionist Speech Accompanied by Antisemitic Speech

1. *Tweet #1: Who goes on Birthright Israel?* In Tweet #1, the TA boasts about deducting points from the grades of Zionist students, including "-5 points for going on birthright." Although the word "Jew" nowhere appears in this tweet, Jews as a class appear in the reference to "birthright," which likely refers to Birthright Israel ("Birthright"), a program that provides Jewish young adults with a free trip to Israel.[70] *Critically*, Birthright's eligibility criteria are based on how Jewish identity is defined by Jewish authorities, such as Orthodox Judaism, the Reform Movement, and the Israeli Supreme Court. These criteria include whether the applicant has a Jewish parent, if they've converted to another religion, or whether a Jewish denomination recognizes them as Jewish.[71] *Also critically,* Birthright does not require applicants to support Zionism.[72] Only Jews (as per Birthright's criteria) go on Birthright trips but only some of them are Zionists. The TA appears to hate them both, i.e., "-2 points just cuz I hate ur vibe in general."

2. *Tweet #2: Zionist tutors.* Tweet #2 asks "why do so many zionists work for the writing center[?]" The website for the UVM Undergraduate Writing Center lists over 40 staff members.[73] Some names sound more stereotypically Jewish than others, and some faces look more stereotypically Jewish than others. The website does not disclose the Zionist affiliations of its staff. Did the TA have an independent source that identified the Zionist staff members? If not, then the TA again equates Jews with Zionists, as well as displaying the antisemitic belief that she can detect if someone is or is not a Jew.

---

70. Taglit Birthright Isr., https://www.birthrightisrael.com/ (last visited Dec. 15, 2024).

71. *FAQ*, Taglit Birthright Isr., https://www.birthrightisrael.com/faq#question_14 (last visited Dec. 15, 2024).

72. One of Birthright's frequently asked questions is, "do my political views affect my eligibility?" Birthright's response is:

> Not at all. We don't ask applicants to share their political views. The Birthright Israel trip is for all Jewish young adults from around the globe. That being said, while on the trip, you'll have the opportunity to ask questions and discuss historical and current events in an organized and educational setting.

FAQ, Taglit Birthright Isr., https://www.birthrightisrael.com/faq#question_105 (last visited Dec 16, 2024).

73. *Meet the Tutors,* Univ. of Vt., https://www.uvm.edu/writingcenters/undergradwriting/meet-tutors (last visited Dec. 16, 2024).

3. *Tweet #3: No opinion on Kristallnacht.* Tweet #3 includes the word "Kristallnacht," a picture of a damaged storefront, and unspecified Hebrew text. This is a reference to an event known as Kristallnacht, an anti-Jewish pogrom that occurred in Nazi Germany on November 9–10, 1938. Tweet #3 does not refer to Israel, which was not established until 1948. Tweet #3 expresses no opinion on Kristallnacht, an event that cries out for commentary.

4. *Tweet #7: A Jew with an Israel connection = a Zionist.* Some American Jews go on Birthright trips, and some have relatives who live in Israel. In the TA's view, both are Zionists.

5. *Antisemitism Radar.* Baddiel reports that at a Free Palestine demonstration in London in May 2021, one of the protesters was carrying a placard with the image of Jesus on it, carrying a cross, with the words "Do Not Let Them Do the Same Thing Today Again." He writes:

> Distinguishing between the two [anti-Zionism and antisemitism] is actually quite simple: look for the ancient trope. One of the things about antisemitism is: it's a very old racism. There are bad myths and bad imagery and bad associations that antisemites have been applying to Jews for centuries, for long before the state of Israel was established. If these are found within a political conversation about the present-day Middle East, then my anti-Jewish racism radar goes off....
>
> "Them" on that placard doesn't mean The Israeli Government ... it means Jews. It expresses the eternal and recurring wickedness of Jews. It must do, as Benjamin Netanyahu, however much of a devil you think he is, was not around in AD 33 cheering for #TeamBarabbas.[74]

Facially Anti-Zionist Speech

1. *Anti-Zionist expression.* In tweets #4 and #5, the TA expresses her anti-Zionism by cyber-bullying Zionists. In tweets #8 and #9, the TA expresses her opposition to Zionism by praising the removal of Israeli flags. These tweets would seem to be not patently antisemitic.

2. *Patently antisemitic, facially anti-Zionist, and mixed messages.* The TA's tweets fell into one of three categories: (a) patently antisemitic; (b) facially anti-Zionist, but not patently antisemitic ("facially anti-Zionist"); and (c) a combination of patently antisemitic and facially anti-Zionist tweets. Should the OCR consider only category (a) tweets when investigating the existence of a hostile environment? If it also considers category (c) tweets, should it redact their facially anti-Zionist elements? If redaction is pursued, how would that process work? Under what circumstances should the entire content be deemed antisemitic?

---

74. David Baddiel, Jews Don't Count 95–96 (2022).

3. The TA's posts were evenly split—a 1 to 1 ratio between patent and non-patent. Now consider teaching assistants R and S. R has four (4) tweets, all of them anti-Zionist and none patently antisemitic. S has five (5) tweets. Four of them, like R's tweets, are anti-Zionist and not patently antisemitic. S's fifth tweet, by contrast, is patently antisemitic. (It may or may not include anti-Zionist content.) In investigating a hostile environment, should the OCR ignore all R's tweets and consider all of S's tweets, even though only one is patently antisemitic? What is the antisemitic status of S's four anti-Zionist tweets? Are they covertly antisemitic? Antisemitic in context? And so forth.

4. *Anti-Zionist versus antisemitic speech.* Concerning the TA's tweets, for what propositions does the UVM case stand?

a. Anti-Zionist speech is conclusively antisemitic if accompanied by patently antisemitic speech.

b. Anti-Zionist speech is presumptively antisemitic if accompanied by patently antisemitic speech, but this presumption is rebuttable.

c. Anti-Zionist speech may be antisemitic, even if not accompanied by patently antisemitic speech.

d. Anti-Zionist speech is presumptively *not* antisemitic if not accompanied by patently antisemitic speech, but this presumption is rebuttable.

e. Anti-Zionist speech is conclusively *not* antisemitic, even if accompanied by patently antisemitic speech.

5. The TA posts anti-Zionist tweets not accompanied by patently antisemitic tweets. Some Jewish students experience these as harassing, i.e., their antisemitism radar goes off. Should the OCR consider the anti-Zionist tweets in its investigation?

6. *Mixed messages offline.* Consider two student protesters standing next to one another at a campus anti-Zionist demonstration. One is holding a patently antisemitic sign and the other a facially anti-Zionist one. Can the former's patently antisemitic message be imputed to the latter? Has the latter engaged in second-degree (reckless) hate speech?

Alyza D. Lewin,
Anti-Zionist Harassment Is Against the Law, Too

10 Sapir (2023)

As president of the Louis D. Brandeis Center for Human Rights Under Law, I speak nearly every day to students on university campuses who are experiencing antisemitism. Here is what they are telling me.

- That trip they took to Israel—it was transformative. It opened their eyes to their Jewish heritage and was among the most meaningful experiences of their lives. But they do not dare post a photo of the trip on social media.

- The items that publicly identify them as Jews—a necklace with a Star of David, a *kippah*, the T-shirt that they got at Hillel with the name of the university in Hebrew letters: They will not wear them. When they do, they become targets of harassment.
- Those student clubs they wish to join to support causes they care about passionately—women's rights, LGBT rights, immigration, climate change, and more—are increasingly demanding that members pledge "no" to Zionism. It is difficult for Jewish students to belong if they believe Israel has a right to exist.
- That office of diversity, equity, and inclusion—the people assigned to increase sensitivity to bias—is often flummoxed by the uniqueness of Jewish identity. Too often, the DEI officers label Jews as "white," do not recognize Jewishness as an ethnicity, and assume that Jews are merely a religious group needing only kosher food and Sabbath accommodations. Worse, some DEI staff have denied Jewish history and perpetuated antisemitic stereotypes by describing Jews as privileged and powerful.

The students simply want to engage in classes and extracurricular activities without being demonized and marginalized. But they find it increasingly necessary to hide their Jewish identity in order to be accepted. As with past generations of Jewish students, they are being pressured to shed some or all aspects of their Jewish identity to gain acceptance. Led to believe that if they abandon what distinguishes them as Jews, they will avoid discrimination or worse, many comply.

According to the Anti-Defamation League, antisemitic incidents on campuses increased 41 percent in 2022, to 219—approximately one college incident on any given day when classes are in session.[75] Universities that receive federal funding (a category that includes nearly all universities in the United States) are legally obligated to protect their Jewish students from such harassment and discrimination. Why, then, are universities so woefully ineffective at protecting Jews?

The problem among university administrators is threefold. Administrators do not understand the nature of contemporary antisemitism. They do not understand Jewish identity and its inextricable relationship with Zionism. And they mistakenly believe that the anti-Zionist animus on campus is simply one side of a good-faith political debate.

As to the first problem: Many administrators today recognize Jew-hatred, such as swastikas spray-painted on a wall or overt denial of the Holocaust, when it comes from white supremacists. Yet, too often, they are unable or unwilling to recognize other forms. They do not understand that antisemitism shows up differently in different

---

75. Editor's note: Ctr. on Extremism, *Audit of Antisemitic Incidents 2022*, The Anti-Defamation League (Mar. 23, 2023), https://www.adl.org/resources/report/audit-antisemitic-incidents-2022. The ADL reports than in 2023, there were 922 antisemitic incidents on colleges and universities, an increase by 321 percent over 2022, most of which occurred after the October 7 terrorist attacks. Ctr. on Extremism, *Audit of Antisemitic Incidents 2023*, The Anti-Defamation League (Apr. 16, 2024), https://www.adl.org/resources/report/audit-antisemitic-incidents-2023.

generations. The one constant of antisemitism is that no matter the century, Jews are always the scapegoat.

In addition to individual Jews, there exists a Jewish collective—the Jewish nation-state.

There are those today who accuse Israel of being the world's worst violator of human rights, while being stunningly indifferent to human rights abuses in countries such as North Korea, Syria, or China. There are those who make accusations against Israel that are not only false but also recall classic antisemitic tropes, such as the idea that Israel deliberately targets Palestinian children or harvests Palestinian corpses for organs. There are those who chant "From the river to the sea, Palestine will be free." This duplicitous plea for Palestinian liberation actually calls for the annihilation of a sovereign state—a call that is never made against any other state. Whereas traditional antisemitism seeks to deny individual Jews their place in society, contemporary antisemitism seeks to do the same to the Jewish collective in the society of nations.

This is contemporary antisemitism. But most university administrators do not recognize or even understand it as such.

This is because of the second problem: Most university administrators do not understand Jewish identity. They do not appreciate that Judaism is an ethno-religion, a belief system inextricably connected to cultural heritage, traditions, history—and land. The connection between Jews and the Land of Israel permeates the Jewish calendar, Jewish life-cycle events, Jewish law, Jewish prayer, and Jewish history. Over half of the 613 commandments in the Hebrew Bible are related to the Land of Israel and can be observed only there. Three of the most important Jewish holidays are connected to the land: Passover is Chag HaAviv, the Spring Festival, when the barley was brought in. Shavuot is Chag HaKatzir, the Festival of Reaping. Sukkot is Chag HaAsif, the Festival of Ingathering, for all the later-ripening fruits. At Jewish marriage ceremonies, Jews customarily break a glass in remembrance of the destruction of the Jewish Temple in Jerusalem.

Jews who consider this ancestral connection to Israel to be part of their Jewish identity are frequently shunned as "Zionists"—deemed pariahs because they believe that Jews have a right to self-determination in their ancestral homeland. But Zionism is as integral to Jewish identity as observing the Sabbath or keeping a kosher diet. It's true that not all Jews are Zionists. But not all Jews are Sabbath-observers, either. Both remain core expressions of Jewish identity. Would university administrators permit student clubs to demand that Catholics disavow the Vatican or that Muslims shed their connection to Mecca in order to be accepted? Or would the administrators recognize that such a demand is discriminatory, biased, and immoral?

The third problem follows directly from the second. Failing to recognize that anti-Zionism is antisemitic, they do not see that ostracizing, marginalizing, or excluding Jews on the basis of the Zionist component of their Jewish identity is not "speech." It is discriminatory and unlawful conduct. Most university administrators who fail to recognize antisemitic rhetoric when the word "Zionist" is substituted for the word

"Jew" appear to believe they are witnessing a good-faith political debate about Israel's policies. And yet, when Jewish students seek to speak with or debate their harassers, they are routinely rebuffed. Increasingly, those who oppose "normalizing" relations with Israel boycott Hillel and other pro-Israel organizations on campus and refuse to speak with Jewish students who support Israel's right to exist.

A recent episode at the University of Vermont suggests a way forward....

The complaint in that case, filed by the Brandeis Center and the Jewish on Campus student advocacy group (JOC), described how Jewish Zionists were being excluded from two UVM student groups, and how a university teaching assistant repeatedly harassed Jewish Zionists online.... The Department of Education Office for Civil Rights (OCR) treated the harassment as a form of national-origin discrimination on the basis of shared ancestry and required UVM, among other things, to revise its policies, procedures, and training to ensure they address it. Jewish students at UVM reported to me that they quickly saw a marked improvement in the way the university responded to their concerns.

The UVM case was the first Biden-administration campus antisemitism case. There were, however, also resolution agreements issued by the Trump administration in campus antisemitism cases at New York University, Duke, and the University of North Carolina at Chapel Hill, and OCR is currently investigating the University of Southern California, the University of Illinois at Urbana-Champaign (UIUC), George Washington University, CUNY Law, and Brooklyn College, among others, in response to Title VI complaints alleging that the universities failed to protect Jewish students from antisemitic harassment and discrimination.

But the first campus antisemitism investigation to be opened by OCR after the National Strategy was announced involves a complaint filed by the Brandeis Center and JOC against SUNY New Paltz. In that case, two Jewish students were kicked out of a group of sexual-assault survivors and then bullied, harassed, and threatened online on the basis of their Jewish and Israeli identities. Leaders of the student organization removed the Jewish students (one of whom had founded the group) after the Jewish students shared on their personal Instagram accounts an infographic that said, "Jews are an ethnic group who come from Israel" and "you cannot colonize the land your ancestors are from." The students were cancelled, stalked, intimidated, and harassed so intensely that they felt compelled to leave campus for their safety. Coming on the heels of the UVM resolution agreement and the release of the National Strategy, the opening of the SUNY New Paltz investigation sends a clear message that OCR is taking this form of antisemitism seriously.

The best antidote to harassment and discrimination is self-confidence and pride. To counter campus antisemitism, we must reject "erasive antisemitism"—defined by the writer Ben Freeman as the erasure of Jewish identity or of Jews as victims of prejudice—and push back against those who ignore or, worse, revise Jewish history and deny the uniqueness of Jewish identity.

No one has the right to demand that Jews shed their sense of peoplehood and repudiate their historic yearning for and connection to Zion (another name for Jerusalem). DEI programs must recognize Jews as both a religious group and a national and ethnic identity. Universities should start, as UIUC did, by issuing statements recognizing that for many students, Zionism is an integral part of their Jewish identity. When Jews are marginalized and excluded on the basis of a fundamental element in their ancestral heritage, society must condemn it as harassment and discrimination. It is time for us to use our legal tools to protect Jews on the basis of not only our religious practice, but also our national, ancestral, and ethnic heritage. The UVM case is just an early drop in the proverbial bucket. But it provides an important model for the ongoing effort to counter campus antisemitism.

University of Illinois at Urbana-Champaign et al., *Joint Statement on Anti-Semitism*

1. *UIUC Statement.* On September 3, 2023, UIUC and several Jewish organizations issued a "Joint Statement on Anti-Semitism."[76] It included the following:

> When Jews are targeted because of their beliefs or their identity, when Israel is singled out because of anti-Jewish hatred, that is antisemitism.
>
> For many Jewish students, Zionism is an integral part of their identity and their ethnic and ancestral heritage....
>
> We deplore anti-Semitic incidents on campus, including those that demonize or delegitimize Jewish and pro-Israel students or compare them to Nazis. This subjects them to double standards that are not applied to others....
>
> All Jewish students should be able to proudly display religious emblems without fear of being targeted by other fellow students. All Jewish students should feel confident that if they encounter a swastika on campus, the university stands with them in rejecting symbols of hate. Anti-Semitism, anti-Semitic forms of anti-Zionism and other forms of discrimination have no place at this university.

In UIUC's view, antisemitic anti-Zionism entails singling out Jews and Israel "because of anti-Jewish hatred." How does UIUC distinguish between this from singling out Jews and Israel not because of anti-Jewish hatred?

2. *Is the Free Exercise Clause the new Title VI?* The case of *Yitzchok Frankel et al., v. Regents of the University of California et al.*, 2024 WL 3811250 (C.D. Cal. Aug. 13, 2024) involved pro-Palestinian protesters at UCLA whose encampment on the cam-

---

76. UIUC announced this in joint statement issued with Jewish United Fund Chicago, Illinois Hillel, Hillel International, Illinois Chabad, Arnold & Porter, and the Louis D. Brandeis Center for Human Rights Under Law. Off. of the Chancellor, *Joint Statement on Anti-Semitism*, Univ. of Ill. Urbana-Champaign (Nov. 16, 2020), https://blogs.illinois.edu/view/6231/1530347443; *see also* Jewish United Fund of Chicago et al., Mutual Understandings (2024), https://brandeiscenter.com/wp-content/uploads/2024/09/UIUC-Mutual-Understandings-and-Attachment-A-09-03-24.pdf.

pus's quad blocked access to various university buildings. People who supported Israel were reportedly kept out of the quad. Plaintiffs were three Jewish UCLA students who asserted that they have a religious obligation to support the State of Israel. One of the plaintiffs reported that he stopped using the quad "because he believed that he could not traverse the encampment without disavowing Israel." Another plaintiff did not enter the quad "because of her knowledge that she would have to disavow her religious beliefs to do so." Plaintiffs alleged that UCLA violated their First Amendment free exercise rights by permitting access to university property to be denied based on a student's religious beliefs. The court, per Judge Marc C. Scarsi, granted the Plaintiffs' motion for a preliminary injunction protecting them against exclusion. Judge Scarsi's opinion opens with the following words:

> In the year 2024, in the United States of America, in the State of California, in the City of Los Angeles, Jewish students were excluded from portions of the UCLA campus because they refused to denounce their faith. This fact is so unimaginable and so abhorrent to our constitutional guarantee of religious freedom that it bears repeating, *Jewish students were excluded from portions of the UCLA campus because they refused to denounce their faith.* UCLA does not dispute this. Instead, UCLA claims that it has no responsibility to protect the religious freedom of its Jewish students because the exclusion was engineered by third-party protesters. But under constitutional principles, UCLA may not allow services to some students when UCLA knows that other students are excluded on religious grounds, regardless of who engineered the exclusion.[77]

3. *Free exercise and secular Jews.* Assume the Free Exercise Clause bars some anti-Zionist student groups from excluding Jews who believe that Judaism requires them to support Israel. What protections would the Free Exercise Clause afford to secular Jews who support Israel as part of their secular Jewish heritage?

D. UC Berkeley School of Law: A Case Study

In August 2022, nine officially recognized student groups at the UC Berkeley Law School (Berkeley Law) adopted bylaws stating that they would "not invite speakers that have expressed and continue to hold views or host/sponsor/promote events in support of Zionism, the apartheid state of Israel and the occupation of Palestine."[78] At the time, two Berkeley professors stated that "happily, just nine out of the more than 100 student

77. Frankel v. Regents of Univ. of Cal., No. 24-CV-04702-PD, 2024 WL 3811250, at *1 (C.D. Cal. Aug. 13, 2024), *appeal dismissed*, No. 24-5003, 2024 WL 4803385 (9th Cir. Aug. 26, 2024).

78. @berkeleylawforpalestine, Instagram (Aug. 21, 2022), https://www.instagram.com/p/Ch-h_43tpLnm/?img_index=1. The nine groups consisted of Law Students for Justice in Palestine, Berkeley Law Muslim Students Association, Middle Eastern and North African Law Students Association, Womxn of Color Collective, Asian Pacific American Law Student Association, Queer Caucus, Community Defense Project, Women of Berkeley Law, and Law Students of African Descent *See* Debra Cassens Weiss, *Anti-Zionist Policies by Student Groups at UC Berkeley Law Fostered Harassment and*

groups at the law school chose to adopt such a bigoted course of action." More student groups followed suit, including the *Berkeley Journal of Gender, Law & Justice* (BGLJ), a student-run feminist journal.

In October 2022, Berkeley Law Dean Erwin Chemerinsky informed the law school community that:

> Student groups have the First Amendment right to adopt this bylaw and may decide what speakers to invite based on their viewpoints.... At the same time, no student group can exclude any speaker on the basis of race, religion, sex, or sexual orientation. That would violate Law School and campus policy, as well as state and federal law.... The Law School has an "all-comers" policy where all student groups and all student events must be open to all students.

In December 2022, the OCR opened a formal investigation into Berkeley Law, asking:

> Whether the University failed to respond appropriately in the fall 2022 semester to notice from Jewish law students, faculty, and staff that they experienced a hostile environment at the law school based on their shared Jewish ancestry when University-recognized student organizations passed a bylaw against inviting speakers who support "Zionism, the state of Israel, and the occupation of Palestine."[79]

On May 3, 2024, the Brandeis Center filed a Title VI lawsuit against Berkeley Law seeking, inter alia, an injunction requiring the university to stop funding or recognizing any student group with the anti-Zionist speakers policy:

> Conditioning a Jew's ability to participate in a student group on his or her renunciation of a core component of Jewish identity is no less pernicious than demanding the renunciation of some other core element of a student's identity—whether based on race, ethnicity, gender, or sexual identity. Imagine, in this day and age, asking members of the LGBTQ community to remain "in the closet" as a condition of membership in an authorized student group. No such imposition is required—or would be remotely tolerated—of other students, who remain free to participate fully in student organizations without disavowing or hiding any part of their identities.

Dean Chemerinsky stated that the school was on "strong legal ground" because student groups have a right to ban speakers based on viewpoints. Both matters are pending.

Hatred, Suit Alleges, ABA J. (Dec. 1, 2023), https://www.abajournal.com/news/article/suit-alleges-anti-zionist-policies-by-student-groups-at-uc-berkley-law-fostered-harassment-and-hatred.

79. For a critical perspective on OCR's investigation, see *Berkeley Students Don't Have to Host Zionists*, PALESTINE LEGAL (Dec. 9, 2022), https://palestinelegal.org/news/2022/12/9/berkeley-students-dont-have-to-host-zionists?rq=berkeley.

Berkeley Journal of Gender, Law & Justice (BGLJ),[80] *Law Students Justice for Palestine Bylaw*

Current through January 19, 2024

[BGLJ amended its bylaws between January 10, 2023, and January 19, 2024. ~~Strike-through~~ indicates deletions and underlining indicates additions from the January 10, 2023 version.]

(a) To include a Palestine-centered and de-colonial approach to holding club activities: The Berkeley Journal of Gender, Law & Justice [BGLJ] is committed to providing a supportive community space for all indigenous peoples globally, including movements for Palestinian liberation. In the rejection of colonialism, imperialism, and other types of oppression, BGLJ is dedicated to wholly boycotting, sanctioning, and divesting funds from institutions, organizations, companies, and any entity that participated in or is directly/indirectly complicit in the occupation of the Palestinian territories and/or supports the actions of the apartheid state of Israel.

(b) Furthermore, in the interest of protecting the safety and welfare of Palestinian students on campus, BGLJ will not invite speakers ~~or publish pieces by authors~~ that have expressed and continued to hold views or host/sponsor/promote events in support of Zionism, the apartheid state of Israel, and the occupation of Palestine. ~~While Law Students Justice for Palestine respects the approach of each individual organization in their implementation of this provision, suggested strategies can include~~ BGLJ adopts this bylaw by publicly stipulating the organization's position of anti-racism and anti-settler colonialism to speakers and prospective authors, ensuring that proposals for speakers and calls for submissions emphasize the organization's desire for equality and inclusion, and informing individuals invited to speak or publish with us of the journal's goals and mission values.

(c) To ensure that solidarity is practiced both in theory and in practice, BGLJ Editorial Board Members ~~agree~~ are encouraged to participate in a "Palestine 101" training held by the Law Students Justice for Palestine to learn ways to create a safe and inclusive space for Palestinian students and students that are in the support of the liberation of Palestine, as well as are encouraged to consider engaging in the BDS movement in the principled manner Palestinians are asking for.

(d) BGLJ is committed to promoting intersectional feminism and critically analyzing interlocked systems of oppression, and involves its membership in ongoing discussions about our understanding of these concepts. The LSJP bylaw frames and contributes to these discussions by decentering oppressive power structures, centering frequently silenced and subordinated voices, and challenging BGLJ members to interrogate their positions in systems of power and knowledge—all core tenets of intersectional feminist pedagogy. The LSJP bylaw also allows BGLJ to explicitly state its commitment to

80. Exhibit F, Brandeis Ctr., Inc. v. Regents of Univ. of Cal. At Berkeley, No. 23-cv-06133 (N.D. Cal. filed Aug. 19, 2024).

intersectional feminist values such as anti-colonialism, anti-racism, and support for indigenous peoples globally. By adopting and acting pursuant to the LSJP bylaw, BGLJ aligns itself with the efforts of countless intersectional feminist scholars, practitioners, and organizations to stand against *all forms of oppression.*

(e) BGLJ understands Zionism as the failed answer to the real question of how to protect Jewish lives from antisemitism. While it has many strains historically, the Zionism that took hold and stands today is a settler-colonial movement. We do not equate the political ideology of Zionism with the religion of Judaism, and standing in opposition to Zionism does not mean we stand in opposition to Jewish people. On the contrary, we understand the political project of Zionism has also made Jewish people less safe, marginalizing Jews of color and subjecting millions to violence under the misnomer of Jewish safety. It is clear that Zionism, in practice, has resulted in massacres of Palestinian people and the systematic separation of Palestinians from their homes, land, and each other—and it is this practice that we oppose.

Analyzing the Journal's Anti-Zionist Speaker Policy

1. *Rationale.* The bylaws present two distinct rationales for the BGLJ's decision not to invite speakers who hold views "in support of Zionism, the apartheid state of Israel, and the occupation of the Palestinian territories and/or supports the actions of the apartheid state of Israel." The first rationale is based on the BGLJ's opposition to Zionism, etc. The second is based on "the interest of protecting the safety and welfare of Palestinian students on campus ..."

2. *Zionist authors versus Zionist speakers.* Is the BGLJ more open to (a) publishing pieces by authors who support Zionism, so long as the piece does not itself express support for Zionism; than (b) hearing speakers who support Zionism, so long as their speech does not itself express support for Zionism? If so, what might account for this differential treatment? [81]

3. *Zionist speech versus Zionist speakers.* The BGLJ's second justification for banning Zionism-supporting speakers has two elements: Zionist speech and Zionist speakers. The journal's apparent goal is to protect Palestinian students from the expression of Zionist viewpoints, which the students might experience as a kind of hate speech with its attendant harms. The second element is that Palestinian students will negatively experience the presence of speakers, a subset of persons, who support Zionism. What harm might Palestinian students experience from the presence of such persons?

4. *Racism as abomination.* Racism is arguably the greatest abomination of our time. Are Jews are abominable insofar as they are implicated in projects that are inextrica-

81. Consider Jeremy Waldron's argument that hateful speech poses the greater threat to its targets when written rather than spoken. Jeremy Waldron, *Dignity and Defamation: The Visibility of Hate*, 123 Harv. L. Rev. 1596, 1604 (2010) ("'What gives the sting to the writing,' said a New York court in 1931, 'is its permanence of form. The spoken word dissolves, but the written one abides and 'perpetuates the scandal.'") (quoting Ostrowe v. Lee, 175 N.E. 505, 506 (N.Y. 1931)).

bly Jewish and irretrievably racist? On this view, are anti-Zionist Jews the only non-abominable ones? What is the presumption: are Jews presumed to be Zionists unless they disavow Zionism? Anti-Zionist unless they profess Zionism? What if (a) being Jewish is a reliable predictor of being a Zionist, i.e., a typical Jew is more likely to be Zionist than anti-Zionist; but (b) being a non-Jew, or a certain class of non-Jews, is not a reliable predictor? Does that make it rational to posit a rebuttable presumption that a given Jew is a Zionist? As a practical matter, what follows from the presumption? Should Jews, but not non-Jews, be required to disavow Zionism in order to be invited to speak? Should there instead be a "Don't ask, don't tell" policy?

5. *Inviting non-Zionists?* Recall Chapter 4's description of Louis Marshall as a "non-Zionist," a viewpoint that entailed:

a. Not supporting the goal of creating a sovereign Jewish state
b. Expressing pride in non-political accomplishments of the Zionist movement, such as advancements in agricultural production
c. Supporting philanthropic projects in the Land of Israel in the fields of education, social welfare, and religion

Would the BGLJ consider inviting a non-Zionist like Marshall to speak? If not, which elements of non-Zionism would the person have to renounce before the BGLJ would consider inviting them?

6. *Zionism and Judaism.* The BGLJ's bylaw states that its members "do not equate the political ideology of Zionism with the religion of Judaism." Posit that some Jews equate a different form of Zionism (e.g., religious Zionism) with their Judaism. See, e.g., *Kestenbaum v. President and Fellows of Harvard College* (D. Mass. 2024), discussed below. What if a secular Jew identifies some form of secular Zionism with their Jewish identity? How do these considerations affect the BGLJ's analysis?

7. *Protecting Jewish lives.* According to the BGLJ's bylaws, Zionism is "the failed answer to the real question of how to protect Jewish lives from antisemitism," and Zionism's project has "made Jewish people less safe ..." Assume it is the case, as Justice Brandeis believed, "the Jews require a state of their own for their continued existence," i.e., Jews are not long for this world without Israel. How would this affect the BGLJ's analysis?

8. *Jews of color.* According to the BGLJ's bylaws, the Zionist project has marginalized Jews of color. This category, known as Mizrahi Jews, comprises Jews with origins in the Middle East and North—roughly half of Israel's Jewish population. The majority of Israel's Mizrahi Jews arrived in Israel following its establishment in 1948, when over 800,000 Mizrahi Jews were expelled from Arab and Muslim-majority countries.[82] Assume the socio-economic gap between Ashkenazi and Mizrahi Jews narrows con-

82. *Mizrahi Jew*, BRITANNICA, https://www.britannica.com/topic/Oriental-Jews (last visited Dec. 16, 2024); *see also* Rachael Gelfman Schultz, *Mizrahi Jews in Israel*, MY JEWISH LEARNING, https://www.myjewishlearning.com/article/mizrahim-in-israel/ (last visited Dec. 16, 2024); *see also Jewish Exodus from the Muslim World*, WIKIPEDIA, https://en.wikipedia.org/wiki/Jewish_exodus_from_the_Mus-

siderably and ultimately disappears. How would that affect BGLJ's analysis? Here recall Schraub's view on the limited utility or edification one can derive by analogizing the Ashkenazi/Mizrahi relationship in Israel to the White/Persons of Color relationship in Europe and the U.S. [83]

9. *An important data point.* Eugene Volokh writes:

> It's important for Jewish students, and for Jews more broadly, to understand the breadth and shape of opposition to Israel among various other groups—including groups that many of those Jews might otherwise see as potential political allies. That a group is willing to exclude a vast range of American Jews as speakers, including many who are on the Left (even far Left) and may well agree with the great bulk of the group's agenda, is an important data point that people should know about the group....
>
> Indeed, my sense is that American Jewish support for Israel stems in part from the view that Jews need a place where they will always be welcome, even when other places turn against them. "Home is the place where, when you have to go there, they have to take you in." Apparently even many ostensible allies and supporters of "diversity, equity, and inclusion" would be willing to boycott what is likely the great majority of Jewish speakers.... That may well move some American Jews more towards the view that alliances with various non-Jewish groups can be dicey and evanescent, and that it's more important to support fellow Jews (and a Jewish country) than to rely on such alliances.
>
> Sometimes "the fitting remedy for evil counsels is good ones" (to quote a famous Jew[84]) because good ideas are the best way (however imperfect it may be) to rebut bad ideas. But sometimes the good counsel can consist of exposing the evil counsel and giving us a better sense of what the evil counsel's advocates really think, so we can more effectively decide what is needed to protect ourselves and those we care about.

10. *UIUC Statement.* UIUC's Joint Statement addressed Zionist excluding student groups as follows: "All Jewish students, including those who identify with Israel or Jewish campus organizations, should be able to participate in campus activities aimed at fighting racism and achieving social justice."[85] This statement does not appear to obligate student groups to include Zionist students or commit the university to facilitate their inclusion.

11. *Credit-awarding activity.* Assuming the typical student organization is entitled to exclude Zionists as members, should the same right extend to official student journals

---

lim_world#:~:text=Primarily%20a%20consequence%20of%20the,these%20Jews%20resettled%20in%20Israel (last visited Dec. 16, 2024).

83. See David Schraub, *White Jews: An Intersectional Approach*, 43 Ass'n for Jewish Stud. 379, 395–401 (2019).

84. Whitney v. California, 274 U.S. 357, 375 (1927) (Brandeis, J., concurring).

85. Off. of the Chancellor, *Joint Statement on Anti-Semitism*, Univ. of Ill. Urbana-Champaign (Nov. 16, 2020), https://blogs.illinois.edu/view/6231/1530347443.

whose members, like the BGLJ's, receive academic course credit from Berkeley Law for their journal work? Should such a journal, for example, be permitted to require members to participate in a "Palestine 101" training or similar activities? Should such requirements only be permitted if they have a sufficient pedagogical nexus to the journal's academic focus? (A law school would presumably not permit a Civil Procedure or a Business Association instructor to require students to participate in a training such as "Palestine 101.") Do the BGLJ's bylaws establish this existence of the requisite nexus? Do the 2024 amendments to the BGLJ's bylaws address concerns specific to credit-awarding activity?

12. *Employers' hiring policies.* Recall Marcus's observation that getting caught up in a civil rights complaint alleging anti-Jewish discrimination "is not a good way to build a resume or impress a future employer."[86] In a similar vein, Dean Chemerinsky has said that:

> I would hope that generally employers wouldn't deny students opportunities because of their free speech activities and that the employers would be very much wanting to protect student speech. But I also understand that there's a point at which an employer says a student who has said certain types of things aren't the ones we want to present to our clients.
>
> And so I think it's a very different situation, as a dean, my position is we want to help all of our students get jobs. But I also say to students in orientation ... that part of being a professional is you should be conscious of what you're putting on social media, you should be conscious of things you're saying because you're going to be evaluated by that, and there's a limit to how much we can protect you.[87]

Dean Erwin Chemerinsky, *Statement to the UC Berkeley Law Community*

April 13, 2024[88]

I write this with profound sadness. Since becoming a dean, my wife and I have invited the first-year students to our home for dinner. We were asked this year by the presidents of the third-year class to have the graduating students over for dinner, because they began in Fall 2021 when COVID prevented us from having dinners for

86. Kenneth L. Marcus, *Standing Up for Jewish Students*, The Jerusalem Post (Sept. 9, 2013, 8:52 PM), https://www.jpost.com/opinion/op-ed-contributors/standing-up-for-jewish-students-325648.

87. Free Speech Unmuted, *The 1st Amendment on Campus with Berkeley Law Dean Erwin Chemerinsky*, Hoover Inst. (May 7, 2024), https://www.hoover.org/research/1st-amendment-campus-berkeley-law-dean-erwin-chemerinsky.

88. Erwin Chemerinsky, *Statement from Dean Erwin Chemerinsky*, Berkeley L. (Apr. 13, 2024), https://www.law.berkeley.edu/article/statement-from-dean-erwin-chemerinsky/; *see also* Josh Blackman, *Berkeley Students Post Anti-Semitic Cartoons, Disrupt Dinner at Dean Chemerinsky's Home*, Reason (Apr. 10, 2024, 5:20 PM), https://reason.com/volokh/2024/04/10/berkeley-students-post-anti-semitic-cartoons-disrupt-dinner-at-dean-chemerinskys-home/.

them. We were delighted to oblige and designated three nights—April 9, 10, 11—that graduating students could choose among. I never imagined that something we do to help our community would become ugly and divisive.

The week before the dinners, there was an awful poster on social media and bulletin boards in the law school building of a caricature of me holding a bloody knife and fork and with blood around my lips, with the words in large letters: "No dinner with Zionist Chem while Gaza starves." I never thought I would see such blatant antisemitism, with an image that invokes the horrible antisemitic trope of blood libel and that attacks me for no apparent reason other than I am Jewish. Although many complained to me about the posters and how it offended them, I felt that though deeply offensive, they were speech protected by the First Amendment. But I was upset that those in our community had to see this disturbing, antisemitic poster around the law school.

The students responsible for this had the leaders of our student government tell me that if we did not cancel the dinners, they would protest at them. I was sad to hear this but made clear that we would not be intimidated and that the dinners would go forward for those who wanted to attend. I said that I assumed that any protest would not be disruptive.

On April 9, about 60 students came to our home for the dinner. All had registered in advance. All came into our backyard and were seated at tables for dinner. While guests were eating, a woman, who led the group responsible for the posters, stood up with a microphone that she had brought, stood on the top step in the yard, and began a speech, including about the plight of the Palestinians. My wife and I immediately approached her and asked her to stop and leave. The woman continued. When she continued her speech, there was an attempt to take away her microphone. Repeatedly, we said to her, that you are a guest in our home, please stop and leave. Our home is not a forum for free speech. Indeed, even if this were held in the law school building, there would be no First Amendment right to disrupt the event. About 10 students were with her and ultimately left as a group.

The dinner, which was meant to celebrate graduating students, was obviously disrupted and disturbed. I am enormously sad that we have students who are so rude as to come into my home, in my backyard, and use this social occasion for their political agenda.

The dinners went forward on Wednesday and Thursday. On Thursday night, about 15 people came to our home and stood on the street in front of it, and then on the path directly next to our backyard. They chanted (some chants were quite offensive) and yelled and banged drums to make noise to disturb the dinner. The dinner continued.

I have spent my career staunchly defending freedom of speech. I have spent my years as a dean trying hard to create a warm, inclusive community. I am deeply saddened by these events and take solace that it is just a small number of our students who would behave in such a clearly inappropriate manner.[89]

89. Chemerinsky, *supra* note 88.

Antisemitism and Free Speech at UC Berkeley Law

1. *Unprotected speech.* According to the Foundation for Individual Rights and Expression (FIRE), the students didn't have a First Amendment right to interrupt Dean Chemerinsky's backyard party. While the First Amendment generally doesn't apply to private settings or non-public forums, the situation becomes more complex if the event was school sponsored. Even in such cases, however, using "forum analysis," the dinner would likely be considered a limited public forum at most. This means that while the hosts (acting as state officials) could restrict speech to casual conversation and limit attendance (content-based restrictions), they couldn't discriminate based on viewpoint (e.g., permitting only pro-Israel advocates to speak).[90] "I have taught First Amendment law for 44 years," writes Dean Chemerinsky, "and as many other experts have confirmed, this is not a close question."[91]

2. *Say the word?* Concerning these events, Professor Brian Leiter writes that "It's pretty clear what's going on: students who feel impotent in the face of the horrors in Gaza are taking it out on a symbolic representative, i.e., their Jewish dean. There's a word for that, and it's not one that reflects well on them."[92] If there's a word for it, why not use it? What criteria should be used to determine when to label someone as an anti-Semite or to describe an act or statement as antisemitic? Are these criteria different when applied by Jews as compared to non-Jews?

3. *Campus officials speaking out.* Six months after Dean Chemerinsky issued this statement, he published an op-ed in the *New York Times,* headlined, "College Officials Must Condemn On-Campus Support for Hamas Violence." He wrote:

> The speech of those celebrating Hamas is protected by the First Amendment on public university campuses and at private universities that choose to adhere to free speech principles, because there is a right to express all ideas, even very offensive ones. But that does not mean universities can or should do nothing.... At the very least, campus officials must issue a simple message: "Those who have praised the terrorism of Hamas on this campus have the right to express their views. But we, as campus officials, have the duty to say that celebrating murder, rape, and taking hostages is deeply offensive and fundamentally inconsistent with what this university stands for." Saying so should not take courage.[93]

---

90. Jessie Appleby et al., *No, the Berkeley Law Student Didn't Have a First Amendment Right to Interrupt the Dean's Backyard Party*, FIRE (Apr. 15, 2024), https://www.thefire.org/news/no-berkeley-law-student-didnt-have-first-amendment-right-interrupt-deans-backyard-party.

91. Erwin Chemerinsky, *No One Has a Right to Protest in My Home,* The Atlantic (Apr. 26, 2024), https://www.theatlantic.com/ideas/archive/2024/04/campus-protest-first-amendment-berkeley/678186/.

92. Brian Leiter, *Some Berkeley Law Students Have Lost Their Minds*, Brian Leiter's L. Sch. Reps. (Apr. 11, 2024) https://leiterlawschool.typepad.com/leiter/2024/04/some-berkeley-law-students-have-lost-their-minds.html.

93. Erwin Chemerinsky, *College Officials Must Condemn On-Campus Support for Hamas Violence*, N.Y. Times (Oct. 20, 2024), https://www.nytimes.com/2024/10/20/opinion/hamas-colleges-free-speech.html.

E. Free Speech and Anti-Discrimination Law

Alexander Kestenbaum and Students Against Antisemitism, Inc. v. President and Fellows of Harvard College

United States District Court, D. Mass.
2024 WL 3658793 (August 6, 2024)

[The case arises from Harvard University's alleged failure to adequately protect Jewish students during campus protests following the October 7, 2023, Hamas attack on Israel. The plaintiffs, a recent graduate and a Jewish advocacy group, filed several claims. The district court, per Judge Richard Stearns, held that plaintiffs plausibly pled a claim of Title VI deliberate indifference. The facts as pleaded, he found, show that "Harvard failed its Jewish students."

The week before issuing this ruling, Judge Stearns dismissed a lawsuit alleging that M.I.T. violated Title VI by inadequately responding to campus antisemitism following the October 7 attack. *StandWithUs Ctr. for Legal Justice v. Massachusetts Inst. of Tech.*, 2024 WL 3596916 (D Mass July 30, 2024). Judge Stearns found that MIT officials demonstrated a proactive and escalating response, for example, by suspending some students from non-academic activities, suspending an "undisciplined" student group, issuing warnings about disciplinary consequences, and ultimately arresting students who violated policies. The university publicly condemned antisemitic actions, launched initiatives to address antisemitism,[94] and enforced its policies against harassment and disruption. This disparity in institutional action led the court to find that MIT's efforts, though imperfect, were not "clearly unreasonable."]

District Judge Stearns.

This case has its roots in an outburst of antisemitic behaviors on the Harvard University campus following the October 7, 2023 terrorist attack by Hamas on Israel. The plaintiffs are Alexander Kestenbaum, a Jewish recent graduate of the Harvard Divinity School, and Students Against Antisemitism, Inc. (SAA), a non-profit "comprised of voluntary members, including students at higher education institutions" founded to defend the rights of individuals "to be free from antisemitism in higher education." Alleging that Harvard affirmatively ignored discrimination against Jewish and Israeli students, plaintiffs sued the University seeking damages and prospective injunctive relief. The Second Amended Complaint (SAC) [alleges] deliberate indifference to ha-

94. These initiatives included *Standing Together Against Hate*, which provides training on antisemitism, Islamophobia, anti-Arab hate, constructive dialogue, managing sensitive conversations, and education about Middle East history and contrasting narratives. *3 Questions: Melissa Nobles on Combating Antisemitism and Islamophobia*, MIT News (Dec. 4, 2023), https://news.mit.edu/2023/3q-melissa-nobles-combating-antisemitism-and-islamophobia-1204.

rassment of ... Jewish and Israeli students in violation of Title VI of the Civil Rights Act of 1964.[95]

Background

On October 7, 2023, the Palestinian Sunni Islamist terrorist group Hamas committed a savage terrorist attack on Israel.[96] The day after the attack, more than thirty Harvard student groups issued a joint statement purporting to "hold the Israeli regime entirely responsible for all unfolding violence." On October 18, 2023, two Harvard student groups organized a metaphorical "die-in" involving hundreds of students at which members of the protesting groups "harassed and physically assaulted Jewish students."

Throughout the fall 2023 semester, Harvard student groups, including Harvard Afro; Boycott, Divestment and Sanctions; Graduate Students for Palestine; Jews for Liberation; and the Palestinian Solidarity Committee (PSC),[97] regularly demonstrated on campus. Protestors marched through campus, staged classroom walkouts, and rallied in campus common areas, at times staying overnight. During these events, demonstrators chanted provocative slogans such as "from the river to the sea,"[98] "free Palestine," and "globalize the intifada." The bullying of Jewish students also spilled into classrooms. For example, a Harvard Law School Torts professor announced a final exam focused on the Israel/Gaza conflict (and only changed course when the Registrar's Office intervened). And a Harvard Law School student who assaulted a Jewish student at the October 18 "die-in" was permitted to remain in his position as a teaching fellow for a first-year Civil Procedure course.

Antisemitic episodes persisted and, if anything, intensified into the spring 2024 semester. On January 2, 2024, Harvard students posted a flurry of antisemitic messages on a University-wide group app called Sidechat.[99] When Kestenbaum reported the messages to Harvard administrators, the official response was to terminate his access to Sidechat and restrict Sidechat membership to current undergraduate students. In late January, posters memorializing Israeli citizens taken hostage by Hamas were van-

95. Editor's note: Plaintiffs also alleged a claim of direct discrimination, which the court dismissed, and claims of breach of contract and implied covenant, which the court allowed to proceed.

96. "Hamas" is an acronym for Harakat al-Muqawama al-Islamiya, which translates roughly in English to Islamic Resistance Movement. In 1997, the U.S. Department of State designated Hamas as a Terrorist Organization under § 219 of the Immigration and Nationality Act, 8 U.S.C. § 1189.

97. Harvard Afro and Boycott, Divestment, and Sanctions are not registered student groups.

98. "From the river to the sea" refers to the area between the Jordan River and the Mediterranean Sea, in which Israel, the West Bank, East Jerusalem, and the Gaza Strip are located. Plaintiffs allege that the phrase is a "genocidal call for the destruction of Israel and its Jewish inhabitants."

99. These messages included students "proudly accept[ing] the label of terrorist," calling a Jewish student a "pedo lover," claiming that "all of you Zionists" are "killers and rapists of children," and referring to a Jewish student's nose as "crooked."

dalized with messages such as "ISRAEL DID 9/11."[100] Soon after, a Harvard employee emailed Kestenbaum inviting him to debate Israel's "role in 9/11."[101]

A flash point ignited in April of 2024, when protesting students erected an encampment in Harvard Yard, an iconic close in the center of the Harvard campus. Harvard had cautioned students that "tents and tables are not permitted in the Yard without prior permission," and that "students violating these policies are subject to disciplinary action." Despite the warnings, Harvard did nothing to stop "people with backpacks, tents, suitcases, and carts" from descending on the Yard on April 24 to create a tent encampment. The encampment was left undisturbed until May 14, when Interim President Alan Garber negotiated with leaders of the encampment over the terms of vacating the Yard. In exchange for an end to the encampment, Garber instructed all Harvard schools to reinstate any student protestors who had been placed on involuntary leave, promised to expedite any administrative hearings against these students, and agreed to conduct the hearings with "leniency." Garber also offered Harvard Out of Palestine, an unregistered student group, meetings with Harvard's governing board to advocate for divestment of any Harvard endowment ties with Israel.

The ongoing tumult caused many Jewish and Israeli students to fear for their personal safety and hindered their ability to complete their academic studies. During one of the protest rallies, demonstrators blockaded Jewish students in a study room, and during another, protestors "surrounded and intimidated" Jewish students. Protesting students embedded in the encampment followed Kestenbaum "every time [he] tried to walk through Harvard Yard." Some students felt compelled to doff clothing that might identify them as Jewish and ceased attending Jewish-sponsored events on campus. Still others feared walking about campus, missed classes, and felt isolated from their classmates.

Plaintiffs further aver that they feel abandoned by Harvard's administration. Although Kestenbaum and SAA members have complained repeatedly to various Harvard offices and administrators, they claim that the situation has not improved. And when asked before the U.S. House of Representatives whether "calling for the genocide of Jews violate[s] Harvard's rules of bullying and harassment," then-President Claudine Gay disconcertingly replied that "it depends on the context."

According to plaintiffs, Harvard's response has been not just simply inadequate but skewed in its bias. For example, after student groups protested for two weeks in Caspersen lounge, a common student area in the Harvard Law School, Jewish students

---

100. Editor's note: On such allegations see Glen A. Tobias & Abraham H. Foxman, The Anti-Defamation League, Unraveling Anti-Semitic 9/11 Conspiracy Theories (2003), https://www.adl.org/sites/default/files/documents/assets/pdf/combating-hate/anti-semitic-9-11-conspiracy-theories.pdf; *see also* The Anti-Defamation League, Antisemitic Conspiracies About 9/11 Endure 20 Years Later (2021), https://www.adl.org/resources/report/antisemitic-conspiracies-about-911-endure-20-years-later.

101. On his social media account "9/11 Guy," the employee identified himself as "an 'anti-Semite' because [he has] no problem with Jews per se, just the ones who think there's a different set of rules for them," and questioned whether the October 7 terrorist attacks had truly occurred. Harvard eventually fired the employee in April of 2024.

asked Harvard deans and administrators if they could also hold a demonstration in the lounge. Only after that request was made did Harvard Law Dean of Students Stephen Ball email the student body that the lounge area is reserved for "personal or small group study and conversation." That edict notwithstanding, Harvard (at least de facto) permitted pro-Palestine protests in the lounge to continue until the end of the semester. Harvard required Chabad, a campus Hasidic Jewish community center, to remove its Hanukkah menorah from campus each night to prevent it being vandalized, but it provided 24/7 security to PSC's "Wall of Resistance." And although then-President Gay appointed an Antisemitism Advisory Group in November of 2023, Garber dissolved the Group before it could make any formal recommendations.[102]

Harvard has a fulsome array of policies that govern student behavior. These include a Non-Discrimination and Anti-Bullying Policy, Protest Rules, a Statement on Rights and Responsibilities, Student Organization Policies, and various student handbooks (together, the Policies). The Policies prohibit "singling out or targeting an individual for less favorable treatment because of their protected characteristic" and "unwelcome and offensive conduct that is based on an individual or group's protected status." They also bar "any unauthorized occupation of a University building, or any part of it, that interferes with the ability of members of the University to perform their normal activities" and "interference with freedom of movement or with freedom from personal force or violence." Violation of the Policies is said to be "subject to appropriate discipline."

Deliberate Indifference

The parties agree that Title VI protects Jewish students from harassment,[103] and discrimination based on actual or perceived Israeli identity is of course discrimination based on national origin.

A deliberate indifference claim has five elements: (1) plaintiffs were "subject to 'severe, pervasive, and objectively offensive' ... harassment"; (2) the harassment "caused the plaintiff to be deprived of educational opportunities or benefits"; (3) the school "knew of the harassment"; (4) the harassment occurred "in its programs and activities"; and (5) the school "was deliberately indifferent to the harassment such that its response (or lack thereof) is clearly unreasonable in light of the known circumstances." Harvard contends that the SAC fails to adequately plead the first and fifth elements.

In evaluating the first element, courts look to a constellation of non-dispositive factors: "severity of the conduct, its frequency, whether it [was] physically threatening or not, and whether it interfered with" the student experience. Taking these factors into account, plaintiffs have plausibly pled that they were subject to severe, pervasive, and objectively offensive harassment. The SAC vividly limns repeated, fear-inducing conduct that amounted to more than "off-color banter," or, in Harvard's words, "offensive

102. Garber subsequently created a Presidential Task Force on Combating Antisemitism.

103. Editor's note: Judge Stearns states that discrimination based on Israeli identity is "of course discrimination based on national origin." Notice he does not assert that discrimination based on Jewish identity is "of course" or obviously constitutes Title VI discrimination based on race and/or national origin.

utterance[s],"[104] The protests were, at times, confrontational and physically violent, and plaintiffs legitimately fear their repetition. The harassment also impacted plaintiffs' life experience at Harvard; they dreaded walking through the campus, missed classes, and stopped participating in extracurricular events.

As to the fifth element, Harvard first argues that it could not, or at least is not legally required to, infringe on protected First Amendment activity. It may be true that, as a policy matter, Harvard has elected not to curtail the protests in the interest of protecting free speech (although as a private institution, it is not constitutionally required to do so). The court consequently is dubious that Harvard can hide behind the First Amendment to justify avoidance of its Title VI obligations. At any rate, whether this argument has any teeth is a decision best reserved for a later day. The record is too thin to determine whether Harvard in fact acted to protect free speech rights as it contends Title VI required it to do and whether the protest activity itself comes within the protections of the First Amendment.

Harvard next contends that it responded to many of the incidents cited in the SAC and, although its response was perhaps less than "ideal," it "cannot plausibly be characterized" as clearly unreasonable. Harvard is correct that the SAC describes a handful of steps that Harvard took in response to antisemitic incidents. But as pled, Harvard's reaction was, at best, indecisive, vacillating, and at times internally contradictory. For example, the day after Dean Ball emailed all Harvard Law students that Caspersen lounge was limited to "personal or small group study and conversation," demonstrators hosted a "vigil for martyrs" in the lounge without any pushback from law school administrators. Rather than call a halt to the vigil, Dean Ball attended it. In another venue, while Harvard police officers were on scene at the encampment, when a Jewish student was openly "charged" and "push[ed]," the officers failed to react. And while Harvard, on April 22, 2024, suspended the PSC until the end of the semester, the short-term suspension proved to be in name alone, as the PSC spearheaded the creation of the encampment in Harvard Yard just two days later.

These are but some of the many examples set out in the SAC documenting Harvard's failure to address what former President Gay and Interim President Garber repeatedly publicly recognized as an eruption of antisemitism on the Harvard campus. Indeed, in many instances, Harvard did not respond at all. To conclude that the SAC has not plausibly alleged deliberate indifference would reward Harvard for virtuous public

---

104. The out-of-circuit district court cases on which Harvard relies to argue the opposite are easily distinguished. In *Mandel v. Board of Trustees of California State University*, 2018 WL 5458739 (N.D. Cal. Oct. 29, 2018), plaintiffs adequately alleged only three "isolated" events, and the remaining alleged events were "vague and lack[ing] substantiating specifics," such as dates, times, and identities of the students allegedly harassing Jewish students. And in *Felber v. Yudof*, 851 F. Supp. 2d 1182 (N.D. Cal. 2011), "a broad swath of the conduct alleged occurred at times and in places where plaintiffs were not present," and plaintiffs did not establish that they were denied access to educational services. Here, the SAC alleges with specificity a myriad of events occurring over seven months that Kestenbaum and/or SAA Members witnessed (or were targets of), many of which caused plaintiffs to be denied educational opportunities.

declarations that for the most part, according to the allegations of the SAC, proved hollow when it came to taking disciplinary measures against offending students and faculty. In other words, the facts as pled show that Harvard failed its Jewish students.

The court will, as it has before, add some concluding thoughts. In assessing the actions taken in similar circumstances by Harvard's sister institution, the Massachusetts Institute of Technology, the court observed that the fault it attributed to MIT was "its failure to anticipate the bigoted behavior that some demonstrators—however sincere their disagreement with U.S. and Israeli policies—would exhibit as events unfolded." *StandWithUs Ctr. For Legal Justice v. M.I.T.* ___ F.Supp.3d ___ (July 30, 2024, D. Mass.) But despite MIT's failure of clairvoyance, it did respond with a perhaps overly measured but nonetheless consistent sense of purpose in returning civil order and discourse to its campus. As the court pointed out, the law expects reasonable and proportionate acts by university officials—the standard is not faultless perfection or ultimate success. Liability attaches only when a school's response is "so lax, so misdirected, or so poorly executed as to be clearly unreasonable under the known circumstances." The facts as alleged in the SAC plausibly establish that Harvard's response failed Title VI's commands....

Unlawful Conduct vs. Protected Speech

1. *Why dubious?* Why, in Judge Stearns's view, is it "dubious that Harvard can hide behind the First Amendment to justify avoidance of its Title VI obligations"?

2. *Understand the interplay.* The Foundation for Individual Rights and Expression (FIRE) filed an *amicus* brief in *Kestenbaum* arguing that while "universities must ensure unlawful conduct does not deprive its students of the benefits of their education... Title VI cannot constitutionally turn schools into censors."[105] It expressed concern that "the current moment presents a real danger of silencing student and faculty expression in the name of anti-discrimination."[106] It asked the court to "evaluate this case in light of the threat to expressive rights and academic freedom presented by misinterpreting harassment obligations."[107]

---

105. Brief for Neither Party at 9, Kestenbaum v. President and Fellows of Harv. Coll., No. 24-cv-10092, 2024 WL 3658793 (D. Mass. filed July 16, 2024), https://www.thefire.org/research-learn/fire-amicus-brief-filed-kestenbaum-v-harvard.

106. *Id.* at 12.

107. *Id.* at 14.

Catherine E. Lhamon, U.S. Department of Education Assistant Secretary for Civil Rights, *Title VI First Amendment Considerations*[108]

May 7, 2024[109]

Dear Colleague:

Title VI's protections against discrimination based on race, color, and national origin encompass antisemitism and other forms of discrimination when based on shared ancestry or ethnic characteristics....[110]

I. Title VI First Amendment Considerations

Nothing in Title VI or regulations implementing it requires or authorizes a school to restrict any rights otherwise protected by the First Amendment to the U.S. Constitution. OCR enforces the laws within our jurisdiction consistent with the First Amendment.

The fact that harassment may involve conduct that includes speech in a public setting or speech that is also motivated by political or religious beliefs, however, does not relieve a school of its obligation to respond under Title VI as described below, if the harassment creates a hostile environment in school for a student or students.

Schools have a number of tools for responding to a hostile environment—including tools that do not restrict any rights protected by the First Amendment. To meet its obligation, a university can, among other steps, communicate its opposition to stereotypical, derogatory opinions; provide counseling and support for students affected by harassment; or take steps to establish a welcoming and respectful school campus, which could include making clear that the school values, and is determined to fully include in the campus community, students of all races, colors, and national origins.[111]

---

108. This is an excerpt from U.S. Department of Education Assistant Secretary for Civil Rights Lhamon's "Dear Colleague Letter." CATHERINE E. LHAMON, U.S. DEP'T OF EDUC., OFF. OF C.R., PROTECTING STUDENTS FROM DISCRIMINATION, SUCH AS HARASSMENT, BASED ON RACE, COLOR, OR NATIONAL ORIGIN, INCLUDING SHARED ANCESTRY OR ETHNIC CHARACTERISTICS (2024), https://www.ed.gov/media/document/colleague-202405-shared-ancestrypdf.

109. *Id.*

110. [FN5] See *T.E. v. Pine Bush Cent. Sch. Dist.*, 58 F. Supp. 3d 332, 353–55 (S.D.N.Y. 2014) (holding that discrimination based on shared ancestry and ethnic characteristics is prohibited by Title VI).... [FN 23] Because Title VI does not protect students from discrimination based only on religion, OCR may refer complaints of discrimination based exclusively on religion, such as a school's denial of a student's request to miss class for a religious holiday, to the U.S. Department of Justice, which has jurisdiction under Title VI to respond to certain complaints of religious discrimination in public schools. See 42 U.S.C. § 2000c-6.

111. See, e.g., *Feminist Majority Foundation v. Hurley*, 911 F.3d 674, 688 (4th Cir. 2018) (to address hostile environment on social media, school administrators "could have more clearly communicated to the student body that the University would not tolerate sexually harassing behavior either in person or online. The University could have conducted mandatory assemblies to explain and discourage cyber bullying and sex discrimination, and it could have provided anti-sexual harassment training to the entire student body and faculty"). A school cannot meet its obligation to address harassment under federal civil rights laws simply by referring matters to the police.

OCR does not interpret Title VI to require any recipient to abridge any rights protected under the First Amendment. For instance, if students at a public university engage in offensive speech about members of a particular ethnic group and that speech contributes to a hostile environment within an education program about which the university knows or should know, the university has a legal obligation to address that hostile environment for students in school. The university may, however, be constrained or limited in how it responds if speech is involved.[112] . . .

II. Expression of Views About a Particular Country

Speech expressing views regarding a particular country's policies or practices is protected by the First Amendment and does not necessarily implicate federal civil rights laws.[113] However, if harassing conduct that otherwise appears to be based on views about a country's policies or practices is targeted at or infused with discriminatory comments about persons from or associated with a particular country, then it may implicate Title VI and should be analyzed on a fact-dependent basis.[114] For example, if a professor teaching a class on international politics references or criticizes the government of Israel's treatment of non-Jewish people,[115] the nation of Saudi Arabia's response to religious extremism, or the government of India's promotion of Hinduism, so long as such comments do not target Israeli, Jewish, Saudi, Arab, or Indian students based on race, color, or national origin, that would not likely implicate Title VI.

By contrast, Title VI protections could be implicated if a professor teaching about international politics refers to Jewish people, Muslim people, or Hindu people using offensive stereotypes based on perceived shared ethnic characteristics or shared ancestry. . . .

---

112. See *id. at* 688–89 (holding that the university could not ignore "the sexual harassment that pervaded and disrupted its campus solely because the offending conduct took place through cyberspace").

113. Such distinctions have been drawn in Title VII cases to distinguish offensive political remarks from discriminatory harassment based on race, color, national origin, religion, and sex. *See Singh v. Town of Mount Pleasant*, 172 Fed. Appx. 675, 681 (7th Cir. 2006) (holding that a supervisor's insensitive comment about how the U.S. should handle a high-profile Cuban refugee was not national origin harassment of an employee under Title VII); *Fair v. Guiding Eyes for the Blind, Inc.*, 742 F. Supp. 151, 156 (S.D.N.Y. 1990) (finding that defendant's remarks "concerned his opinions on various political, moral and social issues" and were not based on plaintiff's gender, so those allegations could not constitute harassment based on sex); *Reichman v. Bureau of Affirmative Action*, 536 F. Supp. 1149, 1176 (M.D. Pa. 1982) (deeming "comments concerning the Arab-Israeli conflict and [the Israeli prime minister] to be political opinions rather than disparagements of Judaism" that would constitute unlawful religious harassment under Title VII). OCR similarly interprets Title VI to not be implicated by conduct based solely on political views.

114. *See* 34 C.F.R. § 100.3(a). *Cf. Kamal v. Hopmayer*, 300 Fed. App'x 37, 38–39 (2d Cir. 2008) (holding that a high school principal's frequent classroom visits to discuss his military service in the first Gulf War did not state a claim under Title VI of race, color, or national origin harassment of an Iranian Muslim student absent evidence of any prejudice or negative sentiments about Iranian people, Muslim people, or any other group during those discussions).

115. Executive Order 13899 provides that federal agencies "shall consider" the non-legally binding IHRA working definition of antisemitism and accompanying examples of antisemitism "to the extent that" any such "examples might be useful as evidence of discriminatory intent."

OCR acknowledges that it may sometimes be difficult to distinguish between alleged conduct based on views regarding a particular country or its policies (which would not implicate Title VI) and alleged conduct based on students' actual or perceived shared ancestry or ethnic characteristics or their citizenship or residency in a country whose residents share a dominant religion or a distinct religious identity (which could implicate Title VI). However, these distinctions help determine when conduct falls within OCR's jurisdiction under Title VI....

Michael C. Dorf,[116]
Free Speech Versus Antidiscrimination in the Scholarship of Eugene Volokh[117]

Following the Hamas-led atrocities in Israel on October 7, 2023, and Israel's ensuing war in Gaza, with its very high number of civilian casualties and suffering, during the 2024 spring semester, college campuses became a key site of conflict between speech and antidiscrimination norms. Some of that conflict has a clear-cut solution. Antisemitic or Islamophobic violence and true threats are unprotected wherever they occur; they can clearly be proscribed on campus, whether by a state university or a private one. But other clashes pose hard questions.

In a made-for-virality confrontation in December 2023, Congresswoman Elise Stefanik grilled the presidents of Harvard, M.I.T., and the University of Pennsylvania as to whether a call for genocide would violate the schools' codes of conduct. The university presidents attempted to give nuanced and legally correct answers. For example, Harvard's then-President Claudine Gay described such speech as "hateful" and contrary to "Harvard's values," but noted that, given the university's commitment to free speech, whether a call for genocide violated the campus code would depend on whether it crossed the line into actual violence, bullying, or harassment. That was not good enough for Stefanik and others; both Gay and University of Pennsylvania President Elizabeth Magill would soon lose their jobs as a consequence of bringing a lawyer to a knife-fight. Even many liberals who recognized Stefanik's bad-faith demagoguery criticized the university presidents for their tone-deafness or worse. Meanwhile, the leaders of other universities rushed to clarify that calls for genocide would indeed violate their codes of student conduct. For example, Stanford University issued a statement on social media condemning "calls for the genocide of Jews or any peoples," which, it said, "would clearly violate Stanford's ... code of conduct for all students at the university."

---

116. Michael C. Dorf is Robert S. Stevens Professor of Law at Cornell Law School. Authoring or co-authoring over one hundred scholarly articles and essays, and the author (with Laurence H. Tribe) of On Reading the Constitution (1991), and No Litmus Test: Law Versus Politics in the Twenty-First Century (2006). This excerpt was initially published in 2024 as Cornell Legal Studies Research Paper No. 24-12, available at https://ssrn.com/abstract=4935040.

117. Eugene Volokh is the Thomas M. Siebel Senior Fellow at the Hoover Institution. For thirty years, he has been a professor at the UCLA School of Law, where he has taught First Amendment law, copyright law, criminal law, tort law, and firearms regulation policy. Volokh is the author of the textbooks, The First Amendment and Related Statutes (7th ed. 2020) and Academic Legal Writing (5th ed. 2016), as well as more than one hundred law review articles.

Volokh pushed back hard in an essay on his eponymous blog. Noting that both Stanford's own commitments and a California statute known as the Leonard Law[118] protect free speech on campus to the same extent that the First Amendment protects non-campus speech,[119] Volokh explained that calls for genocide, absent more, are in fact protected speech. He went on to say ... that respectable arguments could be made for genocide, at least in certain circumstances. His principal examples of genocides that might be justified were the actual U.S. atomic bombing of Hiroshima and Nagasaki if understood as aiming at securing a Japanese surrender without an even greater loss of life and a hypothetical retaliatory nuclear strike as a means of maintaining a deterrent against further nuclear strikes by the aggressor.

Volokh's point was not that, in these examples or any others, genocide would be self-evidently justified. On the contrary, Volokh recognized that what amounts to genocide and whether it is justified are contested. Many of Israel's critics contend that Israel is committing genocide in Gaza; if they are correct, then defenses of Israel's ongoing conduct of the war could be deemed calls for genocide. Meanwhile, some critics of protesters on behalf of Palestinians argue that slogans like "from the river to the sea" and defenses of *intifada* are calls for genocide.[120] However, so long as neither side crosses over into its own violence, true threats, or otherwise unprotected expression or conduct, Volokh argued, standard free speech doctrine—which applies at all campuses in California, including Stanford—protects calls for genocide.

I agree with Volokh's analysis, at least as a descriptive matter. There is no "calls for genocide" exception to the First Amendment. But I am not fully persuaded about the inferences he draws for college campuses outside California.

To be clear, Volokh and I agree that a private university outside of California could, consistent with the Constitution, subject students to discipline or even expulsion for engaging in speech that would be fully protected against general government regulation. However, Volokh thinks private universities *shouldn't* take such measures, because, he says, private universities "do not need more speech restrictions than ... public universities that are governed by the First Amendment." I agree with that proposition

---

118. Cal. Educ. Code § 94367 (West, Westlaw through Ch. 27 of 2024 Reg. Sess.) ("No private postsecondary educational institution shall make or enforce a rule subjecting a student to disciplinary sanctions solely on the basis of conduct that is speech or other communication that, when engaged in outside the campus or facility of a private postsecondary institution, is protected from governmental restriction by the First Amendment to the United States Constitution or Section 2 of Article I of the California Constitution.")

119. To the same extent so far as penalties are concerned, that is. The Leonard Law protects only against discipline.

120. *See, e.g.*, [Holding Campus Leaders Accountable and Confronting Antisemitism: Hearing Before the H. Comm. on Educ. and the Workforce, 118th Cong. 49] (statement of Rep. Stefanik[, Member, H. Comm. on Educ. and the Workforce]) (contending that the term *intifada* is "[a] call for violent armed resistance against the State of Israel, including violence against civilians and the genocide of Jews."); Simon Sebag Montefiore, *The Decolonization Narrative Is Dangerous and False*, Atlantic (Oct. 27, 2023) (arguing that the phrase "from the river to the sea" "implicitly endorses the killing or deportation of the 9 million Israelis").

as well. But I do not fully agree with his assessment of what the First Amendment entails where it applies of its own force, that is, to public universities.

So far as free speech is concerned, the campus setting is a double-edged sword.[121] On one hand, it provides special reasons for solicitude towards speech claims. As I noted some years ago, "one of the very reasons for existence of the college or university is to encourage robust debate through uninhibited expression of views, including controversial ones." And the Supreme Court has left open the possibility that the First Amendment extends some protection to academic freedom. However, and on the other hand, even if special speech-protective constitutional rules and standards apply in many academic settings, they do not apply in all such settings. In some respects, the campus context has the opposite implication: the First Amendment allows even a public university to restrict some speech that would be fully protected if it occurred off campus.

To see why, it is useful to explore other special contexts in which the First Amendment permits restrictions on speech that would be impermissible if imposed broadly by the government as regulator. It is a commonplace that the limitations the First Amendment imposes on government efforts to regulate speech can depend on the relation between the government and the speaker as well as the physical space within which the speech occurs. Consider a few examples.

Although the Supreme Court has "applied the captive audience doctrine only sparingly," it has recognized that in certain settings the government interest in protecting people from unwelcome messages justifies restrictions on speech that would be impermissible in more purely public settings. The leading Supreme Court cases involve speech that intrudes on people in their homes, but the principle is not limited to the home. For example, the United States Court of Appeals for the Second Circuit upheld a prohibition on begging in the New York City subway, where commuters are effectively a captive audience; three years later, that court distinguished "the special conditions of the subway" system in the course of striking down a broader begging prohibition that applied in any public place. The juxtaposition illustrates the commonsense idea that the protection the Constitution affords speech can depend on the characteristics of the space in which it occurs—an idea that also finds expression in the Supreme Court's public forum doctrine.

The workplace is another setting in which speech that could not be the basis for general regulation can be limited by the government as employer. That is not for the reason Oliver Wendell Holmes, Jr., speaking for the Massachusetts Supreme Judicial Court, offered: because the government can condition employment on the waiver of the constitutional right to free speech. Rather, the employee speech doctrine recog-

121. To be more precise, it is a double-edged sword with a flat surface in between. *See* Michael C. Dorf, Disaggregating Free Speech on Campus, Dorf on Law (Nov. 17, 2017). ("In some contexts, the fact that speech claims are made on campus should make them stronger relative to competing claims; in other contexts, the fact that speech claims are made on campus should make them relatively weaker; and in still other contexts, the campus setting should make no difference.")

nizes that government as employer has speech-infringing interests that government as regulator lacks. Among them is the interest in protecting workers—who are in essence a captive audience for the speech of their co-workers—from unwelcome speech. Even if an employer would not choose to offer such protection to its employees absent legal compulsion, employers undoubtedly have an interest in complying with federal law protecting workers from invidious discrimination.

The captive audience concept provides part but not all of the justification for the conclusion that Title VII's proscription of hostile-environment harassment does not contravene the First Amendment. There is also the antidiscrimination policy itself. After all, application of Title VII to bar hostile-environment harassment does not merely protect workers against unwelcome messages. It implements the statutory goal of ensuring equal employment opportunity free of invidious discrimination.

Similar interests justify restricting student expression under Title VI in its application to colleges and universities that receive federal funds, which is to say, every major college and university in the United States. In classrooms and dormitories, students are a captive audience. Indeed, a dormitory is a home, triggering the special considerations associated with the captive audience cases addressing the home.[122]

Meanwhile, just as Title VII aims to ensure equal employment opportunities, Title VI (as applied to colleges and universities) aims to ensure equal educational opportunities. To the extent that a hostile environment based on membership in a protected class interferes with such opportunities, it contravenes the antidiscrimination statute's purpose (and text).

However, while antidiscrimination norms justify some restrictions on campus speech in classrooms and dormitories, students are not a captive audience everywhere on campus. A campus quadrangle is a rough analogue of a public park. On the quad or its equivalent, the university setting should not afford administrators any greater power to censor speech than the government enjoys relative to the general public in parks.[123]

---

122. During the discussion session following my oral presentation of a draft of this essay, Professor Volokh noted that a college dormitory is a home for both speakers and unwilling listeners. Fair enough. For that reason, the decision by Barnard College to ban all signs on dormitory doors as a content-neutral means of protecting other students in the dormitory from hurtful messages seems excessive. If my neighbor displays an offensive sign, it does not intrude into my home, even if my neighbor lives very close nearby so that I cannot avoid seeing the sign each time I enter or leave my home. That is not to say, however, that a speaker's right necessarily prevails over an unwilling listener's right, so long as they are both at home. Quiet hours in the dormitories appropriately privilege listeners. Speech-related disputes between roommates present further questions, although these matters are often more in the nature of interpersonal relations than legal doctrine....

123. To be sure, depending on the campus layout, students and faculty might need to cross the quad to get to class, thus exposing them to speech they might prefer to avoid. But the same could be true of someone who needs to cross a public park (or take a long detour) to get to work. Moreover, streets and sidewalks are traditional public fora no less than are parks. Yet proximity to passersby who cannot completely avoid unwanted messages is not a sufficient reason to deny speech rights on captive audience grounds.

Nonetheless, lawsuits by Jewish students at the University of California at Berkeley, Columbia, Harvard, and elsewhere make Title VI claims in partial reliance on statements by pro-Palestinian protesters in outdoor settings and on social media; the plaintiffs allege that the administrations at their respective schools took insufficient steps to protect them from a hostile environment. While some of the plaintiffs' allegations involve targeted threats, others concern statements that, while wrong-headed or offensive, would clearly constitute protected political speech if made at a rally in a public park.

The claims against universities for not doing enough to rein in allegedly antisemitic speech have gained traction. In the Harvard case, a federal district court rejected a motion to dismiss the complaint without reaching the question whether Title VI, if construed to require a private university to infringe the speech of its students, would violate the First Amendment. Meanwhile, the Department of Education (DOE) Office of Civil Rights has taken a position similar to that of the plaintiffs in the cases described above. For example, in addressing complaints against the University of Michigan, it declared: "While the University may not discipline speakers for protected speech, the University retains a Title VI legal obligation to take other steps as necessary to ensure that no hostile environment based on shared ancestry persists." The suggestion is that statements by students can be instances of protected free speech but also, either on their own or when aggregated with other similar statements or conduct, contribute to a hostile environment for other students in violation of Title VI.

The DOE's stance is not exactly self-contradictory, but it does place universities in an awkward position. Ordinarily, the obligation to prevent or remediate a hostile environment can be satisfied through means such as individual discipline and general training. Yet the DOE itself acknowledges that discipline is not available for protected speech. Thus, training cannot truthfully instruct students that they will face any remedial consequences for protected speech. Training usually consists of dos and don'ts. Given the DOE's acknowledgment that speech can be both protected and also a contributor to a hostile environment, any training would need to consist of dos and please-don'ts.

What, then, can universities do? They can provide tools to support the emotional wellbeing of students who feel besieged by speech they experience as hostile—although doing so invites complaints about coddling oversensitive young adults.[124] Counter-speech by the university administration is another option—although engaging in such counter-speech when the underlying speech concerns divisive issues risks violating the neutrality commitments some universities have made.[125] As of this writing, DOE

---

124. For an insightful defense of campus "safe spaces" against such charges, see Ashutosh Bhagwat & John Inazu, *Searching for Safe Spaces*, Inside Higher Ed (Mar. 20, 2017).

125. See, e.g., Kalven Comm., Report on the University's Role in Political and Social Action 2 (1967). ("There emerges ... a heavy presumption against the university taking collective action or expressing opinions on the political and social issues of the day, or modifying its corporate activities to foster social or political values, however compelling and appealing they may be.")

has not provided clear guidance about what universities should do to counter what it regards as the discriminatory impact of protected speech.

As the latest round of conflicts between free speech and antidiscrimination law works its way through the legal system, lawyers and judges might wish to rethink the DOE position. A simpler solution would be to conclude that if speech is protected (or would be at a public university), it necessarily cannot be deemed a contribution to a hostile environment. That approach would not make all of the difficult tradeoffs go away, but it would simplify the analysis. It would also be very much in the spirit of Volokh's work—which, while invariably attentive to nuance, nevertheless puts a thumb on the scale in favor of both liberty and clear rules rather than vague standards.

Conclusion

"Those who won our independence by revolution were not cowards," wrote Justice Brandeis in his concurrence in *Whitney v. California*, in "what may be the most important judicial opinion ever written on the subject of freedom of speech."[126] It is tempting to read the *Whitney* concurrence and its companion in the canonical precursors of modern free speech doctrine—the dissent of Justice Holmes in *Abrams v. United States*,[127]—as focused on the courage to tolerate disagreeable opinions on the chance that they might usefully dislodge flawed conventional wisdom. It is tempting, in other words, to read Brandeis as extolling the courage to tolerate the offensive views of *others*.

That is surely part of what Brandeis meant, but it is not the whole of it. A culture of free speech requires not only the courage to listen politely while the loudmouths have their say but the courage of thoughtful people to speak up—to take and defend unpopular positions, to follow arguments where they lead, to consider the force of countervailing considerations and give them their due, but no more. As Vincent Blasi has insightfully observed, the essential civics lesson Brandeis sought to convey in *Whitney* was that "the key to a successful democracy lies in the spirit, the vitality, the daring, the inventiveness of its citizens."[128]

Cary Nelson,[129]
The Future of Campus Antisemitism After October 7

September 2024

The flood of campus antisemitism [after October 7] arrived not in response to Israel's declaration of war following Hamas's attacks nor even in reaction to the IDF's

126. Vincent Blasi, *The First Amendment and the Ideal of Civic Courage: The Brandeis Opinion in* Whitney v. California, 29 Wm. & Mary L. Rev. 653, 660 (1988).

127. 250 U.S. 616 (1919).

128. Blasi, *supra* note [126], at 686.

129. Cary Nelson is Jubilee Professor of Liberal Arts and Sciences and Professor of English Emeritus at the University of Illinois Urbana-Champaign. He is an affiliated faculty member at the University of Haifa and the recipient of an honorary doctorate from Ben-Gurion University of the Negev. He was

first bombing runs in Gaza. It came as a form of symbolic participation in the Hamas pogrom itself.... As early as the 1982 Lebanon War, anger at Israel was displaced onto Jews everywhere,[130] but it came in response to images of people dying in Israeli raids. This time, counter-intuitively, "it was the murder of 1,200 people in southern Israel, and the seizing of around 250 hostages, that triggered this outburst of anti-Jewish hatred." That is a watershed development in the normalization of antisemitism. It will not now disappear.

Meanwhile, heightened anxiety has to be grounded in impossible knowledge. Hamas's conduct on 10/7 was fundamentally impossible to understand. The intricate, obscene, intimate brutality, sustained for hours, cannot really be registered in detail. It resembles an endless horror movie more than a series of believable crimes. So we retreat not into denial but into nonrecognition. We cannot remain face to face with the carnage of that day. We cannot hold the violence in our minds as an object of analysis and understanding. And yet we must try....

I thus feel a moral responsibility to approximate at least a glimpse of some of what the victims experienced, though, again, it is almost impossible to put oneself in their place. Fear for themselves and family members, efforts at self-defense, surprise and shock, anger, excruciating pain, disbelief, often intermixed, place the fullness of their experience outside complete comprehension. And these descriptive categories themselves are too familiar, too cliched, to be adequate. Nor are the range of personal experiences interchangeable. A Jewish family under attack in its safe room, twenty Israelis crowded into a roadside shelter, a lightly armed kibbutz defender trying to block access by a murder squad and about to be overwhelmed, a child trying to process a nightmare attack turned real, parents lying on top of their children hoping that they would be shot and their children spared, concert goers gunned down in their cars, IDF soldiers unexpectedly under attack by a superior force, a civilian successfully hiding from the murder squads hearing another victim being tortured, a woman in a field undergoing the most primal sexual assault imaginable: these experiences are at once unitary, collectively designated as 10/7, and unique. The myriad horrors of a day and more, altogether monstrous and immoral on their own, known and unknown alike, combine to form a totality that we can only name clumsily and inadequately.

I always told my Holocaust poetry students that no matter how much you read, no matter how many films you watch, you will not actually approximate, no less enter, the experiential worlds of those in Auschwitz or the other death camps. If you visit camps and see the physical settings it helps bring the horror closer. But a wide gulf between us and that time persists nonetheless. If you visit the room below ground in Buchenwald

---

president of the American Association of University Professors between 2006 and 2012. He is 2024 co-recipient of the Campus Faculty Heroes Award from StandWithUs and Mothers Against Campus Antisemitism. His most recent book is HATE SPEECH AND ACADEMIC FREEDOM: THE ANTISEMITIC ASSAULT ON BASIC PRINCIPLES (2024). He is presently completing ZIONISM CONFRONTS THE ABYSS: THE IMPACT OF THE OCTOBER 7 MASSACRE IN THE DIASPORA.

130. *See* discussion *supra* Chapter 11.

with the ovens intact, see the slide from the outside that Jews were flung down, and the hooks below on which they were hung, the mind peoples the space with Jewish victims. And yet whatever they experienced remains unavailable. The dedication of the SS guards is even more incomprehensible.

And if you could experience the camps as an actual inmate, believing that you were in that nightmare world from which the only release was death, you wouldn't choose to live that way even for a day. But imagining you could enter that world for a day itself entails a misconception. You would not cross the gulf unless you believed the day would never end. I do not think the inner world of the Hamas terrorists of 10/7 is approachable either. No political analysis of indoctrination, no explanation of amphetamine supplements, no historical context for hopelessness or anger, gives access to whatever enabled Hamas terrorists to sustain that intricate, intimate savagery for hours.

The Israelis underestimated what Hamas was capable of. We—all of us in the West—underestimated the depth of antisemitism lying in wait in our cities and on our campuses.

The new base for antisemitic antizionism is this: hatred. Neither a political analysis nor a political proposal. Hatred. That is what our students, staff, and faculty will face going forward.

With hatred replacing politics at center stage, we are entering a newly intensified emotional phase of campus conflict. It is grounded in the recognized psychology of othering and casting out of an enemy group. To be othered as a student or faculty member means no longer feeling welcome on your own campus. You are no longer a fit subject of empathy. You are reborn as Ruth amid the alien corn....

* * *

Students, faculty, and staff whose affinity for Israel partly shapes their identities are going to face increased pressure to disavow the relationship, effectively breaking with themselves. Most undergraduate students are at a vulnerable age when they are in the process of identity formation and consolidation. Zionist students in antisemitic campus settings will suffer assaults on their emerging identities. Indeed, with identity politics now dominating many campus disputes, we need to realize that assaulting Jewish student identities during their vulnerable, impressionable years is a primary goal for Israel's opponents. It often replaces political disagreements over Israeli policy. Virulent attacks on Israel now serve simultaneously as attacks on the Jews in the room.... Israel itself is partly a sideshow, an excuse for attacks on Jewish identity, for global Jihad....

Students in programs with majority Zionist faculty and student membership may be able to withstand these psychological assaults but many others will find the level of psychological safety necessary to do their work difficult to sustain. Universities are not in the business of providing intellectual safety. Intellectual challenges are essential to education, and they are protected by academic freedom. But a sense of psychological safety is necessary if students are to believe they can express their views and debate the strengths and weaknesses of those views without being personally denounced or discriminated against....

* * *

On the Columbia campus, they called out "Disclose! Divest! We will not stop! We will not rest!," "Oh Al-Qassam [Brigades], you make us proud, kill another soldier now!," "One, two, three, four, Israel will be no more!," "Five Six Seven Eight, Israel is a terrorist state," "Israel will fall! Brick by brick, wall by wall!," "Red, black, green, and white, we support Hamas's fight!," "Hamas we love you. We support your rockets too!," "It is right to rebel, Al-Qassam, give them hell!," and "From the water to the water, Palestine is Arab!" [A group] gathered to lead chants wearing keffiyehs, displaying Hamas symbols, and teaching people to chant "Death to Israel," "Death to America," and "Death to the Jews" in Farsi and Arabic....

The most time-honored chant, "From the river to the sea, Palestine will be free" was invoked almost everywhere.... Those who insist it has no eliminationist implications, no implication Palestinians will be free of Israelis and control the land, were more challenged after Hamas launched a genocidal pogrom intended to reach from the sea to the river. [One slogan user] claims she means the slogan to be a call for peace and coexistence.... [A] lone speaker in any case cannot successfully assert an alternative meaning for a slogan chanted by thousands of others.

Speaking from Qatar, Hamas leader and former politburo chair Khaled Mashal was very clear about where the terrorist group stands on the slogan in a January 2024 interview with Kuwaiti podcaster Amar Taki. "From the river to the sea" is an explicit call for Hamas dominance throughout, from east to west and north to south, "Hanikra to Eilat." Any less totalizing reference, he adds, is merely a temporary political deception. It is thus at best ignorant and pathetic for an American student to announce the slogan can usher in a utopia of peaceful coexistence.

But some alternative meanings are clearly disingenuous. When those issuing calls to "globalize the intifada" or chanting "There is only one solution, intifada revolution!" are pressed to realize those are demands for lethal violence, they simply dissemble if they are among the few who know at least a little of the relevant history: "We only mean the first, not the second intifada," whose signature events were the suicide bombings that killed civilians indiscriminately. Of course, the chants cannot escape invoking the core legacy of suicide bombings. That is the one message delivered to Israelis and Jews everywhere....

[What] the ACLU [and others do not] fully grasp as well is the psychological and political impact these chants have on Jewish students, especially at non-Christian institutions where the majority of Zionists are Jewish. Zionism is at the core of their identity. The mass chants are a collective assault not only on their political beliefs but on who they are. They are death chants. The ACLU's April 26 statement about the protests implicitly leaves us with only the traditional liberal recourse: combat bad speech with good speech.[131] But there is no speech that can ameliorate the effect

131. Editor's note: Letter from Anthony D. Romero, Exec. Dir. & David Cole, Nat'l Legal Dir., The Anti-Defamation League (Apr. 26, 2024), https://www.aclu.org/documents/open-letter-to-college-and-university-presidents-on-student-protests.

of a slogan like "Glory to our martyrs" that celebrates the Hamas pogrom. Students confronted by a collective psychological assault from their peers are not merely alienated. To be surrounded by the sound of mass hatred is not merely to be made uncomfortable. Jewish students, faculty, and staff do not simply find this "deeply offensive," as the ACLU would have it; they find it fundamentally threatening, canceling. And that is why the ACLU's reassuring distinction between unacceptable, individually targeted hatred and absolutely protected collective hatred is not only inadequate and unresponsive but also historically ignorant. When Charlottesville Nazi protestors chanted "The Jews will not replace us" it was not merely an idea to be discredited. It was a call for the elimination of the Jewish enemy within. I would not ask for eliminationist language to be prohibited. But I would ask universities to respond to these chants in a way that recognizes their actual destructive power. That means not only rapid denunciation but also long-term educational projects to counter their corrosive and persuasive effects.

Regulating Antisemitic Speech on Campus

1. How does the OCR letter distinguish between criticism of a country's policies and discrimination based on shared ancestry?

2. How does Dorf differentiate between speech restrictions in various campus settings, e.g., classrooms, dorms, and quadrangles? What principles should guide approaches in each space?

3. What is the significance of the "captive audience" concept in Dorf's analysis of campus speech regulation? Does this concept play out differently in the workplace and, if so, what accounts for the difference?

4. How does Nelson differentiate between previous campus antisemitism and post-October 7th manifestations? What specific psychological impacts does he identify for Jewish students facing hostile campus environments?

5. In Nelson's view, what is the significance of eliminationist or threatening chants and slogans like "from the river to the sea" for Jewish students? How do recent events affect the interpretation of such slogans compared to their historical usage? Compare Nelson's analysis to Professor R. George Wright's discussion of the planned neo-Nazi march on Holocaust survivors in Skokie.

6. How do Nelson's observations complicate the traditional "combat bad speech with good speech" approach advocated by free speech advocates? What alternative frameworks might be needed and available?

7. How do OCR, Dorf, and Nelson propose to balance the tensions between the First Amendment protections of free speech and university obligations under Title VI to prevent discrimination and hostile environments?

8. What criteria should universities use to distinguish between speech that contributes to a hostile environment under Title VI and hateful or offensive speech protected by the First Amendment?

9. Re-read the facially non-antisemitic anti-Zionist tweets posted by the UVM teaching assistant. Any new insights?

F. Future Directions for Jews on Campus

Benjamin S. Selznick & Sandra Greene, *Jewish on Campus: Complexity and* Tikkun Olam[132]

New Directions for Higher Education (2024)

In hopes of catalyzing social change, we offer future directions along three dimensions: affirming identity expressions, actualizing institutional priorities to support Jews, and combatting antisemitism....

Affirming identity expressions

Jewishness can be a complex identity space, at once covering presentations of religion, spirituality, race, ethnicity, and gender. Moreover, Jewishness can be a visible or an invisible identity; a self that can be expressed both publicly and privately; a presentation that can be freely expressed or, for reasons that often include personal safety, covered.

What does this identity complexity mean for contemporary higher education practice? To begin, we suggest ... that it is important for Jewishness as an identity space to be fully recognized and valued by colleges and universities. This embrace comes at all phases of a student's higher education journey—from recruitment practices that equitably embrace their identity to valuing Jews as full members of the campus community. Moreover, it proactively (rather than reactively) considers Jewishness both with respect to religiosity and, in the current climate of the United States, to race....

> Race for the Jewish people has never been solidified; they were once considered to be a separate race and now they are seen as being part of the dominant White culture. Although benefitting from White privilege, Jews also possess distinctive traits (e.g., traditions, belief system, physical characteristics), which separate them from the dominant ethnoreligious identities of their fellow citizens.

Such considerations are important at the individual level—especially given the diversity of racial and ethnic expressions held by Jews—and the campus-wide level.

When Jewishness is affirmed, students will have greater success in college and an enhanced sense of belonging; there may also be positive benefits with respect to supporting mental health and wellbeing as Jewish students productively engage the curriculum and co-curriculum. Such support can and should of course emerge from formal Jewish life and organizations (e.g., Chabad, Hillel, Greek life) but can also be woven throughout the institution in important and necessary ways.

---

132. Reprinted by permission of John Wiley and Sons.

Structural and organizational considerations

Accommodations

Accommodations for religious observance and dining are [an imperative] ... for Jewish students. This becomes crucially important when ensuring excused course absences for the observances of Rosh Hashanah and Yom Kippur, which frequently occur early in the fall semester and can be challenging for students, most notably new and/or transfer students, to navigate.

Diversity, equity, inclusion, and belonging (DEIB) emphasis

As colleges and universities devote increasing personnel and attention to fostering supportive and generative climates for DEIB, we encourage that Jewish students ... be an important part of these efforts. This can include increased attention to Jewish students' dietary needs; active leadership involvement and support for Jewish student life through its formal organizations; and directly inviting Jewish students to participate in campus-wide forms of DEIB....

Interfaith exchange

As a related form of fostering inclusion and belonging while valuing diversity, research on Jewish student appreciation consistently demonstrates the importance of creating and sustaining opportunities for interfaith exchange, both formally and informally. We encourage campuses committed to Jewish life to take interfaith [exchange] seriously; to move structured and intentional interfaith dialogue from happenstance and the periphery toward dedicated resources and centrality.

Providing space(s)

It is also important for institutions to not overlook the importance of providing physical spaces for Jewish students to congregate and come together as a community. While nationally, larger campuses with more robust Jewish populations frequently have dedicated spaces via Hillel, Chabad, and/or Greek-letter organizations, this is not always the case. Making sure that Jews always have a space to be Jews matters.

Combatting antisemitism

Most concerning for the psychological and physical safety of Jewish students is a pressing need to combat rising antisemitism in the United States.... *To what extent is existing antisemitism being addressed and proactively combatted*? Such a question has taken on far greater importance amidst ongoing conflict between Israel and Hamas and the substantial disruption this has caused to the safety and security of Jews on campuses across the United States.

Antisemitism can appear in many forms, from microaggressions (e.g., "you don't look Jewish") to overt peer-to-peer threats; from participation in campus engagement (e.g., Jewishness and leadership[133]) to criminal acts such as arson and defacement of

---

133. Editor's note: In February 2015, a Jewish student at UCLA faced scrutiny during her nomination to the student council's Judicial Board. Council members questioned Beyda's ability to remain unbiased due to her Jewish background and involvement in Jewish organizations, initially voting to

property. Antisemitism can also be expressed by staff and faculty—a highly concerning situation when Jewish students feel silenced or, worse, openly harassed in the context of pursuing coursework.[134]

As a roadmap and pathway for campus leaders, we share . . . the three A's: Awareness, Allyship, and Action (2022).[135] Regarding **awareness**, the findings echo our considerations for structural change with respect to direct Jewish inclusion in DEIB initiatives. We supplement this recommendation by suggesting that, for many campuses, awareness must include recognition that antisemitism is a perennial threat to campus climate . . . that can permeate campus life; a proactive rather than reactive approach must be taken.

The second A is **allyship**, which revolves around demonstrating solidarity with Jewish students. We highlight a particular recommendation as it stitches together individual- and structural-level imperatives. Campuses must: "create and maintain regular patterns of connection between administration and Jewish students, including attending in-person events and celebrations important to Jewish students." We comment here that dialogue and attendance sends a message to the entire campus community that decision-makers value the presence of Jews and Jewish life. Such a finding also reflects the importance of including Jewish perspectives when designing and implementing programming connected to Jewish experiences, histories, and cultures.

The third A is **action**. Several steps (e.g., ensuring accommodations) align with what we have previously expressed. . . . We do highlight one step, however . . . institutions should "improve bias reporting policies and procedures, and provide support services for students experiencing antisemitic bias, harassment, and other forms of discrimination." The salience of this point cannot be overstated. If Jews, who may already have to "cover" to protect their psychological and/or physical safety, have no reliable and secure way to report harassment based on their religious identity, they in turn can be left feeling that their campus simply does not care about antisemitism as a distinctive

---

reject her nomination. This decision was later reversed after a faculty adviser intervened. UCLA's Chancellor condemned the incident, calling it a "teaching moment," while the students involved later apologized for their actions. Adam Nagourney, *In U.C.L.A. Debate Over Jewish Student, Echoes on Campus of Old Biases*, N.Y. Times (Mar. 5, 2015), https://www.nytimes.com/2015/03/06/us/debate-on-a-jewish-student-at-ucla.html.

134. Editor's note: In February 2022, OCR opened an investigation into CUNY Brooklyn College's graduate mental health counseling program following allegations that professors and peers subjected Jewish students to anti-Semitic harassment by portraying them as "white and privileged" and complicit in the oppression of people of color. The students claimed that they were bullied in class discussions and on social media, and when they expressed distress, they were told to "get your whiteness in check" or "keep your head down." *U.S. Dept. of Education Opens Investigation Into Anti-Semitism at Brooklyn College*, Brandeis Ctr. (Feb. 3), https://brandeiscenter.com/u-s-dept-of-education-opens-investigation-into-anti-semitism-at-brooklyn-college/. In a Resolution Letter with CUNY, the OCR expressed concern that Brooklyn College allowed a hostile environment for Jewish students to persist despite receiving numerous reports made and concerns regarding the incidents. *Id.*

135. *ACE, AJC, Hillel, Collaborate on Summit to Combat Campus Antisemitism*, Am. Council on Educ. (Apr. 15, 2022), https://www.acenet.edu/News-Room/Pages/ACE-AJC-Hillel-Summit-Campus-Antisemitism.aspx.

form of hate. Such an issue becomes particularly important in creating and sustaining positive campus climates for Jews in the immediate aftermath of reported antisemitic incidents. Here, campuses are encouraged to ask and then activate in response to the following question: How will current and future Jewish students come to know that this campus is a safe place for them to learn, grow, and develop?

Conclusion

What is the responsibility of a higher education institution to its Jewish students?... Our greatest hope for the months and years ahead is that campuses listen to their Jewish communities with more informed ears, fully understand the seriousness of antisemitism, learn deeply from community experiences, and create supportive policies and pathways that embrace religious identities not only for Jews, but for all who wish to fully develop and express their identities in climates of belonging.

A powerful concept across Jewish thought that can light the way is that of *tikkun olam*—the continual practice of repairing a broken world.... The work of repair is often difficult yet always necessary for ensuring that Jews can bring their whole selves into their learning and development and carry the many lessons of college forward toward individual and societal change.

Resources for Jewish Students Experiencing Antisemitism

1. *Campus antisemitism.* According to a 2023 ADL national survey,[136] 73 percent of Jewish college students have experienced or witnessed antisemitism since the start of the 2023–2024 school year. Compare this to a 2021 survey which found that 32 percent of Jewish students experienced antisemitism directed at them. Other survey findings included:

a. *Physical safety*. Pre-October 7, 67 percent of Jewish students said they felt physically safe on campus; after, only 46 percent felt that way.

b. *Emotional safety*. Pre-October 7, 66 percent of Jewish students felt emotionally safe; after, only 33 percent felt that way.

c. *Welcoming and supportive*. Pre-October 7, 64 percent of Jewish students viewed their university as welcoming and supportive of Jewish students; after, only 44 percent felt that way.

d. *Disclosing Jewish identity.* Pre-October 7, 64 percent of Jewish students felt comfortable with others knowing they're Jewish; after, only 39 percent felt that way.

e. *Doing enough*? A majority of students, both Jewish (77 percent) and non-Jewish (67 percent) felt their university was not doing enough to address anti-Jewish prejudice.

---

136. *Nearly Three-Quarters of Jewish Students Experienced or Witnessed Anti-Semitism on Campus, New Survey Finds*, The Anti-Defamation League (Nov. 29, 2023), https://www.adl.org/resources/press-release/nearly-three-quarters-jewish-students-experienced-or-witnessed-antisemitism.

f. *Antisemitic-specific training.* More than half (56 percent) of all students surveyed said they had previously completed DEI training, but only 18 percent of those who had DEI training said that they had completed any training modules specific to anti-Jewish prejudice.

2. *Campus Antisemitism Report Card.* The ADL uses a grading system to assess campus antisemitism at various universities based on administrative action and policies, incidents on campus, and Jewish student life. It gave grades of C to UICU and University of Vermont; D to Columbia and UC Berkeley; and F to Harvard, MIT, and UCLA.

3. *ReportCampusHate.org.* Hillel International, the ADL, and the Secure Community Network operate a portal for Jewish students to report bias incidents on campuses. Information submitted through this form is reviewed by trained personnel who will support the student or reporting party in the incident response process, bringing in local Hillel professionals, the campus administration, and law enforcement as appropriate.

4. *Campus Antisemitism Legal Line (CALL).* In November 2023, a free legal protection helpline was created for university students who have experienced antisemitism. Student, family, faculty, or staff members can go to the CALL website or text "CALLhelp" to 51555 to report incidents of antisemitic discrimination, intimidation, harassment, vandalism, or violence that may necessitate legal action. Lawyers can provide pro bono representation for victims who choose to move forward with specific cases. CALL also provides referrals to support services such as mental health counseling services.

Part Five

Allies Against Antisemitism

Chapter 13

Émile Zola: Antisemitism Is Antithetical to Liberal Democracy

The Dreyfus Affair consisted of a series of sensational trials and related developments in France, following the arrest in October 1894 of Captain Alfred Dreyfus, a Jewish officer charged with delivering military secrets to the German enemy. The affair reached a climax by 1898 with the publication of the famous manifesto, "I accuse!" (*J'accuse!*), by Émile Zola who, baptized and raised Catholic, was one of the most influential French novelists of his era, and a major figure in the political liberalization of France.

In fiery tones, Zola accused France's military authorities—venerated by most of the population—of having wrongfully convicted Dreyfus, who had by then been condemned to life imprisonment on Devil's Island, off the north coast of South America. Zola charged that the evidence produced at Dreyfus's trial was flimsy and some of it fraudulent—to say nothing of the blatant violations of French legal procedures in the delivery of evidence to the prosecution but not the defense.

In the months immediately following Dreyfus's trial, there was no "affair" of passionately differing opinions by Dreyfus's defenders, known as Dreyfusards, and his opponents, known as anti-Dreyfusards. There were indeed expressions of shock and indignation at the news of the crime, but near-unanimous approval of the sentence. A few national leaders did express disappointment, but only that French law did not permit the death penalty for political offenses. The antisemitic press cheered over how, finally, such a high-placed Jewish villain was being punished. Even most Jews believed that justice had been done, but few commented publicly on the matter.

As the only prisoner on Devil's Island, Dreyfus was subjected to unspeakably cruel treatment, including solitary confinement, and forbidden to speak even to his guards. He was often chained to his bed in the grueling tropical heat. It seemed that the death penalty was being applied indirectly—with prolonged torture before the inevitable arrival of death throes. The suffering of this innocent man stands out as one of the many profoundly troubling aspects of this affair. His endurance and survival over more than four years seem miraculous—and were soon termed heroic—but he returned to France white-haired, with limbs resembling those of a human skeleton, barely remembering how to speak after years of enforced silence.

Alfred Dreyfus's case disappeared from public view not long after his imprisonment. However, as evidence began to emerge that another officer, Walsin Esterhazy, was clearly guilty of the crime for which Dreyfus had been convicted, demands for a retrial began to arise. At first, they gained little public support, and France's military authorities refused to budge. For them, the case was closed, period. Crucially, the Minister of War, General Auguste Mercier, a man known for his intelligence and liberal sentiments, assured the French public that the evidence against Dreyfus was overwhelming. He and others also intimated that there was damning information about the case that could not be divulged publicly for reasons of national security. Reports that Dreyfus had confessed when first arrested were widely believed, though they were ultimately revealed to be false.

The man who first discovered the evidence of Esterhazy's guilt, Col. Georges Picquart, was ordered by his superiors to remain silent. Before long, he was sent away on a dangerous foreign mission, then expelled from the military, and finally himself sentenced to over a year in prison. Esterhazy was eventually brought to trial in 1898 but quickly found innocent—to the widespread jubilation of the Anti-Dreyfusards and dismay among Dreyfusards.

When Esterhazy was declared innocent, Zola decided he must speak out. The courts had failed. Now the issue should be brought to the general public. However, rather than being acclaimed by the public, his manifesto provoked antisemitic riots throughout France, and he was subsequently charged and found guilty of criminal libel, with a prison sentence and a heavy fine.

Nonetheless, support for him and demands for a retrial of Dreyfus slowly gathered strength, as French political opinion moved leftward. At Zola's trial, at the conclusion of the attorney-general's address, Zola read a declaration to the jury. The text of Zola's defense at his trial is printed below. After his sentence, he fled to Britain and was never actually imprisoned, but he met an early death in 1902, before Dreyfus's full exoneration in 1906. Zola died of asphyxiation in his sleep, due to a blocked chimney—possibly a murder, but never proven as such.

Dreyfus's final exoneration was part of a general amnesty. Those who blundered and then lied to cover up their conduct were put in the same "forgotten" or "excused" category as Dreyfus himself, who suffered nearly five years of unspeakable misery. Full justice for Dreyfus might have been established in historical memory, but not in the courts of law.

Émile Zola v. Judet and Others

Court of Assizes of the Seine
Feb. 7–23, 1898

Monsieur Zola delivered the following declaration to the jury.

In the chamber, at its session of January 22, M. Méline, president of the cabinet, declared, amid the frantic applause of his obliging majority, that he had confidence in the twelve citizens to whose hands he entrusted the defense of the army. It was of you, gentlemen, that he spoke. And just as General Billot dictated his decree to the council of war, which was charged with the acquittal of Major Esterhazy, uttering from the tribune for the instruction of his subordinates the military countersign of unquestionable respect for the thing judged, so M. Mélme has endeavored to give you an order to sentence me in the name of respect for the army, which he accuses me of having outraged. I denounce to the conscience of honest people this pressure of public power on the justice of the country. These are abominable political practices, dishonoring a free nation.

We shall see, gentlemen, if you will obey. But it is not true that I am here before you by the will of M. Méline. He yielded to the necessity of prosecuting me only in great agitation, in terror of the new step that truth in its march might take. That is known to everybody. If I am before you, it is by my own will. I alone have decided that the obscure, the monstrous matter should be brought before your jurisdiction, and I alone, in the full exercise of my will, have chosen you, the highest and most direct emanation of French justice, that France at last may know all, and decide. My act had no other object, and my person is nothing; I have sacrificed it, satisfied simply to have placed in your hands not only the honor of the army, but the endangered honor of the entire nation.

You will pardon me, then, if your consciences have not been thoroughly enlightened. It is not my fault. It seems that I was dreaming in expecting to bring you all the proofs—in considering you alone worthy, alone competent. They began by taking from you with the left hand what they seemed to give you with the right. They made a pretense of accepting your jurisdiction, but, though they trusted you to avenge the members of one council of war, certain other officers remained unassailably superior even to your justice. Understand it if you can. It is absurd in hypocrisy and furnishes striking proof that they feared your good sense and did not dare to run the risk of allowing us to say everything, and of allowing you to judge everything. They pretend that they desired to limit the scandal. And what do you think of this scandal, of my act, which consisted in laying the case before you, in desiring that the people, incarnate in you, should pass judgment upon it? They pretend, further, that they could not accept a disguised revision, thus confessing that they have only one fear at bottom—that of your sovereign control. The law is completely represented by you, and it is this chosen law of the people that I have longed for, that I profoundly respect, as a good citizen, and not the equivocal procedure by which they have hoped to baffle you.

Thus am I excused, gentlemen, for having turned you aside from your occupations without succeeding in flooding you with the total light of which I dreamed. Light, complete light, that has been my sole, my passionate desire. And this trial has just proved it to you; we have had to struggle step by step against a desire for darkness, extraordinary in its obstinacy. For each shred of truth torn from the unwilling, a fight has been necessary; they have disputed everything, they have refused us everything, they have terrorized our witnesses in the hope of preventing us from proving our case. And it is for you alone that we have fought; that this proof might be submitted to you in its entirety, so that you can pass judgment without remorse and in your conscience. Therefore, I am certain that you will take our efforts into consideration, and that, more-

Cinq Centimes

Directeur ERNEST VAUGHAN

L'AURORE

Littéraire, Artistique, Sociale

JEUDI 13 JANVIER 1898

J'Accuse...!

LETTRE AU PRÉSIDENT DE LA RÉPUBLIQUE

Par ÉMILE ZOLA

LETTRE

A M. FÉLIX FAURE

Président de la République

Monsieur le Président,

Figure 13.1. J'Accuse, open letter about the Dreyfus Affair by Émile Zola, published in *L'Aurore*, January 13, 1898.

over, enough light has been shed. You have heard the witnesses, and you will hear my counsel, who will tell you the true story that maddens everybody and that everybody knows. So, I am at ease; the truth is now with you; it will do its work.

M. Méline thought, then, to dictate your verdict in entrusting to you the honor of the army, and it is in the name of this honor of the army that I myself appeal to your

Figure 13.2. A caricature of Alfred Dreyfus (1859–1935) as a six-headed serpent pierced by a dagger which bears the sign, "the traitor," V. Lenepveu, 1899.

justice. I deny M. Méline's statement in the most formal manner; I have never insulted the army. On the contrary, I have expressed my tenderness, my respect, for the nation in arms, for our dear soldiers of France who would rise at the first threat, in defense of the French soil. And it is equally false that I have attacked the commanders, the generals who would lead them to victory. If certain individuals in the war offices have compromised the army by their conduct, is it an insult to the entire army to say so? Is it not, rather, the work of a good citizen to free the army from all compromise, to sound the alarm, in order that the misdeeds which have forced us to this fight may not be repeated and lead us to new defeats? However, I do not defend myself. I leave to history the judgment of my act, which was a necessary act. But I declare that they dishonor the army when they allow the *gendarmes* to embrace Major Esterhazy after the abominable letters that he has written. I declare that this valiant army is insulted daily by the bandits who, pretending to defend it, sully it with their base complicity, dragging into the mud everything good and great that France still has. I declare it is they who dishonor this great national army, when they mingle the cry of "Long live the Army!" with the cry of "Death to the Jews!" And they have cried "Long Live Esterhazy!" Great God! The people of St. Louis, of Bayard, of Condé, and of Hoche, the people that have won a hundred giant victories, the people of the great wars of the republic and the empire, the people whose strength, grace, and generosity have dazzled the universe, crying "Long live Esterhazy!" It is a shame that only our effort on behalf of truth and justice can be wiped out.

You know the legend that has been created. Dreyfus was condemned justly and legally by seven infallible officers, whom it is impossible even to suspect of error without insulting the entire army. In this avenging torture, he is expiating his abominable misdeed. And, as he is a Jew, a Jewish syndicate has been created, an international syndicate of people without a country, with hundreds of millions at their disposal for the purpose of saving the traitor at the cost of the most shameless maneuvers. Then this syndicate began to heap up crimes, buying consciences, throwing France into a murderous tumult, determined to sell her to the enemy, to set Europe on fire with a general war, rather than abandon this frightful design. It is quite simple, even puerile and imbecilic as you see. But it is upon this poisoned bread that an unclean press has been feeding our people for months, and we should not be astonished at the spectacle of a disastrous crisis, for, when stupidity and lies are sown at such a rate, a crop of madness is sure to be harvested.

Certainly, gentlemen, I do not offer you the insult of believing that you have been caught by this nursery tale. I know you. I know who you are. You are the heart and reason of París, of my great Paris, where I was born, which I love with an infinite tenderness, which I have been studying and singing for forty years. And I know, too, now, what is going on in your brains, for, before sìtting here as an accused, I sat in the seats which you occupy. You represent the average opinion; you aim to be wisdom and justice en masse. Presently I shall be with you in thought in your deliberations in the jury room, and I am convinced that you will endeavor to guard your interests as citizens, which naturally are, according to you, the interests of the whole nation. You may be mistaken, but your purpose will be to insure your own welfare and the welfare of all.

I see you at your homes, at night, under the lamp; I hear you talking with your friends; I accompany you to your shops and stores. You are all workers, some merchants, others manufacturers, and a few professional men. And you are filled with a perfectly legitimate anxiety concerning the deplorable state into which business has fallen. Everywhere the existing crisis threatens to become a disaster, receipts are falling off, transactions are becoming increasingly difficult. So that the thought that you have brought here, the thought that I read on your faces, is that there has been enough of this, and that it must come to an end. You do not say, as many do: "What difference does it make to us whether an innocent man is on Devil's Island? Is the interest of an individual sufficient to warrant the agitation of a great country?" But you do say, nevertheless, that the agitation which we are carrying on, in our hunger for truth and justice, is paid for too dearly by all the evil that they accuse us of doing. And, if you convict me, gentlemen, the sole foundation of your verdict will be the desire to quiet your families, the need of a resumption of business, the belief that, in striking me, you will put an end to a campaign of vindication that is harmful to the interests of France.

Well, gentlemen, you would be utterly mistaken. Do me the honor to believe that I am not defending my liberty here. In striking me, you will only add to my stature. Whoever suffers for truth and justice becomes august and sacred. Look at me, gentlemen. Have I the appearance of one who has sold himself? Do I look like a liar and a traitor? Why, then, should I act as I do? I have behind me neither political ambition nor sectarian passions. I am a free writer, who has given his life to toil, who tomorrow will again take his place in the ranks and will resume his interrupted task. And how stupid are they who call me an Italian! I who was born of a French mother, brought up by Beauce grandparents, peasants in that robust region; I who lost my father at the age of seven, and never went to Italy until I was fifty-four, and then only to get material for a book. Which does not prevent me from being very proud that my father was of Venice, that resplendent city whose ancient glory sings in all memories. And, even if I were not French, would not the forty volumes in the French language which I have scattered by millions throughout the entire world suffice to make me a Frenchman, useful to the glory of France?

So, I do not defend myself. But what an error would be yours, if you were convinced that, in striking me, you would re-establish order in our unhappy country. Do you not understand that that of which the nation is dying is the darkness in which they are bent upon leaving her, the equivocations in which she is agonizing? The mistakes of our governors are piled upon mistakes; one lie necessitates another, so that the mass becomes frightful. A judicial error has been committed, and then to hide it, it has been necessary to commit each day a new attack on good sense and equity. The conviction of an innocent man has involved the acquittal of a guilty man; and now today you are asked to convict me in my turn, because I have cried out in my anguish at the sight of the progress of the country in this frightful path. Convict me, then. It will be one error more added to the others, an error the burden of which you will bear in history. And my conviction, instead of bringing about the peace that you desire, and that we all desire, will only sow the seed of a new crop of passion and disorder. The measure is full, I tell you; do not make it overflow.

Why do you not exactly estimate the terrible crisis through which the country is passing? They say that we are the authors of the scandal, that it is the lovers of truth and justice who are leading the nation astray and urging it to riot. Really, this is mockery. To speak only of General Billot, was he not warned eighteen months ago? Did Colonel Picquart not insist that he should take in hand the matter of revision, if he did not wish the storm to burst and overturn everything? Did not M. Scheurer-Kestner, with tears in his eyes, beg him to think of France, and save her such a catastrophe? No, no! Our desire has been to facilitate everything, to allay everything, and if the country is now in trouble, the responsibility lies with power, which, to protect the guilty, and in the furtherance of political interests, has denied everything, hoping to be strong enough to prevent the light from being shed. It has maneuvered in the shadows on behalf of darkness, and it alone is responsible for the present distraction of consciences.

The Dreyfus case, ah! Gentlemen, that has become a very small matter now. It is lost and far away, in view of the terrifying questions to which it has given rise. There is no longer any Dreyfus case. The question now is whether France is still the France of the rights of man, the France that gave liberty to the world, and that ought to give it justice. Are we still the most noble, the most fraternal, the most generous nation? Shall we preserve our reputation in Europe for equity and humanity? Are not all the victories that we have won called into question? Open your eyes, and understand that, to be in such confusion, the French soul must have been stirred to its depths in face of a terrible danger. A nation cannot be thus upset without imperiling its moral existence. This is an exceptionally serious hour; the safety of the nation is at stake.

And, when you shall have understood that, gentlemen, you will feel that but one remedy is possible—to tell the truth, to do justice. Anything that keeps back the light, anything that adds darkness to darkness, will only prolong and aggravate the crisis. The role of good citizens, of those who feel it to be imperatively necessary to put an end to this matter, is to demand broad daylight. There are already many of them who think so. The men of literature, philosophy, and science are rising on every hand, in the name of intelligence and reason. And I do not speak of the foreigner, of the shudder that has run through all Europe. Yet the foreigner is not necessarily the enemy. Let us not speak of the nations that may be our adversaries tomorrow. But great Russia, our ally; little and generous Holland; all the sympathetic nations of the north; those countries of the French language, Switzerland and Belgium—why are their hearts so heavy, so overflowing with fraternal suffering? Do you dream, then, of an isolated France? Do you prefer, when you cross the frontier, not to meet the approving smile upon your legendary fame for equity and humanity?

Alas! Gentlemen, like so many others, you expect the thunderbolt, the descent from heaven of the proof of the innocence of Dreyfus. Truth does not come in that way. It requires research and intelligence. We know very well where the truth is, where it could be found. But we dream of that only in the secrecy of our souls, and we feel patriotic anguish lest we expose ourselves to the danger of having this proof someday flung in our face after having involved the honor of the army in a lie. I wish also to declare squarely that, though, in the official notice of our list of witnesses, we included certain ambassadors, we had formally decided in advance not to summon them. Our audacity has provoked smiles. But I do not think that there was any smiling in our foreign office, for there they must have understood. We simply intended to say to those who know the whole truth that we also know it. This truth is bandied about at the embassies; tomorrow it will be known to all, and, if it is now impossible for us to seek it where it is protected by formalities that cannot be overstepped, the government which is not ignorant, the government which is convinced, as we are, of the innocence of Dreyfus, will be able, when it likes, and without risk, to find witnesses who will make everything clear.

Dreyfus is innocent; I swear it. I stake my life upon it; I stake my honor upon it. At this solemn hour, before this tribunal that represents human justice, before you, gentlemen of the jury, who are the emanation of the nation, before all France, before the entire world, I swear that Dreyfus is innocent. And by my forty years of toil, and by the authority that this labor has given me, I swear that Dreyfus is innocent. Let it all fall to the ground, let my works perish, if Dreyfus is not innocent. He is innocent.

Everything seems to be against me—the two chambers, the civil power, the military power, the journals of large circulation, the public opinion that they have poisoned. And with me there is but an idea, an ideal of truth and justice. And I am perfectly at ease; I shall triumph.

I did not wish my country to remain in falsehood and injustice. Here I may be condemned; but someday, France will thank me for having helped to save her honor.

A. A Deeper Understanding of the Dreyfus Affair

Over the past century, the Dreyfus Affair has inspired an impressive outpouring: thousands of books, articles, novels, movies, plays, and various works of art. No summary can do justice to the Affair's intricacies, its imposing cast of characters, and its astonishing paradoxes, especially in terms of why Dreyfus's conviction ultimately divided France's population so passionately, most notably the country's intellectual elite, its world-famous intellectuals and artists, centered in Paris.

Over that century, interpretations of the Affair have been divided in revealing ways, highly moralizing on a more popular level, more nuanced in the case of scholars, especially in the last few decades. One recent author has declared the Affair to be "the greatest political scandal and miscarriage of justice in modern history." The words are those of novelist Thomas Harris, acclaimed for his many works of historical fiction. His own novel, based on the Affair, *An Officer and a Spy* (2013), was soon followed by a movie version. He might have added that few historical episodes have been so widely misunderstood, both by right- and left-wing observers.

In several regards, the Dreyfus Affair even exceeded the notorious outbreak of pogroms in Russia as the most influential development in the history of modern antisemitism before the Holocaust, although the story of those pogroms, too, has been characterized by significant shifts in scholarly interpretations.

A deeper understanding of how historians and other scholars have dealt with the Affair requires a consideration of some of the major developments of the nineteenth century, addressed below under the following overlapping headings: France, *La Grande Nation*; Demography and Movement of Peoples; Industrialization and Modernism; Inherited Mindsets; The Rise of the Jews; Personality and Accident.

B. France, *La Grande Nation*

"Greatness" (*grandeur*) was for centuries central to French identity. *La Grande Nation* long stood as Europe's major nation in the number of its inhabitants, but France was also renowned for the richness of its culture and the power of its state. French language became the universal international language by the eighteenth century, and the French empire eventually spread throughout the world. Following the French Revolution of 1789 (and Emperor Napoleon's consolidations), much of Europe fell under French rule. That involved the exportation of French revolutionary laws and institutions, as well as such related matters as the metric system. Revolutionary law also recognized the civil equality of France's Jewish inhabitants, the first European country to do so (in 1791), with long-range implications, both positive and negative, many gaining dramatic expression in the Dreyfus Affair.

Even after Napoleon's defeat, after the end of his European empire, and after the restoration of the Bourbon monarchy in 1815, France still loomed as the major power in Europe. The new king, Louis XVIII, recognized the permanence of the Revolution's most fundamental institutional achievements, including the *Code Napoléon*, with its commitment to Jewish civil equality and its associated ideal of "careers open to talent." That meant that France's Jewish citizens were still promised equality under the law. Their subsequent careers revealed remarkable talents—applauded on the one hand yet resented on the other.

Early in the nineteenth century, Austria's conservative prime minister, Klemens von Metternich, ruefully quipped that "when France sneezes, Europe catches a cold." The Dreyfus Affair qualified as an especially impressive sneeze. The United States and other countries in Europe observed the Affair with keen interest; what came to be termed "the Jewish Question" was preoccupying them as well. Comparable affairs, though of smaller fame and general import, occurred in extremely different places: autocratic Russia (the Beilis Affair, 1913), and liberal-democratic United States (the Leo Frank Affair, 1915). In both, the precedent of the Dreyfus Affair was explicitly stressed, if imperfectly understood.

The experience of the Affair seemed to stress how dangerous to Jews modern antisemitism might become, even for Jews protected by French law. Paradoxically, in Russia, Mendel Beilis was actually found innocent of ritual murder, in a predominantly reactionary, antisemitic environment, while Leo Frank, charged with murdering a young employee of his, was found guilty and later lynched—in the United States, where Jews were widely considered to be securely accepted as equal citizens, protected by the law. What then were the lessons in terms of the law and antisemitism? Not simple or obvious ones.

Large-scale developments in the nineteenth century put France's *grandeur* to repeated tests. The country experienced near-constant upheaval, several major uprisings, a new revolution (and a second brief republic in 1848), a Bonapartist Second Empire in the 1850s and 1860s, a humiliating total defeat in 1871, and the Paris Commune in the spring of that year (a violent, desperate revolutionary episode, with aspects of a civil war, in which the Parisian insurgents were brutally repressed). It resulted in around 60,000 deaths and thousands exiled. A new republic, France's third, emerged from that harrowing experience.

The Third Republic was in power during the Affair, but it had begun unsteadily, with significant factions of monarchists, Bonapartists, and republicans (themselves divided from conservatives to socialists). The new republic was conservative at first, actually with a monarchist majority (divided according to the preferred monarch), but a slow if unsteady leftward trend set in during the 1870s and 1880s. The Affair, often described as *suddenly* dividing France, occurred in an already deeply divided country, one that seemed poised to veer in either a right-wing or left-wing direction.

Laws enacted under the Third Republic were influenced by the desire to counteract the authoritarian rule of Napoleon III's Second Empire (1851–1871). A key concern was protection of individual liberty, especially freedom of the press. A mushrooming of journals and newspapers did occur. However, flagrant irresponsibility also came to characterize a substantial portion of the press under the Third Republic. Liberalizing law seemed to have had unintended consequences. The antisemitic press often spread lies and misinformation, as did the press of other persuasions. A libel law was passed in 1881, but what constituted libel of a criminal nature remained debatable and irregularly enforced—or misused, as in Zola's case in 1898. However, he had been incautious in levying charges against the military that he could not possibly prove; he received a jail sentence and a heavy fine.

Jews were occasionally successful in suing the antisemitic press for libel. One of those occasions was when Jewish butchers sued the Marquis de Morès in reaction to his public charge that Jewish ritual slaughter was unacceptably cruel. The courts of the state ruled otherwise, and the marquis was fined.

Another kind of reaction to the libelous assertions of the antisemitic press was to challenge its authors to meet on the field of honor, in elaborately officiated duels. This was unusual because in most of Europe, Jews were rarely involved in duels.[1] But the leading Dreyfusard, Joseph Reinach, fought thirteen duels in the course of his life. In early 1894, one instance of Jews involved in a duel became especially famous, when

---

1. For an economic analysis of dueling, see Warren F. Schwartz et al., *The Duel: Can These Gentlemen Be Acting Efficiently?*, 13 J. Legal Stud. 321 (1984), http://www.jstor.org/stable/724239.

Captain Armand Mayer, who had also been defamed by the Marquis de Morès, challenged him to a duel. The marquis was a veteran of many duels, and his superior skill with a sword resulted in the death of the young Jewish captain.

Public outrage in reaction to that death stood in thought-provoking contrast to the later antisemitic riots of 1898, protesting Zola's manifesto. De Morès was denounced across the political spectrum. The funeral of Captain Mayer was attended by the largest crowd since the death of the extremely popular leader, Léon Gambetta, a decade earlier. France's Chief Rabbi, Zadoc Kahn, eloquently addressed those assembled at the grave of Captain Mayer. It seemed that the French nation had come together to mourn the tragic death of a young Jewish officer at the hands of an antisemitic brute. (This was, it should be noted, shortly before Alfred Dreyfus was arrested.)

France's precarious pre-eminence in nineteenth-century Europe was repeatedly challenged, most decisively by a new and powerful neighboring nation-state, the Prussian-led German Reich. The final step in the establishment of that nation was completed by a humiliating defeat of France in the Franco-Prussian war of 1870–71. The defeat was so complete that Napoleon III himself was captured on the battlefield. In the ensuing peace settlement, France lost two prized provinces, Alsace and Lorraine, to Germany. That punitive settlement left the French dreaming of *revanche* (revenge)—to "make France great again," so to speak.

In World War I, revenge was at last achieved, though at such a horrendous price that it resembled a tragedy more than a victory. France did not become great again; the country would experience another humiliating defeat by Germany in the opening stages of World War II.

Britain, France's long-standing antagonist across the English Channel, also grew impressively in numbers and power in the nineteenth century, while France's birthrate slowed, and its industrial productivity failed to keep up with the competition from Germany and Britain. Fears of decadence and decline haunted the French during what is now nonetheless known as the Belle Epoque in the decades immediately before World War I. In truth, the Belle Epoque was both beautiful and ominous. The contrasts were especially notable in the tension between Paris and the rural provinces (already expressed as a "civil war" in the Paris Commune of 1871).

Germany's victory over France eventually impelled France's leaders to negotiate in the early 1890s what had previously been considered an impossible alliance—with reactionary Russia—toward the goal of surrounding Germany. That alliance of progressive republican France and reactionary tsarist Russia had many awkward aspects. Russia was notorious for the oppression of its Jewish population, while French Jews considered themselves blessed by the laws of the republic. How could they protest against the internal policies of this new and much-valued ally? Would any protest not put the patriotism of French Jews in question, implicitly placing Jewish interests above French needs?

That was only one of many challenges facing Jews in France. Many Jewish populations in Europe suffered oppression in the nineteenth century, most notably those in

Romania. Again, what was the responsibility of France's Jews, in terms of the contradiction between their long-standing "internationalist" concern for the often-desperate plight of their Jewish kin in other countries, and their more recently acquired French patriotism?

Before modern times, a form of Jewish international solidarity had existed, for example, in rescuing Jewish hostages, or in bribing hostile officials. Jews in those years never considered themselves primarily Poles, Germans, or French. Jews did not become receptive to the idea of actively embracing the nationalism of the countries they lived in until the nineteenth century. Even then, everyone knew about Jewish international sympathies; the power of the Rothschilds, for example, with their representatives in many lands, was famous. Weren't Jews, by their own particularistic identity and centuries-long religious traditions, obviously problematic nationalists in Christian-majority lands?

In France, many prominent Jews had German-sounding names. Aside from Rothschild (meaning "red sign" in German), Reinach (suggesting the German *rein*: pure, and *ach*: "oh!" or wonder), Blum (German: flower) and of course, Dreyfus. That was a common name in France, looking humorously, if deceptively, like the German words for "three foot."

However, many non-Jewish French citizens also had German-sounding names, for example, the antisemitic head of Intelligence, Sandherr; especially those (like his) with origins in Alsace, where the regional dialect was a form of German. "Foreign" Italian names were also common (Gambetta, Zola), to say nothing of Napoleon Buonaparte. France, especially after the revolution, in principle accepted immigrants who embraced French ideals, no matter what their country of origin.

This was true in principle, but not always in practice. Aside from Napoleon (a *very* special case), Gambetta and Zola were actually born in France, with French mothers but Italian fathers; the French Right still cast doubt on the genuineness of their French identity. French law required that Gambetta and Zola undergo formal procedures to acquire citizenship (a French mother was not enough). It is not often recognized that bigotry and violence in nineteenth-century France were much more prominent against Italians than against Jews, in large part because Italians were more numerous and more often desperately poor—and stereotyped as Mafiosi—while Jews were more often law-abiding members of the middle and upper classes.

The problematic issue of the Jews' supposed international solidarity was further muddled by the internal divisions among the Jews themselves. Sephardim looked down on Ashkenazim, western Jews abhorred the Ostjuden (eastern Jews); and those eastern Jews were divided into an array of bitterly contentious factions. The charge of international Jewish solidarity was not only exaggerated but close to the opposite. Nonetheless, most Jews did feel a tug of sympathy for the oppressed Jews in other countries, a stronger tug than that felt by non-Jews, though many prominent nineteenth-century Gentiles publicly expressed sympathy for Jewish suffering in the Russian pogroms. The charge that Jewish leaders often met privately (or secretly) did have some basis, but the meetings were not to plan how to undermine the world of the Gentiles, but rather, how to deal with their many powerful enemies in that world.

A number of questions lingered as the source of lively debate by the eve of the Dreyfus Affair: Did Jews add to France's *grandeur*, or did they undermine it? A related question was, did the French example offer confirmation for the argument that treating Jews fairly would induce them to abandon their offensive habits and ideas? Or did developments in France raise renewed doubts about the ultimate possibility (or desirability) of absorbing Jews into a unified modern nation-state?

Such doubts found expression on the Jewish side, in a new ideology, Zionism, born during the Dreyfus Affair—though they were also fundamental to modern antisemitism. Zionism and modern antisemitism did have certain opinions in common. Theodor Herzl, the founder of political Zionism, noted in his diary that anti-Semites praised him, while most Jews attacked him. Zionism and modern antisemitism also suggested common feelings about the extent to which laws, particularly those that recognized Jewish civil equality and protected minorities, were an effective way of dealing with the Jewish Question. The Dreyfus Affair seemed to suggest that in permitting Jewish success on such an impressive scale, as was the case in France, hatred and resentment were only postponed—or even ultimately intensified, in light of the remarkable extent of that success.

Another related but obdurate question remained about how much French Jews could separate themselves from Jewish religion and tradition before they stopped being Jews. In fact, a fair number of French Jews, as well as Jews in other countries, did just that: sometimes intermarrying, even converting to Christianity, but more commonly, adopting a secular-humanist identity, one that dismissed both Judaism and Christianity as unreasonable remnants of a "medieval" past. That conclusion seemed to be the one reached by Alfred Dreyfus, though some ambiguities about his beliefs lingered, as will be further explored below.

C. Demography and Movement of Peoples

An argument has been made that demographic factors (or rapid population growth and the resulting mass movement of peoples) explain much more about the fate of modern Jews than a strictly intellectual approach to the subject, stressing the independent power of beliefs. Jewish population growth, from the late eighteenth century to the early twentieth, was remarkable, especially since its fastest-growing areas were in backward Eastern Europe, in the Russian Pale of Settlement and the neighboring Austrian province of Galicia. In Western Europe, Jewish numbers in the nineteenth century were rarely more than one percent of the general population; in France, Jews made up less than a quarter of one percent. In total numbers, Jews in Russia by the 1890s outnumbered those in France by something like 100 times. The differences in wealth between Jews in the east and in the west were also great.

The German term for eastern Jews, Ostjuden, acquired negative connotations, often picked up by non-German speakers. Most Ostjuden were poor and religiously traditional. They often shocked western observers in their appearance and behavior: They were deemed "primitive," lacking not only enlightenment but also modern hygiene and norms of civility. As noted, eastern Jews had their own hostile opinions about westerners, including the westernizing Jews. For them, men like Dreyfus were not only bad Jews; they were close to no longer being Jews at all.

Many French people, considering their country's declining birth rate, had mixed feelings about immigrants. Jews in particular could be seen as representing "intellectual capital," bringing fresh ideas and talents, as well as capital in the more conventional sense. Italian immigrants had acquired a somewhat different image, but in the nineteenth century, they had provided such famous Frenchmen as Gambetta and Zola. On the other hand, prejudice—and especially violence—against Italians was greater than against Jews, even after the antisemitic riots of 1898.

Jews moved not only from countryside to cities in Russia; they also moved in substantial numbers out of Russia and Galicia, increasing the population of neighboring European cities to a remarkable extent. In 1860, Vienna counted 6,000 Jewish residents; in 1870, 40,000; by 1910, there were over 175,000.

Paris did not have anything like the number of Jewish immigrants that Vienna and other cities did, but by the 1880s, a few areas of Paris were being settled by Jews primarily from Eastern Europe—to general unease, if not alarm. Those feelings were expressed not only by non-Jewish residents but also by long-resident French Jews. The troublesome developments elsewhere in European cities regarding the Ostjuden impressed many French observers as an unhappy future for France if more Jews from Eastern Europe continued to arrive. That apprehension also played a role in the Dreyfus Affair.

Actually, thousands of Jews did arrive in France after 1871, largely in Paris; they were not Ostjuden but long-term French citizens, moving out of Alsace and Lorraine after those provinces were taken over by the victorious German Reich. Movement to Paris in itself represented a form of upward mobility for those Jews, aside from allowing them to avoid becoming citizens of the German Reich. In fact, the Reich had its own Jewish residents, numerous in Berlin, and they embraced German nationalism as enthusiastically as French Jews embraced French nationalism. German Jews also enjoyed civil equality, though it was only granted to all of them with the unification of Germany. Revealingly, there was no move of German Jews into the upper ranks of the Prussian military, comparable to the move of French Jews into that country's officers' ranks.

Alfred Dreyfus was one of those Alsatian Jews, a teenager when his family moved to Paris after a brief stay in Switzerland. However, many members of his extended family remained in Alsace to manage the family businesses, and Dreyfus maintained regular contact with his family there, making a few border crossings that were technically illegal. Those contacts were listed as suspicious in his indictment: How could one possibly plan *revanche* against the German enemy when one's extended family had become German? (Of course, the same question could be applied to non-Jewish Alsatians who moved to France.)

French anxieties about being swamped by impoverished Jews were paralleled by indignation that extremely rich Jews, again often with German-sounding names, were buying up prestigious dwellings in Paris and elsewhere. Rich Jews in unprecedented numbers also began to appear at France's many elegant and fashionable sites.

Again, Dreyfus became one of these wealthy newcomers. His case was especially notable once he had entered the higher echelons of the French military. He took up residence in exclusive Parisian neighborhoods, and he enjoyed a lavish lifestyle, one that included private stables for his morning rides—to say nothing of regular intimacies with the highest quality courtesans of Paris. (That sort of activity was hardly unusual for officers at the time, though most of them lacked the kind of income that Dreyfus enjoyed from his family's factories—around ten times what a comparable French officer's salary was, and more once Dreyfus married, since his wife belonged to a family that was even richer than his, and she came with a handsome dowry.)

At Dreyfus's trial, a few of his fellow officers claimed that he bragged about the opportunities his riches allowed him, especially with the opposite sex—even after he married. They also reported that he had been seen publicly, wearing his officer's uniform, in the company of women of ill repute. Given Dreyfus's reserved character and his limited friendships with other officers, the charge that he bragged to them about his sexual adventures seems unlikely, but the jealousies of his fellow officers were real, and his tendency to assume a sense of intellectual superiority to them did not help.

The number of Jewish officers in France seems yet more amazing, in that European Jews, long without a nation of their own to defend, had few military traditions or aspirations: no armies, no military schools, no titled nobility with military roles. There were, of course, the mythical heroes of ancient times, but Jewish values and social prestige (*yikhus*) in Europe were more centered on intellectual attainments and moral behavior, not physical prowess and bravery under fire. Traditional Jews tended to be disdainful of such prowess, making a distinction between Gentile *koakh* (brutish physical power) and Jewish *moakh* (brains, mental agility), symbolically present in the twins, Esau and Jacob, in Genesis. The extent to which Dreyfus identified with (or was even familiar with) such matters is unclear, since he rarely discussed them in public, while he did assert a "rationalist" identity.

In tsarist Russia, Jews were drafted into the army for twenty-five years—a special horror when the draftees were young and poor, as they often were. With rare exceptions, those Russian Jews who were drafted did not become part of the tsarist officer corps, except as medics. In France, it was unusual for Jews to become ordinary, non-commissioned foot soldiers, and service in the military was by no means regarded as such a horrible fate. French Jews were moving, by mid-century, into the urban middle and upper classes, and being an officer was more appropriate to their station than being a foot soldier. Jewish military officers also constituted a potent rebuttal to negative stereotypes. Many French Jews seemed to feel the need to prove themselves worthy citizens, ready to sacrifice and even die for the French *patrie* (fatherland). Dying for Mother Russia was decidedly less attractive for Jews, and those who moved out of Russia did not easily or quickly embrace the nationalism of other countries. Many of them were attracted to socialist movements.

D. Industrialization and Modernization

The European industrial revolution was a form of modernization or rationalization of industry. It was a vast process, many aspects of which benefitted Jews, in part because of their historic links to finance and commerce. Industrialization pushed aside old methods and institutions, gradually creating a new elite of monetary wealth and challenging the old elite of traditional lineage and Christian religion. The process might be termed a destructive-creative one, with a definite dark side. Creation in many realms involves destruction—and resentment.

Antisemitism has often been described as an appealing ideology for those who feel threatened or offended by modern times and modernization in general, especially since Jews seemed to thrive so markedly in liberal, modernizing environments. Industrialization in France was more gradual than in Germany, Britain, or the United States, and for some time, it did seem that hostility to Jews had less appeal in France than in Germany. Thus, relatively slow industrialization and gradual modernization were in some regards seen as an advantage for the French. However, slow industrialization was decidedly not an advantage in challenging the new German nation—for which heavy industry was believed necessary.

An extensive literature appeared in France during the nineteenth century, claiming that Jews had become the new rulers of France and other countries by means of their newly acquired wealth as capitalists. A prize-winning book appearing in 1879, titled, *Mon Vieux Paris* ("My Old Paris") was especially notable, and its author, Edouard Drumont, would soon become notorious for his bestselling volumes, titled, *La France Juive* ("Jewish France"), documenting the alleged takeover and ruin of France by the Jews. In *Mon Vieux Paris*, he had lamented the passing of the "old Paris," a place of charming neighborhoods, small shops, and tasteful monuments replaced by Jewish-owned department stores and ugly modern symbols, soon typified by the detested Eiffel Tower (another German-sounding name, though actually not Jewish).

Herzl was one of Drumont's many admirers; he found the notorious anti-Semite to be an "artist," one whose books helped him acquire a liberating way of thinking. Drumont in a sense returned the favor by giving Herzl's book, *The Jewish State*, a highly favorable review. Jean Jaurès, the socialist tribune and late-arriving Dreyfusard, had earlier also praised Drumont for exposing the Jewish miscreants in the notorious Panama Scandals of the late 1880s, one of whom "revealed all" to Drumont before committing suicide.

E. Inherited Mindsets

Hostility to Jews has been termed "the longest hatred." The term has been criticized by some historians as lacking adequate attention to shifting historical context and failing to account for the long stretches of Gentile-Jewish tolerance. Also left hanging, so to speak, is the issue of whether hatred of Jews is entirely a product of the non-Jewish mind, having nothing to do with what Jews really are or do. At any rate, the term has become popular in referring to antisemitism, and certainly any hatred lasting for two millennia, over diverse areas of Europe and much of the rest of the world, might well be considered a major force, even a transcendent, inexorable one—part of a mystical divine plan. God's use of evil to accomplish good is a familiar theme of the Old Testament.

The modern European and purportedly "scientific" version of that longest hatred, which was given the neologism "anti-Semitism" in the nineteenth century, emphasized the power of an enduring *material* reality, the Semitic race, denounced as foreign to Europe and bent on destroying European civilization. In the nineteenth century, even some Jews, while resisting the negative stereotypes of "Semitism," were inclined to describe themselves as "Jews by race, not religion." It is unclear if Dreyfus ever used those words in describing his identity.

The period of the European Enlightenment may be seen as a general effort to elevate rational thought, downgrade revelation, and abolish prejudice—particularly religious-based intolerance. The values of the Enlightenment clashed famously in *La Grande Nation* against traditional, organized religion. Voltaire's words, *Écrasez l'infâme!* ("Crush the infamous thing!"—that is, dogmatic religion, epitomized by the Catholic Church), became a familiar slogan of the Enlightenment. The French Revolution represented a major victory of enlightened values and associated notions of historical progress made possible by reason. Throughout Europe in the nineteenth century, secular rationality began to prevail over religious dogma, perhaps most famously in light of Darwin's theory of evolution, but in many other realms as well. Religious people felt under rising attack—the conservative Catholics in France to an especially great extent.

The Dreyfus Affair came to be regarded as a crucial chapter in the long struggle between modern, rationalist ideals and traditional religious faith. Initially, Dreyfus's conviction was seen as marking a victory for those opposed to Enlightenment ideals, linked to related notions of respecting established authority. The Anti-Dreyfusards were often conservative Catholics, ones who believed that Jews, because of their religion and their centuries-old cultural heritage, should never be allowed to assume positions as military defenders of any Christian nation. For them, France was historically Catholic, and even by the late nineteenth century—despite the French Revolution—Catholics remained the overwhelming majority of France's population, especially in its provincial rural areas. For the traditional peasant population of France, a Jew in a French military uniform was almost as jarring as a Jew would have been in the dress of a Catholic priest. Such a mindset, a *mentalité,* is not easily altered.

By the time of the Third Republic, most French Jews had become politically allied with French Protestants (who represented only about one percent of the total population but were also well represented in the military, if less so than the Jews) and the republican anti-clerical left (much larger and increasing in numbers but difficult to measure). Not surprisingly, Jews, Protestants, and secularists in the Third Republic supported anti-Catholic legislation, including the so-called Ferry Laws, passed between 1879 and 1886, which removed the Catholic Church from primary school education. The explicit long-range goal of the Ferry Laws was to educate France's children in rational, modern ideas, and free their minds from irrational dogma. Catholics felt under siege.

F. The Rise of the Jews

"The Jew is everywhere!" became an antisemitic slogan throughout Europe by the late nineteenth and early twentieth centuries. It was obviously a gross exaggeration, yet it represented a reality for many people. The striking rise in Jewish numbers was one element of that belief, but Jews remained, despite the population explosion in Eastern Europe, only a small part of the total European population. Their mobility was new, and they tended to flock into major urban areas in numbers that were often impressive, but they obviously could not be physically "everywhere."

More substantially, *imagery* about Jews—whether positive or negative—did come to appear almost everywhere, even in places where there were no Jews. The Dreyfus Affair certainly drew attention "everywhere." Charles Péguy, famous liberal Catholic author, poet, and early Dreyfusard, exclaimed that "Dreyfus has become more famous than Napoleon!"

Péguy was not lamenting that fact; he was no enemy of the Jews—more like a philosemite, or at least an admirer of certain prominent Jews. He had formed cordial contacts with some of them before the Affair. Another provocative observation he made, based on those contacts, was that hostile attitudes to Jews were not only widespread among his fellow Catholics; such sentiments were also to be found in three-quarters of the Jewish upper bourgeoisie. Half of the Jewish middle bourgeoisie was also hostile, he asserted, as was one-third of the Jewish petty bourgeoisie. Alfred Dreyfus, of course, belonged to the first of those categories.

Marx, Freud, Einstein: These three Jews rank high among the reigning luminaries of modern times. Their Jewishness was problematic, but they were all recognized as Jews. Their high visibility and fame had no equivalent in premodern Europe. The only partial exception was Baruch Spinoza in the mid-seventeenth century, who was expelled from his own Jewish community and shunned by most observant Jews for being critical of religion and the Bible, but he was eventually admired as a philosopher—his writings increasingly read throughout Europe.

In the course of the nineteenth century, many other individual Jews were admired—much more than Jews had ever been before in European history. In a parallel way, the sympathy of non-Jews for the injustices that Jews faced became more widespread than ever before. Once the Nobel Prize was established (1901), Jews were awarded a notably disproportionate number of them.

Again, speaking of enhanced visibility, not numbers, very famous fictional Jewish characters were to be found in Dickens' Fagin (the notorious pickpocket chief in *Oliver Twist*) and Shakespeare's Shylock (from *The Merchant of Venice,* popular in nineteenth-century Europe). There were many more Jewish protagonists in popular fiction, positive as well as negative.

Among actual historical figures, Benjamin Disraeli became Britain's most famous statesman at a time when Britain's fame and power was unparalleled. Like Marx, he was technically a Christian (obligatory as a British prime minister), but his ancestors were

Jewish, and his name means "of Israel." He did not deny his Jewishness. On the contrary, he famously took pride in his Jewish race, which he described as one of the superior races—one that indeed enjoyed great power, often exercised behind the scenes.

Disraeli was admired by many, including Queen Victoria, but he was poorly informed about Jewish history, and he spread much exaggeration if not pure nonsense about Jewish power. The issue here, however, is not the accuracy of his ideas but rather the extent to which he contributed to Jewish visibility. Everyone in Europe and the United States, at least among the educated, recognized the name Disraeli, just as they did the name Rothschild.

A recent (2019) volume, *The Jewish Century*, by UC Berkeley professor, Yuri Slezkine, makes an intriguing case for the "jewification" of modern times. That term, of course, is part of the vocabulary of antisemitism—and a Jewish century that also witnessed the Holocaust obviously needs some qualification—but Slezkine is himself of Jewish lineage and is by no means self-hating. His somewhat playful and unorthodox definition of "Jewishness" is essential to his argument, since he considers certain castes of Indians to be Jewish, as well Lebanese Arabs, and a few African tribes, such as the Ibos.

The point here, again, is Jewish visibility, but not all visible Jews were angels, and those who were not, as suggested above, also contributed significantly to Jewish notoriety. In this regard, one of the most revealing brief definitions of Jewishness can be found in a typical tongue-in-cheek Jewish witticism: "Jews are like everyone else—only more so." That definition could be cited as a further aspect of the rise of the Jews, in that European Jews in modern times became significantly over-represented in many public or "visible" fields—as doctors, scientists, inventors, lawyers, professors, authors, moneylenders, and millionaires. Jews also made up much more than one percent of stock market con men, bunko artists, and other miscreants. They were particularly known as over-achievers in forgery and contraband, and as entrepreneurs in the trade of "White slavery" (prostitution).

G. Personality and Accident

In the above paragraphs, the main attention has been on major impersonal determinants, or large historical forces and slow-moving deep structures, beyond the ephemeral political noise and shallow surface of "event history" (*histoire événementielle*, to use a term associated with the influential Annales school of history). Those paragraphs are consonant with trends in the writing of history by professional historians. Similarly, "Great Men" history, so prominent in the nineteenth century, has been downgraded by professional historians. The issues are not easily summarized or agreed upon, but an article by a journalist in *Commentary* magazine posed them in succinct and thought-provoking terms. It was titled, "No Hitler, No Holocaust." This was in 1984, before the term "the longest hatred" became popular, but the article argued implicitly against the power of the concept—that the mass murder of Jews in World War II was not inevitable, and that Hitler's personal role was crucial.

Much the same might be said about the Dreyfus Affair, as to whether it was somehow inevitable, an expression of the ever-recurring longest hatred, as distinguished from the influence of individuals. The Affair might also be described as accidental, involving avoidable mistakes and rushed decisions by incompetents, not the result of large impersonal forces. It is not a long stretch. Without Dreyfus's particular personality, there would not have been an affair. Or, if Picquart had initially been in a key position (as he was shortly after Dreyfus was sent to Devil's Island), the Affair would almost certainly have been averted. Take War Minister Paty du Clam out of the picture, and again, Dreyfus might well have been passed over as a possible traitor, given the weakness of the evidence against him.

Alfred Dreyfus was often termed a hero, mostly for enduring unspeakable suffering. But he was no "Great Man" in the way that Napoleon was. In many regards, Dreyfus seemed a conventional bourgeois citizen, an ordinary man of limited horizons, ultimately disappointing many Dreyfusards. His personality calls for special attention.

To the question, "why was Dreyfus so swiftly and stubbornly accused, given the shaky evidence?" the prevailing and plausible answer has been, "because he was a Jew." But there are some uncertainties about that answer, related to defining Jewishness and to how much Dreyfus corresponded to antisemitic stereotypes about Jews. His dreams, already in childhood, of becoming an officer in the French army, stand out especially as different from such stereotypes. He did fit, as an adult, into the stereotype of being extremely rich and living ostentatiously, but why would such a rich man sell minor secrets for paltry sums? The lack of a plausible motive was the strongest point in his defense, although those who arrested him maintained that the motives of a Jew were impossible to understand.

The main—and only substantial—physical evidence for the charges against Dreyfus was that the handwriting on the *bordereau*, or "list" of secrets for sale to the German authorities, largely resembled his handwriting. Experts differed on that point; the expert who argued most confidently that Dreyfus's handwriting and that of the *bordereau* were similar defended that conclusion by asserting that the obvious differences in the two handwritings were the result of Dreyfus's efforts to disguise his handwriting in composing the *bordereau*.

The question of how Jewish this particular Jew was took on special significance in the Affair. Was he more Jewish than French, or more French than Jewish? And could one be less than 100 percent French and still be a reliable French officer? Dreyfus's French identity seemed obvious, but so was his Jewishness. He was Jewish by law, that is, traditional Jewish law (Halakhah), since he was born of a Jewish mother, but also French by French law, since both of his parents were French citizens. His ancestors and relatives were all Jewish; he was married to a Jewish woman in an Orthodox ceremony, officiated by France's Chief Rabbi.

On the other hand, as a self-described "rationalist," Dreyfus rejected Halakhah. Reliable details about the more intimate aspects of his private life and marriage are sparse, but his wife was more attached to Jewish religion and tradition than he was. Still, they both apparently ate food that was not kosher. He did not say daily prayers, and he shaved his beard regularly. The extent to which he participated in traditional holidays such as Passover and Yom Kippur is unclear, but he regularly joined his relatives in observing them.

More significantly, Dreyfus had enough attachment to Jewish tradition and enough Jewish learning to recite the demanding texts of the "Kaddish," the Mourner's Prayer, following the deaths of close relatives—and he travelled to Germany to do so, because that particular traditional obligation (the central theme of which is the sanctification of God's name) was something many other French Jews had stopped observing. They also typically lacked the learning to do it.

In short, while Dreyfus no longer believed in Jewish religion and rejected Halakhah, he still accepted some Jewish traditions, roughly comparable to those lapsed Christians who still celebrated Christmas and Easter, and whose weddings took place in a church. To repeat: Dreyfus did not make a point of being Jewish, but he did not try to hide his Jewishness either. To the question of whether he was more French than Jewish or more Jewish than French, one might say that he was definitely more French—but with footnotes.

Those footnotes impressed the men who charged him with treason.

To change our perspective and consider the issue of Jewishness as it often was posed in the 1890s: Was Dreyfus *racially* a Jew? As noted, some Jews made the distinction of being "Jewish by race but not by religion." Did Dreyfus look or act Jewish? That there was a typical Jewish (or Semitic) physical appearance and behavior was widely accepted by Jew and Gentile alike in the 1890s. However, Dreyfus's brother, Mathieu, was tall, blond, and blue-eyed (similar to the stereotype of the Aryan), and known for his bonhomie, his enjoyment of a wide circle of social contacts, including non-Jews—which was common for French Jews, especially in Paris. It is not often pointed out—and not obvious from photographs—that Alfred Dreyfus was also blond (though balding and beginning to turn grey by the time of his trial) and blue-eyed. He was a few inches shorter than his brother but not actually short (as Jews were stereotyped to be). He was slim, physically fit, and loved horse-riding (again, contrary to racial stereotypes). It is unlikely that he would have been recognized on a Paris street as a Jew, even without his uniform.

However, unlike his brother, Dreyfus was reserved in manner, lacked a sense of humor, and his few friends seem to have been exclusively Jewish. His social life was confined to his extended family. Such qualities could hardly have been considered sure signs of Jewishness or have been considered morally objectionable under normal circumstances. Many members of regional, ethnic, and religious groups tended to restrict their social life to those "like them," and reserved people are found in all such groups.

Dreyfus's customary reserve was also accompanied by a manner suggestive of intellectual arrogance, and his lack of friends had one very negative consequence: he had no *patrons*, higher military acquaintances who could look out for him. It might have been more difficult for a Jew to find a patron, but apparently other Jews had managed to do so, and there were many high-ranking Jews in the army who might have served as Dreyfus's patron. At any rate, there were few among his superior officers who knew him and liked him—and most significantly, few who might have said, "I know Alfred well, and he could not possibly be a traitor." Below, we will hear more about one of Dreyfus's superiors, Georges Picquart, who had supervised him as a student and did not like him.

Another trait with negative consequences, mentioned by friend and foe alike, was Dreyfus's weak voice—variously described as dull, monotonous, and lacking in emotional vigor. He did not possess the commanding presence that was widely believed to be essential in a military officer, and he regularly made a poor impression on the witness stand, in an age when being an effective public speaker was extremely important. (Clemenceau, Jaurès, and Gambetta were among the most admired of such public speakers, but there were many more.)

Dreyfus himself came to recognize, in his letters to his wife while imprisoned, some of his personal flaws, evident also in his memoirs, published after his return to France from Devil's Island. He even implicitly accepted the observation that, given his unshakable respect for his superiors, he might have been an anti-Dreyfusard, so to speak, if another man had been arrested and convicted as he had been. Dreyfus's respect for his superiors was indeed extremely strong—and tragically misplaced!

Dreyfus's memoirs are revealing in other ways as well. By his account, the members of his extended family were all paragons, without exception, while he described himself as "strong and pure in my immaculate conscience." He and his wife were "two pure and honest hearts whose thoughts have been only for our beloved country, for France." (His pure and immaculate conscience felt no need to refer to his marital infidelities—not that this behavior was unusual in France at that time. And his devoted wife, who apparently only learned of his sexual escapades during his trial, seemed to accept them, again in a manner typical for the time and place.)

A closer scrutiny of another recognized hero of the Affair, Georges Picquart, is also revealing. Dreyfus's earlier supervisor was socially conservative, a Catholic (though a lapsed one), and contemptuous of Jews. Although he disliked Dreyfus, he recognized his Jewish student's intelligence and diligence. Picquart remained suspicious and dismissive of the Dreyfus family to the end, once curtly ordering Mathieu from his office, since he believed that Dreyfus's brother was offering him a bribe. In the later celebrations over Dreyfus's exoneration, Picquart refused to shake Dreyfus's hand, and he avoided contact with other members of the family (besides Mathieu), whom he considered typically pusillanimous, unappealing Jews.

At the same time, Picquart showed remarkable fortitude, once he became familiar with the evidence, in insisting that Dreyfus was innocent and Esterhazy guilty. That meant eventually contradicting his superior officers, whom he reluctantly came to realize were implicated in an inexcusable cover-up. It would have been easy for him to have simply remained quiet, obeying orders to drop the case. Instead, he persisted—at great personal cost. He was expelled from the army and spent a year in prison. However, in

1906, after the victory of the Dreyfusards, Picquart achieved the rank of general and became Minister of War.

Was Picquart simply an "exceptional" officer? What gave him the courage to confront his superiors? Was it respect for the law of the land? A transcendent or "fundamental" respect for truth-telling and justice? For her part, Hannah Arendt described him as "no hero" but rather "a simple quiet, disinterested spirit ... that common type of citizen with an average interest in public affairs who, in the hour of danger (though not a minute earlier) stands up to defend his country in the same way as he discharges his daily duties."

How is it possible that a man of unusual moral fortitude was also an anti-Semite? Much obviously depends on how one defines the term, but stranger things have happened. The Affair posed a related puzzle: How could it be that, among the many bigots and "dullards," there were some anti-Dreyfusards who were known not only for their intelligence and artistic accomplishments but also for their honesty and open-mindedness? They were not typical anti-Dreyfusards, but nonetheless, their presence on what has generally been considered the culpable side of the Affair underlines the danger of jumping to facile conclusions. There were millions of anti-Dreyfusards about whom we have little reliable information, only informed speculation about their beliefs. (As the contemporary American novelist, Henry James, wrote, "Never think you have said the last word about the human heart.")

The most famous hero of the Affair was, of course, Émile Zola. His courage has become legendary, but he, too, was more complicated and less heroic than most accounts recognize. Historian Ruth Harris, one of the most perceptive and thorough recent historians of the Affair, portrays Zola as primarily motivated by a sense of adventure rather than of moral outrage, in writing *J'accuse!* Many of his novels included ugly stereotypes of Jews. He once wrote, "It is indeed Jewry as a whole, that stubborn and cold-blooded conqueror, marching toward the sovereign kingship of the world's nations, that it has bought ... with its omnipotent gold."

Another alleged hero deserves mention, the eloquent tribune, leader of the French socialists, Jean Jaurès. He was a late convert to the Dreyfusard cause, and, like Marx himself (in a notorious early essay), Jaurès conflated capitalist egoism and Jewishness. As noted, he had a friendly relationship for a while with the anti-Semite, Drumont, and only later was he able to recognize the difference between Jews as a whole and Jews as capitalists. Seeing admirable traits even in some of the Jewish capitalists who were Dreyfusards was a particularly difficult step for him. That his wife was a devoted Catholic was also awkward for a man so critical of religion, but that awkward situation was typical of many free-thinkers and supporters of the Ferry Laws.

What might be termed the "uncontested villains" of the Affair were many, including, of course, the actual author of the *bordereau*, Esterhazy. However, it seems that incompetence was at least as important as antisemitism in explaining the actions of those who railroaded Dreyfus. Under pressure from the antisemitic press, they ironically demonstrated their lack of a prime military virtue: calm courage under fire. The principle that seemed to guide them most was self-interest, linked to a refusal to consider admitting to a mistake—which, on the battlefield, is also very difficult to acknowledge. That such men so feared being attacked by Drumont suggests the dark side of freedom of the press, but of course, also the power of antisemitism.

To be sure, Commandant Paty de Clam ranks as an unprincipled villain, as much as Esterhazy, though for different reasons. In some regards, Paty de Clam appeared to be a man of learning and experience, but in the Affair, he comes across as a popinjay with influential connections, who somehow was able to pull others along with his confident misreading of the evidence. No doubt he had ready listeners, among them Col. Jean Sandherr, Chief of Military Intelligence and a hard-core anti-Semite, who was more than a willing participant in what finally amounted to an appalling railroading of an innocent man.

General Mercier, the Minister of War who so confidently informed the public that the evidence against Dreyfus was overwhelming, was known as an intelligent modernizer, a free-thinking lapsed Catholic with an English Protestant wife. He was often attacked by the antisemitic press for showing favor to Jews in the military. His public stance against Dreyfus might have reflected his desire to get the antisemitic press off his back more than any personal hostility toward Jews—yet another example of the dark side of a free press.

One final hero of the Affair deserves mention. By the eve of World War I, Charles Péguy, an unusually tolerant Catholic, and an admirer of many individual Jews, had become bitterly disappointed with the Dreyfusards, whom he had joined early. He was even more outraged by the general amnesty of 1906—"forgetting" the crimes of the anti-Dreyfusards, as if they were paralleled by the crimes of Dreyfus, Picquart, and others.

Even Jaurès eventually earned Péguy's profound contempt. When Jaurès was assassinated by a right-wing fanatic as armies were mobilizing in August 1914, Péguy was heard to utter a shout of savage delight. The anti-militarism and anti-Catholicism of the beloved socialist tribune offended Péguy, whose patriotism had grown into something all-consuming and ultimately toxic. He quarreled bitterly with many of his former friends, growing ever more isolated.

Péguy perished under German fire, in the opening battles of World War I. On the German side, Lance Corporal (*Gefreiter*) Adolf Hitler was later wounded but not killed.

Chapter 14

Pope St. John XXIII: Antisemitism Is Antithetical to Christianity

This chapter examines four pivotal moments in which official organs of the Catholic Church took a stand against the persecution of Jews or worked to improve the Church's relationship with Jews: Pope Innocent IV's 1247 papal bull condemning blood libel claims in Germany; Cardinal Lorenzo Ganganelli's 1759 report debunking blood libel claims in Poland; the Second Vatican Council's groundbreaking 1965 declaration, *Nostra aetate*; and the establishment of diplomatic relations between the Vatican and Israel.

The texts examined in this chapter demonstrate the profound connection between theological beliefs and law; they also demonstrate how Christian thought about the Jewish people developed over time. Sadly, these texts also demonstrate how even though legal protections were guaranteed to the Jewish people by the law, antisemitic attitudes could not be stemmed merely by legal responses. The same texts demonstrate that a misunderstanding of official teaching of the Catholic Church was used in popular culture to support antisemitism in Europe, at various times in history. Some Christian theologians openly promoted antisemitic thought in their own works.

The genocidal murder of millions of Jews in the Shoah provided Christian leaders across Europe, specifically, the occasion to reflect more profoundly on how a society primarily populated with men and women of the Christian faith could have allowed such an atrocity to take place and how so many Christians could have actively participated in it. That moment of reflection, at least for the Catholic Church, led not to a political response, but to a profoundly theological one which echoed what the Gospel of John proclaims: salvation comes from the Jews (Jn 4:22). Hence, any form of antisemitism is inconsistent with an authentic expression of Christianity.

A. The Blood Libel Is False

The term "blood libel" refers to the accusation that Jews across Europe engaged in the ritual murder of Christians, typically children. While the earliest known case was said to have taken place in Norwich, England in the year 1144 C.E., similar accusations were made across Europe throughout the entirety of the Middle Ages. In Norwich, William, a young apprentice, died the day before Easter. At the time, the death was considered a murder like any other; however, several years later, a Christian knight,

Simon de Novers, murdered a local Jewish man, named Eleazar, to whom he was in debt. De Novers was put on trial and was defended by the local bishop, who argued that the real crime was not the murder of Eleazar by Simon, but that of William, three years earlier. The defense argued that it was Eleazar who had murdered young William—an argument for which there was no concrete evidence—but all the local Jews were guilty of the crime. The king, who oversaw the trial, was so shocked by this claim that the trial was adjourned, and de Novers was released.

William's "murder" was later popularized by Thomas of Monmouth, who claimed as a source a local Jewish man named Theobald of Cambridge, who alleged that the murder had been a human sacrifice offered to fulfill the "ancient writings of his fathers,"[1] which demanded the annual killing of a Christian. While never an officially recognized martyrdom,[2] the myth of William of Norwich grew, as did similar accusations against Jewish communities across Europe.

There are many factors behind such accusations, but the official response of the Catholic Church was to condemn them consistently, often decrying them as grotesque acts of greed. Sadly, these official responses did little to stem the tide of claims that Jews would kidnap, torture, and kill Christian children, using their blood for magic, sacrilege, or the baking of matzah. A critical theological component to the accusation of blood libel is its connection to the Jewish feast of Pesach (Passover) and the Christian feast of Easter.[3]

While the specific document examined here is not the first Papal intervention[4] against accusations of blood libel and reprisals against Jewish communities for the alleged ritual murder of Christians, the work of Pope Innocent IV is in direct response to a specific accusation of blood libel raised against the Jewish community in Valréas (Vaucluse, France). In March of 1247 C.E., the body of a two-year old girl was found; this became the excuse for sacking the surrounding area, including confiscating the

1. *See* Thomas, of Monmouth, The Life and Miracles of St. William of Norwich 93–94 (Augusts Jessop & Montague Rhodes James eds., & trans., 2011) (1896).

2. A martyr, in the Christian tradition, is a person who dies because of his or her faith in Jesus Christ. The term comes from the Greek and means "witness." The tradition of martyrdom is also known in Judaism. *See* Daniel Boyarin, *Martyrdom and the Making of Christianity and Judaism*, 6 J. Early Christian Stud. 577 (1998), https://dx.doi.org/10.1353/earl.1998.0053.

3. For more information regarding the question of "blood libel," see Magda Teter, Blood Libel: On the Trial of an Antisemitic Myth (2020). *See also Blood Libel: A False, Incendiary Claim Against Jews*, The Anti-Defamation League (Sept. 1, 2016), https://www.adl.org/resources/backgrounder/blood-libel-false-incendiary-claim-against-jews?gad_source=1&gclid=CjwKCAiA9bq6BhAKEiwAH6bqoGDmByGt7JkuMrqVJNV458zPK64CHTyn8CmevzJ2PgpwZG_zmsNTJhoC1k0QAvD_BwE&gclsrc=aw.ds; *see also Blood Libel*, Am. Jewish Comm., https://www.ajc.org/translatehate/blood-libel (last visited Dec. 31, 2024).

4. *See* Innocent III, *Sicut Judaeis* (1199 C.E.). Specifically, beyond the offer of protection, the document forbade compulsory baptism or conversion, which was incorporated by Gratian into his *Concordia discordantium canonum*, better known as the *Decretum*, creating a foundational text for Catholic law prohibiting forced conversions (I, C. 23., q. 4., cap. 16, c).

property of the local Jewish community. The bull[5] or official papal communiqué was sent to bishops throughout France and Germany at the time. Beyond just ecclesiastical authorities, the bull also makes mention of the responsibility of secular authorities. This bull clearly responds to the particular incident in Valréas, while placing it into the larger context of the Church's approach to the Jewish community.

Pope Innocent IV,[6] *The Lamentable Complaint of the Jews*

(Lachrymabilem Judaeorum)
July 5, 1247 C.E.

We have received the lamentable complaint of the Jews of Alemannia, that certain ecclesiastics as well as secular princes and other nobles and powerful individuals of your cities and dioceses, intending impious schemes against them, are thinking up and fabricating various and diverse pretexts in order to unjustly plunder and seize their goods. Without prudent consideration, they falsely impose upon them that during the solemnity of Passover they consume the heart of a murdered child in their rites, believing that the law commands this, whereas the divine scripture among other commandments of the law says 'Thou shalt not kill,' and prohibits them from touching anything that could cause death during the Passover, when it clearly states the opposite to the law, and maliciously throw the dead body of a man at them, if perchance it happens to be found somewhere. And by these and many other fabrications, raging against them without accusations, confessions, or convictions, they strip them of all their goods contrary to God and justice, despite privileges kindly granted to them by the Apostolic See. They oppress them with hunger, prisons, and so many hardships and grievances, afflicting them with various forms of punishment and condemning many of them to a shameful death. These Jews, as if under the dominion of the aforesaid princes, nobles, and powerful individuals of more affluent condition than their fathers under Pharaoh in Egypt, are compelled to miserably exile from the places inhabited by them and their ancestors from a time beyond memory. Fearing their extermination,

---

5. The name "bull" for certain documents generated by popes comes from the Latin term *bulla*, referring to the seal which authenticated the document. It came to be used as an official form of communications of various decisions made by the pope. *See Papal Bull*, Britannica, https://www.britannica.com/topic/bull-papal (last visited Dec. 31, 2024).

6. Born Sinibaldo Fieschi (in the twelfth century), Pope Innocent IV was a student of law in the famed school of Bologna before being ordained as a Catholic priest. He became bishop of Albenga (northern Italy) in 1225 and was elected pope on June 25, 1243. He is most well known in history for his conflict with Frederick II, the Roman emperor who was condemned by the pope and a gathering of bishops in the city of Lyon, France, in 1245. Here, Innocent IV's legal background was evident, in that the emperor was condemned on the triple charge of perjury, sacrilege, and suspicion of heresy. Innocent IV also developed a heightened sense of the universal responsibility of the pope, which led him to have a particular interest in resolving the long-standing conflict among Christians in the eastern empire and in Europe. This also likely contributed to his unique thought that Jews constituted a part of the flock of Christ. For more on Innocent IV's views on Judaism, see Rebecca Rist, *Popes and Jews, 1095–1291* 164–206 (2016).

they have deemed it necessary to seek recourse to the providence of the Apostolic See. Therefore, not willing that the aforementioned Jews be unjustly harassed, whose conversion the Lord, in His mercy, awaits, since, as attested by the prophet, the remnant of them is believed to be saved, we command that you, showing yourselves favorable and kind towards them, should duly revoke through legitimate means whatever has rashly been attempted against the same Jews by the aforesaid prelates, nobles, and powerful persons, restoring them to their rightful state. Henceforth, you shall not allow them to be improperly harassed by anyone concerning these or similar matters, resolving such troublemakers by ecclesiastical censure without possibility of appeal.

Jews Appeal to Pope Innocent IV Concerning Blood Libel Accusations

1. *The lamentable complaint of the Jews.* It is interesting to note that the Jewish community both considered it possible and felt it necessary to communicate directly with the pope, rather than to take up the issue with the local ecclesiastical or civil authorities. The pope's response gives insight into their reasoning, as he indicated that the local authorities were also guilty in the matter. The Jewish community recognized that it had a legal claim it could present to the pope, in his authority as the supreme judicial authority among Christians. While the request presented to Pope Innocent IV does not appear to have survived, by the nature of his response it can be posited that the request was not merely one of desperation, but one based on a knowledge of the recognized rights of the Jewish community, some of which were based on divine law and the principles of justice, while others had been "granted to them by the Apostolic See."

2. *Pretexts to plunder.* Innocent IV recognized the persecution of the Jews, particularly tied to the notion of blood libel, as being a total fabrication with a very specific end. He did not offer any theological commentary on the question, other than to forcefully correct the myth that the Jews had been "commanded" to kill Christians, particularly during Passover. Innocent IV combatted this idea as absurd, pointing to the foundation of all Judeo-Christian law, the Ten Commandments, and the injunction against murder, which had been given by God in a theological text common to both communities. The pope pointed to the particularly insidious nature of the lie or myth of blood libel as an intentional manipulation of the truth, revealed in sacred scripture and aimed primarily at stealing from the Jewish community. While not said expressly in the text, the pope hinted at an underlying theological tension: Christians accused Jews of violating one precept ("thou shalt not kill") as a pretext for Christians to violate another ("thou shalt not steal").

3. *Maliciously throw the dead body of a man at them.* Equally important was the flippant manner in which the pope described the accusations made against the Jews. Innocent IV did not hide how ridiculous he believed blood libel accusations to be. As he had already pointed to the real cause of these accusations—the desire of impious Christians to confiscate Jews' property—he emphasized this point by denigrating the very accusation itself. At no point was any credence given to the possibility that any-

one in the Jewish community mutilated the body of the young girl found in Valréas. Rather, the truth was that a dead body was found—the result of a horrific crime, to be sure—but the accusation that followed was based on fiction and supposition, not fact.

4. *Under the dominion of rulers more powerful than Pharaoh.* The pope returned to a theological context in an effort to shame the Christians who brought the false allegations against the Jews in Valréas. The reader at the time would have immediately made the connection with the unjust treatment of the Jews in Egypt, recorded in the Book of Exodus; the powerful comparison here risks being lost on the modern reader. The Jews came to Egypt because of famine, where they found that Joseph, who had been sold into slavery by his brothers, had risen to a level of authority under the Pharoah such that he was able to convince the leader of Egypt to offer the people of Israel succor. There, they thrived, until "there came a Pharoah who did not know Joseph," when a program was initiated to "oppress them with forced labor" and even commanded that every boy born to a Hebrew mother be killed (Exodus 1:6–16). This led to generations of oppression that only ended when Moses rose and led his people to freedom in the promised land. The Christian leaders who were perpetrating these injustices upon the Jewish people were just as oppressive as the Pharoah, one of the great "villains" of history. As these leaders were Christians and received the teachings of the Gospel, unlike Pharoah, their treatment of the Jewish people should be better than his.

5. *Seeking recourse from the pope.* The notion here is not merely a supplication, but an official legal act. This underscores the fact that the Jewish community was aware of the legal protections afforded by the governing law. While those protections still legitimated forms of discrimination, if properly applied, they would have eliminated any legal prosecution based merely on religion. The fact that the pope responded to this official legal request further demonstrates his understanding that accusations of blood libel were specious and prohibited under the law.

6. *Ecclesiastical sanctions.* The pope made a decision in the matter, based on the applicable law, and informed the necessary authorities. The decision was not only retroactive—that the current persecution should end because the law had already forbidden it—but also prospective, in that it dictated that further harassment would lead to severe ecclesiastical sanctions. To comprehend the weight of these sanctions, it is useful to remember that ecclesiastical courts had tremendous authority in societies of the day and the threat of an unappealable sanction would not only change the condition of people within earthly society, but it would have been thought to put at serious risk their immortal souls. It is difficult to overstate the gravity of the punishment threatened by the pope for any future offenders. This was, in effect, group defamation relief and a hate crimes law before the name, with the penalty enhanced to eternal damnation.

7. *Blood libel accusations persisted.* So, if the pope addressed the question as a legal matter—with significant theological arguments serving as the foundation of the applicable law—and if the threatened penalty for future such actions was so grave, why did this not put an end to the notion of "blood libel?" This is a legitimate question, and it points to the fact that the accusations were not primarily legal, or even authentically

theological, in nature. The pope's response was clear and authoritative. It was based on a sound interpretation and application of the law and of consolidated theological teachings, rooted in the work of St. Augustine. It came close to mocking those who brought such senseless charges against the Jewish community. It condemned the Christian leaders, both civil and ecclesiastical, who used these obviously false accusations as a ruse to fuel their own greed. Nevertheless, this authoritative condemnation by the highest juridical authority in Christendom did not put an end to charges of blood libel. This indicates that there is much more behind these accusations than theological and legal concerns.[7]

Theological Underpinnings of Pope Innocent IV's Papal Bull

1. *The role of Jews in Christian salvation history.* At least since the fourth century C.E., one of the predominant elements of Christian thought about Judaism was that the rejection of Jesus of Nazareth as the Messiah resulted in the loss of the Jewish people's status as God's "chosen people" (cf. Exodus 19:5). This theory—which continues to appear in many different forms throughout history—is commonly referred to as "supersessionism." However, this was not Christianity's univocal position. St. Paul, himself a Jewish convert to Christianity after his dramatic experience "on the road to Damascus" (Acts 9), wrestled with the idea of reconciling the people of Israel's past and their future, after they did not recognize Jesus as the Messiah. For Paul, the problem was very real, but the answer to the problem was equally sure: "Will their infidelity nullify the fidelity of God? Of course not! God must be true" (Rom 3:3–4). To the modern reader, there can be no question of Paul's conviction that the people of Israel continued to have a place in God's plan: "I ask then, has God rejected his people? Of course not! For I too am an Israelite, a descendant of Abraham, of the tribe of Benjamin. God has not rejected his people whom he foreknew" (Rom 11:1–2). For some Christians after Paul, the destruction of the Temple in the first century C.E. and the failed revolt led by Bar Kokhba[8] in 132–135 C.E. provided both a rhetorical framework for the concept of supersessionism, and the concrete evidence of its truth. If Israel had not been replaced by the Christian community as God's chosen people, then the Temple would not have been destroyed.[9]

2. *Contra Iudeaos.* In parts of the ancient world, Jews and Christians worshipped in the same spaces and read from the same scriptures. In this atmosphere, theological disputes between Christians and Jews were commonplace. Many of these dialogues were

---

7. Rist, *supra* note 6.

8. The revolt led by Simon Bar Kokhba was also the last of the uprisings by Jews in Judea against Roman occupation. *See* Benjamin Kerstein, *The Bar-Kochba Revolt*, World Hist. Encyc. (Aug. 30, 2018), https://www.worldhistory.org/The_Bar-Kochba_Revolt/.

9. For a brief introduction to the concept of "supersessionism" in the early days of Christianity, see James Woods, *Augustine and Antisemitism*, Ad Fontes (Nov. 29, 2023), https://adfontesjournal.com/commonwealth/augustine-and-antisemitism/.

written; the Chrisitan variety came to be known by the generic Latin title, *Contra Iudeaos*—Against the Jews. While the title might be startling to a modern reader, it does not carry any negative connotations in Latin. Most often, these dialogues contained both Jewish and Christian voices.[10] The theological disputes in these early dialogues, from a Christian perspective, hinge on the question with which St. Paul struggled, as well as other practical considerations. For example, could you be a Christian and still observe Jewish feasts?

3. *Dialogue.* In the early days of the Common Era, there also existed authentic examples of Jewish-Christian intellectual dialogue. A surprising number of examples of such dialogues survive to this day.[11] These dialogues follow on the encounters between Jesus and the Jewish authorities of his day[12] and early encounters between recent converts to Christianity and local Jewish communities.[13] In the address by Stephen recorded in the seventh chapter of Acts of the Apostles,[14] there is a hint of the kind of language that will become commonplace in the dialogue literature of the early centuries of the Common Era. It must be noted that, in this dialogue literature, the similarities of the communities are also on display, especially their agreement on the composition of their common sacred scriptures.[15] The dialogues of this early era often contain an authentic back-and-forth; the Jewish interlocutors were not (always) "straw men" set up to demonstrate the power of the Christian argument. Nevertheless, the dialogues were always intended as an evangelical tool for Christianity, seeking to convince Jews of the truth of the Messianic status of Jesus of Nazareth.

4. *From dialogue toward a theological definition.* While the dialogue continued for the first few centuries of the Common Era, Christian theology moved forward in defining its unique characteristics, further distinguishing itself from the Jewish community. But the fundamental quandary of St. Paul remained unresolved:

> I have great sorrow and unceasing anguish in my heart. For I could wish that I myself were accursed and cut off from Christ for the sake of my own brothers and sisters, my own flesh and blood. They are Israelites, and to them belong the

---

10. *See, e.g.*, Willliam Varner, Ancient Jewish-Christian Dialogues: Athanasius and Zacchaeus, Simon and Theophilus, Timothy and Aquila: Introductions, Texts, and Translations (2005) (featuring three dialogues between Christians and Jews from the fourth, fifth, and sixth centuries, C.E., respectively).

11. *See* William Horbury, Jews and Christians in Contact and Controversy (1998); *see also* Arthur Lukyn Williams, Adversus Judaeos: A Bird's Eye View of Christian Apologiae Until the Renaissance (1935).

12. *See, e.g.*, *Matthew* 22:15–46; *John* 5:1–47, 7:14–36, 8:12–59, 10:22–39.

13. *E.g.*, *Acts of the Apostles* 2:14–36; 3:11–26.

14. *See Id.* at *7:51* ("You stiff-necked people, uncircumcised in heart and ears, you are forever opposing the Holy Spirit, just as your ancestors used to do").

15. *See, e.g.*, *The Dialogue of Timothy and Aquila*, *in* Ancient Jewish-Christian Dialogues: Athanasius and Zacchaeus, Simon and Theophilus, Timothy and Aquila 143–145 (William Varner trans., 2004). After Timothy lists the books of the Hebrew Scriptures for his Jewish interlocutor (3.7–18), Aquila answers, "And what are the books handed down to you, which you call the 'New Covenant'? The Christian said: Why do you need the names of these? The Jew said: Just as you wish to convince me out of my canon, so do I want to do the same from your 'covenant'" (3.19–21).

> adoption, the glory, the covenants, the giving of the law, the worship, and the promises; to them belong the patriarchs, and from them, according to the flesh, comes the Christ, who is over all, God blessed forever. Amen. (Rom 9:2–5)

5. *Augustine's unique take.* St. Augustine, one of the greatest minds of the early Christian community, also struggled with this reality in his writings. One of Augustine's greatest intellectual interlocutors was Faustus, an exponent of Manichean thought.[16] In Augustine's work, *Contra Faustum Manicheaum,*[17] he laid a foundation for the positive theological status of not only spiritual things, but also things of the flesh. This positive outlook toward the "flesh" set the stage for Augustine to move away from the common dichotomy found in the dialogues and other early Christian literature on the Jews, in which Christianity was portrayed as "spiritual," and heresy, including Judaism, was seen as "of the flesh." Augustine developed an image of the Jews around two figures of the Hebrew Scriptures: Cain and Ham. Cain, in killing his brother, was condemned to wander the earth, but through his supplication to God, was granted protection.[18] Ham, the son of Noah, was cursed for revealing his father's nakedness to his brothers; the curse, however, was for him to become the servant of his brothers.[19] These two figures were key to Augustine's unique presentation of the role of the Jewish people after the life of Jesus. Both provide examples of punishment for transgressions that do not lead to annihilation, but rather to permanently diminished status. Like Cain and Ham, for Augustine, the Jews were marked with a permanently diminished status, because of their failure to recognize in Jesus of Nazareth the prophesied Messiah.

6. *Book-bearers.* Jews' service to Christians, in Augustine's mature vision, was found in their preservation of the Scriptures. Augustine's profound insight was that the continued presence of the Jews after the life of Jesus allowed Christians even greater proof of the veracity of their claims of the Messianic status of Jesus: "Therefore, when they do not believe our Scriptures, their own, which they blindly read, are fulfilled in them, lest perchance any one should say that the Christians have forged these prophecies about Christ which are quoted under the name of the sibyl, or of others, if such there be, who do not belong to the Jewish people."[20] For Augustine, the presence of the Jewish people everywhere there were Christians was a fulfillment of the words of Psalm 59:10–11, which in the Septuagint translation mentions that God "shall not slay" the psalmist's enemies, but rather shall "disperse them" in His might. Their role, then, was to continue to witness the truth that the prophecies of the Scriptures were fulfilled in Christ; they

---

16. The Manicheans were a sect that departed from orthodox Christianity, especially in its radically dualistic vision of the world. Founded in Persia in the third century C.E. by its prophet, Mani (Augustine always refers to him as *Manichaeus*), the religion is synchronistic of many religions of its day. The division between "flesh" and "spirit" is typical of its radical dualism which, for Augustine, became the catalyst for his unique theological interpretation of the Jews. For an English translation, see Saint Augustine of Hippo, *Contra Faustum Manichaeum, in* Augustine: The writings Against the Manichaeans and Against the Donatists 191–482, 400 (Philip Schaff ed., Richard Stothert trans., 1887).

17. *Id.* Composed around the year 400 C.E.

18. *See* Genesis 4, 8–16.

19. *See Id.* at 9:20–27.

20. Augustine, *De Civitate Dei*, Book XVIII, ch. 46.

had not been "superseded" or supplanted by Christians; rather, they remained in God's protection, like Cain, but must serve their "brothers," like Ham.

7. *From theological definition to legislation.* One important development in Augustine's theology that comes to define legislation regarding the exercise of rights afforded to the Jewish people under Imperial and ecclesiastical legislation, stems from his interpretation of Psalm 59, mentioned above. Augustine read in those words an obligation on the part of Christians to protect the Jewish people: "Why of the Jews, Slay not them, lest sometimes they forget Your law? Those very enemies of mine, that have slain me, do not Thou slay. Let the nation of the Jews remain."[21] Rather than find a total prohibition against Jewish property ownership, or other limitations one might expect to find were the supercessionist theory to have totally prevailed, Augustine's explanation of the Jewish people as continually giving witness to the truth of Jesus provided them with a unique, but not unencumbered, status in the law.[22]

The Catholic Church's Legal System and the Pope's Legal Role

1. *The Catholic legal system.* Unlike many other religious groups, the Catholic Church has a legal system with elements recognizable to students of civil law: it is a highly structured system of local courts, with stable judges, prosecutors, and notaries to adjudicate local disputes. At the time of Innocent IV, those courts would have held mixed jurisdiction with local, civil courts. In fact, the Magna Carta offers evidence of some attempts to curtail the use of ecclesiastical courts in favor of state-sponsored courts.[23] Certain basic legal concepts (court records, appeal courts, etc.), after the fall of the western Roman empire, redeveloped first in the Catholic Church, and only later in civil jurisdictions.

2. *The Roman Catholic Church.* The connection between the Catholic Church and the Roman Empire greatly influenced the Church's own legal system. Similarly, especially in the codes of the Emperor Theodosian, Catholic theology also greatly influenced civil law. Once the Roman Empire declared Christianity to be the official religion in 380 C.E.,[24] the form of Christianity that became the official religion was that which followed the teachings of the Council of Nicaea (325 C.E.).[25] Major theological

21. Augustine, *Exposition on Psalm 59*, pt. 1.

22. Kenneth Stow argues convincingly that these restrictions are best viewed from the perspective of "citizenship." That is, in Christian Europe, drawing its legal history from late Roman imperial law, Jews were not understood to have the same status of "citizen" as Christians. *See* Kenneth Stow, *The Catholic Church and the Jews, in* The Cambridge History of Judaism 15–29 (Jonathan Karp & Adam Sutcliffe eds., 2017).

23. For an examination of the Catholic Church and the Magna Carta, see Richard H. Helmholz, *The Church and Magna Carta*, 25 Wm. & Mary Bill Rts. J. 425 (2016).

24. For more on Cunctos Populos, *see* Robert L. Wilken, *The Jews and Christian Apologetics After Theodosius I Cunctos Populos*, 73 Harv. Theological Rev. 451 (1980).

25. The first ecumenical council of Christianity was held in Nicea in the year 325 C.E. Beyond settling the major theological issues of the day, it also created the first universally binding legislation

points became the subject of Imperial legislation; the nexus between the state and Christianity was such that the internal legislation of the Church became a source for civil legislation. Regarding the legal status of the Jews, however, there was no official Church teaching underlying the civil legislation. Rather, what was seen were more ad hoc decisions by the emperors, which came not from an official Church teaching, but from the application of a generalized theological interpretation of the continued presence of the Jews, often drawing from the theology of St. Augustine.

3. *Restrictions* and *rights*. For example, one of the provisions regarding the Jews found in the Theodosian Code dates to 315 C.E. In a letter to a Christian bishop, the Emperor Constantine stated that any Jew who dared to intimidate or attack a Jewish convert to Christianity would be "handed over to the flames."[26] While there was some relationship to the Christian understanding of the indelibility of baptism that loosely grounded this law, it was more of a practical disposition than a theological one. At the same time, the Theodosian Code noted that the Jews had legitimate rights and privileges, unlike heretical Christian sects that were outlawed. It was this balance of restrictions and rights found in Roman Imperial Law that came to serve as the legal foundation for papal decisions like *Lachrymabilem*.

Nearly two centuries after Theodosius II issued the first codified version of Roman law, the Emperor Justinian edited and updated more than three million lines of text, creating the *Corpus Iuris Civilis*.[27] Together with the composition of the Talmud, these two texts represent the greatest legal undertakings of antiquity. The *Corpus Iuris Civilis* was not merely a compilation: many laws were excluded from this text as being outdated or irrelevant; however, the laws pertaining to the rights and restrictions placed on the Jews were maintained, and new legislation was introduced in Justinian's *Novellae*.

4. *What did these restrictions and rights look like?* Jews were forbidden to construct new synagogues, but were permitted to repair old ones.[28] Jews were forbidden from proselytizing Christians,[29] but were protected from forced proselytism by Christians.[30] Intermarriage between Christians and Jews was forbidden,[31] yet it was illegal to "lay hands, under the pretense of religion, on Jews... who live in peace and attempt nothing tumultuous or contrary to the laws."[32] Interestingly, this prohibition had an entirely religious motivation: it was unchristian to do so. This raises the question of whether

---

for all Christians. This council served as a model for future legislative efforts, especially up to the split between Catholic and Orthodox Christianity, which is commonly referred to as the "Great Schism," in 1054 C.E. *See* Richard Mayne, *East and West in 1054*, 11 Cambridge Hist. J. 133 (1954); *see also* Jonathan Harris, *The "Schism" of 1054 and the First Crusade*, 13 Crusades 1 (2014); *see also* Brett Whalen, *Rethinking the Schism of 1054: Authority, Heresy, and the Latin Rite*, 62 Traditio 1 (2007).

26. *See* Code Theod. 16.8.1.pr.

27. *See* Frederick W. Dingledy, *The Corpus Juris Civilis; A Guide to Its History and Use*, 35 Legal Reference Serv. Q. 231 (2016).

28. Nov. 146.8 (553).

29. Code Just., 1.9.16 (Justinian I 527).

30. *Id.* at 1.12.2.

31. Code Theod. 3.7.2, 9.7.5.

32. *Id.* at 16.10.24.

blood libel, or other historical false charges against the Jews, can effectively be legislated against. How effectively does law shape the community?

One peculiar piece of legislation comes from the year 408 C.E., when Jews were enjoined against burning images of the cross during the festival of Purim;[33] at the same time, the law reminded the reader that the Jews were free to worship according to their own faith, but without "contempt for Christian law." The same law also speaks of the "privileges" (rights) the Jews had under the law.[34] This law is contained in a letter from the co-emperors to Anthemius, the praetorian prefect of the Eastern Roman Empire. Was it true that Jews were burning images of the cross during their celebration of the festival of Purim? Or did this law respond to a false narrative that indicated bias against the Jews? While the origin of the law is lost to history, it speaks to the fact that legalized prejudice against the Jews existed much earlier than the "blood libel" accusations of the Middle Ages.

5. *Successor to St. Peter.* While Roman imperial authority declined in the West, papal authority increased, as did the legal dimension of the papacy. The Bishop of Rome, seen as the successor of St. Peter, who was the head of Jesus's twelve apostles, came to be understood as being the ultimate, but not unlimited, authority of Christianity. The pope's authority was not mediated, but direct; he had the authority to intervene in any situation either referred to him or which he called to himself. While each local ecclesiastical authority (bishop) had complete administrative, legislative, and judicial authority within his own territory, the pope's authority superseded that of the local bishop.

6. *Court of last resort.* Over the centuries, legal disputes and theological questions were referred to the pope for definitive responses. The responses often took the form of a bull like *Lachrymabilem*. The pope's legal role invested him with both full legislative and judiciary authority. Many of the fundamental elements of the pope's legal role came to be best expressed in a medieval series of twenty-seven principles that were collectively known as the *Dictatus papae*.[35] Among the ideas expressed therein, two are particularly relevant: a sentence passed by the pope could not be altered by anyone; and no one who appealed to the pope could be condemned.[36] So, the Jews who appealed to the pope for a response were seeking legal protection from the highest judicial authority; in doing so, they demonstrated an understanding of the legal system of the Catholic Church.

7. *The supreme court.* The legal authority of the pope, however, was tied directly to his legislative authority. This is still true today. Where modern political structures include a separation of powers as a system of checks and balances, the Catholic Church is a community based on theological principles that necessitate an ultimate arbiter.

---

33. *See* Book of Esther 8.

34. *Id.* at 16.8.18.

35. *See* Gilchrust JT, *Canon Law Aspects of the Eleventh Century Gregorian Reform Programme*, 13 J. Ecclesiastical Hist. 21 (1962).

36. Dictatus Papae (1075) (*Quod sententia illius a nullo debeat retractari et ipse omnium solus retractare possit* (XVIII). *Quo nullus audeat condemnare apostolicam sedem apellantem* (XX)).

Therefore, the pope is vested with supreme administrative, legislative, and judicial authority. As supreme judge, he is the ultimate arbiter of the law, which he, or his predecessors, have written. The legal response provided by Pope Innocent IV, then, was not based solely on the facts of the situation, but also on a read of the governing law. The law cited in *Lachrymabilem* had its origins in the Roman imperial legislation discussed above and was developed by other popes before Alexander IV. Therefore, the bull served as an application of existing law, which was then enriched for the future by its application molded to this particular context.

8. *A lawful religion.* The most concise formulation of the legal principle for treatment of the Jews came from Pope Gregory I in 598 C.E.: "Even as it is not allowed to the Jews in their assemblies presumptuously to undertake for themselves more than that which is permitted them by law, even so they ought not to suffer any disadvantage in those [privileges] which have been granted to them." This expression hints at the protections guaranteed to the Jews under Roman imperial law, the greatest of which is recognition as a religion (*religio lecita*) rather than as a heretical form of Christianity, which were not allowed to have any public expression.[37] Those protections, while enshrined in the law, were obviously not always enforced by local authorities.

9. *Interpretation and innovation.* While the pope was often interpreting the law in his decisions, he also had the authority to modify it. One such modification in favor of the Jews took place in 1272 C.E. This change relates directly to the legal rights of Jews in the court system. As early as 419 C.E., legislation had existed that prohibited Jews from testifying against Christians in court.[38] This legislation was included in the *Corpus Iuris Civilis*.[39] During the Middle Ages, however, the concept of a trial by one's peers developed, and the pope recognized the incongruence between the standard of law and this ancient prohibition's impact which would, in effect, necessitate that a Jew accused of a crime would never actually have a trial of his peers. Therefore, Pope Gregory X, in 1272 C.E., decreed that "the testimony of Christians against Jews shall not be

37. *E.g.*, Corpus Iuris Civilis 1.5.3. ("Emperors Arcadius and Honorius to Clearchus, City Prefect. All heretics must take notice that they are without question to be deprived of all places, whether held under the name of churches, *diaconia* or ecclesiastical prisons or private houses where opportunity for their meeting is furnished. All these buildings or private structures are to be claimed for the Catholic Church.")

38. Synod of Carthage Canon 129 (419 C.E.). ("To all it seemed good that no slaves or freedmen, properly so called, be admitted to accusation nor any of those who by the public laws are debarred from bringing accusation in criminal proceedings. This also is the case with all those who have the stain of infamy, that is actors, and persons subject to turpitudes, also heretics, or heathen, or Jews but even all those to whom the right of bringing accusation is denied, are not forbidden to bring accusation in their own suits.")

39. Corpus Iuris Civilis 1.5.11 ("As many judges requiring Our advice have consulted Us as to the disposal of litigation, in order that they may be advised what to decide with reference to heretic witnesses, and whether their testimony should be accepted or rejected, We order that no testimony shall be given against orthodox litigants by a heretic, or by those who adhere to the Jewish superstition, whether one, or both parties to the suit are orthodox. We grant permission to heretics or Jews, when they have litigation with one another, to introduce witnesses qualified to testify . . .").

valid unless there is among these Christians some Jew who is there for the purpose of offering testimony."[40]

10. *Blood libel republished.* When local authorities failed to respect the governing law, Jewish communities made recourse to the supreme judicial authority, the pope. Despite the authoritative nature of the responses given by the popes, history shows that the problem of the "blood libel" accusation persists. What is new in *Lachrymabilem*, however, is the fact that the pope responds with a legal document to a situation he recognizes is not actually a question of law. Rather, Pope Innocent IV frames the question as one of greed. This provides one possible explanation for why accusations of "blood libel" persist, despite the repeated condemnations by various popes. Evidence from the very first case of "blood libel" suggests this is the most common motivation, making the accusation more about monetary gain than theology. Nevertheless, the imperial legislation being applied and interpreted by popes in their various judicial responses to inquiry from Jewish communities has theological underpinnings. While the economic motives are documented by historians, the role of Christian theology in such accusations requires further explanation.

Medieval Christian Theology and Jews

1. *Who killed Jesus?* One of the persisting theological accusations against the Jews was that of "deicide": the Jews were responsible for the death of Jesus of Nazareth, the Son of God. One of the most important Christian scriptural passages for this charge is Matthew 27:25. The Gospel of Matthew recounts that the chief priests and elders of the Jewish community bound Jesus and handed him over to Pilate, the Roman governor of Judea, for judgment. Pilate questioned Jesus, who refused to answer. In accord with a custom that had developed in honor of Pesach—that a prisoner would be granted his freedom—Pilate asked the crowd gathered if they wanted him to free Jesus, rather than Barabbas, a murderer who, according to the Gospel of Mark, had participated in an insurrection against the Romans.[41] In the Gospel of Matthew, Pilate recognized Jesus's innocence and the fact that he had been handed over "out of envy."[42] When the crowd agitated all the more for Barabbas's release, Pilate washed his hands and declared of Jesus, "I am innocent of this man's blood. Look to it yourselves."[43] Then, the crowd responded with one of the most problematic phrases in the Christian scriptures in terms of Jewish-Christian relations: "His blood will be upon us and upon our children."[44] This passage provides a theological foundation for those who would claim that "the Jews" killed Jesus and bear collective, generational guilt for his death.

---

40. Gregory X, *Sicut Judaeis* (1272 C.E.).
41. *See Mark* 15:6–7.
42. *Matthew* 27:18.
43. *Id.* at 27:24.
44. *Id.* at 27:25.

2. *Early commentary*. Such language presents itself very early on in Christian works. In a second century dialogue by Justin Martyr,[45] he engaged a Jew named Typho, and exchanged various opinions about the Scriptures and the law. Justin laid this accusation on Typho and the Jewish people:

> For other nations have not inflicted on us and on Christ this wrong to such an extent as you have, who in very deed are the authors of the wicked prejudice against the Just One, and us who hold by Him. For after that you had crucified Him, the only blameless and righteous Man, through whose swipes those who approach the Father by Him are healed, when you knew that He had risen from the dead and ascended to heaven, as the prophets foretold He would, you not only did not repent of the wickedness which you had committed, but at that time you selected and sent out from Jerusalem chosen men through all the land to tell that the godless heresy of the Christians had sprung up, and to publish those things which all they who knew us not speak against us. So that you are the cause not only of your own unrighteousness, but in fact of that of all other men.[46]

Here, the implication of Matthew 27:25 was expressed: it was the Jewish people of all generations who crucified Jesus of Nazareth.

3. *The poet of deicide*. Melito of Sardis,[47] a Christian bishop of the early fourth century C.E., further developed this theme in several of his homilies dedicated to the Christian feast of Pesach (Easter). It must be noted that, in this time, no official Christian doctrine had yet been formulated, beyond what was found in the Scriptures; that would only begin to occur in the year 325 C.E., with the first of what were known as the "ecumenical" councils, gatherings of bishops from around the known world to discuss, debate, and determine official Christian doctrine.[48] Many questions of practice were still debated and Melito belonged to a theological camp known as Quatrodecimans, those who commemorated the death of Jesus on the fourteenth day of the Jewish month of *Nisan*. This practice was contrary to that used in Rome and, therefore, subject to criticism as being "too Jewish." While much of Melito's apparent antisemitism can be contextualized by critiques against his position on the celebration of the Christian feast of Easter, he was the first recognized Christian author who expressly brought the charge of "deicide" against the Jews. Melito wrote:

---

45. Justin Martyr was born around the year 100 C.E., and converted to Christianity around the year 130 C.E. He is known for his two *apologia* and an extant dialogue with a Jew named Trypho. He is recognized as one of the "fathers" of the Church, a leading intellectual figure in the Christian tradition. *See* L.W. Barnard, Justin Martyr: His Life and Thought (1967).

46. Justin Martyr, Dialogue with Typho, ch. XVII (160).

47. For more on Melito of Sardis, see Alistair C. Stewart, Melito of Sardis: On Pascha (St. Vladimir's Seminary Press ed., 2016).

48. *E.g.*, the first of these councils was convoked by the Emperor Constantine and took place in the city of Nicea; one of its official statements is the first "creed," a summary of Christian doctrine, known as the "Nicene Creed" and still recited in worship services, not only in the Catholic Church, but among other Christian denominations. *See Nicene Creed*, Britannica, https://www.britannica.com/topic/Nicene-Creed (last updated Dec. 6, 2024).

> Why, O Israel did you do this strange injustice? You dishonored the one who had honored you. You held in contempt the one who held you in esteem. You denied the one who publicly acknowledged you. You renounced the one who proclaimed you his own. You killed the one who made you to live. Why did you do this, O Israel?... It was necessary for him to suffer, yes, but not by you; it was necessary for him to be dishonored, but not by you; it was necessary for him to be judged, but not by you; it was necessary for him to be crucified, but not by you, nor by your right hand.... This is the one who came to you, the one who healed your suffering ones and who resurrected your dead.... This is the one whom you sinned against. This is the one whom you wronged. This is the one whom you killed. The one who hung the earth in space, is himself hanged; the one who fixed the heavens in place, is himself impaled; the one who firmly fixed all things, is himself firmly fixed to the tree. The Lord is insulted, God has been murdered, the King of Israel has been destroyed by the right hand of Israel.[49]

4. *Lingering effects*. Pope Gregory the Great (d. 604 C.E.) was the first great Western Christian figure of the Middle Ages. During his thirteen years as pope, Gregory addressed the subject of Jews and their communities in more than two dozen letters.[50] For example, in March 591 C.E., a Jewish man complained to Gregory that the Bishop of Terracina (35 miles south of Rome) had expelled the community from its synagogue on multiple occasions. Gregory, in response, admonished the bishop and corrected him: "If such is the case, we wish that your fraternity restrain himself from contention of this sort and that, as we have stated, the place which they acquired with your knowledge for their gatherings be allowed them for their meetings just as was the custom."[51] Yet, at the same time, Gregory's theological position followed that of Augustine, with added urgency that the Jews be converted to Christianity, though through sound preaching and good practice, abhorring the notion of forced conversion.

Much later, writing after the First Crusade, Bernard of Clairvaux (1090–1153 C.E.), one of the most influential Christian writers of the Middle Ages, continued the Augustinian view of the Jews as living witnesses to the truth of the Scriptures. However, Bernard developed his thought on the Jews in various ways. Rabbi Efraim of Bonn recorded Bernard's defense of the Jews against the violence of crusaders: "The Lord heard our outcry, and he turned to us and had pity upon us. In his great mercy and grace, he sent a decent priest, one honored and respected by all the clergy in France, named Abbot Bernard, of Clairvaux in France, to deal with this evil person. Bernard... said to them: It is good that you go against the Ishmaelites. But whosoever touches a Jew to take his life, is like one who harms Jesus himself... for in the book of Psalms it is

49. Melito of Sardis, Homily on the Passover 73, 76, 86, 96 (100).

50. *See* Jeremy Cohen, Living Letters of the Law: Ideas of the Jew in Medieval Christianity 73–94 (1999).

51. *Id.* at 75.

written of them, 'Slay them not, lest my people forget.'"[52] Bernard's unique contribution came from his interpretation of the Jews in light of the scriptural text, *Song of Songs*.

At the beginning of that text, in the Latin Vulgate translation, one reads: *oleum effusum nomen tuum*, "Your name is oil poured out." In explaining this phrase, Bernard spoke of the sin of ingratitude, found particularly among hypocrites; he used the Gospel reference to the Pharisees as a model of such hypocrisy. Bernard developed this metaphor over the course of several homilies, contrasting the synagogue (the Jews) with the Church (the Christians); while individuals of both groups could demonstrate hypocrisy, "whereas the Synagogue, as we have said, grumbles and recalls its own merits ..., the Church remembers his kindness."[53] This remembrance of God's kindness was the Christian response of gratitude, in place of the hypocrisy of the Jews. This response, however, was that of the Church perfected, not of those here on earth. This contrasted with the response of the Jews, who found satisfaction in the material gifts given to them in the land flowing with milk and honey (Exodus 3:8).[54]

Other figures, like Thomas Aquinas, addressed more practical concerns. In 1271 C.E., in response to questions posed to him by Margaret of Flanders about how a ruler should treat Jews living in his/her territory, Thomas composed what is often referred to as his "Letter on the treatment of the Jews."[55] In this letter he responded to eight questions posed, all of which regarded not theological, but practical, matters. Aquinas used the Scriptures, both Christian and Jewish, to formulate his responses, not because he understood the questions to have theological implications, per se, but because he held the Scriptures to be an authoritative source. For example, the eighth question regarded the imposition upon the Jews of distinctive clothing. Aquinas responded that it was appropriate for Jews of both sexes to be required to wear distinctive clothing; in his response, he made reference to a legal text issued by the Fourth Lateran Council, an important legislative effort of the Catholic Church in the year 1215 C.E. However, Thomas also noted, importantly, "this is mandated them by their own law, namely that they make for themselves fringes on the four corners of their cloaks, through which they are distinguished from others."[56]

The Fourth Lateran Council made different legislative provisions regarding the Jews in Christian society. Beyond the imposition of distinctive dress, which the Council recognized "was enjoined upon them [the Jews] by Moses, himself,"[57] it also addressed the topic of usury:

---

52. *See* A. Neubauer and M. Stern, Hebraische Berichte uber die Judenverfolgungen wahrend der Kreuzzuge, Quellen der Geschichte der Juden in Deutschland 2, 59, 221(Jeremy Cohen trans., Berlin, 1892).

53. Cohen, *supra* note 50, at 227.

54. *Id.* at 229.

55. For a comprehensive overview of Thomas of Aquinas's thoughts on the Jews, see John Y.B. Hood, Aquinas and the Jews (1995).

56. Thomas Aquinas, Letter to Margaret of Flanders (The Sacra Doctrina Projects ed., trans., accessed Sept. 16, 2024) (1271), https://thomistica.net/letter-to-margaret-of-flanders.

57. Fourth Lateran Council Canon 68 (1215).

> The more the Christian religion is restrained from usurious practices, so much the more does the perfidy of the Jews grow in these matters, so that within a short time they are exhausting the resources of Christians. Wishing therefore to see that Christians are not savagely oppressed by Jews in this matter, we ordain by this synodal decree that if Jews in future, on any pretext, extort oppressive and *excessive* interest from Christians, then they are to be removed from contact with Christians until they have made adequate satisfaction for the immoderate burden. Christians too, if need be, shall be compelled by ecclesiastical censure, without the possibility of an appeal, to abstain from commerce with them. We enjoin upon princes not to be hostile to Christians on this account, but rather to be zealous in restraining Jews from so great oppression. We decree, under the same penalty, that Jews shall be compelled to make satisfaction to churches for tithes and offerings due to the churches, which the churches were accustomed to receive from Christians for houses and other possessions, before they passed by whatever title to the Jews, so that the churches may thus be preserved from loss.[58]

The notion of the Jews as "blasphemers" also led to a prohibition against holding public office, repeating what had earlier been legislated in a local council in Toledo (633 C.E.): "It would be too absurd for a blasphemer of Christ to exercise power over Christians. We therefore renew in this canon, on account of the boldness of the offenders, what the council of Toledo providently decreed in this matter: we forbid Jews to be appointed to public offices, since under cover of them they are very hostile to Christians."[59] This conflation of theological and practical considerations became common in the Middle Ages, as was already seen in the earliest accusations of "blood libel."

5. *The greater guilt*. The charge of "deicide" lingered in Christian language for centuries. While never the official teaching of the Catholic Church, the notion of collective Jewish guilt for Jesus's death perdured within the Christian community. The Council of Trent (1545–1563 C.E.), which was convoked in the wake of the Protestant Reformation, took up the matter expressly. In the year 1566, a catechism—an explanation of the fundamental elements of the faith—was published by the Catholic Church; as it followed the Council of Trent and synthesized its teachings, it is often referred to as the "Catechism of the Council of Trent."[60] The document was directed toward pastors, as an effort to ensure that they were offering to the faithful an authentic presentation of the Catholic faith, in light of the rise of various strains of Protestant theology. In commenting on a line from the creed speaking about Jesus's suffering and death, the Catechism addressed the reasons he suffered.

58. *Id.* at Canon 67.

59. *Id.* at Canon 69.

60. It is also referred to as the "Roman Catechism" and the "Catechism of Pius V." The Catechism of the Council of Trent 3 (John A. McHugh et al. trans., 1923) (1566), https://www.saintsbooks.net/books/The%20Roman%20Catechism.pdf.

> The reasons why the Savior suffered are also to be explained, that thus the greatness and intensity of the divine love towards us may the more fully appear. Should anyone inquire why the Son of God underwent His most bitter Passion, he will find that besides the guilt inherited from our first parents the principal causes were the vices and crimes which have been perpetrated from the beginning of the world to the present day and those which will be committed to the end of time.... Besides, to increase the dignity of this mystery, Christ not only suffered for sinners, but even for those who were the very authors and ministers of all the torments He endured. Of this the Apostle reminds us in these words addressed to the Hebrews: Think diligently upon him that endured such opposition from sinners against himself; that you be not wearied, fainting in your minds. In this guilt are involved all those who fall frequently into sin; for, as our sins consigned Christ the Lord to the death of the cross, most certainly those who wallow in sin and iniquity crucify to themselves again the Son of God, as far as in them lies, and make a mockery of Him. This guilt seems more enormous in us than in the Jews, since according to the testimony of the same Apostle: If they had known it, they would never have crucified the Lord of glory; while we, on the contrary, professing to know Him, yet denying Him by our actions, seem in some sort to lay violent hands on him.[61]

While the Catechism did not directly address the question of deicide, it clearly indicated that the cause of Jesus's death was not limited to the people of his own day. Rather, the principal causes were "the vices and crimes" of all humanity, "perpetrated from the beginning of the world to the present day and those which will be committed to the end of time." The Jews alone were not responsible for Jesus's death, nor did they bear the greater guilt. That, according to the Catechism—the "more enormous" guilt—belonged to Christians who continued to sin, "making a mockery" of Jesus.

6. *Miserable and accursed people.* While the Catholic Church was offering this teaching tool to its pastors, Martin Luther was offering different advice to his followers. Early in his ministry, as one would expect from someone steeped in the Augustinian tradition, Luther was sympathetic to the Jews. In an essay written in 1523, Luther states the following:

> If the apostles, who also were Jews, had dealt with us Gentiles as we Gentiles deal with the Jews, there would never have been a Christian among the Gentiles.... When we are inclined to boast of our position [as Christians] we should remember that we are but Gentiles, while the Jews are of the lineage of Christ. We are aliens and in-laws; they are blood relatives, cousins, and brothers of our Lord.... If some of them should prove stiff-necked, what of it? After all, we ourselves are not all good Christians either.[62]

---

61. The Catholic Church, The Catechism of the council of trent 55–56 (Theodore Alouis Buckley ed., trans., 1852) (1566).

62. Martin Luther, *That Jesus Christ Was Born a Jew, in* Martin Luther, The Bible, and the Jewish People: A reader 77–83 (Brooks Schramm and Kirsi I. Stjerna eds., trans., 2012) (1523).

His attitude changed over time, as is best on display in his work of 1543, *On the Jews and Their Lies*. This sixty-five-thousand-word pamphlet was published after Luther's protector, John Frederick (1503–1554), elector of Saxony, had issued a mandate prohibiting Jews from engaging in business in the realm (which included the areas of Dresden, Leipzig, and Chemnitz) and from residing within the territory. Luther developed many antisemitic themes in the pamphlet: Jews believed their status as "chosen of God" made them superior and that all non-Jews were like cattle, intended to be slaves; Jews mocked the Ten Commandments; Jews blasphemed Jesus in their synagogues, calling him a "bastard"; they regarded Mary, Jesus's mother, as a "whore" who committed adultery with a smith; Jewish schools were "the Devil's nest"; the Jews had been possessed by the Devil and his angels; the Jews were the most avaricious people in history. Luther stated directly to his reader: "Therefore, dear Christian, be advised and do not doubt that next to the devil, you have no more bitter, venomous, and vehement foe than a real Jew who earnestly seeks to be a Jew."[63] Among their "sins," Luther also cited accusations of "blood libel," though he did not assert the truth of this, or other historical accusations against the Jews.

Luther then prescribed seven courses of action his reader should take. First, synagogues and Jewish schools were to be avoided and others were to be warned against the Jews. Second, Jews should not be allowed to own homes. Third, their books of prayer and copies of the Talmud should be confiscated. Fourth, rabbis should be prohibited from teaching. Fifth, all protection of Jews traveling should be revoked, as "they have no right to be in the land." Sixth, they should be prohibited from practicing usury; it is noteworthy that, of Luther's resolutions, this was the longest and most developed. Seventh, the Jews should be forced into labor, rather than make money through usury.

B. A Missed Opportunity to Debunk the Blood Libel

Beginning in the middle of the seventeenth century, frequent accusations of "blood libel" began to be raised against the Jewish community in Poland. One of the most notorious cases was in Sandomir (in 1698 C.E.), where a Christian woman threw the dead body of her illegitimate child into the yard of an elder of the local Jewish community, to implicate him in the child's death. While exonerated in the first trial, a second one was convoked in the highest court of the land, in Lublin, where the Jewish elder was convicted and sentenced to death. In 1712 C.E., in the aftermath of the trial, the king expelled the Jewish community from Sandomir.[64] After many other such trials, in 1758 C.E., the Jewish communities of Poland sent Jacob Zelig (Selek) as an emissary to

63. Martin Luther, On the Jews and Their Lies 47 (Martin H. Bertram, trans., 2009) (1543).

64. For a thorough history of this and other cases in Poland and Russia, see Simon M. Dubnow, History of the Jews in Russia and Poland, From the Earliest Times Until the Present Day (Israel Friedlaender trans., 2001) (1916).

Rome, to plead with Pope Benedict XIV to issue a bull forbidding the false accusations of "blood libel" against the local Jewish community.

Cardinal Lorenzo Ganganelli, who later became Pope Clement XIV, was a consultor of the Supreme Sacred Congregation of the Roman and Universal Inquisition ("the Holy Office"), the department of the Vatican's central administrative office (a.k.a., curia) founded in 1542 C.E. as a tribunal responsible for adjudicating questions of faith and morals. When Pope Benedict XIV received Zelig's request, he commissioned the Holy Office to investigate the matter and inform him of the veracity of the claims. Ganganelli produced the following report in response.

The text, which was consigned to the Holy Office in late 1759 C.E., is a thorough examination of the history of "blood libel" claims, focusing only in part on the contemporary situation in Poland. It was an internal document of the Holy Office and was not published. The Jews of Poland had hoped that some public statement might be issued, as they knew had been done by other popes in the past.

Two important considerations mark this document as a missed opportunity on the part of the Church. First, given the clear and thorough examination of the history of "blood libel" accusations throughout history, and the near total condemnation of those accusations as spurious, the document offered a well-reasoned rebuttal to any who would believe the accusation to be true. Second, the examination of the situation in Poland in the eighteenth century by Ganganelli could have led to a strong condemnation of the antisemitism of the day. The failure to offer a public response to the supplication of the Jewish community in Poland must be considered a missed opportunity on the part of the Church to offer a clear, comprehensive, and authoritative condemnation of antisemitism, as it had in the past.

While never officially made public, a copy of the text appears to have been in the possession of the Jewish community in Rome; a German translation of this version was published in 1888 by Abraham Berliner.[65]

In 1911, a notorious case of "blood libel" was prosecuted in Kiev. Mendel Bellis, a Jew employed at a local brick-making kiln, was put on trial for the death of a Christian child, whose body had been found near the kiln. In his legal defense, copies of Ganganelli's report and other documents of the Catholic Church were put forward; their authenticity was challenged by a Catholic theologian, Justinus Pranaitis. Lord Nathanial Mayer Rothschild wrote to the Cardinal Secretary of State,[66] seeking to authenticate Ganganelli's report. Only eleven days after Rothschild's request, Cardinal Merry del Val wrote back to Rothschild, confirming its authenticity. While not determinative of the outcome of Bellis's trial, this letter confirms that the extant copies of Ganganelli's report accurately reflect his work.

---

65. *See*, Cecil Roth, The Ritual Murder Libel and the Jew: The Report by Cardinal Lorenzo Ganganelli (Pope Clement XV) (1935).

66. The Vatican's equivalent of the U.S. Department of State.

Cardinal Lorenzo Ganganelli,[67] *Report of Cardinal Ganganelli*

January 10, 1760 C.E.

Not only those who accuse should be believed.

In the year 1758, there was presented to Benedict XIV of glorious memory, by Jacob Selek, a Jew, of Polish nationality, a petition in which he implored from the Pontifical Beneficence an opportune defense against the vexations, imprisonments, extortions, torments, and death to which his unhappy co-nationals were so often subjected on the pretext that when they manufactured their well-known Unleavened Bread they mingled it with human blood, and especially that of Christians. To such an extent has this been the case that, for the past ten years, if the corpse of any Christian were found by chance, murder was immediately suspected, and it was moreover soon believed to have been committed by the Jews of that neighborhood for the above-mentioned superstitious purpose....

But let us leave aside the attempt to indicate unwelcome characteristics peculiar to individual nations, since in some of them we should find vampires and ghosts, whence would follow an open censure of this kind of preconception. I will confine myself simply to pointing out the grave peril which is brought about for many innocent people, should they be judged by anyone who is under the influence of such prejudices.... When the passion of hatred is manifest, it is wrong to imagine that any Judge would let himself be led astray; but when the hatred is concealed under a cloak of zeal, and above all religious zeal, then the judge must exercise all caution that he may avoid being taken by malice unawares.... May God guard me from simply suspecting that the two Polish Bishops and the Apostolic Nuncio wished to conceal the truth by artifice, or that they sent fraudulent information here. It is possible, however, that they may have been not deceivers but deceived....

In the Papal States also, in Viterbo to be precise, on June 13th, 1705, the Jews (we are told) tried to commit a similar act of barbarity against a Christian boy, and in Ancona, in the year 1711, they were accused of having bled and killed a Christian boy.... Now if this crime is imputed to the Jews by so many nations, in nearly every period and place (even where they are subjected to strict control), if it is imputed to them moreover by so many writers, with evident proofs, it is possible for everyone to see on what a basis of truth the information from Poland on this subject must rest....

---

67. Born in Rimini, Italy, on October 31, 1705, Giovanni Vincenzo Antonio Ganganelli joined the Order of Friars Minor Conventual (Franciscans) in 1723 and took as his new name in religious life, Lorenzo. He received a doctorate in theology in Rome, taught for two decades in various theological faculties around Italy and, in 1759, was named a cardinal. This was the year after Ganganelli had been commissioned by the Holy Office of the Roman and Universal Inquisition to investigate the claims of the Jewish community in Poland that they were being persecuted for false accusations of blood libel. *See* Louis-Antoine Carccioli, The Life of Pope Clement XIV (J. Johnson & J.P. Coglhan trans. 1776). Ganganelli's report was read before the pope on Jan. 10, 1760.

So that if Innocent IV[68] accepted the petitions of the Jews of Germany, and defended them from this false imputation, charging the Christian Prelates and Potentates to protect them, it seems that common-sense requires that the Holy See should now take into consideration the defense of the Jews of Poland from whatever injury has come upon them through the above-mentioned false imputation....

In order to give the lie to these most impudent calumniators, it is enough to remember that Gregory IX, in the year 1235, issued an Encyclical "To faithful Christians," and the following year wrote to all the Bishops of France, and that both of the letters were in justification of the Jews in the matter of this same crime which is imputed to them by Poland, or by certain people of that Kingdom. We should reflect also on the Constitution of the Supreme Pontiff Innocent III, *Licet perfidia Judaeorum*, which may be read in Volume I of his letters (letter 300, p. 540). In this we shall see how many other Roman Pontiffs have undertaken to protect this unhappy people. "Although they may wish rather to remain in their stubbornness than to know the prophecies of the Prophets and the secrets of the Law, and to arrive at the knowledge of the Christian faith (says Innocent there); nevertheless, because they demand the help of Our protection and because Christian piety is merciful; We therefore, treading in the footsteps of Our predecessors of happy memory, the Roman Pontiffs, Callixtus, Eugenius, Alexander, Clement and Celestinus, accept their petition and grant them the shield of our protection." However much the Jews may be reproved for their contumacy and obstinacy, yet we never read that they have been reproved by the Holy See for the crime imputed to them in Poland. On the contrary, they have been positively cleared of such an imputation by Gregory IX and Innocent IV; and they were protected with great clemency by Innocent III, following the example of so many of his Predecessors. This would never have happened had they really been guilty of the supposed atrocious crime....

In Verona, then, a certain Jew named Joseph was defended by a celebrated Christian advocate, against the charge on which he had been accused that "he had cruelly killed a child, in order that he might make a mock of the most Holy Death of our Saviour, and put innocent blood to most wicked and nefarious uses, which, as the Prosecutor has attempted to prove, by certain records of circumforaneous history, has been done at other times." However, the said Jew, Joseph, was defended by the Christian advocate from the aforesaid accusation (which is the same as that brought forward in Poland), was declared innocent and, as such, was released. I think, however, that it is necessary to report literally the sentence of acquittal pronounced on February 28th 1603:

> The said Joseph, through his most excellent advocate, as well as in his own legitimate defense, has argued and indeed demonstrated, by bringing forward various passages of the Holy Bible, that the Hebraic rite abhors the shedding of blood. He has indicated moreover that various Princes held this rumor of the use of blood to be "vain and false" and have issued special ordinances to

68. Editor's note: Ganganelli includes his own translation of *Lachryimabilem Iudaeorum* in the report. *See* Ganganelli, *supra* note 65.

> that effect: namely [the Regent] Bona [of Savoy] and Gian Galeazzo Sforza [her son], Dukes of Milan, as appears under the date May 19th, 1479;[1] Pietro Mocenigo, Doge of Venice, dated April 22nd, 1475; and lastly the Emperors Frederick III, Charles V, and Maximilian II, dated March 8th, 1566, in which it is affirmed that in the past the Supreme Pontiffs have forbidden men to believe the accusation of the alleged impious abuse of Christian blood. In consequence of all this, suspicion of such impious wickedness on their part is removed. On this account, the most Illustrious Lord Podestà (at that time Giustiniano Contarino), together with the most Excellent Consulate, has released the aforesaid Joseph.

Wherefore I observe that not only Giulio Morosini, but also D. Paulo Sebastiano Medici, another neophyte from Judaism, personally known by me, put forth various accusations against the Jews. The Jews of Rome printed and published a full vindication against the same, to which this Medici could not reply. At the end of the last century there was issued to the public light from the press of Abraham of Worth a book entitled *An Admonition of Great Profit*. The anonymous author therein makes it evident that it is an utter imposture that the Jews go in search of Christian blood, in order to make superstitious use of it and to knead their Unleavened Bread. He quotes many texts from the Old Testament, various oracles of the supreme Pontiffs, and copious testimonies from well-known writers. . . .

It should then be concluded that, among so many infanticides imputed by writers to the Jews in hatred of our Holy Faith, only two can be said to be true, since these two only can be said to be proved by authentic proofs after much diligent search and a considerable lapse of time. When, therefore, I come to consider the reports from Poland individually, I shall show in a clear light how meagre, doubtful, and uncertain are the proofs adduced of the pretended imputations. Indeed, I wonder whether it may not be reasonably suspected that the whole is an imposture of Christians against the Jews! . . .

I was obliged to make all these observations on the detailed information that came from Poland, because these are supported, as will now be seen, on the basis of pretended facts. These have already been made to disappear and confuted on the authority of historians. Hence, the aforesaid reports in particular ought not, in my opinion, to cause any harm to the Jews.

By order of this supreme tribunal, Msgr. the Nuncio of Poland obtained reports concerning the petition of Jacob Selek the Jew, of Polish nationality, only from the Bishops of Lutzk and Kiev, which are given in the annexed summary, under the letters A, B, and C. With due respect, I will make the necessary observations on the same. In the information of the Bishop of Lutzk (headed B) we read as follows: "We may understand most plainly how many and how great proofs of cruelty towards Christian blood have been given in this kingdom (i.e., Poland) by the perfidious Jewish nation, not only from histories printed all over the world, but also from the judgments in cases of infanticide pronounced before various diocesan courts and also by the executions on the persons of the unfaithful (it is this which gives just offence) that followed in virtue of them from the year 1400 to the present time."

One gathers from the preface to this report that those prejudices about and against which I have reasoned in my first section (comprising "Reflections" upon the reports in general) exist in the mind of Mgr. the Bishop of Lutzk, and that the aforesaid report relies on those same principles on which were fabricated the accusations against the Jews of Germany, France, Venice, Padua, Verona, Viterbo, and Ancona. Therefore, if the Supreme Pontiffs Gregory IX and Innocent IV judged such accusations to be baseless (as I have clearly shown), and if the Jews were declared innocent in the other tribunals of Italy, I cannot see how they can be considered guilty of such a crime in Poland alone....

Now let us discuss these proofs and consider their importance. Who can think it possible that the Jews of Poland, if they had murdered a Christian who was in their service, would afterwards want to leave the body of the dead man displayed to public view, and not bury it safely in a deep and dark grave? For the Jews of Poland know, and know by very painful experience, that a mere suspicion of homicide is enough to make them considered, and sentenced, as guilty!...

But what would the Treasurer of Lutzk say if it were proved that such a monstrous crime has sometimes been (God forbid that it should be always!) committed by Christians—even by the father himself!—and then imputed to the unhappy Jews? I blush at suspecting it, but I am much more embarrassed at producing the authentic record of it marked "D.1." Here, we read that a Christian father mutilated a tender daughter of his in several places with mortal wounds, and, wrapping her in cloths, abandoned her in the manger of a stable in an inn, kept (according to the custom of Poland) by Jews. Here we read that this little girl, surviving by the Divine Will, confessed out of her own mouth that she had been ill-treated, with so many wounds and mutilations, by her own father. Yet suspicion had already been formed against the Jews and it was already desired to proceed against them!... I will only add that we Christians ought to remember that this stain of infanticide and of homicide was imputed against our religion by the Pagans in the first centuries....

From that which has been concluded up to this point, it may be realized with what lively faith we ought to ask God with the Psalmist, "Deliver me from the calumnies of men." For it cannot be denied that "Calumny maketh the wise man mad, and destroyeth the strength of his heart," as Ecclesiastes says (8:7).

I therefore hope that the Holy See will take some measure to protect the Jews of Poland, as St. Bernard, Gregory IX, and Innocent IV did for the Jews of Germany and of France, "that the name of Christ be not blasphemed" by the Jews and, moreover, that their conversion may not become more difficult. I do not venture, however, to put forward any project to liberate these unfortunates from such ill usage, hoping that Jesus Christ will suggest to his Vicar such means as shall be honorable to the Christian name and conducive to the conversion of those unhappy ones.

Cardinal Ganganelli's Unpublished Report Was Exculpatory

1. *Not only those.* Ganganelli begins his report with a telling citation. Taken from the work of an early Christian historian, Theodoret,[69] the citation sets the tone for Ganganelli's primary argument: the repetition of accusations over time, in different places, does not make them truer. Later, he identifies the key to accusations of "blood libel" as residing in a generalized prejudice against Jews, one that necessarily leads to unjust decisions.

2. *The grave peril.* In a style typical of the day, Ganganelli does not immediately address the specific question which gave rise to his report but, rather, places it into a larger context. The foundation of this larger context is the conviction that "the strength of preconception results in a readiness to persuade oneself of the truth of everything that is consistent with it, and at the same time the difficulty in believing the opposite." Ganganelli quickly identifies the accusation of "blood libel" as an expression of prejudice against the Jews; he also astutely points out that such a pervasive prejudice renders justice almost impossible. He cites various examples from both Christian and non-Christian sources: from Seneca's *de Ira*, offering advice warning princes against the tendency to believe the false over the true, to embarrassing examples of fraud perpetrated by Christian leaders by taking advantage of the piety of others.

3. *Under a cloak of zeal.* Ganganelli also identifies the primary reason that accusations of "blood libel" are so convincing, while being not only false but obviously manufactured. No judge would allow himself to be prejudiced against the truth by something obvious. However, were that prejudice masked as something else, such as religious zeal, it would be difficult for a judge to distinguish prejudice from faith, leading to the kinds of unjust decisions Ganganelli documents throughout his report.

4. *Not deceivers but deceived.* The report is composed based on information sent to Ganganelli through the Apostolic Nuncio.[70] The request was officially made through the Sacred and Supreme Roman and Universal Inquisition, asking that the Nuncio compile information from local authorities where the accusations had been made and then forward it to Rome. However, the information received is deemed suspect. Ganganelli uses this line to hint to his audience—the Cardinal members of the Holy Office, who must make recommendations to the pope based on their evaluation of this report—that he does not fully believe the information he has been provided by the

69. Theodoret of Cyrrhus (died c. 458 C.E.) was a theologian and historian of the early Christian Church, especially its monastic tradition. For more about Theodoret of Cyrrhus, see Theresa Urbainczyk, Theodoret of Cyrrhus: The Bishop and the Holy Man (2002). This quote is taken from Theodoret of Cyrrhus, The Ecclesiastical History bk. 1, ch. 31.

70. "Nuncio" is the title given to an official, stable representative of the pope in a particular country. The function is both that of ambassador from the Holy See to that country and representative of the pope among the local Catholic community. *See Nuncio*, Britannica, https://www.britannica.com/topic/nuncio (last visited Jan. 1, 2025).

local ecclesiastical authorities. The implication is that the local authorities have fallen prey to the prejudices about which Ganganelli has already warned his reader.

5. *Most impudent calumniators.* After offering a sample of historical examples of "blood libel" accusations in other places in different eras, Ganganelli names those who would perpetuate these allegations as calumniators. While this may appear to be a random word choice, Ganganelli, as a professor of theology, is well aware of the implications of this word to his audience. From the Latin root, *calvor* (to use artifice; to deceive), calumny is recognized in Catholic moral theology as a particularly grave sin. It is a specific form of lying, in that it is directly aimed to diminish the good name (*bona fama*) of a person, specifically by imputing to him/her a crime or fault of which the speaker knows the person is not guilty. He cites examples from past interventions of popes in defense of Jewish communities throughout Europe as proof that the accusation of "blood libel" has been recognized by the highest moral authority (the pope) to be nothing more than calumny. For Ganganelli, as he states, "such could not have been possible had they been guilty" of this crime.

6. *A Jew named Joseph.* In support of his claim that (almost) all such accusations are not only false but sinful, Ganganelli offers an argument from a secular court. In Verona in 1603, a member of the local Jewish community named Joseph was accused of murdering a young Christian boy. As in prior accusations, the murder was allegedly in order to obtain the young boy's blood, which would then have been put to "wicked and nefarious uses." With the help of a Christian advocate (lawyer), and through citations of the Hebrew Scriptures, the conclusions of secular rulers and the determinations of popes, Joseph was declared innocent of the accusation. This particular example goes directly to the heart of Ganganelli's supposition: if the accusation of "blood libel" is examined in an unbiased manner, innocence can be the only honest conclusion. That the civil court of Verona can arrive at this proper conclusion based on evidence that is universally available and not directly specific to this case also argues that other courts, including the one in Poland, could, and should, have come to the same, correct conclusion.

7. *Personally known by me.* Ganganelli introduces a peculiar, personal element into his report. This is not entirely unheard of, but given the scope of his original assignment, it is very telling that this anecdote is included. As noted above, much of the report is an effort to provide what Ganganelli deemed necessary to place the current question into its broader, historical context. Here, however, the author inserts a personal experience. He is aware of a Jewish convert to Christianity, a certain Paolo Sebastiano Medici, who published a series of (false) accusations against the Jews, to which the local Roman Jewish community published a response. Ganganelli notes that Medici could not rebut the rebuttal of his false claims. This episode appears to be included to reinforce Ganganelli's point that it is not uncommon for Jewish converts to Christianity to raise false accusations against the faith they formerly professed. This further supports Ganganelli's supposition that much of the falsehood behind these, and other, accusations against the Jews is motivated by a misguided expression of religious zeal.

8. *Only two can be said to be true*. Of all the episodes of supposed "blood libel" known to and examined by Ganganelli, he states that "only two *can be said* to be true" for the sole reason that the Church allowed these two children to be venerated as "blood libel" saints. One of these two is Simon of Trent, killed in 1475 C.E.[71] While noting that these two examples are considered authentic, Ganganelli includes significant criticism of Simon's sainthood, including the fact that the pope at the time of Simon's death, Sixtus IV, forbade any public devotion to Simon. (This ban was not lifted until 1588.) The second true-enough accusation is that of Andreas of Brixen, who was killed in 1462. In Andreas's case, no public devotion was allowed until 1753. What causes Ganganelli to speak of these particular accusations as "true" is the Church's apparent official recognition of these two children as saints. For him, such a determination could not be based on a falsehood. The truth adequacy of these accusations is founded on what he describes as "authentic proofs after much diligent search and a considerable lapse of time." In this way, Ganganelli casts doubt on the veracity of the claims made against the Jews in Poland, as these accusations bear none of those hallmarks.

9. *With due respect*. In turning his attention to the accusations that give rise to the report, Ganganelli cites the documentation provided by the Bishop of Lutzk, allowing the reader to notice the contrast between Ganganelli's arguments for setting aside prejudice and the words of the bishop:

> We may understand most plainly how many and how great proofs of cruelty towards Christian blood have been given in this kingdom (i.e., Poland) by the perfidious Jewish nation, not only from histories printed all over the world, but also from the judgments in cases of infanticide pronounced before various diocesan courts and also by the executions on the persons ... that followed in virtue of them from the year 1400 to the present time.

In the opening words of his report, the Bishop of Lutzk makes all of the errors, factual and argumentative, against which Ganganelli has warned his reader. It should be clear to the modern reader, as it must have been to his contemporaries, that Ganganelli offers an implicit, and not subtle, criticism of the work of the Bishop of Lutzk, having already demonstrated the falsehood of historical claims upon which the Bishop of Lutzk wishes to assert the truth of the current accusations against the Jews.

> Then, too, it seems that Mgr. the Bishop of Lutzk has shown himself too prone to believe what cannot be true.... If then in Spain, where they dwelt so long and were so wealthy, the Jews were never accused of such a crime, how can it be credible that when they had scarcely arrived in Poland, they at once began the epoch of infanticide and homicide?

The various examples of Jewish violence against Christians in Poland proffered by the Bishop of Lutzk are dismissed by Ganganelli.

10. *Such a monstrous crime*. The murder of a child is, indeed, a monstrous crime. For Ganganelli, however, the true nature of the crimes being examined are not moti-

---

71. *See* R. Po-chia Hsia, Trent 1475: Stories of a Ritual Murder Trial (1992).

vated by religion and their "monstrous" nature comes from the fact that the attempted infanticide was perpetrated by the father. As he notes, however, "suspicion had already been formed against the Jews" such that not even the testimony of the young girl who survived the attempted infanticide implicating her father was sufficient to prevent the Jewish community from becoming a scapegoat for the crime.

11. *Take some measure to protect the Jews.* Ganganelli does not offer a particular remedy. Rather, he urges the pope to be guided in prayer to find a resolution that both honors the Christian faith and is conducive to the conversation of the Jews. In this, the report echoes the concerns already expressed in earlier theological and legal documents. Protection of the Jewish community is incumbent upon the pope not only because it honors the truth by putting an end to calumnies—which is necessary in any just society—but also because, presumably, it makes their conversion to Christianity more likely.

12. *An "unpublished" report.* It may seem an obvious question to the modern reader to ask why, if the report was so condemnatory of the local ecclesiastical authorities' prejudice against the Jewish community, and did such an eloquent job of situating those false claims within the larger narrative of anti-Jewish attitudes across Europe from the first known accusation of blood libel in 1144 to 1758 C.E. when the report was composed, why it was never published by the Church? The answer is found in the nature of the report. It was never intended to be a public document. The commissioning of a consultor to examine a particular matter and report back to a particular office of the Catholic Church's curia is a regular occurrence. What is extraordinary, however, is that despite this, the local Jewish community in Rome somehow obtained and maintained a copy of the report. The same is apparently the case for other Jewish communities in Italy. Those copies—which in a certain way represent a violation of the confidentiality normally imposed in such matters—are the reason that later scholars became aware of its existence. Had this report followed the course of so many others, it would have lingered in the archives of the Holy Office, at least until the day some scholar happened upon it.

The Report in the Context of Catholic-Jewish Relations of the Day

1. *Little Simon.* While the Middle Ages saw successive popes frequently renew calls for adherence to the legal protections afforded to Jews, what followed was a more complicated relationship. Papal condemnations of accusations of "blood libel" waned. Combined with this apparent silence on the part of the Catholic Church was the notorious case of the "blood libel" accusation in Trent, in 1475 C.E. A young boy known as "little Simon" disappeared in the spring of that year; he was just over two-years old, and his disappearance immediately became a *cause célèbre.* In the background was the work of a Franciscan priest, a renowned preacher in the area, Bernard of Feltre. Bernard and a handful of other notable Franciscan priests were the primary promoters of a new organization known as *monte di pietá* ("mount of piety"), which were intended

as a charity and functioned like a modern-day credit union. This was part of Bernard's work against usury, the charging of high interest rates on loans. For Christians at the time, the understanding of usury included charging any interest on a loan; therefore, control of what is now considered traditional banking fell to the Jewish communities across Europe.

It is easy to imagine that Bernard's preaching against usury contained a high level of antisemitism. In fact, Bernard "predicted" in 1475 C.E. that a Christian child would be abducted and murdered by a Jew at the next Passover. Little Simon disappeared on March 23, 1475. A thorough search of the Jewish quarter of Trent, ordered by the local ecclesiastical authority but executed by the civil authority, failed to reveal Simon's body. Rather, on the day after Easter (26 March 1475), a group of Jewish men found the body of Simon by the river; they immediately went to notify the local bishop, who refused to see them. They then contacted the local civil authority who came to the house, retrieved the body, and arrested those present.

2. *Worse than silence.* Pope Paul III issued the bull, *Cum nimis absurdum* (Since it is absurd)[72] in July 1555, establishing the Jewish ghetto in Rome, and imposing other sanctions on the entire Jewish population of the territory that was controlled by the pope as its civil leader.[73] While some of these sanctions were merely repetitions of previous legislation,[74] others, like the establishment of the ghetto, were entirely new. Scholars differ in opinion as to whether these sanctions were merely punitive, designed to encourage mass conversion to Christianity, or reflective of the attitude of the Catholic Church toward any non-Catholic faith in the time of the Protestant reformation.[75] Regardless of the motive, it is clear that greater restrictions were being imposed on Jews in the sixteenth century, and not only in parts of Italy. The language of *Cum nimis absurdum* reiterates that Jews did not, and could not pretend to, enjoy full citizenship.

3. *A quo primum.* In the year 1751 C.E., Pope Benedict XIV issued a bull, titled *A quo primum*, to the bishops of Poland, on the topic of Jews and Christians living in the same place. This document contains a clear bias against the Jews in Poland. The faithfulness of the Jews to their religion is called a "threat" to the Catholic community, likened to the "various sexts [that] have attempted to establish themselves in Poland and to spread the seeds of their errors, heresies and evil opinions."

72. *See* Pope Paul IV, *Cum Nimis Absurdum* (1555), https://ccjr.us/dialogika-resources/primary-texts-from-the-history-of-the-relationship/paul-iv.

73. Serena di Nepi, Surviving the Ghetto: Toward a Social History of the Jewish Community in 16th-Century Rome (Paul M. Rosenberg trans. 2020).

74. *E.g.*, Fourth Lateran Council Canon 68 (1215). The canons of the Fourth Lateran Council (1215 C.E.) had already included a provision that Jews and Muslims should be required to wear some kind of distinctive dress, such that they would be immediately recognizable as non-Christians.

75. *See, e.g.*, David Berger, *Cum Nimis Absurdum and the Conversion of the Jews*, 70 Jewish Q. Rev. 41 (1979); Kenneth Stow, *The Proper Meaning of "Cum Nimis Absurdum,"* 71 Jewish Q. Rev. 251 (1981).

C. Vatican II: "What Happened in His Passion Cannot Be Charged Against All the Jews"

October 28, 1965

Like the previous text, the one proposed here, *Nostra aetate* ("In our day"), is not expressly legal. However, as the teachings of the Second Vatican Council are the authoritative expression of Catholic belief, the document *Nostra aetate* expresses not only the current teaching of the Church on its relationship to Judaism and Jews, but also, in part, the Catholic Church's understanding of religious liberty, which directly impacts subsequent internal legislation and the role of the Holy See as an actor in international law. It must be noted that Jewish voices played a significant role in the development of this document; Cardinal Augustin Bea, who was tasked with the drafting and coordination of what would eventually become *Nostra aetate*, was a noted Hebrew bible scholar and was very familiar with the work of Jewish intellectuals. As early as 1960, he was in dialogue with scholars like Rabbi Abraham Joshua Heschel.[76] These dialogues, and the continued interaction with Jewish scholars throughout the drafting, played an influential role in the shaping of the final text.

Second Vatican Council, convened by St. Pope John XXIII, Nostra aetate *("In our times")*[77]

Declaration on the Relation of the Church with Non-Christian Religions

1. In our time, when day by day mankind is being drawn closer together, and the ties between different peoples are becoming stronger, the Church examines more closely her relationship to non-Christian religions. In her task of promoting unity and love among men, indeed among nations, she considers above all in this declaration what men have in common and what draws them to fellowship. One is the community of all peoples, one their origin, for God made the whole human race to live over the face of the earth. One also is their final goal, God. His providence, His manifestations of goodness, His saving design extend to all men, until that time when the elect will be united in the Holy City, the city ablaze with the glory of God, where the nations will walk in His light.

76. *See* Julian E. Zelizer, Abraham Joshua Heschel—a Life of Radical Amazement (2021).

77. *Nostra aetate* is the declaration of the Second Vatican Council on the relationship between Catholicism and non-Christian religions. The Second Vatican Council contained various forms of authoritative teachings, including documents known as dogmatic constitutions (*Lumen Gentium*, "on the Church," and *Dei verbum*, "on divine revelation"), pastoral constitutions, decrees, and declarations. While declarations are the least authoritative form of document published by the Council, they are still binding expressions of the teachings of the Catholic Church. For the official text of *Nostra aetate*, see 58 *Acta Apostolciae Sedis* 740–44 (1966).

Figure 14.1. St. Pope John XXIII (1959) (public domain).

Figure 14.2. Rabbi Abraham Joshua Heschel meeting in New York on March 31, 1963, with Cardinal Augustin Bea, who shepherded the process of Catholic introspection that led to *Nostra aetate*. Rabbi Heschel is seen showing Cardinal Bea an issue of *Die Jüdische Presse*, a pre-Holocaust Orthodox German-language publication. Photo courtesy of American Jewish Committee.

Men expect from the various religions answers to the unsolved riddles of the human condition, which today, even as in former times, deeply stir the hearts of men: What is man? What is the meaning, the aim of our life? What is moral good, what is sin? Whence suffering and what purpose does it serve? Which is the road to true happiness? What are death, judgment and retribution after death? What, finally, is that ultimate inexpressible mystery which encompasses our existence: whence do we come, and where are we going?

2. From ancient times down to the present, there is found among various peoples a certain perception of that hidden power which hovers over the course of things and over the events of human history; at times some indeed have come to the recognition of a Supreme Being, or even of a Father. This perception and recognition penetrates their lives with a profound religious sense....

4. As the sacred synod searches into the mystery of the Church, it remembers the bond that spiritually ties the people of the New Covenant to Abraham's stock. Thus the Church of Christ acknowledges that, according to God's saving design, the beginnings of her faith and her election are found already among the patriarchs, Moses, and the prophets. She professes that all who believe in Christ—Abraham's sons according to faith—are included in the same Patriarch's call, and likewise that the salvation of the Church is mysteriously foreshadowed by the chosen people's exodus from the land of bondage. The Church, therefore, cannot forget that she received the revelation of the Old Testament through the people with whom God in His inexpressible mercy concluded the Ancient Covenant. Nor can she forget that she draws sustenance from the root of that well-cultivated olive tree onto which have been grafted the wild shoots, the Gentiles. Indeed, the Church believes that by His cross Christ, Our Peace, reconciled Jews and Gentiles, making both one in Himself.

The Church keeps ever in mind the words of the Apostle about his kinsmen: "Theirs is the sonship and the glory and the covenants and the law and the worship and the promises; theirs are the fathers and from them is the Christ according to the flesh" (Rom. 9:4–5), the Son of the Virgin Mary. She also recalls that the Apostles, the Church's mainstay and pillars, as well as most of the early disciples who proclaimed Christ's Gospel to the world, sprang from the Jewish people. As Holy Scripture testifies, Jerusalem did not recognize the time of her visitation, nor did the Jews in large number, accept the Gospel; indeed not a few opposed its spreading. Nevertheless, God holds the Jews most dear for the sake of their Fathers; He does not repent of the gifts He makes or of the calls He issues—such is the witness of the Apostle. In company with the Prophets and the same Apostle, the Church awaits that day, known to God alone, on which all peoples will address the Lord in a single voice and "serve him shoulder to shoulder" (Soph. 3:9).

Since the spiritual patrimony common to Christians and Jews is thus so great, this sacred synod wants to foster and recommend that mutual understanding and respect which is the fruit, above all, of biblical and theological studies as well as of fraternal dialogues. True, the Jewish authorities and those who followed their lead pressed for the death of Christ; still, what happened in His passion cannot be charged against all the Jews, without distinction, then alive, nor against the Jews of today. Although the Church is the new people of God, the Jews should not be presented as rejected or accursed by God, as if this followed from the Holy Scriptures. All should see to it, then, that in catechetical work or in the preaching of the word of God they do not teach anything that does not conform to the truth of the Gospel and the spirit of Christ.

Furthermore, in her rejection of every persecution against any man, the Church, mindful of the patrimony she shares with the Jews and moved not by political reasons but by the Gospel's spiritual love, decries hatred, persecutions, displays of anti-Semitism, directed against Jews at any time and by anyone. Besides, as the Church has always held and holds now, Christ underwent His passion and death freely, because of the sins of men and out of infinite love, in order that all may reach salvation. It is, therefore, the burden of the Church's preaching to proclaim the cross of Christ as the sign of God's all-embracing love and as the fountain from which every grace flows.

5. We cannot truly call on God, the Father of all, if we refuse to treat in a brotherly way any man, created as he is in the image of God. Man's relation to God the Father and his relation to men his brothers are so linked together that Scripture says: "He who does not love does not know God" (1 John 4:8). No foundation therefore remains for any theory or practice that leads to discrimination between man and man or people and people, so far as their human dignity and the rights flowing from it are concerned.

The Church reproves, as foreign to the mind of Christ, any discrimination against men or harassment of them because of their race, color, condition of life, or religion. On the contrary, following in the footsteps of the holy Apostles Peter and Paul, this sacred synod ardently implores the Christian faithful to "maintain good fellowship among the nations" (1 Peter 2:12), and, if possible, to live for their part in peace with all men, so that they may truly be sons of the Father who is in heaven.

Mutual Understanding and Respect

1. *In our times.* The document makes explicit reference to its historical context, which must be taken into consideration. Published in 1965 as part of the process of *aggiornamento* (updating) of the presentation of the Catholic Church's teachings, as called for by Pope John XXIII, *Nostra aetate* is not unique in seeking to re-present the teachings of the Church to the modern world. However, it is noteworthy that in perhaps its most important feature, the total condemnation of any and all forms of antisemitism, it expressly states that it is not motivated to do so by "political reasons but by the Gospel's spiritual love." Given the temporal proximity to the Shoah, the Fathers[78] of the Council wisely left this marker in the text, lest future generations find

78. In speaking about the bishops and cardinals who had deliberative vote at the Second Vatican Council, it is common to refer to them with the generic term "Fathers." *See, e.g.*, *Second Vatican Council*, Britannica, https://www.britannica.com/event/Second-Vatican-Council (last updated Nov. 15, 2024). This distinguishes them from the *periti*, experts, whose opinions were vital in shaping

in it a specifically politically motivated rebuke of the horrors perpetrated during the Second World War.

2. *A profound religious sense.* The goal of the document is to express the Catholic Church's self-understanding of its relationship to religious traditions that do not accept Jesus Christ as the Son of God. In doing so, the context is set as broadly as possible, relating to the "religious sense" that the Church believes is inherent in all men and women, of all cultures and times. The Council wishes to speak of the human experience of the "other," a notion of a Supreme Being. From this broad, universal context, the document will turn its attention to specific religions.

3. *Abraham's stock.* This section of the document begins a radical theological shift away from Augustine's image of the Jews as "bearers of the book": credible witnesses for the Messianic status of Jesus of Nazareth, in as much as they continue to hold as unfulfilled the prophecies which Christians believed were fulfilled in his life. For more than 1500 years of Christian theology, the rejection of the overwhelming majority of Jesus's Jewish contemporaries of his claims to be the Son of God was often considered to have merited for the Jewish people a punishment, as noted earlier. *Nostra aetate* utterly rejects this claim and affirms the authenticity and enduring nature of God's relationship to the Jewish people. This is the first authoritative teaching of the Catholic Church that builds on St. Paul's image of the olive tree (cf. Rom 11:24), totally rejecting all notions of supersessionism.

4. *Mutual understanding and respect.* The document puts forward a path to continue to build the kind of mutual respect that had been lacking for nearly two millennia. Through academic studies of the sacred texts held in common, Christians and Jews can begin an authentically fraternal dialogue. Here, the text turns toward its most profound theological statement. While acknowledging the historical fact that some leaders of the Jewish community, as recorded in the Gospels and in other historical texts, played some role in the death of Jesus, no blanket charge can be laid at the feet of the Jewish people—not all those alive at the time of Jesus, and certainly not those alive afterwards. While Christians still hold that it is theologically correct to speak of a "new people of God," such does not imply a rejection by God of his chosen people, Israel. Rather, as noted above, the image of the "wild branch" (the Gentiles) grafted onto the olive tree (the people of Israel) itself comes from sacred scriptures; Christianity has always held that the death and resurrection of Jesus reconciled heaven and earth and eliminated distinctions among the peoples of the earth. The Council Fathers are painfully aware that Christian practice and teaching has not always lived up to the truth revealed in sacred scripture. Therefore, this utter rejection of any claim of a collective Jewish responsibility for the death of Jesus, while representing a milestone in authoritative Catholic teaching, does nothing more than reflect the truth that Christians should have always held.

---

the expressions used in the Council's documents. *See An Overview of the Second Vatican Council*, Vatican News (Oct. 11, 2022, 10:01 AM), https://www.vaticannews.va/en/vatican-city/news/2022-10/vatican-ii-council-60th-anniversary-video-history-background.html.

5. *In catechetical work.* While there are many fascinating points in the drafting history of the document,[79] few are as striking as this point. Where the final version includes a generic statement that all catechetical materials should avoid teaching anything contrary to authentic doctrine—a mere truism—the penultimate draft, shared on November 18, 1964,[80] contained much stronger language: "May all, then, see to it that in their catechetical work or in their preaching of the word of God they do not teach anything that could give rise to hatred or contempt of Jews in the hearts of Christians. May they never present the Jewish people as one rejected, cursed, or guilty of deicide."[81] While it is true that the current language necessarily includes the same prohibitions, the prior phraseology more adequately addressed the exact inaccurate teachings that fueled the rhetoric of the blood libel accusations of prior centuries.

6. *Moved not by political reasons.* It is tempting to read the theological content of this section of *Nostra aetate* with secular eyes, and see the condemnation of prior, unauthoritative but popular Christian teaching about the collective responsibility for Jesus's death as nothing more than a political statement against the horrors of the Shoah. While it cannot be denied that those horrors were alive in the minds of the drafters of the document, a political reading of the document would be reductionist and would evacuate this milestone of its true significance. What is contained in these lines is the total rejection not only of bad teaching, but of the centuries of bad practice that led to the persecution of the Jewish people, particularly in the Christian west. The document condemns all forms of persecution but mentions antisemitism by name. Failure to decry persecution of the Jews because of their religious beliefs, the document holds, is against the Gospel; antisemitism is contrary to Christianity, itself. The Catholic Church expressly acknowledges that a good follower of Jesus cannot accuse the Jewish people collectively of the death of Christ; a good Christian also cannot fail to decry the persecution of the Jews.

Internal Changes to the Catholic Church

1. Angelo Giuseppe Roncalli was elected pope on October 28, 1958, taking the name John XXIII. His service in the Vatican diplomatic corps during World War II provided him with a particular preparation that would, in part, be key to the thought expressed in *Nostra aetate*. While serving in the diplomatic corps, Roncalli provided thousands of falsified baptismal certificates to distribute to Jews, in order to protect them from deportation and certain extermination. He has been credited with saving tens of thousands of Jews. Chaim Barlas served as head of the Jewish Rescue Committee in Turkey at the same time Roncalli was the papal representative in that country; years after

79. For a complete drafting history, see *Nostra Aetate Drafts*, Council of Ctrs. on Jewish-Christian Rels., https://ccjr.us/dialogika-resources/documents-and-statements/roman-catholic/second-vatican-council/na-drafts#ges:searchword%3Dnostra%2Baetate%26searchphrase%3Dall%26page%3D1 (last visited Jan. 1, 2025).

80. *Id.*

81. *Id.*

Roncalli's death, Barlas stated: "Much blood and ink have been spilled in the Jewish tragedy of those years, but to the few heroic deeds which were performed to rescue Jews belong the activities of the Apostolic Delegate, Monsignor Roncalli, who worked indefatigably on their behalf."[82] During his first Good Friday[83] services as pope, in 1959, John XXIII spontaneously changed the liturgy, removing an expression that, to modern ears, rang as a condemnation of the Jews. Cardinal Augustin Bea, the Hebrew bible scholar to whom Roncalli entrusted the drafting of the document that would become *Nostra aetate*, later recalled:

> It is and will remain John XXIII's great merit that he realized this touchy problem and understood its great significance. It was he, who with great personal conviction removed from the liturgy of Good Friday, the expression *pro perfidis Judaeis*,[84] source of much misunderstanding. Going further, he gave personal approval to the task of preparing for the Council an appropriate draft. When, in one of his more decisive moments about this question, I had given him my opinion on such a draft, I received, a few days later, a precious note, written in his own hand, in which he stated, "I have read with great attention Cardinal Bea's report, and I agree perfectly about the gravity and responsibility of our approach." It is, therefore, to John the XXIII to whom we must first be thankful in a large measure, if this draft was presented to the Council.[85]

Roncalli was canonized as Pope St. John XXIII on April 27, 2014.

2. On the same day that *Nostra aetate* was approved (October 28, 1965), an exemplary version of one of the important changes called for in that document was already at work in the Diocese of Trent (Italy). As mentioned earlier, one of the alleged victims of "blood libel" was the young boy known as Simon of Trent. He was venerated as a saint by Catholics in the Diocese of Trent for nearly five hundred years; his was one of the two cases mentioned by Ganganelli to be "true."[86] Based on the work of a historian-priest of the Diocese of Trent, Monsignor Iginio Rogger, the cult of Simon

82. For a brief overview of Roncalli's actions on behalf of Jews during World War II, *see* John Rothman, *An incomparable Pope—John XXIII and the Jews (Extended)*, https://insidethevatican.com/magazine/vatican-watch/incomparable-pope-john-xxiii-jews-long/ (last visited Jan. 1, 2025).

83. The Christian holy day remembering the passion and crucifixion of Jesus.

84. The Roman Catholic liturgical memorial of the crucifixion of Jesus includes a series of petitions, one of which was offered *pro perfidis Iudaeis*, later repeating the expression, *Iudaicam perfidiam*. To the modern ear, the Latin adjective *perfidus* and the noun *perfidia* sound like the modern term "perfidious," meaning "deceitful" or "untrustworthy." In Latin, however, the term's primary meaning is "unfaithful." Pope John XXIII intuited this difficulty and likely saw it as an unnecessary source of confusion, thus having the adjective *perfidis* removed, while leaving the prayer "for the Jewish people" as part of the rite. For an interesting examination of the term, see Henri de Lubac, Medieval Exegesis or the doctoral dissertation of Susan G. Sullivan, *Ancient and Medieval Interpretation of the Complaints of Jeremiah* (2013) (Ph.D. dissertation, Catholic University of America) (on file with the University Libraries, Catholic University of America).

85. *See* Civilita Cattolica, 1964, at II, 219–20.

86. *See* Ganganelli, *supra* note 65.

of Trent was officially suppressed.[87] His historical reconstruction of the case demonstrated that the testimony gathered in the trial of the Jews accused of Simon's murder did not answer the pertinent questions about the case raised by an examination of the evidence,[88] but, rather was the fruit of a kind of antisemitic hysteria. Based on Rogger's work, and that of another historian commissioned by the Archbishop of Trent, Father Willehad Paul Eckert, the Archbishop of Trent sent the matter to the appropriate office of the Vatican curia. In response, in a letter dated May 4, 1965, the office described the appropriate process for the declaration of a saint in the 15th century; it was clear from that response that this process was never completed. While the cult of Simon of Trent was approved, there was never any declaration about his presumptive martyrdom.[89] Therefore, the norm of can. 1284 of the 1917 Code of Canon Law was invoked, which required the archbishop to "prudently remove from public cult relics" whose authenticity was uncertain. As Simon had never been proclaimed by the Vatican as a martyr, and in light of the new historical research that cast serious doubt on the legitimacy of the trial of his alleged murderers, Archbishop Alessandro Gottardi officially ended the cult of Simon of Trent on the same day *Nostra aetate* was approved.[90]

3. While some books on the history of Vatican II[91] have neglected to mention the work of Jewish scholars like Rabbi Heschel, his influence, and that of other Jewish scholars, was key to the work of Cardinal Bea.[92] There can be little doubt that Rabbi Heschel was a fundamental player in the crafting of *Nostra aetate*. According to a letter dated April 14, 1982, and signed by the then-Secretary of the Commission for religious relations with the Jews of the Vatican's Secretariat for Promoting Christian Unity, Rabbi Heschel met with Cardinal Bea on four separate occasions, the first of which was on November 26, 1961, and the subject of their meeting is recorded as being "antisemitism."[93] Three of Heschel's books were sent to Cardinal Bea in February 1962, who acknowledged a "strong common spiritual bond" with Heschel.[94] When a new draft of the

87. For a comprehensive list of Monsignor Rogger's work on the question of Simon of Trent, see Emanuele Curzel (a cura di) & Diego Quaglioni (a cura di), *Gli scritti di Iginio Rogger sul caso del "Simonino," in* Studi trentini. Storia 19–42 (2015).

88. For example, the medical commission that examined Simon's wounds said they were still fresh when his body was discovered on the Monday following Easter. The Jews who offered testimony during the trial stated that the boy was killed on Thursday, because his blood was needed to prepare the *matzot* for Passover. These and other historical inaccuracies were brought to light by Monsignor Rogger, and other historians in the 20th century.

89. Curzel & Quaglioni, *supra* note 87, at 34–35.

90. The official notification was given in 91 Revista Diocesana Tridentina, 1965, at 595–96.

91. *E.g.*, Giuseppe Alberigo, History of Vatican II (1995).

92. For a thoughtful reflection on *Nostra aetate* and the theological thought contained therein, *see* Augustin Bea, The Church and the Jewish People (1966). This work includes important contextual notes on *Nostra aetate*, including Cardinal Bea's addresses to the Council.

93. *See* MS-603: Rabbi Marc H. Tanenbaum Collection, 1945–1992, Series C: Interreligious Activities. 1952–1992, Box 23, Folder 8, Heschel, Abraham Joshua, 1982–1989, undated, https://collections.americanjewisharchives.org/ms/ms0603/ms0603.023.008.pdf.

94. *Id.*; *See also* Eva Fleischner, *Heschel's Significance for Jewish-Christian Relations*, 4 Q. Rev. 76 (1984).

document which maintained the traditional Catholic language hoping for the eventual conversion of Jews to Christianity appeared in newspaper articles, Heschel strongly condemned this language as "spiritual fratricide," noting that "Jews throughout the world will be dismayed by a call from the Vatican to abandon their faith in a generation that witnessed the massacre of six million Jews ... on a continent where the dominant religion was not Islam, Buddhism, or Shintoism."[95] The final version of *Nostra aetate* mentions no call for the conversion of the Jews. As noted by Heschel: "The Schema on the Jews is the first statement of the Church in history—the first Christian discourse dealing with Judaism—which is devoid of any expression of hope for conversion."[96] While the true influence[97] of Heschel will never be fully known, his role was significant enough that his thought was quoted publicly by a pope. Shortly after Heschel's death, Pope Paul VI—with whom Heschel had had a private meeting in 1964—stated in a public audience, "even before we have moved in search of God, God has come in search of us," a quote acknowledged in the official version of that speech to have been taken from the writings of Rabbi Abraham Joshua Heschel.[98]

4. Another important historical note around the drafting of *Nostra aetate* was not only the role of prominent Jewish voices, but also that of one of the most prominent Protestant theologians of the 20th century, Karl Barth.[99] Already in his own seminal work, *Church Dogmatics*, he had tried to re-envision a Protestant understanding of the role of the Jews in salvation history. Far from the antisemitic rhetoric of Martin Luther, Karl Barth was a strong critic of the national socialists in Germany and even published theological criticisms of the movement. In 1939, he wrote:

> He who rejects and persecutes the Jews rejects and persecutes Him who died for the sins of the Jews—and then, and only *thereby* for our sins as well. He who is a radical enemy of the Jews, were he in every other regard an angel of light, shows himself, as such, to be a radical enemy of Jesus Christ. Anti-Semitism is sin against the Holy Ghost. For anti-Semitism means rejection of the *grace* of God.[100]

When it appeared that the drafting of *Nostra aetate* was not going to be as strong as some Jewish advocates had hoped, they sought the intervention of Karl Barth.[101] While it is unclear exactly what can be credited to Barth's interventions, his dialogue with concerned Jewish parties, his contact with Catholic experts at the Council, and

---

95. *Id.*

96. *Id.* at 77.

97. *See* Joshua Furnal, *Abraham Joshua Heschel and* Nostra Aetate: *Shaping the Catholic Reconsideration of Judaism During Vatican II*, 7 Religions 70 (2016), https://www.mdpi.com/2077-1444/7/6/70.

98. *See* Am. Mag., Mar. 10, 1973, at 202.

99. For a short biography of Karl Barth, see Thomas Forsyth Torrance, *Karl Barth*, Britannica, https://www.britannica.com/biography/Karl-Barth (last visited Jan. 1, 2025).

100. Karl Barth, The Church and the Political Problem of Our Day 51 (Charles Scribner's Sons ed., 1st ed. 1939).

101. *See* Daniel Herskowitz, *Karl Barth and Nostra Aetate: New Evidence from the Second Vatican Council*, 72 J. Theological Stud. 843 (2021).

his later (mild) criticisms of the document[102] indicate that he strove to understand and reframe what he considered to be the first, and greatest, schism: that between synagogue and church.

5. On November 23, 1970, the International Catholic-Jewish Liaison Committee (ILC) was created and on the same day, a "memorandum of understanding"[103] was composed, which has guided the work of the committee since that time. The memorandum distinguishes two main areas of focus for the committee: questions of the mutual relationship among Catholics and Jews and questions of common concern to both communities. Notably, the first of the questions concerning mutual relationships concerns "manifestations of antisemitism in various parts of the world."[104] The second also treats the question of antisemitism specifically as addressed in *Nostra aetate* § 4:

> Elimination of antisemitism in all its forms as demanded by the Vatican Declaration *Nostra aetate*, particularly in text-books of religious teaching and history in order to present respectfully Judaism according to its own understanding on all levels of teaching and education. Liturgical and para-liturgical texts and expressions should be examined with a view to avoiding offensive references to or representation of Judaism, without compromising the legitimate differences between the Church and Judaism.[105]

6. While the work of the ILC continues,[106] a few years after its founding, on October 22, 1974, Pope Paul VI instituted the Commission for Religious Relations with the Jews. This commission did not supplant the work of the ILC but rather continued to supplement it, primarily through the drafting of documents. The first two documents drafted by this commission relate specifically to the call given in *Nostra aetate* regarding catechetical teachings and liturgical language within the Catholic Church referencing the Jewish people. On December 1, 1974, a relatively terse document titled, "Guidelines and Suggestions for Implementing the Conciliar Declaration *Nostra aetate* (n.4)"[107] was published. As the title of the document indicates, it takes a practical approach to the questions raised in *Nostra aetate* regarding expressions used in theological and liturgical texts, rather than proposing any theological models itself. It calls for attention to be paid to four main points: dialogue; liturgy; teaching and education; and joint social action. The document is noteworthy for its clear and honest assessment of the situation and its call for dramatic action.

---

102. Found in his commentary on the documents of Vatican II, *Ad limina Apostolorum*.

103. *See A Memorandum of Understanding*, Int'l Catholic-Jewish Liaison Comm., http://www.christianunity.va/content/unitacristiani/en/commissione-per-i-rapporti-religiosi-con-l-ebraismo/ilc---international-catholic-jewish-liaison-committee-/incontri/en25.html.

104. *Id.*

105. *Id.*

106. While the committee originally met on an annual basis, the regularity of the meetings slowed over time. The last recorded meeting and statement were in 2019.

107. *See Guidelines and Suggestions for Implementing the Conciliar Declaration "Nostra Aetate" (n. 4)*, Dicastery for Promoting Christian Unity, http://www.christianunity.va/content/unitacristiani/en/commissione-per-i-rapporti-religiosi-con-l-ebraismo/commissione-per-i-rapporti-religiosi-con-l-ebraismo-crre/documenti-della-commissione/en3.html (last visited Jan. 1, 2025).

7. In the United States, for example, a Secretariat for Catholic-Jewish relations was instituted within the bishops' conference. In 1985, it issued its own "Guidelines for Catholic-Jewish Relations."[108] Among the nine principles established in this document, one speaks directly of striving to understand Judaism through the essential traits by which Jews define themselves, in light of their own religious experience. The document connects such an awareness directly to the experience of the Shoah and the birth of the modern state of Israel.

Mechanisms for Enforcing *Nostra aetate*

1. While *Nostra aetate* is an authoritative declaration on the part of the highest teaching authority of the Catholic Church,[109] it falls into a category of teachings that are not considered to be infallible. However, that is not to say that Catholics are not bound to observe it. Specifically, the law of the Catholic Church holds that even for non-infallible, and in fact non-definitive teachings, there are different levels of adherence prescribed, but even the lowest level *obseqium religiosum intellectus et voluntatis* (Latin: a religious submission of the intellect and will) indicates a deferential stance by the believer to the authority that has given such an authoritative, but non-definitive, teaching.[110] Therefore, while it would not be an act of heresy,[111] denial of such a teaching could have disciplinary consequences.

2. Perhaps the most well-known case of such consequences is that of Bishop Richard Williamson.[112] Formally excommunicated on July 1, 1988, along with three others for being consecrated bishops without having received a mandate from the pope, in violation of can. 1387 CIC,[113] Bishop Williamson is outspoken in his denial of the Shoah. In an effort to reconcile with the bishops excommunicated by Pope John Paul II—a move motivated by internal concerns—on January 21, 2009, Pope Benedict XVI lifted

108. *See Guidelines for Catholic-Jewish Relations,* U.S. Conference of Catholic Bishops, https://www.usccb.org/prayer-and-worship/liturgical-year/lent/guidelines-for-catholic-jewish-relations (last visited Jan. 1, 2025).

109. *See* 1983 Code c.749.

110. *See* 1983 Code cc.748–752. For a more complete discussion of the concept of *obsequium*, see Justin Wachs, Obsequium in the Church: Sacred Tradition, Second Vatican Council, 1983 Code, and Sacred Liturgy (2014).

111. *See* can. 1983 Code c.751 ("Heresy is the obstinate denial or obstinate doubt after the reception of baptism of some truth which is to be believed by divine and Catholic faith. . . .").

112. The case of Bishop Williamson is a complex one, which brings into focus various elements of the life of the Catholic Church, including the declaration of schism and the related sanctions imposed on Archbishop Marcel Lefebvre, and four of his followers, among them Bishop Williamson. For a broader view of the matter from a legal perspective, see the Apostolic letter of John Paul II, *Ecclesia Dei*, July 2, 1988.

113. At the time, the canon was 1382; the text, while moved in the reform of the penal code by Pope Francis in 2021, remained unaltered: "Both the bishop who, without a pontifical mandate, consecrates a person a bishop, and the one who receives the consecration from him, incur a *latae sententiae* excommunication reserved to the Apostolic See."

the excommunication of Bishop Williamson and the others.[114] An external firestorm was set off, because Williamson had repeatedly denied the deliberate killing of Jews by Nazis; the presumption of some was that Pope Benedict XVI (a German national) might somehow be endorsing such a view by lifting the excommunication. Internally, there was a fear expressed by some that the move was an attempt to "turn back time" and undo some of the changes introduced into the life of the Catholic Church in Vatican II. In Benedict's own words:

> A gesture of reconciliation with an ecclesial group engaged in a process of separation thus turned into its very antithesis: an apparent step backwards with regard to all the steps of reconciliation between Christians and Jews taken since the Council—steps which my own work as a theologian had sought from the beginning to take part in and support. That this overlapping of two opposed processes took place and momentarily upset peace between Christians and Jews, as well as peace within the Church, is something which I can only deeply deplore.[115]

Benedict went on to thank "all the more our Jewish friends, who quickly helped to clear up the misunderstanding and to restore the atmosphere of friendship and trust" that had marked Catholic-Jewish relations since Vatican II. Williamson was ordered to retract his comments;[116] he was eventually expelled by the government of Argentina, where he was the head of a seminary. He has never reconciled with the Catholic Church.

3. Later that year, Pope Benedict XVI visited Israel. On May 11, 2009, he visited Yad Vashem Memorial. His speech given there was an unequivocal reaffirmation of the Church's position against all forms of antisemitism, as expressed in *Nostra aetate*. He said:

> "I will give in my house and within my walls a memorial and a name . . . I will give them an everlasting name which shall not be cut off" (Is 56:5). This passage from the Book of the prophet Isaiah furnishes the two simple words which solemnly express the profound significance of this revered place: *yad*—"memorial"; *shem*—"name." I have come to stand in silence before this monument, erected to honor the memory of the millions of Jews killed in the horrific tragedy of the *Shoah*. They lost their lives, but they will never lose their names: these are indelibly etched in the hearts of their loved ones, their surviving fellow prisoners, and all those determined never to allow such an atrocity to disgrace mankind again. . . . As Bishop of Rome and Successor of the Apostle Peter, I reaffirm—like my predecessors—that the Church is commit-

114. The date is given in a later clarification issued by Pope Benedict on March 12, 2009. *See* Benedict XVI, On the Remission of the Excommunication of the Four Bishops Consecrated by Archbishop Lefebvre (Mar. 10, 2009), https://www.ewtn.com/catholicism/library/on-the-remission-of-excommunication-of-the-four-bishops-consecrated-by-archbishop-lefebvre-6910.

115. *Id.*

116. See Vatican Note on Bishop Williamson, Vatican Sec'y of State, Vatican (Feb. 4, 2009), https://www.catholicsforisrael.com/articles/jewish-christian-relations/104-vatican-note-on-bishop-williamson.

ted to praying and working tirelessly to ensure that hatred will never reign in the hearts of men again. The God of Abraham, Isaac and Jacob is the God of peace (cf. Ps 85:9).[117]

D. The Relationship Between the Holy See and the State of Israel

Decades after *Nostra aetate* revolutionized Jewish-Catholic relations, and after decades of diplomatic work, including a pilgrimage to Israel by Pope Paul VI in 1964, the Holy See (the name given to the Catholic Church's operations in the diplomatic sphere) signed a Fundamental Agreement (a.k.a., a concordat) with the State of Israel on December 30, 1993 (16 Tevet 5754). The Fundamental Agreement regularized the relationship between the Catholic Church and the State of Israel and addressed various Church concerns.[118] Because the Fundamental Agreement has never been ratified by the Knesset, there remain many unresolved aspects.

The Fundamental Agreement expressly references Israel's founding document, the Declaration of the Establishment of the State of Israel (Declaration), issued on May 14, 1948 (5 Iyar, 5708). The Declaration provides essential context for the Fundamental Agreement and enables a fuller understanding of the developing relationship between the Holy See and Israel and Catholic-Jewish relations more generally.

Below is the complete text of the Declaration, followed by the Fundamental Agreement. The Declaration lays out the central moments in the recent history leading up to Israel's creation. The foundation for the modern state is the "natural right of the Jewish people to be masters of their own fate, like all other nations," which is expressed in their "spiritual, religious, and political identity." The Declaration was issued in Tel Aviv on the eve of the expiration of the British Mandate, which was a post-World War I arrangement for the governance of territories that had previously been governed by the Ottoman Empire.

---

117. Benedict XVI, Pope, Address of his Holiness Benedict XVI (May 11, 2009), https://www.vatican.va/content/benedict-xvi/en/speeches/2009/may/documents/hf_ben-xvi_spe_20090511_yad-vashem.html.

118. The Holy See and Israel also signed an additional protocol relating specifically to the rights and obligations of their respective diplomatic representatives. The full text of the Fundamental Agreement is available online at *Fundamental Agreement Between the Holy See and the State of Israel*, Vatican, https://www.vatican.va/roman_curia/secretariat_state/archivio/documents/rc_seg-st_19931230_santa-sede-israele_en.html (last visited Jan. 1, 2025). Concordats between the Catholic Church and other states date back more than a millennium. While the Holy See has diplomatic relations with 177 nations, it does not have concordats with all of them, including the United States.

Declaration of the Establishment of the State of Israel

Issued at Tel Aviv on May 14, 1948 (5th of Iyar, 5708)

ERETZ-ISRAEL [(Hebrew)—The Land of Israel] was the birthplace of the Jewish people. Here their spiritual, religious and political identity was shaped. Here they first attained statehood, created cultural values of national and universal significance and gave to the world the eternal Book of Books. After being forcibly exiled from their land, the people remained faithful to it throughout their Dispersion and never ceased to pray and hope for their return to it and for the restoration in it of their political freedom.

Impelled by this historic and traditional attachment, Jews strove in every successive generation to re-establish themselves in their ancient homeland. In recent decades they returned in their masses. Pioneers, *ma'pilim* [(Hebrew)—immigrants coming to Eretz-Israel in defiance of restrictive legislation] and defenders, they made deserts bloom, revived the Hebrew language, built villages and towns, and created a thriving community controlling its own economy and culture, loving peace but knowing how to defend itself, bringing the blessings of progress to all the country's inhabitants, and aspiring towards independent nationhood.

In the year 5657 (1897), at the summons of the spiritual father of the Jewish State, Theodore Herzl, the First Zionist Congress convened and proclaimed the right of the Jewish people to national rebirth in its own country. This right was recognized in the Balfour Declaration of the 2nd November, 1917, and re-affirmed in the Mandate of the League of Nations which, in particular, gave international sanction to the historic connection between the Jewish people and Eretz-Israel and to the right of the Jewish people to rebuild its National Home.

The catastrophe which recently befell the Jewish people—the massacre of millions of Jews in Europe—was another clear demonstration of the urgency of solving the problem of its homelessness by re-establishing in Eretz-Israel the Jewish State, which would open the gates of the homeland wide to every Jew and confer upon the Jewish people the status of a fully privileged member of the comity of nations. Survivors of the Nazi holocaust in Europe, as well as Jews from other parts of the world, continued to migrate to Eretz-Israel, undaunted by difficulties, restrictions and dangers, and never ceased to assert their right to a life of dignity, freedom and honest toil in their national homeland. In the Second World War, the Jewish community of this country contributed its full share to the struggle of the freedom- and peace-loving nations against the forces of Nazi wickedness and, by the blood of its soldiers and its war effort, gained the right to be reckoned among the peoples who founded the United Nations.

On the 29th November, 1947, the United Nations General Assembly passed a resolution calling for the establishment of a Jewish State in Eretz-Israel; the General Assembly required the inhabitants of Eretz-Israel to take such steps as were necessary on their part for the implementation of that resolution. This recognition by the United Nations of the right of the Jewish people to establish their State is irrevocable.

This right is the natural right of the Jewish people to be masters of their own fate, like all other nations, in their own sovereign State.

ACCORDINGLY WE, MEMBERS OF THE PEOPLE'S COUNCIL, REPRESENTATIVES OF THE JEWISH COMMUNITY OF ERETZ-ISRAEL AND OF THE ZIONIST MOVEMENT, ARE HERE ASSEMBLED ON THE DAY OF THE TERMINATION OF THE BRITISH MANDATE OVER ERETZ-ISRAEL AND, BY VIRTUE OF OUR NATURAL AND HISTORIC RIGHT AND ON THE STRENGTH OF THE RESOLUTION OF THE UNITED NATIONS GENERAL ASSEMBLY, HEREBY DECLARE THE ESTABLISHMENT OF A JEWISH STATE IN ERETZ-ISRAEL, TO BE KNOWN AS THE STATE OF ISRAEL.

WE DECLARE that, with effect from the moment of the termination of the Mandate being tonight, the eve of Sabbath, the 6th Iyar, 5708 (15th May, 1948), until the establishment of the elected, regular authorities of the State in accordance with the Constitution which shall be adopted by the Elected Constituent Assembly not later than the 1st October 1948, the People's Council shall act as a Provisional Council of State, and its executive organ, the People's Administration, shall be the Provisional Government of the Jewish State, to be called "Israel."

THE STATE OF ISRAEL will be open for Jewish immigration and for the Ingathering of the Exiles; it will foster the development of the country for the benefit of all its inhabitants; it will be based on freedom, justice and peace as envisaged by the prophets of Israel; it will ensure complete equality of social and political rights to all its inhabitants irrespective of religion, race or sex; it will guarantee freedom of religion, conscience, language, education and culture; it will safeguard the Holy Places of all religions; and it will be faithful to the principles of the Charter of the United Nations.

THE STATE OF ISRAEL is prepared to cooperate with the agencies and representatives of the United Nations in implementing the resolution of the General Assembly of the 29th November, 1947, and will take steps to bring about the economic union of the whole of Eretz-Israel.

WE APPEAL to the United Nations to assist the Jewish people in the building-up of its State and to receive the State of Israel into the comity of nations.

WE APPEAL—in the very midst of the onslaught launched against us now for months—to the Arab inhabitants of the State of Israel to preserve peace and participate in the upbuilding of the State on the basis of full and equal citizenship and due representation in all its provisional and permanent institutions.

WE EXTEND our hand to all neighboring states and their peoples in an offer of peace and good neighborliness, and appeal to them to establish bonds of cooperation and mutual help with the sovereign Jewish people settled in its own land. The State of Israel is prepared to do its share in a common effort for the advancement of the entire Middle East.

WE APPEAL to the Jewish people throughout the Diaspora to rally round the Jews of Eretz-Israel in the tasks of immigration and upbuilding and to stand by them in the great struggle for the realization of the age-old dream—the redemption of Israel.

PLACING OUR TRUST IN THE ALMIGHTY, WE AFFIX OUR SIGNATURES TO THIS PROCLAMATION AT THIS SESSION OF THE PROVISIONAL COUNCIL OF STATE, ON THE SOIL OF THE HOMELAND, IN THE CITY OF TEL-AVIV, ON THIS SABBATH EVE, THE 5TH DAY OF IYAR, 5708 (14TH MAY 1948).

Fundamental Agreement between the Holy See and the State of Israel

(*Conventio inter Apostolicam Sedem atque Israelis Statum*)
30 December 1993/16 Tevet 5754

Preamble

The Holy See and the State of Israel,

Mindful of the singular character and universal significance of the Holy Land; Aware of the unique nature of the relationship between the Catholic Church and the Jewish people, and of the historic process of reconciliation and growth in mutual understanding and friendship between Catholics and Jews....

Realizing that such Agreement will provide a sound and lasting basis for the continued development of their present and future relations....

Agree upon the following Articles:

Article 1

§ 1. The State of Israel, recalling its Declaration of Independence, affirms its continuing commitment to uphold and observe the human right to freedom of religion and conscience...

§ 2. The Holy See, recalling the Declaration on Religious Freedom of the Second Vatican Ecumenical Council, *Dignitatis humanae*, affirms the Catholic Church's commitment to uphold the human right to freedom of religion and conscience....

Article 2

§ 1. The Holy See and the State of Israel are committed to appropriate cooperation in combatting all forms of antisemitism and all kinds of racism and of religious intolerance, and in promoting mutual understanding among nations, tolerance among communities, and respect for human life and dignity.

§ 2. The Holy See takes this occasion to reiterate its condemnation of hatred, persecution, and all other manifestations of antisemitism directed against the Jewish people and individual Jews anywhere, at any time and by anyone. In particular, the Holy See deplores attacks on Jews and desecration of Jewish synagogues and cemeteries, acts which offend the memory of the victims of the Holocaust, especially when they occur in the same places that witnessed it....

Article 3

§ 1. The Holy See and the State of Israel recognize that both are free in the exercise of their respective rights and powers, and commit themselves to respect this principle in their mutual relations and in their cooperation for the good of the people.

§2. … The Church recognizes the right of the State to carry out its functions, such as promoting and protecting the welfare and the safety of the people. Both the State and the Church recognize the need for dialogue and cooperation in such matters as by their nature call for it.

§3. Concerning Catholic legal personality at canon law, the Holy See and the State of Israel will negotiate on giving it full effect in Israeli law. …

Article 4

§1. The State of Israel affirms its continuing commitment to maintain and respect the "Status quo" in the Christian Holy Places to which it applies and the respective rights of the Christian communities thereunder …

§3. The State of Israel agrees with the Holy See on the obligation of continuing respect for and protection of the character proper to Catholic sacred places, such as churches, monasteries, convents, cemeteries and their like.

§4. The State of Israel agrees with the Holy See on the continuing guarantee of the freedom of Catholic worship.

Article 5

§1. The Holy See and the State of Israel recognize that both have an interest in favouring Christian pilgrimages to the Holy Land. Whenever the need for coordination arises, the proper agencies of the Church and of the State will consult and cooperate as required.

§2. The State of Israel and the Holy See express the hope that such pilgrimages will provide an occasion for better understanding between the pilgrims and the people and religions in Israel.

Article 6

The Holy See and the State of Israel jointly reaffirm the right of the Catholic Church to establish, maintain and direct schools and institutes of study at all levels; this right being exercised in harmony with the rights of the State in the field of education.

Article 7

The Holy See and the State of Israel recognize a common interest in promoting and encouraging cultural exchanges between Catholic institutions worldwide, and educational, cultural, and research institutions in Israel, and in facilitating access to manuscripts, historical documents and similar source materials …

Article 8

The State of Israel recognizes the right of the Catholic Church to freedom of expression …

Article 9

The Holy See and the State of Israel jointly reaffirm the right of the Catholic Church to carry out its charitable functions …

Article 10

§ 1. The Holy See and the State of Israel jointly reaffirm the right of the Catholic Church to property....

Article 11

§ 1. The Holy See and the State of Israel declare their respective commitment to the promotion of the peaceful resolution of conflicts among States and nations, excluding violence and terror from international life.

§ 2. The Holy See, while maintaining in every case the right to exercise its moral and spiritual teaching-office, deems it opportune to recall that, owing to its own character, it is solemnly committed to remaining a stranger to all merely temporal conflicts, which principle applies specifically to disputed territories and unsettled borders....

The Fundamental Agreement and Its Context

1. *The Holy See and the State of Israel.* It is interesting to note that the only place in the Fundamental Agreement that mention is made of the Jewish religion is in the preamble. While the Holy See as an international actor represents the Catholic Church as a religious entity, and the State of Israel, in its 1948 Declaration of Independence, declared "the establishment of a Jewish state," the Fundamental Agreement does not mention the "Jewishness" of the State of Israel. Rather, this aspect is left primarily to the preamble. This does not diminish the historic nature of the document, nor is it the case that the question of Catholic-Jewish relations is absent from it. The preamble contains rich language that refers to the unique status of the Holy Land and the first articles of the agreement make ample reference to the Holy See's commitment to decrying antisemitism.

2. *Human rights and religious freedom.* While mention of the Jewish religion is not explicit in the document, it is implicit in the fact that the first line of the official text makes reference to the 1948 Declaration, which expressly connects the creation of the modern state of Israel to the historic connection between Judaism and the land (*eretz*) where "they first attained statehood." The reference to the Declaration of Independence is also helpful to place into context the discussion of human rights and religious freedom, as it expressly calls for "full and equal citizenship and due representation" of the Arab (non-Jewish) citizens of the territory, as well as the "economic union of the whole of Eretz-Israel." Express mention is also made of three other documents: the 1948 United Nations Universal Declaration of Human Rights; and two declarations from Vatican II—*Dignitas humanae,*[119] on religious freedom; and *Nostra aetate.*

3. *Appropriate cooperation.* Article 2 of the Fundamental Agreement puts into action the theological claims of *Nostra aetate* §4. It explicitly reiterates the condemnation of all forms of antisemitism, along with more generic forms of racism and religious

119. Paul VI, Pope, Declaration on Religious Freedom (Dec. 7, 1965), https://www.vatican.va/archive/hist_councils/ii_vatican_council/documents/vat-ii_decl_19651207_dignitatis-humanae_en.html.

intolerance. The language of the second paragraph is even more explicit than the first and is limited in scope to the Holy See, whereas the first expresses cooperation between the two states. It includes a total condemnation by the Holy See of all forms of antisemitism, powerfully calling such acts offensive to "the memory of the victims of the Holocaust."

4. *Mutual relations.* In article 3, the unique nature of a concordat is most visible. While what is proper to the State of Israel is easily understood to be those things that a modern nation state must do in its day-to-day operations (economic, diplomatic, security, health, education, and other concerns), what is "proper" to the Holy See relates to the religious mission of the Catholic Church. It is interesting to note that the State of Israel recognizes the autonomy of the Church in training, appointing, and deploying its own personnel, without interference from the state. This is a primary concern of the Catholic Church, in seeking to exercise its own freedom (*libertas ecclesiae*—freedom of the Church).[120] The third paragraph of the article represents an as-yet-unresolved point in the development of Holy See-Israel diplomacy; from the Catholic perspective, the recognition of the legal status of Catholic institutions as determined by internal Church law (known as canon law) is an important part of its own understanding of its free exercise.

5. *Not just personnel.* Article 6 of the Fundamental Agreement moves beyond questions of personnel and speaks of the kinds of institutions that the State of Israel recognizes as being authentically part of the life of the Catholic Church. Beyond those more generally recognized as "religious"—that is, related directly to worship or acts of charity—the State also recognizes the important role that education plays in the life of the Catholic Church, and grants it the right to establish and direct, autonomously, schools of all levels, such that the State and the Church act harmoniously in the field of education.

6. *Common Interest.* Articles 7–9 list a series of areas in which the State of Israel and the Catholic Church express their mutual understanding of a common interest served by the work of the Church. While articles 8–9 list more concrete activities, article 7 is of particular interest, in relation to what was established in *Nostra aetate* and repeated in the preamble to the Fundamental Agreement, namely working toward the elimination of all forms of antisemitism. These articles foresee this happening through shared cultural activities on a global scale, through exchanges among educational institutions. In an indirect manner, this important article speaks to the fundamental role of education in combating antisemitism, particularly through historical research, echoing the role that sound historical research played, for example, in the elimination of the cult of Simon of Trent.

---

120. For a more modern explanation of this medieval concept, see Paul Horwitz, *Freedom of the Church without Romance The Freedom of the Church in the Modern Era*, 21 J. Contemp. Legal Issues 59 (2013), https://scholarship.law.ua.edu/fac_articles/185.

St. Pope John Paul II: Prayer of the Holy Father at the Western Wall

1. *St. Pope John Paul II.* The Fundamental Agreement was signed during the papacy of Pope John Paul II. His relationship with Jewish scholars and believers has been well documented[121] and was often recalled during his visit to Israel in March 2000, the first official visit of a pope to the state of Israel.[122] Prior to that visit, on March 12, 2000, in an unprecedented ceremony known as the "Day of Pardon," during a liturgy in St. Peter's in Rome, Cardinal Edward Cassidy (then the head of Pontifical Council for Promoting Christian Unity, in which the Secretariat for relations with the Jews was still located), offered the following prayer: "Let us pray that, in recalling the sufferings endured by the people of Israel throughout history, Christians will acknowledge the sins committed by not a few of their number against the people of the Covenant and the blessings, and in this way will purify their hearts." To these words, John Paul II responded, "God of our fathers, you chose Abraham and his descendants to bring your Name to the Nations: we are deeply saddened by the behavior of those who in the course of history have caused these children of yours to suffer, and asking your forgiveness we wish to commit ourselves to genuine brotherhood with the people of the Covenant."[123]

2. *St. Pope John Paul II visits the Western Wall.* On March 26, 2000, John Paul II placed that same prayer in the cervixes of the Western Wall (also known as the Wailing Wall).[124] Just days before, in his visit to Yad Vashem, John Paul II recalled his personal experience of the deportation of Jewish friends from Poland during World War II, and honored "the millions of Jewish people who, stripped of their dignity, were murdered in the Holocaust."[125] He also offered this solemn promise to the Jewish people:

> As Bishop of Rome and Successor of the Apostle Peter, I assure the Jewish people that the Catholic Church, motivated by the Gospel law of truth and love and by no political considerations, is deeply saddened by the hatred, acts of persecution and displays of anti-Semitism directed against the Jews by Christians at any time and in any place. The Church rejects racism in any form as a denial of the image of the Creator inherent in every human being (cf. *Gen* 1:26).[126]

---

121. *See, e.g., Pope John Paul II: Relations with Jews and Israel*, Jewish Virtual Libr., https://www.jewishvirtuallibrary.org/pope-john-paul-ii-relations-with-jews-and-israel (last visited Jan. 1, 2025).

122. The visit by Pope Paul VI in 1964 did not have the character of an official state visit.

123. For the prayers from that liturgy, see *Day of Pardon Mass First Sunday of Lent*, Bos. Coll. (Mar. 12, 2000), https://www.bc.edu/content/dam/files/research_sites/cjl/texts/cjrelations/resources/documents/catholic/johnpaulii/day_of_pardon_mass.htm.

124. *See, The "Note" that Pope John Paul II Placed Between the Stones of the Western Wall During His Visit to Israel*, Yad Vashem, https://www.yadvashem.org/artifacts/featured/note-pope-john-paul-ii.html (last visited Jan. 1, 2025).

125. *See* John Paul II, Pope, Speech of John Paul II, Visit to the Yad Vashem Museum (Mar. 23, 2000), https://www.vatican.va/content/john-paul-ii/en/speeches/2000/jan-mar/documents/hf_jp-ii_spe_20000323_yad-vashem-mausoleum.html.

126. *Id.*

During his visit to Israel, John Paul II connected the condemnation of all forms of antisemitism called for in *Nostra aetate* to the historic guilt of Christians for violence against the Jewish people, including their role in the Shoah. This recognition opened the way for an authentic reconciliation which he hoped would lead to "a new future in which there will be no more anti-Jewish feeling among Christians or anti-Christian feeling among Jews, but rather the mutual respect required of those who adore the one Creator and Lord, and look to Abraham as our common father in faith."[127] Pope John Paul II was declared a saint on April 27, 2014, together with Pope John XXIII.

Diplomatic Complexities in the Holy See-Israel Relationship

1. *Theology, politics, and diplomacy*. In a 2009 speech at Boston College, Ambassador Mordechay Lewy, Israel's ambassador to the Holy See, outlined a number of important considerations in evaluating the success of the establishment of diplomatic relations between the two entities.[128] Ambassador Lewy spoke of an inherent "asymmetry" in that the Holy See's representative to Israel (or to any country) is a high-ranking cleric, who has both diplomatic and religious duties, where the representative of Israel operates merely in the diplomatic sphere. In this, diplomatic relations must be distinguished from interreligious dialogue, which more properly takes place between the Apostolic See[129] (as distinguished from the Holy See) and the Chief Rabbinate of Israel. While the two are necessarily interconnected, interreligious dialogue and diplomatic relations are technically different spheres of operation in which the Holy See could utilize the same representative, but the State of Israel cannot. Similar questions of diplomacy and internal Church matters may arise, for example, with a controversial internal Church decision regarding declaring someone a saint, to which the State of Israel might voice opposition.

2. *Contemporary complexities*. Many of the issues that were left undecided in the Fundamental Agreement remain unresolved. The "asymmetry" described by Ambassador Lewy continues to also further complicate matters, given the Holy See's *Pactio*[130] signed with the Palestinian Liberation Organization in 2015, which followed upon the establishment of relations between the two entities in 1994. It must be noted that the Holy See continues to call for a "special statute" for Jerusalem which would guarantee

127. *Id.*

128. Mordechay Lewy, *From Denial to Acceptance: Holy See-Israel Relations*, 4 Stud. in Christian-Jewish Rels. Lewy CP 1 (2009).

129. Where the "Holy See" is the name given to the Catholic Church's operations in the diplomatic sphere, the Code of Canon Law refers to the Church's internal or religious operations, under the name of the "Apostolic See." *Cf.* 1983 Code C.361).

130. This document is referred to as a "Basic Agreement," as opposed to the "Fundamental Agreement" signed with the State of Israel. For the full text, see Basic Agreement Between the Holy See and the Palestine Liberation Organization, Holy See-Palestine Liberation Org., Feb. 15, 2009, https://www.vatican.va/roman_curia/secretariat_state/2000/documents/rc_seg-st_20000215_santa-sede-olp_en.html.

"the proper identity and sacred character of the City and its universally significant, religious and cultural heritage."[131] This stands in obvious contrast to the position taken by the State of Israel. The concern for Jerusalem's unique character also reflects the Holy See's desire to maintain access to Christian holy sites; it is also a diplomatic position based on United Nations General Assembly Resolution 303-IV, adopted on December 9, 1949.[132] This thought had already been expressed by Pope Pius XII on April 15, 1949, when speaking about the desire of Christians to resume pilgrimages to the Holy Land:

> We have never ceased to pray repeatedly for this enduring and genuine peace. And to the end that it might be brought to fruition and permanence at the earliest possible moment, We have already insisted in Our Encyclical letter *In Multiplicibus*, that the time has come when Jerusalem and its vicinity, where the previous memorials of the Life and Death of the Divine Redeemer are preserved, should be accorded and legally guaranteed an "international" status, which in the present circumstances seems to offer the best and most satisfactory protection for these sacred monuments. We cannot help repeating here the same declaration, encouraged by the thought that it may also serve as an inspiration to Our children. Let them, wherever they are living, use every legitimate means to persuade the rulers of nations, and those whose duty it is to settle this important question, to accord to Jerusalem and its surroundings a juridical status whose stability under the present circumstances can only be adequately assured by a united effort of nations that love peace and respect the right of others.[133]

Again, as noted by Ambassador Lewy in his speech at Boston College, while diplomatic agreements are made between governments on a broader scale, the individual items included in the Fundamental Agreement that touch domestic policy for the State of Israel are, nevertheless, considered matters of foreign affairs for the Holy See. It is natural, therefore, to expect disagreement on the best way to concretely implement in domestic policy those things agreed to in an international accord. These disagreements and continued negotiation are not signs of a "return to the past"; rather, the fact that the matters contained in the agreement continue to be debated, despite fundamental disagreements on some major issues, should be seen as a triumph of diplomacy based in the theological recognition of the importance of Judaism to Christianity and, necessarily, to the concerns of the Holy See.

---

131. *Id.*

132. "To restate, therefore, its intention that Jerusalem should be placed under a permanent international regime, which should envisage appropriate guarantees for the protection of the Holy Places, both within and outside Jerusalem and to confirm specifically the following provisions of General Assembly resolution 181 (II): (1) The City of Jerusalem shall be established as a *corpus separatum* under a special international regime and shall be administered by the United Nations. . . ." For the full text, see G.A. Res. 303 (IV), (Dec. 9, 1949), https://digitallibrary.un.org/record/210578?v=pdf&ln=en.

133. Pius XII, Pope, Redemptoris Nostri Cruciatus, nn. 9–10 (Apr. 15, 1949). For the full text, see *Redemptoris Nostri Cruciatus*, Vatican, https://www.vatican.va/content/pius-xii/en/encyclicals/documents/hf_p-xii_enc_15041949_redemptoris-nostri-cruciatus.html (last visited Jan. 1, 2025).

Catholic Zionism and the Church's Support for Israel's Right to Exist

Catholic "Zionism." Given all that has been said in this chapter, is it possible to sustain the hypothesis that the official position of the Catholic Church is one of "Zionism"? The easy answer is yes, if by Zionism one means the political statement of the legitimacy of the existence of the State of Israel. This was made possible by the positive expression of Judaism found in *Nostra aetate.* In *Lachrimabilem Iudaeorum,* Pope Innocent IV expresses that the Jews have received "privileges granted to them by the Apostolic See," as if the Jewish people were subject to the spiritual, and temporal, authority of the Catholic Church. In *Nostra aetate,* Jews are recognized on their own terms, as the "well-cultivated olive tree" onto which the wild branch of the nations have been grafted.[134] This led Pope John Paul II to speak of the Jewish people in 1980 as "the people of God of the Old Covenant, which has never been revoked."[135] In that same speech, he made his own the thought of the German Episcopal Conference: "Whoever encounters Christ, encounters Judaism."[136]

Nostra aetate went beyond merely condemning expressions of antisemitism. It opened the door to an authentic dialogue between Judaism and Christianity, one in which the important concept of "the land"[137] (*ha-aretz*) in relation to the covenant between God and his people has received adequate consideration.[138] This must be considered in the contrasting light of Augustine's biblical interpretation of the Jewish people having been condemned to wander the earth like Cain and serve their brothers like Ham. *Nostra aetate* clearly states the Jewish people have been and remain chosen by God. No punishment can be transposed upon the entire Jewish people for the actions of those who participated in the crucifixion of Jesus.

In his apostolic exhortation on the situation of the Catholic Church in the Middle East, *Ecclesia in medio oriente*, Pope Benedict XVI wrote:

> Relationships between the two communities [Jewish and Christian] of believers bear the marks of history and human passion. Misunderstandings and reciprocal distrust have abounded. Past persecutions, whether surreptitious or violent, are inexcusable and greatly to be deplored. And yet, despite these trag-

---

134. *Nostra aetate*, § 4.

135. John Paul II, Pope, Encounter of John Paul II with Representatives of the Jewish Community (Nov. 17, 1980), https://www.vatican.va/content/john-paul-ii/it/speeches/1980/november/documents/hf_jp_ii_spe_19801117_ebrei-magonza.html.

136. *Id.*

137. For a summary of a Catholic understanding of the "theology of the land" see Phillip Cunningham, *A Catholic Theology of the Land?: The State of the Question*, 8 Stud. in Christian-Jewish Rels. 1 (2013).

138. For example, in the texts from John Paul II's visit to Israel in March 2000, every time the word "land" appears, it is marked with a capital "L"; while it is consistent in the English translations of the documents from that visit, it is less consistent in other translations. See the twenty-eight public speeches of John Paul II in Israel at *Travels 2000*, Vatican, https://www.vatican.va/content/john-paul-ii/en/travels/2000.index.1.html (last visited Jan. 1, 2025).

> ic situations, the interplay between both communities over the centuries proved so fruitful that it contributed to the birth and expansion of the civilization and culture commonly known as Judeo-Christian. It is as if these two worlds, claiming to be different or opposed for various reasons, had decided to unite in offering humanity a noble alloy. This relationship, which both unites and separates Jews and Christians, ought to open both groups to a new sense of responsibility for and with one another.[139]

This new "sense of responsibility for and with one another" remains a work in progress, but it includes a recognition of the right of the State of Israel to exist and a condemnation of all forms of antisemitism.

139. Benedict XVI, Pope, Ecclesia in Medio Oriente, n. 22 (Sept. 14, 2012), https://www.vatican.va/content/benedict-xvi/en/apost_exhortations/documents/hf_ben-xvi_exh_20120914_ecclesia-in-medio-oriente.html.

Index

Note: Page numbers with 'f' denote figures and page numbers with 'n' refer to notes.

I